Teaching English Abroad

Your expert guide to teaching English around the world

Susan Griffith

trotman | t

While every effort has been made to ensure that the information contained in this book was accurate at the time of going to press, some details are bound to change within the lifetime of this edition, especially those pertaining to visa requirements for teachers, exchange rates and the conditions offered by the schools listed in the country directories. Readers are invited to contact Susan Griffith, c/o Crimson Publishing Ltd, 19–21c Charles Street, Bath BA1 1HX, or email her at info@crimsonpublishing.co.uk with any comments or corrections. The best contributions will be rewarded with a free copy of the next edition or any other Crimson title.

DISCLAIMER

The opinions expressed in the case studies set in this style of box are entirely those of the featured organisation. Those in an italic script have been submitted independently, usually by readers of earlier editions of this book.

NOTE: Most wages and prices are given in local currencies. For conversion to sterling and US dollars, use www.oanda.com.

Teaching English Abroad

This edition first published in Great Britain 2015 by Crimson Publishing Ltd, 19–21c Charles Street, Bath BA1 1HX

First edition 1991
Fifteenth edition 2015

© Crimson Publishing 2015

A catalogue record for this book is available from the British Library.

ISBN 978 1 78059 149 0

Typeset by IDSUK (DataConnection) Ltd
Printed and bound in Malta by Gutenberg Press Ltd

CONTENTS

Preface v

Part 1: Introduction

Introduction **3**

Some Definitions 3
Scope of Opportunities 4
Motives for Teaching English 8
Red Tape 10
Rewards and Risks 11

Training **14**

The Value of ELT Qualifications 14
Range of Courses 15
Certificate Courses 15
Directory of Training Courses 27
 CELTA UK 27
 CELTA Abroad 34
 Trinity CertTESOL UK 51
 Trinity CertTESOL Abroad 53
 Short Introductory Courses 56
 Online TEFL Training 57
 Academic Courses 60
 Training Courses in North America 62
 Training Courses Worldwide 64

Finding a Job **79**

TEFL Websites 79
Recruitment Fairs 81
Recruitment Organisations 81
Speculative Job Hunt 94
On the Spot 97
Advertisements 98
Freelance Teaching 99

Preparation **101**

Summer Camps Abroad 101
UK Summer Schools 101
While You're Waiting 104
What To Take 110
Recommended Bibliography 114

Problems **117**

Problems At Work 117
Problems Outside Work 123

Part 2: Country By Country Guide

Western Europe **129**

Austria 129
Benelux 135
 Belgium 135
 Luxembourg 137
 The Netherlands 138
France 141
Germany 158
Greece 174
Italy 186
Portugal 205
Scandinavia 213
 Denmark 213
 Finland 213
 Norway 215
 Sweden 216
Spain 221
Switzerland 248

Central and Eastern Europe **254**

Bulgaria 257
Czech Republic 260
Slovak Republic 270
Hungary 276
Poland 282
Romania 292
Russia 296
The Baltics 306
 Latvia and Lithuania 306
 Estonia 306
Ukraine 308
Moldova 311

The Rest of Europe **312**

Albania 312
Andorra 313
Bosnia-Herzegovina 314
Croatia 314
Cyprus 316
Malta 317
Serbia, Montenegro and Kosovo 320
Slovenia 321

Central Asian and Other Republics **323**

Georgia 324
Azerbaijan 326
Kazakhstan and Kyrgyzstan 328

Middle East **332**

Afghanistan 336
Israel 338
Palestine 339
Kuwait 340
Lebanon 341
Oman 344
Qatar 347
Saudi Arabia 349
UAE 354
Yemen 357
Turkey 358

Africa **371**

Egypt 376
Sudan 380
Kenya 383
Madagascar 385
Morocco 386
Tunisia 388
Libya 390
Mauritania 391
Equatorial Guinea 392
Senegal 393
Other African Countries 394

Asia **396**

China 399
Mongolia 422
Hong Kong 423
Macao 432
Indonesia 434
Japan 441
Korea 464
Indian Subcontinent 477
    India 477

Nepal 481
Pakistan and Bangladesh 484
Tibet 485
Sri Lanka 486
Maldives 488
Malaysia 489
Singapore 493
Brunei 495
Vietnam 496
Cambodia 506
Laos and Burma 509
Taiwan 512
Thailand 521

Latin America **538**

Argentina 543
Bolivia 551
Brazil 555
Chile 561
Colombia 570
Ecuador 574
Mexico 579
Peru 585
Venezuela 588

**Central America and the
Caribbean** **591**

Costa Rica 591
Guatemala and Honduras 596
Nicaragua 598
El Salvador 599
Dominican Republic 600

North America **601**

Australasia **604**

Australia 604
New Zealand 607

Index of Advertisers **609**

PREFACE

Having originally written this book in 1991 and updated it many times since, I am in a good position to take an historical view of the international English teaching business. How things have changed in a quarter of a century! In those early days, job vacancies were mainly uncovered in the lineage adverts of the *Guardian* on Tuesdays. Only a handful of TEFL teacher training centres existed, compared to the hundreds now in places as farflung as Nicaragua, the Philippines and the Galápagos. Included here is the cheapest four-week CELTA course (£700 in Odessa) and the most expensive (£2500 in Caracas).

The destinations have changed as well. The preface of the first edition was written 13 scant months after the fall of the Berlin Wall. In the years that followed, the clamour for the English language knew no bounds in the former Eastern bloc nations. As of 2016, demand in that region has waned as indigenous English teachers have been trained. Twenty-five years ago, China was accepting English teachers exclusively via the education department of the Chinese government. Now there is a dizzying free-for-all of private and public institutions hiring native speaker teachers. Tragically, former receiving countries such as Yemen and Syria are now totally out-of-bounds.

Some linguists believe that English will be the last lingua franca. However, as Anglo-American domination of the world shrinks, so will the influence of its language. But while we are still in its heyday, an ability to teach the English language is the most globally mobile skill there is. Countries that continue to demonstrate a voracious demand for English teachers include Korea, China, Vietnam, Taiwan, Indonesia, Turkey, Saudi Arabia, Russia, Mexico, Chile, Argentina and of course Brazil as it prepares for the Olympics next year. A view that the Japanese market has stagnated is belied by the new inclusion of a chain of language schools that seeks to recruit a thousand teachers. Opportunities are opening in new corners of the world all the time, from Myanmar to Angola, Moldova to Mongolia (all of which have information included for the first time in this edition), and in a thousand more familiar places from Barcelona to Bangkok.

For this edition, I have noticed a proliferation of teaching assistant schemes attractive to students and new graduates. British Council programmes have opened up in India (Generation UK-India) and Thailand (TET Programme). Volunteer teachers are deployed at summer schools in Romania (BREDEX), secondary schools in Colombia (via agencies like Flying Cows) and in state schools in Malaysia (Bright Spark Teachers). North Americans are placed by their thousand throughout state schools in Spain (NALCA). Teaching English after university is a rite of passage for large numbers of Britons and North Americans, and is a great way to begin your professional career.

The TEFL industry has spawned hundreds of specialist websites that cover teacher training forums and publicise current vacancies worldwide. Some might wonder what a book can add. I have tried to create a hand-held tool that makes it easy for the reader to compare at a glance destinations for teachers, institute requirements, visa regulations, possible problems and rewards. This book aims for clarity – to help make sense of the overwhelming clutter of unsifted information online.

Note that the hundreds of language schools and teaching organisations around the world that submitted details of their teaching vacancies have not paid to be included in this book. Shaded text headed by a company name has been supplied by the relevant company, whereas boxed first-hand accounts by named teachers have been freely shared with readers.

In addition to all the hard information and vacancy listings that it includes, this book tries to convey a flavour of life as a teacher abroad, by including first-hand descriptions of everything from the etiquette on first entering an Argentinian staffroom – you kiss rather than shake hands on first acquaintance – to tips on apartment rental agencies in Japan. My aim has always been to make the information as concrete and up-to-date as possible, and to cut the waffle. This book can be the stepping stone to a brilliant year or two of adventure abroad.

Susan Griffith
Cambridge
October 2015

PART 1

INTRODUCTION

INTRODUCTION
TRAINING
FINDING A JOB
PREPARATION
PROBLEMS

INTRODUCTION

A report commissioned by the British Council estimated that the number of English language learners will peak in the next eight years at a staggering two billion. The statistics illustrate the extent to which English dominates our globalised world: three-quarters of the world's mail is written in English, 80% of the world's electronically stored information is in English and well over a third of users of the internet communicate in the language you are reading at this moment. English dominates the world's business, sports, entertainment, aviation, science and technology, which explains why there are an estimated six million teachers of English working worldwide. Mind-boggling statistics aside, the demand for instruction at all levels given by people who happen to speak English as their mother tongue is insatiable.

Just as Latin was the lingua franca of Europe in the Middle Ages, now it is English that is the language used to communicate between persons not sharing a mother tongue. When the newly liberated nations of Eastern Europe sloughed off Russian, they turned in very large measure to English rather than to the other main European languages. In fact, countries as far-flung as Cambodia, Namibia and Turkmenistan are busy making English one of the keystones of their educational systems. In German-speaking Switzerland, there are signs that English is replacing French as the preferred second language at school. English is the international language of science, of air traffic control, and to a very large extent of trade and export. Advertisers around the world often choose English, to avoid expensive multilingual campaigns. Switzerland's national airline is Swissair, not Air Suisse or Luft Schweizer.

This is bad news for all those Germans, Swedes and French Canadians who would like to market their language skills to fund a short or long stay abroad. But it is English speakers, mainly from Britain, Ireland, North America, Australia and New Zealand, who accidentally find themselves in possession of such a sought-after commodity.

SOME DEFINITIONS

The commonly used acronyms ELT, TEFL, TESL and TESOL can be confusing, especially since they are often used interchangeably. ELT, which stands for English Language Teaching, has come to be the mainstream expression in the UK (preferred by such august bodies as the University of Cambridge and by the publishers of the main journal in the field). But most people still refer to TEFL (pronounced 'teffle'), Teaching English as a Foreign Language. TESL stands for Teaching English as a Second Language, and TESOL means Teaching English to Speakers of Other Languages. People learn English as a second language when they need to use it in their day-to-day lives, for example emigrants to the UK and the USA or inhabitants of ex-colonies where English retains official status and may well be the medium of instruction in schools. (English is the official or joint-official language in more than 75 countries.)

As this book is for people who want to travel abroad to teach, the term TEFL is mainly used here, as well as ELT. Teachers of English as a Second Language (ESL) are usually involved with multicultural education. In the USA, the vast majority of English language teaching is of ESL because of the huge demand for English among those people who have emigrated to the USA and whose first language is not English. Therefore the term ESL dominates in American contexts, even when (technically) EFL is meant.

The acronym TESOL covers both situations, yet it is not widely used apart from in institutions which favour the Trinity College London qualifications known as the Certificate and Licentiate Diploma in TESOL (see Training section later) and also in the context of the American organisation TESOL Inc., which is the largest English teachers' organisation in the world, claiming more than 12,000 members.

There is no shortage of other acronyms and sub-categories in the world of TEFL. One of the main ones is ESP, which means English for Specific Purposes. ESP aims to match language teaching with the needs of various professions such as business, banking, tourism, medicine, aviation, science, technology, secretarial, etc. Business English is probably the most important in this category (and 'English for Shopping' as sometimes offered in Japan is the least important). Because a great many learners are motivated by a desire to use English at work, they want their teachers to adopt a functional rather than a structural approach. In other words they want to have lessons in which they can pretend to be telephoning a client, recommending, applying, advising, agreeing, complaining and so on. They are certainly not interested in the subjunctive.

EAP stands for English for Academic Purposes, ie English at an advanced level usually taught to students who are planning to study at foreign universities or English-medium institutions in their own country. EAP is largely in the hands of government-funded programmes, such as those run by the British Council.

Note that the acronym TOEFL can cause confusion. The Test of English as a Foreign Language is a US-based standardised test administered to language learners. Passing a TOEFL exam is widely held to be a reliable indicator of how well an individual can communicate in English. The focus of many language schools abroad is to prepare candidates for the exam, and so many advertise for teachers with 'TOEFL' experience. The UK counterpart, sponsored by the British Council and Cambridge English is IELTS (International English Language Testing System), commonly used by candidates worldwide who want to enrol in English-speaking universities.

SCOPE OF OPPORTUNITIES

The range of locations and situations in which English is in demand covers an enormous spectrum. If TEFL is booming in Kazakhstan and Laos and Colombia, there can be few corners of the world to which English has not penetrated. English has been called a 'barometer of western influence' and only a handful of countries in the world (notably North Korea) have rejected western influence outright. Burma used to fall into this category but not any more, since it is fast opening up to western influences including to the English language. The economic tigers of the BRIC nations (Brazil, Russia, India, China) have been flagging slightly in 2015, but their markets for the English language continue to grow massively. Economists predict that the MINT countries will be the next emerging economic giants: Mexico, Indonesia, Nigeria and Turkey. Apart from Nigeria, these countries already have huge ELT industries, which can only expand.

Many years have passed since the arrival of the single European market, which precipitated a greater expansion of the English language than ever before in Europe's history. There has been an enormous increase in demand, especially from companies and professionals eager to participate in an integrated Europe. At least one German-based multinational has gone so far as to decree that all operations will be conducted in English. The attraction of European Union countries for British and Irish teachers is enhanced by the fact that they have the legal right to work there.

The kinds of people who want to learn English are as numerous as the places in which they live. The worldwide recession saw a certain amount of cutting back in spending from Moscow to Madrid, for example on corporate training budgets, but it is remarkable how resilient the market has remained, even in struggling Greece. In an even more competitive employment market, a command of English is considered so essential that individuals are prepared to fund themselves and their children. The area of the industry that seems to be booming almost everywhere is the teaching of children, known as Young Learners or YL in the trade. Kids as young as 18 months are being immersed in an English-speaking environment and older ones are being sent to private English classes as their parents keep a weather eye on their future career prospects.

People around the world can think of a dozen reasons why they need to sign up for private English lessons.

- A Taiwanese student dreams of studying at UCLA.
- A Bulgarian bus driver, proud to be from a member state of the EU, wants to work in Denmark where he will be able to communicate in English.
- The wife of the Peruvian ambassador in Islamabad wants to be able to speak English at official functions.

- A Greek secondary school student has to pass her English exams in order to proceed to the next year and, like most of her classmates, attends a private tutorial college for English lessons.
- A Turkish youth wants to be able to flirt with tourists from Northern Europe.
- A Mexican waiter wants to get a job in the Acapulco Hilton.
- A Saudi engineer has to be able to read reports and manuals in English for his job.

The list is open-ended, and prospects for hopeful teachers are therefore excellent. There are also hundreds of international schools throughout the world where English is the medium of instruction for all subjects and there may be specific EFL vacancies. These will be of most interest to certified teachers who wish to work abroad.

But the situation is not all rosy for the prospective teacher. As the profile of the English language has risen, so has the profile of the profession that teaches it, and the number of qualified and experienced English teachers has increased along with the rise in demand. The difficult employment situation for new graduates in the UK and elsewhere has prompted some to look abroad, and to equip themselves with a TEFL certificate in order to get some work experience on their CV. The explosion in the availability of training courses means that a much higher proportion of job-seekers have a TEFL certificate than was the case a decade ago, and (quite rightly) foreign language schools are becoming more selective when hiring staff.

People who cruise into a country expecting to be hired as an EFL teacher simply on the basis of being a native speaker are in most cases (though not quite all) in for a nasty shock. Employers at all levels will ask for evidence of the ability to teach their language or at least a university degree as proof of a sound educational background. Certainly without a degree, a TEFL qualification or any relevant experience, the scope of opportunities shrinks drastically.

WHO IS ELIGIBLE TO TEACH?

Anyone who can speak English fluently and has a lively, positive personality has a fighting chance of finding an opening as a teacher somewhere. Geordies, Tasmanians and Alabamans have all been known to be hired as English teachers (not to mention Norwegians and North Africans), though most employers favour native speakers of English without a heavy regional accent. Depending on the economic and cultural orientation of a country, schools will prefer British English or North American English. For obvious geopolitical reasons Europe and Africa incline towards Britain while Latin America and the Far East incline towards the USA and Canada. Many other countries have no decided preference, for example Indonesia and Turkey. Clear diction is usually more important than accent. On the American English versus British English debate, **Sab Will**, one-time Course Director of TEFL Paris training courses, says:

> *I'm not convinced it's a major concern. There are certainly French who find one flavour (or should that be 'flavor'?) easier to understand than the other, and some people want to be taught mainly in one 'accent' based on their intended future use of English. But overall I think it all evens out. Most students are happy with a friendly, competent and enthusiastic teacher who is able to adapt to their needs and supply them with materials and learning situations relevant to their situation. In relation to that, the origin of the teacher pales in comparison. Of course the teacher should be able to 'neutralise' their accent if necessary, whatever their origins, so that the student has a model which will be understood throughout the English-speaking world.*

The US government maintains a website for teachers and learners of American English abroad at http://americanenglish.state.gov.

English language teaching is an industry that is seldom regulated, giving rise to the host of cowboy schools sometimes dubbed the 'McDonald's of English teaching'. The other side of the coin is the proliferation of cowboy teachers, who have no feel for language, no interest in their students and no qualms about ripping them off. The issue of qualifications must be considered carefully. It is obviously unwise to assume that fluency in English is a sufficient qualification to turn someone into an EFL teacher. Many experienced teachers of English come to feel very strongly that untrained teachers do a disservice both to their students and to their language. Certainly anyone who is serious about going abroad to teach English should turn to the relevant chapter to consider the training options. As Groucho Marx said, who would want to belong to a club that would want him as a member if he has no formal qualifications or experience? Among the army of teachers-cum-travellers, there are undoubtedly some lazy, spiritless and ungrammatical native speakers of English who have bluffed their way into a teaching job. Most books and journals about language teaching are unanimous in their condemnation of such amateurs. Yet there are some excellent teachers who have learned how to teach by practising rather than by studying. For certain kinds of teaching jobs, a background in business and commerce might be far more useful than any paper qualifications in teaching. Therefore we have not excluded the unqualified teacher-traveller from our account. As long as they take their responsibilities seriously and bear in mind that their pupils have entrusted them with significant quantities of time and money to help them learn, they need not bring the EFL profession into disrepute. Some untrained teachers we talked to during the research for this book found the responsibility so unnerving that they promptly enrolled in a TEFL course before unleashing themselves on an unsuspecting language-learning public.

Non-native speakers should not assume that their services would not be in demand outside their home countries. **Richard Ridha Guellala** was born in Holland, raised in Tunisia and partly educated in England, and now has one of the most highly respected qualifications in TEFL, the Cambridge Diploma. While teaching in Thailand, he wrote:

> *Most non-native speakers think that a position as an EFL teacher is impossible for them. However, I came to the conclusion that even unqualified non-native speakers are often hired by Asian schools, as long as they project a professional image during the interview, speak clearly, are well-groomed, know the basics of English grammar and are fluent in the language. Scandinavians and Dutch are sometimes even more successful in finding teaching jobs at top schools than native speakers. True, we non-native speakers possess a rather 'heavy' or 'funny' accent but, believe it or not, some Asian employers favour our accents to the native speaker's because we speak more slowly and use very simple basic vocabulary.*

To get a sense of the range of individuals who pursue this course, the site www.teachingtraveling.com carries illuminating interviews with teacher-travellers of all ages and backgrounds.

At an extreme opposite from the casual teacher-traveller is the teacher who makes ELT a career. Only a minority of people teaching English abroad are professional teachers. Career prospects in ELT are in fact not very encouraging. After teachers have achieved a certain level of training and experience, they can aspire to work for International House and then for the British Council. From there, they might become a director of studies at a private language institute, although one is unlikely to become a director without a primary interest in business and administration.

THE OLDER TEACHER

An increasing number of early-retired and other mature people are becoming interested in teaching English abroad for a year or two. Although it may be true that in certain contexts, language institutes are more inclined to employ a bright young graduate, if only for reasons of image and marketing, there are plenty of others who will value maturity, especially the growing number of establishments specialising in teaching young children. **Peter Beech**, Director of Anglo-Hellenic in Corinth, Greece, which trains and places teachers in jobs, has noticed an increasing interest from people who have already had a career in the UK, in teaching or in any field, who want to move abroad.

Whereas only a few companies openly impose an upper age limit, some age discrimination does regrettably take place, more noticeable in some countries than in others. The teacher recruitment agency Teach to Travel Ltd insists that candidates be less than 40 to be placed in Turkey, Thailand, Hong Kong and South

Korea. A government scheme in Brunei accepts teachers up to age 52 for primary schools, 55 for secondary. Saudi Arabia will not issue visas to teachers over 55 and China likewise imposes a maximum age of 55 or 60 for issuing the Z-visa. In Indonesia, the government wants foreign teachers to be aged 25–54.

For older job-seekers it will be a matter of spreading their net as widely as they can by contacting as many relevant organisations, including voluntary ones, as possible. Older applicants may have to work harder to demonstrate enthusiasm, energy and adaptability to prospective employers; but this should be no bar to someone committed to creating adventures later in life. The issue of age will matter less if you can present yourself face-to-face to possible employers (unless you really are a decrepit old geezer or crone). Some keen candidates have volunteered in the first instance which gives them the chance to show their mettle. Others have had success by heading away from the competition of the big cities to focus on quiet backwaters.

Australian journalists **Alexandra Neuman** and **John Carey**, aged 49 and 50 respectively, decided that having worked for 30-odd years it was time to do something different. They didn't want to do the sensible thing and wait until retirement, so started saving and planning, and after a couple of years had saved enough to fund a year in Italy. At first Alex didn't work but when they decided to extend their stay, she needed to find work. The only work available was teaching English, which is what she is doing right now in the lovely town of Bergamo:

> *It won't matter what you read, who you speak to or how much planning you do once you arrive, your experience will be completely different. I have yet to meet one person who had a similar experience to mine, so above all you must bring with you tolerance, flexibility and an upbeat attitude. The rewards are well worth it. I love living here, I have never met such kindness and I know bureaucracy is terrible and I get paid badly but as I sit looking out of my hilltop apartment to the snow-capped Alps and the grapes ripening on the vine just below my bedroom window I think life is pretty wonderful!*

JERRY MELINN

Jerry Melinn enjoyed teaching English at an institute in Athens through Anglo-Hellenic so much that he signed on for another year:

I suppose you could say I don't fit the profile of a TEFL teacher. Usually they are unattached, young and out to see the world after finishing their university studies. I worked in the telecommunications industry in Ireland for almost 40 years and took advantage of an early retirement scheme when I was 56 years old. I didn't want to stop working and, as my four children were grown up, I decided, with the agreement of my wife, to try my hand at teaching English in Greece. I was interested in Greece because we have friends here and had been coming to Greece on holidays for many years.

WHAT EMPLOYERS ARE LOOKING FOR

Between the dodgy operators and the British Council is a vast middle ground of respectable English teaching establishments. Many would prefer to hire only qualified staff, yet they are not always available. On the whole these schools are looking for teachers with a good educational background, clear correct speech, familiarity with the main issues and approaches to TEFL, and an outgoing personality.

A bachelor's degree and/or TEFL certificate is no guarantee of ability as **Marta Eleniak** observed in Spain, where she taught during her gap year (after doing a one-week introductory TEFL course):

I've seen graduate teachers make such a mockery of the enterprise that it's almost criminal. TEFL is creative teaching. Forget about your educational experiences. In TEFL you have got to be able to do an impression of a chicken, you've got to be a performer. And you have to be flexible. If the pupils are falling asleep, conduct a short aerobics class and change tack to something more interesting. A good teacher builds a rapport with the class, and is enthusiastic, patient, imaginative and genuinely interested in the welfare of the pupils.

A sophisticated knowledge of English grammar is not needed, since in most cases, native speakers are hired to encourage conversation and practise pronunciation, leaving the grammar lessons to local teachers. On the other hand, a basic grasp is necessary if only to keep up with your students.

MOTIVES FOR TEACHING ENGLISH

There are perhaps five main types of individual to be found teaching English from Tarragona to Taipei:

- the serious career teacher
- the student of the prevailing language and culture who teaches in order to fund a longer stay
- the long-term traveller who wants to prolong and fund his or her travels
- the philanthropic or religious person sponsored by an aid organisation, charity or mission society
- the misfit or oddball, perhaps fleeing unhappiness at home.

Experienced English teacher **Deryn Collins** wrote from Spain, identifying just three types of folk who teach abroad:

There are people who want to learn about how others live and take part, those who want to put a year out on their CV and those who leave their homeland because they cannot live with their 'own'. Which means you will on occasion work with a weirdo or maybe you are that weirdo. But mostly the mix of personalities is a marvellous thing. You can find good friends in teachers' rooms – some might even find love!

In many countries, English teaching is the most easily attainable employment, in fact the only available employment for foreigners. Anyone who wants to transcend the status of mere tourist in a country such as Thailand, Bolivia or Japan will probably be attracted to the idea of teaching English. The assumption behind some thinking at the snobbish end of the EFL spectrum is that people who do it for only a year or two as a means to an end (eg learning Chinese, studying Italian art, eating French food) are necessarily inadequate teachers.

There are small pockets of people (mainly in the Far East) whose sole ambition is to earn as much money as possible to pay off student debts or fund further world travels. Seldom are these good teachers, if only because they take on so many hours of teaching that they can't possibly prepare properly for their lessons. But for most teachers, making a lot of money is not a priority or, if it was at the outset, they are soon disillusioned.

Salaries in popular tourist destinations (such as Paris, Barcelona, Chiang Mai) may actually be lower than in less appealing neighbouring towns, even though the cost of living is higher. Pay scales are relatively meaningless out of context. For example, high rents and other expenses usually eat up the high salaries paid in Japan, at least in the first year. When converted into sterling a salary in Romania might sound pitiful but will be perfectly adequate there. In some countries such as Kenya or Argentina, a TEFL salary may not be enough to fund anything beyond a spartan lifestyle, and savings from home are essential to fund any travelling. Yet the majority of people who spend time abroad teaching English are able to afford to live comfortably and have an enjoyable time without feeling pinched, although they end up saving little.

A summary of **Barry O'Leary's** round-the-world history as a TEFL teacher might be inspiring to others considering a new direction:

The last time I counted, I'd taught more than 2,300 students in my eight years as a TEFL teacher. That's a lot of lost-looking faces, funny English accents, and spur of the moment questions that I've had to answer. I'm not saying I'm the most intelligent TEFL teacher – only last week I really grasped the difference between subject and object questions – but I can offer some advice to those willing to learn. After doing a TEFL course in London with St Giles College, I bought a one-way ticket to Australia with a stop-off in South America. I left alone and without any job prospects but I was pumping with adrenaline; my new life living abroad was about to start.

My first job was in Quito, Ecuador, where I got paid $2 an hour for teaching feisty Ecuadorian teenagers. I wasn't interested in the money, teaching was fun and I got a buzz from helping them. It was so much better than the pressurised sales jobs I'd escaped from. After three months teaching in Quito I was hooked. I travelled overland to Salvador (getting robbed in Rio on the way) and was lucky enough to get more work just before the Carnival. I stayed for four months and really fell in love with teaching, and Brazil. My time in Sydney wasn't such an adventure, but I learnt a lot teaching vigorous Chinese students. I saved up enough (the pay was pretty good) for an amazing three-week trip up the east coast, and shot off to Bangkok where I'd lined up a job.

I was met by a strict Catholic nun, my new boss, who pummelled me into shape, or at least she tried, and that's where I first learnt how to teach younger learners. Despite being in Thailand for the Tsunami, which I almost ended up in, my seven months teaching was amazing. I loved teaching tiny, funny kids who were smiling all day. I saved up enough for a six-week overland trip through Laos, Cambodia, Vietnam, China, and then to Moscow on the Trans-Mongolian Railway. I returned to England a new man. I'd travelled the world and had become a teacher, but my thirst for adventure continued. After the summer teaching in London, I headed for Seville, Spain, where I've been ever since. This year I married my Spanish wife who, incidentally, used to be my student (she was 21 and I was 25 before you ask). In my six years here I've really learnt how to teach, thanks to some excellent training and a stiff hand from my boss. I know how to teach now, I get excellent results and my students like my classes, well, the majority of them who can be bothered to learn.

Barry is a blogger and has self-published a book, *Teaching English in a Foreign Land* (www.teachingenglish inaforeignland.blogspot.com.es).

OXFORD TEFL

Barcelona, Prague, London, Cadiz, Malaga and Kerala

4 and 5 week Trinity Cert. TESOL courses

Internationally recognised around the world

Oxford TEFL is one of the most popular and respected providers of accredited TEFL courses in Europe. Over the last 15 years we have built an enviable reputation as a first-class teacher training academy. Our qualified and experienced tutors give optimum support to our trainees in a friendly and professional environment. Our accredited courses are awarded by Trinity College London which means their quality is recognised worldwide and by the British Council.

We can help you find a job and obtain visas and arrange comfortable and low-priced accommodation. Many of our trainees find a job on course completion as a result of our free careers service and go on to fund their travels. Come and join us in one of our centres to take the next step to becoming a TEFL teacher!

'I really enjoyed my course. The four weeks were very intense, but the support and guidance from the teacher trainers was excellent throughout. I'd never taught before so I was quite nervous at first, but the course gave me the knowledge and teaching techniques I needed to build my confidence. I was really happy to be offered a job at the end of my course.' Talia Lash

'The Oxford TEFL course really exceeded my expectations in every way. Although it was intense and stressful at times, the tutors were always supportive and the atmosphere was always great.' Rebecca Stent

'I can't imagine moving abroad to teach English without having the training I received at Oxford TEFL. I feel that I now have the head-start I need to be an effective English teacher from my very first day on the job. The course is challenging and extremely informative. It's worth all of the time, money and effort!' Bryan McPhail

'I have met other teachers who have struggled to find work, as they hold a less credible qualification, but the Trinity Cert TESOL from Oxford TEFL has always impressed potential employers.' Grace Cunnington

Email: tesol@oxfordtefl.com

Skype: tesoloxfordteflbcn

Tel: +34 93 174 0062

RED TAPE

The European Union (EU) consists of the UK, Ireland, the Netherlands, Belgium, Luxembourg, Denmark, Sweden, Finland, Austria, Estonia, Latvia, Lithuania, Poland, Czech Republic, Slovakia, Hungary, Slovenia, Croatia (as of 2013), Malta, Bulgaria, Romania, the Greek populated area of Cyprus, France, Germany, Italy, Greece, Spain and Portugal, the latter six of which have enormous EFL markets. Within the EU, the red tape should be minimal for all nationals of member states who wish to work in any capacity. Outside the EU, legislation varies from country to country. In theory there is also 'free reciprocity of labour' within the European Economic Area. The EEA takes in those Western European countries that have decided to stay outside the Union, viz. Iceland, Liechtenstein, Norway and Switzerland.

All of this means that British and Irish nationals have a significant advantage over Americans, Canadians, Australians, New Zealanders and South Africans when job-hunting in Europe. Although not impossible for other nationalities, it is difficult for them to find an employer willing to undertake the task of proving to the authorities that no EU citizen is available or able to do the job. **Brian Komyathy** from Long Island, New York, was disappointed when he made enquiries about moving to an EU country:

> European walls of regulations do not exactly bespeak, 'Americans welcome aboard'. I'm technically eligible to acquire Irish and hence EU citizenship through my grandparents, so as soon as various documentary records are located and processed I'll not have the problems I do now. A slew of phone calls convinced me of the necessity of taking this course.

Within the landmass of continental Europe, the Schengen Agreement means that there are no border controls among the 26 participating countries. Non-EU citizens who enter Europe are permitted to stay in one or more countries of the Schengen zone for up to 90 days within a six-month period. In the past, long-stay residents of European countries would cross the border to leave the Schengen Area to renew their tourist visa. However, when the regulations changed to limit stays to 90 days in six months, many non-EU semi-residents had to depart. As of May 2014, Schengen visa applications must be registered in advance on the central database Visa Information System (VIS). Applicants will be required to provide their biometric data (fingerprints and a digital photograph) when applying for a Schengen visa. The price of the visa is currently €60. Non-Europeans should be careful not to overstay the 90-day limit on their Schengen visa. If it is picked up on departure, they will be liable for a huge fine. Some potential employers like English language summer camp companies accept North Americans and Antipodeans because the job lasts less than 90 days. A small number of European language schools will accept non-Europeans on an intern basis (ie unpaid or badly paid) for periods of less than 90 days.

Other Americans find ingenious ways to stay legal. In some cases non-Europeans with a student visa are permitted to work up to a certain number of hours, in France, for example and in Germany, where international students on a student visa are permitted to work 240 part-time days a year. International and student exchange organisations may be able to assist. Some US-based organisations cooperate with partner agencies in various countries to place native speaker teachers in schools or institutes, often as volunteers or as live-in tutors. For particulars, see page 91 of the Finding a Job chapter.

The immigration authorities of many countries accord degree-educated English teachers special status, recognising that their own nationals cannot compete as they can for other jobs. Other countries may lack the mechanism for granting work visas to English teachers and so will often turn a blind eye to those who teach on tourist visas, since everyone knows that locals are not being deprived of jobs, rather they're being given an advantage by having the chance to learn English.

Some organisations have developed a study-and-teach solution. While you are learning Russian in Moscow or Spanish in Caracas, you do some English tutoring on the side. Since your status is primarily as a student, it is unnecessary to obtain a full work authorisation. Teachers who find a job before leaving home can usually sort out their visas or at least set the wheels in motion before arrival, which greatly simplifies matters. You can only start the process after finding an employer willing to sponsor your application, preferably one that is familiar with the processes. There is no point applying to the embassy or consulate until you have found an employer. The majority of countries will process visas only when they are applied for from outside the country. So if you have to visit your chosen country on a tourist visa in order to find a job (which is the usual process), you will have to leave the country to apply for the work visa, though often this can be done from a neighbouring country rather than your country of residence. The restrictions and procedures for obtaining the appropriate documentation to teach legally are set out in Part 2 of this book, country by country. A website for lawyers has a handy chart of country-by-country work permit/residency regulations at http://us.practicallaw.com.

STAYING ON THE RIGHT SIDE OF THE LAW
Prospective teachers should contact the relevant consulate for the official line. If you do get tangled up in red tape, always remain patient with consular officials. If things seem to be grinding to a halt, it may be helpful to pester them, provided this is done with unfailing politeness.

REWARDS AND RISKS

The rewards of teaching abroad are mostly self-evident: the chance to become integrated in a foreign culture, the pleasure of making communication possible for your students, the interesting characters and lifestyles you will encounter, a feeling of increased self-reliance, a better perspective on your own culture and your own habits, a base for foreign travel, a good suntan . . . and so on. In Paul Theroux's recent travel book about southern Africa, *The Last Train to Zona Verde*, the venerable grandaddy of travel writers identifies the particular rewards of becoming a teacher, as he did in Angola:

> *Over the following days I became a part-time teacher at the Instituto Superior de Ciencias da Educacao in Lubango. My students were all . . . teachers themselves, improving their skills, many of them intending to return to their own schools, or to use their proficiency in English to study abroad for a further degree – two of them wanted to study law elsewhere. Nothing is more satisfying in travel than to land in a place and assume an occupation, even a temporary one, as a teacher; to cease being a voyeur and have a purpose and a routine, especially one that involved interacting with intelligent students. I had once been a contented teacher in Africa, so I happily slipped into the role and was comforted with a sense of belonging.*

A longer lasting benefit is to your CV: in future job applications and interviews you can highlight how teaching abroad has enhanced your ability to think on your feet and explain things clearly, bolstered your confidence when presenting information to groups, improved your inventiveness and so on (which will all be true).

Yasmin Peiris, away from home for the first time and teaching in China, sums up the highs and lows:

> *Looking back on the last 12 months, some experiences stand out very clearly. Unfortunately, that includes times when you fall ill or feel homesick, or even feel lonely. Homesickness is natural and is a phase that passes very quickly. This is my first time away from home and I feel like the past year has been a massive achievement personally and professionally. It's been great having my own apartment, making friends from all over the world, learning Chinese, and more importantly, realising my own strengths, limits and skills through my time here. The work experience gained and the friendships made will be the most precious souvenir – that I know won't get lost or confiscated by customs. I already knew that I had to come into this experience with an open mind, and I'm glad I did because China surprised me at every turn, constantly giving me something weird or wonderful to write home about.*

Good teachers often find their classes positively fun and place a high value on the relationships they form with their students. Teaching is a lot of fun when it's done right. One-to-one teaching can also be enjoyable since you have a better chance to get to know your students or clients. (By the same token, it can be a miserable experience if you don't get on, since there is no escape from the intimacy of the arrangement.) Off-site teaching provides glimpses into a variety of workplaces and private homes, perhaps even resulting in hospitality and friendship with your students.

As competition for jobs has increased, working conditions have not improved. There is a growing tendency for EFL teachers to be offered non-contract freelance work, with no guarantee of hours, making it necessary for them to work for more than one employer in order to make a living. Job security is a scarce commodity. Part-time freelancers of course miss out on all the benefits of full-time work such as bonuses, holiday pay, help with accommodation in some cases, and so on.

Uninitiated teachers run the risk of finding themselves working for a shark or a cowboy who doesn't care a fig about the quality of teaching or the satisfaction of the teachers, as long as students keep signing up and paying their fees. 'Client satisfaction' is their only criterion of success; business takes complete precedence over education. Exploitation of teachers is not uncommon since the profession is hampered by a lack of both regulation and unionisation.

The job of teaching English is demanding; it demands energy, enthusiasm and imagination, which are not always easy to produce when you are confronted with a room full of stonily silent faces. Instead of the thrill of communication, the drudgery of language drills begins to dominate. Instead of the pleasure of exchanging views with people of a different culture, teachers become weighed down by sheaves of photocopies and visual aids. Like most jobs when done right, teaching English is no piece of cake and is at times discouraging, but invariably it has its golden moments. It offers opportunities for creativity, learning about other cultures and attitudes, making friends and of course travelling. Not a bad job in many ways.

Roberta Wedge writes amusingly on a possible spin-off from a teaching contract abroad:

> *TEFL is one of the most sex-balanced job fields I know (though the Director of Studies is usually a man) and, for those who are interested, the possibilities of finding your one true love appear to be high. 'Thrown together in an isolated Spanish village, eating tapas in the bar, hammering out lesson plans together – we found we have so much in common.' And a year later they were married. (A true story.)*

On a more serious note, teachers should inform themselves about the political situation before offering their EFL services and take stock of their particular sensitivities concerning issues such as political freedom, democracy, human rights, religion and so on. To take a couple of examples, teachers in China have been shocked by the overt racism. For instance a Ghanaian teacher working in a small city not that far from Beijing had to get used to the local people coming up to him to rub his skin to see if the black would come off. In the Central Asian Republics, home to ethnically diverse populations, certain groups are treated shamefully. If you are concerned by these matters, check the Washington-funded Freedom House website at www.freedomhouse.org for updates. Additional insight can be gained from Reporters Sans Frontières (Reporters without Borders) at www.rsf.org. With regard to 'press freedom' their Worldwide Press Freedom Index rates countries according to the freedom of their press; in 2015 Finland and Norway were at the top, Eritrea and North Korea at the bottom of the list. China and Vietnam are both near the bottom.

TRAINING

THE VALUE OF ELT QUALIFICATIONS

Training in teaching English as a foreign language is not absolutely essential for successful job-hunting; but it makes the task easier by an order of magnitude. Anyone with the Cambridge Certificate (CELTA) or the Trinity Certificate in TESOL (both discussed in detail below) is in a much stronger position to get a job in any country where English is widely taught. These certificate courses provide a rigorous introduction to teaching English in just one month full-time (admittedly at considerable expense) or part-time over a period of months, and so anyone interested in spending some time teaching abroad should seriously consider enrolling on a certificate course. There are numerous other kinds of qualifications available, some obtainable after a weekend course and others after years of university study; many are described briefly in the Directory of Training Courses below.

However, the Cambridge and Trinity certificates should not be thought of as a magical passport to work. Increasingly, even certificate-holders are struggling to find a decent job, mainly because so many more people now have the qualification than in the past; more than 10,000 candidates enrol on a CELTA course each year. Many language schools, especially in France and Germany, will not want to hire a novice teacher and are unlikely to be tempted to take on anyone who does not present a dynamic and energetic image. Still, the certificate training continues to give applicants an important edge over the competition.

Increasing your marketability is not the only reason to get some training. The assumption that just because you can speak a language you can teach is simply false. There may be plenty of people who have a natural flair for teaching and who can do an excellent job without the benefit of a certificate or any other ELT qualification. (As mentioned earlier, the term ELT has come to be preferred to TEFL in many contexts.) There are, however, many other people who, when faced with a class full of eager adolescents, would not have a clue where to begin. Doing a TEFL course cannot fail to increase your confidence and provide you with a range of ideas on how to teach and (just as important) how not to teach. Even a short introductory course can usually illustrate methods of making lessons interesting and of introducing the range of teaching materials and approaches available to the novice teacher. What is needed more than theory or academic attainment is an ability to entertain and to dramatise, but not without a framework into which your classroom efforts can be placed.

A perpetual problem that a TEFL course solves is the general level of ignorance of grammar among native speakers. Native-speaker teachers often find that their students, who are much better informed on English grammar than they are, can easily catch them out with questions about verb tenses and subjunctives, causing embarrassment all round. Some training courses can also introduce you to the cultural barriers you can expect to encounter and the specific language-learning difficulties experienced by various nationalities (many of which will be touched on in the country chapters).

Some go so far as to see training almost as a moral obligation. Completely untrained teachers may end up being responsible for teaching people who have paid a great deal of money for expert instruction. This is of special concern in countries that have been inundated with 'tourist-teachers', while the ministries of education may be struggling to create all-graduate teaching professions. If you happen not to be a natural in the classroom, you may well fail to teach anything much to your students, whether they be young children in Hong Kong or businessmen in Portugal.

Not satisfied that a one-week course was enough to qualify him as a teacher, **Ian Abbott** went on to do the Cambridge Certificate at International House in Rome and summarises his view of TEFL training:

I wouldn't recommend teaching English as a foreign language without investing in a course first. You've got to remember that the people coming along to your lessons are desperate to learn your language and it is costing them a small fortune. It is only fair that you know what you are doing and can in the end take that money without guilt, knowing you haven't ripped them off to increase your travel funds.

One of the practical advantages of joining a TEFL course is that many training centres have contacts with recruitment agencies or language schools abroad and can advise on, if not find, a job abroad for you at the end of the course. Training centres differ enormously in how much help they can offer. If the 'after-sales service' is important to you, shop around before choosing which training course to patronise.

Even in countries where it may be commonplace to work without a formal TEFL qualification (for example Cambodia and Japan), teachers who lack a specific grounding in TEFL will often be at a disadvantage. In some cases, the jobs available to the unqualified tend to be at the cowboy end of the market and may therefore offer exploitative conditions. In some countries (such as Turkey) a TEFL certificate is a prerequisite for a work visa, which is yet another justification for doing some formal training before setting off.

RANGE OF COURSES

There is a bewildering array of courses available, at vastly different levels and costs, so it is wise to carry out some careful research before choosing. If you need help funding a training course, you may be eligible for a Professional and Career Development Loan, which is a bank loan where the government covers the interest for the duration of the course and for the first month after the course finishes. After that you have to pay it back in the normal way within five years; further details can be found at www.gov.uk/career-development-loans or by phoning +44 800 100900.

The British Council has administered an English Teaching Graduate Scheme whereby unemployed graduates received grants to cover half the fee of a CELTA or Trinity Certificate course. Unfortunately the scheme is not running in 2016. If it is revived the information will be posted at http://englishagenda.britishcouncil.org/english-teaching-graduate-scheme.

When choosing a course, it is worth asking certain questions that will indicate how useful the qualification will be at the end of it; such as, is there any external validation of the course and how much opportunity is there for teaching practice? Also find out what size of class you will be in (10–12 is much better than 15–20) and what qualifications and experience the tutors have. Cactus TEFL (www.cactustefl.com) is a mine of information about all things TEFL related. It offers a useful advice, orientation and admissions service for prospective TEFL teachers. The online and telephone support offers personal guidance on courses and allows you to apply directly to a wide range of TEFL course providers worldwide.

The Directory of Training Courses in this chapter organises the courses available under various headings: the 120+-hour certificate courses externally validated by the University of Cambridge and Trinity College London, first in the UK and then worldwide, 'Short Introductory Courses', 'Online TEFL Training', 'Academic Courses', which are primarily full academic courses offered at universities (this list is far from comprehensive) and, finally, a selection of courses offered around the world, 'Training Courses in North America' and 'Training Courses Worldwide'.

CERTIFICATE COURSES

The most useful qualification for anyone intending to spend a year or more abroad as an English teacher is a certificate in English language teaching validated by one of the two examination bodies active in the field of ELT: University of Cambridge English Language Assessment and Trinity College London. The Certificate qualification is acquired after an intensive 120–130-hour course offered full-time over one month or part-time over several months. Since 2011 Cambridge, in association with International House London, has been offering a CELTA course online that combines online study with live teaching practice (described below).

Most centres expect applicants to have the equivalent of university entrance qualifications, ie three GCSEs and two A levels, and some require a degree. Admission to the course is at the discretion of the course organiser after a sometimes-lengthy selection process. Places on courses at the well-established centres may be difficult to get at short notice, especially in summer, though the proliferation of training centres means that most are not as oversubscribed as they once were.

Applicants should be able to demonstrate a suitable level of language awareness and convince the interviewer that they have potential to develop as a teacher. Some centres won't consider applicants under the age of 20. Past academic achievement is less important than aptitude; even a PhD does not guarantee acceptance. Most schools will send you a task sheet or grammar research activity as part of the application. Sample questions might be 'How would you convey the idea of regret to a language learner?' or 'Describe the difference in meaning between "I don't really like beetroot" and "I really don't like beetroot"'.

Courses are not cheap but should be viewed as an investment and a potential passport to a worthwhile profession in many different countries. In fact, prices have been coming down over the past couple of years, with many centres trying to survive amid keen competition. The range is about £1000 to £1,400 for a full-time or part-time course with an average of £1,250. Most centres include the validation body's fee, variously called assessment, moderation or examination fee, which in 2015 was £130 (Trinity) or £140 (Cambridge).

Many colleges of further education offer the Trinity or Cambridge certificate part time and these are usually less expensive. Timetables for part-time courses vary, but the norm is to attend classes one or two evenings a week for one or two terms of the academic year plus occasional full days for teaching observation and practice. The further education sector has been hit hard by government cuts in the UK, and a number of FE colleges are no longer offering certificate courses in TEFL, particularly those that used to offer the Trinity CertTESOL course. As one former convenor of a part-time course in a Home Counties college of FE explained in 2015:

> *'It was getting increasingly expensive for learners, and more and more seemed to want an intensive pro-gramme or at least one with fewer hours of classroom learning. I think more demanding work lives and more free time options have also had an impact, as they have on most areas of adult education . . . Many FE colleges are not well set up for intensive TESOL programmes (no classroom space available wholly just for 5 weeks; few students available for micro-teaches from June–early October in many cases) . . . So unfortunately we no longer offer the course.'*

Some institutes of higher education, such as Anglia Ruskin University in Cambridge and the University of Hull, no longer offer a certificate course to all comers but embed the course into university modules on for example a BA course in English Language Teaching.

Once accepted onto a certificate course, you will usually be given a pre-course task to familiarise yourself with some key concepts and issues before the course begins. Full-time courses are very intensive and 100% attendance is expected, so you need to be in a position to dedicate yourself completely to the task in hand for four weeks. The standard of teaching is high, the course rigorous and demanding and the emphasis is on the practice of any theory taught. One of the requirements is that participants teach a minimum of six hours of observed lessons to authentic English language students.

Trinity's CertTESOL and the Cambridge CELTA are accredited by the Office of Qualifications and Examinations Regulation (Ofqual), the national body for the regulation of vocational qualifications outside the higher education sector. On the Qualifications and Credit Framework for England, both certificate courses have been accredited as a Level 5 qualification, which is considered equivalent in difficulty to the second year of an undergraduate degree course. CELTA and Trinity CertTESOL graduates may receive credits towards degree programmes at the discretion of the institution. The British Council has adopted the terminology 'TEFL-1 qualified teachers', which means they have a CELTA/CertTESOL or equivalent, and TEFL-Q which means they have a BEd, PGCE with Qualified Teacher Status or a DELTA.

INTERNATIONAL HOUSE BARCELONA

'I studied English for many years and had finally achieved a very advanced level, so I decided to do something with my English: teaching was the obvious job for me. I was offered a job in a small school where I'm from in the north of Spain even though I had no training as a teacher, but the school was awful: the owner was unprofessional and seemed uninterested in the students and I had the impression she was just in it for the money.

'However, I did my best but after eight months I realised I needed training and support if I was ever going to be a professional teacher.

'An English friend told me about the Cambridge CELTA and told me that International House Barcelona was the best, most professional and prestigious place to take the course so I applied and was accepted.

'I am now halfway through the course and am extremely happy that I was accepted. The tutors are amazing; right from the first day we all felt we were members of a special, very supportive group. There is no competition, we all help each other and we all feel we are learning an incredible amount and getting really supportive, constructive feedback on our work in the teaching practice classes when we teach real students who are here to learn English. The way the tutors teach us was a real eye-opener right from the start when we had an Arabic lesson – no English was used in the class and by the end of the lesson we were acting out role plays in Arabic confidently. The tutors don't lecture, they practise what they preach and their input sessions are fun as well as being very informative. The tutors put us in the students' shoes and the focus is very much on learning outcomes and how the teacher can help the students achieve these.

'When I finish the course I want to take the CELTYL extension course at IH Barcelona so that I feel confident teaching children as well as adults and then I'm going back to my hometown to open a small English language school of my own. My school will be nothing like the school I mentioned above. I will put into practice all that I've learned at International House Barcelona and I hope my students will soon be speaking fluent English.'

Karla

CAMBRIDGE CELTA

Cambridge CELTA (Certificate in English Language Teaching to Adults) has established itself as a key passport to teaching opportunities overseas. It has a solid reputation in the international teaching community and high levels of recognition among employers around the world. CELTA is administered and regulated by

Cambridge English (1 Hills Road, Cambridge CB1 2EU; +44 1223 553997; www.cambridgeenglish.org) and is sometimes referred to simply as the Cambridge Certificate. Many believe that CELTA is the most reliable route to jobs with better rates of pay and with employers who are willing to give more support to novice teachers.

You don't have to stay in the UK to take CELTA. Administered and regulated by the assessment wing of the University of Cambridge, CELTA courses are offered at 46 centres in 61 countries. For example, the British Council runs courses in Milan, Naples, Kuwait, Kiev, Dhaka, Casablanca and many others; CELTA courses are offered by 24 centres in Australia and New Zealand and steadily climbing in North America so that there are now 25 CELTA course providers in the USA and eight in Canada. A full list is available at the Cambridge English website: www.cambridgeenglish.org/find-a-centre/find-a-teaching-centre. International House Worldwide is one of the key providers, accounting for more than half of all CELTA courses taken.

The CELTA Online blends self-study with teaching practice. The course has been produced in partnership with International House, London and leads to the same internationally recognised certificate as the face-to-face CELTA course. Candidates still have to do at least six hours of observed teaching practice in person, and the course will be carried out over at least 10 weeks. Note that it is no cheaper than the original; in fact there is often an extra charge of about £80 for course materials. Currently, 70 CELTA centres offer the CELTA Online, including 25 in the UK, five in Italy, three in Canada and four in Australia.

Securing a place on a CELTA course isn't automatic. Course providers are selective in order to ensure standards are kept high – and as a result, the pass rate is usually at least 90%. Grades available are Pass, Pass 'B' and Pass 'A', giving candidates the chance to distinguish themselves. CELTA provides a foundation of theory but focuses on effective teaching skills and practical tools for teaching English to adult learners. You'll gain hands-on teaching practice and the experience and support to build confidence in the classroom.

Many teachers believe that a CELTA plus some teaching experience is the perfect recipe for securing a good teaching job, as **Doug Burgess** wrote while teaching in Chile:

If you are interested in job security and acquiring a work visa, it is highly advisable that you complete the CELTA and try to get some experience as it will give you flexibility and options when you are here so that you can have the most comfortable and enjoyable time possible.

Some people have voiced surprise that a course which qualifies people to teach only adults is still so dominant, when much of the demand for English comes from young learners. Cambridge English also offers an extension to the CELTA course for people who want to teach young learners, called the YL extension; however this is to be discontinued from December 2016.

SAXONCOURT TEACHER TRAINING

Why CELTA?

CELTA is an internationally recognised ELT qualification. It is accredited by Cambridge University's ESOL department and is sought by reputable schools worldwide as the benchmark entry-level certificate for new teachers.

Why Saxoncourt?

Saxoncourt is a well-established CELTA centre with over 15 years' experience of delivering high-quality training in a variety of formats. We run four-week full-time intensive courses and part-time courses over 12 weeks enabling trainees to develop new skills and opportunities while still holding down their current jobs. We have a dedicated team of highly experienced and qualified tutors who work hard to ensure that trainees get the best possible introduction to the challenges and rewards of EFL teaching.

What's the course like?

In a word 'intense' – but also incredibly rewarding. The learning curve is steep and the demands it places on trainees in terms of time and energy are high, but the benefits usually come pretty quickly too: you learn about teaching – the course's main focus is methodology; you learn about the English language – there's no surer way to learn than to teach; you learn about other cultures – you'll be teaching students from all over the world; you learn about yourself – if you've never taught before, the course gives you plenty of real and practical experience, and most people find their confidence improves as they find they *can* do it.

What does it involve?

Trainees must complete six hours of assessed teaching, write four assignments and plan lessons. They also have at least 60 hours of input where they learn the key elements of effective and successful English teaching.

What do I get out of it?

Passing the course means you are CELTA qualified. This means, quite literally, that a world of opportunities opens up. You will be equipped to start a career enabling you to travel, meet new people and make a real contribution to their lives – what are you waiting for?

TRINITY COLLEGE LONDON

The other principal initial Certificate in TESOL is awarded by Trinity College London (89 Albert Embankment, London SE1 7TP; +44 20 7820 6100; tesol@trinitycollege.co.uk; www.trinitycollege.co.uk). The Trinity Certificate (CertTESOL) has international recognition, is highly regarded by employers in the UK and around the world and is considered to have equal academic standing to CELTA. Currently there are about 100 centres worldwide offering CertTESOL training full or part-time. Nearly a third are outside the UK, with eight centres in Spain, two in New Zealand and centres in other countries such as Canada, Hong Kong, Czech Republic, Ireland, Italy, Malta, Japan, Argentina and Uruguay.

Trinity stipulates a minimum of 130 hours offered intensively over a minimum of four and often five weeks or part time over a longer period. All intensive courses must have a pre-course learning component in addition to the minimum hours. The course content includes grammar and phonology, a range of teaching approaches and methodologies, classroom management and motivation, hands-on experience of teaching aids (from blackboards to computers), introduction to the learning of an unknown language (in which trainees receive four hours' instruction and lesson planning). In addition, they must complete a minimum of six hours of observed and assessed teaching practice and spend at least four further hours observing experienced teachers of English.

The CertTESOL is accepted by the British Council as an appropriate initial TESOL qualification in its accredited English language teaching organisations in the UK and its own teaching centres overseas. In fact, British Council offices in Recife and Sao Paulo in Brazil and Valencia in Spain offer the course. All courses meet the core Trinity requirements but there are variations in course delivery across the different providers to reflect different in-house practices and philosophy. Trinity seeks to ensure that its qualifications are in line with those of other comparable awarding bodies – principally Cambridge English.

A graduate of the Trinity Certificate course remembers her experience:

I got good grades for my four A levels and wanted to take a year out abroad. I did some research on the net – found out a bit about teaching English ('TESOL') – but realised that a weekend course wouldn't be cheap, or actually give me the qualification for a decent job. I looked into online teacher training – but I really wanted the experience of meeting other would-be teachers and experienced trainers. I therefore chose a five-week intensive Trinity CertTESOL course – I could have done it part-time, but I was in a hurry! I was warned about how very intensive it would be – how I should tell my friends that I'd be really busy for five weeks – and sure enough when I was accepted for the course I had to start reading straightaway for some written tasks to complete beforehand.

The course itself was an extraordinary experience. I started (and finished!) by feeling very enthusiastic and energetic. There were written assignments ('journals') to prepare over the four weeks and I was corrected on my grammar, punctuation and spelling, which was a surprise at first. I had to plan my time carefully – what I would do in the evenings and at the weekend, how much I could read. The most demanding but exciting part was the teaching practice with real students from different nationalities. It had never occurred to me I would feel so nervous. The first time I stood up in front of them I realised they expected to learn something from me, and I kept forgetting that there was no point in explaining difficult words or ideas in English – I had to learn very specific techniques to teach my own language. Overall . . . my own communication skills improved enormously, my students were very kind and I learnt to respect their feelings, the other trainees were (all bar one) very supportive, I learnt to manage a heavy workload in and out of school, and finally I feel I developed as a teacher and as a person – all in five weeks!

CHOOSING A COURSE

It is up to prospective trainees to weigh up the pros and cons of the courses available to them and to establish how rigorously each course under consideration is monitored. One reservation that a few employers abroad have expressed is that the proliferation of providers of certificate courses, whether on behalf of Cambridge, Trinity or independents, has made it more difficult to maintain a uniform standard, especially since so much of the assessment of candidates is subjective. The general decline in standards of literacy in Britain and North America has also prompted some to complain of a decline in quality of TEFL training.

When it comes to workload, trainees in both CELTA and Trinity TESOL courses complain of a punishing schedule. But most come away claiming that the course elements are superb. At the time, participants sometimes feel as though they are drowning in information, but realise that the course has to pack a great deal of material into four brief weeks. When trying to identify differences between them, one view is that the CELTA concentrates more on the structure of language and classroom management, and Trinity on the use of authentic materials and practical teaching techniques. The majority who go on to teach abroad are very grateful for the training it gave them, as in the case of **Andrew Sykes**, teaching in Bordeaux:

As for the certificate course that I did in Leeds it was certainly one of the most stimulating, challenging and interesting things I have ever studied for. Initially I felt a bit out of place – I had a background of science A levels, a maths degree and two years as a (failed) accountant. The course was professionally run and there were good teacher-student relations. Most people had never taught anybody anything before in their life, but we were gradually eased into teaching by the supportive teaching staff who were refreshingly (and diplomatically) critical when required to be. A criticism which some students had was that there wasn't enough feedback about what was expected to gain a pass, let alone achieve an A or B. The best recommendation for the course is perhaps that I would never have felt comfortable teaching without it.

So even if your social life disappears for a month and all you can talk about at weekends is phrasal verbs and English idioms, the consensus is that it is worthwhile.

Many certificate courses are offered by independent companies outside the Cambridge and Trinity folds and these are more difficult to assess. For many, one of the key factors will be cost. Generic certificate courses are available in dozens of countries and the cheapest ones are offered in the cheapest countries. **James Clarke** and his girlfriend Sally were looking for a course for under $1,000 inclusive in South America and ended up at one in Peru, which has since gone out of business, though that did not prevent them from thinking it gave them a good grounding:

We took (and both passed) a TEFL training course in Trujillo, Peru that cost $900 for four weeks including a homestay and all food – much cheaper than anywhere in Buenos Aires where we had been before. It was a very good experience, with only one other student on the course, unlike a rival course we observed in Cusco, Peru, where there were maybe 14 students. Every day of the first week we observed four hours of classes (with participation) as well as four hours of theory from 9am to 1pm. In the second week, the observation turned into actual teaching of the classes with the same theory lessons. The third week involved observation of a higher standard of classes and then the fourth week was teaching, but four hours per day instead of two hours in the second week. We taught grammar, conversation and pronunciation, all using games, activities, dynamics and motivational techniques using music. There was one drawback that we suspect was down to the price of the course – we did not receive any original textbooks, just photocopied pages from textbooks.

Possible advantages of doing a TEFL training course abroad are that you may already be teaching or living in that country and want to upgrade your qualifications locally; the course and cost of living may be cheaper than in your home country; and successful course participants will almost certainly be put in touch with local employers, making it much easier to land a job in that place.

Jonathan Davies, who runs a well-regarded TEFL training course in Toulouse, comments on the difficulties of choosing the right course, especially when the big international chains dominate the google rankings:

If you do some googling for TEFL courses, you will often find a course in an attractive French location offered. But when you click on it suddenly you are back to a home page and being offered a discount on a course on the other side of the world. Or you find that the course is not externally accredited, online, only over a weekend ... Suddenly the TEFL course and your new life in France is just being sold as a working holiday for young American backpackers. 'We are not running our Bordeaux course – how about Thailand?'

Teaching practice is key. Busy colleges such as Ealing, Hammersmith and West London College offer an insight into the diversity of ELT work because they teach such a wide range of students, to whom their CELTA trainees are exposed during teaching practice sessions.

OTHER RECOGNISED QUALIFICATIONS

In 2005, Cambridge English introduced the Teaching Knowledge Test (TKT), a new accessible test about teaching English to speakers of other languages, delivered to international standards. The test, which can be taken by both practising and aspiring teachers, involves three modules that cover the background to language learning and teaching, planning lessons/using resources and managing the teaching and learning process. Hundreds of TEFL training centres worldwide are offering short courses to candidates who want to prepare for TKT, which is more accessible than CELTA and does not include teaching practice as part of the assessment. A final module of interest to current teachers with no formal qualifications is called TKT Practical and requires no course work but an assessment of practical teaching abilities. Note that this option will be discontinued from December 2016. Further information is available at www.cambridgeenglish.org/TKT.

Beyond CELTA is the Diploma. Whereas CELTA is considered an initial qualification, the Diploma (as distinct from any old diploma with a lower case) is an in-service modularised course for experienced English language teachers. The Cambridge Diploma in English Language Teaching to Adults (DELTA) and the Trinity Diploma (Dip TESOL) are high-level qualifications usually open to graduates who have at least two years of recent ELT classroom experience. The Diploma course is available intensively over a minimum of eight weeks but more usually part-time over several months or a year. A Distance DELTA option supported by International House (IH) and the British Council is increasingly popular (www.thedistancedelta.com) because it can be combined with full-time teaching work. The fees – currently £2,950 plus £321 in assessment fees – are sometimes subsidised by employers. Of the three modules, you can do the second one face-to-face at International House in London intensively over six weeks or less intensively over 16 weeks. This is known as the Blended DELTA.

TEACHING HOUSE NEW YORK

The Blended Delta Program by Erica Lederman

'After two years of teaching English as a second language to adults, both in my home country of the United States and in Russia, I became stuck in a rut. Lessons were overly predictable and my knowledge of language ceased to expand. In 2010 I began working for International House/Teaching House New York, which coincidentally was beginning to offer the Blended Delta programme that same year. It was the perfect opportunity for me to pull myself out of that rut and learn more about language, methodology and curriculum design.

'The Blended Delta is composed of three separate components: a written exam, a face-to-face course and a written thesis. Although it is possible to do these components in any order, it's highly recommended that candidates complete the modules separately and in sequence so that they can get the full benefit and devote the time necessary to each task. The Blended Delta programme at Teaching House treats the first and third modules as distance courses and the second module as an on-site, intensive course. This allows a lot of flexibility for candidates, who can participate from all over the world.

'Although thoroughly challenging and, at times, extremely stressful, the Delta was an invaluable experience. After completing the programme I have a better understanding of the teacher's role in the classroom and the beliefs that underlie every word and action spoken during a class. I am also more confident experimenting with different methodologies and techniques, as I am able to evaluate them critically and predict how they might work with my group of learners.

'Furthermore, the Delta has opened up other avenues in ELT besides classroom teaching, such as publishing materials and teacher training. For anyone who wants to pursue a long-term career in the ELT industry, the Delta is a worthwhile investment.'

Universities (especially the former polytechnics) from Brighton to Belfast offer their own certificate or diploma in TEFL. Most are one-year or two-year courses, full or part-time, and tend to be more theoretical than Cambridge and Trinity courses. It is important to do some research before committing yourself to a course so that you are sure that the qualification you obtain will be recognised by employers both in the UK and overseas. Once again find out if there is some form of external assessment and whether the course includes a reasonable amount of teaching practice.

Stephen Curry felt let down by the course he chose:

> I called my local university to see what courses were available and was advised that they could provide a course consisting of two modules, one from the PGCE and one from the MEd programme, which would be equivalent in status to a one-month certificate and would be 'recognised'. The course of study took from May to February to complete. It was a lot of hard work, research based and absolutely no fun whatsoever. I did the course on the understanding that it would lead to a stand-alone TEFL certificate. I have since tried to get the university to confirm in writing that this module carries the recognition they claimed it would but they now say that they cannot do this. Unfortunately it was not until the latter stages of the course that I (and others) began to see that the eventual outcome would be a qualification that was unlikely to be recognised in the eyes of anyone outside the university, let alone as being equivalent to the Cambridge/Trinity certificate.

A number of undergraduate institutions such as Central Lancashire, Nottingham Trent and Portsmouth offer TESOL as part of an undergraduate course; the UCAS directory lists all university courses in the UK and can be consulted online at www.ucas.com, or in any careers or general library. MA courses in ELT and Applied Linguistics are offered at dozens of universities and colleges. Some offer a master's by distance learning aimed at practising ELT teachers worldwide. Arguably, there is a world oversupply of MAs; however, an MA is a prerequisite for many posts in some countries, especially in the Middle East.

Anyone who wishes to specialise in the highly marketable field of Business English should enquire about specialist courses such as the First Certificate for Teachers of Business English (FTBE) validated by the London Chamber of Commerce & Industry or LCCI (www.lcci.org.uk/teaching-qualifications.asp) or the 50-hour blended Cert IBET (International Business English Training) validated by English UK and Trinity college. Yet another possibility is to undertake the course online for example with the Consultants-E Ltd (www.theconsultants-e.com) which charges £695 for 70 hours over 10 weeks.

TEFL ORG UK

Katrin Winter had always wanted to see the world, travel and experience different cultures and ways of life. Now in her mid-twenties she has decided to take the plunge and finally take a gap year. She enrolled on the 140-hour Premier TEFL Course in July.

'The instructor miraculously managed to make the English grammar sound like the most interesting thing in the world. He was an experienced teacher himself and shared a lot of his knowledge with us. When the course was over, I soon received my certificate in the post. I used TEFL Org UK's website to look for jobs as I was looking to go to China. I found a job within three days of finishing the course and I am now in Xi'an.'

Despite vast cultural differences, which she admits sometimes can be a struggle, she said:

'I meet wonderful people every day, in and outside of the school; there is so much culture and so many experiences to be had here. I won't even try and start describing the wonderful food I've had! I work at a language school, so my working day usually starts at 2pm and lasts until 8.30pm. My weekend is Wednesday and Thursday, which is actually quite nice as most people will be at work and the city less hectic. The students at school are very motivated to learn and respect their teachers a lot. Older students are also keen to find out about where I am from, and more about my culture and traditions. We often have discussions on local affairs.

'It's been a very rewarding experience so far. I have had some maddening days when people can't understand me due to the language barrier and I miss home comforts and familiar faces, but those days are offset by so many more wonderful days full of learning new things and experiencing a whole different way of living.'

INTRODUCTORY COURSES

Although the Cambridge and Trinity certificates are sometimes referred to as 'introductory courses', cheaper, shorter and less rigorous introductions to the subject are available. With the dramatic rise in the popularity of certificate courses there has been a decline in what might be considered as more amateurish courses, though these do have a role to play, for example for school leavers who would not be accepted onto a certificate course or for the curious who do not want to commit themselves to a month-long course or pay £1,000+ until they have had some preliminary exposure to the field.

Because there are some commercial enterprises and 'cowboy' operators cashing in on the EFL boom, standards vary and course literature should be studied carefully before choosing. Most people who have done a TEFL training course claim that the most worthwhile part is the actual teaching practice, preferably to living, breathing foreigners rather than 'peer-teaching' in mock lessons to fellow participants. The fact is that most short introductory courses do not allow for much chance to do teaching practice. On the other hand they can provide lesson ideas and some hand out useful manuals full of lesson plans.

The more upmarket introductory courses often present themselves as an opportunity to sample the field to see whether you want to go on to do a certificate course at a later stage. Others make their course sound as if it alone will be sufficient to open doors worldwide. Some in the industry consider weekend courses to be money-spinning machines and their claims to dispense 'internationally recognised' certificates to be highly contentious. It would be unreasonable to expect a weekend or five-day course to equip anyone to teach, but most participants do find them helpful. After seeing an advertisement in the New York subway advertising for English teachers, **Roger Blake** was prompted to seek out some training. Back in England, Roger, who admits to being a not particularly academic type, enjoyed the 'crash' weekend training he did with i-to-i so much that he enrolled in a home-study module of a further 20 hours. Later, when he was asking about local teaching possibilities in Addis Ababa, he felt more confident being able to show two course certificates.

The majority of residential courses last a weekend or for four to five days and cost between £250 and £500, not counting accommodation. Almost all will issue some kind of certificate that can sometimes be used to impress prospective employers. Anyone who wants a job after doing a short course should aim to do it in the spring when the majority of jobs are advertised for the following academic year. Many people who complete an introductory or 'taster' course go on to do an intensive certificate, often at the same centre.

A number of private language centres offer their own short courses in TEFL, which may focus on their own method, developed specifically with the chain of schools in mind (for example Berlitz) or may offer a more general introduction. You may come across schools looking for teachers to teach the Callan Method. But many people in the industry are sceptical (to put it mildly) about its efficacy, including an American teacher who worked at a participating school in Poland, a country where the Callan Method is popular:

> *The Callan Method is little more than a fraud. The material is so pedagogically and linguistically outdated that no well-informed student would ever use it. Further, the book is excessively morbid. I couldn't, in good faith, teach the Callan Method again.*

A number of accrediting bodies and monitoring organisations exists, but competition between them does not make the task much easier. It is strongly recommended that you ensure that an independent body accredits the course for which you are applying.

As a part of the general move within the profession to monitor standards and offer assurances of quality, the College of Teachers (www.collegeofteachers.ac.uk) is an important awarding body. It has a Royal Charter, is based within the Institute of Education in London and is a registered charity.

The International Accreditation of TESOL Qualifying Organisations (IATQuO) is another monitoring organisation, which has been run by an individual in Bristol since 2005 and has validated a handful of TESOL certificate courses in Europe; details from IATQuO in Bristol (ADMoller@aol.com; www.iatquo.org).

ONLINE AND DISTANCE LEARNING

The rise of the internet and increased use of electronic communications has made online TEFL training courses far more popular than the old distance learning and correspondence courses. Providers of face-to-face courses are suffering from the competition from cheap online courses, and some are cancelling courses due to low take-up rates. Not only is an online course much cheaper but it can also be done in the candidate's own time and/or in any part of the world.

Typically, online courses at the professional end of the spectrum involve at least 150 hours of tutor-led home study, as required for Level 5 of the Qualifications and Credit Framework. Some 'hybrid' or 'blended' courses including the CELTA Online offer distance learning in combination with a residential element. A new entrant to the profession is faced with a bewildering array of distance courses to choose from but does not always possess the knowledge or experience to judge between them.

Among accrediting bodies, which mostly operate as commercial enterprises, some specialise in online courses, for example Accreditat in Edinburgh (www.accreditat.com), which accredits TEFL/TESOL providers for both face-to-face and distance/online courses.

ACTDEC, the Accreditation Council for TESOL Distance Education Courses, was established in 1993 to improve on standards of distance TESOL/TEFL programmes. A copy of the ACTDEC code of practice and other details, including a list of accredited members, can be viewed online at www.ACTDEC.org.uk. It is not always easy to ascertain the levels of quality control. Newer accrediting bodies have yet to prove their rigour, such as OTTSA (Online TESOL and TEFL Standards Agency; www.ottsa.org) and ALAP (Awarding Language Acquisition for Professionals; www.alapuk.org).

A NOTE ABOUT ACCREDITATION
Distance training varies enormously in quality. Some companies are successful primarily because of their advertising campaigns and skill with social media but offer very mediocre courses. Others offer good quality courses and receive excellent feedback on course work. Careful research is needed before choosing where to spend your money on an online course. Obviously a 100-hour online certificate that can be bought through groupon for $40 is going to be of limited value.

People considering the distance learning route to TEFL training should be cautious. Some of the promotional literature does not inspire confidence: I spotted some egregious errors recently which stated that their course 'is designed to suit you're learning speed' and another offering, a 'life-long career gaurantee.' The most obvious disadvantage is the lack of face-to-face teaching practice, though some courses are more interactive, providing opportunities for blocks of teaching practice plus plenty of tutor feedback. Be aware that some employers, including ones whose details are included later in this book, specify that they will not consider applications from people with online certificates. For example Dave Fox, Director of Lexis TESOL Training Centres in Queensland, Australia, explained the situation in a recent interview: 'These days I come across lots of people looking for work who have "qualifications" from weekend-long TEFL courses or online courses with no practical element and I can't offer them anything. It's really important that you make sure your TEFL/TESOL certificate meets the criteria for work in your country of choice.' **Annabelle Laker** got in touch from Vietnam to report that the 120-hour TEFL course she had done in England before leaving did not really count for much, but fortunately she had also undertaken a 20-hour practical weekend TEFL course and had also worked as a teaching assistant in a school in England, which was experience valued more highly by her prospective employers.

A new development for distance students of TESOL is that they may be able to get actual teaching practice online or via Skype. If you are not satisfied with the course but have paid your money (typically £400+ for a certificate course), you have little recourse, though some such as the English Training Centre (www.englishtc.co.uk) offer a 21-day full refund to dissatisfied candidates. One way of ascertaining the worth of a distance learning course you may be considering is to ask to be put in touch with past students.

Details of introductory, online and distance training courses both in Britain and abroad are provided in the Directory of Training Courses that follows.

TRAINING IN THE USA

Until 10 or 15 years ago, there were virtually no short intensive courses in TEFL available in North America. That has now changed. In addition to the 25 Cambridge CELTA providers in the USA (an increase of eight from two years ago), a number of independent TEFL training organisations offer four-week intensive courses (see Directory of Training Courses below). The major providers like Transworld are well connected with language schools abroad, particularly in Latin America and the Far East. Competition is keen among the schools, and prices remain fairly consistent at about $2,300–$2,800 for a four-week course, with the odd course available for around $2,000.

The American Language Institute in San Diego has been praised by its graduates, such as **Bryson Patterson** writing from Costa Rica:

> *The ALI TEFL course is a solid teacher training programme encompassing methodology, live classroom practice, grammar and job placement. A day would begin with four hours of methodology (the theory and practice of second language acquisition). Trainees are then instructed in the ins and outs of lesson planning, and annual planning. Mock classes are video taped, helping students to evaluate their own performance. Afternoons are spent working as assistants for mentor teachers in live EFL classrooms and rotating through all the levels of EFL classes at the ALI.*

If one of your main criteria is the after-course job advice, make sure you investigate properly. **Melanie Twinning** felt let down by the choice she made:

> *Despite being at least $1,000 more expensive than the competition, the course I chose really didn't do everything it promised. It has really no job placement to speak of and the man in charge of job placement is actually rather mean. Luckily I had your book and a bit of confidence and was able to find positions on my own but if you're paying $3,000 for a TEFL course I think you should get what it promises. I have to say the course itself was incredibly well done and the director is phenomenal. They just won't help you at all unless you are going to Korea.*

It is easier to get practical experience of teaching English (without a qualification) by joining one of the many voluntary ESL programmes found in almost every American city, run by community colleges, civic organisations and literacy groups. For a first hand account see the chapter on North America at the end of this book. The membership organisation ProLiteracy Worldwide (www.proliteracy.org) operates in most states and offers volunteer tutors training workshops and access to specialist ESL materials that it publishes.

Note that the Peace Corps is developing a 120-hour TEFL training programme which it is piloting in Armenia and elsewhere in 2015. Davinna Artibey from Oregon is serving as a TEFL teacher and trainer in Nicaragua until November 2017, and was concerned that such a new qualification would not be widely recognised after she leaves the Corps. Its goals are different from those of commercial language schools, in encouraging cooperation with local teachers and engagement with the community, and focusing less on classroom management, as the CELTA does, for example.

DIRECTORY OF TRAINING COURSES

CAMBRIDGE CERTIFICATE (CELTA) IN THE UK

The following is a reasonably comprehensive (though not exhaustive) list of CELTA courses offered in the UK. In addition, various universities including Bath, Bristol, Nottingham Trent and Sunderland, plus many colleges of further education and adult education centres in London and around the country, plus some English language institutes offer occasional full-time or part-time CELTA courses. All are linked from www.cambridgeenglish.org/find-a-centre/find-a-teaching-centre.

ACTION ENGLISH LANGUAGE TRAINING LTD: Leeds; ✆ +44 113 244 9403; www.aelt.co.uk; full-time and online; rough frequency 12 per year. £1,250.

ACTION ENGLISH, LEEDS

'A year after graduating from university and following several months of deliberation, I finally decided to enrol on a CELTA course. For me, choosing where to do the course was a fairly easy decision. I had studied in Leeds for three years and knew of people who had finished university and gone on to complete a CELTA at a small, friendly and well-located school called Action English. I had only heard excellent things and after contacting them and organising an interview, I knew that it would be the ideal place to take the course. I must say, there were certainly no surprises!

'The course offered an excellent mixture of theory and practice, with mornings focusing on grammar and teaching skills, and afternoons set aside for teaching practice. I was thrown into teaching on day three and although nervous, I still felt that I was well prepared, despite the fact that I had not taught a lesson in my life! I would say that this was almost entirely due to the wonderful staff (and students) at Action English. The course is renowned for its intensity, and although this was apparent from the start, the warm and friendly staff ensured that I had as pleasant (a word not associated with the course too often) a journey as possible. They were always willing to go the extra mile! Their support was fantastic and this was a feeling that was shared by all on the course. How could I have survived without the many cups of tea? Oh, and let's not forget "Cake Fridays"! The atmosphere created was perfect and at the times when stress levels were rising, there was somebody on hand to help you through.

'Since completing the course, I have taken part in some volunteering at Action English and have found a job in China. I cannot recommend the school enough; the help I received whilst on the course, and the help I have received since finishing, has given me the perfect grounding needed to ensure that I will succeed in achieving my goal of forging a successful career as an EFL teacher.'

Joe D

ANGLO-CONTINENTAL TEACHER TRAINING CENTRE: Bournemouth; ℂ +44 1202 557414; www.anglo-continental.com; full and part-time; rough frequency 6 per year. £1,296.

BASIL PATERSON COLLEGE: Edinburgh; ℂ +44 131 225 3802; www.basilpaterson.co.uk; full-time; rough frequency 8 per year. £1,195.

BELFAST METROPOLITAN COLLEGE: Belfast; ℂ +44 28 9026 5142; www.belfastmet.ac.uk; part-time; rough frequency 2 per year. £1,450.

BELL LANGUAGE SCHOOL: Cambridge; ℂ +44 1223 275598; www.bellenglish.com/teachers; 5 full-time; from £1,395.

BELL LONDON: London WCI; ✆ +44 207 440 6770; www.bellenglish.com/London.Twice a year. From £1,395.

BLACKBURN COLLEGE: Blackburn; ✆ +44 1254 292500; www.blackburn.ac.uk; part-time. £1,100.

BOLTON COLLEGE: Bolton; ✆ +44 1204 907333; www.boltoncollege.ac.uk; part-time.

BRASSHOUSE CENTRE: Birmingham; ✆ +44 121 303 0114; www.brasshouse.birmingham.gov.uk/; part and full-time; rough frequency 3 per year. £1,200.

BRITISH STUDY CENTRES: Oxford; ✆ +44 1865 263200; www.british-study.com/teacher-training/ centres/oxford; full-time; rough frequency 12 per year. £1,245.

BROMLEY COLLEGE OF FURTHER & HIGHER EDUCATION: Bromley; ✆ +44 20 8295 7000, ext 7127; www.bromley.ac.uk; part-time.

BROOKLANDS COLLEGE: Weybridge, Surrey; ✆ +44 1932 797774; www.brooklands.ac.uk; part-time; rough frequency 4 per year. £1,175.

CANTERBURY CHRIST CHURCH UNIVERSITY: Canterbury; ✆ +44 1227 767700, ext 2129; www.canterbury.ac.uk; full and part-time January to May; rough frequency 1 per year; £1,280.

CARDIFF & VALE COLLEGE: Cardiff; ✆ +44 2920 250400; www.cavc.ac.uk/celta; 1 full-time in summer, 2 part-time per year; £1,500.

CITY OF BATH COLLEGE: Bath; ✆ +44 1225 312191; www.bathcollege.ac.uk; part-time; £1,496.

CITY OF BRISTOL COLLEGE: Bristol; ✆ +44 117 312 5886; www.cityofbristol.ac.uk; part-time over 8 or 10 weeks, or 18 weeks if online. £1,495.

CITY OF OXFORD COLLEGE: Oxford; ✆ +44 1865 550550; www.cityofoxford.ac.uk. Full-time in July. £1,288.

CONCORDE INTERNATIONAL STUDY CENTRE: Canterbury; ✆ +44 1227 451035; www.concorde-int.com; full-time, 5 per year. £1,163.

EALING, HAMMERSMITH & WEST LONDON COLLEGE: London; ✆ +44 207 565 1283; www.wlc.ac.uk; full-time 7 times a year and part-time. £1,150.

EMBASSY CES NEWNHAM: Cambridge; ✆ +44 1223 345650; www.embassyenglish-com/celta; full-time; roughly 3 per year. £1,450.

ENGLISH LANGUAGE HOUSE: Milton Keynes; ✆ +44 1908 694357; www.englishlanguagehouse.co.uk; full and part-time; rough frequency 4 per year. £1,350.

GLASGOW CLYDE COLLEGE: Glasgow; ✆ +44 141 272 3638; www. glasgowclyde.ac.uk; 1 full-time in June, 1 part-time October-February. £1,150.

GLOUCESTERSHIRE COLLEGE: Cheltenham; ✆ +44 1242 532144; www.gloscol.ac.uk; full and part-time; rough frequency 4 per year.

GREENWICH COMMUNITY COLLEGE: London; ✆ +44 20 8316 6610; www.gcc.ac.uk; part-time only with various start dates. £1,250.

ILS ENGLISH: Nottingham; ✆ +44 115 969 2424; www.ilsenglish.com; full-time in June, August, September, and October. £1,200 including moderation fee.

INTERNATIONAL HOUSE BELFAST: ✆ +44 28 9033 0700; www.ihbelfast.com. £1,230.

INTERNATIONAL HOUSE BRISTDL: tt@ihbristol.com; www.ihbristol.com. 7 times a year. £1,350.

INTERNATIONAL HOUSE LONDON: ✆ +44 20 7611 2414; www.ihlondon.com; infott@ihlondon.com; full and part-time; rough frequency 11 per year. This is the largest CELTA and DELTA centre in the world. £1,495.

INTERNATIONAL HOUSE NEWCASTLE: ✆ +44 191 232 9551; www.ihnewcastle.com; 6 per year; £1,300. Also offers IH Cert in Teaching Younger Learners and Teenagers (TYLT). 1 week, £320.

INTERNATIONAL HOUSE LONDON

'Studying for a qualification to teach English as a foreign language was something I had always planned to do and when I was made redundant earlier in the year I decided it was now or never. It had been a long time since I was in full-time education, and thankfully methods and techniques have changed a lot, so it was with some trepidation that I signed up for my course.

'Everything I read and the people I spoke to all suggested that the CELTA course was very "full on" and hard. Having worked in a variety of sales and marketing roles in IT, and then in fundraising for an international charity, I wondered just how hard could it be?

'Well, it was like trying to drink from a fire hose, there was so much information to absorb, and you didn't want to spill a drop. There is a large volume of work to do throughout the four weeks, with the assignments and lesson preparation, and it certainly required some organisational skills that I didn't know I had.

'The combination of theory followed each day by teaching practice, with real students, allowed you to immediately try out what you were learning and get feedback. The feedback from the tutors was invaluable, allowing us to benefit from their vast experience, but the feedback from the students' faces was immediate and a good indicator of how the lesson was going. The opportunity to observe experienced teachers also gave a good insight as to how it should be done.

'There was a real mix of people on the course and you certainly get to know each other very well in a very short space of time! International House was a great place to do a CELTA course since it has great resources and support. It felt very slick, well organised and efficient.

'Getting a CELTA qualification feels a bit like passing your driving test, you think you know how to drive, but the real learning comes when you start driving. I am looking forward to teaching and building on this experience.'

Sally Colwell

ISE HOVE: Sussex; © +44 1273 384800; www.isehove.com; full-time (7 times a year), part-time (twice a year). £925-£1,075.

ITTC: Bournemouth; © +44 1202 516289; www.ittc.co.uk; full-time and part-time; rough frequency 12 per year; £1,371.

LAL TORBAY: Torbay, Devon; www.lalschools.com; 5 full-time courses a year. £1,250.

ITTC

Lisa D – a-not-so-average CELTA candidate

'I originally come from Canada, but came to England in 2002 and got work in an office. The monotony got to me and I searched around for a CELTA course and decided on ITTC. I'm glad I chose ITTC as the course was so practical and the tutors on the course were really good role models who tried to get the best out of everyone.

'I was lucky to be offered work at BEET/ITTC straight after the course, and I worked the whole summer for them before I went to teach overseas. I've taught in private language schools, I've set up and organised English immersion camps for teenagers where I had to design the whole course as well as produce materials, I've worked in secondary schools overseas and also trained up to be an examiner for English language examinations. So far I've spent time in Switzerland, Italy and Colombia, and I come back to England regularly to work on summer programmes.

'Having the CELTA has given me an opportunity to use my brain more than I ever did working in an office. I love working with people from different cultures, and it has also allowed me to learn other languages more easily. I still don't like being asked to teach areas I haven't been trained for and I'm not much of a disciplinarian – but this hasn't really been a problem, as my students always seem so motivated.

'In 2013 I decided I'd like to complete the Cambridge Delta so I studied at ITTC and in Argentina and now I'm a Delta qualified teacher.'

Lisa D. wrote this while in Bournemouth, but she is currently working for the British Council in Colombia.

LANGUAGE LINK TRAINING: London; ℭ +44 20 7370 4755; www.languagelink.co.uk; full-time offered monthly; part-time 2 times a year; £1,100–£1,150.

LANGUAGE TEACHING CENTRE BRIGHTON: Hove, East Sussex; ℭ +44 1273 735975; www.ltc-brighton.com; full-time; rough frequency 4 per year. £995.

MANCHESTER ACADEMY OF ENGLISH: Manchester; www.experienceenglish.com/celta; full and part-time; rough frequency 11 per year. £1,350.

MANCHESTER CENTRAL SCHOOL OF ENGLISH; Manchester; ℭ +44 161 236 7575; www.manchestercse.co.uk; 9 intensive courses plus 2 part-times/online.

NEWCASTLE COLLEGE: Newcastle; ℭ +44 191 200 4538; www.ncl-coll.ac.uk; part-time. £1,250.

NOTTINGHAM TRENT UNIVERSITY: Nottingham; ℭ +44 115 848 6156; www.nlc.ntu.ac.uk part-time. £1,380.

NILE TEFL: Norwich; ℭ +44 1603 664473; www.nile-elt.com; full-time; rough frequency 8 per year. £1,431.

NILE TEFL, NORWICH

Thom talks about his career in ELT, which all started with a CELTA:

Little did I know when I first enrolled for a CELTA that it would lead to a postgraduate degree and a leading role at one of the largest teacher training institutes in Europe.

In my case, CELTA lead to two years' teaching in Portugal, where a friend had told me he "played football on the beach in the days and taught English in the evenings". I still had the travel bug, so I returned to Britain for a year, finding work in ESOL classes at higher education colleges, and saved money to travel to Australia. During a year there, I taught in Surfer's Paradise and Sydney, and started to understand how people were making an interesting and fulfilling career from TEFL, rather than doing it as a means to an end.

I moved to Thailand from Australia, and after a year or so working at a university, I started at the British Council, where I was encouraged to think more long-term about teaching, and did the Delta by distance. This modular qualification is now one of a selection of online courses offered by NILE, and is done by distance learning with online and local supervision. I did really well with this qualification, and started to become involved in more and more interesting projects, and to develop an interest in teacher training. It was time to leave Thailand, however, and life then took me to Santiago de Chile where my work led me to take a Master's Degree in Language Testing, and the opportunity to develop in the area of Educational Technology.

I've been working in language testing, teacher training, technology in and out of the classroom, and language teaching and learning for the last seven years.

These days I work closely with the professional development and post-graduate students at NILE in Norwich, and enjoy a working environment that offers net-working possibilities for teachers at every stage of their ELT career. Somewhere along the way I stopped playing football on the beach, but I haven't missed it as much as I once would have thought!

As Director of NILE I have had the opportunity to meet many teachers from around the world, all with different perspectives on what makes a good training course, and my team and I are constantly striving to improve our courses, from CELTA to our Master's Degree, in order to be able to continue to deliver world-class professional development. With experienced tutors, extensive resources onsite and home-stay accommodation near the course centre, NILE makes the perfect place to follow the CELTA course.

OXFORD HOUSE COLLEGE: London; ✆ +44 20 7580 9785; www.oxfordhousecollege.co.uk; part and full-time; rough frequency 12 per year. £1,325.

RANDOLPH SCHOOL OF ENGLISH: Edinburgh; ✆ +44 131 226 5004; www.randolph.org.uk; part and full-time; rough frequency 9 per year. £990.

READING COLLEGE: Reading; ✆ +44 1189 554319; www.reading-college.ac.uk; part-time October to February. £1,284.

READING OPEN CENTRE: English Language & Teacher Training Centre, Reading, Berkshire; ✆ +44 118 939 1833; www.telc-reading.co.uk; semi-intensive; rough frequency 3 per year. £1,300.

ST GILES BRIGHTON: Brighton; ✆ +44 1273 682747; www.stgiles-international.com; full-time; rough frequency 11 per year. £1,230.

ST GILES INTERNATIONAL LONDON HIGHGATE: London; ✆ +44 20 8340 0828; www.stgiles-international.com/teacher-training; full-time; rough frequency 18 per year. £1,230.

SAXONCOURT TEACHER TRAINING: London; ✆ +44 20 7499 8533; 20 7491 1911; www.saxoncourt.com; full and part-time; rough frequency 12 per year. £1,199.

SKOLA TEACHER TRAINING: London; ✆ +44 20 7287 3216; www.skolacelta.co.uk; part-time; 3 times a year part-time. £1,295.

SOLIHULL COLLEGE: Solihull; ✆ +44 121 6787295; www.solihull.ac.uk; part-time. £1,391.

SOUTH THAMES COLLEGE: London; ✆ +44 20 8918 7366; www.south-thames.ac.uk; 3 full-time and one part-time. £1,250.

STANTON TEACHER TRAINING: London; ✆ +44 20 7221 7259; www.stanton-school.co.uk; full-time; rough frequency 12 per year. £1,311.

STUDIO CAMBRIDGE: Cambridge; ✆ +44 1223 369701; www.studiocambridge.co.uk; full-time; rough frequency 2 per year. £1,400.

SUSSEX DOWNS COLLEGE: Eastbourne; ✆ +44 1323 637240; www.sussexdowns.ac.uk; intensive course offered over 4.5 weeks in the summer; £1,100; also part-time over 11 weeks from February and September; £950.

TEACHING HOUSE LONDON: London; ✆ +1 800 756 2003; www.teachinghouse.com/london; full and part-time; 6 courses per year. £1,384.

UNIVERSITY OF GLASGOW, EFL Unit: Glasgow; ✆ +44 141 330 6521; www.glasgow.ac.uk/langcent full-time and part-time. £1,200.

UNIVERSITY OF SHEFFIELD, ENGLISH LANGUAGE TEACHING CENTRE: Sheffield; ✆ +44 114 222 1780; www.sheffield.ac.uk/eltc. Full-time in June/July and August/September plus part-time, blended and online. £1,450.

WESTMINSTER KINGSWAY COLLEGE: London; ✆ +44 20 7802 8813; www.westking.ac.uk; part-time; rough frequency 1 per year.

CAMBRIDGE CERTIFICATE (CELTA) ABROAD

The following centres, listed alphabetically by country, offer the Cambridge Certificate in English Language Teaching to Adults.

ARGENTINA

INTERNATIONAL HOUSE BUENOS AIRES: Buenos Aires; ✆ +54 11 4788 1788; www.ih-buenosaires. com. Full-time offered monthly plus 2 part-time courses a year. $1,260 plus registration fee $190.

ARMENIA

ESOLARM: Yerevan; ✆ +374 60 509 709 or 99 166 599; www.esolarm.org; 1 full-time course in July. €1,150.

AUSTRALIA

AUSTRALIAN TESOL TRAINING CENTRE (ATTC): Sydney, Brisbane and Perth; ✆ +61 2 8252 2821/1300 730 466; info.ATTC@navitas.com; www.attc.edu.au; full and part-time; rough frequency 12 per year.

CURTIN UNIVERSITY: Perth; ✆ +61 8 9266 4224; www.english.curtin.edu.au; full-time; rough frequency 2 per year. starting June and November. AUS$2,850-$3,100.

HOLMESGLEN LANGUAGE CENTRE: Chadstone (Victoria); ✆ +61 3 9564 1779; www.holmesglen. vic.edu.au; full and part-time; rough frequency 4 per year.

HOLMES INSTITUTE TEACHER TRAINING: Melbourne; ✆ +61 3 9662 2055; www.holmesinstitute. edu.au; full-time; rough frequency 4 per year.

INSEARCH UNIVERSITY OF TECHNOLOGY, SYDNEY (UTS): Sydney; ✆ +61 2 9218 8646; www.in-search.edu.au/teacher-training; full and part-time; rough frequency 3 of each per year. AUS$3,090.

INSTITUTE OF CONTINUING & TESOL EDUCATION (ICTE): Brisbane; ✆ +61 7 3346 6734; www.icte. uq.edu.au/celta; full and part-time; rough frequency 4 per year. AUS$2,995 plus moderation fee.

INTERNATIONAL HOUSE SYDNEY: Sydney; ✆ +61 2 9279 0733; www.training.ihsydney.com; full-time courses offered monthly, 5 part-time; AUS$3,150 plus $250 Cambridge assessment fee.

LEXIS TESOL TRAINING CENTRE (LTTC): Maroochydore, Queenland; ✆ +61 7 54792272 or 5447 4448; www.lexistesoltraining.com/sunshine-coast; CELTA on Sunshine Coast. Full-time from February, May and July; 10 weeks part-time from September; $2,750.

MELBOURNE TRAINING ASSOCIATES: Carlton, Melbourne; ✆ +61 3 9041 5341; www.melbtraining. com.au; 5 full-time courses, and part-time blended courses. $3,100-$3,300.

MILNER INTERNATIONAL COLLEGE OF ENGLISH: Perth; ✆ +61 8 9325 5444; www.milner.wa.edu. au/CELTA; full and part-time; rough frequency 5 per year. AUS$2,890.

PHOENIX ENGLISH LANGUAGE ACADEMY: Perth; ✆ +61 8 9227 5538; www.phoenix.wa.edu.au/ teachertraining; 5 full-time (130 hours), 3 part-time per year; AUS$2,945-$3,100.

RMIT ENGLISH WORLDWIDE: Melbourne; ✆ +61 3 9657 5876; www.rmitenglishworldwide.com; full and part-time; rough frequency 3 per year. AUS$3,100.

SOUTH AUSTRALIAN COLLEGE OF ENGLISH (SACE Adelaide): Adelaide; ✆ +61 8 8410 5222; www.sacecoll.sa.edu.au; full-time; rough frequency 4 per year. AUS$3,100.

TASMANIAN COLLEGE OF ENGLISH (SACE Hobart and SACE Whitsunday): Hobart, Tasmania; ✆ +61 3 6231 9911; www.tas.sace.com.au; full-time; rough frequency 1 per year in October. AUS$3,100.

TEACHING HOUSE MELBOURNE: Melbourne; ✆ +1 800 756 2003; www.teachinghouse.com; full and part-time courses year round. AUS$2,800.

AUSTRIA

BFI VIENNA: Vienna; ✆ +43 1 811 78 10152; www.bfi.at/english/courses/celta; 1 full-time and 2 part-time courses per year. €2,000.

BAHRAIN

BRITISH COUNCIL, BAHRAIN: Manama; ✆ +973 1726 1555 ext 229; www.britishcouncil.org/me; 1 full-time from mid-May. 850 dinars (£1,450).

BELARUS

INTERNATIONAL HOUSE: Private Educational Institution Study Centre, Minsk; ✆ +375 44 7784328; www.ih.by. 2 full-time in summer; £850.

BELGIUM

LANGUAGE TEACHER TRAINING IN BELGIUM: Brussels; ✆ +32 488 516 955; www.lttb.eu; 5 full-time, 4 part-time; €1,680.

BRAZIL

ALLIANCE, Manaus, Amazonia; ✆ +55 92 35843764; www.alliancegroup.com.br.

BRITANNIA INTERNATIONAL ENGLISH: Rio de Janeiro; ✆ +55 21 2143 7630; www.britannia.com.br; full-time and part-time; R$4,300 (£885).

CULTURA INGLESA: Sao Paulo, Belo Horizonte, Bahia, Natal, Belém and João Pessoa; www.culturainglesasp.com.br. Occasional part-time courses mainly for Brazilian teachers. Sample price R$3,540 + R$480 Cambridge fee.

SEVEN ENGLISH: Sao Paulo; ✆ +55 11 2392 0017; www.sevenidiomas.com.br; full and part-time both twice a year; R$3,440 plus US$211 Cambridge fee.

TARGET LANGUAGE SERVICES LTDA: São Paulo; ✆ +55 11 3207 5400; www.targetlanguage.com.br; 2 full-time, 2 part-time.

UP LANGUAGE CONSULTANTS: Terreo; ✆ +55 11 5105 0200; www.uplanguage.com.br; 1 part-time.

BULGARIA

AVO-BELL SCHOOL OF ENGLISH: Sofia; ✆ +359 2 944 032; www.teflcertificates-avo.com; full-time; rough frequency 5 per year; £975-£1,020 for course alone, £1,235-1,280 including self-catering accommodation.

CANADA

ENGLISH CANADA WORLD ORGANIZATION: Halifax; +1 902 429 3636; www.celta.ca.

GLOBAL VILLAGE: Calgary; ✆ +1 403 543 7300; www.celtacalgary.ca; full-time 3 times a year, part-time twice a year; C$2,500.

GLOBAL VILLAGE: Vancouver; ✆ +1 604 684 1010; www.gvcareer.com; full-time; rough frequency 5 per year. C$2,500.

GREYSTONE COLLEGE: Toronto; ✆ +1 416 323 1770; www.greystonecollege.com/celta-program-toronto. 3 part-time courses a year.

INTERNATIONAL HOUSE CAREER COLLEGE: Vancouver; ✆ +1-604-739-9836; www.tesl-vancouver.com; 8 full-time courses a year; C$2,345 plus $150 registration fee.

INTERNATIONAL LANGUAGE SCHOOLS OF CANADA – MONTREAL: Montreal; ✆ +1 514 876 4572; www.celta.ilsc.ca; full-time; rough frequency 7 per year. Also part-time and online with practicum. C$2,500.

LSC INTERNATIONAL COLLEGE: Toronto; ✆ +1 416 488 2200; www.ecenglish.com/en/teacher-training/toronto-celta; full-time every month. C$2,500.

SOL SCHOOLS: Toronto; ✆ +1 416 322 3405; www.solschools.com; 4 part-time courses. C$2,500.

TEACHING HOUSE TORONTO: Toronto; ✆ +1 800 756 2003; www.teachinghouse.com; part-time courses year round. C$2,500.

CHINA

EDUCATION FIRST: Beijing; ✆ +86 6586 5550.

INTERNATIONAL HOUSE BEIJING: Beijing; ✆ +86 188 106 039 01; www.ihbeijing.com; 2 full-time in the summer. RMB11,500.

LANGUAGE LINK CHINA TRADE CENTER: Beijing and Shanghai; ✆ +86 10 5169 5583; www.celtachina.com.cn; full-time; rough frequency 10 per year. RMB 12,500.

SYDNEY INSTITUTE OF LANGUAGE AND COMMERCE (SILC): Shanghai; ✆ +86 21 6998 0003; www.insearch.edu.au/Teacher-Training/CELTA-SILC-details; course is run once a year in August by Insearch in Sydney (entry above). RMB 15,550.

COLOMBIA

BRITISH COUNCIL BOGOTÁ: Bogotá; ✆ +57 1 325 9090; www.britishcouncil.co; full-time and blended. 4,300,000 pesos.

INTERNATIONAL HOUSE BOGOTÁ: Bogotá and Medellin; ✆ +57 1 336 4747; www.ihbogota.com; full-time 7 times a year; $1,795-$1,895.

CYPRUS

SHERIDAN PRIVATE INSTITUTE: Nicosia; ✆ +357 22590 556; www.sheridan.com.cy; full-time in summer.

CZECH REPUBLIC

AKCENT – INTERNATIONAL HOUSE: Prague; ✆ +420 2 6110 9225; www.akcent.cz; full and part-time; rough frequency 10 per year; £1,049 (£898 early bird discount). Also offered in Brno and in Bratislava summer only; £989 + £290 in self-catering flat.

EVROPSKE CENTRUM JAZYKOVYCH: Ceske Budejovice; ✆ +420 387 204 662; www.celta-training.eu; 5 full-time courses May to Sept. £828 if booked more than 3 months in advance.

HELLO LANGUAGE CENTRE OSTRAVA: Ostrava; ✆ +420 261 109 249; www.akcent.cz.

MASARYK UNIVERSITY: Brno; ✆ +420 54 949 7785; http://cic.muni.cz/en; part-time over 15 weeks in autumn and spring. 35,000 crowns.

ECUADOR

BSL (BRITISH SCHOOL OF LANGUAGE): Montañita and Cuenca; ✆ +593 9 9885 4399; www.celtainecuador.com; offered 8 times a year in Montañita at eco-lodge by Pacific Ocean and 3 times a year in Cuenca. $2,595 in Montañita includes accommodation and meals; $1,595 in Cuenca without accommodation.

KAMALA EDUCATION AND TRAINING GALAPAGOS: Santa Cruz, Galapagos; ✆ +593 99 27 90079; www.CELTAgalapagos.com; minimum 4 full-time courses a year; $2,350, with last minute reduction to $1,700 recently. Packages available that include a month of volunteering after the course.

EGYPT

BRITISH COUNCIL: Cairo; ✆ +20 2 3300 1845; www.britishcouncil.org/egypt; full-time; frequency 6 per year; 16,000 Egyptian pounds (£1,340).

FRANCE

BRITISH COUNCIL PARIS: ✆+33 1 49 55 73 07; teacher.training@britishcouncil.fr; www.british council.fr; offered in Paris and Lyon; €1,850.

CIEL BRETAGNE, Le Relecq Kerhuon, Brittany; www.esolbrittany.com. New 5-week course running 4 times between May and October 2016. €1,700.

ESOL STRASBOURG: Strasbourg; ✆ +33 7 62 99 17 22; www.esolstrasbourg.com; 5 per year full-time; €1,500 winter; €1,600 high season.

ILC FRANCE (INTERNATIONAL LANGUAGE CENTRE): Paris; ✆ +33 1 44 41 80 20; www.ilcfrance. com/teacher-training; full-time; rough frequency 9 per year; €1,800.

ILC FRANCE-IH PARIS

ILC France- International Language Centre France

Delighted Celta candidates give a snapshot of the ILC France Celta Teacher Training in central Paris:

The CELTA course is grueling but if you can give it all that you have, you'll come out of it with a **highly respected and marketable qualification that will last you a lifetime**. I thought **ILC France** delivered a great course. It was very organised and well taught by two highly trained and committed trainers. I've done many courses in my lifetime (in the UK, France, Singapore, China, Malaysia) and this was, without a doubt, the hardest, but the best course I've ever attended. **Angie 2015**

The CELTA course delivered at **ILC France** provides you with transferable skills, I came out of the class learning something new every day from the well balanced timetable of informative seminars on current teaching methodology as well as plenty of teaching practice. Despite the intensive nature of the course and the daily stress it was quickly forgotten by the unending support of the first class tutors and the **ILC France** teachers. **Kate 2015**

ILC France Celta tutors have a great reputation, you can check with Cambridge English who assesses all the Celta centres. My tutors were great and I wouldn't have been able to get through the four weeks without them. The course is intensive but **ILC France** have designed the programme of seminars and teaching practice in a very manageable way, the learning experience for both trainees and students was excellent. I can't thank the centre enough for helping me develop professionally as a teacher. I'm now working in a private language school in Paris. I would highly recommend **ILC France** to anyone thinking of doing the CELTA in Paris. **Paul 2014**

I did the CELTA **at ILC France** two years ago and I'd certainly recommend it. A great experience. The 2 teacher trainers were excellent: detailed, interactive classes, constructive feedback, plenty of teaching time. **Plus you're not going to get a better location in Paris! Steven 2013**

GEORGIA

EDUCATION & TRAINING INTERNATIONAL LTD: Tbilisi; ✆ +995 32 225 0945; www.eti.uk.com

INTERNATIONAL HOUSE TBILISI: Tbilisi; ✆ +995 32 294 0515; www.ihtbilisi.ge/en/celta; full-time in the summer (provisional), part-time in the autumn and online CELTA; all £780.

GERMANY

BERLIN SCHOOL OF ENGLISH: Berlin; ✆ +49 30 229 0456; www.berlin.school-of-english.de; 8 full-time per year and two part-time; €1,595 (including exam fee).

HAMBURG SCHOOL OF ENGLISH: Hamburg; ✆ +49 40 480 2119; www.hamburg.school-of-english. de; 3 full-time per year; €1,595.

INTERNATIONAL HOUSE FRANKFURT: Kaiserstr. 12, 60311 Frankfurt; www.suarez.de/celta-frankfurt; 8 per year; €1,595.

MUNCHNER VOLKSHOCHSCHULE: Munich; ✆ +49 89 48006 6265; www.mvhs.de/celta; full and part-time; rough frequency 2 per year (August/September); €1,595.

GREECE

BRITISH COUNCIL ATHENS: Athens; ✆ +30 210 369 2339; www.britishcouncil.gr; 4 full-time courses a year; €1,425 plus €150 Cambridge fee.

CELT: Athens; ✆ +30 210 330 2406; www.celt.edu.gr; 4 full-time, 2 part-time; €1,450, plus €160 Cambridge assessment fee; also offers its own TEFL certificate course (€1,300).

STUDY SPACE: Thessaloniki; ✆ +30 231 026 9697; www.studyspace.gr; part-time October to January or February to May; full-time in June; €1,800 including accommodation.

HUNGARY

INTERNATIONAL HOUSE: Budapest; ✆ +36 1 345 7046; www.teacher-training.hu; monthly full-time; 1 part-time per year; £899 for early booking; £999 otherwise.

INDIA

THE BRITISH COUNCIL ENGLISH LANGUAGE TEACHING CENTRE: New Delhi; ✆ +91 1800 102 4353; www.britishcouncil.in; full-time offered in Mumbai, Kolkata and Chennai as well as Delhi; Rs130,000 (£1,300).
PLANET EDU: Gurgaon, Haryana; ✆ +91 124 4684 800; www.theplanetedu.com; full-time in summer; Rs130,000.

INDONESIA

THE BRITISH INSTITUTE (TBI): Jakarta; ✆ +62 21 300 27988; www.tbi.co.id; 3 full-time in Jakarta, 1 in Bali; $1,800.

IRELAND

INTERNATIONAL HOUSE: Dublin; ✆ +353 1 635 5850; www.ihdublin.com; monthly and 1 part-time course; €1,750 inclusive.
KAPLAN INTERNATIONAL COLLEGE: Dublin; ✆ +353 1 672 7122; Dublin@Kaplan.com. 5 part-time. €1,700.
THE ENGLISH ACADEMY: Dublin; ✆ +353 1 872 6600; www.theenglishacademy.ie; 9 full-time courses a year; €1,600.
UNIVERSITY COLLEGE CORK, Language Centre: Cork; ✆ +353 21 490 3883; www.ucc.ie/esol; part-time twice a year, semi-intensive (7 weeks) in spring and one intensive course in June; €1,750.

ITALY

ANGLO-AMERICAN CENTRE: Cagliari, Sardinia; ✆ +39 070 654 955; www.angloamericancentre.it; 2 full-time over summer; €1,600.
BRITISH COUNCIL: Naples; ✆ +39 081 578 8247; www.britishcouncil.it; full-time in June/July; €1,850.
GIGA INTERNATIONAL HOUSE: Catania, Sicily; ✆ +39 095 715 2243; www.gigact.com. 4 full-time; €1,600-€1,750.
INTERNATIONAL HOUSE: San Donato Milan; ✆ +39 02 527 9124; www.ihmilano.it; full-time; rough frequency 3 per year. €1,880.
INTERNATIONAL HOUSE PALERMO: Palermo; ✆ +39 091 584954; www.ihpalermo.it; full-time; rough frequency 1 per year. €1,550.
INTERNATIONAL HOUSE ROME/ACCADEMIA BRITANNICA: Rome; ✆ +39 06 7047 6894; www.ihromamz.it; full-time and semi-intensive 5 per year. €1,800. Also run YL extension and DELTA modules.

INTERNATIONAL HOUSE ROME

'I am completely satisfied with the course and especially the course tutors. Their professionalism and expertise are admirable. The content of the seminars was incredibly educational and interesting. I have been given the tools for further self-improvement and I have been given the opportunity to improve my teaching skills. I have got what I hoped for! Thank you all for your effort!' **Rachel B.**

'These have been the most constructive and satisfying weeks of my professional life.' **Luke T.**

'It was challenging, fruitful and inspiring. I learned a completely new perspective on teaching and the structure of the course was absolutely perfect to make me achieve all that, especially the fact that we were immersed in teaching practice (mine or my colleagues') every single day!' **Lisa E.**

'The course was far more difficult at the start than I'd expected, but it gradually became easier to follow. I thank my tutors for having put all their effort to back me up through such a complex and energy consuming practice of teaching (learning how to teach), and I must say each did brilliantly, helping me to develop my teaching skills from quite different yet complementary points of view.' **Shariat H.**

'I really enjoyed the course, although it was intense and sometimes stressful. I feel the support from the trainers was great, they were very encouraging and provided very constructive feedback. They also acted as good role models in terms of their attitudes and teaching styles. Thank you!' **Sarah F.**

'It was really what I was looking for. It was very concrete, and I learnt about many useful teaching methodologies I hadn't known before. The tutors were fantastic, especially responding to the students' needs. It will certainly be one of the best points in my curriculum vitae.' **Matthew H.**

'The course was worth every penny, and I would recommend this specific language school to anyone else interested in taking a CELTA course. Thanks for the experience!' **Daniel B.**

THE CAMBRIDGE SCHOOL: Verona; ℂ +39 45 800 3154; www.cambridgeschool.it; full and part-time; rough frequency 2 per year.

JAPAN

LANGUAGE RESOURCES: Kobe; ℂ +81 78 382 0394; www.language-resources.org; part-time. 290,000 yen plus Cambridge fee.

JORDAN

BRITISH COUNCIL AMMAN: www.britishcouncil.org/jordan; full-time twice per year (January and August); 1,750 dinars.

KAZAKHSTAN

INTERPRESS INTERNATIONAL HOUSE: Almaty; ℂ +7 727 315 25 25; www.ihkazakhstan.com; www.celta.kz; full-time in summer; 390,000 tenge.

KOREA

INTERNATIONAL GRADUATE SCHOOL OF ENGLISH IGSE: Seoul; ℂ +82 2 6477 5151; http://sce. igse.ac.kr/community/TheCambridgeCELTA. Summer intensive; 2,350,000 won.

KUWAIT

BRITISH COUNCIL KUWAIT: Kuwait City; ✆ +965 2251 5512; www.britishcouncil.com.kw/en/teach/celta; intensive course in August; 850 Kuwaiti dinars.

LATVIA

INTERNATIONAL HOUSE RIGA-SATVA: Riga; ✆+371 6722 6641; www.ihriga.lv; full-time in July and August; €1,050.

LEBANON

ALLC INTERNATIONAL HOUSE BEIRUT: Beirut; ✆ +961 1 500978; www.allcs.edu.lb; full-time; rough frequency 2 per year in the summer; one in Beirut, the other in Saida (Sidon). $1,800.

MACEDONIA

SOUTH EAST EUROPEAN UNIVERSITY LANGUAGE CENTRE: Skopje; ✆ +389 70 321 985; www.seeu.edu.mk/sites/celta; 1 intensive in June; €975.

MALAYSIA

THE BRITISH COUNCIL LANGUAGE CENTRE: Kuala Lumpur; ✆ +60 3 2723 7900; www.britishcouncil.org/my; part-time over 10 or 20 weeks or full time in August. 9,275 ringgits (£1,660).

MALTA

IELS MALTA: Sliema; ✆ +356 2132 0381; www.iels.com.mt; 3 full-time a year; €1,400.
NSTS ENGLISH LANGUAGE INSTITUTE: Valletta; ✆ +356 2558 8500; www.nsts.org; full-time; rough frequency 3 per year.

MEXICO

INTERNATIONAL HOUSE: Mexico City, Guadalajara and Quintana Roo; www.ihmexico.com. Mostly full-time. $1,795.

MOROCCO

BRITISH COUNCIL CASABLANCA: Casablanca, Rabat and Tangier; ✆ +212 802 001045; www.britishcouncil.ma/en/teach; full-time and part-time; 25,000 dirhams (£1,650).

MYANMAR

BRITISH COUNCIL BURMA: Yangon; ✆ +95 1 246789/256290; www.britishcouncil.org.mm; full-time in May; 2,000,000 Kyat (£1,150).

NEPAL

BRITISH COUNCIL TEACHING CENTRE NEPAL: Kathmandu; ✆ +977 1 441 0798; www.britishcouncil.org.np/teach/courses-qualifications/celta. Full-time September; £1,400.

NETHERLANDS

BRITISH LANGUAGE TRAINING CENTRE: Amsterdam; ✆ +31 20 622 3634; www.bltc.nl; 2 full-time and 2 part-time courses offered annually; €1,925 inclusive.
BRITISH SCHOOL NETHERLANDS: Den Haag; ✆ +31 70 315 4080; www.britishschool.nl; part-time on 18 Fridays from September; €2,250.

NEW ZEALAND

AUT INTERNATIONAL HOUSE, Auckland; ✆ +64 9 921 9630; www.aut.ac.nz; 2 part-time; NZ$2,150.
CAMPBELL INSTITUTE: Wellington; ✆ +64 4 803 3434; www.campbell.ac.nz; full-time in June; NZ$3,195.
CHRISTCHURCH COLLEGE OF ENGLISH: Christchurch; ✆ +64 3 343 3790; www.ccel.co.nz; full-time; rough frequency 3-5 per year. NZ$3,050.
CHRISTCHURCH POLYTECHNIC INSTITUTE OF TECHNOLOGY: Christchurch; ✆ +64 3 940 8296; www.cpit.ac.nz; 4 part-time per year.
LANGUAGES INTERNATIONAL: Auckland; ✆ +64 9 309 0615; www.languages.ac.nz; full-time; rough frequency 6 per year. NZ$3,200.
NEW ZEALAND LANGUAGE CENTRES: Auckland; ✆ +64 9 303 1962; www.nzlc.ac.nz; 5-week courses run 5 times a year; NZ$3,200.
UNIVERSITY OF AUCKLAND: English Language Academy, Auckland; ✆ +64 9 919 7666; www.ela. auckland.ac.nz; 4 full-time, 2 part-time; NZ$3,300.
UNIVERSITY OF WAIKATO PATHWAYS COLLEGE: Hamilton; ✆ +64 7 858 5600; www.waikato.ac.nz; full-time; rough frequency 4 per year. NZ$3,300.

OMAN

BRITISH COUNCIL OMAN: Muscat; ✆ +968 2468 1000; www.britishcouncil.om/en; part-time; 1,000 Omani rials (£1,660).
INTERNATIONAL HOUSE MUSCAT: Ruwi, Muscat; enquiry@polyglot.org; www.pi.om; full-time in August. 1,050 Omani rials (£1,750).

POLAND

BRITISH COUNCIL KRAKOW: Krakow; ✆ +48 12 428 5930; www.britishcouncil.pl/en/celta; 6 full-time courses per year; 5230 zloty.
BRITISH COUNCIL WARSAW: Warsaw; ✆ +48 22 695 5900; www.britishcouncil.pl/en/warsaw; 3 full-time courses in summer, 1 part-time throughout the year; 5400 zloty (early booking discount available).
GAMA COLLEGE OF ENGLISH: Krakow; ✆ +48 12 6341259; www.gamacollege.pl/teacher-celta.html.
INTERNATIONAL HOUSE-INTEGRA KATOWICE: Katowice; ✆ +48 32 259 9997; www.ih.com.pl; 2 full-time in summer.
INTERNATIONAL HOUSE WROCLAW: Wroclaw; ✆ +48 71 781 7290; www.ih.com.pl; full-time; rough frequency 9 per year; from £805 if booked early.
LANG LTC: Warsaw; www.lang.com.pl/celta; twice full-time in summer and part-time in spring and autumn; 5,200 zloty (£900).

PORTUGAL

INTERNATIONAL HOUSE LISBON: Lisbon; ✆ +351 21 315 1493/1494/1496; www.ihlisbon.com; full and part-time; rough frequency 10 per year. €1,500.

QATAR

INTERNATIONAL HOUSE DOHA: www.ihdoha.com; 2 full-time in summer; 11,500 Qatari rials (£2000+).

ROMANIA

SHAKESPEARE TRAINING SRL: Bucharest; ✆ +40 744 314 437 or +40 21 230 2006; www.celtatraining.ro; 2 full-time, 1 part-time; £1100.

INTERNATIONAL HOUSE LISBON

'Taking the CELTA course at IH Lisbon has been a life-changing experience. It is, without a doubt, an incredibly intense course, but ultimately, very rewarding. No sooner have you observed a veteran teacher in the classroom, than you are teaching your first class. The tutors, however, provide you with all the advice, support and encouragement you need to get through those first few nerve-wracking lessons. Feedback is constant, fair and endlessly helpful. In addition, all the reference materials you could possibly need are either located in the school library, or accessible from the computer room. IH Lisbon provided me with the solid foundations on which to start my teaching career, and I would highly recommend the school to anyone wishing to undertake the CELTA certificate.'

Louise Marques

RUSSIA

BKC-EDUCATION WITHOUT LIMITS: Moscow; www.bkcih-moscow.com; full-time; rough frequency 7 per year; from £850.
LANGUAGE LINK ROSTOV-ON-DON: Taganrod, Rostov; ✆ +7 863 200 1444; www.languagelink.ru. Full-time in July/August. £900.
LANGUAGE TESTING PROFI (LT-PRO): St Petersburg; ✆ +7812 2445488; www.lt-pro.ru; 2 full-time in summer. 85,000 roubles (+ £135 Cambridge fee).
URAL FEDERAL UNIVERSITY CENTRE OF LANGUAGE EXCELLENCE (UCLEX): Ekaterinburg; ✆ +7 902 267 0986; www.uclex.urfu.ru. Intensive course in July; £1,200.

SERBIA

INTERNATIONAL HOUSE BELGRADE: Belgrade; ✆ +381 11 3612 218; www.ihbelgrade.co.rs; 4 full-time per year; £900.

SINGAPORE

THE BRITISH COUNCIL SINGAPORE: Napier Road; ✆+64 6473 1111; www.britishcouncil.sg; 2 full-time, part-time; S$5,900.
CA INTERNATIONAL COLLEGE: Singapore; ✆ +65 6536 2193; www.tesol.edu.sg; full-time (4 weeks) and part-time (8 weeks). S$5,100.

SLOVENIA

MINT INTERNATIONAL HOUSE: Ljubljana; ✆ +386 1 300 4300; www.mint.si; 2 full-time in summer; €1,250 plus €250/€350 for a month's accommodation.

SOUTH AFRICA

DURBAN LANGUAGE CENTRE: Durban; ✆ +27 31 201 3448; www.durbanlanguage.com.
GOOD HOPE STUDIES: Cape Town; ✆ +27 21 683 1399; www.ghs.co.za; full-time; rough frequency 6 per year; $1,690.

INTERNATIONAL HOUSE CAPE TOWN: Seapoint, Cape Town; ✆ +27 21 433 0546; www. ihcape-town.com; 6 full-time, 1 part-time; 14,250 Rand.

INTERNATIONAL HOUSE JOHANNESBURG: Johannesburg; ✆ +27 11 339 1051; www.ihjohannesburg.co.za; full-time; rough frequency 6 per year.

SPAIN

CAMBRIDGE ENGLISH: London School of Languages, San Sebastian; www.languagetestingservices.com; 3 full-time courses; €1,550.

CAMBRIDGE SCHOOL: Granollers, Barcelona; ✆ +34 93 870 2001; www.celta-delta.com; 5 weeks full-time; rough frequency 4 per year; €1,535.

CAMPBELL COLLEGE: Valencia; ✆ +34 96 362 8983; www.cambridgeceltavalencia.com; 5 per year; €1,450.

CHESTER SCHOOL OF ENGLISH: Madrid; ✆ +34 91 401 9729; www.chester.es; full-time offered July, August, September, November, February and May; €1,450 including the Cambridge fee.

CLIC INTERNATIONAL HOUSE: Seville; ✆ +34 95 450 01316; training@clic.es; www.tefl.es; full-time; rough frequency 12 per year; €1,575. Also available 4 times a year in Malaga. Spanish courses ✆ +34 95 450 2131; www.clic.es.

CLIC INTERNATIONAL HOUSE SEVILLE

Emily Turner's testimonial

'When I arrived at CLIC IH on the first day of the CELTA course, I was painfully aware of the weight of the decision that I had made: I had willingly given up a secure job in the middle of a recession to pursue a career in EFL teaching. My former colleagues thought that I was mad!

'Now my only regret is that I didn't take the leap earlier! I have a job that I love which is both challenging and rewarding and gives you the opportunity to travel all around the world . . . although why anyone would ever want to leave Seville is beyond me!

'I will always remember the first of the CELTA course as the day that my new life began. All my nerves evaporated after the warm welcome that I received from the staff at CLIC IH and I soon felt at home. The most memorable part of that day was watching our tutors teach a lesson, observing them filled me with the determination to study hard and to one day teach as inspirationally as them.

'And study hard I did! The CELTA course is demanding, after all you only have a few weeks to be moulded into the teachers of tomorrow. It is testament to the quality of the course that after a month I felt filled with the confidence to teach an engaging, informative lesson to students of any age and ability.

'This intensive nature of the CELTA means that it is a bond for life! My class-mates and I became a family; we were all there to offer encouragement as each of us took our turn to stand in front of a class and teach for the first time. Although now we are scattered all over the world we all stay in touch and are planning a reunion. Equally, my tutors have remained important in my life and two months after the course has ended, they are regularly in contact, tracking my progress and continuing to offer support and advice.

'Now to my great delight, I work for CLIC IH and I couldn't be happier. CLIC IH isn't just a language school, it's a community of people that have made a commitment to learning and development. It is a lively place to study and work and is bursting with interesting people and ideas. Just ask anyone in Seville and they will tell you themselves.'

EL CENTRO BRITÁNICO: Santiago de Compostela; © +34 981 597490; http://www.elcentrobritanico.es /celta; 3 full-time a year; €1,590.

EXAMS CATALUNYA: Barcelona; © +34 93 411 1333; www.exams-catalunya.com; full-time in August; €1,625.

HYLAND LANGUAGE CENTRE: Madrid; © +34 91 431 9757; www.hylandmadrid.com; 4 full-time (June, July, August and September) and part-time; €1,570.

INSTITUTE OF MODERN LANGUAGES: Granada; © +34 958 225536; www.celtagranada.com; 6 per year; €1,350.

INTERNATIONAL HOUSE BARCELONA: Barcelona; © +34 93 268 3304; www.ihes.com/bcn; full-time, part-time and online; rough frequency 19 per year; €1,650.

INTERNATIONAL HOUSE BARCELONA

Why International House Barcelona?

Part of a worldwide organisation

IH Barcelona's Teacher Training Department is part of the London-based IH world organisation, the largest and widely regarded as the best independent language teaching and teacher training organisation in the world.

Solid reputation and prestige

People come to IH Barcelona because of its reputation as a centre of excellence. Around 75% of students sign up because the school has been recommended to them by a friend. Our trainers are all experts and are well known in the EFL world. Since 1974, around 6000 teachers of English have been trained with us, making us one of the largest ELT training centres in Europe.

Huge teacher training courses programme

IH Barcelona has a huge teacher training courses programme ranging from the **CELTA, CELTYL Extension, to the DELTA and specialised courses for Managers, Trainers, Directors of Studies**, along with online courses covering areas such as 'using technology in the classroom', teaching pronunciation, etc. We also run regular workshops throughout the year and offer consultation services to schools around the world.

Cambridge English Language Assessment examining centre

In 2006, IH Barcelona became a Cambridge ESOL Examining centre for their prestigious range of English Language Exams. In 2014 we became a Platinum Examining centre, thanks to our work ethic, growth and reliability.

Modern facilities

We have a well-stocked library, interactive whiteboards in most classrooms, a computer/internet centre, wi-fi access throughout and a snack bar inside the building with its own sun terrace, a great place to relax at the end of the day.

Central location

We are situated in a large modernist building in the centre of the city, only about a 10-minute walk from Plaza Catalunya.

Finding work

IH Barcelona is well known in the EFL world. According to an independent survey on IH Barcelona, 20% of trainees who take the CELTA course here are offered work before they have completed the course, whilst 70% are working as teachers within four weeks of finishing.

Why Barcelona?

Barcelona has the largest Gothic quarter in Europe, modernist buildings designed by Gaudi, miles of beaches and offers art museums, opera halls, music festivals, and one of the best football clubs in the world! This combined with shops, fabulous tapas and wine bars, makes Barcelona one of the greatest cities to visit! Why not combine all this with an EFL course?

International House Barcelona Teacher & Translation Training Department

C/ Trafalgar, 14. 08010 Barcelona; Tel +34 93 268 3304; Fax +34 93 268 0239.

training@bcn.ihes.com; translation@bcn.ihes.com; www.ihes.com/bcn.

INTERNATIONAL HOUSE MADRID: Madrid; ✆ +34 91 319 7224 or 91 310 1314; www. ihmadrid.com; full and part-time; rough frequency 3 per year; €1,610.

INTERNATIONAL HOUSE MADRID

'Not being a native speaker of English, I had certain reservations and wondered how I would fit in with the others on the course. But my nerves disappeared after the first day's teaching practice when the tutor assured me that not only was my level of English good enough, I had a very important strength: my knowledge of Spanish students' problems in learning English – both the grammar and their difficulty with pronunciation.

'The training was pitched at just the right level and the support that both tutors gave me helped build my confidence to learn about teaching and enjoy it! The tutors never used the word "weaknesses", they only spoke about more effective teaching. I thoroughly enjoyed the teaching practice and learned so much by watching others that I actually looked forward to feedback because I knew I would have something positive to say about my colleagues and whatever they had to say about my lessons, it would only help me improve.

'IH Madrid's CELTA centre is right in the heart of the city and each classroom of the newly designed CELTA wing of this impressive three-storey building has video projector, wi-fi and state-of-the-art equipment which allowed audio to be played straight from my mobile phone. Madrid can be hot in the summer so I was so glad they had air conditioning and a great library to do a bit of quiet studying in the evening before heading to a *terraza* for a cool drink.

'Everyone told me it was going to be intensive and it was. But I'm still amazed at how much I learnt in just four weeks. By the end of the course I really felt prepared to go into class, which was essential because I wanted to start work straight after the course.

'I suppose I could sum up my CELTA like this. I learnt that with the right support and training from people who know their business inside out, you can achieve anything. I arrived a trainee, made some great friends and left ready to start my own classes. No more feedback, no more support, just me – an English teacher!'

INTERNATIONAL HOUSE PALMA: Palma; ✆ +34 971 726408; www.ihes.com/pal; full-time; rough frequency 4 per year. €1,545.
INTERNATIONAL HOUSE SANTANDER: Santander; ✆ +34 942 233 664; www.ihsantander.com/cursos/cursos-profesores.
IRISH ACADEMY: Palmas de Gran Canaria; www.theirishacademy.com; 5 per year; €1,530.
LENGUAS VIVA: Valencia; www.celtavalencia.com; €1,470-€1,520.

SRI LANKA

BRITISH COUNCIL: Colombo; www.britishcouncil.org/srilanka; intensive course every August; 375,000 rupees (£1,800).

SWITZERLAND

ACADEMIA SCHWEIZ: Basel; ✆ +41 61 260 2020; www.academia-basel.ch; 1 full-time in July, 1 part-time October-January.

BELL LANGUAGE SCHOOL, SWITZERLAND: Geneva; ✆ +41 22 749 1616; www.bell-school.ch; full-time in July and 3 part-time courses per year; SFr3,950.

CAMBRIDGE ENGLISH: St. Gallen; ✆ +41 71 278 0040; www.celta.ch; 1 part-time; SFr3,500.

FLYING TEACHERS: Zurich; ✆ +41 44 350 3344; www.flyingteachers.ch.

SL&C CELTA CENTRE: Lausanne; ✆ +41 21 310 0300; www.supercomm.ch; full-time in July; online from September; SFr3,800.

TLC, THE LANGUAGE COMPANY: Baden; ✆ +41 56 205 51 78; www.tlcsprachschule.ch; part-time over 10 weeks, starting September; also offers one full-time course in July; SFr4,200 in both cases.

THAILAND

ECC (THAILAND): Chiang Mai; ✆ +66 2 655 3333; www.eccthai.com; full-time; rough frequency 2 per year; $1,600; also offered with an extra week of teaching young learners.

INTERNATIONAL HOUSE BANGKOK: Bangkok; ✆ +66 2 6326 790; www.ihbangkok.com; also offered in Chiang Mai and Phuket; $2,100 in Bangkok, $2,495 in Chiang Mai and $2,595 in Phuket, including accommodation.

TUNISIA

INTERNATIONAL HOUSE TUNIS: Tunis; ✆ +216 71 145 300; www.britishcouncil.tn/en/teach/celta; full-time in summer. 4,040 Tunisian dinars.

TURKEY

BRITISH SIDE: Istanbul; ✆ +90 212 327 2701; www.britishside.com; 2 full-time in summer, several part-time. £1,200.

INSTITUTE OF LANGUAGE STUDIES - INTERNATIONAL HOUSE: Izmir; ✆ +90 232 484 2490; http://english.ilsizmir.com/index.php/teacher-training/celta. 4 and 6-week formats 5 times a year. £1,080.

INTERNATIONAL MEDITERRANEAN ACADEMY (IM ACADEMY): Fethiye; ✆ +90 252 616 64 06; www.im-academy.org; full-time in summer; £1,100.

INTERNATIONAL TRAINING INSTITUTE: Levent, Istanbul; ✆ +90 212 283 6466/6426; www.iti-istanbul.com; full and part-time offered frequently; £1,200. Also offering the first CELTA in Bursa, summer 2015 in partnership with Uludag University.

IZMIR UNIVERSITY OF ECONOMICS: Izmir; ✆ +90 232 279 2525; www.ieu.edu.tr; 1 full-time, 9 part-time. £1,026 full-time; £899 part-time.

UKRAINE

GRADE EDUCATION CENTRE: Kiev; www.grade.ua; 2 full-time in summer; $1,299/$1,399.

INTERNATIONAL HOUSE KYIV: Kiev; ✆ +380 44 238 9870; www.ih.kiev.ua; 3 full-time and 2 part-time per year. $1,389 ($100 discount for early booking).

INTERNATIONAL HOUSE SEVASTOPOL: Sevastopol; ✆ +380 692 944 100; www.ih-sevastopol.com.ua; 2 full-time in summer. £1,000.

LONDON SCHOOL OF ENGLISH: Odessa; ✆ +380 48 777 50 15; www.lse.ua; 1 full-time in July; £700.

UNITED ARAB EMIRATES

THE BRITISH COUNCIL, ABU DHABI: Abu Dhabi; ✆ +971 2 691 0600; www.britishcouncil.ae; full and part-time; also in Sharjah and Dubai. 10,000 dirhams.

HIGHER COLLEGES OF TECHNOLOGY: Many locations; ✆ +971 2 681 2070; www.hct.ac.ae.

USA

DENVER BRIDGE TEFL: Denver; ✆ +1 303 785 8864 ext 862; www.bridgetefl.com; full-time; rough frequency 7 per year. $2,495.

ELS LANGUAGE CENTERS: Tacoma, Washington; ✆ +1 253 680 7296; celta@els.edu; www.els.edu; 9 full-time per year; $2,550.

INTERNATIONAL HOUSE SAN DIEGO: San Diego; ✆ +1 619 260 1113; www.ihsandiego.com; full-time; 5 courses per year. $2,695.

ST GILES INTERNATIONAL: San Francisco; ✆ +1 415 788 3552; www.stgiles-usa.com; full-time; rough frequency 8 per year. $2,495.

MISSOURI STATE UNIVERSITY CELTA CENTER: Springfield; ✆ +1 417 836 6540; www.international.missouristate.edu; 5-week courses 4 times a year. $2,450.

ST GILES NEW YORK CITY: New York; www.stgiles-usa.com; 6 full-time courses a year. $2,495.

SOL SCHOOLS MIAMI BEACH: Miami; ✆ +1 305 763 8520; www.solschools.com; 5 full-time courses per year. $2,500.

TEACHING HOUSE ATLANTA: Atlanta; ✆ +1 800 756 2003; www.teachinghouse.com; full-time; 4 courses per year.

TEACHING HOUSE BOSTON: Boston; ✆ +1 800 756 2003; www.teachinghouse.com; full and part-time; rough frequency: 8 full-time courses per year and 2 part-time courses per year.

TEACHING HOUSE BROOKLYN: Brooklyn; ✆ +1 800 756 2003; www.teachinghouse.com; full-time; 2 courses per year.

TEACHING HOUSE CHICAGO: Chicago; ✆ +1 800 756 2003; www.teachinghouse.com; 11 full-time and 3 part-time courses per year.

TEACHING HOUSE DETROIT: Detroit; ✆ +1 800 756 2003; www.teachinghouse.com; full-time; 2 courses per year.

TEACHING HOUSE HOUSTON: Houston; ✆ +1 800 756 2003; www.teachinghouse.com; full-time; 2 courses per year.

TEACHING HOUSE LOS ANGELES: Los Angeles; ✆ +1 800 756 2003; www.teachinghouse.com; full-time; 10 courses per year.

TEACHING HOUSE MIAMI: Miami; ✆ +1 800 756 2003; www.teachinghouse.com; full-time; 6 courses per year.

TEACHING HOUSE MINNEAPOLIS: Minneapolis; ✆ +1 800 756 2003; www.teachinghouse.com; full-time; 2 courses per year.

TEACHING HOUSE NEW YORK: New York; ✆ +1 800 756 2003; www.teachinghouse.com; full and part-time; rough frequency 28 per year.

TEACHING HOUSE NEW YORK

Opening Doors to Opportunities – Teaching House CELTA

'Index finger outstretched, breath held, continents and bodies of water flashing before my eyes, fast at first then slower, as the outlines of countries became clearer, the oceans became visible. Slower still, as the spinning sphere began to reveal the names of places I'd learned long ago. Losing its momentum, the globe breathed one final breath, jerking to a stop, leaving the tip of my index finger trembling above the spot where I would spend the next year and a half of my life: Vietnam. I closed my eyes, submitted my résumé, completed a phone interview, accepted their offer, bought a one-way ticket, packed up my life into two small suitcases, hugged my family goodbye, held back tears, and fell asleep on the 24-hour flight to the other side of the world. I opened my eyes to find myself struck by two very intense feelings: fear and heat. There I was, alone, scared, and sweating outside international arrivals at Tan Son Nhat airport in Ho Chi Minh City. That was all it took to change my life: the blink of an eye . . . and my CELTA.

'I was very grateful for everything that I learned during my CELTA course. The foundation it gave me allowed me not to feel like a total fraud as I stepped into my first real class. Whether I was teaching three-year-olds the ABC song, listening to the latest Taylor Swift single with my teenage students, or delving into the depths of American culture with adults, my CELTA course at Teaching House prepared me to be creative and retrospective. It helped me to develop into the teacher I am proud to have become.

'Like most people who uproot their lives to take on new and challenging adventures, I found myself in a state of constant self-discovery. I realised that I loved teaching English, and that I wisely (or unwisely) invested so much of myself into my classes that my students had the power to affect me long after I went home for the night. I realised that I had the ability to bridge cultural barriers, developing relationships with those I had very little in common with except the desire to grow. I realised that every choice I had made in my life had led me to that point, that time, that place, and I was happy.

'My departure came in late Spring, just as the dark clouds of rainy season were descending upon Vung Tau. The heavy rains seemed to wipe my slate clean, leaving my future open to just about anything. I could once again take out my globe, give it a spin, and hold my breath as my future lies just under the tip of my index finger.'

TEACHING HOUSE PHILADELPHIA: Philadelphia; ✆ +1 800 756 2003; www.teachinghouse.com; 4 full-time courses per year.

TEACHING HOUSE PHOENIX: Phoenix; ✆ +1 800 756 2003; www.teachinghouse.com; 2 full-time courses per year.

TEACHING HOUSE PORTLAND: Portland; ✆ +1 800 756 2003; www.teachinghouse.com; 2 full-time courses per year.

TEACHING HOUSE SALT LAKE CITY: Salt Lake City; ✆ +1 800 756 2003; www.teachinghouse.com; 2 full-time courses per year.

TEACHING HOUSE SAN DIEGO: San Diego; ✆ +1 800 756 2003; www.teachinghouse.com; 3 full-time courses per year.

TEACHING HOUSE SAN FRANCISCO: San Francisco; ✆ +1 800 756 2003; www.teachinghouse.com; 5 full-time courses per year.

TEACHING HOUSE WASHINGTON DC: Washington DC; ✆ +1 800 756 2003; www.teachinghouse.com; 11 full-time, 2 part-time courses per year.

UNIVERSITY OF TEXAS AT AUSTIN CELTA CENTER: Austin; ✆ +1 512 471 2480; www.world.utexas.edu/celta; 6 full-time courses a year; $2,595.

VENEZUELA

BRITISH COUNCIL VENEZUELA: Caracas; ✆ +58 212 952 9965 Ext: 248; celta@britishcouncil.org.ve; www.britishcouncil.org.ve; full-time in January; 25,000 Bolivars (£2,500).

VIETNAM

APOLLO EDUCATION: Hanoi and Ho Chi Minh City; ✆ +84 4 3943 2053; www.teachatapollo.com; 4 full-time courses in both Hanoi and Ho Chi Minh City; 3,440,000 dong (£1,000).

INTERNATIONAL LANGUAGE ACADEMY (ILA): Ho Chi Minh City; ✆ +84 1207 267 159; www.teachenglish.ilavietnam.com; full-time; rough frequency 9 per year. $1,750.

LANGUAGE LINK VIETNAM: Hanoi; ✆ +84 4 3974 4999; www.llv.edu.vn; full-time; rough frequency 4 per year. $1,600.

TRINITY COLLEGE CertTESOL IN THE UK

A+ ENGLISH LANGUAGE SCHOOL: Sheffield; ✆ +44 114 209 6292; www.aplusenglish.co.uk; 9 full-time courses, 1 part-time course. £1,050 plus £195 admin and moderation fee; 15% early booking discount.

ATHENA TEACHER TRAINING: Bournemouth; ✆ +44 1202 544166; www.tefl-training.co.uk. 4 full time courses a year. £1,074 plus moderation fee.

BOLTON COLLEGE: Bolton; ✆ +44 1204 482460; Suzannah.Redmond@boltoncc.ac.uk; www.boltoncollege.ac.uk; part-time courses from September and February. £1,350.

CITY COLLEGE PETERBOROUGH: Peterborough; ✆ +44 1733 761361 Ext. 241; www.citycollegepeterborough.ac.uk. Part-time from January (6 hours a week for 6 months); £1,395.

COLCHESTER INSTITUTE: Colchester; ✆ +44 1206 712487; www.colchester.ac.uk; part-time 20 weeks from September. £1,500.

ENGLISH IN MARGATE: Margate, Kent; ✆ +44 1843 227700; Jake.Castaldi@leolanguages.com; www.traintoteachenglish.com; part of International Language Homestays; 130-hour course delivered 4 times a year; £1000 plus £50 registration fee. Accommodation £600.

ENGLISH NATURALLY: Winchester; ✆ +44 1962 859700; www.english-naturally.com; 2 full-time in summer (£990); 2 part-time (£1200) plus moderation fee of £125. Host family accommodation for £102 per week.

EUROSPEAK: Reading; ✆ +44 118 958 9599; trinity@eurospeak.org.uk; ww.tefl-certification.net; full-time monthly; £1,195.

GLASGOW CLYDE COLLEGE: Glasgow; ✆+44 141 272 3664; www.glasgowclyde.ac.uk; part-time for 36 weeks from end of August followed by 10 half days of teaching practice at Langside Campus; £1,100 plus £155 moderation fee and £80 for textbooks.

GOLDERS GREEN COLLEGE TEACHER TRAINING CENTRE: London; ✆ +44 20 8905 5467; www.teachertraininglondon.com; full-time; 2 times per year; £969.

INLINGUA: Cheltenham; ✆ +44 1242 250493; www.inlingua-cheltenham.co.uk; full-time; 6 times a year; £1,155 + £135 moderation fee.

DOMINIC HARRIS

'It was in September 2009 that I found myself at Bergamo train station in North Italy bound for Lecco, a small town near Lake Como. And as I stood alone on that platform in the early evening sunshine, with barely a word of the mother tongue and not entirely sure whether I definitely had somewhere to stay when I arrived there, I reflected on how I had got myself into this situation.

'It all started in November 2008 when I was sitting with my fellow fresh TEFL-ites awaiting the beginning of our five-week TESOL guidance into the world of international EFL teaching. The course was as challenging and fulfilling as anything I had ever done. Along the way, I taught students from no fewer than 20 different countries, learnt rudimentary Japanese, taught, reflected, analysed, learnt about different languages and cultures, taught, made new friends, played the most international games of football ever, taught again and had a marvellous time whilst doing it all.

'Now at the end of my eight months in Italy I have had a chance to reflect once again on how it has developed me as a teacher. Teaching abroad swept me out of my comfort zone and gave me a deeper connection with the plight of the language learner. Professionally, it has stretched and challenged me, with my having to integrate and, perhaps more essentially, assimilate into a new professional set up and "way of doing things". It has been tough at times indeed, and a zeal for the job at hand, ie teaching, is essential. But, in short, by making the jump into the unknown of international EFL teaching, I have come out a more fulfilled and better teacher than when I stood alone on the platform of Bergamo train station.'

KEELE UNIVERSITY: Keele; ✆ +44 1782 733013; elu@keele.ac.uk; www.keele.ac.uk. One intensive course in summer.

LANGUAGES TRAINING & DEVELOPMENT: Witney, Oxfordshire; ✆ +44 1993 708637; www.ltd-oxford.com; full-time; rough frequency 6–12 per year. LT&D has Erasmus partnership with school in Hungary and part of the course is delivered in Szekszard. Erasmus funding available; £950 to non-EU participants.

LEEDS ENGLISH: Leeds; ✆ +44 113 275 1964; www.leedsenglish.com; 20 weeks part-time from January £950 plus £49 admin fee.

LEWIS SCHOOL OF ENGLISH: Southampton; ✆ +44 2380 228203; www.lewis-school.co.uk; 5 times a year full-time, £995; 1 time part-time £1,200; plus moderation fee of £130.

LIVERPOOL SCHOOL OF ENGLISH: Liverpool; ✆ +44 151 706 0730; www.lse.uk.net; 4 intensives per year.

THE MANCHESTER COLLEGE: Manchester; ✆ +44 161 203 2100; www.themanchestercollege.ac.uk.

NORTHAMPTON COLLEGE: Northampton; ✆ +44 1604 1232344; www.northamptoncollege.ac.uk; part-time, 1 per year. £700 for trainees under 24, £1,400 otherwise.

NORTHBROOK COLLEGE: Northbrook, Sussex; ✆ +44 845 155 60 60; www.northbrook.ac.uk; part-time 3 times a year (1 evening a week for 13 weeks) £1,575.

OPEN DOORS INTERNATIONAL LANGUAGE SCHOOL: Plymouth; ℂ +44 1752 258770; www.odils. com; 1 full-time, 1 part-time a year. £995 plus moderation fee.

OXFORD INTERNATIONAL EDUCATION GROUP: Greenwich, London; ℂ +44 20 8239 1444; www. isistefl.com; full-time; rough frequency 9 per year. Part-time courses offered at other Oxford International (formerly ISIS Education) locations in Oxford, Brighton and Central London; £995-£1,095 with possible discounts.

OXFORDTEFL LONDON: London; tesol@oxfordtefl.com; www.oxfordtefl.com; 6 full-time and 1 part-time course per year; £1,225; course also offered in Spain, Czech Republic and India.

ST BRELADE'S COLLEGE: St Aubin, Jersey; ℂ +44 1534 741305; www.stbreladescollege.co.uk; full-time; rough frequency 2 per year; £1,250 including exam fee.

ST GEORGE INTERNATIONAL: London; ℂ +44 20 7299 1700; www.tesoltraining.co.uk; 11 full-time and 3 part-time per year. £895 full-time, £995 part-time.

ST GILES EASTBOURNE: Eastbourne; ℂ +44 1323 729167; www.stgiles-international.com; full-time; rough frequency 3 per year. £995 plus £130 moderation fee.

ST GILES LONDON CENTRAL: London; ℂ +44 20 7837 0404; www.stgiles-international.com; full-time; rough frequency 7 per year plus one part-time. £1,095 + £130.

SIDMOUTH INTERNATIONAL SCHOOL: Sidmouth, Devon; ℂ +44 1395 516754; efl@sidmouth-int. co.uk; www.sidmouth-int.co.uk; full-time; 3 per year; £1,250 including moderation fee; accommodation arranged on request.

SUSSEX CENTRE FOR LANGUAGE STUDIES: University of Sussex, Brighton; ℂ +44 1273 877485; www.sussex.ac.uk; full-time in summer. £1,270.

SUSSEX COAST COLLEGE HASTINGS: Hastings; ℂ +44 1424 458342; www.sussexcoast.ac.uk; 6 months part-time starting January and September; £1,290.

SUTTON COLLEGE: Sutton, Surrey; ℂ +44 20 8770 6901; www.scola.ac.uk; part-time 1 per year; £950.

TAMESIDE COLLEGE: Greater Manchester; ℂ +44 161 908 6789; www.tameside.ac.uk; part-time, £1,300.

TEFL LAB LONDON: Bloomsbury, London; ℂ +44 20 7637 3813; www.tefllab.co.uk; full-time monthly; £840 plus £110 moderation fee.

THE LANGUAGE INSTITUTE/TLI ENGLISH LANGUAGE TRAINING: Edinburgh; ℂ +44 131 226 6975; www.tlieurope.com; full-time; rough frequency 3 per year; £990.

TRAINING 4 TEFL: Rose of York Language School, London; ℂ +44 20 7637 2212; www.training4tefl.com; frequent full-time courses throughout the year; £830-£945.

UNIVERSAL LANGUAGE TRAINING (ULT): Woking, Surrey; ℂ +44 1983 853808; www.universal-language.co.uk; 2 full-time courses in summer, one in Woking, one at Royal Holloway University in Egham, Surrey; £845 plus £130 moderation fee.

UNIVERSITY OF CENTRAL LANCASHIRE: School of Languages and International Studies, Preston; ℂ +44 1772 894241; cenquiries@uclan.ac.uk; www.uclan.ac.uk; full-time in August, £1,295. Also offers university-level courses in TESOL.

UNIVERSITY OF MANCHESTER LANGUAGE CENTRE: Manchester; ℂ +44 161 306 3397; www.ulc. manchester.ac.uk/english/certtesol; twice a year; £1,480.

WE BRIDGE INTERNATIONAL LTD: Cardiff; ℂ +44 2920 225656; www.we-bridge.co.uk; 4 times a year; £1,250.

TRINITY COLLEGE CertTESOL ABROAD

ARGENTINA

CASA DE INGLÉS: Resistencia-Chaco; ℂ+54 362 432 2953; lauraalvarez@arnet.com.ar or casade ingles@ymail.com; part-time course between April and October.

AUSTRIA

ABCi: Gmunden; www.abci-english.at.

BRAZIL

THE BRITISH COUNCIL: Recife; trinitycert@britishcouncil.org.br; www.britishcouncil.org.br; course takes place at Cultura Inglesa Boa Viagem, Recife.

CULTURA INGLESA: Rio de Janeiro; ✆ +55 21 2528 8734; www.culturainglesa.net/wps/portal/inicio; courses also available in Goiânia and Sao Paulo.

CANADA

COVENTRY HOUSE INTERNATIONAL: Toronto; ✆ +1 416 929 0227; www.study-at-coventry.com; full-time; rough frequency 2 per year; C$999 (with discount).

CHINA

EF EDUCATION FIRST: Beijing, Shanghai and Guangzhou; jake.whiddon@ef.com; www.ef-teachers.com.

CZECH REPUBLIC

OXFORD TEFL: Prague; www.oxfordtefl.com; full-time; rough frequency 10 per year; €1,300 if booked early.

GREECE

AMERICAN COLLEGE OF GREECE: Athens; www.acg.edu; 2 part-time over 8 weeks, 1 full-time in July blended with online; €2,000.

HONG KONG

THE EDGE LEARNING CENTER LTD: Causeway Bay; ✆ +852 92791395; www.theedge.com.hk.

ENGLISH FOR ASIA: Sheung Wan, Hong Kong; ✆ +852 2392 2746; www.englishforasia.com; full and part-time; rough frequency 10–12 per year; HK$25,000 (£2,070).

INDIA

OXFORDTEFL: Kerala; www.oxfordtefl.com; full-time 8 times a year. €1,300 if booked in advance.

ST GEORGE INTERNATIONAL: New Delhi; www.stgeorge.co.in; full-time.100,000 rupees (£1000).

INDONESIA

IALF BALI (INDONESIA AUSTRALIA LANGUAGE FOUNDATION): Bali; ✆ +62 361 225243; www.tesolbali.com; full-time; rough frequency 4 per year; $1,900.

IRELAND

ATLANTIC SCHOOL OF ENGLISH AND ACTIVE LEISURE: Schull, County Cork; ✆ +353 28 28943; www.atlantic-english.com; full-time; rough frequency 3 per year; €1,450 plus accommodation can be arranged for €80–€150 per week.

ITALY

BRITISH SCHOOL VICENZA: Vicenza; ✆ +39 0444 542190; www.britishschoolvicenza.net/tefl-teacher-training; full-time in summer; €1,450. Course exported from St George International of London.

TEFL IN ITALY Rome; ✆ +39 06 92919464; www.tefl-in-italy.com. 4+ full-time courses a year. €1,749 (or €1,549 with discount).

JAPAN

SHANE ENGLISH SCHOOL: Tokyo; ✆ +81 3 5275 6756; sophia.mcmillan@shane.co.jp; www.tefljobsinjapan.com. Full-time in summer.

MALTA

EUROPEAN SCHOOL OF ENGLISH: St Julian's; ✆ +35 621 373789; www.esemalta.com.
EC MALTA: St Julian's; ✆ +35 621 388500; www.ecenglish.com.

MEXICO

ICLS (INTERNATIONAL CHRISTIAN LANGUAGE SCHOOL): Guadalajara; ✆ +52 33 38 25 97 65; www.icls.mx; course exported from ODILS, Plymouth, UK.

NEW ZEALAND

EDENZ COLLEGES: Auckland; ✆ +64 9 309 5208; www.edenz.ac.nz; intensive (5 weeks) and semi-intensive (10 weeks) with monthly start dates.
INTERNATIONAL PACIFIC COLLEGE: Palmerston North; ✆ +64 6 354 0922; www.ipc.ac.nz/fesol-courses.html; full-time 2 per year.

PARAGUAY

STAEL RUFFINELLI DE ORTIZ – ENGLISH: Asuncion; ✆ +595 21 226062/207017; www.stael.edu.py; part-time February to November.

SPAIN

ACTIVE LANGUAGE: Cadiz; ✆ +34 95 6 221426; training@activelanguage.net; www.activelanguage.net; 2 full-time in the summer, 1 part-time through the academic year; €1500 (€150 discount for early booking).
APP ACADEMIA DE IDIOMAS: Gandia, Valencia; ✆ +34 96 286 7281; www.appformacion.com.
BRITISH COUNCIL VALENCIA: Valencia; ✆ +34 963392981; www.britishcouncil.org/es; full-time in July, €1,595.
FUNDACIÓ INSTITUT D'ESTUDIS NORD-AMERICANS: Barcelona; ✆ +34 93 240 5110; teacher training@ien.es; www.ien.es.
LANGUAGE CAMPUS: Laguna, Tenerife; ✆ +34 922 630 302; www.lcidiomas.com. Part-time from January; €1,400.
OXFORDTEFL: Barcelona, Malaga and Cadiz; ✆ +34 93 1740062; www.oxfordtefl.com; full-time; rough frequency 12 per year; €1,400.
TEFL-IN-SPAIN: Malaga; ✆ +34 951 956 784; www.tefl-in-spain.com; full-time most months. €1299 if booked 3 months in advance, otherwise €1450.
TESOLSpain: Granada; ✆ +34 664 60 2846; www.tesolcourse.com/tesol/spain-granada. Not certain that the course will run.

THAILAND

ST STEPHEN'S INTERNATIONAL SCHOOL: Nakhon Ratchasima 30130; ✆ +66 86 4688040; www.trinitytesolthailand.com; 4-week residential course includes private accommodation and meals in the national park area of Khao Yai, Thailand. 6 times a year. £1,499.

TURKEY

INKAŞ AŞ: Istanbul; ✆ +90 212 496 1010; efikri@superonline.com.

URUGUAY

DICKENS INSTITUTE: Montevideo; ✆ +598 2 710 7555 ext 105; www.dickens.edu.uy; part-time.

SHORT INTRODUCTORY COURSES

BERLITZ WORLDWIDE: http://careerservices.berlitz.com; all newly hired teachers (who must be university graduates) must join free 2-week training in-house in the Berlitz Method.

EF ENGLISH FIRST TEACHER TRAINING: 1 or 2 week course offered in Boston, Paris, Munich or Malaga; ✆ +44 20 7341 8500; www.ef.co.uk/tz; approx $920–$1,100 for 1 week, and just under double for 2 weeks; cost varies depending on location.

FLYING CLASSROOMS: Norwich Study Centre, Norwich; ✆ +44 1603 619091; www.flyingclassrooms.co.uk. 2-week 45-hour Introduction to TEFL. £350 p.w. Also specialist 1-week course in teaching Young Learners, Business English, Drama Techniques for Creative Language Teaching (12 hours in 3 days, £300).

GLOBAL LANGUAGE TRAINING LTD: London EC1; ✆ +44 203 435 6821; www.globaltefl.uk.com. 2-day weekend courses in London, Birmingham, Manchester and Sheffield throughout the year. £150/£180.

i-to-i: Leeds, UK; ✆ +44 800 093 3148; www.i-to-i.com or www.onlinetefl.com; 20-hour weekend courses in London, Birmingham and Sydney; £149.Can be combined with online options.

ITTC: Bournemouth; ✆ +44 1202 516289; www.ittc.co.uk; TEFL taster day £70 including lunch; frequency 10 per year. Fee can be credited to CELTA if booked.

KRISTAL INTERNATIONAL: Carmarthen, Wales; ✆ +44 1994 231145; www.tefl-course.net; modularised 30-hour courses which combine on-site and home study; weekend courses offered in various UK locations; prices from £199 for Module 1.

SAXONCOURT TEACHER TRAINING: London; ✆ +44 20 7499 8533; www.saxoncourt.com; mainly a CELTA provider but run taster days with a grammar booster workshop for £59.

STAR TEFL: www.star-tefl.com; weekend courses throughout the year in various cities from Cardiff to Cambridge; £200.

TEFL ORG UK: ✆ +44 1349 800600; info@tefl.org.uk; www.tefl.org.uk; classroom, online and combined TEFL courses throughout the UK, from 20 to 150 hours.

TEFL ORG UK

Rebecca is 18 years old and originally from Cambridgeshire. She took a 50-hour TEFL Course in April, and saw it as a great option for travel and work upon leaving school.

'My first TEFL job has been in Sant Sadurni D'Anoia, a small town in Catalunya (Spain) which is the birthplace of Cava. I'm working as a conversation assistant (alongside the English teacher) and living with local families. I teach children aged 7 to 16. It is very challenging, but so rewarding; we have a lot of fun too! I work 20 hours a week, but I am in school 9–5 most days. My main job is organising speaking activities, but I'm also involved in lots of other things and do private English classes; I currently do four hours a week but I am considering doing more. It's so wonderful to live in another culture: the food, the parties (they love their parties here) and it's the best way to learn another language and where I live there are two languages which is even better. Taking a TEFL Org UK course was one of my best decisions. I left school in June with average grades and started work in September. Being given such an opportunity in this economic climate is rare. I could not be happier. I intend doing a degree in a few years but for now, I am going to work and get the life experience that university cannot teach you. I'm currently planning where I want to go next – I am hoping France!'

Rebecca has just enhanced her qualification by completing a 100-hour Advanced TEFL Course, allowing her to specialise in teaching young learners, teaching business English and teaching English online.

UK-TEFL: Lytham, Lancashire; ✆ +44 871 222 1231; www.uk-tefl.com. Intensive standard and advanced 2 or 3 day courses throughout the UK but mainly in the London area, Birmingham and Manchester. Held on weekends and weekdays, £200–£250; summer 2015 discounted prices £133/£167.

ONLINE TEFL TRAINING

AMERICAN CULTURE UK/TESOL TURKEY: Antalya, Turkey; www.onlinetesol.com; £1,416.

AMERICAN TESOL INSTITUTE: Tampa, FL, USA; ✆ +1 813 975 7404 and 877 748 7900; www.americantesol.com; from $295.

ANGLO CENTRES: Calle Unió, 41, bajo, Tarragona, Spain 43001; ✆ +34 977 251 437; www.tefl.anglocentres.com. 150-hour online course (£315) or combined with teaching practice (£750). Endorsements for Business English or Young Learner teaching can be added. Also offer 4-week intensive course in Tarragona.

CIEE (COUNCIL ON INTERNATIONAL EDUCATIONAL EXCHANGE): Portland, Maine, USA; tefl@ciee.org; www.ciee.org/tefl. Online TEFL course.

ENGLISH TRAINING CENTRE: Birmingham, UK; ✆ +44 121 449 2221; www. englishtrainingcentre.co.uk or www.tesol-direct.com; online courses at three levels: 250, 150 and 110 hours costing £465, £355 and £299 respectively with last minute discounts sometimes available. Also offer certificate courses in Teaching Business English (TBE) and Teaching English to Young Learners (TEYL).

ENJOY TEFL: Harrogate; www.enjoytefl.com; 120-hour course and access to two mindfulness courses for £90/$135.

ESL CERTIFIED: ✆ +1 888 661 8005; www.eslcertified.com, 100-hour ($350) and 120-hour ($425) instructor-led online courses. Free demo lesson available online.

AMERICAN TESOL INSTITUTE

American TESOL Institute (ATI) was incorporated in 2004 to meet the global demand for professionally trained English teachers, and provides TESOL certification courses. American TESOL Institute's mission is the standardising of an introductory English teacher training programme for individuals wishing to teach English, and to raise awareness about teaching abroad opportunities for US citizens.

American TESOL Institute's vision is innovating and growing with technologies that are changing the paradigm of teaching and learning, and to certify 100,000 plus English teachers to work abroad and online by the year 2021.

ATI is known for providing a quality and cutting edge learning experience, and for being a leader in the global education market. ATI is building on existing strengths to maintain an international reputation as a trusted provider of high quality TESOL education and teachers.

Upon completion of an American TESOL certification course you can teach English as a second language worldwide. In the global economy jobs teaching English as a second language are available in most countries. American TESOL graduates receive optional job placement teaching English abroad. American TESOL graduates teach non-native English speakers the basics of English while living and working abroad. TESOL and TEFL teachers are trained to meet general academic requirements for teaching ESL, which provides opportunities for ATI teachers to excel in a variety of environments. English as a Second Language courses are offered globally in most public and private school systems. There is a high demand for American TESOL teachers at schools and universities worldwide.

After becoming certified with American TESOL Institute, a job placement support team helps you in obtaining a teaching job. TESOL Job Placement provides teaching opportunities in Asia, the Middle East, Europe, Latin America or anywhere else in the world where ESL positions are available. ATI provides volunteer and paid teaching jobs at schools or private organisations abroad, and paid or volunteer internships inside the USA. American TESOL graduates also have the option to pursue online and freelance teaching jobs. Job placement is optional with TESOL certification.

American TESOL certification provides a smooth transition to teaching English abroad in countries all over the world. TESOL courses provide a base knowledge in teaching English as a second language with focus on methods and approaches to TESOL.

Discover resources for teachers, professional development webinars, teaching jobs, and TESOL certification courses online at www.AmericanTESOL.com (+1 877 748 7900; info@americantesol.com).

TRINITY COLLEGE LONDON Approved Service Provider

TRINITY COLLEGE LONDON Validated Course Provider 2911

English for ASIA

Trinity Cert TESOL & Dip TESOL

- Supportive training
- Excellent centre facilities and comprehensive teaching resources
- Immediate post course employment opportunities
- **Over 1000 teachers trained since 1999**
- **Higher than 99% pass rate in 2015**
- **92% of trainees received A or B passes in 2015**

Cert TESOL full-time 2016 courses (applicable for student visas)

- 11 Jan – 6 Feb
- › 15 Feb – 12 Mar
- › 14 Mar – 9 Apr
- › 11 Apr – 7 May
- 16 May – 11 Jun
- › 4 Jul – 30 Jul
- › 1 Aug – 27 Aug
- › 5 Sep – 1 Oct
- 3 Oct – 29 Oct
- › 14 Nov – 10 Dec

Cert TESOL part-time 2016 courses

- 19 Mar – 12 Jun
- › 18 Jun – 11 Sep
- › 17 Sep – 11 Dec

Dip TESOL blended online/ face-to-face courses

- Nov – Aug
- › Feb – Feb

'The Trinity CertTESOL can be a demanding but also richly rewarding experience for trainee teachers. We do all we can to create a positive, supportive environment for all of those who train with us, using a blend of approaches to cater for the different types of trainee that we work with on the course, from experienced teachers to those entering a new career in teaching.'

Tom Garside, Director of Teacher Training
BA(Hons.) CELTA, DELTA, PGDipTESOL, MATESOL

E tesol@englishforasia.com   **T** +852 2366 3792   www.englishforasia.com

The Trinity Certificate in TESOL and Diploma in TESOL are recognised and accepted by the British Council. The Certificate in TESOL registered under the Non-local Higher and Professional Education (Regulation) Ordinance (Course Registration 250562). It is a matter of

GLOBAL ENGLISH: Exeter, Devon, UK; ✆ +44 1392 411999; www.global-english.com; from £210 for 70 hours to £475 for 250-hour course; offers additional specialist components in Young Learners and Business English plus flexible teaching practice local to the trainee.

GLOBAL LANGUAGE TRAINING: London and New York; ✆ +44 203 435 6821 (UK), +1 646 688 2927 (US); www.globaltefl.uk.com. 150-, 120-, 60- and a variety of short 40-hour courses available for £189, £139, £79 and £59.

ICAL: London, UK; ✆ +44 845 310 4104; www.icaltefl.com £155; offers practical teaching placement; cost is £245.

INTENSIVE TEFL COURSES (ITC): Darlington, UK; ✆ 0845 644 5464; www.tefl.co.uk; distance course for £135, nominated as Part 2. Part 1 should be a face-to-face weekend course but not being offered at present.

INTERNATIONAL TEFL ACADEMY: Chicago headquarters; www.internationalteflacademy.com. 170-hour online certificate course offered over 11 weeks including 20 hours of classroom observation and teaching to be arranged locally. $1,395.

INTERNATIONAL TEFL TRAINING INSTITUTE: New York, Sao Paulo, London; ✆ +1 646 762 6361; www.becomeenglishteachers.com. 120 hours, US$350 with tutor support: US$235 without tutor. Can be combined with onsite tuition in many cities worldwide ($1,600+).

INTERNATIONAL TEFL INSTITUTE: London W1; ✆ +44 20 7129 1063; admin@itefli.com; www.itefli.com. 120-hour Certificate (£115), 180-hour Diploma (£135) and 250-hour Master Diploma (£169) plus short specialised TEFL/TESOL courses.

INTESOL WORLDWIDE LTD: Northwich, Cheshire, UK; ✆ +44 1606 871001; www.intesoltesoltraining.com; online and onsite courses (since 1993), costing from £175 to £1,260; 120-hour Cert TEFL with TEYL (Young Learners) allows you to take up Intesol-arranged jobs in Cambodia, China, India, Japan, Korea, Nepal, South America, Thailand, UAE or Vietnam.

i-to-i: Leeds, UK; ✆ +44 800 093 3148; www.i-to-i.com, www.onlinetefl.com; 140-hour course combines 20 hour face-to-face weekend course with 120 hours follow-up online, £349 with occasional internet reductions. Range of online courses from £149 for a foundation course. Also Level 5 EDI CertTEFL accredited by Ofqual that includes 6 hours of assessed teaching practice. Current price is £1,195.

ITTT (INTERNATIONAL TEFL & TESOL TRAINING): www.teflcourse.net or www.teflcorp.com; range of online courses from $190 to $1500 when combined with teaching practice. Now affiliated to TEFL International, which offers 4-week in-class courses worldwide.

LearnTEFL: London SW19; ✆ +44 208 123 1585; and Chicago, +1 888 234 9318; www.learntefl.com; 60-hour foundation course (£125), 120-hour course (£225), 150 hours (£275).

LINGUAEDGE: Beverly Hills, CA, USA; ✆ +1 888 944 3343; www.linguaedge.com; 50-hour, 100-hour or 150-hour online courses; $149, $249, and $349.

LONDON TEACHER TRAINING COLLEGE: London, UK; ✆+44 20 8133 2027; lttc@teachenglish.co.uk; www.teachenglish.co.uk; 60 and 120-hour certificate courses (£175/£285 by download, £310 by post); 180 hour Diploma (£325).

LOVETEFL.COM: Leeds, UK; ✆+44 113 829 3300; info@lovetefl.com; www.lovetefl.com; 120, 180 and 300 hours: £129, £169 and £239 (2015). Job and intern placement in Thailand, China, etc.

MIDWEST EDUCATION GROUP: Chicago, IL, USA; ✆ +1 773 382 1567; contact@midwested.us; www.midwested.us; 120-hour online TESOL training programme certified by Illinois Board of Higher Education with optional 30-hour practicum; shorter option 60 hours with tutor support.

MYTEFLWORLD: www.myteflworld.com. 100-hour TEFL course accredited by ACCREDITAT. £195.

NORWOOD ENGLISH: Laois, Eire; ✆+353 087 94 10148; www.norwoodenglish.com; from €160 for 120-hour distance course; does not offer practical teaching placement. Other specialist courses on Grammar for EFL (€100), teaching Business English (€175), etc. New joint online course and teaching practice in Vietnam.

ONTESOL: Toronto, Canada; ✆ +1 416 929 0227; toll-free in Canada +1 877 778 3749; toll-free UK +44 808 101 3459; info@ontesol.com; www.ontesol.com; online courses developed via Coventry House lasting 100, 120 or 250 hours; C$349 for 120-hour course.

TEACHING ENGLISH IN ITALY: Florence, Italy; sheila@teachingenglishinitaly.com; www.teaching englishinitaly.com; Basic Online TEFL/TESOL English Teaching Certificate course (120 hours), $265/€200; Grammar course (20 hours) with guided tutor support, $110; Teaching Business English and Teaching English to Young Learners, both 30 hours, and both cost $220.

TEACH TEFL FIRST: London; ✆ +44 207 247 5820; www.teachteflfirst.com/contact. Part of recruitment company Teachtotravel.co.uk. Range of online courses: the Traveller (80 hours), Adventurer (100 hours) and Explorer (140 hours); £160–£200.

TEFL 247: London and Co. Cork, Ireland; ✆ +44 8444 905078; tefl247.com; very cheap self-guided on-line courses starting at £30. Organise 'TEFL bursts' i.e. short tasters of teaching in China, Thailand or Poland.

TEFL CAMBRIDGE: ✆ +44 208 816 8212; www.teflcambridge.com; 5 TEFL training courses ranging from 20 to 140 hours. Accredited by ACCREDITAT.

TEFL EXPRESS: ✆ +44 20 3287 7796; www.teflexpress.co.uk; 150-hour online courses costing £349–£469. Affiliated to Language Link and course provides passport to jobs and internships in their network of 100+ schools worldwide.

TEFLINK: ✆ +44 208 144 6901; www.teflink.com; range of 8 online TEFL courses; accredited by ACCREDITAT.

TEFLSTOP: www.teflstop.com; part of Intesol Worldwide (above); online course aimed at backpackers; £295 for 100-hour course; guaranteed jobs or internships in China.

TEFL TRAINING COLLEGE: London W1; ✆ +44 20 7129 1063; admin@go-tefl.com; www.go-tefl.com. Certificates/Diplomas of Educational Studies in TEFL from 100 to 300 hours, costing £115–£219. Sister company to International TEFL Institute above.

TESOL-DIRECT: Birmingham; ✆ +44 121 449 2221; www.tesol-direct.com; 110-hour certificate course (from £325) and 150-hour course (from £495) plus specialist 65-hour courses on teaching Business English (£350) and English for Young Learners (£295).

THE CONSULTANTS-E LTD: Weymouth; ✆ +44 1305 788523; www.theconsultants-e.com; specialise in online courses in International Business English Training. Also some in-person courses, e.g. 10 week Cert IBET (Certificate in International Business English Training), £695 plus moderation fee of £160.

TRAIN-TO-TEFL: Bolton; www.train-to-tefl.com. 120-hour online certificate course. Online interactive modules (17 units) written by experienced teacher and trainer Suzannah Redmond with regular assessment so that trainees can gauge their progress. £99. Can be blended with 2-day face-to-face TEFL introduction course in Manchester.

TUTORGROUP ONLINE TESOL TRAINING INSTITUTE: Taipei, Taiwan; www.TGOTTI.com. 70-hour course.

UNIVERSITY OF TORONTO: Toronto, Canada; ✆+1 416 628 1386; http://teflonline.teachaway.com; online TEFL course offered in association with respected teacher recruitment agency Teachaway; 100-hour, 120-hour or 150-hour options ($995, $1,295 and $1,495).

WORDS LANGUAGE SERVICES: Dublin, Ireland; ✆ +353 1 6392984; www.wls.ie; 100-hour course for €225; grammar course for €50; does not offer practical teaching placement.

ACADEMIC COURSES

This represents a small selection of university courses in TEFL/TESL in the UK. On the www.ucas.com site, you can search by subject and find courses in TEFL/TESOL usually offered in combination with another subject such as a modern language or tourism.

ANGLIA RUSKIN UNIVERSITY: East Road, Cambridge CB1 1PT; ✆ +44 1245 493131; efl@anglia.ac.uk; www.anglia.ac.uk; offers BA in English Language teaching and an MA in Applied Linguistics and TESOL.

ASTON UNIVERSITY: Languages and Social Sciences Unit, Aston Triangle, Birmingham B4 7ET; ✆ +44 121 204 3762; lss_pgadmissions@aston.ac.uk; www.aston.ac.uk; MSc in Teaching English to Speakers of Other Languages (TESOL), MSc in Teaching English for Specific Purposes (TESP), MSc in Teaching English to Young Learners (TEYL), MSc in Educational Management in TESOL (EMT), part-time, 2–5 years, £8,000; MA in TESOL studies, MA in TESOL and Translation, MA in Applied Linguistics, all £5,250.

CANTERBURY CHRIST CHURCH UNIVERSITY: North Holmes Road, Canterbury CT1 1QU; ✆ +44 1227 767700 (Department of English and Language Studies); languagestudies@canterbury. ac.uk; www.canterbury.ac.uk; offers Diploma/MA in TESOL; full (12 months) or part-time; also offers the CELTA (see entry).

LONDON METROPOLITAN UNIVERSITY: 166–220 Holloway Road, London N7 8DB; ✆ +44 20 7133 4202; humanities@londonmet.ac.uk/admissions@londonmet.ac.uk; www.londonmet.ac.uk; MA TESOL and Applied Linguistics (for experienced teachers). Full-time one-year course; £7,650 for EU students or £11,400 for non-EU students.

SHEFFIELD HALLAM UNIVERSITY TESOL CENTRE: Sheffield; ✆ +44 114 225 5515; www.shu. ac.uk/tesol/teaching; MA in TESOL (full-time); M.Ed. in TESOL by distance learning; Postgraduate Certificate in Teaching English for Academic Purposes.

UNIVERSITY COLLEGE PLYMOUTH ST MARK & ST JOHN: Plymouth; www.marjon.ac.uk; MSc TESOL offered full-time for 12 months; £5,000 for UK/EU students and £10,000 for overseas; good honours degree or equivalent required for admission.

UNIVERSITY OF BEDFORDSHIRE: Park Square, Luton, Bedfordshire LU1 3JU; ✆ +44 1234 400400; www.beds.ac.uk; BA (Hons) in English Language Studies with Teaching English as a Foreign Language (TEFL), BA (Hons) in English Language for Business, BA (Hons)/Diploma in English for International Communication, MA in Applied Linguistics (TEFL), TEFL Certificate (summer school, £1200), TEFL Certificate (part-time evening).

UNIVERSITY OF BIRMINGHAM: Centre for English Language Studies, Westmere, Edgbaston Park Road, Edgbaston, Birmingham B15 2TT; ✆ +44 121 414 3239/5696; www.birmingham.ac.uk; MA in TESOL, on-site or distance learning or in Applied Linguistics.

UNIVERSITY OF BRIGHTON: School of Languages, Falmer, Brighton, East Sussex BN1 9PH; a.pickering@brighton.ac.uk; www.arts.brighton.ac.uk; offers Diploma and MA in TESOL; 1 year full-time or part-time; these are both post-graduate courses; applicants must have some English teaching experience for the MA and 2 years for the Diploma; also offers a MA in English Language Teaching, 1 year full-time or part-time, for teachers with a limited amount of experience. The one-year Diploma course costs £1,750 (full-time) while the MA fees are £5,580.

UNIVERSITY OF CENTRAL LANCASHIRE: School of Languages and International Studies, Preston, PR1 2HE; ✆ +44 1772 892400; cenquiries@uclan.ac.uk; www.uclan.ac.uk; BA (Hons) in Teaching English to Speakers of Other Languages, BA (Hons) in TESOL and Modern Languages, MA in TESOL and Applied Linguistics.

UNIVERSITY OF EDINBURGH: 21 Hill Place, Edinburgh EH8 9DP; ✆ +44 131 650 6200; www.ed. ac.uk; MSc or Post-Graduate Diploma or Certificate in TESOL.

UNIVERSITY OF EXETER: School of Education and Lifelong Learning, St Luke's Campus, Heavitree Road, Exeter EX1 2LU; ✆ +44 1392 264837; ed-student@exeter.ac.uk; EdD/PhD/MPhil/MEd/ TESOL; full-time, part-time and intensive summer study.

UNIVERSITY OF LEEDS: Leeds; www.education.leeds.ac.uk; MA in TESOL with choice of specialities, eg Young Learners and ICT.

UNIVERSITY OF MANCHESTER: Postgraduate Admissions Office, School of Education, Faculty of Humanities, Oxford Road, Manchester M13 9PL; ✆ +44 161 275 3463; education-enquiries@ manchester.ac.uk; www.manchester.ac.uk; offers MA TESOL or MA Educational Technology and TESOL in 3 modes of study: 1 year full-time or part-time, UK/EU £6,500 and overseas £14,500;

and 3 years distance, £2,667 a year; entry requirements include 3 years' teaching experience; the university also offers an introduction to TESOL as part of an undergraduate degree (one term).

UNIVERSITY OF READING: Department of English Language & Applied Linguistics, Whiteknights, PO Box 218, Reading RG6 6AA; ✆ +44 118 378 8512; a.j.horn@reading.ac.uk; http://bit.ly/NrUkaC; MA ELT in both campus-based and distance-study modes, with an additional study track for novice teachers; also, MA in Applied Linguistics.

UNIVERSITY OF STIRLING: Institute of Education (CELT), Stirling FK9 4LA; www.stir.ac.uk; MSc in TESOL (Teaching English to Speakers of Other Languages); MSc in TESOL and CALL (Computer Assisted Language Learning) and PhD and EdD in TESOL Education available; General English, IELTS Preparation, English for University Study, Short Courses for Teachers, and a Summer School in August are also offered.

UNIVERSITY OF SUSSEX: Sussex Centre for Language Studies, Falmer, Brighton, East Sussex BN1 9RH; ✆ +44 1273 678416; UG.Admissions@sussex.ac.uk (for bachelor's degree programme) or PG.Admissions@sussex.ac.uk (for master's programmes); www.sussex.ac.uk; BA in English Language Teaching; 3 or 4-year joint major in ELT with English, English Language, Language(s) or Linguistics; includes opportunity to take Trinity TESOL Certificate as part of degree; MA in English Language Teaching; MA in International English Language Teaching and a Postgraduate Diploma in ELT (full-time 1 year, part-time 2 years).

UNIVERSITY OF WARWICK: Centre for Applied Linguistics, Coventry CV4 7AL; ✆ +44 24 7652 3200; appling@warwick.ac.uk; www2.warwick.ac.uk/fac/soc/al/; MA in ELT/ESP/English for Young Learners (all post-experience), English Language Teaching (Studies and Methods) (less than 2 years' experience), ELT (Multimedia) (either pre- or post-experience); one-term Postgraduate Certificate in any of the MA specialisms (January to March), 2 terms for a Postgraduate Diploma.

UNIVERSITY OF WOLVERHAMPTON: Wolverhampton; www.wlv.ac.uk; International Academy offers BA (Hons) in Linguistics and TESOL.

TRAINING COURSES IN NORTH AMERICA

USA

AMERICAN LANGUAGE INSTITUTE: San Diego State University, 5250 Campanile Drive, San Diego, CA 92182 1914; ✆ +1 619 594 5907; ali@mail.sdsu.edu or rhillier@mail.sdsu.edu; www.ali.sdsu.edu; TESL/TEFL Certificate validated by SDSU Dept of Education (3 graduate credits); 4 weeks, 130 hours, offered in January and June, and part-time in autumn and spring; $2,725; dormitory/homestay/apartment accommodation can be arranged through the ALI housing office. Job placement assistant programme.

BOSTON ACADEMY OF ENGLISH: 59 Temple Place, 2nd Floor, Boston, MA 02111; ✆ +1 617 338 6243; info@bostonacademyofenglish.com; www.teflboston.com; 4-week intensive 120-hour CTE-FL course, $2,550; part-time over 12 weeks, $2,400.

BOSTON LANGUAGE INSTITUTE: 648 Beacon St, Boston, MA 02215; ✆ +1 617 262 3500; www.bostonlanguage.com; intensive 4-week TEFL Certificate course (120 hours) offered monthly; 12-week Saturday programmes also offered 3 times a year; special TEFL Certificate Programme for Non-Native Speakers of English also offered: course includes additional training on pronunciation, American culture and other relevant topics; tuition of $2,465 includes fees, all study materials and lifetime job assistance.

ETON INSTITUTE: New York; www.americas.etoninstitute.com; TESOL/TFL programme leads to City and Guilds Access Certificate in English Language Teaching (ACE), a TESOL qualification in communicative and modern language methods; 120 hours over 6 weeks. £2,480.

HAMLINE UNIVERSITY: TEFL Certificate Program, School of Education, 1536 Hewitt Avenue, St Paul, MN 55104; ✆ +1 651 523 2429; education@hamline.edu; www.hamline.edu; intensive 1-month courses in July and January and part-time extensive courses autumn and spring; current tuition $3,230; focus is on developing communicative language teaching strategies; ongoing career counselling provided. Graduate credit granted; course can be used towards Hamline's MA in ESL; advanced TEFL option offered.

HUNTER COLLEGE CONTINUING EDUCATION: New York; ✆ +1 212 772 4000; www.hunter.cuny.edu/ce/certificates/tesol. Intensive course with 20 hours of practice teaching in ESOL classrooms. $3,800.

INTERNATIONAL TEFL ACADEMY: Boston, Chicago, Honolulu, New York, San Diego and Seattle. 4-week course given at various intervals, e.g. 9 times a year in Chicago; from $1,995 in Chicago to $2,550 in Hawaii (at the Intercultural Communications College Honolulu).

LADO TEFL CERTIFICATE: 401 9th Street, NW, Suite C 100, Washington, DC 20004; ✆ +1 202 223 0023; tefl@lado.edu; www.tesol.com. 135-instructional-hour professional teacher training programme. Intensive courses offered monthly; semi-intensive courses in spring, summer and autumn. $1,950.

MIDWEST TEACHER TRAINING PROGRAM: 19 N. Pinckney Street, Madison, WI 53703; ✆ +1 800 765 8577 or +1 608 257 8476; info@mttp.com; www.mttp.com; practical, hands-on 5-week TEFL Certificate Course (130 hours including 10 hours of teaching practice) in a progressive university city; 4 times a year; tuition and course materials $2,595; housing arranged if needed; integrated with an ESL school providing an international environment; job placement assistance including resource library, job search workshop and personal résumé editing; graduates have found jobs in 40 countries.

NEW SCHOOL: New York; www.newschool.edu/matesol14; Masters in TESOL offered on-campus or online.

OXFORD SEMINARS: Santa Monica and New York; ✆ +1 800 779 1779; www.oxfordseminars.com; TESOL/TESL courses held in cities around the USA, usually on university/college campuses; 60 hours over 3 consecutive weekends; $1,095.

SCHOOL OF TEACHING ENGLISH AS A SECOND LANGUAGE (in cooperation with Seattle Pacific University): 9620 Stone Avenue. N., Suite 101, Seattle, WA 98103; ✆ +1 206 781 8607; STESLinfo@spu.edu; www.schooloftesl.com; offers both a TESOL/TEFL certificate and a Washington State ELL Endorsement programme. The certificate consists of four classes which may be taken in a 4-week intensive format or via evening and/or online classes. Tuition for all formats is $245 per credit (2015). Credits can be transferred into master's degree programmes in either the Seattle Pacific University School of Education or College of Arts and Sciences (MA-TESOL). Bachelor's degree required for admission. Local housing list available on request; personal advising; employment seminars, graduates' networking services and an onsite ESOL class.

SIT GRADUATE INSTITUTE: Brattleboro, Vermont 05302-0676; ✆ +1 802 258 3310; tesolcert@sit.edu; www.graduate.sit.edu. 130-hour TESOL Certificate course taught intensively at various times throughout the year in New York, Houston and locations in Latin America including Costa Rica, Guatemala and Ecuador. Affiliated to nonprofit World Learning and the Experiment in International Living. Cost from $1,400 in Caserta, Italy to $2,595 in New York.

TRANSWORLD SCHOOLS: TESOL Certificate training courses at Transworld Schools, 551 Sutter Street, 6th Floor, San Francisco, CA 94102; ✆ +1 415 928 2835; transwd@aol.com; www.transworldschools.com; Comprehensive TESOL Certificate (4 weeks full-time, 10 weeks part-time, $2,100); TESOL Certificate (3 weeks full-time, 10 weeks part-time $1,900); Intensive TESOL Certificate (for experienced ESOL teachers: 2 weeks full-time; 7 weeks part-time, $1,700); Advanced TESOL Certificate (for experienced ESOL teachers: 1 week full-time; 4 weeks part-time, $900); Distance Learning TESOL Certificate with 1 week on-site residency $1,000; all courses internationally recognised; approved by State of California, BPPE (Bureau for Private Postsecondary Education) and accredited by ACCET, Continuing Education Credits awarded; high-quality training, low tuition, and lifetime job placement worldwide; accommodation ($650–$1580 for 4 weeks); courses include evaluated Teaching Practice, teaching children and adults, grammar, Business English, TOEFL and syllabus design; facilities include multi-media lab, video and internet.

WASHINGTON ACADEMY OF LANGUAGES: TESL Graduate Certificate/Endorsement Program, 521 Wall St, Seattle, WA 98121; info@wal.org; www.wal.org; Graduate TEFL Certificate offered in conjunction with University of Seattle; 8 courses for total of 24 quarter credits; offered intensively as 8-week summer course, or online. Tuition for each course is $400 or $600.

WESTERN WASHINGTON UNIVERSITY TESOL PROGRAM: Bellingham, WA 98225; © +1 360 650 4949; www.wce.wwu.edu/TESOL; full-time and part-time university courses starting in September, with a summer intensive option; interdisciplinary course work and practical experience lead to a certificate of achievement and a supporting endorsement in teaching ESL; distance education and overseas practicum experiences in Mexico available. Fees total $6,750.

CANADA

Note that the website of TESL Canada (www.tesl.ca) has links to a large number of approved teacher training programmes across Canada.

GLOBAL TESOL: Edmonton, Canada; © +1 888 270 2941; info@globaltesol.com; www.globaltesol.com; office/training centres across Canada, and in many countries worldwide; world's largest TESOL Certificate and Diploma granting programme as described in a free Travel-and-Teach information package; 40,000 graduates teaching English in 85 countries; range of Canada Government certified TESOL Certificate and Diploma courses held regularly in cities throughout Canada and other countries; 5-day intensive format, or online and correspondence study options available worldwide; overseas job guaranteed; prices range from C$695 to C$3,495; 16 specialisation course options; 120-hour to 600-hour programme available; other courses offered online or by correspondence include Teaching Business English, Teaching TOEFL Preparation, Teaching Grammar, Teaching Children, Teaching Adults, Tourism English, Teaching CALL Computer English and more; accommodation can be arranged; franchises available; email for details.

GREYSTONE COLLEGE: 560 Granville St, 3rd Floor, Vancouver, BC V6C 1W6; www.greystonecollege.com; TESOL130 Certificate programme; 1 month full-time, offered monthly or 12 weeks part-time. Practicum arranged after the course. C$1,620.

INTERNATIONAL HOUSE CAREER COLLEGE: 200–215 West Broadway, Vancouver, BC V6H 167; © +1 604 739 9836; www.tesl-vancouver.com; IH Career College offers IH Certificate (130 hours and online) starting 4 times a year. C$1,650 (C$1,000 online).

INTERNATIONAL LANGUAGE ACADEMY OF CANADA (ILAC): 920 Yonge St, 4th floor, Toronto M4W 3C7; © +1 416 961 5151 and 688 West Hastings, 3rd floor, Vancouver, BC V6B 1P1; © +1 604 484 6660; www.ilactesol.com; 4-week, 100-hour certificate courses offered 7 times a year in both cities. C$990.

OXFORD SEMINARS: 131 Bloor St West, Suite 200–390, Toronto, ON M5S 1R8 and 10405 Jasper Ave, Suite 16–21, Edmonton, AB T5J 3S2; www.oxfordseminars.ca; 60-hour course held over 3 consecutive weekends. C$995 (plus GST).

PEAK TESOL: College of the Rockies, Cranbrook, BC; www.cotr.bc.ca/TESOL; online course or blended, with optional 20-hour practicum. C$1,995.

SOL SCHOOLS INTERNATIONAL: Toronto; www.solschools.com. 4-week TESL diploma offered monthly. C$1,450.

STUDY AT COVENTRY: Toronto; www.study-at-coventry.com. 5-week TESOL Certificate, recognised by TESL Canada. 8 times a year C$999.

TRAINING COURSES WORLDWIDE

WORLDWIDE

BRIDGE: Head office: 915 South Colorado Blvd, Denver, CO 80246; © +1 303 785 8864; toll-free (USA and Canada): © +1 888 827 4757 or +44 808 120 7163 (UK); www.bridgetefl.com; intensive

140-hour TEFL courses offered in centres in Argentina, Brazil, Chile, Peru, Colombia, Costa Rica, Guatemala, Mexico, Czech Republic, UK (Northern Ireland and London), Greece, Italy, Spain, Hungary, Russia, Thailand, Turkey, Vietnam, Cambodia, UAE, South Africa and USA; on-site TEFL course tuition starts at $1,695. Online and blended-learning courses also available worldwide starting at $184.

EBC INTERNATIONAL: Headquarters, Madrid; ℂ +34 91 555 3975 plus toll-free numbers in UK, US and Canada; www.ebcteflcourse.com; 4-week certificate course offered at frequent intervals in Madrid, Buenos Aires, Boracay (Philippines), Chania, Prague and Phuket. Course alone costs from €1000 but can also book accommodation

GLOBAL TESOL COLLEGE: main website www.globaltesol.com and headquarters in Canada: 7712, 104 St, Edmonton, AB T6E 4C5; in North America: ℂ +1 888 270 2941/+1 780 438 5704, tesol@globaltesol.com; US-East in North America: ℂ +1 866 837 6565, tesol@tesol world.com; US-West in North America: ℂ +1 888 837 6587, info@globaltesolusa.com; Australia: ℂ +61 7 3221 5100, teachenglish@sarinarusso.com.au; China: ℂ +86 134 0508 0034, info@teflcoursechina.com; Greece: ℂ +30 274 302 9012, Georgia@globaltesol.gr; for accommodation: info@linguisticlab.com; India: ℂ +91 172 269 2682, info@tesolindia.com; Malaysia: ℂ +60 85 413778, joanne@globaltesol.com.my; Mexico: ℂ +52 818 368 2410, linda@engcanada.com; New Zealand: nz@globaltesol.co.nz; Philippines: ℂ +632 910 1438, global@edulynxcorp.com; Singapore: ℂ +65 6221 3957, info@globalelt.org; Taiwan: ℂ +886 2 2369 1181 (24 hrs), anne@globaltesol.com.

LANGUAGE CORPS: Stow, MA; ℂ +1 978 562 2100; toll-free (North America): +1 877 216 3267; www.languagecorps.com; 4-week TESOL training course offered in many places worldwide from Crete to St Petersburg, Rio to Phnom Penh, followed by job-placement assistance; courses accept school leavers; cost varies according to location but typically $1,750–$2,000 with varying options for paying more for extra services, eg guaranteed job placement.

PARADISE TEFL: www.paradisetefl.com; based in Cambodia with intensive courses offered in multiple locations in Cambodia, Vietnam, Laos, Malaysia, Thailand and Mexico; frequent start dates.

SIT (SCHOOL FOR INTERNATIONAL TRAINING) GRADUATE INSTITUTE: Kipling Road, PO Box 676, Brattleboro, VT 05302; ℂ +1 800 257 7751; tesolcert@sit.edu; www.sit.edu/tesolcert; full-time; 130-hour SIT TESOL Certificate course offered in various locations in the US and worldwide including Chicago, IL and Rohnert Park, CA, Quito (Ecuador), Oaxaca (Mexico), Bangkok and Chiang Mai (Thailand), Guatemala City and Quetzeltanango (Guatemala), Kharviv (Ukraine) and others; fees vary from $1,400 in Thailand to $2,295 in the US.

TEFL INTERNATIONAL: admin@teflinternational.org.uk; www.teflinternational.org.uk; USA Head office: 1200 Belle Passi Rd. Woodburn, OR 97071; TEFL International TESOL Certificate, 120-hour including observed Teaching Practice; available worldwide: full-time, part-time and distance learning; Special Projects with guaranteed work or internship (including volunteer projects); TEFL International World Wide Locations: Buenos Aires, Beijing, Hong Kong, Shanghai, Zhuhai, Manuel Antonio, Prague, Alexandria, Brittany, Corinth, Calcutta, Florence, Rome, Tokyo, Kathmandu, Cebu (Philippines), Lubin, Seoul, Barcelona, Seville, Ban Phe, Chiang Mai and Phuket, London, New York, Woodburn, Ho Chi Minh City; most centres offer the course every month; prices vary slightly from $1,390 to $1,790, but with regular specials and discount programmes.

VIA LINGUA: info@vialingua.org; www.vialingua.org; Proprietary 120-hour Certificate course (Via Lingua CTEFL) accredited by the College of Teachers and franchised to language institutes worldwide; moderated by ELT Institute, Hunter College, City University of New York; course available in Arequipa (Peru), Budapest, Buenos Aires, Guzmán (Mexico), Crete, Florence, Ho Chi Minh City, Istanbul, New York, Panama, Pattaya (Thailand), Phnom Penh (Cambodia), Porto (Portugal), Rio de Janeiro, St Petersburg, Santiago (Chile) and Sardinia; prices vary according to location from €1,175 course fee in Florence to $2,100 in New York.

ARGENTINA

ÍBERO TEFL SCHOOL: 113 Piedras Street, Buenos Aires; © +54 11 6023 8375; info@iberotefl.com. ar; www.iberotefl.com; intensive 4-week TEFL certificate courses offered monthly; $990; can be combined with 3 weeks' Spanish tuition for $1,365; claim 99% of graduates find paid jobs after gaining certificate.

MENTE ARGENTINA: Av. Santa Fe 3192 piso 4'b', C1425, Buenos Aires; © +54 11 3968 7861 (Argentina); +1 858 926 5510 (USA); +44 20 3286 3438 (UK); info@menteargentina.com; www.menteargentina.com; 4-week TEFL certificate course offered monthly; 150 hours including 24 hours of teaching practice; all-in prices including accommodation from $2,690 for student residence to $3,250 for private apartment, all in the best areas of Buenos Aires such as Palermo, Belgrano, Barrio Norte and Recoleta; Spanish course can also be arranged.

ROAD2ARGENTINA: Buenos Aires; © +54 11 4826 0820; www.road2argentina.com/tefl-argentina; partner of EBC above with follow-on volunteer teacher placement programme (for a fee).

AUSTRALIA

AUSTRALIAN TESOL TRAINING CENTRE (ATTC): Sydney: Level 1, 31 Market Street, Sydney, NSW 2000; © +61 2 9389 0249; Brisbane: Level 1, 295 Ann Street, Brisbane, QLD 4001; © +61 7 3229 0350; train@attc.edu.au; www.attc.edu.au; CELTA centres that offer Foundation in TESOL course (4 weeks) full and part-time courses throughout the year; accommodation service available; internet enrolment AUS$1,500.

ENGLISH LANGUAGE SERVICES: Adelaide Institute of Technical and Further Education (part of the Government Department of Education, Training and Employment), 5th Floor, Renaissance Centre, 127 Rundle Mall, Adelaide, South Australia 5000; © +61 8 8207 8805; els.tesol@tafesa.edu.au; http://els.sa.edu.au; Certificate IV in TESOL; 315-curriculum hour course AUS$3,300; TESOL for overseas teachers and TESOL online.

GLOBAL TESOL AUSTRALIA: Sarina Russo Centre, 82 Ann Street, Brisbane, Queensland 4000; © +61 7 3221 5100; teachenglish@sarinarusso.com.au; www.globaltesol.com; 120-hour to 600-hour programmes available; tuition fees AUS$995–$2,300; all courses can be completed in-class, online or by correspondence; job overseas guaranteed.

LANGUAGE TRAINING INSTITUTE (LTi): PO Box 1061, Nambour, Queensland 4560; © +61 7 5442 3511; admin@LTi.edu.au; www.LTi.edu.au; Certificate IV in TESOL; 5 weeks full-time or up to 12 months part-time. Course can be completed on-site at several centres in Victoria, NSW and Queensland (and also Singapore and Tehran) or by distance education (either online or traditional using printed textbooks and workbooks). AUS$2,000–$3,000.

LEXIS TESOL TRAINING CENTRE (LTTC): Maroochydore, Queensland; © +61 7 54792272 or 5447 4448; www.lexistesoltraining.com/sunshine-coast; Intro to TESOL; 1 or 2 weeks in Maroochydore, Brisbane, Byrons Bay, Noosa and Perth. $499 or $999. Maroochydore centre also offers the CELTA.

TEACH INTERNATIONAL: Head Office, Level 2, 370 George Street, Brisbane, Queensland 4000; © +61 7 3211 4633 ext 4; www.teachinternational.com; Foundation in TESOL, 100 hours, AUS$1,695; Certificate III in TESOL, 110 hours, AUS$2,295, and Certificate IV in TESOL, 220 hours, AUS$2,995, accredited by Australian government; offered throughout the year.

BRAZIL

INTERNATIONAL TEFL ACADEMY: Rio de Janeiro; www.internationalteflacademy.com; Monthly, $1,995.

TEFL INTERNATIONAL: Natal; www.teflinternational.org.uk; 2 full-time courses a year in January and July. $2000 excluding accommodation.

CAMBODIA

LANGUAGECORPS: ✆ +1 877 216 3267 toll-free (US); www.languagecorps.com; 4-week TESOL courses available monthly in Cambodia; $1,750.

TEACHERS IN CAMBODIA: Phnom Penh; http://teachersincambodia.com/tefl-course; in partnership with Learning Jungle International School 4-week TEFL training course programme that includes 20 hours of classroom observation, 20 hours of monitored classroom teaching experience and employment.

CHILE

INTERNATIONAL TEFL ACADEMY: Av. Las Urbinas 68, Providencia, Santiago; ✆ +56 9 976684301; info@tefl-academy.com; www.tefl-academy.com; 120-hour certificate course, 9 times a year; $1,995; life-long job assistance.

CHINA

APPLIED CAREER TESOL (ACT): Guangzhou; www.appliedtesol.com; on-the-job training with Canadian company; 160-hour TESOL Cert and 300 hours' teaching practice; $200 to start and then work is paid while learning.

BUSINESS ENGLISH SOLUTIONS INTERNATIONAL, LLC: Zhejiang, China and 10 Pine Ridge Lane, Mansfield CTR, CT 06250; ✆ +1 860 553 6666 (Connecticut); ✆ +86 13757252787 (China); info@journeyeast.org; www.journeyeast.org; TEFL Certification and iTEFL (Intensive TEFL China Certification); $1,800–$2,800 including accommodation; ESL Job Placement Service.

TEFL IN CHINA: Room 50307, Friendship Hotel, Beijing 100873; ✆ +86 10 828 50464; tefl@safea. gov.cn or service@chinajob.com; http://tefl.chinajob.com; 7-day intensive course offered 17 times a year usually in Beijing but also in Guangzhou, Shanghai and Chengdu. RMB3000.

TEFL INTERNATIONAL: At Gateway Language Village, Xiangzhou Culture Plaza, Ningxi Road, Zhuhai; ✆ +86 756 229 8967; admin@teflinternational.org.uk; www.teflinternational.org.uk; 120-hour accredited TESOL certificate course in Zhuhai and Beijing; good job and internship prospects all over China with the job placement assistance programme; course runs monthly and costs $1,690 (excluding accommodation) which costs $250–$300 in a shared dorm.

COLOMBIA

FUNDACION EDUCATIVA PERSONAL GROWTH: Bogota; www.pgrowth.com; training course in communicative teaching available in San Andres Island, Bogota and Cartagena (all in Colombia).

ISSO – INTERNATIONAL STUDENT SERVICES ORG: Cali; www.estudiosexterior.com; training centres in Bogotá, Cali, Medellin and Barranquilla. 120-hour course, semi-intensive and intensive. $950.

COSTA RICA

CENTRO ESPIRAL MANA: Invu de Peñas Blancas village, San Isidro de Peñas Blancas, near Chachagua, between San Ramon and La Fortuna; admin@espiralmana.org; www.espiralmana.org; School for International Training's TESOL Certificate Course; 1-month intensive offered monthly. Contact Mary Scholl.

COSTA RICA TEFL: Heredia and Playa Samara; info@costaricatefl.com; www.costaricatefl.com; offers 10 TEFL Certification courses per year, 160 hours' contact time; costs $1,485, including job placement assistance, course materials, course portfolio and text and access to local cultural events as well as a 10% discount on Spanish classes at Intercultura; the core instructors all have masters degrees and/or higher in education and in teaching English as a second or foreign language with more than 22 years of professional teaching experience; Heredia courses affiliated to Intercultura Costa Rica; www.interculturacostarica.com; see entry in Central America chapter.

INTERNATIONAL TEFL ACADEMY: Heredia; www.internationalteflacademy.com; 4-week course given 5 times a year between July and December. $1799 including online discount. Board and lodging with family cost $550.

MÁXIMO NIVEL EXECUTIVE LANGUAGE CENTER: de la Farmacia la Bomba 75m sur, San Pedro, San Jose (HQ in Cusco, Peru); ✆ +1 800 866 6358; info@maximonivel.com; www.maximonivel.com; 150-hour TEFL/TESOL Certificate (over 4 weeks) for $1,400–$1,700 offered monthly except December; 50-hour TEIB (Teaching English for International Business) Certificate and TIEEP (Teaching International English Exam Preparation) Certificate (over 3 days), $400 each; rough frequency 4 times a year; housing arranged with families, in shared apartments, hostels, etc from $225 for 4 weeks; lifetime job-finding assistance; an average of 5 graduates are employed by Máximo Nivel each month.

TEFL INTERNATIONAL: TEFL International, S.A. Apartado #161 Quepos, Manuel Antonio 6350 Costa Rica; admin@teflinternational.org.uk; www.teflinternational.org.uk; 120-hour TESOL; optional Spanish as a Second Language Course; monthly start dates; course fee $1,790. Homestays for $400.

CYPRUS

INTESOL: Limassol; UK office: ✆ +44 1565 631 366; info@intesolinternational.com; www.intesolinternational.com; 4-week TESOL course with teaching practice; lifetime job guidance. €1,260.

CZECH REPUBLIC

HELLO ACADEMIES: Tyrsova 1832/7, Prague 12000; ✆ +420 607 733334; s.madl@smallerearth.com; www.helloacademies.com; 4-week course offered monthly; $1,480. IATQuO-accredited.

INTERNATIONAL TEFL ACADEMY: Prague; www.internationalteflacademy.com; 6 times a year. $1,465.

ITC INTERNATIONAL TEFL CERTIFICATE: Frantiska Krízka 1, Prague 170 00; ✆ +420 224 817530; www.itc-international.eu; ITC trains English speakers during a 2-week course held 6 times a year. EU grant money may be available for this; contact your National Agency for Lifelong Learning Programme, or lukas@itc-international.eu.

LIVE TEFL: Prague; www.liveteflprague.com. 4-week course offered monthly. €1200. Accredited by the College of Teachers. Graduates of the course are given a 6-month full-time contract with salary guarantee with its parent company, the large language school Spěváček.

TEFL IN PRAGUE: Edua Languages, U Pujcovny 2, 110 00 Prague 1; ✆ +420 739 540930; info@teflinprague.com; www.teflinprague.com. 4-week TEFL courses with job guarantee and visa support in the Czech Republic. €1,550 including 39 days of accommodation. Under the umbrella of EDUA Group, the biggest private educational institution in the Czech Republic.

TEFL INTERNATIONAL: Prague; admin@teflinternational.org.uk; www.teflinternational.org.uk; 120-hour TESOL; optional Czech Language Course; 5 times a year; from £1,221 plus accommodation from €300.

TEFL WORLDWIDE PRAGUE: Freyova ul. 12/1, 190 00 Prague; ✆ +420 603 486 830; info@teflworldwideprague.com; www.teflworldwideprague.com; British and American-owned school offering 4-week TEFL course in Prague; courses offered monthly; job assistance worldwide; €1,300 plus accommodation.

THE LANGUAGE HOUSE: Education Center SPUSA, Na poříří 1038/6, 110 00 Prague 1; ✆ +420 224 210 813; info@thelanguagehouse.net; www.thelanguagehouse.net; 4-week course offered 10 times a year; €1300 or €1550 with housing included (€100 discount February–May and November). IATQuO-accredited.

TEFL WORLDWIDE

Ginny Thompson remembers her experiences from the October 2006 course with TEFL Worldwide:

"When I think back about my two years living abroad, it's amazing to realize how much my four-week experience with TEFL Worldwide Prague has impacted my life. With a bag packed for only those four weeks, I arrived in Prague with an open mind and a desire to experience a life and culture outside of the States. Little did I know, I would end up living in the Czech Republic for two years, working in Spain, South Korea and Peru, travelling the world, developing lifelong friendships and most importantly experiencing illuminating *growth*.

Although I had travelled and studied abroad before, I still arrived in Prague full of anxiety, a pounding heart and thoughts like, "How can I possibly teach English to someone who doesn't understand English?" These thoughts were quickly comforted by a lovely welcome to the city from TEFL Worldwide Prague from the moment I arrived at my accommodation. It was reassuring to arrive in a completely foreign place and feel so well cared for and encouraged by TEFL Worldwide to truly make the most of my certification experience. The instructors were patient, competent and extremely knowledgeable in the TEFL field. As I had never taught a class before in my life I was shocked at how by the end of the four weeks I felt confident to walk into any classroom anywhere in the world and teach an engaging, successful lesson.

I will always treasure memories like cooking dinner with friends while laughing over creative lesson ideas, the smile on my Czech student's face when she finally understood a grammar point, and the clinking of champagne glasses at the end of an incredible experience. TEFL Worldwide provided a program that not only gave me an excellent skill-set but also the freedom to be creative in my teaching, the support to find a job and home, and the encouragement to go out and explore the world. I've always said the most difficult part of leaving your comfort zone and moving abroad is that initial decision to pack your bags and get on a plane. After that first step, the world you enter will be an exciting, adventure filled place full of experiences you can't even imagine. From then on your world will expand horizons beyond horizons and you will be so thankful you took that initial risk. TEFL Worldwide Prague welcomed me into that world, taught me to embrace it and will forever hold a special place in my heart."

WATTSENGLISH: Rohacova 77, Prague 3; www.wattsenglish.com; UK-registered company with franchised summer camps teaching young children throughout the Czech Republic and Slovakia. Offer their own International TEFL Certificate (WITC) specialising in teaching English to young learners; 10,000 Czech crowns but free if candidate teaches a complete season with Wattsenglish.

ECUADOR

CEC-EPN (CONTINUING EDUCATION CENTER): National Polytechnic School, Quito; www.cec-epn.edu. ec/idiomas/tefl; 150 hours in September including cross-cultural awareness module; $1,395. Job placement assistance.

CENTRO DE ESTUDIOS INTERAMERICANOS/CEDEI: Casilla 597, Cuenca; ℭ +593 7 283 9003; info@cedei.org; www.cedei.org; summer TEFL programme, $3,225 including accommodation.

EGYPT

AMERICAN UNIVERSITY IN CAIRO: PO Box 74 New Cairo 11835; ℭ +20 2 2797 4978; teflinfo@ aucegypt.edu; www.aucegypt.edu; US enquiries to 420 Fifth Avenue, 3rd Floor, New York, NY 10018 2729; ℭ +1 212 730 8800; offers MA in Teaching English as a Foreign Language (MA/ TEFL); American-style education in an overseas setting.

TEFL INTERNATIONAL: 4, Shohdy Basha Street, Stanly, Alexandria; admin@teflinternational.org.uk; www.teflinternational.org.uk; 120-hour TESOL; monthly start dates; course fee $1,690; optional teaching Internship programme with Arabic language and cultural programme, $1,990; steady supply of jobs in Cairo.

FRANCE

TEFL INTERNATIONAL: 275 rue Saint-Jacques, 75006 Paris; admin@teflinternational.org.uk; www.teflinternational.org.uk; 120-hour TESOL; monthly start dates; course fee $600+€950. Accommodation from €250.

TEFL TOULOUSE: 9 Allees Frederic Mistral, 31400 Toulouse; ℭ +33 5 61 54 76 67; www.tefltoulouse. com; 4-week TEFL Certificate (validated by IATQuO); 9 per year; €1,600; accommodation costs €350–€600 with host family, in studio flat, etc; specialist sessions on Business English, teaching Young Learners and how to set up as a freelance teacher in France. Lifetime job guidance.

THE LANGUAGE HOUSE: Montpellier Espace Langues, 5 ter avenue Saint Lazare, 34000 Montpel-lier; ℭ +33 6 8483 8559; info@teflanguagehouse.com; www.teflanguagehouse.com; affiliated schools in Nice (English American Center, 22 rue d'Alsace Lorraine, 06000 Nice), as well as in Marrakesh (Morocco) and Antalya (Turkey); 4-week TEFL Certificate Program and 1-week Teaching Business English Program (also offered online); French programmes validated by IATQuO; offered monthly; Cert. course costs €1,290, and Business course €690 on-site, €390 online; homestays, single studios and shared apartments can be arranged; job assistance focuses on Mediterranean countries. Contact Gyl Golden.

GREECE

ANGLO-HELLENIC TEACHER TRAINING: 13 Vasilou St, Corinth 20006; ℭ +30 27410 53511; info@ teflcorinth.com; www.teflcorinth.com; delivers training course for TEFL International; accommoda-tion in Vrahati, 20 minutes from training centre.

CELT: 77 Akademias St, 106 78 Athens; ℭ +30 210 330 2406; www.celt.edu.gr; €1,300; 100+ hour Certificate course offered intensively in the summer months and part-time starting October, January, March and April; also offer CELTA course, €1,450.

TEFL INTERNATIONAL: Corinth; www.teflinternational.org.uk; 120-hour TESOL course over 4 weeks; 5 times between May and September; course fee $600+€920; accommodation for €250–€350; 10 hours' teaching practice with Greek children and adults; teacher placement service via Anglo-Hellenic Teacher Recruitment (www.anglo-hellenic.com).

VIA LINGUA CRETE: Chrysanthou Episkopou 48, 73 132 Chania, Crete; ✆ +30 28210 57438; maria@vialingua.org; www.teflgreece.com or www.vialingua.org; 5 offered per year between May and October; €1590 including shared accommodation.

GUATEMALA

MÁXIMO NIVEL EXECUTIVE LANGUAGE CENTER: 6a Avenida Norte #16 y 16A, La Antigua (HQ in Cusco, Peru); ✆ +1 800 866 6358; info@maximonivel.com; www.maximonivel.com; 150-hour TEFL/TESOL Certificate (over 4 weeks) for $1,400–$1,700 offered monthly except December; 50-hour TEIB (Teaching English for International Business) Certificate and TIEEP (Teaching International English Exam Preparation) Certificate (over 3 days), $400 each; rough frequency 4 times a year; housing arranged with families, in shared apartments, hostels, etc from $225 for 4 weeks; lifetime job-finding assistance; an average of 5 graduates are employed by Máximo Nivel each month.

HONG KONG

CHINESE UNIVERSITY OF HONG KONG: 23/F, Tower, B, School of Continuing and Professional Studies, The Chinese University of Hong Kong, Mongkok Town Centre, 90 Shantung Street, Mongkok, Kowloon; ✆ +852 2209 0235; http://english.scs.cuhk.edu.hk/scs/course/lang/eng/ab/doc/071-393000-01?disp=en; two courses on offer: Diploma Programme in Teaching English as a Second Language, 10 months, tuition fee HK$13,500 plus HK$100 enrolment fee; Master of Arts Programme in Teaching English to Speakers of Other Languages (jointly organised by School of Continuing and Professional Studies, The Chinese University of Hong Kong and Lancaster University), 2 years, tuition fee HK$89,800 plus HK$200 enrolment fee; contact Carol To, Programme Coordinator.

FIRST CLASS INTESOL: 6th Floor, Kailey Tower, 16 Stanley Street, Central, Hong Kong ✆ +852 2526 9156; http://intesol.firstclass.edu.hk; online certificate programmes (including Level 5) which can be supplemented with practice teaching.

HEADSTART GROUP LTD: Hong Kong & Macao; ✆ +852 2155 9602; http://tefl.headstartgroup.co; online course based on 120-hour or 160-hour diploma course, costing HK$6,800 or HK$15,800. Option of adding 40 hours of paid and assessed teaching practice in Headstart partner schools (at a cost of HK$11,800).

HK TESOL INSTITUTE: Unit 802, New Kowloon Plaza, Olympic, Kowloon, Hong Kong; ✆ +852 2880 5080; hk.tesol.ins@gmail.com; www.hk-tesol.org; Compact TESOL certificate course offered monthly; 3 weeks, 60 hours including 10-week practicum with affiliated Dramatic English (see entry in Hong Kong chapter); US$1,599; added week of cultural immersion including 5 days in Beijing for US$3,999.

HUNGARY

KATEDRA LANGUAGE SCHOOLS: Anderköz 1-3, 1061 Budapest; teacher.training@katedra.hu; intensive CELT (4 weeks) and semi-intensive (6 weeks) throughout the year; £760; cheaper if booked early.

VIA LINGUA BUDAPEST: Tavasz u. 3, 1033 Budapest; ✆ +36 1 368 1156; budapest@vialingua.org; www.via-lingua.hu; 4-week intensive Certificate in TEFL course offered 4 times a year; €1,275 plus £120 membership in College of Teachers plus €250–€420 for accommodation; course run by Tudomany Nyelviskola (see entry in Hungary chapter).

INDONESIA

TEFL INTERNATIONAL: Surabaya; www.teflinternational.org.uk; monthly; $1600 plus $150-$250 for accommodation.

IRELAND

ALPHA COLLEGE OF ENGLISH: 4 North Great George's Street, Dublin 1; ℭ+353 1 874 7024; admin@alphacollege.com; www.alphacollege.com.

CENTRE OF ENGLISH STUDIES: 31 Dame Street, Dublin 2; ℭ+353 1 671 4233; info@ces-schools.com; www.ces-schools.com.

CLARE LANGUAGE CENTRE: Erasmus Smith Building, College Road, Ennis, Co Clare; ℭ +353 65 684 1681; clarelc@iol.ie; www.clarelc.ie.

CORK LANGUAGE CENTRE INTERNATIONAL: Wellington House, 16 St Patrick's Place, Wellington Road, Cork; ℭ +353 21 455 1661; info@corklanguagecentre.ie; www.corklanguagecentre.ie.

DORSET COLLEGE: 66 Lower Dorset St, Dublin 1; ℭ +353 1 830 9677; info@dorset-college.ie; www.dorset-college.ie.

DUBLIN SCHOOL OF ENGLISH: Dollard House, 2–5 Wellington Quay, Temple Bar, Dublin 2; ℭ +353 1 677 3322; admin@dse.ie; www.dse.ie.

GALWAY LANGUAGE CENTRE: The Bridge Mills, Galway; ℭ +353 91 566468; info@galwaylanguage.com; www.galwaylanguage.com.

INTERNATIONAL HOUSE DUBLIN: 66 Lower Camden Street, Dublin 2; ℭ +353 1 475 9011/3; info@ihdublin.com; www.ihdublin.com.

INTERNATIONAL TEFL COLLEGE OF IRELAND: 29 Northumberland Avenue, Dun Laoghaire, Co. Dublin; ℭ +353 1 280 7001; info@itci.ie; www.itci.ie; 100-hour TEFL training courses; several courses run throughout the academic year (September to May); €500; teaching practice with foreign students free of charge.

MEI (MARKETING ENGLISH IN IRELAND): 1 Lower Pembroke Street, Dublin 2; ℭ+353 1 618 0910; www.mei.ie; is an association of recognised schools and a representative body (similar to English UK); many MEI schools provide teacher training courses (CELT) and ACELS-accredited courses.

NORTH MON LANGUAGE INSTITUTE: North Monastery Road, Cork; ℭ +353 21 439 4458; info@nmli.ie; www.nmli.ie.

U-LEARN: 97 St Stephens Green, Dublin 1; ℭ +353 1 878 7339; www.ulearnschool.com.

ITALY

ACLE (ASSOCIAZIONE CULTURALE LINGUISTICA EDUCATIONAL): Via Roma, 54, 18038 Sanremo; ℭ +39 184 506070; info@acle.org; www.acle.org; 5–6 day intensive TEFL-TP (Through Theatre and Play) introductory course with full board and lodging included; €150 course fee; successful students work as paid tutors, teaching English at camps throughout Italy (see Italy chapter); this project offers a combination of theory plus invaluable practical experience with emphasis on drama and child-centred learning activities; tutors receive an introductory TEFL Certificate at the end of the working period.

CENTRO TOSCAN DI LINGUE: Piazzale Porta al Prato 14, 50144 Florence; www.centrotoscano.com; venue for TEFL International's 4-week certificate course given monthly. $500 + €1190.

INTERLINGUE LANGUAGE SYSTEM/ROME TEFL COLLEGE: Via Lucrezio Caro 67, 00193 Rome; info@interlingue-it.com; www.interlingue-it.com/tefl; TEFL International Certificate courses run 9 times a year. €400 deposit plus €1000 without accommodation; accommodation from €400.

TEACHING ENGLISH IN ITALY: Florence; www.teachingenglishinitaly.com; 3-day weekend TEFL courses (20 hours, Friday to Sunday) offered every other month at Europass, Florence; €195. 1-week TEFL Teacher Refresher (€500) and 2-week Creative Classroom courses also in collaboration with the Europass teacher training Centre, Florence (€820).

VIA LINGUA FLORENCE: Via Brunelleschi 1, 50123 Florence; ✆ +39 055 283161; florence@vialingua.org; www.cteflflorence.com; 1-month intensive; approximately 9 a year; course fee €1,195 plus from €650 for accommodation.

JAPAN

TEFL INTERNATIONAL: 4-25-16 Minamimizumoto, Katsushika-ku, Tokyo 125-0035; admin@teflinternational.org.uk; www.teflinternational.org.uk; 120-hour TESOL; monthly start dates; course fee $2,390; paid teaching work arranged.

VOLTA ASSOCIATES: Chiyoda-ku, Tokyo 101–0054; www.volta-associates.com/tesol-course.html; 30-hour in-class TESOL training (affiliated to American TESOL) for 60,000 yen including handbook.

MALTA

ETI MALTA: Teacher Training & Development, St Julian's, Malta; www.etimalta.com; range of short Continuing Professional Development courses offered.

INLINGUA MALTA: Sliema; www.inlinguamalta.com; 45-hour TEFL Certificate offered in-house. TEFL Course Coordinator, Donovan Gatt.

MEXICO

DUNHAM INSTITUTE: Avenida Zaragoza 23, Chiapa de Corzo, Chiapas; ✆ +52 961 616 1498; academic-coordinator@dunhaminstitute.com; www.dunhaminstitute.com; 4-week TEFL course in conjunction with Spanish courses and language exchange and tutoring of local students; minimum commitment 8 weeks if tutoring local students or 5 months if teaching in schools; $1,600 includes free homestay with local family.

HESLINGTON LANGUAGE PROGRAM / HELP ENGLISH MEXICO: Tehuacán; www.helpenglishmexico.org/tesol-certification-program; 4-month American TESOL course combined with intership, starting August, January and April. $2,500.

INTERNATIONAL TEACHER TRAINING ORGANIZATION: Madero No. 469, Guadalajara, Jalisco 44100; ✆ +52 33 3658 5858; toll-free from UK: ✆ +44 800 404 9800; toll-free from USA: ✆ +1 866 514 7479; www.tefl.com.mx. 4 weeks offered monthly; $1,490. Guaranted job placement.

INTERNATIONAL TEFL ACADEMY: www.internationalteflacademy.com; Ciudad Guzman (3 times a year), Puerto Vallerta (6 times) and Guadalajara (8 times).

TEACHERS LATIN AMERICA: Plaza Galerías, Circuito Interior (Calz. Melchor Ocampo) 193 Local J-11, Miguel Hidalgo, 11300 Ciudad de México; ✆ +52 155 1496 0227; www.teachers-latin-america.com; 80-hour plus TEFL Certificate Programme offered monthly; 40 hours' in-class study, 10–20 hours of instructor-assessed student teaching and at least 25 additional hours of self-study on grammar, lesson planning, etc; $1,190 including accommodation; job assistance throughout Latin America.

TEFL INTERNATIONAL: Chiapa de Corzo; www.teflinternational.org.uk/mexico.html; Monthly $1,690. Volunteer teachers programme $1,950.

TEFL TRAINING MEXICO: Jalisco; ✆ +52 341 412 8090; www.tefl-trainingmexico.com; 130 hours, including 16 hours of private Spanish tuition; total $1,500; $400 for homestay accommodation. Affiliated to Via Lingua.

NETHERLANDS

BRITISH SCHOOL NETHERLANDS: Vrouw Avenweg 640, 2493 WZ Den Haag; ✆ +31 070 315 4080; www.britishschool.nl; 5-day intro to TEFL offered in mid-July; €502; also offer CELTA course.

NICARAGUA

INTERNATIONAL TEFL ACADEMY: Leon; ✆ +1 505 2311 7411; www.nicaraguatefl.com; face-to-face as well as online and blended; $1899 (discounts for early booking).

PERU

INTERNATIONAL TEFL ACADEMY: Arequipa; www.internationalteflacademy.com; offered in July and October, $1,550.

MÁXIMO NIVEL EXECUTIVE LANGUAGE CENTER: Avenida El Sol 612, Cusco; ✆ +51 84 581800; info@maximonivel.com; www.maximonivel.com (see also Costa Rica and Guatemala); 150-hour TEFL/TESOL Certificate (over 4 weeks) for $1,400–$1,700 offered monthly except December; 50-hour TEIB (Teaching English for International Business) Certificate and TIEEP (Teaching International English Exam Preparation) Certificate (over 3 days), $400 each; rough frequency 4 times a year; housing arranged with families, in shared apartments, hostels, etc from $225 for 4 weeks; lifetime job-finding assistance; an average of 5 graduates are employed by Máximo Nivel each month.

RUSSIA

BENEDICT SCHOOL: 4 Admiraltejskaya Embankment, St Petersburg 190000; ✆ +7 812 325 7574; www.eng.benedict.ru; 4-week Via Lingua course offered 4 times a year. €1300 plus 18,000 roubles for accommodation. 13-week Work-Study programme in autumn and spring, which combines 2-week introductory TEFL training with Russian language course and job guidance. £690.

SLOVAKIA

CANADIAN LANGUAGE SCHOOL: Nitra; ✆ +421 904 371 050; info@canadian.sk; www.canadian schoolnitra.sk or www.facebook.com/Canadian.Language.school.NITRA; 2-week 'Teach the Teacher' summer course for new ESL teachers who are not confident about grammar and teaching techniques; 2 weeks of intensive lessons (8 hours per day, 80 hours) with various start dates in July and August; £320 including materials but not accommodation.

SPAIN

ANGLO CENTRES: Calle Unió, 41, bajo, Tarragona 43001; ✆ +34 977 546309; www.tefl.anglocen tres.com; 4-week residential Certificate course, accredited by College of Teachers; offered 6 times a year; £1,040; also offer online and blended courses. Contact Vince Ferrer or Rob Bianchi.

CANTERBURY TEFL: Calle Covarrubias 22, 2° Derecha, 28010 Madrid; ✆ +34 91 838 0082; www.canterburytefl.com; 40 hours of teaching theory supplemented by 40 hours of lesson planning, 20 hours class observation and 20 hours paid internship; €1,275 reduced by €280 for paid teaching.

EBC INTERNATIONAL: Orense 16, 2E, 28020 Madrid; ✆ +34 91 555 3975; www.ebcteflcourse.com; offered monthly; approx €1,275. 1-year visa option for non-EU participants is a possibility.

EUROPE TEFL TEACHER TRAINING: Salvador Espriu 91, 08005 Barcelona; ✆ +34 932 215515 info@europetefl.com; www.europetefl.com; 4-week intensive full-time; TEFL courses run throughout the year in Barcelona, Seville and many other locations in Europe and Latin America; €1,300, including all course materials, expert job guidance, alumni network and more; accommodation in the city centre and close to the schools can be arranged, €400–€500 a month. Contact Kevin Cline.

INTERNATIONAL HOUSE BARCELONA: Calle Trafalgar 14, 08010 Barcelona; ✆ +34 93 268 3304; training@bcn.ihes.com; www.ihes.com/bcn; Business English Teachers course, 36 hours over 2 weeks, July only, €450; also, Director of Studies Training Course and Trainer Training Course, both 1 week in July, €555; and the International Diploma in Language Teaching Management (IDLTM), 2-week on-site course in July followed by 8 months of online assignments, €3,150; help given with finding accommodation.

OXBRIDGE BARCELONA: Numancia 47 entl 2, 08029 Barcelona; ✆ +34 93 532 7565; UK: +44 20 8133 0043; tefl@oxbridge.es; www.oxbridgetefl.com; Oxbridge International TEFL Certificate with employment opportunities; 120 hours including 20 hours of real teaching practice; subsidised course price after a successful interview in Barcelona, with reduction of €400 from full price of €1,250.

OXBRIDGE MADRID: Corredera Baja de San Pablo 39, 28003 Madrid; ✆ +34 91 523 4243. As above.

TEFL IBERIA: Barcelona; www.tefl-iberia.com; 4 week course throughout the year, but more in summer. €1350 (€1200 with early booking discount).

TEFL INTERNATIONAL: in Seville and Barcelona; admin@teflinternational.org.uk; www.teflinternational.org.uk; 120-hour TESOL; monthly start dates; course fee from €1,390.

TTMADRID: C/ Montesa, 35 (esc dcha) 2° dcha, 28006 Madrid; ✆ +34 91 572 1999; info@ttmadrid.com; www.ttmadrid.com; 4-week intensive courses accredited by the College of Teachers; courses run 9 times a year; course fee €1,375. interviews with teaching agencies arranged on graduation; course emphasis on teaching Business English; real teaching experience with adults and elective inputs on how to teach children. Non-EU nationals may obtain student visa while combining this course with Spanish; €2,750.

THAILAND

AYC INTERCULTURAL PROGRAMS: 9/197, 7th Floor, GOT Building Soi Ratchadaphisek 29, Ratchadaphisek Road, Chatuchak, Bangkok, 10900; ✆ +66 2556 1533; h_r@aycthailand.com; www.aycthailand.com; 120 hour TESOL course validated by INTESOL; course runs in Bangkok, Koh Samui and Phuket and costs $799 ($999 with accommodation); job guarantee for native English speakers under 52 years of age, holding a bachelor's degree.

CHICHESTER COLLEGE, THAILAND: 1st Fl., Muangthai Phatra Complex, 252/193 Ratchadaphisek Rd., Bangkok 10320; ✆ +66 2 693 2901; www.chichester.ac.th; TESOL certificate and distance diploma courses in cooperation with Chichester College UK; 4-week certificate course runs monthly; $1,595; accommodation offered at a private lodge near the Chichester Training Centre in Bangkok, and provided at a special subsidised rate of $150 for the entire duration of the full-time course only; graduates are provided teaching placements through Spencer International, which has links with schools in Thailand, Cambodia, Vietnam, Myanmar, Indonesia and China.

FEECHERS TEACHER TRAINING: Thailand; http://feechers.weebly.com; teacher recruitment company that arranges free 6-day teacher training in cooperation with various training centres, and job placement programme in the coastal provinces of Suratthani, Chumphon and Prachuap Khiri Khan in southern Thailand and various locations in the north and northeast of Thailand.

GREEN TEFL: Chiang Mai; ✆ +66 53 226718; www.greentefl.com. 120 hours, offered 5 times a year, including considerable on-the-job training experience teaching in local NAVA school; 38,500 baht if booked early, 45,000 baht otherwise.

ISLAND TEFL: Phuket, also in Koh Samui, Surin and Bangkok. Monthly. 120 hours over 3 weeks ($999), 150 hours in 4 weeks ($1,490). Job placement programme $795.

PARADISE TEFL THAILAND: ✆ +66 840 513655; www.paradisetefl.com or http://tefltesolthailand.com; franchise in Koh Phangan of international network of training courses; 9 per year; 32,000 baht.

PENNIES FOR PAPA FOUNDATION: Chiang Rai 57240; ✆ + 66 84 756 3900; www.penniesforpapa.org or www.volunteer4thailand.org; 120-hour online TESOL course combined with 4 or 12 week internships teaching Akha people in a Northern Thai village; 4 weeks for $999; 12 weeks for $1,997.

SEE TEFL (Siam Educational Experience): Chiang Mai; ✆ +66 53 266295/6; info@seetefl.com; www.seetefl.com; 4-week training course; 10–15 times a year; $1,495 (or $1,295 if booked early). Accommodation can be provided for extra $350–$400; job guarantee and also internship programme.

TEFL CAMPUS: Phuket or Chiang Mai; ✆ +66 81 968 9334; www.teflcampus.com; 4 weeks.$1,690 or $1,790 with accommodation in Chiang Mai.

TEFL EAST/GLOBAL TRAINING ACADEMY, tefleast@gmail.com; www.englishjobsthailand.com. Affiliated to American TESOL Institute. 7-day teaching orientation in Bangkok ($500) followed by placement throughout Thailand for 4-5 months, for degree-holders only. Monthly salary 30,000 baht per month.

TEFL INTERNATIONAL: 32/185 Phunphon Road, Talad Neua Ampur Muang, Phuket 83000; admin@teflinternational.org.uk; www.teflinternational.org.uk; 120-hour TESOL certificate course at Chiang Mai and Phuket; $1,690 excludes accommodation.

TESOL COURSE THAILAND: Bangkok and Phuket; www.tesolcoursethailand.com; 120 hours (3 weeks) in-class course followed by 4–5 months of teaching in Thailand with free accommodation; course fee $1,590. Affiliated to American TESOL Institute.

TEXT AND TALK ACADEMY: 1961 Phaholyothin Road (opposite Mayo Hospital), Lardyao, Chatuchak, Bangkok 10900; ✆ +66 2 561 3443; info@teflteachthai.com; www.teflteachthai.com; 6-week certificate courses (about $1,495), upgrade and refresher course, 16-week diploma course, 8-week TEYL course, 8-week advanced skills course and home study course. Acts as hiring agent at end of course.

UNITED EDUCATIONAL CONSULTANTS CO. LTD: 4th Floor, Silom Plaza, Silom Road corner Narathiwat Road, Bangkok 10500; ✆ +66 2 233 2388; info@teflthai.com; www.teflthai.com; 120 hours over 5 weeks with 10 start dates throughout the year; 44,500 baht; course earns eligible graduates 9 US graduate credits in education; US master's degree can be completed in 1 year while teaching in Thailand; also offers graduate diploma in teaching; 3 and a half-year part-time bachelor's degree in education, and weekend study for 1 and a half-year dual US and Thai accredited master's degree (www.uecthai.com), including required Thai teaching licence.

UNITEFL THAILAND: T.Suthep, A.Muang, Chiang Mai 50200; ✆ +66 88-402-8217; www.unitefl.com; 120-hour course offered monthly in Chiang Mai and 7 times per year in Phuket; 45,000 baht (£820/$1,4950); affiliated to TEFL International.

WECI TEFL: 70/145 Soi; 112, Nongkae, Hua Hin, Prachuap Khiri Khan 77110; ✆ +66 32 900464; www.wecitefl.com; 120-hour course in seaside town 2 and a half hours south of Bangkok; starting from 36,000 baht with other options to include placement or preparation for ED (educational) visa.

TURKEY

ONLINETESOL TURKEY: Antalya; http://onlinetesol.com; American Culture U.K. TESOL 150-hour course including a teaching practicum in Turkey; TL1300 (including tax).

VIA LINGUA ISTANBUL: Kent English, Bahariye Cad. 15/2, Kadiköy, 34710 Istanbul; ✆ +90 216 347 2791/2; istanbul@vialingua.org; www.tefl-turkey.com; 4-week CTEFL course offered 6 times a year; €1,275 plus €300 for accommodation.

VIETNAM

MIDWEST EDUCATION GROUP: 4633 N. Western Ave., Suite 207, Chicago, IL 60625; ✆ +1 847 496 7919; contact@midwested.us; www.midwested.us; 4-week classroom-based TESOL programme in Vietnam; MEG has satellite offices in the two major cities plus Can Tho south of Ho Chi Minh City; course cost is $1,100.

TEACHING ENGLISH - VIETNAM: Go Vap District, Ho Chi Minh City; ✆ +84 933883731; peter@teaching english-vietnam.com; www.teachingenglish-vietnam.com; Australian government accredited TEFL-TESOL programme offered monthly; 150 hours over 4 weeks with minimum 20 hours of practice teaching of 'real' language learners; Fee of US$1,499 includes free accommodation near the school and guaranteed paid employment.

INTERNATIONAL HOUSE

Teacher Training with International House

Choosing the right training course or applying for your first teaching job abroad can be a daunting prospect. There are so many courses available and potential job opportunities to consider that it is hard to know where to start – and you want to make the right choice as this is your future!

If you choose International House, you don't need to worry.

The International House (IH) network is committed to continually driving excellence in both language teaching and teacher training. International House led the way in creating the first training course specifically for English as a Foreign Language for teachers in 1962, which formed the basis for the current CELTA qualification, so we really are the experts.

As a network of 155 affiliated schools in 52 countries globally, International House is a fantastic option for both teacher training and a career in teaching English. We offer training courses for every stage of a teacher's career, delivered both face to face and online.

Why should you train with International House?

■ IH has over 50 years of experience in developing and training teachers

■ IH courses are moderated by the IH Assessment Unit and recognised globally

■ The IH name is widely respected in the field of language teaching, and teachers that have trained with IH are widely sought after by employers

■ Course participants who train with an IH school in any location within our network will receive the same high standard of training and assessment

■ Training with IH means you are guaranteed to train with dedicated professional trainers

Why should you work for an International House school?

When starting a new career it is essential you begin with the right foundations and IH schools have the systems and support in place to help you.

You can progress with International House and work with other teachers that feel as passionately about teaching as you do. Our schools only employ professional teachers with recognised teaching qualifications and our quality charters ensure that all teachers receive regular training and support from academic managers.

We are a network of schools committed to the same values and quality standards, not a franchise, so each school has its own unique character and local flavour.

Many of our teachers started their career with one IH school and have moved around the network. So International House really can be a career choice for life.

For more information please visit ihworld.com/teachers or email info@ihworld.com.

FINDING A JOB

You have only two choices: to search for a job from afar or go to the country of your choice and look around. Having a job arranged before departure obviously removes much of the uncertainty and anxiety of leaving home for an extended period. It also allows the possibility of preparing in appropriate ways: sorting out the right visa, researching the course books in use, etc. Others prefer to meet their employer and inspect the school before signing a contract. It is always an advantage to meet or make contact with other teachers to get the real lowdown on a particular employer and place, rather than accepting a job in complete ignorance of the prevailing conditions. But of course this is not always feasible.

Employers usually choose their staff several months before they are needed, so most schools advertise between April and July for jobs starting in September. If you want to look for a job in person, you will either have to go on a reconnaissance mission well in advance of your proposed starting date or take your chances of finding a last-minute vacancy.

FINDING A JOB IN ADVANCE
There are three ways of finding a teaching job in advance:

- *by answering an online advertisement*
- *using a recruitment agency or the large international English teaching organisations such as International House*
- *conducting a speculative job search, ie making contact by email or telephone with all the schools whose addresses you can find in this book or from any other source, including social networks like LinkedIn.*

TEFL WEBSITES

For schools, a website advert offers an easy and instantaneous means of publicising a vacancy to an international audience. Teachers looking for employment can use search engines to look for all pages with references to EFL, English language schools and recruitment. CVs can be emailed quickly and cheaply to advertising schools, who can then use email themselves to chase up references. The internet has very quickly taken over as the primary means of recruitment.

Arguably it has become a little too easy to advertise and answer job adverts online. At the press of a button, your CV can be clogging up dozens, nay, hundreds of computers. It is interesting to note that some of the schools that corresponded with this book for the current edition said that they seemed to get a more reliable brand of teacher from readers of this book and that they are more impressed with a job-seeker who goes to the trouble of assimilating the information from a book than the ones who spend their days skating over the internet. But basically, recruitment via the internet is here to stay.

While opening up an enormous range of possibilities, the internet can be a bewildering and discouraging place to job-hunt. A host of websites promise to provide free online recruitment services for English teachers. Because many sites are struggling on the margins, they often seem to offer more than they can deliver and you may find that some offer little more than general waffle or that the number and range of jobs posted are disappointing, either undated (and therefore meaningless) or with dud links. That being said, everywhere you look on the internet, potentially useful links can be found. For many years Dave Sperling's 'Dave's ESL Cafe' (www.eslcafe.com) dominated the field and it is still the first port of call for many to check job vacancies and investigate further. Often the job discussion forums are invaluable, for example if you are considering signing a contract with a training company in Kazakhstan; although some of these forums tend to be quite a few years old. In any case 'Dave' provides a mind-boggling amount of material and many links to specific institutes and chains in each country.

Another key international site is www.tefl.com, which has gained in authority and popularity over recent years. When subscribing (for free), you can specify whether you want to be notified of vacancies by email on a daily or weekly basis. The site claims to have more than 21,000 registered employers. At the time of writing the countries with the most vacancies listed were China (70) and Spain (95).

It is possible to register your details as a job-seeker. **Fergus Cooney** learnt the hard way not to be too general on ESL Cafe:

> *I posted a message simply stating 'Qualified teacher seeking job'. Within two days I was inundated with many dozens of replies requesting my CV and, more surprisingly with job offers everywhere, although the majority were from Korea, Taiwan and China. 'Jackpot,' I thought (I have since realised that many schools/agents must have an automatic reply system which emails those who advertise in the way I did). I quickly began sifting through them, but not as quickly as they kept arriving in my inbox. Before a few more days had passed, I had become utterly confused and had forgotten which school was which, so I deleted them all, got a new email address and posted a second, more specific message on Dave's.*

In almost all cases, employers will only contact an applicant if they wish to proceed with their application, so do not expect any politely worded refusals.

While these two giants of the TESL world (www.eslcafe.com and www.tefl.com) have pushed some other sites out of business, many rivals survive and flourish.

Here is a brief survey of some of the key recruitment sites.

- www.englishjobsabroad.com: clear layout with range of dated and archived job postings with email addresses revealed.
- www.mytefljobs.com: range of vacancies, though not very numerous.
- http://teflen.com/tefl-tesol-jobs-board-employment-job-portal.html: mainly recruitment agencies with live vacancies.
- www.tefl-jobs.co.uk: recruitment website from the 247recruit stable, with undated postings.
- www.tefljobs.net: dated vacancies with possibility of clicking through to contact details; free to register but must upload a CV in order to apply.
- www.esl.com/jobs: newcomer with an impressive searchable directory of language schools and job listings.
- www.gooverseas.com/teach-abroad: searchable online directory of opportunities to teach, study, volunteer and intern abroad, based in Berkeley, California. Includes some first-hand reviews of employers and programmes.
- www.glassdoor.co.uk/index.htm: claims to be the only job search with a view from the inside. Covers all kinds of work as well as English teaching. Includes some reviews posted by employees.
- http://tesljobs.com: dated vacancies.
- www.esl101.com: database of recent job postings minus contact details.
- www.ihworld.com/jobs: International House maintains clear website with links to its 159 affiliated schools in 52 countries with email addresses of directors and directors of studies. The recruitment and training sections of the website are accessible to all; enquiries to worldrecruit@ihworld.com.
- www.eslbase.com/schools: reasonably reliable links to language schools, country by country and www.eslbase.com/jobs has current vacancies. Useful TEFL forum.
- www.totalesl.com: part of the Icon Group of Thailand, which also owns Tesall.com and www.esljobfeed.com. Strongest in vacancies in Asia.
- www.teflsearch.com: has an alphabetical directory of potential employers as well as dated vacancies with contact details.
- www.teachinghouse.com/english-teaching-jobs: huge TEFL jobs database with dates and email addresses.
- www.onlinetefl.com/tefl-jobs-abroad/tefl-jobs-board: maintained by i-to-i (part of the giant tour operator TUI). Most listings are for the obvious recruiters.

- www.tefllogue.com: discursive site with links to blogs and other sites that might be useful (but no current vacancies). Part of the BootsnAll travel network.
- www.eslteachersboard.com: vast site and free community for EL teachers with current job postings (dated and with email addresses revealed) and teachers' CVs.
- www.eslemployment.com: good selection of dated vacancies.
- www.tefl.org.uk: TEFL Scotland Ltd has some current vacancies; contact details available after registering.
- www.onestopenglish.com: teachers' resource site maintained by the educational publisher Macmillan An annual subscription costs £42/$68.
- www.jobsabroadbulletin.co.uk: jobs board has a 'Teaching & TEFL' section, which remains archived and is easy to access.
- www.teflcourse.net/tefl-jobs: good, easy to navigate with historic dated vacancies (part of online training company ITTT).
- http://worldoftefl.com: Quinn's World of TEFL has a TEFL jobs board and ESL resources.

Other websites that are country specific, eg www.ohayosensei.com (jobs in Japan) or www.ajarn.com (teaching in Thailand) are listed in the relevant country chapters.

RECRUITMENT FAIRS

In an ideal world, prospective teachers could meet a range of employers all at once. Certified classroom teachers looking for vacancies in international schools have access to this kind of event (see section on Certified Teachers below). But it is not very common in TEFL. The energetic **Aidan O'Toole**, long-time resident of Andalucía, describes the advantages of the annual job fair he has spearheaded in Córdoba, where Spanish language schools can meet job-seekers in May:

> *The first Spainwise recruitment fair in 2009 was a success with many teachers and language schools attending. Each side invests a small amount of money into getting a job, which is far more efficient than teachers flying out from England for just one or two interviews. The chance to meet face-to-face is tremendously useful for both sides. Of course tefl.com (and similar) have transformed the recruitment process and the typed CV and letterbox seem to belong to another era. But it is just too easy for newly qualified teachers to lean on the wrong button on their computer and send out hundreds of CVs, sometimes in answer to adverts they haven't even read.*

Aidan thinks that meeting a range of job-seekers makes it much easier for language school owners to spot the best candidates than rifling through a pile of CVs from new CELTA graduates. Meeting face-to-face also allows candidates who do not fit the perfect profile a chance to shine.

RECRUITMENT ORGANISATIONS

Major providers of ELT and teacher placement organisations of various kinds may be able to assist prospective teachers in English-speaking countries to find teaching jobs. Some are international educational foundations; some are voluntary organisations such as the Peace Corps or charities; some are major chains of commercial language schools; and others are small agencies that serve as intermediaries between independent language schools abroad and prospective teachers. The companies and organisations listed in this chapter have been assigned to the following categories (though there is some blurring of distinctions):

- international ELT organisations (including the major language school chains)
- commercial recruitment agencies
- voluntary, gap year and religious organisations
- North American organisations, which cater primarily (though not exclusively) to citizens of the USA and Canada
- placement services for British and American state-qualified teachers.

Note that agencies and organisations that operate only in one country or one region are described in the country chapters in the second part of this book.

It is hardly worthwhile for a family-run language school in Northern Greece or Southern Brazil to pay the high costs which most agencies charge schools just to obtain one or two native-speaker teachers. Vacancies that are filled with the help of agencies and recruitment consultants tend to be either at the mass-market end where there are large numbers of unfilled entry-level positions or at the elite end of the ELT market for specialised or high-level positions.

HOW AGENCIES WORK
Agencies make their money by charging client employers; the service to teachers is usually free of charge. By law in the UK, no fee can be charged to job-seekers either before or after placement, except if a package of services is sold alongside (eg insurance, visas, travel, etc). Note that different rules apply in other countries, so that placement fees are the norm in the USA. Some of the best recruitment organisations to deal with are ones that specialise in a single country and are located in situ, such as Ray English TEFL Recruitment in Xi'an or Anglo-Hellenic Recruitment in Corinth (see China and Greece chapters). They tend to have more first-hand knowledge of their client schools.

Bear in mind that the use of an intermediary by foreign language institutes is no guarantee of anything. Small independent recruiters, especially in the context of Korea or the Middle East, are sometimes trying to fill vacancies that no one in the country who is familiar with the employer would deign to fill. As the American **Rusty Holmes** said of his employer in Taiwan: '*The school was so bad it had to recruit from America.*' If you are in any doubt about the reliability of an agency or the client he/she represents, it is a sensible precaution to search online and ask for the name of one or more current or recent teachers whom you can ask for a first-hand account. It is a bad sign if the agency is unable or reluctant to oblige.

The hiring of teachers for chain schools abroad is done either at a local level, especially when they are franchises (so direct applications are always worthwhile), or centrally, if the school has trouble filling vacancies.

One way in which recruitment agencies work is to create a database of teachers' CVs and to try to match these with suitable vacancies as they occur. In order to be registered with such an agency it is almost always essential to have a relevant qualification, often at least the Cambridge or Trinity Certificate, since agencies tend to deal with high-level, difficult-to-fill vacancies. Smaller agencies may have fewer vacancies on their books but they can often offer a more personal service. A good agency will provide a full briefing and information pack on the school in particular and the country in general, and will make sure that the contract offered is a reasonable one.

One London-based recruitment agent, David Taylor of the Anglo-Pacific Asia Consultancy, has noticed that an advert will elicit a good response, say 30 replies. He will follow up on no more than about a third of those and reported that in a recent case he heard nothing back from a single one, which means he had gone to a lot of trouble sifting through applications to no avail and still had an unfilled vacancy. As a result he publicises his phone number for interested teachers to contact, but not his email address.

Volunteer English teachers are in demand by dozens of commercial sending agencies which routinely charge volunteers £800–£2,000+ for placement and related services. Before her final year at university, **Susannah Kerr** took up one of these placements in Thailand, which she found to be less structured than the agency literature had promised. She felt that the school to which she was assigned did not really need English-speaking volunteers and she suspected that they invited foreigners merely as status symbols. With hindsight she felt that she had been naïve to assume that the school would be grateful for her efforts. She was allowed to teach whatever she liked, so naturally she concentrated on spoken English and taught no grammar and only occasional writing exercises. She was given no lesson plans and was not required to prepare the students for exams. When the teachers saw that the volunteers were coping, they took a holiday.

THE BRITISH COUNCIL

The British Council (www.britishcouncil.org) is the largest ELT (English language teaching) employer in the world. The Council represents the elite end of the ELT industry. At its own 70 or so teaching centres in 53 countries, it offers the highest quality language teaching available in those countries and employs the best qualified teachers, so it is important to understand that the British Council does not generally welcome applications from very inexperienced or unqualified teachers. The British Council is a very professional organisation and its jobs tend to come with attractive terms and conditions. However in a few locations, the Council has been recruiting 'apprentice' teachers or teaching assistants with a qualification but without experience.

The Council's offices abroad are usually well informed about opportunities for English language teaching locally. Most maintain a list of private language schools (especially if they are exam centres), which is often a useful starting point for a job search.

Contact details for the offices worldwide are listed online at www.britishcouncil.org/organisation/our-global-network. The charter of the British Council defines its aims as 'to promote a wider knowledge of the United Kingdom and the English language'. It is non-profit-making and works non-politically. It employs over 7,000 staff overseas, a good 2,000 of whom are involved with the teaching of the English language in some capacity. Other work that the Council carries out includes the running of libraries, the organisation of cultural tours and exchanges, etc. But language teaching and teacher recruitment remain among its central concerns.

A useful starting place for qualified EL teachers is to check the list of current vacancies at https://jobs.britishcouncil.org. British Council teaching centres recruit both through London and locally. They especially welcome applications from teachers with experience or an interest in specialist areas such as Young Learners, Business English, skills through English, IELTS exam preparation, etc.

Most of the contracts offered through the website above are for two years and an attractive salary and relocation package (airfares, allowance for shipping belongings, etc). Many teachers value all the intangible benefits such as the security of working for an established institution, and encouragement of professional development with possible perks such as receiving a subsidy to study for a Diploma qualification or other training grants. Once you have secured one job with the Council, it is possible to move to other jobs in other offices. Internal vacancies are described separately at the jobs portal.

A completely separate programme run by the British Council is the placement of language assistants in schools for an academic year. The Language Assistants team administers exchange programmes with 14 countries worldwide. Applicants for assistant posts must be native speakers of English who have completed their secondary education and at least two years of degree-level study in the UK, often but not necessarily in the language of the destination country. In some countries (especially China and countries in Latin America) posts are of particular interest to graduates interested in a career in TEFL. The website is open for applications from October and the deadline for submission is the end of November (for posts starting the following summer/autumn). For more information see the Languages Assistants website (www.britishcouncil.org/language-assistants/become/where-can-I-go) or contact the team by emailing language.assistants@britishcouncil.org or phoning the British Council on +44 161 957 7755.

In conjunction with the BBC, the British Council also maintains a website called Teaching English (www.teachingenglish.org.uk) which is a free resource for teachers and includes lesson plans, worksheets, teaching tips, webinars, apps, etc.

The British Council is a large and complex institution with two headquarters: one at 10 Spring Gardens, London SW1A 2BN (+44 20 7930 8466) and the other at Bridgewater House, 58 Whitworth Street, Manchester M1 6BB (+44 161 957 7755).

INTERNATIONAL ELT ORGANISATIONS

Bell English, Hillscross, Red Cross Lane, Cambridge CB2 0QU (+44 1223 278800; www.bellenglish.com/jobs). Bell recruits teachers for senior ELT posts in its associated schools in Thailand, Macao, China, Jordan and Switzerland.

Bénédict Network International Sarl (www.benedict-international.com). Dozens of franchised business and language schools in Europe (15 in Germany, 8 in both Switzerland and Italy), plus several in Russia and Ecuador. Recruitment is not centralised.

Berlitz (www.berlitz.com/Careers/33; links to Berlitz sites for countries worldwide some of which indicate current job vacancies). Berlitz is one of the largest language training organisations in the world with about 550 franchised locations in 70 countries. It is also one of the oldest, founded in 1878. The company's core business is language and cultural training, and teacher vacancies occur most often in Germany, Turkey and Korea. All Berlitz teachers are native, fluent speakers and university graduates; all must undergo training in the 'Berlitz Method', a direct 'see-hear-speak' teaching approach that does not rely on translation. Berlitz is known for supervising its teachers' techniques very closely, and deviation from the method is not permitted. Berlitz schools abroad employ teachers directly, usually on a part-time basis initially, after they have completed a training course in the Berlitz Method. Berlitz has been expanding its summer programmes for young learners in Germany, Spain, etc.

Cactus TEFL (www.cactustefl.com) is a consultancy that advises on TEFL training courses but is of little help in job finding.

CfBT Education Trust, 60 Queens Road, Reading RG1 4BS (+44 118 902 1000; www.cfbt.com or http://careers.cfbt.com). Has English teaching programmes in Brunei and Oman that recruit for and manage EFL/EAP/ESP/Primary/Secondary teachers and instructors for various projects and contracts. The website contains contact details for each office and information on how to apply.

EF English First Teacher Recruitment and Training, 1st Floor, Jiu An Plaza, 258 Tongren Road, Shanghai, China 200040 (+86 21 6039 5870; efrecruitment@ef.com; www.englishfirst.com/trt and for China only www.ef-teachers.com). Recruitment of teachers for 200 EF schools in China, Russia and Indonesia.

ELS Language Centers, Princeton, NJ (www.els.edu/en/careers). ELS, now owned by Berlitz, is the world's largest network of campus-based English language instruction and university preparation centres. ELS has links with English teaching centres at universities in China, Korea, Malaysia, Turkey, Saudi Arabia, Panama, etc, but does not recruit teachers itself.

ICC – The European Language Network, Germany (info@icc-languages.eu; www.icc-languages.eu). Umbrella organisation and NGO for adult education associations (eg Volkshochschulen, folk high schools or Universities of Applied Sciences) in about a dozen European countries cooperating in the learning and teaching of foreign languages in Europe. A list of member organisations and contact names can be found on their website. The ICC runs specialist training courses for foreign language teachers in adult, continuing and vocational education. A teacher certification scheme (EUROLTA: European Certificate in Language Teaching to Adults) is also in operation.

IH World Organisation, Unity Wharf, 13 Mill Street, London SE1 2BH (+44 20 7394 2147; worldrecruit@ihworld.com; http://ihworld.com/jobs). International House (IH) is one of the largest and oldest groups of language schools, teaching English as a foreign language (and 25 modern languages) in 155 affiliated schools in 52 countries worldwide. IHWO Recruitment Services is based in London at the International House World Office, which is the co-ordinating body for all International House affiliated schools. It is responsible for managing the recruitment of teachers, trainers and senior staff for IH schools and annually expects to assist in the recruitment of between 350 and 400 teachers for International House schools worldwide. The minimum qualification requirement for teaching posts is the Cambridge CELTA or Trinity TESOL Certificate. All IH schools adhere to internal quality standards that provide strict guidelines on terms and conditions, working hours and working environment. (Note: IH London, a language school and teacher training centre, is a separate company; see training directory.)

Inlingua (www.inlingua.com). International chain of 352 language centres that operate autonomously in 35 countries across Europe, Africa, Asia, North and South America. Link to jobs on website especially in Germany, Italy and the Middle East.

Language Link, 6 Duke's Road, London WC1H 9AD (+44 20 3214 8250; info@languagelink.co.uk; www.languagelink.co.uk). Training and recruitment agency that places about 200 qualified (including newly qualified) teachers in its network of affiliated schools in Russia, China, Vietnam, and Uzbekistan. Usually minimum qualifications are TEFL Certificate or PGCE or experience but visit the website of the country you wish to work in as the agency may be running in-service training courses over the period of the contract. Local pay rates. Shared apartment accommodation is usually provided at no additional cost or deduction from the salary. (See Training chapter for details of Language Link's CELTA courses.)

Marcus Evans Linguarama, 7 Elm Court, 1 Arden Street, Stratford-upon-Avon CV37 6PA (+44 1789 203910; personnel@linguarama.com or dannycoughlan@linguarama.com; www.linguarama.com/employment). Linguarama specialises in providing language training for professionals. Applicants for jobs in Linguarama language schools abroad must have at least a degree and a Cambridge/Trinity Certificate (or equivalent). Linguarama finds placements for 50–100 teachers at 21 centres in six European countries; in June 2015, they were advertising vacancies in Germany, France, Netherlands, Spain and Italy.

Richard Lewis Communications, Riversdown House, Warnford, Southampton, Hampshire SO32 3LH (+44 1962 771111; www.riversdown.com/careers). RLC has a network of offices worldwide, especially in Finland, Sweden and Germany, specialising in cross-cultural training and language teaching.

Saxoncourt, 59 South Molton Street, London W1K 5SN (+44 20 7491 1911; recruit@saxoncourt.com; www.saxoncourt.com). One of the largest UK-based recruiters of EFL teachers, Saxoncourt places several hundred teachers per year in schools worldwide. Clients are based in Japan, Taiwan, China, Italy, Vietnam, Malaysia, Peru, Saudi Arabia and Turkey. Applications are welcome, particularly from candidates with a Cambridge CELTA, Trinity TESOL or equivalent qualifications. Interviews are held in London, where possible. Interested candidates should register online at www.saxoncourt.com. The Saxoncourt website features a regularly updated current vacancies page, online registration and country-specific sections with downloadable information packs.

SAXONCOURT RECRUITMENT

A case study from one of our teachers

Why Taiwan?

'Taiwan is a unique and beautiful country. You can be in the centre of Taipei and then within 30 minutes you can be in the mountains. It has everything from beaches to mountains to bustling cities. Life goes on all night as there are many 24-hour shops and the retail stores are open till late into the night. Whether you want a nice relaxed coffee, a beer in a pub or a wee dance in a club the Taiwanese cities have it all.

'The food is cheap, tasty and there is something for everybody. You can go to the night markets where there is a lot a variety or you can to one of the many restaurants that have food from all over the world.'

How did your recruitment company help you?

'Saxoncourt was very useful. It took the majority of the stress away and left me to concentrate on my teaching. Once I was recruited I was in constant contact with the recruiter who was constantly asking what I needed and giving me close support. Everything from my visa documents to my arrival pickup was organised for me and this left me feeling very supported as going to Asia for the first time was quite a scary prospect.'

How is the teaching?

'Teaching in Taiwan is a very rewarding experience. The majority of classes are Young Learners; however, there are other classes such as adults, teenagers and full-time kindergarten. The Taiwanese students are a lot of fun once they get to know you, and they work very hard at their schools all day, so appreciate the more active and fun classes here at Shane English School Taiwan (SEST).'

What are you doing now?

'Currently I'm working as the Human Resource Assistant Director of Studies (HRADoS) of SEST. The promotion opportunities are there at SEST for those who work hard and show a good attitude. I am now in charge of recruitment for the whole country and also play an integral role in scheduling for the teachers.'

Wall Street English International (teach@wallstreetenglish.com; www.wallstreetenglish.com). Now owned by Pearson, Wall Street operates both company-owned and franchised centres, and employs more than 2,000 teachers in nearly 450 centres in 29 countries and territories in Asia (China, Indonesia, Hong Kong, South Korea, Malaysia, Thailand and Vietnam), Europe (France, Germany, Italy, Portugal, Spain, Switzerland, Czech Republic, Russia, Turkey), Latin America (Argentina, Brazil, Chile, Colombia, Ecuador, Mexico, Nicaragua, Peru, Venezuela), the Middle East (Israel, Saudi Arabia) and Africa (Morocco). The most recent location to open is Luanda in Angola. The countries with almost continuous vacancies are China, Russia, Ecuador, Saudi Arabia, Turkey and Indonesia. Applicants should have at least a bachelor's degree and the appropriate professional qualifications of a CELTA or equivalent TEFL certificate. One year's teaching experience is an advantage. Due to restrictions and visa legislation in many countries within the network, Wall Street prefers teachers from the UK, Ireland, USA, Canada, Australia, New Zealand and South Africa. The interview process is as follows: a first-round interview is a 'get to know you' interview that will probably last around 45 minutes. Some countries will consider doing this on the phone with offshore applicants. A second-round interview will involve discussing a lesson plan created by the applicant and giving a brief teaching presentation of approximately 15 minutes. This interview will also last approximately 45 minutes. Qualified applicants can apply online.

COMMERCIAL AGENCIES

If you have a TEFL background, you can send a CV with covering letter via email or post to the relevant agencies. Agencies that specialise in a single country are not included in this chapter, but are mentioned in the country chapters.

Anglo-Pacific (Asia) Consultancy, Suite 32, Nevilles Court, Dollis Hill Lane, London NW2 6HG (+44 20 8452 7836). Educational consultancy specialising in recruitment in Thailand, Taiwan, China and Indonesia. Also offers careers guidance to TEFL teachers returning from overseas. Welcomes approaches from graduates (or people with an HND/equivalent higher qualifications) who have a recognised TEFL certificate. Places teachers at all levels in the public and private sectors and provides teachers with background information about their destination country including teaching tips and cultural information.

Astute Education, Nottingham (+44 115 905 0148; colin@astuteeducation.co.uk; www.astute education.co.uk). Specialise in recruiting contracted and permanent staff for nurseries, primary, secondary and tertiary education establishments around the world, with occasional TEFL/TESOL vacancies, especially in the Middle East.

BBD Education, Dubai (+971 56 724 2373; recruitment@bbd.ae; http://bbdeducation.com). Recruits teachers mainly for international schools but occasional TEFL posts in Turkey, the Middle East, Asia and Africa.

Beyond Borders Staffing and Consulting LLC, Chicago (beyondbordersjobs@gmail.com; www.beyondbordersesl.com). New agency owned by James Soller (who also runs teaching blog www.jimmyesl.com). 50+ vacancies in China, 5-10 in Korea and Saudi Arabia. Skype interviews. Must have 4-year degree for entry level positions and 2+ years teaching experience plus a TEFL qualification for more advanced posts.

Carfax Education Recruitment, 48 Langham Street, London W1W 7AY (+44 20 7927 6200; www.carfax-recruitment.com). Offices in Dubai, Moscow, Baku and London. EFL-qualified freelance tutors recruited from the UK to tutor children in Russia, Azerbaijan, Dubai, etc. Tutoring mainly in English but also in other core subjects needed for studying abroad.

English in Action, 2 Hawks Lane, Canterbury CT1 2NU (+44 1227 818250; recruitment@english inaction.com; www.englishinaction.com). Native speaking teachers based in UK with minimum CELTA/Trinity travel out to Europe, for short periods of 1–8 weeks to deliver specialised active programmes to children. Recent destination countries included Austria, Germany, Slovenia and Turkey.

English Language Company, Sydney, Australia (+ 61 2 9267 5688; www.englishlanguagecompany.com/other-elc-programs-worldwide). ELC Sydney runs a range of programmes around the world which may need native speaker teachers including an English language summer camp in Singapore, plus teacher or teaching intern placement in Vietnam, Malaysia, China and India (Jaipur).

ESL Certified Recruiting Services, Colorado (+1 888 661 8005; teach@eslrecruitme.com; www.eslrecruitme.com). Recruitment of native speaker teachers for China, Korea, Vietnam, Ecuador, Georgia and Uzbekistan.

ESLstarter Ltd, Northwich, Cheshire (+44 161 818 2191; www.eslstarter.com). Recruits teachers, interns and volunteers for clients in Korea, China, Thailand, Vietnam, Argentina, etc. normally after they complete 120-hour proprietary online TEFL course. Training followed by placement incurs fees, e.g. £495 for Cambodia in 2015.

Evocation EFL, Bon Marché Centre, 241–251 Ferndale Road, Brixton, London SW9 8BJ (+44 20 7274 8441; efl@evocationefl.net; www.evocationefl.net). Annually recruits about 200 teachers from English-speaking countries, after a face-to-face interview in the UK. Candidates must have CELTA/Trinity TESOL, first degree and at least some relevant experience. The majority of job vacancies are in Italy.

Footprints Recruiting (www.footprintsrecruiting.com). A proactive and principled teacher recruitment agency based in Vancouver, Canada with vacancies mostly in Korea and China but also in Abu Dhabi, and other countries.

Global Education Logistics, London (www.globaleducationlogistics.com). Mainly recruits QTS teachers for international schools, but some openings for ESL teachers in Saudi Arabia, Russia, etc.

Global Recruitment Solutions (UK) Ltd, Wales; +44 77 9047 9238; recruitment@globalrecruitsolutions.co.uk or alison.recruitment@gmail.com; www.globalrecruitsolutions.co.uk. Sole proprietor, Alison Morgan, interviews and places teachers in Saudia Arabia, UAE, Europe and Asia. University degree required plus a teaching qualification such as PGCE + QTS or CELTA/TEFL for ESL positions.

Gold Star TEFL Recruitment, Taiwan (jim.althans@goldstarteachers.com; www.GoldStarTeachers.com). Independent English-owned TEFL recruitment agency filling vacancies for a variety of English schools across China and less often for Indonesia and Saudi Arabia.

Hunt ESL, London (+44 208 144 1233; teachabroad@intesoltesoltraining.com; www.huntesl.com/apply-paid-tefl-job). Part of the international training organisation Intesol. Vacancies in China, Korea, Thailand and Russia.

Intesol Worldwide Ltd in partnership with ESLstarter Ltd (above); www.intesolinternational.com. Teaching practice follows Intesol training courses in franchise schools in Cyprus, Hong Kong, Spain, South Africa, Singapore, Vietnam, Japan, Thailand, Bolivia, Iran, Dubai, Sharjah, Qatar, Moscow, Vladivostok, Turkey and Shrewsbury. TEFL jobs and internships worldwide.

Language Solutions, 11 Coldbath Square, London EC1R 5HL (+44 20 7689 1900 or +44 7725 497166 barry.shorten@langsols.com; simon.macartney@langsols.com; www.langsols.com). Global network of privately owned schools that specialise in teaching working adults in industry (especially the energy industry); welcomes applications from highly qualified and experienced EFL teachers for Budapest, Baku (Azerbaijan), Algeria, Qatar, Libya and Jubail Industrial City (Saudi Arabia) among others. Minimum requirement is a CELTA certificate.

LoveTEFL.com, TEFL House, Suite 1, Chantry House, Victoria Road, Leeds LS5 3JB (+44 113 829 3300; info@lovetefl.com; www.lovetefl.com). Online TEFL training provider that places fee-paying interns and teachers in Thailand, China, Cambodia, India, Venezuela and Colombia.

My ESL Recruitment (+966 540 717260; www.myeslrecruitment.com). Recruits for highly paid positions in the Middle East, etc.

Norwood English, Laois, Eire (+353 57 875 6325; info@norwoodenglish.com; www.norwoodenglish.com/jobs). TEFL training centre in Ireland that places teachers in, for example, China, Vietnam, India, Italy, Georgia, etc.

Oxford Vision Education Ltd, 10 Maddox St, London W1S 1PF (+44 20 3214 9920; info@oxfordvision.com; www.oxfordvision.com). London and Istanbul-based consultancy that recruits TEFL teachers for international network of private schools and language centres in the Islamic world, with partner offices in Kazakhstan, Tajikistan and Kyrgyzstan.

Prime Teachers International, York Science Park, Heslington, York YO10 5NP (+44 1904 567673; info@primeteachers.com; www.primeteachers.com). UK-based recruitment consultancy for the education sector with vacancies in Turkey, the Middle East, China, nurseries in Moscow, etc. Recruitment manager is Georgina Tognola.

Reach To Teach, head office in Iowa, USA (+1 201 467 4612; UK +44 20 3286 9794, Australia +61 2 8011 4516; www.ReachToTeachRecruiting.com). One of the largest human resource companies for teachers in Asia, primarily Korea, China, Taiwan, Vietnam and Russia. All services are free to teachers.

Teachaway, Toronto and Vancouver, New York and Edinburgh (www.teachaway.com). Recruits for employers in Korea, China, Japan, Hong Kong, Saudi Arabia, Mexico, Kazakhstan and others. Appointed recruiters for state-qualified teachers to work in the public school system of Abu Dhabi among others.

Teach to Travel Ltd, Room 4, Third Floor, Duru House, 101 Commercial Road, London E1 1RD (+44 20 096 1214/7193 2546; hr@teachtotravel.co.uk; www.teachtotravel.com). 300 English teachers placed in Turkey, South Korea, China, Hong Kong, Saudi Arabia and Thailand (200 to

Turkey – see entry; the rest divided among the Asian countries). TEFL/CELTA and university degree required. Recruitment Consultant is Fiona Mendoza, and director is Geoffrey Thomas.

TEFL Express (+44 20 3287 7796; jobs@teflexpress.co.uk; www.teflexpress.co.uk). TEFL training course provider and affiliate of Language Link. Recruitment and internships in Russia, China, Thailand, Hong Kong, Indonesia and others. Candidates must be TEFL/CELTA trained; two years of experience is required for some positions.

TEFL Heaven, Experience Teaching Abroad Ltd., Weston super Mare (+44 20 8133 3885; teachabroad@teflheaven.com; www.teflheaven.com). Hundreds of interns placed in Thailand, Vietnam, China, Costa Rica, Peru and Guatemala, normally after doing a 2-week or 4-week in-country TEFL training course. Affiliated to TEFL Blue Pty Ltd in Melbourne, Australia and Echo English Ltd (see entry in Thailand chapter)

TEFLOne (www.teflone.com). Since 2006, Taipei-based TEFLOne has been recruiting TEFL-certified teachers for Shane schools among others in Taiwan, Japan, China, Vietnam and Indonesia. Positions start every month in all countries, and teachers can be placed well in advance. Positions can be teaching young learners, adults or a combination. All positions offer a competitive salary with training, academic and welfare support and opportunities for career progression. TEFLOne carries out the whole recruitment process from pre-screening for visa/work permit eligibility, interviewing, reference checking, visa and flight liaison and arranging arrival time. Due to the requirements of the schools, TEFLOne can proceed only with teachers who are native English speakers from the UK, USA, Canada, South Africa, Ireland, Australia or New Zealand and holders of a recognised degree and a TEFL qualification. Most successful candidates will have completed an intensive 120-hour classroom-based TEFL course that includes at least six hours' observed teaching practice. Contact David Coles (david.coles@teflone.com) for more information.

VOLUNTARY, GAP YEAR AND RELIGIOUS ORGANISATIONS

Christians Abroad (+44 300 012 1201; recruit@cabroad.org.uk; www.cabroad.org.uk). Ecumenical charity providing information and advice to people of any faith or none who are thinking of working overseas, whatever their circumstances, whether short or long-term, voluntary or paid. Occasional openings for TEFL teachers, eg in India, Tanzania, Kenya, Zambia, etc.

VSO (Voluntary Service Overseas), 317 Putney Bridge Road, London SW15 2PN (+44 20 8780 7500; enquiry@vso.org.uk; www.vso.org.uk). VSO is a professional organisation that works in more than 30 countries in Africa, Asia and the Pacific. It receives requests, including some in English language teacher training. Volunteer requirements vary but the usual commitment is two years. Most placements are for skilled and qualified professionals aged 18–75 from a variety of backgrounds. VSO recognises the Trinity TESOL and Cambridge CELTA qualifications. The VSO package for its volunteers includes airfares, medical cover, National Insurance contributions, rent-free accommodation and a modest salary in line with local pay rates. VSO also provides full in-country support including pre-departure training and briefing, basic language and cultural orientation on arrival prior to starting placement.

A number of companies charge school-leavers and others to arrange volunteer placements abroad, known as voluntourism, many of which are in schools where volunteers teach English. Several of those listed here are founder members of the Year Out Group (www.yearoutgroup.org), formed to promote well-structured gap year programmes.

AIESEC (www.aiesec.co.uk). Acronym for the International Association for Students of Economics and Management, a student organisation with links to over 100 countries. AIESEC can organise placements in any of its member countries for students and recent graduates in many fields including education. Participation fee in UK is £350.

BUNAC (www.bunac.org.uk). Teaching internships in partnership with Love TEFL above, in China, Thailand, Cambodia, Nepal, South Africa and Colombia. Prices from £745 include 120-hour online TEFL course.

Global Crossroad, Irving, TX (+1 866 387 7816; www.globalcrossroad.com). Volunteer teaching and internships in 18 countries, from Uganda to Peru. Paid teaching in China (minimum six months). For volunteer programmes in many countries, application fee of $299 plus varying weekly fee.

Global Nomadic, London (+44 20 7193 2652; www.globalnomadic.com). Tries to minimise costs in its placements worldwide, including paid teaching in Thailand, China, Spain and Costa Rica, sometimes in conjunction with an in-country training course. Volunteer teaching placements in Peru, Madagascar and other countries.

Inspire Volunteer Abroad, Newbury (+44 1635 45556; www.inspirevolunteer.co.uk). Volunteer teaching placements from two weeks to six months in India, Nepal, Cambodia, Romania, Peru, Thailand and Tanzania. Prefers older candidates with teaching experience. Costs start from about £900 for a 1-month placement in Cambodia or six weeks in Romania. All accommodation and some meals are included.

Integrate Hands, London (www.integratehands.org/projects.htm). Fellowships for fluent English speakers to work with NGOs in post-conflict societies such as Ethiopia, Iraqi Kurdistan and Uganda, mainly teaching English to children, teachers and parents.

International Volunteer HQ, New Plymouth, New Zealand (+64 6 758 7949; info@volunteerhq.org; www.volunteerhq.org). Short-term volunteer teaching in many countries for varying fees.

IST Plus, Churcham House, 1 Bridgeman Road, Teddington TW11 9AJ (+44 20 7788 7877; www.istplus. com). IST Plus administers Teach in China and Teach in Thailand programmes (see respective chapters).

i-to-i Volunteer Travel, 261 Low Lane, Leeds LS18 5NY (+44 113 205 4610; info@i-to-i.com; www.i-to-i.com/about-volunteer-travel). i-to-i offers intensive TEFL/TESOL training weekends for £149 at venues in UK/Eire cities or online courses, with paid TEFL internships in China, Thailand and Vietnam plus many teaching placements worldwide for paying volunteers. The company (a brand of TUI Travel) is moving away from the volunteer market and towards more professionalism.

Lattitude Global Volunteering, 42 Queen's Road, Reading, Berkshire RG1 4BB (+44 118 959 4914; volunteer@lattitude.org.uk; www.lattitude.org.uk). Overseas volunteering opportunities for 17–25 year olds, including teaching in Argentina, China, Ecuador, India and Vietnam. Posts are for between three and five months and cost the volunteer from £2,300 plus airfare, insurance and medical costs. Board, lodging and (sometimes) a living allowance are provided.

Love Volunteers, New Zealand (www.lovevolunteers.org). Voluntourism teaching worldwide including Albania, Cambodia, Cameroon, Ethiopia and Honduras.

Plan My Gap Year, Down Farm Barn, Lamberhurst, Tunbridge Wells, Kent TN3 8HF (+44 1892 890473; www.planmygapyear.co.uk). Choice of volunteer teaching projects, mainly from two or four weeks to 24 weeks in Cambodia, Ghana, India, Morocco, Nepal, Romania, South Africa, Sri Lanka, Tanzania, Thailand and Vietnam. Prices for a fortnight are mainly £200–£400 plus registration fee of £149.

Projects Abroad, Aldsworth Parade, Goring, Sussex BN12 4TX (+44 1903 708300; info@projects-abroad.co.uk; www.projects-abroad.co.uk). Sends up to 4,000 people abroad annually on a variety of projects in developing countries, with English teaching projects in Ethiopia, Peru, Sri Lanka, Thailand among others. Projects start from two weeks in length, with an average volunteer spending three months. Three-month placements start at about £2,700, excluding travel costs but including accommodation, food, insurance and in-country support.

Starfish Volunteers (+44 330001 0807; www.starfishvolunteers.com). UK company that places volunteers of all nationalities in teaching projects in Thailand and India.

The Project Trust, Hebridean Centre, Ballyhough, Isle of Coll, Argyll PA78 6TE (+44 1879 230444; info@projecttrust.org.uk; www.projecttrust.org.uk). Sends school leavers (aged 17–19) to teach English as a second language in Senegal, Cambodia, China, Japan, India, Malaysia, Sri Lanka, Thailand, Chile, Dominican Republic and Honduras. Participants must fundraise to cover part of the cost of their 12-month placement, at present £6,200 (2016).

Travellers Worldwide, 2A Caravelle House, 17/19 Goring Road, Worthing, West Sussex BN12 4AP (+44 1903 502595; info@travellersworldwide.com; www.travellersworldwide.com). Provides teaching as well as many other work experience and volunteer placements worldwide. Prices start from £845 for a short two-week stint.

Travel to Teach (T2T), Thailand (www.travel-to-teach.org). Thai-based organisation that provides volunteer teaching opportunities (among others) in Thailand, Cambodia, Laos, Vietnam, China, Bali, Sri Lanka, Maldives, India, Costa Rica, Guatemala, El Salvador, Nicaragua and Mexico. Fees start at £515 for a month.

Usit, 19/21 Aston Quay, Dublin 2, Ireland (+353 1 602 1742; volunteer@usit.ie; www.usit.ie). In addition to paid teaching placements in China, Usit also places paying volunteers who do not need to have qualifications to teach in developing countries, ie Nepal, India, Thailand, Vietnam, Sri Lanka, Ghana and South Africa. Prices are from €939 for a month.

Volunteering Solutions (+44 800 014 8160; info@volunteeringsolutions.com; www.volunteering solutions.com/teaching-volunteer-projects). Teaching placements in many countries in Africa, Asia and South America, from teaching monks in Galle, Sri Lanka to children in Honduras. Agency is based near Delhi.

OPPORTUNITIES FOR NORTH AMERICANS

Although the companies, agencies and charities listed here are based in the USA and cater primarily to North Americans, some may be in a position to help overseas applicants. Recruitment agencies in the USA have stronger links with Latin America and the Far East than with Europe. As in Britain, some organisations are involved primarily with English-medium international schools following an American curriculum, and are looking to recruit state-certified teachers; these are listed separately at the end of this section.

A Broader View, Pennsylvania, +1 215 780 1845; www.abroaderview.org. A non-profit active in 24 countries with teaching placements in many locations including Cameroon and the Galapagos. An average price for eight weeks is US$1,700.

Center for Intercultural Education and Development (CIED), Georgetown University, Washington, DC (www.elprograms.org). The English Language Fellow Program, administered by the CIED, is a 10-month fellowship sponsored and funded by the US Department of State. Participants must be US citizens, have an MA in TESOL or a related field and some classroom teaching experience. Participants receive a stipend, living allowance to cover food, housing, local transportation and utilities. Pre-departure briefings take place in August. The 50 or so destinations include unusual countries like Algeria, Mauritania and Turkmenistan.

CIEE (Council on International Educational Exchange), 300 Fore Street, Portland, ME 04101 (www. ciee.org/teach). Administers teaching in Chile, Peru, China, Spain, Dominican Republic, Mexico, South Korea, Vietnam and Thailand. Participants are placed in local schools where they teach English and are compensated with a local salary and temporary or permanent housing.

Council for International Exchange of Scholars, 1400 K St, Suite 700, Washington, DC 20005 (+1 202 686 6245; scholars@iie.org or DGipson@iie.org; www.cies.org). The Core Fulbright Scholar Program, administered by the US Department of State, provides up to 60 grants for teaching English in over 50 countries, open to people active in the field. Candidates with a doctorate in Applied Linguistics or TEFL may consider the Specialist Program. Applicants must be US citizens.

Fulbright English Teaching Assistant (ETA) Program, Institute of International Education, New York (+1 212 984 5525; http://us.fulbrightonline.org/eta-program-charts or http://exchanges.state.gov/us/program/fulbright-english-teaching-assistant-program). Recent college graduates and young professionals are placed as English teaching assistants for 6–12 months in primary and secondary schools or universities overseas to improve foreign students' English language abilities and knowledge of the United States. Candidates must have a BA and knowledge of the host country's language.

Greenheart Travel, Chicago (www.greenhearttravel.org). Cultural exchange organisation that arranges teaching jobs in South Korea and China; and offers fee-paying volunteers placements in schools in Indonesia, Thailand, Costa Rica, Myanmar and Italy, and homestay tutoring in Colombia, France, Italy, Spain and Brazil.

InterExchange, 161 Sixth Avenue, New York, NY 10013 (+1 800 597 3675; workabroad@interexchange. org; www.interexchange.org). Arranges homestays with 15 hours a week of English tutoring of the family in France, Spain, Italy, Austria and Germany (for 1–3 months), plus paid EFL teaching posts in Chile, China, Thailand and Vietnam. Programme fees from $795 for live-in positions in Europe and varying fees for further afield.

LanguageCorps, Sudbury, MA (+1 978 562 2100; toll-free (North America): +1 877 216 3267; www. languagecorps.com). Company offers 4-week TESOL training course in many places worldwide, and then job placement in South-East Asia, Latin America, etc.

American English, US Department of State, Washington DC (http://americanenglish.state.gov). The State Department promotes understanding of American language, society, culture, values and policies around the world. Educational exchange programmes for English language teachers and students are administered by Regional English Language Offices (RELOs) of which there are 25 around the world. Some RELOs provide English language instruction at American Language Centers, as do binational centres, which work closely with American embassies. Most teachers are hired directly by the centre in question; addresses are linked from the website given above. ESL professionals with an MA/PhD may consider the 10-month English Language Fellow Program or the shorter-term English Language Specialist Program.

Peace Corps, Washington, DC (+1 855 855 1961; www.peacecorps.gov). TEFL has historically been one of the major programme areas of the Peace Corps, which currently has programmes in 64 countries. Just less than 40% of the 6,818 volunteers work in the education sector, with many involved in ELT. Volunteers, who must be US citizens, over age 18 and in good health, are sent on 27-month assignments. All expenses, including airfare and health insurance, are covered. Peace Corps volunteers teach at both secondary and university level, and some become involved with teacher training and curriculum development. It can take 9–12 months between application and departure. Education volunteers must have a college degree (not necessarily in education) and varying levels of experience of ESL tutoring one-to-one or classroom teaching.

Scotia Personnel, 6045 Cherry St, Halifax, NS B3H 2K4, Canada (+1 902 422 1455; scotiap@ ns.sympatico.ca or info@scotia-personnel-ltd.com; www.scotia-personnel-ltd.com). Teaching placements in Korea and China; live-in tutoring in France, Italy and Spain. C$672 service fee.

TESOL International Association, Alexandria, VA (+1 703 836 0774; info@tesol.org; www.tesol.org). A key organisation for professional ESL/EFL teachers worldwide, TESOL is an association offering various publications and services to 12,000 members in 120 countries. Full individual membership costs $98 per year, or $60 for those who have been in the field for less than three years. Members can receive assistance from TESOL's Careers Service and attend the Job MarketPlace, an ESL/EFL job fair held during TESOL's annual convention. Teaching vacancies are published at careers.tesol. org/jobs.

WorldTeach, Cambridge, MA (+1 857 259 6646; www.worldteach.org). Non-profit organisation that provides college graduates with one-year contracts (EFL or ESL) in American Samoa, Colombia, Costa Rica, Ecuador, Guyana, Namibia, the Marshall Islands, China, Bangladesh, Chile, Pohnpei (Micronesia) and Thailand. Summer programmes are available in Costa Rica, Ecuador, Haiti, Poland, Namibia, Morocco, Nepal, Micronesia and South Africa. Participants pay a volunteer contribution ranging from zero to $4,590; several programmes are fully funded by the host country including Samoa, the Marshall Islands and Micronesia.

As mentioned earlier in the introductory section about Red Tape, Americans are permitted to travel in continental Europe, known as the Schengen Area, for up to 90 days at a time in a six-month period. Some summer jobs as English teachers on language camps are shorter than 90 days, and tutors and counsellors do not require a work visa. In some countries like Germany, employers are able to help some nationalities with visas. For example when **Brandon Howard** was 22 and finishing up his last semester at Montana State University in global and multicultural studies, he came across vacancies with the German summer camp company LEOlingo on a work abroad website:

> *My application process for LEOlingo was straightforward and dynamic. I was asked anything from how many children's songs do you know, to are you good at riding a horse? I had no previous English teaching experience per se, but had multiple years of backcountry guiding for youth. Work permits were not as difficult to obtain as I had originally thought. After working closely with my German boss we found that the proper steps could be taken once I had landed in Germany. At the foreigners' registration office I had to present all required documents such as my work contract and the €50 transaction fee.*

CERTIFIED TEACHERS

Certified primary and secondary teachers who want to work in mainstream international schools abroad should be aware of the following agencies and organisations, which match qualified candidates with vacancies. Most of the hiring for primary and secondary schools abroad (often referred to in the American context as K–12: kindergarten to grade 12) is done at recruitment fairs included in the list below. The files of job-seekers are added to a database that can be consulted by recruiters, who then choose whom they want to interview. Candidates who successfully land a job abroad with the help of a US agency may have to pay a placement fee of $300–$600, though in some cases the employer underwrites this expense.

Council of International Schools, Leiden, Netherlands (EducatorRecruitment@cois.org; www.cois.org). Educator Recruitment Service for certified teachers (BEd or PGCE) with at least two years' teaching experience. The agency hosts at least one recruitment fair in London in January, and has a searchable database online of accredited international schools.

Gabbitas Education, London SW1 (www.gabbitas.co.uk/). Established for 143 years, Gabbitas maintains a register of qualified and experienced teachers available for teaching posts in South America, Europe, Asia, etc. Gabbitas generally recruits subject-specialist teachers for English-medium schools. It has offices in China, Japan, South Korea and Russia.

International Schools Services, Princeton, NJ (www.iss.edu). Offers teaching opportunities for educators in private American and international schools around the world. ISS hosts three international recruitment centres (IRCs) annually, where interviews are conducted by international school administrators. Applicants must have a bachelor's degree and relevant K–12 experience. IRC registration materials are provided on approval of application.

Queen's University, Kingston, ON (ed.careers@queensu.ca; http://info.educ.queensu.ca/torf/index.php). Organises the Teachers' Overseas Recruiting Fair. Fair takes place in late January. Teacher certification required plus at least two years' K–12 teaching experience. Registration opens in September.

Search Associates (www.searchassociates.com). 13 job fairs worldwide for fully qualified primary and secondary teachers with relevant experience. Search Associates is not usually appropriate for TEFL teachers who have no school experience but offers information and placement assistance for teachers with at least some mainstream school experience (with pupils aged 3–18). Long-term positions only (one to three-year contracts, renewable).

Seek Teachers (www.seekteachers.com). Educational consultancy for international teaching jobs, mainly in primary and secondary schools, but also advertise some ESL teaching jobs mainly in the Far and Middle East.

Teach Anywhere (www.teachanywhere.com). Online recruiter of licensed teachers for positions worldwide, mostly in international schools.

Teacher Recruitment International (Australia), Sydney, Australia (www.triaust.com). Places teachers in primary and secondary school posts in international schools in Europe, Asia, the Middle East and, to a lesser extent, South America. Initial registration fee of A$77 but no placement fee.

University of Northern Iowa, Overseas Placement Service for Educators, Cedar Falls, IA (overseas. placement@uni.edu; www.uni.edu/placement/overseas). UNI is a non-profit organisation and it does not charge any placement fees to schools or teaching candidates. Recruiting fair is held in early February. Educators must hold current certification in elementary or secondary education.

SPECULATIVE JOB HUNT

The vast majority of language schools do not publicise their vacancies internationally and instead depend on local adverts, word of mouth, personal contacts and direct approaches. Because there is quite a high turnover of staff in TEFL positions, a speculative job search has a better chance of success than in many other fields of employment. For a successful campaign, only two things are needed: a reasonable CV and a list of addresses of potential employers. But always bear in mind that the majority of language schools won't offer you work until they have interviewed you, normally via Skype if you are not in the country.

APPLYING IN ADVANCE

Entire books and consultancy companies are devoted to showing people how to draw up an impressive curriculum vitae (CV, or résumé as it is called in the USA). But it is really just a matter of common sense. Obviously employers will be more inclined to take seriously a well-presented document than something scribbled on the back of a dog-eared envelope. Obviously any relevant training or experience should be highlighted rather than submerged in the trivia about your schooling and hobbies. If you lack any TEFL experience, try to bring out anything in your past which demonstrates your 'people skills', such as voluntary work, group counselling, one-to-one remedial tutoring, etc and your interest in (and ability to adapt to) foreign countries. If you are targeting one country, it would be worth drawing up a CV in the local language; **Judith Twycross** was convinced that her CV in Spanish was a great asset when looking for teaching work in Colombia. If you get the job, however, be prepared for your new employer to expect you to be able to speak the vernacular.

School websites very often have a recruitment or 'work for us' icon, and increasingly applications are invited online. The necessary steps and required documents should all be explained clearly. Customs differ. In France, for example, many companies ask for a 'motivation letter'.

Attitudes and personality are probably just as important as educational achievements in TEFL, so anything that proves an aptitude for teaching and an extrovert personality will be relevant, especially if you are going after a job teaching children. This is easier to convey over Skype than in the old-fashioned paper application.

The other essential ingredient is the names and contact details of language institutes. Each of the country chapters in this book provides such a list and recommends ways of obtaining other addresses, for example by contacting a federation of language schools (if there is one) or specialist recruiters in your destination country. Note that the embassy or British Council is unlikely to be able to help. For example in some countries the US embassy website states categorically that 'the US Embassy does not maintain a database, either formal or anecdotal, of English schools or recruitment agencies.' The most comprehensive source of addresses of language schools is usually the *Yellow Pages*, which in many cases can be consulted online. Just type 'Yellow Pages' and your destination country into a search engine and then search for 'Scuole di Lingue' in Italy, 'Jazykova Skola' in the Czech Republic and so on. Some countries are much better than others, for example, the online Portuguese *Yellow Pages* are very helpful whereas the Russian are not.

Of course it has to be stressed that accepting a job offer without meeting the employer face-to-face carries risks. In some cases, a language school has to be fairly desperate to hire a teacher it has never met for a vacancy that has never been advertised. On the other hand, job-hunting in situ is not a realistic possibility for many. If applying from home, it is a good idea to follow up any hint of interest with a phone call. The best time to phone language school directors is six or seven weeks before the beginning of term. Perhaps the school has a contact in your country who would be willing to conduct an informal interview on its behalf or will be willing to give you a chance to show your stuff on Skype.

If your credentials are not the kind to wow school directors, it might still be worth sending off a batch of warm-up letters, stating your intention to present yourself in person a couple of weeks or months hence. Even if you don't receive a reply, such a strategy may stick in the mind of employers, as an illustration of how organised and determined you are.

INTERVIEWS

Whether you are interviewed at home or abroad, slightly different rules apply. For example, smart casual dress, neither flashy nor scruffy, is appropriate in Britain, while something more formal might be called for in certain cultures such as France or Japan. Even if all your friends laugh when you pack a suit before going abroad, you may find it a genuine asset when trying to outdo the competition. As **Steven Hendry**, who has taught English both in Japan and Thailand with none of the usual advantages apart from traveller's canniness, says:

> *You may not need a tailor-made suit but you definitely need to be able to present a conservative and respectable image.*

As with the CV, so at interview: highlight anything that is remotely connected with teaching even if it has nothing to do with the English language, and do it energetically and enthusiastically. Yet keenness will seldom be sufficient in itself. You don't have to be an intellectual to teach English; in fact the quiet bookish type is probably at a disadvantage. An amusing illustration of this is provided by **Robert Mizzi**'s description of his interview for the JET Programme in the Japan chapter (see page 444).

DON'T HAVE A TEFL BACKGROUND?

Do a certain amount of research, eg acquaint yourself with some of the jargon such as 'notional', 'communicative-based', etc. It is not uncommon for an interviewer to ask a few basic grammar questions. To help you deal with this eventuality, see the list of recommended reading in the chapter on Preparation. Visit the ELT section of a bookshop to begin familiarising yourself with the range of materials on offer. Always have some questions ready to ask the interviewer, such as 'Do you favour the Oxford or Cambridge course books?', 'What audio materials do you have?' 'Do you encourage the use of songs?' or 'Do you teach formal grammar structures?'

An interesting post was published on a Teaching English in Berlin blog recently that set out some of the questions that you should have ready to ask at an interview. Don't be shy to ask the obvious:

- How much freedom will I have to plan classes?
- How many hours can I realistically expect to get?
- How many teachers do you employ?
- Is there a teacher's room or preparation area?
- Is there a photocopier?
- What resources are available?
- What's your teaching methodology?

- Is there any training or career development available?
- How much administration or paperwork will I have to do?
- How much is the pay? Is travel pay included?

You will certainly be asked how long you intend to stay and (depending on the time of year) nothing less than nine months will be considered. They will also want to know whether you have had any experience. With luck you will be able to say truthfully that you have (at least) taught at a summer school in Britain or elsewhere (again, see chapter on Preparation). Some applicants who are convinced that they can do a good job make a similar claim, untruthfully, knowing that at the lower end of the TEFL spectrum this will never be checked. Similarly some candidates claim to have done a TEFL course and pretend to have left the certificate at home. A certain amount of bluffing is inevitable in most interviews, so you'll just have to decide how far you are prepared to go. Bear in mind that the true depths of your ignorance could easily be plumbed. Another skill you might be tempted to exaggerate is your knowledge of the local language. **Philip Dodd** was hired by a language teaching agency in Madrid on the understanding that he could speak fluent Spanish and on his first assignment was sent out to give English lessons to a young child living in a wealthy suburb. He was greeted at the door by the mother, who wished to make sure of a few things before she entrusted her precious offspring to this stranger. Not able to follow her voluble stream, Philip nodded affably and said *sí* whenever he guessed it was appropriate. After one of his affable *sí's*, the woman's face turned grey and she ordered him out of her house. He still doesn't know what he said that was so shocking. On the other hand, a certain inflation of your abilities may be expected, and will be met with distortions of the truth from the employer as you both decide whether you are going to hit it off.

Of course many applicants avoid potential embarrassment at interview by preparing themselves for a stint as a teacher. If you have done a TEFL course of any description, be sure to take along the certificate, however humble the qualification. Even schools in far-flung places are becoming increasingly familiar with the distinctions between various qualifications and are unlikely to confuse a Cambridge certificate with an anonymous distance learning 'certificate'. In Asia especially, nothing short of the original will do, since there are so many counterfeit copies around.

If you have a university degree, be sure to take the certificate along. Even if the interviewer is prepared to take your word for it, the school administration may need the document at a later stage either to give you a salary increment or to obtain a work permit. If needed for a work permit, prepare to pay to have the document notarised or apostilled (authenticated). **Adam Hartley**, who taught English in China, hadn't realised that his MA would have earned him a higher salary; although he arranged for two separate copies to be sent from Britain, neither arrived and he had to be content with the basic salary. Americans should take along their university transcripts; any school accustomed to hiring Americans will be familiar with these. Also take along any references; something written on headed paper will always impress, even if your previous jobs were not in teaching.

Once the interviewer indicates that you are a strong contender, it is your turn to ask questions. Ask about the details of pay, hours and conditions and take notes (see the section on Contracts below). Often there are disappointing discrepancies between what is promised in the early stages and what is delivered; at least if these things have been discussed at interview, you will be in a stronger bargaining position if the conditions are not met.

Unrealistic expectations are a genuine hazard when contemplating an exciting stint of working abroad. A recruitment consultant in the field offers the following sensible advice:

> Teachers should be made aware that they are being employed to do a professional job and it is hard work and long hours. They should not underestimate the cultural differences even in countries they think they know. These often lead to misunderstandings and dissatisfied teachers. I am also constantly surprised by teachers who take jobs without knowing the first thing about the place, the job, the sort of classes they will have, etc. They should make a checklist of questions and if they are making applications on their own they should ask to speak to teachers who are there at the time or who have just left.

Research is the key. You wouldn't apply for a job in the UK without knowing something about it so why do so when you're going to another country? Google can reveal a lot about a potential employer. Check feedback on forums such as www.eslcafe.com and eslbase.com. The site www.reddit.com/r/TEFL carries reviews of some employers and a busy TEFL forum. Occasionally an embassy or consulate will assist, as in the case of the US Embassy in Seoul, which keeps a file of language schools about which it has received persistent complaints. More commonly, someone will have set up a web page where this kind of inside information can be obtained (again, common in Korea).

Professional English language teachers often try to attend a regional conference sponsored by TESOL Inc (tesol.org) or IATEFL (International Association of TEFL; iatefl.org) where a jobs market is hosted. **Sandeha Lynch** describes the TESOL Arabia Conference he attended in Al-Ain:

> *These are serious ELT conferences not only as marketing fairs for publishers, booksellers and software companies, but also as an open job shop for the local employers. Teachers from all over the Gulf try to get there to socialise, look for a new job or just absorb enough academic wisdom to last them another year. If teachers are looking for a job then most of the time they'll be making appointments, checking off their interview scorecards and watching the clock. All of the local colleges and recruiting agencies have stands there, and they are busy from morning to night giving interviews to anyone who knows the local scene and has the right qualifications.*

ON THE SPOT

It is almost impossible to fix up a job in advance in some countries, due to the way the TEFL business operates. For example, written applications to the majority of language schools in Ecuador or Peru or Vietnam would be mostly a waste of time since the pool of expat teachers and travellers on the spot is usually sufficient. Even in countries such as Spain and Germany, for which adverts appear in the UK, the bulk of hiring is done on the spot.

When you arrive in a likely place, your initial steps might include some of the following.

- Check job ads on Craigslist, Gumtree, Kijiji or equivalent.
- Transcribe a list of schools from the *Yellow Pages*.
- Read the classified column of the local newspapers, including local English language papers and magazines.
- Check noticeboards in likely locations such as the British Council, US Embassy/Cultural Centres, universities, TEFL training centres, English language bookshops (where you should also check which EFL materials are stocked) or hostels which teacher-travellers frequent.

Once you have prepared a CV, email it to yourself as an attachment so it will always be accessible. That way you don't have to carry it around with you and you can easily modify it in any internet café. A reconnaissance trip is a good idea if possible, although **Andrew Whitmarsh** didn't even realise he was looking for a new job, when one found him in Indonesia:

> *As often happens, I didn't find my job, my job found me. I was standing on top of a volcano in Indonesia when a gentleman in my hiking group asked me what I did for a living. Upon my reply of 'English Teacher', he declared that this was wonderful news to hear and he had just the job for me. The gentleman just happened to be the President Director of Wall Street Institute – and he needed teachers.*

With a little more purpose and a little less serendipity, **Fiona Paton** found a job teaching English in France. On her way back from a summer holiday in Spain, she broke her return journey in Vichy long enough to distribute her CV to several language schools, which resulted in a job for the academic year.

After obtaining a list of potential employers and before contacting them, get hold of a detailed map and guide to the public transport network so you can locate the schools. Phone the schools and try to arrange a meeting with the director or director of studies (DOS). Even if an initial chat does not result in a job offer, you may learn something about the local TEFL scene, which will benefit you at the next interview, especially if you ask lots of questions. You might also be able to strike up a conversation with one of the foreign teachers, who could turn out to be a valuable source of information about that school in particular and the situation generally. It is very common to have to begin with just a few hours a week. Make it clear that you are prepared to stand in at short notice for an absent teacher. The longer you stay in one place, the more hours will come your way and the better your chances of securing a stable contract.

This gradual approach also gives you a chance to discover which are the fly-by-night schools, something that is difficult to do before you are on the scene. The British Council has called for an EU-wide recognition scheme for language schools to force rogue schools out of business. But this is a long way off, and in the meantime disreputable schools flourish in Europe just as they do in other parts of the world. It is not always easy to distinguish them, though if a school sports a sign 'Purrfect Anglish' you are probably not going to need an MA in Applied Linguistics to get a job there. Working for a cowboy outfit may not be the end of the world, though it often spells trouble, as the Problems chapter will reveal. But without many qualifications you may not have much choice.

ADVERTISEMENTS

The monthly *EL Gazette* (www.elgazette.com) is a source of news and developments in the ELT industry for all interested individuals even though it is pitched at the professional end of the market and carries few job ads. An annual print subscription costs £33 in the UK, and £55 worldwide, though much of its content is available free in the digital edition. Job vacancies appear year round on the main TEFL websites, though schools that advertise in February or December are often advertising a very urgent vacancy, eg 'to start immediately, good salary, air fares, accommodation'; but these are exceptional.

Almost all adverts specify TEFL training/experience as a minimum requirement. But there is always a chance that this is merely rhetorical. Those who lack such a background should not feel defeated before they begin, since a TEFL background may turn out not to be essential. A carefully crafted CV and enthusiastic personality (not to mention a shortage of suitable applicants) could well persuade a school that it doesn't require a Cambridge or Trinity certificate with two years' experience after all.

Advertisements will sometimes include a contact name or company in the UK to which enquiries should be addressed for posts abroad. This may be a recruiting agency, TEFL training centre or a language school in the UK that is in contact with language schools abroad or it may just be an ex-employee who has agreed to do some recruitment for a commission fee. Note that none of these middle men is allowed to charge the job-seeker any fee. When discussing terms and conditions with an agent, bear in mind that the agent may be more interested in collecting a commission for finding someone to fill the vacancy than in conveying all the seamy facts.

Occasionally cases crop up of misleading or even fraudulent ads. A case a few years ago resulted in this headline in the *Times Educational Supplement*: 'Thousands conned by Botswana job hoax'. A conman placed adverts for teaching jobs in a fictitious school in Botswana, sent a letter of acceptance to all who applied and a request for $100 as a visa processing fee. Even if this sort of bare-faced fraud is rare, it is best to be sceptical when interpreting ads, including on the internet, where promises of earning huge salaries, particularly in less than affluent countries, are usually pie-in-the-sky. Never send money to an employer on the promise of a job. The rule of thumb is if it sounds too good to be true, don't believe it.

> Based on his experience of answering advertisements placed by Turkish language schools, one cynical job-hunter has drawn up a glossary of terms, helping new applicants to 'read between the lines'.
>
> ■ 'Dollar Linked Salary': paid in the local currency and only linked to the dollar every three or six months.
> ■ 'Free Accommodation': no way can you afford to rent a place of your own. You have no say in who your flat-mates are.
> ■ 'Paid Flight': this is usually for a one-way flight.
> ■ 'Leading School': all the schools say this about themselves.
> ■ 'Provides In-Service Training': could be weekly, monthly or annually.
> ■ 'Degree and Cert essential': that's what the Ministry of Education wants. Will recruit anybody if desperate (good schools) or anybody at all (cowboys).
> ■ 'Central Location': near all the good pubs.
> ■ 'Young and Dynamic Team': be like a student again.
> ■ 'Teachers are encouraged to use their own materials and be creative': there isn't much in the way of resources.

ELT training centres often have numerous links with foreign schools and may have a noticeboard with posted vacancies. Unless you are a trainee at the relevant centre, it will probably be tricky consulting such a noticeboard, but a cooperative secretary might not mind a *potential* trainee consulting the board. University careers offices may also have contacts with schools abroad to which their graduates have gone in the past, so if you have a university connection, it is worth making enquiries.

FREELANCE TEACHING

Private English lessons are usually more lucrative than contract teaching simply because there is no middleman. Learners may prefer them as well, not only because of the more personal attention they receive in a private lesson but because it costs them less. As a private tutor working from your own home or visiting students in theirs, you can undercut the big schools with their overheads. But at the same time you deprive yourself of the advantages of working for a decent school: access to resources and equipment, in-service training, social security schemes and holiday pay. The life of a freelance teacher can be quite a lonely one. Usually teachers working for a school take on a small amount of private teaching to supplement their income, provided this is allowed in their contract. Most employers do not mind unless your private teaching is interfering with your school schedule or (obviously) if you are pinching potential clients from your employer.

In order to round up private students, you will have to sell yourself as energetically as any salesperson. Turn to the section on 'Freelance teaching' in the Spain chapter for some ideas that have worked in Spain but could work anywhere. It might be possible to persuade companies to pay you to run English classes for employees during the lunch hour or siesta (if appropriate), though you would have to be a confident teacher and dynamic salesperson to succeed. You are far more likely to find one or two students by word of mouth and build from there.

SELF-PROMOTION IS ESSENTIAL
Steven Hendry *plastered neatly printed bilingual notices all over town in Chiang Mai in Northern Thailand.*
Ian McArthur *made a large number of posters (in Arabic and English) and painstakingly coloured in the Union Jack by hand in order to attract attention in Cairo. (Unfortunately these were such a novelty that many posters were pinched.)*

Putting a notice on appropriate noticeboards (in schools, universities, public libraries, popular supermarkets) and running an advertisement in the local free ads community website like Gumtree/Craigslist are good ideas; you will also need a reliable mobile phone and frequent access to your email. These methods should put you in touch with a few hopeful language learners. Once you've made a good start, word will spread and more paying students will come your way, though it can be a slow process.

Counterbalancing the advantages of higher pay and a more flexible schedule are many disadvantages. Everyone, from lazy Taiwanese teenagers to busy Barcelona businessmen, cancels or postpones one-to-one lessons with irritating frequency. People who have taught in Latin countries complain that the problem is chronic. Cancellations among school and university students especially escalate at exam time. It is important to agree on a procedure for cancellations that won't leave you out of pocket. Although it is virtually impossible to arrange to be paid in advance, you can request 24 hours' notice of a cancellation and mention politely that if they fail to give due warning you will insist on being paid for the missed lesson. But you can't take too tough a line, since your clients are paying above the odds for your flexibility. Another consideration is the unpaid time spent travelling between clients' homes and workplaces.

Teaching by Skype or some other online system is now a common supplement or even full-time teaching possibility. A growing number of companies recruit teachers anywhere in the world to teach remotely from their homes, for example the Spain-based ISUS (http://jobs.ispeakuspeak.com), www.gofluent.com, which recruits in the US, Europe and the Philippines, and the German-based www.learnship.de for business English. A bold and ambitious advert was run recently on tefl.com by SpeakPlus (www.speakplus.fr) based in Lyon, France. This start-up wants to recruit 3000 entry level online EFL teachers around the world by the end of 2020 to join a marketplace that connects language learners with 'coaches'. The startling wage mentioned was £36 an hour, though most online teaching pays far less than that. With more and more people having fast internet connections and not enough time (or money) to attend in-person lessons, this is a fast-growing market. New technologies make it straightforward to be beamed into a classroom on the other side of the world via Google Hangouts which allow up to 10 people to join in a video call. Other suggestions for getting started as an online teacher can be found in an article by Emily Segev on the British Council blog (http://blog.britishcouncil.org/2014/06/18/how-to-get-started-as-an-online-teacher-of-english).

If you are more interested in integrating with a culture than in making money, exchanging conversation for board and lodging may be an appealing possibility. This can be set up by answering (or placing) small ads in appropriate places (the American Church in Paris noticeboard is famous for this). **Hannah Start**, a school-leaver from Merseyside, put up a notice at her local English language school indicating that she wanted to exchange English conversation for accommodation in Paris; a businesswoman on an intensive English course contacted her and invited her to stay with her.

PREPARATION

The preceding chapters on ELT training and job-hunting set out ways in which you can make yourself more attractive to potential employers. One of the best ways in which to prepare for a stint of teaching abroad is to teach English locally. Relevant experience can usually be gained by volunteering to tutor language learners in your home town; this is particularly feasible in the USA, where literacy programmes take place on a massive scale. It might also be a good idea to contact the director of a local commercial language school and ask to sit in on some lessons and to talk to teachers. A polite note expressing your interest in TEFL would probably meet with a positive response. EFL teachers are like everyone else; they are experts at what they do and don't mind sharing that knowledge with interested outsiders.

SUMMER CAMPS ABROAD

More prolonged exposure to TEFL can best be gained by working at a language summer school in the UK or a language summer camp abroad. **Rona Mackenzie**, who has now been teaching English in Southern Spain for a few years, started this way:

> *My first ESL teaching post was a fun, but gruelling, eight-week summer school in the south of England, where I cut my teeth. It was a baptism of fire, but something I would recommend. I didn't have to deal with a new country and a new language, as well as my first teaching job. Teaching classes of 14 unruly teenagers as a new teacher wasn't easy, but it was an invaluable experience. Next came the real deal. A move to Spain, a new job, a new life.*

You don't have to confine your hunt for a summer teaching post to the UK either. Summer camps that combine English tuition with sports and activities are held from the mountains of Romania to the Basque country. **Emma Lander** is another graduate who wanted to test the TEFL waters by accepting a summer position in the middle of a Finnish forest next to a lake:

> *I recommend working at a summer school if you're new to TEFL and you're not sure about it as a career. The informal approach to work and the freedom you are given in the classroom is an excellent way to ease in to teaching and see if it's right for you.*

Emily's employer was Nordic School (see entry in Scandinavia chapter).
This is the way **Ross O'Brien** from Ireland also started out, but at the opposite end of Europe, in Andalucía:

> *A word of advice: teaching English is a challenging, demanding job and I'd recommend working in a summer camp before you commit to a year round contract in an academy. My summer experience in TECS proved invaluable, and I really felt confident in my abilities starting in Blue Door, despite the fact they offer very different things.*

Both TECS and the Academia Blue Door have entries in the directory of employers following the Spain chapter.

UK SUMMER SCHOOLS

Language courses take place throughout the British Isles in the summer, especially in tourist areas. It is estimated that there are 600–800 English language schools in operation in Britain during July and August, mainly catering for foreign students, especially from France, Spain, Italy and other EU countries, and increasingly from further afield, such as Russia and Turkey. Many of these schools advertise heavily in the spring, eg 'Teach English on the English Riviera'. Quality varies of course. The British Council has an accreditation scheme and a searchable database at www.educationuk.org/english, which allows you to search by region and type, eg junior vacation courses in Southern England. A sister organisation, English UK, also has links to its 470 members at www.englishuk.com. Schools are located throughout the UK including Wales and Scotland, but are concentrated in the South East, Oxford, Cambridge and coastal resorts such as Bournemouth and Hastings.

Newly qualified EFL teachers are often hired for these summer positions which not only provide a chance to find out whether you will enjoy English teaching for a longer period, but may put you in touch with people who are well informed on overseas possibilities. The pace is likely to be hectic with a full programme of extracurricular activities which might include anything from producing a magazine to chaperoning trips to the theatre in Stratford.

Resources may be limited, though not many of the kind of employer **Marta Eleniak** found herself working for some time ago have survived:

I have got nothing good to say about my employer. We were expected to do nearly everything including perform miracles, with no support and pathetic facilities. I can only liken it to being asked to entertain 200 people for four hours with a plastic bowl. The pupils got a raw deal too because of false promises made to them.

She does admit though, that it was on the basis of this three-week job that she got a job in a Madrid language school.

Recruitment of summer teachers gets underway in the new year and is usually well advanced by Easter. The short-term nature of the teacher requirements means that schools sometimes have difficulties finding enough qualified staff. Wages are higher than for most seasonal summer jobs. The average starting salary for teachers with a TEFL certificate is about £300–£400 per week in addition to board and lodging at residential schools, and some salaries top £450 a week. Time off is normally non-existent in these intensive summer schools, and you may be asked to sign a waiver form regarding the 48-hour maximum working week. Since most schools are located in popular tourist destinations, private accommodation can be prohibitively expensive and the residential option attractive. Without a TEFL certificate or any TEFL background it is easier to get taken on as a non-teaching sports and activities supervisor, which at least would introduce you to the world of TEFL. EFL teachers must expect a number of extracurricular activities such as chaperoning a group of over-excited adolescents to a West End theatre or on an art gallery visit. In most cases, you will be required to obtain an enhanced DBS criminal records check.

Some of the major language course organisations that offer a large number of summer vacancies are listed below.

Anglo Continental Educational Group, 29–35 Wimborne Road, Bournemouth BH2 6NA (+44 1202 557414; jhaine@anglo-continental.com; www.anglo-continental.com).

Anglophile Academics, 140–144 Freston Road, London W10 6TR (+44 20 7603 1466; tutors@ anglophiles.com; www.anglophiles.com). Teachers needed for summer camps and schools in England and one or two in Ireland.

Ardmore Language Schools, Hall Place, Berkshire College, Burchetts Green, Maidenhead, Berkshire SL6 6QR (+44 1628 826699; jobs@theardmoregroup.com; www.theardmoregroup.com or www. ardmore-language-schools.com/working_for_ardmore.aspx). Successful applicants will be DBS-checked to work in one of 19 residential summer centres.

Bell Summer Schools, Red Cross Lane, Cambridge CB2 0QU (+44 1223 275594; www.bellenglish.com/jobs). Schools in Cambridge and St Albans, plus Oxfordshire and Berkshire. Pay rate for CELTA-holder is £363 per week plus statutory holiday pay of £43.81.

Concorde International Summer Schools, Arnett House, Hawks Lane, Canterbury, Kent CT1 2NU (+44 1227 451035; recruitment@concorde-int.com; www.concorde-int.com/recruitment).

Discovery Summer, 33 Kensington High St, London W8 5EA (+44 20 7937 1199; www.discovery summer.co.uk/employment.php). EFL teachers for various locations in England such as Radley (Oxfordshire) and Shrewsbury (Shropshire).

EC English Language Centres (jobs.ecenglish.com). International company with UK summer schools in Brighton, London, Oxford, Cambridge, Bristol and Manchester. Teaching rate of about £16 per hour (including holiday pay).

EF Language Travel, 22 Chelsea Manor Street, London SW3 5RL (+44 20 7341 8612; www. ef.co.uk/ summer-jobs). Centres in Oxford, Torbay, Brighton, Hastings, London, etc.

EJO, Eagle House, Lynchborough Road, Passfield, Hampshire GU30 7SB (+44 1428 751549; www.ejo.co.uk/work-with-us).

Embassy English (http://jobs.embassysummer.com). Teachers and other staff needed for 2–8 weeks at many summer schools. Also summer teaching jobs at three Embassy Academies.

International Quest Centres, 7 Trinity, 161 Old Christchurch Road, Bournemouth BH1 1JU (+44 1202 296868; jobs@internationalquest.co.uk; www.internationalquest.co.uk/summer-jobs). 13 summer schools in the UK, Ireland and the US.

Kent School of English, 10 and 12 Granville Road, Broadstairs, Kent CT10 1QD (+44 1843 874870; enquiries@kentschool.co.uk; www.kentschoolofenglish.com).

LAL UK Summer Schools, Conway Road, Paignton, Devon TQ4 5LH (+44 1803 558555; jobs. england@lalgroup.com; careers.lalschools.com). Summer schools held in Torbay, Tavistock, Taunton, Winchester and Twickenham. Part-time hourly wage of £15.61 in London, from £12.21 elsewhere.

OISE Youth Language Schools, OISE House, Binsey Lane, Oxford OX2 0EY (+44 1865 258325/29; ylsrecruit@oise.com; www.oiserecruitment.com). 120 summer teaching jobs at 10 summer schools.

Oxford International, 259 Greenwich High Road, London SE10 8NB (recruitment@oxfordinternational. com; www.oxfordinternational.com/recruitment). 800 teachers, activity leaders, etc.

Pilgrims Young Learners, 38 Binsey Lane, Oxford, OX2 0EY (+44 1865 258336; recruitment@ pilgrims.co.uk; www.pilgrims.co.uk).

Plus International, 8–10 Grosvenor Gardens, London SW1W 0DH (+44 20 7730 2223; recruitment@ plus-ed.com; www.plus-ed.com). 120 summer teaching positions in the UK plus Dublin. Weekly wage of £220 with less than two years' experience.

Project International, 19 Catherine Place, London SWIE 6DX (+44 20 7916 2522; recruitment@ projectinternational.uk.com; www.projectinternational.uk.com/employment). Jobs at 12 centres from Dover to Stafford.

Stafford House Study Holidays, 19 New Dover Road, Canterbury, Kent CT1 3AS (+44 1227 811506; recruitment@staffordhouse.com; www.staffordhouse.co.uk). Part of Cambridge Education Group, with 14 centres.

SUL Language Schools, 31 Southpark Road, Tywardreath, Par, Cornwall PL24 2PU (+44 1726 814227; claires@sul-schools.com; www.sul-schools.com/teachers).

Thames Valley Summer Schools, 13 Park Street, Windsor, Berkshire SL4 1LU (+44 1753 852001; recruit@thamesvalleysummer.co.uk; www.thamesvalleysummer.co.uk/working-for-us.html). Salary from £355 per week.

Roberta Wedge found that working for a large summer school organisation was not only good preparation for a teaching contract in Italy, but was fun for its own sake:

> *The big language mills in Britain are a good way to see the country. I signed up with OISE in Exeter because I wanted to tramp the moors. It's possible to spend the whole summer jumping around fortnightly from contract to contract, all arranged ahead of time through the same organisation.*

WHILE YOU'RE WAITING

After you have secured a job, there may be a considerable gap which will give you a chance to organise the practicalities of moving abroad and to prepare yourself in other ways. If you are going to a country that requires immigration procedures (the majority of cases unless you're an EU citizen planning to work in another member state) your employer can start the visa procedures. You may have to do a lot of running around to embassies, getting your degree certificate legally endorsed, getting police clearance (ACPO or DBS disclosure, in the UK). In addition to deciding what to take and how to get to your destination, you should think about your tax position and health insurance, plus find out as much as you can about the situation in which you will find yourself.

If you are entering the world of TEFL as a beginner, you might want to get a little experience. While still in his home town of Portsmouth and before taking up his gap year placement in China in 2013, **James Butcher** showed considerable enterprise:

> *I volunteered at a local primary school so that I had an idea of how the classroom environment worked and it also gave me ideas on how to control and motivate the class. I also had the chance to work with a Moldovan lady living in England and I helped her develop her English.*

If finding local opportunities is difficult, go online to sites such as LiveMocha, Verbling, LRNGO or iTalki in order to get some teaching experience.

ELT professionals should consider joining the International Association of Teachers of English as a Foreign Language (IATEFL, Kent; www.iatefl.org). Membership, which costs £55 to individuals, £35 to students or retirees and £171 to institutions, entitles teachers to various services including six newsletters annually and access to special interest groups, job alerts, conferences, workshops and symposia.

The more information you can find out about your future employer the better. **Kathy Panton** thinks that she would have been a more effective teacher in her first year in the Czech Republic if she had asked more probing questions beforehand:

> *Now that I have a better idea of what to teach I think I could handle it, but a first-year teacher should ask a lot of questions; such as, what books the students have used, teacher continuity, very detailed report of what the students can do (as opposed to what they have studied), and most of all what they will be expected to accomplish during the school year. If the report is vague, I don't think anyone should take the job unless they are really confident that they'll be able to develop the framework themselves. I would look for a school that said something like, 'You'll guide the students through Hotline 1 textbook, and also give them extra vocabulary and speaking exercises to supplement the text. You'll also work with a phonics text for a few weeks, because these students have poor pronunciation. You'll probably find it useful to bring some old magazines but the school has several ESL textbooks already.' This would show that the school takes both curriculum and organisation seriously.*

An invaluable source of information is someone who has taught at the school before; ask your employer for a couple of email addresses or (better) phone numbers. Past teachers often pass on priceless minutiae, not only recommending pubs, bakeries, etc but (if the accommodation is tied to the job) to arrive early and avoid the back bedroom because of the noisy plumbing or to take your wellies since winter rains turn the streets to rivers.

CONTRACTS

This is the point at which a formal contract or at least an informal agreement should be drawn up. Any employer who is reluctant to provide something in writing is definitely suspect. Horror stories abound of the young unsuspecting teacher who goes out to teach overseas and discovers no pay, no accommodation and maybe even no school. For this reason you should not only sign a contract but also have a good idea about what you are committing to.

WHAT A CONTRACT SHOULD COVER
The following items should be covered in a contract or at least given some consideration.

- ■ *Name and address of employer.*
- ■ *Details of the duties and hours of the job. (A standard load might be 24 contact teaching hours a week, plus three hours on standby to fill in for an absent teacher, fill all the board markers in the staff room, etc).*
- ■ *The amount and currency of your pay. Is it adequate to live on? How often are you paid? Is any money held back? Can it be easily transferred into sterling or dollars? What arrangements are there if the exchange rate drops suddenly or the local currency is devalued?*
- ■ *The length of the contract and whether it is renewable.*
- ■ *Help with finding and paying for accommodation. If accommodation is not provided free, is your salary adequate to cover this? If it is, are utilities included? Does the organisation pay for a stay in a hotel while you look for somewhere to live? How easy is it to find accommodation in the area? If it is unfurnished what help do you get in providing furniture? Can you get a salary advance to pay for this and for any rent deposits?*
- ■ *Your tax liability.*
- ■ *Provisions for health care and sick pay.*
- ■ *Payment of pension or national insurance contributions.*
- ■ *Bonuses, gratuities or perks.*
- ■ *Days off, statutory holidays and vacation times.*
- ■ *Paid flights home if the contract is outside Europe, and mid-term flights if you are teaching for two years.*
- ■ *Luggage and surplus luggage allowance at the beginning and end of the contract.*
- ■ *Any probationary period and the length of notice which you and the employer must give.*
- ■ *Penalties for breaking the contract and circumstances under which the penalties would be waived (eg extreme family illness, etc).*

Obviously any contract should be studied carefully before signing. It is a wise precaution to make a photocopy of it before returning to avoid what happened to **Belinda Michaels**, whose employer in Greece refused to give her a copy when she started to dispute some points. In some cases the only contract offered will be in a foreign language (eg Arabic or Kazakh) and you will either have to trust your contact at the school for a translation or consider obtaining an independent English translation. **Amanda Moody** signed documents that were only in Japanese and later found out that she'd been diddled out of her end-of-year bonus.

HEALTH AND INSURANCE

Increasingly, the immigration authorities abroad will not grant a teacher a work permit until they have provided a medical certificate. Many countries such as Russia and Korea may insist on an HIV test and various other health checks, including for syphilis and tuberculosis. General practitioners (GPs) make a charge, often a hefty one, for carrying out these tests, whether you do it before you leave home or after arrival.

Reputable schools will make the necessary contributions into the national health insurance and social security scheme. Even if you are covered by a national scheme, however, you may find that there are exclusion clauses such as dental treatment, non-emergency treatment, prescription drugs, etc or you may find that you are covered only while at work. Private travel insurance can be very expensive. Most insurance companies offer a standard rate that covers medical emergencies and a premium rate that covers personal baggage, cancellation, etc. On a 12-month travel policy, expect to pay roughly £20–£25 per month for barebones cover and £35–£40 for more extensive cover. One of the cheapest policies is offered by Coe Connections International (www.coeconnections.co.uk), which offers 12 months of basic cover for just £189 for people working abroad or just travelling. Unusually, it can be purchased after you have left home. Note that annual travel policies do not cover a single long stay, but will cover a number of trips with a maximum stay of 30 or 70 days or whatever the limit is.

Within Europe private insurance is not absolutely essential because European nationals are eligible for reciprocal emergency health care within the EEA. The European Health Insurance Card (EHIC) entitles EU citizens to emergency health care in any member state; however, this would not cover repatriation in the case of a serious problem. Specialist expatriate policies might be worth investigating, though these may exceed £400 for one year. Bespoke insurance policies can be drawn up by brokers such as Campbell Irvine (www.campbellirvine.com). Off-the-peg policies are of course cheaper – try Direct Travel Insurance (www. direct-travel.co.uk) or Ace Traveller Insurance (www.aceinsure.com), which covers work and study abroad and includes a gap year policy for people up to age 44. Policies designed for expats are available from Abrams Insurance Agency in Virginia (www.aia-international-insurance.com).

The EHIC scheme entitles European citizens to free medical treatment in public hospitals within the 27 EU member states, plus Iceland, Liechtenstein, Norway and Switzerland. You can apply online for it via the NHS or by phone (+44 300 3301350) quoting your National Insurance number. The card is free, so be careful to use an official site such as www.nhs.uk/ehic, avoiding the tricksters who put up official-looking sites but charge a fee. Even if your employer will be paying into a health scheme, cover may not take effect immediately and it is as well to have the ordinary tourist cover for the first three months.

No matter what country you are heading for, you should check the travel advice available from the NHS. The Department of Health has discontinued its leaflet *Health Advice for Travellers* but go to www.nhs.uk/healthcareabroad for links to country-by-country information. Increasingly, people are carrying out their own health research on the internet; check, for example, www.fitfortravel.nhs.uk and www.travelhealth.co.uk. The website of the World Health Organization (www.who.int/ith) has lots of information, including a listing of the very few countries in which certain vaccinations are a requirement of entry, primarily a Yellow Fever certificate, if you are travelling from an affected country.

A company that has become one of the most authoritative sources of travellers' health information in Britain is MASTA (www.masta-travel-health.com). It maintains a database of the latest information on the disease situation for all countries and the latest recommendations on the prevention of tropical and other diseases. Customers can book a telephone consultation or visit one of MASTA's travel clinics that administer inoculations (see website for prices) and sell medical kits and other specialist equipment like water purifiers, mosquito nets and repellents. Note that arguably the advice errs on the side of caution (which means it also makes more profit). A worldwide searchable listing of specialist travel clinics is maintained by the International Society of Travel Medicine (www.istm.org) although many cities and some countries are not included.

NATIONAL INSURANCE CONTRIBUTIONS, SOCIAL SECURITY AND PENSIONS

Nationals of the EEA countries working in another member state are covered by European Social Security regulations. Information about national social security arrangements in Europe can be read online at http://ec.europa.eu/social/main.jsp. Similarly, contributions made in any EEA country count towards benefit entitlement when you return home. The UK also has social security agreements with other countries including Croatia, Israel, Jamaica, Turkey and the USA. The international section of the Department for Work and Pensions at Newcastle (helpline +44 191 218 7777; www.gov.uk/international-pension-centre) should be able to advise.

If you don't make national insurance contributions while you are out of the UK in a country with no reciprocal agreement, you will forfeit entitlement to benefits on your return. You can decide to pay voluntary contributions in the UK at regular intervals or in a lump sum in order to retain your rights to certain benefits. Unfortunately this entitles you only to a retirement/widow's pension, and not to sickness benefit or unemployment benefit.

The question of pensions may seem irrelevant if you are just taking off for a year or two to teach English abroad. However, anyone who remains in the job for more than a couple of years should give some thought to starting or maintaining a pension. Because most English language teachers move between countries, it makes sense to pay into a personal pension scheme in your home country and also to maintain your right to a state pension by keeping up voluntary contributions. The question becomes vexed in those countries where state pension contributions are compulsory, as in Germany. Regulations of course vary from country to country so that, for instance, you are entitled to receive a pension after paying into the German scheme for five or more years, but in Portugal you have to contribute for 17 years. If you pay into a scheme and leave before you are entitled to claim a pension, you will have to try to reclaim some of the money you paid in. In Germany you won't get back more than half. If you work in a number of countries you may find that you spend your retirement corresponding with national pension authorities, something that long-term expat teachers are understandably worried about. According to one who has lobbied the European parliament to consider the predicament of peripatetic English teachers:

> *Social security regulations vary from country to country, so it is important to look into whether you will be entitled to a pension later if you intend spending any length of time in one place and have to pay pension contributions in a state scheme.*
>
> *It's nice to hop around when you are young and full of energy and ideas. It's not so nice to find out that you have paid a lot of money into a scheme that won't pay you a pension later. English teachers are adventurers, but I'm afraid too many of us are forgetting a fundamental problem: how do we survive when we are old? We have managed to get the EU to realise that there is at least one group of professionals, ie TEFL teachers, who are living up to the European ideal of mobility of labour, but may well find they face a bureaucratic nightmare when they retire and apply for a state pension.*

TAX

Calculating your liability to tax when working outside your home country is notoriously complicated so, if possible, check your position with an accountant. Everything depends on whether you fall into the category of 'resident' or 'domiciled'. Most EFL teachers count as domiciled in the UK since it is assumed that they will ultimately return. Legislation has removed the 'foreign earnings deduction' for UK nationals unless they are out of the country for a complete tax year. Since most teaching contracts operate from September, this means that the vast majority of EFL teachers, including teachers on high salaries in the Middle East or on the Japan Exchange and Teaching scheme which were formerly tax-free, are liable to UK tax. If you are out of the country for a tax year, you will be entitled to the exemption, provided no more than 62 days (ie one-sixth of the year) have been spent in the UK. Anyone who is present in the UK for more than 182 days during a particular tax year will be treated as resident with no exceptions. HM Revenue & Customs has set out the requirements in the document RDR1 'Residence, Domicile and the Remittance Basis' (see www. hmrc.gov.uk).

If the country in which you have been teaching has a double taxation agreement with Britain, you can offset tax paid abroad against your tax bill at home. But not all countries have such an agreement and it is not inconceivable that you will be taxed twice. Keep all receipts and financial documents in case you need to plead your case at a later date. HMRC has a good website if you have the patience to look for the information you need (www.hmrc.gov.uk).

If US citizens can establish that they are resident abroad, full-time for 12 months less up to 35 days spent in the US, the first $99,200 of overseas earnings is tax-exempt in the USA, though it is compulsory for all Americans to submit a tax return.

TRAVEL

London is the cheap airfare capital of the world and the number of online and office-based agencies offering discount flights to all corners of the world is seemingly endless. General websites such as www.cheapflights. co.uk, www.travelsupermarket.com, www.skyscanner.net, www.expedia.com and www.opodo.com are good starting points, though comparison shopping this way can be time consuming and frustrating. Even after long hours of surfing, the lowest internet fares can often be undercut by a good agent, particularly if your proposed route is complicated, so don't hesitate to get on the phone. Alternatively, consult specialist travel magazines such as *TNT* (free in London) plus the Saturday edition of the *Independent* or other national papers. The major student and youth (under 26) travel agency STA Travel is usually a good starting place. For bookings and enquiries call STA Travel on +44 333 321 0099 or log on at www.statravel.co.uk to find fares and check availability. Other reliable agencies specialising in long-haul travel include Trailfinders with 29 branches in Britain and Ireland (www.trailfinders.com) and Travel Nation in Hove (www.travelnation. co.uk), which is staffed by real experts who specialise in finding the best deals on round-the-world flights, discounted long-haul flights and multi-stop tickets.

Within Europe, rail is often the preferred way of travelling, especially since the months of September and June when most teachers are travelling to and from their destinations are among the most enjoyable times to travel. Good discounts are available to travellers under 26. Websites to check include www.uk.voyages-sncf. com; www.traineurope.co.uk (+44 871 700 7722) or the marvellous site for train travellers everywhere: www.seat61.com.

Thousands of travel websites in the US compete for custom. Discounted tickets are available, for example, from Air Treks in San Francisco (www.AirTreks.com). When **Cara McCain** was looking for a cheap flight from Texas to Korea to take up a teaching job, she booked one on www.vayama.com.

HOSPITALITY EXCHANGES

If you are planning to travel and conduct a speculative job hunt, you might want to take advantage of one of the hospitality exchanges that flourish over the internet, the best known of which is the Couchsurfing Project (www.couchsurfing.com). Like so many internet-based projects, the system depends on users' feedback, which means that you can check on a potential host's profile in advance and be fairly sure that dodgy hosts will be outed straightaway. Airbnb.com started out as a website for individuals to rent out lodgings, usually a spare room in their house but is now more commercial, but always worth checking.

Roving English language teacher **Bradwell Jackson** had been mulling over the possibility of travelling the world for about a decade before he finally gave up his job as a drug abuse counsellor in Florida to take off. On his earlier travels he had discovered the benefits of joining Servas (www.usservas.org in the USA; www. servasbritain.net in the UK) and two other hospitality exchange programmes Global Freeloaders (www. globalfreeloaders.com) and the Hospitality Club (www.hospitalityclub.org). His first destination was Mexico, where to his amazement he found English teaching work at the first place he happened to enquire in Mexico City:

I really must say right away that Servas is not simply for freeloading in people's homes. However, once you take the plunge and commit to wandering the earth, things just start to fall into place. If you belong to clubs such as Global Freeloaders, Hospitality Club, or any of the other homestay organisations, don't be surprised if the family you stay with invites you for an extended stay. The first such family I stayed with in Mexico invited me to stay for six months. All they asked was that I help with the costs of the food they prepared for me and the hot water I used.

Bradwell has continued his couchsurfing travels in some unlikely locations. His host in Bamako, Mali, let him stay for two months in exchange for two hours of English lessons a day. He was a wealthy man who gave Bradwell all his meals, internet access, laundry and so on. He commented that *'once one lands into a dream situation like this, you are apt to feel a bit guilty, and such hospitality takes time to get used to. Still, I am certainly not complaining'*. More recently, en route to his teaching job in China, he stayed with a host in Hong Kong.

MAPS AND INFORMATION

Good maps and guides always enhance one's enjoyment of a trip, which no number of apps and GPS on your smartphone can replace. Most people you will meet on the road will probably be carrying a *Rough Guide* or a *Lonely Planet*. These are both excellent series, though try not to become enslaved by their advice and preferences. Even though so much advance information is available over the internet, nothing can compete with a proper guidebook to pore over and take away with you. If you are going to be based in a major city, buy a map ahead of time. Visit the famous travel bookshop Stanfords, with a branch in Bristol as well as the mother-store in Covent Garden, London; its searchable catalogue is available online at www.stanfords.co.uk. The Map Shop in Worcestershire (www.themapshop.co.uk) and Maps Worldwide in Wiltshire (www.mapsworldwide.com) both do an extensive mail order business in specialised maps and guidebooks.

The Foreign & Commonwealth Office (FCO) regularly updates its travel advice for every country in the world and includes risk assessments of current trouble spots; go to www.gov.uk/foreign-travel-advice. If you are living in a country with poor security, you will want to keep abreast of developments. The FCO has ended its 'Locate' scheme on which British nationals could register their details so they could be contacted in a national crisis. Britons abroad are now expected to follow FCO advice on social media via Twitter or Facebook, or subscribe to the free email alert service.

LEARNING THE LANGUAGE

GIVE AND TAKE
Even if you will not need any knowledge of the local language in the classroom, the ability to communicate will increase your enjoyment many times over. After a long hard week of trying to din some English into your students' heads, you probably won't relish the prospect of struggling to convey your requests to uncomprehending shopkeepers, neighbours, etc. A refusal to try to learn some of the local language reflects badly on the teacher and reinforces the suspicion that English teachers are afflicted with cultural arrogance.

If there is time before you leave home, you might consider learning the language of the place you are going to by enrolling in a part-time or short intensive course of conversation classes at a local college of further education or using a self-study programme with books and tapes or an online course. This will also have the salutary effect of reminding you how difficult it is to learn a language. Take a good dictionary and a language course at a suitable level, for example the *Oxford Take Off In . . .* series from Oxford University Press (global. oup.com/takeoff in) as MP3 downloads, the BBC (www.bbc.co.uk/languages), Linguaphone (www.linguaphone.co.uk) and Pimsleur (www.pimsleur.com), an audio-based learning system whose courses consist of half-hour sessions every day. Also, check out noticeboards in local cafés, etc or on Facebook for info about language exchanges. A great resource is www.gumtree.com, which has a skills/language swap section. If you're lucky, your conversation partner might also be able to help you with advice/contacts for your trip or your job hunt.

Of course it is much easier to learn the language once you are there. Some employers may even offer you the chance to join language classes free of charge or swap English lessons for those in the local language; if you are particularly interested in this perk, ask about it in advance. Some cities, such as Barcelona and Istanbul, have regular informal 'English café' evenings (*intercambio*), although people you meet this way will be more interested in improving their English than your Spanish. Check out the site www.lingobongo.com, which focuses on language exchanges in Berlin, Madrid and Barcelona as well as teaching jobs.

Minna Graber, who fell in love with the Romanian culture and language, has been trying to improve her Romanian while teaching English in Bucharest, but her colleagues and acquaintances are not making it easy for her:

My main problem was that the English teaching staff were completely unable to understand that my main reason for being there was to improve my Romanian. They, in the main, refused to converse with me in anything other than English and on frequent occasions made fun of my efforts. This is despite the fact that I am at around level C1 in this language. They seemed to believe that if you know English you don't have to learn other languages. The other assumption was that English speakers can't learn other languages. This attitude was often replicated elsewhere in the town and I had to fight quite hard to persuade my Romanian friends that I was not a walking English conversation lesson.

Signing up for language classes on location is a good way of finding out about local teaching openings, as **Till Bruckner** found:

The first thing I do when I arrive somewhere new is to get myself language lessons. The teacher will have met many other foreigners, have local connections and speak some English. In other words he or she is the natural starting point in your job hunt. If you make clear that you can only continue paying for your lessons if you earn money too, you've found a highly motivated ally in your search for work.

Surprisingly, it is not always an advantage to know the language, as **Jamie Masters** discovered in Crete:

About speaking Greek. Well, no one told me. I assumed that they'd be quite pleased to have a Greek-speaking English teacher, best of both worlds. It's useful for discipline; the kids can't talk about you behind your back; you can tell when they're cheating on their vocab tests; and, I stupidly thought, you can explain things more clearly, really get them to understand . . . Well, I was wrong, and was laboriously reprimanded for it when they finally worked out what I was doing. But by that time it was too late: the kids knew I could understand Greek, and so they knew they didn't have to make the effort to speak to me in English. No amount of my playing dumb worked.

WHAT TO TAKE

The research you do on your destination will no doubt include its climate, which will help you choose an appropriate range of clothing to take. But there is probably no need to equip yourself for every eventuality. EFL teachers usually earn enough to afford to buy a warm coat or boots if required. Be sure to pack enough smart clothes to see you through the academic year; jeans are rarely acceptable in the classroom.

SAVE BEFOREHAND!
Even though you are expecting to earn a decent salary, you should not arrive short of money. It is usual to be paid only at the end of the first month. Plus you may need sizeable sums for rent deposits and other setting-up expenses.

A generous supply of passport photos and copies of your vital documents (birth certificate, education certificates, references) should be considered essential. Recreational reading in English may be limited, so you might consider taking an e-reader since a supply of novels will weigh you down. It could take time to establish a busy social life, so a laptop or iPad are *de rigueur*. BBC radio can be accessed online around the world but the fantastic BBC iPlayer sadly isn't available when you're abroad (though there are ways round it by using a secure proxy). The BBC's free iPlayer app is currently available in Austria, Australia, Belgium, Canada, Denmark, Finland, France, Germany, Ireland, Italy, Luxembourg, Netherlands, Portugal, Spain, Sweden and Switzerland, though not all programming is available in all countries.

A wi-fi-enabled smartphone will probably do everything that you need, ie send emails and browse the web, not to mention take photos, play music and of course make phone calls (though roaming charges can be astronomical). To avoid floating off into a news vacuum, some people subscribe to the BBC daily email service, which sends out a selection of news stories according to the interests you register. Others relish the prospect of no longer having a clue who is who in the Cabinet or what scandal has befallen footballers and their wives. A further advantage of having access to the BBC is that you can record programmes for use in the classroom.

Find out from returned travellers what items are in short supply or very expensive. Some items that recur on teachers' lists of what they wish they had taken from home include their favourite cosmetics, vitamin tablets, a deck of cards, ear plugs and thermal underwear.

TEACHING MATERIALS

Try to find out which course your school follows and then become familiar with it. Depending on the circumstances, there may be a shortage of materials, so again enquire in advance about the facilities. (For example, English texts being used in a few places in Cambodia dated from 1938 and contained such useful sentences as 'I got this suit in Savile Row'.) When **Rebecca Mallinson** went to Sudan to teach English through a London-based charity, SVP (see Africa chapter), she was none too impressed with the course books:

> *English is taught in Sudan using the world's most boring textbook, entitled SPINE. It was seemingly produced to put the next generation off English and ensure that they will not have any speaking skills. Teachers are expected to rush through the chapters . . . regardless of whether the students have understood anything or not. When I queried this with one of the supervisors, he looked at me with total lack of comprehension, as though actually 'learning English' was not an aim at all.*

For new teachers the most useful thing is to have a really good course book to work from, with teachers' books and good supplementary materials like Jill Hadfield's *Communication Games* as invaluable support. Material from such sources can save a lot of preparation time when planning your own task-based lessons.

If you are going to have to be self-reliant, you may want to contact the major EFL publishers, primarily Oxford University Press, Cambridge University Press, Longman, Macmillan, and Heinemann to request details of their course books with a sample lesson if possible, and the address of their stockist in your destination country. For information, advice and free teaching resources, you can join the Oxford University Press Teachers Club at http://elt.oup.com. Online professional development is available from OUP's Teachers' Academy (www.oup.com/elt).

Before leaving home, browse a specialist ELT catalogue either in the EFL department of a bookshop or online. KELTIC (www.keltic.co.uk) operates a specialist mail order service from Oxfordshire, offering an extensive range of ELT materials. You can use its user-friendly website anywhere in the world to get information and advice or to order materials or you can contact KELTIC by telephone (+44 1869 363589) or email (keltic@btol-uk.com).

Another major stockist of ELT materials is BEBC, the Bournemouth English Book Centre in Dorset (www.bebc.co.uk). The company supplies books, CDs and ELT software by mail order to teachers worldwide. For a list of recommended titles, see the next section.

Dave's ESL Café devotes a page to ESL publishers. The publisher Delta (www.deltapublishing.com) has an ESL catalogue online that may be helpful.

Here is a list of items to consider packing which most often crop up in the recommendations of teachers of conversation classes in which the main target is to get the students talking. Teachers expecting to teach at an under-resourced school might think about taking authentic materials including some of the following:

- good dual language dictionary, picture dictionary
- appropriate pop music downloaded on an iPod with speakers so that you can play songs with clear lyrics such as the Beatles or early Billy Bragg to your classes
- games and activities book
- illustrated magazines such as the *National Geographic* or unusual publications, for example old comic books, teen mags or the *Big Issue*
- maps (for example of London)
- tourist guides to your home country, travel brochures, blank application forms
- flash cards (which are expensive if bought commercially; homemade ones work just as well)
- grammar exercise book
- old Cambridge exam papers (if you are going to be teaching from its suite of exams).

Postcards, balloons, stick-on stars and photos of yourself as an infant have all been used to good effect. If you know that there will be a shortage of materials, it might even be worth taking general stationery such as notebooks, carbon paper, Blu-Tack, plastic files, large pieces of paper, coloured markers, etc.

Koober Grob spent an enjoyable time in Russia trying to hone the conversation skills of her highly motivated students. Her main regret was that she hadn't brought with her a 10-page list of possible discussion topics to help them practise their colloquial English, because she found that she was sometimes at a loss for topics (which may account for the conversation one day turning to chocolate-covered ants in Africa).

Richard McBrien, who taught English in China, recommends taking a collection of photos of anything in your home environment. A few rolls shot of local petrol stations, supermarkets, houses, parks, etc can be of great interest to students in far-off lands. It may of course be difficult to anticipate what will excite your students' curiosity. The anthropologist Nigel Barley, who has written amusing books on his fieldwork, describes in his book *Not a Hazardous Sport* (now out of print, alas) being enlisted to attend an impromptu English conversation club in a remote corner of Indonesia:

> *I answered questions about the royal family, traffic lights and the etiquette of eating asparagus, and gave a quick analysis of the shipbuilding industry. At the end of the evening, I fled back to the hotel.*

EFL teachers cannot escape so easily, so you should be prepared to be treated like a guru of contemporary British or American culture. If you know in advance that you will have to perform in this capacity, you might get hold of *Britain: For Learners of English* by James O'Driscoll (Oxford University Press, 2009; £33.50), which provides historical and cultural background of British society and institutions, as well as the private daily life of the British people.

ONLINE RESOURCES

More and more TEFL teachers are making use of the vast number of teaching resources available online. Also more schools are installing interactive whiteboards in classrooms, which can be a godsend for teachers. After getting used to using them at a well-equipped school in Kazakhstan, **Anthony Cook** concluded that *'they tend to inspire a lot of new ideas and approaches, especially in terms of incorporating video into lessons'*. He says that it's like having a cinema screen in the classroom, which makes it so much nicer than getting 10 people to crowd around a laptop.

A lightweight pack of basic teaching resources, including flashcards, counters, dice, an activity book with ideas and games, and a portable white board, has been designed by a British TEFL volunteer who experienced first-hand having to teach a classful of children with no resources. Multi-kit sets cost £29.95 from TripKits (www.tripkits.co.uk).

Teachers can access online a range of actual lesson plans and printable materials for immediate use with students as well as teacher forums and job sites. **Sab Will** was Course Director and main trainer on a TEFL training course in Paris. He has a special interest in English-learning websites and language blogs and has provided some of the information for this section. He started his first website for teachers in 1997 and currently runs www.hotchpotchenglish.com, which includes a teacher training forum, in-depth ELT book reviews and free interactive exercises for students.

Macmillan's onestopenglish.com is a good example of a useful website offering free teaching materials, although practically all the major ELT publishers now offer something similar. Here you will find masses of materials, either linked in to existing course books or stand-alone exercises, often with recordings, printable sheets, videos and teacher's notes. Along the same lines are websites which are not linked to publishers but which offer very much the same thing – masses of exercises of all types. Again, there is usually a surprisingly rich free section, and a more comprehensive paying option, often aimed at organisations. The British Council's www.teachingenglish.org.uk is a good place to start, while www.eslprintables.com and www. enchantedlearning.com for children offer helpful printouts and worksheets. Try also EnglishZone and Babel-Zone from LCF clubs (www.lcfclubs.com) which can be sampled in a free trial. Experienced TEFL teachers have generously shared masses of English teaching resources, like the non-profit site http://tomstefl.com or http://tefltastic.wordpress.com ('news, views and reviews from TEFL lifer Alex Case, plus 1,000 worksheets and 500 articles via the drop-down menus'). You can of course pay for good teaching ideas too: membership of TeachitWorld (www.teachitelt.com) gives you access to 10,000 pages of lesson plans and materials; access to pdfs is free whereas a proper membership costs £50 for a year. Then there are websites that are not specifically for English teachers or learners but that house much which teachers can make use of, such as the major newspaper and television sites, or cultural sites like www.visitbritain.com or www.royal.gov.uk. Some of these, such as the BBC and Voice of America even have special sections where they have created mini-websites full of exercises for English learners based on their own up-to-date content, which is great for keeping lessons fresh and stimulating. Check out www.bbc.co.uk/learningenglish, and Voice of America's http://learningenglish.voanews.com. Bite-size news reports at www.englishnewslessons.com are sure to stimulate classroom discussion.

Hot on the heels of the resources above comes a whole raft of websites which are not explicitly for English teaching, have no derived exercises for use in class, are not always appropriate, and yet they offer incredible potential for the innovative and adventurous English language teacher. These belong to the online world of YouTube (free videos), Flickr (free photos), Wikipedia (free knowledge), Deezer (free music), the BBC (free news) and Google Earth (free maps). Once you have learnt how to adapt real English to your classroom and to your students you will find these sites to be an absolute goldmine which will help you inject some marvellously unexpected and highly appreciated moments into your classes.

An abundance of free little programs is available to make life easier, at least for tech-heads. With the legendary Hot Potatoes (http://hotpot.uvic.ca) you can create your own interactive exercises such as gap-fills, crosswords and multiple choice questions. Audacity (http://sourceforge.net/projects/audacity) allows you to record high-quality audio. With Google's Blogger (www.blogger.com) or alternative user-friendly blogging tools like WordPress (http://wordpress.org), Blogspot (www.blogspot.com) and Tumblr (www.tumblr. com), you and your students can create blogs and use them to extend their English learning to their outside class activities. The virtual world 'Second Life' (http://secondlife.com) is being used ever more creatively by teachers to hold 'in-world' English classes in a unique, fun environment. And sites such as Amazon and eBay can be used to assess buying opportunities, read product reviews, discover the auction process and why not spend a few pennies as a group to buy something for the class! The possibilities are endless.

Last, but not least, scores of teacher forums come and go for new and experienced teachers alike. These typically cover teaching techniques, difficult situations needing solutions, or simply mention useful new teaching resources which have come to light recently. JimmyESL.com was started by James Soller, an ESL teacher and blogger. It offers real advice about teaching abroad and an honest outlook of the ESL/TEFL industry. He is offering to pay $25–$50 for articles he uses on his site.

In reality, there is such an enormous amount of great stuff out there that the examples mentioned are a drop in the ocean. The best way to discover others is simply to type in 'English teacher training forum' or 'English teaching jobs Taiwan' or 'free English teaching resources' or whatever it is you're interested in and start surfing away. Googling for something specific will also provide useful leads, anything from ideas for teaching young learners (http://esl4word.wordpress.com) to preparation for IELTS (www.ielts.org). A good source of links is provided by an experienced teacher in Spain at http://eflbytes. wordpress.com.

RECOMMENDED BIBLIOGRAPHY

There is such a plethora of books and materials that the choice can be daunting to the uninitiated. Every teacher should have a basic manual of grammar handy, such as:

Oxford English Grammar Course by Michael Swan and Catherine Walter (Oxford University Press, 2011; Basic: £21; Intermediate: £22.50; Advanced: £26.50). Short bite-sized grammar

OXFORD TEACHERS' ACADEMY

Inspiration online today. Ideas for class tomorrow

For many people, teaching abroad is one of the most enriching and inspiring experiences in their professional lives, from learning about new cultures and languages to meeting new people and helping them to succeed. Sometimes, however, professional development opportunities are not easy to access, and informal professional networks can be difficult to maintain.

This is why Oxford Teachers' Academy could be the perfect companion in your teaching travels.

Oxford Teachers' Academy offers a programme of online self-study courses, which you can follow in your own time and, at your own pace, and in any location, for up to 12 months. The courses provide guidance in the areas of professional development that are most relevant to English language teachers, offering 30 hours of media-rich material that includes videos from experts, essential theories, and access to the latest ELT research. The community elements of the programme, such as peer chat and discussions, facilitate sharing between the participants and help build useful networks.

This means you're never alone, and you're never short of ideas.

Get ready to be inspired!

explanations with plenty of practice. The 'Pronunciation for grammar' CD-ROM helps students with the rhythm, stress and intonation of grammar structures.

Practical English Usage by Michael Swan (3rd edition, Oxford University Press, 2005; £32.50; intermediate to advanced). The world's most trusted reference grammar. Indispensable guide to problem points in the English language as encountered by learners and their teachers with clear, practical information and examples. Now also available Practical English Usage, an app for iPad, iPhone, Windows and Android, which is quick and easy to use. (See www.oup.com/elt/fingertips.)

Teaching Grammar by Jim Scrivener (Oxford University Press, 2003; £12). Part of the Oxford Basics series.

Grammar for English Language Teachers by Martin Parrott (Cambridge University Press, 2010; £27.20).

Understanding and Using English Grammar by Betty Azar (Pearson Education, 2009; £40).

English Grammar in Use by Raymond Murphy (Cambridge University Press, 2012; with answers and CD ROM, £26.50; plus supplementary exercises with answers: £13.10).

Advanced Grammar in Use by Martin Hewings (Cambridge University Press, 2013; £21.20; with answers).

Collins English Grammar (Collins Gem, 2006; £4.99; genuinely pocket-sized). Dubbed by at least one novice as 'the teacher's friend'.

Here is a selected list of recommended books and teaching aids which you could consider.

Oxford Advanced Learner's Dictionary (8th edition, Oxford University Press, 2015; £36). The world's best selling advanced learner's dictionary. Helps develop all language skills with information on collocations, synonyms and writing. Available with DVD and premium online access code.

Collins Cobuild Advanced Learner's English Dictionary (Collins, 2014; £28). Collins publishes a range of dictionaries for the language learner.

Cambridge Advanced Learner's Dictionary (Cambridge University Press, 2013; £35.50). Available with a CD-ROM.

Freestanding by Maurice Jamall (Abax Publishing, 1998; out of print). Elementary to upper intermediate. Teachers' resource book suitable for children and young adults.

Grammar Practice Activities by Penny Ur (Cambridge University Press, 2009; £29.20). Paperback with CD-ROM. Teaching classic for all levels and ages. Includes photocopiable worksheets and visuals.

Grammar Games by M. Rinvolucri (Cambridge University Press, 1985; £27.50). Includes activities for all levels.

The Practice of English Language Teaching by Jeremy Harmer (4th edition, Longman, 2007; £36). A well-known core reference work for teachers from the author of *How to Teach English* (£36.10), a straightforward introduction to TEFL for new teachers.

Oxford Basics is a series of 11 short accessible books for teachers who are new to ELT or who are looking for new creative ways of teaching with limited resources. The series includes *Introduction to Teaching English* by Jill and Charles Hadfield (Oxford University Press, 2008; £20), a practical guide with lesson plans for new teachers of English, and *Simple Speaking Activities* by the same authors (Oxford University Press, 1999; £12).

The English Language Teacher's Handbook by Joanna Baker and Heather Westrup (VSO, 2000; £14.99). How to teach large classes with few resources.

Lessons from Nothing by Bruce Marsland (Cambridge University Press, 1998; £21.70). From the Cambridge Handbooks for Language Teachers series.

Children Learning English by Jayne Moon (Macmillan, 2005; £24.20). Introduces the theory behind good classroom practice with examples from around the world.

Learning Teaching by Jim Scrivener (Macmillan, 2011; £35.20).

How Languages are Learned by Patsy M. Lightbrown and Nina Spader (4th edition, Oxford University Press, 2013; £24.50). A prize-winning, readable introduction to research in language acquisition and how it relates to the classroom.

Oxford Basics for Children is a series of five titles for teachers of young learners which provides adaptable teaching ideas in an easy-to-follow format. Series includes *Starting and Ending Lessons* by Naomi Moir (Oxford University Press, 2009; £12), *English Through Music* by Jane Willis and Anice Paterson (Oxford University Press, 2008; £14.50).

Ladybird Key Words Reading Scheme (Ladybird's Books for English Learning). Inexpensive series for teaching young children.

PROBLEMS

Potential problems fall into two broad categories: personal and professional. You may quickly feel settled and find your new setting fascinating but may discover that the job itself is beset with difficulties. On the other hand the teaching might suit but otherwise you feel alienated and lonely. Those who choose to uproot themselves suddenly should be fairly confident that they have enough resources to rely on themselves, and must expect some adjustment problems. Only you can assess your chances of enjoying the whole experience and of not feeling traumatised. Women may encounter special problems in countries where women have low status. An informative site is www.journeywoman.com, among many others.

PROBLEMS AT WORK

Anyone who has done some language teaching will be familiar with at least some of the problems EFL teachers face. Problems encountered in a classroom of Turkish or Peruvian adolescents will be quite different from the ones experienced teaching French or Japanese business people. The country chapters attempt to identify some of the specific problems which groups of language learners present.

Although you are unlikely to be expected to entertain 200 people for four hours with a plastic bowl, there may be a fairly complete lack of facilities and resources. The teacher who has packed some of the teaching materials listed on pages 111–112 will feel particularly grateful for his or her foresight in such circumstances. Some schools, especially at the cowboy end of the spectrum, go to the extreme of providing very rigid lesson plans from which you are not allowed to deviate and which are likely to be uncongenial and uninspiring. Even when reasonable course texts are provided, supplementary materials for role play and games can considerably liven up classes (and teachers). You can obtain extra teaching aids after arrival from the nearest English language bookshop or make them yourself, for example tape a dialogue between yourself and an English-speaking friend or cut up magazines or use postcards to make flashcards. If the missing facilities are more basic (eg tables, chairs, heating, paper, pens) you will have to improvise as best you can and (if appropriate) press the administration for some equipment.

PROBLEMS WITH STUDENTS

A very common problem is to find yourself in front of a class of mixed ability with incompatible aims. How do you plan a lesson that will satisfy a sophisticated business executive whose English is fairly advanced, a delinquent teenager and a housewife crippled by lack of confidence? A good school will of course stream its clients and make life easier for its teachers. But this may be left to you, in which case a set of commercially produced tests to assess level of language acquisition could come in very handy. Alternatively you can devise a simple questionnaire for the students to describe their hobbies, studies, family or whatever. This will not only display their use of English but also give you some clues about their various backgrounds. One way of coping with gross discrepancies is to divide the class into compatible groups or pairs and give tasks which work at different levels. Subdividing a class is in fact generally a good idea especially in large classes.

In some places you may even have to contend with racial or cultural friction among students, as **Bryn Thomas** encountered in Egypt:

> *One of the problems I found in the class was the often quite shocking displays of racism by the Egyptians towards their dark-skinned neighbours from Somalia. Vast amounts of tact and diplomacy were required to ensure that enough attention was given to the Somalis (who tend to be shy, quiet and highly intelligent) without upsetting the sometimes rowdy and over-enthusiastic Egyptians.*

Your expectations of what teaching is supposed to achieve may be quite different from the expectations of your students. Foreign educational systems are often far more formal than their British or American counterparts and students may seem distressingly content to memorise and regurgitate, often with the sole motivation of passing an exam. But this doesn't always operate. Many teachers have had to face a class that doesn't seem to care at all about learning any English and merely wants to be entertained.

In many countries free discussion is quite alien, whether because of repressive governments or cultural taboos. It is essential to be sensitive to these cultural differences and not to expect too much of your students straightaway. The only way of overcoming this reluctance to express an opinion or indeed express anything at all is to involve them patiently and tactfully, again by splitting them into smaller units and asking them to come up with a joint reply.

Discipline is seldom a serious problem outside Europe; in fact liberal teachers are often taken aback by what they perceive as an excess of docility, an over-willingness to believe that 'teacher is always right'. In some cases, classes of bored and rebellious European teenagers might cause problems (especially on Fridays), or children who are being sent to English lessons after school simply as an alternative to babysitting for working mothers. Unfortunately, a couple of troublemakers can poison a class. You may even have to contend with one or two downright uncontrollable students as **Jamie Masters** did in Crete:

> At least two of my pupils were very malevolent. There was one, Makis, who used to bring a 'prop' to every lesson, some new way of disrupting the class: an air pistol, a piece of string with a banknote tied to it, a whistle, white paint. He used to slap my cheeks, hug me and lift me off the floor, was quite open about not wanting to work . . . and then claimed I was picking on him when I retaliated. Well, call me a humourless unfeeling bastard, but . . .

One teacher in Turkey found the majority of his students 'bouncy, bright, enthusiastic and sharp' but with one class he was always amazed that they walked upright when they got out of their chairs. It often turns out that each class develops a certain character.

Marta Eleniak, who taught in Spain, recommends taking a hard line:

> Be a tyrant at the start. The kids can be very wicked and take advantage of any good nature shown. Squash anyone who is late, shouts, gossips, etc the first time or it'll never stop. The good classes make you love teaching. The bad make you feel as if you want to go back to filing.

Each level and age group brings its own difficulties. Anyone who has no experience of dealing with young children may find it impossible to grab and hold their attention, let alone teach them any English. A lack of inhibition is very useful for teaching young children, who will enjoy sing-songs, nursery rhymes, simple puzzles and games, etc. A firm hand may also be necessary if **Aine Fligg**'s experience in Hong Kong is anything to go by. She was bitten on the ankle by one of her less receptive students. When the headmaster came in and remonstrated (with Aine!), the child bit him on the nose. The brat was then incarcerated in a cupboard, and emerged somewhat subdued.

Blogger and world traveller **Travis Ball** from California gradually learnt how to cope with young children at the rural language school at which he taught in Japan:

> I was brand new to teaching, so it was really rough getting started. With very little training, I was thrown in and expected to swim. I had 27 classes a week, 18 of them on different lesson plans. My youngest student was five while my oldest was 61. The sheer diversity of age and language experience threw me for a loop. In the first two weeks, I made two separate children cry, which I felt awful about. This was a cultural thing that I had to get used to. The first occasion involved my youngest student. We were doing a warm-up drawing activity and at the end I asked for the coloured pencils back so we could get onto the next game. The one word this child knew was 'no' which he kept repeating. I tried to take the pencil and move on with the class, which caused him to cry. I handed back the pencil and he basically coloured for the whole class.

The other instance involved this little boy's sister. I was attempting to teach the class the difference between the sound 'B' and 'V'. I started with one student and had her watch my lips as I said the word 'vanilla' and after a few attempts, succeeded in getting her to say the correct sound. Then I came to the next student and she tried twice and broke into tears on the third failed attempt. Not sure what to do, I kept going around the circle and the crying student calmed down after a few minutes, and was laughing with the next game minutes later. By the end of my nine months there, I was close to all my students, young and old. Leaving was especially rough with a few of the kids, and some of the adults as well.

Only 18 years old himself, **Sam James** had to teach a variety of age groups in Barcelona during his gap year and despite the problems, ended up enjoying it:

The children I taught were fairly unruly and noisy. The teenagers were, as ever, pretty uninterested in learning, though if one struck on something they enjoyed they would work much better. Activities based on the lyrics of songs seemed to be good. They had a tendency to select answers at random in multiple choice exercises. On the other hand they were only ever loud rather than very rude or disobedient. The young children (8–12) were harder work. They tended to understand selectively, acting confused if they didn't like an instruction. Part of the problem was that the class was far too long (three hours) for children of that age and their concentration and behaviour tended to tail off as the time passed.

Beginners of all ages progress much more rapidly than intermediate learners. Many teachers find adolescent intermediate learners the most difficult to teach. The original fun and novelty are past and they now face a long slog of consolidating vocabulary and structures. (The 'intermediate plateau' is a well-known phenomenon in language acquisition.) Adolescents may resent 'grammar games' (which are a standard part of EFL), thinking that games are suitable only for children.

It may be necessary to manage the unrealistic expectations of your students, something that a blogger in Budapest encountered again and again (https://budabeats.wordpress.com/tag/english-teachers):

Common in nearly every initial class, be it in a business contracted by the two schools I now work for . . . or private individuals who have sought my tutelage through the internet classifieds, is the goal of perfection. 'I want to sound like a native speaker.' 'I would like to not have an accent.' 'I want to be understood perfectly.'. . . Of course, this is absurdly impossible to achieve in the short amount of time in which they would like to reach this goal (which puts tremendous pressure on me as well).

The worst problem of all is to be confronted with a bored and unresponsive class. This may happen in a class of beginners who can't understand what is going on, especially a problem if you don't speak a word of their language. It can be extremely frustrating for all concerned when trying to teach some concept or new vocabulary without being able to provide the simple equivalent. If this is the case, you'll have to rely heavily on visual aids. Whole books have been written to show EFL teachers how to draw, for example *1,000+ Pictures for Teachers to Copy* by Andrew Wright (available second-hand). For a very low-level class, you may need to resort to your bilingual dictionary for lesson plans. But some enjoy the challenge: 18-year-old **Hannah Bullock** found teaching her class of Czech beginners good fun 'because each lesson was like an invigorating game of charades'. Many new teachers make the mistake of doing all the talking. During his year of teaching in Slovenia, **Adam Cook**, like many others before him, came to the conclusion that silence is one of the teacher's most effective tools.

TIPS FOR DEALING WITH A LETHARGIC CLASS
The best way to inject a little life is to get them moving around, for example get them to do a relaxation exercise or have them carry out a little survey of their neighbours and then report their findings back to the class. A reluctance to participate may be because the students do not see the point of it.

A blogger called Emma provides some ESL teaching tips:

> *Having a number of icebreakers up your sleeve can be incredibly useful. Entering a new class can be daunting, but starting with an icebreaker is a sure way to make yourself and the class feel more at ease. They can be used initially to warm up a class or to form a break between sections of a lesson. They can be used as a way to introduce yourself to a new class or to introduce a new topic. Short engaging icebreaker activities can be in the form of songs, games, rhymes or drama.*

For some of her practical suggestions of games and songs that work well, see www.vesl.org/2013/06/ice-breakers-progress.

In many countries foreign teachers come to feel like a dancing bear or performing monkey, someone who is expected to be a cultural token and an entertainer. If the students are expecting someone to dance a jig or swing from the chandelier (so to speak) they will be understandably disappointed to be presented with someone asking them to form sentences using the present perfect. At the other extreme, it is similarly disconcerting to be treated just as a model of pronunciation, and you may begin to wonder whether your employer might be better off employing a tape recorder.

PROBLEMS WITH YOURSELF

Lessons can fizz or fizzle. The latter may be the fault of the students but more often it is down to the teacher. One of the most common traps into which inexperienced teachers fall is to dominate the class too much. Conversational English can only be acquired by endless practice and so you must allow your students to do most of the talking. Even if there are long pauses between your questions and their attempts to answer, the temptation to fill the silences should be avoided. Pauses have a positive role to play, allowing students a chance to dwell on and absorb the point you have just been illustrating. Avoid asking 'Do you understand?' since the answer is meaningless; it is much more useful to test their comprehension indirectly.

> *A native speaker's function is seldom to teach grammar, though he or she should feel comfortable naming grammatical constructions. You are not there to help the students to analyse the language but to use it and communicate with it. It has been said that grammar is the highway code, the catalogue of rules and traffic signs, quite useless in isolation from driving, which gets you where you want to go. Grammar is only the cookery book while talking is cooking for other people to understand/eat. Persuading some students whose language education has been founded on grammar rather than communication that this is the priority may be difficult, but try not to be drawn into detailed explanations of grammatical structures.*

Being utterly ignorant of grammar can result in embarrassing situations. You can only get away with bluffing for so long ('Stefan, I don't think it matters here whether or not it's a subjunctive') and irate students have been known to report to school directors that their teachers are grammar-illiterate. One useful trick suggested by **Roberta Wedge** is to reply with 'Very good question – we're going to deal with that in the next class.' Usually it will suffice to have studied a general grammar handbook such as *Practical English Grammar* or *Practical English Usage* (see the bibliography in the previous chapter). If you contradict yourself between one lesson and the next, and an eager student notices it, take **Richard Osborne**'s advice and say 'Ah yes, I'm sorry about that. You see, that's the way we do it at home. Bizness is often spelled with a Z in Canada.'

The worst fate that can befall a teacher is to run dry, to completely run out of ideas and steam before the appointed hour has arrived. This usually happens when you fail to arrive with a structured lesson plan. It is usually a recipe for disaster to announce at the beginning of the lesson 'Tonight let's talk about our travels/hobbies/animals' or whatever. Any course book will help you to avoid grinding to a halt. Supplementary materials such as songs and games can be lifesavers in (and out) of a crisis. If you are absolutely stuck for what to talk about next, try writing the lyrics of a popular song on the board and asking the class to analyse it or even act it out (avoiding titles such as 'I Want Your Body'). Apparently songs which have worked well for many teachers include George Michael's 'Careless Whispers', the Beatles' 'Here Comes the Sun' and 'When I'm 64' and 'Perfect Day' by Lou Reed. The site http://lyricstraining.com/game2043.htm attempts to provide an easy method to learn and improve foreign languages skills through music and lyrics. Another way of stepping outside the predictability of a course book might be to teach a short poem that you like, or even a short story (eg by Saki) if the class is sufficiently advanced.

LESSON STRUCTURE

A very popular way to structure a lesson is in 'notions'; you take a general situation like 'praising' or 'complaining', teach some relevant vocabulary and structures and then have the class put them into practice in role-play situations. Unfortunately repetition is the key to language learning, though you have to avoid boring drills, which will kill any interest in the language.

When a lesson goes well, it can be deeply satisfying. **Philip Tomkins** did his TEFL training in Greece in 2010 and identified the high point of his teaching experiences as sharing a joke in English with a class and all having a fit of the giggles. The low point was inadvertently using technical jargon in his first lesson, which temporarily killed it dead, and being faced with blank looks.

Culture shock is experienced by most people who live in a foreign country in whatever circumstances (see below), but can be especially problematic for teachers. Unthinkingly you might choose a topic which seems neutral to you but is controversial to the students. A little feature on the English pub, for example, would not be enjoyed in Saudi Arabia. A discussion about whaling might make a class of Norwegians uncomfortable. Asking questions about foreign travels would be tactless in many places where few will be able to afford international travel.

One of the more subtle problems is knowing how to approach teaching, as **J. W. Arble** discovered:

I was caught up with trying to work out how to present myself to my students: whether to assume the role of friend, exotic or mentor; whether to be 'charismatic' or reserved, enthusiastic or dry, serious-minded or idiot savant. Given the limited time, I persuaded myself the aim was to make the subject interestingly different; with the hope a few might be triggered into curiosity. Less worthily, I just wanted to be liked.

One of the hardest problems to contend with is teacher burn-out. If you invariably arrive just as the class is scheduled to begin, show no enthusiasm and glance at the clock every 90 seconds, you will not be a popular teacher. Getting hold of some new authentic materials might shore up your flagging enthusiasm for the enterprise. If not, perhaps it is time to consider going home (bearing in mind your contractual commitments).

PROBLEMS WITH EMPLOYERS

All sorts of schools break their promises about pay, perks and availability of resources. The worst disappointment of all, however, is to turn up and find that you don't have a job at all. Because schools which hire their teachers sight unseen often find themselves let down at the last moment, they may over-hire, just in the way that airlines overbook their flights in the expectation of a certain level of cancellation. Even more probable is that the school has not been able to predict the number of pupils who will enrol and decides to hire enough teachers to cover the projected maximum. Whatever the reason, it can be devastating to have the job carpet whipped from under your feet. Before you have got to this stage, you should have done an online search for feedback about your employer. Social media and sites like reddit, glassdoor and gooverseas.com can be very useful if your prospective employer has been reviewed. Sometimes an employer is bad enough for former teachers to set up their own facebook page like one created by some disgruntled ex-employees of an institute in Kuwait, which did not beat around the bush: 'If you want to work for liars, work around violent types, work around drug users, work around colleagues who will spy on you and report your every move to your boss, and work around those teaching on false credentials, this is your place.'

Most employers are not this bad and merely fail to deliver some of the promised perks. Having a signed contract helps. It may also be a good idea to maintain contact with the school between being hired and your first day of work. If the worst does happen, you could try losing your temper, threatening to tarnish its good name and demanding a month's pay and your return airfare. Or you could try playing on the guilt of the director and ask him or her to help you get a last-minute job in another school.

Just because a school does not belong to the EFL establishment does not mean that teachers will be treated badly (and vice versa). However, the backstreet fly-by-night school may well cause its foreign teachers anxiety. The most common complaints revolve around wages – not enough or not often enough or both. Either you will have signed a contract (possibly in ignorance of the prevailing conditions and pay levels) or you have nothing in writing and find that your pay packet does not correspond with what you were originally promised. It is probably not advisable to take up a confrontational stance straightaway since this may be the beginning of a year of hostility and misery. Polite but persistent negotiations might prove successful. Find out if there is a relevant teachers' union, join it and ask it for advice (though EFL is notorious for being non-unionised). As the year wears on, your bargaining clout increases, especially if you are a half-decent teacher, since you will be more difficult to replace mid-term.

One recourse is to bring your employer's shortcomings to the attention of the British Council or, in extreme cases of exploitation, your embassy/consulate. If you are being genuinely maltreated and you are prepared to leave the job, delivering an ultimatum and threatening to leave might prompt improvements in your working conditions. Remember that if there are cowboy schools, there are also cowboy teachers. Many honest and responsible employers have fallen victim to unreliable and undisciplined individuals who break their promises, show up late and abuse the accommodation they are given. Try not to let your employer down unless the provocation is serious.

Language schools must function as businesses as well as educational establishments and in some case the profit motive overtakes everything else. In those cases, teachers soon realise that they matter less to the people in charge than the number and satisfaction of students. You may be asked to conduct a conversation class in a room not much smaller than the Albert Hall. Some employers leave you entirely to your own devices and even look to you for teaching ideas. Others interfere to an annoying degree; we've heard of one school director in Spain who bugged the classrooms to make sure the staff were following his idiosyncratic home-produced course outlines. **Jayne Nash** worked for a chain of schools in France that use their own method; clients learnt basic phrases and words for everyday situations in parrot fashion:

> *The courses were aimed at local business people, therefore students learnt mostly spoken English to introduce themselves, their company or product, language for meetings, telephone conversations, etc. The method seemed very effective, but can prove extremely tedious for the teacher. After you have repeated a word 10–20 times with 10 students, four times a day, five days a week . . .*

One of the most commonly heard complaints from teachers concerns the schedule. Eager only to satisfy clients, employers tend to mess around with teachers' timetables, offering awkward combinations of hours or changing the schedule at the last moment, which is extremely stressful. A certain amount of evening work is almost inevitable in private language schools, where pupils (whether of school or working age) must study

English out of hours. Having to work early in the morning and then again through the evening can become exhausting after a while. It can also be annoying to have several long gruelling days a week and other days with scarcely any teaching at all (but still not days off).

> **H.P.W. = HOURS PER WEEK**
> *One trick to beware of is to find that the 24 hours a week you were told you would be working actually means 32 45-minute lessons (which is much harder work than teaching 24 one-hour lessons). Even if the number of hours has not been exaggerated, you may have been deluded into thinking that a 24-hour week is quite cushy. But preparation time can easily add half as many hours again, plus if you are teaching in different locations, travel time (often unpaid) has to be taken into consideration.*

In some situations teachers may be expected to participate in extra-curricular activities or marketing exercises such as dreary drinks parties for pupils or asked to make a public speech. Make an effort to accept such invitations (especially near the beginning of your contract) or, if you must decline, do so as graciously as possible. There might also be extra duties, translating letters and documents, updating teaching materials, etc for which you are unlikely to be paid extra.

PROBLEMS OUTSIDE WORK

Your main initial worry outside your place of employment will probably be accommodation. Once this is sorted out, either with the help of your school or on your own, and you have mastered the essentials of getting around and shopping for food, there is nothing to do but enjoy yourself, exploring your new surroundings and making friends.

CULTURE SHOCK

Enjoying yourself won't be at all easy if you are suffering from culture shock. Shock implies something which happens suddenly, but cultural disorientation more often creeps up on you. Adrenaline usually sees you through the first few weeks as you find the novelty exhilarating and challenging. You will be amazed and charmed by the odd gestures the people use or the antiquated way that things work. As time goes on, practical irritations intrude and the constant misunderstanding caused by those charming gestures – such as a nod in Greece meaning 'no' or in Japan meaning 'yes, I understand, but don't agree' – and the inconvenience of not being able to do simple tasks without the help of a local will begin to get on your nerves. Unless you can find someone to listen sympathetically to your complaints, you may begin to think you have made a mistake in coming in the first place.

Experts say that most people who have moved abroad hit the trough after three or four months, probably just before Christmas in the case of teachers who started work in September. A holiday over Christmas may serve to calm you down or, if you go home for Christmas, may make you feel terminally homesick and not want to go back. Teachers who survive this often find that things improve in the second term as they cease to perceive many aspects of life as 'foreign'.

You're bound to suffer from low spirits occasionally, but remember not to broadcast your feelings randomly. Feeling contempt and hostility towards your host country is actually part of the process of adjusting to being abroad. If you feel you have to let off steam about the local bureaucracy or the dishonesty of taxi-drivers or the shockingly bad accent of the local English teachers, remember to do so in private, in emails or when there are no local people around. This is especially important if you have colleagues who are natives of the country. They may find some of the idiosyncrasies of their culture irritating too but, unlike you, they have to live with them forever.

The best way to avoid disappointment is to be well briefed beforehand, as emphasised in the chapter on Preparation. Gathering general information about the country and specific information about the school before arrival will obviate many of the negative feelings some EFL teachers feel. If you are the type to build up high hopes and expectations of new situations, it is wise to try to dismantle these before leaving home. English teaching is seldom glamorous.

> **TOP TIP**
> Don't go around saying 'In my country, we do this . . .' You're not in your country now, so let go of the things that frustrate you, and just enjoy the journey.

Some native-speaker teachers have found an unpleasant rift between local and foreign staff, which in some cases can be accounted for by the simple fact that you are being paid a lot more than they are. Sometimes new foreign teachers find their local colleagues cliquey and uncommunicative. No doubt they have seen a lot of foreigners come, and make a lot of noise, and go, and there is no particular reason why they should find the consignment you're in wildly exciting and worth getting to know.

LONELINESS

Creating a social life from scratch is difficult enough at any time, but becomes even more difficult in an alien tongue and culture. You will probably find that many of your fellow teachers are lots of fun and able to offer practical help in your first few weeks (especially any who are bilingual). If you find yourself in a one-foreigner village, surely there's another lonely teacher across the mountaintop. You could meet for a drink at the weekend to commiserate and to draw up a charter and call yourselves 'The Wonga Plateau EFL Teachers' Association' (and remember to put yourself down as founder the next time you are revising your CV). You may even want to take some positive steps to meet people and participate in activities outside the world of English language instruction. This may require uncharacteristically extrovert behaviour, but overcoming initial inhibitions almost always pays worthwhile dividends.

If you are tired of conversations about students' dullness or your director of studies' evident lunacy, you could try to meet other expatriates who are not EFL teachers. The local English language bookshop might prove a useful source of information about forthcoming events for English speakers, as will be any newspapers or magazines published in English. Seek out the overseas student club if there is a university nearby (though when it discovers what line of work you are in it may well have designs on you). Even the least devout teachers have found English-speaking churches to be useful for arranging social functions and offering practical advice. If there is a bar in town which models itself on a British/Irish pub or American bar, you will no doubt find a few die-hards drinking Guinness or Budweiser, who might be more than willing to befriend you.

The most obvious way to meet other foreigners is to enrol in a language course or perhaps classes in art and civilisation. Even if you are not particularly serious about pursuing language studies, language classes are the ideal place to form vital social contacts. You can also join other clubs or classes aimed at residents abroad, for example some German cities have English amateur dramatics groups.

Making friends with locals may prove more difficult, though circumstances vary enormously according to whether you live in a small town or a big city, with some gregarious colleagues or by yourself, etc. The obvious source of social contact is your students and their friends and families (bearing in mind that in certain cultures, a teacher who goes out to a bar or disco with students risks losing their respect). As long as you don't spend all your free time moping at home, you are bound to strike up conversations with the locals, whether in cafés, on buses or in shops. Admittedly these seldom go past a superficial acquaintance, but they still serve the purpose of making you feel a little more integrated in the community. Local university students will probably be more socially flexible than others and it is worth investigating the bars and cafés frequented by students. If you have a particular hobby, sport or interest, find out if there is a local club where you will meet like-minded people; join local ramblers, jazz buffs, etc – the more obscure, the more welcome you are likely to be. You only have to become friendly with one other person to open up new social horizons if you are invited to meet their friends and family. Also make an effort to organise some breaks from work. Even a couple of days by the seaside or visiting a tourist attraction in the region can revitalise your interest in being abroad and provide a refreshing break from the tyranny of the teacher's routine.

COMING HOME

For some, teaching abroad can be addictive. The prospect of returning home to scour the local job adverts becomes distinctly unappealing as they drink Retsina, eat sushi or spend the weekend at a Brazilian beach. Once you have completed one teaching contract, it will be very much easier to land the next one, and it can be exhilarating to think that you can choose to work in almost any corner of the globe. By the same token, many people who go abroad to teach English get burned out after a year or two. The majority of English teachers do not think of TEFL as a long-term proposition. They talk about their colleagues who move on to other things as getting a 'proper job', ie one that does not require an early start followed by a long idle morning, where shabby treatment by bosses is not the norm and where you do not have to correct anyone's phrasal verbs.

Homesickness catches up with most EFL teachers and they begin to pine for a pub or bar where repartee is quick and natural and for all the other accoutrements of the culture of their birth. The bad news is that there are few jobs in EFL in Britain except at summer schools. Even professional English language teachers can find it difficult to land a reasonable job in the UK. American teachers will probably fare better due to the growth industry of ESL in the US, though the majority of openings are part-time with few fringe benefits and opportunities for career development. The good news is that a stint of teaching English abroad is an asset on anyone's CV/résumé. Employers of all kinds look favourably on people who have had the get-up-and-go to work at a respectable job in a foreign land. On returning home from teaching in Chile, **Heidi Resetarits** began looking for jobs and found that having international work experience on her résumé was invaluable. Potential employers were intrigued by the fact that she'd lived in Chile. Such experience can always be presented as valuable for increasing self-assurance, maturity, a knowledge of the world, communication skills and any other positive feature which comes to mind. Very few teachers have regretted their decision to travel the world, even if the specific job they did was not without its drawbacks and difficulties.

PART 2

COUNTRY BY COUNTRY GUIDE

WESTERN EUROPE
CENTRAL AND EASTERN EUROPE
THE REST OF EUROPE
CENTRAL ASIAN AND OTHER REPUBLICS
MIDDLE EAST
AFRICA
ASIA
LATIN AMERICA
CENTRAL AMERICA AND THE CARIBBEAN
NORTH AMERICA
AUSTRALASIA

AUSTRIA

The market for ELT in Austria is largely dominated by English for the business community, so teachers with any kind of experience of the business world have a sharp advantage over those with experience only of teaching general English.

As in Germany and Switzerland, most private language institutes depend on freelance part-time teachers drawn from the sizeable resident international community. An estimated 90% of EFL teachers in Austria are freelancers, which means that they do not have a contract with just one school and must pay tax as self-employed workers.

Teachers might consider joining the TEA (Teachers of English in Austria, www.tea4teachers.org/joomla), which costs €33 a year (€19 for students) although it doesn't help job-seekers.

FINDING A JOB

The British Council in Vienna has a list of English language institutes in Vienna and occasionally posts teacher vacancies on its noticeboard. Job ads and relevant employment information for English speakers appear on the site www.virtualvienna.net/jobs.

The online Yellow Pages for Austria are straightforward to use (www.herold.at). Search for *'Sprachschulen u-unterricht'* in the city or region in which you are looking for work.

Most of the 240 *Volkshochschulen* offer English courses in their programmes of general adult education. The co-ordinating office for the provinces in Austria is situated in Vienna. Browse www.vhs.or.at for more information. See the list of employers for details about salary/working conditions for Vienna's adult education centres.

More than 200 English language teaching assistants from the UK and USA are placed in Austrian secondary schools from 1 October to 31 May by the British Council and the Fulbright Commission. The British Council annually looks for about 100 assistants with a decent level of German to work 13 hours a week for €1,134 net per month (www.britishcouncil.org/language-assistants/become/austria). The Fulbright Commission is responsible for recruiting about 140 American graduates with a working knowledge of German and interest in teaching for the same scheme. Detailed information and an application form can be downloaded at www.usta-austria.at and submitted between 15 November and 15 January.

A newer placement scheme for volunteers is operated by ABCi, the non-profit Austrian Bilingual Classroom Initiative (www.abcienglish.at). Participating native speaker teachers must be graduates in education or a related subject and have a driving licence and knowledge of German to enable them to travel round Austria offering free lessons at various schools located in Eisenstadt, Graz, Innsbruck and other cities. Some of the programme is delivered online as well. The aim of the programme is to reach every Austrian pupil with native speakers from English-speaking countries by 2020.

New arrivals in Austria should visit a number of institutes and try to piece together a timetable. After working for three or four schools, it is better to cultivate just one or two since it is unrealistic to work for any more than this on a longer-term basis. A smart appearance and confident manner are always assets when looking for work teaching within the business community. Most Austrians will have an intermediate or higher level of English.

To give an idea of qualifications needed, MHC Business Language Training in Vienna asks for teachers who have some business background, ideally in a specialised area such as marketing, finance or law; it does not insist on a degree but welcomes a teaching certificate such as the CELTA. By contrast English Connection in Salzburg requires a TEFL qualification plus at least three years' teaching experience, whereas experience and/or knowledge of business, law, medicine, tourism, etc are seen as useful bonuses.

The rate at reputable institutes starts at €18–€20 per lesson (normally 45 minutes) and more for 60-minute lessons (€20–€30). This is none-too-generous when the high cost of living in Vienna is taken into account, although taking seminars can pay fairly well (between €300 and €400 per 7+ hour day). Life in the provinces is less expensive of course. At the interview stage, always find out whether quoted rates are gross or net, if travelling time is covered, and when you will be paid. Some schools pay after the course has finished, which will leave you a pauper for an extended period.

TEACHING CHILDREN AND AT SUMMER CAMPS

The demand for teachers of children and young people is very strong in Austria as elsewhere in Europe. Summer camps provide scope for EFL teachers, as indicated in the entries for English for Children and English for Kids. Another major player is The Kids English Company (Kagraner Platz 8, 1220 Vienna; +43 1 263 8931; www.kidsco.at/working.htm) which mounts language courses for children aged 3–10. More than 30 native speaker teachers work at its language centre in Vienna plus teach lessons in kindergartens, private homes, etc. Recruitment takes place between May and September, and pay is generous, €28 per hour. Another company to try is LETA (Learn English Through Action; www.leta.co.at/en/careers) which runs summer camps in Salzburg and Vienna. A Slovakian company, Sidas School (www.sidaschool.com), employs native English speakers for its Active English Weeks and Summer Day Camps which run in neighbouring countries including Austria (see entry in chapter on Slovakia).

REGULATIONS

There is no problem for British and Irish teachers; however, applications for work permits for non-EU citizens (*Beschäftigungsbewilligung*) are almost never granted. All schools claim that they will not hire a non-EU citizen unless they already have a work permit. According to American **Tom Clark**, who has taught English all over the world:

> *Austria is a hard nut to crack with all its red tape and its xenophobic attitude. I have been trying to find a way for seven years to get a job, preferably in Feldkirch, where my daughter lives, but it is a nightmare.*

A language institute there told him he needed to be married to an Austrian before he could be eligible for a work permit. However, that was before Austria introduced a flexible new immigration scheme in 2011 whereby highly qualified workers or skilled workers in shortage occupations may obtain a 'Red-White-Red Card' valid for an initial 12 months; more details of this can be found at www.migration.gv.at/en/types-of-immigration/permanent-immigration-red-white-red-card.html. A hefty percentage of earnings (typically 17%) will be deducted at source (or should be) of any non-resident teacher who earns more than €2,000 in a tax year. The only people entitled not to have these deductions made are licensed translators (certified in Austria), who are permitted to take care of their contributions independently.

Austria (like Germany) has many bureaucratic layers. New arrivals need to register with the police, organise a bank account (into which their wages will be paid directly) and get a tax number from the local tax office. Everyone also needs a *Meldebestätigung* or registration of residence.

GEOFF NUNNEY

Geoff Nunney, knowing that his job at a language school in Slovakia would end with the academic year, was anxious to sort out a summer job and had positive responses to his enquiries to summer employers in Austria, Italy and Spain, mostly sourced through this book. He accepted an invitation to Vienna, which is as accessible from where he was located in Nitra, as London is from his native Birmingham.

I walked away with the job on the day, which is a good feeling, and you couldn't wipe the smile off my face. I got six weeks' work with English for Kids, two in Vienna, and four in Linz. The programme is a mixture of English teaching, sports coaching and lots of things. It was quite a detailed application process: three lesson plans, two references, and then the director invited me to interview in Vienna. So I have more work than I did last summer, more time between camps and will be working in a beautiful country. Also, they pay travel expenses to Austria, and there are four days of training, before you start. It's not even the end of April but I have my summer sorted. I can highly recommend them. The employer also responded positively to an admission of a chronic health problem I have, asked a couple of questions, not unreasonable, and checked if I have private health insurance, which I do (with Ace Travel Insurance).

LIST OF EMPLOYERS

ABCi

Austrian Bilingual English Classroom Initiative für Projektarbeit und Sprachkompetenz, Brunnenweg 2. 4810 Gmunden

☎ +43 7612 65040

✉ office@abcienglish.at

🖥 www.abcienglish.at

NUMBER OF TEACHERS: 35 volunteer teachers.

PREFERENCE OF NATIONALITY: British. Also American, Canadian, Australian, New Zealand and Irish.

QUALIFICATIONS: Degree in education or similar teaching qualification.

CONDITIONS OF EMPLOYMENT: 3–5 months; 6–8 hours per day.

SALARY: Unpaid.

FACILITIES/SUPPORT: Accommodation is provided. No assistance with permits.

RECRUITMENT: Adverts in the *Guardian*. Interviews by Skype or phone.

CONTACT: Frank L. Carle, Managing Director.

BERLITZ AUSTRIA GmbH

Graben 13, 1010 Vienna

Also Mariahilferstrasse 27, 1060 Vienna; Schlosshoferstr. 13–15, 1210 Vienna; Getreidegasse 21, 5020 Salzburg, etc.

✉ katharina.gruensteidl@berlitz.at

🖥 www.berlitz.at

NUMBER OF TEACHERS: No fixed number, teachers work on a freelance basis in Vienna, the Tirol, etc.

PREFERENCE OF NATIONALITY: None but it is very hard for non-EU citizens to obtain work permits.

QUALIFICATIONS: Perfect command of English and a talent for teaching. Academic background preferred; pedagogical experience is helpful but not vital. Any other background (business, engineering, IT, etc) is welcome.

CONDITIONS OF EMPLOYMENT: Freelance contract with no fixed hours. Schools are open Monday to Friday, 8am–8pm.

SALARY: Starting salary is €24 for a double unit (80 minutes).

RECRUITMENT: Interviews are essential.

CONTACT: Ms Katharina Grünsteidl, Salzburg office.

BERLITZ AUSTRIA GMBH KIDS & TEENS

Schlosshofer Strasse 13-15, 1210 Vienna

erika.eckwolf@berlitz.at

www.berlitz.at/en/kids_teens

PREFERENCE OF NATIONALITY: Native speakers with EU nationality.

QUALIFICATIONS: Communicative personality and flexibility. TEFL training and childcare experience advantageous.

CONDITIONS OF EMPLOYMENT: Day camps in Vienna, and 5-day residential camps throughout Austria in July and August. Camp staff participate in sports and evening programme. Opportunities may arise to teach adults as well.

FACILITIES/SUPPORT: Initial training (4 days) in Berlitz Method given in late April, and specialised training for teaching children (3 days) in Vienna in early May.

RECRUITMENT: Application deadline mid-April.

CONTACT: Erika Eckwolf.

BIKU GmbH & Co KG

English Project Weeks and Summer Camps, Schneckgassse 14, 3100 St Pölten

+43 2742 77561

playandlearn@biku.at or office@biku.at

www.biku.at

NUMBER OF TEACHERS: 15–20.

PREFERENCE OF NATIONALITY: British, American, Australian, New Zealander, South African and Irish, but must have the legal right to work in Austria.

QUALIFICATIONS: Minimum TEFL certificate. Must be willing to travel.

CONDITIONS OF EMPLOYMENT: Freelance, so dates are flexible. Trainers travel around the country on project weeks on which they teach 6 lessons a day, during the school week.

SALARY: Negotiable.

FACILITIES/SUPPORT: No help with visas given.

RECRUITMENT: Interviews are essential and carried out in Austria.

CONTACT: Frau Mag. Doris Wieder.

COLE ENGLISH CENTRE FOR KIDS

Weingartnerstrasse 108, 6020 Innsbruck, Tirol

+43 664 371 6063

admin@cole.at

www.cole.at

NUMBER OF TEACHERS: 2 pre-school teachers or teaching assistants and 2 QTS (Qualified Teacher Status) primary school teachers.

PREFERENCE OF NATIONALITY: British.

QUALIFICATIONS: PGCE with English/German, or BA in English Language/Education. Well spoken British English.

CONDITIONS OF EMPLOYMENT: 1-year contract with either 10 or 20 hours per week.

RECRUITMENT: Usually via adverts on teaching and TEFL websites. Interviews are essential and can be conducted by phone; 1 month probationary period.

CONTACT: Rosie Ladner-Cole, Proprietor.

DELPHIN SPRACHSERVICE

Jeneweingasse 17, 1210 Vienna

+43 1 585 5347

delphin@dolphin.at

www.dolphin.at

NUMBER OF TEACHERS: 17 for one-to-one lessons, some of which are conducted in Viennese coffee houses.

PREFERENCE OF NATIONALITY: British, Irish, American.

QUALIFICATIONS: Charisma and competence, experience and appearance, resourcefulness and reliability, diligence and dynamics.

CONDITIONS OF EMPLOYMENT: Stage 1: freelance contracts from 1 to 6 months, starting at 1 hour/week; Stage 2: fixed contract (including health care and pension), open ended, starting at 10 hours/week.

SALARY: Stage 1, €15–€35 per unit (55 minutes); stage 2, €10–€25 per hour.

FACILITIES/SUPPORT: Centres provide preliminary accommodation for the first weeks and help teachers find a place on their own. Assistance with work permit only after a trial period.

RECRUITMENT: Interview essential: face-to-face, over the phone, review of references.

CONTACT: Mr Adrian Krois, Recruitment Officer.

DIE WIENER VOLKSHOCHSCHULEN

Lustkandlgasse 50, 1090 Vienna

info@vhs.at

www.vhs.at

16 Vienna Adult Education Centres (VHS, life-long learning). English courses according to CEFR levels, 60 different languages offered, European language portfolio for adults, Cambridge Exams in collaboration with British Council Vienna, TELC Certificates.

NUMBER OF TEACHERS: Varies according to demand. All teachers are freelance.

PREFERENCE OF NATIONALITY: None, but normally hire teachers living locally.

QUALIFICATIONS: EUROLTA (ICC, The European Language Network, Die Wiener Volkshochschulen), EUROLTA-EUROVOLT Diploma (ICC, The European Language Network, Die Wiener Volkshochschulen), CELTA, DELTA and/or university training, or varied extensive experience of language teaching in upper secondary/adult/university education (at least 2 years' work experience).

CONDITIONS OF EMPLOYMENT: Self-employed freelancers. Minimum commitment 15 weeks (one term). Teaching hours Monday–Saturday between 6am and 9pm.

SALARY: €18 per 50-minute lesson. Maximum: approx €540 per month.

FACILITIES/SUPPORT: Workshops and other in-service training courses available. Library and media facilities.

RECRUITMENT: Courses are planned 6 months in advance. European CV (google 'Europass' for information on the standard format), letter of intent and local interview essential.

ENGLISH FOR CHILDREN (EFC)/ENGLISH LANGUAGE DAY CAMP (ELDC)

Jägerstrasse 28, 2230 Gänserndorf

scott.matthews@englishforchildren.com or
office@englishforchildren.com

www.englishforchildren.com

NUMBER OF TEACHERS: EFC: varies according to need. ELDC: about 25 counsellors.

PREFERENCE OF NATIONALITY: None, but must be a native English speaker.

QUALIFICATIONS: Minimum age 20. Experience of teaching children is required.

CONDITIONS OF EMPLOYMENT: EFC: freelance 10-month contract (September to June). Most of the work is part-time in kindergartens and home groups. ELDC: the summer camp runs in Vienna during July for 4 weeks.

FACILITIES/SUPPORT: For the EFC programme teachers need to be living in Austria. Full training given, free of charge, before and during contract. All course materials provided. Housing not provided. ELDC: 4-week summer camp programme, lunch provided during camp days, 5 days a week, housing not provided; however, relevant contacts to student housing, hostels etc available.

RECRUITMENT: Direct applications by email and telephone interviews.

CONTACT: Scott Matthews, Director.

ENGLISH FOR KIDS

A. Baumgartnerstrasse 44/A7042, 1230 Vienna

+43 1 667 4579

magik@e4kids.co.at

www.e4kids.at.

NUMBER OF TEACHERS AND CAMP COUNSELLORS: 6–8 for full-immersion residential summer camp in Lachstatt near Linz in Upper Austria; 8–12 for day camps in Vienna.

PREFERENCE OF NATIONALITY: EU or others with work permit for Austria.

QUALIFICATIONS: CELTA or Trinity Certificate (minimum grade B) and some formal teaching preferred/required. Camp counsellors require no formal training/experience but must be outgoing, enjoy working with children and should like outdoor activities and sports.

CONDITIONS OF EMPLOYMENT: Duration: mid-July to end August. 2 weeks in Vienna and 3 weeks in Upper Austria. Pupil groups aged from kindergarten to age 10, and 10–15. Full-immersion courses with in-house methods following carefully planned syllabus and teachers' manual, supplemented with CD-ROMs etc. Pre-camp teacher training is mandatory.

SALARY: Varies depending on qualifications. Up to €1,650 per month gross, plus travel costs within Austria, full board and accommodation.

FACILITIES/SUPPORT: Good standard of accommodation and full board provided for teachers. Computer room, internet and video room available.

RECRUITMENT: www.e4kids.at/txt/jobs/apply/job_opportunity.html.

CONTACT: Irena Köstenbauer, Principal.

ENGLISH IS FUN CAMP

Hausgartenweg 20, 2122 Riedenthal

+43 1 369 6833

claudia_millwisch@chello.at

www.englishisfun.at

PREFERENCE OF NATIONALITY: English native speakers (also Spanish, Italian and French native speakers). Must have permission to work in Austria.

QUALIFICATIONS: Experience of working with children needed.

CONDITIONS OF EMPLOYMENT: Hours according to demand. Freelance basis.

RECRUITMENT: Personal interviews held.

CONTACT: Claudia Millwisch, Director.

MHC BUSINESS LANGUAGE TRAINING GmbH

Wiedner Hauptstrasse 54/13A, 1040 Vienna

+43 1 603 0563

office@mhc-training.com

www.mhc-training.com

NUMBER OF TEACHERS: 50 for Vienna, Innsbruck, Linz, Salzburg, Graz and Klagenfurt. Also operate business language training in Bratislava (see entry in Slovakia chapter).

PREFERENCE OF NATIONALITY: Any.

QUALIFICATIONS: MHC trainers have an understanding of business experience, often specialising in areas such as marketing, finance, pharmaceutical or law. A degree is not necessary, although a teaching certificate such as CELTA would be of value.

CONDITIONS OF EMPLOYMENT: Freelance, teaching 15–25 hours per week.

SALARY: €26–€32 per 60 minutes, depending on experience and development with MHC. Seminars pay between €300 and €400 per day (7–9 hours). Trainers are responsible for paying their own taxes (about 21%) and social security (variable).

FACILITIES/SUPPORT: Resource library, photocopying, trainer development, course books for courses supplied for trainers. Trainers from non-EU countries require working papers.

RECRUITMENT: Interviews are essential and usually take place at premises. Possibility of Skype interviews if the applicant is based abroad.

CONTACT: Mark Heather, Managing Director (mark.heather@mhc-training.com).

MIND & MORE, MANAGEMENT AND EDUCATION SERVICES GmbH
Goldschmiedgasse 10, 3rd floor, 1010 Vienna
+43 1 535 9695
office@mindandmore.at
www.mindandmore.at/jobs.html

Management and Education Services is also the Representative Office of the British Open University and OU Business School in Austria, South Germany, Slovenia and Hungary.

NUMBER OF TEACHERS: About 70 language trainers in Vienna and more in many locations around the country and across the borders, plus management skills faculty trainers.

PREFERENCE OF NATIONALITY: None.

QUALIFICATIONS: Minimum university degree plus CELTA or TESOL and teaching experience; preferably also business experience.

CONDITIONS OF EMPLOYMENT: Freelance contracts. Hours vary.

SALARY: Language training: min €22 per 45-minute unit/€28 for 60-minute units; more for specialised language training and seminars; market rates for management skills training.

FACILITIES/SUPPORT: Support given.

RECRUITMENT: Via internet, personal recommendations, partner institutions including British Council, BFI and related institutions. Send cover letter, CV in EU-format and copies of certificates and references. Face-to-face interview essential.

CONTACT: Mag. Walter Grubanovitz (w.grubanovitz@mindandmore.at).

SPIDI SPRACHENINSTITUT
Franz-Josefs-Kai 27/10, 1010 Vienna
+43 1 2361 717
office@spidi.at
www.spidi.at

NUMBER OF TEACHERS: About 50 Business English/ESP trainers for Vienna, Tirol and Vorarlberg.

PREFERENCE OF NATIONALITY: EU citizens.

QUALIFICATIONS: Minimum CELTA or equivalent. Business English and ESP teaching experience preferred.

CONDITIONS OF EMPLOYMENT: Freelance. Flexible hours.

SALARY: €26–€28 per hour, depending on qualifications and experience.

FACILITIES/SUPPORT: No assistance with accommodation. Library with PCs for trainers. Monthly teacher development sessions.

RECRUITMENT: Local interview essential.

CONTACT: Martina Groh (martina.groh@spidi.at).

THE ENGLISH CAMP COMPANY LLC
Via Della Madonna Delle Grazie, Santa Maria Degli Angeli, Assisi (PG) 06081, Italy
+39 331 586 7751/320 3722 106
info@theenglishcampcompany.com
www.theenglishcampcompany.com

NUMBER OF TEACHERS: 15–25 for summer camps in Austria (and Italy).

PREFERENCE OF NATIONALITY: None.

QUALIFICATIONS: Previous teaching experience or experience working at summer camps with children.

CONDITIONS OF EMPLOYMENT: 2-month contract between June and early September. Working hours 9am–5pm. Compulsory 1-week orientation in Assisi must be attended in early June.

SALARY: €175 per week.

FACILITIES/SUPPORT: All teachers are housed with host families.

RECRUITMENT: Closing date for applications beginning of April. Applications open in October.

CONTACT: Ashleigh McLean (ashleigh.mclean@theenglishcampcompany.com) and Nate Poerio (nate.poerio@theenglishcampcompany.com). Founders and Directors.

BENELUX

Belgium

As one of the capitals of the EU, there is a huge demand for all the principal European languages in Brussels. Yet, despite the enormous amount of language teaching in Belgium, there are also a large number of well-qualified expatriates and spouses who take up teaching. This may meet some demand, but not all. To find contact details for language schools in Belgium, the online *Yellow Pages* is a useful tool. A search for 'language schools' in the Brussels Region on www.goldenpages.be will turn up about 85 institutes.

Newcomer is a bi-annual publication which remains in print, though its sister English language monthly magazine *The Bulletin* ceased publication in June 2012 in order to go entirely digital (www.xpats.com). *Newcomer* contains information and contact addresses of interest to the newly arrived teacher, including a listing of major language schools (look for it in newsagents).

The casual teacher will encounter a lot of competition from highly qualified candidates in Brussels and other cities, and will probably steer clear of schools that teach senior EU bureaucrats. Telephone/Skype teaching is popular in Belgium, especially among French learners of English; for example see Phone Languages (www.phonelanguages.com).

Several language teaching organisations are represented in more than one Belgian city, especially Berlitz, which employs about 225 freelance teachers in 14 branches. Linguarama Belgium also recruits freelance native speaker teachers with a TEFL teaching qualification and at least two years' experience of teaching non-native adults. CVs and letters of application can be emailed to personnel@linguarama.com. CLL (Centre de Langues), based in Louvain-la-Neuve, employs about 100 teachers to work on a freelance basis.

As throughout continental Europe, children attend summer camps which focus on language learning. Companies such as Kiddy & Junior Classes (part of Language Studies International) and Ski Ten International organise holiday English courses. Pro Linguis is another company that arranges week-long residential language courses in Thiaumont, a remote southern corner of Belgium near Luxembourg (+32 63 220462; www.prolinguis.be) and which employs some native English speaker teachers who must be willing to keep themselves amused. Courses are put on for all ages including children, so teachers may also be given pastoral duties patrolling dorms, etc.

Social security payments are very high in Belgium. A full-time teacher should expect to be charged about €800 every three months. The first €7,070 can be earned free of tax; thereafter the rates are high.

FREELANCE TEACHING

It is feasible to put up notices in one of the large university towns (Brussels, Antwerp, Ghent, Leuven, Liège, etc) offering conversation practice. Almost all foreign teachers who begin to work for an institute do so on a freelance basis and will have to deal with their own tax and social security. Officially they should declare themselves *indépendants* (self-employed persons) and pay contributions that amount to up to one-third of their salary. In fact many English teachers take their gross salary without declaring it, and don't work long enough to risk being caught. Once a teacher has worked black (*en noir/in het zwart*), it is difficult to regularise his or her status, since they then have to declare all previous earnings. Therefore anyone who plans to spend more than a few months teaching in Belgium should consider this issue.

LIST OF EMPLOYERS

BERLITZ LANGUAGE CENTRES

Avenue Louise 306–310, 1050 Brussels

+32 2 626 9593

joke.vandaele@berlitz.be

www.berlitz.be

NUMBER OF TEACHERS: About 225 (for Brussels, Waterloo, Namur, Charleroi, Liège, Antwerp, Bruges, Mouscron-Tournai, Ghent, Hasselt, Tienen, Mechelen and West Flanders).
PREFERENCE OF NATIONALITY: British or Irish.
QUALIFICATIONS: University degree.
CONDITIONS OF EMPLOYMENT: Freelance – flexible hours (mornings, evenings plus Saturday morning).
SALARY: €15 per 40-minute teaching unit.
FACILITIES/SUPPORT: No assistance with accommodation. In-house training lasts 8 days.
RECRUITMENT: Via adverts and direct applications.
CONTACT: Joke Van Daele, Country Manager of Instruction.

CALL INTERNATIONAL

Avenue Louise 65, 1050 Brussels

+32 2 644 9595

brussels@callinter.com

www.callinter.com

Centre for Accelerated Language Learning in Belgium (Brussels, Waterloo, Tournai and Liège).
NUMBER OF TEACHERS: 150.
PREFERENCE OF NATIONALITY: None.
QUALIFICATIONS: Degree necessary. Experience an advantage. Good communication skills needed.
CONDITIONS OF EMPLOYMENT: Freelance with a car. Flexible hours.
FACILITIES/SUPPORT: No assistance with accommodation.
RECRUITMENT: All year through.
CONTACT: Sylvie Laurent.

CLL CENTRE DE LANGUES

Place de l'Université 25, 1348 Louvain-la-Neuve

+32 10 470628/470629

jobs@cll.ucl.ac.be or eujobs@cll.ucl.ac.be

www.cll.be

NUMBER OF TEACHERS: 100 trainers for European institutions in Brussels, plus adult and business classes in Brussels and Wallonia.

PREFERENCE OF NATIONALITY: From English-speaking countries.
QUALIFICATIONS: Experience in teaching English as a foreign language and, if possible, with a degree in languages.
CONDITIONS OF EMPLOYMENT: Freelance, variable hours (daytime, evenings, Saturdays, etc).
SALARY: €22.10–€27.50 per hour according to experience.
FACILITIES/SUPPORT: None.
RECRUITMENT: Interviews in Belgium essential, followed by an integration session.
CONTACT: Sabine Thirion, Recruitment Coordinator.

LANGUAGE STUDIES INTERNATIONAL / KIDDY & JUNIOR CLASSES

Boulevard Clovis 83, 1000 Brussels

Adult school: +32 2 217 2373

info@lsi-be.net

www.lsi-be.net

Children's school +32 2 218 3920

info@kiddyclasses.net

www.kiddyclasses.net

NUMBER OF TEACHERS: 30–60.
PREFERENCE OF NATIONALITY: None.
QUALIFICATIONS: For the adult school: qualified university level teachers with TEFL experience. For the children's school: qualified teachers or would-be teachers with experience in children's entertainment.
CONDITIONS OF EMPLOYMENT: Freelance, although 1–2 month contracts during the summer. Adult school hours: 9am–8pm; children's school: 9am–5pm.
SALARY: Varies.
FACILITIES/SUPPORT: None, although for the 2-month summer contract assistance is given finding accommodation.
RECRUITMENT: Via internet, newspaper, universities, company brochure. Interviews essential unless excellent references received. Interviews are carried out in Brussels.
CONTACT: Mme Sylvaine Drablier, Director of children's school; Mme Christelle Denay for adult school.

LC LANGUAGE CENTRE

Avenue de Broqueville, 113, 1200 Brussels

+32 2 771 7131

language.centre@skynet.be

www.lclanguagecentre.com

NUMBER OF TEACHERS: 20 (for English).

PREFERENCE OF NATIONALITY: UK and USA.

QUALIFICATIONS: TEFL or TESL and experience.

CONDITIONS OF EMPLOYMENT: Freelance/flexible contracts and work hours.

SALARY: Flexible.

FACILITIES/SUPPORT: None.

RECRUITMENT: Direct application. Interview essential.

PRO LINGUIS

Rue de l'Eglise 228, 6717 Thiaumont

secretariat@prolinguis.be

www.prolinguis.be

NUMBER OF TEACHERS: 14 (freelancers) to work near Arlon close to the Luxembourg border.

PREFERENCE OF NATIONALITY: British.

QUALIFICATIONS: Kindergarten teacher or summer camp counsellor, primary school teacher, EFL training, BA in English or any other language, in business, law or social studies.1 year's teaching experience needed for summer positions.

CONDITIONS OF EMPLOYMENT: Minimum 1-year contract, or 2-month contract in summer; 7 hours per day, 4–5 days per week.

SALARY: €12.50–€14 per hour plus free board and lodging on campus.

RECRUITMENT: Personal contacts and websites. Phone interviews. Summer recruitment carries on until mid-June.

CONTACT: Edward Young, Academic Director.

SKITEN INTERNATIONAL

Chateau d'Emines, 45 rue de Rhisnes, 5080 Emines la Bruyere, Namur

+32 81 213051

skiteninternational@gmail.com

www.skiten.com

NUMBER OF TEACHERS: 2 for English (plus 1 for tennis).

PREFERENCE OF NATIONALITY: None.

QUALIFICATIONS: Experience with children. Some knowledge of French useful. Mostly aged 18–25.

CONDITIONS OF EMPLOYMENT: Student contract for July or August. 6 hours of work per day including teaching and 'animation', ie supervising camp activities.

SALARY: €1,200 per month.

FACILITIES/SUPPORT: Board and lodging provided at camp.

RECRUITMENT: University exchanges, word of mouth.

CONTACT: Martine Goffinet, Directrice, or Stéphanie de Bellefroid, Manager.

Luxembourg

With only a handful of private language schools in the country, Luxembourg does not offer much scope for ELT teachers. Fiona Hynd, the *Responsable Pédagogique* for the English World Institute Luxembourg, recently described the typical situation:

> *We do not recruit from outside the Grande Région of Luxembourg and the neighbouring regions in Germany, France and Belgium. When actively recruiting we do so locally and from CVs sent in on spec by people already living in the area. I think this is more or less true for most of the language schools here as Luxembourg is not a hot spot on people's lists of places to go. The cost of living is quite high and the work is mostly freelance and rarely full-time. I believe we are one of the few remaining schools to offer contracts.*

The national employment service (l'Administration de l'Emploi) at 10 rue Bender, L-1229 (Jobseekers' hotline +352 247 88888; www.adem.public.lu) has a EURES adviser who may have information about language teaching openings.

Informal live-in tutoring jobs are possible. Luxembourg Accueil Information (10 Bisserwee, L-1238 Luxembourg-Grund; +352 241717; www.luxembourgaccueil.com) is a centre for new arrivals and temporary residents. It provides a range of services on its premises from October to May, including workshops and language courses, and might possibly be able to advise on teaching and tutoring possibilities. Annual membership costs €20.

Inlingua and Berlitz have centres in Luxembourg City (www.inlingua.lu and www.berlitz.lu), and the Prolingua Language Centre hires professionally turned out teachers with a driving licence to teach in businesses (www.prolingua.lu/en/prolingua/employment-at-prolingua). Prolingua also runs language summer schools for school children.

Netherlands

Dutch people have a very high degree of competence in English after they finish their schooling. Educated Dutch people are so fluent in English that the Minister of Education once suggested that English might become the main language in Dutch universities, a suggestion which caused an understandable outcry. However, the schooling system has become increasingly international and university staff are being challenged to lecture and publish in English and to advance their English-language skills.

Yvonne Dalhuijsen, manager at UvA Talen (see list of employers), sees an increasing need for advanced levels of English within both companies and universities. She is always on the lookout for teachers who are native speakers of English. On the other hand, a few long-standing employers of freelance corporate trainers have ceased English teaching operations because of insufficient demand.

What private language schools there are tend to provide specific training in Business English and to be looking for language trainers with extensive commercial or government experience as well as a teaching qualification and – particularly outside the capital – some fluency in Dutch. Business English, Legal English and Academic English (writing papers, abstracts, etc) are subjects in high demand. So many native English speaking citizens have settled in the Netherlands, attracted by its liberal institutions, that most companies depend on long-term freelancers. Candidates with just a CELTA and some teaching experience can try to pick up part-time work taking IELTS or other Cambridge preparation classes for example with the Centre for British English in Rotterdam (www.cbelanguages.nl/jobs).

Most of your competition will already have the VAR-WUO document that many employers expect to see. This is a Declaration of Independent Contractor status which must be applied for from the tax office (Belastingdienst). When applying you will have to estimate how many hours and how many employers you expect to have in a year, which is difficult if you are starting out. You are likely to fall into the part-time category which is under 1,225 hours a year (average 23 hours a week). Obviously freelancers will have to be responsible for covering their own social security. The standard monthly contribution to a health insurance scheme is €100.

It might be possible to fix up some informal freelance lessons with university students from non-Dutch backgrounds, including Spanish, whose level of English is less advanced than their local counterparts'.

The Yellow Pages are easy to search online (www.detelefoongids.nl) under the rubric *Talenonderwijs* (Language Training). The site of NRTO (www.nrto.nl), the Dutch Council on Training and Education, links to a handful of English-training institutes. The British Language Training Centre in Amsterdam offers the CELTA course (see Training chapter) and may be able to give advice to qualified job-seekers and recommend other institutes to try for work. Linguarama Nederland has a sizeable operation in the business training field with centres in Amsterdam, the Hague and Soesterberg; enquiries may be sent to personnel@nl.linguarama.com. Only applicants with a full TEFL/TESOL or CELTA qualification will receive a response (www.linguarama.com/nl/vacatures).

Outside the mainstream language institutes, it might be possible to arrange some telephone teaching. Try, for example, Dialogue Talen in the Hague (www.dialoguetalen.nl).

Another possibility for those not interested in a corporate atmosphere is the network of *Volksuniversiteit*, adult education centres. Branches that teach English – 48 in all – can be found throughout the country, all listed at www.volksuniversiteit.nl.

LIST OF EMPLOYERS

BERLITZ LANGUAGE CENTRES

- info@berlitz.nl
- www.berlitz.nl

Branches in Amsterdam, Den Haag, Maastricht, Rotterdam and 19 others.

NUMBER OF TEACHERS: 39.

PREFERENCE OF NATIONALITY: None.

QUALIFICATIONS: Minimum bachelor's degree and if possible TEFL and/or business-related work experience.

CONDITIONS OF EMPLOYMENT: 1-year contract. Working hours are between 7.30am and 9.45pm.

SALARY: €1,000–€2,500 per month depending on qualifications and hours worked.

RECRUITMENT: Via the website or on the spot. Interviews essential.

CONTACT: Joke Van Daele, Country Manager of Instruction (joke.vandaele@berlitz.be).

BOGAERS TALENINSTITUUT B.V.

Groenstraat 139–155, 5021 LL, Tilburg

- +31 13 536 2101
- admin@bogaerstalen.nl
- www.bogaerstalen.nl

NUMBER OF TEACHERS: 5 foreign out of total of 50.

PREFERENCE OF NATIONALITY: British.

QUALIFICATIONS: Degree and TEFL certificate. Experience in teaching conversational and Business English preferred. Candidates preferred with valid VAR-WUO.

CONDITIONS OF EMPLOYMENT: From 1 week to 9 months.

SALARY: €22.50 per hour.

FACILITIES/SUPPORT: Will help with accommodation if needed.

RECRUITMENT: Speculative CVs and applications.

CONTACT: Marion Bernard, Training Coordinator.

LANGUAGE PARTNERS

Sarphati Plaza, Rhijnspoorplein 24, 1018 TX, Amsterdam

- +31 20 685 2991
- afke.derijk@languagepartners.nl
- www.languagepartners.nl

Offices also in The Hague, Rotterdam, Amersfoort, Zwolle, Breda and Nijmegen.

NUMBER OF TEACHERS: Approximately 200 (freelance and contract).

PREFERENCE OF NATIONALITY: None.

QUALIFICATIONS: Native speakers, CELTA or TEFL qualifications, and relevant experience in business-to-business training.

CONDITIONS OF EMPLOYMENT: 6–12 months. Variable hours.

FACILITIES/SUPPORT: No help with accommodation or visas.

RECRUITMENT: Online recruitment and word of mouth. Interviews are essential.

CONTACT: Ms. Afke de Rijk, HR Manager.

PCI – PIMENTEL COMMUNICATIONS INTERNATIONAL

Bachlaan 43, 1817 GH Alkmaar

- +31 72 512 1190/515 6518
- hrdepartment@pcilanguages.com
- www.pcilanguages.com

NUMBER OF TEACHERS: 50+.

PREFERENCE OF NATIONALITY: Mostly British, Irish or North American. Australians, New Zealanders and South Africans also welcome.

QUALIFICATIONS: Experience in business and technical English. Cross-cultural communication skills and familiarity with modern teaching methods needed. Should have a VAR-WUO or be eligible to apply for one.

CONDITIONS OF EMPLOYMENT: Freelancers working mostly in-company nationwide.

SALARY: Starts at €27 per hour.

FACILITIES/SUPPORT: Most teachers are already living in the Netherlands.

RECRUITMENT: Advertisements, word of mouth and recommendations.

CONTACT: Ms Iona de Pimentel.

UvA TALEN

Roetersstraat 25, 1018 WB Amsterdam

- +31 20 525 4637
- trainers@uvatalen.nl
- www.uvatalen.nl

Independent language institute, affiliated to the Universiteit van Amsterdam, and consisting of a translation agency and a training centre.

NUMBER OF TEACHERS: Varies, only freelance.

PREFERENCE OF NATIONALITY: None, provided native English speaker (with widely understood dialect).

QUALIFICATIONS: Experience in teaching adults and registered at the Dutch Chamber of Commerce as a freelancer, with a VAR-WUO. Working knowledge of Dutch and/or the level system of the Common European Framework of Reference (A-B-C) is required.

CONDITIONS OF EMPLOYMENT: Freelance assignments only.

SALARY: From €25 per hour, plus compensation for preparation work or marking.

FACILITIES/SUPPORT: No assistance with accommodation or work permits. Project manager monitors content of the courses and is happy to advise teachers on content and materials.

RECRUITMENT: Teachers submit CVs and cover letter; face-to-face interviews required on arrival.

CONTACT: Yvonne Dalhuijsen, Operational Manager (YDalhuijsen@uvatalen.nl).

FRANCE

The French used to rival the English for their reluctance to learn other languages. A Frenchman abroad spoke French as stubbornly as Britons spoke English. But things have changed, especially in the business and technical community. French telephone directories contain pages of English language training organisations and the law continues to put pressure on companies to provide ongoing training for staff. The *Droit Individuel à la Formation (DIF),* meaning the individual's right to vocational training, stipulates that companies have to devote a prescribed minimum of their gross payroll to employee training. English and computing are the most popular objects of investment, and therefore many private language institutes cater purely to the business market. In fact a quick browse through the entries in the List of Employers at the end of this chapter will lead you to the conclusion that the majority of adult language training in France is business oriented, with most of it taking place on-site and the rest taking place in business and vocational schools. In this setting the term *formateurs* or 'trainers' is often used instead of English teachers. Private training companies involved with *formation* often produce very glossy brochures which look more like the annual report of a multinational corporation than an invitation to take an evening course. Most offer one-to-one tuition.

Interestingly, registered unemployed French citizens are entitled to access training paid for by the state. Those who have been made redundant can arrange through their local employment office (*Pôle Emploi*) to sign up for language (or other) courses at €15 an hour. Others who are out of work and who haven't used up their DIF (training) entitlement can use it while unemployed.

Many of the thousands of non-profit Chambres de Commerce et d'Industrie (CCI) around France have their own Centres d'Etude des Langues. In addition, a considerable number of town councils (*mairies*) offer simple English courses to locals for a reduced rate, or allow associations to offer courses using their premises, so you might be able to pick up a few hours of teaching this way. Recently the chamber of commerce of Tarn et Garonne was paying €22 an hour gross.

Teaching children has traditionally been left mostly to French teachers of English, helped sometimes by foreign language assistants placed in schools (see later). According to the director of TEFL Toulouse, the teaching of Young Learners is on the up in France, with a current trend for teaching toddlers. Jonathan Davies speculates that teaching teenage groups after school will continue to take off, as it did in Spain in the 1990s. Teaching by Skype or other online system is now a common supplement or even full-time teaching possibility in a growing market.

PROSPECTS FOR TEACHERS

Advanced ELT qualifications seem to be less in demand in France than solid teaching experience, particularly in a business context. Few schools accept candidates on the basis of being a native speaker and candidates may be asked to provide official certificates to show the educational level they have reached. However, anyone who has a university degree in any subject and who can look at home in a business situation (and possesses a suit/smart clothes) has a chance of finding teaching work, particularly if they have a working knowledge of French.

All respectable language schools in France now want to see solid evidence of experience and competence, or at least a strong drive to work in the teaching field. A good CV showing past experience and a TEFL certificate from a reputable training organisation are almost guaranteed tickets at least to the interview stage.

Ironically, more 'serious' qualifications such as a BEd, PGCE or even the DELTA are not always a help. The fact is that language schools fight for contracts on price, and ordinary clients tend not to differentiate and believe language lessons are the same from whichever school. Therefore a teacher's experience and qualifications have little to do with schools winning training contracts. How much language schools have to pay teachers is a major issue. In other words, an enthusiastic new teacher clutching a shiny new TEFL

Certificate may actually be more attractive than someone with a weight of experience and qualifications who expects to be paid accordingly. Salary scales are relatively fixed in France, and experience and advanced qualifications don't really give you much bargaining power. The situation is made worse by the rapidity with which language teachers move on, and language schools know that there are plenty of other good candidates hungry for work and experience, and more or less ready to work for the basic rate.

In some circles it is fashionable to learn American English, which means that, despite the visa difficulties for non-EU citizens, it is possible for Americans to find work as well. Many institutes claim to have no preference as to the country of origin of their native-speaker teachers though most expect to hire foreigners already resident in France with appropriate working papers. Most French students are happy with a friendly, competent and enthusiastic teacher, whatever their nationality, who is able to adapt to their needs and supply them with materials and learning situations relevant to their situation.

FINDING A JOB

IN ADVANCE

France is such a popular and obvious destination for British and Irish people and also for North Americans that a job hunt from abroad can be disappointing. Major language-teaching organisations receive speculative CVs every day and can't promise anything until they meet the applicant.

A comprehensive list of English language institutes in France is hard to come by. The *Pages Jaunes* (Yellow Pages; www.pagesjaunes.fr) are a useful search engine; search under the heading *Ecoles de Langues* and your desired destination.

The British Council offices in Paris, Lyon and Marseilles (www.britishcouncil.fr) teach English to adults, and to children and teenagers during the school holidays, and may have vacancies for well-qualified teachers, mainly to work part-time at their partner schools in Paris suburbs such as Vaucresson (teacherrecruitment@ britishcouncil.fr). **Sab Will**, long-term English resident of Paris, worked at the British Council in Paris for several years and says to get in you will have to convince them you are good, with relevant experience and qualifications. It also has a useful online teaching resource centre (www.britishcouncil.fr/en/teach/online-resources) which offers a weekly collection of links to free materials from British Council websites.

The Centre International d'Etudes Pédagogiques (CIEP) in France offers thousands of assistantships in France for students from many different countries (+33 1 45 07 60 00; www.ciep.fr). Enrolled undergraduates and graduate students aged 20 to 30 (35 in the UK) can spend an academic year working as English language assistants in secondary and (increasingly) primary schools throughout France. In return for giving conversation classes 12 hours a week, providing classroom support and teaching pupils about their country, assistants receive a gross allowance of approximately €965 a month (€794 net) for seven months, beginning 1 October. Those who want to carry on teaching through the summer may apply to teach lycée students (aged 15–18) on intensive language summer courses fully funded by the French government. Similar posts for the academic year are also available in other francophone countries such as Belgium, Canada (Québec) and Switzerland.

Assistants must have a working knowledge of French, so modern languages students are encouraged to apply. Applications are considered from students who have at least AS level, Higher Grade or equivalent in French. Some posts in primary schools require degree-level French because any help offered by colleagues and all discussion of pupil progress, curriculum, lesson planning, etc is likely to be in French. British applicants should contact the Language Assistants Team, British Council (10 Spring Gardens, London SW1A 2BN; language.assistants@britishcouncil.org; www.britishcouncil.org/language-assistants).

American students can participate in the scheme by applying through the Assistantship Program at the French Embassy in Washington; for further information contact assistant.washington-amba@diplomatie. gouv.fr or browse http://highereducation.frenchculture.org/teach-in-france.

In some cases the description language 'assistant' is a misnomer in schools where there isn't much support from the rest of the staff. Whereas some might relish the responsibility, others might find the job quite isolating.

EMILY SLOANE

Emily Sloane from America was posted as an assistant to a small town in Lorraine (where the quiche comes from), unknown to any English language guidebook that she could find.

I taught English to about 170 students in three different primary schools, two 45-minute sessions per class per week, for a total of 12 hours of work each week. In general, the teaching and lesson planning were thoroughly enjoyable, although I wasn't given much guidance and received no feedback throughout the year, so I'm sure the fact that I was already comfortable and experienced with teaching and working with children made a big difference in my enjoyment. The kids, although adoring and very enthusiastic, were a lot rowdier than I had expected, and I was obliged to spend a lot more time on behaviour management than I'd anticipated. The kids were never mean, just excitable and chatty, especially so because my class offered a break from their usual blackboard-and-worksheet style routine. The fact that I was the only assistant in my town meant that my French improved noticeably, especially my slang and listening comprehension, although it made for some lonely weekends, because I was forced to get by in French all the time.

The Alliance Française (AF) is a venerable organisation, analogous to the British Council, with a large teaching operation in London and centres worldwide. Favourable reports circulate of people getting useful information or contacts from it. Anyone who can converse in French might find it useful to make contact before leaving home. Most centres have a noticeboard where requests for tutors, au pairs, etc are occasionally posted.

There is also demand for experienced English teachers from French universities (*grandes écoles*), although you really need to be living in France to stand a chance of securing a job. The university has various systems of employment. For example Lyon 2 employs about 45 native English teachers by a system called '*vacataire*' (independent contracting), which means you need to have a principal employer. There is also another system called '*travailleurs indépendants*' where teachers can work at two/three/four universities, but are classed as self-employed and have to pay their own social security, which amounts to about 20% of gross earnings of €40–€60 an hour. Toulouse has five universities which are often looking for teachers and pay up to €50. The disadvantage of working at the universities is that although they pay relatively well with good conditions of employment, they often pay late; you could be waiting for up to six months.

TESOL-France (www.tesol-france.org) posts mostly high-level job announcements which are accessible to members. Membership costs €49 a year (€27 if a student or unemployed) and brings other networking advantages.

When applying to a training organisation, try to demonstrate your commercial flair with a polished presentation including a business-like CV (omitting your hobbies) preferably accompanied by a hand-written letter in impeccable French.

Although English teachers can still get away with more relaxed dress codes and a certain '*originalité*' is tolerated, you will still give yourself the best chance of employment if you follow typical French conventions: dress very smartly for interviews, be positive and enthusiastic, ask questions as well as answer them, and don't sell yourself too cheaply if you have a qualification or experience which is relevant to what they are looking for. Watch out for language schools trying to make you believe that working evenings or Saturdays is absolutely normal. You may not be able to get paid more for agreeing to do this, but you might be able to negotiate other concessions, such as more time off during the week.

The technique of making a personal approach to schools in the months preceding the one in which you would like to teach is often successful. On the strength of her Cambridge Certificate from International House, **Fiona Paton** had been hoping to find teaching work in the south of France in the summer but quickly discovered that there are very few opportunities outside the academic year. On her way back to England, she disembarked from the train in the picturesque town of Vichy in the Auvergne just long enough to distribute a few self-promotional leaflets to three language schools. She was very surprised to receive a favourable reply from one of them once she was home, and so returned a few weeks later for a happy year of teaching.

Make it really easy for language schools to contact you by acquiring a French mobile phone (www.mobile. free.fr charges from €16 a month). Feature the number prominently on all your CVs and motivational letter (often requested by employers and recruiters).

Teaching English in exchange for room and board is not uncommon though it is normally combined with looking after the family's children or doing some domestic chores in order to pay for studies. The strings attached to a free room should be made very clear from the outset, or the candidate (quite often a young woman) might be in for an unpleasant surprise once installed if the family starts heaping on some decidedly non-linguistic tasks (ironing, washing, taking the kids to school). The University of London Institute in Paris at 9–11 rue de Constantine has a noticeboard advertising very occasional teaching vacancies as well as live-in tutoring and au pair jobs.

While looking for something to do in her gap year, **Hannah Start** was put in touch with a French bank executive who had done an English language course in Hannah's home town and who wanted to keep up her English at home in Paris by having someone to provide live-in conversation lessons. So, in exchange for three hours of speaking English in the evening (usually over an excellent dinner), Hannah was given free accommodation in the 17th arrondissement.

ANDREW SYKES

Andrew Sykes felt that he owed the success of his job-hunt to his misguided and unsuccessful accountancy training rather than to his TEFL certificate.

I wrote to more or less all the schools from your book in France and elsewhere that didn't stipulate 'experience required' and was fairly disheartened by the few, none-too-encouraging replies along the lines of 'if you're in town, give us a call'. Sitting in a very cheap hotel bedroom halfway down Italy in early November feeling sorry for myself and knowing that I was getting closer and closer to my overdraft limit and an office job back in the UK, I rang the schools that had replied and so picked up the phone and rang through to a company in Tours. 'Drop in', the voice said, 'and we will give you an interview'. So I jumped on the next train, met the director on Monday and was offered a job on the Tuesday morning, initially on an hour-by-hour basis and then in December on a contract of 15 hours which was later increased to 20 hours a week.

OK, I was very lucky. I have since learned that the school receives several phone calls and letters per week; it's an employer's market. What got me the job was not my TEFL certificate nor my very good French. It was the fact that I was an ex-accountant. I had been one of the thousands enticed by the financial benefits of joining an accountancy firm after graduation. But I hated the job and failed my first professional exams. Ironically the experience gained during those two and a half years of hell was invaluable. Whereas in Italy they want teaching experience, in France they want business experience.

You will in the end be teaching people not objects, and any experience you can bring to the job (and especially the job interview) will help. However ashamed you may be of telling everyone in the pub back home that you were once a rat catcher, it may be invaluable if the school's main client is 'Rent-o-kil'.

TEACHING CHILDREN

The state Education Nationale system is highly regimented and difficult to get into without passing a very challenging test called the CAPES, and later on the Aggrégation. Native-speaker teachers might be able to find an opening in a specialised school such as a Montessori school, often run by expats. The British Council has a large and successful English teaching operation in Paris. Individual tutoring is most likely to take place on Wednesdays (when state schools are closed) and Saturdays.

It will be much easier to arrange part-time work tutoring children in a family context. An innovative company called the Speaking Agency recruits up to 1,000 native speakers over 18 to work for a few hours a week either babysitting children aged 3–12 focusing on teaching English through play, or teaching older children. These are all live-out positions so the company is interested in hearing from people already living in France. As well as in Paris, it places tutors in Lyon, Lille, Bordeaux, Nantes, Toulouse, Montpellier, Aix-en-Provence and Nice. The hourly rate is €10–€12.50 for the childcare positions, €13–€20 for the tutoring, depending on number of children and travel distance. Details of the online application procedure are at www.facebook.com/jobinfrance.

Anyone who is interested in obtaining a childcare qualification and learning French while at the same time earning €1,000 a month by tutoring children in English from September to June should investigate a programme run by the Paris Institute of Childcare Training (www.parisict.com/jobs.html).

If you are hoping to land a contract with an institute that teaches children, for example with the British Council, you must have relevant experience, aptitude and (ideally) qualifications, as the criteria are stricter than for teaching adults. They take most new teachers on just in advance of the school year so will probably be looking to replace people around June or July ready for *la rentrée* (start of the academic year) in September. Another possibility is holiday courses, of which there are many, and for which extra teachers are needed in summer, winter and at Easter.

French kids can be rowdy, though if you have a small class, 'crowd control' shouldn't be too much of an issue. If you are having trouble managing a private class, it is difficult to complain to parents because they won't be too impressed to hear that their little cherubs are messing around and wasting their money.

ON THE SPOT

Prospective teachers should not automatically head for Paris but bear in mind that provincial cities have many language schools too. Due to the many French companies that have decided it is more cost effective to relocate in the provinces, many regional centres such as Orléans, Lyon, Marseilles, Toulouse, Lille and Rouen are crawling with medium and large international companies, all needing English-speaking staff, as confirmed mid-2014 by **Jonathan Davies**, Director of the TEFL training company TEFL Toulouse (www.tefltoulouse.com): *'The good news is that outside Paris and some touristy and Mediterranean areas, most of France is still FAR from being saturated with qualified TEFL teachers, just at a time when the whole of France finally seems to want to learn English!'*

SARA BREESE

Sara Breese described her job-hunt in Paris and the style of life teaching can pay for.

Finding work in France is a rather arduous process; however, with determination and zeal one can easily find work. I moved to Paris in September as a jeune fille au pair and doing side work teaching children English. The next year I decided to get my ESL teaching certificate at TEFL Paris which was one of the best decisions I ever made. Not only did I love the process of getting my certificate, but I also discovered a love for teaching. ESL is probably the number one industry for Anglophones and is your best investment in terms of success in the job search. In order to find a teaching job I looked in the FUSAC [mentioned below] and applied to every English teaching organisation in the magazine. After about two weeks, I received some calls asking for interviews. I interviewed with three different places, accepting a job where I still work. I am paid €20 per hour gross, €16 after taxes. I immediately signed a CDII which is the ideal type of contract for a Business English teacher in Paris. It translates to basically a long-term intermittent contract meaning that you will receive work when it is available but you will not stop being considered an employee.

I have not been able to save money because Paris is very expensive. I can make anywhere between €1,000 and €1,600 a month. Rent in Paris is very high and I have never heard of a teaching organisation providing housing for their teachers. When I first moved to Paris I lived in what they call a chambre de bonne (maid's quarters). These are rented for about €450 per month, so as a teacher you can expect at least half your pay cheque to go to rent.

Not only is it hard to find work in Paris, but of course rents are very high in the capital. If you do decide to give it a go in Paris, watch for adverts in the *Metro* for English language courses, since these are usually the biggest schools and therefore have the greatest number of vacancies for teachers. Certain streets in the 8th arrondissement around the Gare St Lazare abound in language schools including some cowboy outfits whose standards are not always what they should be. Again, schools which insist on a TEFL certificate and use a rigorous recruitment process are probably the safest bet. If you are desperate, you might want to go for less reputable or well-known schools but be ready to be disappointed.

FREELANCE TEACHING

Well-off parents of French school children often pay for private lessons for their kids. Business people with a pressing need for English, which they are reluctant to reveal to their employer, and worried exam students are other big markets for freelance English tutors. Private lessons are a very good supplement to an official contract and it is worth spending a bit of time putting notices up and spreading the word that you are available for this sort of work. **Sab Will** has charged €30 an hour for a minimum of two hours at a time and people seem to accept this if you can convince them you are well-qualified, experienced and pleasant to be with. In general €20 is considered a decent fee for an hour's private tuition, and should be the minimum charged in Paris by anyone with qualifications or experience. Many people advertise and then have to find a suitable public place to meet clients. Rather than choose a café where you might end up spending a couple of euros on a drink, the Luxembourg Gardens or other parks make a good meeting place in the summer. Outside Paris, you may do better charging €15, especially in places like Nice where there are so many English tutors.

A category of legal worker was introduced in 2009, the 'auto-entrepreneur', which is open to anyone officially based in France (ie with French bank account, working papers and French social security number). Individuals can set up as a one-man or one-woman company and sell their services. This is attractive to teachers because it can be accomplished quickly, including online, and also to employers because they do not have to pay social security contributions.

Long-time teacher in France **Jonathan Davies** of TEFL Toulouse describes the trend:

> Many teachers are now setting themselves up as freelancers or auto-entrepreneurs, which has added flexibility. You can bill language schools for hours you do for them, and also bill individual clients that you find yourself. You can even be both a freelancer and have contracts – you don't have to choose one or the other. Of course if you are a freelancer you can choose your own rates and conditions too. It's a fun time to set up business in France, and really not that complicated. Auto-entrepreneurs get taxed about 25% of what they make though, so you need to hike up your hourly rate if you choose this route. Make sure your French TEFL course helps you with all this. One of our ex-trainees with a background in marketing refused to charge under €90 an hour – and got plenty of work!

Self-employed workers (*travailleurs indépendants*) are obliged to register at the social security office (www.urssaf.fr/independants/). The hourly fees (*honoraries*) paid to freelance teachers should be significantly higher than to contract workers (*salariés*), since they are free of deductions. There are many *panneaux* or noticeboards (see below) that might prove useful to someone looking for private tutoring. This is especially appealing to Americans who do this without worrying too much about visas.

As part of a well-organised teaching job hunt in Marseilles, American **Bradwell Jackson** tried to arrange to teach some private lessons:

> Besides searching for jobs in schools, I also tried my hand at the tutoring market. I put up **petites annonces** in the local boulangeries and bars, and I also put an ad in a free local paper called **13** (treize), also called **Top Annonce** (www.topannonces.fr). The cost of placing the ad was not free, but it wasn't expensive (maybe €10). This did turn out to be fruitful, as I did get responses. My big disadvantage was that I didn't have a cell phone, and I was told that the French are not inclined to respond to someone only by email. I decided to counteract this by putting in a very low asking price, only €10 per hour. With that price, I got several responses, even with only an email address advertised. The problem was that there was a time lag of two weeks between my placing the order and its appearance, by which time I had booked a plane ticket back to Mexico. I also advertised on a free website service called Kelprof (www.kelprof.com). It was indeed free, but to contact referrals you have to use a password and 08 numbers which, I learned the hard way, are very expensive.

According to an American blogger and school *assistant* called Kelsey, using sites like this takes patience, as she reported in 2013:

> All of us assistants, myself included, had high hopes for finding students online using sites like KelProf.com and Cherche-Cours.com [now www.superprof.fr]. Unfortunately, we were nearly all disappointed. I don't think any

of my friends have found jobs through those sites; there are just so many English-speakers in Nice that there's no shortage of English teachers. I did find one student through Cherche-Cours, but after I went on vacation he dropped off the face of the earth . . . not sure what happened there! My disappearing student was a complete beginner, which made for a lot of work on my end, so I'm kinda glad he just stopped showing up for lessons. . . Since leaving France, I've gotten several emails from Kelprof/Cherche-Cours with requests from students for lessons. So maybe just be patient and the students will come!

There are expatriate grapevines all over Paris, very helpful for finding teaching work and accommodation. The noticeboard in the foyer of the Centre d'Information et de Documentation Jeunesse (CIDJ) at 101 Quai Branly; +33 1 44 49 12 00; www.cidj.com (métro Bir-Hakeim) is good for occasional student-type jobs, but sometimes there are adverts for a *soutien scolaire en Anglais* (English tutor). Access hours to the CIDJ without an appointment have been reduced to 1pm–6pm Tuesdays to Saturdays.

The other mecca for job and flat-hunters is the American Church at 65 Quai d'Orsay (métro Invalides), which has very active noticeboards upstairs, downstairs and outside. There is a charge for posting a notice and they are kept up to date. In the basement, the free corkboard is much more chaotic; it can take about half an hour to rummage through all the notices.

The American Cathedral in Paris (23 Avenue George V; www.americancathedral.org), near the métro stations Alma Marceau and George V, also has a noticeboard featuring employment opportunities and housing listings. The free bilingual newsletter *France-USA Contacts* or *FUSAC* (www.fusac.fr) is now only online and carries dozens of teaching adverts. An advert under the heading 'Work Wanted in France' starts at €36 for 20 words. **Sab Will** recalls placing his own small ad in FUSAC when he first arrived in Paris and getting responses from prospective students. It is also effective at providing ways to get into the English-speaking expat community in Paris.

It may be worth including a reminder here that anyone who advertises their services should exercise a degree of caution when arranging to meet prospective clients.

Outside the bigger cities, your chance of picking up freelance work is greatly improved. Working as a language assistant in a small town in Lorraine, **Emily Sloane** had no problem finding freelance work:

Through word of mouth and no active self-promotion, numerous townspeople contacted me about private English tutoring. By the middle of the school year I had five private students, whom I taught once a week each for a modest fee, with sometimes a meal on top. It was nice to be able to work through more complicated material with older students and really nice to have an inside look into various French households. Plus, the tutoring sessions kept me busy. I also earned some extra cash by doing freelance writing work for the mother of one of my students, which helped to supplement my fairly meagre salary and allowed me to take long and stress-free vacations during the numerous school breaks.

Despite not really needing French to teach – good teaching technique rarely involves having to translate or explain in French – many schools still prefer you to be able to speak some. Also you will get more private students if you can explain your prices and conditions over the phone. Some TEFL courses can offer a French course at a discount rate.

REGULATIONS

EU CITIZENS

For more than 10 years, EU citizens have been free of the obligation to obtain residence permits to live and work in other EU countries so the *carte de séjour* is now obsolete for them. Long-stayers may choose to apply for one since it can be a useful piece of ID, but they will have to be prepared to provide a battery of translated documents.

Once you take up paid employment in France, your employer must complete all the necessary formalities for registering you with social security (*sécu*) and you will be issued with a registration card and then pay a percentage of your wages as contributions. French red tape is a pain in the neck, but once you've got it over and done with you are into quite a nice system of benefits and help on anything from unemployment and housing aid to child benefit and income supplements if you don't earn much one year.

NON-EU CITIZENS

In France, it is much more difficult for Americans, Canadians, Australians and all other non-EU citizens to get a work permit than it is for EU teachers. However, people with initiative are able to get at least some legal work, at least for a limited period. The easiest way (apart from marrying a French national) is to enrol in a French course at an official provider like the Alliance Francaise and acquire a student visa, which allows the holder to engage in up to 20 hours of paid work a week, which is a typical teaching contract anyway, for up to one year. Possibilities exist for Americans who want to act as counsellors and activity leaders at English immersion summer camps in France, for example with companies like NACEL International (www.american-village.fr/en/recruitment/recruitmentnews.php) and Telligo (www.telligo.fr).

One American who did a TEFL training course in Paris describes the outcome of a well-organised job hunt:

*I went to Paris on the big TEFL job hunt, and thought I might share my advice on how to get a job. They say it's 'almost impossible' for Americans to get a work visa or a good job in France, and I'd like to prove that theory wrong. Come prepared. Get a TEFL certificate. Bring your birth certificate and CV in both French and English, handwritten cover letters in both languages, passport photos and college transcripts. On the third day of my search, I got an interview. A few days later, I showed up and got the job. Overall I'd say it was not **nearly** as bad as I was warned it would be. Of course, I had to go back to the US for three months to get my work visa, but there's no other way to do it, besides working illegally (something I wasn't willing to do).*

Another American, aged 22, took the student route, but doesn't mention what fees were payable for enrolling in a university. This advice is of use mainly to Americans who genuinely want to study for an MA:

Initially I decided to pursue a master's degree in a French university. Luckily, I had a professor who had studied at Paris III, so I emailed him and asked how I could apply, but if you contact the head of the department at any Parisian university and send a proposal (CV plus motivation letter), you can ask for an application. I started this process around March/April of last year for the fall semester. Getting accepted into a French university should not be too hard if you have a bachelor's degree. It helps to speak French, but if you don't, there may be some universities with French classes or you can consider an Anglophone university such as the American University in Paris. If and when you are accepted, you will receive a letter of enrolment with which you can apply for a visa in the States. Since you can only get a student visa before going to France, this letter is very important. I received this in about June/July. A law requires you to go through CampusFrance (www.campusfrance.org) for which you will probably need a translation of your diploma, etc. Applying for a student visa requires a lot of patience and setting up an appointment at the consulate weeks in advance. The important thing is never to get discouraged, have a lot of patience and remember – where there's a will, there's a way.

The website of the Speaking Agency mentioned above, which employs a large number of non-EU people on a part-time basis, has good information on the student visa route (just google 'Speaking Agency' and 'Sorbonne').

More questions on long-stay visas for studies will be answered on the French consulate website, for example at www.consulfrance-losangeles.org. One possibility open to some Americans with Irish or Greek ancestry is to obtain a passport from an EU member state. An easier route is to teach on a voluntary or occasional basis; or you can always work on the 'black market', which is not really easy or advisable, but is something that the French, as well as foreigners, continue to do all the same. A long-time Nice-based expat offers an advisory service to prospective incomers on legal and financial questions and charges transparent fees; her website www.monamiandy.com relaunched September 2015.

CONDITIONS OF WORK

Teaching 'beezneezmen' is not everyone's cup of tea, but it can be less strenuous than other kinds of teaching. Provided you do not feel intimidated by your students' polished manners and impeccable dress, and can keep them entertained, you will probably be a success. As mentioned above, one-to-one teaching is increasingly common – with some schools in Paris it constitutes 70% of their business – for which ELT training (including the CELTA or Trinity Certificate) does not prepare you. However, if you develop a rapport with your client, this kind of teaching can be most enjoyable as **Sara Breese** describes:

> *I have enjoyed teaching as most of my students are adults who have chosen to take English classes, either for pleasure or to advance their career. The majority of them are nice and very motivated, thus making my job a pleasure. The teaching is mostly one-on-one and you are allowed to teach in whichever style you please. I appreciate this freedom to be creative with my students. However, this freedom is becoming more and more rare as schools are imposing their personalised TEFL methods. I have friends who work for other companies and it makes them feel like robots repeating the same lesson over and over again. The only problems I have encountered in my time as a teacher have been in the planning. I am travelling constantly all over Paris which means your day is never dull, but also can make it rather stressful. As a mobile teacher I have to carry all of my teaching materials with me. I am often seen running through the metro with a backpack full of books, CDs and a stereo.*

Language schools which offer this facility to clients, especially those in small towns rather than big cities, may well expect you to drive, perhaps even own, a car so that you can give lessons in offices and other workplaces. Most schools pay between €18 and €25 (gross) per lesson.

Salaried teachers should be covered by a nationally agreed and widely enforced *Convention Collective*, which makes stable contracts, sick pay, holiday pay, etc compulsory as well as guaranteeing a monthly salary. Until a few years ago, there were two types of typical teaching contract with French language schools. The first was a CDD (*contrat à durée déterminée*), a fixed-length contract, and a CDI (*contrat à durée indéterminée*), an open-ended contract. This obliges employers to pay teachers for a minimum number of hours (typically 20), even when they don't have enough clients to create that much work, as during the economic crisis. This resulted in a number of schools going bust. To tackle this problem a new kind of contract has emerged and is becoming the norm: a CDII (*contrat à durée indéterminée intermittent*). This guarantees a low minimum such as 10 hours and pays an hourly rate for hours worked above that. A good language school should be able to allocate 20–25 hours a week to those who want them, but they are protected against paying for hours not taught when times are tough.

The annual holiday allowance for full-time teachers is five weeks plus an extra five days off. An unusual feature in France is that some schools calculate the salary according to a certain number of teaching hours per 9 or 12 months, and will pay overtime for hours worked in excess of this. Obviously the total can't be calculated until the end of the contract, which is a drawback for anyone considering leaving early.

Another legislated benefit when working for a French company is that between 24 and 150 paid hours a year must be released for training. As of 2014, employees can open a 'Personal Training Account' (*Compte Personnel de Formation* or CPF) online at www.moncompteformation.gouv.fr. **Sab Will** put this law to good use:

My TEFL Diploma was paid for this way. But once I got it my employer didn't give me an extra centime more for my efforts. The three of us who had done the diploma stayed the obligatory year after the qualification and then left. So the language school lost its three most qualified teachers. Language schools that pay significantly more for experience or advanced qualifications are rare beasts.

Telephone and internet teaching are popular for their convenience and anonymity, and a growing number of companies such as Phonalangue (www.phonalangue.fr/recrutement.php) and World Speaking affiliated to Berlitz (www.telelangue.com/en/about/careers) specialise in this and employ native-speaker trainers. For many people, making mistakes over the phone is less embarrassing than face-to-face, though the lack of personal contact is felt by some to be detrimental to the learning experience. Many have been surprised by the good results. It is not necessary to be able to speak French and possibly even an advantage to be monolingual, so you won't be tempted to break into French in frustration. The basic requirements for phone trainers are normally an address in France, education to university level and experience in business. The standard rate of pay for telephone teaching is about €17–€19 an hour.

Partly because of France's proximity to a seemingly inexhaustible supply of willing English teachers, working conditions in France are seldom brilliant. You can survive in France, and even Paris, on a typical 20-hour-a-week contract, but to live more than a basic existence you will need to supplement this with extra hours from somewhere else.

Although **Andrew Boyle** enjoyed his year teaching English in Lyon and the chance to become integrated into an otherwise impenetrable community, he concluded that even respectable schools treated teachers as their most expendable commodity. By contrast, **Fiona Paton** was well looked after and had no trouble finding a comfortable and affordable flat in Vichy (which is often easy in popular holiday resorts outside the summer season). Her impression was that flat-sharing is not as commonplace in France as in other countries.

EMILY SLOANE

Emily Sloane discovered that although the French do not often come across as the most approachable of people, having a slightly firmer sense of privacy than is common in some countries, they can be great company:

I joined the French Alpine Club, which had a thriving and spirited branch in my village. In addition to weekly indoor rock climbing sessions, I accompanied club members on various weekend hikes and climbing trips in the Jura and Vosges Mountains in France and Switzerland and even attended a 10-day climbing clinic in Northern Provence. Learning French climbing vocabulary while suspended 100 feet above the ground, when misunderstandings could have pretty serious consequences, was an experience I won't soon forget. The club members were fantastic people who generously shared the tight space of their homemade 'camping cars' and handcrafted liqueurs. I even convinced them to dress as Americans and speak English one night at the climbing wall. In return for their effort, I provided American snacks and music and a cheat sheet of useful American slang and insults that they enthusiastically tried out on each other. Through the club I even found my very own French lover, which proved to be the most efficient way to improve my language skills.

LIST OF EMPLOYERS

ANGLESEY LANGUAGE SERVICES (ALS)

1 bis, 3 Avenue du Maréchal Foch, 78400 Chatou

☎ +33 1 3480 6515

✉ als@alschatou.com

🖥 www.als-formationlangues.com

Company established 1978, located just outside Paris.

NUMBER OF TEACHERS: 50.

PREFERENCE OF NATIONALITY: Native speakers.

QUALIFICATIONS: CELTA plus 2 years of experience preferred but possibilities for trainees. Intermediate level or above in French an advantage. Ideally, teachers have a specialist area, such as finance or engineering. Car owner/driver an advantage.

CONDITIONS OF EMPLOYMENT: 10-month renewable contract. 15–25 hours per week. Pupils are adults and many are taught in their workplaces. Recent expansion, so group lessons at all levels offered in evenings and during the day. Some evening and Saturday work available.

SALARY: €18.50 per hour plus 12% on top for holiday pay. Travel expenses.

FACILITIES/SUPPORT: Some help with finding accommodation is available. No initial training but help with preparation provided plus ongoing professional development provided for teachers.

RECRUITMENT: Initial contact by email then one-to-one interviews held in school or in Anglesey (Wales).

CONTACT: Mike Webster.

APPLILANGUE

16 E rue du Cap Vert, 21800 Quetigny

☎ +33 3 8052 9898

✉ contact@appli-langue.com

🖥 www.appli-langue.com

NUMBER OF TEACHERS: 12+.

PREFERENCE OF NATIONALITY: None.

QUALIFICATIONS: TEFL diploma and/or business experience.

CONDITIONS OF EMPLOYMENT: Open-ended contracts. Hours of teaching between 8.30am and 7.30pm.

SALARY: €1,449 per month starting, less about 20% for contributions.

FACILITIES/SUPPORT: School has contact who rents rooms while teachers are looking for an apartment. Help given with work permit applications including recommending a registered translator.

RECRUITMENT: Spontaneous CVs, word of mouth from former teachers.

CONTACT: Karen Longley (karen.Longley@appli-langue.com).

ATRIBORD

62 bis rue des Peupliers, 92100 Boulogne Billancourt

☎ +33 1 46 10 94 40/3

✉ atribord@atribord.com

🖥 www.atribord.com

NUMBER OF TEACHERS: 33 business language teachers (all languages).

PREFERENCE OF NATIONALITY: None.

QUALIFICATIONS: Degree and TEFL needed plus good experience or real initiative (ideally both). Teachers should be able to go into companies and talk to their students as equals, sensitive to the demands of professional life.

CONDITIONS OF EMPLOYMENT: Open-ended contract. 15–25 hours of work a week depending on availability.

SALARY: €20–€30 an hour depending on experience.

FACILITIES/SUPPORT: No accommodation or visa help.

RECRUITMENT: Local ads e.g. FUSAC and interviews.

CONTACT: Niall Bickersteth, Partner.

BABYLANGUES

19 rue Pavée, 75004 Paris

☎ +33 1-42 74 23 34

✉ recruitment@babylangues.com

🖥 www.job-in-france.babylangues.com

Operates in Bordeaux, Lyon, Lille and Nantes as well as Paris.

NUMBER OF TEACHERS: 450 per year.

PREFERENCE OF NATIONALITY: None.

QUALIFICATIONS: Instructors must be native English speakers and must have had some professional experience working with children. No minimum level of French and no teaching experience are required, as instructors receive free training in Babylangues' innovative methodology.

CONDITIONS OF EMPLOYMENT: Normally 1 academic year (September–June). Minimum stay is 4 months covering one semester. Flexible hours from 5 to 25 a week, based around instructors' availabilities. Usual slots are weekdays 4pm–8pm and Wednesday/Saturday 9am–5pm.

SALARY: €10.45–€16.50 net per hour.

FACILITIES/SUPPORT: Free medical check-up and possibility of full free coverage by French Social Security. Instructors receive a list of recommended rental agencies and websites for searching for accommodation. Babylangues does not sponsor visas for non-EU applicants.

RECRUITMENT: Adverts on FUSAC. Ongoing recruitment via video-conferences. If successful at this stage, candidates must also attend a meeting with the agency in France, to finalise paperwork, confirm availability and receive their teaching schedules.
CONTACT: Mathias Benoit-Levy, Director.

LE BUS BILINGUE

2 bus Rue Jules Breton, Paris 75013
+33 782 75 41 67
jobs@busbilingue.com
www.lebusbilingue.com

NUMBER OF TEACHERS: 25.
PREFERENCE OF NATIONALITY: None, though so far all teachers have had the legal right to work in France.
QUALIFICATIONS: Experience teaching children aged between 3 and 12 years at a school, as a private tutor, etc. Teacher training would be ideal: TEFL, PGCE, etc.
CONDITIONS OF EMPLOYMENT: Rolling contracts with no fixed end point. 5-8 hours per week.
SALARY: €25 (gross) per hour. Deduction for tax and social security is 21% (which means net wage is less than €20).
FACILITIES/SUPPORT: Advice given on accommodation.
RECRUITMENT: Mainly via FUSAC, personal recommendations and word of mouth. 2-stage interview process whereby the candidate is interviewed by two members of the Bus Bilingue team and later observed in a classroom/lesson setting.
CONTACT: Ruth Skitt, Assistant Director (rskitt@busbilingue.com).

BUSINESS & TECHNICAL LANGUAGES

82 blvd Haussmann, 75008 Paris
+33 1 4293 4545
recrute@btl.fr
www.webbtl.com/fr

NUMBER OF TEACHERS: 70.
PREFERENCE OF NATIONALITY: British citizens for seconded contracts. EU citizen or candidate with working authorisation secured.
QUALIFICATIONS: TEFL training/experience, excellent communication skills, English mother tongue or equivalent are all needed. Business experience, good IT skills and French a definite plus.
CONDITIONS OF EMPLOYMENT: Full-time posts are available as well as part-time, and may include extensive travelling around greater Paris to meet up with clients.
SALARY: On application.
FACILITIES/SUPPORT: Homestay accommodation is arranged for the first 2 weeks, while teacher looks for accommodation. No help with work permits.
CONTACT: Shelli Chavet, Head of Pedagogical Coordination.

CITYLANGUES

Bât. C, Le Triangle de l'Arche, 11, cours du Triangle, Le Faubourg de l'Arche, Secteur Arche Nord, 92937 Paris La Défense Cedex; also 8 rue Louis Blériot, 92500 Rueil Malmaison
+33 1 5591 9670 (La Défense) and +33 1 4749 7946 (Rueil Malmaison)
ms@citylangues.com
www.citylangues.com

NUMBER OF TEACHERS: 25 for business clientele.
PREFERENCE OF NATIONALITY: None, but employ only teachers resident in Paris with French working papers.
QUALIFICATIONS: Degree and TEFL certificate.
CONDITIONS OF EMPLOYMENT: Teaching represents 72% of total paid hours as per French law.
SALARY: According to profile, graded accorded to experience.
FACILITIES/SUPPORT: No assistance with accommodation. Training available in how the French system works, emphasis on team work in school.
RECRUITMENT: Local interviews essential. Adverts on FUSAC.
CONTACT: Stefan Wheaton, president of the Language Commission of the French Training Federation.

ENGLISH POINT

Head Office: 14E rue Pierre de Coubertin, Parc de Mirande, Dijon 21000
+33 820 626064
t.holland@englishpoint.fr
www.englishpoint.fr

NUMBER OF TEACHERS: 14.
PREFERENCE OF NATIONALITY: British, New Zealander, American, Canadian, South African.
QUALIFICATIONS: Preferably a CELTA or equivalent and/or significant teaching experience plus business work experience. The majority of courses are business-based so knowledge of how a business works is essential. Also, being an objectives-based school you should be able to think from the client's perspective and adapt your teaching accordingly.
CONDITIONS OF EMPLOYMENT: Contracts are from 3 months – permanent. Teaching hours 8am–9pm, Monday–Friday (possible Saturday mornings).
SALARY: €20–24 per hour depending on age/experience/flexibility etc.

153

FACILITIES/SUPPORT: School can help find accommodation for teachers, from organising viewings to full accommodation management.

RECRUITMENT: Through websites, training schools, word of mouth, etc. Telephone interviews essential followed by face-to-face meeting.

CONTACT: Tony Holland, Director.

FONTAINEBLEAU LANGUES & COMMUNICATION

47 Boulevard Marechal Foch, 77300 Fontainebleau

✆ +33 1 6422 4896

🖰 recruitment@flc-int.com or dianne.riboh@flc-int.com

💻 www.flc-int.com

NUMBER OF TEACHERS: 12 English teachers, 35 in total.

PREFERENCE OF NATIONALITY: British/Irish. Australians, Canadians and Americans or other native English speakers with EU citizenship or French working papers.

QUALIFICATIONS: TEFL training (eg CELTA). Must be dynamic, creative, versatile and able to work in a team. Previous business experience a plus.

CONDITIONS OF EMPLOYMENT: 1 year minimum. Majority of teaching takes place in company premises so owning a car is necessary (transport costs reimbursed at €0.45 approx. per km). Variety of teaching situations including groups, one-to-one lessons and Business English. Hours are grouped as much as possible between 9am and 7pm, Monday to Friday.

SALARY: Starting at €19 per hour which includes 12% holiday pay. Social security deductions are about 22%.

FACILITIES/SUPPORT: Training workshops held regularly. Large teachers' library.

RECRUITMENT: Interview essential – usually by phone.

ICB EUROPE

45 rue d'Aboukir, 75002 Paris

✆ +33 1 4455 3831

🖰 declankehoe@icbeurope.com

💻 www.icbeurope.com

NUMBER OF TEACHERS: 50 full-time and part-time.

PREFERENCE OF NATIONALITY: None but native English speaker.

QUALIFICATIONS: Prefer candidates who are TEFL/TESOL/CELTA qualified with a couple of years of business experience, ideally within the financial/insurance sectors. Working use of French needed. Excellent presentation and communication skills.

CONDITIONS OF EMPLOYMENT: Open-ended contracts. Trainers who can stay for at least 1 year are preferred. To teach during normal office hours Monday to Friday.

SALARY: Trainers who are available at all times can be guaranteed 800 teaching hours a year with an average remuneration of about €1,600 per month plus a monthly bonus programme based on student satisfaction and lesson observations. 21% deductions for tax and social security.

FACILITIES/SUPPORT: No assistance given with visas or accommodation.

RECRUITMENT: Adverts in FUSAC. Group interview involves candidates introducing themselves, a grammar test and some group discussion about different teaching techniques. If successful at this stage the candidate then goes on to have a one-to-one interview with the owner of ICB Europe, Eric Wrobley.

CONTACT: Declan Kehoe, Recruitment Manager/Résponsable Pédagogique.

ILC FRANCE (INTERNATIONAL LANGUAGE CENTRE)

13 Passage Dauphine, 75006 Paris

✆ +33 1 4441 8020

🖰 info@ilcfrance.com

💻 www.ilcfrance.com/recrutement

NUMBER OF TEACHERS: 34.

QUALIFICATIONS: CELTA or approved equivalent. Experience of business world essential.

CONDITIONS OF EMPLOYMENT: Teaching hours between 8.30am and 7pm. Contracts according to French labour laws. 80% of teaching is in-company.

SALARY: Variable according to contract.

FACILITIES/SUPPORT: Assistance with finding accommodation, teacher development and training. ILC offers full-time and part-time CELTA courses (see Training chapter).

RECRUITMENT: Spontaneous CVs and local adverts, although priority given to IH network. Interviews in Paris essential.

CONTACT: Marlene Regaya, Director (marlene.regaya@ilcfrance.com).

INLINGUA PARIS

109 rue de l'Université, 75007 Paris

✆ +33 1 4551 4660/4946 1501

🖰 inlinguaparis@inlinguaparis.com

💻 www.inlinguaparis.com

NUMBER OF TEACHERS: Many teachers for corporate students required for seven branches in Paris area (others at Bastille, La Défense, Roissy, Etoile, Vélizy and Saint-Denis).

PREFERENCE OF NATIONALITY: None.

QUALIFICATIONS: TEFL plus minimum 2 years' experience preferably with professional adults. Preferred minimum age 25. Candidates must be creative, independent, flexible, of excellent appearance and with a good cultural background.

CONDITIONS OF EMPLOYMENT: Minimum 12 months; open-ended contracts. Flexible hours, with guaranteed minimum, mostly 20–30 hours per week.

FACILITIES/SUPPORT: Assistance with accommodation, work permits and training possible.

RECRUITMENT: Adverts in FUSAC. Interviews essential in France.

CONTACT: Philippe Fouque, General Manager.

LINGUARAMA

Tour Eve, 7è étage, 1 Place du Sud, La Défense 9, 92806 Puteaux Cedex

+33 1 4773 0095

paris@linguarama.com

www.linguarama.com

NUMBER OF TEACHERS: 30.

PREFERENCE OF NATIONALITY: Native speakers with working papers for the EU.

QUALIFICATIONS: Recognised TEFL qualification (CELTA or Trinity Cert) plus 1 year's teaching experience required. Driving licence useful.

CONDITIONS OF EMPLOYMENT: Full-time teachers work 25 hours per week September to June. Part-time teachers work flexible hours. Teaching is Business English, taught in-company and at school.

SALARY: Approx. €1,725 per month.

FACILITIES/SUPPORT: Advice on finding accommodation. Regular training available.

RECRUITMENT: Via Linguarama in England and also locally.

CONTACT: Jo Dennison, Pedagogical Manager (JoDennison@linguarama.com).

PARIS CORPORATE LANGUAGE CENTER

59 rue Meslay, 75003 Paris

+33 1 5301 8150

otilghman@parisclc.com

www.parisclc.com

NUMBER OF TEACHERS: 15 (10 in Paris).

PREFERENCE OF NATIONALITY: Native speaker, with working papers for France.

QUALIFICATIONS: TEFL/CELTA/TESOL certificate and observed teaching experience.

CONDITIONS OF EMPLOYMENT: Minimum 1 year. CDI (open-ended contract). Approximately 25 teaching hours a week.

SALARY: To be discussed at interview.

FACILITIES/SUPPORT: No assistance with accommodation or work permits.

RECRUITMENT: Adverts in FUSAC and other sites. Face-to-face interviews in Paris are essential. For positions outside Paris, telephone interviews are held.

CONTACT: Olivia Tilghman-Osborne, Director of Methodology.

SPEAKING AGENCY / BABY-SPEAKING

27 rue du Chemin Vert, 75011 Paris

+33 1 8395 4176; +33 6 6218 8624

developpement@speaking-agency.com; paris.recruitment@speaking-agency.com; paris.recruitment@baby-speaking.fr

www.speaking-agency.com; www.baby-speaking.fr

Babysitting and teaching positions with French families in Paris, Lyon, Lille, Bordeaux, Nantes, Toulouse, Montpellier, Nice and Aix-en-Provence.

NUMBER OF TEACHERS: Up to 500 live-out part-time tutoring positions from autumn, 200 from January; up to 1,000 altogether. To work either with young children aged 3–12 or older children 12–18.

PREFERENCE OF NATIONALITY: Applicants must be native speakers and EU citizens or hold a student/working holiday/working visa for France.

QUALIFICATIONS: No specific diploma is required but applicants need to have experience in working with children (babysitting and/or tutoring). No minimum level of French language is required. Minimum age 18.

CONDITIONS OF EMPLOYMENT: Minimum stay 4 months. Starting September/October or January. All part-time positions. Flexible work schedules: 'Baby-speakers' choose the number of hours they want to work according to their availability, normally between 5 and 20 per week. Tutors for older children work 2–8 hours per week.

SALARY: Mostly €10–€12.50 per hour. For tutoring positions of adolescents, the range is €13–€20 per hour, depending on the number of children, location and the number of hours worked.

FACILITIES/SUPPORT: No accommodation provided, although agency has partnership with residences which offers a discount. Selected applicants are trained in an innovative early language acquisition method developed by specialists in child bilingualism.

This counts as a declared job in France so tutors are entitled to French health insurance.

RECRUITMENT: Online application to HR Team. Skype interviews.

SYNDICAT MIXTE MONTAIGU-ROCHESERVIERE
35 Avenue Villebois, Mareuil, 85607 Montaigu
- +33 2 5146 4545
- anglais@sm-montaigu-rocheserviere.fr
- www.gapyear-france.com

NUMBER OF TEACHERS: 5.

PREFERENCE OF NATIONALITY: British.

QUALIFICATIONS: Ages 18–26. Experience of and interest in teaching and a love of France.

CONDITIONS OF EMPLOYMENT: Standard contract length 9 months, to teach 20 hours per week.

SALARY: €207 per month.

FACILITIES/SUPPORT: Accommodation provided with local host families/resident project coordinator.

RECRUITMENT: Interview essential, possibly in UK or in France (Vendée April–June).

CONTACT: Julie Legrée, Project Coordinator.

TELAB LANGUAGE COURSES BY TELEPHONE
3 Place de la Poste, 71520 Tramayes
- +33 3 8550 5858
- s.evans@telab.com
- www.telab.com

Specialises in teaching English by phone.

NUMBER OF TEACHERS: 60.

PREFERENCE OF NATIONALITY: None but must be native English speaker, resident in France and with necessary working papers.

QUALIFICATIONS: Language teaching qualifications (TEFL or equivalent), at least 2 years' experience in teaching languages to company employees, work experience in or knowledge of a specific field (eg marketing, finance, medical, technical, etc), excellent communication abilities, independent, organised and rigorous at work. Must have a computer and know how to use the internet.

CONDITIONS OF EMPLOYMENT: Teachers work from home, flexible hours between 7am and 9pm. There is a trend for more teachers to work full-time rather than part-time.

FACILITIES/SUPPORT: Assistance given with social security registration (about 20% of gross salary is taken at source as contributions). No help with work permits or accommodation.

RECRUITMENT: Referrals, internet, press. CVs can be faxed to +33 1 3080 4458.

CONTACT: Emmanuel Fays (e.fays@telab.com).

TLC – THE TURNER LEARNING CENTER
33&62 rue des Renaudes, 75017 Paris
- +33 1 8364 5400
- job@tlc-fr.com
- www.tlc-fr.com/job

NUMBER OF TEACHERS: 40.

PREFERENCE OF NATIONALITY: Native English speakers.

QUALIFICATIONS: University qualification, TEFL or CELTA trained, appreciation for corporate English, experience of ESOL exams preferred and for some courses fluent French is needed. Non-EU citizens must have a French work permit valid until the end of the academic year.

CONDITIONS OF EMPLOYMENT: 10-month contract September to the end of June. 10–25 hours a week of classes, depending on their specialism, experience and availability, though most teach 12–15 hours. TLC offers most of its lessons, some in clients' homes, between 5pm and 7.30pm, with all day Wednesday and Saturday possibilities. Timetabling is compatible with teachers already working in the French school system as well as the corporate English sector.

SALARY: Teachers working for TLC hold either a CDI work contract or, if they wish, are registered as independent. The CDI contract includes French national health insurance with an attractive hourly wage bringing the net salary up to a possible €21 an hour, depending on experience, qualifications, quality and promptness of class reporting, completion of contract and training attendance if deemed necessary. Independent teachers have the same wage conditions but can see their hourly rate reach €32 because they pay their own contributions. They must provide TLC with an *attestation de vigilance* every trimester ensuring that they have settled their social taxes, which provides them with social insurance coverage.

FACILITIES/SUPPORT: No assistance with accommodation or work permits.

RECRUITMENT: Monthly hiring drives. Adverts online and in magazines. Timetable of application and interview dates is posted at www.tlc-Fr.com/job. Skype interview in first instance then face-to-face interview in Paris.

CONTACT: Marina Duchêne, General Manager.

TRANSFER

15 rue de Berri, 75008 Paris

+33 1 5669 2230

info@transfer.fr

www.transfer.fr

Also: 20 rue Godot de Mauroy, 75009 Paris.

NUMBER OF TEACHERS: 90.

PREFERENCE OF NATIONALITY: None.

QUALIFICATIONS: Either professional or technical experience (law, finance, etc) or solid teaching experience, Cambridge CELTA or similar qualification and degree.

CONDITIONS OF EMPLOYMENT: Short-term, long-term or permanent. Teaching takes place generally from 9am to 6pm and some evenings.

SALARY: On application. About 20% deducted for tax and social security.

FACILITIES/SUPPORT: Americans must have their own work papers as no assistance is given with arranging these.

RECRUITMENT: Application and CV. Interview.

CONTACT: Marian Casey (mcasey@transfer.fr).

WALL STREET INSTITUTE

www.wallstreetinstitute.fr/recrutement

NUMBER OF TEACHERS: Varies; 58 franchised branches (addresses can be found on website). Largest ones are in Paris (with 6 branches), Amiens, Reims, Orleans and French Riviera.

PREFERENCE OF NATIONALITY: EU or with valid working papers.

QUALIFICATIONS: CELTA or TESOL certificate. BA or 2+ years' teaching experience.

CONDITIONS OF EMPLOYMENT: Permanent contracts offered. To work part-time hours or full-time if necessary up to 136 hours per month.

SALARY: €1,470 per month plus bonuses; €16 per hour.

RECRUITMENT: Via local advertising and the internet, eg in FUSAC. Online application procedure via recruitment site www.keljob.com.

CONTACT: HR Manager, 2 Patio de la Pyramide, Puteaux 92800; +33 1 5813 8964; recrutement@wsiparis.com.

GERMANY

The excellent state education system in Germany ensures that a majority of Germans have such a good grounding in English that very little teaching is done at the beginner level. If German students want exposure to a native speaker they are far more likely to enrol in a language summer course in Britain than sign up for extra tuition at a local institute. Furthermore, many secondary schools in Germany employ native speakers of English to assist in classrooms (programme details below). English is also offered at *Volkshochschulen* or adult education centres where various subsidised courses are run.

Cities in the former East Germany such as Leipzig, Dresden and Erfurt are less popular destinations for job-seeking teachers than Munich, Berlin and Freiburg, and may therefore afford more opportunities, especially since provision of English in the schools lags slightly behind that of Western Germany.

The greatest demand for English in Germany continues to come from the business and professional community, and with the continuing strength of the German economy, demand for English has held up well. Throughout the country the language teaching scene is remarkably stable. That does not mean that it is easy to walk into a job. Most firms that send English trainers into companies work with a stable list of expat freelancers resident in Hanover or Munich or wherever it is. However, highly paid in-company positions for EFL and ESP teachers can still be found, and the agencies and consultancies which supply teachers to business clients have increased the number of native-speaker freelance teachers they recruit. Demand is greatest outside cities such as Munich, where teachers complain about a lack of work.

PROSPECTS FOR TEACHERS

Many of the companies that market in-company English courses are desperate for good teachers and trainers, though there is no shortage of inexperienced teachers looking for teaching opportunities. Any graduate with a background in economics or business who can speak German has a good chance of finding work in a German city. A TEFL certificate and a university degree have less clout than relevant experience, as **Kevin Boyd** found when he arrived with his brand new Cambridge certificate at the beginning of the academic year:

> *I was persuaded by a teaching friend to go to Munich with him to try to get highly paid jobs together. As he spoke some German and had about a year's teaching experience, he got a job straightaway. Every school I went to in Munich just didn't want to know as I couldn't speak German and only had four weeks' teaching experience. After two days of this I decided to try my luck in Italy.*

Experience in business is often a more desirable qualification than an ELT qualification. The question is not so much whether you know what a past participle is but whether you know what an 'irrevocable letter of credit' or a 'bank giro' is. Many schools offer *Oberstufe*, advanced or specialist courses in, for example, Banking English, Business English, or for bilingual secretaries, etc. Full-time, vocationally oriented courses in languages for business and commerce are called *Berufsfachschule* and this is by far the most buoyant part of the market. Cambridge or Trinity Certificates or even a Diploma are not regarded as appropriate training for any of these. However, the more serious schools and the regional English Language Teachers' Associations (ELTAs) have been moving to professionalise the industry and to offer and require more training in ELT skills. Qualifications such as a degree in physics may also impress and lead to scientific translation work, according to **Penny**, a teacher in Berlin.

Very few schools are willing to consider candidates who can't speak any German. Although the 'direct method' (ie total immersion in English) is in use everywhere, the pupils may expect you to be able to explain things in German. Penny was not put off so easily:

At the beginning they all expected me to talk to them in German. True to my CELTA training I insisted on English except in emergencies and they got used to it!

If the school prepares its students for the London Chamber of Commerce exams (LCCI), the teacher will be expected not only to understand the syllabus but to interpret and teach it with confidence. There is still a preference for British English, but the increasing number of course participants working for global or American companies prefer Canadian/American English.

Fees charged to companies by the most established and specialist teachers and trainers can be very high, which means few openings occur in this sought-after sector. These teachers also have high overheads and a staggeringly large percentage of their incomes will disappear in compulsory contributions (described below) and expenses. One further requirement of many employers is a driving licence, so that teachers can travel easily from one off-site assignment to another.

FINDING A JOB

Up to 300 posts as English-language classroom assistants are available at secondary schools throughout Germany. Applications are encouraged from students who have at least AS level, Higher Grade or equivalent in German. UK applicants should contact the Language Assistants Team at the British Council (assistants@britishcouncil.org; www.britishcouncil.org/language-assistants/become/germany). The salary is €800 a month (net) for 12 hours of work a week, unchanged for many years. Language assistants such as **Sarah Davies** (who was sent to a small town in the east) advise against agreeing to teach in a small village where conditions may be basic and the sense of isolation strong.

Other nationalities can also participate through Pädagogischer Austauschdienst (PAD; www.kmk-pad. org). About 140 American students and graduates are accepted as English Teaching Assistants through the Fulbright Program (administered by the Institute of International Education, 809 UN Plaza, New York, NY 10017-3580). Candidates planning to go on to become teachers of German are strongly preferred; contractual arrangements are as above plus help with travel and insurance.

Like so many embassies, the German Embassy in London is not noted for its helpful attitude to aspiring teachers or other job-seekers. Apart from directing students to enquire about the exchange programme run by the British Council and providing addresses of the state ministries of education, it recommends applying to the Zentrale Auslands-und Fachvermittlung (International Placement Services), ZAV, part of the German Federal Employment Agency (Villemombler Strasse 76, 53123 Bonn; +49 228 713 1313; zav@arbeitsagentur.de). All applications from abroad are handled by this office. Although people of any nationality can apply through the ZAV, only citizens of old EU countries (who have German language skills) are entitled to expect the same treatment as a German. As usual, it is much more difficult to arrange a job by sending written applications and CVs from the UK than by presenting yourself in person to language school directors and training companies, CV in hand. Determination, qualifications, experience and being on the spot are often deciding factors when an employer has to choose between large numbers of similarly qualified applicants.

The best source of language school addresses is once again the *Yellow Pages* (*Gelbe Seiten*), which can be consulted online (www.gelbeseiten.de), or try www.goyellow.de and search for *Sprachschulen*. Another way of accessing potential employers is via the local English Language Teachers Association, a branch of which can be found in most major cities. The Munich branch (MELTA) is especially vigorous and carries a few job vacancies and a page of employers (www.melta.de/jobs-listing). There is also a forum for English teachers in Germany, including advice for newbies, which can be found at http://elt.yuku.com. Look for English-language magazines aimed at expats and you may come across some relevant adverts.

All the major language school chains have a significant presence in Germany including Berlitz, 34 of whose schools were advertising vacancies for native English speaker instructors at the time of writing (June

2015), Inlingua (with 70 training centres), Linguarama, specialising in language training for business in a number of cities, and Wall Street Institute, which keeps expanding. Rates of pay vary, however. Some employers pay inexperienced teachers in the range of €12–€16 for a 45-minute lesson, whereas more senior positions are paid €18–€30+ an hour.

Throughout Germany, more than 2,000 adult education centres or *Volkshochschulen* teach the English language (among many other courses) to adults. Native speakers with teaching experience might find a role within the Deutscher Volkshochschul-Verband e.V (www.vhs.de).

One of the easiest entrées to the TEFL world is as a tutor on a language summer camp. These have mushroomed in Germany, and take on lots of native speakers to help kids improve their English through interactive play, sports, music, etc during the school holidays. Try for example:

Berlitz Kids: www.berlitz.de. See entry in List of Employers.

Camp Adventure: www.campadventure.de. English camps in various locations. Instructors must be over 19 year old and have training.

LEOlingo Sprachcamps: www.leo-lingo.de. See entry in List of Employers.

Oskar Lernt Englisch: www.oskar-lernt-englisch.de. Native-speaker teachers and counsellors should have a working knowledge of German and an *Erweitertes polizeiliches Führungszeugnis* (enhanced police clearance less than six months old).

Penguin Camp: www.penguincamp.de. See entry in List of Employers.

Sphairos: +49 89 187 03156; www.sphairos.de. They claim on their Facebook page that their 'melting pot' of teachers have 'charm and vigour'.

Sprachcamp Allgäu: www.sprachcamp-allgaeu.de. Looking for native English speakers also interested in outdoor education.

Sunflower Sprachcamps: www.sunflower-sprachcamps.eu. See entry in List of Employers.

The summer of 2013 was **Sarah Paschke**'s third summer of working for LEOlingo in Bavaria. She first applied after finishing her degree in the US when she knew she wanted to live in Europe and had to find something to justify this decision to her father. So she googled 'summer camps', knowing that she wanted to work for a small personal outfit rather than one of the giant language camp companies. To further overcome her parents' possible objections, she wanted to find a summer job that paid a wage and would assist with the visa issue:

LEOlingo was delightful and timely in the application process. A couple of the 'megas' sent automated rejection replies to my email account or I never received any word back at all. After sending my résumé and questionnaire, a Skype interview was scheduled within a matter of two weeks. I had a background of teaching and tutoring youth; however, nothing with the intensive responsibilities of directing children 24/7. When I was applying around Europe, I was disappointed that so few employers offered a wage in addition to accommodation and food. LEOlingo pays well and gives you accommodation and food, which allowed me to save money to travel after camp.

The LEOlingo programme is a balance of language games, sports and crafts to keep the campers engaged, excited and interested in the topics. From writing and acting mini-dramas, to playing a camp-wide game of Capture the Flag, there is little time for campers to be bored! I knew it was going to be demanding, a high-energy and 'on-top-of-your-game' sort of job, and I was up for that challenge. LEOlingo really pushed me to interact with the German culture from the start since from the start we were staying with German host families in town. I don't speak German so I was lucky to have a family that knew English and was equally interested in me as I was in them. I still keep in contact with my host family and go to visit them a couple times a year when I can. Encounters with my pupils were always unpredictable, and they never failed to amaze me. Germans in general have a higher knowledge and capacity to learn English. Schools teach it well and the students at the summer camps are highly motivated and intrigued by the LEOlingo staff. Last summer my fellow teachers and counsellors represented all but two English-speaking countries. The highlight of camp is the correspondence between cultures, whether it is between counsellor and camper, or counsellor and counsellor. I learned so much about my own culture.

After her first summer as a LEOlingo teacher, Sarah decided to get her TEFL certification and then went on to teach in the Czech Republic, for which the training and experience in Germany were invaluable. Several other LEOlingo staff, Brandon Howard from the US and Laura Nichol from Bristol, also wrote to say how much they had enjoyed their summer employment in Bavaria.

INTERVIEWS

Most schools and institutes in Germany cannot, under normal operating circumstances, hire someone unseen merely on the basis of his/her CV and photo. Applicants should arrange for a face-to-face interview and should be prepared to make themselves available at a moment's notice. Professional presentation is even more important for securing work in the German business world than elsewhere. Vacancies occur throughout the year since businessmen and women are just as likely to start a course in April as in September. Germans tend to be formal, so dress appropriately and be aware of your manners at an interview. Also good references (*Zeugnisse*) are essential.

A good starting place is Frankfurt am Main, sometimes nicknamed 'Bankfurt' or 'Mainhattan'. Frankfurt has the highest concentration of major banks and financial institutions in the country and a correspondingly high number of private language schools. It is helpful, though not essential, to have some basic knowledge of German and business experience. In a job interview with a language school director, demonstrating a detailed knowledge of a handful of commonly used textbooks may be more important than business experience.

You can also impress a potential employer by showing some familiarity with current major German business news (bank mergers, etc). This can be done by following the financial news on Bloomberg or downloading the BBC's *World Business Report*. Language schools are looking for teachers who can pose intelligent questions to business students about their jobs. There is a considerable demand from the business community for guidance on conducting 'small talk' in English, which is crucial in building rapport with clients and colleagues.

NINO HUNTER

Nino Hunter decided to go to Berlin, a city which is both exquisitely trendy and reassuringly relaxed, and one that appeals most to people in search of European culture at its finest. Despite his recent degree in Modern languages from the University of Bath, he found it a struggle.

I did find it extremely difficult to find teaching posts in Berlin. I think the main reason would be the sheer number of English speakers in Berlin, many of whom wish to stay in this amazing city. Given the lack of industry, they have little alternative but to fall back on teaching English, with or without a CELTA/TEFL certificate. The English community is huge in Berlin (check Toytown Berlin at www.toytowngermany.com/berlin which has new postings every day). There are of course a huge number of schools in Berlin but given the number of teachers and the decreasing demand over the last two years due to the global economic crisis many of them have become exceptionally picky about who they choose to take on, often asking for at least two years' experience, etc. There was a particular demand for English teachers able to teach advanced students (Cambridge levels 1 and 2) and a few schools simply wouldn't take people on who didn't have experience teaching higher level students.

All of which means that the market in Berlin is extremely saturated and sending a CV off to each and every school usually doesn't help. The best way of finding teaching positions in the city is putting on a suit and going to the schools with a CV, introducing yourself and trying your hardest not to get fobbed off by a secretary, but rather to get an actual interview where they offer you a course. This obviously requires a little courage and a fair amount of energy but is the only way of being sure your CV isn't deleted immediately and is in fact the only way I or any of my colleagues got jobs at private language schools.

The teachers at the Berlin School of English where I did my CELTA course assured me that no one would pay less than €15 for 45 minutes to a teacher with a CELTA. My first school paid me just €12 and it took me 10 weeks to get up to €14, which was not at all uncommon.

Two pieces of advice I could give would be firstly to try to get on the lists for the Volkshochschulen (I think there are about seven in Berlin), as these pay more (if you have a university degree even more) and the classes are large and quite fun. I would also recommend joining ELTABB (English Language Teacher's Association (www.eltabb.com/main/index.php) which costs €40 a year but is undoubtedly the best place to network and sometimes perfect positions come up. Basically one needs to be as proactive as possible and not be too fussy. If Wall Street or Berlitz offers you a course, take it.

Last year a British teacher newly arrived in Berlin set up a blog https://teachingenglishinberlin.wordpress.com with tips on job-hunting and settling into the city plus ideas for lesson-planning.

FREELANCE TEACHING

The majority of native speakers teaching for commercial institutes are not on contracts, but are employed on a freelance basis (*Honorarvertrag*) to work for between two and 20 hours per week. Schools employing freelance teachers are not in a position to make deductions, because they cannot know a teacher's full expenses. Teachers may also work for several different schools. Freelance teachers are responsible for paying their own tax, pension insurance contributions and (crucially) health insurance.

Upon successful completion of a Trinity TESOL certificate course in England, **Ann Barkett** from Atlanta went to Munich to look for freelance work, but found it tough going:

During the period from December to March, I was putting up flyers for private and group lessons but received no response. I finally answered an advert for a private student whom I taught for a few weeks, but there just wasn't enough work or money coming in and I grew tired of trying at that point.

Many freelance teachers find themselves for the first time required to design an ESP course (English for Specific Purposes), individually tailored to the needs of their business students. **Nathan Edwards** found that he got better at this:

Experience has shown me that such a syllabus must be flexible, open to change and short-term adjustment so as to accommodate the complex and evolving needs of students who are also full-time working professionals. Students and their employers must be given the assurance of a clearly structured course outline, but this must be partly generated by an ongoing negotiated process with all the participants. Finally don't forget that the students themselves can be a valuable source of ESP course material such as authentic English email messages, business letters and company brochures from their offices.

REGULATIONS

EU citizens are free to travel to Germany to look for and take up work, but like all German nationals must register their address with the relevant district authority (*Einwohnermeldeamt*) or local *Bürgeramt* within a week of finding permanent accommodation. For this they will need proof that they are living locally, eg a copy of a contract with a landlord, and possibly proof of employment or funding. This office then liaises with the immigration authority, which issues a certificate of free movement, *EU-Freizuegigkeitsbescheinigung*, which isn't an absolute requirement but can be a useful bit of paper to have.

Useful guidance for the red tape affecting freelance teachers is available on the internet, for example on the relevant forums of ELTABB, MELTA, etc. Also try www.expatica.com/de/main.html and the Legal Guide to Germany at www.lg2g.info, which cover topics such as taxation, pensions and insurance.

NON-EU CITIZENS

Any non-EU citizen who wants to stay in Germany for more than the 90-day validity of a Schengen visa must obtain a residence permit (*Aufenthaltsgenehmigung*). Citizens of the USA, Australia, Canada, Israel, Japan, New Zealand and Switzerland may apply for a residence permit within a week of arrival in Germany. Citizens of other countries are required to obtain a visa prior to entry at a German embassy or consulate in their country of residence. Residence permits are handled by the local immigration office (*Ausländerbehörde*).

The normal procedures would be to find a job and to obtain a work permit before applying for a residence permit.

To apply for a work permit you need a valid passport, a letter from your employer stating what the position you have been offered is, what your projected income will be and the completed application form for a work permit. Once you have the work permit you can then apply for a residence permit, for which you will need:

- the completed application form
- valid official ID or passport
- an up-to-date passport photograph
- accommodation: proof of sufficient room for all members of the family and statement of rental costs (including heating, water and electricity) and mortgage (where applicable)
- work permit
- employees: proof of employment (written statement by employer or a contract)
- self-employed applicants: statement of registration of business
- proof of sufficient means to support yourself
- detailed statement and proof of regular income (wages for the past three months, wages of spouse and children, if they have an income)

- proof of health insurance in Germany
- students: statement of matriculation and proof of sufficient means to support yourself (a written statement from your parents stating they will support you is sufficient).

According to the Residence Act of 2004 (*Aufenthaltsgesetz* or *AufenthG*) that governs residence permits for non-EU citizens, applicants must prove that they have a secure and regular income, which is next to impossible for freelance teachers. The only exceptions are if you can show that you can invest at least one million euros and/or create at least 10 new jobs and/or prove that the business will benefit the region economically.

German immigration laws require discretionary decisions from the individual authorities, so prospects for non-EU freelancers will differ from region to region. Only a work permit which has been issued by the district/city you live in is valid.

American and Canadian students or recent graduates who find an employer while still in North America might seek advice on documentation from Cultural Vistas (formerly CDS International) in New York (www.culturalvistas.org), which can facilitate the red tape for individuals to work as interns in Germany for up to a year.

TAX, HEALTH INSURANCE AND SOCIAL SECURITY CONTRIBUTIONS

About 95% of all the EFL teaching work in language schools and companies in Germany is offered on a freelance or self-employed basis. The hourly rates you are offered might sound good, but freelancers and self-employed teachers lose roughly 40% after paying tax and contributions. A trainer-recruiter in a small town near Frankfurt succinctly described the trade-off: '*Germany is comparable to Scandinavia in that you can expect to lose 40%. . . However, for this you get great health cover, a pension and some of the best social support in the world.*' Half of stoppages are payments into the German pension scheme. This is a compulsory contribution for all freelance teachers regardless of whether they already have a private pension scheme. These 'expenses', plus tax and rent, mean that most hard-working teachers are left with very little disposable income. **Sylvia Weismiller**, Director of Euro-Lingua, based in Freiburg, writes:

> Yes, it's very complicated, and lots of grey areas, unenforced requirements, etc. One of my American teachers is having problems getting his permits renewed. They said if he paid his pension contributions, they would renew it. What those two have to do with each other is a mystery! However, I don't know any foreigners who pay it, even though it is an official policy. At the moment the responsible government offices are swamped with applications from Eastern Europe so it's a huge plus if the applicant has an EU passport.

Sylvia also mentions solidarity tax (about 5.5% of your income tax) and church tax (8%–9% of income tax), which you can avoid by registering as an atheist. However, medical insurance can be painful, particularly if you're a woman:

> Official health insurance depends on age, sex, etc. Also complicated. Women pay about double (for instance as a female in my 40s I was paying more than €400 per month). It doesn't depend on your income. If you are a registered student, however, you can get a much lower rate, I think €80 per month. As a student you can only work a limited number of hours, but as there aren't any tuition fees it's not a bad idea. There are also expat programmes which charge, I believe, €90 per month. They are limited to five years. You have to have health insurance to get your residence permit extended.

If you are a non-EU citizen you can ask the Deutsche Rentenversicherung (German pension authority) to repay the contributions you have made if you have paid into the state scheme for less than five years, ie have paid less than 60 pension contributions.

Foreigners working in Germany no longer need a physical tax card but must register with ELStAM (electronic PAYE).

CONDITIONS OF WORK

You can almost guarantee that you will be teaching adults except at summer camps, since school children receive such a high standard of English tuition at school. Contracts for full-time work are usually at least a year long, often with a three-month probation period. But it is rare to be *Angestellt*, ie fully employed by a school with guaranteed minimum hours, sick pay, holiday pay, etc.

Hourly rates can be high: typically €17–€25 per lesson and double that and more for established teachers of Business English. Off-site teaching hours often incur a premium of €2–€5 to compensate for travel time, or sometimes employers pay 'three hours for two'. Freelancers who earn high incomes have normally been in Germany a long time, speak excellent German and have invested in acquiring relevant specialisations, resources, materials, etc. They have built up their clientele and reputation over years and defend their patch with understandable vigour. The majority of newcomers gain their initial experience at franchise language schools where the pay is much lower, sometimes on a par with cleaners, and where poor working conditions and no job security prevail. A 30-hour working week could consist of 40 45-minute lessons, which would be a very heavy workload.

However, after walking into a tiny English school on her street in Berlin and asking the owner if she needed any help, Penny, a British widow in her 50s, built up an enviable client base. She describes her experiences in Berlin:

> *I do two classes a week, one in the morning and one in the evenings. The morning class is made up of retired ladies who come for fun and I have difficulty keeping them speaking English. I keep reminding them that I am being paid to teach them English and not to learn German from them. We have a good relationship and go out to the cinema occasionally. The members of the evening class are slightly more serious about learning English. Some of them sometimes join in the cinema outings.*
>
> *The classroom has a table with eight chairs, which limits the size of the class. There is a blackboard – I would dearly love a whiteboard – and a CD/tape player. Most of my work, however, is one-to-one teaching, which I originally obtained through the school. I charge €14 and pupils come to me. Now, many pupils are recommended by a former or current pupil, so I have several German-Russians and several art historians together with some business ladies – there is a big demand for Business English.*

Penny doesn't depend on her teaching, because otherwise her standard of living would be much lower than it is. If you are depending solely on one employer for your income try to find an institute which guarantees a monthly minimum number of hours. Monthly salaries for full-time *Angestellter* (employees) can be from €1,200 to €2,000 gross, with the possibility of paid overtime. Considering that a one-bedroom flat in one of the big cities can easily cost €450–€600 per month, excluding bills, salaries need to be high. Quite a few schools assist with accommodation. Teachers often turn to rental agencies, though their fees can be very steep, as much as two or three months rent plus VAT. Try answering ads on a classified ads website or the local *mitwohnzentralen*, which charges a more reasonable fee (usually one month's rent) for finding flats, though it may charge less if you end up renting a room or flat from owners who are temporarily absent. It is customary to pay your rent directly out of a bank account, so open a basic current account (*girokonto*) as early as you can. By law, the deposit you pay (usually three months' rent) is put in a bank account, which should be a joint savings account in the tenant's and landlord's name, so that neither can withdraw money without the approval of the other.

LIST OF EMPLOYERS

ACADEMY OF EUROPEAN LANGUAGES
Kölnstrasse 19, 53113 Bonn

✆ +49 228 242 5840

🖰 karriere@academy-bonn.de or
info@sprachakademie-bonn.de

💻 www.sprachakademie-bonn.de

NUMBER OF TEACHERS: 200 in most German cities.

PREFERENCE OF NATIONALITY: None.

QUALIFICATIONS: Advanced qualifications needed and much experience.

CONDITIONS OF EMPLOYMENT: Negotiable hours; open freelance contracts.

SALARY: €20+ for a 45-minute lesson.

FACILITIES/SUPPORT: Help can be given with accommodation and work permits if necessary.

RECRUITMENT: Personal recommendations.

CONTACT: Tony Westwood, Director (t.westwood@ sprachakademie-bonn.de).

BERLIN SCHOOL OF ENGLISH
Checkpoint Arkaden, Charlottenstrasse 81, 10969 Berlin

✆ +49 30 229 0455

🖰 info@berlin.school-of-english.de

💻 www.berlin.school-of-english.de

NUMBER OF TEACHERS: 30–40.

PREFERENCE OF NATIONALITY: None, but must be a native English speaker.

QUALIFICATIONS: University degree plus TEFL/CELTA Certificate and minimum 1 year's experience.

CONDITIONS OF EMPLOYMENT: Minimum 1 year on freelance basis. Between 16 and 30 hours per week. Focus on Business English and ESP in a diverse range of professions and industries.

SALARY: Details given at interview stage.

FACILITIES/SUPPORT: In-house training provided: accredited Cambridge CELTA Centre, regular teaching workshops and seminars, internet access for teachers, school library.

CONTACT: John Wills, School Manager (john.wills@berlin. school-of-english.de).

BERLITZ DEUTSCHLAND GmbH
Hahnstraße 68–70, 60528 Frankfurt

✆ +49 69 666 089 258

🖰 jobs@berlitz.de

💻 www.berlitz.de

Hiring is done locally by one of the 60+ schools in Germany. All contact information is linked from www.berlitz.de. At the time of writing, more than 30 Berlitz schools had vacancies but most were open to people already residing in the vicinity or having the required documents to work in Germany (visa and work permit).

NUMBER OF TEACHERS: Varies depending on the size of the language centre. Over 1,000 instructors employed in Germany.

PREFERENCE OF NATIONALITY: Native English speakers preferred.

QUALIFICATIONS: Teaching abilities, a professional attitude, good communication skills, willing to work a flexible schedule, and preferably have a business background.

CONDITIONS OF EMPLOYMENT: Open-ended, freelance contracts. Flexible hours between 8am and 9.30pm.

FACILITIES/SUPPORT: Training in the Berlitz Method given before start. Assistance with accommodation and work permits occasionally given.

RECRUITMENT: Adverts and personal referral.

CONTACT: Judith Schminke, Teamleader HR (judith.schminke@berlitz.de).

BERLITZ KIDS & TEENS – BERLITZ DEUTSCHLAND GmbH
Königin-Elisabeth Strasse 52, 14059 Berlin

✆ +49 30 3030 8479

🖰 laurie.castrocamargo@berlitz.de

💻 www.berlitz.de

NUMBER OF TEACHERS: 250.

PREFERENCE OF NATIONALITY: Native English speakers.

QUALIFICATIONS: Experience working with children aged 7–17 and also experience of teaching English preferred.

CONDITIONS OF EMPLOYMENT: Freelance work in English holiday camps during German school holidays (Easter 1–2 weeks, summer 4–8 weeks, autumn 2–4 weeks). Camp programmes run all day from 8am to 11pm.

SALARY: €450 per week. Freelancers have to deal with tax and health insurance independently.

FACILITIES/SUPPORT: No help with accommodation. If required an employer's letter of intent can be provided to non-EU citizens. Support will be given in dealing with the German authorities.

RECRUITMENT: Advertising in local magazines and word of mouth. Interviews are desirable and can be carried out over the telephone.

CONTACT: Laurie Camargo, Kids Director (Quality and Training).

CAMBRIDGE INSTITUT

Hildegardstr 8, 80539 Munich

☎ +49 89 221115

✎ info@cambridgeinstitut.de

🖥 www.cambridgeinstitut.de

NUMBER OF TEACHERS: Approximately 30.

PREFERENCE OF NATIONALITY: British.

QUALIFICATIONS: Formal teaching qualification essential, eg PGCE (preferably in modern languages).

CONDITIONS OF EMPLOYMENT: 11-month contracts, renewable for a further 11 months. 26 hours per week. Lessons 9am–11.45am and 5.30pm–9.10pm.

SALARY: €2,600 per month less social security and income tax payments.

FACILITIES/SUPPORT: Assistance with accommodation. Induction course and ongoing workshops.

RECRUITMENT: Interview in UK or Munich essential.

CONTACT: Philip Moore, Principal.

CONTEXT SPRACHEN – UND MEDIENDIENSTE

Elisenstr 4–10, 50667 Cologne

☎ +49 221 925 4560

✎ teaching@contextinc.com or office@contextinc.com

🖥 www.contextinc.com.

NUMBER OF TEACHERS: 15–20.

PREFERENCE OF NATIONALITY: None.

QUALIFICATIONS: Must be native English speakers with academic education and experience.

CONDITIONS OF EMPLOYMENT: Freelance basis. Hours vary between 8am and 8pm, Monday to Friday.

SALARY: Varies according to qualifications/experience and degree of difficulty of class taught.

FACILITIES/SUPPORT: Accommodation and visas are responsibility of teachers. Some training given.

RECRUITMENT: Newspaper adverts, followed by local interviews.

DAVID BERRY LANGUAGES

Florastasse 2, 13187 Berlin-Pankow

☎ +49 30449 9025

✎ ped@dbl-berlin.de

🖥 www.dbl-berlin.de

NUMBER OF TEACHERS: 10–15.

PREFERENCE OF NATIONALITY: None.

QUALIFICATIONS: Minimum CELTA with preferably 2 years' experience.

CONDITIONS OF EMPLOYMENT: Freelance contract with flexible working hours.

SALARY: Negotiable depending on travel/course requirements.

FACILITIES/SUPPORT: Will refer teacher to the local ELTA for help with accommodation.

RECRUITMENT: Interviews are essential.

CONTACT: David Berry-Lichtenberg, Director of Studies.

DESK

Blumenstr. 1, 80331 Munich

☎ +49 89 263334

✎ info@desk-sprachkurse.de

🖥 www.desk-sprachkurse.de

NUMBER OF TEACHERS: 30 native speakers (70 teachers in total). For central Munich or Herrsching on Ammersee.

PREFERENCE OF NATIONALITY: None.

QUALIFICATIONS: Degree with TEFL experience of adult education (in-class or online).

CONDITIONS OF EMPLOYMENT: Duration of contract to suit. One of the few schools in Munich offering a full contract, rather than freelance conditions. Flexible teaching hours mainly early mornings and evenings.

SALARY: €22 per 45-minute lesson.

FACILITIES/SUPPORT: No help with accommodation.

RECRUITMENT: CV and interview.

CONTACT: Erwin Schmidt-Achert, Owner (e.schmidtachert@desk-sprachkurse.de).

DIE NEUE SCHULE

Gieselerstrasse 30a, 10713 Berlin

☎ +49 30 873 0373

✎ bewerbung@neueschule.de

🖥 www.neueschule.de/jobs.htm

NUMBER OF TEACHERS: 80.

PREFERENCE OF NATIONALITY: British, American, Irish, Canadian.

QUALIFICATIONS: Cambridge or TEFL certificate and teaching experience needed. Mostly adults (ages 25–40) in small groups of no more than 8.

CONDITIONS OF EMPLOYMENT: Open-ended freelance contracts and some employed teachers. Variable hours in the daytime (9am–3pm) and evenings (6pm–9.15pm).

SALARY: Approx. €19 per hour.

FACILITIES/SUPPORT: Help with accommodation.

RECRUITMENT: Personal interview necessary, application link on website.

CONTACT: Martina Grebe, Director of Studies (Grebe@neueschule.de).

EURO INGOLSTADT
Esplanade 36, 85049 Ingolstadt
+49 841 17001
sw@euro-ingolstadt.de
www.euro-ingolstadt.de

State-recognised vocational language college.

NUMBER OF TEACHERS: 25.

PREFERENCE OF NATIONALITY: British, American, Canadian.

QUALIFICATIONS: At least a bachelor's degree (main focus must be German). PGCE preferred. At least 3 years' experience.

CONDITIONS OF EMPLOYMENT: Permanent contracts. Part-time work possible. 30 hours per week.

SALARY: Based on German state salary scale.

FACILITIES/SUPPORT: Assistance given with accommodation and work permits.

RECRUITMENT: Interview in Ingolstadt necessary.

CONTACT: Stuart Wheeler, Headmaster.

EURO-LINGUA
Beuggenerstr. 12, 79618 Rheinfelden-Nöllingen
+49 179 693 1898
info@euro-lingua.de
www.euro-lingua.de

Also has branch in Riehen, Switzerland near Basel.

NUMBER OF TEACHERS: 5.

PREFERENCE OF NATIONALITY: None, but native English speakers preferred.

QUALIFICATIONS: University degree, teaching experience, foreign language ability, preferably TOEFL or teacher training.

CONDITIONS OF EMPLOYMENT: Freelance.

SALARY: €15 per 45-minute lesson starting salary.

FACILITIES/SUPPORT: Advice given on local accommodation agencies. Non-EU teachers applying for a work permit outside Germany can be supplied with statement of projected income,

etc. Support available as needed for lesson planning, books and other materials.

RECRUITMENT: Word of mouth, local ads, contact with schools abroad.

CONTACT: Sylvia Weismiller, Director.

FINER ENGLISH
Friedrich-Naumann-Strasse 19, 34131 Kassel
+49 561 766 9236
Joe.Finer@Finerenglish.com
www.Finerenglish.com

NUMBER OF TEACHERS: 25 for two branches in Kassel.

PREFERENCE OF NATIONALITY: British, Canadian, American.

QUALIFICATIONS: University degree plus a teaching qualification, if possible, plus at least 2 years' relevant teaching experience. However, personality is more important than a stream of qualifications.

CONDITIONS OF EMPLOYMENT: Teachers work as freelancers who teach only on clients' premises. School is looking for teachers able to commit for at least 1 year. Most teachers have a weekly timetable of about 17 90-minute classes.

SALARY: Teachers invoice Finer English for hours worked. Typical monthly earnings are €2,200–€3,000. Freelancers are paid in full but must organise the payment of income tax and health insurance.

FACILITIES/SUPPORT: Full teacher support provided including finding accommodation and dealing with red tape. Teachers need to arrange a medical examination with a German doctor in order to obtain medical insurance which is a pre-condition of receiving a work permit.

RECRUITMENT: Via internet. Intensive telephone interviews conducted from Kassel, Germany.

CONTACT: Joe Finer, Director or Oliver Grund, Director of Studies (Oliver.Grund@Finerenglish.com).

GERMAN AMERICAN INSTITUTE TUEBINGEN
Karlstrasse 3, 72072 Tübingen
+49 7071 795260
mail@dai-tuebingen.de
www.dai-tuebingen.de

NUMBER OF TEACHERS: 20–30.

PREFERENCE OF NATIONALITY: North American.

QUALIFICATIONS: College degree (minimum requirement BA or BSc). Applications from candidates holding a certificate in TESOL, TESL or TEFL are especially welcome. Candidates with a driver's licence valid in Germany are needed.

CONDITIONS OF EMPLOYMENT: Freelance positions only. Average workload 3–9 hours per week, teaching adults and high school students. Also summer camps for 10–14 year olds.

SALARY: Hourly wage.

RECRUITMENT: Local interview required.

CONTACT: Stephanie Krenze, Language Program Co-ordinator (07071 795 2614; stephanie.krenze@dai-tuebingen.de).

HAMBURG SCHOOL OF ENGLISH

Eppendorfer Landstr. 93, 20249 Hamburg

+49 40 480 2119

info@hamburg.school-of-english.de

www.hamburg.school-of-english.de

NUMBER OF TEACHERS: 60–70.

PREFERENCE OF NATIONALITY: British, North American.

QUALIFICATIONS: University degree plus ELT certificate. Preferred minimum 1 year's experience.

CONDITIONS OF EMPLOYMENT: Minimum 1 year on freelance basis. Between 16 and 30 hours per week.

SALARY: Approx. €29–€45 for 90-minute teaching session.

FACILITIES/SUPPORT: Assistance given with finding accommodation and obtaining work permits. Cambridge CELTA course provider.

RECRUITMENT: Via local or telephone interviews.

CONTACT: Bill Cope, Director of Studies (bill.cope@hamburg.school-of-english.com).

HARDIE INTERNATIONAL LANGUAGE TRAINING & COACHING

Fasanenweg 3, 59174 Kamen

+49 50 33 911455

info@hardie-iltc.com

www.hardie-iltc.com

NUMBER OF TEACHERS: 15.

PREFERENCE OF NATIONALITY: None.

QUALIFICATIONS: Highest possible. Usually branch specialists are retrained as coaches, consultants or trainers.

CONDITIONS OF EMPLOYMENT: Open freelance contracts. Lessons take place 7 days a week between 7am and 10pm.

SALARY: Above average (depending on qualifications and experience).

FACILITIES/SUPPORT: Accommodation can be provided or at least advice given.

RECRUITMENT: Through partner organisations. Interviews compulsory and sometimes carried out in UK or by telephone.

CONTACT: Gudrun Hardie, Owner.

ICC SPRACHINSTITUT

Am Nordplatz 9, 04105 Leipzig

+49 341 5502 2460

info@icc-sprachinstitut.de

www.icc-sprachinstitut.de

NUMBER OF TEACHERS: 50.

PREFERENCE OF NATIONALITY: None.

QUALIFICATIONS: University degree, CELTA and preferably TEFL experience with corporate clients.

CONDITIONS OF EMPLOYMENT: Fixed term or freelance. Teaching in-company business courses, intensive and evening courses. Internships also available.

SALARY: €15–€20 per 45-minute lesson.

FACILITIES/SUPPORT: Assistance with accommodation and work permits (if necessary). Induction and regular training included. Good career prospects throughout the ASSET group.

RECRUITMENT: Walk-ins mainly though email applications welcome. Local interview essential.

CONTACT: James Parsons, Director (james.parsons@icc-sprachinstitut.de) or Mrs Teresa Lang, Educational Director (teresa.lang@icc-sprachinstitut.de).

INLINGUA SPRACHCENTER KIEL

Alter Markt 7, 24103 Kiel

+49 431 981380

info@inlingua-kiel.de

www.inlingua-kiel.de

NUMBER OF TEACHERS: Approximately 10 trainers.

PREFERENCE OF NATIONALITY: None.

QUALIFICATIONS: Degree, CELTA certificate and some teaching experience preferred.

CONDITIONS OF EMPLOYMENT: 6-month probationary period. Teaching hours Monday to Friday between 8am and 9pm and extra Saturday hours possible 8am–5pm. Full-time contract guarantees 100 teaching hours per month.

SALARY: From €12 per teaching hour.

FACILITIES/SUPPORT: Information is provided about the best way to find accommodation in Kiel. Necessary paperwork is provided for non-EU employee to take to foreigners' office to obtain a work permit.

RECRUITMENT: Through online advertisements and by receiving speculative CVs.

CONTACT: Armando Lizarzaburu (a.lizarzaburu@inlingua-kiel.de).

INLINGUA SPRACHSCHULE HANNOVER

Andreaestrasse 3, Ecke Schillerstrasse, 30159
Hannover

✆ +49 511 324580

🖱 info@inlingua-hannover.de

💻 www.inlingua-hannover.de

NUMBER OF TEACHERS: 15.

PREFERENCE OF NATIONALITY: English, American, Canadian; other native English speakers.

QUALIFICATIONS: Degree in any subject and minimum 1 years' TEFL experience.

CONDITIONS OF EMPLOYMENT: Minimum 12 months. Average at least 25 school lessons (45 minutes each) per week.

SALARY: Approx. €15 per lesson.

FACILITIES/SUPPORT: Assistance finding accommodation.

RECRUITMENT: Newspaper adverts and internet.

CONTACT: Ms Heiki Gleichmann.

INTERACT! LANGUAGE CONNECTS

Osdorfer Landstrasse 11, 22607 Hamburg

✆ +49 40 2199 0400

🖱 info@interact-experts.com

💻 www.interact-experts.com

NUMBER OF TEACHERS: 42.

PREFERENCE OF NATIONALITY: None.

QUALIFICATIONS: CELTA plus experience, business background and very good references.

CONDITIONS OF EMPLOYMENT: Various hours, Monday to Saturday, mornings and evenings.

SALARY: Approx. €18–23 per hour.

FACILITIES/SUPPORT: Assistance given with accommodation. Training. Access to internet/materials.

RECRUITMENT: Via adverts, agencies, internet and word of mouth.

CONTACT: Kerstin Hansen, Manager (kerstin.hansen@interact-experts.com).

LEOlingo SPRACHCAMPS FÜR KINDER

Seitzermühle 1, 92369 Sengenthal, Bavaria

Werderstrasse 35, 19055 Schwerin, North Germany

✆ +49 9181 904755 (Bavaria); +49 385 581 5430 (North Germany)

🖱 baer@leo-lingo.de (Bavaria); goerner@leo-lingo.de (North Germany)

💻 www.leo-lingo.de

Summer language camps for children in North-Eastern Germany (Hamburg, Baltic Sea, Mecklenburg-Vorpommern) and Bavaria.

NUMBER OF TEACHERS: 20–25 in Bavaria; 10–15 in North Germany.

PREFERENCE OF NATIONALITY: English-speaking countries (USA, UK, Canada, Australia, etc).

QUALIFICATIONS: Applicants should have previous experience of working with children, preferably as a camp counsellor or in similar fields such as teaching, au pairing, sports coaching, etc.

CONDITIONS OF EMPLOYMENT: Mid-July to beginning of September in Bavaria; 6–7 weeks from mid-June till beginning of August in North Germany. Day counsellors work 9am–5pm Mon-Fri. Night counsellors work 5pm–9am Sun/Mon–Fri, although the actual programme time is only 7–9.30pm.

SALARY: €200 per week for day counsellors plus either bed and breakfast or full bed and board. The salary for a night counsellor is €100 per week, plus full bed and board.

FACILITIES/SUPPORT: Counsellors are provided with free accommodation during their working weeks (including the weekends), either with a German host family or at places such as youth hostels. If counsellors have a week off, they must arrange their own accommodation. For non-Europeans who are hired, LEOlingo sends the necessary information about work permits and they are responsible for the application process themselves, which usually involves arranging an appointment at their nearest German consulate and handing over the required documents, for example, completed visa application form, passport photo, copy of the working contract, proof of residence, proof of health insurance/funds. 8-day compulsory training is unpaid.

RECRUITMENT: Via job websites and university careers services. Application form followed by possibility of video interview.

CONTACT: Andrea Bär (Bavaria); Sabine Görner (North Germany).

LINGUA FRANCA

Mauerstrasse 77, 10117 Berlin

✆ +49 30 8639 8080

🖱 info@lingua-franca.de

💻 www.lingua-franca.de

NUMBER OF TEACHERS: 50.

PREFERENCE OF NATIONALITY: None.

QUALIFICATIONS: University degree plus TEFL experience and/or certificate. Experience in ESP preferred.

CONDITIONS OF EMPLOYMENT: Freelance only. Can generally give good teachers as many lesson hours as they want.

FACILITIES/SUPPORT: No help with accommodation. Will write the necessary letter to the employment office to support work permit application. In-house training available.

RECRUITMENT: Local interviews.

CONTACT: Douglas Werner, Director of Studies.

MARCUS EVANS – LINGUARAMA SPRACHENINSTITUT DEUTSCHLAND

✆ personnel@linguarama.com

💻 www.linguarama.com

NUMBER OF TEACHERS: From 25 Business English trainers in the smaller Linguarama schools to 70 in the larger ones; Linguarama schools located in Berlin, Cologne, Dusseldorf, Frankfurt, Hamburg, Leipzig, Munich, Stuttgart, and many smaller towns. Vacancies at the time of writing in Cologne and Dusseldorf, and often vacancies in Munich at Sendlinger-Tor-Platz 7, 80336 Munich; +49 89 2000 0930; munich@linguarama.com.

PREFERENCE OF NATIONALITY: Native English speakers only who must have valid working papers for the EU.

QUALIFICATIONS: Minimum university degree or equivalent and a basic TEFL qualification (eg CELTA). 2 years' experience of teaching Business English is preferred with a keen interest in business as a minimum.

CONDITIONS OF EMPLOYMENT: Mixture of contract and freelance teachers. Freelance teachers work variable hours, usually early mornings and evenings. Contract teachers usually contracted for 1 year, extendable to 2 years, but occasionally shorter contracts available. 23 days paid holiday per 12-month contract.

SALARY: €1,660–€1,915 per month depending on experience.

FACILITIES/SUPPORT: Contract teachers are given an initial 2-week accommodation entitlement and assistance with finding permanent accommodation. Travel expenses to the city are paid from the UK if recruitment is through head office. Help is given with obtaining a residence permit, etc. All teachers are given an induction course and paid training is held monthly.

RECRUITMENT: Usually interviews locally for freelance teachers. Contract staff are sometimes recruited locally or via Linguarama Group Personnel Department, 1 Elm Court, Arden Street, Stratford-upon-Avon CV37 6PA (see introductory section, Finding a job).

CONTACT: Danny Coughlan, Personnel Manager.

PENGUIN CAMP

Tempelhof 3, 74594 Kressberg

✆ +49 7957 9239 122

✉ info@penguincamp.de

💻 www.penguincamp.de

NUMBER OF TEACHERS: 5-10 freelance language counsellors for day camps around Munich and some overnight camps in several locations in Bavaria.

PREFERENCE OF NATIONALITY: None.

QUALIFICATIONS: Native English or bilingual students, teachers, performing artists, etc with creativity, independence, stamina, humour and organisational skills. Experience with children and some knowledge of German helpful.

CONDITIONS OF EMPLOYMENT: 4-day camp at Easter and Monday-to-Friday day and residential camps during the summer. Counsellors work 9-16 hour days.

SALARY: €240–€450 per week depending on hours and experience with Penguin.

FACILITIES/SUPPORT: Advice can be given on accommodation (hostels, etc) in or near Munich and on permits (if non-EU). Counsellors are independent contractors so are responsible for their own tax and social security.

RECRUITMENT: Via websites and word of mouth. Skype interviews.

CONTACT: Claus Reimers, Director.

PET-SPRACHEN

Baaderstr. 3, 80469 Munich

✆ +49 89 2006 2090

✉ team@pet-sprachen.de or info@pet-sprachen.de

💻 www.pet-sprachen.de

NUMBER OF TEACHERS: 100 freelancers for 14 branches throughout Germany and occasionally in Austria and Switzerland.

PREFERENCE OF NATIONALITY: None.

QUALIFICATIONS: TEFL qualification and/or degree preferable, as are business experience and friendly, outgoing disposition.

CONDITIONS OF EMPLOYMENT: Travelling to companies to hold in-company courses on a freelance basis.

SALARY: Minimum €21 per teaching unit (45 minutes) plus travel.

FACILITIES/SUPPORT: No assistance with accommodation. Materials support given. Teachers' workshops held.

RECRUITMENT: Direct applications. Local interviews necessary.

CONTACT: Paul Bacon, Owner/Manager (paul.bacon@pet-sprachen.de).

SPRACHZENTRUM SUD

Bahnhofplatz 2, 83607 Holzkirchen

✆ +49 8024 1733

✉ info@sprachzentrum-sued.de

💻 www.sprachzentrum-sued.de

NUMBER OF TEACHERS: 15 general and business trainers.

PREFERENCE OF NATIONALITY: British, Irish, American, Australian.

QUALIFICATIONS: Teaching certificate (eg CELTA, DELTA) or university degree. Teaching experience needed, especially in Business English.

CONDITIONS OF EMPLOYMENT: Freelance; employment possible after 1 year of successful freelancing. Also freelance teachers needed for summer camps in Munich, Jofestal and Spitzingsee.

SALARY: Between €15 and €25 per hour, depending on the qualification and contract.

RECRUITMENT: Telephone interviews possible. Candidates in Europe will be invited to interview and to teach a practice lesson with volunteer students.

CONTACT: Dr Karin Wiebalck-Zahn, Managing Director. Summer camp applications to Anissa Nasser (anissa.nasser@sprachzentrum-sued.de).

STEVENS ENGLISH TRAINING

Essen: Rüttenscheiderstr. 68, 45130 Essen

Cologne: Hohenstaufenring 29–37, 50674 Cologne

Dortmund: Westenhellweg 112, 44137 Dortmund

Münster: Olferstrasse 6, 48153 Münster

C +49 201 877 0770

office@stevens-english.de

www.stevens-english.de

NUMBER OF TEACHERS: Approx. 80 full and part-time corporate language trainers.

PREFERENCE OF NATIONALITY: None but should be native English speakers.

QUALIFICATIONS: TEFL certificate or experience of the business world. Should be EU national with basic German and a driving licence, as well as a degree and CELTA if possible.

CONDITIONS OF EMPLOYMENT: 2-year contracts. Hours between 7.30am and 8.45pm Monday to Friday. Minimum 80 hours per month guaranteed. 80% of teaching is in-company with high element of ESP.

SALARY: Paid on points system per 45-minute session. Guaranteed minimum.

FACILITIES/SUPPORT: Furnished flats available at certain locations (eg Essen) for trainers recruited from the UK. Extensive workshop training programme for trainers. Free training for the LCCI exam 'First Certificate in Teaching Business English' (FTBE). Extensive library of teaching materials. Use of company car may be available.

RECRUITMENT: Interviews essential and can be by Skype. Candidates receive €100 towards travel expenses and one night's accommodation provided.

CONTACTS: Michael Stevens, Managing Director.

SUNFLOWER SPRACHCAMPS

Ruhrallee 69, 44139 Dortmund

C +49 231 5346 1758

office@sunflower-sprachcamps.eu

www.sunflower-sprachcamps.eu

NUMBER OF TEACHERS: Up to 6 for Dusseldorf area.

PREFERENCE OF NATIONALITY: Great Britain, Ireland and Malta are preferred. Non-EU citizens will need a work permit.

QUALIFICATIONS: Students, undergraduates and graduates with love of and practical experience working with children and teenagers.

CONDITIONS OF EMPLOYMENT: 4–7 weeks from mid-July to early September, including 1 week of training. 35 hours per week (day camp) plus preparation time.

SALARY: €220 per week (paid cash in hand) plus free accommodation and transport to the campsites.

FACILITIES/SUPPORT: Accommodation provided. Assistance given to foreign candidates to obtain a work permit.

RECRUITMENT: Via internet job portals and cooperation with universities. Applicants must complete an application form and solve tasks.

CONTACT: Theresia Kreul, Director and Owner.

TARGET TRAINING GmbH

Kopernikusstr 13, 63071 Offenbach

C +49 69 848 4790

jobs@targettraining.eu

www.targettraining.eu

NUMBER OF TEACHERS: 43 trainers.

PREFERENCE OF NATIONALITY: None.

QUALIFICATIONS: Look for trainers with a university degree, CELTA (or equivalent) and 5 years' EFL experience (including some business/corporate EFL training).

CONDITIONS OF EMPLOYMENT: Initial contract is 2 years. 40 hours per week, during normal office hours.

SALARY: €2,700 per month (after completing a 6-month probation period). DELTA trainers receive a higher rate. Deductions amount to about 40% (depending on personal circumstances).

FACILITIES/SUPPORT: Relocation budget offered plus assistance with finding accommodation. Target proactively supports all staff in acquiring the necessary paperwork (EU and non-EU alike). Applicants receive a detailed overview during the interview process.

RECRUITMENT: Via tefl.com, social media (such as Xing and LinkedIn) and through website. Two telephone interviews followed by a task-based interview conducted face-to-face in Germany.

CONTACT: Helen Sinclair, Trainer Recruiter.

WALL STREET INSTITUTE / WSI EDUCATION GmbH
ZHd. Teacher Recruitment, Rosental 5, 80331 Munich or Postfach 330911, 80069 Munich
✆ +49 89 552 9890 or +49 89 239 6050
  or 0800050 8050
🖰 recruiting@wallstreetinstitute.de
🖵 www.wallstreetinstitute.com/de

NUMBER OF TEACHERS: Approximately 150, at 27 locations.

PREFERENCE OF NATIONALITY: None, but it is easier to employ EU citizens due to visa restrictions.

QUALIFICATIONS: Teachers must be native English speakers with ESL/TEFL or equivalent qualification, experience in teaching English as a second language, ability to work within an existing, structured teaching method, excellent organisational and interpersonal skills, and be motivated, energetic and dedicated.

CONDITIONS OF EMPLOYMENT: Contracts of at least 1 year, usually unlimited (if residency permit has been obtained). No freelance contracts. Between 15 and 25 hours per week, plus paid overtime.

SALARY: Depends on the city. There is also the opportunity to earn bonuses and be paid commission.

FACILITIES/SUPPORT: Can help teachers find accommodation through informing them about various reputable websites and

organisations when they arrive in the city of employment. Also, if the applicant does not speak German, WSI may accompany them to the immigration office and help them register and obtain their work permit. WSI gives a letter of intent to the employment authorities. Once the employment authorities have given their permission, the applicant receives a contract.

CONTACT: HR department.

XCHANGE SERVICES
Hornschuchpromenade 20, 90762 Fürth
✆ +49 911 950 990 10
🖰 jobs@xchange-services.de
🖵 www.xchange-services.de

Incorporating English Studio. Also arranges summer camps (summercamp@xchange-services.de; www.englishsummercamp. de).

NUMBER OF TEACHERS: 15–20.

PREFERENCE OF NATIONALITY: Native English speakers. Work permit required.

QUALIFICATIONS: Minimum teaching/training qualification, eg PGCE, CELTA/Trinity, TEFL/TESOL certificate. Relevant business experience and commercial/industrial training experience also considered.

CONDITIONS OF EMPLOYMENT: Open-ended contract for freelancers; 24 contact hours per week; teaching hours between 7.30am and 8pm.

SALARY: Hourly rates to be negotiated.

FACILITIES/SUPPORT: May be able to advise on accommodation.

RECRUITMENT: Word of mouth. Interviews essential.

CONTACT: Thomas Hintze (thomas.hintze@xchange-services.de).

GREECE

For the past five years, Greece has been inching towards the cliff-edge of eviction from the Eurozone and then retreating. At the time of writing, the situation looked dire with Europe losing patience with the serial bail-outs and with crisis talks predicted to fail. The unemployment rate remains stubbornly high at 25%. Swingeing austerity has had a deeply detrimental effect on the Greek economy. Every business has suffered, especially private language schools, because when money is tight, language learning is one of the first things to get the chop. Public sector workers have had to accept drastic pay cuts, job losses, and an end to favourable pension payouts. It will still be a long time before travelling teachers will be able to step easily into a job. Many schools have shut down and many more are planning to shut down. Taxes are so high that school owners are finding it difficult to make a profit and don't see the point of staying open, especially as they generally have a problem collecting the fees from parents. This has led to a situation in which there is a serious over-supply of teachers compared to positions available.

English teacher **Jerry Melinn** has been able to observe the changes over the past nine years that he has been living in Athens, and his assessment makes for depressing reading:

> *There is no doubt that the financial crisis has had a very negative effect on the Greek people. Businesses – including foreign language schools – are closing daily and unemployment is at record levels. The number of students in language schools is falling and where students still attend, some parents don't pay the fees or are late paying. Competition among schools and from private teachers has increased. Private teachers have dropped their prices significantly and some parents are now finding it as cheap, if not cheaper, to hire a private teacher than to send their children to a private language school. There is also huge pressure on school owners to enter the students for the exams as fast as possible so the parents can save money. This is a big problem because if the students are not ready and fail the test the reputation of the school will suffer, which will result in a reduction in the number of new students.*
>
> *Taking a medium to long-term view, I believe the ESL industry in Greece will continue to decline further from its peak eight or so years ago. There will probably be little or no recruitment into the public service for a long time and employment in this area was one of the drivers for ESL. Tourism plays an important role in the economy and this will continue to stimulate demand but conversational English would be the main requirement here perhaps and not Lower or Proficiency certificates.*

The number of candidates sitting the Michigan Lower and Proficiency exams is declining. On the other hand there has been a spike in interest in the IELTS test, probably because Greeks see this as a route to finding work or study opportunities abroad. As for leisure pursuits, Jerry Melinn has noticed that cheap 'recession pastimes' like cycling and running have become popular, inspiring Jerry to buy a road bike on which he does up to 250km a week.

The fact remains, teachers like Jerry Melinn continue to enjoy teaching in Greece. Schools continue to operate and the teacher recruitment agencies (see directory) remain in business. Thousands of private language schools – the term *kentra xenon glosson* has been replacing the term *frontisteria* – continue to supplement the language education of most children aged 6–16. A few years ago the state school system lowered the age when students begin to learn English, so parents want very young children to get ahead of the game and have a good grounding in English before they start their state school lessons. Secondary school students are all in pursuit of higher scores in the Panhellenic exams that determine university entrance.

Greek language schools are often run by local entrepreneurs and because they are limited to three or four classrooms are often housed in buildings which were not purpose-built as schools. Secondary school pupils in Greece are obliged to study 15 subjects, all of which they must pass before being allowed to proceed to the next year. In most areas the teaching of English in state schools is considered inadequate so that the vast majority of pupils also attend *frontisteria*, and it is not uncommon for a 15-year-old to have two or three hours of lessons a day (in other subjects as well as English) in one or more private establishments to supplement the state schooling. Despite this gruelling timetable, the students are usually motivated and generally participate enthusiastically in their lessons, reaching a high level of proficiency by age 16.

English language teaching in Greece has been described as an exam industry, and there is fierce competition among the international exam bodies. At one time Cambridge First Certificate and Cambridge Proficiency examinations dominated though they have had intense competition from the University of Michigan exams and more recently by the Pearson Test of English and the English Speaking Board (ESB) which won a tender for ESOL work from the beginning of 2014. The different exams are administered by two rival associations of language schools mentioned below, PALSO and EUROPALSO. A newcomer has just arrived on the scene in Greece, City & Guilds English (www.cityandguilds.gr), which is aggressively marketing its exams. In fact, there are now 15 exams to choose from, all administered by different examining boards, and the terminology can be confusing. A certificate in one of these exams earns points to help the applicant get on the waiting list for a job in the civil service or in a state school. Some teachers and students still refer to the exams by exam board names such as First Certificate and Proficiency (Cambridge), Michigan and Michigan Proficiency, Edexcel, etc. A structure for language learning and assessment has been laid down by the European Union (called the Common European Framework of Reference for Languages) which has gained widespread acceptance in Greece. B2 denotes someone who can function in English as an 'Independent User' and C2 denotes the highest level 'Mastery' of English.

PROSPECTS FOR TEACHERS

The employment situation for teachers is undeniably more difficult than it was in the boom years when schools were opening left, right and centre. **Jain Cook**, long-time Director of Studies at a successful language school in Patras paints a depressing picture:

> *Things have changed a lot here, and it's much more difficult to find work. A lot of schools have shut down, so there are some very experienced teachers out there looking for work. The Koutsantonis school has been lucky because our student numbers haven't really dropped. The problem is parents not paying the fees, and this applies to all private schools. I finished at the school two weeks ago, and have already had 17 phone calls from ex-teachers or someone who is a friend of someone I know, asking me for work in September. I've had teachers asking for a job who are willing to work for two or three euros an hour! People are desperate for work. This also applies to private lessons, which are practically non-existent now and if you do get a student, you cannot charge much more than €5 an hour – and that's if you are a native speaker.*
>
> *In some ways it's depressing here. Every time you go out another shop has shut down and people look miserable. It's really not the best place to come at the moment to work, especially when just under half of 18–25 year olds are unemployed and there is a lot of bad feeling towards foreigners, although more towards illegal immigrants.*

Yet prospects for EU citizens with a university degree and a TEFL qualification are not hopeless, particularly outside Athens. A fairly recent development is that ESP classes are becoming more popular in Greece and institutions organising company classes are sometimes on the lookout for professional, highly trained teachers.

A qualification is becoming essential, though not necessarily experience. The government stipulates that in order to obtain a teacher's licence, English teachers must have at least a BA in English Language and Literature or Education, so virtually all schools expect to see a degree certificate. Note that the government enforces a quota on all employers: for every foreigner they hire, they must employ 10 Greeks.

Having a TEFL qualification, as always, will make the job hunt easier. Given the size of the ELT market in Greece, it is surprising that so few training centres offer the CELTA or the Trinity TESOL certificate in Greece. The main teacher training organisations in Greece tend to concentrate on training Greek speakers to become English teachers, though Anglo-Hellenic in Corinth and Via Lingua in Crete run courses mainly attended by native English speakers. The main ELT training organisations in Greece are listed below:

American College of Greece/DEREE, 6 Gravias St, Aghia Paraskevi, 153 42 Athens (+30 210 600 2208; www.acg.edu). 2 part-time Trinity CertTESOL courses held over 8 weeks in spring and full-time course in July blended with online studies. €2,000.

Anglo-Hellenic, 13 Vasilou St, 200 06 Corinth (+30 27410 53511; www.anglo-hellenic.com; www.tefl.gr). TEFL International Certificate course (www.teflcorinth.com) held monthly between Easter and November; also offered part-time. Fee is €1,295. Accommodation is located in Vrahati on the seaside near Corinth. Shared accommodation €250; private room €350.

CELT, 77 Akademias St, 10678 Athens (+30 210 330 2406/1455; info@celt.edu.gr; www.celt.edu.gr). Offers its own 4-week certificate course for €1,300, CELTA (€1,450 plus Cambridge assessment fee of €160) and range of other courses. Also available part-time.

Study Space, D Gounari 21, 54622 Thessaloniki (+30 231 026 9697; www.studyspace.gr). Cambridge-approved centre whose CELTA package includes assistance with employment in its partner schools in Thessaloniki and throughout Northern Greece. Fee for full-time course (held in June) is €1,800 and includes accommodation.

Via Lingua Crete, Chrysanthou Episkopou 48, Chania, 73132 Crete (+30 28210 57438; www.teflgreece.com or www.vialingua.org). 5 times a year between May and October. €1,590 including shared accommodation.

Americans and other non-EU citizens will find it difficult to find a school willing to hire them, purely because of immigration difficulties. The government can impose stiff penalties on employers who break the rules and few, at least in the major cities, will risk it, as **Tim Leffel** found out some years ago: '*We had planned on teaching in Greece, but as Americans, we were not exactly welcomed with open arms in Athens; they told us to try the countryside.*' Tim moved on to Turkey instead.

A further complicating factor is the high number of Greek emigrés to North America and Australia who have returned (or whose children have returned) to Greece. In many cases, they are virtually native speakers of English but are favoured because of their ancestry. Of course there will always be schools prepared to hire Americans and others if well qualified, such as the Hellenic American Union, which has one of the largest programmes in adult EFL in Athens. The Betsis School in Piraeus (see Directory) accepts one or two American TEFL graduates as interns who stay no more than the 90-day validity of their Schengen visas.

One reason why EU citizens with basic qualifications can expect to land a job in Greece is that wages are not high enough to attract many highly qualified EFL teachers. Greece tends to be a country where people get their first English teaching job for the experience and then move to more lucrative countries. Also, few schools place any emphasis on staff development or provide in-house training, so serious teachers tend to move on quickly. The majority of advertised jobs are in towns and cities in mainland Greece. Athens has such a large expatriate community that most of the large central schools at the elite end of the market are able to hire well-qualified staff locally. But the competition may not be so keen in Edessa, Larissa, Preveza or any of the numerous towns of which the tourist to Greece is unlikely to have heard.

FINDING A JOB

IN ADVANCE

Unless you elect to register with one of the recruitment agencies (that deal primarily with Certificate-qualified teachers), it may not be worthwhile trying to find a job in advance, since so much in Greece is accomplished by word of mouth. Getting a list of language schools from outside Greece is not easy. A considerable proportion of *frontisteria* belong to the Pan-Hellenic Federation of Language School Owners (PALSO Headquarters, 2 Lykavitou St, 106 71 Kolonaki, Athens). There are local branches of PALSO all over Greece though they are unlikely to offer much help to job-seeking teachers until they are looking on the spot. Note that the Athens association of language school owners has split from PALSO and now calls itself EUROPALSO (Akademias 98–100, Athens 106 77; +30 210 383 0752; www.europalso.gr). EUROPALSO consists of hundreds of schools in the Athens area and keeps a file of applications submitted by teachers (europalso@europalso. gr) or you can visit in person to see if any school owners have registered an interest in hiring teaching staff. PALSO-Chania has a separate web presence (only in Greek) at www.palso-chania.gr (Partheniou Kelaidi 72, Chania 73136; +30 28210 92622), while the Heraklion branch is at www.palsoher.gr.

An alternative association of language schools is QLS (Quality in Language Services), which aspires to be a Panhellenic Association of Accredited Language Schools. Overseeing its 24 member schools, the main office is in Volos; links to schools can be found on www.qls.gr.

The internet is not as useful for the job-seeker in Greece unless you can easily read the Greek alphabet. The *Yellow Pages* can be accessed in English at www.xo.gr/dir-az/F/Foreign-Language-Schools/?lang=en. Occasional job ads appear in English on the site of the ELT News (www.eltnews.gr/news). For example in the past, the Omiros Association of Foreign Language Schools has invited experienced English teachers (prefer-ably native) to submit their CVs to s-omiros@otenet.gr for the academic year.

Most schools do their hiring for the following academic year between May and July. Obviously the major chains of schools offer the most opportunities, and it is worth sending your CV in the spring to organisations such as the Strategakis Group, which has about a hundred schools in Northern Greece (www.strategakis.gr). Another major organisation is The Scholars Group (www.the-scholars.gr).

Fortunately there are several active recruitment agencies that specialise in Greece with offices in Greece and/or Britain. These recruitment agencies are looking for people with at least a bachelor's degree and normally a TEFL qualification and/or experience (depending on the client school's requirements). All cli-ent employers provide accommodation. Long-established agencies Anglo-Hellenic Teacher Recruitment and Cambridge Teachers Recruitment both have entries in the Directory below.

When discussing your future post with an agency, don't be lulled into a false sense of security. It is wise to check contractual details for yourself and verify verbal promises. Check to see whether you are entitled to any compensation if the employer breaks the contract and similarly whether you will have to compensate the school if you leave early. Find out if there will be any other native English-speaking teachers in the area, and ask about the possibility of contacting your predecessor in the job.

After graduating from the TEFL Corinth certificate course, **Jerry Melinn** (aged 56) began working for the Katsianos School of Foreign Languages in Athens, where he remained teaching for four great years. As he developed as a teacher, he moved on to a different school where he is left mostly to his own devices and is allowed to cover the whole course including grammar:

> *I read some horror stories on the internet about teaching in Greece but my experience has been great. The TEFL course in Corinth prepared me well for teaching. I have learned so much, made many new friends and grown very attached to the students. I have nothing but admiration for them as they come to lessons twice a week after Greek school and the vast majority are well behaved and good humoured.*
>
> *I am still happy teaching here though things are more difficult as a result of the financial crisis. I now rent my own apartment and work on a contract for 15 hours a week at a school about 15 minutes by bus from my apartment. I occasionally work some extra hours especially coming up to exam time. I have much more autonomy as a teacher now and I like the responsibility of teaching exam classes on my own. The financial crisis has taken its toll and my pay has been reduced but I was able to negotiate a rent reduction, which offset my pay cut.*
>
> *I still enjoy teaching and in my free time I go cycling, swimming and to the gym. As usual, my wife and I have holidays at Easter, June and September and I go home to Ireland for the summer and for Christmas.*

Phil Tomkins graduated from the Corinth TEFL course mentioned above and took up his first TEFL post on the small island of Kea in the Cyclades. His 'interview' with the director of the Kea school simply involved catching a bus to Athens and meeting her for an informal chat over coffee at a street café.

Given how many children study English outside school, it is surprising there are very few summer language camps or English programmes in Greece. The Russian-based Nordic School that operates English language camps in Finland has recently expanded operations to Crete (contact details may be found it its entry in the Scandinavia chapter).

IAN PARR

Ian Parr is yet another mature candidate who trained in Corinth and found work straight afterwards, in his case at a chain of three language schools in a suburb of Athens called Vyronas.

This has been my first job as an EFL teacher, having previously worked as a laboratory scientist in England for 10 years. I decided I wanted a new challenge and to travel so I completed the TEFL International course at Corinth. I first heard about this school in Athens through a contact I made on a Living in Greece website. I rang the school and spoke to the owner who asked me to come to Athens for an interview the same week. I met the school owner who was friendly and who checked my degree and teaching certificates, asked me a few questions about myself and told me that she expects her teachers to act professionally at all times whilst at the school. She then told me she would have work for me from January until the end of the school year in June, around 20 hours a week and that she would pay me €10 an hour. On returning to Greece after the Christmas holidays I soon found a small apartment to rent in the centre of Athens.

As is usual, the Greek teachers teach the younger children and also teach grammar to the older students. Native-speaker-teachers teach everything except grammar. This is common in Greece apparently and is a little frustrating as teaching grammar was a challenge I was looking forward to. Altogether my hours only added up to 12 hours a week which was disappointing considering I'd been promised 20. Over the months I have worked extra hours covering classes, doing mock speaking tests and giving extra classes close to the exams. The biggest difficulty has been surviving financially in what is an expensive city. Eventually it has gotten easier as I now have a private lesson and do some editing work for a local English man who owns a publishing company. I have been offered a full-time contract to work at the same school for next year and will take it as I have enjoyed my time here and want to learn more of the culture and language here in Greece.

ON THE SPOT

So many *frontisteria* rely on agents or personal contacts to find teachers for them that it can be difficult to walk into a job. The majority of schools have filled all their vacancies by July, so September is usually too late for prospective teachers to be looking for work. One of the best times to look is January. Greece is far less attractive in mid-winter than in summer, and many foreign teachers do not return to their posts after Christmas. Finding work in the summer is virtually impossible; most English language summer courses in resorts or on the islands are staffed by people who have taught for an academic year. **Will Brady** is one of the co-founders of Atlantis Books on the island of Santorini (www.atlantisbooks.org). He picked up a teaching job on the island:

> *It was just an opportunistic thing. I knew that I needed to earn some money so having recently got a TEFL qualifi-*
> *cation I thought I'd try my hand at a bit of TEFL teaching. I wandered around Fira and asked if there were any lan-*
> *guage schools, discovered that I was facing one, and walked in. I met a very strange man, who was the manager*
> *(the owner didn't speak English). This guy had studied psychology in England. I think he took a liking to me be-*
> *cause I was English. I asked if I could do some work for them and he more or less told me straight away that I could,*
> *but kept things on very vague terms. Whilst I was back in England to arrange a few things, I negotiated with him*
> *over the phone. Then when I got back to the island I just went in and started. There was no interview whatsoever.*

Although Will had enquired about working legally, he concluded that advice from the Greek Embassy in London '*seemed to lead to no certain conclusions about what was the correct protocol*'. He ended up working under the table, an arrangement that suited both himself and the school owner, and was paid a wage equivalent to the British minimum. Work was part-time, teaching (or assisting in the classroom) about 2–3 hours a day, 3–4 times a week. The language school had never hired a native English speaker before and all the Greek teachers would defer to Will on grammatical points, something he found 'quite strange', because he was considerably younger.

Although **Jamie Masters** knew that October was not prime time for job-hunting, that is when he arrived in Heraklion to look for work, some years ago now:

> *I advertised (in Greek) in the Cretan newspapers, no joy. I lowered my sights and started knocking on doors*
> *of frontisteria. I was put onto some guy who ran an English-language bookshop and went to see him. Turned*
> *out he was a linch-pin in the frontisterion business and in fact I got my first job through him. Simultaneously,*
> *I went to the PALSO office and was given a list of schools which were looking for people. The list, it turned out,*
> *was pretty much out of date. But I had insisted on leaving my name with them (they certainly didn't offer) and*
> *that's how I found my second job.*

Once you arrange an interview, be sure to dress well and to amass as many educational diplomas as you can. This will create the right aura of respectability in which to impress the potential employer with your conscientiousness and amiability. Decisions are often taken more according to whether you hit it off with the interviewer than on your qualifications and experience. Jamie Masters found that no one cared a fig about his PhD in classics.

When you elicit interest from a language school owner or a family, take your time over agreeing terms. Greece is not a country in which it pays to rush, and negotiations can be carried out in a leisurely and civilised fashion. On the other hand, do not come to an agreement with an employer without clarifying wages and schedules precisely. Make sure you read your contract very carefully so that you are familiar with what you should be entitled to. Anglo-Hellenic provides a detailed four-page contract in Greek and English, a sample of which is available on its website (http://anglo-hellenic.com/schools/contract.htm).

FREELANCE TEACHING

Private lessons are not as easy to find as they used to be. Established EFL teachers might now have three or four private pupils when before they had as many as 15. This is partly because of the falling birth rate in Greece and also because the middle classes have less disposable income and prefer to send their children to the local *kentro xenon glosson* or to someone they know locally who has passed the B2 level examination and who charges much less than a native English speaker, sometimes as little as €4–€5. This is a huge contrast with the going rate for qualified private tutors of €25 per hour for B2 tuition, and €30 per hour for C2, probably more in Athens.

Private tutoring jobs seem to materialise either from the language schools (whose directors seldom seem to mind their teachers earning on the side) or from conversations in a café-bar. It is a good idea to pin your card up at private schools, local shops and so on.

Trading English lessons for board and lodging is a common form of freelance teaching in Athens and else-where. Sometimes contracted teachers are offered free accommodation in exchange for tutoring their boss's children. In Athens, the rich suburbs of Kifissia and Kolonaki are full of families who can afford to provide private English lessons for their offspring. The suburbs of Pangrati and Filothei are also well-heeled. It is also possible to start up private classes for children, provided you have decent accommodation in a prosperous residential area, though this will usually be too expensive if your only source of income is private teaching.

REGULATIONS

Long-term English teachers are meant to obtain a teacher's licence and the bureaucratic procedures in-volved can be stressful, even with a supportive employer. The Ministry of Education considers a BA or higher degree in English Literature or a degree in Education a sufficient qualification, though a TEFL certificate strengthens your application of course. You must have your degree certificate officially translated and nota-rised/apostilled, either before you leave home (which is usually cheaper) or in Greece.

If and when the teacher's licence arrives from Athens, the teacher must take it along with his or her pass-port, photos and a lot of patience to the police station to apply for a residence permit, which should come through in about a month. The health certificate and residence permit must be renewed annually, though if you protest loudly enough you can usually get away with just having a chest X-ray. Keep photocopies of all forms.

Frontisteria usually tend to leave all the bureaucratic legwork to the teachers. If teachers work illegally, they will not be paying insurance contributions so will not be eligible for unemployment benefits, bonuses, pension, etc. Employers will take on the necessary transactions only if they are convinced that a candidate will be an asset to their school. Officially, applicants with non-EU passports must obtain a letter of hire from a language school which must be sent to an address outside Greece. The teacher takes the letter to the nearest Greek consulate and applies for a work permit; the procedures take at least two months.

It is mandatory for Greek employers to register full-time employees with the Greek national health insur-ance scheme, which has changed its name from IKA to EOPYY, which covers less than it used to. For exam-ple everyone has to pay more for medicines and contribute 15% to the cost of medical tests, treatments, etc. School owners have always been reluctant to pay contributions for their staff, especially when the rate of contribution rose to 30% of salary in the wake of Greece's financial catastrophe, while the employee's con-tribution of 16%–20% should be deducted at source. Many Greeks no longer see the point of paying, since it is much more expensive for them than it used to be and covers less. It is necessary to qualify for a pension but many are wondering if there will be any pensions in the future. Freelance teachers who teach privately will not be covered by social security unless they choose to pay TEBE contributions to the OAEE (insurance for the self-employed), which will be a minimum of €250 a month regardless of earnings.

CONDITIONS OF WORK

Standards vary among employers. Legislation that used to protect teachers is being watered down so that the government can cut its expenditure. Again **Jain Cook** provided a bleak account of recent changes and their impact on teachers:

There is no longer a legal minimum wage. Our teachers took a 15% pay cut and another 20%–22% a year later. Married teachers used to get an extra 10% per hour, but this has been abolished. That means that the income of a married woman will have been reduced by 45% over two years. Things are not easy! As salaries have dropped, so have rents. Some rents in Patras have dropped from €350 per month to €150, and there are hundreds of empty flats. Everything else though, has gone up.

The standard recommended hourly wage is €8.13 (gross), €6.84 (net).

In general the large chains are better, probably for no other reason than that they have a longer history of employing native English speakers. You also have some back-up if you have been hired through a mediating agency. Some of the small one-man or one-woman schools are run by barely qualified entrepreneurs who have had little contact with the English language; their teaching techniques involve shouting (usually in Greek) at their students and getting them to recite English irregular verbs parrot fashion. In fact this kind of school is on the decline, and standards have been rising.

The average number of hours assigned to teachers has been shrinking, to 18 per week or even as low as 12, which means reduced earnings and the possibility that the school will not be obliged to pay contributions. Teachers with superior training or experience may be able to ask for more hours and a higher rate. Schools that recruit from abroad tend to pay €700–€1,000 a month in addition to free accommodation. The custom in Greece has been to supplement low basic wages with a range of statutory benefits, eg holiday pay and Christmas and Easter bonuses. However, the recent austerity measures threaten the survival of many of these compensatory perks. So far the long-established compulsory bonuses paid at Christmas, Easter and at the end of a contract have not been abolished in the private sector, though they have been abolished in the public sector. There are also plans to abolish unemployment benefit for teachers who have worked for an eight-month academic year.

Teachers must find their rewards elsewhere, as 45-year-old recently qualified TEFL teacher **Phil Tomkins** did while teaching on the small island of Kea:

> *Regarding finances, I long ago reconciled myself to the fact that I would never be a millionaire (certainly not from teaching!) and for some time have been re-adjusting what I want out of life. Peace and contentment, for me, far outweigh the benefits of the rat race and I am happy to live in comfortable 'poverty' on a sunny Greek island doing a job I enjoy, rather than working my fingers to the bone chasing the almighty dollar, and giving whoever is the current architect of our doom a big, fat slice of it. To measure one's successes solely in pounds, shillings and pence is a sure way to depression, disappointment and stress. Friends and family have all been very enthusiastic and supportive of me 'doing a Shirley Valentine' – and not a little jealous that even now, at the end of November, I'm still to be found at the beach most days. So far I have been thoroughly enjoying it, though I am missing my two main dietary requirements: curry and beer.*

The teaching year has been shrinking, so that an increasing number of schools now start their courses at the beginning of October and finish at the end of May. So some schools offer eight-month contracts rather than the nine months that used to be standard. Teachers should always check beforehand the date up to which they will be paid. Native English speakers are often employed to teach exam classes that finish before the end of May. Teachers should check that they will be paid until the end of the month if they are not going to continue at least a few hours a week doing oral work with their students. Schools have been known to break the contract by paying off teachers as soon as their classes have taken the exams.

Employers who have suffered from staff desertions in the past may hold back some of your monthly pay as a bond (*kratisi*) against an early departure. Teachers with insufficient hours are forced either to work at more than one school (which school owners are not keen on) or to take on private students. Split shifts are now very uncommon except in technical colleges or universities. Almost all teaching at *frontisteria* takes place between 5pm and 10pm.

It is not unusual to be expected to teach in two or more 'satellite' sites of the main school in villages up to 10 miles away. Local bus services are generally good and cheap but you could find yourself spending an inordinate amount of (unpaid) time in transit and standing around at bus stops.

All areas have a local workers' office, where you can go if you are in dispute with your employer or fear that you are being ripped off.

PUPILS

Most native English speakers are employed to teach advanced classes, usually the two years leading to Cambridge or other exams. Because of the Greek style of education, pupils may not show much initiative and will expect to be tested frequently on what they have been taught. **Andrew Boyle** found the prevailing methodology of 'sit 'em down, shut 'em up and give 'em lots of homework' was moderately successful.

Another problem is that there is a great deal of pressure to assign pass marks just to retain the students' custom. Some school owners are so profit motivated, they have euros for eyeballs. Students expect to be told the answers and bosses want their teachers to be lenient with the marking so that the students all pass and parents will re-enrol them.

Will Brady, teaching on the island of Santorini, found the pupils quite challenging, particularly the girls:

The job was littered with problems because the kids, for a start, were pretty uninterested. They were the off-spring of hotel owners on the island, for the most part, whose only reason for having their kids learn English was so that they could be of use in the family business when the tourists came in summer. They had a level of MTV English but that was about it. They weren't motivated to learn and it was quite difficult to get them interested in the subject. I had a particular problem with a class of 15- to16-year-old girls who were quite difficult to discipline. For some lessons I was alone and they took advantage of the fact that I didn't speak Greek. They were not even bothering to whisper, but talking openly to each other, and playing footsie with me under the table, and it was very difficult to know how to handle that. The manager took me aside and told me in no uncertain terms that I should not respond to any of the advances. Thankfully, I hadn't entertained the idea.

ACCOMMODATION

Since many schools provide a flat or at least help in finding a flat, teachers are often not too concerned about their living arrangements. Placements arranged by the recruitment agencies offer free accommodation in addition to the full salary. It is definitely worth checking in advance about furnishings. Flats are sometimes quite spartan but some of the better ones are comfortably furnished and may have a washing machine and television in addition to the essentials. However, some flats, especially in Athens, are unfurnished, which is a serious nuisance for someone on an eight-month contract.

Utility bills come every two months, and winters in Greece can be surprisingly cold. Even in a small flat, the electricity bill will run to hundreds of euros. Water bills are very cheap, however. Before taking over accommodation, try to find out if the bills have been paid. Changing the name is such a major hassle (involving tax returns, etc) and unfortunately it is not uncommon for tenants to move on without paying their bills and the new tenant becomes liable. Non-payment of electricity and phone bills (but not water bills) will result in disconnection, and no final reminders are sent out.

LEISURE TIME

Teachers in Athens should have no trouble constructing a social life. Outside Athens, the social order is still fairly conservative. A further problem is the enormous language barrier in a country where it will take some time to learn how to read the alphabet. Watching Greek television is a good way to learn the language plus Greek lessons are run free of charge in many locations. **Cassandra**, based in the north of Greece, found that *'teaching was a bit more difficult and isolating than I expected, but once I was used to the lifestyle I enjoyed it . . . with hindsight I would have enrolled in Greek lessons sooner and tried to get out and meet more people.'*

Most teachers find the vast majority of Greek people to be honest, friendly and helpful and are seldom disappointed with the hospitality they receive. As anyone who has visited Greece knows, the country has countless other attractions, not least the very convivial tavernas. Eating out is no longer the bargain it once was. With the increase in VAT, many goods and services have risen in price, and even wine, which used to be exempt, is now taxed. Travel, particularly ferry travel, is affordable and a pure delight out of season. Despite all the hassles, most people enjoy a year in Greece.

LIST OF EMPLOYERS

ANGLO-HELLENIC TEACHER RECRUITMENT
13 Vasilou St. 200 06 Corinth
- +30 27410 53511
- applications@anglo-hellenic.com
- www.anglo-hellenic.com or www.tefl.gr

NUMBER OF TEACHERS: About 80 vacancies every year in a wide choice of locations.

PREFERENCE OF NATIONALITY: British.

QUALIFICATIONS: University graduates with a TEFL certificate. Graduates of TEFL Corinth course are given priority.

CONDITIONS OF EMPLOYMENT: Most vacancies are in September, several in January and a few throughout the year.

SALARY: 9-month contracts pay the going rate of €700–€1,000 per month plus bonuses and 4-weeks' paid holiday.

FACILITIES/SUPPORT: Accommodation in a furnished flat. A four-page contract will be provided by agency (specimen copy available beforehand). Anglo-Hellenic also takes care of the bureaucratic essentials, and encourages meetings and exchange visits of its teachers and provides interactive web-based facilities for information, opinion and social chat. Several TEFL certificate courses (120 hours) are run every summer, with shorter professional development courses also being offered throughout the year.

RECRUITMENT: Interviews are conducted in London, Athens or Corinth, throughout the summer.

CONTACT: Peter Beech, Recruitment Director.

BETSIS LANGUAGE SCHOOLS
Thivon 109, 18542 Piraeus
- +30 210 490 8926
Second site: Pyrgou 31, 18542 Piraeus
- abetsis@otenet.gr; abetsis@hol.gr;
  lmamas@yahoo.com

NUMBER OF TEACHERS: 15–20, also for two branches in small town of Drosia, north-west of Piraeus.

PREFERENCE OF NATIONALITY: British and Irish. As of April 2013, offering short internships to US nationals who have completed Anglo-Hellenic certificate course mentioned above.

QUALIFICATIONS: Bachelor's degree and Cambridge exams.

CONDITIONS OF EMPLOYMENT: 8-month contracts. 18–24 hours per week. Also opportunities for teachers to work at the publishing company, Andrew Betsis ELT, specialising in ELT exam books. Positions are available in the editorial and marketing departments.

SALARY: €9,000–€10,000 per year.

FACILITIES/SUPPORT: School helps teachers find rental accommodation and with the bureaucracy involved in applying for a work permit.

CONTACT: Lawrence Mamas, Director of Studies.

CAMBRIDGE TEACHERS RECRUITMENT
8 Daskalou-Kitsou, Maroussi, 15124 Athens
- +30 210 258 5155 or +30 697 222 8893 (mobile) or
  +30 694 655 8217
UK contact address of main interviewer (August only):
53 Green Acres, Parkhill, Croydon CRO 5UX, UK
- +44 20 8686 3733
- macleod_smith_andrew@hotmail.com

NUMBER OF TEACHERS: 25+ per year.

PREFERENCE OF NATIONALITY: British or EU.

QUALIFICATIONS: Degree and TEFL certificate, a friendly personality and conscientious attitude.

CONDITIONS OF EMPLOYMENT: Contracts usually between September and May, although some summer work. Usual hours are Monday to Friday between 4pm and 10pm (25 hours per week).

SALARY: Roughly €650–€800 net per month plus flat, bonuses, 4-weeks' holiday pay and pension contributions.

FACILITIES/SUPPORT: Accommodation is provided (not necessarily free) plus health insurance and pension. Holiday pay is given at Christmas and Easter. Applicants can expect to receive plenty of information about working in Greece.

RECRUITMENT: Comprehensive interviews are conducted between mid-June and the end of August. Interviews are held in hotels in Central London.

CONTACT: Andrew Macleod-Smith.

KOUTSANTONIS SCHOOL OF LANGUAGES

35 Gounari Ave, 26221 Patras

✆ +30 2610 273925

✉ kapaflc@otenet.gr

NUMBER OF TEACHERS: Out of 35 staff in 9 schools, only 1 is British.

PREFERENCE OF NATIONALITY: Native English speakers with Greek ancestry.

QUALIFICATIONS: University degree. Preferably a teaching qualification and some experience.

CONDITIONS OF EMPLOYMENT: 8-month contracts. 10–12 teaching hours per week, evenings only, Monday–Friday.

SALARY: The legal minimum of €9 gross has been abolished so it is up to school owner and teacher to agree a rate.

FACILITIES/SUPPORT: School owner will help with search for an apartment and might be able to lend furniture.

RECRUITMENT: Generally teachers leave their CVs in person and are called back for interview when a vacancy occurs.

CONTACT: Cindy or Connie Koutsantoni (kapaflc@otenet.gr).

LAMBRAKI FOREIGN LANGUAGES CENTRES

Kamarioti 4, 71414 Gazi, Heraklion, Crete

✆ +30 2810 822292

✉ info@lambraki.eu or lambraki.gazi@gmail.com

🖥 www.lambraki.gr or www.lambraki.eu

NUMBER OF TEACHERS: 10.

PREFERENCE OF NATIONALITY: Britain.

QUALIFICATIONS: University degree and TEFL qualification.

CONDITIONS OF EMPLOYMENT: Most teachers stay 2–3 years. 18–25 hours per week.

SALARY: From €700 per month (negotiable), less 16% deductions.

FACILITIES/SUPPORT: Assistance given in finding accommodation. School assists with residence permit after teacher provides a verified copy of his/her degree; official translation can be done in Heraklion.

RECRUITMENT: Via newspaper adverts, personal contact and PALSO Association. Telephone interviews.

CONTACT: Irene Lambraki, School Director.

LORD BYRON SCHOOL

104, Tsimiski St; Diagonbios, 54622 Thessaloniki

✆ +30 2310 278804

✉ school@lordbyron.gr or lordbyron@lordbyron.gr

🖥 www.lordbyron.gr

Member of QLS.

TEACHERS: 3–5 native English speakers.

PREFERENCE OF NATIONALITY: EU citizens.

QUALIFICATIONS: University degree, TEFLA, CELTA and EFL teaching experience.

CONDITIONS OF EMPLOYMENT: Standard contract 8 months. 24–26 hours per week. 40% of clients are adults or university students.

SALARY: €800 to €1,000 according to qualifications. 17% deductions for tax and social security.

FACILITIES/SUPPORT: Assistance finding accommodation and obtaining a legal status/teaching permit.

RECRUITMENT: Via detailed CV, interview, model lesson (with lesson plan). Interviews are carried out in Thessaloniki every May and June.

CONTACT: Harry J. Nikolaides, School Director (harry@lordbyron.gr).

PAPAELIOU SCHOOLS OF FOREIGN LANGUAGES

111 Karaiskou Str, 185 32 Piraeus-Athens

✆ +30 210 417 3892

✉ karaiskou@papaeliou.edu.gr

🖥 www.papaeliou.edu.gr

Branches in Piraeus and Nikea.

NUMBER OF TEACHERS: 45.

PREFERENCE OF NATIONALITY: British. Majority are Greek-Americans or Greek. Must possess a valid visa.

QUALIFICATIONS: Minimum age 21. Bachelor's or master's degree and teacher training.

CONDITIONS OF EMPLOYMENT: 1–3 year contracts to teach at least 4 hours a day. Hours extend late into the evening.

SALARY: Approx. €850 net; €382 deductions.

FACILITIES/SUPPORT: No help with accommodation.

RECRUITMENT: Interviewees teach a demo lesson. Successful candidates must then complete the in-service training programme and sign a probationary 3-month contract.

CONTACT: Ms Ino Panayotou, Director of Studies.

NUMBER OF TEACHERS: 6.

PREFERENCE OF NATIONALITY: None, but EU member state passport preferred.

QUALIFICATIONS: minimum BA plus TESOL certificate and experience. TESOL courses offered at Linguistic Lab.

CONDITIONS OF EMPLOYMENT: Standard contract period 1 year. To work 18–25 hours per week. Classes begin early September and finish in May/June. Summer classes may run in June and July.

SALARY: €700 a month; no deductions made.

FACILITIES/SUPPORT: Free accommodation is provided: furnished 2-bedroom apartments, to be shared between 2 teachers. Utilities are the responsibility of teachers. Option to have a private apartment, with a lower salary.

RECRUITMENT: To apply send a CV, copies of diplomas and passport, reference letters and a recent photo to the above address.

CONTACT: Bob Filis, Owner.

ITALY

The economic woes that have afflicted Southern Europe are not hitting the English language teaching market as hard as they were including among companies specialising in corporate training. The younger end of the spectrum is holding up particularly well, with many children and teenagers being entered for externally moderated exams like the Cambridge suite, for which they often turn to private tutoring companies. Chances are always better in towns and cities which cannot boast leaning towers, gondolas or coliseums. Small towns in southern Italy and Sardinia, in the Dolomites and along the Adriatic have more than their fair share of private language schools and institutes, all catering to Italians who have failed to learn English in the state system. (English teaching in Italian schools is generally acknowledged to be inadequate.)

PROSPECTS FOR TEACHERS

A complete range of language schools can be found in Italy, as the *Yellow Pages* will confirm. At the elite end of the market, there are the 34 schools which belong to AISLi, the Associazione Italiana Scuole di Lingue (www.aisli.it) which is involved with teacher employment (www.aisli.it/recruiting.html). Prospective teachers can submit their CVs to AISLi (aisli@aisli.com) who will circulate them round all member schools. Only ultra-respectable schools can become AISLi members so there are thousands of good schools outside the association. AISLi schools normally expect their teachers to have decent qualifications and in return offer attractive remuneration packages and conditions of employment.

At the other end of the spectrum, there is a host of schools which some might describe as cowboy operations, though these are decreasing in number. The CELTA is widely recognised and respected in Italy (unlike in France, for instance) as are other certificates. The days of finding work without a qualification are all but over. US qualifications are less well known for the simple reason that work permits are very difficult for non-EU citizens to obtain. There are so many job-seekers with TEFL training that qualifications are necessary in order to compete with all those native English speakers so keen to live, work and teach in Italy. A healthy number of schools can be seen advertising on the main ELT websites like www.tefl.com.

Strict employment regulations and red tape in Italy make small companies reluctant to offer full-time 'Italian' contracts or help with legal paperwork. Increasingly, schools are hiring teachers only on a freelance basis, whom they pay by the hour and offer no benefits. For example, Caledonian Communications in Milan commented: '*Unfortunately due to the economic situation in Europe we have had to change our staffing policy. We therefore no longer offer contracts, teachers are hired on a freelance basis.*' This means that most English teachers work for more than one private language school and also teach freelance lessons to make ends meet. However, these are exceptions. Another training company in Milan, The Language Grid (see entry) offers Italian contracts to long-term staff.

A few schools offer a British contract (ie one that is not subject to Italian legislation) in which the wages are lower than on an Italian contract but the benefits may be good and the red tape much less (see entries for Alpha Beta Piccadilly and Caledonian Communications for example).

The British and Irish recruitment agency, Evocation EFL, has a specialist section that places certified TEFL teachers with employers throughout Italy (www.evo.jobs). They are employed on a British contract and the agency maintains that the net earnings are equivalent to their Italian counterparts, but much cheaper for the employer.

Compulsory contributions for social security and expensive perks make hiring a permanent member of staff very costly so most of the jobs available are eight or nine-month contracts, October to May. The majority of English teachers in Italy work with no long-term job security, which is acceptable for those who want to spend only one or two years in the country. A lot of teaching work in Italy is paid under the table. Contracts shouldn't be expected at the start though they are more likely to be given by private language schools in smaller out of the way places.

Some private schools are contracted to provide teaching staff to state schools, but are trying to get away with paying teachers the same low wage from €12. If you are offered off-site work in the state sector (normally available only if you know Italian), do plenty of research and try to negotiate an hourly wage of at least €25 and read any contract carefully before signing.

A useful starting place for resources and information on training and teaching English in Italy is www.teachingenglishinitaly.com, a site maintained by **Sheila Corwin,** an American resident in Florence who has been working and living as an English language teacher and teacher trainer in Italy (on and off) since 2002. The company offers affordable online options in basic TEFL certification (from €200/$265), a 20-hour weekend TEFL course in Florence (€195) about six times a year and other teacher refresher courses; details from sheila@teachingenglishinitaly.com. Another repository of tips for teaching in Italy is www.tjtaylor.net with up-to-date resources in the Careers section covering qualifications, visas, tax and so on.

FINDING A JOB

IN ADVANCE

There is no single compendium of the hundreds of language school addresses in Italy. The relevant Yellow Pages, *Pagine Gialle*, are user friendly: go to www.paginegialle.it and choose the handy English version of the site. Typing in 'language schools' will produce more than 2,400 entries. The search engine allows you to search by city or more generally by region.

International language school groups such as Benedict Schools, Linguarama, Berlitz and inlingua are major providers of English language teaching in Italy. International House has a dozen affiliated schools throughout the country most of which teach English. Wall Street Institute now has 70 centres in Italy and actively recruits native English speakers. Occasional vacancies are posted at www.wallstreet.it/jobs; in most cases applications should be sent directly to the school, whereas other recruitment is done by head office in Milan (staff@wallstreet.it). Applications to Berlitz should be sent to the individual schools hiring, eg workinrome@berlitz.com and workinmilan@berlitz.com.

A considerable number of Italian schools advertise vacancies on www.tefl.com; for example there were 37 job postings at the time of writing (June 2015). Several Italian-based chains of language schools account for a large number of teaching jobs. Many operate as independent franchises. For example you can get contact details for all 160+ British Institutes on the website www.britishinstitutes.it (click on 'Sedi'). Smaller chains to investigate include My English Schools (www.myenglishschool.it) which hire teachers for Bari, Bologna, Florence, Milan, Modena, Palermo, Rome, Turin and Verona; Morgan Schools (www.morganschool.it) with a network of 20 schools around Italy, and Millenium [sic] Language Schools (www.milleniumlanguage.it).

Other chains include the British Schools Group (www.britishschool.com/forms/teaching-opportunities. htm) with nearly 70 member schools. The Oxford Group (www.oxford.it) also has a centralised recruitment department (see entry for International School of Europe). Most language schools in Italy seem to incorporate the word British, English, Oxford or Cambridge randomly combined with Centre, School or Institute, which can result in confusion, especially when it comes to the British School Group (www.britishschool.it/job_opportunities. php) which is quite separate from the British Schools Group.

American citizens have a lot of problems finding work in Italy, largely because it is so difficult to obtain a work permit. However, a solution suggested by **Carla Valentine**, an English teacher in Venice, is to try working for one of the Department of Defense US army schools on the military bases in Italy. Under these circumstances, work permits are processed in the USA.

ON THE SPOT

The online *Yellow Pages* is probably still the best source of possible employers. Italians like face-to-face contact and, according to **Sheila Corwin**, director of www.teachingenglishinitaly.com, stopping by a school to meet the director often works better than blindly sending out résumés through snail or electronic mail. She urges job-seeking teachers to leave their CVs with directors even if the school is not hiring at the time because schools sometimes call back one or even three months later when they need a teacher. It is also a good ploy to offer to teach a few free lessons to their students to help get a foot in the door.

Often a few hours' teaching can gradually be built up into a full-time job by those willing to say yes. If you're there when they need you, you can usually get something. Most find that the longer they stay, the more hours they get, though there is still no job security working this way.

ALEX NEUMAN

Alex Neuman, a globetrotting journalist, describes how she set about finding teaching work in the town of Bergamo, where she and her partner had decided to spend a year or two.

The first step these days is to go online. I quickly found three or four English schools in Bergamo: Shenker, Wall Street, Inlingua and two small local firms run by individuals. I decided I should also look in Milan since it is only 45 minutes by train from Bergamo.

This is where you quickly realise this is not like job hunting in your own country and in your own language. Few Italians answer emails from strangers. You have to pick up the phone - a challenge when your language is rusty but as these were English schools most had an English speaking receptionist. Then I discovered the vagaries of the private teaching system, which basically is out to make as much money as possible while paying as little as possible to teachers and expecting infinite flexibility on the teacher's part and no flexibility on the school's part!

You will need patience and a sense of humour at this stage. I quickly got an interview with Wall Street Institute and Shenker and was accepted at Shenker. Being accepted is not a problem it's actually getting onto the payroll and teaching that takes time. It was three months before I got on a two-week training course where I was promised €150 a week. In fact I received this money in December - two months after I'd done the course and five months after the initial interview. So it is best to have plenty of spare cash to see you through the first six months of finding work.

Shenker was good for me because I had no formal teaching qualification and it is based around a system so all your lesson plans are provided, you simply turn up and teach the system. For this you will be paid about €13.50 an hour before tax. I get about 15 hours of work a week, although they promised 20. But as I started working for them during the financial crisis their student numbers were considerably down.

They do offer 30 hour-a-week contracts but at a much reduced rate of pay. This will suit some people as it means you can stay in the country if you have a work contract. However, the pay is truly abysmal and you have to do the 30 hours a week, which can often involve split shifts including working till 8.30pm every evening and Saturday mornings. Plus these contracts only run from September to July so you don't get paid in August.

The upside to teaching is that the Italians working in the schools are great on the whole. Everyone knows that the system is bad and tries to help each other through it. The students are also great and if you have a class you get to know, teaching can be really fun. It's a good way to get to know people and the Italians are by and large extremely friendly and always willing to help you out if they can. It also gives you a sense of belonging and really getting involved.

Melanie Drake had much better luck in Bari:

Italy has been a very positive experience for the most part, though living in the south without knowing the language can be quite problematic! It is really pretty easy to get work in Italy once TEFL-qualified, as the English level here is low (in the south especially). Money isn't fantastic but it balances out as life is fairly cheap, particularly if, like me, you can walk to work. Often accommodation is included with the contracts offered too. Ironically I am earning half of what I got in London, though here I can save fairly easily as my outgoings are halved. It works out pretty well.

Scouring adverts in English language newspapers has worked for some. The fortnightly publications *Wanted in Rome* (www.wantedinrome.com) and *Wanted in Milan* (www.wantedinmilan.com) are very useful (particularly in the spring) as is the Italian-language classified ads paper *Porta Portese*. If you happen to see a request for 'mothers only', this means that they are looking for a teacher whose mother tongue is English (*Insegnanti madrelingua*), not a female with small children. Other publications with useful classifieds include *The Florentine* and *Easy Milano*.

FREELANCE TEACHING

Another possibility is to set up as a freelance tutor, though a knowledge of Italian is even more of an asset here than it is for jobs in schools. A participant on a *Guardian* web forum on ELT careers wrote in an encouraging vein for older job-seekers:

I'm a career changer in my mid-50s and have had no problems here in Italy. I don't teach in language schools but contract direct with local state schools, libraries and private students, but that is based on having had means of support until I developed the requisite contacts.

Alex Neuman is another teacher in middle life who has found Italy, and Bergamo in particular, a welcoming place. She supplemented her hours at local academies with private students:

Italians are desperate to speak English so getting private students isn't that hard. The best students I have got are through word of mouth. A very friendly neighbour is always recommending me to friends and colleagues and I have managed to find myself three or four that keep me busy. I got my very first student by putting up a notice on the university noticeboard in Bergamo but have never had to do more than that. When writing an ad for private students you must always use the words 'mother-tongue speaker' – even though 'native English speaker' is more correct English! Rates for private students vary between €15 and €25 an hour.

University students looking for private tuition might consult university noticeboards such as the one at the Città Universitaria in Rome, main campus of La Sapienza University of Rome.

Porta Portese is also a good forum in which to advertise your availability to offer English lessons in Rome; adverts placed by women should not betray their gender and meetings with prospective clients should not take place in private homes. As long as you have access to some premises, you can try to arrange both individual and group lessons. Whatever way you decide to look for work, remember that life grinds to a halt in August, just as it does in France. Competition is keenest in Florence and Venice, which are both saturated, so new arrivals should head elsewhere.

Freelance teaching can be very lucrative and you can expect to make around €20 an hour, which is still undercutting most of the language agencies (which charge around €26 per hour and keep half themselves). New entrants to the market may have to offer lessons for €15 until they become established.

SUMMER WORK

Paid work is available at a number of summer camps offering English instruction, a good opportunity for young people to spend a summer in Italy and learn more about teaching English to young learners. A number teach through the medium of theatre, so anyone interested in drama will be attracted by this idea. This opportunity is open to non-European nationalities, since the work period is less than three months and therefore within the duration of a Schengen visa. Some teacher training is often provided by the schools and companies that run these camp programmes. Most of these companies pay about €200 a week (less for city day camps). Successful summer teachers are often offered contracts for the academic year.

See entries at the end of this chapter for ACLE, Canadian Island, The English Camp Company, Kid's World, Lingue Senza Frontiere and International House in Campobasso. Other summer employers include:

Alice in Città Milan, (www.aliceincitta.org). Summer camps are based in Italian primary and secondary schools during summer holidays. Italian children learn English through games, art, sports, songs and acting.

Language Network, Feltre, Belluno (www.feltre-online.com). Energetic TEFL-qualified staff needed June/July. Pay is €1,000 for 25 days of work.

Berlitz Italy (louise.thorne@berlitz.it or summercamps@berlitz.it; www.berlitz.it). Candidates must be native English speakers and experienced with children to work at two camps in Tuscany. Two-week minimum stay in June/July.

The English Experience (englishcamps@englishexp.co.uk). Advertising two-week summer contracts in 2015. Interviews in Norwich in June.

Horizons Language Services, Largo Brindisi 18, int. 11; 00182 Rome (+39 677 201534; www.horizons.ie). Summer camp tutors needed mid-June and July. Ideally aged 20–35 with CELTA and experience with young children. Teachers already resident in Rome preferred.

M B Scambi, Padua (www.mbscambi.com). Summer camp for month of July held on the beach at Lignano Sabbiadoro in the Venice area. Experienced teachers are paid €390 (gross) per week plus free room and board in shared en suite rooms.

Newbeetle Viaggi Studio, Jesi (www.newbeetleviaggistudio.it). Language camps in the Marches. €300 net per week plus hotel accommodation and all meals.

Smile Modena (www.smilemodena.com). Employs summer tutors to mount English language theatre productions with groups of children. Summer staff are chosen after auditioning, including in London in October.

Scotia Personnel, Halifax, Canada (+1 902 422 1455; scotiap@ns.sympatico.ca or info@scotia-personnel-ltd.com; www.scotia-personnel-ltd.com). This North American agency runs an organised scheme whereby young North Americans are recruited to tutor English in families. Wage of €100–€200 per week.

REGULATIONS

The bureaucracy for citizens of EU member states has been simplified in recent years. EU citizens intending to stay in Italy longer than 90 days are required to register at the *anagrafe* office of the local town hall. Those who intend long stays of five years should apply for a *carta di soggiorno* or *certificato di residenza* (residence certificate). To obtain this, they must take proof of income (employment contract, financial backing from home) and must pass an Italian language test.

PHILIP LEE

Philip Lee from New Zealand wanted to spend his summers working in Europe. After a successful camp job in Switzerland, his attention turned to Italy. Although he didn't have direct experience of teaching English as a foreign language, he had worked with children and given tuition and revision classes. Here he describes the highs and lows of the job.

I searched online for work over the summer in Italy. There were a lot of random jobs that didn't really lead to anything and a lot of misleading job adverts. However, I found some English teaching websites that were credible and I applied. After completing a written application on my background and experience in teaching, working with children and art/drama/games/sport and providing references, I was hired by Lingua Senza Frontiere. I taught English through various indoor and outdoor activities. About 90% of my time was spent playing a game/sport or completing an activity that was explained and conducted in English and there was very limited traditional 'classroom' teaching. The focus was to do as much as possible in English, including the instructions for each activity. Depending on the children's age and their familiarity with English, it was possible by using simpler words, shorter sentences and demonstrating my instructions at the same time. Teaching was very physical: I spent most of my day - about five hours of teaching and two of supervision - standing. Because a lot of the children were not very familiar/comfortable with English I had to be very energetic, positive and supportive throughout the day to keep them encouraged.

Lunch was up to two hours long and we were always treated to a good and big Italian lunch. Most schools were happy to cater to special diets as long as they were given prior notice. I stayed with the most hospitable and generous families, most of whom lived by the seaside. While living with the host families, who often had children in the camp as well, I was given my own room and sometimes my own bathroom. The families were very accommodating and understood that non-Italians did do some things differently, such as eating more than one biscuit for breakfast. They also understood that I wanted to experience as much of Italy as possible and took me out on numerous occasions. We went to vineyards, restaurants, farms, relatives' houses, shops, the beach, holiday homes, bars and clubs with the older host brothers and sisters, the pool, concerts and neighbouring towns and cities. They were also quite happy when I went out to socialise at night.

The wages are not high, however, I considered the English camp as a working holiday and was not aiming to leave with many savings. The biggest problem was the language difficulties with the children and at the schools. This was because it was uncommon for any of the tutors to speak much Italian. Any tutor who spoke Italian was instructed not to make this known so that the children would not take advantage of it. The difficulty in communication made our job harder, but arguably it gave the children a better learning experience. The training sessions that the camp organisation provides are really vital and it would have been a great benefit if I had written down all the ideas for games and activities for future reference.

There were a few behavioural problems with some children but we were not expected to deal with these. Each camp had a local Italian teacher in charge of the camp and we would tell her of any problems. If she did not handle it, we could inform our employer, who would communicate directly with the school.

Altogether it was a great opportunity to meet people from all over the world as well as Italians, to spend time in Italy not as a tourist, and incredible fun working with children, as all day is spent playing games or doing activities.

As mentioned earlier, non-EU citizens have very little chance of getting their papers in order for a longer-term job unless they are dual nationals or receive a firm offer of a permanent job while they are still in their home country. In the words of the recruitment agency, Evocation EFL: 'Please, don't waste your time (and ours) by applying if you are from outside the EU (we cannot get visas if you are from the US, Canada, etc.).' Detailed information can be found at www.portaleimmigrazione.it including templates of the forms needed to apply for the *permessi*. According to the Italian Embassy in Washington, language teachers from the USA need a visa for *lavoro subordinato*. To qualify they must first obtain from their employer in Italy an authorisation to work issued by the Ministry of Labour or a Provincial Office of Labour (*Servizio politiche del lavoro*) plus an authorisation from the local *questura*. The originals of these plus a passport and one photo must be sent to the applicant's nearest embassy or consulate.

These procedures can take up to a year to complete and, as **Carla Valentine**, an English teacher in Venice, points out, '*no school director in his right mind is going to bother going through that process when there are plenty of British teachers here who can work without visa red tape*'. It is for this reason that so many Americans and other non-EU citizens work in Italy without work visas. However, there are two legal alternatives for US citizens. The first is to go to Italy on a student visa, which allows you to work for up to 20 hours a week (enough to live on). Interested Americans and other nationalities can contact private language schools that offer Italian classes to find out whether they can sponsor candidates signing up for a course of long duration. This is the route that Carla took some years ago:

> *Getting a student visa is very easy. I enrolled for a year at Istituto Venezia to learn Italian. With a letter of enrolment from the school I was able to get a student visa from the Italian Consulate in Boston for one year (whether or not I attend classes is irrelevant, although obviously I do).*

Long-term language courses are expensive, but prices differ radically. **Sheila Corwin** provided a snapshot of the options in Florence, where she lives and trains TEFL teachers:

> *A standard 20-hour Italian course runs €220 per week at Europass, the private Italian language school in Florence where I hold my weekend TEFL courses, but I am sure a cheaper quote would be offered for a longer stay (www.europass.it). The Istituto Europeo where I've studied Italian offers a year-long Italian course for €5,180 which covers 960 lessons for a duration of 48 weeks (www.istitutoeuropeo.it/indexENG.html). The Centro di Cultura per Stranieri, which offers Italian language courses through the University of Florence, is a lower-cost option. They offer 10-week courses in each of the four seasons costing €500-€650 (www.ccs.unifi.it/changelang-eng.html). Finally, the Centro di Internazionale Studenti Georgio La Pira offers the Italian-in-Florence programme, which is almost certainly the cheapest available. They offer semi-intensive month-long courses (40 hours) for €160 (www.centrointernazionalelapira.it).*

The second option is to become an independent contractor. This involves getting an expensive tax code number (*partita IVA*) from the local town government, which you have to do once you are earning more than €5,000, and work for more than one private language school. To get this number, you need a *codice fiscale* (similar to a social security number), which is available from the local town hall upon presentation of a passport or may also be obtainable online from the Agenzia delle Entrate (Revenue Agency).

With this number it is possible to obtain the *partita IVA* from the municipal authorities, though it will be necessary to use the services of an accountant. With these numbers you can find work and get paid, even though technically without a *permesso di soggiorno* you are still an illegal immigrant. Australian and New Zealand citizens aged 18–30 plus Canadians aged 18–35 are eligible for a 12-month working holiday visa in Italy. Holders are not meant to work for more than six months during the year.

Tax is a further headache for long-stay teachers. As soon as you sort out the work documents, you should obtain a tax number (*codice fiscale*). The rate of income tax (*Ritenuta d'Acconto*) is usually about 23% in addition to social security deductions of 8%–9%. You'll be better off if you can work out an arrangement whereby the private language school deducts an amount from your wages in order to cover the taxes that you'd pay if you had a *partita IVA*.

CONDITIONS OF WORK

A typical salary for a full-time timetable would be about €1,300 net per month (roughly £1,000), though novice teachers sometimes earn not much more than €1,000. Staff on a *contratto di collaborazione* are paid by the hour, normally ranging from €12 to €19 net. Always find out if pay scales are quoted net or gross, since the two figures are so different. Take-home pay is not as high as might have been expected because of the high cost of compulsory national insurance, social security and pension contributions. Salaries tend to be substantially higher in Northern Italy than in the south to compensate for the much higher cost of living. Business English, as always, can be very lucrative. Intensive Business English, based in Milan (see List of Employers) offers a gross salary of between €1,800 and €3,250. However, some teachers in Rome, Milan, Bologna, etc have had to reconcile themselves to spending up to half their salaries on rent. Even for Italians, salaries are low when compared with the cost of living.

Only professional teachers will benefit from the industry-wide agreement or *Contratto Collettivo Nazionale del Lavoro* (CCNL), which sets a high salary for a regulation 100-hour working month. Because of the high costs of legal employment, there is a lot of dubious practice in Italy and prospective teachers should try to talk to an ex-teacher before committing themselves, especially if offered a job before arrival.

Few teachers complain about their students. Even when pupils attend English classes for social reasons (as many do in small towns with little nightlife) or are generally unmotivated, they are usually good natured, hospitable and talkative in class. In contrast to Greece, many language school directors are British rather than local.

LEISURE TIME

Italian culture and lifestyle do not need to have their praises sung here. A large number of teachers who have gone out on short-term contracts never come back – probably a higher proportion than in any other country. While rents are high, eating out is fairly cheap and public transport is quite affordable. Women teachers should be prepared to cope with some Mediterranean machismo, particularly in the south, and may have to contend with unwanted male attention.

Compared with many languages, Italian is easy to learn, though courses are expensive. It may be possible to swap English lessons for Italian ones, which might lead to further freelance teaching.

LIST OF EMPLOYERS

A.C.L.E. (ASSOCIAZIONE CULTURALE LINGUISTICA EDUCATIONAL)
Via Roma 54, 18038 San Remo
℡ +39 0184 506070
✉ info@acle.org
🖥 www.acle.org

NUMBER OF TEACHERS: 750 for 400 city day camps and residential camps all over Italy from Sicily to the Dolomites.
PREFERENCE OF NATIONALITY: Native English speakers between 19 and 30 years of age.

QUALIFICATIONS: Minimum age 19. Must have experience working with children and the ability to teach English through the use of theatre and outdoor activities. A fun-loving personality and genuine interest in children, high moral standards and a flexible attitude to work required, preferably with some experience of living and travelling abroad.
CONDITIONS OF EMPLOYMENT: Camps start in June and run until September. Minimum of 3-weeks commitment required. The average tutor works for 4 weeks or more. Tutors change location every week or fortnight.
SALARY: €225 (city camp) and €275 (summer camp) per week, plus full board and homestay accommodation. Transport between camps provided plus insurance.

FACILITIES/SUPPORT: Intensive 5/6-day introductory TEFL-TP (Teaching English to Foreign Learners through Theatre and Play) course is compulsory and provided for fee of €150 usually deducted from wages.

RECRUITMENT: Application online at www.acle.org. Recruitment season for following summer opens 1 October. Deadline for applications is the middle of March, though recruitment can continue into June if vacancies remain.

CONTACT: Jake, ACLE Recruitment Office (jake@acle.org).

ALPHA BETA PICCADILLY
via Talvera/Talfergasse 1a, 39100 Bolzano/Bozen
☏ +39 0471 978600
✉ info@alphabeta.it
💻 www.alphabeta.it

NUMBER OF TEACHERS: 10–15 also for branch in Merano/Meran, also in South Tyrol.

PREFERENCE OF NATIONALITY: Must have a passport from an EU member state.

QUALIFICATIONS: Minimum CELTA or equivalent. DELTA plus at least 2–3 years' TEFL experience preferred.

CONDITIONS OF EMPLOYMENT: 9-month contract with 18–22 contact hours per week.

SALARY: Around £1,530–£1,650 per month gross based on a British contract, depending on qualifications and experience. Standard UK income tax and social security deductions are made.

FACILITIES/SUPPORT: School has 2 flats available for teachers to share. Assistance given with work permits; however, these are relatively straightforward.

RECRUITMENT: Usually via www.tefl.com. Interviews are essential and are occasionally held in the UK.

CONTACT: Peter Marsh-Hunn, Director of Studies, English (marsh-hunn@alphabeta.it).

ANDERSON HOUSE
Via Bergamo 25, 24035 Curno, Bergamo
☏ +39 035 463074
✉ p.anderson@andersonhouse.it
💻 www.andersonhouse.it

AH is a language school specialising in corporate language training and management training for companies (TIP, DPI, ICE and intercultural communication). It also offers courses to children and adults in preparation for Cambridge exams, and is a centre for language testing and certifications (Cambridge, BULATS, TOEIC and TOEFL). Anderson House is a founder member of SIETAR Italia (www.sietar-italia.org).

NUMBER OF TEACHERS: 4 full-time; 6 part-time for English; 10 part-time for other languages.

PREFERENCE OF NATIONALITY: British and Irish. European passport essential.

QUALIFICATIONS: Degree plus CELTA (minimum grade B), TESOL, DELTA or CertIBET (Trinity's Certificate in International Business English Training) and minimum 3 years' experience.

CONDITIONS OF EMPLOYMENT: Couples with car a bonus. Contracts from October to June (8/9 months) or from January for 5 months. All contracts renewable. To work 25 hours per week, 8am–10pm (one period of the day free). Some Saturday morning work; some summer work (June, July, September).

SALARY: €1,300 net for qualified teachers with 3 years' experience. Salary negotiable for those with more experience.

FACILITIES/SUPPORT: Italian lessons at cost. 70% is company work (general and business) both on and offsite. School has 3 small company cars and helps teachers with accommodation. Excellent facilities, staff resource centre, free internet access.

RECRUITMENT: Via www.tefl.com and direct application.

CONTACT: Peter Anderson, Director and Owner (p.anderson@andersonhouse.it).

ANGLO-AMERICAN CENTRE
Via Mameli 46, Cagliari 09124, Sardinia
☏ +39 070 654955
✉ angloamericancagliari@gmail.com
💻 www.angloamericancentre.it

Member of AISLi.

NUMBER OF TEACHERS: 20.

PREFERENCE OF NATIONALITY: Must be native speakers of English and have legal status to work in the EU.

QUALIFICATIONS: CELTA or Cert TESOL, 2 years' post-CELTA, reasonable Italian language competence, experience especially with younger learners, knowledge of Cambridge ESOL exams. Valid driving licence preferred.

CONDITIONS OF EMPLOYMENT: 1 October to 30 June for new teachers. 25 hours' contact time per week. Also summer school in July and possiblilty of contract renewal.

SALARY: €1,150–€1,300 per month (net of contributions).

FACILITIES/SUPPORT: School helps teachers to make contact with landlords and may accompany new arrivals to viewings. References can be provided to landlords and loans to cover initial deposit if necessary. Flight contribution.

RECRUITMENT: Direct applications, via TEFL.com or the AISLi website. Interviews are held face-to-face in Cagliari or via Skype.

ASSOCIAZIONE ITALO BRITANNICA

Piazza della Vittoria 14/22, 16121 Genoa

- +39 010 591605
- mzacco@italobritannica.it
- www.italobritannica.it/en

NUMBER OF TEACHERS: Approximately 15.

PREFERENCE OF NATIONALITY: None.

QUALIFICATIONS: Degree and CELTA or equivalent.

CONDITIONS OF EMPLOYMENT: Teachers are freelancers with approximately 12–15 hours' work per week.

SALARY: €14 per hour net, VAT is paid by the school.

FACILITIES/SUPPORT: Help may be given to find accommodation.

RECRUITMENT: Interviews may be held in London but preferably in Genoa.

CONTACT: Marina Zacco, Director.

BENEDICT SCHOOL

Dell'Industria Via 87, 41012 Carpi

- +39 059 695921
- info@benedict-carpi.it
- www.serverbenedict.com

NUMBER OF TEACHERS: 14.

PREFERENCE OF NATIONALITY: British, American, Irish. Minimum of 2 years' TEFL experience.

QUALIFICATIONS: Minimum TEFL (CELTA or equivalent certification).

CONDITIONS OF EMPLOYMENT: Mid-September until mid-July. Minimum 90 hours per month guaranteed (average 120 hours). 60% of work is with companies; 40% with private students.

SALARY: To be discussed at interview.

FACILITIES/SUPPORT: Accommodation provided by school.

RECRUITMENT: Internet and recruitment agency.

CONTACT: Ing. Philippe Bernet, General Manager and Owner.

BRITISH INSTITUTES – NEW SCHOOL

Via de Ambrosis 21, 15067 Novi Ligure

- +39 0143 2987
- noviligure@britishinstitutes.it
- www.britishinstitutes.it/novi-ligure

NUMBER OF TEACHERS: 8.

PREFERENCE OF NATIONALITY: British, American.

QUALIFICATIONS: TEFL Diploma/degree plus 1 year's experience.

CONDITIONS OF EMPLOYMENT: 9 months, renewable. Average of 25 hours per week.

SALARY: €11 per hour net.

RECRUITMENT: Via www.tefl.com.

BRITISH LANGUAGE SERVICES/LINGUAVIVA

Via C. De Cristoforis 15, 20124 Milan

- +39 02 659 6401
- segreteria@linguaviva.net
- www.linguaviva.net

NUMBER OF TEACHERS: Approximately 20.

PREFERENCE OF NATIONALITY: British and Irish.

QUALIFICATIONS: Minimum CELTA or equivalent, degree plus some experience. Must be dynamic. Preference given to teachers with accommodation in the Milan area.

CONDITIONS OF EMPLOYMENT: October to June/July. 15–25 hours per week.

SALARY: Freelance rates.

RECRUITMENT: Adverts followed by personal interviews in Milan. Send full CV with photo and email addresses of 2 referees.

BRITISH s.r.l.

Via XX Settembre 12, 16121 Genoa

- +39 010 593591
- britishsrl@libero.it
- www.britishgenova.it

NUMBER OF TEACHERS: 12.

PREFERENCE OF NATIONALITY: EU, American, Australian and Canadian.

QUALIFICATIONS: Bachelor's degree plus CELTA and some experience.

CONDITIONS OF EMPLOYMENT: 25+ hours per week between mid-September and mid-June.

SALARY: Variable according to hours worked.

FACILITIES/SUPPORT: Assistance given with accommodation, teaching materials and course programming.

RECRUITMENT: Interviews essential, usually take place in Italy or by phone.

CALEDONIAN COMMUNICATIONS

Viale Vigliani 55, 20148 Milan

- +39 02 4802 0486/1086
- info@caledonian.it
- www.caledonian.it

NUMBER OF TEACHERS: 15–20, depending on time of year.

PREFERENCE OF NATIONALITY: EU citizens or others with permits already. British nationals can be hired on UK contract and given help to find accommodation. First 2 weeks are provided free and in some cases up to 1 month.

QUALIFICATIONS: Degree (preferably in a business subject) and TESOL, CELTA or DELTA. Prefer candidates who have worked in business for 5 years, have 2 years EFL experience and a driving licence.

CONDITIONS OF EMPLOYMENT: All teachers are freelancers, and paid on an hourly basis.

SALARY: Varies according to age and experience.

RECRUITMENT: Word of mouth, newspapers, magazines, internet and CVs sent on spec.

CONTACT: Maria McCarthy, Managing Director (maria@caledonian.it).

THE CAMBRIDGE SCHOOL
Via Rosmini 6, 37123 Verona
- +39 045 8003154
- info@cambridgeschool.it
- www.cambridgeschool.it

NUMBER OF TEACHERS: 12-15.

PREFERENCE OF NATIONALITY: None, provided they are native speakers with a valid EU passport/visa.

QUALIFICATIONS: Cambridge CELTA or Trinity CertTesol is essential. Minimum 2 years' experience as a teacher and experience with Cambridge English exam preparation is an advantage.

CONDITIONS OF EMPLOYMENT: 9 months, October-June, renewable with opportunities to work in the summer. 25 hours a week between Monday and Saturday lunchtime.

SALARY: Approximately €1,300 a month, net.

FACILITIES/SUPPORT: Medical insurance is provided. School usually knows of 2-3 flats as potential teacher accommodation or will accompany teacher to estate agents to ease the language barrier.

RECRUITMENT: Preliminary Skype interview and final face-to-face interview at the Cambridge School.

CONTACT: Vanes Marzaroli, Director of Studies & Teachers' Coordinator (vanes.marzaroli@cambridgeschool.it).

CANADIAN ISLAND
Via Gioberti 15, 50121 Florence
- +39 05 567 7567
- info@canadianisland.com
- www.canadianisland.it

NUMBER OF TEACHERS: 12 for summer camps.

PREFERENCE OF NATIONALITY: None.

QUALIFICATIONS: Overnight camp experience and an overall love and enthusiasm of working with children.

CONDITIONS OF EMPLOYMENT: 4 weeks. Working round the clock.

SALARY: €200 a week plus room and board.

FACILITIES/SUPPORT: Accommodation provided.

RECRUITMENT: Ads in university career website. All interviews by Skype.

CONTACT: Maria Rocco, Director.

CLM BELL
Via Pozzo 30, 38122 Trento
- +39 0461 981733
- clm-bell@clm-bell.it
- www.clm-bell.com

NUMBER OF TEACHERS: 25 approximately, also for Riva del Garda.

PREFERENCE OF NATIONALITY: Native English speakers.

QUALIFICATIONS: Minimum 2 years' experience with CELTA/DELTA qualification.

CONDITIONS OF EMPLOYMENT: 9-month contracts. To work 23 hours per week, can be extended. Positions also available at summer camp.

SALARY: €1,350-€1,550 per month.

FACILITIES/SUPPORT: Single subsidised accommodation on a limited basis. Help provided with work permits. Workshops given by teacher trainers.

RECRUITMENT: Via TEFL.com or direct applications. Interview required.

CONTACT: Ivana Ferrari, Centre Manager, or Jane Nolan, Centre Manager for English.

DARBY SCHOOL OF LANGUAGES – ROME – MILAN
Via Mosca 51, Villino 14, 00142 Rome
- +39 06 5196 2205
- darby@darbyschool.it
- www.darbyschool.it

NUMBER OF TEACHERS: 40–50, also for Milan.

PREFERENCE OF NATIONALITY: None, but must be native English speaker.

QUALIFICATIONS: TEFL certificate CELTA.

CONDITIONS OF EMPLOYMENT: Freelance. Teachers for both Rome and Milan can choose their hours which usually are an average of 20–25 hours per week. More hours available if wanted.

SALARY: The average salary of about €1,400 is sufficient and more to live on in Italy.

FACILITIES/SUPPORT: New teachers are helped to find accommodation.

RECRUITMENT: Relevant CVs and interviews.

CONTACT: Gilda Darby.

EUROPLACEMENTS ITALY SRL – RECRUITMENT AGENCY

Piazzale Biancamano 8, 20121 Milan

📞 +39 02 6203 3060

✎ info@europlacements.it or
  g.taccone@europlacements.it

💻 www.europlacements.it

NUMBER OF TEACHERS: 50–70.

PREFERENCE OF NATIONALITY: English-speaking countries; EU citizens preferred for visa purposes.

QUALIFICATIONS: BA in Education with specialisation in subjects for upper school.

CONDITIONS OF EMPLOYMENT: 12 or 24-month contracts. Hours are 9am–4pm Monday–Friday.

SALARY: €1,400 per month (net) on average.

FACILITIES/SUPPORT: Some schools assist with accommodation.

RECRUITMENT: Advertisements on targeted websites plus many spontaneous applications. Preliminary interviews by Skype. Face-to-face interviews held in London three times a year or when necessary.

CONTACT: Gianna Taccone, Director of Educational Division and Family Division for English Mother Tongue Recruitment.

IIK ANCONA SCUOLA DI LINGUE

Scalo Vittorio Emanuele II, 1, 60121 Ancona

📞 +39 071 206610

✎ info@iik.it

💻 www.iik.it

NUMBER OF TEACHERS: 5–6.

PREFERENCE OF NATIONALITY: British preferred; EU citizens.

QUALIFICATIONS: Minimum 3 years' teaching experience and TEFL/TESOL certificate. (Taster weekend courses and distance learning courses without observed and assessed teaching practice will not be considered.)

CONDITIONS OF EMPLOYMENT: Generally from September until end of June. Guaranteed minimum 25 hours per week. Teaching takes place between 8.45am and 9pm.

SALARY: €10 net per hour.

FACILITIES/SUPPORT: Assistance given with finding accommodation but teacher responsible for paying rent. School advises EU teachers on getting residence permit, fiscal code and enrolling in health services.

RECRUITMENT: Direct contact and www.tefl.com.

CONTACT: Maria Margherita Gargiulo, Director of Studies.

INTENSIVE BUSINESS ENGLISH

Corso Buenos Aires 7, 20124 Milan

📞 +39 02 6900 2017

✎ info@ibeschool.com

💻 www.ibeschool.com

NUMBER OF TEACHERS: 45, for Milan, Bologna, Turin, Rome Venice and online.

PREFERENCE OF NATIONALITY: British, Irish, Australian, and New Zealander, already living in Italy.

QUALIFICATIONS: Minimum 3 years' experience and relevant certificate/qualification. Previous experience of Business English.

CONDITIONS OF EMPLOYMENT: 12-month contract. Usual hours are 9am–7pm, Monday to Friday. Teaching corporate clients in-company and online.

SALARY: Between €1,800 and €3,250 gross depending on type of contract and experience. 20%–30% deductions for taxes.

FACILITIES/SUPPORT: Accommodation in flats owned by the school at very low rates. Cost of training with TeacherTraining.it may be reimbursed after 2 years' employment.

RECRUITMENT: On the internet, advertising in local magazines and through the teacher network in Milan. Interviews essential.

CONTACT: Gordon Doyle, Director of Studies.

INTERLINGUE LANGUAGE SYSTEM COLLEGE – TEFL INTERNATIONAL

Via Lucrezio Caro 67, 00193 Rome

📞 +39 06 321 5740

✎ info@interlingue-it.com

💻 www.interlingue-it.com

NUMBER OF TEACHERS: Approx. 20.

PREFERENCE OF NATIONALITY: None.

QUALIFICATIONS: Minimum TEFL certificate, university degree, some teaching experience.

CONDITIONS OF EMPLOYMENT: 9-month contracts, working between 20 and 30 hours per week.

SALARY: €12.50–€19 per hour, depending on contract.

FACILITIES/SUPPORT: Support in searching for accommodation. Also runs intensive training courses.

RECRUITMENT: Via students on their TEFL course, online application form and other methods. Interviews required, final interview must be carried out in Rome.

CONTACT: Angela Giordano, General School Manager.

INTERNATIONAL CLUB

P.le A. Moro, 6, 20034 Giussano

✆ +39 0362 354057

🖱 info@internationalclub.it

💻 www.internationalclub.it

NUMBER OF TEACHERS: 25.

PREFERENCE OF NATIONALITY: British, Irish, or any other native English speaker in possession of EU citizenship or *Permesso di Soggiorno* (work visa).

QUALIFICATIONS: For adult classes: CELTA/TESOL or any other TEFL qualification plus at least 1 year's experience with teaching groups at all levels. For children's classes: any qualification for teaching children (not necessarily as an EFL teacher) and experience with teaching children. Must have a driving licence. Other skills advantageous such as sports, music, arts or drama.

CONDITIONS OF EMPLOYMENT: Standard contract is 9 months or longer. Permanent teachers welcome. Sometimes teachers are employed shorter term and summer contracts from June to July are offered. Teachers work 25–35 hours per week.

SALARY: €12.50 net per hour.

FACILITIES/SUPPORT: Accommodation in flats owned by the school at very low rates. Free seminars for teachers.

RECRUITMENT: By direct contact or recruitment agencies. Interviews can be carried out on the phone or by internet. Occasionally interviews arranged in the UK or USA during the summer.

CONTACT: Mary Sposari, Director of Studies.

INTERNATIONAL HOUSE (CAMPOBASSO) ITALY

Via Zurlo 5, 86100 Campobasso

✆ +39 0874 481321

🖱 risoreumane@ihcampobasso.it and info@ihcampobasso.it

💻 www.accademiabritannica.it

NUMBER OF TEACHERS: 20 for summer camp in Italy.

PREFERENCE OF NATIONALITY: British/American.

QUALIFICATIONS: CELTA qualification and experience teaching children and teenagers essential.

CONDITIONS OF EMPLOYMENT: Contract 2/4 or 6 weeks from end of June to August. 6 hours' teaching per day. Pupils aged 8–16.

SALARY: Approximately €65 per shift.

FACILITIES/SUPPORT: Accommodation and all meals provided.

RECRUITMENT: Direct application.

CONTACT: Mary Ricciardi, Director.

INTERNATIONAL HOUSE (PALERMO)

Via Quintino Sella 70, 90139 Palermo

✆ +39 091 584954

🖱 ihpalermo@ihpalermo.it or dos@ihpalermo.it

💻 www.ihpalermo.it

NUMBER OF TEACHERS: 9 plus 1 Director of Studies and 1 Children's Coordinator.

PREFERENCE OF NATIONALITY: British; others considered (only those holding a passport from an EU member state).

QUALIFICATIONS: Degree, CELTA (minimum grade 'B'), DELTA. School interested in career teachers only.

CONDITIONS OF EMPLOYMENT: 8-month contracts. 25 hours per week, usually 1pm–9.30pm.

SALARY: From €1,200 plus increments.

FACILITIES/SUPPORT: Assistance with finding accommodation (rent €350–€400 per month). Weekly seminars and workshops. School will subsidise in-service diploma course by distance learning for suitable candidates. Italian survival lessons. CELTA courses offered in June every year.

RECRUITMENT: Via IH World Organisation or directly. Interviews essential.

CONTACT: Jonathan Ingham, Director of Studies.

KEEP TALKING

Via Roma 60, 33100 Udine, Friuli-Venezia Giulia

✆ +39 0432 501525

🖱 info@keeptalking.it

💻 www.keeptalking.it

NUMBER OF TEACHERS: 6.

PREFERENCE OF NATIONALITY: None, but must be native speakers.

QUALIFICATIONS: University degree and CELTA or equivalent required plus minimum 1 year of experience. Driving licence essential to carry out work in local companies.

CONDITIONS OF EMPLOYMENT: 9-month contracts (*contratto di lavoro a progetto*, which means an hourly paid contract with a guaranteed minimum number of hours). Minimum 750 contact hours over 9 months. 25 hours per week. Lessons mostly at lunchtimes and evenings and Saturday mornings.

SALARY: Starting hourly wage of €14.50–€16.50 (net); monthly €1,200–€1,330 depending on qualifications and experience.

FACILITIES/SUPPORT: Training seminars once a month. Excellent facilities. Income tax, pension, medical/accident insurance paid by employer. Accommodation provided. 30 hours of survival Italian.

RECRUITMENT: Face-to-face interview normally essential in Udine or in London in July. Candidates who are successful at interview will be told within about 2 weeks if they have been successful. Adverts via internet (www.tefl.com).

CONTACT: Kip Kelland, Director (kip@keeptalking.it).

KID'S WORLD
Via Lucrino 22a, 00199 Rome
✆ +39 06 8621 2471
✉ info@kidsworld.it
🖥 www.kidsworldenglish.com

NUMBER OF TEACHERS: 40 to teach children aged 7–13 at summer camps.

PREFERENCE OF NATIONALITY: None.

QUALIFICATIONS: Teachers should be dynamic and sporty.

CONDITIONS OF EMPLOYMENT: Summer camp period lasts 4–6 weeks between mid-June and the end of July. Teachers work around 8 hours a day.

SALARY: Approx. €900 per fortnight, less deductions of 25%.

FACILITIES/SUPPORT: Accommodation and meals are provided.

RECRUITMENT: Via local adverts for English teachers. Candidates applying from abroad can be interviewed by telephone or Skype.

CONTACT: Simon Charlesworth, Director (s.charlesworth@kidsworld.it).

LANGUAGES INTERNATIONAL SRL
Via Ippolito D'Aste 1/12, 16121 Genoa
✆ +39 010 595 8889
✉ robertson@languagesinternational.it
🖥 www.languagesinternational.it

NUMBER OF TEACHERS: 35–70 (depending on the time of year) in schools in Genoa and Rome.

PREFERENCE OF NATIONALITY: Native English speakers with passport from EU country.

QUALIFICATIONS: Prior teaching experience, university degree and recognised TEFL/TESOL certificate.

CONDITIONS OF EMPLOYMENT: Between 24 and 34 working hours per week, depending on which city the teacher is based in and their flexibility.

FACILITIES/SUPPORT: Assistance is given with accommodation, ie appointments to visit rooms are set up.

RECRUITMENT: Usually via the internet or word of mouth. Interviews are carried out over the phone if the candidate is not in Rome, Milan or Genoa.

CONTACT: Millica Robertson, Director of Studies.

LINGUE SENZA FRONTIERE
Corso Inglesi 172, 18038 – San Remo
✆ +39 0184 533661
✉ info@linguesenzafrontiere.org or
niamh.lsf.application@gmail.com
🖥 www.linguesenzafrontiere.org/work-with-us.html

NUMBER OF TEACHERS: Approximately 200 per summer for English immersion camps for children 7–14.

PREFERENCE OF NATIONALITY: Native English speaker.

QUALIFICATIONS: TEFL certificate or equivalent useful and/or relevant experience. Must be a native speaker with a bubbly personality and have a genuine interest in working with children. Italian is not required but is useful.

CONDITIONS OF EMPLOYMENT: 2-week contract plus a free 4–5 day training course, which is compulsory. Working hours are 8.45am–4.15pm, Monday to Friday. Some English-speaking actors are employed for the academic year as well.

SALARY: €450 net per 2-week camp all-in.

FACILITIES/SUPPORT: Accommodation is provided from beginning to end of contract. Online pre-training then 4-day on-site training course, when accommodation is in shared rooms. During camp, tutors stay with an Italian host family.

CONTACT: Niamh Miller, Tutor Coordinator.

LIVING LANGUAGES SCHOOL
Via Magna Grecia 2, 89128 Reggio Calabria
✆ +39 096 533 0926
✉ info@livinglanguages.it
🖥 www.livinglanguages.it

Also: via Madonna, 21 Gallico, 89135 Reggio Calabria

NUMBER OF TEACHERS: 8.

PREFERENCE OF NATIONALITY: Native English speakers.

QUALIFICATIONS: TEFL, CELTA.

CONDITIONS OF EMPLOYMENT: 9-month renewable contracts. British contract. Teaching hours 3pm–9pm, Monday to Friday.

SALARY: Approx. €826 (net) per month for an inexperienced teacher.

FACILITIES/SUPPORT: Help given with accommodation.

RECRUITMENT: Via adverts. Some interviews carried out in UK.

LONDON SCHOOL
Corso Rosmini, 66, 38068 Rovereto
✆ +39 046 442 1285
✉ info@londonschoolrovereto.it
🖥 www.londonschoolrovereto.it

NUMBER OF TEACHERS: 4–5.

PREFERENCE OF NATIONALITY: British.

QUALIFICATIONS: Degree, and excellent command of English language. Pronunciation and grammar must be perfect. Teachers who also speak Italian are preferred. For summer work, training or experience in teaching young learners is preferred, eg online TESOL plus TEYL course (via www. teachingenglishinitaly.com).

CONDITIONS OF EMPLOYMENT: 1-year contract which may be renewed. 20–25 working hours per week. Summer vacancies are also available at children's courses held between mid-June and mid-August at the BluHotel in Folgaria in the mountains of Northern Italy. Summer teachers work between 2 and 9 weeks.

SALARY: €12–€15 per hour. Summer teachers earn €300 (net) a week in addition to full board and hotel accommodation; wages are paid at the end of the contract.

FACILITIES/SUPPORT: Help is given to find accommodation. Work permits are taken care of by the school's accountant.

RECRUITMENT: References, detailed CV and interviews essential.

CONTACT: Gordana Marjanovic, Owner.

LORD BYRON COLLEGE

Via Sparano 102, 70121 Bari

+39 080 523 2686

johncredico@lordbyroncollege.com

www.lordbyroncollege.com

One of the largest independent language schools in Italy, with 40 years' experience and an annual attendance of nearly 2,000 students of all levels and ages. Authorised by the Italian Ministry of Education and member of EAQUALS (European Association for Quality Language Services).

NUMBER OF TEACHERS: 30 full-time, 30 part-time. Summer position: July 1st – August 8th.

PREFERENCE OF NATIONALITY: UK nationals. Canadian, American, Australian and South African applicants can be considered only if they have dual European citizenship.

QUALIFICATIONS: Degree, TEFL qualification, at least 1 year's teaching experience and knowledge of Italian or another foreign language.

CONDITIONS OF EMPLOYMENT: UK contracts for 8 months from October to June or 5 months from January, renewable. National insurance and pension coverage. 27.5 hours per week including paid training and development hours. Students of all ages and levels. Salary and conditions: starting salary from €1,000 net per month in school year, €1,300 total for summer school. Paid orientation week. 5 weeks' paid holiday.

FACILITIES/SUPPORT: Free in-house DELTA course for teachers with minimum 1,200 hours' teaching experience. Teacher training and development programme for all teaching staff. Large self-access centre with video club, cinema, large TEFL resource centre and library and staff internet access. Participation in school's film dubbing and voiceover programme. Free Italian course. City centre accommodation found but not paid for.

RECRUITMENT: Online application form in the Teaching Opportunities section of the website can be submitted by email or post with full CV, recent photograph, names and email addresses of 2 teaching-related references, copies of degree, TEFL qualification and passport from an EU member state. Interviews and hiring in June for October start and in December for January.

CONTACT: John Credico, Director of Studies (johncredico@lordbyroncollege.com).

LUCKY LION SCHOOL SRL

Via della Libertà 191 c/d/e, 90143 Palermo

+39 091 986 5100

info@luckylion.it

www.luckylion.it

NUMBER OF TEACHERS: 4.

PREFERENCE OF NATIONALITY: None.

QUALIFICATIONS: Native English speakers with CELTA or equivalent.

CONDITIONS OF EMPLOYMENT: Contracts are generally less than 1 year but are renewable. Approximately 25 hours per week depending on the time of year.

FACILITIES/SUPPORT: Help provided to find private accommodation.

RECRUITMENT: Face-to-face interview and demonstration lesson essential.

CONTACT: Jacqueline Louise Scott, Director of Studies.

MAC LANGUAGE SCHOOL

Formazione OK, Via Alessandro Cruto 8, 00146 Rome

+39 06 8366 4460

info@maclanguage.it

www.formazioneok.com

NUMBER OF TEACHERS: 57 for positions nationwide.

PREFERENCE OF NATIONALITY: None if native English speaker.

QUALIFICATIONS: 3 years' experience or certified teachers.

CONDITIONS OF EMPLOYMENT: 4–8 hours per day.

FACILITIES/SUPPORT: None.

RECRUITMENT: Internet, newspapers, other. Interviews essential. Sometimes phone interviews can be arranged.

MADRELINGUA SCHOOL OF ENGLISH
Via San Giorgio, 6–40121 Bologna
+39 051 267822
info@madrelinguaenglish.com
www.madrelinguaenglish.com

NUMBER OF TEACHERS: Around 10.
PREFERENCE OF NATIONALITY: None, but must be eligible to work legally in Italy.
QUALIFICATIONS: Degree plus CELTA (or equivalent) essential, YL qualification and/or DELTA preferred. The school contributes to course fees for staff wishing to extend their qualifications.
CONDITIONS OF EMPLOYMENT: Academic year is October to June. Teachers work evenings and Saturday mornings. Some permanent positions available.
SALARY: Depending on experience but above average for the local market. Minimum €20 per hour gross. Taxes are around 20%.
FACILITIES/SUPPORT: The school can arrange a 'homestay' on a temporary basis. English teachers may take subsidised Italian language courses.
RECRUITMENT: Speculative CVs.

OXFORD GROUP
International Campus Baranzate, Via I Maggio 20, 20021 Baranzate (MI)
+39 02 872581
info@oxford.it
www.oxford.it

A group of schools affiliated to the International School of Europe (www.internationalschoolofeurope.it) that offers an English-medium education to children aged 3-18.
NUMBER OF TEACHERS: 200+ ESL teachers for Milan, Rho, Florence, Bergamo, Asti, Seregno, Rome, Varese, Lecco, Merano, Brescia, Castiglione delle Stiviere (MN) and Reggio Emilia.
PREFERENCE OF NATIONALITY: EU passport required.
QUALIFICATIONS: Degree + TEFL certificate (or equivalent, including a teaching certificate). Experience and/or willingness to teach the younger age ranges needed.
CONDITIONS OF EMPLOYMENT: Normal term is mid-September until the end of July. Working hours vary, but average at 25 contact hours per week.
SALARY: To be discussed.
FACILITIES/SUPPORT: Schools may help teachers find accommodation but teachers pay their own rent.

RECRUITMENT: Via recruitment agencies, websites and newspapers. Interviews can be arranged by video conferencing or occasionally in the UK.
CONTACT: Ian George Bolton, Head of Language Department (igbolton@oxford.it).

OXFORD SCHOOL OF ENGLISH s.r.l.
Administrative Office, Via S. Pertini 14, 30035 Mirano, Venice
+39 041 570 2355
oxford@oxfordschool.com or employment@oxfordschool.com
www.oxfordschool.com or www.oxforditalia.it

NUMBER OF TEACHERS: 20–30 for 15 schools in North-East Italy; most are independent franchises (60–70 teachers employed altogether). Oxford School Venice was advertising for EL teachers June 2015.
PREFERENCE OF NATIONALITY: British.
QUALIFICATIONS: Degree, TEFL and knowledge of Italian needed. Candidates must be holders of an EU member state passport.
CONDITIONS OF EMPLOYMENT: 9-month contracts or longer, 22 hours per week.
SALARY: Varies according to hours and length of contract but generally €1000–€1300. Tax deductions of about 23% give minimum health and welfare cover.
FACILITIES/SUPPORT: Accommodation at teacher's own expense, but school will help to find it.
RECRUITMENT: Interviews in London from mid-May or in Italy.
CONTACT: Philip Panter, Administrator.

QUAGI LANGUAGE CENTRE
Via Manzoni, 100/C, Erice C. Santa, 91100 Trapani, Sicily
+39 0923 557748
quagi@quagi.com
www.quagi.org

NUMBER OF TEACHERS: 7.
PREFERENCE OF NATIONALITY: Native English speakers with an EU member state passport.
QUALIFICATIONS: Preferably 2 years' experience, a degree and CELTA or TESOL certificate are required.
CONDITIONS OF EMPLOYMENT: Usually 8 months, October to the end of May. 4-month contracts also offered (January to May).
SALARY: €1,200 guaranteed base salary per month.
FACILITIES/SUPPORT: Modern school offering training to become an official Cambridge ESOL oral examiner and/or

invigilator. In-house training is provided before courses start. Perks include internet, a large range of resources and a return flight to the UK at the end of the contract term and holidays are fully paid. The school will also help teachers find fully furnished accommodation, arrange tax file numbers and medical visits.

RECRUITMENT: Direct. Telephone interviews possible.

CONTACT: Teresa Matteucci, Director.

THE BRITISH LANGUAGE CENTRE
Largo Pedrini 2, 23100 Sondrio

📞 +39 0342 216130

🖱 info@thebritish.it

💻 www.thebritish.it

NUMBER OF TEACHERS: 6–7.

PREFERENCE OF NATIONALITY: British.

QUALIFICATIONS: CELTA (good grade) and minimum of 3 years' experience. DELTA preferred. Full driving licence is essential.

CONDITIONS OF EMPLOYMENT: UK-based contract is for 10 months from September 1st. 25 hours teaching per week plus meetings, admin, etc.

SALARY: £1,100 (gross) per month. Deductions come to about €300.

FACILITIES/SUPPORT: Assistance given with finding accommodation, eg helping to sort through ads and accompanying teacher to see possible places. Paid holidays. Outbound flight and setting in allowance given.

RECRUITMENT: CV and interview face-to-face or by Skype.

CONTACT: Steve Marsland, Director.

THE ENGLISH CAMP COMPANY LLC
Via Della Madonna Delle Grazie, Santa Maria Degli Angeli, Assisi (PG) 06081

📞 +39 075 804 1402

🖱 info@theenglishcampcompany.com

💻 www.theenglishcampcompany.com

NUMBER OF TEACHERS: 15–25 for summer camps throughout Italy.

PREFERENCE OF NATIONALITY: None.

QUALIFICATIONS: Previous teaching experience or experience working at summer camps with children.

CONDITIONS OF EMPLOYMENT: 2-month contract. Working hours 9am–5pm. Compulsory 1-week orientation must be attended in early June.

SALARY: €175 per week.

FACILITIES/SUPPORT: All teachers are housed with host families.

RECRUITMENT: Closing date for applications beginning of April.

CONTACT: Ashleigh McLean and Nate Poerio, founders and directors.

THE ENGLISH CONVERSATION CLUB
Via Giousè Carducci 5/1, 16121 Genoa

📞 +39 010 540964

🖱 enquiry@thetrainingcompany.org or smurrell@thetrainingcompany.org

💻 www.thetrainingcompany.org

NUMBER OF TEACHERS: 12.

PREFERENCE OF NATIONALITY: None.

QUALIFICATIONS: CELTA/DELTA or equivalent. Online certificates are not acceptable.

CONDITIONS OF EMPLOYMENT: 10-month contract. 100 working hours per month.

SALARY: €1,100–€1,300 per month net.

FACILITIES/SUPPORT: Assistance given to find accommodation prior to arrival.

RECRUITMENT: Usually via the internet. Interviews are essential and can be carried out over the phone or occasionally in the UK.

CONTACT: Stephen Murrell, Director.

THE LANGUAGE GRID
Via Carducci 35, 20123 Milan

📞 +39 0349 7633507/034 016 7235

🖱 info@thelanguagegrid.com

💻 www.thelanguagegrid.com

NUMBER OF TEACHERS: 14 trainers for this company which specialises in the banking and finance sector.

PREFERENCE OF NATIONALITY: Must be native English speakers, ie born and raised in an English-speaking country, with legal permission to stay in Italy.

QUALIFICATIONS: University degree (preferably in business or finance) and TEFL experience (or willing to learn).

CONDITIONS OF EMPLOYMENT: Long-term full-time Italian contract. 38 hours per week.

SALARY: National Contract with legislated benefits (no freelancers). Approximately €25,000–€30,000 (gross) per year, plus bonus. Deductions can amount to 46% in total for social security, taxes, etc.

FACILITIES/SUPPORT: Holiday and sick pay entitlements, etc included in salary package. No assistance given with accommodation or visas.

RECRUITMENT: Internet, head hunter, word of mouth. Applications in writing with cover letter, CV and recent photo. Interviews take place face-to-face in Milan only.

CONTACT: Zoe Veronica Avlonitis, Managing Director.

TJ TAYLOR LANGUAGE TRAINING
Via Appiani 12, 20121 Milan
✆ +39 02 4300 19075
🖱 work@tjtaylor.net or info@tjtaylor.net
💻 www.tjtaylor.eu

NUMBER OF TEACHERS: 12.

PREFERENCE OF NATIONALITY: Native speakers of English with right to work in Italy.

QUALIFICATIONS: Minimum is a recognised TEFL qualification (CELTA or Trinity plus a few other recognised qualifications) and minimum 3 years' experience (5–10 preferred), with a strong preference for corporate training experience. Most new recruits comfortably exceed this minimum.

CONDITIONS OF EMPLOYMENT: 1 year if starting in January or September. 25 contact hours a week, Monday to Friday.

SALARY: From €1300, after all taxes deducted. Freelancers have to invoice.

FACILITIES/SUPPORT: New teachers are assigned a local 'buddy' from the teaching staff, though the majority of teachers are already in Milan or the surrounding area.

RECRUITMENT: Ads on website, Twitter, Facebook and LinkedIn profiles, and normally also on www.tefl.com. Interviews essential and always held in Milan as positions tend to be long term.

CONTACT: Alex Taylor, Managing Director.

UNITED COLLEGE
Ronco a Via Von Platen 16/18, 96100 Siracusa
✆ +39 0931 22000
🖱 info@unitedcollege.it or
   carolyn.davies@unitedcollege.it
💻 www.unitedcollege.eu

NUMBER OF TEACHERS: 10.

PREFERENCE OF NATIONALITY: British (work contracts for non-Europeans much more difficult to arrange).

QUALIFICATIONS: Degree plus Trinity or Cambridge certificate, plus 1 year's experience. Basic knowledge of Italian preferable.

CONDITIONS OF EMPLOYMENT: Mid-September to mid-June. Hours between 3pm and 9pm.

SALARY: Approximately €1100 net per month (depending on experience). Italian contract with contributions paid.

FACILITIES/SUPPORT: Accommodation arranged and paid for by school. Car available.

RECRUITMENT: Through www.tefl.com.

CONTACT: Carolyn Davies, Director of Studies.

WINDSOR INTEGRATED LANGUAGE & BUSINESS SOLUTIONS
Via Molino delle Lime 4/F, 10064 Pinerolo
✆ +39 0121 795555
🖱 cv@windsorpinerolo.it
💻 www.windsorpinerolo.it

NUMBER OF TEACHERS: 6–9.

PREFERENCE OF NATIONALITY: British or EU applicants only.

QUALIFICATIONS: Minimum Certificate in TEFL, experience of teaching Military English.

CONDITIONS OF EMPLOYMENT: 9–10 months (October to June).

SALARY: About €1,000 net per month.

PORTUGAL

As the weakest Eurozone country after Greece, Portugal has been following a path of strict austerity in order to win back the confidence of international markets, which inevitably has held back its economy. However its economy improved enough for it to grow by nearly 1% in 2014 and for the country to exit the European bailout. Unemployment is still high at 13% but that is down two percent from the previous year. The northern region around Porto has traditionally been the country's economic powerhouse and it especially looks set on a road to recovery, which means that there should be more disposable income around for English courses. High unemployment among those under 25 (currently 31.2%) might encourage some of them to enhance their skills base by improving their English.

Teaching opportunities persist, especially in the teaching of young learners. Relations between Portugal and Britain have always been warm and a preference for British teachers remains strong. Most language institutes cater for anyone over the age of seven, so you should be prepared to teach children. The Portuguese government has been pushing for English to be taught from first grade and as a result parents are eager to start their children very young in private English classes. The enrolment for children's courses continues strong and a number of language institutes serve a student body that is 90% under the age of 17. Language schools often find it hard to recruit teachers who have experience of teaching children and a basic knowledge of Portuguese, which is useful when teaching young children. A new trend is for established institutes to offer intensive summer courses. A job teaching on one of these is easier to secure and can provide a useful route into longer-term teaching.

In fact, some schools organise courses in nursery/primary schools for children from the age of three, sometimes as part of the Ministry of Education's 'Teaching and Understanding of the first level of basic English' programme. For example the Windsor School in Ovar, south of Porto, offers courses to 'toddlers' (www.windsorschool.ws/carrer.html).

The vast majority of British tourists flock to the Algarve, along the southern coast of Portugal, which means that many Portuguese in the south who aspire to work in the tourist industry want to learn English. Schools such as the Wall Street Institute in Faro (www.wsenglish.pt) and the Centro de Línguas in Lagos cater for just that market. But the demand for English teachers is greatest in North and Central Portugal. Jobs crop up in historic centres such as Coimbra, Braga and Viseu and in small seaside towns like Aveiro and Póvoa do Varzim. These can be a very welcome destination for teachers burnt out from teaching in big cities, first-time teachers who want to avoid the rat race, or teachers who simply want to secure a steady wage and accommodation. The British Council (www.britishcouncil.pt) has nine English language centres in Coimbra, Greater Lisbon, Porto, etc and recruits teachers, usually on a part-time basis initially, who are locally engaged rather than hired through the Council's Teacher Recruitment department in London (teachingjobs@pt.britishcouncil.org). Candidates must have a degree, TEFL certificate and two years' post-TEFL qualification EFL teaching experience. CVs are kept on file for six months.

FINDING A JOB

Most teachers in Portugal have either answered adverts or are working for one of the large chains. International House (www.ihportugal.com) has 11 affiliated schools in Portugal. Wall Street Institute (www.wsenglish.pt) is well represented with 32 centres, some of which are always looking for dynamic teachers; CVs can be emailed to hr-recruitment@wsenglish.pt.

About three-quarters of all IH students in Portugal are children, so expertise with young learners is a definite asset and the British Council in Lisbon offers occasional CELTA extension courses in teaching young learners. IH and the British Council, among others, also offer 'courses to help professionals', so expertise in law/finance and business should also prove helpful when trying to secure a job.

Outside the cities where there have traditionally been large expatriate communities, schools cannot depend on English speakers just showing up and so must recruit well in advance of the academic year (late September to the end of June). The Bristol School Group (see entry) offers the only possibility of which we have heard for working in the Azores, so if you want to work in the most isolated islands in the Atlantic Ocean – more than 1,000km west of Portugal – this is your chance. Small groups of schools, say six schools in a single region, is the norm in Portugal. A number of the schools listed in the directory at the end of this chapter belong to such mini-chains. One of the most well established is the Cambridge Schools group that every year imports dozens of teachers.

A company that specialises in teaching children aged 3–13 is Fun Languages/Kids Club (www.kidsclub.pt), with dozens of clubs throughout the country. It is possible to submit an online application form, which is circulated round all the clubs and any with vacancies will make contact.

Many schools are small family-run establishments with fewer than 10 teachers, so sending off a lot of speculative applications is unlikely to succeed. As is true anywhere, you might be lucky and find something on the spot. The Cambridge CELTA is widely requested by schools and can be obtained at IH in Lisbon.

REGULATIONS

The red tape for EU citizens working in Portugal is reasonably painless. All that is required (as throughout the EU) is to register locally and obtain a *Certificado de Registo* (Registration Certificate) after an initial three-month stay by taking documents to show proof of accommodation, health insurance and means of support. If you are employed, you must show that you have been registered in the social security system and are not being paid less than the Portuguese minimum wage (€ 589 per month in 2015). These must be presented to an immigration office – Serviço de Estrangeiros e Fronteiras (SEF; www.sef.pt) – or at your local Town Hall (*Câmara Municipal*). Forms can be downloaded from the SEF site, and the fee is €15.

Non-EU residents will have a much more difficult time trying to work in Portugal. Obtaining a work permit is next to impossible and therefore getting a contract job is out of the question for most. Self-employed teachers from outside Europe can work on what used to be called 'green receipts' for the hours they taught, which was a way of making their tax status legal. In 2013, these were replaced by electronic invoice receipts called *faturas-recibo*. Like green receipts, these are necessary before you can be paid, but you aren't eligible to obtain them until you have an NIF (*Numero Identificação Fiscal*), for which you will need to be a legal resident. Without a contract, the only way to qualify is to have a Portuguese citizen sponsor you. For a detailed account of the bureaucratic battles fought by English teacher **Andrea Smith** from Washington DC, see http://americaninportugal.blogspot.it/2012/02/so-you-want-to-move-to-portugal-heres.html. She could achieve legal status only with the ongoing help of her Portuguese boyfriend.

The other alternative is to seek employment with schools that prefer American speakers: any school with 'American' in the title is probably a good bet. Try the American School of Languages (see entry) or CAA (Centro Anglo-Americano) in Chaves and Vila Real (www.caaenglish.com). The latter is a family-run school that prefers to hire EU citizens because they are cheaper, although it would make an exception for qualified candidates (who rarely apply).

Since most teachers working for nine months are working on a freelance basis, they are responsible for paying their own taxes and contributions. There are seven income tax brackets ranging from 10.5% to 42% and an array of tax deductions, credits and special benefits. Tax laws and regulations are frequently subject to change. The tax retention rate for the self-employed has risen from 21.5% of earnings to 25%. The first 12 months of self-employment are exempt from social security payments.

CONDITIONS OF WORK

The consensus seems to be that wages are low, but the cost of living, at least outside the major cities, is reasonable. Imported consumer goods are taxed and expensive and the cost of domestic fuel and tolls on roads and bridges are high, but local produce such as olive oil, fruit, vegetables and wine is still relatively inexpensive. Public transport is quite cheap, as well as eating out. Working conditions are generally relaxed and students are generally helpful, as **Rachel Beebe** discovered:

Most students had a good attitude and tried very hard to speak the language. I spoke virtually no Portuguese in encounters or classes, and the students made every effort to use what they were learning to communicate with me.

The normal salary range is €700–€1,000 net per month. Full-time contract workers are entitled to an extra month's pay after 12 months, which is partly why most teachers are employed on 9–10 month contracts. Some schools pay lower rates but subsidise or pay for flights and accommodation. Several provide free Portuguese lessons. Teachers being paid on an hourly basis should expect to earn €10–€17, but they will of course not be eligible for the 13th-month bonus or paid holidays. Rates per hour can sink as low as €7, which isn't enough to live on unless you can also secure free accommodation. If you are living in an urban centre, then you'll also need to factor in any unpaid travel time to find out how much you are 'really' getting paid.

LIST OF EMPLOYERS

AMERICAN SCHOOL OF LANGUAGES
22 – 1° Avenida Duque de Loulé, 1050 090 Lisbon
☏ +351 21 314 6000/+351 967 907035
✎ admin.asl@mail.telepac.pt
💻 www.americanschooloflanguages.com

NUMBER OF TEACHERS: 5–10.
PREFERENCE OF NATIONALITY: EU citizenship is a plus but not essential.
QUALIFICATIONS: University degree, TEFL training course (preferably CELTA), EFL experience with adults preferable but not essential.
CONDITIONS OF EMPLOYMENT: Contract runs from October to June with some summer work an option. Contract is renewable for the next academic year, 21–24 working hours per week.
SALARY: €1,200–€1,600 per month with adjustments for inflation and opportunities for advancement.
FACILITIES/SUPPORT: Some assistance given to find accommodation, ie help making phone calls to prospective landlords, etc.
RECRUITMENT: Interviews in Lisbon are essential.

BRISTOL SCHOOL GROUP PORTUGAL
Bristol School – Instituto de Línguas da Maia,
Trav. Dr. Carlos Pires Felgueiras, 12–3°, 4470 158 Maia
☏ +351 22 948 8803
✎ bsmaia@bristolschool.pt
💻 www.bristolschool.pt

Comprises a group of 9 language schools in Portugal: 4 in Oporto area, 2 in the Azores and 3 inland (Castelo Branco, Fundão and Colvilha). Addresses and email contacts all at www.bristolschool.pt.
NUMBER OF TEACHERS: 25.
PREFERENCE OF NATIONALITY: British and Irish (couples preferred).
QUALIFICATIONS: Bachelor's degree and TEFL qualification. EFL experience essential.
CONDITIONS OF EMPLOYMENT: Minimum period of work 15 September to 30 June. Full-time contract of 25 hours per week. Students aged from 8.
SALARY: Basic salary plus Christmas bonus and end-of-contract bonuses plus tax rebate. Legal contract of work.
FACILITIES/SUPPORT: Assistance with accommodation given.
RECRUITMENT: Direct application preferred.

CAMBRIDGE SCHOOL
Avenida da Liberdade 173, 1250 141 Lisbon
☏ +351 21 312 4600
✎ info@cambridge.pt or av.liberdade@cambridge.pt
💻 www.cambridge.pt

Portugal's largest private language school with 9 centres, 5 in Lisbon and one each in Porto, Coimbra, Almada and Funchal (Madeira).

NUMBER OF TEACHERS: 90–110.

PREFERENCE OF NATIONALITY: EU citizens or in possession of a Portuguese *Autorizacao de Residencia*.

QUALIFICATIONS: Bachelor's degree plus CELTA, Trinity CertTESOL or an equivalent EFL qualification. Online qualifications are not acceptable. EFL experience preferred, however, newly qualified applicants may be successful.

CONDITIONS OF EMPLOYMENT: All contracts are Permanent Employment Contracts for full-time work, with a minimum commitment of 9 months, from 1 October to 30 June. 22 50-minute lessons a week. Also summer course teaching available.

SALARY: In a typical month, most starting teachers will average between €1,200 and €1,300 after deductions and extras. All staff receive a monthly meal subsidy of €141 and are included in the Portuguese National Health scheme. The school employs its own medical officers. One month paid summer holiday. Christmas and summer bonuses are paid.

FACILITIES/SUPPORT: All schools have 2–3 senior staff.

RECRUITMENT: Adverts on tefl.com. Applicants should send CV, recent photograph, contact telephone number and copies of degree and EFL certificate. Interviews are usually held in London in May and possibly mid-summer depending on requirements. Visitors to Portugal can be interviewed in Lisbon by prior arrangement.

CONTACT: Jeffrey Kapke, Adrian Mather, Robert Hart or Tony Hilzbrich, Pedagogical Administration.

CENTRO DE INGLES DE FAMALICAO

Edificio dos Correios, n° 116–4° Dto, Rua S. Joao de Deus, 4760 162 V.N. de Famalicao

C +351 252 374233

@ centroinglesfam@gmail.com

🖥 www.fameli.pt

NUMBER OF TEACHERS: 3.

PREFERENCE OF NATIONALITY: Native speakers from UK or Ireland.

QUALIFICATIONS: Degree and CELTA (or equivalent) essential; experience an advantage but not essential. Online qualifications are not accepted.

CONDITIONS OF EMPLOYMENT: 9-month renewable contracts from late September to end of June. 24 contact hours per week, Monday to Friday only.

SALARY: At least €948 per month (net). Paid holidays at Christmas, Easter and Carnival. Travel expenses of €150 paid at beginning and end of contract.

FACILITIES/SUPPORT: Fully furnished flat near school provided rent free, sharing with other teacher(s). Help given with work permit procedures. Lessons are regularly observed and feedback given.

RECRUITMENT: Via adverts on the internet (www.tefl.com). Interviews essential, normally in London in July.

CONTACT: David Mills, Director of Studies.

CIAL – CENTRO DE LINGUAS

Avenida Republica 14–2, 1050 191 Lisbon

C +351 213 533733; mobile +351 918 500300

@ linguas.estrangeiras@cial.pt

🖥 www.cial.pt

Also branch in Faro.

NUMBER OF TEACHERS: 15–17.

PREFERENCE OF NATIONALITY: EU citizens.

QUALIFICATIONS: University degree, CELTA, EFL teaching experience to adults (minimum 2 years); Business English teaching experience.

CONDITIONS OF EMPLOYMENT: Contracts October to June. Early morning, lunchtime and evening teaching hours.

SALARY: Depends on work agreement. Possibility of full-time, part-time or hourly basis. Monthly performance evaluation bonus paid as well as free Portuguese lessons and free health insurance as fringe benefits.

FACILITIES/SUPPORT: Family accommodation can be arranged for first 4 weeks if requested.

RECRUITMENT: Pre-selection through detailed CV; personal interviews compulsory.

CONTACT: Isabel Coimbra, Director (isabelcoimbra@cial.pt).

ENGLISH LANGUAGE CENTRE CASCAIS

Rua da Palmeira 5, 1A/B, Cascais

C +351 21 483 0716/916 060170

@ caroline.darling@elc-cascais.com

🖥 www.elc-cascais.com

NUMBER OF TEACHERS: 9.

PREFERENCE OF NATIONALITY: Native speakers only, preferably from the UK.

QUALIFICATIONS: University degree and CELTA or equivalent.

CONDITIONS OF EMPLOYMENT: 10-month renewable contract from 1 September. 15–18 hours per week. Also part-time work teaching Young Learners from age 5.

SALARY: €850 per month (for teaching a basic 15 hours per week).

FACILITIES/SUPPORT: Recruitment locally; pedagogical support – regular training workshops.
RECRUITMENT: Through tefl.com/local adverts. Face-to-face interviews essential normally held between April and June.
CONTACT: Caroline Darling, Director (caroline.darling@ elc-cascais.com).

ESE – ENGLISH SCHOOL ÉVORA
Praça da Muralha, 12–1° esq. 7005 248 Évora
☎ +351 266 743231/938 512574
✉ jobs@ese.com.pt
🖥 www.englishschoolevora.com

NUMBER OF TEACHERS: 3.
PREFERENCE OF NATIONALITY: EU citizens, native English speakers.
QUALIFICATIONS: Degree, CELTA or equivalent, minimum 2 years' experience. Knowledge of Portuguese or a Latin language an advantage.
CONDITIONS OF EMPLOYMENT: 9-month renewable contract on freelance basis, October 1st-June 30th. 24 hours plus possible overtime. Most teaching in evenings till 10pm plus Saturday mornings.
SALARY: €1,664 (gross) per month. €16 per hour.
FACILITIES/SUPPORT: Some assistance with finding accommodation. 10 days' holiday at Easter/Christmas.
RECRUITMENT: Through the internet. Interviews are often on Skype.
CONTACT: Michael W. Lewis, Director.

FUN LANGUAGES – KIDS CLUB VISEU
hua Estevão Lopes Morago, Lote 326, 3510 085 Viseu
☎ +351 232 426978
✉ sandy@funlanguagesviseu.net
🖥 www.funlanguagesviseu.pt

One of 20 franchised branches throughout the country. HQ in Lisbon (geral@kidsclub.pt).
NUMBER OF TEACHERS: 9.
PREFERENCE OF NATIONALITY: Native speakers from Britain or North America.
QUALIFICATIONS: University education, teaching experience and teaching qualification preferred, although if a candidate shows potential, the employer is willing to train.
CONDITIONS OF EMPLOYMENT: Period of work September to July. 30 teaching hours per week.
SALARY: Variable, depending on rent, bills, qualifications and circumstances. Arrangement will be discussed during the interview process. Teachers work freelance which means deductions are not made at source.

FACILITIES/SUPPORT: Accommodation is always provided for teachers moving to Portugal. Rent and bills are included in salary. The school registers teachers and takes care of permits, bank account and other issues involved in relocation.
RECRUITMENT: Advertising and headhunting at EFL summer camps in Britain. Online application form. Interviews are essential, and sometimes take place in the UK as well as Portugal.
CONTACT: Sandy Albuquerque, Director of Studies.

ILC CENTRO INTERACTIVO DE LINGUAS
Rua Mouzihno de Albuqerque 56 1° esq., 2400 193 Leiria
☎ +351 244 830950
✉ Sergio.g@il-c.com.pt
🖥 www.il-c.denki.pt

Also has centres in Batalha and Fátima, in the same region.
NUMBER OF TEACHERS: 12.
PREFERENCE OF NATIONALITY: None.
QUALIFICATIONS: Degree.
CONDITIONS OF EMPLOYMENT: Standard contract is 10 months with 25 working hours per week.
SALARY: €12 per hour.
RECRUITMENT: Interviews carried out in Portugal.
CONTACT: Sérgio Gomes, Director.

INSTITUTO DE LINGUAS DE S. JOAO DA MADEIRA
Rua Durbalino Laranjeira S/N, 3700 108 S. João da Madeira
☎ +351 256 833906
✉ institutodelinguas@gmail.com
🖥 www.institutodelinguas.net

NUMBER OF TEACHERS: 14 working in schools/companies outside the Institute; 5 working at the Institute.
PREFERENCE OF NATIONALITY: British.
QUALIFICATIONS: DELTA/COTE plus 2 years' experience.
CONDITIONS OF EMPLOYMENT: 9-month contracts from mid-September.
SALARY: Dependent on qualifications.
FACILITIES/SUPPORT: No help given with accommodation, work permits; training sessions, workshops, seminars at the British Council Oporto.
RECRUITMENT: Interview essential.
CONTACT: Dr Helena Nicolau, Director.

INTERNATIONAL HOUSE (LISBON)

Rua Marquès Sá da Bandeira 16, 1050 148 Lisbon

✆ +351 21 315 1493/4/6

✉ info@ihlisbon.com

🖥 www.ihlisbon.com

NUMBER OF TEACHERS: 18.

PREFERENCE OF NATIONALITY: Native English speakers.

QUALIFICATIONS: CELTA minimum.

CONDITIONS OF EMPLOYMENT: Standard length of stay is 9 months. Flexible working hours to include evening and Saturday work. Pupils range in age from 8 to 80. Standard working week is 18 hours.

SALARY: €1,3440 per month for first year teachers, based on 18 hours per week teaching.

FACILITIES/SUPPORT: Assistance with finding accommodation. CELTA and IHCYL courses offered regularly (see Training chapter).

RECRUITMENT: Local advertisements and by IH, London.

CONTACT: Colin McMillan, Director.

INTERNATIONAL HOUSE (PORTO)

Porto: Rua Marechal Saldanha 145–1° Foz do Douro, 4150 655 Porto

✆ +351 22 617 7641

✉ info@ihporto.org or info@ihleca.com

🖥 www.ihporto.org or www.ihleca.com

Matosinhos: Leça da Palmeira, Rua Oliveira Lessa 350, 4450 751 Matosinhos

✆ +351 22 995 9087

✉ business@ihporto.org

NUMBER OF TEACHERS: 10.

PREFERENCE OF NATIONALITY: British, Canadian, Australian, New Zealander and American.

QUALIFICATIONS: CELTA/Trinity.

CONDITIONS OF EMPLOYMENT: 1-year contracts, 22 hours per week, pupils aged from 7.

SALARY: Depending on qualifications and experience.

FACILITIES/SUPPORT: Assistance with accommodation. Portuguese lessons available. Training provided.

RECRUITMENT: Direct application.

CONTACT: Shawn Severson, Educational Projects Manager (shawnseverson@ihporto.org).

INTERNATIONAL LANGUAGE SCHOOL

Av. Republica Guiné-Bissau, 26 A, 2900 588 Setubal

✆ +351 26 524 1605

✉ ilssetubal@gmail.com

🖥 http://ils.pai.pt

NUMBER OF TEACHERS: 6.

PREFERENCE OF NATIONALITY: Native English speakers.

QUALIFICATIONS: CELTA or equivalent, 1 year's experience or more.

CONDITIONS OF EMPLOYMENT: October–July, 25 teaching hours per week.

SALARY: Approximately €1,300 per month (gross).

FACILITIES/SUPPORT: Accommodation provided.

RECRUITMENT: Via www.tefl.com. Direct applications by email with CV and photo are welcome. Interviews can be conducted by phone.

CONTACT: Tanya Garcia, Director.

LANGUAGE PROJECT – INSTITUTO DE LINGUAS

Rua de Camões 4, Quinta Nova de Sao Roque, 2670 513 Loures

✆ +351 219 823084

✉ info@language-project.com

🖥 www.language-project.com

NUMBER OF TEACHERS: 3.

PREFERENCE OF NATIONALITY: None.

QUALIFICATIONS: CELTA or equivalent, relevant degree and 2 years' experience including with young learners.

CONDITIONS OF EMPLOYMENT: Contract is 9 months (1 academic year) with 22–24 contact hours per week.

SALARY: €1,200 gross per month.

FACILITIES/SUPPORT: Assistance given with finding accommodation if necessary.

RECRUITMENT: Usually via adverts in schools, word of mouth or local websites. Interviews are essential either face-to-face or via Skype.

CONTACT: Christine Fonseca. Director (lproject@sapo.pt).

NOVO INSTITUTO DE LINGUAS

Avenida das Tulipas, N° 20B, 1495 159, Miraflores, Lisbon

✆ +351 21 412 0929 or 21 943 5238

✉ admin@nil.edu.pt

🖥 www.nil.pt

NUMBER OF TEACHERS: 8 or 9 English teachers for 3 schools in and around Lisbon; branches in Miraflores, Portela and Massamá.

PREFERENCE OF NATIONALITY: British.

QUALIFICATIONS: Experienced and inexperienced graduates who have successfully completed a recognised minimum 4-week TEFL course.

CONDITIONS OF EMPLOYMENT: 9-month (1 October to 30 June) contract that is renewable, 24 contract hours per week (Monday–Friday). No Saturday hours.

SALARY: Depends on experience.

FACILITIES/SUPPORT: Secretarial and administrative help in finding permanent accommodation. Week-long orientation course end of September to aid teachers in the classroom.

RECRUITMENT: Website advertising (eg www.tefl.com) followed by possibility of UK interviews in June/July and September

CONTACT: Nicholas Rudall, Director of Studies.

OXFORD SCHOOL

Lisbon: Rua D. Estefania, 165–1°, 1000 154 Lisbon

✆ +351 21 354 6586/796 6660

✉ info1@oxford-school.pt

Cacém: Av. Bons Amigos, 37–1°Dto, 2735 077 Cacém

✆ +351 21 914 6343

💻 www.oxford-school.pt

Member of AEPLE .

NUMBER OF TEACHERS: About 40 employed at two branches in Lisbon and one in Cacém; 6 new hires per year.

PREFERENCE OF NATIONALITY: British.

QUALIFICATIONS: Minimum TEFL course (eg CELTA), qualifications and some experience.

CONDITIONS OF EMPLOYMENT: October–June. Hours mainly 1pm–3pm and 5pm–9pm.

SALARY: Minimum €17 per 1 teaching hour or €1,400 per month for 20 teaching hours per week. Deductions for taxes and social security approx. 15%.

FACILITIES/SUPPORT: Help given with finding a shared flat.

RECRUITMENT: Direct application. Interviews essential in Lisbon or London.

CONTACT: Zilda Amaro, Manager (Zildamaro@oxford-school.pt).

ROYAL SCHOOL OF LANGUAGES – ESCOLAS DE LINGUAS, LDA

Rua José Rabumba 2, 3810 125 Aveiro

✆ +351 234 429156 or 234 425104

✉ rsl@royalschooloflanguages.pt

💻 www.royalschool.pt

Schools also in Porto, Agueda, Guarda, Ovar, Viseu, Ilhavo, Sever do Vouga and Paredes. Languages taught: English, French, German, Italian, Spanish and Portuguese.

NUMBER OF TEACHERS: 30–35 in the whole group.

PREFERENCE OF NATIONALITY: British, Australian, Canadian and American.

QUALIFICATIONS: University degree plus TEFL/TESOL certificate.

CONDITIONS OF EMPLOYMENT: 9-month contracts. 25–27 teaching hours per week.

FACILITIES/SUPPORT: Assistance with accommodation and working papers. 5-day training course with Global TESOL College.

RECRUITMENT: Via CVs or interviews, which sometimes take place in UK.

SCHOOLSTOP

Rua de Santa Quitéria 34B, 1250 212 Lisbon

✆ +351 918 615364

✉ want-to-teach@schoolstop.pt

💻 www.schoolstop.pt

NUMBER OF TEACHERS: 6.

PREFERENCE OF NATIONALITY: British.

QUALIFICATIONS: CELTA.

CONDITIONS OF EMPLOYMENT: Standard contract is 1 year with 6 working hours per day.

SALARY: Variable.

RECRUITMENT: Interviews are not essential.

SELF ESCOLA DE LINGUAS

Rua Bela de São Tiago n° 20, 9060 400 Funchal, Madeira

✆ +351 291 222894 or 962 192323

✉ info@e-self.net

💻 www.e-self.webnode.pt

NUMBER OF TEACHERS: 2 full-time and 3 freelancers (working on green receipts).

PREFERENCE OF NATIONALITY: Native speakers of English with permission to work.

QUALIFICATIONS: Teachers with teaching or other degree, TEFL or formal teacher training or experience.

CONDITIONS OF EMPLOYMENT: Full-time teachers for 9-month contracts sometimes needed from beginning of academic year. Most vacancies are for part-time teachers to give short-term intensive courses.

SALARY: Variable.

FACILITIES/SUPPORT: School can assist teachers in finding accommodation and has been known to assist financially.

RECRUITMENT: CVs can be submitted by email in Microsoft Word or posted.

CONTACT: Rebeca Jardim, Director of Studies (rebeca.jardim@gmail.com).

SPEAKWELL ESCOLA DE LINGUAS

Head office: Praça Mário Azevedo Gomes, N.421, 2775 240 Parede

☎ +351 21 456 1771

✉ speakwell@speakwell.pt

💻 www.speakwell.pt

NUMBER OF TEACHERS: 12 full-time and 40 part-time.

PREFERENCE OF NATIONALITY: None, but must be native English speakers.

QUALIFICATIONS: TEFL certificate, preferably plus some business experience, or experience teaching children.

CONDITIONS OF EMPLOYMENT: Freelance, with the possibility of full-time hours. School opening times are weekdays and Saturdays. Business trainers and qualified school teachers also required.

SALARY: Above the average hourly rate for Portugal.

FACILITIES/SUPPORT: Good pedagogic and administrative support. Can help new teachers find accommodation through contacts, etc.

RECRUITMENT: Internet, local advertising, word of mouth.

CONTACT: Sue Munnion, Director.

SCANDINAVIA

Certain similarities exist in ELT throughout Scandinavia. The standard of English teaching in state schools is uniformly high, as anyone who has met a Dane or a Swede travelling abroad will know. Yet many ordinary Scandinavians aspire to fluency, so keep up their English by attending evening classes, if only for social reasons. Sweden, Denmark and Norway have excellent facilities for such people, which are variations on the theme of 'folk university', a state-subsidised system of adult education. Classes at such institutions are the ideal setting for enthusiastic amateur teachers.

But as elsewhere in Europe the greatest demand for the English language comes from the business community, particularly in Finland. Enthusiastic amateurs tend to be less in demand in this setting than mature professionals. Yet Scandinavia is not a very popular destination for such teachers, despite its unspoilt countryside, efficient public transport and liberal society. So there is scope for most kinds of teacher to work in Scandinavia.

Since Finland and Sweden are EU members, red tape is straightforward for EU teachers. But even in Norway, whose people voted by a referendum not to join, the formalities are straightforward for EU citizens and language institutes employ foreign teachers.

Denmark

There is little recruitment of English teachers outside Denmark, apart from the Cambridge Institute Foundation, which is Denmark's largest EFL institution with a number of branches that specialise in Business English. The Danish government has tightened up the immigration laws, making it virtually impossible for non-Europeans to get working permits. Many schools expect their teachers to speak Danish, and there seem to be almost enough fully bilingual candidates resident in Denmark to satisfy this requirement. It is worthwhile for any native English speaker with an appropriate background who is staying in Denmark to enquire about part-time openings.

Like Scandinavians generally, Danes are enthusiastic self-improvers, which means that evening classes in English (and hundreds of other things) are very popular. These are purely recreational and are meant to be fun and informal (*hygge* in Danish). *Folkehøjskoler* (folk high schools) offer residential courses of varying lengths where working conditions are generally so favourable that there is very little turnover of teaching staff. The tradition of voluntary organisations, including trade unions, running courses is still strong in Denmark. It might be worth tracking down one of the voluntary organisations that run evening classes countrywide such as the Danish equivalent of Workers' Education, Arbejdernes Oplysnings Forbund or AOF (www. aof.dk). Addresses of the Danish Folkeuniversitet can be found on its website at www.folkeuniversitetet.dk.

Wages in Denmark are set by law and teaching English is no exception. The minimum is DKK170 an hour, and that is what most new arrivals earn. However, once you're established you can expect to earn about DKK220 an hour teaching in the state sector (which is much better funded and resourced than its UK counterpart). Denmark has among the highest taxes in the world, ie over 50% until you acquire a tax card (*frikort*), whereupon the rate drops and only earnings over a certain limit are taxed.

Finland

Although Finland's second language is Swedish, English runs a close second (or third). Finns are admirably energetic and industrious in learning foreign languages, possibly because their own language is so impenetrable (belonging to the Finno-Ugric group of languages along with Hungarian and Estonian). English is taught in every kind of educational institution from trade and technology colleges to universities, in commercial colleges (*kauppaloulu*) and in Civic and Workers' Institutes. Private language schools flourish too and traditionally have not been too fussy about the paper qualifications of their native English-speaker teachers.

They seldom teach straight English courses but tailor-make courses for clients, eg 'English for presentation skills', so they are not looking for young first-timers to teach their wealthy corporate clients. Still, some private schools (such as Berlitz) may take on native English speakers without a teaching qualification.

Children start their primary education at age seven, and many children between the ages of three and seven are sent to private kindergartens, many of which are English (as well as German, American, etc). These sometimes welcome a native English speaker with experience of teaching children. (The only skill that concerned one of these nurseries-cum-kindergartens looking to hire a young British graduate was singing.) Local teachers all have an MA degree since this is the minimum requirement. Provision of English is so good in state schools that there is little scope for picking up slack from disgruntled school leavers who feel they can't speak enough English. Neither is there much demand from an immigrant population since there are few foreigners or refugees in Finland compared with Norway or Sweden.

FINDING A JOB

Branches of the long-established Federation of Finnish-British Societies promote local language courses and publicise the availability of freelance tutors; its website www.finnish-britishsocieties.com carries links to English clubs and societies around Finland.

Another big player in the provision of English language teaching is Richard Lewis Communications (RLC), with offices in Finland and Sweden as well as England (see entry). RLC draws most of its students from senior management in both the public and private sectors, and also provides cross-cultural training. Of course not all the teaching takes place in the capital. There is a significant demand for freelance teachers for business in Turku, Oulu and other cities.

Teachers without European nationality will encounter serious problems. American university students and recent graduates (within two years) over 21 can apply to the American-Scandinavian Foundation (58 Park Avenue, New York, NY 10016; +1 212 779 3587; www.amscan.org/work.html) for work permits to cover a self-arranged internship. At one time there was a well-developed programme of teaching placements in Finland but that programme has expired. It is still worth asking ASF about TEFOL traineeships in Finland for the academic year, from the end of August until the end of May.

The Nordic School based in St Petersburg (see entry) mounts an ambitious series of children's summer schools at 11 different colleges in Finland (several of them Christian establishments) plus one in Sweden, for Russian children aged 7–17 learning English (age range varies among camps). Up to 80 native English speakers are recruited to implement an intensive programme of conversation lessons, at 24 fortnight-long camps. Teachers are given free accommodation and meals plus a wage at the end of each camp, and also offered transport to another location for those working at consecutive camps. The programme has expanded into the other seasons as well as summer. **Anthony Cook** has enjoyed three summers with Nordic School and hopes to do more in the future, which is a positive endorsement:

> *I heard about the job from a colleague in Moscow who had previously worked for Nordic School. Although I am an experienced EFL teacher, it took me a couple of attempts before a vacancy came up. Since then, however, the school has sent me a list of available camps every year. Although I'm Australian and don't have an EU passport, there were no red tape problems; I suspect it's because staff are technically employed in Russia, which nicely avoids the Eureaucracy.*
>
> *There are opportunities to use different spaces – including the Finnish outdoors – as your classroom. The lack of a set syllabus makes it essential to bring your own 'bag of tricks'. After my first year I arrived with a large folder full of stuff that I thought might be useful for various ages and levels, which made the experience much easier and more enjoyable.*
>
> *The biggest challenge is that you're dealing with four groups: the students of course, the Nordic School management (who are very approachable and helpful – though some of the managers on-site have limited*

English), the camp instructors and the Finnish staff at the rural colleges where most camps take place. Some camps are very remote, and isolation can be an issue. Ruokolahti camp, for example, is situated far from any town, at the end of a long promontory miles from the mainland, surrounded by a lake. The location is gorgeous – you've never taught anywhere prettier than this! – but the conveniences of city life are quite inaccessible.

I like the fact that Nordic School employs other professionals to look after the students outside of teaching hours. You'll never find yourself staying with a homesick child at night, dealing with minor injuries or removing a teenage girl from a teenage boy's sleeping quarters at 2am – that's someone else's job. If one of the camp instructors is a newbie, the school usually pairs them with a more experienced colleague, so there's generally someone there who knows how to deal with the tricky situations that can arise in camp.

Another fan of Nordic School is freelance writer, blogger and sometime English teacher **Emma Lander,** who spent one summer after university in Finland:

My school sat next to one of Finland's many lakes so in our free time we were able to swim, row boats and explore the forest area around the camp on bikes. As there was nothing around the area (and the bikes and boats were free for teachers) there was nothing really to spend money on, which made it a great place to save the €500 we were paid at the end of each two-week camp. The atmosphere at the school was great; everyone was always excited, active and happy to be there and the students were fun to teach. Because it was a summer school we were free to teach what and how we wanted and we often joined classes together to create big treasure hunts and other fun games.

CONDITIONS OF WORK

Back in the corporate world of Finnish cities, freelance arrangements have largely replaced contracts. A teaching unit of 45 minutes is the norm, with less evening work than elsewhere. Wages are high, but so is the cost of living. Some schools compress the teaching into four days a week, leaving plenty of time for weekend exploration of the country.

Taxes are high and are usually the responsibility of the teacher, whereas contributions should be paid by the employer; social security and unemployment insurance deductions will amount to at least 6% of the salary. Note that there is virtually no possibility of accepting payment 'under the table'. The system is highly controlled and everybody pays his or her taxes.

The Finnish Embassy in London's website (www.finemb.org.uk) has limited information about living and working in Finland. Helsinki has about 35 museums and art galleries plus a high density of sports facilities, ice rinks, etc. The long dark winters are relieved by a wide choice of cheerful restaurants, cafés, bars and clubs in the cities, and saunas almost everywhere.

Norway

The trend in Norwegian EFL is similar to that in Denmark, and most schools rely on a pool of native English speakers already resident in Norway. The instructional supervisor for Berlitz Norway says that he finds it next to impossible to recruit teachers from abroad because: '*They don't have a place to stay, a bank account, a work permit, can't attend interviews or training "next week". On top of this I have so many applicants who have all of these things in place and are in the Oslo area.*' Most jobs are for part-time work and of course do not offer accommodation. At least things are easier from an immigration point of view than they used to be. Although Norway is not a member of the EU, it does allow the free reciprocity of labour so that EU citizens are allowed to work in Norway without a work permit. Immigration restrictions on non-EU teachers remain stringent.

The *Yellow Pages* for Norway is available online at www.gulesider.no, though typing in *sprakinstitut* produces only a handful of results, of which one is Berlitz. As throughout Scandinavia, the Folkuniversity of Norway plays an important role in language tuition and hires native English speakers, mostly on an occasional basis for evening classes (www.folkeuniversitetet.no). There are branches in several hundred Norwegian municipalities, with fairly major teaching operations in Stavanger, Skien, Kristiansand and Hamar. Berlitz (see entry) hires native English speakers with no TEFL background provided they are graduates and successfully complete the Berlitz Instructor Training.

The basic hourly wage is about NOK160, though this can double for high-level business teaching. Expect to lose about a third in deductions.

Casual opportunities may crop up in unpredictable places. **David Moor** was simply intending to spend a month on holiday skiing in Norway, but then he saw an advert in a local supermarket for a native English teacher and jumped at the chance:

A teacher put me up and fed me. I'd intended to stay in the hostel or a cheap hotel, but was finding Norway expensive. I was just working for keep, teaching three days a week, so I had lots of spare time. I had a fantastic time, much better than a normal holiday.

Sweden

For many years the EFL market has been in a slow but inexorable decline, as standards of English among school leavers have improved. The Folkuniversity of Sweden has a long-established scheme (since 1955) by which British and other native English speakers may be placed for nine months (one academic year) in a network of adult education centres throughout the country, but it no longer has a policy of actively recruiting applicants from abroad. It takes on new staff who are already resident in Sweden and even then, the work is part-time, at least initially (www.folkuniversitetet.se; look under 'Lediga Jobb').

Originally the teaching at the Folkuniversity (FU) consisted of evening classes called a 'study circle', an informal conversation session. Circumstances have changed, however, and the range of pupils can be very varied, from unemployed people to business executives, as well as people who want to prepare for Cambridge examinations or IELTS. People who need English at work are in the majority these days.

FINDING A JOB

Advertisements almost never appear on EFL job sites. Teachers with a solid ELT background might try the main state universities that put on English courses or the language schools listed in the *Yellow Pages* of Stockholm, Malmö, Gothenburg, Orebro and Uppsala. **Charlotte Rosen** decided to do a TEFL course in London before going to Sweden to be with her Swedish fiancé:

I had visited Sweden several times before going to Gothenburg to work. After I'd been in Sweden for about six weeks, I looked through the Yellow Pages for language schools and sent off my CV in English, which wasn't a problem because everyone speaks English really well. I was offered several interviews, including by the British Institute. Many of them said they were interested but the terms only start in September and January so you have to time your applications quite carefully.

Another possibility is to try some of the private schools in Sweden (not fee paying, as in Britain), particularly if you are interested in staying in Sweden longer term. The Swedish school system has changed dramatically over recent years and private schools (*friskolor* – free schools) are now plentiful. There are a few English schools within the state system but most of them are independent. Internationella Engelska Skolan (www. engelska.se) is one of Sweden's leading independent English-medium schools, founded by an American, and branches have opened all over the country. The website has detailed information about teacher recruitment which applies primarily to certified subject teachers. The schools follow the Swedish curriculum, are authorised by Skolverket and are free for the students.

Cathryn Lock, who has a Swedish fiancé and a degree from an English university, started working at a secondary school a couple of years ago. She found the job through the national employment service, Arbetsförmedlingen (www.ams.se), sent in a letter of application and was interviewed by the headmaster. Cathryn has since gone on to pass a teacher exam in Sweden and she believes that it is quite possible to get a job if you come from the UK.

Although a business background will stand you in good stead, some of the private language schools accept certification, or even just a degree. The British Institute sometimes has vacancies for teachers with the CELTA. Making a breakthrough as a freelancer is difficult without a knowledge of the language, or the Swedish labour market and a functioning network of contacts.

CONDITIONS OF WORK

Teachers must pay tax in Sweden on a scale that varies according to the municipality. Swedish income tax is notoriously high, and the FU estimates that teachers lose about 30% in deductions. However, the upside of paying lots of tax is that Sweden is famous for the quality of its public services, its generous childcare and sick-day policies and its efficient and moderately priced public transport system. Although Swedes groan about tax, they do not often express frustration that their money is 'wasted'. Constructing a lively social life can be a challenge. **Ann Hunter** points out that it can be difficult to make Swedish friends:

> *The only Swedes you meet regularly are your pupils and the professional relationship can make it awkward to socialise, though after your first term you can get to know ex-pupils quite well. Learning Swedish, if it is possible, is a good way to meet people, though your fellow students are foreigners of course.*

Andrew Boyle had mixed feelings about Sweden and Swedish people:

> *Sweden is a pleasant place to live, if a little dull at times. It is a generally liberal place, although the increasingly multicultural nature of society is causing Swedes to have to face up to their own prejudices. The students are generally of a high level and although initially quiet not unfriendly and even chatty after they know you a little better.*

Still, once you meet one outgoing Swede you'll find yourself quickly drawn into a group, which manages to avoid the horrific cost of dining out/drinks by sticking to meals and parties in people's homes, trips to free galleries and museums and various meetings of social clubs/interest groups. There are also of course cheaper places to eat out, which you'll discover once you're able to find your way around. Stockholm has a great vibe, although the stylishness of its inhabitants can sometimes be intimidating. Gothenburg has a younger feel, and is the city of choice for hip young Scandinavians (and other nationalities, since the Swedish government is remarkably supportive of promising artists).

Outside the major cities, especially further north, you have to be independent and comfortable with your own company for long periods to enjoy Sweden. During the seven months of the winter the locals either hibernate or devote all their leisure to skiing. Anyone who enjoys outdoor activities will probably enjoy a stint in Sweden, especially ramblers and hill-walkers, who take advantage of the *Allemannsrätt*, the law that guarantees free access to the countryside for everyone. Island hopping around the (car-free) Stockholm archipelago with a tent is an excellent and cheap way to enjoy nature, eat far too many cinnamon buns and lie around in the sun. Summers are usually very warm, certainly more so than in Britain, which is why so many Swedes have an enviable golden tan.

LIST OF EMPLOYERS

DENMARK

BERLITZ LANGUAGE SERVICES SCANDINAVIA
Borgergade 28, 1300 Copenhagen
- ✆ +45 70 215010
- ✉ teaching@berlitz.dk
- 🖥 www.berlitz.dk

NUMBER OF TEACHERS: Varies for openings in Norway, Finland, Sweden and Denmark, usually Greater Copenhagen and Southern Sweden.

PREFERENCE OF NATIONALITY: None.

QUALIFICATIONS: Minimum bachelor's degree and/or business-related work experience.

CONDITIONS OF EMPLOYMENT: Freelance basis and mostly part-time. All new trainers must attend compulsory one-week Berlitz training course. Timetable changes from week to week; most teaching takes place in mornings and evenings.

FACILITIES/SUPPORT: No assistance with accommodation given.

CAMBRIDGE INSTITUTE FOUNDATION
Vimmelskaftet 48, 1161 Copenhagen K
- ✆ +45 33 133302
- ✉ info@cambridgeinstitute.dk
- 🖥 www.cambridgeinstitute.dk

NUMBER OF TEACHERS: 26.

PREFERENCE OF NATIONALITY: British, Irish.

QUALIFICATIONS: Bachelor's degree, TEFL qualification and at least 1 year's TEFL experience abroad.

CONDITIONS OF EMPLOYMENT: 7-month renewable contracts (October to May). Minimum 20 hours per week, students aged 18–70.

SALARY: DKK270 (approx. £29) per teaching hour.

FACILITIES/SUPPORT: Furnished accommodation available in central Copenhagen. Training given.

RECRUITMENT: Direct application from teachers to email address above.

SANWES SPROGINSTITUT APS
Kokholm 1, 6000 Kolding
- ✆ +45 75 517410
- ✉ sanwes@sanwes.dk
- 🖥 www.sanwes.dk

Also branches at Andkaervej 19, 7100 Vejle (+45 75 724610), and Fredericia Uddannelsescenter, Mosegardsvej 2, 7000 Fredericia (+45 75 941411).

NUMBER OF TEACHERS: 20–22.

PREFERENCE OF NATIONALITY: British, American, Australian.

QUALIFICATIONS: Should have some business background, be open-minded, cheerful and have lots of initiative.

CONDITIONS OF EMPLOYMENT: Freelance; preferred minimum period 6 months; daytime hours; total number depends on clients.

SALARY: Approximately DKK172 (about £20) per hour.

FACILITIES/SUPPORT: No assistance with accommodation. Pre-service training from other teacher. Help given with work permits.

RECRUITMENT: Local interviews.

CONTACT: Tina McCaffery, Partner (tina@sanwes.dk).

FINLAND

AAC GLOBAL
Porkkalankatu 20, 00180 Helsinki
- ✆ +358 9 4766 7800
- ✉ recruitment@aacglobal.com
- 🖥 www2.aacglobal.com

NUMBER OF TEACHERS: With growing operations in Sweden and Denmark, the company has over 300 trainers (80 native English speakers) and a total of 7 offices in Finland, ie Helsinki, Tampere, Turku, Jyväskylä, Kouvola, Vaasa and Oulu. It trains over 10,000 professionals yearly.

PREFERENCE OF NATIONALITY: British, American and Canadian.

QUALIFICATIONS: University degree plus CELTA/TEFL or equivalent or degree plus business background; teaching experience preferred. Driving licence is an asset.

CONDITIONS OF EMPLOYMENT: Trainers expected to deliver an interesting range of challenging language courses with a multicultural perspective.

FACILITIES/SUPPORT: Possibility of one-way airfare being paid. Induction training provided and a system of head trainers to support the trainers in each language.

RECRUITMENT: Direct application (see careers page of website), newspaper ads and recruitment websites.

MARK RICHARD'S BUSINESS ENGLISH OY
Kaisaniemenkatu 4 A, 00100 Helsinki
- ✆ +358 9 6124 0362
- ✉ office@mrbe.net
- 🖥 www.mrbe.net

NUMBER OF TEACHERS: 7.

PREFERENCE OF NATIONALITY: British, Australian or American.

QUALIFICATIONS: Degree plus CELTA or equivalent or PGCE.

CONDITIONS OF EMPLOYMENT: Teachers are freelance.

SALARY: €22–€28 per 45 minutes. Tax rate starts at 20% plus pension contribution of 4.5%.

RECRUITMENT: Interview is essential.

CONTACT: Mark Burton, Managing Director.

NORDIC SCHOOL

15 Komissara Smirnova Street, Office 301, Saint Petersburg, Russia 194044

📞 +7 812 303 8696; mobile +7 911 295 3187

📧 lena1909@mail.ru or elena@nordicschool.ru

💻 www.nordicschool.ru

Russian language school that has been hiring teachers to teach English to Russian children aged 8–16 in camps in Finland since 2000 (and more recently in Russia).

NUMBER OF TEACHERS: 50–80.

PREFERENCE OF NATIONALITY: UK, Canada, USA, Australia, New Zealand.

QUALIFICATIONS: Teachers should ideally have experience of working with teenagers and should be familiar with conversational teaching/TEFL methods.

CONDITIONS OF EMPLOYMENT: 2–8 weeks for summer camps from mid-June. 1–2 weeks for winter camps; 1 week in spring and autumn camps. Teaching 5–6 hours a day from 9am to 2.15pm or 3.15pm with few breaks. 5 days per week.

SALARY: €200–€250 per week (net) depending on season and number of teaching hours. No transport costs are covered.

FACILITIES/SUPPORT: Full-board accommodation provided in twin rooms and 3–5 meals per day provided.

RECRUITMENT: Mostly through TESL websites, job boards and TESL schools. Applicants should submit CV, letter, scan of passport and recent photo. Skype or phone interviews acceptable.

CONTACT: Ms Lena Kostenyuk, Director.

RICHARD LEWIS COMMUNICATIONS

Länsituulentie 10, 02100 Espoo, Helsinki

📞 +358 9 4157 4700

📧 info.finland@rlcglobal.com

💻 www.riversdown.com/careers

Offices also in Turku, Tampere, Oulu and Kuopio (contacts on website); and in the UK: Riversdown House, Warnford, Southampton, Hampshire SO32 3LH.

RLC has a network of offices worldwide, especially Scandinavia, specialising in cross-cultural and communication skills training and language teaching.

PREFERENCE OF NATIONALITY: British, American, Australian, New Zealander or any native English speaker.

QUALIFICATIONS: University degree and TEFL preferred.

CONDITIONS OF EMPLOYMENT: Freelance work only.

FACILITIES/SUPPORT: Assistance with finding accommodation. New teachers are given thorough training in RLC's methods and cross-cultural tools/courses.

RECRUITMENT: Apply online.

CONTACT: Helen Teppo, Office Co-ordinator (helen.teppo@rlcglobal.com).

NORWAY

BERLITZ A/S

Akersgata 16, 0158 Oslo

📞 +47 22 331030 / 23 003360

📧 teaching@berlitz.no

💻 www.berlitz.no

NUMBER OF TEACHERS: Varying number of freelancers only. Also has branch in Stavanger.

PREFERENCE OF NATIONALITY: None. Non-Europeans must obtain a contract after the compulsory one-week Berlitz training course and take it to the Ligningskontoret to have 3-month tourist visa extended.

QUALIFICATIONS: Minimum bachelor's degree and/or business-related work experience. Must be energetic, outgoing, creative and open to web-based instruction.

CONDITIONS OF EMPLOYMENT: Freelance basis and mostly part-time. Timetable changes from week to week; most teaching takes place in mornings and evenings. Offer crash courses in summer.

FACILITIES/SUPPORT: No assistance with accommodation given.

CONTACT: Thea Melberg, Instructor Coach (thea.melberg@berlitz.no).

FOLKEUNIVERSITETET/FRIUNDERVISNINGEN OSLO

Torggata 7 (P.B. 496 Sentrum), 0181 Oslo

📞 +47 22 476000

📧 info.ost@folkeuniversitetet.no

💻 www.folkeuniversitetet.no

NUMBER OF TEACHERS: 2 full-time, 8–12 part-time.

PREFERENCE OF NATIONALITY: None, but must be native English speaker.

QUALIFICATIONS: TEFL experience and/or qualification(s) (min. CELTA or equivalent).

CONDITIONS OF EMPLOYMENT: No contracts. Non-EEA residents will need a work permit. Students aged 18–65.

SALARY: Varies according to course (NOK270–300 per 45-minute lesson).

FACILITIES/SUPPORT: No assistance with accommodation, monthly teacher development workshops. Possibility of working at other centres around Norway.

RECRUITMENT: Local interviews only.

CONTACT: Wayne Kelly, Supervisor of English courses (Wayne.Kelly@fuost.no).

LINGU SPRÅKSENTER
Madlaveien 10, 4008 Stavanger
- +47 40 300040
- stavanger@lingu.no
- www.lingu.no

NUMBER OF TEACHERS: 6 for clients in Oslo and Stavanger.

PREFERENCE OF NATIONALITY: British, American, Australian, etc.

QUALIFICATIONS: TEFL certification, if not a degree in teaching/ English language. Experience with adults as private students and in groups is valuable.

CONDITIONS OF EMPLOYMENT: Freelance. Hours vary according to availability. Some teachers work full-time (28 teaching hours per week) while others work part-time.

SALARY: Hourly pay according to teacher's education and experience.

FACILITIES/SUPPORT: Advice given on finding accommodation but it is not provided.

RECRUITMENT: Vacancies are posted online. Good candidates are called in for an interview and teach a mini-lesson as part of the recruitment process. Skype interviews also possible.

SWEDEN

RICHARD LEWIS COMMUNICATIONS
Riversdown House, Warnford, Hampshire SO32 3LH, UK
- maria@rlcglobal.com
- www.rlc.se

NUMBER OF TEACHERS: 40 in Stockholm, Göteborg, Malmö and Helsingborg.

PREFERENCE OF NATIONALITY: Must be native English speakers.

QUALIFICATIONS: Degree and recognised TEFL qualification essential. Teaching experience in Business English and some personal business experience would be an advantage.

CONDITIONS OF EMPLOYMENT: Various locations in Europe, mainly UK, Finland, Sweden and Germany. Full-time and freelance positions available.

SALARY: Depends on location and experience.

FACILITIES/SUPPORT: Varies depending on location.

RECRUITMENT: Send CV to info@crossculture.com with a covering letter.

CONTACT: Maria Johnsson, Director.

SPAIN

Despite having been hit hard by the global recession, or maybe even because of it, Spain continues to offer plenty of opportunities for native English teachers. Language schools continue to attend to the massive demand from young adults just out of school or university who cannot find a job (youth unemployment is estimated to be a heart-sinking 50%) and who are keen to fill their time productively and improve their CVs. Demand is also strong from parents who continue to send their young children and teenagers to English classes and summer camps, to help them pass school exams and eventually cope with a job market that demands fluency in English more than ever.

The national push to introduce English early continues; it is compulsory in state schools from the first year of primary school. In conjunction with the Spanish Ministry of Education and Science, the British Council has been recruiting teachers, mostly with qualified status, to work in primary schools (www.britishcouncil.org/spain/en/bilingual-schools-project-0). This trend has filtered through to private language providers, many of whom offer courses to very young children. Spanish government-funded schemes to deploy native-speaking conversation assistants throughout the education system have been gathering pace. For example the Madrid Commune employs 1,880 native English speakers as assistants (*auxiliaries*) in both private and public bilingual institutions.

The fastest growing sector of the market is in teaching young children. In fact there is a special category of teacher being sought by CALAC, an association of four language schools in Andalucia, which is of Very Young Children (VYC), as young as three.

Another development that has benefited the English teaching industry is the increasing popularity of applying for European funds to put on English classes in the workplace, as administered by the Fundación Tripartita.

Thousands of foreigners teach English in language schools (*academias*), from the Basque north (where there is a surprisingly strong concentration) to Andalucía in the south and Galicia in the west as well as Madrid and Barcelona. The entries for language schools occupy many pages of the Madrid *Yellow Pages* and in the whole country total about 800 listings in the online *Yellow Pages*. Almost every main street in every Spanish town has an *Academia de Inglés*. *Academias* are privately run and are not regulated by the Ministerio de Educación.

Spain has always been a popular destination for EFL teachers. Who can fail to be attracted to the climate, scenery, history and culture? Economic expansion and increased prosperity in some quarters have brought about a dynamic, fast-paced society, while traditional stereotypes of flamenco and bull-fighting are completely outmoded. New arrivals discover that the various regions, from Asturias to Andalucia, have their own culture and do not consider themselves primarily Spanish at all.

With so many new schools opening to meet rising demand, in some places the ELT business has become very competitive, with academy owners competing for both teachers and students. Some do their best to squeeze out every last euro of profit, which can lead to poor working conditions. In some of the bigger cities a teacher's salary does not go all that far, although it is still possible to have a three-course meal (*menu del dia*) with wine for €8 outside the big cities. In many parts of Andalucía, if you ask for a *caña* (a small glass of beer) or a glass of *tinto* you're given a decent tapa for free.

While teaching wages probably won't allow you to save, they are usually enough to support a tolerably comfortable lifestyle. These are points to bear in mind when visions of paella and beaches dance before your eyes.

PROSPECTS FOR TEACHERS

The days are gone when any native speaker of English without a TEFL background could reasonably expect to be hired by a language academy. Almost all respectable schools these days require a solid TEFL certificate, while short/distance learning courses are often frowned upon. Many schools in some major cities echo the discouraging comments made by the director of a well-established school in Barcelona who said that he has found that there is a large supply of well-qualified native English speakers on hand so that his school cannot possibly reply to all the CVs from abroad that it receives as well. Schools report that the number of applications from candidates with a recognised TEFL certificate has increased simply because so many more centres in the UK and worldwide are churning them out.

Opportunities for untrained graduates have all but disappeared in what can be loosely described as 'respectable' schools, though there are still language academy directors who might be prepared to hire someone without qualifications, particularly part-time. A number of schools fall into this category. To take a random example, the expatriate director of a well-established school in Alicante estimated that of the 20 or so schools in town, only four operate within the law (ie keep their books in order, pay social security contributions for their staff, etc).

Many Britons and Irish people with or without TEFL qualifications still set off for Spain to look for work on spec, preferably before the summer begins or in early September, visiting, calling in and emailing their CVs once they get there. While in the past many employers did much of their recruitment locally at the last minute, and a high percentage of schools depended on word of mouth and local walk-ins for their staff requirements, in recent years schools have been turning more and more to the internet to source teachers. Anyone with some experience and/or a teaching qualification should find it fairly easy to land a job this way. While speaking Spanish is not a must for most jobs, some knowledge of the language is a plus, both for job prospects and quality of life. The usual process in the big cities is to put together a timetable from various sources, and teachers in this situation should be reconciled to the fact that some or all of their employers in their first year will exploit them to some degree. Having said that, those who choose smaller cities or towns, or who stay on for a second or further years, can be choosier.

The situation for Americans and other non-EU citizens has become almost impossible if they want to work legally in the private sector (see section on Regulations below). An important exception is the NALCA programme operating throughout Spain where a 'bilingual schools' campaign has been implemented. Native English speakers from North America work as assistants in state and private schools, both at the primary and secondary levels. The NALCA programme (North American Language and Culture Assistants in Spain) is administered by the Spanish Ministry of Education (details at www.mecd.gob.es/eeuu/convocatorias-programas/convocatorias-eeuu/auxiliares-conversacion-eeuu.html) and places about 4000 Americans and Canadians in schools for the academic year October to May. Applicants must have a degree and at least an intermediate knowledge of Spanish; applications open in early January and are due by the end of March. Assistants receive a monthly allowance (*ayuda mensual*) of €700 (€1,000 in Madrid). Note that mediating agencies such as CIEE (www.ciee.org/teach/spain) ease the application process for a fee of $2,000. Various companies and organisations are involved with recruitment of native-speaker assistants, such as Multilingual Education Development & Support in Navarra (www.meddeas.com/en), UP International Education (www.upinternatinaleducation.com), which places graduates as assistants in private schools throughout spain and rewards them with grants of up to €845 per month, the BEDA programme which works with Catholic schools in the Madrid region (www.ecmadrid.org/en/language-assistant), and CAPS (has a directory entry).

The Meddeas programme recruits English speakers at three levels: Advanced are those with a BA in English and education, or a BA plus TEFL Certificate, who receive €900 a month; Graduate level are candidates with any degree, whose grant is €850; and the Speakers Program is for school leavers. Graduates may choose to receive half the grant in addition to accommodation with a host family. Participants on the Speakers Program earn €300 in addition to homestay accommodation and have a lighter load of conversation practice.

Summer language camps are popular, in which sport and language learning are interwoven for children aged 5–18. For these, native English speakers are recruited in large numbers in March and April to teach the language and to coach sports and/or supervise swimming. Companies to try include ModLang in Zaragoza (www.modlang.es), Red Leaf with camps in Galicia (www.redleaf.es), English YA (www.englishya.es), Eurobridge International (www.eurobridge.net), McGrogans Summer School (www.mcgroganschool.com) and TECS (see entry).

FINDING A JOB

Because schools run the whole gamut from prestigious to rough-and-ready, every method of job-hunting works at some level. Many independent language schools are run by expatriate Britons and Irish people, and quite a few of these will offer guidance and support for newer teachers, as well as opportunities for further professional development.

IN ADVANCE

Candidates who know that they want to teach in Spain should consider doing their TEFL training with an organisation with strong Spanish links such as OxfordTEFL in London with schools in Barcelona and Cadiz (see the Training chapter for details of the Trinity Cert TESOL courses). Better still, do your training in Spain, which will allow you to get to know the country and the specific needs of the students, to take advantage of the job guidance of trainers that know the local job market well, as well as being on the spot for job vacancies. This option is often even cheaper than staying in the UK, given the lower cost of living and the fact that many centres offer a package that includes low-priced accommodation. International House has centres in Barcelona, Madrid, Santander and Palma, Mallorca offering the CELTA course, as do CLIC in Seville, Chester School and Hyland Language Centre in Madrid, and Campbell College in Valencia, among others around Spain.

A great number of vacancies are advertised online, especially in May/June for an autumn start. For example the key site tefl.com was carrying 83 schools and companies advertising jobs in Spain (June 2015). The websites of Spanish language institutes tend to be reasonably transparent (unlike for Portuguese schools) and the majority display an icon 'Work with us' or 'Trabaja con nosotros'.

For a listing of English language schools in Spain, one source is the *Yellow Pages*, which can be accessed on the internet (www.paginasamarillas.es) – you simply type in '*Academias de Idiomas*' and the city or town of interest. You can find a list of members of FECEI, the national federation of private language schools, on the Spainwise website (www.spainwise.net). Also on the Spainwise site you'll find current job offers in FECEI schools and details of the annual Spanish TEFL Jobs Fair. Held in mid-May, the fair is a showcase for FECEI schools. Schools from different parts of Spain have stands where teachers can meet employers face-to-face and find out about job opportunities for the following academic year. The fair is a good opportunity to meet lots of employers under one roof, compare what different locations have to offer and conditions offered by different schools, as well as attend talks on such issues as legalities and paperwork, adapting to life in Spain, etc. It's free so, if you're the type who likes to look before you leap, this fair could provide the answers to many of the questions on your mind. For further details, contact Aidan O'Toole (info@spainwise.net).

ANDY HEATH

Andy Heath tells how he made good use of the Spanish TEFL Jobs Fair.

Fresh out of my CELTA course and with very little idea of what to do next, I was lucky enough to hear about the Spainwise Recruitment Fair, a kind of one-stop shop for TEFL jobs across the country. The only problem was I had already booked a return ticket home. Attending the fair would involve travelling to and from Spain twice in a month, difficult on a teacher's salary, almost out of reach of an unemployed one. I was serious about teaching, though, and equally serious about finding a good place to do it. I'd heard all the scare stories about exploitation, fly-by-night schools and shady *operators. The chance to meet dozens of potential employers face-to-face and size them up while they did the same to me seemed too good to pass up.*

A month later, as I mulled over three job offers, each in a different province of Spain and each from someone I was sure I would enjoy working with, I knew I'd made the right decision. The school I chose, Academia Blue Door in Córdoba, eased me through all the red tape and helped me with accommodation, as all the schools involved in Spainwise had offered to do. The job itself involved longer hours than you would ever teach without a break in England, but I appreciated the way that teaching in the evenings left mornings and afternoons free to sleep or enjoy life in a new city. A 10 o'clock finish coincides with when most Spaniards finish their dinner and start thinking about which bar to visit afterwards, so you don't miss much nightlife.

The recruitment agency EES Madrid run by Richard Harrison is closing in Madrid, but may be re-established in 2016 in London and possibly Dublin; email richardinmadrid@gmail.com for details.

Successful candidates from TtMadrid (see entry in Directory of Training Courses Worldwide; www. ttmadrid.com) are directed to several Madrid agencies such as Pembroke Educational Consultants (www.peceducacion.com). Another teaching agency to try is Training Express (www.trainingexpress.es/ recruitment), which also offers teaching by telephone and has its principal offices in Madrid, Bilbao and Barcelona. Entry-level interships lasting three months are available through the training company Hands-on TEFL (spain@handsontefl.com).

ON THE SPOT

Most teaching jobs in Spain are still found on the spot. While trying to flee recession in his native Ireland, **Ross O'Brien** was persuaded to give up on his plan to fix up a teaching job in Spain before leaving home:

Mistakenly, I'd decided that I didn't want to leave Ireland until I had secured a job abroad, so every time I opened the advert for the May job fair in Córdoba (sponsored by Spainwise), I would close it again almost instantly, not even considering it. Then my dad talked some sense into me: 'You have to speculate to accumulate!' He was right and I knew it. Cheap Ryanair flights booked, CV uploaded to the Spainwise website and three weeks later I found myself in Córdoba attending the fair.

Many language schools stipulate that they interview all candidates in person before hiring. With increasing competition from candidates with solid TEFL qualifications, it is more and more difficult for the under-qualified to succeed. The best time to look is between the end of the summer holidays and the start of term, which falls in the first two weeks of October, although you can find jobs in late October too. Since some teachers do not return to their jobs after the Christmas break and schools can find themselves left in the lurch, early January may also be possible. Try outlying towns and suburbs if work is scarce in the city centres. In Madrid there are usually at least part-time jobs going most months of the academic year, though after Easter demand dies down. Many schools shut over the summer, but there is some work to be had in those that remain open, since most of their teachers disappear over the summer too, or teach kids in a number of English summer camps dotted around the country.

Once in Spain, the local press can be useful, for example newspapers such as the twice-weekly *Cambalache* in Seville, *La Vanguardia* on Sunday and the daily *Segundamano*. In *El Pais* look in the classified section of the salmon-coloured supplement '*Negocios*', under '*Idiomas*', and in *Segundamano* under '*Ofertas de Empleo – Profesores*'. The classified advert papers *Cambalache* and *Segundamano* are also good for flat hunting, as is the webpage www.loquo.com, which also carries some teaching jobs in its employment listings (can be viewed in English).

The website www.madridteacher.com is a comprehensive source of information about teaching opportunities in Madrid (specifically), and also in the rest of Spain. It is run by a group of freelance teachers who teach in small and mid-sized companies, academies, schools and with private students in Madrid. The website www.lingobongo.com is also recommended for both Madrid and Barcelona for teaching jobs and language exchanges. The Expatriate Café website (www.expatriatecafe.com/forums) contains links to potential employers, as well as useful information about TEFL training, certification and ESL.

Local magazines may advertise the possibility of *intercambio*, which means an exchange of English for Spanish or Catalan conversation practice – a great way to meet locals. Some Irish pubs not only offer the opportunity to meet other expats but often organise weekly *intercambio* nights, which will be listed in the English-speaking press. Recommended expat teacher hang-outs in Madrid include J&J Books & Coffee on Wednesdays, Thursdays and Saturdays, Carmencita Bar (which has '*Cañas and Conversation*' sessions on Tuesdays), the Irish Rover and the Triskel Tavern. English language bookshops sometimes have a noticeboard with relevant notices, as do the EOIs (*Escuelas Oficial de Idiomas*) in major cities (these are enormous state-sponsored official language schools with up to 10,000 students).

After finishing their A levels, **Sam James** and **Sophie Ellison** were hoping to spend their gap year in Barcelona if possible. After acquiring their Trinity TESOL Certificates in their destination city, they did the rounds of the language schools:

> *Though tedious, this did work and we doubt we would have found work any other way. Job availability didn't seem that high in Barcelona when we were looking in October and we both accepted our only job offers. (Our age may have put off some employers.) Most schools seem to have recruited in September, so October was a bit of a lean month. I got my job by covering a class at two hours' notice for a teacher who had called in sick. When this teacher decided to leave Barcelona, I was interviewed and offered her classes on a permanent basis. I got the job permanently about a fortnight after handing out CVs. Sophie was asked to her first interview after about three weeks of job-hunting. She was selected but then had to wait for several more weeks while her contract was finalised.*

Conventional wisdom says that summer is the worst time to travel out to Spain to look for work since schools will be closed and their owners unobtainable. However, **Sam James** handed round his CV again in May (when his hours were cut) and was given some encouragement. He thinks that because so few teachers look for work just six weeks before the end of the academic year, employers are sometimes in need of replacements and this might well be a way for teachers to get ahead of the queue for September jobs. With the recent boom in language learning (especially English) more and more schools are head-hunting for the following academic year before the summer break. With so many no-frills cheap flights on the market, a reconnaissance trip might be worth a gamble.

When knocking on doors, bear in mind that most language academies will be closed between 2pm and 4pm, when directors are invariably away from their desks. Leave a smartly produced CV with a local mobile telephone number. It is a very good idea to buy a mobile or at least an inexpensive local SIM card with a local number for your own phone. A serious director will probe into claims of experience and will soon weed out any bogus stories. Other directors are just checking to see that you are a reasonable proposition or at least not a complete dud.

For qualified teachers, opportunities abound. For the untrained, a more probable scenario is that they will elicit some mild interest from one or two schools and will be told that they may be contacted right at the beginning of term and offered a few hours of teaching as course start dates loom. It can become a war of nerves; anyone who is willing and can afford to stay on has an increasingly good chance of becoming established.

The great cities of Madrid and Barcelona act as magnets to thousands of hopeful teachers. **Sam James** blamed his lack of job security and bitty hours on Barcelona's popularity, '*the result of the great supply of willing teachers here keeping working conditions down and making it hard to exert any leverage on an employer when one is so easily replaced*'. For this reason other cities and towns may answer your requirements better. There are language academies all over the country and a door-to-door job hunt in the area of your choice might pay off.

LIVE-IN POSITIONS

Some excellent programmes exist to place young people in families to do some tutoring in exchange for board and lodging. A UK company that matches Spanish families with English speakers for short or long stays is ELA Scotland/Spain (englishassistance@btopenworld.com). People from outside the EU who want to experience Spanish culture might like to consider a live-in position with a family who wants an English tutor for its children or a voluntary position as an English assistant on summer language/sports camps. Further details may be sought from Relaciones Culturales, the youth exchange organisation at Calle Ferraz 82, 28008 Madrid (+34 91 541 7103; www.worktravelstudyinspain.com), which places native English speakers aged 18–40 with Spanish families who want to practise their English in exchange for providing room and board; the placement fee is €300.

Several American organisations, including InterExchange in New York (www.interexchange.org), arrange Teach in Spain programmes whereby fee-paying young Americans (mainly women) live with a family in exchange for speaking English and providing 15 hours of tutoring a week for 1–3 months; fees start at $795.

CHRISTOPHER WEEKS

On New Year's Day 2013, Chris Weeks noticed an advertisement for www.myfamilyabroad.com on the useful job site www.jobsabroadbulletin.co.uk and decided 'New year: new start'.

I was impressed by the www.myfamilyabroad.com website and thought the volunteer programme would suit someone like me with no prior TEFL experience (though I had done a 140-hour online TEFL course with i-to-i). After a phone interview with the agency, I waited a few days whilst my profile was sent out to some Spanish families to see if I was suitable for their requirements. I was then emailed the details of a family with an 8-year-old boy and 3-year-old girl which seemed a perfect fit for myself.

In exchange for a room and food (all freshly home-cooked by the father of the family, José), I was expected to undertake English-speaking activities with the children for 15 hours each week. These ranged from homework help to English language games. The only problem I faced was tantrums and tears on occasion from the three-year-old, but she was cute so all could be forgiven.

My teaching was in the evenings so I was able to explore Madrid by day and undertake Spanish lessons at a great academy (on which we received a discount through myfamilyabroad.com). I got to meet the extended family including Grandma, and went *on holiday with the family to Andalucía, which was a great experience. I was made to feel very welcome despite my lack of Spanish. The low point was the weather. Unfortunately 2013 saw the coldest winter on record - it even snowed in Madrid in March, which was unheard of.*

The company is now called Culture Go Go and leaves subscribers to arrange their stays directly with host families (see entry). After his volunteer placement, Chris investigated finding paid work in Madrid and had plenty of offers of interviews. But he had a ticket to Glastonbury that he didn't want to sacrifice and this made it hard to land a longer-term job. He concludes: *'Madrid is a vibrant and exciting city which I may well return to in the future to live and work.'*

FREELANCE TEACHING

As usual, private tutoring can pay better than contract teaching because there is no middle man. **Stuart Britton** easily found private pupils to supplement his school income in a small town in the un-touristy north of Las Palmas de Gran Canaria. However, when his employer found out, he was told to drop them or risk being sacked, even over the summer when the school was closed, and Stuart had no other source of income. He resented this so much that he advises not bothering with small schools, and simply concentrating on obtaining private students.

As always, it is difficult to start up without contacts and a good knowledge of the language; and when you do get started it is difficult to earn a stable income due to the frequency with which pupils cancel. The problem is particularly acute in May when undergraduates and school pupils concentrate on preparing for exams and other activities fall by the wayside. Spaniards are fond of taking off extra days to link a mid-week fiesta with the weekend, known as *puente*, meaning bridge.

Getting private lessons is a marketing exercise and you will have to explore all the avenues that seem appropriate to your circumstances. Obviously you can advertise on noticeboards at universities, EOIs, community centres (*centros cívicos*), public libraries, corner shops and wherever you think there is a market. Major stores are a good bet, for example Alcampo supermarkets. A neat notice in Spanish along the lines of '*Profesora Nativa de ingles da clases particulares a domicilio*' might elicit a favourable response. Introduce yourself at local state schools and ask them to pin up a notice broadcasting your willingness to ensure the children's linguistic future. Compile a list of addresses of professionals (eg lawyers, architects, etc) as they may need English for their work and have the wherewithal to pay for it. Try export businesses, distribution companies, perhaps even travel agencies. Make the acquaintance of language teachers who will know of openings and advertise your availability on free ads websites, Craigslist, etc.

> *Because private classes can be better paid than institute teaching, they are much in demand, including by contract teachers, some of whom are engaged in some private tutoring. You could arrange a school contract with no more than 15 or 20 hours and supplement this with private classes, which are lucrative though unstable.*

REGULATIONS

All EU teachers working on contract should possess a resident permit (*Certificado de registro de ciudadano de la Unión*) with a tax number (NIE), which can be obtained from the Foreigners' Office (Oficina de Extranjeros) in the province of residence or at a designated police station (www.mpt.gob.es/es/servicios/extranjeria.html). A contract will not be issued until you have applied for an NIE (*Número de Identidad de Extranjero*). The application charge is €15. Since 2012, it has been necessary to demonstrate that you have medical insurance while in Spain and that you have an income of at least €400 a month, either from your employer, as a registered self-employed worker or from independent means (a credit card might be sufficient accompanied by a letter from your bank that you are well under the credit limit). If you are working legally, you will automatically be registered with the Social Security system for medical treatment; otherwise you will have to show a private policy that satisfies their requirements.

At present, the procedure for applying for a first-time Residency Certificate and NIE is as follows: go to the Oficina de Extranjería (which in Madrid can be found at Calle Manuel Luna, 29, 28020 Madrid near metro station Tetuán; +34 912 72 95 00) preferably after booking an appointment, though this is not always necessary. Beforehand you should download, fill out and print the form EX-15, the *Solicitud de Número de Identidad de Extranjero (NIE) y Certificados*. Otherwise pick up and complete the form on arrival. At the office you will be given a form to fill out, again with your personal information, which you must take to the nearest bank and pay the required fee. Return to the office to wait to collect your NIE, initially valid for three months but which can be extended to five years. With your NIE and passport, you can then go to the Social Security Office (Seguridad Social) to apply for a Social Security Number, with completed form *Modelo TA1* (www.seg-social.es). Your employer should be able to advise you on all the steps. The NIE is an important form of identification for filing taxes, establishing a business, opening a bank account and so on. All people with an address in Spain, including foreigners, are obliged to register at the *padrón* office in their local town hall (*ayuntamiento*), which is free of charge.

Many long-stay foreigners engage a specialist lawyer called a *Gestoria Administrativa* to assist in navigating the bureaucracy. Spain Expat (www.spainexpat.com) has pages of useful information about living and working in Spain, while the online community www.eyeonspain.com has some busy forums. Alternatively, teacher recruitment agencies like Spainwise can advise.

The immigration situation for people from outside Europe is going from bad to worse. Most of the institutes that once hired North Americans now refuse to tackle the lengthy procedures involved in obtaining work permits, mainly because the tax and social security authorities have been doing frequent inspections. If they discover illegal workers, the penalty for the company can be as much as €20,000. Berlitz cautions: '*Unfortunately, the European Union (EU), of which Spain is a part, seldom issues work permits to non-EU citizens unless they are married to an EU citizen.*' Americans with Irish or Italian ancestry often prefer to chase the papers that will get them a passport from an EU member state.

As mentioned above, the main exceptions for North Americans are the NALCA programme for Canadian and American graduates, and also summer schools where the period of work is shorter than the 90-day validity of a Schengen tourist visa. Non-EU citizens may also live with Spanish families free of charge in exchange for tutoring the children in English. The Youth Mobility visa allows Canadians (18–35) and New Zealanders (18–30) to work for up to a year; the Canadian quota for the year is 1,000.

The TEFL training company TtMadrid mentioned above has designed a combination of TEFL training course with Spanish language tuition which makes non-EU nationals eligible for a student visa and therefore able to live and work in Spain for up to 12 months. This option costs a cool €2,750; see further details at www.ttmadrid.com/the-spanish-programme.php.

None of this means that there aren't any Americans or other nationalities teaching in Spain without permits. According to Jon Loop, many post-Hemingway Americans go to Spain for a year to learn Spanish and 'find themselves man' (or maybe even find themselves a man). The teacher-training schools in major cities are full of American as well as British trainees, and Americans, Australians and New Zealanders also find work, not just teaching private classes but through numerous intrepid academies that hire them off-contract and send them off to teach in companies rather than on school premises. Anyone who works on a tourist visa will have to renew it every three months by leaving the Schengen zone for 90 days. A new independent company called COMO Consulting run by two young American expats can advise on moving to Spain to live and work (www.comoconsultingspain.com) for varying consultation fees.

Social security (*seguridad social*) contributions are between 4% and 7% of earnings, typically 6.4%. Together with taxes, the total deductions from a gross wage average 8.5%. Tax residents will need to pay income taxes in Spain and are generally defined as those who live in Spain for more than 183 days in each calendar year. However, www.spainexpat.com suggests that in many cases you only need to file a tax return in Spain when you make more than €22,000 per year; unlikely if you are a language teacher. Spain and Britain have a double taxation treaty so Britons can't be taxed twice. Under EU legislation, language schools must give contracts and make contributions for all staff, whether full-time or part-time. In practice, this does not always happen. After a few months of teaching for one academy, **Jon Loop** asked for a contract and was given a special 11-hour contract (though at the time he was teaching 20 hours a week). Contracts for fewer than 12 hours a week do not require more than minimal social security contributions. **Joanna Mudie** from the Midlands describes the situation that results from this:

> There's a great deal of uncertainty and insecurity about all aspects of work: hours, days, rates of pay, insurance, etc. Contracts (if you're lucky enough to get one) are a load of rubbish because employers put down far fewer hours on paper to avoid paying so much insurance, and also to protect themselves if business dwindles. My advice is, forget your English sense of honesty and obeying the law. 'When in Rome . . .' Relax and simply don't worry about the legalities. It usually seems to work out okay, and if not, well, it's a nice life in the sun.

Schools that sidestep the regulations and do not pay contributions to cover their employees' social security might well be the ones willing to employ non-Europeans and pay cash in hand. Teachers interested in long-term prospects should try to get work with the respectable schools that do issue contracts and pay contributions.

CONDITIONS OF WORK

Most schools offer €1,100–€1,300 gross for 25 hours of teaching a week. Perks at the better schools include 2-3 weeks of paid holiday. A standard hourly wage for starter teachers would be €14, although some pay more. Better hourly wages are paid to registered freelancers sent out to firms.

Spanish TEFL is no different from TEFL in other countries in that there are always some employers who offer low pay, long hours and poor conditions. For example, teachers have discovered that pay has been deducted when they have been unavoidably absent or that their bonuses have been withheld with no explanation. **Sam James** was taken aback when his hours were drastically cut by his employer in Barcelona with no notice. The simple explanation was that Sam was working without a contract, which would have guaranteed a certain number of hours. He advises getting a contract if at all possible, even on a lower rate of pay, since contracts bring security, a reliable income and holiday pay (which he knows because his girlfriend Sophie had one).

BARRY O'LEARY

Barry O'Leary wrote from Seville in his third year of teaching there. In his first year he worked for a slightly disorganised and crafty academy where there was no mention of a contract, classes started at 8am and staggered throughout the day until 10pm and it was difficult to predict how much he would earn from month to month because he wasn't paid for local holidays. Luckily, in his second year, after mingling with the other expat teachers, he was able to land himself a job with a more professional establishment. He now works fixed hours from 4pm until 10pm, Monday to Thursday, leaving the mornings free, and there are excellent ongoing training sessions on Friday mornings. The language school is one of the most successful in Seville with 12 academies scattered throughout the city and it takes care of its teachers, offering fixed contracts with long-term prospects.

The students, who are often passionate and keen to learn English, range in age from six to sixty so there is never a dull moment. Classes have a maximum of twelve, all material is provided and there is scope to move away from the syllabus now and then. A lot of extra work is necessary in February and June when the exams take place but it's worth the agony.

Life in Seville is fun and varied, with an abundance of festivals including the religious Semana Santa and the livelier Feria. The city is a great place to live and a base for exploring Andalucia. Evenings can be spent in the many bars enjoying tapas, watching flamenco or Sevillanas (a local dance) or just mingling with the locals. Seville is generally safe and with the year round blue skies, it's a great place to brush up on your Spanish and experience a different way of life.

As always, you can gain an idea of an employer's integrity by talking to other teachers as well as by using your intuition at the interview. Asking lots of questions is a good idea since then you can find out your pay and maximum hours so that you will be in a stronger position to argue, should your employer try to mess you around. But realistically, many new arrivals feel exploited at least in some respects in their first year. **Laura Phibbs** was spared the possibility of being exploited, since her promised job evaporated overnight:

> *The Madrid school director rang me to inform me that I had got the job and I was to start nine days later. When, as instructed, I rang to confirm the arrival time of my plane, I was told that there was no job for me after all since the school had gone bankrupt. I think what really made me angry was that I had rung him rather than the other way round. He did not even say sorry or sound in the least remorseful.*

It is possible that the bankruptcy was just an excuse in the face of insufficient pupils. There's far less demand for English during the summer months (apart from at summer camps), hence the near-universality of nine-month contracts. Most people find it impossible to save enough in nine months to fund themselves abroad for the rest of the year. Most pay agreements also already include the bonuses (*pagas extraordinarias*) that have already been adjusted pro-rata, of which there are two or three a year. Legal schools will pay *finiquito* (holiday pay) at the end of a contract, which should be equivalent to the pay for two and a half days of every month worked, based on your base (not full) salary.

The experience of teaching at a summer camp can be enjoyable and lucrative. The pay is generally fair (say, €800–€1,000 for a four-week stint plus free board and accommodation, rising to €1,200, including accommodation, if you're particularly fortunate) though some organisations offer little more than accommodation, meals and pocket money. **Glen Williams** describes his summer job at a summer language camp in Izarra in the Basque Country:

The children learned English for three hours in the morning with one half-hour break (but not for the teacher on morning snack duty trying to fight off the hordes from ripping apart the bocadillos). Then we had another three or four hours of duties ranging from sports and/or arts to shop/bank duty. For many of us, inexperienced with dealing with groups of kids, there were a few problems of discipline. It was the kids' holiday and they quickly cottoned on that we English teachers in general were a bunch of hippie types.

PUPILS

For a long time, Spaniards had the reputation for being somewhat challenged at learning languages. But now in the main cities, so many people speak decent English that foreign teachers find it hard to practise their Spanish. Often adult learners are more motivated than children. This was one of **David Bourne**'s biggest problems and one that he thinks is underestimated, especially as a high proportion of English teaching in some academies is with children and teenagers:

I have found that a lot of the younger students only come here because their parents have sent them in order to improve their exam results. The children themselves would much rather be outside playing football. There are days when you spend most of the lesson trying (unsuccessfully in my case) to keep them quiet. This is especially true on Fridays. I have found it very hard work trying to inject life into a class of bored 10-year-olds, particularly when the course books provided are equally uninspiring.

In such cases it might be a good idea to change your aim from teaching them English to entertaining them (and paying your rent). If students don't want to learn, you will only break your heart trying to achieve the impossible.

Adults are usually an easier proposition, willing to listen and think and with a good sense of humour. In general the Spanish will welcome opportunities to speak animatedly in class and express their opinions. A good knowledge of Spanish is helpful if not essential when teaching junior classes, as **Peter Saliba**, director of a language school in Malaga, explains:

We need teachers with a fluent command of Spanish, not the typical grasp of elementary phrases which may get them by in a social context. On a limited two or three hours per week teaching timetable, there simply is not time for cumbersome English explanations of English grammar and vocabulary. It is worse still with young learners and teens, who will 'run riot' or at the very least run circles round non-Castilian speaking teachers.

Needless to say, Spaniards are a nation of talkers. If things seem to be going awry in your classes, for example students turning up late or being inattentive, don't hesitate to make your feelings known, just as Spaniards do.

ACCOMMODATION

Rents usually swallow up at least a quarter of a teacher's income, more in the big cities and much more if you don't share. In small towns, it is not uncommon for schools to arrange accommodation for their teachers at least for an initial period. The director at a language school in the small Galician town of Marin estimates a modest starting rent of €150 per person in a shared flat, plus bills. Many Spanish students want to live with English students, so check language school, EOI and university noticeboards for flat shares. Some teachers even arrange to share a flat rent-free in exchange for English lessons.

When renting a flat expect to pay a month's rent in advance, plus one or two months' rent as deposit. Since your first pay cheque may not arrive until November, you should arrive with £1,000+ to tide you over. Try to avoid using an *inmobiliaria* (letting agency), which will charge a further month's rent (at least). Be aware of the agencies or associations with seedy premises that charge you a fee before showing you anything. You will quickly distinguish their ads from private ones in the classifieds. In Madrid and Barcelona many people use the free ads paper *Segundamano*; if you do decide to compete for a flat listed in this paper, get up early, since most decent flats are snapped up quickly. When **Barry O'Leary** was looking for a two-bedroom apartment to rent in Central Seville, he advertised in Spanish on a community noticeboard, now http://sevilla.olx.es. It is easier flat hunting in July/August than in September/October or February.

LEISURE TIME

Once you acquire some Spanish, it is very easy to meet people, since Spaniards are so friendly, relaxed and willing to invite newcomers out with them. Of course there is also a strong fraternity of EFL teachers almost everywhere. With luck you will end up socialising with both groups in bars, at parties, *romerías* (pilgrimages), fiestas, etc.

If you're looking for traditional Spanish culture, don't go to Madrid, and certainly don't look for it in Barcelona, which is not Spanish at all but Catalan. Seville, Granada and Valencia are lovely Spanish cities. While teaching in Andalucía, **Joanna Mudie** appreciated the chance to learn about the traditional but still very much alive dances of Spain, eg Sevillanas, Malagueras and Pasadoble.

Rona Mackenzie was clearly enjoying a good quality of life while teaching at the Academia Blue Door in Córdoba:

> *So here I am, a few years down the line, loving my life in Spain. I still get driven to distraction by certain things. I will never get used to the lack of queuing, and the haphazard way in which certain things are dealt with can be very frustrating. But the climate, the wonderful people, the laid-back lifestyle, the food and the fiestas more than make up for that. Everything they say about Spain is pretty much true and I love this country. If you want to teach in Spain, go for it. Come with an open mind, a relaxed attitude, a willingness to learn the language and a serious commitment to hard work and you will doubtless love it. ESL teaching can be for anyone, at any age, as long as your attitude is right. I still miss a Sunday roast sometimes, but the food here's amazing. And I've found a shop where they stock Tetley's tea!*

Glen Williams describes his spare-time activities in Madrid, a city with an enormous variety of nightlife where he was clearly enjoying himself to the full:

> *Madrid is a crazy place. We usually stay out all night at the weekend drinking and boogying. During the gaps in my timetable (10am–2pm and 4pm–7pm) I pretend to study Spanish (I'm no natural) and just wander the back streets. I suppose I should try to be more cultural and learn to play an instrument, write poetry or look at paintings, but I never get myself in gear. I think most people teach English in Spain as a means to live in Spain and learn the Spanish language and culture. But there is a real problem that you end up living in an English enclave, teaching English all day and socialising with English teachers. You have to make a big effort to get out of this rut. I am lucky to live with Spanish people (who do not want to practise their English!).*

A few schools offer free or subsidised Spanish lessons as a perk to teachers. Otherwise investigate the government-run Escuela Oficial de Idiomas.

If the idea of teaching in Spain appeals at all, it is almost always a rewarding and memorable way for people with limited work experience to finance themselves as they travel and live abroad for a spell.

CLIC INTERNATIONAL HOUSE SEVILLE

Mark Hennigan's testimonial

'In the year 2011, a simpler time, a young(ish) man was faced with that reality that has become all too commonplace these days. His job was no longer there where he had left it, and suddenly he had to find a new way to make a living. Fortunately, this was an instance where life had happened whilst he had been busy making other plans. He was fluent in an important and beautiful language (if you're willing to overlook a West Ireland accent) and he was willing to stand up in front of children, teenagers and adults alike and potentially make a fool of himself in order to learn how to stand up in front of children, teenagers and adults alike and potentially not make a fool of himself.

'I was that man. And my plan was to do the CELTA. Of course the decision of where had yet to be made. I was in Ireland and needed a change. There's only so much walking in the rain and the resultant wet socks I could take and I had taken a lot that year. My friend had moved to Seville two years previous to live with his Spanish girlfriend and word drifted back to the old country about a place where the pace is easy, life is out on the street and there's a giant ball of fire in the sky that keeps people warm. It sounded strange and wonderful. I was in.

'So I did my Skype interview, packed my Barry's tea and said goodbye to the folks back home and then arrived in warm, sunny Seville – and suddenly it was all very real that within 24 hours I'd be standing in front of a classroom full of people that did not speak my language, and I most certainly did not speak theirs. That first day felt like a week and that first week a month. By the time the course had finished I wasn't the same man that had arrived five weeks and a thousand years before in Seville. I had worked those once-wet socks right off. I was exhausted. I was also exhilarated.

'The CELTA is one of the best things I've ever done. It's intense, but in all the right ways. I learned an amount that's difficult to measure. I met people that I would count among my closest and best friends. I encountered a way of life I hadn't known before. And somewhere along the way I had become a TEFL teacher.

'Of course, one of the best things about doing the CELTA, and certainly one of my principal reasons for doing the course, is the incomparable freedom to travel that it gives you. And so it's been 14 months since and I'm still here in Seville, which is odd because I could have sworn that my plan was to leave after six weeks. That plan had changed at some point to four months as I was enjoying myself so much that I wanted to stay – but just for the summer. Then the plan was to leave after 11 months so I could stay – but just for an academic year. As it stands, I'll depart this beautiful city, with all it has to offer, to travel with the freedom that the CELTA has given me at some point next year. That's the plan anyway.'

LIST OF EMPLOYERS

ACADEMIA ANJO

Rosalía de Castro 73-2D, 27880 Burela, Lugo

+34 639005046

angela.clare.ball@hotmail.com

www.academiaanjo.es

NUMBER OF TEACHERS: 4.

PREFERENCE OF NATIONALITY: None, but must have EU passport.

QUALIFICATIONS: Ideally candidates will have a view to a career in teaching and have teaching experience, a degree in languages and/or a reputable TEFL qualification.

CONDITIONS OF EMPLOYMENT: 9-month contract; working hours normally 3.30-9/9.30pm.

SALARY: €900-€1,300 (net) depending on experience, with accommodation provided.

FACILITIES/SUPPORT: Accommodation is provided; teachers pay for utilities. School helps teachers obtain a NIE and register for social security. Contributions are made amounting to €300-€400 a month.

RECRUITMENT: Via ads on tefl.com. Skype or telephone interviews.

CONTACT: Angela Clare Ball, Director.

ACADEMIA BLUE DOOR

C/Alhaken II, 6, 14008 Córdoba

+34 957 491535

recruitment@bluedoorspain.com; info@spainwise.net

www.bluedoorspain.com

NUMBER OF TEACHERS: 12.

QUALIFICATIONS: Native speakers of English with university degree and TEFL qualifications.

CONDITIONS OF EMPLOYMENT: Student groups no larger than 6. Contracts are from the end of September to the end of June.

SALARY: School offers a competitive package with salary above national pay agreements plus full national health and social security cover.

RECRUITMENT: Blue Door is a member of ACEIA and FECEI, and recruits at the Spainwise annual recruitment fair in May (www.spainwise.net).

CONTACT: Aidan O'Toole, Director (+34 692 613687).

ACADEMIA BRITANICA (INTERNATIONAL HOUSE CÓRDOBA)

C/Rodriguez Sanchez, 15,14003 Córdoba

+34 957 470350

info-cordoba@acabri.com

www.cordoba.acabri.com

NUMBER OF TEACHERS: 20, also for branch in Huelva.

PREFERENCE OF NATIONALITY: EU member state passport holders who can get residence permits easily.

QUALIFICATIONS: A or B in CELTA plus minimum 1 year's experience, especially in teaching younger learners.

CONDITIONS OF EMPLOYMENT: 9-month contracts, mid-September to mid-June, 22–25 hours per week. Majority of students are aged 4–17.

SALARY: Monthly average around €1,600 gross. Average 12% tax; 6.5% social security deductions.

FACILITIES/SUPPORT: Help with finding accommodation. Residence permits are applied for by the school and the teacher is accompanied to the permits office soon after arrival.

RECRUITMENT: Through IH recruitment system, or locally. Interviews in the UK for teachers recruited through IH World.

CONTACT: Simon Armour, Director of Studies (simon@acabri.com).

AMERICAN LANGUAGE ACADEMY

Plaza Conde del Valle de Suchil 15–17, 28015 Madrid

+34 91 445 5511

efl@americanlanguage.es

www.americanlanguage.es

NUMBER OF TEACHERS: 30 for summer and academic year positions.

PREFERENCE OF NATIONALITY: North American though with permission to work or with student visa.

QUALIFICATIONS: Native speaker with BA degree or currently enrolled as an undergraduate, and language teaching qualifications (CELTA or TEFL). Prefer minimum 1 year's experience, though entry level positions open to candidates willing to take academy's own intensive training course.

CONDITIONS OF EMPLOYMENT: 1-year contract in first instance. Mostly block hours in mornings or evenings for a maximum of 28.5 teaching hours per week. To start July or October. Mostly teaching adults.

SALARY: Minimum €1,200-€1,350 per month (net) for average 26.5 hours per week.

FACILITIES/SUPPORT: No help with accommodation. Visa advice given to North American teachers. Lots of teacher resources and support.

RECRUITMENT: CV (no later than April), application form and personal or skype interview in Madrid including brief demo class. Interviews are held up to the end of May for positions beginning in October.

CONTACT: Jeffrey Locey, Director of Studies, Sergio Domene, Academic Coordinator and Language Consultant.

ASTEX SERVICIOS LINGUISTICOS
C/Hermanos Bécquer 7–6°, 28006 Madrid
✆ +34 91 590 4921
✉ aslpedagogico@astex.es
🖥 www.astex.es

NUMBER OF TEACHERS: ASTEX employs around 350 ESL teachers at any one time, and usually hires 30 new teachers each September/October, with vacancies needing to be filled throughout the year. More than 50% of its classes are phone lessons which can be given from anywhere in the world.

PREFERENCE OF NATIONALITY: Native English speakers with EU citizenship or permission to work.

QUALIFICATIONS: Require CELTA or equivalent and minimum 2 years' EFL teaching experience. For telephone classes a specific training course (2 sessions of 3 hours) must be completed.

CONDITIONS OF EMPLOYMENT: 9-months contract/20–25 hours per week.

SALARY: Contracted teachers earn €17–€17.50 gross; freelancers earn €23–24 gross.

FACILITIES/SUPPORT: Teachers' room: library, computers (free internet) and printer. Free workshops for teachers.

RECRUITMENT: Ads on madridteacher.com. Interview required.

CONTACT: Fran O'Hara, Recruitment Manager (fohara@astex.es).

BERLITZ (ESCUELAS DE IDIOMAS BERLITZ DE ESPAÑA)
HQ, Enrique Granados 6, Complejo Empresarial IMCE, 28223 Pozuelo de Alarcón. Recruitment office: Calle Jose Ortega y Gasset 11, 1° Izq, Barrio de Salamanca, 28006 Madrid
✆ +34 91 577 7259
✉ teach@berlitz.es
🖥 www.berlitz.es

Nine centres in Spain comprising 4 in Madrid and region, 2 in Barcelona, 1 in Seville, 1 Palma de Majorca, and 1 in Valencia.

NUMBER OF TEACHERS: Berlitz Spain employs approx. 100 native speakers.

PREFERENCE OF NATIONALITY: EU (for paperwork reasons).

QUALIFICATIONS: Degree level of education; no teaching qualification required as Berlitz provides training.

CONDITIONS OF EMPLOYMENT: 9-month contracts. Depending on contract type, hours range from an average of 9 (smallest part-time) to 28 hours (full-time) per week, but can vary. Schedules are also quite varied.

SALARY: Depends on which of 6 contract types. Sample contract pays €1,400 (gross). For first-year teachers, total deductions are around 8%.

FACILITIES/SUPPORT: Compulsory training usually in early October. No assistance with accommodation.

RECRUITMENT: Via adverts on various Spanish websites. Face-to-face interviews essential.

CONTACT: Simon Williamson, Country Manager of Instruction.

BRITISH SCHOOL
Plaza Ponent, 5–2nd floor, 43001 Tarragona
✆ +34 977 211605
✉ british@bstarragona.com
🖥 www.bstarragona.com

NUMBER OF TEACHERS: 5.

PREFERENCE OF NATIONALITY: Native English speakers with EU member state passport.

QUALIFICATIONS: University degree, CELTA or Trinity EFL teaching qualification and minimum 1 year's experience teaching English abroad.

CONDITIONS OF EMPLOYMENT: October to June, 21 class hours per week.

SALARY: Gross salary €1,158.34 per month for 21 class hours a week; new-year bonus €260 and end-of-contract holiday pay €662 and travel expenses €228.

FACILITIES/SUPPORT: First week's accommodation paid in hotel; school video and book libraries.

RECRUITMENT: Internet with telephone interview.

BVRNS ACADEMY
Kalebarria 44–46 bajo, Durango, 48200 Vizcaya
✆ +34 946 203668
✉ info@bvrnsacademy.com
🖥 www.bvrnsacademy.com

NUMBER OF TEACHERS: 5.

PREFERENCE OF NATIONALITY: British, native English speakers; also bilingual French-English.

QUALIFICATIONS: Degree, TEFL qualification and experience. Teachers should be cheerful, lively, genuinely interested in teaching and enjoy working with both children and adults. Some knowledge of Spanish preferable.

CONDITIONS OF EMPLOYMENT: Standard 9-month contract. Students vary from young children to mature adults. Courses are grouped according to their level and age and take place mainly in the afternoon and evening (some in the morning). Maximum 8 in a class. 23 teaching hours per week.

SALARY: €1,325 per month for academic year. Bonus at the end of the course €500 on successful completion of contract.

FACILITIES/SUPPORT: Shared furnished room in a flat available for rent of about €270 monthly plus bills.

RECRUITMENT: Initial enquirers should send CV and recent photograph. Telephone interview required.

CONTACT: Ana Lopez, Director.

CAMBRIDGE ENGLISH STUDIES
Avenida de Arteixo 8–1°, 15004 A Coruña
+34 981 160216
www.cambridgeenglishstudies.com

NUMBER OF TEACHERS: 12 teachers, 8 in Coruña and 4 in Ferrol.

QUALIFICATIONS: Teachers must be EU citizens and hold a recognised TESOL qualification (eg CELTA/Trinity College London/RELSA).

CONDITIONS OF EMPLOYMENT: Contracts run from mid-September to end June, teaching 25 hours per week.

SALARY: Basic net salary is €1,000 per month plus increments for experience and qualifications. Taxes and social security paid by the school.

RECRUITMENT: Interviews required, but telephone interview is acceptable.

CAMBRIDGE HOUSE
C/Lopez de Hoyos, 95 1°A, 28002 Madrid
+34 91 519 4603/681 346677
teachers@cambridge-house.com
www.cambridge-house.com

NUMBER OF TEACHERS: 35 for 5 schools in central Madrid.

PREFERENCE OF NATIONALITY: British or Irish teachers. In the case of non-EU teachers, they must already have their working papers.

QUALIFICATIONS: University degree, CELTA certificate and a minimum of 6 or 12 months' teaching experience.

CONDITIONS OF EMPLOYMENT: The average length of contract is 9 months (October to June) but summer work is available to teachers who want to stay on. Contact hours are between 22 and 26 with 3 hours' paid preparation. Most teaching is in evenings till 10pm but early finish on Fridays at 7.30pm and no Saturdays.

FACILITIES/SUPPORT: Advice offered on accommodation and help in all matters of social security and residency application. Full social security payments and a work contract guaranteed. Workshops and staff meetings are held regularly to inform teachers of any extra courses available.

RECRUITMENT: Applications are received by email and acknowledged immediately. CVs are kept on file for future vacancies that crop up.

CONTACT: Penny Rollinson, Director of Studies.

CAMBRIDGE SCHOOL
Placa Manel Montanya 4, 08400 Granollers, Barcelona
+34 93 870 2001
alistair@cambridgeschool.com
www.cambridgeschool.com/en/work-with-us.html

NUMBER OF TEACHERS: 65 for 7 schools in Barcelona area.

PREFERENCE OF NATIONALITY: Native English speakers who can legally work in Spain, ie EU members or non-EU members with a work permit.

QUALIFICATIONS: At least CELTA or equivalent. Clean driving licence, experience of teaching children or adolescents and/or experience of the business world would all be assets.

CONDITIONS OF EMPLOYMENT: Contract length September to June or possibly July, 20 contact teaching hours per week.

SALARY: Average salary is €1,300 a month for 20 contact hours per week.

FACILITIES/SUPPORT: Assistance with accommodation, weekly seminars and workshops are part of the job, school library, teachers' room and extensive teachers' materials available. Offer the CELTA course 5 times a year.

RECRUITMENT: Teachers should send their CV to admin@cambridgeschool.com and will be interviewed either face-to-face or by phone.

CONTACT: Alistair Jones, Director.

CANADIAN LANGUAGE INSTITUTE
c/ París N° 25, Montequinto, 41089 Seville
+34 95 412 9016
rrhh@canadianli.es
www.canadianli.es

NUMBER OF TEACHERS: 10 for 3 branches in Seville.

PREFERENCE OF NATIONALITY: Any English-speaking country. EU member state passport essential.

QUALIFICATIONS: BA in Linguistics or Education. Experience with TPRS (Teaching Proficiency through Reading and Storytelling) and CI-based approaches.

CONDITIONS OF EMPLOYMENT: 1 or more years. 20–25 hours a week.

SALARY: €1,300 per month.

FACILITIES/SUPPORT: Advice on accommodation given.

RECRUITMENT: Via posts on EFL boards. Local interview essential.

CONTACT: Victoria Mantecon, Director of EFL Department.

CAPS (CONVERSATION ASSISTANT PROGRAMME FOR SCHOOLS)

Riereta 2, 08184 Palau-Solità i Plegamans, Barcelona
+34 93 864 8886
caps@hometohome.es
www.hometohome.es/CAPS

NUMBER OF TEACHERS: 150 for Catalonia and Valencia.

PREFERENCE OF NATIONALITY: Native English speaking countries, eg UK, USA, Australia and Canada.

QUALIFICATIONS: Minimum of A level or equivalent, and a native level of English. Most are aged 18–25. Must also have a desire to work with children. Desirable extras would include TEFL certificate or similar, some teaching experience and a desire to pursue teaching as a career.

CONDITIONS OF EMPLOYMENT: 9-month contract, though some come for shorter periods, eg 2 months. 25 hours per week.

SALARY: €200 per month, which is considered a study grant. All deductions covered.

FACILITIES/SUPPORT: Participants live with families who are part of the programme. If a student visa is required, information is given.

RECRUITMENT: Marketing/advertising on various websites, eg www.loquo.com. CAPS representatives actively recruit in the UK, USA and Canada for example the Almondbury Agency in London recruits assistants for up to 250 schools (www.aupair-agency.com/Teaching-English-in-Spain.htm). All interviews are carried out via video conferencing.

CENTRO EDIMBURGO IDIOMAS

Edificio Edimburgo, Plaza Niña, 21003 Huelva
+34 959 263821/263862/250168
info@centroedimburgo.com
www.centroedimburgo.com

NUMBER OF TEACHERS: 20.

PREFERENCE OF NATIONALITY: Must be EU citizen or hold work permit for Spain.

QUALIFICATIONS: Degree, CELTA plus 1 year's experience. Must speak conversational Spanish.

FACILITIES/SUPPORT: School helps find flats.

RECRUITMENT: Recent photograph and 2 references must be sent with application. Interviews essential.

CHALMORE LANGUAGE SOLUTIONS

Calle Orense, 32 esc. izq. Oficina 1, 28020 Madrid
+34 91 555 1510
cv@chalmore.com
www.chalmore.com

NUMBER OF TEACHERS: 15.

PREFERENCE OF NATIONALITY: Must be native speakers of English, and be EU citizen.

QUALIFICATIONS: CELTA or TEFL (no online courses) and a minimum of 1 year's teaching experience.

CONDITIONS OF EMPLOYMENT: September–June. About 25 hours per week.

SALARY: On application. Taxes and social security paid by school.

FACILITIES/SUPPORT: No assistance with accommodation or work permits.

RECRUITMENT: Adverts in specialist media. Interviews are essential and are carried out in Madrid.

CONTACT: Frank Moerman, Director/CEO.

CIC

Via Augusta 205, 08021 Barcelona
+34 93 200 1133
iccic@iccic.edu
www.iccic.edu

NUMBER OF TEACHERS: 80 for 4 centres in Barcelona.

PREFERENCE OF NATIONALITY: Mix of native English speaking and teachers with 'native competence' from all around the world.

QUALIFICATIONS: Cambridge/Trinity certificate and 1 year's experience.

CONDITIONS OF EMPLOYMENT: Most new teachers are given a temporary 9-month contract running from October to June.

SALARY: Discussed during interview.

FACILITIES/SUPPORT: In-house training and professional development if funded by school.

RECRUITMENT: CVs via internet, all suitable candidates are interviewed.

PREFERENCE OF NATIONALITY: English native speakers from UK, Ireland, USA and Canada.

QUALIFICATIONS: No qualifications or experience necessary but candidates require enthusiasm to work with children.

CONDITIONS OF EMPLOYMENT: Flexible length of stay from a weekend to a year, according to agreement between host family and live-in tutor. Usually stays last 4-10 weeks. Recommended number of hours of language assistance is 15 per week.

SALARY: No wages are paid, only an exchange of food and accommodation for tutoring help.

RECRUITMENT: Interested candidates become members for a year (£15/$25/€20) which allows access to host contact details throughout Spain.

CONTACT: Tim Arnaudy, Co-founder.

Incorporates Pueblo Ingles programme of language holidays, in which an informal exchange of English conversation takes place over 8 days in various holiday resorts in Spain, where native English volunteers interact and converse with Spanish clients who want to improve their English. Native-speaking participants receive free room and board, and transport from Madrid.

NUMBER OF TEACHERS: 80 for Madrid and Seville, and suburbs.

PREFERENCE OF NATIONALITY: Native speakers who already have NIE (residence card) and are registered as *autónomos* (freelancers who pay their own tax and social security).

QUALIFICATIONS: CELTA or equivalent plus 2 years' experience.

CONDITIONS OF EMPLOYMENT: Teaching mainly for companies face-to-face in small classes or online.

SALARY: From €19 per hour gross.

FACILITIES/SUPPORT: Compulsory training at beginning.

RECRUITMENT: Adverts in madridteacher.com. Interviews can be by phone.

CONTACT: Iñaki Cornago. HR Coordinator.

NUMBER OF TEACHERS: 2.

QUALIFICATIONS: Bachelor's degree in English or languages and some teaching experience with children desirable. Driving licence.

CONDITIONS OF EMPLOYMENT: 9-month contract; 12 hours per week mostly in the evenings.

SALARY: €12 per hour plus bonus for holidays at the end of contract; 8% tax and social security deduction.

FACILITIES/SUPPORT: Room in school apartment offered for €250 per month plus bills.

RECRUITMENT: Interview essential.

CONTACT: Ruth Farpón Largo, Director.

NUMBER OF TEACHERS: 9.

PREFERENCE OF NATIONALITY: EU citizens.

QUALIFICATIONS: Applicants must have the CELTA or TrinityTESOL certificate, a university degree and a minimum of 1 year's experience.

CONDITIONS OF EMPLOYMENT: 9 months. A full-time contract is 34 hours per week comprising 23 contact teaching hours and 11 hours on-site preparation, marking and meeting time.

SALARY: Minimum starting salary is €1250 per month (net). Settling-in allowance of €200 paid in second term.

FACILITIES/SUPPORT: New teachers are provided with up to 1 week's free accommodation organised by the academy and are assisted by the school to find more long-term accommodation. A representative of the school will arrange and accompany new employees when applying for all necessary permits, which usually include: application for residency and a national identity number (in the provincial capital Foreign Affairs Department), application for a social security number (local Social Security office) and also assistance with opening a local bank account.

RECRUITMENT: Via Spainwise.net and tefl.com. Skype interviews are acceptable.

CONTACT: Paul Hillman, Director.

EL CENTRO DE INGLES

C/Caldereros 7, 23740 Andújar, Jaén

direccion@elcentrodeingles.es

www.elcentrodeingles.es/employment

Sister school in nearby Bailen.

NUMBER OF TEACHERS: 2–4 new teachers required every year for September start.

QUALIFICATIONS: CELTA/Trinity and 2 years' experience, especially valued if with children.

CONDITIONS OF EMPLOYMENT: 9.5-month contract. 21–24 contact hours per week (full-time 34-hour contract to cover class preparation, meetings and teacher training, etc). Holiday bonus on completion of contract.

SALARY: Basic starting salary (21 teaching hours) is €1,316.45 gross, about €1,200 net. Bonus for DELTA-qualified teachers.

FACILITIES/SUPPORT: Help with accommodation, paperwork, settling in, induction. Full medical cover.

RECRUITMENT: Interviews in Spain or England (as notified on website). Also recruit via www.spainwise.net.

CONTACT: Julie Hetherington, Director.

ENG-AGE LANGUAGE CENTRE

Calle Mendez Nuñez 51, Oficina 3, 36900 Marin, Pontevedra (Galicia)

+34 619 267765

eng-age@hotmail.com

www.eng-age.es

NUMBER OF TEACHERS: 4.

PREFERENCE OF NATIONALITY: UK, Ireland and native speakers from other English speaking countries if they hold a passport from an EU country.

QUALIFICATIONS: University degree and English teaching qualification are essential. One year's experience is an advantage.

CONDITIONS OF EMPLOYMENT: 9-month contract from 1 October with possibility to extend till end of July. 20–25 teaching hours per week.

SALARY: €868–€1,100 per month gross, less 6.4% social security and 2% tax. Minimum 20 hours per week.

FACILITIES/SUPPORT: Manager accompanies teacher on flat-viewing trip and to government offices to translate and

help with obtaining a NIE and registering for social security.

RECRUITMENT: Via tefl.com and other sites. Skype interviews essential.

CONTACT: Mercedes Vivero Enjamio, Manager.

ENGLISH 1

Marqués del Nervión 116, 41005 Seville

+34 95 464 2098

info@english1sevilla.com

www.english1sevilla.com

NUMBER OF TEACHERS: 6.

QUALIFICATIONS: Degree and TEFL certificate (or diploma) and experience, especially with young learners preferred.

CONDITIONS OF EMPLOYMENT: 23 contact hours per week, Monday to Thursday only, teaching children, teenagers and adults. 9-month contract from October to June.

SALARY: Starting salary €1,100 gross plus extra payments for Cambridge exam preparation classes.

FACILITIES/SUPPORT: In-house training and great support in a very friendly and harmonious working atmosphere. Lots of assistance in finding accommodation.

CONTACT: Jennifer Fricker, Owner.

ENGLISH LANGUAGE TRAINING

Avd País Valencià, 129–131, 03820 Cocentaina (Alicante)

+34 96 559 2204

info@qeltcocentaina.com

www.qeltcocentaina.com

NUMBER OF TEACHERS: 3.

PREFERENCE OF NATIONALITY: British.

QUALIFICATIONS: CELTA or TESOL qualification (not short online introductory courses) and a minimum of 1 year's teaching experience.

CONDITIONS OF EMPLOYMENT: 9 months October to June. 25 hours a week.

SALARY: €950–€1,000 (net) according to experience.

FACILITIES/SUPPORT: Assistance offered with finding accommodation. Assistance given with obtaining identification documents for Spain.

RECRUITMENT: Via online advertising. Interviews are usually carried out over the phone or on Skype, but if the candidate is in the area a face-to-face interview is preferable.

CONTACT: Michaela Aylott, Director.

ENGLISH TEACHERS COLLECTIVE (ETC)

C/ Joaquin Costa 15, 28002 Madrid

☎ +34 902 090166

✉ info@etcspain.com

🖥 www.etcspain.com

NUMBER OF TEACHERS: 35. Most vacancies in Madrid and Barcelona, in company and private classes.

PREFERENCE OF NATIONALITY: British or American.

QUALIFICATIONS: CELTA/TrinityTESOL qualification plus 1 year's experience.

CONDITIONS OF EMPLOYMENT: 9-month contracts. 15 hours per week.

SALARY: €1,000 per month net.

FACILITIES/SUPPORT: No help with accommodation. Help given with residency permit and obtaining social security number. Monthly internal teacher training seminars.

RECRUITMENT: New post alerts via Facebook and Twitter. Local interviews essential.

CONTACT: Paul Hevicon, Director General.

ESIC IDIOMAS

Sancho el Fuerte 38, Bajo, 31011 Pamplona

☎ +34 948 173011

✉ idiomas.pam@esic.es

🖥 www.esic.edu/idiomas

NUMBER OF TEACHERS: 28 (some part-time). Centres in Seville, Malaga, Zaragoza, etc as well as Pamplona.

PREFERENCE OF NATIONALITY: Native English speakers.

QUALIFICATIONS: Recognised TEFL qualification and relevant experience.

CONDITIONS OF EMPLOYMENT: 9-month contract; 24 hours per week.

SALARY: €1,240–€1,320 depending on experience; €18 per hour self-employed.

FACILITIES/SUPPORT: Help is given to find accommodation and paperwork necessary to work in Pamplona. An initial induction course, with accompanying handouts, is given and various training and information sessions are given throughout the academic year.

RECRUITMENT: Sometimes interviewed by phone.

CONTACT: Fay Williams, Coordinator (fay.williams@esic.es).

EUROLANGUAGE CONSULTANTS (ELC)

Calle Alfredo Marquerie, 5 (bajo), 28034 Madrid

☎ +34 91 740 5911

✉ recruitment@eurolanguage.org

🖥 www.eurolanguage.org

NUMBER OF TEACHERS: 20 natives, 18 non-natives.

PREFERENCE OF NATIONALITY: No preference, but EU working papers are necessary.

QUALIFICATIONS: TEFL, CELTA or TESOL certificates preferred, but also value other experience and interest in teaching.

CONDITIONS OF EMPLOYMENT: 9-month academic year. Part-time or full-time positions available.

FACILITIES/SUPPORT: Normally no help given with accommodation, but if a teacher does not speak Spanish employer can help with phone calls and general orientation.

RECRUITMENT: Web contacts, eg MadridTeacher, Lingobongo and Bolsa de Trabajo. Face-to-face interviews in Madrid.

CONTACT: Kerry Davis, Director of Studies (kerry. davis@eurolanguage.org).

EUROSCHOOLS

Plaza de la Independencia, Regueiro 2, 36211 Vigo

☎ +34 986 291748 / 986 378600

✉ info@euroschools.eu

🖥 www.euroschools.eu

NUMBER OF TEACHERS: 15.

PREFERENCE OF NATIONALITY: Must be EU.

QUALIFICATIONS: Good degree preferably in English, Spanish or modern languages, TEFL qualification, some experience preferred. Must have knowledge of Spanish and outgoing, friendly personality.

CONDITIONS OF EMPLOYMENT: 9 months from October 1st. 25 class hours per week.

SALARY: Competitive plus allowances are paid for university degree and TEFL teaching qualifications in proportion to qualifications.

FACILITIES/SUPPORT: Assistance given with finding accommodation. Holiday entitlement is 2+ weeks at Christmas, 1 week at Easter, 2 days at Carnaval. Access to internet and school computer network available to teachers.

RECRUITMENT: Good references needed plus CV, photo (which is essential) and Skype interview.

CONTACT: Mr John Moriarty, Managing Director.

HOT ENGLISH LANGUAGE SERVICES

Paseo del Rey 22, 1 Planta, Oficina 1, 28008 Madrid

☎ +34 91 543 3573

✉ business@learnhotenglish.com or
teacherinfo@hotenglishmagazine.com

🖥 www.learnhotenglish.com

NUMBER OF TEACHERS: 40–50 per year.

PREFERENCE OF NATIONALITY: Native speakers, must be legally authorised to work in Spain because employer does not at present sponsor candidates for a work permit.

QUALIFICATIONS: TEFL/TESOL/CELTA or equivalent is a must. Teachers without formal qualifications, but possessing substantial verifiable experience, will also be considered. Candidates must be resident in Spain and have already applied for and received a Spanish NIE and social security number. Exceptions could be made in the future for teachers hired to teach telephone/Skype classes.

CONDITIONS OF EMPLOYMENT: September/October to 30 June. Minimum 8–10 hours up to as many hours as the teacher's schedule allows.

SALARY: €14–€18 per hour (gross), with adjustments based on class length and location. Deductions average 8.5%

FACILITIES/SUPPORT: Hot English has a flat available for rent; otherwise, it can point new arrivals in the direction of where to look for a flat.

RECRUITMENT: Adverts on local websites such as www.madridteacher.com and www.lingobongo.com. For Madrid positions, interviews must be held in person. For positions in other Spanish cities, interviews are held over the phone, as long as the candidate is already residing in the relevant city.

CONTACT: Mely Armstrong, Teacher Coordinator or Thorley Russell, Managing Director.

IDIOMASTER LANGUAGE CENTRES

C/Juan Rico 8, 14900 Lucena, Córdoba

+34 957 591678

recruitment@idiomaster.es

www.idiomaster.es

NUMBER OF TEACHERS: 9 for a group of schools.

QUALIFICATIONS: Must be friendly and enthusiastic. University degree, CELTA or Trinity and at least 1 year's experience, preferably with children. Less experience acceptable if candidate achieved A/B on certificate course.

SALARY: Minimum monthly gross salary €1,250 plus end of contract bonus of 2.5 days' salary per month worked. Full social security and national health insurance cover.

FACILITIES/SUPPORT: Ongoing internal teacher training and support plus external teaching conferences and courses. Digital classrooms with interactive whiteboards. Help with finding accommodation. Preparation centre for the Cambridge suite of exams. A registered Trinity College, London examination centre and member of ACEIA, FECEI and CALAC (Central Andalusian Language Academies; www.calacschools.es).

INLINGUA SANTANDER

Avenida de Pontejos 5, 39005 Santander

+34 942 278465

inlingua.santander@inlingua.com

www.inlinguasantander.com

NUMBER OF TEACHERS: 12.

PREFERENCE OF NATIONALITY: EU native English speakers or having a work permit for Spain.

QUALIFICATIONS: TEFL certificate and/or teaching experience, university degree.

CONDITIONS OF EMPLOYMENT: Contract for academic year or summer, full-time contract: up to 26 teaching hours a week.

SALARY: Minimum net €1,057.

FACILITIES/SUPPORT: Assistance with finding accommodation, inlingua Method course, workshops, school library. Free Spanish lessons.

RECRUITMENT: Via tefl.com, etc, interview by phone.

CONTACT: Mrs Ingrid Antons, Director.

INSTITUTE OF MODERN LANGUAGES

Puerta Real 1, 18009 Granada

+34 958 225536

info@imlgranada.com

www.imlgranada.com

NUMBER OF TEACHERS: 20.

PREFERENCE OF NATIONALITY: British, other native English speakers.

QUALIFICATIONS: University degree, TEFL qualification and relevant experience.

CONDITIONS OF EMPLOYMENT: Contract for the academic year, contract for part-time work, national insurance, social security.

FACILITIES/SUPPORT: Good resources, Examination Centre for University of Cambridge ESOL Examinations in Granada, Almería and Málaga. Offer CELTA course.

RECRUITMENT: EFL teachers are recruited from among the best qualified in Granada at the time. Initial short-list drawn up by director of studies from available CVs, then school owner carries out second interviews of short-listed candidates.

CONTACT: Monika Czernek (monika.czernek@imlgranada.com).

INTERLANG

C/Velázquez, 117, 1a, 28006 Madrid

+34 91 515 8422

empleo@interlang.es

www.interlang.es

NUMBER OF TEACHERS: 90.

PREFERENCE OF NATIONALITY: None but must be native speaker and have EU working papers if non-EU citizen.

QUALIFICATIONS: CELTA plus 2 years' TEFL experience and sound knowledge of business English.

CONDITIONS OF EMPLOYMENT: Registered freelancers, or school offers standard 9-month contracts. Typical teaching hours 8.30am–10am/1pm–6pm.

SALARY: €18.50 per hour gross on contract, €24 per hour gross for registered freelancers. Tax deductions vary, but for freelancers there's a 7% deduction for the first two years and then 15%.

RECRUITMENT: Via the company website or via permanent advert at www.madridteacher.com. Candidates are asked to send recent CV and colour photo to empleo@interlang.es. A face-to-face interview in Madrid is essential before an offer of work can be made.

CONTACT: Sean O'Malley, Director of Studies.

INTERNATIONAL HOUSE MADRID
Calle Covarrubias 1, 28010 Madrid
- +34 91 319 7224
- selection@ihmadrid.com
- www.ihmadrid.com

NUMBER OF TEACHERS: 190 for 4 centres in Madrid.

PREFERENCE OF NATIONALITY: No preference, but applicants must have permission to work permanently in the EU.

QUALIFICATIONS: Candidates must have the Cambridge CELTA or Trinity CertTESOL. Applicants without one of these qualifications will not be accepted.

CONDITIONS OF EMPLOYMENT: Initially posts are for the academic year from October to June. 19–22 hours of teaching per week.

SALARY: Competitive salary for the market in Madrid. More details on application. As a rough guide teachers on around 20 hours a week can expect to receive around €1,100–€1,200 net depending on experience and qualifications (after deductions of 6% for social security and 10%–11% for income tax).

FACILITIES/SUPPORT: No assistance with accommodation; there is a plentiful supply in Madrid. No assistance with work permits.

RECRUITMENT: Advertising through IH World organisation, other recruitment sites such as tefl.com, IH Madrid website, word of mouth and email applications to the above address. Face-to-face interviews in Madrid essential.

CONTACT: Mr Alex Bishop, Human Resources.

ISE TENERIFE (ISE LANGUAGE LTD)
Calle Obispo Rey Redondo 52, 38201 San Cristobal de la Laguna, S/C de Tenerife
- +34 922 194744
- sindi@ise.uk.com
- www.isetenerife.com

NUMBER OF TEACHERS: 3.

PREFERENCE OF NATIONALITY: UK, US.

QUALIFICATIONS: Any teaching certificate. Must be able to speak a little Spanish.

CONDITIONS OF EMPLOYMENT: Long-term work. From 12 hours per week.

SALARY: €12 per hour (net).

FACILITIES/SUPPORT: Advice given on finding accommodation and on applying for residence permits.

RECRUITMENT: Partner school of ISE Hove (www.ise.uk.com) that offers CELTA courses. Skype interviews are fine.

CONTACT: Sindi Ferrera Martínez, Director and Owner.

KEDARO INTERNATIONAL
Calle Murillo 8, 21001 Huelva
- +34 959 87 37 12
- info@kedaro.com
- http://kedaro.com

NUMBER OF TEACHERS: 15-20.

PREFERENCE OF NATIONALITY: EU passport holders or valid work permit holders.

QUALIFICATIONS: CELTA or TESOL and 1 year's experience; less experienced candidates are considered with pass A or B.

CONDITIONS OF EMPLOYMENT: 9-10 months with optional summer work. 24 hours a week.

SALARY: €1000 net with 3 hours of Spanish lessons included.

FACILITIES/SUPPORT: Assistance given with flat-hunting.

RECRUITMENT: Via tefl.com, Dave's ESL Cafe and Spainwise. Always 2-3 Skype interviews.

CONTACT: Richard McCulloch, Director of Studies (rich@kedaro.com).

KIDZ IN ACTION
Calle Cuesta 13, Majadahonda, 28220 Madrid
- +34 912 540 554
- info@kidzinaction.es
- www.kidzinaction.es

NUMBER OF TEACHERS: 3.

PREFERENCE OF NATIONALITY: None.

QUALIFICATIONS: Ability to communicate at the level of young learners.

CONDITIONS OF EMPLOYMENT: 1–2 years. Usual hours are 12pm–8.30pm.

SALARY: €1,200 per month after tax.

FACILITIES/SUPPORT: Advice and contacts given for accommodation. No help given with visas.

RECRUITMENT: Interviews in Spain.

CONTACT: Jonathan Lipschitz, Owner.

KLEINSON: LA CONSULTORA DE IDIOMAS

C/Apodaca 7, bajo izquierda, 28004 Madrid

+34 91 140 0570

info@kleinson.es; formacion@kleinson.es

www.kleinson.es

NUMBER OF TEACHERS: 22 native English speakers out of 50 for companies throughout Spain.

PREFERENCE OF NATIONALITY: None whatsoever, although Kleinson does not provide work visas.

QUALIFICATIONS: Teachers become 'consultants' after working with Kleinson. Ideally, candidates come with at least 2 years' experience and/or a CELTA. Candidates who hold the company's values and are hard workers but with very little teaching experience can still be considered. It is important that staff share Kleinson's professional values and embrace diversity.

CONDITIONS OF EMPLOYMENT: Average contract is from September/October to June/July. All consultants start with morning, lunchtime or evening hours. After at least a year and receiving solid feedback they are moved up to block hours.

SALARY: All consultants, regardless of experience, start at €20 per hour gross (which is €15 net) for classes in the city centre. For classes outside the centre contract teachers can receive up to €25 per hour net. Teachers officially signed up as freelancers are paid €20 per hour and can go up to €30. It's important to know that by law in Spain, 9% of wages are retained for tax from freelancers (*autonomos*) in addition to social security contributions. Rewards paid to teachers who bring in new clients.

FACILITIES/SUPPORT: All consultants are required to attend a training session. Informal advice given on finding accommodation. No assistance with work permits.

RECRUITMENT: Word of mouth, online ads or collaborations with TEFL academies throughout Spain and the USA. Online application procedure, 3-step interviews take place only in Madrid: telephone interview first followed by a group interview and finally an individual one.

CONTACT: Shiva Roofeh, Head of Training.

LA ACADEMIA DE INGLÉS

Avda. de Moratalaz 139 (Lonja), 28030 Madrid

+34 91 430 5545

info@idiomastop.com

www.idiomastop.com

NUMBER OF TEACHERS: Approx. 40 per course.

PREFERENCE OF NATIONALITY: EU citizens or people with legal status.

QUALIFICATIONS: University degrees + TEFL + good level in the Spanish language.

CONDITIONS OF EMPLOYMENT: 9–10 months. Any hours between 8am and 10pm, but mainly 4pm–9pm. Also run residential immersion camps in Asturias in July. Volunteers receive living expenses and transport from Madrid.

FACILITIES/SUPPORT: No help with accommodation.

RECRUITMENT: Interviews are essential and are always carried out in Madrid.

CONTACT: Ana Aparicio, Director.

LINC, ENGLISH FOR LIVING

Calle Genaro Parladé, 4. Bajo B, 41013 Seville; also Calle Los Balbos S/N, 11009 Cadiz

+34 954 500459

sevilla@linc.es

www.linc.es/tefl-jobs-seville-cadiz

NUMBER OF TEACHERS: 15–20.

PREFERENCE OF NATIONALITY: Must be an EU member state passport holder and native English speaker.

QUALIFICATIONS: Degree plus EFL qualification (CELTA or Trinity) and 1-2 year's teaching experience. Some knowledge of Spanish helpful.

CONDITIONS OF EMPLOYMENT: Standard contract is 9/10 months from September/October to June. Full and part-time contracts available. Full-time is 24 contact hours per week. Some summer work available.

SALARY: €1,200 (gross) per month for full-time contracts.

FACILITIES/SUPPORT: Help is given with finding accommodation, particularly if the teacher can't speak Spanish. Regular in-service training programme. Free Spanish classes.

RECRUITMENT: Interviews held via Skype or phone.

MCGINTY SCHOOL OF ENGLISH

Avda, Cabo de Gata, 54, 04007 Almeria

+34 950 259745

dos@mcgintyschool.com

www.mcgintyschool.com

NUMBER OF TEACHERS: 26 in total.

PREFERENCE OF NATIONALITY: None. Must be national of EU member state or have valid work permit.

QUALIFICATIONS: Minimum CELTA or PGCE, preferably language graduate with 3 years' relevant teaching experience.

CONDITIONS OF EMPLOYMENT: 1-year contract from early September with the possibility of summer work and contract renewal. Maximum 25 teaching hours per week, mainly between 4pm and 9.30pm, Monday–Friday.

SALARY: Starting full-time salary is €1,175 net per month but may increase depending on experience and qualifications. Bonus paid on completion of contract.

FACILITIES/SUPPORT: Assistance provided with finding accommodation and registering for social security, etc. Regular training and development sessions in school; support to attend training and conferences. Free Spanish lessons.

RECRUITMENT: Usually via internet (www.tefl.com). Applicants should send CV and photo in first instance. Interviews are essential and can be conducted in Spain or over the phone.

CONTACT: Angus McGinty, Director.

MAUCAL SL
Pol. Argualas Nave 35, 50012 Zaragoza
+34 976 350 205
maucal@maucal.com
www.maucal.com

Language consultancy with branches in Huesca and Granada as well.

NUMBER OF TEACHERS: Approximately 4.

QUALIFICATIONS: EFL qualification and bachelor's degree (with honours) preferable.

CONDITIONS OF EMPLOYMENT: Contracts of 9–10 months; from 12 to 34 hours a week.

SALARY: Depends on hours a week.

RECRUITMENT: Application via www.tefl.com or CV. Interview essential.

MERIT SCHOOL
Campo Florido 54–56, 2a, 08027 Barcelona
+34 93 243 1524
dos@meritschool.com
www.meritschool.com

NUMBER OF TEACHERS: 40–50 for 8 branches.

PREFERENCE OF NATIONALITY: Native English speakers. Must have EU member state passport or current work permit for Spain.

QUALIFICATIONS: University degree, TEFL certificate (preferably

grade B or higher), 1 year's experience. Classroom experience with young learners or teenagers an advantage.

CONDITIONS OF EMPLOYMENT: Most contracts run from October to June with the possibility of extension into July for summer courses. Number of teaching hours varies – part-time and full-time teachers are sought.

SALARY: €15–€18 per hour. Travelling fee for off-site classes.

FACILITIES/SUPPORT: 3 centres plus in-company department: Campo Florido and Sant Cugat campuses (Young Learners, Teenagers, Adults), UPC campus (University students and staff) and in-company department (Business and General English for adults off-site in companies). Regular in-house workshops, financial assistance to attend external training events, good library of teaching resources, peer observation scheme, regular observations and feedback by senior staff. Spanish classes.

RECRUITMENT: Mostly local (internet sites like www.loquo.com) but sometimes on international sites like www.tefl.com. Applications from interested teachers are always welcome. Face-to-face interview required. Best time to apply is late May to July or in September.

CONTACT: Michael Terry, Director of Studies or David Corp.

PREMIER SCHOOL OF ENGLISH
C/ Perafán de Rivera 1 – Local, 41710 Utrera, Sevilla
+34 955 861951
info@premierenglish.es
www.premierenglish.es

Member of ACEIA, FECEI and CALAC.

NUMBER OF TEACHERS: 7.

PREFERENCE OF NATIONALITY: No real preference as long as they are native speakers and have EU residency permit.

QUALIFICATIONS: Must have a CELTA or Trinity TESOL plus 1 year's experience.

CONDITIONS OF EMPLOYMENT: 9-month contracts. Maximum 24 hours of teaching mostly in the afternoons and evenings: 4pm–9.45pm Monday to Thursday, 4pm–6.15pm Friday.

SALARY: Starting salary €1,300 (gross) which could increase depending on experience and qualifications. Deductions total about €100 a month. 2 weeks paid holiday at Christmas and 1 week at Easter.

FACILITIES/SUPPORT: School actively helps teachers find flats and negotiate with landlords, etc. Help given with red tape (the procedures vary from year to year). Paid one-week induction.

RECRUITMENT: Through recommendations, www.spainwise.net and other internet sites. Interviews essential.

CONTACT: Francis Rodriguez, Director of Studies.

SPEAK ENGLISH SCHOOL

Cimadevilla 17 Ent F, 33003 Oviedo, Asturias

✆ +34 985 226136

✉ speakschool@hotmail.com

🖥 www.speakschool.com

PREFERENCE OF NATIONALITY: British.

QUALIFICATIONS: TEFL certificate and a minimum of 2 years' experience.

CONDITIONS OF EMPLOYMENT: 9-month contracts, to work 25 hours per week.

SALARY: €1,200 per month (net) plus end-of-contract bonus.

FACILITIES/SUPPORT: The school can help with finding accommodation.

RECRUITMENT: Interviews essential, but can be carried out in the UK. Sometimes, telephone/Skype interviews can be arranged.

CONTACT: Mick Gordon, Director of Studies.

TECS (THE EDUCATIONAL CONSORTIUM OF SPAIN)

The English Centre, Apdo. Correos 85, 11500 El Puerto de Santa María, Cadiz

✆ +34 956 853000

✉ tecscamp@tecs.es

🖥 http://recruit.tecs.es

NUMBER OF TEACHERS: 15–20 teachers required throughout the year for 4 language centres on the Costa de la Luz in southwest Spain. More than 130 staff employed in summer (60 teachers, 80 monitors plus management and support staff) at five residential camps in Andalucía and one in Madrid region.

QUALIFICATIONS: Employees must be team players who are young at heart and full of energy, with a mature and responsible personality. EFL teachers require a 100-hour TEFL qualification or normal school teaching qualification (if candidate has experience working with foreign-language children). Police check required.

CONDITIONS OF EMPLOYMENT: Minimum 4 weeks (2 fortnight-long camps); academic year runs from 15 September or 1 October to 12 June.

FACILITIES/SUPPORT: 5 days' pre-camp training.

SALARY: €550 per fortnight. Free board and lodging. Salary during year is €863–€1,368 (gross). Hourly rate if teaching less than 12 hours is €12 (gross).

RECRUITMENT: Online and via Spainwise.com jobs fair in May. Recommended dates to apply are February/March.

CONTACT: Douglas Haines, Summer Camp Recruitment; Gillian Thompson, Director of Language Centres.

THE FARM SUMMERCAMPS

Barrio Elizalde 11, 01193 Erentxun, Alava

✆ +34 945 063234

✉ info@campamentosthefarm.com

🖥 www.campamentosthefarm.com

NUMBER OF TEACHERS: One for each 6–7 children on various camps in Basque country, ie in Gorozika, Lurkoi, plus one in Asturias.

PREFERENCE OF NATIONALITY: All, including fluent speakers of English from Scandinavia and Holland as well as Britons and Irish, Canadians and Americans.

QUALIFICATIONS: Experience desirable; must have good communication skills. Counsellors should find living communally a positive and inspiring experience, show flexibility and creativity when it comes to teaching workshops and classes and have maturity and sensitivity in helping to prevent and resolve conflicts.

CONDITIONS OF EMPLOYMENT: Camp takes place in July.

CONTACT: Mascha Snoijink (mascha.thefarm@gmail.com).

TICK IT ENGLISH

Calle Doctor Marañón, 1, Entr, 24402 Ponferrada, León

✆ +34 987 088256

✉ tickitenglish@yahoo.es

🖥 www.tickitenglish.com

NUMBER OF TEACHERS: 4.

PREFERENCE OF NATIONALITY: British.

QUALIFICATIONS: CELTA and 2 years' teaching experience, especially with young learners (ages 4–16).

CONDITIONS OF EMPLOYMENT: 9-month contract. 25 hours per week.

SALARY: €1,350 per calendar month, less approximately €100 in contributions.

FACILITIES/SUPPORT: Help given to teachers to find suitable accommodation. One flat is available to rent through the school. Help given to EU citizens to register with the local authorities and obtain the necessary paperwork.

RECRUITMENT: Adverts on www.tefl.com. Some interviews held in the UK.

CONTACT: Derek Holloway, Director of Studies (derek@tickitenglish.com).

TRAINING EXPRESS S.L.

Plaza del Cordón N° 1, 28005 Madrid

✆ +34 91 521 1554

✉ jobs@trainingexpress.es

🖥 www.trainingexpress.es/recruitment

Madrid-based language consultancy. Affiliated to the online language teaching company Ispeakuspeak.com which hires virtual trainers worldwide.

NUMBER OF TEACHERS: 200 in Spain.

PREFERENCE OF NATIONALITY: Must have EU passport or work and residency permit for Spain. Internship programme for Americans.

QUALIFICATIONS: Minimum 2 years' experience plus TEFL certificate and degree. Minimum age 22. Must have a relevant degree for many posts.

CONDITIONS OF EMPLOYMENT: 9-month contracts in Spain, full-time and part-time.

SALARY: €1,000–€1,200 per month gross. Standard deductions of about 6%.

FACILITIES/SUPPORT: Assistance given with accommodation through a relocation agency. Help given with obtaining the necessary permits, including liaising with local state ministry.

RECRUITMENT: Via international websites such as www.tefl.com and local sources. Interview required.

CONTACT: Rebecca Webb, Chief Learning Officer for Training Express Recruitment.

UCETAM (Union de Cooperativas de Enseñanza de Trabajo Asociado de Madrid)
Programa Bilingüe Ucetam (PBU), San Bernardo 97–99, bis edificio Colomina, 28015 Madrid
☎ +34 91 448 0622
✉ bicucetam@ucetam.es or applications@ucetam.es
🖥 www.ucetampbu.es (English version)

NUMBER OF TEACHERS: About 136 native speakers who assist classroom teachers as 'native auxiliaries' in the Madrid region.

PREFERENCE OF NATIONALITY: Mainly American and British.

QUALIFICATIONS: University degree, not necessarily in education.

CONDITIONS OF EMPLOYMENT: One academic year (5 September until 22 June) with the possibility of extension for a further year. 18 or 26 hours per week (in the classroom) and one additional hour for staff meetings (two hours from 2015).

SALARY: €981 for 18 hours a week; €1,441 for 26 hours a week. Free lunch at the schools. Schools cover social security costs and repatriation insurance but EU teachers must pay contributions of 2%; US teachers have no deductions.

FACILITIES/SUPPORT: No assistance with accommodation. Assistance given with red tape. The scholarship scheme is run in conjunction with Madrid local educational authority and assistant teachers work on a student visa. UCETAM presents documents to the immigration authorities, then non-EU participants are called for fingerprints.

RECRUITMENT: Via website. Interviews via Skype or in Madrid. Deadline for applications: 24 February. Decisions will be communicated in March or April.

CONTACT: Sarah Mackin, Program Coordinator.

VAUGHAN SYSTEMS
Edificio Eurobuilding 2, Calle Orense 69 – 1º planta, 28020 Madrid. Also offices in Barcelona, Valladolid, Vigo, Valencia, Seville and Santander.
☎ +34 91 748 5960, ext 4370
🖥 www.vaughanenglishteachers.com/the-vaughan-systems-job-center

NUMBER OF TEACHERS: 96 (mostly for Madrid).

PREFERENCE OF NATIONALITY: None but EU or work permit required.

QUALIFICATIONS: No experience needed; training given during free 2-week training course in the company's methods, in one of the cities where they have an office.

CONDITIONS OF EMPLOYMENT: Freelance and a few contract positions for an academic year. Mostly teaching in-company with a lot of travelling between workplaces.

SALARY: Teachers are all self-employed and bill Vaughan at the end of the month for the hours they have taught.

FACILITIES/SUPPORT: Teachers look after their own social security contributions. No accommodation.

RECRUITMENT: Online application system.

CONTACT: Natasha Pascua and Marta Martinez, Teacher Recruitment & Training Coordinators.

VAUGHAN TOWN
Edificio Eurobuilding 2, Calle Orense 69 – 1° planta, 28020 Madrid
☎ +34 91 748 5950
✉ anglos@vaughantown.com
🖥 http://volunteers.grupovaughan.com

Intensive 6-day cultural exchange programme or 'talk-a-thon', from a Sunday to a Friday, held almost every week year round. 15 Spaniards and 17 English speakers are put together in a relaxed environment, accommodation in 4 picturesque locations within 2 hours of Madrid, to re-create an English-speaking village. The programme is based on both one-to-one sessions and group activities, as well as excursions, parties and walks in the countryside.

PREFERENCE OF NATIONALITY: All native speakers welcome.

SALARY: None for 1-week language exchange, but free food, accommodation, and transport from Madrid to hotel are provided.

CONTACT: Vaughan Volunteers Recruitment Manager.

WAYMAN ENGLISH INTERNATIONAL, S.L.

Calle Narcisos 62-A, 28016 Madrid (Registered office)

wdarcy@waymanenglish.com;
jobs@waymanenglish.com

www.waymanenglish.com

NUMBER OF TEACHERS: 20 freelancers teach English.

PREFERENCE OF NATIONALITY: Mainly native speakers only. No assistance given with work, residency or student visas.

QUALIFICATIONS: CELTA, TEFL or other recognised qualification and a university/college degree are needed. Qualifications, teaching expertise (technique and classroom management skills) etc are all desirable, but Wayman English also assesses personality, character, professionalism and a love for teaching. Candidates should provide an updated CV – preferably with a current photo – and confirm they already reside in Spain and have the ability to legally work in Spain. Ideally the candidate has a minimum of 5 years' teaching experience, especially with business English, though company sometimes takes on teachers with less experience (eg 2–3 years) in whom employer sees potential and is willing to mentor. Intermediate level of Spanish will be valued.

CONDITIONS OF EMPLOYMENT: Normally, teachers work throughout the academic year (September to June) but sometimes on a case-by-case basis depending on the client's demands or needs. Most work is part-time. Hours normally from 8am and/or from 1pm to 5pm Monday to Friday. Number of hours varies from 25 to 90+ a month. Timetables normally fill up once the teacher has demonstrated his or her ability.

SALARY: Gross hourly rates for freelance teacher are €18–€21 for phone teaching; €21–€25 for one-to-one and group classes. Rates depend on the client, duration of assignment, volume of hours and whether they are block hours or not.

FACILITIES/SUPPORT: No help with accommodation, though advice will be given on most convenient areas of Madrid to live, to take advantage of teaching opportunities in the city centre and in the numerous companies in the northern part of the city.

RECRUITMENT: Mostly word of mouth and personal recommendation. Specific jobs are advertised on teaching websites and local newspapers in Spain. All plausible candidates are given a personal interview. The candidate needs to be in Madrid as business needs may mean the candidate needs to start immediately.

CONTACT: Wayne D'Arcy, Programme Development Director and Co-owner.

SWITZERLAND

The status of English is unassailed in multilingual Switzerland, where English is the preferred language of communication between people from different regions. The tourist industry and the presence of many international organisations and businesses make a knowledge of English an absolute priority. English has been compulsory throughout the curriculum in all Swiss schools since 2010, which involved retraining Swiss teachers on a massive scale and somewhat more demand for foreign teachers of English.

Yet prospects are gloomy for people who fancy the idea of teaching the gnomes of Zurich or their counterparts in other parts of Switzerland, unless they are ultra-qualified. Although immigration regulations are not as restrictive as they once were (see the next section), Switzerland will not suddenly be welcoming an army of foreign language teachers. Teachers may also like to consider whether they wish to face the barrage of regulations that are part and parcel of living in Switzerland, from attempting to open a bank account without possessing a small fortune, to falling foul of strict rubbish disposal regulations.

The Swiss economy remains solid, but is not as invincible as it was once considered to be, as the director of a *Sprachschule* in Basel explained:

> *As a small language school in a country and region which has been experiencing severe withdrawal symptoms (from full employment, job and financial security), it is unlikely that we will be recruiting staff from outside Switzerland, especially as there is a large reservoir of potential candidates here in the Basel region and work permits for staff from outside Switzerland are now a rarity.*

This was corroborated by **Estelle Bieri** of the chain of Migros Club Schools (www.ecole-club.ch):

> *In order to teach English, we require teachers to be either native speakers or to have a C2 level of English, preferably with a good Cambridge Proficiency pass. Teachers must have a B residence permit. In addition, they require a qualification in teaching English as a foreign language to adults, for example a CELTA or equivalent, or higher. This is valid for any Swiss school which is Eduqua validated (Eduqua is an independent body for quality control). Many of our teachers have university qualifications. Teaching experience is welcome, particularly with regard to teaching certain levels and types of classes (ESP, etc).*

There are nine Wall Street Institutes and eight Bénédict Schools in Switzerland; a list of addresses is available at www.wallstreetinstitute.ch and www.benedict-international.com. At the time of writing (June 2015), the St Gallen, Geneva and Lausanne branches were advertising vacancies for 'talented and motivated new teachers' with a valid Swiss work permit; check www.wallstreetinstitute.ch/en/jobs. One of the biggest Wall Street schools is the one in Lausanne at Rue du Simplon 34, 1006 Lausanne (+41 21 614 6614; wsi.lausanne@wallstreetenglish.ch). If you are hired by a Swiss language school, wages are high: ranging from SFr30 to SFr60 for a 50-minute lesson.

Private tutoring is a possibility for those who lack a permit, as the American world traveller and free spirit **Danny Jacobson** discovered when he was living with his Swiss girlfriend in Bern:

> *A Swiss friend advised me to apply at one of the English schools but I didn't think it would work without a permit. So I just made my own flyer and put it up around town and the next thing I knew I had a bunch of people calling me up to help with proofreading seminar papers/assignments and to give private lessons. I figured I'd go for quantity and low-ball the market, charging only SFr20 per hour. But I found a few adverts for people looking for teachers and with those, I went with their offered price, which was much more.*

A qualified teacher can charge about SFr80 an hour in the cities, so even SFr40 might be considered a bargain.

The English Teachers' Association in Switzerland (www.e-tas.ch) operates a jobs board with a few vacancies, mainly for part-time trainers for business or for summer programmes. For example, the Boston School in Zurich (www.thebostonschool.com) was advertising for an in-company trainer whilst Languages for Fun in Coppet on Lake Geneva (www.languagesforfun.ch) was advertising for part-time mother-tongue teachers for children. The newsgroup http://groups.yahoo.com/group/swissenglish is aimed at EFL teachers already in Switzerland, not those enquiring about job opportunities.

REGULATIONS

No permit is needed for EU citizens who stay for less than three months though there is an obligation to register online. If they want to stay beyond that, eg to continue job-hunting or to do a seasonal job, they must obtain an L-permit (labour permit) for jobs lasting less than a year. If they are able to submit an employment contract from a Swiss employer, the Migration Office can complete residence formalities and no additional work permit is required.

If the contract of employment is going to extend beyond one year, it is necessary to apply for a B-permit, valid for between one and five years. There are strict quotas which were reduced in 2015 due to anti-immigrant feelings within Switzerland. So they are available only to highly qualified people for senior positions.

Detailed information about the regulations is published by the Federal Office of Migration (www.bfm.admin.ch) and is sometimes available from the cantonal authorities, for example downloadable brochures about living and working in Zurich are available at www.awa.zh.ch. The canton of Zurich also allows foreigners to apply for a work permit online (in German language only), which shortens the application time. The searchable forum www.englishforum.ch can also be helpful on technical matters.

As a result of Switzerland moving towards integration with Europe, non-EU citizens are finding it harder to gain legal access to Switzerland's English-teaching market unless they apply in special categories like spouse or trainee. If a non-European does find an employer willing to sponsor their application, the applicant will have to collect the documents from the Swiss embassy in his or her home country.

VACATION WORK

More possibilities for teaching English exist at summer camps than in city language institutes, as can be seen from the programmes listed in the directory below. There are a number of international schools in Switzerland, some of which run English language and sports summer schools. The Swiss Federation of Private Schools produces a list of summer schools in Switzerland held at its member schools, indicating which ones teach English. This is available at www.swiss-schools.ch. Watch for occasional ads on this site or, if you are in Switzerland, make local enquiries.

In addition to the organisations with entries below, the following organisations offer summer language courses between June and September and may need teachers or monitors (or some combination of the two):

Aiglon College Summer School, 1885 Chesières-Villars (+41 24 496 6171; www.aiglon.ch).
Collège Alpin International, Beau Soleil Holiday Language Camp, 1884 Villars-sur-Ollon (www.beausoleil.ch).

PHILIP LEE

Philip Lee from New Zealand spent his summers during university working at English language summer camps on the Continent, including one summer with Village Camps (see entry). The application for the position of counsellor involved a formal application and phone interview, plus he had to complete a basic first aid/CPR course (CPR etc) at his own expense. This opportunity is open to non-European nationals, as Philip reported recently.

There wasn't much of a visa problem as most tutors from outside the EU (US/Canada/Australia/NZ) had a three-month tourist visa I believe. I never encountered any problems in relation to my visa and working and even when I was working in Switzerland, where I expected more regulation and controls, there wasn't a problem at all. I worked in Switzerland for a two-week camp. But there were people who stayed there for up to 12 weeks working without problems.

I was paid cash in hand for the Swiss camps. I think payment was always a bit of concern for people working in this line of work for the first time, in the sense that there were no 'employment rights', but at the organisations I worked with, payment was always managed very professionally.

Alpadia Summer Camps, 1820 Montreux (www.alpadia.com/en/about-us/jobs.htm). Holiday language courses in Leysin, Ascona and Zug, for which it hires tutors and activity leaders for the summer season.

Institut Le Rosey, Camp d'Eté, 1180 Rolle (+41 21 822 5500; summercamp@rosey.ch; www.roseysummercamps.ch/jobs). Qualified or experienced EFL teachers over 20 for co-educational summer camps with sports coaching in Gstad and Rolle on Lake Geneva. Teachers must be capable of carrying out boarding school duties.

Institut Monte Rosa, 57 Avenue de Chillon, 1820 Montreux-Territet (+41 21 965 4545; info@monterosa.ch; www.monterosa.ch).

International Camp Suisse is a British-based language camp with an office in West Yorkshire and the camp held in Torgon (www.campsuisse.com). Activity leaders and language teachers are needed to fill many summer positions.

Les Elfes in Verbier (www.leselfes.com/about-us/jobs). Another camp operator looking for seasonal summer or winter staff, most of whom will be over 20, though younger candidates are eligible to do work experience.

Leysin American School in Switzerland, 1854 Leysin (www.las.ch/summer/staff). Contact the director of Summer Programs.

St George's School in Switzerland, 1815 Clarens/Montreux (www.st-georgescamp.ch).

Surval Mont-Fleuri, Route de Glion 56, 1820 Montreux 1 (www.surval.ch). For teenage girls.

TASIS (The American School in Switzerland), Summer Language Programs, Via Collina d'Oro, 6926 Montagnola-Lugano (+41 91 960 5151; http://summer.tasis.com/page.cfm?p=303). Hiring takes place between January and March. Net salaries are SFr2,600 for counsellors and SFr4,000 for teachers. American staff may be eligible for a SFr1,400-1,500 contribution to their transatlantic airfares and Europeans up to SFr500.

LIST OF EMPLOYERS

BERLITZ SCHOOL OF LANGUAGES AG
Gerbergasse 4, 4051 Basel
- +41 61 226 9040
- basel@berlitz.ch
- www.berlitz.ch/en/basle/job_vacancies

NUMBER OF TEACHERS: 15.

PREFERENCE OF NATIONALITY: Must be living in Basel and have residence permit.

QUALIFICATIONS: Bachelor's degree or professional experience, eg business, banking. Berlitz is looking for motivated and enthusiastic employees who can openly engage with others, have a love of language and culture, and a positive disposition. Must have teaching experience with adults and be a communicative person.

CONDITIONS OF EMPLOYMENT: No limit on contract length. Candidates must be available for at least 20 hours per week. Flexible hours of work. Pupils are adults whose average age is between 30 and 40.

SALARY: SFr22.50 per 40-minute lesson plus 10%–20% supplements for some programmes.

FACILITIES/SUPPORT: No assistance with accommodation. Training provided.

RECRUITMENT: Through adverts. Local interviews essential.

CONTACT: Martijn Morren (martijn.morren@berlitz.ch).

HAUT-LAC CAMP
Ch. de Pangires 26, 1806 St-Légier
- +41 21 555 5000
- camp@haut-lac.ch
- www.haut-lac-camp.ch

NUMBER OF TEACHERS: Teachers/monitors needed for summer, spring and winter language camps for adolescents.

PREFERENCE OF NATIONALITY: Native English speakers, preferably with a passport from an EU member state.

QUALIFICATIONS: TEFL, CELTA or equivalent plus it is useful to have experience in sports, drama, art or games organisation.

CONDITIONS OF EMPLOYMENT: Language and sports summer camp (late June to end of August); winter ski camp (end of December to early April); spring camp (early April to early May).

FACILITIES/SUPPORT: Full board and lodging provided in single, twin or three-bedded rooms. Help given with travel expenses. Free laundry facilities and use of sports equipment.

RECRUITMENT: Send for an application form to jobs@haut-lac.com.

CONTACT: Steve McShane, Director.

INLINGUA – BASEL
Dufourstrasse 50, 4052 Basel
- +41 61 278 9933
- sprachkurse@inlingua-basel.ch
- www.inlingua-basel.ch

NUMBER OF TEACHERS: 50–55.

PREFERENCE OF NATIONALITY: Must be a Swiss or EU citizen and be in possession of a Swiss residence permit.

QUALIFICATIONS: University degree is essential. If the degree is not a teaching degree then CELTA or equivalent is required in addition (online courses are not accepted).

CONDITIONS OF EMPLOYMENT: Generally open-ended contracts but a two-year minimum commitment is expected. Lessons are held from 7am to 9.30pm and the teachers' workload depends on their availability.

SALARY: Starting full-time salary is approximately SFr5,500. Salary is directly dependent on number of lessons taught. It could take a few months before a full-time workload is built up.

FACILITIES/SUPPORT: The school handles all paperwork for work permits. No help with accommodation.

RECRUITMENT: Usually via ETAS (English Teachers' Association of Switzerland), advertising online or unsolicited applications. Interviews are essential. First round is conducted via telephone followed by one or two rounds of personal interviews held at the school.

CONTACT: Ms Anja Georg, Personnel Assistant (anja.georg @inlingua.com).

THE CAMBRIDGE INSTITUTE
Seidengasse 6, 8001 Zurich
- +41 44 221 1212
- zuerich@cambridge.ch
- www.cambridge.ch

PREFERENCE OF NATIONALITY: Native English speaker who is already resident in Zurich.

QUALIFICATIONS: English teaching certificate or diploma (eg CELTA or equivalent). The candidate must have already obtained the required permits to live and work in Switzerland.

CONTACT: Roger Bourne, Director of Studies.

THE LANGUAGE FACTORY
Bionstrasse 4, 9015 St Gallen
- info@thelanguagefactory.ch
- www.thelanguagefactory.ch

NUMBER OF TEACHERS: 3.

PREFERENCE OF NATIONALITY: None.

QUALIFICATIONS: CELTA.

CONDITIONS OF EMPLOYMENT: Open-ended period of employment.

SALARY: Depends on qualifications and experience.

FACILITIES/SUPPORT: No help with accommodation. Most teachers are already resident.

RECRUITMENT: Job ads, mainly on e-tas.ch (English Teachers' Association in Switzerland). Interviews carried out via Skype or face-fo-face.

CONTACT: Judith Vogt, Teacher Trainer.

TLC–INTERNATIONAL HOUSE
Bahnhofstrasse 44, 5400 Baden
- +41 56 205 5178
- info@ihbaden.ch
- www.ihbaden.ch

NUMBER OF TEACHERS: 25.

PREFERENCE OF NATIONALITY: Native English speakers.

QUALIFICATIONS: Minimum CELTA plus experience teaching English to adults. Some business experience is preferable.

CONDITIONS OF EMPLOYMENT: Open-ended contract. Classes start at 8am and finish at 9.30pm. If the teacher is flexible in terms of location and time they can work up to 26 hours per week.

SALARY: SFr60–SFr72 depending on qualifications, experience and range of teaching.

RECRUITMENT: Usually through ETAS (English Teachers' Association of Switzerland), adverts on websites such as www.jobs.ch or through word of mouth. Interviews are essential. Preliminary interview can be done by phone and successful candidate will need to take a trial lesson in Switzerland.

CONTACT: Andrea Merki, HR Manager (Andrea.Merki@ ihbaden.ch).

VERBIER LANGUAGE SCHOOL
Centre de l'étoile, Rue de Médran 6, CP 475, 1936 Verbier
- +41 79 653 2227
- info@verbierlanguageschool.com
- www.verbierlanguageschool.com

NUMBER OF TEACHERS: 2 full-time and varying numbers of part-time staff depending on the season.

PREFERENCE OF NATIONALITY: None.

QUALIFICATIONS: Teachers must be bi or tri-lingual. Obviously it's better if potential employees have experience, but language skills and personality are highly important. Classes do not always focus on grammar but should make learning fun and relaxed. Conversational skills are paramount.

CONDITIONS OF EMPLOYMENT: Seasonal contracts are June to August and December to April. Usual teaching hours are 9am–12pm and 4pm–7pm.

SALARY: SFr25 per hour. Less deductions required by Swiss law (pension, second pension, accident insurance, taxes).

FACILITIES/SUPPORT: Teachers must find their own accommodation but employer provides list of agencies and people who may be able to offer help. Assistance given with work permits.

RECRUITMENT: Selection made from CVs received and interviews arranged, by Skype if necessary.

CONTACT: Rosi Pickard, Director (rosimoment@hotmail.com).

VILLAGE CAMPS
14 Rue de la Morache, Nyon, 1260 Vaud
- +41 24 493 3064
- personnel@villagecamps.com
- www.villagecamps.com

Language summer camp at Leysin near Lake Geneva in French-speaking Switzerland (also in York, England and Cyprus).

PREFERENCE OF NATIONALITY: European, North American, Australian and New Zealand passport holders may apply.

QUALIFICATIONS: Applicants must be at least 21 years of age, possess a recognised qualification in language teaching (minimum 4 weeks) and be a native English speaker. Must have proven teaching experience of at least a year. A second language is desirable and experience in sports, creative and/or outdoor activities is essential. A valid first aid and cardiopulmonary resuscitation (CPR) certificate is required while at camp.

CONDITIONS OF EMPLOYMENT: Employment periods vary from 3 to 8 weeks between June and August. Unpaid orientation (last week of June) must be attended.

SALARY: Room and board, accident and liability insurance and a weekly allowance of SFr425 provided.

RECRUITMENT: Starts in January. There is no deadline to submit applications, but positions are limited. Interviews are by telephone. For information on dates, locations, and positions available and to apply directly online, visit www.villagecamps.com.

CONTACT: Personnel Director.

WALL STREET ENGLISH

Rue du Simplon, 34, 1006 Lausanne

☎ +41 21 614 66 14

✉ brad.elliott@wallstreetenglish.ch

🖥 www.wallstreetenglish.ch

Head office of WSI Switzerland which comprises 9 schools.

NUMBER OF TEACHERS: 12 in Lausanne, 60 in Switzerland.

PREFERENCE OF NATIONALITY: None. Due to restrictions on work permits, candidates who are already established in Switzerland are preferred.

QUALIFICATIONS: CELTA or equivalent is a minimum.

CONDITIONS OF EMPLOYMENT: Open-ended contract. Variable hours but usually evenings 5pm–8pm.

SALARY: SFr37–60 per hour, depending on type of lesson given. Tax deducted at source for non-long-term residents plus various insurance deductions.

FACILITIES/SUPPORT: Assistance given with obtaining insurance card and sorting out tax but only after candidate has arranged his or her own work permit.

RECRUITMENT: Teachers for other WSI branches in Switzerland and the Czech Republic are generally recruited by a team leader in each school individually, and therefore candidates are encouraged to apply directly to their chosen school/area. Interviews are essential and occasionally conducted via Skype.

CONTACT: Brad Elliott, National Academic and HR Director.

CENTRAL AND EASTERN EUROPE

The transition to a market economy throughout Eastern and Central Europe initially resulted in a huge demand for professional assistance, especially in improving the skills of communication in English. In the 1990s and early 21st century this was matched by an enthusiastic demand from young westerners to live and work in Eastern Europe. But it seems that curiosity about Eastern Europe has waned. At the same time, the standard of state language education has improved to the extent that there are now many more competent homegrown teachers in Hungary, Poland and so on. Obviously schools, especially in the state sector, prefer to hire locals for whom they don't have to provide accommodation. And with the improvements in state provision of language teaching, fewer Eastern Europeans feel compelled to invest in private instruction.

Very few of the agencies and organisations abroad that once placed volunteers and teachers in the region are still active. SOL in Devon, which has been recruiting native speaker teachers for many years, announced in 2015 that its move to support teacher training of local teachers in Eastern Europe had completely taken over its recruitment activities.

While Russia and many of its former satellites have continued to wrestle with their political and economic demons, the more stable Central European states of Hungary, Poland, the Czech Republic, Slovakia, the Baltic States and more recently, Bulgaria and Romania, have been welcomed into the European fold by acceding to the EU. As a result, thousands of their citizens have had the chance to move to the UK or Ireland to earn some money and improve their English, again contributing to the contraction of the market back home.

Yet despite having moved past making 'Western' synonymous with 'desirable', the majority of Central European people are still remarkably welcoming to Britons and Americans. Thousands of temporary and longer-term visitors continue to fall under the spell of famous destinations such as Prague, Budapest, Kraków, as well as many other beautiful towns in Slovakia and Bulgaria. Even those who find themselves in the less prepossessing industrial cities usually come away beguiled by Central European charm. The English language teaching industry in these countries has grown up, and hires native speaker teachers with proven experience or an appropriate qualification. For qualified English teachers the market is now more stable, realistic and developed.

The explosion in the number of training centres for TEFL/TESL teachers in all English-speaking countries means that the pool of certified available teachers is fairly large. Teachers who can claim to specialise either in teaching Young Learners or in teaching Business English are especially attractive since both these areas of ELT are buoyant. Tourism training colleges in Hungary, the Czech and Slovak Republics and the Baltics are especially keen on encouraging conversational English. The easiest way to become more employable is to acquire a TEFL qualification, which could prove especially useful (and incidentally cheaper) if obtained in Eastern Europe. For example International House in Prague, Budapest, Katowice and Wroclaw all offer the CELTA course, while ITC Prague offers a TESOL certificate (see the Directory of Training Courses), as do many others.

North Americans will find that the accession of some of the former Eastern bloc countries to the EU has resulted in immigration regulations favouring English teachers from Britain and Ireland. Language institutes understandably do not want to become involved with the delays and expense of supporting non-EU candidates to obtain a residence permit, though some are willing. One of the first language-teaching organisations to break into Eastern Europe has continued to be one of the most active and energetic in the region, International House. IH-affiliated schools are flourishing in Belarus, Lithuania, Latvia, Estonia, Ukraine (where there are six), Poland, Romania, Bulgaria, Hungary, Russia and Slovakia, among others. The affiliation agreement with all IH schools states that the schools can employ only teachers who have passed the CELTA course. Similarly the British Council is often in need of suitable candidates to fill vacancies in its teaching centres in Bulgaria, Romania, Ukraine, etc.

Local salaries can seem absurdly low when translated into a hard currency. Some schools pay what is usually a generous salary by local standards but which can leave little after paying for food and accommodation. It is difficult to generalise, but a typical package would include a monthly net salary of £500–£600 in addition to free or subsidised accommodation and possibly some other perks such as a travel stipend. The best-paid jobs are for firms that teach in-company courses, especially in Poland, though they are unlikely to offer accommodation.

A host of private language schools that are either independent or part of larger language-teaching organisations are represented in Eastern and Central Europe. Most of the Central European schools listed in the directory are well established and offer above-average working conditions. In the more volatile climate of Russia and former Soviet republics (which are several years behind the stable democracies of Central Europe), locally managed schools come and go, and tend to choose their teachers from the pool of native English speakers on the spot, who also come and go. Intrepid travellers visiting the Central Asian Republics with no intention to work are still sometimes invited to stay a while and do some English teaching, as was happening in off-the-beaten-track towns in Poland and the former Czechoslovakia in the 1990s.

One interesting option for those who do not wish to commit themselves for a full academic year is to work at one of the many language summer camps which are offered to young people, usually in scenic locations from Lake Balaton in Hungary to Lake Baikal in Siberia to the Black Sea resorts of Bulgaria.

CONDITIONS OF WORK

The financial rewards of working in the old Russian Empire are usually so negligible that trained/experienced teachers cannot be enticed to teach there unless they have an independent interest in living in that part of the world or are supported by a voluntary organisation. Even the large language chains which offer reasonable working conditions (eg flat provided, plenty of support) do not pay high enough wages to allow ordinary EL teachers to save any money. Russia itself can offer reasonable wages, but the cost of living can be very high in Moscow and St Petersburg and inflation continues to be a problem.

Most of the Central European cities and larger towns have sprouted western-style supermarkets – Tesco stores are proliferating in Hungary, Poland, etc – and other consumer outlets, often to the disgruntlement of the older generations who have a fondness for their local shops. Living in these cities begins to feel not so very different from living in France or Italy, particularly with the influx of international companies. The nightlife of Budapest rivals that of Berlin. Smaller towns and rural areas can still be a very different proposition (until you come across expats who have bought property on the cheap in Bulgaria, etc).

FINDING A JOB

Far fewer vacancies in Central and Eastern Europe are being advertised in the educational press and on the internet, especially in Poland, but it is still worth checking the main EFL job sites such as www.tefl.com, which at the time of writing carried job ads for 57 different employers in the region, with the majority of 25 being in Russia. The possibility of creating your own job in the more obscure corners of this region still exists. Much of what takes place happens by chance, and protocol is often given a back seat to friendly encounters. Obtaining work often comes down to the right (or wrong) hairstyle or whether you've got any Polish/Lithuanian/Slovak/Azerbaijani ancestry. Looking professional, being persistent and asking as many questions as you answer, rather than sitting back on your heels, usually pays off. EU teachers will have an advantage in EU member countries, although other nationalities do succeed in finding employers willing to take on the expense and hassle of applying for the documentation.

Michael Todd from the US describes a typical trajectory for the TEFL teacher taking his or her first tentative steps into Eastern Europe to becoming established. When he arrived, he had done one undergraduate course in teaching English and a tutoring seminar for volunteer teachers, both back in Michigan. Initially he spent nine months near Katowice in Poland teaching the Callan Method, then two years at the Technical University of Liberec in the Czech Republic, and after five years in Bratislava he became a Senior Teacher. Along the way he acquired a CELTA from International House Budapest (which he wishes he had done earlier), and a Business English Teaching certificate (BET) from International House Bratislava:

> *I found my first job in Slovakia online. I don't remember which site. They turned out to be bloodsuckers, so after a year I moved to International House Bratislava. Another teacher and I walked into IH and asked for an interview. The DOS promptly interviewed us. Because I didn't have a CELTA, the DOS had me do a teaching demonstration a few days later. Having impressed her in the teaching demo, we discussed the contractual terms. I decided, stupidly, to return to my first employer, but IH was still willing to hire me for the following fall.*

According to Michael, teaching one-to-one at international businesses around Bratislava gave him lots of autonomy and variety. Some of his students just wanted to chat but most were looking for competently delivered lessons and they expected to be corrected often. Students over the age of 45 tend to be more difficult to teach, and they complain about how hard the language is. It would be easier to save money if it wasn't so tempting to visit nearby Vienna, Budapest and Prague. Fortunately there is a healthy market for private lessons, so it is not difficult to supplement your income.

In addition to International House, the major chains have some franchise schools in the region, chief among them EF English First, which sends many teachers to Russia, and Language Link with affiliated schools in Russia, Uzbekistan and one school in Kazakhstan (www.languagelink.co.uk). The Peace Corps (toll-free +1 855 855 1961; www.peacecorps.gov) provides volunteer teachers on 27-month contracts to many countries in Eastern Europe. Until April 2014, the largest programme was in Ukraine but volunteers were evacuated and the programme is still suspended. Other destination countries for Peace Corps teachers are Armenia, Georgia, Kyrgyz Republic, Azerbaijan and Moldova. Candidates must be US citizens, have a degree and be in good health. All expenses, including airfare and health insurance, are covered. Volunteers teach at both secondary and university level and become involved with teacher training and curriculum development.

The rest of this chapter is organised by country. Bulgaria, Czech Republic, Slovak Republic, Hungary, Poland and Romania are followed by Russia and its former satellite states (the Baltic States and Ukraine and Moldova). The former Yugoslav republics of Slovenia, Croatia, Bosnia-Herzogovina, Serbia and Montenegro are included in the chapter 'The Rest of Europe' along with Albania, Cyprus and Malta. Finally the Central Asian Republics are covered.

BULGARIA

Since Bulgaria joined the EU in 2007 it has attracted more EU tourists as well as property speculators and foreign businesses. The demand for English teachers is substantial, although opportunities in the private sector are still relatively scarce. Almost all schools ask for at least a degree and teaching certificate.

FINDING A JOB

A Bulgarian agency of long standing appoints 60–80 native speakers to teach in specialist English-language secondary schools for one academic year for which the deadline is 31st May. Details are available from Teachers for Central and Eastern Europe (21 V 5 Rakovski Boulevard, Dimitrovgrad 6400; +359 391 24787; tfcee@usa.net; www.tfcee.8m.com). Graduates, preferably with a TEFL background, are accepted from the USA, UK, Canada and Australia to spend an academic year teaching. The weekly teaching load is 19 40-minute classes per four-day week. The salary in Bulgarian leva is equivalent to $400. Benefits include free furnished accommodation, 60 days of paid holiday, paid sick leave and work permit. A summer programme is also available at Black Sea resorts for which the application deadline is 20th June. TfCEE charges an application fee of $60. A number of other companies offer English-language summer schools and camps at resorts near Varna. A recent advertisement for teachers was placed in tefl.com by the Orange House English Language Centre in Varna (www.orangehousevarna.com) offering to pay about £1,000 for the nine-week summer stint.

The British Council in Sofia has a thriving English centre, which offers courses for young learners, adults and businessmen and women; to enquire about any forthcoming teaching vacancies email learnenglish@britishcouncil.bg. Pharos is the biggest chain of foreign-language and computing schools in Bulgaria, and affiliated to the Strategakis Schools network of Northern Greece; however, this book has never heard of any native speakers being hired by a Pharos school and its website is only in the Cyrillic script.

Outside the official education system a reasonable number of language institutes and educational establishments are on the look-out for well-presented, confident candidates. One of the first private schools to be established after the revolution of 1990 was the AVO-3 School of English, with two schools in Sofia affiliated to Bell Worldwide. It runs CELTA courses that are at the cheaper end of the scale for Europe (see entry in the Directory of Training Courses) and often advertises for native English-speaking staff who must have a degree, preferably in English and at least a year of teaching experience, preferably with young learners (www.avo-bell.com/work_offers). The current rate of pay is €750–€900 per month before deductions of approximately 15%.

American teachers with at least a master's degree could try the AUBG, a private American-style liberal arts university located in Blagoevgrad (www.aubg.edu). All classes are in English and the university's English Language Institute prepares future AUBG applicants for the TOEFL and SAT exams, as well as teaching courses every semester to absolute beginners and intermediate students.

EFL vacancies hardly ever crop up on the internet, but this does not mean that they do not exist, as **Darren Quinn** reported:

> *Before I came to Bulgaria I had no idea what the job market was really like. All the information and advice I found online was negative. However, when I arrived here, even though I didn't speak the language very well, I walked into every school I could find and asked them for work. I had obtained my CELTA and had worked in South Korea for one year before I moved here, though it would have been possible to work at some schools here without the CELTA. Within a few months I was working part-time at four different schools and also had some private students. Work was a difficult grind for a long time here. However, two years ago, my wife and I were able to open our own small school, which has since grown into one of the biggest in the city (see entry for ABC School).*
>
> *I would have to say that overall my experience in Bulgaria has been a very good one. The students are excellent and the Bulgarian people are very friendly and relaxed. The culture is fascinating and varied. Many people*

are put off coming to Bulgaria, perhaps because they think there are few job opportunities and much of the information online concerning employment is quite negative. From my own experience, I can say that this is not true: if you put in the leg-work you can find work here and if you aren't worried about making a fortune, this is a very enjoyable place to teach English.

REGULATIONS

Bulgaria's accession into the EU has made it easier for teachers in terms of red tape. EU citizens only need a letter from their employer in order to get permission to stay for one year. It's a little time consuming, but basically unproblematic, and is done at the local police station. US citizens, on the other hand, need a visa obtained from one of the four Bulgarian consulates in the US. For this reason the Real English School (see entry), among others, employs only EU citizens or non-EU citizens who have a right to stay for some other reason (eg marriage to a Bulgarian). The English Academy, however, will consider employing US citizens, who are responsible for their own visas, although some assistance is given with paperwork.

LEISURE TIME

Vicky Williams, co-director of the Real English School based in Veliko Turnovo and Pleven, finds that living in Bulgaria is never dull:

As for living and working in Bulgaria, it is a country that is changing rapidly. There are still some vestiges of communism around in terms of architecture, cars, bureaucracy and lack of choice in shops, etc, but on the other hand there is a huge amount of building going on and many people now do have a lot of money. It's a fascinating place to live at the moment – it is a country of contrasts.

The current minimum wage in Bulgaria is 360 leva a month, about €184, the lowest in Europe. Since a month's rent for a one-bedroom flat can cost more than that, the majority of Bulgarians live together in family units, often with several generations squashed together in one house.

Most big cities are well equipped and Bulgaria is striving to meet the guidelines put in place since joining the European Union. In town, you'll find everything you would expect from a modern European city. In rural areas, on the other hand, wages are still much lower and living conditions can be more traditional, for example in the countryside you can still see peasants with donkeys and carts and stooped old ladies lugging branches of trees home to burn for firewood. In these areas indoor toilets may be something of a luxury. The Bulgarian countryside, especially mountain areas, is expansive and unspoilt, with plenty of affordable opportunities to hike or ski in the winter. The Black Sea coast is mostly built up as holiday resorts and is a popular place for a cheap seaside break.

LIST OF EMPLOYERS

ABC ENGLISH LANGUAGE CENTRE
23 Marno Pole Street, Veliko Tarnovo
+359 899 950 318
abc-bg@hotmail.com
www.abcenglish.eu

NUMBER OF TEACHERS: 4.
PREFERENCE OF NATIONALITY: EU passport holders only.
QUALIFICATIONS: CELTA.
CONDITIONS OF EMPLOYMENT: 1 year minimum. Variable hours between 9am and 9pm.

FACILITIES/SUPPORT: Assistance given with accommodation and work permits.

RECRUITMENT: Website advertising, followed by interview.

CONTACT: Darren Quinn, Director.

ENGLISH ACADEMY PLOVDIV

28 Gladston Street, Plovdiv 4000

☏ +359 32 623457

✉ plovdiv@englishacademybg.com

🖥 www.englishacademybg.com

NUMBER OF TEACHERS: 4.

PREFERENCE OF NATIONALITY: Only native English speakers.

QUALIFICATIONS: Recognised teaching certificate such as the Cambridge CELTA.

CONDITIONS OF EMPLOYMENT: 3, 6 and 12-month contracts. Full-time: Tuesday to Friday, 5.40pm–9.40pm and Saturday 9am–1pm and 2pm–6pm. Part-time: less than 24 hours per week within the same time frame.

SALARY: 15 Bulgarian leva per hour.

FACILITIES/SUPPORT: Arranges with local agents for accommodation viewings and assists with translation. Non-EU citizens are responsible for their own visas although the school gives assistance.

RECRUITMENT: Telephone and/or in-person interviews.

CONTACT: Mark A Faulkner, Director of Studies (markfaulkner@englishacademybg.com).

ENGLISH ACADEMY VARNA

48 Preslav Str, Nezavisimost Square, Varna 9000

☏ +359 52 622351

✉ varna@englishacademybg.com

🖥 www.englishacademybg.com/en/varna-jobs

NUMBER OF TEACHERS: 14 for academic year and summer school.

PREFERENCE OF NATIONALITY: Only native English speakers.

QUALIFICATIONS: Degree in any subject and teaching certificate are essential, 3 years' experience preferred. Must be friendly and outgoing.

CONDITIONS OF EMPLOYMENT: 12-month contracts preferred starting in July (over 4 terms), 20–24 teaching hours a week, 5 days a week (Monday to Friday at summer school or Tuesday to Saturday during academic year, although a lot of teaching takes place at weekends). Part-time positions 12+ hours. July/August summer schools run in association with charitable foundation (www.arkutino-school.eu).

SALARY: 23 leva per hour, more for technical/non-standard teaching. 10% flat rate tax. Summer teaching rate is 20 leva per hour net with a guaranteed minimum of 18.

FACILITIES/SUPPORT: Free shared accommodation given for full-time summer work.

RECRUITMENT: Over the internet (mainly www.tefl.com). Interviews essential, either by telephone/Skype or face-to-face. Non-EU citizens are responsible for their own visas, but assistance given with the relevant paperwork.

CONTACT: Mark Mctaggart, Director of Studies (mark@englishacademybg.com).

THE REAL ENGLISH SCHOOL

21 Hadji Dimitar Street, Veliko Turnovo 5000

☏ +359 62 605749/886 171753

✉ information@realenglishschool.eu

🖥 www.realenglishschool.eu

NUMBER OF TEACHERS: 6. Also 3 or 4 teachers for Pleven branch (Office no. 1, Turgovski Complex Maxi, Ul. Tsar Boris III no. 12, 4th Floor, Pleven; tel +359 64 806363).

PREFERENCE OF NATIONALITY: Must have EU member state passport, native English speakers only.

QUALIFICATIONS: CELTA or equivalent, prefer minimum 1-year's experience. Without CELTA, must have BA/MA in English or PGCE plus 2 years' TEFL experience. Experience teaching any exam courses (FCE, CAE, CPE, TOEFL, SAT, IELTS, ILEC) will be an advantage. The school teaches General and Business English (students are aged from 8 to adult).

CONDITIONS OF EMPLOYMENT: 1-year standard contract. 24 contact hours a week. Also summer vacancies on Black Sea coast between early July and late August.

SALARY: 1,000 Bulgarian leva per month (net).

FACILITIES/SUPPORT: Free Bulgarian lessons. Assistance with locating accommodation and registering with the police, etc.

RECRUITMENT: Through www.tefl.com, www.eslbase.com and local hire. Interviews are essential, and can be by phone.

CONTACT: Colin and Vicky Williams, Directors.

CZECH REPUBLIC

The proliferation of TEFL-qualified teachers has allowed language schools to become far more discerning, especially in Prague. Language institutes generally do not accept online TEFL certificates, and adhere to the international standard of looking for teachers who have had at least 106 class hours in a four-week on-site programme, with at least six hours of observed teaching practice. Smaller Czech towns, including some rather uninspiring places in the steel-producing heart of the country and the Moravian capital Brno, offer interested teachers more scope for employment than the tourist-clogged capital. Be prepared for living and working conditions to change significantly once you leave the capital, especially for EFL teachers. Prague offers low pay, split shifts and intense competition between language schools that leads to job insecurity for teachers. Teaching private lessons is the most lucrative but the most difficult to fix up for new arrivals. Private lessons can be charged at 350+ crowns an hour, but most teachers working for a run-of-the-mill institute start at a base rate of 200–250 crowns which has not risen in some years. A good way to attract students initially is to charge at the lower end of the scale but to teach in groups of three or four.

FINDING A JOB

Most schools prefer a mixture of accents though British and Irish people have a red tape advantage because of their EU membership. But there are plenty of Americans, Canadians and Australians who are generally well received partly because of the large number of Czechs who emigrated to Australia.

STATE SCHOOLS

Qualified teachers are seldom recruited to teach in Czech primary and secondary schools as they once were. However the centralised contact, the Academic Information Agency (AIA) in Prague (see entry), part of the Ministry of Education, continues to offer a placement service into one-year positions. Any positions that are registered with the AIA are likely to be in smaller towns rather than Prague. The school year runs for 10 months from 1 September to 30 June, though some vacancies occur in January between semesters. In some cases, TEFL qualifications are not required, though normally the minimum requirements accepted are BA/MA in English/Applied Linguistics, a teaching qualification and experience. Applications should be submitted before the end of April. The AIA simply acts as a go-between, circulating CVs and applications to state schools that have requested a teacher. Schools then contact applicants directly to discuss contractual details. **Brian Farrelly** spent a very successful year some time ago teaching in state schools:

> *I taught in two state schools in the Czech Republic and had a really great time in both. I felt really privileged to teach the students there. In my first job in a 'gymnasium' secondary school in a small town called Sedlcany, south of Prague, the staff and students made me tremendously welcome. I also greatly enjoyed the freedom to teach as I saw fit, although I felt initially very daunted by the lack of guidance regarding what I should be doing with the students.*

One British teacher with extensive teaching experience in Slovakia was delighted and relieved to be hired by the Technical University of Liberec. On application he was upfront about having failed the CELTA course the previous summer and also about having severe epilepsy, and was 'really encouraged by the Director's promotion of equal opportunities and non-discrimination'.

PRIVATE INSTITUTES

A wide range of well-established academies offers high standards of instruction. The main international chains of language schools such as Berlitz have large established operations in the country. Most teachers are recruited locally, often through a TEFL training centre, such as TEFL Worldwide Prague (www.tefllworldwideprague.com), or via noticeboards, for example at the British Council and English-language bookshops.

It is not difficult to find contact details for English-language institutes in Prague and elsewhere. The most established schools which are externally vetted and their quality standards monitored belong to ACERT (Asociace Certifikovanych Jazykovych Skol; http://en.acert.cz) and/or AJSA (Asociace Jazykovych Skol a Agentur CR; www.ajsa.cz). Member schools could be worth approaching since many of them include teacher recruitment information in English on their websites. Also the *Yellow Pages* (Zlaté Stránky; www.zlatestranky.cz) are an excellent source of addresses under the heading *Jazykove skoly* as is the listing of schools at www.expats.cz/prague/directory/language-schools.

Of the institute websites that are available in English, a selection that provide teacher vacancy information, and in some cases online application forms, include the Gulliver Group (www.skolagulliver.cz), James Cook (http://jcl.cz), Lexis (www.lexis.cz), Sophia (www.sophia-cb.cz) and Tutor (see entry) plus:

Cloverleaf Group, Ostrava: www.cloverleaf.cz
English Link s.r.o., Prague: www.englishlink.cz
Glossa skola jazyku: http://glossa.cz
International House, Brno: www.ilcbrno.cz
Tandem Jazykove, Prague: www.tandem.cz/work-for-tandem.

Even though most schools in Prague claim to receive plenty of CVs on spec from which to fill any vacancies that arise, their willingness to describe their recruitment procedures online (in contrast to the main language schools in Poland) indicates that the demand for teachers is still strong. Anyone who is well qualified or experienced should have few difficulties in finding a job on the spot, particularly if they are lucky with their timing. The market in Brno is booming too, with more than 120 language schools listed as operating in the country's second-largest city (many will be one-person outfits), catering to a population of less than 400,000. Most people wait until they arrive in Prague before trying to find teaching work, which is what **Linda Harrison** did:

> *The best time to apply is before June. I arrived in September, which was too late, but if you persevere there are jobs around. A lot of teaching work here seems to be in companies. Schools employ you to go into offices, etc to teach English. After a short job hunt, I was hired by a company called Languages at Work which paid well and provided food and travel vouchers as well as helping with accommodation.*

Languages at Work has since morphed several times and is now the Spevácek Education Centre (see entry). People end up teaching in Prague via the most circuitous routes, as **Anne Morris** from the USA describes:

> *Although I'm near retirement age, I'm still a free spirit and am living in Prague now more or less by chance. I ran into an American couple at a jam-packed event in Old Town Square on a visit to Prague two years ago who said they were teaching English here. I've always loved this city so I asked how one would get a job like that and they scratched out a website on the back of an envelope (TEFL Worldwide). I lost them in the crowd but on return to the US came across the envelope in a coat pocket and decided to check it out – and now here I am teaching English. Just wish I'd made this discovery much earlier in my life!*

Outside of Prague, chances are reasonable of finding jobs in the private sector all year round, with the greatest selection available in late August through to November and in January/February. Those without qualifications or experience will find it very difficult because they will be competing with all those keen new graduates of TEFL training courses in the Czech Republic (see Directory of Training Courses). Unlike state schools, private schools in Prague do not offer accommodation, and will give preference when hiring to anyone who is already resident.

If you are stuck for a job during the summer months, a good option is to work in a summer camp until the school year starts. There are a number of summer camp options available, particularly teaching children, as well as intensive one-week courses for adults at holiday resorts. Children's camps do not generally pay very well, but food and accommodation are included, and many teachers use the camps as an opportunity to get to know a bit more of the country before going back to their city jobs in September. One to try is a British company, Wattsenglish, which runs residential and city summer camps as well as children's schools in Prague, Liberec, Usti nad Labem, Teplice, Karlovy Vary, Sokolov, Pardubice, Olomouc, Ostrava and Mlada Boleslav (www.wattsenglish.cz/for-teachers/employment-opportunities).

There are some advertisements for teaching jobs in the local English language online press, primarily at www.expats.cz, with fewer in the *Prague Post* (www.praguepost.com). It may be worth advertising your speciality as an English tutor (eg marketing, law, etc) ahead of time. **Kathy Panton** suggests enlisting the help of a Czech friend to translate 'Native speaker will tutor English to intermediate or advanced students', and send it to a free ads site such as *Annonce* (www.annonce.cz).

REGULATIONS

Since accession, EU citizens no longer have to apply for a visa or work permit. As throughout the EU, those who intend to stay more than 90 days must obtain a residence certificate from the regional office of the Ministry of the Interior; see the Immigration section at www.mvcr.cz for contact details or phone the information hotline on +420 974 832421.

Correspondingly it has become more problematic for non-EU citizens to obtain the necessary permission to live and work in the Czech Republic. The sought-after document is the blue card, which entitles foreign nationals with good qualifications (minimum university degree) to both live and work in the country. This requires gathering a raft of documents including employment contract, proof of accommodation, health cover of at least €60,000, etc and presenting it at the Czech embassy in your country or, in some circumstances, to the Ministry of the Interior. Foreigners do sometimes pick up work on their Schengen tourist visa but, before it expires after 90 days, the holder must exit the country and is not allowed to return until a further 90 days have elapsed.

The Czech Republic has Youth Mobility agreements with New Zealand and Canada which allow young people aged 18–35 who meet the acceptance criteria to reside in the Czech Republic for up to 12 months (www.mzv.cz/ottawa and www.mzv.cz/sydney); the administration fee is currently 2,500 crowns.

EU citizens who want to set up as self-employed freelancers should obtain a Business Licence (*zivnostensky list*) as **Martin Filla** did:

> It took me about 6 months to get a business licence. Before then some people took me on just as a temporary teacher and without a contract. After I got my business licence, more schools were willing to give me work and also a (standard) contract with it. According to law, it took me about three years to get my permanent residence visa and this also shows schools I plan to live in the Czech Republic.

CONDITIONS OF WORK

People teaching at private institutes in Prague, where there is a definite glut of foreign teachers, attracted by the cultural chic of the city, have been called the 'sweat shop labourers' of the TEFL world because of the low wages that employers can get away with paying. Salaries in the capital are sometimes lower than in smaller cities such as Brno, even though the cost of living is higher.

Working conditions in state schools are generally better than in private schools, though opportunities are far fewer than they used to be. The guaranteed salary at state schools, even if you're sick or there is a holiday, is a definite advantage. If you are lucky enough to be teaching mostly final-year students, your working hours in the exam month of June will be minimal, even though the teaching day at a state school might start at 8am. This counts as a lie-in compared with teaching in private companies, which is often underway by 7am or 7.30am. And of course in state schools there is no evening or weekend work.

The monthly wage range in state schools of 20,000–35,000 crowns gross is catching up with wages in the private sector. If you are renting on the open market, expect to spend between a fifth and a quarter of your earnings on simple accommodation. Hourly fees start at roughly 200 crowns net, though a more usual wage is 230–250 crowns. A full-time salary should be adequate to live on by local standards but will not allow you to save anything, unless you take on lots of private tutoring.

The scramble for getting teaching hours did not appeal to the 40-something Australian author Rachael Weiss whose long stay in Prague resulted in the amusing and revealing book *The Thing About Prague* published in 2015. Her spin on English teaching is more negative than most:

> *I suppose I could have got a teaching certificate and joined the hordes of Brits and Americans working for horrible cowboy outfits for a pittance, but two things stopped me. First. I don't have what it takes to work for a horrible cowboy outfit. There are plenty of them in Prague. 'Schools' set up by glassy-eyed bandits, mainly from Russia and America - men who'd arrived in Prague like rats off a cargo ship that'd washed up on a tropical paradise, filled with vulnerable foreigners who had no other way of earning a living, and natives desperate to learn the language of the internet. Living was cheap, wages were low and labour was plentiful.*
>
> *I heard tale after tale of teachers working for minimal rates a few hours a week, having to travel three hours for every one they worked and not getting paid for their travel time, being done out of their pay, being promised visas that never materialised. I kept hearing of jobs lost with no notice and of ghastly bosses.*
>
> *Second, I didn't want to teach English because that was the job that all the expats did, and I didn't want to be in the expat crowd. I didn't want to work with a whole lot of Americans and Brits, where I'd have to talk endlessly about the food and television we'd left at home. I wanted a job, any job, one that was more like an ordinary job.*

In Brno, wages nearly match those of Prague, but you should expect less in smaller cities such as Olomouc, Xlin, Hradec Kralove, etc. However, outside the Czech Republic's major cities the cost of living drops and many teachers in smaller cities and towns find that they are able to save more despite actually earning a lower monthly salary.

The majority of private language school clients are adults who are available for lessons after work, so most teaching takes place between 4pm and 8pm, Monday to Thursday. Long-time resident **Martin Filla** (originally from Australia but with a passport from an EU member state) reported that two years ago was a struggle for him due to the financial crisis and a reduction in the number of students. He now teaches only 25 hours a week, with half his students from language schools, and 40% in private lessons. Martin encounters the problem familiar to all EFL teachers, trying to balance encouragement of students to speak with trying to get them to speak accurately, as he reported while working for David's Agency (see entry) in the Moravian spa town of Luhacovice:

> *Most of the teaching was conversation based, to students who were intermediate or upper intermediate. One great challenge was to make it comfortable and interesting for everyone to speak, and help the students overcome their shyness. It was difficult to make every lesson interesting for everyone, and I was unsure about how much I should correct the students' bad grammar habits. Adult students especially have bad habits from earlier learning and these are very difficult to correct.*

ANNE MORRIS

Anne Morris warns that it will take time to find your financial feet in the Czech Republic.

Do not plan on living on your income for several months at least. Schools usually only give you a few classes to start out. Also you are not paid when classes are cancelled for one reason or another or school is on vacation (I found this out the hard way in February when classes stopped during winter break) and there are a lot of initial expenses involved in housing, agency fees, health insurance, phone, internet, etc so best to have a bit of a stash to fall back on.

One reward has been the opportunity to, if not totally assimilate, be a part of the native culture to some extent. An example was last night when I attended my high school's prom or 'ball' as they call it. Such fun to compare this universal ritual to a US prom! For starters, it was held in a palatial hall by any standards - not a crepe paper decorated basketball court as I remember high school dances and, heaven forbid, alcohol was served! A definite no-no in the US. And of course the kids outdid themselves with originality of style and sophistication. Really fun to be an onlooker.

Accommodation in Prague is more plentiful than it used to be. If you have a friend to translate for you, you can try the accommodation listings in *Annonce*, the Prague free ads paper, or Craigslist in English (http://prague.craigslist.cz). Most employers are prepared to help newcomers to find accommodation, usually a room in a small shared flat or university hostel. In the rest of the country there is less competition for affordable accommodation. However, those moving to Brno or Zlin will find that the real-estate agents have taken over the market, so those without local support may find themselves having to pay one month's rent to the agent as a finder's fee. On the other hand, agents do offer the advantage of providing a wide selection of furnished flats covering a range of budgets and in a variety of neighbourhoods. Many people place an advert in the local *Inzert Expres* or classifieds in other magazines, looking for accommodation. Many Czech students welcome the opportunity to share a flat with a native-English speaker in order to practise their English for free.

Students are reported to be 'a delight to teach, alert, intelligent, fun-loving, keen and interested'. Many English teachers avail themselves of the excellent resource centres run by the British Council in Prague and Brno. The British Council's teaching centre in the centre of Prague has very occasional openings for teachers who are TEFL certified with two years' relevant experience. One of the strongest motivations among secondary school (*gymnasium*) students to learn English is the prospect of the 'Maturita' (school-leaver's) exam. At the beginning of the year they are given 25 topics (eg the British Royal Family, the influence of the media) and at the end of the year they must talk in English about one topic (chosen at random) for 15 minutes. This is a very good incentive for class participation.

LEISURE TIME

The cost of living in Prague continues to creep up, though most things are still affordable in other towns. For example a decent midday meal at a Brno restaurant (soup, main course and beer) will cost 100 crowns, whilst rents for one-bedroom flats outside the Brno city centre start at 8,000 crowns a month. It is possible to survive on 600+ crowns a day. Prague has a vibrant nightlife with clubs and cafés, cinema, opera, poetry and dance. There is so much expat culture that a new arrival serious about getting into Czech culture will encounter many distractions.

In Prague theft is a problem, though walking the streets is reasonably safe. In small towns, however, English teachers are more likely to be treated as honoured guests with occasional offers of hospitality and invitations, for example to join skiing trips (which are very cheap), as **Hannah Bullock** from Oxford discovered in her year out between school and university in the town of Strakonice:

> *I've got some great Czech friends here. A colleague of mine has been very kind (as I've found most Czechs are) and has been like a mentor-cum-grandpa to me, taking me to visit castles, nearby towns, beautiful little villages and to walk in the mountains which border Germany. Most of this would have been very difficult without a car (the trains go very infrequently and at unsociable hours). I've spent many weekends in Prague since it's only one and a half hours by bus. I had to do double takes on hearing English spoken and seeing the Guardian being passed round the bars. Now instead of seeing Prague as the opening to Central Europe with its old-fashioned trams and cobbled streets as I did when I first arrived in September, I think of it as the door back to Westernisation.*

One final tip: if you play a musical instrument, take it with you since it's a great way to make local friends.

LIST OF EMPLOYERS

ACADEMIC INFORMATION AGENCY (AIA)
Centre for International Cooperation in Education (Dum zahranicníspoluprace), Na Porici 1035/4, 110 00 Prague 1
- +420 221 850504
- aia@dzs.cz
- www.dzs.cz/cz/akademicka-informacni–agentura/english-teachers-6

NUMBER OF TEACHERS: Teachers needed for state primary and secondary schools throughout the Czech Republic though numbers have been decreasing over the years.

PREFERENCE OF NATIONALITY: Native English speakers from UK, Canada, USA, Australia.

QUALIFICATIONS: Professional teachers are preferred for teaching at primary and secondary schools. All candidates are required to have a college or university-level degree, preferably in English or in a related field. Additional qualification in teaching English as a foreign language (eg CELTA) is necessary for applicants who are graduates of courses in non-related subjects. Previous experience in teaching English in a classroom setting is greatly welcomed. High motivation is expected.

CONDITIONS OF EMPLOYMENT: 10-month contracts, 1 September to 30 June, 24 hours per week.

SALARY: Same as local Czech teachers.

FACILITIES/SUPPORT: Accommodation provided by schools (free or subsidised). Non-EU citizens – work and residence permits organised before arrival.

RECRUITMENT: Interested applicants register their availability with AIA, which circulates details to schools looking for a teacher.

CONTACT: Karla Benesová.

AKAIA JAZYKOVÁ AGENTURA
Benátská 1078, 570 01 Litomyšl
- +420 731 103727
- akaia@akaia.cz
- www.akaia.cz

NUMBER OF TEACHERS: 4.

PREFERENCE OF NATIONALITY: EU preferred but other nationalities are also welcome.

QUALIFICATIONS: CELTA or equivalent plus degree and at least 1 year's experience.

CONDITIONS OF EMPLOYMENT: 10 months, renewable. 30 hours per week.

SALARY: 27,000–30,000 crowns less 2,000 crowns for social security.

FACILITIES/SUPPORT: School has a flat and information about other flat rentals. Assistance given with red tape. All teachers need a criminal record check; EU citizens must register with the different authorities; non-EU teachers have to get a visa.

RECRUITMENT: Interviews generally by Skype.

CONTACT: Tomáš Fila, Director.

AKCENT INTERNATIONAL HOUSE PRAGUE

Bitovská 3, 140 00 Prague 4

✆ +420 2 6110 9218

🖱 info@akcent.cz

🖥 www.akcent.cz

NUMBER OF TEACHERS: 100.

PREFERENCE OF NATIONALITY: None (need to comply with Czech immigration laws).

QUALIFICATIONS: Degree plus CELTA or equivalent (minimum).

CONDITIONS OF EMPLOYMENT: 10 or 12 months from September/October. Approximately 22 contact hours per week (ie 26 45-minute lessons). Mostly teaching General English to adults, though some YL teaching. Teaching both on-site and in-company.

SALARY: 10,000–14,000 crowns (before tax) per month plus shared accommodation, end-of-contract bonus and other benefits.

FACILITIES/SUPPORT: Health insurance covered and 25 days paid holidays per calendar year. Contribution made to cost of travelling to Prague. Offers CELTA/DELTA courses plus courses in teaching Young Learners and Business English.

RECRUITMENT: Helena Linková, Teacher Recruitment (helena. linkova@akcent.cz).

BRNO ENGLISH CENTRE

Starobrnenska 16/18, 602 00 Brno

✆ +420 541 212262

🖱 martin@brnoenglishcentre.cz

🖥 www.brnoenglishcentre.cz

NUMBER OF TEACHERS: 16.

PREFERENCE OF NATIONALITY: Native English speakers with EU citizenship or valid visa.

QUALIFICATIONS: A university degree plus an internationally recognised TEFL/TESOL qualification (not online), together with a minimum of 1 year's teaching with a similar institution.

CONDITIONS OF EMPLOYMENT: Standard contract is from September to May (9 months). Up to 24 lessons (45 minutes) per week, plus preparation, training and meetings. Contracts may be renewed.

SALARY: Around 24,600 crowns per month (gross) for average of 24 teaching hours a week. The average teacher would take home about 18,000–19,000 crowns.

FACILITIES/SUPPORT: Centre finds affordable accommodation (eg monthly rent of 7,000 crowns), pays the fees associated

with this and advances the first month's rent. Work permits are generally not a major problem. It is more problematic gaining the residence permit needed for non-EU citizens, although the centre provides assistance.

RECRUITMENT: Normally by direct application. The centre does not go through agencies or intermediaries. Interviews are essential and can, in theory, be carried out in the UK or else by phone.

CONTACT: Martin Kleinwächter, Director.

CALEDONIAN SCHOOL

U Půjčovny 2, Prague 1

✆ +420 210 084221

🖱 jobs@caledonianschool.com

🖥 www.caledonianschool.com

NUMBER OF TEACHERS: 100 in various locations in Prague and in schools around the Czech Republic (also in Slovakia).

PREFERENCE OF NATIONALITY: Teachers with EU citizenship preferred due to visa requirements.

QUALIFICATIONS: Teachers must have TEFL/TESOL/CELTA qualification with or without teaching experience.

CONDITIONS OF EMPLOYMENT: One year contract, usually from September, with possibility of renewal. 22 to 26 45-minute lessons a week. School teaches adults and young adults, in-school and in-company.

SALARY: Approx 18,000–20,000 crowns per month (after 15% deduction for tax) for qualified teachers, depending on number of hours worked. Pay rise after 6 months. Health insurance must be arranged independently.

FACILITIES/SUPPORT: Personal assistance in finding accommodation is not provided; however, there are a few tips at www.caledonianschool.com/jobs-teaching-english-accomodation. html. Free Czech lessons. Transport reimbursed to full-time teachers. Affiliated to TEFL training courses lasting 4 weeks offered by teflinprague.com.

RECRUITMENT: Interviews carried out in person or via Skype. Applicants must complete a lesson plan task as part of the interview. School hires year round.

CONTACT: HR Department.

DAVID'S AGENCY

Dr. Veseleho 1042, 763 26 Luhacovice

✆ +420 603 346618

🖱 catto@davidsagency.cz

NUMBER OF TEACHERS: 2 in Zlin, 2 in Luhacovice spa town and 1 in Uherske Hradiste.

PREFERENCE OF NATIONALITY: British or other native English speakers.

QUALIFICATIONS: University degree and TEFL.

CONDITIONS OF EMPLOYMENT: 10-month contracts, 8am–noon and 1pm–4.30pm.

SALARY: 24,000 crowns (gross) less about 25% for tax, health insurance and social benefits.

FACILITIES/SUPPORT: Accommodation arranged for 5,000 crowns per month. Assistance with work visa process. Training given in Czech language and culture.

RECRUITMENT: Via email. Early application encouraged to allow visa-processing time. Interviews are held in Britain in the summer.

CONTACT: David Catto, Director.

EDCENTRE SCHOOL S.R.O.
1414 Jasenicka, 755 01 Vsetin
- +420 775 115039
- lance@edcentre.cz
- www.centrumjazyku.cz/job-opportunity

NUMBER OF TEACHERS: 6 for schools in Vsetin and Valasske Mezirici.

PREFERENCE OF NATIONALITY: None, but EU member state passport or residence preferred.

QUALIFICATIONS: Bachelor's degree, EFL qualification (CELTA or equivalent) and 1–2 years' experience teaching abroad. Good knowledge of grammar needed.

CONDITIONS OF EMPLOYMENT: 10–12 months from September. 30–35 45-minute 'teaching hours' a week which fall between 7am and 8pm with a large gap in the middle of the day. Most teachers are on *Zivnostensky* list (sole trader's business licence).

SALARY: From 220 crowns per 45 minutes, depending on qualifications, experience and whether teacher is on *Zivnostensky* list. Deductions for registered self-employed teachers approximately 15% of earnings.

FACILITIES/SUPPORT: School accommodation is sub-let to teachers. Help given with red tape.

CONTACT: Lance Adam LaSalle, Co-director.

P.A.R.K. SCHOOL OF ENGLISH
8c Stankova, 602 00 Brno
- +420 5 4121 1900
- infobrno@skolapark.cz
- www.skolapark.cz

NUMBER OF TEACHERS: 15.

PREFERENCE OF NATIONALITY: None.

QUALIFICATIONS: Normally CELTA or Trinity CertTESOL plus a degree.

CONDITIONS OF EMPLOYMENT: 1-year contract. Teaching hours are between 7.30am and 8.30pm. School tries to avoid assigning split shifts.

SALARY: Varies according to experience. Deducted contributions usually amount to 10% of salary.

FACILITIES/SUPPORT: Office staff help teachers find the right flat or room. Assistance willingly given with obtaining visas, though it is a long process for non-EU teachers.

RECRUITMENT: Mostly local or direct approach from recently qualified TEFL teachers.

CONTACT: Ralph Davies, Director of Studies, or for locations outside Brno: Roman Koznar, Managing Director.

POLYGLOT SPOL S.R.O.
Mecislavova 8, 140 00 Prague 4
- +420 241 740566
- skola.praha@polyglot.cz
- www.polyglot.cz

NUMBER OF TEACHERS: Approximately 50 for branches in Prague, Brno, Ceske Budejovice, Plzen, Ostrava, Jihlava and Liberec and for summer programme.

PREFERENCE OF NATIONALITY: None.

QUALIFICATIONS: CELTA/TEFL or other certification of at least 120 hours of training plus experience.

CONDITIONS OF EMPLOYMENT: Between 7 and 20 hours' teaching per week depending on whether the employee teaches in the morning or afternoon.

SALARY: 200–300 crowns per hour.

RECRUITMENT: Interviews are not always essential.

CONTACT: Katerina Kamberska, Director of Studies (katerina. kamberska@polyglot.cz).

SPEVACEK EDUCATION CENTRE
Namesti Miru 15, 120 00 Prague 2
- +420 222 517869
- centrum@spevacek.info
- www.spevacek.info

Member of Czech Association of Language Schools (www.acert.cz). ISO 9001, and AJSA (www.ajsa.cz).

NUMBER OF TEACHERS: 150.

PREFERENCE OF NATIONALITY: Must be a native English or Czech/Slovak speaker. EU citizens only unless non-EU candidate already holds a valid visa.

QUALIFICATIONS: Minimum requirements are university degree and a recognised TEFL certificate. Online TEFL training is not acceptable unless combined with extensive experience. Formal EFL teaching experience is valued and rewarded. Professionalism, reliability, enthusiasm and smart appearance expected.

CONDITIONS OF EMPLOYMENT: 10-month renewable contracts. 80–90 teaching units per month (more if requested). Minimum 17–20 hours a week teaching all sorts of courses: adults, mainly in-company General and Business English, public courses, pre-school courses, post-secondary courses, small groups and individuals. Teaching kindergarten children, teenagers or (optional) public courses in a sister school. More experienced teachers may get 25 hours of work. Hours normally 7.30am–10am and 3pm–7pm. Lots of public transport involved. Summer work also available.

SALARY: Teaching is paid on an hourly basis. Approx. 23,000 crowns (gross) per month plus bonus.

FACILITIES/SUPPORT: Affiliated to sister school for TEFL training, Live TEFL Prague. Orientation training in September. Full academic support with teacher development workshops. Free Czech lessons.

RECRUITMENT: School recruits year round but main recruiting time is June–August. Résumés/CVs and cover letter welcomed via career web page. Interviews conducted in Prague or via Skype.

CONTACT: Ms Ria Korcová, DOS (ria.korcova@spevacek.info).

STATE LANGUAGE SCHOOL BRNO
Jazyková skola s právem státní jazykové zkousky, Kotlárská 9, 602 00 Brno
🖰 kucerova@sjs-brno.cz
💻 www.sjs-brno.cz

NUMBER OF TEACHERS: 2.
PREFERENCE OF NATIONALITY: British.
QUALIFICATIONS: Must have TEFL qualification.
CONDITIONS OF EMPLOYMENT: 1 academic year (September to June). Approximately 20 hours per week.
SALARY: About 18,000 Czech crowns per month.
FACILITIES/SUPPORT: Assistance with finding accommodation, full help with work permits and training available at staff meetings.
RECRUITMENT: Liaise with other schools.
CONTACT: Iveta Kucerová, Deputy Director.

SWALLOW SCHOOL OF ENGLISH
Mrštíkova 399/2a, 460 07 Liberec III
✆ +420 603 829171
🖰 info@swallow.cz
💻 www.swallow.cz

NUMBER OF TEACHERS: 15, mostly for young learners.
PREFERENCE OF NATIONALITY: EU citizens, or others with permission to work in EU.
QUALIFICATIONS: CELTA + 1 year's experience.
CONDITIONS OF EMPLOYMENT: 10 months. Teaching 26 45-minute lessons per week about half on-site and half off-site.
SALARY: Approx. 20,000–25,000 crowns per month (gross) less about 3,000 crowns in contributions.
FACILITIES/SUPPORT: Advice given on finding affordable accommodation in the range of 4,000–7,500 crowns per month. Assistance with paperwork given to non-EU teachers.
RECRUITMENT: Via tefl.com. Interviews mainly by Skype.
CONTACT: Richard Hunter, Director.

THE PHILADELPHIA ACADEMY s.r.o.
T.G.M. 916/111, 293 01 Mladá Boleslav
✆ +420 326 733386
🖰 philadel@philadel.com
💻 www.philadel.com

Member of AJSA.
NUMBER OF TEACHERS: Approx. 40 in total.
PREFERENCE OF NATIONALITY: None (though visas for Canadian and Australian citizens are problematic).
QUALIFICATIONS: BA/MA in English plus TEFL/TESOL/CELTA.
CONDITIONS OF EMPLOYMENT: 1 school year at least. About 25 hours per week (20 guaranteed – more is possible).
SALARY: 200 crowns per hour. Deductions depend on agreement.
FACILITIES/SUPPORT: Fully furnished flat with satellite dish, DVD player, etc located 15 minutes walking distance from the school building – paid for by school, except for utilities.
RECRUITMENT: Internet advertising. Interviews essential.
CONTACT: Dana Zbíralová, Owner.

TUTOR SCHOOL
U Půjčovny 2, Prague 1
✆ +420 210 084210
🖰 jobs@tutor.cz
💻 www.tutor.cz

Part of EDUA Group (www.eduagroup.cz) and associated with Caledonian School (see above entry) though a separate legal entity.

NUMBER OF TEACHERS: Most vacancies in Prague and Brno.

PREFERENCE OF NATIONALITY: Teachers with EU citizenship preferred due to visa requirements.

QUALIFICATIONS: Teachers must have TEFL/TESOL/CELTA qualification with or without teaching experience.

CONDITIONS OF EMPLOYMENT: 1-year contract, usually from September, with possibility of renewal. 22 to 26 45-minute lessons a week. Most teaching takes place in-company.

SALARY: Approx 18,000–20,000 crowns per month (after 15% deduction for tax) for qualified teachers, depending on number of hours worked. Health insurance must be arranged independently.

FACILITIES/SUPPORT: Assistance in finding accommodation is not provided.

RECRUITMENT: Interviews carried out in person or via Skype. Applicants must complete a lesson plan task as part of the interview. School hires year round.

VISTA WELCOME
Volsinach 2300/75 (Atrium House), Strašnice,100 00 Prague 10
✆ +420 284 862345
✉ vista@iol.cz
🖥 www.vista-welcome.cz

NUMBER OF TEACHERS: 6 native speakers. 32 Czech teachers.

PREFERENCE OF NATIONALITY: British, Canadian and American.

QUALIFICATIONS: TEFL certificate and/or proven ELS teaching experience. Mature teachers preferred, though enthusiasm important. School does not want to hire people who are just looking for a way to see the world. Experience in teaching Business English a plus.

CONDITIONS OF EMPLOYMENT: 1-year contract minimum. Teaching hours vary. Full-time teachers guaranteed at least 20 lessons (45 minutes each) per week. Courses aimed at firms and organisations looking for in-house courses. Teachers often work for more than one school to get enough teaching hours.

SALARY: 230 crowns per hour plus medical and social insurance; or 320 crowns without insurance.

FACILITIES/SUPPORT: No accommodation provided though advice may be given to new arrivals.

RECRUITMENT: Adverts in the local English-language newspaper for expats, the internet and via other schools in Prague.

SLOVAK REPUBLIC

Slovakia has been somewhat neglected not only by tourists but by teachers as well. As one language school director put it a couple of years ago:

Many teachers head for Prague, which is why Slovakia stands aside of the main flow of the teachers. That's a pity as Prague is crowded with British and Americans while there's a lack of the teachers here in Slovakia.

Another wrote from a small Slovakian town: '*It would be wonderful if through your book more native speakers come to Slovakia.*' The density of private language schools in the capital, Bratislava, and in the other main cities such as Banska Bystrika makes an on-the-ground job hunt promising.

Once considered a backward part of Europe, huge resources have been poured into the country's development including into increasing access to English instruction. The European Social Fund has targeted groups who need English and provided subsidised or even free courses for people working in education or the civil service. As a result, a substantial demand exists for native English teachers, although the wages are fairly low so many teachers tend to take on private students and/or economise. The salary range for teachers is €550–€800 net, €750–€1,100 gross. Many schools pay by the lesson, which should start at around €12. Schools that provide free accommodation of course offer a lower wage. The flat rate of tax in Slovakia is 20%.

It used to be a level playing field for English-speaking foreigners wanting to teach in Slovakia, but now EU citizens have a clear advantage, needing only to confirm residency for tax purposes. Registration can be done at the local police station. In order to obtain a trade licence, which is necessary for self-employed freelancers, you will have to supply a sworn declaration that you have not been convicted of any crimes for the previous 10 years, something that can be done at the British Embassy in Bratislava (for a fee). Many teachers go freelance after one or two years of working for a school, which is advantageous for both schools and teachers. Freelancers may have less security but earn more.

For candidates from outside the EU, the Slovak visa process is expensive and time consuming. The main costs are getting a criminal record check from the teacher's home country (cost varies) and the visa fee. The applicant will have to submit a medical certificate, evidence of accommodation (ie a document from your landlord/lady) and so on. A blood test must be carried out at the Oddelenie cudzokrajnych chorob, Fakultna Hospital in Bratislava, Martin or Kosice, as a pre-requisite for a residence permit. All documents will have to be translated, notarised and/or apostilled. Most employers guide their teachers through the process but not many will cover the cost.

A programme open to non-EU candidates as well as Europeans is run by Edulink Language School (see entry). This semi-volunteer programme recruits native speakers to teach English for an academic year.

The British Council at Panská 17 in Bratislava's old town (www.britishcouncil.sk) sometimes advertises vacancies for freelance teachers to start in September. The English-language weekly newspaper, the *Slovak Spectator* published on Mondays, doesn't carry many adverts of interest to people looking for teaching work. However, it does publish its Career Guide every February for €5 and also online the very useful business directory the Green Pages; see http://greenpages.spectator.sme.sk/en/c/language-schools.html which includes a list of about 60 language schools with full contact details.

Although wages can be low, prices for food and meals out are not expensive. Accommodation in Bratislava is about twice as expensive as in small towns in Central Slovakia.

Budapest, Vienna and Prague are all within easy reach. Slovakia also offers good conditions for mountain walking in the Tatras along thousands of miles of hiking routes up to an altitude of 2,500m and for mountain cycling.

Michael Todd, who was a senior teacher at IH Bratislava, enjoyed living in Slovakia, but had a few reservations:

Typically, teachers stay one or two years and move on to another country. Bratislava is more a place to get experience. It's nice enough, well located, but turnover is very high as Bratislava just doesn't have enough to hold teachers, unless of course, they start dating a local. I've met a lot of people from different countries, seen a lot of interesting places around Bratislava and have been introduced to literatures I hadn't known about. It's rewarding that I'm helping people and can believe in my work rather than working for some company that sells some product. But the pay is low and the hours can be long. Accommodation is ok but it's kind of like being in university again as we share apartments with other teachers and tend to have hand-me-down furniture. Landlords/ladies are often controlling and seem to view your renting from them not as a business arrangement but as if they are doing you some personal favour. On a further note, I wouldn't have stayed in Slovakia as long as I have except that I've been dating an Austrian woman and, as an American, moving to Austria just wasn't an option. Bratislava is ok, it's not hard to live here but it's not in the league of Prague or Budapest. Usually when I visit some nearby city, I feel a little depressed coming back to Bratislava.

GEOFF NUNNEY

Geoff Nunney enjoyed a stint in Slovakia so much that he stayed on for several years. First he worked at Vages School (www.vages.sk), then at Lingua School (www.lingua-english.sk) in Nitra and the Rain School in nearby Šala (www.rainschool.sk), both east of the capital, and finally at a bilingual *gymnázium* or grammar school in Čadca, which had been arranged through the excellent UK-based organisation SOL (which is no longer recruiting teachers as of 2015).

It's thanks to your book that I found Slovakia. I teach at two local schools and two businesses here, including a brewery, in Nitra. The people here are great and were incredibly supportive when I lost both parents last year and also when I returned to England for treatment for a chronic health problem.

During the school's opening hours (7am-8pm) I teach kids, teenagers and adult conversation classes. The school provides good teaching resources, internet, copying and up-to-date textbooks. The recruitment processes were very thorough, consisting of a face-to-face interview with the head teacher, who was very informative, approachable and asked relevant questions.

The best thing you need in Slovakia is a sense of humour. I have been in school plays, and they are a very friendly nation of people. Their standard of English is very good, and they are great fun to teach. For example last Friday, a student stopped me and said, 'Geoff, the walls have ears' to demonstrate his mastery of an English idiom. Oh yes, I am even dating a Slovak teacher, who asked me out - very forward people the Slovaks - she stole my business card, rang my mobile, and we had a night out at the Irish Pub in Nitra. So things are definitely looking up.

Teaching wages in Slovakia allow you to cover the basic cost of living, but not much else. You can survive, pay the bills, but don't expect to save a lot. Although wages aren't great here, the locals and the scenery and the supportive staff make up for it. I speak a little Slovak, and if you immerse yourself, you will get the rewards. I love it out here, and it has stunning mountains and walking country. I would describe it all as a Slovak adventure!

LIST OF EMPLOYERS

ACADEMIA ISTROPOLITANA NOVA
Prostredna 47/A, 900 21 Svaty Jur
+421 2 4497 0451
ruth@ainova.sk
www.ainova.sk

NUMBER OF TEACHERS: 6.
PREFERENCE OF NATIONALITY: UK citizens.
QUALIFICATIONS: University graduates preferably with pedagogical degree or holders of CELTA, TEFL or other internationally recognised certificate.
CONDITIONS OF EMPLOYMENT: 1-year contract, 80 teaching hours per month. Part-time teachers to work on trade licence (*živnosť*) or on an agreement basis (*dohoda*) in and around Bratislava.
SALARY: By agreement.
FACILITIES/SUPPORT: Assistance given in finding accommodation but teachers pay rent.
RECRUITMENT: Personal recommendation and ELT training centres. Phone interviews possible.
CONTACT: Ruth Zorvan, Head of Professional Communication and Language Programmes.

AGENTÚRA VZDELÁVANIA s.r.o.
Pečnianska 6, 851 01 Bratislava
+421 910 787 089 (mobile)
info@agenturavzdelavania.sk
www.agenturavzdelavania.sk

NUMBER OF TEACHERS: 6 part-timers.
PREFERENCE OF NATIONALITY: None.
QUALIFICATIONS: Higher education, teaching experience. Having some expertise in a specific profession, such as law, medicine, accounting, finance or marketing is an advantage.
CONDITIONS OF EMPLOYMENT: Open-ended employment. 6–10 hours a week.
SALARY: €12–€25 per 60-minute lesson. All taxes and levies are paid by the teacher.
FACILITIES/SUPPORT: No help with accommodation or visas.
RECRUITMENT: Internet job boards, interviews.
CONTACT: Alžbeta Rigáňová, Managing Director.

AKADEMIA VZDELAVANIA – ACADEMY OF EDUCATION
Gorkého 10, 815 17 Bratislava
+421 2 5441 0033
www.akademiavzdelavania.sk

Non-profit adult education association.
NUMBER OF TEACHERS: Approximately 20 full-time posts in branches throughout Slovakia. Branches recruit individually and are linked from website.
PREFERENCE OF NATIONALITY: Native English speaker holding an EU member state passport.
QUALIFICATIONS: CELTA or TESOL qualification (or recognised equivalent) and degree. Energy, enthusiasm and an interest in people required. Must be willing to teach a range of classes, including teenagers or young learners.
CONDITIONS OF EMPLOYMENT: 1 academic year (mid-September to end of June). Teachers' contracts are for a maximum of 22.5 contact hours per week.
SALARY: Competitive salary plus accommodation allowance, local travel pass, health insurance, luncheon vouchers and contribution to airfares.

FACILITIES/SUPPORT: Work and residence permits arranged and paid for. Academic and pastoral support, regular seminars and workshops; orientation for new teachers.

CONTACT: Director of Studies.

CALEDONIAN SCHOOL
Vltavská 24, Prague 5
+421 2 5731 3650
jobs@caledonianschool.com
www.caledonianschool.com

Teachers hired for schools in Slovakia as well as the Czech Republic – see entry in chapter on Czech Republic.

CANADIAN LANGUAGE SCHOOL NITRA
Kupecká 6, Nitra 949 01
+421 904 371 050 (Office)
info@canadian.sk or phil@canadian.sk
www.facebook.com/Canadian.Language.School.
NITRA

NUMBER OF TEACHERS: Currently 6, but intending to expand to 8.

PREFERENCE OF NATIONALITY: EU citizen (due to slow and expensive bureaucratic processes in Slovakia). Teachers must have clear English.

QUALIFICATIONS: TESOL/CELTA is generally the minimum; however, director is more interested in finding exciting and effective teachers with 'the right stuff' who will never be boring.

CONDITIONS OF EMPLOYMENT: Minimum 6 months with ongoing opportunities. 35 actual hours per week, spread across the spectrum of the day.

SALARY: Above the average local salary to attract and retain the best teachers.

FACILITIES/SUPPORT: All taxes, health and social insurance and flat are provided from the gross salary. Non-EU teachers have to pay their own visa-related expenses, including waiting up to 3 months to see if their visa will be approved, prior to being able to start work. School offers intensive 2-week 'Teach-the-Teacher' summer courses.

RECRUITMENT: Skype interviews are possible.

CONTACT: Philip Le Mottee, Director.

EDULINK LANGUAGE SCHOOL S.R.O.
Radlinského 4, Trnava 917 01
+421 910 428 281
trnava@edulink.sk
www.edulink.sk/jobs

NUMBER OF TEACHERS: 4 semi-volunteers to teach English (or French) for an academic year to adults and children in Trnava and Bratislava.

PREFERENCE OF NATIONALITY: Countries where English is spoken as a first language.

QUALIFICATIONS: TEFL certificate and a can-do attitude.

CONDITIONS OF EMPLOYMENT: 1 academic year. 38 'scholar hours' (each hour is 45 minutes).

SALARY: €500 a month.

FACILITIES/SUPPORT: Homestay or shared accommodation is arranged and paid for, plus medical insurance, visa support and holidays. Guidance given on how to apply for documentation in their home countries to apply for work permit; red tape within Slovakia is paid for by school.

RECRUITMENT: International TEFL websites or referrals. Skype interviews.

CONTACT: Pero Hattingh, Owner/Director.

EUROTREND 21
Namestie slobody 16, 811 06 Bratislava
+421 2 5249 4350
info@eurotrend21.sk or office@eurotrend21.sk
www.eurotrend21.sk

NUMBER OF TEACHERS: 4.

PREFERENCE OF NATIONALITY: None.

QUALIFICATIONS: Minimum university degree, TEFL certificate and experience.

CONDITIONS OF EMPLOYMENT: Minimum contract 6 months. Hours are available mornings, afternoons and evenings.

SALARY: Dependent on experience. Starts at €12 per 45-minute lesson.

RECRUITMENT: Interviews are essential and are carried out on-site.

CONTACT: Coordinator of Language Courses.

HARMONY SCHOOL
26 Kapitulska, 917 01 Trnava
+421 33 534 4982
info@harmony.sk
www.harmony.sk; www.lal.sk

NUMBER OF TEACHERS: 15 full-and part-time teachers.

PREFERENCE OF NATIONALITY: EU citizens.

QUALIFICATIONS: CELTA/DELTA or equivalent.

CONDITIONS OF EMPLOYMENT: 1-year contract with 25 teaching hours and 10 admin hours per week.

SALARY: €1,000–€1,200.

FACILITIES/SUPPORT: Assistance given with finding accommodation.

RECRUITMENT: Interviews are essential.

CONTACT: Jana Chynoradska, Managing Principal (jana@harmony.sk) or Eva Paršová, Adviser (eva@harmony.sk).

INSTITÚT EURÓPSKYCH JAZYKOV

Nam. Osloboditelov 10, 071 01 Michalovce

 +421 907 448 408

 institut.ej@gmail.com

 www.institut.sk

NUMBER OF TEACHERS: Rolling vacancies.

QUALIFICATIONS: Must be university graduate. School is looking for professionalism, strong educational background, experience, personality, and communication and people skills. Teachers should be patient, enthusiastic, good team players, with a sense of humour.

CONDITIONS OF EMPLOYMENT: Semesters start mid-September, early January and early April. 90-minute lessons. Many clients are graduates and civil servants, since the European Social Fund pays for free English courses for these categories.

FACILITIES/SUPPORT: Accommodation provided and help given with settling into local area.

CONTACT: Petra Gondkovicova, Owner/Manager.

INTERNATIONAL HOUSE BRATISLAVA

Namestie SNP 14, 811 06 Bratislava

 +421 2 5296 2674

 info@ihbratislava.sk

 www.ihbratislava.sk

NUMBER OF TEACHERS: 20, especially young specialists.

PREFERENCE OF NATIONALITY: EU citizens.

QUALIFICATIONS: Minimum Cambridge CELTA/Trinity Cert and preferably 1 year's experience in YL teaching or Cambridge exam preparation. A degree is not essential.

CONDITIONS OF EMPLOYMENT: 10 months. Average 25 teaching hours per week (no weekends). Mainly off-site teaching. plus children's classes, general and business English.

SALARY: Full-time contract teachers are paid €752–€1,011 per month gross unless they want to live in a shared, school flat, in which case pay is reduced to €536–€795 gross (€433–€614 net). Freelance contracts pay more but the teacher pays for his/her own contributions.

FACILITIES/SUPPORT: Full-time teachers are offered rent-free accommodation in shared flats. Assistance given with red tape. Workshops and training sessions.

RECRUITMENT: Via www.tefl.com. Interviews are essential and can be carried out be telephone/Skype.

CONTACT: Jon de la Fuente, Director of Studies (dos@ihbratislava.sk).

JAZYKOVÁ SKOLA START

Miestnost c71, Kriva 18, 040 01 Kosice

 +421 917 642230

 recruitment@jazykova.sk

 www.jazykova.sk/jobs.php

Also has a branch in Presov.

NUMBER OF TEACHERS: 10.

PREFERENCE OF NATIONALITY: Native English speakers, mainly British, American, Australian.

QUALIFICATIONS: TEFL or previous experience is an advantage.

CONDITIONS OF EMPLOYMENT: 1 academic year, extendable to a permanent contract. Usual hours are 3pm–8pm with some morning lessons.

SALARY: By negotiation.

FACILITIES/SUPPORT: School finds accommodation for teachers. School assists logistically but not financially with visas (eg €170). EU citizens do not require visas.

RECRUITMENT: Via the internet. Also, a number of teachers come to Slovakia because they are in a relationship with a local and their partners make the initial contact in response to advertising. Interviews are carried out by phone or Skype. In the case of teachers already in Slovakia they are carried out in person.

CONTACT: Richard Swales, Director.

MHC BUSINESS LANGUAGE TRAINING s.r.o.

Zamocká 30, 811 01 Bratislava

 +43 1 603 0563 (HQ in Vienna)

 office@mhc-training.com

 www.mhc-training.com/en/jobs

Sister school of MHC in Austria.

NUMBER OF TEACHERS: 25.

PREFERENCE OF NATIONALITY: Any.

QUALIFICATIONS: MHC trainers have an understanding of business experience, often specialising in areas such as marketing, finance, pharmaceuticals or law. A degree is not necessary, although a teaching certificate such as CELTA would be of value.

CONDITIONS OF EMPLOYMENT: Freelance, teaching 15–25 hours per week.

SALARY: €16–€20 per 60 minutes, depending on experience and development with MHC. Seminars pay between €200 and

€250 per day. Trainers are responsible for paying their own taxes (about 19%) and social security (variable).

FACILITIES/SUPPORT: Resource library in Vienna, photocopying at clients' premises, trainer development. Books required for courses. Trainers from non-EU countries require working papers.

RECRUITMENT: Interviews are essential and usually take place at premises. Possibility of Skype interview if the applicant is based abroad.

CONTACT: Mark Heather, Managing Director (mark.heather@ mhc-training.com).

SIDAS LANGUAGE SCHOOL
P.C. Strojar, Juzna Trieda 93, 040 01 Kosice
✆ +421 905 853127
✍ schofield@sidaschool.com
🖥 www.sidaschool.com

Also operate in the Czech Republic and Austria.

NUMBER OF TEACHERS: 15-20 for both set-location and peripatetic posts.

PREFERENCE OF NATIONALITY: British and Irish, but native speakers from other countries welcome.

QUALIFICATIONS: Ideally applicants will have a first degree and TEFL qualifications. Training and assistance are provided to people with no real experience.

CONDITIONS OF EMPLOYMENT: Three programmes: Natives in Schools in which teachers teach primary and secondary school children as part of the normal English-medium curriculum in all subjects; Active English Weeks, which require teachers to travel town-to-town for a minimum of 4 weeks delivering week-long courses of active English to children of mixed abilities; and children's Summer Day Camps in varying towns which involve sport, drama and very little classroom teaching. Also after-school opportunities in nursery schools for teachers based in one town for the academic year. Hours for set-location teachers typically 8am-2pm Monday to Friday, but some work 1pm-7pm.

SALARY: Competitive local salary that can increase over time.

FACILITIES/SUPPORT: Free accommodation during the working week. Company finds a flat, usually shared with fellow Sidas teachers, for teachers in set locations. Help given with permits. Training provided before and during the working period.

RECRUITMENT: Via tefl.com, etc. Skype interviews.

CONTACT: Dave Schofield, Managing Director.

THE ENGLISH CLUB
Pri Suchom mlyne 36, 811 04 Bratislava
✆ +421 904 415490
✍ oravecmartin@ba.telecom.sk
🖥 www.theenglishclub.sk

NUMBER OF TEACHERS: 2–4.

PREFERENCE OF NATIONALITY: British.

QUALIFICATIONS: University degree plus TEFL/TESL/CELTA and 1 year's experience.

CONDITIONS OF EMPLOYMENT: 10-month contract from September to June. Working hours between 7am and 9.45pm, 30 hours per week.

SALARY: From €7 per 45 minutes.

FACILITIES/SUPPORT: Shared flat with wi-fi is available. All necessary paperwork for work permits is completed by the school.

RECRUITMENT: Usually via the internet. Interviews are essential.

CONTACT: Martin Oravec, Director.

HUNGARY

English is compulsory for all Hungarian students who wish to apply for college or university entrance, and university students in both the arts and sciences must take courses in English. The Hungarian education system has much to be proud of, not least the efficacy with which it retrained its Russian teachers as English teachers after the return to democracy in 1989. The network of bilingual secondary schools (*gimnazia*) has produced a large number of graduates with a sophisticated knowledge of English. In cities and even some small towns, bilingual schools now operate at the elementary level as well. From first grade onwards, students study basic subjects in English and Hungarian. The vast majority of private language schools are owned and run by Hungarians rather than expats. Even though the calibre of Hungarian teachers is very high, some schools still seem keen to employ native English teachers.

The invasion of foreigners in Budapest was never as overwhelming as it was (and is) in Prague, but still Budapest has a glut of teachers, among them some who have fled over-crowded Prague. The opportunities that do exist now are mostly in the provinces. Even in the more remote parts of the country, formal academic qualifications are important. It is a legal requirement that the bilingual schools employ a native English speaker as lector. Most *gimnazia* liaise with the Fulbright Commission or the Central European Teaching Program and take on Americans, though Britons are also eligible.

Teachers are poorly paid in Hungary, aside from in the top-notch private schools. Rents in Budapest are high and take a major proportion of a teacher's salary; some schools help by subsidising accommodation, or it may be possible to arrange accommodation in return for English lessons. Teachers through the Central European Teaching Program (see entry) have housing and utilities provided. Low as the salaries may seem, native English speakers can console themselves with the thought that they are usually better paid than Hungarian university lecturers.

FINDING A JOB

Very few jobs in Hungary are advertised in the international TEFL press and only a handful of teaching companies publish information for job-seekers on their sites, for example Cambridge Schools (www.cambridge.hu), Angol Intezet (English Institute) with seven branches in Budapest (www.angolintezet.hu) catering for corporate clients, M-Prospect (www.m-prospect.hu/job) and Berlitz (recruiting@berlitz.hu). In the USA, recruitment of conversational English teachers and sometimes of other academic subjects as well takes place via the Central European Teaching Program (CETP, see entry). The programme offers 'cultural immersion through teaching' and is open to anyone with a university degree, preferably some experience of TEFL and overseas teaching/study experience and a willingness to pay the programme fee. CETP liaises with the relevant government department in Hungary to place teachers in state schools as well as in some parochial schools throughout the country. Hungary has a network of Dual Language Grammar Schools in which English is the medium of instruction for some subjects.

The website of the Hungarian Association of Language Schools (NYESZE) has a searchable listing of member schools at www.nyelviskola.hu.

AFTER ARRIVAL

The British Council in Budapest (www.britishcouncil.hu) operates teaching centres on both the Buda and Pest sides of the capital. In 2015 it was looking to hire 'high performing hourly-paid teachers of English' particularly of young learners (teaching@britishcouncil.hu).

Of interest to Americans is the Regional English Language Office located in the Public Diplomacy section of the US Embassy (Szabadság tér 12, 1054 Budapest; RELOBudapest@state.gov; http://hungary.usembassy.gov/relo.html). Unlike the British Council, the Regional Office receives English language specialists and fellows from the US.

PRIVATE SCHOOLS

While it has become increasingly difficult for foreigners to find teaching jobs in Hungarian state schools, private institutes provide more scope, primarily to meet the needs of the business community and also for children whose parents are keen for them to supplement the English teaching at state schools. It is estimated that there are over 100 private language schools in Budapest alone and 300 around the country, both very fluid numbers since schools open and close so quickly. Many private schools use native English speakers as live commercials for the schools, though nowadays they want to advertise the qualifications of their teachers too.

Anyone with a recognised TEFL Certificate and experience of the business world has a chance of finding at least some hourly teaching after arrival in Budapest or elsewhere. Institutes catering to the business market seem to have weathered a national policy change that stipulated that language training did not count as vocational training for the purposes of state subsidies. Companies that had received some funding to send employees to English courses have had to retrench.

To find the less well-established schools on the spot, keep your eyes open for the flyers posted in the main shopping streets or check out the English-language weeklies. Occasionally teaching jobs are advertised on English-language sites such as www.budapestjobs.net and www.xpatloop.com/classifieds.

Private tutoring provides one way of supplementing a meagre salary. Freelance teachers may find a developing market for their linguistic expertise among company executives. The Department of Commerce, for example, employs teachers to train bankers, traders and top electrical engineers. A UK-based online service was launched in 2014 to match prospective native-speaker tutors with learners in Budapest: LearnEnglishBudapest.com vets aspiring teachers and, once approved, posts mini-biographies on their site for Hungarians to contact directly. They have fixed prices for lessons in the range of 3000-6000 forints an hour, according to qualifications and experience as well as location and time of lessons. Another company that connects freelance teachers with adults, children and companies seeking private tuition is PENNA Native English Teachers (www.AnyanyelviAngolTanarok.hu). Obviously these companies do not assist with teaching premises, so you will have to find a suitable place for your tutorials. Apparently upstairs at Burger King is a favourite. Note that Hungarian taxes quickly become a headache for freelance teachers, since the government by law takes 26% of earnings.

REGULATIONS

Since Hungary is a full member of the EU, EU citizens do not require a residence permit, and immigration procedures have been much simplified. However, before the 93rd day of their stay, they should report their presence to their nearest regional Office of Immigration and Nationality. The office will issue a registration certificate, which permits indefinite stays. EU citizens working full-time in Hungary are subject to the same social security and pension obligations as Hungarians. Employees must make payments into the National Health Insurance Fund and into a pension fund.

Non-EU citizens must arrange a visa before leaving their country of residence and then apply for a work/residence permit. A foreign employee cannot be legally paid until she or he has a work permit (which costs 5,000 forints). This fee has been waived for those applying to teach through the Central European Teaching

Program (CETP). Those nationals who require a work permit must find a Hungarian employer who is entitled to apply for a work permit from the relevant Regional Employment Office.

To obtain a one-year residence permit, non-EU nationals must jump through a series of hoops, and provide everything from a title deed for their accommodation to bank statements. An American teacher and blogger set out all the steps he took a couple of years ago; he rose to the challenge of what he describes as a 'highly ordered scavenger hunt' and helpfully describes the process at https://budabeats.wordpress.com (search for 'Residence').

CONDITIONS OF WORK

Salaries vary, but teachers at private institutes tend to earn from 2,500 forints (€8) an hour or 250,000 forints a month. It is essential to find out whether pay is net or gross since Hungarians lose more than a quarter of their already meagre wages in tax and contributions. It is also important to check whether your employer is taking out insurance on your behalf: an insurance mix-up turned **Ellen Parham**'s 'satisfactory' high-school salary into something worse than meagre.

American graduate and CETP participant **Genevieve Pierce** found that teaching teenagers in a state school could be challenging:

> *They were totally uninterested in learning, didn't complete their homework, and lacked any opinion or view-point. This is a result of the political situation in Hungary and the low salaries. I am sure my students overhear their parents complain about money and politics constantly, which has to drain the students' hope for a future. I think they feel trapped in Hungary. One student even said, 'Why should I do my homework when I'm going to live in Hungary and be a shop clerk like my mother?'*

On a more positive note, Genevieve found that going to class with a topic that everyone could talk about and allowing lessons to evolve was a more successful teaching strategy than following a strict lesson plan. In general students in the rural areas of Eastern Hungary are better behaved than their counterparts in Budapest, though their level of English will be lower. This kind of problem won't arise if you are teaching in the business community.

LEISURE TIME

The Opera House in Budapest is one of the most beautiful in the world, the Széchenyi thermal baths are the perfect place to unwind graciously and the cutting-edge 'ruin bars' set up in derelict buildings make for a fantastic and arty nightlife. It is easy to make a strong argument for living in Budapest, but there are downsides, as long-stay American teacher **Ellen Parham** explains:

> *Everything is convenient for me here in Budapest, but some of the others in the CETP programme who are teaching in smaller towns are treated like celebrities and everyone knows them. Living in a big city is hindering my ability to speak Hungarian, too. Everyone speaks English and I am never forced to speak Hungarian.*

Being made to speak this notoriously difficult language, however, can be a mixed blessing, as **Genevieve Pierce** discovered while living in a quaint city on the Romanian border:

> *Teaching in a place where you don't speak the language is difficult because you feel like a child. I seriously need a babysitter if I'm going to do anything of grave importance (ie visit the doctor, purchase a bicycle, arrange a*

postage delivery). Though, with all that said, teaching abroad has been the best experience of my life. I love to see students' faces when they finally realise what I'm talking about. I have enjoyed all the school functions such as dances, initiation ceremonies and graduation. The best part has been learning about another culture, understanding their way of life. It's like nothing I could learn from a book.

LIST OF EMPLOYERS

AMEROPA LANGUAGE SCHOOL
Oktobér Huszonharmadika u. 5, 1117 Budapest
- +36 1 209 3993
- ameropa@ameropatraining.hu
- www.ameropatraining.hu

NUMBER OF TEACHERS: 60.
PREFERENCE OF NATIONALITY: None.
QUALIFICATIONS: Minimum bachelor's degree and teacher training (TEFL, CELTA or equivalent).
CONDITIONS OF EMPLOYMENT: Ongoing contracts, usually between 6 and 24 months with 10–20 working hours per week.
SALARY: Competitive.
FACILITIES/SUPPORT: Assistance given with work permits.
RECRUITMENT: Interview and demonstration lesson are essential.

CENTRAL EUROPEAN TEACHING PROGRAM
3800 NE, 72nd Avenue, Portland, OR 97213, USA
- +1 503 287 4977
- mary.cetp@gmail.com; hildie.cetp@gmail.com; hajni.cetp@gmail.com
- www.cetp.info

NUMBER OF TEACHERS: 90–100.
PREFERENCE OF NATIONALITY: Native English speakers: USA, Canada, the UK and native English-speaking Europeans.
QUALIFICATIONS: Minimum: bachelor's degree plus 40-hour online TEFL certificate. Retired people welcome.
CONDITIONS OF EMPLOYMENT: Standard contract 10 months (1 school year), although teachers can sometimes be placed for winter semester only. To teach 22–26 hours per week.
SALARY: $450–$750 per month after taxes, paid in local currency.
FACILITIES/SUPPORT: All teachers receive a furnished apartment with utilities paid. Apartments range from a small studio to a spacious 1 or 2-bedroom flat. All are equipped with TV and washing machine, among other amenities. CETP provides teachers with all necessary documents for residence and work permits and health insurance cover. A week-long orientation is provided in Budapest prior to the start of the school term. A Hungarian director and her assistant oversee CETP teachers throughout the year.
RECRUITMENT: Via word of mouth, the internet and university placement offices. CETP programme fee is $1,800–$2,500 for an academic year, $1,500–$1,800 for one semester. The lower fees are for primary schools in rural areas.
CONTACT: Mary Rose, Director.

FUNSIDE ASSOCIATION
Villanyi ut 14, 1114 Budapest
- +36 1 950 950 2
- tabor@funside.hu
- www.funside.eu

NUMBER OF TEACHERS: 5–6 per summer season for 20 international children's camps on Lake Balaton and in Budapest (as well as in Austria).
PREFERENCE OF NATIONALITY: None as long as they are native English speakers.
QUALIFICATIONS: Teaching English as a second language experience, as well as experience working with children. Camp experience preferred. University students and teachers staying in Budapest are welcome to apply. A criminal records check may be required.
CONDITIONS OF EMPLOYMENT: 5 weeks during summer period, long hours.
SALARY: Agreed on an individual basis. Some expenses covered.
FACILITIES/SUPPORT: Accommodation and meals provided (at overnight camps only).
RECRUITMENT: Only via online application form from January. Interviews are essential between February and May, preferably in person, alternatively on Skype.
CONTACT: András Kittka, Director (+36 30 9776 111).

INTERNATIONAL HOUSE BUDAPEST

Language School & Teacher Training Institute, Vermezo
u. 4, 1012 Budapest

☎ +36 1 212 4010

✉ dos@ih.hu

🖥 www.ih.hu

NUMBER OF TEACHERS: 40.

QUALIFICATIONS: Minimum: Cambridge CELTA.

CONDITIONS OF EMPLOYMENT: Contracts are for 25 contact
hours per week including in-company teaching, teaching young
learners, groups, one-to-one and special projects.

SALARY: 198,000 forints per month (net).

FACILITIES/SUPPORT: Assistance given with finding
accommodation. In-service teacher development.

RECRUITMENT: Through direct application. Interviews essential,
conducted if necessary by telephone or Skype.

CONTACT: Mark Tansey, Director of Studies.

KARINTHY FRIGYES GIMNAZIUM

Thököly ucta 7, Pestlorinc, 1183 Budapest

☎ +36 1 291 2072

✉ bognaraniko1@gmail.com

🖥 www.karinthy.hu

NUMBER OF TEACHERS: About 70.

PREFERENCE OF NATIONALITY: Native English speakers.

QUALIFICATIONS: MA in English (preferred) or TEFL/TESL
qualification.

CONDITIONS OF EMPLOYMENT: 1–2 year contracts, 22 lessons
a week.

SALARY: National salary plus all costs of accommodation in a
pleasant, fully furnished and equipped flat near the school. 10%
taxes and social security deduction.

FACILITIES/SUPPORT: Assistance with work permits; authorised
copies of degrees and/or certificates are needed by the end of
June.

RECRUITMENT: Application directly through agencies and
foundations. Interviews preferred and conducted via Skype,
webcam or telephone.

CONTACT: Ms Aniko Bognar, Deputy Head.

KATEDRA LANGUAGE SCHOOL NETWORK

Anker köz 1–3, 1061 Budapest

☎ +36 1 700 0137

✉ tanar@katedra.hu

🖥 www.katedra.hu

NUMBER OF TEACHERS: 15 for franchised schools in 37 towns
plus 10 locations in Budapest.

PREFERENCE OF NATIONALITY: Native English speakers.

QUALIFICATIONS: CELTA, DELTA or equivalent.

CONDITIONS OF EMPLOYMENT: Standard contract is 6–12
months, 12 to 16 45-minute lessons per week.

SALARY: From 2,750 to 3,250 forints per lesson.

FACILITIES/SUPPORT: Assistance given with applying for work
permits. Also offer teacher training certificate courses (see
Training Directory).

RECRUITMENT: Interview and mock lesson in Budapest is
essential.

CONTACT: Ildikó Tóth, Director of Studies (tothildiko@katedra.hu).

LIVING LANGUAGE SEMINAR

Eló Nyelvek Szemináriuma, Fejér György u. 8–10, 1053
Budapest

☎ +36 1 317 9644

✉ info@elonyelvek.hu or elonyelv@t-online.hu

🖥 www.elonyelvek.hu

NUMBER OF TEACHERS: 3–5 native English speakers.

PREFERENCE OF NATIONALITY: British, American,
Canadian.

QUALIFICATIONS: A great deal of ESL teaching experience,
registered City & Guilds, Local State Examinations centre.
Preparation for City & Guilds, Cambridge and local ITK-Origó
exams, TOEFL iBT, business English.

CONDITIONS OF EMPLOYMENT: Contracts from 3 months.
Negotiable hours. Mainly teaching adults (aged 16–40).

SALARY: High by local standards.

FACILITIES/SUPPORT: No assistance with accommodation at
present.

RECRUITMENT: Through adverts. Interviews required.

CONTACT: Paul Biró, Director.

MANHATTAN LANGUAGE SCHOOL

Örs vezér tér 25/C, 1106 Budapest

☎ +36 1 431 8630

✉ info@manhattannyelvstudio.hu

🖥 www.manhattannyelvstudio.hu

NUMBER OF TEACHERS: 8–10 depending on the term. Also for
branch in Pest: Kiscelli utca 7–9, 1032 Budapest.

PREFERENCE OF NATIONALITY: None.

QUALIFICATIONS: Teaching qualification (preferably CELTA or
equivalent) and some teaching experience.

CONDITIONS OF EMPLOYMENT: Teachers work on freelance basis. Working hours depend on the type of course that is taught, eg company courses can start as early as 7am or in-house courses can finish after 8pm.

SALARY: €7–€11 per hour depending on the level taught and location of the course.

RECRUITMENT: Face-to-face interview although on rare occasions a phone interview may suffice. Candidates must also conduct a mock lesson.

TUDOMANY NYELVISKOLA
Tavasz u.3, 1033 Budapest

- +36 1 368 1156
- info@tudomanynyelviskola.hu
- www.tudomanynyelviskola.hu

Sister school is Európai Nyelvek Stúdiója at Tavasz ut 2 (www.enys.hu/english).

NUMBER OF TEACHERS: 10–15.

PREFERENCE OF NATIONALITY: British and American.

QUALIFICATIONS: TEFL/TESL preferred.

CONDITIONS OF EMPLOYMENT: 10-month contracts, hours vary.

FACILITIES/SUPPORT: Assistance with accommodation not usually given. Training sometimes available. Affiliated with ELT training centre Via Lingua Budapest (see Training listings). Discount on course given to those who obtain a distinction or merit and then teach for 2 years.

RECRUITMENT: Local interviews essential. Must teach demo lesson.

CONTACT: Ms Krisztina Tüll (dos@europainyelvek.hu).

POLAND

Prospects for English teachers in Poland, eastern Poland in particular, remain reasonable, even if the seemingly insatiable demand for English teachers that has characterised the past 25 years is now a thing of the past. Poles are still keen to learn English, but with the explosion of no-frills flights and the opening of borders, millions of Poles simply get on a plane and come to Britain or Ireland, to acquire the language while they work.

This is gradually having a knock-on effect on the quality of Polish English teachers working in their home country, although the reverence for 'native speakerhood' still runs high. A famous Polish poet described (in perfect English) how his teenage daughter and her friends largely communicate in English, or at least a form of English picked up from TV shows and pop songs, and that some of the older generation are worried that Poland is becoming swamped by the English language and western culture. Like the rest of Europe, Poland is also moving to introduce English to very young learners from the age of three, so experience of teaching children is highly prized.

For now, certain types of English classes, largely taught by native English speakers, are still popular; according to one director of studies: 'realistic' conversation classes teach Poles how to rent a flat or order a drink, while others teach students how to fill in forms (good luck to them).

Major cities such as Warsaw, Wroclaw, Krakow, Poznan and Gdansk are possible destinations, especially for people with experience of preparing for Cambridge exams or those looking for in-company work. The smaller towns in eastern Poland and in Silesia in southern Poland are more promising destinations, where the competition for jobs will be less intense and you may still receive preferential 'foreigner' treatment if you gain a dependable reputation as a teacher. A contributor to www.polishforums.com wrote to an enquirer:

> *You should be looking at smaller places, less competition for jobs and less competition means more money for you. I live in Katowice and know that schools around here are always looking for teachers. However . . . how to put this . . . it ain't no Paris. Kato has a bad image, but once you know the places to go it's fine. And it's only a 45–60 min drive from Krakow.*

An even more extreme view was posted on the same site: *'The market here in Poland is truly saturated. There are plenty of private language schools in Warsaw now and Krakow is stuffed with native speakers all chasing the same work. The best bet is to look at somewhere in the back woods.'*

Foreign teachers usually find their students friendly, open and keen to learn more about the world. Discussion classes are likely to be informed and lively, with students well up to date on developments and very well motivated to practise their English. In some companies, promotion depends on the level of English achieved, which spurs students from the business world to be especially committed. On the other hand, if the company is paying for an employee's lessons, there may be little incentive to attend regularly or with enthusiasm.

FINDING A JOB

Interested teachers should not expect to be snapped up unless they have at least a TEFL certificate and some sort of teaching experience. International House has a big presence in Poland, with major schools in Bielsko-Biala, Katowice, Torun and Wroclaw among others; vacancies are posted at www.ihworld.com/jobs. Bell Schools can be found in Gdansk, Gdynia, Szczecin and Warsaw. These high-profile ELT organisations are founding members of PASE, the Polish Association for Standards in English, which promotes ethical practices in the private sector. PASE (www.pase.pl) has about 25 member schools. PASE members employ almost exclusively teachers with a recognised teaching qualification and the vast majority have graduated from universities in Poland. Schools approved by the Polish Ministry of Education insist that their teachers have a university degree and a teaching qualification.

In 2015 the British Council was advertising for self-employed English teachers for Warsaw and Wroclaw. Teachers based in Poland were invited to send a CV, covering letter and copy of their TEFL certificates to teach@britishcouncil.pl. The Council also recruits teachers of children and adults for residential summer camps.

ON THE SPOT

Semesters begin on 1 October and 15 February, and the best time to arrive is a month beforehand. After arrival, try to establish some contacts, possibly by visiting the English department at the university. Although some school directors state a preference for British or American accents, many are neutral provided you are a native English speaker.

Private language schools can be found everywhere, catering for all kinds of English. The Warsaw *Yellow Pages* carries several pages under the heading *Jezykowe Kursy, Szkolenia.* Alternatively you can trawl for language schools at www.przewodnik.pase.pl. Check out www.nativespeaker.com.pl where individuals advertise private tuition and some language schools post vacancies. Another possibility is the Polish employment site www.praca.money.pl and search for Lektor jobs. The very busy British Council in Warsaw (near Central station) and the smaller partner offices and libraries in other cities may be able to assist personal callers.

While some institutes have high standards in those they hire, others are looking more for personality, as a rather jaundiced online poster complained on www.polishforums.com:

> It's a sad fact that the English teaching market in Poland is driven by price not quality. School owners want bright and bouncy 21-year-olds straight off a degree, ideally with a CELTA, who are going to entertain the customers and not have an opinion on teaching. They'll complain that 'natives are unreliable' when these 21-year-olds stay in the pub till 2 in the morning on a weekday but it's a fair trade at the end of the day because they won't start demanding better standards like a more experienced teacher would (eg Being paid. On time. As agreed).

If you base yourself in Warsaw and wish to advertise your availability for private English tuition, try advertising in *Gazeta Wyborcza*'s Warsaw section and also Gumtree, which carry small ads in Polish including language teachers. It might also be worth placing a notice just to the right of the main gate of Warsaw University. A further idea is to visit Irlandzki Pub 3 at ul. Miodowa 3 near the castle, which many English speakers use as their watering hole.

Freelancing is popular, and there is demand for tailor-made one-to-one courses, though the economic crisis saw the corporate market shrink. When **Kathy Cooper** was based in the small town of Raciborz in Silesia she worked for three language schools over seven years and also freelanced on the side. She found that once her name was established around town, she had a waiting list of willing students. Banks are likely clients and often pay well by Polish standards. Kathy also taught corporate clients (signed through the school), including in the fields of '*food/chocolate, cement, power plants, furniture, steel, industrial cleaning and sanitation, automotive, banking, industrial equipment, manufacturing, legal profession, doctors, and hotel industry. Yes, I am in Poland, land of opportunity for teachers.*'

Competent freelancers ask for at least 50 zloty an hour though corporate clients pay 90–150 zloty. In cities where there is a glut, some foreigners have been giving lessons for as little as 30 zloty. As usual, private students can be unreliable, so try to get them to pay for a block of lessons in advance. For this work, teachers should have enough ELT awareness to be able to devise their own syllabus. They will also have to put up with early or late hours (8am/9pm) and the inevitable cancelled lessons as business execs reschedule due to important meetings. Kathy Cooper got around this problem simply by calling another business client who wanted to make up lost hours.

HOLIDAY LANGUAGE CAMPS

Some private language-teaching organisations run short-term holiday courses in summer and occasionally winter, requiring native English speakers.

To take one example, the Perfect English private language school (www.perfectenglish.pl) in southern Poland has been seen advertising vacancies for its summer courses held in the mountains or on the seaside, as well as for the academic year. American young people might be interested in volunteering to work at one of the several English-language immersion camps run by the Kosciuszko Foundation's Teaching English in Poland Program (www.thekf.org/programs/teaching_english_in_poland). The three to four-week programme takes place in July. American Ashley Kosciolek blogged on www.independenttraveler.com about her successful summer on the programme:

> *I applied through the Kosciuszko Foundation in New York and spent one month of my first post-college summer at an English immersion camp, instructing teens in the tiny town of Limanowa. The program paid for everything but my flights: housing, food, and trips to places like Krakow, Warsaw and Zakopane on weekends. It even provided a small stipend, which was a welcome surprise at the end of my time there. I made tons of amazing friends with my fellow American teachers, as well as the Polish staff. I'm still in touch with several of them and with many of the students I taught. I quickly adapted to a life with no air-conditioning, no baseball (although we did try to teach the students how to play), crosses on the walls of every classroom, and surpluses of churches and vodka. I took a semester of Polish in college before embarking on the adventure, but my ability to actually speak it improved markedly with each day.*

Short holidays in which paying language learners mingle and interact with native speakers who are given free room and board and transport from the nearest city are organised by Angloville (see entry).

REGULATIONS

Poland's requirements for EU teachers are broadly in line with the rest of Europe. Teachers wishing to stay for more than three months must register their address at the town hall to obtain a *Zameldowanie*, which can then be used to apply for a social insurance number (ZUS) and a tax number (NIP). The latter will be needed in order to be paid by an employer if on a real contract (*umowa o pracy*) or to issue invoices if a registered independent contractor (i.e. freelancer). Employers should assist with the documentation and the necessary translation of official documents into Polish. The minimum monthly ZUS contribution from teachers is 300 zloty, for the first two years.

Non-EU citizens who want to stay for more than 90 days and for less than a year will have to jump through the usual hoops prior to departure from their home country. The required documents must be presented in person to a Polish Consulate: a valid work permit certificate issued by the Office of Wojewoda in Poland or a promissory work permit from your Polish employer, your passport, two photos, a completed application form and the current fee for a work visa. In order for your employer to obtain permission to employ a foreign teacher, he or she will have to submit originals or notarised copies of your degree diploma and TEFL certificate (if applicable) with official translations. After arrival with the visa, you will need to obtain a work permit. Most schools will assist with the documentation but may not bear the financial cost. When the initial visa expires (after three months), it is possible to apply for a residency card from inside Poland, which will be valid for two years. Most employers who take on foreign teachers are well aware of the procedures which, according to one, could fill a book on their own. The Polish Embassy in Washington can provide further details (www.polandembassy.org).

CONDITIONS OF WORK

Generally speaking, private language schools in Poland offer reasonable working conditions. Instead of hearing complaints from teachers about employers, it tends to be more often the other way round, as the Director of Studies of a private language school makes clear:

> *My boss, who has been employing British native speakers for seven years and who has proved to be a very patient person, could provide you with some hair-raising stories of teachers signing their contracts and withdrawing at the very last minute (having probably found a more lucrative job in Asia), teachers returning a couple of days late after the Christmas break without presenting any adequate excuse (or not returning at all), not to mention the state of flats and equipment which, after being used for nine months, are often left in a wrecked condition.*

Wages are higher than they used to be, but the cost of living has really risen too. The current average wage in the private sector is about 45–60 zloty an hour less about a fifth in tax. That means that a teacher working 20 hours a week is likely to clear not much more than $1,000 a month. However, it is becoming more uncommon for overtime to be paid to teachers for hours worked in excess of the contracted number (typically 24) and for transport perks to be offered. Even the most respectable institutes are sometimes guilty of paying their teachers late, as they struggle with cash-flow problems. If you have to rent on the open market, expect to pay the equivalent of at least $300 a month for a small studio flat that may or may not include utilities and internet access. Food bought in supermarkets is cheap but eating out has become more expensive, as have bars unless you stick to beer and Polish vodka.

Heidi Rothwell-Walker enjoyed company teaching, which was a contrast with the basic adult education she had been doing in Britain.

> *I was expected to work any time from 7am to 6pm. Sometimes the early hours (especially in the long winter) can get you down, but you will be rewarded financially for starting at 7am. There was a lot of travelling and waiting at bus stops, but working conditions in the companies were excellent. Not every company gave you access to a whiteboard or overhead projector but they could be made available upon request.*

KATHY COOPER

Kathy Cooper is an American grandmother who suddenly decided to live in Europe. Immediately after obtaining a Trinity certificate in TESOL in the UK, she was offered a job in southern Poland and has fallen in love with her life there, the chemical-free foods, the teaching and the culture. She began her Polish teaching career in the town of Opole, where she was thrown in at the deep end. With time, she was able to refine her teaching schedule.

Teaching varies from school to school, and from classroom to classroom. Starting out, I was thrown immediately into a range of beginning children to executive business and British Council exam classes. It was either to be my death or destiny. I now specialise in only executive business and exam classes. Periodically, I embark on a student who wants to attend either high school or university in America, hence I teach TOEFL exams for both. SLEP (Secondary Level English Proficiency) testing is the new format for high school entrance in America, it is part of the TOEFL system. I can proudly relate that my last student attending a foremost university in the States has just been asked to return, and on scholarship, to obtain her MA in Graphic Design. She was their first Pole of several thousand foreign students. Teachers are a mix of English-speaking nationalities; I have worked with all, including other Americans. It is most common you will teach with Polish teachers. In my case, again, I have some executives and advanced students that require only native speakers because of their language level. Facilities vary; I've been lucky to have had beautifully renovated and comfortable buildings and classrooms. It's not always the norm. Your resource library can often depend on the age of the company. I am with a young school now, and we are stocking year by year.

Despite a considerable amount of disorganisation at many schools, no one complains of a lack of hospitality from the Poles. Poles even seem to have the ability to crack jokes in English when their English is very elementary, so lessons are not usually dull. On the whole they are also very well motivated and hard working, including adolescents. One teacher warns against working for a school that employs a regimented learning method like Callan or Avalon which takes a lot of the fun out of teaching.

LEISURE TIME

Poland offers no shortage of sights to see, pubs to visit, museums, theatres and parks to enjoy. Films are usually in English with Polish subtitles. Travelling is fairly cheap and easy. The transport system in Warsaw and some other cities looks complicated at first glance but is in fact straightforward. People in shops and so on can seem rude and abrupt, though this should not be taken personally.

Kathy Cooper has fallen for the food:

> *Poland yields the most amazing hams, kielbasas and bacon that have ever melted in my mouth. Add the dense and daily purchased homemade breads that taste like my grandmother's, the variety of local and international cheeses, harvests of the freshest chemical-free fruits and vegetables that can be found, plus ice creams, baked goods and phenomenal yoghurts abound. Need I say more?. . .*

Although Kathy does go on to say that the western plague of hypermarkets, including Tesco, has led to the closure of traditional small shops.

Heidi Rothwell-Walker is convinced that she made the right decision when she chose to work for a school in Poland rather than at one of the other schools around the world that offered her a job:

> *The language is difficult, comprising such wonderful names as 'Sczcyrk', a tiny ski village, but it can make for a good atmosphere in the classroom as you struggle with Polish pronunciation whilst your students try to get their tongues round English words.*
>
> *Poland can seem a bit of a backwater, but it's a tremendous experience. It'll change your thinking completely and you'll either love it (like 98% of people) or hate it, but you must try it. I have just renewed my contract for another year because I have been very impressed by them and am very happy here.*

LIST OF EMPLOYERS

ANGLOSCHOOL
ul. Klaudyny 12, 01–684 Warsaw
+48 22 833 2100
klaudyny@angloschool.com.pl
www.angloschool.com.pl

NUMBER OF TEACHERS: 10–12 native English speakers in 5 centres in Warsaw and Lomianki.

QUALIFICATIONS: CELTA or equivalent and a BA or MA. Teaching experience preferred. Experience of teaching children is valued.

CONDITIONS OF EMPLOYMENT: 9-month contract from mid-September, up to 28 hours per week teaching 3pm–8.30pm Monday to Friday. Some morning classes 8.30am–10am.

SALARY: Competitive. School pays taxes and social security (45%).

FACILITIES/SUPPORT: Accommodation is provided by the school in the form of two- or three-roomed shared flats or single rooms in a house. Accommodation includes all necessary facilities, ie furniture, a phone, cable TV, a washing machine, kitchen with necessary equipment. Initial training course and ongoing workshops.

RECRUITMENT: Cooperates with schools running CELTA, TEFL courses, which provide a job placement service. Advertising in newspapers, internet (www.tefl.com) and recruitment agencies. Direct application with CV and photo welcomed.

CONTACT: Ms. Agnieszka Heintze, Director of Studies (agnieszka@angloschool.com.pl).

ANGLOVILLE
Al. Niepodleglosci 147/25, 02–555 Warsaw
+48 533 655 147
info@angloville.com; apply@angloville.com
www.angloville.com

NUMBER OF TEACHERS: 20 a month for short language exchanges. Also provide native speaker teachers to language institutes in Warsaw, Krakow and Poznan.

PREFERENCE OF NATIONALITY: None.

QUALIFICATIONS: No experience/qualifications. Must be a native speaker of English and at least 18. Must be enthusiastic conversationalist willing to engage in English conversation for at least 12 hours a day.

CONDITIONS OF EMPLOYMENT: 6-day language exchange programme operates year round at three scenic locations around Poland, including one in the Bug River National Park. Variable hours of English conversation time mainly with business executives.

SALARY: None, but free board and hotel accommodation are given. Hotel has swimming pools, spa, tennis courts and other facilities.

RECRUITMENT: Application process is online. Occasionally interviews take place by telephone. Processing of applications takes up to three weeks.

CONTACT: Magdalena Janowska, Programme Co-ordinator (biuro@angloschool.com).

BRITISH CENTRE S.C. – ENGLISH LANGUAGE COURSES
ul. Dabrowskiego 8/6, 42–202 Czestochowa
+48 34 361 5914
office@britishcentre.pl
www.britishcentre.pl

NUMBER OF TEACHERS: 2.

PREFERENCE OF NATIONALITY: British.

QUALIFICATIONS: CELTA and experience with preparing students for Cambridge ESOL exams.

CONDITIONS OF EMPLOYMENT: 1-year contract with between 15 and 20 lessons per week.

SALARY: 35 zloty per lesson (45 minutes). 25–26 zloty after tax and social security deductions.

FACILITIES/SUPPORT: Room provided in English teacher's house.

CONTACT: Ms Henryka Rabenda, Co-owner.

ELS-BELL EDUCATION
ul. Targ Drzewny 3/7, 80–886 Gdansk
+48 58 308 4777
gdansk@belt.edu.pl
www.bellschools.pl

In association with Bell Educational Trust of Cambridge.

NUMBER OF TEACHERS: 90 for centres in Gdansk, Gdynia, Bydgoszcz, Szczecin and Warsaw. One Bell affiliate is Program Bell in Poznan (office@program-bell.edu.pl).

PREFERENCE OF NATIONALITY: British and Irish. Non-EU considered with relevant experience.

QUALIFICATIONS: CELTA or Trinity TESOL plus university degree. Minimum 1 year's experience.

CONDITIONS OF EMPLOYMENT: September to June, 20–26 hours a week. Annual workload is 680 hours. Part-time contracts also available. Also runs summer camps for young learners (aged 9–17).

SALARY: 2,400–2,800 zloty net per month, plus end-of-contract bonus of 1,000 zloty. Warsaw wages are higher: 3,000–3,600 zloty.

FACILITIES/SUPPORT: Accommodation assistance. Costs of obtaining work permits and visas are reimbursed by school. Health insurance taken out. In-house teacher development programme. Warsaw centre also runs CELTA and DELTA courses.

RECRUITMENT: Ads on internet. Interviews necessary, usually by phone.

CONTACT: Ludka Kotarska, Managing Director.

ENGLISH COLLEGE
ul. Zeromskiego 31, 26–600 Radom
☎ +48 385 8033
✉ biuro@englishcollege.pl
🖥 www.englishcollege.pl

Centres located in Radom and 6 nearby towns including Kozienice, Itża, Pionki and Zwoleń.

PREFERENCE OF NATIONALITY: Native speakers of English with clear standard British, Irish or North American accent.

QUALIFICATIONS: Degree (preferably in education or TESOL), TEFL/TESOL Certificate and experience. Should be enthusiastic, energetic, open minded and enjoy contact with people and eager to learn new things. Could be teaching kindergarten or adults.

CONDITIONS OF EMPLOYMENT: 9-month contracts (30 teaching weeks) from end of September. 22–24 hours per week, teaching all ages: children, teenagers and adults. Hours mainly 3pm–8.30pm.

SALARY: 20,000–22,000 zloty per contract depending on the hours. Monthly advance of 2,000 zloty plus contract completion bonus (up to 10% of salary).

FACILITIES/SUPPORT: Single furnished studio flat provided free, but not utilities. Cost of work permit covered by school (including courier delivery) but not visa if required. Transport paid for to off-site schools (30–40 minutes away from Radom) by bus or company car. Half of the cost of health insurance will be reimbursed.

RECRUITMENT: Application form, photo and copies of teaching certificates to be submitted and 2 references received directly before Skype interview is arranged.

CONTACT: Anna Machlarz, Director of Studies.

ENGLISH LANGUAGE CENTRE 'RIGHT NOW'
Pszczynska 17, 44–240 Zory, Silesia
☎ +48 32 434 2929
✉ info@rightnow.com.pl
🖥 www.rightnow.pl/jobopp.php

NUMBER OF TEACHERS: 1–2.

PREFERENCE OF NATIONALITY: EU member state passport holder.

QUALIFICATIONS: TESOL certificate or equivalent, and at least 1 year's teaching experience to speakers of other languages.

CONDITIONS OF EMPLOYMENT: 10 months mid-September to mid-June. 12 90-minute lessons per week plus private tuition.

SALARY: About 2,500 zloty per month after deductions and taxes.

FACILITIES/SUPPORT: Subsidised accommodation at school's flat within walking distance of the school. Assistance with work permits.

RECRUITMENT: Internet ads followed by interviews in person or by telephone.

CONTACT: Rafal Zurkowski, Owner/Manager.

GLOBAL VILLAGE
Al. Legionów 42, 25–035 Kielce
☎ +48 41 362 1393
✉ office@gv.edu.pl
🖥 www.gv.edu.pl

NUMBER OF TEACHERS: 7. Also for branches in Kielce, Starachowice and Skarzysko.

PREFERENCE OF NATIONALITY: EU citizens preferred.

QUALIFICATIONS: Bachelor's or master's degree plus a CELTA, DELTA or TEFL certificate.

CONDITIONS OF EMPLOYMENT: Standard contract length 1 academic year, to work 3pm–8pm, Monday to Friday.

SALARY: Competitive.

FACILITIES/SUPPORT: The school organises accommodation.

CONTACT: Urszula Szczepanczyk, Director (urszula@gv.edu.pl).

INTERNATIONAL HOUSE INTEGRA BIELSKO
ul. Zielona 32, 43-300 Bielsko-Biała
☎ + 48 33 822 33 30
✉ bielsko@ih.com.pl
🖥 www.ih.com.pl; www.facebook.com/IHBielsko

School has bilingual Kindergarten and primary school.

NUMBER OF TEACHERS: 11.

PREFERENCE OF NATIONALITY: EU candidates preferred (as they do not require a visa to live and work in Poland). In view of extra costs and administration involved in employing non-EU citizens, only particularly strong applicants can be considered.

QUALIFICATIONS: CELTA or equivalent, degree and 1 year's teaching experience required, especially of young and very young learners.

CONDITIONS OF EMPLOYMENT: 9 months. 21 hours a week. In-school group teaching is mostly from 3.30pm to 8.30pm. One-to-one lessons and in-company classes are in the mornings, afternoons and evenings, but teachers are not required to teach outside a 12-hour band during the day.

SALARY: 2900–3700 zloty depending on qualifications and experience. Tax deductions differ between nationalities (eg 0% for Britons, 18% for Irish).

FACILITIES/SUPPORT: The school assists new teachers with finding accommodation. If a non-EU teacher is employed, the school covers the costs of obtaining the visa (excluding travel and hotel costs). 20 days paid holiday.

RECRUITMENT: International House World Organisation; www.tefl.com. Interviews are carried out via Skype (with a webcam) or in person.

CONTACT: Katarzyna Jakielaszek, Director of Studies (katarzyna.jakielaszek@ih.com.pl).

INTERNATIONAL HOUSE TORUN
ul. Legionów 15, 87–100 Torun
+48 56 622 5081
Standish.torun@inthouse.pl
www.inthouse.pl

NUMBER OF TEACHERS: 10.
PREFERENCE OF NATIONALITY: None.
QUALIFICATIONS: CELTA needed. Experience not essential.
CONDITIONS OF EMPLOYMENT: 9 months.
SALARY: 1,600–1,875 zloty (net) depending on experience.
FACILITIES/SUPPORT: Shared accommodation provided. Help given with registration of EU teachers who stay more than 3 months, and to non-EU teachers who need work permits.
RECRUITMENT: Through IH World and also direct contact to school. Interviews necessary and sometimes carried out at IH London.
CONTACT: Glenn Standish, Director of Studies.

INTERNATIONAL HOUSE – WROCLAW
ul. Leszczynskiego 3, 50–078 Wroclaw
biurowroc@ih.com.pl
www.ih.com.pl

NUMBER OF TEACHERS: 8. Also for Bielsko-Biala and Wroclaw.
PREFERENCE OF NATIONALITY: EU citizens, but non-EU citizens may also be considered.
QUALIFICATIONS: Minimum CELTA or Trinity certificate. 1 year's experience or CELTA Pass 'A' or 'B' preferred.
CONDITIONS OF EMPLOYMENT: 9-month standard contract, 21 contact hours per week.

SALARY: 2,600–3,400 zloty per month net (in first year) depending on qualifications and experience.
FACILITIES/SUPPORT: The school helps new teachers find suitable accommodation before and on arrival.
RECRUITMENT: Via IH Human Resources in London or direct at wrocdos@ih.com.pl. Interviews are carried out by IH Human Resources in London or else directly in Wroclaw in person or by phone.
CONTACT: John Fowler, Director of Studies (wrocdos@ih.com.pl).

LEKTOR SZKOLA JEZYKOW OBCYCH
ul. Olawska 25, 50–123 Wroclaw
biuro@lektor.com.pl
www.lektor.com.pl

NUMBER OF TEACHERS: 70.
PREFERENCE OF NATIONALITY: British, Irish, American, Canadian and Australian.
QUALIFICATIONS: Certificate in TEFL required (CELTA, DELTA or equivalent).
CONDITIONS OF EMPLOYMENT: Contracts for 1 or more years, 20–25 lessons per week. Students are young adults. Company organises intensive summer courses and language camps as well.
SALARY: From 55 zloty per hour.
FACILITIES/SUPPORT: Assistance with finding accommodation and obtaining work permit if necessary.
RECRUITMENT: Adverts on www.tefl.com. Personal interviews essential.

MCGREGOR LANGUAGE SCHOOLS
ul. Jagietty 2, 32–400 Myslenice
+48 12 372 2895
jobs@mcgregor.home.pl
www.mcgregor.net.pl

NUMBER OF TEACHERS: 8–10. Also for other branches in Limanowa and Wadowice.
PREFERENCE OF NATIONALITY: None.
QUALIFICATIONS: A successful candidate must have completed an ESL/EFL training course. Experience is not necessary but is an advantage.
CONDITIONS OF EMPLOYMENT: Length of stay October to June. 24 teaching hours per week between 3pm and 9pm.
SALARY: 2,800 zloty gross per month, less 19% for income tax and social security contributions.
FACILITIES/SUPPORT: Free fully furnished accommodation provided, 5 minutes walk from school. The school takes care of all

paperwork and covers the cost of the work permit, as well as providing full support to non-EU citizens to obtain a residence visa (though teachers cover the cost, currently 1,800 zloty (£50).

RECRUITMENT: Applications should include CV, 2 referees and copies of degree and TEFL certificates. Skype or face-to-face interviews.

CONTACT: Maria Garczynska-Payne, Academic Manager.

MULTISCHOOL SZKOLA JEZYKOW OBCYCH
ul. Niedzwiedzia 46, 02–666 Warsaw
+48 22 638 2339
biuro@multischool.pl
www.multischool.pl

NUMBER OF TEACHERS: 45 in 3 branches in Warsaw for kindergarten, primary and middle school pupils.

QUALIFICATIONS: TEFL course, higher education; experience not necessary. Must have degree or master's in early childhood education.

CONDITIONS OF EMPLOYMENT: 12 months. Teaching hours 8am–3pm and 3pm–8pm.

SALARY: $1,000 a month average, varies according to timetable. Less 10% for deductions.

FACILITIES/SUPPORT: Help given in finding a flat to rent and in obtaining a work permit.

RECRUITMENT: Prefer to interview candidates but can rely on CVs, letters of motivation and telephone conversations.

SPEED SCHOOL OF ENGLISH
ul. Zwyciestwa 14, 44–100 Gliwice
+48 32 331 5874
gliwice@myspeed.pl
www.myspeed.pl

NUMBER OF TEACHERS: About 40 for Gliwice, Bielsko-Biala, Krakow, Tychy, Opole and Wroclaw.

PREFERENCE OF NATIONALITY: English-speaking countries.

QUALIFICATIONS: Ideally a BA degree plus CELTA, TESOL or equivalent. Experience is not essential but considered an asset.

CONDITIONS OF EMPLOYMENT: 10-12 months starting July or September. Afternoon and evening shifts plus mornings on a rotational basis.

SALARY: About 3,000-3,500 zloty per month (net). Airfare allowance paid on completion of contract.

FACILITIES/SUPPORT: Accommodation is ready for teachers' arrival. Full assistance given with work visa application including

official translations and trips to the Labour Department on teachers' behalf. Free 5-day teacher training course.

RECRUITMENT: Internet, walk-in, cooperation with British organisations. Interviews take place face-to-face or by Skype.

CONTACT: Martyna Olszowska, Recruitment Coordinator.

STUDIUM JEZYKÓW OBCYCH 'NEW ENGLAND'
ul. Pomorska 34, 66-400 Gorzów Wlkp.
+48 95 7323087
newengland@pro.onet.pl
www.newengland.pl

NUMBER OF TEACHERS: 1.

PREFERENCE OF NATIONALITY: None, but prefer EU citizens.

QUALIFICATIONS: BA plus TEFL or equivalent. No experience needed.

CONDITIONS OF EMPLOYMENT: 10-month contract. Usual hours are 2pm–9pm.

SALARY: Decent local salary, depending on experience and qualifications.

FACILITIES/SUPPORT: School finds accommodation for teacher.

RECRUITMENT: Skype interview.

CONTACT: Beata Kulik, Owner.

WARSAW INTERNATIONAL TRILINGUAL SCHOOL
Karowa 14/16 lok 6; 00-324 Warsaw; also at ul. Cicha 5, 00-353 Warsaw
+48 503 072 119
amjup2000@yahoo.com
www.3languages.pl

NUMBER OF TEACHERS: 5.

PREFERENCE OF NATIONALITY: None.

QUALIFICATIONS: Early years education certified teachers.

CONDITIONS OF EMPLOYMENT: 3-year contract. Hours of work 7.30am–1pm or 1pm–6.30pm.

SALARY: US$1,000 per month (net).

FACILITIES/SUPPORT: Shared flats provided. Full assistance given with red tape.

CONTACT: Anna Maliszewska, Pre-school Founder and Owner.

YORK SCHOOL OF ENGLISH
ul. Bursztynowa 20–22, 31–214 Krakow
+48 12 415 1818
info@york.edu.pl
www.york.edu.pl.

PASE (www.pase.pl) and Quality English (www.quality-english.com) recognised school, City & Guilds and LCCI approved examination centre. Has branches in Bochnia and Brzesko as well.

NUMBER OF TEACHERS: 30, including approximately 10 full-time native English speakers.

PREFERENCE OF NATIONALITY: British and Irish, also American, Canadian or Australian (EU visa holders preferred).

QUALIFICATIONS: BA/MA (preferably in English or Linguistics). TEFL certificate (CELTA/Trinity or equivalents). Minimum 1 year ELT experience preferred, references.

CONDITIONS OF EMPLOYMENT: 9-month full-time renewable contract (September to June). Average 26 hours per week.

SALARY: Monthly average salary 3,000 zloty gross depending on qualifications and experience. Paid overtime.

FACILITIES/SUPPORT: Free accommodation for the first 3 days. Help given with accommodation. Bonuses. Professional development, regular workshops and conferences.

RECRUITMENT: www.tefl.com.

CONTACT: Ewa Krupska, Director of Studies (e.krupska@york.edu.pl).

ROMANIA

Since the collapse of communism, English has been taught in Romanian primary schools all the way through, so most people under 30 can communicate reasonably well. The vast majority of English teaching is carried out by Romanian teachers, who seem to do a splendid job, judging from the extremely high pass rate their students achieve in the Cambridge exams. Young Romanians possess an enthusiasm for the English language that dates from the arrival of the Cartoon Network in their country and which is driven, as throughout Europe, by the ubiquity of English-language films and music. Teenagers are also motivated to learn English if they harbour an ambition to live and work abroad. Since January 2014 restrictions have been lifted on the right of Romanians (and Bulgarians) to work in the UK, which may spur even more to master English. Yet there are relatively few private language institutes in Romania at present, partly because of the small size of the corporate sector. The arrival of western investment and global companies and hotel chains has created more demand for commercial English though not necessarily the prosperity to pay for it.

The Ministry of Education in Bucharest does not recruit EFL teachers directly, though it cooperates with the British Council to improve standards of local teachers and place unpaid interns. The British Council (www.britishcouncil.ro) has been active in promoting English in Romania at all levels and runs its own Teaching Centre in Bucharest at Calea Dorobantilor 14 (+40 21 307 9600) and also in Iasi. Further along the same street in the capital is the expanding K-12 Cambridge School at number 39 (www.cambridgeschool.ro), which advertises for experienced teachers when it has a vacancy. A foreign language exam is compulsory for graduating from school and university, which has boosted demand for private tuition.

QUEST Romania (www.quest.ro) is the Romanian Association for Quality Language Services, which operates as a quality control system on the basis of an inspection scheme. Its website has been updated recently and links to its dozen or so full members and four observer members. These Language Centres tend to employ well-qualified teachers (most of them Romanian). A few are privately owned, whereas others are NGOs. For example, the Access Language Centre in Cluj-Napoca (www.access.ro) is an NGO supported by the British Council.

Some language schools are listed under the heading *Limbi Straine – Cursuri* in the *Golden Pages* (www.paginiaurii.ro), but these are unlikely to employ a native English speaker. Romanian language schools find it next-to-impossible to attract native English-speaker teachers because they simply can't afford to pay them.

As the director of one QUEST member school wrote:

> *While we would welcome having native English teachers on our staff (we do occasionally receive enquiries from interested people), it is true that given how small our school is (approximately 400 students a year altogether) we cannot afford spending too much on employing them. For the moment, we only employ highly qualified local teachers on part-time contracts. I do not want to mislead people before we reach a more secure position and financial situation, in a very unstable country, economically speaking.*

MINNA GRABER

Many years ago, Minna Graber arrived in Romania to celebrate the New Year and has been besotted with the country ever since.

We went straight into a Carpathian village at the top of a mountain complete with gypsy fiddlers and not an internal combustion engine for miles around. I fell for the place hook, line and sinker and haven't been able to kick the habit. I wanted to teach in the north-east of the country and so contacted the British Council in Iasi, who in turn referred me to SOL. I met the director, Grenville Yeo, at a café and we talked for a long time about the challenges, rewards and requirements. In the end the job offer was with one of the best schools in Bucharest where the students all go on to university (and a significant minority are these days applying for British university places). I work for 18 teaching periods a week. I am not supposed to teach grammar, which at least in my school is seen as the Romanian English-language teachers' prerogative partly, I fear, because they assume native speakers are not capable of this. This is despite the fact that I am fully trained to do so.

The wages sound terrible – 1,100 lei a month after deductions for tax and National Insurance. The other teachers have to pay for accommodation out of this so in comparison I have a big advantage (the school's parents' association provides and pays for my very simple small studio flat and for the running costs). I am very good at living frugally but find that I still have to take on a couple of private students to make ends meet. The rest of the staff work long hours, giving these private lessons.

According to Minna, native speakers of English can command a high fee for giving private tuition. She charges around 60 lei an hour (£11.50). If you work in a private kindergarten, as she did at one point, you can charge even more. Despite her modest earnings, she is far from discontent with her lifestyle:

I go to all the best concerts, have private lessons in Romanian, attend martial arts classes and choir every week and travel a lot. I am even able to put a little by at the end of the month. My students are all completely delightful. I love teaching them. They are respectful and talented. I do have to mother them a little over matters such as getting work in on time. Occasionally they, and their parents, try to exert pressure on me over marks. If a form tutor asks my help in rescuing a student who has problems or who might otherwise get expelled I always do so, otherwise I resist changing marks.

As for leisure time, many a Saturday has been spent haring up the mountains with Bucharest's enormous and enthusiastic mountain club. As a result of my wanderings over the mountains in the summer I made friends with some traditional shepherds and peasant farmers and am always welcome to visit. The times spent with these friends in the countryside are like a journey back into a far distant past. Of course, for all of this a command of the Romanian language is essential.

Nobody knows anything about Romania and the upside of this is that it is a very tourist-free area and you enjoy status as a visitor from the outside world. People are interested and welcoming largely because there are so few visitors. Catch it whilst it still lasts.

A few British exchange organisations and charities recruit volunteers for summer language camps. For example, BREDEX (British Romanian Educational Exchange) is a volunteer student-led organisation which sends about a dozen university students from the UK to five cities in Romania to teach conversational English (see entry), starting in early July; details on its Facebook page. DAD International UK-Romania in Iasi (+40 772 201399; www.dad.ro) sends volunteer teachers to six camps in mountain or seaside locations around Romania. Flights and accommodation are paid, and those who stay for the whole summer season (June 20th-August 30th) are rewarded with a six-day holiday on the Black Sea coast.

Projects Abroad in Sussex (www.projects-abroad.co.uk) recruits paying volunteers to work as English language teaching assistants for the summer or during the academic year in Romania, the only European country among its 29 worldwide destinations. No TEFL background is required. Packages cost from £1,895 for one month to £3,295 for three months and include placement, accommodation, three meals a days, full medical and travel insurance and 24 hour staff support.

Since the accession of Romania to the EU in 2007, red tape for Europeans has become simpler. Any teacher wishing to stay for longer than 120 days should apply for a temporary resident permit. Romania has so far not been allowed to join the Schengen Area. When it does, non-EU citizens will be allowed a maximum stay of 90 days within 6 months unless they obtain a work/resident's permit.

Romania is not a particularly expensive place to stay, but not dirt cheap either. According to the director of the Bredex programme, a recent teacher estimated a total outlay of about £1,000 for the summer including flights, but goes on to qualify this: '*Considering her frenetic travel and impressive/spectacular beer and pizza consumption, we would confidently say that is an upper-end estimate.*'

LIST OF EMPLOYERS

BREDEX (BRITISH ROMANIAN EDUCATIONAL EXCHANGE)

41 Penge Road, London E13 0SL, UK

- +44 7956 946786
- ridwanatbredex@gmail.com
- www.facebook.com/BREDEX.info

Programme for British university students to teach conversational English in summer programmes, founded by Oxford students in 1991 but now open to all UK universities.

NUMBER OF TEACHERS: About 12 volunteers.

PREFERENCE OF NATIONALITY: Native speakers (or with native proficiency) at British universities.

QUALIFICATIONS: Must be students or recent graduates in any discipline from a British university. Candidates should be keen on fostering the educational development of others. Enthusiasm, intellectual curiosity and a willingness to get involved in something different are necessary.

CONDITIONS OF EMPLOYMENT: 7 weeks from early July. 3 weeks of teaching, 1 week to travel and explore Romania, 3 more weeks of teaching. Minimum of 3 hours of teaching on week days but usually 2 teaching sessions a day of 3 hours each.

SALARY: Unpaid. Teachers cover their own travel costs and pay an admin fee of around £40.

FACILITIES/SUPPORT: Free accommodation is provided at Romanian university dorms for the duration of the programme. Prior to the programme, participants receive a cheat sheet of resources from previous years to help plan their lessons but teachers have complete creative control of their classes. The weekend before teaching begins is spent in Bucharest, where participants are given a crash-course introduction to Romanian culture and nightlife, with discussions on teaching.

RECRUITMENT: Contact with universities during autumn and spring terms, via student volunteering bodies, posters and the Bredex Facebook page. A short personal statement, followed by a telephone interview or a meet-up, location permitting.

CONTACT: Ridwan Ibrahim, Director.

PROFESSIONAL LANGUAGE CENTRE

4/1 Semanatorilor St, Targu-Mures 4300

- +40 265 251180; mobile +40 723 241042
- acotoara@gmail.com
- www.professionalcentre.ro

Full member of QUEST, Romanian Association of Quality Language Schools.

NUMBER OF TEACHERS: 1.

QUALIFICATIONS: Bachelor's degree or equivalent.

CONDITIONS OF EMPLOYMENT: 1-year contract. To work 4pm–8pm, 5 days a week.

SALARY: $7 per hour. Taxes and social security paid by the school.

FACILITIES/SUPPORT: Assistance with finding accommodation and acquiring work permits.

RECRUITMENT: Interview required.

CONTACT: Angela Cotoara, Director.

RUSSIA

While the economy and geopolitics remain difficult in Russia, the rouble made a surprising comeback in 2015. Economists predict that inflation will continue to rise slowly, and that growth will not be dramatic, and yet the situation looks relatively stable. If growth is to be maintained, Russia must encourage more foreign firms to invest, which tends to result in a boost to the demand for English, already soaring in the corporate sector. Both old and new language training businesses are eagerly recruiting teachers via advertisements abroad. Hosting the 2018 FIFA World Cup may act as a spur just as the Winter Olympics of 2014 did.

Russians are still basically conservative and awareness of the internet as a learning tool remains low in Russia, so private language schools continue to be popular. The large chains such as Language Link, BKC-International House and EF English First are constantly recruiting teachers for their schools. Rather than employ an underqualified native English teacher, most language schools would rather turn to home-grown English teachers for whom teaching English is a profession and not simply a one- to two-year pastime. Russian English teachers are also far cheaper and do not require visa support and other costly add-on benefits such as accommodation, health care and travel allowances.

However, exceptions are made for qualified candidates, eg native English teachers with a CELTA or Trinity College TESOL certificate. Most schools will also accept applicants who hold TEFL certificates obtained on credible 100+ hour training courses with teaching practice. If you do not hold a certificate but have gained valuable experience teaching General English, Business English and/or international examination courses (IELTS, FCE, CAE and their like) and you have taught both adults and children, you should have little difficulty finding a job teaching English in Russia.

Robert Jensky, Managing Director of Language Link Russia, is convinced that high standards are essential:

I have personally seen many unqualified teachers fail because they did not fully realise the difference between speaking English and teaching English. Although Russians can vary in temperament and personality, they share a respect for education. Russians who under communism did not have to pay for education have come to accept the fact that it is now necessary to do so. There is little debate among Russians as to the significance of the English language both domestically and globally. Their only concern is that they get their full money's worth from each and every lesson. Russian students are demanding and place high expectations on their teachers, and so do the companies that employ them (including those that hire EFL teachers illegally). Given these circumstances, it is strongly recommended that any teacher coming to Russia has with them a good grammar book, a dictionary and a concise guide to TEFL methodology.

Many young Russians are already fairly competent in the language and want to become more conversant with western culture, not just for its own sake but to enhance their career prospects. Jobs in international firms are often advertised only in English. Russians young and not-so-young who want to work in advertising, banking, computing and so on need to speak English and therefore are drawn to the intensive English courses advertised all over the Moscow metro and on lamp posts.

There are also plenty of jobs tutoring and looking after young children, as affluent parents hope to give their children a head start by showing off at the same time. This sector is definitely expanding, with several companies and individuals posting adverts in newspapers and websites such as www.expat.ru; for example, an advert seen in 2015 for one-to-one tutoring jobs with the Native Speakers Club (hr@nativespeakers. ru) offered 1,800 roubles (£21) a lesson. Kindergartens and specialist companies that offer tutors, nannies and governesses for children have also realised that native English speakers '*create a good image for your company*', according to the director of Little Angels Kindergarten in Moscow (see List of Employers). Other specialist agencies include Gouverneur International (www.guvernior.ru), Duke & Duchess International (www.dukeandduchess-int.com) and Bonne International with offices in London and Moscow (www.bonne-int.com). Both take on native English speakers for a number of vacancies, mainly in and around Moscow. ESL-qualified native candidates are needed to tutor children aged 3 to 12 years.

FINDING A JOB

Finding a vacancy in Russia shouldn't be too difficult. Russia is, after all, the largest country on earth, spanning 11 time zones. You only need to decide where in Russia you'd like to settle down to teach English. As a rule, salaries can drop the further you go from Moscow. A lower salary, however, is usually more than made up for by the lower costs of living found in many of the big cities away from Moscow; and a lower cost of living usually means a higher standard of living. Likewise, you're more likely to experience real Russia and real Russians.

Rob Jensky cautions against focusing your job hunt entirely around salary and perks:

> *For newly qualified teachers, academic support can mean the difference between success and failure as a teacher. And speaking of success as a teacher, having tons of personality is imperative. Students want to like their teachers and the way to gain their affection is by truly liking them back. Teachers who like their students will spend the time needed to prepare for their lessons adequately and this is where the value of proper academic support cannot be overestimated. The availability of a good Director of Studies and other experienced teaching staff who can help you with lesson preparation is a benefit that cannot be counted in terms of dollars and cents or pounds and pence.*

Teachers who are capable of performing in a variety of EFL classroom settings (Young Learners, adults, General, Business English, examination preparation) are in the greatest demand. Likewise, teachers who are prepared to be flexible with regard to teaching schedules will find a far greater number of employment opportunities. This is especially true in the great metropolitan areas, where the number of both business and one-to-one clients is on the rise, many of whom want to be taught before or after the working day.

The two most popular international websites used by Russian employers looking to hire English teachers are www.tefl.com and www.eslcafe.com. A typical advert might read: '*British-owned and managed school based in the centre of Moscow is always looking to recruit teachers of English (and other European languages) to work with large Russian and multinational companies from the oil and gas industry and other spheres such as finance, banking and investments, market research, IT and pharmaceuticals.*'

When considering potential employers in Russia make sure that the company has the right to invite and employ teachers in Russia (see visa section for details), check whether the salary is net or gross and ask if accommodation is free/included. An estimated 900 tertiary institutes offer English courses, and many employ one or two highly educated native speakers to assist. Most universities and polytechnics offer free or subsidised accommodation and a civilised timetable but usually can't pay more than a couple of dollars an hour.

Some of the main language chains recruit abroad, including Language Link and EF English First, which recruits large numbers for 35 language schools in Russia on reasonable terms with return flight, medical insurance and visa costs included. Many foreign teachers prefer the security of working for a western-owned company. Even if the wages are not brilliant, the support and fringe benefits usually make up for it. Language Link (see entry) offers an array of different employment opportunities designed to fit the needs of most EFL applicants from qualified to unqualified willing to be interns or volunteers. Reach to Teach, the TEFL recruitment agency, has teaching positions in all the major cities of Russia.

Barry Robinson spent a number of years in Moscow working the EFL circuit and has provided a snapshot of the main employers. He admits that his opinions are totally subjective and are meant purely as a guide:

> *EFL in Moscow can often be more rewarding financially on a freelance basis, but for those who prefer to tie in with an all-inclusive contract, here is some info on what's on offer. BKC has an excellent reputation for teacher development and you get loads of professional support. They always pay on time and for work finished, and they are a decent company who will always look good on your CV. The same applies to Language Link, who are friendly, fair, very supportive and will find you a flat. EF English First probably offers the best contract. They allow teachers to find their own flat (and pay for temporary accommodation during house-hunting) and their schools are always well equipped. They insist that you stick to the EF book so there isn't much room for teacher development.*

A thriving English-language press has established itself in Moscow and St Petersburg. Check adverts in *The Moscow Times* (www.themoscowtimes.com). Check the online message board community for English speakers living in Moscow on www.expat.ru, which at the time of writing carried lots of clearly set out adverts for native English-speaker teachers.

Since 1992 the Serendipity Russian-English Program has been sending Americans to work at the American Home in Vladimir Russia, a city 180km north-east of Moscow. In addition to teaching regular classes, the American teachers give lectures on American society and participate in other activities. Contracts last nine to 11 months (renewable) starting in the second week of August. The annual deadline for applications is 15th March. Complete application information is at www.serendipity-russia.com.

Jim Clost from Canada did not have a TEFL certificate when he went to Russia but he had studied the language at university and so joined a voluntary teaching scheme organised by a local travel agency:

I was required to work between four and six hours a day, only conversation and listening. Accommodation and meals were provided with a local family (normally one of the students); however, no wages were paid as the position was voluntary. I met wonderful students, kids and adults and made friends that I go back to see regularly. The pupils were in general quite shy but some were ready to speak up and chat with me right away. Once we got to know one another conversation flowed more freely. Many of my students were quite eager to have me in their home for dinner. This is normal in Russian society, where meeting with foreigners on a personal basis is a rarity. In my free time, I skated, swam, visited friends for tea and dinner, walked and talked.

Students of Russian should investigate the programme run by the Pro-Ba Centre in St Petersburg where four or eight weeks of intensive study of Russian is followed by a period of work in schools, kindergartens or summer camps (www.russian-learning.com/studyandwork.html). Fees are €2,750 for two months and €3,750 for four months.

The youth exchange company CCUSA (www.ccusa.com or www.ccusa.co.uk) recruits volunteers for English-immersion summer camps in Russia whereby teacher/counsellors from the USA and UK are placed in youth camps in Russia lasting four or eight weeks between mid-June and mid-August. Participants must have experience of working with children and/or abroad, and have an interest in learning about the Russian language and culture. Camps are widely scattered, from Lake Baikal in Siberia to the shores of the Black Sea. The programme fee of $3,145 from the US and £999 from Britain includes return flights to Moscow and onwards to your assigned camp, insurance, orientation on arrival and room and board. Applicants of all ages are accepted: the CCUSA record so far was a 63-year-old American woman who worked at a Russian camp.

PAUL JONES

Australian Paul Jones spent the summer in Russia.

I worked as a counsellor in a summer camp near the city of Perm. When I first arrived, my heart sank because it looked like a gulag (for which the area around Perm is famous!) But you soon forget the physical conditions, mostly anyway. If I didn't like the food at the start, I definitely learnt to like it by the end and now reminisce about the worst of it! My job, as with American summer camps for kids, was to help lead a group of up to 30 children for their three-week stay at the camp. Because I did not speak the language, I was placed with two other leaders so my services weren't really necessary. However, this region of Russia doesn't exactly get many international visitors so the role I played at camp sometimes felt more like being a rock star! The types of activities the kids did ranged from football, basketball and swimming (the colour of the pool was scary) to singing, dancing and crafts. But while I tried as best I could to lead my group of kids in their daily activities,

> every single kid in the camp wants a piece of you because you're the foreigner! So a lot of the job is to just be there and share a different culture with the kids (and their parents sometimes), other Russian counsellors and the Camp Director. I found that a few words in Russian go a long way to bridging the culture gap. And if possible take some souvenirs for the kids. Even a pack of cards with the British flag on them provides 52 little gifts.

CONDITIONS OF WORK

The majority of language schools that recruit teachers from abroad offer a package that includes a salary, free accommodation, subsidised flights, and support for a multiple entry visa. The accommodation will usually be shared with other teachers and the contribution to travel expenses might be 20,000 roubles within Europe, 35,000 roubles for teachers from outside Europe. The net wage range is normally 40,000-65,000 roubles. Reach to Teach offers the higher figure, but that includes a housing stipend. When you see salaries of up to 90,000 roubles advertised, check to see if any perks are offered. Outside the cities, starting wages will be closer to the lower end, and may possibly dip down to 35,000 roubles.

For those who choose to (or have to) live out, the housing market has calmed down somewhat and it is no longer as difficult as it was for foreign teachers to find independent accommodation. Rooms in shared houses in Moscow are in good supply on craigslist, where rents are usually quoted in dollars. Of course, as you leave the bright lights of Moscow and St Petersburg, rental costs come down.

Teachers need to be flexible in their approach to the working world in Russia and be prepared to compromise and adapt to an unfamiliar working environment. **Katherine Hyvärinen** found travelling around the vast city of Moscow to teach in different locations tiring but also exhilarating. She found the rhythm of life to be very fast but ended up enjoying her explorations of '*the mysterious, cultural and chaotic city of Moscow*'.

A cultural difference which many newcomers find difficult to accept is the apparent unfriendliness of the Russian people. However, the cold face of Russian officialdom could not be in starker contrast to the warmth that will greet you when you get to know Russians better. **Elizabeth Bearman**, a teacher in Moscow, goes some way to unravelling the mystery of the cold Russian exterior:

> *The Russian man in the street does not smile unless he is happy, he does not engage complete strangers in meaningless conversation and he does not suffer fools gladly. There is a Russian proverb that perhaps sums it up: 'Only a fool smiles all the time'. However, while Russians can appear rude and unfriendly, when you get to know them they are considerate, helpful, generous and well . . . friendly. The Russian concept of friendship is much deeper and less superficial than elsewhere.*

The clichéd cold exterior of the Russian is nothing compared to the literal cold of the Russian winter, as described by **Travis Boyle** who worked in Moscow (and is from Texas!):

> *The hardest thing about my job is probably the weather. Because I work in-company, I have to trek to all of my students' offices, and because this is Moscow, that means that nine months of the year are cold, snowy, and icy. But the students almost always offer hot tea or coffee.*

Moscow winters last a good four or five months, when temperatures regularly fall below minus 15°C.

Not surprisingly, the younger generation seems more willing to embrace new communicative teaching methods than the older one, according to the director of the Sunny Plus English School in Moscow (www.sunnyplus.ru), which has a constant need for native English-speaker teachers:

Adults cause headaches. They get upset with grammar. Many of them can't easily accept modern methods of teaching. The progress is very slow. For many weeks they can't understand a teacher. They demand changing him. Their pronunciation is terrible, but during classes they keep silent.

By contrast, **Travis Boyle** was pleased with both the quality of his students and the working conditions at IPT Moscow (see entry):

I wanted a part-time teaching contract, and that is what I got with IPT. I wanted time in the middle of the day to study Russian, apply for graduate school, teach private students and so on, so this job has afforded me a framework in which to pursue those tasks. All my students are educated, polite, middle and upper-class business people. I teach in-company, so their offices are, in some ways, my office. They are all well organised, clean, well stocked and quiet enough for lessons.

One of his colleagues, **Katherine Hyvärinen**, was similarly delighted with her adult students in Moscow, whom she described as '*enthusiastic, motivated and with a positive and at times humorous attitude*' towards her lessons. Their boss **Tim Newton,** MD at IPT, has no complaints about the intermediate and advanced students he has taught in Moscow, who are mostly sponsored by their companies and are committed, hard working and dedicated. He compares his school favourably with some of the alternatives:

Don't be fooled into believing that just because you choose to work for a chain school, you are going to be working in either a large school or one staffed by native English-speaking teachers. Many major chains operate small teaching operations in far-flung locations. Proximity to good health care cannot be taken for granted, and could be an issue for people with medical conditions. If proximity to cultural and recreational outlets such as theatres, cinemas, museums, parks, circuses and other tourist attractions is important to you psychologically, then be sure to investigate locations prior to accepting a job.

REGULATIONS

Legalising your status as a teacher has always been fraught with difficulties, particularly for the companies that employ foreigners, who must keep abreast of constantly changing legislation. Established employers licensed by the Federal Migration Service to sponsor visas will know the procedures and make it as painless as possible for you by issuing you with the appropriate letter of invitation by post. In order to qualify for a multiple entry work visa, teachers must provide apostilled (legally certified) copies of their passport, TESOL certificate and university degree certificate, and must undergo an HIV test. The proof of being HIV-negative must be dated within three months of the visa application. You will have to collect your visa from the Russian Embassy in your home country. If your employer is not being particularly helpful, specialist visa agencies may be able to advise such as Real Russia (www.realrussia.co.uk) and VFS Global (http://ru.vfsglobal.co.uk), both with offices in London. Agencies such as Legal Stay (www.legalstay.ru) advertise in Russia their ability to provide working visas for teachers for a colossal fee (eg €1,450 a year).

Some teachers work on multiple entry business visas, though it is not legal to do so. Most foreigners entering the country on one-year multiple entry business visas may remain on Russian soil for a maximum of 90 days before having to leave Russian territory for at least 90 days; in other words, they may remain in Russia for only three months during any six-month period and this is being enforced. Americans are now permitted stays of six months at a stretch.

From the beginning of 2015, employers are supposed to deduct pension contributions from employees who have contracts of more than six months, and apparently this is being enforced.

LIST OF EMPLOYERS

AAA SGI ENGLISH

Bldg 6/7, No 8 Staromonetniy Pereulok, Moscow 119180

+7 495 951 7038

info@aaaenglish.ru

www.aaaenglish.ru and www.stgeorges.co.uk/
sgi-global-group

School is a joint venture between AAA English and St George International in London; both are British owned and managed.
NUMBER OF TEACHERS: Up to 15 for about 300 students (2012) at 2 locations in Moscow (second location at Building 2, No 16 Prospect Mira, Moscow 129090; +7 495 951 7038).
PREFERENCE OF NATIONALITY: British.
QUALIFICATIONS: 1-year minimum teaching experience, first degree, CELTA/TESOL/TEFL.
CONDITIONS OF EMPLOYMENT: 1 year. 40 academic hours per week. Also liaise with Russian summer camp organisation to provide native-speaker teachers for the vacation.
SALARY: 60-75,000 roubles net per month for 160 academic hours (40 per week). However, salary does not depend on doing a minimum of 40 hours per week. The school policy is to find enough students to keep the teaching staff fully occupied. Hours taught above 40 are paid an overtime rate of 500 roubles.
FACILITIES/SUPPORT: Employer finds apartments for staff and pays the finder's fee and security deposit. First return flight from London to Moscow is also paid. Assistance with work permits given. AAA English is licensed by the Moscow City Government as an education establishment and authorised by the Russian Foreign Migration Service to invite and issue work permits and contracts direct to teachers. The school covers the cost of the issue of the work visa and permit.
RECRUITMENT: Via www.tefl.com. Interviews normally conducted by Webex video over the internet.
CONTACT: Michael Lang, General Director/Owner/Head Teacher.

BKC – INTERNATIONAL HOUSE Moscow

3–5 Gazetny Pereulok, Office No 8, Moscow 121019

+7 495 737 5225

recruit@bkc.ru

www.bkcih-moscow.com

NUMBER OF TEACHERS: Approximately 200 contract and hourly paid teachers in Moscow, 50 teachers in the Moscow region. 38 schools in total.

PREFERENCE OF NATIONALITY: None.
QUALIFICATIONS: CELTA, Trinity TESOL, SIT Tesol, TESL Canada or any 100–120 hour onsite course. Higher qualifications such as degree in business/economics needed for some posts along with 2 years' experience.
CONDITIONS OF EMPLOYMENT: 6 or 9 months.
SALARY: Up to 40,000 roubles (net) for 30 hours per week over 9-month contract; from 31,500 roubles for 24 hours a week (9-month contract). End-of-contract bonus of up to 30,000 roubles.
FACILITIES/SUPPORT: The school provides visa support (pays for multiple-entry work visa), shared accommodation, airfare reimbursement, health care, paid holidays and 50% discount for Russian classes. Opportunities for professional development – an active in-house training programme, consisting of regular monthly training seminars and different workshops.
RECRUITMENT: All year round, though main intake for end of August/beginning of September.
CONTACT: Ms Svetlana Ryzhenkova, Recruitment Manager.

CAPITAL & LETTERS ACADEMY

Tverskaya 16-1-809, Moscow 125009

+7 495 777 97 57

info@c-n-l.ru

www.c-n-l.ru

NUMBER OF TEACHERS: 2 at present, hoping to increase to 6–8.
PREFERENCE OF NATIONALITY: British, American, Canadian.
QUALIFICATIONS: CELTA/TEFL and at least 3 years of experience.
CONDITIONS OF EMPLOYMENT: 3-month trial period preceding open-ended stay. 40 working hours a week: Monday–Friday 9am–6pm with a one-hour lunch-break. Roughly 20 hours of teaching, 20 hours of lesson preparation and admin.
SALARY: Minimum 60,000 roubles per month (net), paid fortnightly. Possibility of salary increase every 4 months depending on performance.
FACILITIES/SUPPORT: School offers teachers a choice of apartment to suit their price/comfort level. Assistance given with permits.
RECRUITMENT: Interviewing people in Moscow and seeking candidates abroad.
CONTACT: Alexander Abramov, Senior Project Manager.

CARFAX PRIVATE TUTORS

Kutuzovsky prospekt, 7/4, Moscow 121248

Head office: 48 Langham Street, London W1W 7AY, UK.

☏ +7 495 775 4260; London: +44 20 7927 6200

✉ russiarecruitment@carfax-tutors.com

🖥 www.carfax-tutors.com/become-a-tutor and www.
carfax-recruitment.com

Offices also in St Petersburg, Baku, Dubai and London.

NUMBER OF TEACHERS: 25–30 freelance tutors for school-age children, plus nannies and governesses for pre-school children.

PREFERENCE OF NATIONALITY: British.

QUALIFICATIONS: Good standard of education, eg good degree plus CELTA or Trinity TESOL. Experience needed for some posts.

CONDITIONS OF EMPLOYMENT: Part-time positions are always available to candidates living for up to 6 months in St Petersburg. Flexible timetabling. Up to 20 hours per week with 2-day weekend.

SALARY: £20 an hour. From 45,000 roubles (net) for full-time work.

FACILITIES/SUPPORT: Depends on location. Temporary accommodation provided for initial period or assistance given. Visa invitation is generated after receiving copy of passport. All costs are reimbursed, including flights.

RECRUITMENT: Via TEFL websites such as www.tefl.com. Interviews can be held in London office or via Skype.

EF ENGLISH FIRST

Citydel Business Center, Zemlyanoy Val 9, 3rd Floor, Moscow 105064

☏ +86 21 6133 6133 (in Shanghai)

✉ efrecruitment@ef.com

🖥 www.englishfirst.com/trt/teaching-jobs-in-russia.
html and www.ef-russiateachers.com

NUMBER OF TEACHERS: About 40 for 35 schools in 20 cities (including 20 in Moscow and others in St Petersburg, Stavropol, Rostov, Tyumen, Nizhny Novgorod, Novosibirsk, etc).

PREFERENCE OF NATIONALITY: British, Irish, North American, Australian, New Zealander or South African.

QUALIFICATIONS: CELTA/TESOL/EF TEFL certificate plus a university degree (preferably in English, linguistics or arts), minimum 1-year ESL teaching experience. Minimum age 22.

CONDITIONS OF EMPLOYMENT: 9 months September–May or 12-month renewable contracts. Schools open 9am–9pm, Monday to Friday, and 9am–6pm, Saturday. 28 teaching hours per week within a 40-hour working week.

SALARY: 65,000 roubles (gross) a month.

FACILITIES/SUPPORT: Modern classrooms all fitted with computers and LCD screens with online supplementary materials. Support with finding accommodation. Visas and work permits arranged. Up to 28 days' paid holidays. Annual flight allowance of up to 42,000 roubles. Orientation upon arrival and ongoing training. Medical insurance provided.

RECRUITMENT: All online.

ENGLISH CENTRE ANGLETICA

54 Mira St, Krasnodar 350000

☏ +7 952 832 5480 or +44 7817 902134
(Bournemouth)

✉ klc.angletica@mail.ru

🖥 www.angletica.ru

School in Moscow as well as Krasnodar.

NUMBER OF TEACHERS: 3–9 per year, depending on contract duration.

PREFERENCE OF NATIONALITY: British.

QUALIFICATIONS: Candidates should be well organised, enthusiastic, able to communicate with adults and children alike. Previous work experience is not necessary, as full training is provided on arrival.

CONDITIONS OF EMPLOYMENT: 3 weeks to 9 months. Minimum 22–24 hours per week over 6 days.

SALARY: From £5 per hour net.

FACILITIES/SUPPORT: Free accommodation provided. Candidate covers cost for Russian visa application process but visa support and letter of invitation are arranged. The school pays for the cost of registration upon arrival. Reimbursement for travel by public transport.

RECRUITMENT: Via direct search, eg internet and newspaper adverts in the UK, eg on www.jobsabroadbulletin.co.uk. Recruitment between January and 1 June for early October start. Face-to-face interviews preferred but can be via Skype for global applicants.

CONTACT: Mr Stanislav Sukhanov, General Manager.

GLOBUS INTERNATIONAL

Makarenko St 5, Building 1A, 3rd floor, Office 5, Moscow 105062

Also Myasnitskaya 40/6, Moscow 101000

☏ +7 495 645 2158/421 3112

✉ info@globus-int.ru

🖥 www.globus-int.ru

British-owned company.

NUMBER OF TEACHERS: 26 corporate language trainers for branches in Moscow, St Petersburg, Pushkin, etc.

PREFERENCE OF NATIONALITY: British, Irish, Australian, New Zealander, Canadian, American.

QUALIFICATIONS: Minimum CELTA or equivalent, plus ideally 2 years' experience in corporate environment.

CONDITIONS OF EMPLOYMENT: 12-month standard contract, up to 26 academic hours per week. Lots of travelling within Moscow.

SALARY: From US$1,600 (net) per month, depending on experience.

FACILITIES/SUPPORT: A housing manager helps to accommodate all teachers based on what they would like. Centre organises a work visa invitation, then when the teacher is in Russia, organises all the necessary documents to make sure the teacher is fully registered and has all correct documentation. Medical insurance, survival Russian and in-house teacher training.

RECRUITMENT: Through TEFL websites. Telephone interviews are essential. If possible the school tries to set up face-to-face interviews in London.

CONTACT: Crichton Brauer, Director.

GLORY SCHOOL FOREIGN LANGUAGES
46 Gorokhovaya St, Off 5, St Petersburg 190005
+7 812 438 3083
edu@gloryschool.ru
www.gloryschool.ru

NUMBER OF TEACHERS: 10.

PREFERENCE OF NATIONALITY: British, American or Canadian.

QUALIFICATIONS: Native speaker with higher education and some experience. Prefer candidates with 3 years or more EFL teaching experience or EFL certificate.

CONDITIONS OF EMPLOYMENT: 1-year contract. Part-time in-company classes available.

SALARY: $20 per hour.

FACILITIES/SUPPORT: Assistance is given with renting a flat and applying for work permits and visas. Russian-language lessons can be exchanged for English conversation practice.

RECRUITMENT: Usually via the internet.

IPT (INTERNATIONAL PROFESSIONAL TRAINING) LTD
Office 207, Petrovka Ulitsa 15/13, Moscow 107031
+7 495 228 3513
info@iptrussia.ru
www.iptrussia.ru

NUMBER OF TEACHERS: 40 native speaker corporate trainers out of total staff of 200 in Moscow. IPT also teaches in over 50 regional cities across Russia.

PREFERENCE OF NATIONALITY: Native speaker (or Russian national). Company is British-owned and managed.

QUALIFICATIONS: University degree and certified EFL teaching qualification, plus minimum 3–5 years' EFL experience, ideally including Business English and/or Corporate Language Teaching. Previous experience in Russia or Eastern Europe preferred, but not essential. Experience of financial or legal presentations would be valuable.

CONDITIONS OF EMPLOYMENT: 16-20 academic hours per week. Part-time contract according to Labour Code regulations. Schedule of minimum 80 academic hours per month. Students are all at intermediate level or above. Hours mainly 8am–9:30am and 6pm–7:30pm with some afternoon classes.

SALARY: Negotiable. All salaries are paid net of tax; employer pays all income taxes and social fees. Flight cost reimbursement.

FACILITIES/SUPPORT: Free accommodation given on arrival, and assistance given in search for accommodation, with agents and transport provided. All teachers receive a 12-month, multiple-entry, fully legal teaching visa, which is registered through the company for the duration of the contract. IPT provides native-speaker teachers with free Russian lessons (subject to availability) and teaching workshops on different themes. Free Moscow travel card.

RECRUITMENT: Telephone interviews (at least 3), references, qualifications check, receipt of sample lesson plans.

CONTACT: Tim Newton, Managing Director (tim.newton@iptrussia.ru).

ISTRA SCHOOL
6 Revolution Square, Istra, Moscow Region 143500
+7 496 314 5321; +7 985 915 6319
info@istra-english.ru
www.istra-english.ru

NUMBER OF TEACHERS: 2.

PREFERENCE OF NATIONALITY: British, American, Australian.

QUALIFICATIONS: Minimum 2 years' teaching experience plus CELTA or TEFL certificate.

CONDITIONS OF EMPLOYMENT: 9–10 month contracts. Normal load is 86 hours in a 4-week period which may include Saturdays and Sundays. This comprises 78 hours of teaching (equivalent to 104 academic 'hours' which last 45 minutes) plus 8 normal hours for other duties, eg stand-by, placement testing, paperwork, meetings, seminars, open days, English clubs and presentations.

SALARY: $1,500 per month (net) plus annual bonus. Compulsory insurance contributions paid by school.

FACILITIES/SUPPORT: School arranges invitation and other documents to enable teacher to obtain the visa in their country of residence. The school will reimburse all fees and expenses. Free accommodation is provided in a two-room shared flat. Guidance is given on legal requirements, eg in organising doctor's examination and HIV test; school covers expenses. Teachers are enrolled in free Russian state health care scheme (which does not cover medications or dental services).

RECRUITMENT: Adverts on www.tefl.com. Interviews by Skype.

CONTACT: Tatiana Krouglova, Director.

LANGUAGE LINK RUSSIA
Moscow
job@languagelink.ru
www.jobs.languagelink.ru

NUMBER OF TEACHERS: 200 for 60 schools throughout Russia (Moscow, Moscow Region, St Petersburg, St Petersburg Region, Volgograd, Samara, Toliatti, Ufa, Rostov na Donu, Stavropol, Orenburg etc).

PREFERENCE OF NATIONALITY: British, American, Canadian, Australian, New Zealander and South African.

QUALIFICATIONS: CELTA or Trinity Certificate/Diploma (or equivalents) required unless teachers apply with relevant EFL/ESL experience. Candidates without a 100-hour TEFL qualification may enter Language Link's Teacher Internship Programme. Openings also available to those without experience or qualifications as volunteers or summer camp staff. All applicants should be enthusiastic, cheerful and open-minded.

CONDITIONS OF EMPLOYMENT: 6, 9 or 12-month contracts, 25 teaching hours per week, usually 4 hours a day, 5 days a week. Adult classes, children's classes and in-company. Also runs a number of English-language summer camps near major cities (camps@languagelink.ru) starting the beginning of June.

FACILITIES/SUPPORT: All teachers provided with free accommodation in 2-room flat (for 2 teachers). Paid time off, paid medical services, full work visa support and academic support.

RECRUITMENT: Application is online. Minimum 2 professional references. Telephone/Skype interviews are compulsory unless carried out by Language Link in London.

CONTACT: Robert Jensky, Managing Director.

LITTLE ANGELS KINDERGARTEN
St Novocheremushkinskaya no 49, Office 12, Moscow
+7 8495 332 1603
litang@mail.ru
www.littleangels.ru

Bilingual kindergarten for children aged 1.5 to 7.

NUMBER OF TEACHERS: 5.

PREFERENCE OF NATIONALITY: British, Canadian or Australian.

QUALIFICATIONS: A strong background in early childhood education and a TEFL qualification. Also he/she should have experience of teaching.

CONDITIONS OF EMPLOYMENT: Standard 1-year contract, usual hours are 9am–5pm.

SALARY: Depends on qualification and experience but at least $1,500. If the employee has a work permit from Little Angels, 13% of the tax is deducted from their salary.

FACILITIES/SUPPORT: No help with accommodation or work permit at the moment. Usually, teachers already have a work permit from a company or agency.

RECRUITMENT: By interview, filling in a questionnaire and taking a class. Interviews are essential.

MOSCOW INNOVATIVE LANGUAGE CENTRE
Landyishevaya str., bld.14, Kurkino, 125466 Moscow
+7 911 773 3677/+7 495 997 2365
mail@milcentre.ru
www.milcentre.ru

Private kindergartens offering bilingual education to young children.

NUMBER OF TEACHERS: 2.

PREFERENCE OF NATIONALITY: UK, Canada, USA.

QUALIFICATIONS: Higher/college degree in Humanities/ Psychology/Education/Social Studies; a certificate in TESL/ TEFL would be a bonus. Minimum of 1 year's experience of teaching English to children of pre-school and primary school age, preferably abroad (eg South Korea). If candidate has only TEFL/TESL certificate, 1–2 years' experience of teaching English to young children is obligatory. Knowledge of early development of children and of teaching methodology needed. Supplementary skills and abilities welcome, eg in art, music, sports or acting. Looking for young optimistic and hard-working teachers with experience. New 2-week training programme offered free of charge to those without qualifications, open to Britons and North Americans aged under 45 with a humanities degree.

CONDITIONS OF EMPLOYMENT: Minimum 1 year. 10-hour days starting at 8.30am, 9am or 11am with hour off for lunch. 2 days off per week. Summer camp work may be available.

SALARY: Around 60,000 roubles basic per month.

FACILITIES/SUPPORT: Foreign teachers are provided with comfortable accommodation (separate or shared) close to the school. Full work visa sponsorship and reimbursement.

RECRUITMENT: Ads on ESL/EFL websites. Skype interviews obligatory.

CONTACT: Elena Panfilova, CEO (e.panfilova@milcentre.ru).

PREMIUM ENGLISH

Chistopolskaya 20A, Kazan 420111, Republic of Tatarstan

☎ +7 843 518 6060

✉ info@premiumenglish.ru

💻 www.premiumenglish.ru

British-owned and managed.

NUMBER OF TEACHERS: 12–15.

PREFERENCE OF NATIONALITY: None. School is British owned.

QUALIFICATIONS: CELTA or equivalent plus degree and 1 year's ELT experience. Young Learners' experience an advantage.

CONDITIONS OF EMPLOYMENT: September to July, or 12 months from September. 25 clock hours per week, 5 days a week (2 consecutive days off: Sat/Sun or Sun/Mon). To teach children and adults in the business and professional community both in-company and on school premises.

SALARY: Approx. $1,000 per month after tax.

FACILITIES/SUPPORT: The school provides furnished single accommodation. Employer provides teachers with a multiple-entry work visa. Teachers need to provide apostilled copies of passport and qualification. An HIV test is required for the visa. Survival Russian lessons given. Weekly teacher training.,Contribution to travel expenses given on completion of contract.

RECRUITMENT: Via www.tefl.com.

CONTACT: Steven Mott, Director of Teaching.

WINDSOR ENGLISH LANGUAGE SCHOOL

7 Komsomolsky Prospect, Moscow 119146

☎ +7 495 221 0832

✉ job@windsor.ru

💻 www.windsor.ru/eng/tefl

NUMBER OF TEACHERS: Vacancies almost all year round, especially for part-time teachers experienced with IELTS preparation.

PREFERENCE OF NATIONALITY: British, Canadian, Irish, American, Australian and New Zealander.

QUALIFICATIONS: Bachelor's degree or higher (preferred) and a TEFL certificate essential (CELTA, Trinity College TESOL, etc). Minimum 1-year's experience of teaching in Europe.

CONDITIONS OF EMPLOYMENT: Part-time teaching mainly, but also 9–12 month contracts from August/September. Most teaching takes place on mornings and weekends. Summer openings in Siberia (Abakan in the Republic of Khakasia).

SALARY: From 1,600 roubles per 80-minute lesson. Starting salary for contract work 30,000 roubles per month (approx. $1,000) net, for 26 academic hours per week; 36,000 roubles for 30 hours per week. Overtime hours paid.

FACILITIES/SUPPORT: The school provides good-quality shared accommodation and fully assists and pays for work visas. Employer pays for utilities, health insurance, monthly travel card and bonus. Full in-house academic support.

RECRUITMENT: Via adverts on www.expat.ru, www.tefl.com, etc. Interviews are absolutely essential, usually done by telephone or Skype.

CONTACT: Polina Romashkina, Human Resources.

ZOLOTERRA

Kommuny Street 133, Chelyabinsk 454080

☎ +7 (351) 200 40 10

✉ info@zoloterra.ru

💻 www.zoloterra.ru

NUMBER OF TEACHERS: 5.

PREFERENCE OF NATIONALITY: British.

QUALIFICATIONS: CELTA or Trinity.

CONDITIONS OF EMPLOYMENT: One year contract. Approximately 30 academic hours per week with the possibility of paid overtime.

SALARY: Average US$900–$1200 per month (net, after 13%–30% has been deducted for taxes and social security).

FACILITIES/SUPPORT: Accommodation is provided and all bills are paid by the company. Full working visas are provided and the cost reimbursed. A letter of invitation is provided so the applicant can apply (in person) in London or Edinburgh. An HIV certificate is required.

RECRUITMENT: Adverts on Tefl.com and Dave's ESL Cafe, followed by Skype interview.

CONTACT: Dr S. Zolotykh, Director.

THE BALTICS

Arguably the most Westernised part of the old Russian Empire, the Baltic countries of Lithuania, Latvia and Estonia all became fully fledged members of the EU in 2004. This has significantly eased the bureaucracy for passport holders from EU member states, while other citizens will need to apply for a work permit, which can take many months. For this reason and due to extra costs, most schools strongly prefer to employ EU citizens. A number of budget airlines as well as national carriers operate to the region (eg Ryanair to Kaunas and Riga, Tallinn and Vilnius) plus Wizz Air to Riga and Vilnius. Despite new business and tourism links, the market for English-language teachers has not been expanding, and few vacancies are advertised abroad.

Latvia and Lithuania

Of the three Baltic States, Latvia has been slowest to embrace change, although its beautiful capital, Riga, has become a mecca for a certain type of British tourist (at the lager-lout end of the spectrum). English is increasingly necessary for anyone working in the hospitality sector, although there are still relatively few commercial language schools and virtually no job postings on the TEFL sites.

Qualified ELT teachers could make contact with the Latvian Association of Teachers of English (LATE) in Riga (www.late.lv), though it doesn't get involved with job assistance and is mainly for professional development of English teachers at gymnasiums and other state schools.

One Latvian language school that may be able to offer decent facilities is the Language Centre International House Riga-Satva (www.ihriga.lv), which can also help with visas, flat-finding and teaching support. It does its hiring in April–May for a September start. Berlitz has a presence in Riga.

The market in Lithuania seems to have shrunk in recent years, with EF English First scaling back and the ILS franchise having closed down. The only vacancies seen advertised recently were for English for Academic Purposes and summer courses at a private Christian university in Klaidepa (www.lcc.lt) affiliated to the heavy-duty proselytising City Church.

Estonia

Estonia is arguably the most progressive of the three Baltic countries. The demand for native English-speaker teachers is not very high, as illustrated by the language institute in Tallinn that communicated with this book to say that it already has plenty of native-speaking English teachers in its database, with few vacancies. However once in a while a private institute advertises on an international TEFL site: for example In Down-Town Language School in Tallinn was looking to recruit well-qualified teachers for an August 2015 start and offering a decent monthly salary of €800–€1200 gross.

LIST OF EMPLOYERS

AMERICAN ENGLISH SCHOOL
Naugarduko 4, 01141 Vilnius, Lithuania
📞 +370 5 279 1011
🖳 vilnius@ames.lt
🖥 www.ames.lt

NUMBER OF TEACHERS: 40 for 8 branches throughout the country.
PREFERENCE OF NATIONALITY: None.
QUALIFICATIONS: TEFL certificate required in addition to background in pedagogy.

CONDITIONS OF EMPLOYMENT: 5 days per week (mornings and afternoons). Other conditions negotiable. Students are teenagers, adults and corporate clients, private and public sector.

SALARY: $9–$12 per contact hour.

FACILITIES/SUPPORT: Initial in-house training provided; continuous in-house training and teacher support provided.

RECRUITMENT: Demo class to be taught after the interview.

CONTACT: Ms Egle Kesyliene, Director.

INTERNATIONAL LANGUAGE SERVICES

Roosikrantsi 8B, 10119 Tallinn, Estonia

© +372 627 7170

🖱 info@ilstallinn.ee

💻 www.ilstallinn.ee

NUMBER OF TEACHERS: 7 full-time and 3 part-time.

PREFERENCE OF NATIONALITY: Locally based freelancers preferred.

QUALIFICATIONS: Minimum CELTA or Trinity certificate plus 1 year's experience. Some business knowledge preferred.

CONDITIONS OF EMPLOYMENT: 9 months from 1 September with a good chance of staying on for summer work. 96–120 45-minute lessons per month.

SALARY: €850 per month net, rising to €900 in second year. Teachers must be registered with the tax authorities to be eligible for tax-free allowance.

FACILITIES/SUPPORT: Regular seminars and teacher-development programme leading to LCCI Further Certificate in Teaching Business English. Sponsorship for the Trinity DipTESOL by distance for teachers on longer contracts. No accommodation since plenty of rental accommodation is easily available; a 1-bedroom flat should cost €225–€300 a month, more if it is within walking distance of the school.

RECRUITMENT: Internet ads (www.tefl.com) usually in March. Phone interviews.

CONTACT: Phil Marsdale, Director.

UKRAINE

After the February revolution of 2014, hopes ran high that a closer alliance to the west would gradually strengthen and reform democratic institutions and boost the economy. However, after the humiliating annexation of Crimea by Putin's Russia, and pro-Russian separatist violence in the east of Ukraine which has so far resulted in nearly 6,500 deaths, the road ahead does not look smooth. The economy plummeted in the first two quarters of 2015, with the decline attributed to the military conflict. Inflation is becoming a serious problem. Revenue that might have been devoted to improving the education system is being diverted into defence spending. The Peace Corps was so alarmed by the conflict that in April 2014 it took the decision to suspend its programme and therefore pulled out all of its 300+ volunteers, including many English teachers who have not returned.

The vast republic of Ukraine's EFL market is no longer in its infancy, with a reduced demand for English surviving the recent crisis. Many native English teachers, made nervous by the unrest and also deterred by the persistent low wages, have departed while certain sections of the market (especially corporate) have collapsed.

On the positive side, native English-speaking teachers in Ukraine often remark on the enthusiastic reception they receive from students. Many of the younger pupils express an adoration for the teachers, which can at first be quite overwhelming, and prospective teachers in out of the way places can expect to receive occasional invitations to students' homes in order to meet their families. Although this can initially be a little unnerving, most teachers find that the generous hospitality is one of the things that makes teaching in Ukraine such a worthwhile experience.

After more than a decade in Kiev, **John Hall** is full of the rewards of teaching in Ukraine:

> *You may ask, why teach in this part of the world and not sunnier climes? Well, I did a degree in English Lit and Russian at the University of Westminster. For part of the course I enjoyed nine months in St Petersburg and got hooked on the Slavic mentality, people, culture, literature and general way of life. I guess that feeling has never left me.*
>
> *My situation in Ukraine is not typical, but not unusual either. I have worked for three private language schools since my arrival here, most recently the London School of English and now International House Kyiv, where I have been promoted to Assistant Director of Studies. I have also been married to a lovely Ukrainian woman for the last eight years. The reason for my long stay and subsequent happiness in Kyiv is mainly down to the friendly atmosphere within the city and the pleasing and professional work conditions I have encountered here. The social life is quite lively, though to master the language is a life-long goal!*
>
> *Please don't get me wrong. Ukraine is not the easiest place to live. There are many schools out there that are not as foreigner friendly as my current school. Work permits and visas are a constant nightmare. But here at IH, everything is done legally, which is a major plus, which everyone admires and respects. The students are lovely, polite and hard working on the whole. There are some who fit the first two qualities, but not the latter, and that's to be expected everywhere in the world. They are generally inquisitive and have high expectations of their teachers, which comes out of the national character. They are paying – sometimes quite highly – for a service and expect the teachers to deliver top-notch lessons and answer all their questions confidently. This can be a bit daunting for some teachers, but a challenge and a happy one for most. Children aged 5–16 make up more than half of the overall student number and this has a huge bearing on planning, timetabling and recruitment, as all teachers are expected to be capable of teaching all these groups.*

For professional opportunities, well-qualified candidates can try the British Council in Kiev, which has a teaching centre and hires freelancers on an ongoing basis (job.applications@britishcouncil.org.ua). In addition to the Kiev branch where John Hall works, International House has a strong presence in the country, with vacancies from time to time at its schools in Dnipropetrovsk, Kharviv, Odessa, Sevastopol, Poltava and Lviv (the latter has an entry below).

The British-owned Educational Solutions Group is Ukraine's largest privately owned chain of ELT schools, with a centralised Human Resources office. The group comprises six London Schools of English (see entry) and two Language Academies, in various cities. Teachers with a minimum of a degree, CELTA or equivalent and a little experience will not find it difficult to be hired on 12 or 18-month contracts. US nationals must obtain the IM–1 visa, for which they will need a labour authorisation form (*dozvil na pratsevlashtuvannia*) from their employer.

As in Russia, the process for schools of getting permission to hire foreigners is both expensive and labyrinthine. Business visas for British teachers cost twice as much as for other nationalities. For years, many schools didn't bother and asked their teachers to leave the country every three months and re-enter as tourists. However, the same rule now applies as in the Schengen Area, which is that you are permitted to stay 90 days in 180, and cannot re-enter straightaway. The fine for overstaying is a modest 850 hryvnias (£25) which permits you to stay for a further 90 days.

As is noticeable throughout Europe and elsewhere where English is in high demand, English-language summer camps have arrived on the scene. This huge country has many beautiful landscapes for hosting such camps, from the Carpathian mountains to the Black Sea. Two companies seen advertising for summer staff are Dec Camp Ltd (www.dec-camp.com), which runs an English-immersion activity camp at a recreational centre 70km south of Lviv in Western Ukraine; and the Celyn-abc-camp in Novye Sanzhary, Poltava Province (www.celyn-abc-camp.com), which wanted native-speaker teachers and counsellors to work for between two weeks and three months. The Dec Camp is run by the Dec School in Kiev (www.dec-school.com/dec-school/vakansii.html), which hires teachers for the academic year.

LIST OF EMPLOYERS

INTERNATIONAL HOUSE – KYIV
7 Vandy Vasilevskoy Street, Kyiv 03055
☎ +380 44 238 9870
✉ dos@ih.kiev.ua or school@ih.kiev.ua
🖥 www.ih.kiev.ua/en

Note that as of May 2015, there was a hostile take-over of the school and its future is uncertain.

NUMBER OF TEACHERS: 27–30.
PREFERENCE OF NATIONALITY: Native English speakers.
QUALIFICATIONS: Minimum TEFL/CELTA certificate.
CONDITIONS OF EMPLOYMENT: 1-year contracts. Teach up to 25 hours per week.
SALARY: $1,000–$1,500 a month based on experience, paid in Ukrainian hryvnia.
FACILITIES/SUPPORT: The school provides the teacher with a single room or shared apartment.

INTERNATIONAL HOUSE LVIV
3 Petrushevych Square, Lviv 79005
☎ +380 32 225 5190
✉ ihlviv@gmail.com
🖥 www.ihlviv.com

NUMBER OF TEACHERS: 15.
PREFERENCE OF NATIONALITY: None, but should be native English speakers.
QUALIFICATIONS: CELTA/TESOL/IHC/Trinity certificate.
CONDITIONS OF EMPLOYMENT: 10 months plus 3 weeks' paid holidays. 24 teaching hours per week plus one meeting/seminar.
SALARY: From 6,800 hryvnias ($800 approx.) per month, depending on experience.
FACILITIES/SUPPORT: $400 of return ticket covered by the school. Furnished accommodation is provided for up to $200. Half the cost of the D-type visa and apostille is covered. The cost of the work permit, translation and registration is fully covered by school.
RECRUITMENT: Locally, via the internet and through IHWO recruitment services.
CONTACT: Marianna Ilyina, Director (marianna_ilyina@mail.ru).

LARISA SCHOOL OF LANGUAGE
Sovietskaya and Shevchenko 63, Second Floor, Nikolaev
☎ +380 512 7171 96; +380 94 944 0196
✉ larisaschooloflanguage@gmail.com
🖥 www.larisaschooloflanguage.com or www.larisaschooloflanguage.net

Main office and language school for the LSL Education Network.

NUMBER OF TEACHERS: 10.

PREFERENCE OF NATIONALITY: American, British or Canadian.

QUALIFICATIONS: TEFL/TESL/CELTA.

CONDITIONS OF EMPLOYMENT: Minimum 3-month contract depending on the time of year. Usual working hours are Monday to Saturday, late afternoons and evenings.

FACILITIES/SUPPORT: Assistance is given with finding accommodation and applying for work permits.

RECRUITMENT: Usually via the internet. Interviews are essential and can be carried out through Skype.

CONTACT: Larisa Nemchenko, Director, and Bill Green.

THE LONDON SCHOOL OF ENGLISH GROUP

Room 105, Building 19, 39 Politekhnichna Street, Kyiv 03056

Also: The Language Academy, 14 Lunacharskogo Street, Kyiv 02002 📞 +380 503 801 390

The London School of English Odessa. Office 20, 14 Ekaterininskaya Street, Odessa 65026

📞 +380 44 277 8654 (LSE Kyiv); +380 44 541 0602 (Language Academy); +380 48 777 5015 (LSE Odessa)

📧 admin@lse.kiev.ua (LSE Kiev); lacademy@lse.kiev.ua (Language Academy); office@lse.od.ua (LSE Odessa)

💻 www.lse.ua/vacancies

Part of British-owned Educational Solutions Group.

NUMBER OF TEACHERS: 25–35 at several schools around Ukraine.

PREFERENCE OF NATIONALITY: None.

QUALIFICATIONS: CELTA or Trinity TESOL certificate required (other certificates will not be considered). Degree needed. Minimum 1 year's teaching experience preferred but newly qualified teachers are welcome.

CONDITIONS OF EMPLOYMENT: 12 or 18 months starting late August to October. 24 hours per week. Also summer contracts.

SALARY: 14,400–17,200 hryvnias per month, depending on experience and qualifications. Employees holding a higher TEFL qualification (MA, DELTA) and five years' experience can earn 21,000+ hryvnias.

FACILITIES/SUPPORT: Fully furnished rent-free apartment is provided. Sponsorship on the Cambridge DELTA (in second year of employment) and or YL extension courses is available. Assistance given in obtaining work permit and long-term visa which are paid for by school. Free return flight from UK.

RECRUITMENT: Via www.tefl.com. Initial phone/Skype interview followed by a face-to-face interview, sometimes held in London in summer as well as Ukraine. Walk-in candidates will be given an interview whatever the time of year.

CONTACT: Adam Rudrum, HR Manager.

MOLDOVA

Few people can find Moldova on the map (between the Ukraine and Romania) and fewer know that it is famous for its wine. It languishes at the bottom of the table of the poorest countries in Europe which means that a few agencies recruit paying volunteers. For example Love Volunteers (www.lovevolunteers.org/programs/volunteer-moldova) cooperates with a Moldovan NGO to place volunteer teachers to help school children with conversation practice. Participants stay with families in Causeni. Programme fees start at $340 for one week.

And yet, a handful of commercial language schools is in business and occasionally one will seek to employ a native speaker or two. Sharp-eyed readers of the international TEFL websites will spot the occasional appeal for a teacher, for example at a language summer camp with My English Planet or with the well-respected International Language Training Center in the capital, Chisinau (see entry).

LIST OF EMPLOYERS

INTERNATIONAL LANGUAGE TRAINING CENTER (ILTC)
43 Petru Rares str., Chisinau 2005

📞 +373 22 29 29 88

📧 iltcmoldova@gmail.com or iltcmoldova.hr@gmail.com

💻 http://iltc.md/teaching

NUMBER OF TEACHERS: 3–4 to teach General English to young learners, teenagers and adults, Business English and TOEFL preparation.

PREFERENCE OF NATIONALITY: UK and USA, and other English-speaking countries.

QUALIFICATIONS: CELTA/TESOL/TEFL Certificate.

CONDITIONS OF EMPLOYMENT: 10-month contracts. 24 hours a week, mostly in afternoons and evenings.

SALARY: Fixed salary of US$650 a month (net).

FACILITIES/SUPPORT: Shared or single accommodation is provided by the school, or monthly accommodation allowance of US$300. Support given in obtaining a work and residence permit. Teachers must bring their degree certificate, CELTA or equivalent and criminal background check all apostilled in their home country. The process takes about two months. End-of-contract contribution of US$750 to travel expenses. ESL workshops and teacher mentoring.

RECRUITMENT: Web adverts and Skype interviews.

CONTACT: Oksana Malcenco, Director of Studies.

THE REST OF EUROPE

Outside the mainstream European nations, demand for native speakers of English obviously exists though immigration problems often occur. This chapter contains a miscellany of European opportunities in some quite obscure corners of the continent.

ALBANIA

Information about teaching in this European country wedged between Greece, Macedonia, Serbia and Montenegro has not always been easy to find, but Albania is now fairly stable and offers some opportunities for teachers keen to escape the traditional EFL circuit. The number of paid teaching jobs is still limited by the country's poverty, but Albania is signatory to a Stabilisation and Association agreement with the EU, so there is hope that demand will increase if the country's economy slowly continues to grow.

English is certainly the favoured foreign language and is compulsory from the fifth grade through to university. Some language schools at least aspire to employ a native English-speaking teacher, although few can currently afford it. There is a need for volunteer teachers to come to Albania to expose children from deprived backgrounds to English spoken by a native. The Language Schools in Albania Foundation (LSIA) is the largest non-profit private language tuition provider in Albania, founded in April 1994 by a group of Albanian university teachers and students. It currently operates in 14 locations across Albania and Macedonia and has a little (out-of-date) information on the 'Careers' page of its website (www.lsiaal.org). Volunteers may be offered local accommodation and LSIA will also assist with the red tape. **Blerina Gjonaj**, who used to work for the foundation, suggested for a previous edition that volunteering could lead to a paid job:

> The demand for native English speakers is increasing every day, and the same can be said for paid employment, although that is not yet at the level that everybody wants. It is still easier to find a teaching job if you are a volunteer (maybe at the beginning), and then you can get involved as a paid employee. Albanian people are very interested in learning English. Language schools in Albania enrol children, mature students, adults and even parents of the students.

Albania is still considered to be close enough to a developing country to have a sizeable contingent of Peace Corps volunteers in place, including a number who are teaching English at foreign-language high schools and other institutes. **Margaret Sheridan** was a Peace Corps volunteer, who said: '*I had a terrific experience, teaching English in high school and to adults, then opening a TOEFL test site, the first in Southern Albania, with a terrific Albanian colleague.*'

Other institutions that may be worth contacting are the Memorial International School of Tirana (Ish Shkolla e Partise, Rruga Dritan Hoxha Nr.1, Tirana; +355 4 223 7375; www.mist.edu.al), which currently employs a handful of Americans, Britons and Canadians as ESL teachers. The school's minimum requirement is that teachers have some years of experience in their own fields, although the majority have completed university courses with components in education. A language school in Vlora called the Smart Center (www.smartcenter.al) has been seen advertising a vacancy at a monthly salary of $500. The only commercial institute we have heard of hiring native speakers is the Lincoln Center of Albania (see entry).

Visa guidelines can be checked at the Embassy of the Republic of Albania in the UK or USA. If a European's stay is going to be less than 90 days, they do not need to apply for a visa. It is not possible to cross out of Albania and straight back in again to renew your tourist visa. If you intend to stay longer than 90 days, you must apply for a residency permit. US nationals can stay for up to a year without a permit.

Living costs are very cheap by US and UK standards, though choice can be limited. One volunteer teacher complained that he had to travel five hours by bus to Tirana to buy ketchup. Albania has plenty of scenic attractions, including rugged mountains, ancient Greek ruins and a marvellous stretch of Adriatic coastline, blissfully free of package-holiday tourists.

LIST OF EMPLOYERS

ABRAHAM LINCOLN PROFESSIONAL STUDIES CENTER
Rruga Qemal Stafa Nr. 184, Tirana; also at Rr Ismail Qemali 31
- +355 4 223 0880
- info@lincoln.org.al
- http://lincolnalbania.org

School has a Christian board of directors.

NUMBER OF TEACHERS: Few native English speakers for the 3 branches.

PREFERENCE OF NATIONALITY: American and others.

QUALIFICATIONS: Degree or TEFL certificate required; MA preferred.

CONDITIONS OF EMPLOYMENT: Part-time teachers for courses offered at all levels and special English programmes for several professional institutions in Albania.

RECRUITMENT: Mainly via www.anegino.gen.al (recruitment site in Albanian).

CONTACT: Edita Nikolla (enikolli@lincoln.org.al).

AMERICAN TRAINING CENTER LTD
Rruga Ismail Qemali, Godina 29, Kati III, Tirana
- +355 4 2 257075
- tirana@atcentre.org
- www.atcentre.org

Franchise of the Midwest Education Group in Chicago, offering American English language teaching, TESOL Certification for English Teachers, soft-skills training, etc in Tirana, Korca and Fier.

NUMBER OF TEACHERS: 3.

PREFERENCE OF NATIONALITY: Americans (English native speakers).

QUALIFICATIONS: Experience is a plus, but teachers are usually newly graduated from Midwest's online TESOL training course.

CONDITIONS OF EMPLOYMENT: Minimum 1 year, renewable. 20 hours of teaching a week + 10 hours preparation between 8am and 8pm.

SALARY: US$1,000 per month full-time. US$10 an hour, part-time. Deductions according to law.

FACILITIES/SUPPORT: Assistance given with finding accommodation. Visas can be obtained by Americans without difficulty after arrival.

RECRUITMENT: Via American community in Albania, TESOL Certified Teachers or Midwest Education Group database (www.midwested.us).

CONTACT: Ms Adeila Makashi, Administrator/CEO (adeila.makashi@ande-lm.com.al).

ANDORRA

Andorra lies in the heart of the Pyrenees, between Spain and France, and can be seen as an extension of both countries, though it has its own elected government. It is too small to have many language schools, but the two listed here are possibilities (and you would be there over the skiing season). Technically, Andorra is not a member of the EU so it is necessary to obtain a work permit which involves completing forms in Catalan.

LIST OF EMPLOYERS

CENTRE ANDORRA DE LLENGUES (CALL)
Av del Fener 17, 1-F/G, 500 Andorra-la-Vella
- +376 804030
- idiomes@call.ad
- www.call.eu.com

NUMBER OF TEACHERS: 2.

PREFERENCE OF NATIONALITY: British, Irish and North Americans.

QUALIFICATIONS: BA in English or a foreign language plus TEFL qualification and 2–3 years' experience abroad most welcome. A good knowledge of Spanish and/or French can help. Non-smokers preferred.

CONDITIONS OF EMPLOYMENT: 9–10-month renewable contract that runs from October to June. 27 hours per week, 5 days a week. Teaching hours spread throughout the day. Teaching very young learners (6–7 years) and all other ages including professionals.

SALARY: €1,800 per month (plus overtime if any available).

FACILITIES/SUPPORT: Board and lodging available within walking distance costs from €550 per month. Work permit arranged and paid for by the school.

RECRUITMENT: Direct application with CV and photo by email.

CONTACT: Claude Benet.

INLINGUA ANDORRA
Carrer de la Vinyeta 2, AD500 Andorra la Vella
+376 807060
inlingua@inlingua.ad
www.inlingua.ad

NUMBER OF TEACHERS: 10 for four branches.

PREFERENCE OF NATIONALITY: None.

QUALIFICATIONS: University degree and TEFL certificate needed plus 2 years of experience.

CONDITIONS OF EMPLOYMENT: 9.5 month contracts. 25 teaching hours a week.

SALARY: €1,300 a month less 10% deductions.

FACILITIES/SUPPORT: Assistance given with red tape; teachers must provide criminal record check and university diploma and transcripts with the Hague apostille. No help given with accommodation.

RECRUITMENT: Spontaneous applications, inlingua HQ and other web portals. Skype interviews.

CONTACT: Ferran Costa, Director.

BOSNIA-HERZEGOVINA

There are still few private language schools in Bosnia, and most operate on a small scale. As usual, you could check the list of 27 schools provided at www.eslbase.com/schools/bosnia for leads.

LIST OF EMPLOYERS

NEW ACADEMY
Muharem Suljanovic Street, 79101 Prijedor
+387 65 586469
new_academy@yahoo.com
www.new-academy.com

PREFERENCE OF NATIONALITY: None.

QUALIFICATIONS: 2 years' TEFL experience.

CONDITIONS OF EMPLOYMENT: 1-year contract with working hours between 4pm and 10pm. Also offers summer courses.

RECRUITMENT: Interviews are essential.

CONTACT: Zoran Beric, Principal.

CROATIA

In July 2013 Croatia celebrated its acceptance into the European Union. This is unlikely to have much immediate impact on its struggling economy, but long-term integration will boost business and lead to more demand for a high standard of English.

Building on its strong indigenous English teaching infrastructure, Croatia's private language schools flourish in Zagreb, Varazdin and Karlovac, as well as in other towns. For many schools, the idea of employing a native English-speaker teacher is very attractive; particularly given Croatia's popularity as a British tourist destination, accessible by cheap flights. Teachers who go to work in Croatia are likely to find themselves being made welcome and treated well, certainly outside the usual tourist hot spots. Salaries are likely to be quoted in euros even though the national currency is still the kuna.

The market for private teaching is strong; however, native English teachers need to be well qualified to se-cure a job. The Foreign Language School, Ziger, is fairly modest in size, with only one or two native-speaker teachers, but it still asks for a degree, at least one year's experience, and a CELTA or DELTA certificate.

Non-EU citizens wishing to work in Croatia must apply to the Embassy of the Republic of Croatia for a visa. An application form must be completed by your employer and returned together with a passport, two photographs and details of the job (eg a copy of your contract, length of employment, type of work, location and full address of employer).

The British Council in Zagreb can offer informal assistance to prospective teachers and should be able to put you in touch with the Association of Croatian Teachers of English (HUPE), which organises teacher-development activities but can't help foreign teachers to find jobs.

With its beautiful coastline and accessibility, Croatia has developed summer camps, some of which teach English. The exchange company CCUSA sends volunteer counsellors to Camp California in Pakostane near Zadar on the Adriatic, though counsellor-teachers here pay a programme fee of $245 (www.ccusa.co.uk) but get free room and board. **Geoff Nunney** wanted to find a summer job after the academic term finished at the language school in Slovakia, where he had spent the year. He got a job at Euroclub on Solta, an island off the coast near Split (www.euroclub.hr), the largest international youth camp on the Adriatic:

I have a return invitation for this year, kids of all nationalities from 10 to 20. There's a big mixture of teachers – I was known as the 'Crazy Teacher'. Lots of sports, lessons and a holiday atmosphere. I did four weeks there, and the pay is enough to live on.

LIST OF EMPLOYERS

FOREIGN LANGUAGE SCHOOL – ZIGER
S. Vraza 37, 42000 Varazdin
+385 42 330385
info@skola-ziger.hr
www.skola-ziger.hr

NUMBER OF TEACHERS: 1–2.
PREFERENCE OF NATIONALITY: British, American and Canadian.
QUALIFICATIONS: At least 1 year's experience, CELTA/DELTA, university degree.
CONDITIONS OF EMPLOYMENT: Minimum 1-year contract, teaching hours are usually late afternoon and evenings.
FACILITIES/SUPPORT: Assistance with finding accommodation and work permit (school applies and translates documents).
RECRUITMENT: Via email contact. Interviews by phone.
CONTACT: Irena Ziger, Director.

MHC BUSINESS LANGUAGE TRAINING
Petrinjska 26, 10 000 Zagreb
+385 99 793 6363
zagreb@mhc-training.com
www.mhc-training.com

NUMBER OF TEACHERS: 15.
PREFERENCE OF NATIONALITY: Any.
QUALIFICATIONS: MHC trainers have an understanding of business experience, often specialising in areas such as marketing, finance, pharmaceuticals or law. A degree is not necessary, although a teaching certificate such as CELTA would be of value.
CONDITIONS OF EMPLOYMENT: Freelance, teaching 15–25 hours per week.
SALARY: €10–€15 per 60 minutes, depending on experience and development with MHC. Seminars between €100 and €150 per day. Trainers are responsible for paying their own taxes (12%–25%) and social security (variable).
FACILITIES/SUPPORT: Trainer preparation room, resource library, photocopying, trainer development and social networking events. Trainers require working papers.
RECRUITMENT: Interviews are essential and usually take place at premises. Possibility of Skype interviews if the applicant is based abroad.
CONTACT: Bashkim Fazliu, Regional Director South East Europe (bashkim.fazliu@mhc-training.com).

CYPRUS

A visitor to the Republic of Cyprus will be struck by the similarities with Greece – cuisine, architecture, landscapes, culture, economy on the skids – but then be surprised at the relative prominence of English. Signs are printed in both Greek and English, many (if not most) local people even outside the cities speak some English, and the British influence can be noticed everywhere. Because of the long-standing relationship between Cyprus and Britain, the English language is given much prominence in the state educational system. As a result the density of *frontisteria* is not as high as it is in Greece, though there are still a fair number of private institutes preparing children for external examinations. At least one organisation is trying to market Cyprus to Germans, Russians, etc as a destination (like Malta) in which to learn English. In a joint venture with the British language school Malvern House London, The Language Explorer Cyprus (cyprusadmin@malvernhouse.com; www.thelanguageexplorer.eu) was founded in 2007 to put on holiday English courses for children, adults and families. Its sister school in Limassol, the English Learning Centre (www.englishlearningcentre.com.cy), employs a number of native English-speaking teachers. The long established language camp company Village Camps in Switzerland recently inaugurated an English language camp in Droushia in the west of the country, for which it employed one counsellor for every six campers. The promised pay was €245 per week for the two weeks of the camp, plus €225 in travel expenses.

Cyprus has a small population of just over a million and therefore opportunities are not extensive. Also a large number of Cypriot students leave the island each year to study in the UK and USA, although there are still a number of afternoon language schools in the cities and towns.

To find an ELT job in Cyprus before you arrive is extremely difficult because very few of the ELT schools advertise on the internet and there is a sizeable expat community, from which native English-speaker teachers can be drawn. Some expats will also informally help Cypriot friends with their English over a glass of beer.

Sending speculative CVs is unlikely to succeed. It is more fruitful to visit schools in person and hand them round. Furthermore, state school jobs are extremely hard to come by for foreigners as you need at least a three-year degree in the relevant subject (eg English Literature for teaching English) as well as a good knowledge of Greek. Therefore, most foreign teachers aim to find a job in a language school in the private sector, which will probably mean working in the afternoons or evenings, although some schools also have morning classes. One freelance opportunity might be to approach businessmen and women in the property sector, who have (or would like to have) English and American clients. You'd need a solid business background to succeed, and would be required to provide specialist vocabulary ('grouting', anyone?).

Since Cyprus joined the European Union, visas are no longer a major hurdle. Nationals of all the other 26 EU countries have the automatic right of residence in Cyprus. Those who intend to work and stay in the country are obliged to apply for a registration certificate within four months of arrival. In Nicosia this can be done at the Migration Department; elsewhere applicants must visit the Immigration Police. The fee for registration is a modest €8.54; however, the fine for failing to register is in excess of €2,500.

If you wish to advertise your services as a tutor on English-language sites, try www.cyprus.angloinfo.com or www.cy.bazaraki.com. Most schools offer a contract of 20–25 working hours a week for the academic year September to May/June. The hourly pay is above average for Southern Europe, usually in the range €12–€16 per hour. As in Greece, there are usually two paid holidays during the academic year: two weeks over Christmas and two weeks for the Greek Orthodox Easter.

Most Cypriot schools have very good facilities, although they may be lagging behind somewhat in technology. Teacher support is readily available, with regular free seminars organised by various publishers. In language classrooms, there is a wide range of levels for all ages. The majority of children enrol at language schools when they are about eight and finish around the age of 16, attending lessons twice a week. However, there is a growing demand for children as young as four to start learning English as a foreign language, so schools are introducing classes for younger children. A lesson can last from one to two hours for higher levels. Young students and adults are usually motivated and love interactive teaching. However, those teaching teenagers will need to be firm and to make lessons particularly interesting.

People move to Cyprus nowadays more for the lifestyle than for cheap living. The downside is that eating out, etc is not cheap; however, the improved infrastructure (like the very good motorways) makes life easier. Note there is no train service on the island. Government plans to take the country upmarket by building more marinas and golf courses have had to be set aside because of the recession. The global downturn saw a sharp decline in the number of tourists arriving in Cyprus and many small businesses were forced to close. If reunification with the Turkish north takes place on the island (a long way off but positive moves have been made), then the country could really flourish.

A decent studio apartment can be rented for €350–€450 per month. By opening the English-language newspapers, you will be able to find out what's on and where to meet new friends. If you want to find out more about life in Cyprus for expats, visit the forums at www.cyprusliving.org and www.easterncyprus.com.

TURKISH CYPRUS

There are six private universities, four private schools and at least two language schools in the Turkish Republic of Northern Cyprus (TRNC). The main industry in Northern Cyprus is tourism, largely catering for an English-speaking clientele, so there is local demand to master the languages for employment purposes. However, it should be pointed out that the expatriate community numbers more than 4,000, so there is already a substantial pool of native English speakers on hand to fill any teacher vacancies that occur.

MALTA

Although somewhat off the beaten track and although English is an official language of the tiny island, EFL is booming in Malta. A number of private language schools cater to groups coming from other Mediterranean countries on short courses in the spring, summer and at other times. The National Tourist Office of Malta even distributes a leaflet called 'Learning English in the Sun', or you can check the list of language schools on www.visitmalta.com (which devotes a whole section to 'language learning'). The Ministry of Education also publishes online a list of 42 licensed language schools. The interests of the mainstream English-language institutes are represented by FELTOM, the Federation of English Language Teaching Organisations Malta (+356 2131 0927; www.feltom.com); the site has good links to the 19 member schools and basic information about teaching on the island. Many of the schools have teacher recruitment information on their websites, for example Malta Lingua in St Julian's (www.maltalingua.com/jobs). Another member school in that same resort, EC English Language Centre (http://jobs.ecenglish.com), offers summer jobs to entry-level teachers provided they are able to do an intensive induction course for the first half of June.

All EU citizens have the right to live and work in Malta, although it is necessary to obtain an EFL teaching permit from the EFL Monitoring Board of the Ministry for Education and Employment. In order to be eligible for the permit, a candidate must have an A level in English (grade C or above) from a recognised institution and have completed a TEFL course such as a CELTA. A 60-hour TEFL Induction Course is offered by the majority of FELTOM schools and also satisfies the government requirement. All teachers also need a clean police conduct certificate. Note that self-employed freelancers do not need to obtain a work permit. Australians and New Zealanders under the ages of 25 and 30 respectively may apply for a working holiday visa to Malta, valid for one year.

Wages are paid hourly and are in the €8–€12 bracket, with a steady average of €10. Many professional teachers join MATEFL, the Malta Association of TEFL (www.matefl.org). Membership costs a modest €20. The NSTS English Language Institute in Gzira (HQ, 220 St Paul St Valletta VLT07;+356 2558 8000; http://.

nsts.org/vacancies) markets its English courses in conjunction with sports holidays for young tourists to Malta. NSTS runs weekly vacation courses from June to August, and it might be worth approaching it for a job, particularly if you are a water sports enthusiast. NSTS was keen to hire **Robert Mizzi** from Canada once it learned that he was half-Maltese:

> I was offered a job quite casually when NSTS found out I was volunteering conversational English in the main youth hostel in Valletta. Perhaps one reason they wanted to hire me was they knew the visa would not be a problem. However, I was surprised by how relaxed the offer was. It was just mentioned in passing rather than at an actual interview. I guess it is the Maltese way: once you are one of them, then everything is gravy.

JESSICA STONE

Three years ago Jessica Stone decided to leave the States to embark on a Mediterranean adventure, even though she was older than most who entertain such dreams.

I feel extremely lucky: after carefully examining all the countries I was interested in visiting/teaching/travelling in, I selected Malta as my first choice. I sent out about 15 letters and résumés and received roughly six responses. Three of them asked me to touch base when I arrived, saying they could probably give me part-time work in the summer. One made a definite appointment to meet and one asked if I could do a Skype interview. The latter ended up offering me an excellent position as the Executive Director of Academic Programme Development and Marketing, a far cry from the teaching job I'd originally applied for. Just happened to have the skill set they were looking for at the time. I should say that I am 58 years old and hold a Masters and PhD in Communications, and have taught Business and Business Communications at US universities for over 20 years. In preparation I did a 100-hour TESOL course with LCC in Seattle.

So now I'm living in Malta, have a great flat with a view of the Med and a super job. The school is going to get the work permit for me, which will result in a one-year residency visa to follow on from the initial three months as a tourist. From my understanding, the issues with visas are the same everywhere - lots of paperwork and rubber stamps and moaning about not being able to get one, but anyone who really wants one gets one. And the schools hire people right and left even though you can't officially work without a work permit. The money you earn teaching English is not very good, especially for people my age. But the adventure and cultural experience are truly priceless.

LIST OF EMPLOYERS

AM LANGUAGE STUDIO
299 Manwel Dimech Street, Sliema SLM 1054
+356 21 324242
info@amlanguage.com
www.amlanguage.com

NUMBER OF TEACHERS: 3.
PREFERENCE OF NATIONALITY: British.
QUALIFICATIONS: CELTA or CertTESOL.
CONDITIONS OF EMPLOYMENT: Teachers are employed on a freelance basis and are required to work from July to August with 22.5–30 hours per week.
SALARY: €11 per hour.
FACILITIES/SUPPORT: As teachers are freelance they just have to register as self-employed with the local authorities and do not need to apply for a work permit.
RECRUITMENT: CV and telephone interview.
CONTACT: Edwina Caruana Galizia, Director of Studies.

ELANGUEST ENGLISH LANGUAGE SCHOOL
Keating House, Ross Street, St Julian's STJ 3243
+356 21 374777
dos@elanguest.com
www.elanguest.com

PREFERENCE OF NATIONALITY: British, Canadian and Australian.
QUALIFICATIONS: TEFL course plus A level in English. Applicants with CELTA or DELTA are given preference.
CONDITIONS OF EMPLOYMENT: No contract; however, applicants who can work all year round are given preference. Between 4.5 and 5.5 working hours per day.
FACILITIES/SUPPORT: Assistance given with work permits.
RECRUITMENT: CV, photo and telephone interview.

GLOBAL VILLAGE ENGLISH CENTRE
St George's Street, St Paul's Bay SPB 3476
+356 21 573417
info@gvmalta.com
www.gvmalta.com

NUMBER OF TEACHERS: All staff are native speakers of English.
PREFERENCE OF NATIONALITY: None.
QUALIFICATIONS: Experience and TEFL qualification needed plus minimum 1-year's experience.

CONDITIONS OF EMPLOYMENT: Open-ended contracts. 15–20 hours per week in low season, 20+ hours per week in peak season.
SALARY: Varies according to experience and qualifications.
FACILITIES/SUPPORT: Advice given on rental accommodation.
RECRUITMENT: Mainly via teacher-training courses run on-site. Interviews are essential and are usually carried out face-to-face with the Director of Studies and include analysis of lesson planning.
CONTACT: Mrs Gaby Huhn, Head of School.

IELS MALTA
Matthew Pulis Street, Sliema SLM 3052
+356 21 320381
hr.malta@iels.com.mt
www.lalschools.com or www.ielsmalta.com

NUMBER OF TEACHERS: 60.
PREFERENCE OF NATIONALITY: None.
QUALIFICATIONS: Minimum CELTA but no experience required.
CONDITIONS OF EMPLOYMENT: Open-ended contract with 15 or 22.5 hours per week, depending on preference and availability.
SALARY: €10.50 per hour.
FACILITIES/SUPPORT: Assistance given with work permits.
CONTACT: Angie Conti, Academic Manager (angie.conti@lalgroup.com).

INLINGUA SCHOOL OF LANGUAGES
9 Triq Guzi Fava, Off Bisazza St, Sliema SLM 1632
+356 20102000
dos@inlinguamalta.com
www.inlinguamalta.com

Cambridge accredited centre. Member of FELTOM.
NUMBER OF TEACHERS: 30–100+ depending on time of year.
PREFERENCE OF NATIONALITY: Native speakers if they are able to work in Malta. (inlingua does not apply for work permits.)
QUALIFICATIONS: Matriculation standard of education, A level English and TEFL qualification minimum. Holders of CELTA qualification or higher will be given preference.
CONDITIONS OF EMPLOYMENT: Casual and freelance employment only.
SALARY: Depends on qualifications.
RECRUITMENT: Local interviews essential.
CONTACT: Donovan Gatt, Course Coordinator.

SKYLARK SCHOOL OF ENGLISH
29, Victor Denaro Street, Msida MSD 1604
- +356 21 316604
- info@skylarkmalta.com
- www.skylarkmalta.com

NUMBER OF TEACHERS: 30 freelancers.
PREFERENCE OF NATIONALITY: EU citizenship preferred though willing to consider any CV as long as teachers are native English speakers.
QUALIFICATIONS: Minimum of a TEFL course and a high school-level qualification in English Language (A level or equivalent).

However, a CELTA/DELTA/TESOL certificate is preferable.
CONDITIONS OF EMPLOYMENT: Freelance basis only. Flexible timetable according to teacher's availability. Normally 15–30 class hours a week.
SALARY: €8–€12 per hour.
FACILITIES/SUPPORT: Non-local teachers are given assistance in finding housing as close to the school as possible and at the best rate possible.
RECRUITMENT: Face-to-face interview and on occasion class observation. Occasionally telephone interviews are conducted.
CONTACT: Sigo, Director of Studies.

SERBIA, MONTENEGRO AND KOSOVO

With the short-lived union of Serbia and Montenegro breaking down, followed by Kosovo's declaration of independence from Serbia in 2008, the dissolution of the former Yugoslavia is absolute, with much underlying tension remaining.

The ELT industry has been developing but mainly supplied by local teachers. International House has been affiliated to Cambridge Centar in Podgorice since 2008, the only IH school in Montenegro. One possible lead is the Bejza Education Centre (Kosovska 39, 3rd Fl, 11000 Belgrade, Serbia; +381 11 334 3077; www.bejza.edu.rs).

In order to get a residence/work permit for Serbia, you must submit a contract of employment and a translated copy of your diploma. Further information on the regulations for entering and working in Serbia can be found at www.london.mfa.gov.rs.

The first group of approximately 20 Peace Corps Kosovo volunteers arrived in June 2014 in order to teach English at local secondary schools after three months of cross-cultural, language and technical training.

LIST OF EMPLOYERS

ANGLOLAND LANGUAGE SCHOOL
Starine Novaka 19/I, 11000 Belgrade, Serbia
- +381 11 334 4188
- angloland@sbb.rs or office@angloland.rs
- www.angloland.rs

NUMBER OF TEACHERS: 1–2.
PREFERENCE OF NATIONALITY: None.
QUALIFICATIONS: Bachelor's degree plus CELTA minimum. DELTA or MA in TESOL/Applied Linguistics and/or long-standing experience preferred.
CONDITIONS OF EMPLOYMENT: Two 90-minute lessons per week in some cases.

FACILITIES/SUPPORT: Assistance may be available for accommodation, and work permits may be possible.
RECRUITMENT: Interviews arranged on basis of submitted CV.
CONTACT: Natasha Jovanovich.

OXFORD CENTAR
64 Rimiski trg, 81000 Podgorica, Montenegro
- +382 20 234425
- oxfordcentar@t-com.me
- www.oxfordcentar.com

Language centres also in Bar, Budva, Bijelo Polje, Niksic and Cetinje.

NUMBER OF TEACHERS: 6.

PREFERENCE OF NATIONALITY: British, American, Australian, New Zealander and Canadian.

QUALIFICATIONS: 3–5 years' practical experience. Staff are graduate philologists, some with an MA or PhD.

CONDITIONS OF EMPLOYMENT: 4- or 9-month contract with 22 to 27 working hours per week.

SALARY: €750–€850 per month plus flat allowance of €200 per month.

FACILITIES/SUPPORT: School pays for 2 nights in a hotel as teacher looks for accommodation. Assistance also given with applying for work permits.

RECRUITMENT: Usually via adverts on www.eslbase.com or www.tefl.com. Interviews are essential and can be via phone or Skype.

SLOVENIA

As in Croatia, there are plenty of private schools and opportunities can be created by energetic native English speakers both as freelance teachers for institutes and as private tutors. Slovenia is a sophisticated little country with high standards of education and many well-qualified native teachers of English.

The English Studies Resource Centre at the British Council in Ljubljana has a list of private language schools throughout the country. The Council remains closely in touch with language schools and may be able to refer qualified candidates to possible employers, though the Ljubljana office is not open to the general public. The average hourly wage should start at €10.

As one of the countries that joined the EU in May 2004 and the Schengen Agreement in 2008, Slovenia now has fairly straightforward regulations for EU members. All EU citizens are able to work in Slovenia under the same conditions as Slovene citizens in their countries. However, teachers should obtain a temporary residence permit within three months of entering the country, and will need a valid passport whose expiry date exceeds by at least three months the intended period of stay, health insurance, sufficient means of subsistence and a legitimate purpose for their residence (like a job).Your school should report your post to the Employment Service of Slovenia (*Zavod za zaposlovanje*) in Ljubljana within eight days of starting the job. Canadians aged 18–35 can apply for a Youth Mobility visa that will allow them to work for a year, while New Zealand citizens up to the age of 30 can do likewise.

LIST OF EMPLOYERS

BERLITZ LANGUAGE CENTER
Gosposvetska 2, 1000 Ljubljana
+386 1 433 1325
berlitz.ljubljana@berlitz.si or workinslovenia@berlitz.si
www.berlitz.si

Also centres in Maribor, Kranj, Novo Mesto and Celje. Also organise summer camps in the ski resort of Krvavec and at the seaside at Debeli Rtic.

NUMBER OF TEACHERS: 60.

PREFERENCE OF NATIONALITY: EU or candidates already with permission to work in Slovenia. Candidates should be already living in Slovenia.

QUALIFICATIONS: Tertiary educational background, good communication skills, professional attitude and appearance.

CONDITIONS OF EMPLOYMENT: Minimum 1 year. All work on freelance basis. Number of hours assigned on merit; no guaranteed minimum. Good teachers work 20–40 hours per week.

SALARY: From €10+ per unit (40 minutes).

FACILITIES/SUPPORT: No assistance with accommodation. Compulsory training in Berlitz Method offered twice a year. Regular support through observations and workshops.

RECRUITMENT: Adverts and personal recommendation. Applications welcome at any time and are kept on file for 6 months. Face-to-face interviews are compulsory.

CONTACT: Gregor Sergan, Director.

EVROPA BLED d.o.o.

Finzgarjeva 15, 4260 Bled

+386 45 741563/644988

cilka@evropa-bled.com

www.evropa-bled.com

NUMBER OF TEACHERS: 1–2.

PREFERENCE OF NATIONALITY: None.

QUALIFICATIONS: Experience essential. Teacher training course for TEFL required.

CONDITIONS OF EMPLOYMENT: School year from October to May. Minimum 30–40 lessons a month.

FACILITIES/SUPPORT: Help is given with finding accommodation but the rental charge is borne by the teacher.

RECRUITMENT: Contacts through the British Council.

CONTACT: Cilka Demsar, Director.

NISTA LANGUAGE CENTER

Smarska C.5D, 6000 Koper

+386 5625 0400

info@nista.si

www.nista.si

Located on the Adriatic not far from Trieste, Italy.

NUMBER OF TEACHERS: 15.

PREFERENCE OF NATIONALITY: England, Scotland, New Zealand and Australia.

QUALIFICATIONS: Bachelor's degree (Hons) and TEFL certificate plus a year's teaching experience. Business background useful.

CONDITIONS OF EMPLOYMENT: Minimum 10 months September to June (preferably longer). Usual 24–26 hours' contact time per week. Also part-time openings.

SALARY: About €13 per lesson. No tax or social security deductions.

FACILITIES/SUPPORT: The school finds accommodation for teachers and provides necessary documents for them.

RECRUITMENT: Email, internet.

CONTACT: Mrs Alenka Rajčič, Director.

PANTEON COLLEGE

Linhartova 11, 1000 Ljubljana

+386 1280 3220

info@panteon.si

www.panteon.si

NUMBER OF TEACHERS: 5.

PREFERENCE OF NATIONALITY: British.

QUALIFICATIONS: English teacher with a variety of TEFL experience (TEFL or CELTA certificate).

CONDITIONS OF EMPLOYMENT: Standard length of contract 1 year. 20–30 hours per week including morning, afternoon and evening lessons.

SALARY: €10 per hour (45 minutes of teaching).

FACILITIES/SUPPORT: Help is given with finding accommodation and acquiring the necessary permits.

RECRUITMENT: CV must be submitted. Successful applicants will be invited to attend an interview.

YURENA

Glavni Trg 11, 8000 Novo Mesto

+386 7 337 2100

yurena@siol.net

www.yurena.si

NUMBER OF TEACHERS: 2–3.

PREFERENCE OF NATIONALITY: English.

QUALIFICATIONS: TEFL qualification.

CONDITIONS OF EMPLOYMENT: 1-year contracts. 25–30 hours per week.

SALARY: Approximately €1,000 per month.

FACILITIES/SUPPORT: Accommodation and help with work permits provided.

RECRUITMENT: Interviews essential.

CONTACT: Marija Trunkelj.

CENTRAL ASIAN AND OTHER REPUBLICS

The former Soviet republics have gradually resumed their own national and regional identities. Whereas the Baltic States (Estonia, Lithuania and Latvia) desire few if any ties with Russia, other former Soviet republics, especially those in North Central Asia (Kazakhstan, Kyrgyzstan, Tajikistan, Turkmenistan and Uzbekistan), have joined with Russia (and China) to form a number of economic and security-related treaty organisations. In between these two extremes are the eastern European states such as Belarus and Moldova and the Caucasian States (Armenia, Azerbaijan and Georgia) that drift from one side to the other depending on the nature of the area of cooperation. Prospective EFL teachers seeking to find employment in this vast region would do well to study their atlases carefully and then investigate the prevailing influences affecting the particular country or area in which they are interested at the time of their job search.

Prospective incomers should give some thought as to whether they will be able to tolerate different attitudes to human rights, religious freedoms, etc. On the question of the religious flavour, not to say fervour, of the republic in question, as a general rule, the former western republics are mostly eastern Orthodox Christian and the Southern Central Asian Republics are Sunni Muslim, so there are noticeable differences (including among individuals) between levels of tolerance in matters of sexual freedom, alcohol, dietary habits and even smoking.

An internet job search should yield a few results, for example a post teaching corporate English in Northern Tajikistan or another teaching teenagers in Pavlodar region of Kazakhstan. Many established institutes operating in the various countries of the former Soviet republics are off the radar of search engines. It is not difficult to find contact details for institutes of higher education, technical colleges and pedagogical institutes, some of which may employ native English-speaking teachers at various times. It can also be worth trying international schools. English teaching is still largely delivered by the state. University faculties often have their own international relations office, which may have two or three vacancies for highly educated foreign specialists; try, for example, the Kazakh-British Technical University in Almaty where Louise Wheeler works (see her account below in the section on Kazakhstan). The US government deploys a number of Language Teaching Assistants to most of the countries of the region, from Armenia to Tajikistan, through the Fulbright Program (http://exchanges.state.gov/us/program/fulbright-english-teaching-assistant-program). Assistants are university graduates in their 20s who are normally placed in universities, but also in schools and other venues, to serve as a resource for conversation, vocabulary and reading and writing courses.

Another source of ELT employment can be the NGOs operating in a number of former Soviet republic countries. In response to the increase in demand for English, the Peace Corps sends a substantial number of volunteer English teachers to various nation-states such as Kyrgyz Republic and Armenia.

Much of the demand has been spurred by the influx of businesses connected with the Caspian oil industry, which has particularly affected Kazakhstan, Uzbekistan, Turkmenistan and Azerbaijan. Opportunities with international companies exist for professional teachers where the salaries are approaching those of the oil-rich states of the Middle East. One that puts on intensive language courses for engineers employed by BP in Baku was recently advertising a net monthly salary of $2,350 plus accommodation allowance.

Chain schools such as Language Link, EF and International House can provide sources of TEFL employment. For example Language Link operates teaching centres in Atyrau, Kazakhstan (atyrau@languagelink.ru) and Tashkent, Uzbekistan (www.languagelink.uz) and may in future open others, as long as the petrodollars flow.

Both International House and the Soros Foundation have also been active in opening up the region to English-language learners. IH's partner in Almaty, Kazakhstan is Interpress, which does some of its own teacher hiring (see entry). Try also Study Innovations Language Schools (www.studyinn.kz) in Almaty, Astana, Karaganda, Shymkent and Kostanay.

Belarus is another republic with various language-teaching opportunities, for example at International House Minsk (www.ih.by) and SOL Minsk (www.sol.by). The International Language Training Center in Chisinau, Moldova (www.iltc.md) might be persuaded to hire a native speaker teacher. Another US-oriented school in Chisinau is the American Language Center (http://alc.md), though it tends to hire only local staff. Few foreigners would be able to survive on the low monthly stipend it offers.

A base in Central Asia allows you to explore this fascinating region, as **Anthony Cook** did when he was working in Almaty in Kazakhstan:

> *I tended to try and save up a bit, then splurge on one or two longer trips each year. Travelling around Central Asia is quite the adventure. To mention just two of the 'stans': Kazakhstan itself has a unique multicultural history and awe-inspiring, dramatic landscapes, with wide regional variation (though you have to make a real effort to get to the good bits, because they're separated by vast stretches of nothingness and the transport infrastructure is not the best!). Uzbekistan has some of the world's most impressive Islamic architecture, plus the desert of Karakalpakstan in the west, dotted with ancient, deserted fortresses. The Uzbek people are an added bonus; they're every bit as warm and eccentric as the Kazakhs, and a lot chattier and more inclined to strike up a conversation with strangers. So you meet a lot of 'characters' when you visit their country. If I were to go back to the region, I'd definitely want to continue exploring – the list of intriguing destinations is quite long.*

In searching for a job, perhaps the best advice might be to limit your search to a couple of countries and thereafter do your research. A thorough understanding of the country, its culture and its regard for foreigners is absolutely essential. And be sure to check out the legality of any employment that you are thinking to engage in. As **William Kinsey** found out while working in Almaty, things are not always what they seem:

> *Our school was raided by the police, who demanded our visas and claimed incorrect registration. Our boss/owner was useless and two of my fellow teachers were brought to the police station and had their apartment raided. Further, the boss asked us to lie on his behalf and say that we are not paid, rather we are only English consultants not accepting salary. I can only speculate, but I surmise it creates a tax escape for him.*

Given this, teachers are well advised to check with consulates rather than potential employers as to how legal working status is obtained. As laws change often, employers may not be lying to potential teachers, they may simply be out of date in their current thinking.

GEORGIA

Four years ago the Ministry of Education took the dramatic decision to fund a native English-speaker teaching programme called Teach and Learn with Georgia (TLG). Semester start dates fall in August and January/February. The programme offers foreigners the chance to teach in state schools throughout the country, as part of a cultural exchange programme. Airfares, homestay accommodation, medical insurance and a round-trip ticket for one vacation are all covered by the programme plus a modest stipend (see entry below). Full details are on the TLG website www.tlg.gov.ge.

Reviews of the programme on sites like www.gooverseas.com are generally favourable, like this one posted by Emily, while others focus on the disorganistion:

> *Georgia has been a wonderful experience. The people are very friendly and welcoming. Most of the villages and schools are just excited that they have an English speaker and are very cooperative. Georgia has its share of discomforts: most volunteers are placed in smaller villages (mine has about 1,000 people); bathroom facilities are low tech, which means showers once a week and sometimes Turkish toilets; schools are limited in what materials they have, expect little to no technology used in classrooms. All of that said, the people more than make up for these minor discomforts! Everybody in my village talks to me when we meet. I've received three bouquets of flowers this week already and I got more apples and nuts than I could eat during the fall. The teachers in my*

school got some useful phrases translated and hung them in our coffee room. And it's always great to hear kids improve their reading and become more confident. The little boys I live with delight in using their English, like yelling from the bathroom 'I want toilet paper!' to saying 'Let's go!' as we leave the house. Even now they are hovering around, asking me what I'm doing. I would not trade my time in Georgia for anything.

Teachers are also employed in the private sector, eg by International House (www.ihtbilisi.ge/en/recruitment) and the London School of English (www.londonschool.ge), both in Tbilisi; the latter hosts intensive English summer courses for young learners and professionals, for which it recruits native-speaker teachers. Another language camp organiser is Education & Training International (sales@eti-georgia.ge).

From September 2014, Georgia fell into line with Europe by instigating a policy of allowing foreigners to stay for 90 days in 180 days. Those staying longer need to apply for a D1 (work) immigration visa from outside Georgia.

LIST OF EMPLOYERS

TEACH AND LEARN WITH GEORGIA (TLG)

1 Gmir Kursantta str, Tbilisi 0167

✆ +995 322 200 220 ext 4855

✐ info@tlg.gov.ge or applications@tlg.gov.ge

🖳 www.tlg.gov.ge

NUMBER OF TEACHERS: 50+.

PREFERENCE OF NATIONALITY: British, American, Canadian, Australian, New Zealander, Irish and South African are preferred, but all native speakers will be considered.

QUALIFICATIONS: Minimum 2 years of post-secondary education. A TEFL qualification and teaching experience are not required. Must have criminal record check and medical test including HIV.

CONDITIONS OF EMPLOYMENT: All job placements are full-time positions. One or two semesters, renewable. Teaching schedules vary but are generally through daytime hours Monday–Friday.

SALARY: Volunteers are paid a monthly stipend of 750 lari per month. After taxes are withdrawn and the host family are paid 200 lari to cover food and utilities, only 400 lari are left for spending (about US$175). Free return airfare is paid upfront. Teachers who commit to a year-long contract receive an additional flight ticket equal in value to their tickets to and from Georgia.

FACILITIES/SUPPORT: Visa guidance, airport collection, teacher orientation, etc. are provided.

RECRUITMENT: After initial application enclosing photo and letter of motivation, applicants are interviewed by videoconference.

AZERBAIJAN

Tucked away between Georgia, Iran and the Caspian Sea, the republic of Azerbaijan produces great oil wealth. Because of the capital, Baku's, key role in the production and distribution of oil and gas, language institutes have a lot of money to throw around, and have been offering more than comfortable salaries to teachers. Yet teacher retention is not very high, partly because of the hardships of living in Central Asia and because the employers have not provided enough pastoral support to new arrivals. Many teachers arrive in Baku with no idea how to do the job well or to adapt to the culture.

John Gahan had a head start since he had spent two years as a volunteer with the Peace Corps in Gumlag Village in the Oghuz Rayon of Azerbaijan before deciding to move to the big city:

> While I was completing my last couple of months in my village for Peace Corps, a friend of mine and I decided to seek employment in Baku because we heard the salaries were good, and we felt the adjustment wouldn't be terribly difficult. I found out about English First, arranged an interview, taught a trial lesson to a large group of children and was offered a job. EF had me working immediately, since my visa from Peace Corps hadn't expired and EF arranged my work visa for me within that time. Having completed Peace Corps, I was expecting to roll into Baku and live a comfortable, lucrative life with all the cultural bases already covered. It didn't exactly happen that way because, as many people can attest, there's a big difference between volunteer and 'real' work. I had to make that adjustment rather quickly.
>
> Thus far, the working conditions have been pleasant (well-equipped classrooms with whiteboards and computers and so on) and wages have been satisfactory for a single male on a modest budget. As long as my expenses haven't gotten out of hand, I've been able to save around a thousand dollars a month after student loan payments. I can count on one hand the number of times I've had to deal with behavioural problems, which were efficiently dealt with by the school. Nonetheless, the 'orientation period' at EF is essentially non-existent. Though I had two years of volunteer teaching in a village under my belt, I had no idea about the expectations in the classroom at EF, and I had not taught in a setting like this before. This made my first groups mediocre at best, and particularly scary towards the ends of the levels because I was in a panic that the paying students weren't prepared for their final tests. I was also unaware of what I needed to do to get tests effectively graded and student reports and certificates completed. At this point, however, those problems are water under the bridge, and I fully enjoy working here now. For my own work, help is always available if I ask for it.
>
> When a group of students clicks, it's really wonderful, and the students are extremely grateful for what you do for them. The biggest issue with students here is getting them to think outside the box and discuss topics other than national meals and weddings. For most of them, they want English as a skill, so they can 'find a good job' or study abroad. Teaching here forces idealistic foreign teachers to face the reality of many places, namely that people wish to adopt a language ability from you, but that does not mean that they want to adopt ideas or culture from you. Any strong, independent-minded teacher who wants to save some money and be in a fascinating region can do well in Baku. It's not the liveliest city, but it is changing rapidly, with new buildings going up all the time.

Several British and international companies recruit qualified teachers for Azerbaijan, such as Language Solutions (barry.shorten@langsols.com; www.langsols.az), Teachaway, and Carfax Recruitment with an office in Baku. One of their tutors working in Baku in 2014 blogged on their site:

> After having graduated last summer, I began looking for a job which would offer me the opportunity to teach the subjects I love with a little adventure on the side! I chose to work in Baku, Azerbaijan, with Carfax Education because I knew little about the country, but had always been fascinated by the various cultures of the former Soviet empire, and I wanted to learn more about the former Soviet Republics. So far I have thoroughly enjoyed my time here and find the work very rewarding.

Carfax Baku has an office on the outskirts of the city, though I do most of my teaching at students' homes. This means using taxis to get between lessons – a daily battle with traffic and the frequent road closures caused by the president's convoy! Such time is not wasted, however, because they pepper my day with 15-minute Russian and Azeri lessons. Taxi drivers make great teachers and I now have a very colourful vocabulary.

For a capital city with 2 million people, Baku feels more like a large village. It really seems as if everyone knows each other. This has made making friends much easier than I expected. On top of this the city has a great selection of small coffee shops, bookshop cafés and old style tea houses in which to hang out. I'm truly glad of the opportunity to work in this part of the world. Between Russia and the Middle East lies a country defined by its proximity to both but with an intrinsic national identity and complex history. Luckily I have six more months here to explore it!

LIST OF EMPLOYERS

CARFAX PRIVATE TUTORS
Head office: 48 Langham Street, London W1W 7AY, UK
☎ +44 20 7927 6200
🖥 www.carfax-recruitment.com

Offices also in Russia, Monaco and Dubai.
International private tutors to work in Baku, tutoring
candidates for entrance to schools in the UK and Switzerland.

LINE-LEADER IN EDUCATION LANGUAGE CENTER
Shafayat Mehdiyev 83, 4th Floor, AZ 1141, Baku
☎ +994 12 539 3396/97
📧 info@bakuline.com
🖥 www.bakuline.com

NUMBER OF TEACHERS: 1.
PREFERENCE OF NATIONALITY: British, North American,
Australian, and New Zealander.

QUALIFICATIONS: EFL/ESL certificate.
CONDITIONS OF EMPLOYMENT: 9-month contract from October.
Schools open 9am–9pm, Monday to Saturday, 24 contact hours
per week. Mainly adult students.
SALARY: $2,000 per month.
FACILITIES/SUPPORT: Modern facilities, teacher library,
computer laboratory, guidance and support of academic
coordinator, flights paid on completion of contract, paid
holiday, orientation and ongoing seminars and development.
Assistance given with finding flat (not shared). Medical
insurance and visa provided.
RECRUITMENT: Applications through English First (EF) teacher
recruitment in offices worldwide.
CONTACT: Lala Talishli, Director of Studies.

KAZAKHSTAN AND KYRGYZSTAN

Kazakhstan is another prospering Central Asian Republic where the demand for IELTS preparation continues to soar and the market among young learners is also expanding. Culturally, the country is changing away from the one that was referenced in the film *Borat* (full title: *Borat: Cultural Learnings of America for Make Benefit Glorious Nation of Kazakhstan*).Yet Kazakhstan has not enjoyed a very positive reputation amongst the ELT community, something which **Anthony Cook** thinks is undeserved.

Since obtaining his CELTA a few years ago, Anthony (originally from Australia) has had three contracts with Interpress-IH, which, on balance, he says is probably his favourite school, and Almaty is definitely one of his favourite places to live in.

I first went to KZ to work for Interpress IH the year after Borat was released, with no specific expectations except that it probably wouldn't be quite what Sacha Baron Cohen had depicted. I know the school often has trouble enticing teachers to Kazakhstan, so I'd like to say why I think they're worth considering as employers. There's no such thing as a perfect language school in this world, of course, but I really enjoyed working there and hope I might have the chance to go back one of these days.

Overall, the hours are pretty good, and it's a relief to discover that, unlike in some other countries, there are no Kazakhstani people mad enough to request lessons at 7.30 in the morning! It can be a bit scary for a teacher who has never taught exam prep before to be thrown in at the deep end, but the 'teachers' room culture' is generally very good, with people around who are willing to help you get your head around unfamiliar material.

The students in KZ are probably the best I've taught anywhere. They're lively and talkative, and noticeably more 'worldly' than students in other ex-Soviet republics I've worked in. That's probably because KZ was historically a dumping ground for the USSR's unwanted, from North Koreans to Azeris and everyone in between, so now it's a relatively multicultural place, and the people there like it that way. Kazakhstani students are also keen on the more technical sides of learning a language – they want to master the grammar of English, because they see a connection between speaking correctly and getting the respect of those they speak to. They're inclined to bond well with classmates and, if you're a capable teacher, they'll be grateful for your presence in the classroom and you'll feel their loyalty. Also, in contrast to some Asian countries, in KZ it's considered acceptable and even good to be outspoken, so you generally don't have to struggle to wring opinions out of your students (excluding the occasional surly teenager, of course!). They are also generally quite sociable, and the culture doesn't have the 'barriers' between teacher and student that limit out-of-classroom interaction elsewhere. So it's not difficult to hang out with the locals and make some friends if you want to.

LOUISE WHEELER

With a Masters in TEFL and eight years of teaching experience, Louise Wheeler is also happily working in Almaty, at the Kazakh-British Technical University with which she had had previous contact through her university:

Whilst it is not essential for foreign staff, it can help to bear in mind that personal connections are often important for employment in Kazakhstani society. Therefore, it can help for potential international applicants to at least make a good impression on a personal level, as well as professionally. My job at the university involves teaching English to students between the ages of 17 and 22 in General, Academic, Business and Professional English aimed at supporting them in their study of Business, Oil and Gas, Chemical Engineering or IT subjects in English. I really enjoy working with KBTU students. Like many Kazakhstani students they are enthusiastic, creative, active and willing to share their opinions in class. We are lucky here, in as far as the students are generally pre-intermediate level and above, but the level can be much lower in less prestigious institutions and as you move outside the main cities of Almaty and Astana. The only problem I have experienced with Kazakhstani learners is in motivating them to do independent work out of class. Many have no experience of being asked to work independently prior to university and unfortunately, it can be a challenge to combat certain practices such as plagiarism and cheating in written work.

The wages are definitely good in comparison with many local wages and even with many other organisations employing foreigners in Kazakhstan. I was able to save money and maintain a comfortable quality of life. The thing I love about teaching in Kazakhstan is the 'can do' attitude and enthusiasm to try new things. My colleagues and managers have always been open to new ideas and are generally supportive of teachers who want to implement new systems and projects. It's a fantastic and challenging environment in which to develop as a teacher.

In Almaty we are lucky to have the stunning Alatau mountain range just 15 minutes away by bus, so it is easy to get out to mountains for walking and picnicking in the summer and skiing and skating in the winter. In town there are lots of parks in the centre, which are especially good if you enjoy running. There is a good selection of restaurants and bars in the city too. I personally enjoy the chance to explore different parts of this varied and multicultural city, especially the bazaars. In addition, I have found it a very rewarding experience to learn some Kazakh and Russian. This really helps you to get under the skin of Kazakhstan's culture and society.

Winters in Almaty can seem very long, dark and cold at times. Moreover, Christmas is not celebrated and for our university the 25th is a normal working day. For this reason, my first Christmas period spent in Kazakhstan was a bit of a low point. However, the next year I organised to take a trip home at this time (as most of the expat community do). On the other hand, the Kazakh spring festival of Nawrus, in late March, is a wonderful time. Normally people have a week off and there are lots of cultural events happening around the city and beyond. It is a great chance to see traditional yurts, people in national costumes, try Kazakh speciality foods, watch traditional games and listen to folk music. Moreover, it's a time when you are most likely to experience the much celebrated 'Kazakh hospitality', with local colleagues and friends keen to invite you to their homes. Kazakhstan remains an exciting, multicultural, friendly and fascinating place to live and work.

Visas and work permits need to be sorted out before arriving in Kazakhstan but the school should handle all or most of the paperwork. One thing that may present an obstacle is the relative scarcity of Kazakh embassies and consulates around the world, and their possible lack of cooperativeness. The one in London has a dreadful reputation: it randomly refused to renew one returning teacher's visa, without offering any explanation, and the subsequent appeal process dragged on for weeks. Anthony Cook has had better luck applying in Seoul and Bangkok.

Louise Wheeler confirms that the process can cause difficulties:

The visa must be applied for on your behalf through the organisation you work for. You will be asked to submit notarised, apostilled copies of degrees, masters degrees and teaching certificates (with transcripts), police record checks, a medical certificate and three years of references (stamped by HR departments or equivalent). This process can be very time consuming – up to two years in my experience – and be prepared for the Ministry to change its requirements or processes without warning.

After being issued with a work permit and visa you are also required to get a blood test for HIV/AIDS. However, whilst your application for a work visa is being processed, your employer may make arrangements for you to stay under the terms of a business visa. This kind of visa is valid for three months, provided you leave the country every 30 days.

A large English language school in Reading, England with multiple links to Kazakhstan recently opened a school in Almaty for which it was hiring native speaker teachers to start September 2015. The offered salary was 260,000 tenge plus a housing allowance to cover a studio flat and other benefits (www.eurospeak.kz).

LIST OF EMPLOYERS

KAZAKHSTAN

GANUC INTERNATIONAL LEARNING INSTITUTE
Imanova 13, Astana 010000
+7 717 291 7704
marcelo@ganuc.com or info@ganuc.com
www.ilearninginstitute.net

NUMBER OF TEACHERS: 2.
PREFERENCE OF NATIONALITY: British.
QUALIFICATIONS: CELTA/DELTA with at least 1 year's experience. Young Learner experience valued.
CONDITIONS OF EMPLOYMENT: 1-year contract. Usual hours are 9am–12pm and 3pm–8pm.
SALARY: Equivalent of $1,000 net.
FACILITIES/SUPPORT: Accommodation is provided. Full assistance given with obtaining permits. Teachers must send all documents including copy of passport, diplomas, certificates, medical report and letters of recommendation. The process takes about 6 weeks before the permit can be sent to the candidate, who then takes it to the embassy and gets the visa.

RECRUITMENT: Interviews are essential and are sometimes carried out in the UK.
CONTACT: Marcelo Lopez Lara, Managing Director.

INTERPRESS-INTERNATIONAL HOUSE – ALMATY
InterPress-International House, Keremet 7, Almaty 050040
+7 727 315 2525
recruit@ihkazakhstan.com
www.ihkazakhstan.com

Largest English language school in the country.
NUMBER OF TEACHERS: About 60 foreign and local teachers employed, 35–40 new ones taken on each year for branches in Astana and Karaganda.
PREFERENCE OF NATIONALITY: Native English speakers from UK, USA, Ireland, Canada, Australia.
QUALIFICATIONS: Cambridge CELTA, IHC, Trinity TESOL, MA in TESOL as a minimum and at least 1 year of post-qualification teaching experience preferred. Young Learners qualification and

experience in teaching for exam preparation (IELTS and TOEFL) are preferable.

CONDITIONS OF EMPLOYMENT: 9 or 12-month contracts from September/October. Teaching load 120 hours (or 100 teaching hours) monthly plus 8 hours per month set aside for teachers' meetings, workshops and standby hours.

SALARY: 200,000–240,000 tenge net ($1,000–$1,250) in Almaty, and 220,000–260,000 tenge ($1,150–$1,400) in Astana, depending on qualifications and experience. Overtime hourly rates paid after 1,080 contracted hours. Bonus paid on completion of contract amounting to 150 tenge per hour taught (eg could be total of 216,000 tenge for 12-month contract). Paid holidays: 20 days in 12 months, 15 days in 9 months. Free survival Russian course.

FACILITIES/SUPPORT: Airfare allowance of 120,000 tenge if from Europe, 180,000 tenge if from North America or Australia. Free shared accommodation, all bills paid by the school (excluding long-distance telephone calls, cable TV and internet) or accommodation reimbursement. Airfare allowance. The school assists and covers the costs of a multiple-entry 1-year work visa. Limited health care and 24-hour hotline emergency assistance. Opportunities for promotion and transfer in one of the world's leading educational organisations.

RECRUITMENT: Direct applications to the school and through IHWO Recruitment Services (www.ihworld.com) and online advertising. Phone/Skype interviews essential.

CONTACT: Yelena Olshans Kaya, Central Office Manager and Recruitment Manager.

LANGUAGE LINK KAZAKHSTAN
1a Kulmanova St, Atyrau 060002
(phone) +7 7122 272907
(email) jobs@languagelink.ru
(web) www.jobs.languagelink.ru

CONDITIONS OF EMPLOYMENT: Similar to Language Link Russia mentioned above.

CONTACT: Svetlana Akhmetova, Administrator.

KYRGYZSTAN

CALLAN SCHOOL
49a Suumbaeva Street, Bishkek 720000
(phone) +996 312 040589
(email) callanschool@mail.ru
(web) www.callanschool.in.kg

NUMBER OF TEACHERS: 10 for work in English-language conversation clubs and workplace lessons.

PREFERENCE OF NATIONALITY: American or British.

QUALIFICATIONS: Native speakers of English only, though relevant background would be appreciated.

CONDITIONS OF EMPLOYMENT: 3 months to a year. Variable number of lessons that last 85 minutes.

SALARY: $6 per lesson. Out-of-office lessons pay $8. Total earned is $300-$700 per month depending on number of hours worked (which is more than enough to live in Kyrgyzstan). Tax is about $8 per month.

FACILITIES/SUPPORT: Free homestay accommodation; private room in family home. Assistance given in obtaining a work permit, which will cost the teacher $150 (if they are staying for a year). Opportunities to join excursions organised by Callan School, eg Saturday horse treks for picnics and barbecues.

RECRUITMENT: Interviews normally done through Skype.

CONTACT: Sabira, Manager.

LONDON SCHOOL IN BISHKEK
Baitik Baatyr 39, Bishkek 720005
(phone) +996 312 544474/545430
(email) info@londonschool.kg
(web) http://thelondonschool.org/en/tefl-jobs.php

NUMBER OF TEACHERS: 8.

PREFERENCE OF NATIONALITY: American and British native English speakers.

QUALIFICATIONS: Degree, CELTA and at least 1 year's teaching experience. Teachers without experience also would be considered. Must be aged under 40.

CONDITIONS OF EMPLOYMENT: Minimum 6 months starting all year round. 22 hours per week, 5 hours per day, 4 days a week plus 1-hour interview with new students four times a month. Also has volunteering programme, teaching English to village children.

SALARY: From $650 to $800 a month with free accommodation and monthly cultural excursions within the country all year round.

FACILITIES/SUPPORT: Free room provided plus all accommodation expenses. Help given with work permits for which teachers must have CELTA certificate and 2 references from previous teaching jobs.

RECRUITMENT: Online application. Teachers hired on basis of CV and references.

MIDDLE EAST

Oil wealth has meant that many of the countries of the Middle East have long been able to afford to attract the best teachers with superior qualifications and extensive experience. Most employers can afford to hire only professionals and there are few opportunities for newcomers to the profession. MENA, the common acronym for the Middle East and North Africa, is a region with a lot of recruitment activity. However, the tangled web of explosive conflicts throughout the Middle East has caused many teachers to look elsewhere. Multiple wars have undoubtedly destabilised the area and fanned the flames of Islamic distrust of the West. In fact some radicalised groups are opposed to the teaching of English.

With the tragic disintegration of Syria, bombs exploding in Yemen and alarming reports of Sunni–Shia hostilities and the resurgence of Al Qaeda in the Arabian peninsula, some countries have been rendered completely off-limits. Ongoing tensions between Israelis and Palestinians and an escalation of anti-western sentiment have resulted in many prospective teachers being in fear for their personal security.

The main exception is Turkey, where thousands of native English-speaking teachers find work. Despite its adherence to Islam, Turkey does not fit comfortably into a chapter on the Middle East. But despite its aspirations to join the EU and its secular government, neither does it fit logically into a section on Europe. But whatever its geographical classification, Turkey is a very important country for EFL teachers, whatever their background, and is treated at length later in this chapter.

On the one hand, the wealthy countries of Saudi Arabia, Oman and the Gulf states generally employ teachers with top qualifications. On the other hand, countries such as Jordan may have more casual opportunities. Anyone interested in teaching English to the Palestinians scattered throughout the Arab world is likely to be working on a voluntary basis or for accommodation and a local stipend, rather than for expatriate salaries.

A huge number of Middle Eastern young people aspire to study abroad. For this they need a high standard of English, and many universities and colleges throughout the region offer one-year Foundation Programmes that employ a staggering number of native speakers.

Teachers who sign contracts in a strict Islamic country should be aware of what they are letting themselves in for. People usually spend a year or two teaching in Saudi Arabia to make some money, rather than because they enjoy the lifestyle (unless they are students of Arab culture). When the amount of money accumulating back home is the principal or only motivation, morale can degenerate. The situation can be especially discouraging for women. Yet not everyone is gasping to get home to freely available alcohol, etc. A high percentage of teachers are recruited locally from a stable expatriate community. Demand for native English-speaker teachers continues strong in Saudi Arabia, mainly due to the opening of new colleges and universities, both in the public and private sector, some of which employ scores of ESL teachers and lecturers. Note that many of them accept only online applications. A useful list of institutes of higher education with, in some cases, links to current job vacancies can be found at www.university-directory.eu.

Middle Eastern language schools are also more likely to recruit non-native English speakers, specifically well-heeled teachers with pristine qualifications. **Ahad Shahbaz**, CEO of Interlink Language Center, asks: '*If a non-native speaker is highly educated, has earned his credentials from the Harvards of ESL teacher training institutions, and has near-native and at times superior proficiency and eloquence in the language, should we not be hiring him or her?*'

FINDING A JOB

Unless you are more or less resident in the Middle East, it is essential in most cases to fix up a job in advance. Casual teaching is not a possibility in most countries for a number of reasons, including the difficulty of getting visas, the prohibitively high cost of staying without working and the whole tradition of hiring teachers.

There are a few countries that can be entered on a tourist visa (eg Qatar and the United Arab Emirates) if you want to inspect potential employers, but this would be an expensive exercise. Visa difficulties vary from country to country. In Jordan, for example, schools that would like to hire foreign teachers are often put off by the cost of securing a work permit and paying the attendant lawyers' fees.

As always, it is worth checking with the British Council office in the country that interests you. The British Council has teaching centres in Bahrain (Manama), Jordan (Amman), Lebanon (Beirut), Oman (Muscat), Qatar (Doha), Saudi Arabia (Riyadh, Jeddah and Dammam), Kuwait and the United Arab Emirates (Abu Dhabi, Dubai, and Sharjah). The Council was advertising posts for teachers and senior teachers for the region in 2015; enquiries should be made to the Regional Teaching Centre Recruitment Manage (jalpa.trivedi@ae.britishcouncil.org). Like major ELT organisations, the British Council has a sizeable presence at the Recruitment section of the annual TESOL Arabia conference held every March (www.tesolarabia.net).

American teachers should investigate the US-sponsored Regional English Language Offices, some of which are involved with delivering English-language courses. The RELO in Bahrain is also responsible for Kuwait, Yemen, Qatar, UAE and Oman; and Saudi Arabia comes into the orbit of the RELO in Cairo. The RELO in Amman delivers English-language courses through its American Language Center that employs some native English-speaking teachers (+962 6 552 3901; info@alc.edu.jo).

America-Mideast Educational & Training Services or Amideast is a private, non-profit, non-government organisation with headquarters in Washington DC which provides English-language test preparation and other professional training through its network of operations throughout the Middle East (and North Africa). Recruitment of teachers is done by the individual centres, linked from www.amideast.org.

The usual suspects are active in the region. International House has schools in Dhahran and Jeddah in Saudi Arabia, one in Iran, two in Lebanon, one in Qatar, one in Syria and one in Oman. Berlitz has schools in Bahrain, Beirut, Oman, Qatar, UAE and others.

In Saudi Arabia and other strict Islamic countries, jobs are advertised by gender. Males probably have the advantage because there are openings for them in military academies, aeronautical colleges, etc. But female-only institutions are on the increase and at the time of writing the Middle East recruiter m2r Global was advertising multiple positions for female ESL teachers with schools, colleges and universities in Riyadh, Mecca, Dammam and Jeddah. The remuneration promised to the most highly qualified was $50,000 plus free housing. But in some respects, women continue to be treated as second-class citizens since the adverts firmly warn: '*A female CANNOT sponsor her family*'.

Job adverts regularly appear on websites such as www.tefl.com, www.esl101.com and in specialist journals. Try for example www.gulftalent.com, advertising 'jobs for professionals' and www.seekteachers.com with an office in Qatar. The largest display ads in the British educational press are quite often for Middle East vacancies, many placed by recruitment agencies on behalf of high-spending Saudi clients. A requirement often mentioned in job details is experience of the Middle East, in acknowledgment of the culture shock that many foreigners encounter in adapting to life under Islam. It is also worth checking regional newspapers such as the *Khaleej Times* (www.khaleejtimes.com) from the UAE.

RECRUITMENT AGENCIES

In theory, being hired by an established recruitment agency in your own country should offer some protection against problems. However, it sometimes seems to be the case that people working on commission will say anything to reach their recruitment targets, and will shamelessly exaggerate conditions, such as the distance from accommodation compound to workplace. Check the fine print of any contract, looking for a get-out clause for the employer such as '*the parent company may amend or re-issue benefits, policies and procedures pertaining to the better conduct of its business*'. Such a contract means nothing because the employer reserves the right to change whatever they like. A few years ago an educational consultancy with an office in Toronto recruited a large number of EFL teachers to work for the United Arab Emirates military.

When a dispute arose between client and recruiter, the teachers were the ones to suffer, since they weren't paid promised salaries and their contracts were not honoured.

A typical agency advert for corporate language instructors for the Middle East might read: '*Client seeks applications from male instructors for its corporate training programmes in the petrochemicals, utilities and heavy industries sectors. We can consider UK, Canadian, American, Irish, New Zealander, South African, Egyptian, Jordanian and Filipino nationals. Applied language practice is more important than descriptive language or grammar-bound approaches to language teaching. Applications from enthusiastic candidates who are interested in multimedia are especially welcome. We have projects available in several cities.*'

Reputable agencies to check out include Teachaway (www.teachaway.com), which at the time of writing was recruiting licensed teachers for many positions in Abu Dhabi, among others, the UK-based m2r Global (see entry), Footprints Recruiting (UAE and Kuwait), Tefl.org.uk, English Today Recruitment (www.englishrecruitment.com), In Advance Recruitment (www.inadvance.uk.com), Red Chair Recruitment in Ireland (www.redchairrecuritment.ie) and many others.

LEISURE TIME

The majority of teachers live in foreigners' compounds provided by their employers. Most of these are well provided with sports facilities such as tennis courts and swimming pools. In some locations, such as Jubail in Saudi Arabia, water sports are a popular diversion. Some have described expat life in the Middle East as a false paradise.

The principal pastimes are barbecues, reading out-of-date copies of the *International New York Times*, playing with computers (which are cheaply available) and complaining about the terrific heat and the lack of alcohol (Saudi Arabia and Kuwait are completely dry states). Others of course try to learn some Arabic and make local friends, always taking care not to offend against local sensibilities. The constraints of living under Islam are well known. For example, in some countries anyone found eating, drinking or smoking in a public place during the month of Ramadan could face a jail sentence, large fine and/or deportation. Teachers may be expected to work very unsocial hours during Ramadan, ie starting class at sunset.

LIST OF EMPLOYERS

BRITISH COUNCIL – MENA
MENA-TeacherRecruitment@ae.britishcouncil.org
www.britishcouncil.org/jobs/careers/english

The British Council – Middle and Near East, and North Africa has teaching centres in Bahrain, Iraq, Kurdistan, Kuwait, Lebanon, Oman, Qatar, Saudi Arabia, United Arab Emirates, Jordan, Morocco, Tunisia and Egypt.

NUMBER OF TEACHERS: Fluctuating vacancies across the region, but mostly in Saudi Arabia (ksa.recruit@sa.britishcouncil.org) and Egypt.

PREFERENCE OF NATIONALITY: Most countries will accept applications from teachers across the globe providing they have the required qualifications and a high level of English, if English isn't their first language. Exceptions to this are stated in individual post information.

QUALIFICATIONS: Minimum CELTA or Trinity Cert plus 2 years' full-time (1,600 hours) ELT experience, for hourly teaching. DELTA or Trinity Diploma may be needed for more senior posts. Maximum age 60.

FACILITIES/SUPPORT: Accommodation arranged in some countries plus medical insurance.

RECRUITMENT: Some via British Council Recruitment Unit in Dubai. Also TESOL Arabia conference in March and IATEFL Jobs Market in April each year.

CONTACT: Ms. Jalpa Trivedi (MENA-TeacherRecruitment@ae.britishcouncil.org).

m2r LTD

24 Cheapside, Wakefield, West Yorkshire WF1 2TF

+44 1924 201973

info@m2rglobal.com or charlotte@m2rglobal.com

www.m2rglobal.com

Global recruitment consultancy.

NUMBER OF TEACHERS: 50 per year, sent to various organisations and employers in the Gulf Cooperation Council (GCC) region, ie Bahrain, Kuwait, Saudi and the UAE.

PREFERENCE OF NATIONALITY: Native speakers of English only.

QUALIFICATIONS: Minimum BA degree, ideally in English Language, recognised ESL qualification and 1-year's experience. Overseas experience is preferred also.

CONDITIONS OF EMPLOYMENT: Minimum 1-year contract, renewable. 40 hours per week, though number of contact hours varies.

SALARY: Minimum $30,000 plus benefits such as housing and flights. Saudi salaries up to $42,000 tax-free.

RECRUITMENT: Video or telephone interview can be arranged if face-to-face interview in Yorkshire is not possible.

CONTACT: Charlotte Watson, Recruitment Account Manager, or Mr Munir Mamujee, Managing Director (munir@m2rglobal.com).

AFGHANISTAN

This information may not be of interest to anyone of a nervous disposition. **Tom Clark** from the USA taught here several years ago, and this information is largely based on his account (note that the situation may have changed since he was there). He concludes that Afghanistan is a great place '*for a journalist, spy or madman*'.

TOM CLARK

While teaching in Kuwait, Tom Clark saw an advert on Dave's ESL Cafe that he followed up much later. It turned out that the American University in Kabul (the first private university in the country) was desperate to get teachers in place for a summer project funded by USAID. Since the US government controlled the programme, his visa was sorted out quickly. According to Tom, you could get a lot of stories about the funding and where it was going and how it got disbursed . . . It wasn't so much red tape as corruption, but that is everywhere in Afghanistan. The job was teaching at the university prep programme, plus he was doing extra work for the UN and a human rights organisation. Tom describes the job.

The contract with the university was the best I have had in the ESL world. It paid $5,000 a month with danger pay and other bonuses. It was better than Saudi. It offered holiday pay, housing, transportation, laptop, cell phone, we could fly on UN planes, etc. We stayed in a guesthouse with a beautiful garden, had security guards 24/7 and were fenced in, and we had electricity more than four hours a day. Our money went a long way, as the cost of living was so low there and the American dollar was welcome. Transferring money in and out was not easy, nor setting up bank accounts. Security was a problem, as we were not free to travel around or mix with the locals. If an aid worker was killed, we would be on lock-down/house arrest for weeks at a time. Sometimes we wore bulletproof vests, were always in the presence of security guards, had to be very careful associating with local people and would have to come up with colourful stories to get out and about into the 'field'.

The workplace was quite unorganised and a lot of people were disgruntled. We wanted to teach different subjects, but things were always censored there. My fellow teachers were of a higher calibre than I was used to. All had masters in specialised areas and I had the feeling they all worked for organisations they did not mention on their CVs. They spoke multiple languages and seemed to have alternative agendas other than just teaching. Many of them had prior links to the State Department. It was an odd assortment at best.

The pupils were the cream of the crop. They were not from typical backgrounds, they were from high-ranking military, intelligence and diplomatic families. Occupying our spare time was difficult since we always had to get permission to go anywhere, unless we hid under the radar. There were a handful of 'safe' establishments for foreigners, but after a while you got bored with those and had to find a way to entertain yourself. If it were not for the money, it would be quite hard to stay and live there, unless you really liked reading books all the time.

Employment information about the university can be found at www.auaf.edu.af, where current openings for native-speaking English instructors are listed. Several public universities in the Afghan capital are in the process of transitioning to teaching in English as part of an Afghan Ministry of Higher Education and British Council agreement concluded in October 2013. Most advertised positions are with government agencies and NGOs such as ACBAR in Herat (Agency Coordinating Body for Afghan Relief) at www.acbar.org; many involve computer as well as language training.

In such an unstable setting as Kabul, things change fast and anyone who stays teaching for more than a year is likely to move up quickly. The British Council has a teaching programme in Afghanistan but in keeping with a policy to build capacity they employ mainly qualified local Afghan teachers. Needless to say Afghanistan has a rich and complex history and the people are friendly, warm and wonderfully hospitable once you have gained their trust.

ISRAEL

Because of the large number of English-speaking Jews who have settled in Israel from the USA, South Africa, etc, many native speakers of English are employed in the state education system and there is little active recruitment of foreign teachers. There are a number of private language schools, for example about a dozen Wall Street Institutes and nine Berlitz schools. WSI has opened branches in Netanya on the coast and Nazareth for which it has been recruiting. The one in Nazareth is the first branch of Wall Street Israel in the Arab sector. The British Council (www.britishcouncil.org.il) maintains a small presence in Israel and has teaching centres in Ramat-Gan (Tel Aviv), West Jerusalem and Nazareth, which recruit qualified EFL teachers mainly from the local English-speaking population to teach business English and IELTS preparation.

The going rate for private language tutoring is NIS80–160 per lesson. Finding opportunities and sorting out the red tape for living in Israel is difficult unless you speak fluent Hebrew.

TOM BALFOUR

Tom Balfour discovered there were openings in Israel, shortly after reacquainting himself with a girl he knew in Tel Aviv.

I sent emails with my CV to various English schools, mostly branches of the two big companies Berlitz and Wall Street Institute, explaining my situation - that I would be leaving Israel in a week to return to England for my summer job, but that I wanted to come back in September and teach English in Tel Aviv. Most of the schools simply sent me a reply saying 'get back to us when you return' but Wall Street Institute Tel Aviv invited me for an interview. In the interview I was asked various questions about teaching, and then the director pretended to be a low-level student and asked me to explain various words to her. When she asked me what a model was, I said 'Naomi Campbell, Kate Moss' and then got up and did a pretend catwalk round the room. Although I'm sure that my qualifications helped, I think that might be what got me the job: knowing how to keep explanations simple, and being prepared to look silly if it helped. She told me that if I came back I would be offered a contract.

I had heard (from this book in fact!) that with the high number of native English-speaking immigrants in Israel there wasn't really a market for English teachers. I think, however, that my Trinity qualification and my planned work at the summer school made me stand out from the native candidates, some of whom were hoping for a job simply on the strength of being English speakers.

One difficulty that native English speakers may run into is getting a visa. You improve your chances by being in a relationship with an Israeli or Jewish foreigner.

Israel is an amazing country and Tel Aviv is a great, cosmopolitan city with a good beach and fantastic nightlife.

PALESTINE

Education is all but impossible for many Palestinians in the West Bank and Gaza and the situation is very difficult for teachers. Although the demand is there, the circumstances do not allow the vast majority of Palestinians to achieve their ambition. Like most international organisations, the British Council withdrew from the Palestinian Territories for a time but has now resumed its educational activities in Nablus, Ramallah, Gaza, Hebron and East Jerusalem (www.britishcouncil.ps). The US non-profit organisation Amideast is also active in the same range of towns (www.amideast.org/west-bank-gaza) and was advertising six posts in spring 2015.

The charity UNIPAL (Educational Exchange with Palestinians – see entry in Lebanon section) operates an educational and cultural exchange with Palestinian communities. The political situation has made it impossible for projects to continue in Gaza and also in the other Palestinian territories, so now its projects carry on only in Lebanon. Another charity that arranges for English tutors to spend the summer in Nablus or nearby refugee camps for Palestinians is Project Hope (see entry). Palestinian schools struggle on and anyone who supports their cause might be prepared to become a volunteer teacher. Senior people who can set up programmes would be especially welcome.

LIST OF EMPLOYERS

PROJECT HOPE (Humanitarian Opportunities for Peace and Education)

00970 29 An-Najah, Al Qadim St, Nablus

+970 9233 7077

recruiter@projecthope.ps; nablus@projecthope.ps

www.projecthope.ps

Canadian-registered charity. Non-profit volunteer organisation that supports children denied access to basic services in the refugee camps and villages of the Nablus region of the Northern West Bank.

NUMBER OF VOLUNTEER TEACHERS: 15–30 for the largest provider of free English classes in the West Bank (1,000 students enrolled per month).

PREFERENCE OF NATIONALITY: None.

QUALIFICATIONS: Teachers must have a TEFL qualification or teaching experience along with experience of working with groups of children and young people. Minimum age 21.

CONDITIONS OF EMPLOYMENT: 5 weeks to 1 year, 20–25 hours of teaching a week, with 2 full days off.

SALARY: None. Volunteers must make financial contribution to cover accommodation in a shared apartment of 500 shekels ($150) per month

RECRUITMENT: Teachers fill in an application form and are then interviewed over the telephone (the recruiter calls the teacher).

CONTACT: International Volunteer Recruiter.

KUWAIT

Although teaching salaries are no longer in the stratosphere, as some were more than a decade ago, many organisations still seek to lure expat teachers with favourable terms. Educational standards are variable, as encountered by **B. P. Rawlins** in Kuwait:

> *There are simply too many schools in Kuwait acting like pigs at a trough, all of them out there for the money. They dare not criticise any anti-social behaviour by pupils, parents or adult students for fear of losing fees in a competitive market. Professionalism is viewed with hostile suspicion in some quarters.*

This negative view is not subscribed to by all who have spent time in the region. Many agree that English learners in Kuwait, as throughout the Arab world, can be a pleasure to teach because they are so eager to communicate, and so unhesitant to speak English in class.

As well as keeping an up-to-date list of the many international and English-medium schools in Kuwait, the British Council (PO Box 345, Safat 13004; +965 2205 2300; info@kw.britishcouncil.org) employs teachers year round and for July/August summer courses.

LIST OF EMPLOYERS

AMIDEAST

Mail: PO Box 44818, Hawalli 32063, Kuwait

Physical Address: Ahmed Al-Jabeer St, Opp. Al-Awadhi Mosque, Commercial Bank Building, 2nd Fl, Sharq

📞 +965 2247 0091

✉ kuwait@amideast.org

🖥 www.amideast.org/kuwait

PREFERENCE OF NATIONALITY: North American. AMIDEAST emphasises American-style English.

QUALIFICATIONS: BA/BEd and MA in TESL are essential. 5 years of teaching experience are required.

CONDITIONS OF EMPLOYMENT: Hired as part-time independent contractors. Contracts are usually 6 weeks long and renewable according to demand. Average 2 hours a day, 3 days a week; generally evenings.

SALARY: Depends on qualifications and experience.

RECRUITMENT: Newspaper ads and referrals.

CONTACT: Ms Samar Khleif, Country Director (skhleif@amideast.org).

LEBANON

Lebanon has traditionally been an important commercial hub for the Middle East, a forward-thinking, artistic and entrepreneurial country. However, progress is being set back by sectarian tensions that have escalated with the deepening crisis in Syria. Hezbollah, the main Shi'ite party in Lebanon, has a close alliance with Syria's Bashar al Assad, while the vast majority of Lebanese Sunnis support the mainly Sunni-led uprising in Syria. Furthermore, fear of cross-border strikes from Israel is never far below the surface. There continues to be a heavy UN presence in the south and many foreign embassies advise against non-essential travel to the area.

Most teaching jobs in Lebanon are found in Beirut. Locals are generally open minded and many speak three languages: English, French and Arabic. Male and female teachers will find it relatively easy to adjust (compared to the major culture shock experienced in other Middle East destinations), although the pace of life is slower and more conservative outside Beirut. In 2015, a new programme was implemented in Lebanon called 'Accessing Education: Language Integration for Syrian Refugee Children' funded by the EU and assisted by the British Council. This ambitious English language teaching programme for children aged 8–14 who arrive from Syria with almost no English is being carried out mostly by local teachers after receiving specialised training.

Finding an English teaching job in Lebanon can be difficult as there is a local pool of qualified teachers. A few schools advertise abroad and recruit on teaching websites, but most do not. A further impediment is mentioned by Amideast's Programme Manager, which is that work permits are expensive in Lebanon. Occasionally Amideast hires expatriates who are already in Lebanon taking classes at the American University of Beirut or living with friends or relatives.

If you cannot find a posting, find the contact information of any school online and start sending off your CV. Most full-curriculum schools are English or French, with the other language plus Arabic taught as second languages, although English continues to gain ground over French, to the chagrin of the French. The popularity of English is increasing due to its status as the international language of business and also to a strong tradition of Lebanese emigration to the USA and Australia.

However, even schools that do not use English as the medium of instruction employ English teachers. The website www.schoolnet.edu.lb/schools.htm has links to some private schools around Lebanon; www.lebweb.com is an online directory for everything from banks to schools in Lebanon and the classified section of www.dailystar.com.lb carries occasional teaching vacancies (but check daily). For info about teaching English to adults try the American Lebanese Language Center (see entry) or the British Council (www.britishcouncil.org/lb), which hires teachers on an hourly part-time basis and sponsors suitable candidates to do the Distance DELTA. It's perhaps also worth trying the Lebanese American University (PO Box 13–5053, Chouran, Beirut 1102 2801; www.lau.edu.lb).

While the demand for teachers exists, the wages can be low unless you are lucky enough to be hired by a large, foreign-operated school or university. The minimum wage is about $500 per month and local teachers earn about $750 per month as a starting salary. Foreign teachers can expect to earn about $900–$1,500 a month, depending on credentials, experience and how the contract is negotiated. Contact hours are often high and teachers may be assigned additional tasks. Lebanon has 20 official holidays.

A few larger schools offer on-site housing and those that do not will help teachers find decent accommodation. Finding a flat from abroad is difficult, although some English websites and newspapers list private and shared accommodation.

RED TAPE

Schools will manage your work visa, but expect this to take time. Teachers generally arrive at the airport on a tourist visa. After arrival, the school begins processing work papers, which may take between two weeks and more than two months. Lebanon is a developing country, paperwork is not always straightforward and government offices are not easy to negotiate (if they ever are). Note that teachers from the UK and USA are sometimes preferred simply because their visas are half the price of Canadians' and Australians'. However, **Shelley Beyak-Tarabichi**, who used to work for International House in Beirut, provides words of reassurance: '*Canucks and Aussies still get hired!*' Shelley is originally from Canada and has provided much of the information for this chapter.

Increasingly it will be worthwhile investigating possibilities in this tiny but fascinating country. While accompanying her husband on a short-term contract in Lebanon, **Anne Cleaver** (an early-retired teacher) easily found work (albeit voluntary) at a new Special Needs Centre just outside Beirut:

> *Even during my short period there, I was tentatively offered a full-time post at a neighbouring school and even an opening in Abu Dhabi. There is a real eagerness to learn English in Lebanon. I found Lebanese educationalists, parents and children most welcoming and enthusiastic. Being a British teacher there made me feel more valued, I regret to say, than back in the UK.*

Good education is extremely important and costly in Lebanon and families pay large sums to ensure their child attends a distinguished school and also invest in tutoring outside of school. Children are expected to study hard inside and outside of school, as government tests are difficult.

A very different experience would be to teach in the Palestinian refugee camps. As mentioned, the charity UNIPAL (Universities' Trust for Educational Exchange with Palestinians) operates a summer volunteer teaching programme for teenagers in Palestinian refugee camps located in Lebanon. Volunteers must be native English speakers, based in the UK and at least 20 years old. Previous work with children is essential, and previous teaching experience preferred. TEFL/TESL qualifications are an advantage, but not necessary. The approximate cost of the programme is £550 to cover airfare and insurance as well as food and accommodation for five weeks.

LEISURE

Shelley Beyak-Tarabichi came to appreciate life in Lebanon:

> *Lebanese hospitality is renowned, the food is fantastic (healthy and vegetarian friendly) and the weather is comfortable. You can swim at a beach resort in the summer, ski in the winter and hike all year round. There are gyms, malls, outdoor groups, concerts, art schools and mountain resorts along with traditional Arabic cafés, monasteries, mosques and historical sites dating back thousands, if not millions, of years. While the political situation in Lebanon is termed unstable, it is not evident on a day-to-day level as one would expect.*

LIST OF EMPLOYERS

ALLC IH BEIRUT
American Lebanese Language Center – International House Beirut, Dimitri El Hayek St, Confidence Center, 7th Floor, Sin el Fil, Beirut
℘ +961 1 500978; +961 70 944684
✆ recruitment@allcs.edu.lb
🖥 www.allcs.edu.lb.

Branches also in Dbayeh, Jounieh, Byblos, Saida, Tripoli and Zahle.
NUMBER OF TEACHERS: Approx. 20.
PREFERENCE OF NATIONALITY: American, British.
QUALIFICATIONS: CELTA or approved equivalent, 2+ years' post-CELTA experience. Business English experience essential.
CONDITIONS OF EMPLOYMENT: 12-month standard contract. 26 contact hours per week, split shift between 9am and 9.30pm.

SALARY: $1,000–$1,500, depending on experience and qualifications. No deductions.

FACILITIES/SUPPORT: The Centre finds suitable accommodation but does not pay for it. The Centre deals with all paperwork relating to work and residency permits. Health insurance provided.

RECRUITMENT: Normally through IHWO recruitment page, unsolicited applications and emails. Interviews are essential, usually carried out via Skype.

CONTACT: Elaine Kniveton, Academic Director (elainek@allcs.edu.lb).

UNIPAL
BCM Unipal, London WC1N 3XX, UK
info@unipal.org.uk
www.unipal.org.uk

NUMBER OF TEACHERS: 30 volunteers for summer camps in Palestinian refugee camps.

PREFERENCE OF NATIONALITY: Native English speakers and living in the UK.

QUALIFICATIONS: Experience with children or teaching. TEFL a bonus. Volunteers should have sensitivity, tolerance and political awareness. Must be at least 20 at time of application.

CONDITIONS OF EMPLOYMENT: 3–5 weeks between mid-July and end of August. 5 hours a day.

SALARY: None: volunteers pay £300 plus flights, etc.

FACILITIES/SUPPORT: Simple accommodation provided. Compulsory pre-departure training days held in UK.

RECRUITMENT: Application forms are downloadable from website from November and are due mid-February for interviews in March and training days in mid-April and July.

CONTACT: Brenda Hayward, Director.

OMAN

According to experienced American teacher **Tom Clark**, who has worked in Afghanistan, Egypt, Syria, Turkey, Kuwait and Saudi, Oman is '*the best in the Middle East for being friendly and open and laid back*'. Tom thinks Oman has been experiencing a boom in tourism and employment and is growing and developing very fast. It may be that as more luxury hotels are built and local residents are moved from the beaches, it will become a different country. Technical colleges such as the Salalah College of Technology, where Tom worked – alongside 59 other ESL teachers – have periods of hiring on a big scale.

Since the 1970s Oman has had to import the majority of its skilled labour, including teachers. Teachers of English are employed from Sudan, Sri Lanka, India and North Africa, which means that there is a much broader mix of accents than usual. Positions for native English speakers from the UK etc become available each year with the British Council and Amideast in Muscat, and the major employers of western teachers are the Ministry of Higher Education, Sultan Qaboos University (who hire primarily through TESOL conventions in Dubai and the US each spring) and CfBT Education Trust. The latter supplies expertise in Education and Training for various public and private sector clients including the Ministry of Education, the Ministry of Higher Education and Petroleum Development Oman (PDO).

Despite an expanding EFL market, there's no room at all for visiting job-seekers, since a tight hold is kept on tourist visas. It will make it much easier to land a job if you have an MA in TESOL or Applied Linguistics (or at least are enrolled in a distance learning ELT master's degree) with at least three years' experience, preferably at university level. IH Muscat (Polyglot Institute) in Oman asks for teachers with a BA (English major), CELTA or Trinity TESOL, plus three to five years' EFL experience post-CELTA. If the first degree is a BSc, the approving body requires five years' experience post-CELTA. The main recruiting season begins in March, just prior to the annual TESOL Arabia conference. TATI, the Technical & Administrative Training Institute in Medinat Qaboos (+968 24605086 ext 25; www.tatioman.com) does some hiring of well-qualified native speaker instructors for Salalah mentioned above as well as six other colleges of technology around Oman. The advertised wage is 1000 rials a month basic plus a housing allowance and free flights to Muscat.

Exactly why an MA in TESOL should be necessary is not very clear. One wry description of students in higher education could apply equally to students throughout the Middle East:

> *Unfortunately there is a widespread idea that experts in linguistics and the like have what it takes to teach English. It can come as a bit of a shock, therefore, for teachers who have studied phonics, syllabus design, methodology and socio-linguistics to discover that they are teaching 'Headway Elementary' units 1 to 5 to groups of up to 40 students per class. Not exactly what the MA prepares you for. One could say that the school-leavers who come to the colleges and higher institutes are ill prepared.*

On the other hand Tom Clark found his students to be polite and really engaged with their studies. This is not life in the fast lane of academic endeavour but something of an academic lay-by. If you choose to work in one of the colleges of higher education, you may find that the concept of rigorous academic standards is imperfectly understood, and therefore rarely applied.

Itinerant teacher **Bradwell Jackson** investigated possibilities at Polyglot (www.polyglot.org) and reported that it is both the oldest and the largest school in Muscat. According to the school's marketing manager, the market for English is ever expanding, possibly as much as 13% year on year. The students prefer British English to American, partly for political reasons and also because they are more likely to go to Britain for further studies. Teachers are paid $2,500 a month for working 4pm–9pm Saturday through Tuesday, with no morning classes. Bradwell concludes: '*In the very short time I have been here, Oman strikes me as a very pleasant place to live. It seems a very well-kept secret. Everyone is talking about UAE, as Oman quietly and slowly gains more and more gravitas. The city is very clean and surprisingly modern. I would love to work here myself.*'

Tom Clark also described the favourable quality of life. Newly arrived teachers were presented with a choice of places to live, from villas in the mountains to plantations in the woods, luxury apartments in the suburbs to places on the beach. It is possible to acquire a drinking licence for the five bars in town. Other recreations include scuba diving, boating, desert camping Bedouin-style, picnicking in the mountain valleys, camel racing or just haring around in a 4WD. The countryside and coasts are stunning, and if you can handle the heat and at times the humidity, mountain walking is popular. Just try not to get bored with these activities. There are no others, unless you happen to live near Muscat, where you can indulge in wandering around glossy shopping malls, watching Hindi movies and eating sushi.

LIST OF EMPLOYERS

AMIDEAST OMAN
Al Jama'a Al Akhbar Street, Building 93, Airport Heights, Ghala (Muscat)
℡ +968 2 2459 0309
✉ oman@amideast.org
🖥 www.amideast.org/oman

NUMBER OF TEACHERS: 10 part-time EFL instructors for on and off-site assignments. Based on a memorandum of understanding with the Ministry of Education, AMIDEAST is one of the only institutes legally able to employ teachers on a part-time basis.
PREFERENCE OF NATIONALITY: Americans and other native English speakers.
QUALIFICATIONS: Bachelor's degree plus recognised international certificate in TEFL/TESL and a minimum of 2 years' successful experience teaching English to non-native speakers. Teachers are usually on family visa because their spouse or parent is working in Oman, or have full-time work with local colleges or universities.
CONDITIONS OF EMPLOYMENT: Mostly freelancers. General English classes for children, teenagers and adults held between 8am and 9pm. Business English and other ESP courses conducted for public and private sector organisations on a per contract basis.
SALARY: 10 rials per hour ($25).
FACILITIES/SUPPORT: AMIDEAST will offer assistance in locating affordable housing. All visa-related fees and procurement will be managed by AMIDEAST upon arrival.
RECRUITMENT: Via www.amideast.org plus regional and international TEFL conferences.
CONTACT: Paul Steele, Director of Training Programs (psteele@amideast.org).

CfBT OMAN LLC
PO Box 2278, Ruwi, PC 112, Muscat, Sultanate of Oman
℡ +968 24560239
✉ gen@cfbtoman.com or menaenquiries@cfbt.com
🖥 www.cfbt.com

Subsidiary of CfBT Education Trust.
NUMBER OF TEACHERS: About 12 in British Training Institute in Muscat; over 40 in projects with Ministries of Education and Higher Education.
PREFERENCE OF NATIONALITY: British, North American, Australian, New Zealander.
QUALIFICATIONS: Usually DELTA. Salary increments paid for MA and PhD.
CONDITIONS OF EMPLOYMENT: 1 year renewable, 1 September to 31 August. Up to 25 teaching hours a week. Short-term contracts for consultants.
SALARY: Market rate. Tax free.
FACILITIES/SUPPORT: Free accommodation or accommodation allowance; work permit; annual return flight.
RECRUITMENT: Normally through advertisements on internet (www.tefl.com, www.jobs.edufind.com), agents abroad; CfBT database and www.cfbt.com.
CONTACT: Juliet Cowley (jcowley@cfbtoman.com or gen@cfbtoman.com).

IH MUSCAT / POLYGLOT INSTITUTE OMAN LLC
PO Box 221, Ruwi, Post Code 112, Sultanate of Oman
℡ +968 24 666 666
✉ vacancy@polyglot.org
🖥 www.pi.om

NUMBER OF TEACHERS: 15.

PREFERENCE OF NATIONALITY: UK, Australia, South Africa, USA.

QUALIFICATIONS: First degree (English major), RSA CELTA or equivalent (IHWO standard), minimum 2 years' EFL teaching experience post-CELTA.

CONDITIONS OF EMPLOYMENT: 1–2 years. 26 contact teaching hours per week from a 40-hour working week.

SALARY: Dependent on qualifications and experience.

FACILITIES/SUPPORT: Shared, furnished accommodation is provided for all teachers recruited from abroad. All documentation is arranged and organised by HR team, according to legal requirements.

RECRUITMENT: IH website and interviews normally carried out by IH Recruit Services.

CONTACT: Mrs Jean Scopes, Director of Studies.

MODERN COLLEGE OF BUSINESS & SCIENCE (MCBS)
PO Box 100, Al-Khuwair, 133 Sultanate of Oman
(phone) +968 24583583 / 24583538
(email) jobs@mcbs.edu.om
(web) www.mcbs.edu.om

NUMBER OF TEACHERS: Full-time teachers, faculty positions and interns.

QUALIFICATIONS: Minimum of relevant bachelor's degree and 2 years teaching for some positions, new graduates with CELTA qualification considered to teach in General Foundation Program.

CONDITIONS OF EMPLOYMENT: Starting in autumn or spring.

SALARY: According to qualifications and experience.

SUR UNIVERSITY COLLEGE
PO Box 440, Postal Code 411, Sur, Oman
(email) job@suc.edu.om
(web) www.suc.edu.om

PREFERENCE OF NATIONALITY: Native English speakers.

QUALIFICATIONS: Bachelor's or master's degree in English or related areas, TEFL or CELTA certificate plus minimum 2 years' experience of teaching adults.

CONDITIONS OF EMPLOYMENT: 1 year renewable. 21 hours per week. To teach on foundation course for Omani students who want to study business, IT or engineering at university.

SALARY: $2,000–$2,500 per month basic salary, tax free. 40 days' paid summer holiday.

FACILITIES/SUPPORT: Free furnished accommodation and assistance with work permit. Transport provided, medical insurance, utilities allowance and annual round-trip air ticket.

CONTACT: Professor Ahmad Sharieh (ahmadsharieh@suc.edu.om).

QATAR

The tiny traditional emirate of Qatar is surrounded by Saudi Arabia, Bahrain, the United Arab Emirates and Iran, and has a stable ELT industry. Past reforms by the Emir of the state, Sheikh Hamad bin Khalifa Al-Thani, promoted English over Arabic as the medium of instruction in the state school curriculum, while trying to balance respect for the heritage and conservative nature of Qatar's people.

As a country high in natural gas and oil reserves, Qatar has a per capita income that exceeds some of the leading industrial countries of Western Europe, and as such offers some enticing expatriate packages to teachers. Because of Qatar's booming economy, prices are rising quickly, particularly for accommodation, and it is increasingly difficult to afford a decent place to live. A standard expat housing allowance for a single person might be 5,500 rials a month (as paid by the Ta'alum Group of Schools in 2015 for the first two months of a contract) which is enough to rent a small studio flat only.

After completing a Master of Education in Canada, **Arshiya-Nageen Ahmed** went to Qatar to teach and to research education practice in the Middle East:

I was actively looking for careers related to my field while volunteering to gain additional experience. After receiving three job offers I had to decide my best option. The interview procedures were long, however, I got the job in Qatar and have been working ever since. Students are hesitant to speak English at times since they do not want to make mistakes. Thus the best way is to build good student-teacher rapport so that the students become comfortable in an English-language environment. I was already aware that students would find some difficulty in adjusting to a foreign accent but from their feedback, they seem at ease in understanding a Canadian accent. Furthermore, it is important to encourage students to speak English with their peers so that they stay in practice.

The main teaching opportunities are to be found in the state schools and post-secondary education institutes. There are also opportunities for in-company development of Business English for those with the appropriate qualifications. The British Council has an English language centre in Doha (99 Al Sadd Street, PO Box 2992, Doha; general.enquiries@qa.britishcouncil.org) offering English courses to adults and children and possible advice on finding teaching work.

There are also possibilities within private language institutes: Inlingua Qatar is partnered with Score Plus Education to help candidates gain admission to foreign universities.

LIST OF EMPLOYERS

EDUCATE LEARNING CENTER
Aamal Tower, 1st Floor, West Bay, Doha (PO Box 24635, Doha)
- +974 4417 7103
- info@educate.com.qa
- www.educate.com.qa

NUMBER OF TEACHERS: 8–10.
PREFERENCE OF NATIONALITY: Canada, US, UK, New Zealand, Australia.

QUALIFICATIONS: Must be a native English speaker with a diploma or degree for post-secondary education. Some knowledge of Arabic is preferred. Junior trainers with 6 months' to 5 years' experience are generally preferred for their fresh approach. Employer is looking for candidates who are extroverts, highly organised, professional and with a positive attitude. They should have the ability to teach upper management in corporate settings.
CONDITIONS OF EMPLOYMENT: Minimum 1 year. 40 hours per week: 20–24 hours' teaching time, the rest for lesson planning and preparation.

SALARY: 6,000–10,000 riyals per month, depending on experience and qualifications. No deductions because Qatar is a tax-free country.

FACILITIES/SUPPORT: Accommodation is provided or an allowance in lieu if teachers choose to find their own accommodation. Employer covers costs and takes responsibility for the processes involved in obtaining a work permit after teachers provide the necessary documentation (ie proof of higher education, valid passport etc) and pass the Qatar medical examination.

RECRUITMENT: Referrals, online advertising, via AIESEC International. Interviews are completed over Skype or by telephone.

QATAR AERONAUTICAL COLLEGE
PO Box 4050, Doha
📞 +974 4440 8813
✉ careers@qac.edu.qa or doha.hr@gmail.com
💻 www.qac.edu.qa

NUMBER OF TEACHERS: 35–40.

PREFERENCE OF NATIONALITY: Native English speakers.

QUALIFICATIONS: Bachelor's degree, CELTA, DELTA, TEFL certificate or master's plus minimum 3 years' experience.

CONDITIONS OF EMPLOYMENT: Length of contract is 6–12 months. Working hours are 7am–2pm.

SALARY: $3,600–$4,000 per month.

FACILITIES/SUPPORT: Furnished accommodation, government health card and assistance with work permits provided.

RECRUITMENT: Interviews required, usually carried out in the UK.

CONTACT: Hester Drewry, Training Manager of Foundation Programme (hdrewry@qac.edu.qa) or HR department.

SAUDI ARABIA

Recruitment of English teachers is booming and the recruitment websites are full of advertised vacancies. Whereas at one time employers had very high standards and expected their teachers to have many years of experience, now there are some teachers in the kingdom who don't even have a university degree. Part of the problem is that the country is so wealthy that many from the elite classes know that they will never have to work for a living and do not particularly value education. The teaching is not always very serious and there is an expectation that everyone will 'pass', no matter what. The days of fabulously high salaries are also over, and rising persecution of foreigners has acted as a further disincentive. But expatriate packages are still attractive, with substantial salaries, free airfares and accommodation plus generous holidays and other perks.

Teaching in a naval academy or petrochemical company while living in a teetotal expatriate ghetto is not many people's idea of fun, especially after a request for an exit visa has been denied. Women who get jobs as teachers (at a women's college) may live to regret it when they find that Saudi women are prohibited by law from driving a car and must not appear in public without being covered from head to foot.

Specialist ELT recruiters like Desert Recruiting Services (www.desertrecruiting.com) in Canada which specialises in the Middle East, Global Recruitment Solutions in Wales (www.globalrecruitmentsolutions.co.uk), GoldStar TEFL Recruitment (www.GoldStarTeachers.com), D1 Resourcing in Ireland (www.d1resourcing. com) and Education-Experts in Saudi Arabia (www.edu-experts.com) all advertise vacancies, sometimes urgently. Other recruiters active in Saudi include TQ Education & Training, part of the Pearson Group (www. tq.com), Teach to Travel (www.teachtotravel.com) and Language Solutions (www.langsols.com). Experienced recruiters warn that mobilisation to Saudi Arabia takes three to four months from the interview. There are also recruitment companies operating in Saudi Arabia like Quality Education Holding Company in Riyadh (www.qehc.edu.sa) and Al Rajhi Co. for HRD (www.al-rajhi4hrd.com), but they often operate mainly in Arabic, so dealing with them is not straightforward. One more recruiter to try is based in Sicily: English Language Services (englishlanguageservices59@gmail.com).

TOM CLARK

Tom Clark has also taught in Saudi Arabia. He describes the interview process in the UK with a large group of recruiters who rush the applicants through like cattle and then make them wait around all day to hear the outcome as an 'awful experience'.

Saudi is by far the oddest place to get paperwork done. The embassy people are not friendly and really try your patience. Every day they told me to come back, which meant I was paying for a hotel and paying for taxis and food, etc, waiting for nothing. Yet the company told me the visa was all ready and signed by the Ministry.

I have worked in Saudi on three separate occasions, with Aramco, M-Trading and most recently with the Binladin Group. The contract means nothing, as everything is done by favours and whom you know. Accommodation is normally in a compound, some of which have pretty high security with maybe three different checkpoints, jeeps with machine guns, barricades, etc. The job in Jeddah put us up in a hotel though, where there was no security at all.

I hate to be negative about any place, but Saudi is not an easy place. Depending on where you are, you could be in a very conservative place where shops close for two hours every prayer time. You need to keep covered and to be careful about what you say about most topics, but especially religion, politics and even history. There is no drinking and forget talking to the opposite sex. It is a very regimented lifestyle and you need some pretty tough skin to stay there. The religious police are everywhere, and as a foreigner in the kingdom you are always being watched by someone. I had an all-women's class that by law had to be in a separate building. The students could see me on a screen, but I couldn't see them. An official was present to censor my lesson and shut down the power if I got off topic, even talking about how some battles were fought and won.

Depending on where you are, it is pretty slim pickings to find things to do in your spare time. Even to go around the country is not easy without proof of being Muslim. To the best of my knowledge there is only one cinema in Riyadh, for mothers and children only. Jeddah offers some variety with the beaches and old town and more liberal culture. If you are going to be anywhere, try to be in Jeddah.

Teachers educated to bachelor level can expect to earn US$28,000–US$37,000 per year, while a typical salary range for employees with MAs in English/TESOL/Linguistics is $37,000–$44,000.

Professional teachers tempted by the money should bear in mind the drawbacks, as **Philip Dray** did:

> *I decided against Saudi Arabia. The money was most appealing, but I couldn't think myself into a situation where there was no nightlife and limited contact with women. A year may seem short when you say it fast, but you could get very depressed in a situation like that. Money is nearly everything but it can't buy you peace of mind. So I opted for a job at a school for boys in the UAE that, from the description, sounded sociable, inviting and accessible.*

Morris Jensen points to the good things about Saudi Arabia, including the hospitality, ease of finding lucrative private work, excellent sports facilities, shopping and accessibility of places of interest in the Middle East. He also acknowledges the problems, such as the religious and cultural clashes that arise in the classroom and the frustrating bureaucracy.

Among the documents required for a work permit are a medical certificate notarised by the Foreign & Commonwealth Office in London, an authorisation from the Saudi Ministry of Foreign Affairs, copies of diplomas, a contract of employment and accompanying letter from the sponsoring company. You must also provide a statement of religion; atheism is not an option. The maximum age is 60 for visa purposes. The fee payable before leaving your home country is only the beginning. Your passport is held by your sponsoring employer, while you carry around an official copy as identification, at least until you are issued with an *iqama* (resident visa) by the Ministry of the Interior. Every time you want to leave the country you must request an exit and re-entry visa, which is given at the discretion of your employer. Some foreign workers have reported having to pay a very substantial sum for an exit visa.

The US State Department publishes cautionary guidelines for English teachers at http://photos.state.gov/libraries/saudi-arabia/768382/yoderja/guide.pdf, advising all prospective employees to obtain an official Arabic translation of any contract before signing. Verbal assurances and covering letters are not binding under Saudi law. In the case of an employment dispute, an employee cannot just leave the country (because the employer holds the passport). 'Absconding' is a crime that can result in a heavy monetary fine, detention, deportation and a five-year ban.

LIST OF EMPLOYERS

BERLITZ LANGUAGE CENTRES AL-AHSA

Qatar Road, Hofuf and Mulhim Tower, Thurayat Road, Mubarraz 31982

- +966 3 581 131
- recruitment@berlitz-ksa.com
- www.berlitz-ksa.com

NUMBER OF TEACHERS: Variable for four language centres (two male, two female) in Al-Ahsa in the eastern province of the country.
PREFERENCE OF NATIONALITY: British preferred. Must be native speaker of English.
QUALIFICATIONS: Minimum BA or MA in any subject plus 2 years' teaching experience; or BA + CELTA or equivalent + 3 years' experience; or PGCE + 1 year's teaching experience. Experience of TOEFL preparation would be useful. Married couples preferred.
CONDITIONS OF EMPLOYMENT: Summer-only or one-year renewable contracts. 8 hours per day, all but half an hour of timetabled teaching. At busy times, teachers will be required to work overtime (up to 11 hours per week), which will be paid at one and a half times normal salary.
SALARY: From 96,600 riyals to 123,000 riyals per year tax-free.
FACILITIES/SUPPORT: Furnished single person's or family accommodation provided rent free. Travel allowance covers air travel to and from Saudi Arabia. Full training in Berlitz Method is given. Compulsory training workshops are held.
RECRUITMENT: Online application.

EUROPEAN CENTRE

PO Box 60617, Riyadh 11555
- +966 11 455 0505

NUMBER OF TEACHERS: 20–40 corporate instructors in various cities across Saudi Arabia.
PREFERENCE OF NATIONALITY: British, Irish, Canadian and American.

QUALIFICATIONS: Most positions are for males only. Bachelor's degree in a language-related field as a minimum plus a CELTA/Trinity or equivalent teaching certificate with at least 2 years of previous experience.
CONDITIONS OF EMPLOYMENT: Standard 12-month contract renewable, 7.45am–4.00pm, 5 days per week. Average load of 27 contact hours per week.
SALARY: Salary details on application. The range is from 8,600 riyals gross to 11,300 riyals gross with additional 3,600 riyals or 7,200 riyals per month overtime available in certain locations. Salary scales undergo periodic review.
FACILITIES/SUPPORT: Free, fully furnished accommodation and transport allowance provided. Company provides valid work visas and residence permits (*iqamas*) at company cost and medical cards (*Tawuniya*) for private medical cover with £80 approx of the annual fee paid by the employee. The company also refers candidates at point of hire to a visa broker who does all the necessary paperwork for visa processing. The company covers the broker and visa medical charges, as well as the cost of the actual visa. Prepaid flights are provided. British management. Centre uses labs, tactile learning and simulator facilities, plus Adobe format materials for projectors and smart boards. On-the-job training provided.
RECRUITMENT: Adverts on www.tefl.com. Via recruitment agency Al Rajhi Co. for HRD (www.al-rajhi4hrd.com). CV with scanned copies of qualifications and a photo should be sent by email. A comprehensive PDF information pack is usually sent out to a candidate within 48 hours of receipt of a suitable application. Candidates may apply at any time of year.
CONTACT: Aidan Chalk, Managing Director.

GOLD STAR TEFL RECRUITMENT

Taipei, Taiwan
- apply@GoldStarTeachers.com
- www.GoldStarTeachers.com

PREFERENCE OF NATIONALITY: Native English speakers from UK, Ireland, USA, Canada, Australia, New Zealand or South Africa to teach communicative English to adults for 17 Wall Street International institutes around the country.

QUALIFICATIONS: Bachelor's degree in English, TEFL, Linguistics or Literature. TEFL experience and/or certificate preferred but not required. Must be male teacher or a couple (government regulation for visa). Outgoing sociable personality.

CONDITIONS OF EMPLOYMENT: Minimum 2-year commitment. 30 days paid holiday after 12 months of work.

SALARY: $2,100 per month plus flight, housing allowance and other perks. Total package worth 12,375 riyals per month (salary of 8,000 riyals, flight paid upfront, housing contribution 2,000 riyals and transport allowance 800 riyals).

FACILITIES/SUPPORT: Legal work visa obtained (but fees paid by teacher). Ongoing training. Medical insurance provided.

INTERLINK LANGUAGE CENTERS
Al Yamamah University, PO Box 45180, Riyadh 11512
esl@interlink.edu
www.interlink.edu or www.yu.edu.sa

NUMBER OF TEACHERS: About 50, 80%–85% of whom are native English speakers.

PREFERENCE OF NATIONALITY: Visa regulations stipulate that teachers must have a passport from Australia, New Zealand, Canada, US, UK, Ireland or South Africa.

QUALIFICATIONS: MA in TESL, at least 2 years' EFL/ESL teaching experience with adult learners, and good cross-cultural background, either working or living in another culture.

CONDITIONS OF EMPLOYMENT: Minimum 2-year contract, longer preferred. 20–25 hours per week, plus participation in programme of activities.

SALARY: $38,000–$40,000, tax-free.

FACILITIES/SUPPORT: Free furnished housing, medical insurance and round-trip transport to Saudi Arabia.

RECRUITMENT: Résumés collected through multiple websites. Interviews are essential and can be organised by conference call.

CONTACT: Larry Davies or Dr Nebila Dhieb-Henia, General Director.

JUBAIL UNIVERSITY COLLEGE
English Prep Year Programme, PO Box 10074, Jubail Industrial City 31961
+966 3 342 9000 ext 1008
ucjjobs@gmail.com or jobs@ucj.edu.sa
www.ucj.edu.sa

NUMBER OF TEACHERS: 25+.

PREFERENCE OF NATIONALITY: British, Irish, American, Canadian, South African, Australian, New Zealander.

QUALIFICATIONS: BA in English, Linguistics or TESOL; or bachelor's degree in any discipline from an internationally recognised Anglophone university plus a CELTA/Trinity TESOL certificate. All teachers must have at least 2 years' full-time ESL/EFL/EAP/ESP teaching experience at university/college level and be a native English speaker, or have near-native competency. Maximum age 50.

CONDITIONS OF EMPLOYMENT: Initially 2-year contracts, renewable annually thereafter. 40 hours per week (20 contact teaching hours, 10 prep hours, 10 office hours).

SALARY: Varies depending on qualifications and experience. Salary is tax-free.

FACILITIES/SUPPORT: Free furnished accommodation provided. Full details are supplied to teachers when salary offer accepted on how to get medical clearance and visa application.

RECRUITMENT: Web-based advertising. Interviews conducted by Skype or telephone.

CONTACT: Mike Creed, Academic Recruiting Co-ordinator.

KING FAHD UNIVERSITY OF PETROLEUM & MINERALS
Preparatory English Program, College of Applied and Supporting Studies, Box 5026, Dhahran 31261
+966 3 860 0000
recruite@kfupm.edu.sa
www.kfupm.edu.sa

NUMBER OF TEACHERS: 90 (further 24 teachers are employed in the University English Program; Eldjobs@kfupm.edu.sa).

PREFERENCE OF NATIONALITY: American, Australian, British, Canadian, Irish, New Zealander. Male teachers only for all-male university.

QUALIFICATIONS: Master's degree or full-time postgraduate diploma in TESOL/Applied Linguistics, or Cambridge DELTA, plus minimum 4 years' overseas experience. Cambridge CELTA or equivalent may be acceptable with particularly relevant experience.

CONDITIONS OF EMPLOYMENT: Male, native speakers of English. 2-year contracts starting September and February. 20-hour teaching week Saturday–Wednesday. Students aged 18–20.

SALARY: 124,000–180,000 riyals ($30,000–$42,000).

FACILITIES/SUPPORT: On-campus furnished accommodation with all services available for married or single status. Annual airfares. Local education. Contract completion bonus.

RECRUITMENT: Send cover letter and CV by email to recruite@kfupm.edu.sa. Videoconference interviews are required.

CONTACT: Paul Brown, Director of the Preparatory English Program (pbrown@kfupm.edu.sa).

SKYLINE GLOBAL SOLUTIONS

1055 Westlakes Drive, Berwyn, PA 19312, USA

℮ +1 610 230 0296

positions@skylinetechsolutions.com

www.skylinetechsolutions.com

NUMBER OF TEACHERS: 200+ for positions in Riyadh and Dammam universities, etc.

PREFERENCE OF NATIONALITY: American, British, Canadian, South African, Australian, Irish and New Zealander.

QUALIFICATIONS: BA degree minimum. TEFL/TESL/CELTA qualification. Some positions are available only to females.

CONDITIONS OF EMPLOYMENT: 1-year contract, 20–25 contact teaching hours, total of 40 working hours per week.

SALARY: Tax-free salary of $2,600–$4,200 per month.

FACILITIES/SUPPORT: Furnished shared accommodation provided or stipend for those who live independently. Recruiter manages the visa process and works with local visa agencies to get visas processed.

RECRUITMENT: Print media and internet. Interviews are essential and are conducted in the US.

UAE (UNITED ARAB EMIRATES)

The oil-rich UAE consists of seven emirates or principalities, each governed by a hereditary emir (Muslim ruler). The most important are Abu Dhabi the capital, Dubai and Sharjah. The great draw for TEFL teachers is the money that can be made, as **Ben Naismith** admitted not long after moving to Dubai:

Having spent a number of years working in countries that English teachers typically flock to (Costa Rica, Thailand, etc), my wife and I decided it was time to earn more than the usual ELT pittance. So after a brief look at the available options, we settled on the UAE and Dubai. As with many teaching professionals, this decision was made in the hopes of finding a balance between financial stability and quality of life. And, although we have been here only a relatively short time, our expectations have thus far been pleasantly exceeded.

In terms of the schools, there are a number of the usual chains including Berlitz and the British Council. In addition, there are plenty of teachers working at high schools, colleges and universities. Although I personally work full-time for one school, it seems that the majority of the teachers I have met freelance at a number of different places. Getting a work visa is a bit tricky though, as you need to either be sponsored exclusively by one employer (or else be married to someone who is) or pay to get an office in a free zone.

Regarding the make-up of classes, Dubai truly is a modern cosmopolitan city, and the learners come from all over the world, with the majority either from around the Middle East, South Asia, or South-East Asia. Due to the massive demand for English speakers, there are all types of classes ranging from Young Learners, to General English, to Business English, to ESP – truly something for everyone.

One of our greatest fears moving here, a common one I'm sure, was how we would adapt to the local sur-roundings. Prepared for an extremely conservative society, we were amazed at how liberal it is here in terms of clothing, attitudes, etc. The people are also, by and large, extremely friendly, probably as they too are mostly immigrants in a foreign land! What did live up to the hype though was the heat, which is truly unlike anything I have experienced before, so be prepared.

The huge diversity of nationalities that makes up the population of the Emirates means that English is the lingua franca, and almost everyone is eager to improve his or her knowledge of the language. The respected organisation Amideast (www.amideast.org/uae), with offices in Abu Dhabi, Dubai and Sharjah delivers In-tensive English and TOEFL programmes, for which it recruits experienced English-language teachers.

Many institutes hire only teachers who are already living locally with a residence visa, drawing from a pool of freelance teachers and never hiring from abroad except for occasional senior positions.

Most advertised jobs in the UAE, as throughout the Gulf, say that they require three to five years of EFL experience, and in some cases a master's degree as well. You will be at an advantage if your teaching experi-ence covers exam preparation, TOEFL-iBT, academic and Business English.

STEPH FUCCIO

When Steph Fuccio and her husband (whom she met on the international EFL circuit) applied to universities and similar in Oman and the UAE, most places cited the lack of an MA as the reason their applications were not

moved forward. In the end they were hired in any case by Abu Dhabi University.

This is the first place I've lived where the British Council does not pay the highest English teaching wage, although it has a nice location on the island and still offers its high standard of organisation and good professional development. The rule of thumb for getting on here, much like Italy and some other countries I've been in, is it depends on who you know; no matter what your experience and education are. 'Wasta' is key here: it's who you know, your connections, that get things done, including internet service, speeding tickets and teaching jobs.

The pace in the classroom, much like the pace of life here in general, is slower than most western institutes. Adult students expect a lot of personal attention (not to be confused with correction) but usually this dedication is not expected of them in return, ie they rarely will do any work outside of class, and sometimes will come up with amazing reasons not to do work even in class. Overall, they are good humoured. Although their sense of humour is different from mine, there is always an intersection of silliness that is available. They will always be late for class and want many breaks. They will usually have their 3-4 cell phones on the seat next to them, ready to take a call at the first ring. Emiratis are very well taken care of by their government. Although 80% of the population of the UAE is comprised of foreign nationals, it is the Emiratis who get the best jobs with the highest salaries and best benefits.

I wish I could make it sound more glamorous and inviting. The weather is great for the region, the low humidity is a relief after living in South-East Asia. The food is amazing. The money is spoiling and the lifestyle isn't as strict as in neighbouring Saudi and Bahrain. But this isn't for the faint of heart or first-timer.

Once again, the financial rewards are the principal attraction and make the red tape hassles bearable. Entry-level jobs pay about 8,000–10,000 dirhams (US$2,200–US$2,700) per month tax-free plus free housing. The cost of living is surprisingly inexpensive, so most people can save a lot of money. Abu Dhabi and Dubai look very western and familiar, though these similarities are only skin deep. After Philip Dray's arrival at the Oasis Residence in Dubai, he was well pleased with his decision to move to the UAE, since living conditions in his luxury apartment complex, complete with pool, steam room, squash court and gym, were just as lavish as he would have been given in Saudi.

Certified primary and secondary school teachers might want to investigate the recruitment drive currently underway by the Abu Dhabi Education Council (ADEC), which is attempting to reform the UAE educational system and place expat teachers in public schools throughout the country. Footprints Recruiting acts as an intermediary for this programme (http://adec.footprintsrecruiting.com) as does TeachAway Inc. Note that International House Dubai closed at the end of 2014 when the owner died and his heir decided running a school was not as profitable as real estate.

LIST OF EMPLOYERS

BERLITZ LANGUAGE CENTER

PO Box 47120, Abu Dhabi

✆ +971 2 667 2287

✉ berlitz@emirates.net.ae or info@berlitz-uae.com

🖥 www.berlitz.ae/careers

Centres also in Dubai (PO Box 71453, Dubai; +971 4 344 0034) and Sharjah (+971 6 572 1115).

NUMBER OF TEACHERS: 45.

PREFERENCE OF NATIONALITY: None.

QUALIFICATIONS: University graduates with teaching diplomas. For candidates with non-education or teaching university degrees, a CELTA or TEFL certificate is essential. All instructors need to undergo and successfully complete training in the Berlitz Method of instruction.

CONDITIONS OF EMPLOYMENT: Minimum contract is 2 years. Usual hours are Sunday to Thursday, between 7.30am and 9pm, Saturdays between 9am and 1.30pm. A weekly schedule is provided by the Centre Director specifying working days and hours.

FACILITIES/SUPPORT: Accommodation is provided in a shared teachers' apartment. A work visa and labour card are issued to new candidates on full-time contracts. Original degrees/diplomas and a reference describing the candidate's experience is necessary, with attestation from the UAE Embassy or Ministry of Foreign Affairs in country of origin, plus copy of passport and passport photos.

RECRUITMENT: Through email applications, referrals and adverts in newspapers or websites. Applications should include letter of intent, updated CV and recent passport photo. Interviews are important; for international applicants phone interviews are carried out.

CONTACT: Manal Mahshi Azar, Director, Abu Dhabi (manal.mahshi@berlitz-uae.com); Reem Shehab, Director, Dubai; Sereen Masri, Director, Sharjah.

HIGHER COLLEGES OF TECHNOLOGY

✆ +971 2 692 2635

✉ recruit@hct.ac.ae

🖥 http://recruit.hct.ac.ae

NUMBER OF TEACHERS: Up to 450 English faculty teachers involved in teaching ESL in 15 colleges throughout the UAE.

PREFERENCE OF NATIONALITY: None. Should be native or near-native speaker for English faculty positions.

QUALIFICATIONS: English faculty minimum requirements are master's degree in TEFL (preferred) or bachelor's degree and TEFL diploma; 3 years' teaching experience (tertiary preferred); practical teaching qualification (DELTA preferred); knowledge of contemporary teaching practices and computer-assisted learning.

CONDITIONS OF EMPLOYMENT: Teaching year is from September to June. To teach 20 classes a week (Sunday to Thursday).

SALARY: Tax-free income. Salary based on experience and education. Annual rises are given upon receiving positive performance evaluations.

FACILITIES/SUPPORT: Visa arranged by HCT. Singles and families welcome. Unfurnished accommodation and a furniture allowance, excellent benefit package offered – details provided upon request or to short-listed candidates.

RECRUITMENT: Online HCT application required. Interviews can be conducted via video teleconference.

CONTACT: Robin Smith, Recruitment Manager (robin.smith@hct.ac.ae).

YEMEN

While some people in the past have found Yemen to be the most beautiful and interesting of all Middle Eastern states, the situation at present is too unpredictable and dangerous. As of 2015, both the FCO in the UK and the US State Department advise against all travel to Yemen and those already in Yemen to leave. British diplomatic staff were withdrawn in February 2015.

It is hard to ascertain whether any ESL schools, of the hundred or so that used to flourish in the capital, Sana'a, are still in business. The US Embassy-backed YALI (Yemen-American Language Institute, www.yaliefl.org) which for some time had the lion's share of the market is presumed closed, since the US embassy suspended operations. Other professional schools include Amideast and the British Council, both of which are closed.

TURKEY

Turkey is a wonderful country to travel in, with a wealth of historic sites like Troy and Ephesus, and an economy in reasonable shape. However, tensions have been escalating between the secular liberal parties and the Islamist agenda being promoted by the longstanding prime minister Erdoğan. The government's authoritarian tactics against journalists, minority parties, etc. have made it seem unlikely that Turkey will be admitted to the European Union by 2023, the centennial anniversary of the Turkish Republic. The Turkish currency, the lira, hit a record low in June 2015 after the ruling party lost its majority in an election.

Turkey's ELT industry continues to absorb an enormous number of globe-trotting English teachers and the country is a good choice of destination for fledgling English teachers with a university degree and a TEFL certificate, both of which are required for visa reasons. Over the years, pay and perks have been cut back to some extent. However, every teacher who has complained about employers breaking their promises, run-down accommodation and so on has concluded by saying that Turkish people are amazingly hospitable and the country fascinating. By describing below the problems which some teachers have encountered on short teaching contracts in Turkey, it is to be hoped that readers can guard against them.

PROSPECTS FOR TEACHERS

Turkey's prosperous classes are more eager than ever to learn English and, furthermore, seem to have the money to pay for it. The boom in English is not confined to private language schools (*dershane*), which have proliferated in the three main cities of Istanbul, Ankara and Izmir. In order to prepare students for an English-language engineering, commerce, tourism or arts course, many secondary schools hire native-speaker teachers. Hundreds of private secondary schools (*lises*) consider as one of their main priorities the teaching of the English language. Similarly at the tertiary level, some universities, both private and public, use English as the medium of instruction and offer intensive English preparatory programmes.

A few institutes still offer a package which includes free accommodation and free airfares (London–Istanbul) on completion of a contract. All of these employers want to see a university degree and a TEFL Certificate of some kind, preferably the Cambridge CELTA or equivalent. Both a degree and a specialist qualification are required by the Turkish Ministry of Education before it will approve a work permit (see Regulations below).

The bias in favour of British English over American is not particularly strong. Many schools claim to have no preference and yet, because they advertise on UK-based sites and are more familiar with British qualifications, there is a preponderance of British teachers. Also, the requirement that work visas be applied for in the country of origin makes matters more difficult for teachers from the USA, Australia, etc.

FINDING A JOB

IN ADVANCE

International recruitment agencies sometimes seek entry-level and more experienced teachers for chains of private and public schools in Turkey, especially the capital, Ankara. Try for example Teach to Travel in London (www.teachtotravel.com) and Prime Teachers (www.primeteachers.com) in York. Teacher placement agencies based in Turkey have clients from kindergartens to universities, for example Teachers in Turkey (see entry) and

Marmaris Recruitment (www.marmarisrecruitment.com) who at the time of writing were advertising for native speaker English teachers for the 2015/2016 academic year. The latter charges a fee of £40 to register.

English-medium universities employ considerable numbers of language instructors, such as Bilkent in Ankara and Istanbul Sehir University (see entries for both). Many of the major chains like EFINST and English Time have entries in the directory. Just English (http://justenglishtr.com) and Bank Street (www.bankstreet.org) have also been advertising recently, while one of the largest companies is Amerikan Kultur Dernegi, which with dozens of schools claims to have the biggest network in Turkey. Telephone and online teaching is a large part of its business. Teacher recruitment information is not easily accessible on the websites of these companies, which tend to be only in Turkish and have only a basic web form for applications.

The British Council offices in Istanbul and Ankara have lists of private language schools, primary schools and high schools and may even maintain a Job File where local institutions advertise for TEFL teachers. When it closed down its teaching operations in Turkey, some ex-Council teaching staff set up British Side (www.britishside.com), which hires highly qualified teachers on a full-time basis, as well as others hired on an hourly basis, who are well paid.

The CELTA training centre ITI Istanbul (www.iti-istanbul.com) administers a recruitment service for language schools in Turkey and can send notification of current vacancies to subscribers to their mailing list free of charge. The job search website TurkeyTalent.com might also be of use. Quite a few ads for Turkish schools appear on the main TEFL job sites like www.tefl.com and www.seriousteachers.com in the spring and through the summer. Also check out http://englishjobsturkey.com, the Istanbul expat site http://yabangee.com/category/jobs and the job search site http://kariyer.net (where for example Wall Street Institute frequently advertises for teachers).

Another avenue to explore is to teach in a large company: for example the Marriott Hotel in Ankara sometimes looks for teachers. A lucky few will find summer work in a coastal resort, for example with the International Mediterranean Academy in Fethiye (www.im-academy.org).

Some ads specify that they are looking to hire teachers already in Turkey, though some offer travel expenses. If you are considering accepting a job with an advertiser, ask for the name and telephone number of a previous teacher for an informal reference before accepting. An even better indication is if it has been able to keep its teachers for two or more years. If the school is reluctant to provide this kind of information, be suspicious. It may also be worth phoning the British Council office in the relevant city, since it keeps a file of complaints about language schools.

ON THE SPOT

Although not the capital, Istanbul is the commercial, financial and cultural centre of Turkey, so this is where most of the EFL teaching goes on. On the negative side, there may be more competition from other teachers here and also in Izmir than in Ankara or less obvious cities.

Given the huge demand for native-speaker teachers, Turkey is one country where scouting out possibilities on the ground can pay off, rather than signing a contract at a school you have never seen. After **Bruce Lawson** had a terrible experience with a private language-teaching organisation in Istanbul (*'their contract was a fiction that Tolstoy would have been proud of'*), he concluded that he could have earned half as much again if he had been employed by a school that interviewed and hired locally.

Tim Leffel and **Donna Marcus** from New Jersey were amazed by the ease with which they made their way as English teachers:

> *There's a huge demand for teachers (any nationality really) in Istanbul. We lined up work on our second day of interviews. We interviewed at three schools and all of them offered us positions. We chose one in Bakirköy because there were two jobs available in the same place and we were allowed to wear anything within reason (no ties, no new clothes to buy). They were satisfied that we could only commit ourselves for four months. We did see a lot of applicants turned away, even when there was a need for new teachers, because they lacked TEFL credentials.*

FREELANCE TEACHING

The standard Ministry of Education contract prohibits private teaching outside the bounds of the signed contract. In fact, unless you are blatantly pinching students from the institution that employs you, most employers turn a blind eye. University English departments might be a place to look for private students. The top rate of pay goes over £20 an hour, though a more usual hourly rate would be less than half that, ie 35 lira.

In Istanbul there is a flourishing English Spoken Café where Turkish language learners can meet up near Istanbul university with native speakers informally (though with their dictionaries at the ready). Join the Facebook group to find out where and when events are being held, and also check the Istanbul English Teachers Network on Facebook.

REGULATIONS

Since 10 April 2014, it is no longer possible to process the residence/work permit after arrival in Turkey. You must now apply to the Turkish Consulate in your home country, with the originals of crucial documents, ie the job offer from a Turkish employer, your university degree diploma, teaching/TEFL certificate plus a police check, all of which will be forwarded to the Ministry of Labour. If approved, you must enter the country within 90 days and then apply for a residence permit from the Ministry of the Interior within 30 days of arrival. This process must be repeated every year. A network of General Directorate of Migration Management offices is taking over the role of processing from the Foreigners' Police. For information see www.turkishconsulate.org.uk/en/work_visa.asp. The current fee for Britons to obtain entry clearance and a work permit is £321. The fine levied on foreign employees without the necessary permits is TL695 and ten times that on an employer.

In the past, teachers without a work visa could leave Turkey every three months and renew their tourist visa by crossing back in. However, the regulations have been tightened up and are now in line with the Schengen system, which is that foreigners are allowed to stay 90 days within a period of 180 days. This means that the days of the 'visa run' over the land border to Bulgaria or to Northern Cyprus are now pretty well over. If you are planning to enter as a tourist, be aware that, as of 2014, tourists must obtain an e-visa online, whereas for years it was possible to buy the visa at the border or airport of arrival. Prices differ among nationalities, so check www.evisa.gov.tr for information: the fee for Britons and Americans is $20, whereas Canadians pay $60. If you overstay, you become liable for a hefty exit fine.

All salaries in Turkey are quoted net of deductions, which amount to about 25% for contributions and tax. If the school makes social security contributions on your behalf, you will have medical cover from the first day your work visa becomes valid. The scheme pays all your doctor's bills and 80% of prescriptions. Once again it is prudent to confirm that your employer keeps any promises he or she makes. More than one teacher has realised at a critical moment that, despite assurances, insurance premiums have not been paid by the school.

A complication for people who intend to teach English in a *lise* (state secondary school) or *kolej* (private school) is that the Ministry of Education rules specify that teachers of English should have a university degree in English, Linguistics or related degree and preferably a PGCE or a BEd with English as a main subject. However, this is not strictly enforced.

CONDITIONS OF WORK

The normal deal is a one-year contract (which can usually be broken with one month's notice), free or subsidised shared accommodation and a monthly salary in Turkish lira starting at about £500 in private language schools, or primary and secondary schools. For example EFINST, with three branches in Istanbul, offers from 2,300 to 4,000 lira per month, which may be supplemented by a relocation allowance, free accommodation and insurance. Hourly employment used to be fairly unusual in Turkey, but increasingly employers are finding it more profitable to pay by the hour, especially during low seasons, when the number of teaching hours decreases dramatically.

Over the years many employers have come in for criticism, with words such as 'cowboy', 'unprofessional' and 'untrustworthy' being bandied about by disappointed teachers. Browsing the web will eventually bring you to sites which name and shame schools that sack their teachers to save money, slash wages or pay late, fail to honour contracts, assign inflated marks to students to keep or attract custom, withhold certificates to prevent staff from leaving prematurely and so on. It is not always easy to establish how current some of this information is, plus some of it must be taken with a pinch of salt. One poster on the web forum www.turkeycentral.com holds out against the tide of negativity:

I'm working at a language school in Taksim, Istanbul, and with no experience teaching and a freshly acquired CELTA. I have to admit I couldn't be happier. My school has walked me through the residence permit and now I have a work permit too. On top of that I've made a bunch of good friends, and the students are super enthusiastic. Our school hires on a rolling basis, but the salary is nothing to brag about. It's a beginner's salary, though it can be supplemented by giving your own private lessons, but it's a start. And if you consider it temporary, a really good start at that! I should note that my school, in particular, had terrible reviews all over the net. That said, I still came to check it out when I got an interview. And I can testify that life in a language school is what you make of it – don't believe everything you read online about them. Just visit and find out.

Some people in the ELT business believe that the situation is gradually improving, and that with increased regulation, there are fewer dodgy operators and swashbuckling and unscrupulous employers. One of those optimists is the director of studies at a major Istanbul school:

I have worked for approximately four years in Turkey, in Istanbul and in a small remote town in the south. Prospective teachers always hear many horror stories about working in Turkey and to an extent they are well founded. In the past, schools and employers openly abused teachers' rights. But this is definitely changing. There are many good, up-and-coming organisations which can be trusted. Teachers should ask around, be careful about contracts and conditions, and not agree to the first job they are offered without checking out the school, its size, reputation, etc.

It is important to remember that some teachers have a marvellous time, as **Raza Griffiths** had at the first school he worked for, which was in the town of Ordu on the Black Sea coast:

It would be no exaggeration to say that as a native English person in a region of Turkey unused to foreigners, I enjoyed celebrity status, with lots of inquiring eyes and lots of invitations to dinner. Although the town did not exactly have a thriving cultural life as we would understand it, this was more than compensated for by the sociableness of the people and their deep desire for communication. Because it was a private school, money was not in short supply and the facilities were excellent, with computers, etc. The free furnished flat I was given was large and very comfortable, and there was a free school minibus service that took teachers to the school. On either side of the school there were hazelnut gardens, behind there were mountains and in front the Black Sea, all quite idyllic, especially in summer. The other teachers (all Turkish) were very welcoming from day one, despite the fact that I was less experienced and was getting four times their salary. I could live very comfortably on my salary and still have a lot left over for spending on holidays and clothes.

The standard paid holiday allowance for teachers is 15 days. At inferior schools, national holidays must be taken out of this annual leave, including Muslim holidays such as Seker Bayrami, usually celebrated at the end of Ramadan, and Kurban Bayrami. The former lasts three days, the latter four days, and it is customary to make the bridge to a full week. Christmas is not observed much and you may be offered very little time off, especially in smaller schools where the majority of the staff is Turkish. Big chains of schools, where native English speakers are in the majority in the staff-room, tend to close for a week or a bit more. Most things can usually be negotiated in Turkey, be it the price of a carpet or the terms of a contract, so it is wise to shop around carefully before accepting a job. One non-negotiable condition in some schools is a proscription on facial hair for men and revealing clothing for women.

THE STUDENTS

The major schools are well equipped with computers, language labs and course materials. But better than the back-up facilities is the enthusiasm of the students, who are usually motivated, conscientious and well-behaved, and enjoy group discussions. Teachers should not, however, expect too much interaction between teacher and pupil, as **Tara Dermot**, a teacher in Istanbul, describes:

> *Walk into a classroom in Turkey and you are likely to find every kind of student that you would find all over the world: the eager, the shy, the lazy, the clever one . . . What sets Turkish students significantly apart in my experience is their passivity. Turks grow up in an incredibly teacher-centred learning environment so that is what they are expecting. Having them participate in a far more student-centred, communicative course can therefore be frustrating, but given time and perseverance they will soon see the benefits and the fun to be had.*

'*Willing if unimaginative*' was one teacher's description of her students. One undesirable aspect of Turkish education is that many *lises* (high schools) are too strongly oriented to exam preparation and university entrance. On the whole, however, the friendly openness of young Turks may cause a foreign teacher to forget that Turkey is still an Islamic country where dress is conservative and where only 25% of women are in the workforce. Teachers are still regarded as important figures in society and as such are expected to dress fairly conservatively.

Student behaviour differs radically, depending on what kind of institution you teach in. Private secondary schools tend to be populated with spoiled and immature kids who do not always respect their teachers. **Joan Smith** found this hard to stomach at the private school in Kayseri where she taught:

> *Turkish parents indulge their children something rotten. Rich spoilt students abound in my classroom and discipline goes out the window. Foreign teachers are regarded as inferior and are given even less respect than the Turkish teachers.*

Joan did not think that she should have to tolerate some of the innuendos her male students were getting away with, but had little hope of justice if they and their friends denied her allegations.

DICK BIRD

Dick Bird's (and others') experiences have been very different. Dick, a veteran EFL teacher, taught in Turkey a long time ago but his description of his pupils is still apt:

I have found women students defer to a far higher level of male chauvinism than would be acceptable anywhere in the West. Turkish women also seem to have exceptionally quiet voices and I can't help feeling that this irritating characteristic is somehow related to their role in society – a case of being seen but not heard until you are very, very close perhaps? Sometimes my students know too much grammar to be able to express themselves freely. As their own language is radically different to Indo-European languages they have a lot of difficulty adapting to the sentence structure of English: they regard relative clauses as a perversion and are baffled, if not mildly outraged, by the cavalier way English seems to use any tense it fancies to refer to future actions but is puritanically strict about how one may describe present and past events. Another difficulty Turks have is that we EFL teachers like to use a lot of words in our meta-language (ie language about language, eg adjective, verb) which do not have cognates in Turkish as they do in other European languages, for example a teacher may inform their students that 'will' expresses probability, not intention; this will be readily under-stood by an elementary-level Spaniard but is total gibberish to a Turk (as I suspect it is to a great many native speakers of English).

Dick's analysis of Turkish EFL students ends with a light-hearted description of their irrepressible energy and enthusiasm. I have retained it for many editions of this book since it is so much fun:

Whenever the class is asked a question they would fain prostrate themselves at their teacher's feet were it not that years of instilled discipline keep them penned by invisible bonds within the confines of their desks until the ringing of the bell, whereat pande-monium breaks loose as a thousand berserk adolescents fling themselves across the (highly polished) corridor floors and down the (marble) steps headlong into the play-ground. (This phenomenon may help to explain why fire drills are not a regular feature of Turkish school life.)

A past Director of Studies at Dilko English in Bakirköy agrees that Turkish students are fun to teach but identifies a few of the problems he has encountered:

They have several major problems with English, especially mastering the definite article, the third person singular and the present perfect, none of which exists in Turkish. On the whole, their pronunciation is good, but they do have difficulty with words that have three consonants back to back. (My own surname Gallantry inevitably gets pronounced 'Galilantiree'.) If I have to be critical of my students, it is that they neither listen to, nor read, instructions: five minutes into an exercise there is always someone asking 'What am I supposed to do?' Also a recurring problem is that some students merely come to a language school in order to use it as a social club. They're more interested in meeting someone of the opposite sex than learning English, and this can have a demoralising effect in class.

ACCOMMODATION

If accommodation is provided as part of your contract, it may be located close to the school in a modern flat which you will have to share with another teacher or it may be some way away, possibly in an undesirable neighbour-hood. Fortunately not many teachers are assigned accommodation as gruesome as **Philip Dray**'s in Izmir:

Cockroaches, centipedes, noisy neighbours, a filthy shower room and a fitted kitchen circa 1920 – I was slowly adjusting to it all. But one day, while I was having a shower, I saw a rat looking at me from the ventilation shaft and I knew that my patience had run out. I asked for a new flat but they said they couldn't get a new one before May. So, reluctantly (as there were some very nice people at the school) I had to leave.

If the school doesn't provide a flat it should help you find one and act as go-between with the landlord. Most provide some kind of rent subsidy, since rents in Turkey are high relative to the cost of living. The situation in over-crowded Istanbul is especially tight. One agency estimates that shared accommodation will cost at least 500 lira a month in smaller towns but 600–800 lira per person in Istanbul. It is not uncommon to bargain over the rent as if you were buying a second-hand car. Flats and rooms in shared apartments are advertised on Craigslist etc, or there are estate agencies called *emlak,* but these tend to charge a month's rent. Foreigners are usually considered an attractive proposition as they tend to be undemanding tenants.

In Istanbul, the nicest flats are along the Bosphorus, where the air is clean, the views stunning and a lot of the buildings are older properties with a lot of character; this is why they have been snapped up by well-heeled diplomats and multinationals. The Asian side of the city might have less charm but it also has less pollution and many people prefer it.

LEISURE TIME

Even if you are earning a salary at the lower end of the scale, you should be able to afford quite a good life, especially if you eat a lot of bread, drink local wines and use public transport. Basic meals and food, transport, hotels and cinemas (most films are subtitled rather than dubbed) are still very reasonable, especially away from the seaside and Istanbul. Depending on your smartphone can be problematic. Since January 2015, foreign visitors are prohibited by law from using their own mobile devices after the first 60 days without registering them, for which you must show a residence permit and pay a fee. You can buy used mobiles for 70–100 lira and a SIM card for about 40 lira.

With the benefit of hindsight, **John Boylan** decided the hassles of life in Turkey weren't so bad after all:

Recognise why you are in Turkey – for the experience – and try to enjoy that. You have a chance to live in a fascinating city for a year on the basis of a one-month certificate. You may live near Taksim and, let's be honest, could you afford to live a stone's throw from the equivalent in London or New York? Don't fall into the trap of mixing only with EFL teachers. Broaden your horizons and don't spend all your time in expat bars with a clique of English teachers. Socialising all the time with the same teachers can lead to a climate of moaning. Constructive criticism/advice is fine but too many teachers become bitter and vengeful. Most Turks are OK. If you want to make Turkish friends, get involved in sport or something where you'll see the same people regularly.

Dick Bird points out the advantages of living in Ankara:

It's safer than any European capital (except maybe Reykjavik) and although it may not hum at night, there are enough clubs etc to keep you going for a year, plus very cheap classical concerts and cinemas. And the air pollution is not as bad as it was.

Travel in Turkey is wonderfully affordable. The efficiency, comfort and low cost of Turkish bus travel put the coach services of most other countries to shame (though not their safety record). There is very little crime in Turkey.

Turkey generally is a great place to live and work. It's a fascinating country, full of contradictions, as befits a land that is the bridge between East and West.

LIST OF EMPLOYERS

ABC DIL OKULLARI

Esra Sk. No: 11, 34337, Etiler, Istanbul

+90 212 287 4351

ik@abc-languageschool.com

www.abc-okullari.com

NUMBER OF TEACHERS: 2–5.

PREFERENCE OF NATIONALITY: USA, UK.

QUALIFICATIONS: MA in TESOL, DELTA/CELTA and minimum 4 years' experience.

CONDITIONS OF EMPLOYMENT: 1-year contract. 20–25 hours a week teaching General and Business English (all levels), TOEFL, IELTS and organising an English Conversation club. Classes conducted on and off-site.

SALARY: $1,000–$2,500 per month depending on qualifications and experience. Deductions made for SKG (social security)

FACILITIES/SUPPORT: No assistance given with accommodation or visas.

RECRUITMENT: Adverts in mass media and relevant internet sites, eg www.iti-istanbul.com. Interviews and presentation essential after submitting letters of reference.

BILKENT UNIVERSITY SCHOOL OF ENGLISH LANGUAGE

06800 Bilkent, Ankara

+90 312 290 5401

intrec@bilkent.edu.tr

www.bilkent.edu.tr/~busel

Privately funded not-for-profit English-medium university, part of the national university system, within the Times Education Worldwide Top 50 New Universities.

NUMBER OF TEACHERS: 280 EFL/ESP teachers in preparatory and freshman programmes.

PREFERENCE OF NATIONALITY: Bilkent employs Turkish nationals and native English speakers from Australia, Canada, Britain, USA, South Africa and Ireland.

QUALIFICATIONS: Must be degree holder, preferably BEd or language degree; previous teaching experience not essential but a distinct advantage.

CONDITIONS OF EMPLOYMENT: Contracts from September to August. 20 contact hours per week.

SALARY: Salary quoted net in US dollars and Turkish lira, starting at approximately $900 plus 1,450 lira per month.

FACILITIES/SUPPORT: Free accommodation on campus, private health insurance, airfare and baggage allowance, residence permit, work visa, etc. Good facilities and opportunities for career advancement, eg to study for an ICELT, DELTA and/or MA on full scholarship.

RECRUITMENT: Directly via www.bilkent.edu.tr/~busel/interrec/index.html. Recruitment process for EFL/EAP instructors begins in February each year.

CONTACT: Vanessa McDonagh, Head of Teacher Services.

EARLY AMERICAN ENGLISH

Gaziosmanpasa Branch, Mevlana Mah 869/1, Sok No:62/A, Gaziosmanpasa, Istanbul

+90 212 650 4650

gaziosmanpasa@erkeningilizce.com

www.erkeningilizce.com/gaziosmanpasa

NUMBER OF TEACHERS: Up to 3.

PREFERENCE OF NATIONALITY: Good clear accent for teaching young learners aged 7–14.

QUALIFICATIONS: Must be cheerful and communicative.

CONDITIONS OF EMPLOYMENT: 1 year contract. To work 6 days a week, 8.30am–4pm with some variation in weekday and weekend schedules.

SALARY: Depends on whether hired as a full or part-time teacher. School normally pays a retainer plus a fee per lesson taught.

FACILITIES/SUPPORT: No assistance with accommodation or visas.

CONTACT: Dincer Demir, Head Teacher of ELT Department.

EFINST – FLORYA BRANCH

Florya Plaza 88, Kat. 3, Florya, Istanbul

+90 212 571 6424

NUMBER OF TEACHERS: 10.

QUALIFICATIONS, CONDITIONS OF EMPLOYMENT etc: As for Levent branch below.

CONTACT: Tim Luckhurst, Director of Studies (tim@efdilokulu.com) or Mrs Zeynep Gunduzyeli (zgunduzyeli@efdilokulu.com).

EFINST INTERNATIONAL HOUSE – LEVENT BRANCH

Aydin Sok. F Blok No. 12/1, Levent, Istanbul 34300

+90 212 282 9064

www.ihistanbul.com.tr or www.efinsthr.com

Affiliated to International House.

NUMBER OF TEACHERS: 30 full-time and part-time.

PREFERENCE OF NATIONALITY: Must be native speaker or Turk.

QUALIFICATIONS: Must be from a country where the primary official language is English. Minimum requirements: university degree and a CELTA/TESOL certificate. At least 1 year's post-CELTA teaching experience desirable; Business English experience especially useful. Turkish teachers need degree as English teacher and pedagogy certification.

CONDITIONS OF EMPLOYMENT: 9, 10, or 12-month contracts based on a 5-day working week with 2 consecutive days off and 30 contact hours teaching per week. Part-time contracts are also available. Paid holiday, number of days depending on the length of the contract, plus state and religious holidays.

SALARY: 2,300–4,000 lira monthly, depending on experience and qualifications, including accommodation allowance of 500 lira. Relocation allowance of up to $750. Full private health and life insurance.

RECRUITMENT: IH Recruitment or via internet or direct application. Interviews essential but can be by telephone/ Skype. Some recruitment via www.iti-istanbul.com (email olga@ iti-istanbul.com).

CONTACT: Mrs Zeynep Gunduzyeli, Director of Studies (zgunduzyeli@ihistanbul.com) or Mr Bora Gunduzyeli, Director.

EFINST– SUADIYE BRANCH
Kazim Ozalp Sok. 15/4 Saskinbakkal, Kadikoy 34740, Istanbul
✆ +90 216 302 7250

NUMBER OF TEACHERS: 18.
QUALIFICATIONS, CONDITIONS OF EMPLOYMENT etc: As above.
CONTACT: Deirdre Costello, Director of Studies or Mrs Zeynep Gunduzyeli (zgunduzyeli@ihistanbul.com).

ENGLISH LIFE LANGUAGE SCHOOLS
Kapani Ishani, Konak, Pier Karsisi, TEB ustu Kat 2, Daire 2, Konak, Izmir
✆ +90 232 441 1111
📧 info@dilokulum.com or www.englishlife.com.tr

Group of schools in Izmir, Denizli, Kusadasi, Konya and Usak in Western Turkey, affiliated to Deren & Koray International Tourism and Education Center.

NUMBER OF TEACHERS: 7.
PREFERENCE OF NATIONALITY: English, Scottish, American, Australian, Canadian and New Zealander.
QUALIFICATIONS: Schools licensed by the Ministry of Education require teachers to have at least a 2-year university/college degree, however, a 4-year bachelor's degree is preferred. Those with a 2-year degree or bachelor's degree in a non-relevant field require a TEFL/TESOL certificate. This can be obtained online (preferably TEFL/TESL certification module and a special grammar

module). Outgoing personality needed, with the ability to work in a team. The Callan Method of teaching English requires a sense of urgency, the use of miming and gesticulation, and the presentation of a clear accent with excellent pronunciation skills.

CONDITIONS OF EMPLOYMENT: 1-year contract, renewable for a second year, 20–25 hours per week.

SALARY: Salary is calculated either on hourly or salary-package basis. This varies by school and location, and will be discussed with candidate. All teaching positions have a 6-month probationary period with an increase in pay provided after successfully competing the probationary period.

FACILITIES/SUPPORT: Free accommodation for at least a month. Once teacher finds own accommodation, accommodation allowance of 250 lira is paid. Help with work permits and expense met. Intensive 1-week teachers' training programme via the Callan Method given at time of hire and before starting teaching.

RECRUITMENT: Via www.eslcafe.com and others.

CONTACT: Koray Altan MSc (Manager) and Chuck Militello (Education Group Coordinator).

ENGLISH TIME LANGUAGE SCHOOLS
Time Education Group (TEG), Istiklal Caddesi, Örs Turis-tik s Merkezi No:151, Taksim/Beyoğlu, Istanbul 34300
✆ +90 212 293 9723
🖳 www.englishtime.com

NUMBER OF TEACHERS: 200+ for 15 branches including Izmir, Izmit, Antalya, Bursa, Ankara and Eskisehir.

PREFERENCE OF NATIONALITY: US, Canada, UK, South Africa, Australia, New Zealand.

QUALIFICATIONS: Teachers must have a university degree and a TEFL, TESOL or CELTA certificate. Experience is preferred.

CONDITIONS OF EMPLOYMENT: Full-time teachers are offered a 6 or 10-month contract based upon experience. Classes run 7 days a week. Choice of 4 programmes: weekday morning course (10am–2pm for 6 weeks); weekday evenings (7–10pm for 8 weeks); weekend mornings (9am–1pm for 15 weeks) and weekend afternoons (3–7pm for 15 weeks). Rolling start dates according to when classes fill rather than according to semesters or terms. Part-time work also on offer.

SALARY: Hourly salary 16–18 lira (£4.50–£5) net, housing or housing support, end-of-contract bonus and travel allowance.

FACILITIES/SUPPORT: Furnished housing provided on arrival and then help with accommodation search. Help with red tape given.

RECRUITMENT: Internet job searches, blogs, current teachers' recommendations, word of mouth. Interested applicants to complete online application form and send CV and photo. Interviews carried out by phone or Skype.

ENGLISH WEST/DEREN KORAY GROUP

Cumhuriyet Bulvari, No 36 Kapani Ishani Kat 2, Konak,
Izmir (Pier Karsisi, Konak-Izmir)

℡ +90 232 489 4747

✉ info@englishwest.com or info@derenkoray.com.tr

NUMBER OF TEACHERS: 36.

PREFERENCE OF NATIONALITY: English, Scottish, American, Canadian, New Zealander and Australian.

QUALIFICATIONS: Schools licensed by the Ministry of Education require teachers to have at least a 2-year university/college degree, however, a 4-year bachelor's degree is preferred. Those with a 2-year degree or bachelor's degree in a non-relevant field require a TEFL/TESOL certificate. This can be obtained online (preferably TEFL/TESL certification module and a special grammar module). Outgoing personality needed, with the ability to work in a team. The Callan Method of teaching English requires a sense of urgency, the use of miming and gesticulation, and the presentation of a clear accent with excellent pronunciation skills.

CONDITIONS OF EMPLOYMENT: 1-year contract, renewable for a second year, 20–25 hours per week.

SALARY: Salary is calculated either on hourly or salary-package basis. This varies by school and location, and will be discussed with candidate. All teaching positions have a 6-month probationary period with an increase in pay provided after successfully competing the probationary period.

FACILITIES/SUPPORT: Free accommodation for at least a month. Once teacher finds own accommodation, accommodation allowance of 250 lira is paid. Help with work permits and expense met. Intensive 1-week teachers' training programme via the Callan Method given at time of hire and before starting teaching.

RECRUITMENT: Via www.eslcafe.com and others.

CONTACT: Koray Altan MSc (Manager) and Chuck Militello (Education Group Coordinator).

GENCTUR

Istiklal Cad. No.108, Aznavur Pasaji, Kat: 5, 34430
Galatasaray, Istanbul

℡ +90 212 244 6230

✉ workcamps@genctur.com or workcamps.in@genctur.com

🖥 www.genctur.com.tr, www.upegem.com

NUMBER OF TEACHERS: 10 volunteers for summer camps in Izmir.

PREFERENCE OF NATIONALITY: Native (or good) English speakers.

QUALIFICATIONS: Experience with children, workcamp or teaching experience is preferred.

CONDITIONS OF EMPLOYMENT: Volunteering for teaching English to children aged 12–17 at summer camps for 2 weeks, through outdoor activities, games and songs.

SALARY: Free board and lodging. Volunteer registration via IVS £210.

RECRUITMENT: Only through partner voluntary organisations abroad (eg IVS GB, Thorn House, 5 Rose Street, Edinburgh EH2 2PR; +44 131 243 2745; info@ivsgb.org; www.ivsgb.org).

CONTACT: Zafer Yilmaz (zafer.yilmaz@genctur.com) or Kevser Cimenli (kevser@upegem.com).

iNKUR ENGLISH LANGUAGE INSTITUTE

Ankara Cad. No: 8 izmit, Kocaeli

℡ +90 262 321 5325

✉ inkur@inkur.com

🖥 www.eng.inkur.com

NUMBER OF TEACHERS: 3–8.

PREFERENCE OF NATIONALITY: EU and OECD countries are preferred (easier visa procedure).

QUALIFICATIONS: Minimum qualifications are a bachelor's degree and TEFL/TESOL certificate.

CONDITIONS OF EMPLOYMENT: 9-month contracts, 28 teaching hours per week.

SALARY: $500–$700 per month.

FACILITIES/SUPPORT: Free accommodation available. School applies for the work permit with teacher's academic document copies.

RECRUITMENT: Face-to-face and/or telephone interviews, sometimes carried out in the UK or USA.

CONTACT: Mrs N. Gökçiçek Dogan, Owner and Director.

INTERNATIONAL HOUSE IZMIR

Necatibey Bulvari No 19 K5, Cankaya, Izmir

℡ +90 232 484 2490

✉ info@ilsizmir.com

🖥 http://english.ilsizmir.com

NUMBER OF TEACHERS: 4.

PREFERENCE OF NATIONALITY: None.

QUALIFICATIONS: Degree and CELTA Certificate (or equivalent).

CONDITIONS OF EMPLOYMENT: 1 year. 24 hours per week.

SALARY: Varies according to experience.

FACILITIES/SUPPORT: Advice given on finding accommodation. Help given with obtaining work permit after original degree and CELTA certificates plus passport are provided; school covers all costs.

RECRUITMENT: Carried out locally because local interviews needed.

CONTACT: Billy Hasirci, Director of Studies (bhasirci@ilsizmir. com).

ISTANBUL SEHIR UNIVERSITY SCHOOL OF LANGUAGES ENGLISH PREPARATORY PROGRAM

Istanbul Sehir University, Dogu Kampusu, Kusbakisi Cad. No:27, Altunizade, Uskudar, 34662 Istanbul

✆ +90 444 4034

✉ sepp@sehir.edu.tr

🖥 www.sehir.edu.tr

NUMBER OF TEACHERS: 10–15 per year.

PREFERENCE OF NATIONALITY: None.

QUALIFICATIONS: BA + CELTA or TESOL certificate is minimum requirement. MA in ELT or Applied Linguistics is preferable.

CONDITIONS OF EMPLOYMENT: 1-year contracts. Hours of teaching 8.30am–5.30pm with an afternoon off in the week.

SALARY: 3,500–4,500 lira (£975–£1,250) per month.

FACILITIES/SUPPORT: No assistance with accommodation. The HR Department is in charge of work and residence permits.

RECRUITMENT: Via ads posted on International Training Institute (ITI) Istanbul Joblist (http://jobs.iti-istanbul.com) and British Council mailing lists. Face-to-face interviews are essential; Skype interviews are not possible.

CONTACT: Dr Ilke Buyukduman, Director (ilkebuyukduman@sehir. edu.tr).

KENT SCHOOL OF ENGLISH – ISTANBUL

Bahariye Caddesi No. 15/2, 34710 Kadiköy, Istanbul

✆ +90 216 347 2791 / 347 2792

✉ info@kentenglish.com

For job applications:

✉ dos@kentenglish.com

🖥 www.kentenglish.com

NUMBER OF TEACHERS: 10+.

PREFERENCE OF NATIONALITY: Native speakers of English from the USA, UK, Canada and Australia.

QUALIFICATIONS: Bachelor's degree and TEFL certificate required. Priority given to candidates with teaching experience.

CONDITIONS OF EMPLOYMENT: 8, 10 or 12-month contracts. Weekend, weekday and evening classes in and away from school

premises (in-company training programmes). Weekly teaching hours 25+.

SALARY: Average $1,200 per month.

FACILITIES/SUPPORT: Work and residency permits arranged. Some training provided. Paid vacation. Health insurance. Intensive CTEFL course (Via Lingua) available for those without a teaching certificate.

RECRUITMENT: Local interviews, telephone, fax, mail.

OXFORD VISION EDUCATION & VISA CONSULTANCY

Inebolu Sokak Sozer Apt. No: 9/6 kat: 2, Kabatas-Istanbul

✆ +90 212 293 8350

✉ istanbul@oxfordvision.com

🖥 www.oxfordvision.com

NUMBER OF TEACHERS: 35.

PREFERENCE OF NATIONALITY: USA, UK, Canada, Australia, New Zealand.

QUALIFICATIONS: Minimum 3 years' experience in primary or secondary school with BA degree in any subject and TEFL, TESOL or CELTA certificate.

CONDITIONS OF EMPLOYMENT: 8–9 months. 25 hours a week.

SALARY: Approximately $1,600 per month net.

FACILITIES/SUPPORT: Assistance given in finding accommodation. Government requires employers to apply for work permits after submitting original degree and TEFL certificates.

RECRUITMENT: Via Skype or local interviews.

CONTACT: TEFL Recruitment Manager.

SDM LANGUAGE SCHOOL AND EDUCATION AGENCY

Halaskargazi Caddesi No: 336/1 Kat:3–4, Sisli 34456 Istanbul

✆ +90 212 233 0999

✉ akin@sdm.com.tr or sdm@sdm.com.tr

🖥 www.sdm.com.tr

PREFERENCE OF NATIONALITY: Native English speakers.

QUALIFICATIONS: University graduate, ELT qualification and experience of teaching adults.

CONDITIONS OF EMPLOYMENT: 6-day working week (with Fridays off). Working hours between 10am and 10pm. To teach mainly professionals.

FACILITIES/SUPPORT: Assistance with work permit given.

CONTACT: Akin Isik.

TEACHERS IN TURKEY

Fulya Mah. Buyukdere Cad., Defne Apt. No: 56 9/19, 34394 Mecidiyekoy, Sisli-Istanbul

☎ +90 212 347 0348

✆ tt@teachersinturkey.com, info@teachersinturkey.com

💻 www.teachersinturkey.com

NUMBER OF TEACHERS: 100–150 per year for private schools, kindergartens, primary schools, secondary schools and universities throughout Turkey. Also summer camps.

PREFERENCE OF NATIONALITY: UK, USA, Canada, Australia, New Zealand, Ireland, South Africa.

QUALIFICATIONS: Native English speaker, undergraduate degree, and teaching certificate (eg TEFL, TOESL, CELTA).

CONDITIONS OF EMPLOYMENT: September/October to June. 30 teacher hours per week normally Monday–Friday 8.30am–5pm. Pay day is 15th of month.

SALARY: Starting at 2,500 lira (£600) per month. Completion bonus of 2000 lira.

FACILITIES/SUPPORT: Assistance given in locating suitable housing, connecting roommates and translation help with contracts/landlords. Visa fees of $300–$500 will be reimbursed. Museum card given for free or discounted museum entrance nationwide. Orientation and teacher training seminars organised where possible.

RECRUITMENT: Via internet and in association with Teach to Travel agency in London (www.teachtotravel.co.uk). Personal interviews in UK and Turkey or Skype interviews.

CONTACT: Lara Natario, Academic Coordinator (lara@teachersinturkey.com).

TURCO-BRITISH ASSOCIATION

Bestekar Sokak No. 32, Kavaklidere, 06680 Ankara

☎ +90 312 419 1844

✆ admin@tba.org.tr or dos@tba.org.tr

💻 www.tba.org.tr

NUMBER OF TEACHERS: 20–30.

PREFERENCE OF NATIONALITY: British.

QUALIFICATIONS: Degree plus EFL qualification. Experience desirable.

CONDITIONS OF EMPLOYMENT: 2 years, 27 contact hours per week (45 minutes each lesson).

FACILITIES/SUPPORT: Shared, fully furnished accommodation, paid utilities, close proximity to school (about a 5-minute walk). Assistance with travel costs at the beginning and end of a 2-year contract. Residence and work permit procedures undertaken

and costs met. 4 weeks' paid annual leave, Christmas holiday, national Turkish holidays. Settling-in bonus, national social security covered. TBA is the only association in Turkey acting as an independent Cambridge English Language Assessment Authorised Centre.

RECRUITMENT: Via the *Guardian*, internet and locally.

CONTACT: Ms Özlem Fraser, Administrative Co-ordinator.

TURKISH-AMERICAN ASSOCIATION

Güvenevler, Cinnah Cd. No:20, 06690 Çankaya/Ankara

☎ +90 312 426 26 44

✆ vural@taa-ankara.org.tr

💻 www.taa-ankara.org.tr

NUMBER OF TEACHERS: 7–8 per year.

PREFERENCE OF NATIONALITY: American, British, Canadian, Australian.

QUALIFICATIONS: All candidates need to have a higher education degree in language teaching or a TEFL/TESOL certificate. Candidates must be comfortable with the Communicative Approach.

CONDITIONS OF EMPLOYMENT: 1 year contracts can be extended upon mutual agreement. Flexible hours with courses running mornings and evenings during the week, and all day at weekends. 2 days off per week.

SALARY: 2,140 lira for a 120-hour month, 2,500 lira for working 150 hours, both paid net.

FACILITIES/SUPPORT: Social security, housing and lunches are provided plus airfare upon completion of the contract. Shared housing is provided free of charge (not including domestic expenses). TAA runs the necessary paperwork in Turkey for visas.

RECRUITMENT: Via websites such as www.tefl.com and professional recruitment companies. Interviews can take place online.

CONTACT: Vural Erkec, Academic Director.

UKLA ACADEMY LANGUAGE SCHOOLS

Dikkaldirim MH. Zübeyde Hn Cd. 15/A Demir Apt 16090 Osmangazi – Bursa

☎ +90 224 232 1440

✆ english@ukla.com.tr

💻 www.ukla.com.tr; http://tr-tr.facebook.com/ UKLAACADEMY

NUMBER OF TEACHERS: 15–20 per year. Branches also in Eskisehir and Izmir.

PREFERENCE OF NATIONALITY: Must be native speakers as this is government policy for foreign English teacher employment.

QUALIFICATIONS: Bachelor's degree and CELTA or equivalent certification. Relevant experience is an advantage; minimum 2 years experience for certain posts.

CONDITIONS OF EMPLOYMENT: 1-year contract from August/September, with 28–30 classroom hours per week.

SALARY: Starting at 2,000 lira per month (after tax).

FACILITIES/SUPPORT: Fully furnished shared housing, work visa, residence permit, health insurance, professional development support (seminars and workshops), airfares reimbursed.

RECRUITMENT: Process involves an application essay, lesson plan and a final interview carried out over the phone or by Skype.

CONTACT: Ms Jennifer Dodds, Director of Studies.

VOICE OF LANGUAGES

Atasehir Bulvari, 38 Ada Atasehir 34756 Istanbul

- +90 216 458 22 00
- gdogan@volintr.com
- www.volintr.com

NUMBER OF TEACHERS: 5.

PREFERENCE OF NATIONALITY: American, British, Australian and Canadian native speakers.

QUALIFICATIONS: University degree + CELTA / TEFL or equivalent certification + experience with adult learners, especially of teaching Business English. Females only for some positions.

CONDITIONS OF EMPLOYMENT: 12-month contracts. Mostly evening and Saturday classes, though there might be some morning classes if preferred.

SALARY: 25–50 lira (net), according to experience and level of preparation needed. Support given for obtaining work permits.

FACILITIES/SUPPORT: Help with accommodation may be negotiable.

RECRUITMENT: Networking, references, advertising on sites such as http://yabangee.com. Face-to-face or Skype interviews.

CONTACT: Ms Gülsah Doğan.

Contradictions abound in a continent as complex as Africa, and one of them pertains to the attitude to the English language. On the one hand, the emergent nations of Africa want to distance themselves from their colonial past. On the other hand, they are eager to develop and participate in the world economy and so need to communicate in English. Yet, linguistic questions are often eclipsed by various humanitarian crises and ongoing conflicts. Chaos in Congo and Somalia, government collapse in Libya, the Ebola outbreak, communal violence in the world's newest state, South Sudan, emergence of terrorist groups like Boko Haram in North-Eastern Nigeria and al-Qaeda in the Maghreb in Mauritania . . . none of these adds to Africa's allure. Scrolling through the Foreign & Commonwealth Office's travel warnings with their repeated 'advice against all but essential travel' in many regions is enough to put off many. Tunisia was a good-news story until March 2015 when terrorists killed 21 people, most of them European tourists, in the Bardo National Museum.

What makes much of Africa different from Latin America and Asia (vis-à-vis English teaching) is that English is the medium of instruction in state schools in many ex-colonies of Britain, including Ghana, Nigeria, Kenya, Zambia, Zimbabwe and Malawi. A few countries, such as Gambia, are rejecting English because it is seen as a colonial relic, without knowing which African language to use in its stead. As in the Indian subcontinent, the majority of English teachers in these countries are locals. But there is still some demand for native English speakers in the secondary schools of those countries. The only countries in which there is any significant scope for working in a private language institute are the Mediterranean countries of Morocco, Tunisia and Egypt.

The drive towards English extends to most parts of the continent. Across Southern Africa, the dominant language of business and commerce and the language of university textbooks is English. It is typical that when Namibia acquired independence, it decided to make English its official language to replace Afrikaans. Ethiopia at present is pursuing a policy of improving the levels of English across the country and, with an economy growing at a rate of 10%, is investing in language programmes. A demand for hundreds of native English speakers, mainly at the advanced teacher-trainer level, is created from time to time, which organisations such as the Department for International Development, VSO and Skillshare Africa attempt to supply. Until 2016, the British Council in Dar es Salaam is running a large-scale project (funded by DfID) in 34 training colleges across Tanzania to improve the English-language proficiency and teaching skills in the country. Candidates with a CELTA or Trinity Certificate, a degree in any subject, plus at least two years' teaching experience are invited to apply for two-year (or shorter) contracts.

To balance the picture, it must be said that in some countries (such as Zambia, Nigeria, Sudan) the demand for English teachers has fallen off in favour of science, maths, technology and other languages. Even in ex-colonies of France (Morocco, Tunisia, Senegal, Mali, etc) and of Portugal (Mozambique), English is a sought-after commodity. World traveller **Bradwell Jackson** several years ago discovered paid on-the-spot teaching opportunities in Mali, Mauritania and Senegal.

PROSPECTS FOR TEACHERS

Few language schools exist in most African countries and even fewer can afford to employ expatriate teachers. The British Council maintains offices in most African countries and its assessment of the prospects for teachers is not very encouraging:

> *The English language is taught from a very early stage in many countries and, as a result, there are no institutes which specifically teach it. However, you may want to consider the university and colleges as institutions that teach English, even though it is at an advanced level.*

Because a high proportion of teaching opportunities in Africa are in secondary schools rather than private language institutes, a state teaching certificate is often a prerequisite. Missionary societies have played a dominant role in Africa's modern history, so many teachers are recruited through religious organisations, asking for a Christian commitment even for secular jobs. Apart from work with aid or missionary agencies, there are quite a few opportunities for students and people in their gap year to teach in Africa. Students and other travellers have also stumbled upon chances to teach on an informal basis.

FINDING A JOB

Many organisations, including a range of gap-year agencies, send people to Africa to teach English. These postings are normally regarded as 'voluntary' since wages, if paid at all, will be on a local scale though positions often come with free housing. In some cases a substantial placement fee must be paid. For links to smaller local charities that charge no placement fee, search the listing of Volunteer Programs in Africa at www.truetravellers.org/free-volunteer-programs-in-africa for teaching opportunities. See the chapter 'Finding a job' in Part 1 of this book for further details of the general agencies that send students such as **Sarah Johnson** from Cardiff who went to Zanzibar to teach English and geography at a rural secondary school. Once she started work Sarah discovered that:

> *The expectations which Zanzibari children have from school are worlds away from those of British school children. They expect to spend most of their lessons copying from the blackboard, so will at first be completely nonplussed if asked to think things through by themselves or to use their imagination. I found that the ongoing dilemma for me of teaching in Zanzibar was whether to teach at a low level which the majority of the class would be able to understand, or teach the syllabus to the top one or two students so that they would be able to attempt exam questions, but leaving the rest of the class behind. Teaching was a very interesting and eye-opening experience. I believe that both the Zanzibari teachers and I benefited from a cultural exchange of ideas and ways of life.*

Networks like Couchsurfing (www.couchsurfing.com) have hosts registered all over Africa, who might be interested in exchanging hospitality for English lessons. **Bradwell Jackson** stayed with a couchsurfing host in Bamako, Mali for two months:

> *He is a wealthy man who lives in a nice house, and I get all my meals, internet, my laundry and a few other odds and ends done for free. I teach him two hours every day, which leaves me lots of time to explore Bamako and do whatever else I like.*

Just one word of caution about internet offers: if you see a job advertised that looks too good to be true, do not be tempted to investigate further. Although thankfully rare, scams aimed at 'greedy' foreigners can be sophisticated and seemingly plausible.

PLACEMENT ORGANISATIONS

Africa & Asia Venture (www.aventure.co.uk). Offers students and recent graduates the chance to spend three to five months teaching a wide variety of subjects, especially English in Africa (Uganda, Kenya, Tanzania, Malawi and South Africa). The 2016 participation fee ranges from £1,645 for a 5 week summer programme to £3,285 for 16 weeks plus airfares.

Link Ethiopia (www.linkethiopia.org/volunteering). London-based charity that places volunteers (including gap-year students) for one to six months in partner schools in Ethiopia. Fee for standard three-month placement is £495 plus an equal amount to be fundraised to help the schools.

Peace Corps, 1111 20th St NW, Washington DC 20526 (+1 855 855 1961 toll-free; www.peacecorps. gov). More than a third of Peace Corps volunteers are posted to Africa, many of whom teach on 27-month assignments in 26 African countries, ranging from Mali to Mozambique. Must be US citizen, over 18 and in good health. All expenses, including airfare and health insurance, are covered.

Projects Abroad (www.projects-abroad.co.uk). Work placements in schools in Ethiopia, Ghana, Kenya, Morocco, Senegal, South Africa, Tanzania, Togo and Uganda.

Project Trust (www.projecttrust.org.uk). Sends school leavers (aged 17–19) to teach (often other subjects as well as English) in schools in seven African countries including Namibia, Botswana, Senegal and Swaziland. Participants must fundraise to cover part of the cost of their 12-month placement, at present £6,200 (2016).

Sazani Associates, thereza@sazaniassociates.org.uk. A charitable not-for-profit with offices in Wales and Zanzibar that recruits volunteers with a TEFL qualification to act as teaching assistants in nurseries and state schools in Zanzibar, or to assist adults develop their language skills.

Travellers (www.travellersworldwide.com). Placements to teach conversational English in Ghana, Morocco, South Africa and Zambia, plus other teaching in Zimbabwe.

Village-to-Village (http://v2vtanzania.org/volunteers). Volunteers are sent to the Kilimanjaro region of Tanzania to assist on various projects including teaching English in primary schools and orphanages, teacher training as well as construction and sustainable agriculture projects.

Village Africa, Hampshire (www.villageafrica.org.uk). Teaching volunteer programme in the West Usambara Mountains of Tanzania suspended in 2012 due to changes in the immigration rule, but visitors still welcome on 90-day tourist visa to help children practise their English.

WorldTeach, One Brattle Square, Suite 550, Cambridge, MA 02138, USA (+1 857 259 6646; www. worldteach.org). Non-profit organisation that recruits volunteers to teach English in Namibia, Morocco and South Africa, among other countries around the world. A 12-month placement in Namibia costs $3,990.

ON THE SPOT

The best chances of picking up language-teaching work on the spot are in North Africa, in Egypt, Morocco or Tunisia (treated separately below). Language schools are thriving in South Africa, staffed in large measure by English-speaking South Africans but also by foreigners. Tourists can enter South Africa on a tourist visa for three months, renewable for a further three (for a fee) at an office of the Department of Home Affairs.

If teachers (British as well as American) are prepared to travel to an African capital for an interview with one of the US State Department-sponsored English teaching centres in Africa (often attached to American embassies), they may be given some freelance opportunities. Virtually all hiring of teachers in these government-run language programmes takes place locally, so speculative applications from overseas are seldom welcome. This is how one American got her foot in the door and went on to become the director:

Work in an American Cultural Center is a great way to start off. I myself did it five years ago and am now running a programme. It allows a person to work in Africa but also provides up-to-date material which teachers in the national programmes are often forced to go without. Classes are small and the hours are not too heavy but can usually be increased, depending on the capabilities of the teacher. We also do outside programmes in specialised institutions and thus give teachers experience in ESP (hotels, oil companies, Ministries). People with degrees in EFL are very much in demand.

At the opposite end of the spectrum, grassroots voluntary organisations may have teaching positions. For example The Volta Aid Foundation (www.voltaaidfoundation.org) places teaching volunteers in the eastern province of Ghana. Volunteers stay with local Ghanaian families and cover their living expenses by paying $500 for the first month and $350 for subsequent months.

Till Bruckner is a veteran world traveller who has a decided preference for fixing up teaching and voluntary placements independently:

> *My advice to anyone who wants to volunteer in Africa (or anywhere else) is to go first and volunteer second. That way you can travel until you've found a place you genuinely like and where you think you might be able to make a difference. You can also check out the work and accommodation for yourself before you settle down. If you're willing to work for free, you don't need a nanny to tell you where to go. Just go.*

Opportunities crop up in very obscure corners of the continent. Travel blogger **Kim Reuter** spent several years exploring possibilities in Africa:

> *There are a ridiculous number of job positions just waiting to be filled in Africa . . . but you have to be THERE to find them. For example, while living in Madagascar, I visited the local university and was offered a teaching position on the spot because of my English speaking skills. This position, never advertised online, will only become available to you if you are in the right place at the right time. Obviously the 'right place' is not your faux leather couch in South-West Florida.*

Even further off the beaten track is the island of La Réunion, a département of France between Madagascar and Mauritius. Apparently there is a market for freelance teachers; consider advertising in the paper *Quotidien* (www.lequotidien.re).

PROBLEMS AND REWARDS

If teachers in Finland and Chile suffer from culture shock, teachers in rural Africa often find themselves struggling to cope at all. Whether it is the hassle experienced by women teachers in Muslim North Africa or the loneliness of life in a rural West African village, problems proliferate. Anyone who has fixed up a contract should try to gather as much up-to-date information as possible before departure, preferably by attending some kind of orientation programme or briefing. Otherwise local customs can come as a shock. On a more basic level, you will need advice on how to cope with climatic extremes. Even Cairo can be unbearably hot in the summer (and surprisingly rainy and chilly in January/February).

One unexpected problem is when locals are overawed by foreigners, as **Mary Hall** describes:

> *A white person is considered to be the be-all and end-all of everyone's problems for whatever reason. It's quite difficult to live with this image. Stare and stare again, never a moment to yourself. I'd like to say the novelty wore off but it never did. Obviously adaptability has to be one of the main qualities. We had no running water, intermittent electricity and a lack of such niceties as cheese and chocolate.*

A certain amount of deprivation is almost inevitable; for example teachers, especially volunteers, can seldom afford to shop in the pricey expatriate stores and so will have to be content with the local diet, typically a staple cereal such as millet usually made into a kind of stodgy porridge, plus some cooked greens, tinned fish or meat and fruit. The cost of living in some African cities such as Freetown and Douala is in fact very high, and a teaching wage does not normally permit a luxurious lifestyle. **Peter Kent** taught in Tanzania and kept a journal throughout his stay:

Bit worried about the food situation, only seems to be tomatoes, onions and potatoes at the market so a pretty boring diet. Sijaona is, if I understand her right, going to show us where you can buy more exotic veg . . . Taught standard one (ie year 1) today for the first time since they started this term. There are 105 kids, five or six to a bench which fits three normally. Quite a sight really, 105 bright-eyed kids staring expectantly at you. Mrs Msigwa, their teacher, seems really nice, keen and capable. We may get somewhere between us. You get the impression that if you stuck with them for years to come they'd be speaking English.

But of course volunteer teachers can't stick around that long and after less than a year it was time for Peter Kent to bid farewell to his school amidst present giving, choir singing and emotional speeches.

Health is obviously a major concern to anyone headed for Africa. The fear of HIV-contaminated blood or needles in much of Central Africa prompts many teachers to outfit themselves with a complete expat medical kit before leaving home (see Introduction). Malaria is rife and there is an alarming amount of mosquito resistance to the most common prophylactics, so this too must be sorted out with a tropical diseases expert before departure.

The visa situation differs from country to country of course but is often a headache. Whereas in Cameroon it is not really necessary to obtain a work permit, in Ethiopia it is much more problematic. The rules in Tanzania are complicated too: whether on a three-month tourist visa or two-month visa (both $50 for Britons at the border) you are not permitted to work or volunteer. For working for less than 90 days you must apply for a CTA (Conducting a Temporary Assignment), for which you will need a letter of invitation from your sponsor and the fee of $200.

If all that Africa could offer was a contest with malaria and a diet of porridge, no one would consider teaching there. But anyone who has seen David Attenborough's 'Africa' series can imagine how the continent holds people in thrall. A chance to see the African bush, to climb the famous peaks of Kilimanjaro or Kenya, to frequent the colourful markets, these are the pleasures of Africa which so many people who have worked there find addictive.

TEFL training can lead to unexpected opportunities in Africa. After graduating from York University **Miranda Crowhurst** was pleased to be accepted for one of the 12 places on a CELTA course in her home-town of Cambridge with the Bell School, and really enjoyed the course. While searching for jobs abroad she came across an intriguing opening in Tanzania to teach the young children of two expat families, and secured the seven-month position. She sent back descriptions of her life and adventures, divided between a prospering avocado farm and the nearby town of Mbeya, in a picture postcard Africa:

The farm is just in front of Rungwe volcano and right up against the jungle – you would not believe how beautiful it is looking out over the mountains from my cottage. At dawn when we set off for town, the sun rises spectacularly, lighting up trucks piled with farm labourers, forested mountains silhouetted against the pink sky, and sweeps of mist lying lazily over the villages. I also love walking round town – lots of people say hello in Swahili, and hi, and good afternoon. I'm the only white person I ever see and it makes me feel a little bit like a light bulb, but although people definitely notice me, no one hassles me, is pushy or unfriendly.

EGYPT

The aftermath of the Arab Spring has decidedly failed to bring about the move to democracy that Egyptians who demonstrated hoped to achieve. The situation in 2015 has been calmer than the previous year but the economy is flagging and the politics still polarised.

However, media reports can present an unduly negative image of everyday life in Egypt, and there is anything but hostility to the English language. The director of English at the British Council reported that their English teaching operations were expanding with new partners in suburban Cairo and a resumption of teaching at their offices in Alexandria. Of Egyptians who want to learn English, a large percentage are from the business community, though there is also a demand among university students and school children. Many young Egyptians who aspire to work in their country's computing or tourist industry want to learn English. Students at computer training schools or at tourism training centres like the one in Luxor might be looking for some private tuition from a native speaker.

Check the online *Yellow Pages* in English at www.yellowpages.com.eg; a search for 'Language schools and instruction' reveals more than 500. At one end of the spectrum there are the British Council's Teaching Centres in Alexandria and Cairo (Agouza, Heliopolis, Nasr City and a new centre in Sheikh Zayed City, 40km west of the city centre). At the other there are plenty of dubious establishments. Whereas you will need a professional profile for the former, back-street schools will be less fussy.

The British Council employs more than 100 teachers at five centres in Egypt. For many years Cairo has been one of the few large teaching centres in the British Council network where a recently qualified EL teacher has a good chance of being hired and quickly promoted. The minimum requirements are native English-speaker status, UK passport, CELTA or Trinity TESOL and two years' post-qualification teaching experience. If you are already in Egypt and there are suitable vacancies you will be invited for an interview and demonstration lesson (having sat in on another class beforehand). Summer is a good time to look, when the regular teachers tend to go away to escape the heat. During exam time there is also a need for one-to-one tutors and paid invigilators. The British Council (as always) has a great library and is a good place to teach. The main branch is located centrally in Agouza with another large centre in Heliopolis, which is quite a way from the centre of town and therefore has its own social world. The El-Alsson International School in Giza (www.alsson.com), out near the Pyramids, employs a number of expat teachers.

When **Dan Boothby** spent time in Cairo he found it almost alarmingly easy to find work:

> *I taught one-to-one lessons to several people and got about five hours a week work and charged £10 an hour. Frankly this was much more than I was worth but if you charge less than the market rate then it is felt that you are an amateur. I taught an isolated and lonely five-year-old, son of the Georgian Consul, where I was more a babysitter than a tutor. I felt so guilty about the fee I was charging that I spent an hour trying to get him to learn something. I didn't feel so guilty charging to tutor the Georgian Ambassador, since he probably passed the bill on to his government.*
>
> *I got a lot of students through friends that I made who were teaching at the international schools. The kids at these schools are often in need of extra tuition towards exam times when their parents realise that they've been mucking about all year and are close to failing. The problem is that the kids tend to be very uninterested and so it is difficult to make them concentrate. But I enjoyed one-to-ones. You could build up a large group of students and earn a decent wage but equally teach less hours and have more time – one of the reasons for getting out of England.*

Cairo seems to be a city where work seeks out the casual teacher rather than the other way round. Taxi drivers and hotel staff may ask you, unprompted, if you are available to teach. Most of these are genuine offers but it is best (especially for women) to be cautious. Most job-seekers find that potential bosses are not as interested in their educational background and experience as in how much confidence they can project. It is not unknown for an interview to take place over a game of chess and plenty of glasses of tea so that your general demeanour can be assessed. Jobs seem to be available year round, so there is no right or wrong time to arrive.

Language schools are not all located in Central Cairo but also in the leafy, prosperous residential areas such as Heliopolis, Maadi and Zamalek. Residential areas are also the best areas to look for private clients, as **Ian McArthur** found:

> In Cairo I sought to work as a private English tutor. I made a small poster, written in English and Arabic, with the help of my hotel owner. I drew the framework of a Union Jack at the top, got 100 photocopies and then meticulously coloured in the flags. The investment cost me £3. I put the posters up around Cairo, concentrating on affluent residential and business districts. I ended up teaching several Egyptian businessmen, who were difficult to teach since they hated being told what to do.

More recently an American traveller about to start law school posted the following on Lonely Planet's Thorn Tree forum:

> Back in December I posted a message asking people if they thought it was possible to get short-term jobs abroad or if it was a good idea to possibly make tutoring flyers to put up around town. Both were ideas to supplement the money I already had saved and to have some new adventures/meet locals while travelling. I got a ton of negative responses telling me those ideas wouldn't work, etc, etc. Just wanted to post back on here six months later that it IS possible and my friend and I just did it. We got teaching jobs in Egypt that paid fairly well, without having work permits, without having TEFL, and the classes were for business professionals and thus were short term (five weeks). Also, we put up tutoring flyers all over Cairo and made a decent amount of money doing private tutoring.

The American University, centrally located at the eastern end of the now famous Tahrir Square, is a good place to find work contacts though teaching for the AUC itself is difficult; only five candidates a month are granted an interview so they can afford to be highly selective. Also try the noticeboards at the Community Services Association (CSA No. 4, Road 21, Maadi, Cairo; www.livinginegypt.org), where a range of services for expats is offered including a tutor referral list. In fact beginners' English and conversational English are taught on the premises.

The best places to meet other expats and find out about work opportunities are expat meeting places like El Horreya Café downtown, or the Ace Club in Maadi. Also try the café-bars near the American University and the BCA (British Community Association) with several clubhouses in Cairo (www.bcaegypt.com), where you can only go as the guest of a member.

STUDENTS

In a 2014 article in the *EL Gazette*, Jonathan Gayther of the British Council Cairo described their students as '*lively, welcoming, and always ready to venture an opinion*'. Another teacher describes his Egyptian students at a language institute in the north-west suburb of Sahafeyeen as '*rowdy and sometimes a little over-enthusiastic*'. Having just obtained a Cambridge Certificate in London, he went to visit some friends in Cairo and was immediately offered a three-month summer contract where they were desperate for a teacher. He had to adapt his lessons to please both the ebullient Egyptian youths and a group of shy and industrious Somalis and describes his predicament with such a mixed class:

> Different religions, different ways of thinking and (as I learnt in my first week at the school) different modes of dress must all be taken into consideration. One of the problems that English students in this area have

difficulty with is hearing the difference between B and P. The exercise for this is to hold a piece of paper in front of the mouth and repeat the letters B and P. Since more air is exhaled during the sounding of the letter P than with B, the paper should fly up when P is said, and move only a little with B. The first time I made the students do this we went round the class, first Hamid the engineer from Alexandria, then Mona who was trying to get a job at the reception in the Hilton and then we came to Magda from Mogadishu (the capital of Somalia). All the Egyptians started to laugh – her whole face apart from her eyes was covered with a yashmak. I decided that this should not impede the exercise so if the yashmak moved it was a P, and not a B!

Living expenses are creeping up, as are taxes, though a teacher's salary still permits a comfortable lifestyle. The CELTA course offered by the British Council in Cairo used to be one of the cheapest in the world; however, the current fee of 16,000 Egyptian pounds works out at £1,370.

Most teachers enter Egypt on a tourist visa and then ask their school to help them extend it. The multiple-entry tourist visa is valid for a maximum of six months and costs £32. However, a business visa can be issued if you have a letter of invitation from a company (£65 for single entry, £105 for multiple). This is valid for six months and schools will help to extend it. British citizens can find up-to-date visa information at www.egyptianconsulate. co.uk. Work permits must be applied for by your employer to the Ministry of the Interior in Egypt.

LIST OF EMPLOYERS

AMIDEAST EGYPT

Cairo Office: 38 Mohie El Din, Abou El Ezz Street, Dokki-Giza, Cairo

- +20 2 19263
- HR-egypt@amideast.org; egypt@amideast.org
- www.amideast.org.egypt/careers

Alexandria Office: 15 Abdel Hamid El Abbady, Roushdy, Alexandria

- alexandria@amideast.org
- www.amideast.org/egypt/careers

NUMBER OF TEACHERS: 15–22.

PREFERENCE OF NATIONALITY: North American, but all native English speakers are welcome to apply.

QUALIFICATIONS: Minimum CELTA or TESOL certification, university degree and preferably 2–3 years of teaching adults.

CONDITIONS OF EMPLOYMENT: Local term-to-term hire agreements according to student numbers. 8–15 hours per week, 9 5-week sessions per year. Students are working adults and university students.

SALARY: $5.50–$8 an hour (paid in local currency). Contracted teachers earn $13, less 17.65% for tax and contributions.

FACILITIES/SUPPORT: Good teachers' resources, internet access, friendly working environment. Operates out of three historic mansions on the Mediterranean. No financial assistance with

accommodation given, but temporary housing can be arranged with no cost. No assistance given with work permits.

RECRUITMENT: Pre-interview questions sent to applicants via email, and then a classroom demonstration.

CONTACT: Quincy Dermody, Assistant Country Director.

BRITISH COUNCIL EGYPT

192 El Nil Street, Agouza, Cairo. Also in Heliopolis and Alexandria.

- +20 2 33001666
- MENA-TeacherRecruitment@ae.britishcouncil.org or information@britishcouncil.org.eg
- https://jobs.britishcouncil.org/Login.aspx or www. britishcouncil.org.eg

NUMBER OF TEACHERS: 100+ employed in Alexandria and Cairo area to teach 4,000+ adults and 1,650 young learners at centres in Agouza and Heliopolis, with branches in Nasr City and Sheikh Zayed City. Also take on trainee teachers newly qualified.

PREFERENCE OF NATIONALITY: British (or Egyptian).

QUALIFICATIONS: UK passport, CELTA or Trinity TESOL and 2 years' post-qualification teaching experience. For visa reasons candidates must be less than 60. Enhanced DBS disclosure is mandatory.

CONDITIONS OF EMPLOYMENT: 2-year contracts from mid-August. Classes offered 7 days a week, though most teachers teach either over 5 days each week or 4 days with 1 (non-teaching) work day. 25 contact hours per week.

SALARY: Local annual salary from about 8,700–12,000 Egyptian pounds (net) paid monthly into an Egyptian bank account plus sterling supplement to teachers recruited outside Egypt paid into a UK bank account. Airfares, visa costs and medical insurance are also provided.

FACILITIES/SUPPORT: Compulsory in-service training offered. Assistance given with pursuing DELTA, IBET or YL extension. Help given with accommodation and visas.

RECRUITMENT: Ads are placed many months in advance of vacancies but recruitment is ongoing.

CONTACT: Carol Ashen (Carol.Ashen@britishcouncil.org.eg).

SUDAN

According to the constitution of the Republic of Sudan, drawn up in 2005, the two official languages are Arabic and English. After many years of diplomacy, South Sudan achieved national autonomy in July 2011 and its official language is only English, though most people speak Arabic or dialects of Arabic.

The long-established NGO the Sudan Volunteer Programme, based in London and Khartoum (see entry), sends volunteers to help young Sudanese improve their English through contact with British volunteers. The volunteer's responsibilities might include running discussion groups, providing support for teachers at universities, training for public servants, teacher-training course design and developing course materials for English for legal purposes. Other volunteers have run General English courses and helped with English clubs, especially for pre-sessional and inter-sessional groups of university students. Some volunteers have produced and participated in radio programmes for learners of English and done editorial work for an English-language newspaper, so there is plenty of scope for pursuing individual talents and interests. In collaboration with the Sudan Ministry of Education, SVP has been developing a programme for volunteers to teach in secondary schools where the emphasis is on teaching the teachers and setting up English Clubs.

This is all good news for a country in which the current government has shown little inclination to support the teaching of English as a second language and has instead promoted the Arabisation of the country's educational system. As a result, the general standard of English has sharply declined over the past generation. Some are worried about their personal security, based on media coverage and FCO travel warnings. The FCO continues to warn against all travel to Darfur in western Sudan and reiterates its belief that terrorism is an ongoing threat. The director of the Sudan Volunteer Programme complains about what he sees as the FCO bias: *'We continue to be dogged by the negative and, I believe, misleadingly indiscriminate travel advice issued by the FCO which puts off potential volunteers, or more particularly their families.'*

Undaunted by bad publicity, **Rebecca Mallinson**, a mature-aged volunteer, described in her revealing blog her motivations and feelings on the eve of departure for Khartoum:

> I am now at a stage of life where my children have left home and have their own lives. This is the first time in my adult life that I have been footloose. I decided to re-train as a TEFL teacher and look at possible places to go. I got a wonderful book out of the library called **Teaching English Abroad** that contains details of many countries and mentioned Sudan and SVP. I did a bit of background reading about Sudan and was hooked. It is a country with a lot of archaeology and interesting and diverse cultures. It is a country with a lot of problems, both war and poverty. SVP sends volunteers to enhance understanding of the outside world in Sudan and at the same time increase understanding of Sudan elsewhere. As they are a very small charity, this is obviously a drop in the ocean, but at least it is a start.
>
> I have spent the last nine months preparing to go. I have achieved my TEFL qualification, had some lessons in Sudanese Arabic, reverted to my maiden name, bought suitable clothes for an Islamic country and had a large number of vaccinations. I have also got rid of most of my possessions as I intend this to be a lifestyle change, hopefully doing alternate years of volunteering and paid work for the foreseeable future. As from Thursday I have rented out my home (a boat on the Thames). It is almost time to say 'Goodbye boat, salaam alekum (peace be with you) Sudan!'

Since leaving Sudan, Rebecca has taken up a new volunteering challenge in South Sudan and as of summer 2015 is reporting about the experience at http://nimule-blog.blogspot.co.uk.

MARK TANNER

Mark Tanner, a New Zealand adventurer, found out about the Sudan Volunteer Programme by searching the web and was accepted onto the scheme.

While some volunteers were required to use the syllabus as a guide, I had a free rein over what I taught and how. This prompted me to ask the students to suggest topics that were of interest to them and allowed me freedom to encourage discussion about parts of the Sudanese culture I was interested in. The main objective was to provide the students with a native English speaker and get them used to conversation. We were encouraged to do less-formal sessions called the English Club. For example we themed the cooking class, as our university was all female and cooking was something they considered important. Some classes stand out in my memory such as the one where we tried to teach the students to juggle. The classrooms could be quite hot and were equipped with blackboard and chalk, although we used teaching aids based on our own initiative.

The lodgings provided were basic, but by Sudanese standards good. The stipend was enough to subsist in Sudan, living like the Sudanese. As lovely as the Sudanese are, things are not as organised in the country as we would expect in the West. Yet it would be difficult to find more hospitable people than the Sudanese and there is never a shortage of offers for dinner or to visit a village, which provided a fantastic opportunity to experience the culture in a way many other NGO workers never saw.

There are many interesting things to see in Khartoum, such as Nuba Wrestling, fish markets, Dervish dancing and museums. SVP has a deal with the Blue Nile Sailing Club which allows students to try their luck at sailing on the Nile. Many of the volunteers did other voluntary work for NGOs. I helped an NGO with marketing and to develop a website. My principal motivation for being in the Sudan was to paddle through Sudan on the Nile, and I spent a lot of my spare time trying to source permits for this.

One of the highlights for me was seeing the English of the students improve and the relationships develop from that. Teachers are greatly respected in the Sudan so volunteers are revered and treated with respect.

Not everyone is so positive about being placed by an agency, especially if their motives are strictly philanthropic. The placement that was fixed up for **Till Bruckner** in Sudan didn't live up to his expectations:

> They'd told me at my interview in London that I'd be teaching international politics but when I arrived the local branch didn't know what I'd come for and wanted me to teach conversational English at a university in Khartoum. I figured that if I was going to teach English to kids from well-off families while living in a city of outstanding natural ugliness, I might as well go elsewhere and get paid for it. There'd be no problem finding

work as an English teacher in Sudan. There's great demand and little supply as nobody (including most Sudanese) wants to live there. In a country with poverty on that scale, there's more useful things you can do with £500 than pay for a scheme to tutor English. If you want fun, go elsewhere; if you want to help, put the £500 in an Oxfam charity box.

However, that is just one point of view and many people have felt that their contribution as a volunteer teacher has not been futile, either from the point of view of broadening their own horizons or of helping others.

The SVP site carries illuminating first-hand accounts by recent volunteers, pointing out some of the highs ('the overwhelming friendliness and hospitality of the people') and lows ('the oppressive heat').

LIST OF EMPLOYERS

SUDAN VOLUNTEER PROGRAMME

34 Estelle Road, London NW3 2JY, UK

☎ +44 7910 940819 or +44 20 7485 8619

✉ david@svp-uk.com

🖥 www.svp-uk.com

UK registered charity which promotes English teaching among university students and other adults.

NUMBER OF TEACHERS: 10–20 at any time in and outside Khartoum.

PREFERENCE OF NATIONALITY: None but should be native speakers of English and if not, they should be qualified English-language teachers.

QUALIFICATIONS: TEFL certificate, experience of travelling in developing countries and some knowledge of Arabic are helpful but not obligatory. Volunteers must be over 22, in good health and have some university education.

CONDITIONS OF EMPLOYMENT: Preferred minimum 8 months to tie in with university semesters: October–January or January–May. Secondary school terms run June to February/March.

SALARY: SVP pays subsistence (800 Sudanese pounds/£85), modest accommodation and insurance beyond the initial 3 months. Volunteers must raise the cost of the airfare to Sudan (currently £430) plus £80 (towards the cost of the first 3 months' insurance). Wage can be supplemented by private teaching.

FACILITIES/SUPPORT: Accommodation with self-catering facilities is arranged.

RECRUITMENT: Applications accepted year round. Two referees are also required. Prior to departure, medical check-up required plus selection interviews, orientation and briefings take place. Volunteers are required to write a report of their experiences and to advise new volunteers.

CONTACT: David Wolton.

KENYA

Kenya is another country with a chronic shortage of school teachers. Since 2003, when the government kept its promise to abolish school fees for primary schools, there has been a steady increase in student numbers. The worst teacher shortages are in Western Province. English is the language of instruction in many Kenyan primary schools, so not knowing Swahili need not be an insuperable barrier for foreign teachers. The Kenyan Ministry of Education restricts jobs in the state sector to those who have a university degree, teaching certification and at least one year of professional teaching experience. The few private language institutes that there are in Nairobi are not subject to this restriction. The British Council in Nairobi at Upperhill Road (information@britishcouncil.or.ke) may be able to offer advice. One institute which carries information about year round job openings on its website is the Language Center (see entry), which hires native speakers with a degree and a recognised TEFL qualification.

According to the Kenyan High Commission in London (45 Portland Place, London W1B 1AS; +44 20 7636 2371), all non-Kenyan citizens who wish to work must be in possession of a work permit issued by the Principal Immigration Officer, Department of Immigration, PO Box 30191, Nairobi before they can take up paid or unpaid work. Teachers who have been offered employment should apply for a Class A permit, aimed at those who are suitably qualified and 'whose engagement in that employment will be of benefit to Kenya'. The school should apply for work permits for the teachers even before they enter Kenya. Proof of professional qualifications is required. However, it is not certain that immigration regulations would be strictly enforced in the case of native English speakers looking for teaching work on the spot. Certainly in the past it was possible to fix up a teaching job by asking in the villages, preferably before terms begin in September, January and April. Be prepared to produce your CV and any diplomas and references on headed paper.

Also ascertain before accepting a post whether or not the school can afford to pay a salary, especially if it is a Harambee school, ie non-government, self-help schools in rural areas. A cement or mud hut with a thatched or tin roof will usually be provided for the teacher's accommodation plus a local salary, which would be just enough to live on provided you don't want to buy too much peanut butter or cornflakes in the city. Living conditions will be primitive, with no running water or electricity in the majority of cases. The Kenyan version of maize porridge is called *ugali*. In Daisy Waugh's book *A Small Town in Africa* (no longer in print) she describes how, when she arrived at the village of Isiolo (a few miles from Nairobi) where she had arranged to teach, she was told that they didn't need any teachers and there were no pupils. She patiently waited and, five weeks into term, her class arrived.

People who choose to teach in Kenya do it for love, not money. In the words of **Ermon O. Kamara**, PhD, former Director of the American Universities Preparation Institute in Nairobi:

> *Candidates must view being in Kenya as a holiday with pay. The cost of living and corresponding local salaries sound quite low to foreigners. Consequently they must think of the opportunities to enjoy Kenya's beaches, mountains and game parks as well as experiencing a new and interesting culture. During weekends and holidays, one can travel the breadth of Kenya. Also the proximity to other countries in East and Southern Africa permits a traveller to see a good deal of our continent.*

A Kenyan NGO in the Rift Valley, AHADI (www.ahadicommunity.org) runs a Reach & Teach Project in which volunteers teach in rural schools in Western Kenya. The cost to volunteers is US$300 a week.

LIST OF EMPLOYERS

THE LANGUAGE CENTER LTD

Ndemi Close/Ndemi Road off Ngong Road, PO Box 40661, 00100 Nairobi

(phone) +254 20 386 9531, 386 9532, 387 0610, 387 0612

(email) tlc@language-cntr.com

(web) www.language-cntr.com

NUMBER OF TEACHERS: Approximately 6.

PREFERENCE OF NATIONALITY: British, American.

QUALIFICATIONS: Minimum first degree plus CELTA, TEFL or any other recognised teaching qualification.

CONDITIONS OF EMPLOYMENT: Standard length of contract is 2 years. Normal working hours are 8.30am to 4pm.

SALARY: Around $8.50–$11 per hour for the first year plus medical insurance and gratuity. PAYE tax deductions of 20%–30% of salary.

FACILITIES/SUPPORT: Employer will handle the application process for work permits and pay half of the total expenses.

RECRUITMENT: Online application form or word of mouth. Interviews are essential and are conducted locally.

CONTACT: Mrs Agnes W. Ngugi, Managing Director.

MADAGASCAR

KIM REUTER

Kim Reuter from Florida is primarily interested in conservation and development, but during her long stay in Madagascar she couldn't help but notice how many opportunities there are to teach English both formally through institutions and informally to individuals.

It is not difficult to find teaching work and to my knowledge there is not a significant administrative burden, especially if you are teaching privately or in certain English schools. Many work without an official contract. There may be more red tape if you plan to teach at the university level. Usually you do not need any sort of certification, apart from being a fluent speaker. Teaching materials are extremely hard to find, so be ready to create your own lessons or bring your tools into the country with you. It is also much easier to find these positions if you know some working French (very few people speak any English and it is helpful to know French, if just enough to set up appointments with students). Note that English-French dictionaries are hard to come by.

I was offered a contract job teaching English at the university level in Madagascar. Do not expect to get help in finding accommodation, though this is easily set up in-country either staying in the house of a local family, or in a cheap hotel/apartment. The wages paid for a good private instructor of English are enough to live on (food, accommodation and sightseeing). You should establish early on the teacher-student relationship, especially as a woman, since there are stigmas associated with being a foreigner in Madagascar. It could be that your students perceive your friendly and open attitude (which is normal in western countries) as an invitation for flirtation or a romantic relationship. However, being upfront about the student-teacher relationship can discourage these encounters.

In your spare time, there are so many things to do in Madagascar. It is one of the most amazing places in the world and there is no shortage of things to see. The people here are some of the friendliest I have ever met - expect to meet your students' families, be invited to their school graduations, etc. I highly recommend teaching in Madagascar, and you will find that there are a lot of unexpected perks ... like learning French or Malagasy, as you go through the process of teaching English.

MOROCCO

Although Morocco is a Francophone country, English is a requirement for entrance to university or high-ranking jobs, and there is strong demand from the business communities of the main cities. Like so many African countries, Morocco has sought to improve the standards of education for its nationals, so that almost all teaching jobs in schools and universities are now filled by Moroccans. But outside the state system there is a continuing demand for native English speakers.

The Moroccan Ministry of Employment stipulates that the maximum number of foreign staff in any organisation cannot exceed 50%. It also insists that all foreign teachers have at least a Bachelor's degree in TESOL or a degree plus TESOL/TEFL certificate before they can be eligible for a work permit. The maximum age is 60. Work permits are obtained after arrival by applying for authorisation from the Ministère de l'Emploi, Quartier des Ministères, Rabat. You will need copies of your diplomas, birth certificate and so on. Although a knowledge of French is not a formal requirement, it is a great asset for anyone planning to spend time in Morocco.

A number of commercial language schools employ native English speakers. The hourly rate of pay at most schools is less than £10 (equivalent in dirhams). The American Language Centers are located in the main cities of Morocco and most hire native speakers; see the website www.aca.org.ma/jobs for details. They are private institutes but are affiliated to and partially funded by the US State Department. Two are included in the list of employers, including the Casablanca branch, which recruits native English-speaker teachers from a number of courses including academic institutes in the USA such as the University of North Texas, which offers a graduate certificate in TESOL. Other branches to try are in Marrakech (alcmarr@aca.org.ma) and in Mohammedia (director@alcmohammedia.com).

The workcamps movement is active in Morocco and some of these summer volunteer projects take place on English-language camps for Moroccan adolescents (see CSM entry below).

LIST OF EMPLOYERS

AMERICAN LANGUAGE CENTER
1 Place de la Fraternité, Casablanca 20000
+212 522 277765
casa_dir@aca.org.ma
http://casablanca.aca.org.ma/en/test-efl-jobs

NUMBER OF TEACHERS: 12–15 full-time teachers (mostly native speakers) plus about 40 part-time Moroccan teachers.
PREFERENCE OF NATIONALITY: North American, but British teachers are also welcome to apply.
QUALIFICATIONS: Bachelor's degree, TEFL Certification (CELTA preferred) and a minimum of 1 year's EFL overseas teaching experience.
CONDITIONS OF EMPLOYMENT: A standard contract is for 12 months from 1 October to 30 September. 18 contact hours a week are standard for the Adult Program, mostly evenings and weekends. However, some teachers have additional classes, including Young Learners.

SALARY: 188–208 dirhams per hour (£12.50–£14) according to qualifications and experience. There is also a tax-free housing allowance of up to 3,000 dirhams per month plus a 10,000 dirhams settling-in allowance (over $1,000), which is also tax free. Taxes on a monthly salary amount to about 15% of earnings. Complete medical insurance (80% reimbursable) is provided for all full-time teachers. A ticket to the teacher's residence in the USA (for North Americans) or UK (for British teachers) is provided if a teacher successfully completes 1 year at the centre. There is also an end-of-contract bonus equal to 1 month's pay.
RECRUITMENT: Send CVs with photo, scanned copies of first page of passport and original diplomas and 2 letters of recommendation. All paperwork necessary for teachers to obtain work permits is done by administration staff. New teachers have to bring a copy of their birth certificate and their original university diplomas and certificates.
CONTACT: David Neuses (casa_dir@aca.org.ma).

AMERICAN LANGUAGE CENTER, RABAT

4 Zankat Tanja, Rabat 10000

☏ +212 537 767103

✎ dir@alcrabat.org

🖥 www.alcrabat.org/en/employment/

NUMBER OF TEACHERS: 20 full-time and 25 part-time teachers.

PREFERENCE OF NATIONALITY: Applicants should be from a country where English is the first language.

QUALIFICATIONS: BA preferably in Education, TESOL, or related field; knowledge of French or Arabic highly desirable. TEFL certification required (not online).

CONDITIONS OF EMPLOYMENT: 1-year renewable contracts. 18–22 contact hours per week full-time. Hours of work generally between 2pm and 9pm weekdays (Tuesday to Friday) and 9am and 5pm on weekends. Students aged from 7, mostly aged 14–35.

SALARY: Approximately $1,500 per month (gross) for October to July school year. Possibility of paid overtime. Paid sick leave and medical insurance provided as well as vacation allowance and round-trip airfare upon completing 2 years.

FACILITIES/SUPPORT: Free housing/homestay provided for 2 weeks while permanent accommodation is sought. Pre- and in-service training fully supported. Free access to high-speed internet, free language classes (French and Arabic) and other benefits.

RECRUITMENT: Through TESOL convention in early spring in the US and some local hiring. Video-conference interviews are also used.

CONTACT: Michael McMillan, Director.

AMIDEAST

35 Rue Oukaimeden, Agdal, Rabat

☏ +212 537 67 50 75/81/82

Also: 3 Boulevard Al Massira Al Khadra, Maarif, Casablanca

☏ +212 522 259393

✎ anovelli@amideast.org

🖥 www.amideast.org/morocco

NUMBER OF TEACHERS: Approximately 35.

PREFERENCE OF NATIONALITY: Must be native English speakers.

QUALIFICATIONS: TEFL qualification.

CONDITIONS OF EMPLOYMENT: 1-year contracts, preferably with a view to extending. To work around 70–100 hours per month.

FACILITIES/SUPPORT: Settling-in allowance. Assistance with apartment search and work visas, which must be acquired within 3 months of arrival.

RECRUITMENT: CV and cover letter to knorris@amideast.org. Telephone interview required.

CONTACT: Alex Novelli, Director of Programs.

CHANTIERS SOCIAUX MAROCAINS (CSM – ICYE MOROCCO)

33 Bloc 3 Youssoufio 10000, Rabat

✎ csmmorocco@gmail.com or Badr_Yah@hotmail.com

🖥 Badr_yah@hotmail.com

NUMBER OF TEACHERS: Around 40 volunteers for summer teaching workcamps in Rabat, Salé, Kenitra, Casablanca, etc.

QUALIFICATIONS: Skills teaching children are required. French or Arabic an advantage. Independent attitude and the ability to work in difficult circumstances with little support.

CONDITIONS OF EMPLOYMENT: Voluntary work teaching English to Moroccan youths aged 15–18 from modest or poor families on summer workcamps in July or August. Volunteers teach 25–30 students for 4 hours a day, Monday to Friday.

SALARY: Voluntary work. Volunteers pay for their own flights, insurance, induction and administration.

FACILITIES/SUPPORT: Local host families provide board and lodging. For summer projects, pre-camp orientation at the beginning of July.

RECRUITMENT: Online application through CSM website or through partner agencies such as Volunteers for Peace in the US (www.vfp.org), which charges a registration fee of $500 plus €80.

TUNISIA

Like its neighbour in the Maghreb, Tunisia is turning away from the language of its former colonial master and embracing the dominant language of prosperous and democratic Europe. Although the young generation speak fluent French because they have been taught it in school, many teenagers prefer English. Both Amideast (see entry) and the British Council Tunis Teaching Centre employ qualified native English-speaker teachers. The latter runs a summer school in June and July with extra vacancies; teachers earn £1,800 for the whole period plus accommodation and flights.

ROGER MUSKER

Roger Musker found that people would be interested in paying you for lessons, even though you plan to be in the country for a relatively short time. He was in Tunisia for one winter.

I decided to take a month off work as a kind of sabbatical and, if well planned, at no cost. I found all young people in Tunisia keen to practise and speak English whenever possible. I had one good contact in Sousse, who worked for the Tunisian Tourist Agency. I wrote to him from England and he replied that he could line up students on my arrival, which included himself and his 10-year-old daughter (who turned out to be my best student). At their house I was plied with extremely sweet tea and sticky cakes, which you are obliged to eat. Altogether I had eight keen fee-paying students, including a blind telephone operator, a teacher of English on a revision course and students from the Bourguiba Institute at Sousse University, which claims to be the second-oldest university in the world. For the latter it was necessary to get permission from the Ministry of Education via the headmaster.

Every day I tutored 8-10am and 5-7pm. The hourly rate was about £8, allowing me to cover basic costs while having a working holiday. Even without the contact and knowing Arabic, work is there for the asking. It just takes initiative. Go to any official institute, the tourism or municipal offices, demonstrate your availability and enthusiasm, give them your contact number and await replies.

The Bourguiba Institute in Tunis (47 Av. de la Liberté, 1002 Tunis; www.iblv.rnu.tn) occasionally hires well-qualified teachers.

LIST OF EMPLOYERS

AMIDEAST TUNISIA

22 Rue Al Amine Al Abassi, B.P. 351, Cité Jardina 1002, Tunis

☎ +216 71 145 700
✉ elteachers@amideast.org
🖥 www.amideast.org/tunisia

NUMBER OF TEACHERS: 50 full or part-time independent contract TEFL/TESL teachers. Also for Sousse.

PREFERENCE OF NATIONALITY: Native or near-native speakers of English.

QUALIFICATIONS: Ideally a degree and accredited 100+-hour international certificate in TEFL/TESL. 1 year's successful experience of teaching English to non-native speakers would be a plus. Should have knowledge of US standardised tests like TOEFL and GMAT.

CONDITIONS OF EMPLOYMENT: Minimum 9 months. Classes for children, teenagers and adults held between 8.30am and 9pm. Courses also run for public and private sector organisations.

SALARY: 20.28–23.40 dinars per hour depending on qualifications and experience.

FACILITIES/SUPPORT: Hotel accommodation provided on arrival for up to 15 days until teacher finds accommodation (with help of school). During the 4 months that American and Canadian citizens are allowed to stay as tourists, the school handles arrangements for getting a work permit and visa. A 500-dinar travel grant is paid at the end of the 1-year contract.

RECRUITMENT: Via www.amideast.org plus regional and international TEFL conferences.

CONTACT: Mariem Salhi, EL Coordinator (msalhi@amideast.org).

BRITISH COUNCIL TUNISIA

87 Avenue Mohamed V, BP 96 Le Belvédère, 1002 Tunis

☎ +216 71 145 302
✉ ian.bowman@tn.britishcouncil.org
🖥 www.britishcouncil.tn

QUALIFICATIONS: Minimum certificate in EFL (CELTA or Trinity) plus 2-years' post-certificate teaching experience in EFL. Demonstrable ability to teach across the range of courses offered including adults and young learners. Experience of IELTS and Cambridge Exams desirable. Maximum age 58 for visa reasons.

CONDITIONS OF EMPLOYMENT: 2-year full-time contracts. Also run summer school programme for which they need teachers for 8 weeks (June/July).

SALARY: Flights, baggage, medical insurance and pension contributions in addition to salary for full-time work. Salary for 2-month summer school is £2,000 plus flights, accommodation and medical insurance.

CONTACT: Ian Bowman, Deputy Teaching Centre Manager.

ENGLISH CULTURAL CENTRE

Av 14 Janvier Imm Itkan, 3000 Sfax

☎ +216 74408949
✉ contact@englishculturalcenter.com
🖥 www.englishculturalcenter.com

NUMBER OF TEACHERS: 4.

PREFERENCE OF NATIONALITY: British or American.

QUALIFICATIONS: 3 years' experience.

CONDITIONS OF EMPLOYMENT: 6 months or annual contract. Most classes are in the afternoon/evenings, 4pm–6pm and 6.30pm–8.30pm.

SALARY: 28 dinars (£9.50) per 2 hour lesson.

FACILITIES/SUPPORT: Assistance given with applying for work permits.

RECRUITMENT: Interview is essential and can be conducted on the phone or Skype.

CONTACT: Ahmed Zayani, Administrative and Financial Manager.

LIBYA

On 23 October 2011, the National Transitional Council (NTC) proclaimed the liberation of Libya after more than 40 years under Colonel Gaddafi, who had isolated himself and his country from the western world for so long. Many hoped that this potentially prosperous little country would cohere and flourish after the revolution. Unfortunately the country has descended into chaos and is often in the news for being the unpoliced jumping-off point for migrant boat people from Africa and the Middle East, so many of whom drown in the Mediterranean. The Foreign Office advises against all travel to the country and has closed the British Embassy. It warns of Islamic State-affiliated groups carrying out bombings and kidnappings in 2015. The brief flowering of institutes offering English instruction that came in the wake of the Libyan revolution was soon extinguished, and many fledgling schools and organisations like the English Teachers' Forum for Libya are now defunct. Of the two dozen or so English and international schools listed by the American Libyan Club in 2013/4, only two or three are hanging on by their fingernails, and the club itself no long exists.

If at some point in the future the country stabilises, demand for native-speaking teachers is bound to increase, in the oil, gas and engineering sectors as well as the population at large.

LIST OF EMPLOYERS

ALMAQAR IT & ENGLISH LANGUAGE TRAINING

Al-Fornaj, across from Tripoli Medical Centre, next to the General Mills Company, Tripoli

- +218 21 462 8507; mobile: +218 91 632 9708 / +218 92 486 7908
- english@almaqar.ly
- www.learnenglishlibya.blogspot.co.uk; https://www.facebook.com/AlmaqarITC

NUMBER OF TEACHERS: 8.

PREFERENCE OF NATIONALITY: No preference.

QUALIFICATIONS: CELTA, TESOL, DELTA, or the equivalent.

CONDITIONS OF EMPLOYMENT: 6–12 months. Mornings or evenings. Part-time positions available for freelance teachers.

FACILITIES/SUPPORT: Documents provided to support application for the required visa.

RECRUITMENT: Via internet adverts, local newspapers and English Teachers' Forum, Libya. Interviews essential, can be carried out by Skype.

CONTACT: Therese Martin (Khadija), Director of English Language Studies.

AWARDBRAND LIBYA

Al Noufleen, Tripoli

- +218 21 340 9590
- enquiries@awardbrand.co.uk
- www.awardbrand.ly

NUMBER OF TEACHERS: The school seems to be operating at the time of writing but it could not be ascertained whether they are hiring native speaker teachers.

PREFERENCE OF NATIONALITY: None.

QUALIFICATIONS: Minimum 1st degree + CELTA / CertTESOL.

CONDITIONS OF EMPLOYMENT: 12 months. 25 contact hours per week.

SALARY: Dependent upon qualifications/experience.

FACILITIES/SUPPORT: Accommodation provided. Company organises the visa. Once it is approved, the teacher's passport has to be submitted to the local Libyan Embassy, where it takes 3–7 days to be stamped.

RECRUITMENT: Internet, word of mouth and referrals. Interviews are essential and sometimes take place in the UK.

CONTACT: Head of Tripoli Training Centre, Awardbrand Libya.

MAURITANIA

After gaining some popularity among travellers overlanding from Morocco to Senegal, Mauritania has dropped off the radar again. The FCO advises against all travel to most of the country and all but essential travel to the south, including the capital, Nouakchott. However, it is not considered as dangerous as Mali, where the threat of terrorism is rated as 'high', in possible retaliation for the French intervention in the conflict in Mali in 2013.

When **Bradwell Jackson** visited before the rise in terrorist attacks in the Western Sahara, he was surprised by how few westerners he saw: '*It seems as though this country is up and coming as one of those unexplored gems that travellers haven't yet discovered.*'

Bradwell, who supplied information several years ago, found a teaching job by a '*happy accident of fate*'. On striking up a conversation with a westerner walking on the other side of the street in Nouakchott, he asked her about English language schools, and was promptly taken to the front door of The English Language Centre (now called Sahara English – www.saharaenglish.com):

> *I was lucky enough to speak with the owner right away. I was talking to her while she was busy doing some other things, so it was not a formal interview. I did not have to fill out an application, though she asked me to write a letter explaining why I wanted to work in Mauritania. She seemed very interested, and asked me to come back in a couple of days to do a mock class in front of her teachers. I was hired based on this.*

Bradwell's wages started at 50,000 ouguiyas (now worth $150) a month and increased to 68,000 ouguiyas ($210) a month. He was told that a person hired from within the country is paid much less than a person hired from outside. Getting a work permit was refreshingly simple. The school simply took his passport to the employment office and paid for a one-year work permit.

Bradwell found the students to be a joy to work with, because they were 'serious' and hungry to learn. The coordinator of the Center (which is affiliated to the Université de Nouakchott and the US Embassy) hires 6–8 teachers, one or two of whom he would like to be native English speakers, although this would depend on the school's income. Teachers are paid 1,500–2,500 ouguiyas per hour (about $4.60–$7.75/hour). British English is as popular as American English.

EQUATORIAL GUINEA

After 12 editions of this book came the first report of possibilities for teaching English in the former Spanish colony of Equatorial Guinea, now one of the smallest countries of Africa, surrounded by Cameroon and Gabon. Although **Kim Reuter** has no first-hand experience of teaching English here, she did run a non-profit organisation in the country, so is familiar with the small but growing market for English teachers:

> *It is basically impossible to get a job before you land in country, but you can easily find one in the capital city of Malabo. There are several small English schools that will hire English speakers, and you can also set up English classes through the Spanish and French cultural centres in Malabo. You do not need formal training in teaching English, though you need to be a fluent English speaker and you should bring your teaching tools with you. It is very difficult to enter the country unless you are American because Americans do not need visas. You are technically required to get a resident permit if you plan to stay for more than three months but I do not know of many people who have gone through that long and costly process. I have heard it costs $1,000, but I am still unclear as to what the process is.*

The hours at the English schools are mostly part-time, and pay is approximately $25 per hour. The wages are more than enough to live on in Malabo, though the capital is very expensive (eg $10 to eat, and rent can be around $900 for a one-bedroom apartment). You may or may not have a contract, but you will be expected to teach English courses from start to finish. Finding accommodation can be hard in Equatorial Guinea, but there are a few non-profits that will house you at very low cost, and the English schools may help you find accommodation in the house of a local family (though you should not rely on this). The fellow teachers are usually Equatoguineans who have had English training, which is why native English fluency is so prized. Working in Equatorial Guinea can be very difficult, so be sure to do thorough research on the country before arriving. On the other hand it will pay dividends for years to come. Once you are there, people can be extremely kind and giving. You will be invited into their homes and most students (if you teach at a school) will respect the student–teacher relationship. The upside about Equatorial Guinea is that it is a place that almost no one goes to. Your English-language skills will be prized, you will find that you are one of only a handful of foreigners and you are guaranteed to have experiences that are unmatched in any other country.

SENEGAL

The British Council has a flourishing teaching centre in Dakar (Rue AAB–68, Amitie Zone A et B, BP 6232; +221 33 869 2700; information@britishcouncil.sn) that actively recruits teachers. It will want to see your CV and certification, although **Bradwell Jackson** reports that it will consider hiring non-UK citizens and may leave you 'wriggle room' if you don't quite have the qualifications it officially requires.

The British Senegalese Institute in Dakar (http://britishbsi.com) is the oldest English teaching centre in the country. It does not require teachers to have a specific certificate or experience, although these are certainly desirable. The average hours per week are 15, and the pay is around 3,500 CFA ($6) per hour. Another possibility is the Centre Africain d'Etudes Supérieures en Gestion (Boulevard du General De Gaulle, B.P. 3802, Dakar; courrier@cesag.sn). The school is located in a large, official complex and tends to cater for more affluent students. Bradwell Jackson spoke to the Chef du Departement Langues, who said that no specific certificate was required, just a good knowledge of the language.

The English Language Program run by the US Embassy (RELO-Dakar@state.gov) in Senegal continues to recruit. Although Dakar is an interesting city of contrasts, Bradwell was not tempted to stay. He found the city sprawling and unwieldy, as well as expensive.

OTHER AFRICAN COUNTRIES

LIST OF EMPLOYERS

MOZAMBIQUE

LYNDEN LANGUAGE SCHOOL
Av Zedequias Manganhela 267, JAT Building, 2nd Floor
(PO Box 456), Maputo
📞 +258 21 360494
✉ info@lynden.co.mz
🖥 www.lynden.co.mz

NUMBER OF TEACHERS: 5.
PREFERENCE OF NATIONALITY: British, Australian, South African, etc.
QUALIFICATIONS: CELTA or Trinity plus 2 years' experience.
CONDITIONS OF EMPLOYMENT: 1 year, 25 hours per week.
SALARY: $1,000; half paid in the local currency (meticals).
FACILITIES/SUPPORT: School finds and pays for accommodation. School applies to Ministry of Labour for work permit once teachers gather necessary documents.
RECRUITMENT: EL Gazette, internet or via recruitment partners www.tefl.org.uk. References checked by phone.
CONTACT: Denise Lord or Lynne Longley, Co-Directors.

SOUTH AFRICA

INTERLINK SCHOOL OF LANGUAGES
Suite 501, The Equinox, 154 Main Road, Sea Point, Cape Town 8005
📞 +27 21 439 9834
✉ info@interlink.co.za
🖥 www.interlink.co.za

Member of EduSA, the national association of quality English language centres in South Africa (www.edusouthafrica.com).
NUMBER OF TEACHERS: 10.
PREFERENCE OF NATIONALITY: South Africans preferred but will consider native English speakers with permission to work in South Africa.
QUALIFICATIONS: Recognised TEFL qualification, CELTA preferred.
CONDITIONS OF EMPLOYMENT: Full-time contracts last for 1 year. Part-time contracts reviewed weekly according to demand.

SALARY: Varies according to experience and qualifications. Part-time salary 70 rand per hour.
RECRUITMENT: Interview required.
CONTACT: Luanne McCallum, Manager.

TANZANIA

INDIGENOUS EDUCATION FOUNDATION OF TANZANIA
PO Box 54, Monduli, Arusha Region, Tanzania
US address: PO Box 300067, Jamaica Plain, MA 02130
📞 +1 617 390 8752
✉ volunteer@ieftz.org or info@ieftz.org
🖥 www.ieftz.org

Non-profit, community-collaborative organisation that provides affordable educational opportunities to an under-served population of youth in rural Tanzania.
NUMBER OF TEACHERS: 10 volunteers of whom 1–3 are English teachers for Orkeeswa School.
PREFERENCE OF NATIONALITY: All native speakers.
QUALIFICATIONS: Minimum BA and ESL qualification. Preferably with classroom ESL teaching experience, and an understanding of the challenges of teaching to an exam-driven curriculum while trying to broaden the students' skills. Ideally certified English teachers with experience teaching EFL. Average age is 27.
CONDITIONS OF EMPLOYMENT: Minimum 1-year commitment if teaching forms 1–6. 3–4 months for English Immersion Programme from the end of August to December. School hours are 7.30am–5.30pm with some Saturday classes.
SALARY: None for volunteers. A living stipend is available for volunteers who commit to a full year.
FACILITIES/SUPPORT: Shared housing with basic utilities/amenities is provided for all volunteers. Orientation provided on arrival. Volunteer covers other expenses, including return airfare to Tanzania, visa fees $200 for CTA (Conducting a Temporary Assignment) visa that covers less than 2 months, $1,000 for a resident permit if staying more than 3 months. Basic living expenses (food, travel, etc).

RECRUITMENT: Online. Interview and orientation with US Volunteer Coordinator via email/Skype/phone.

CONTACT: Lisa Heinert, US Volunteer Coordinator.

SERIAN UK
PO Box 19, Monduli
charley.nussey@gmail.com
www.serianuk.org.uk

Serian means 'peace' in Kimaasai.

NUMBER OF TEACHERS: 15–20 teaching assistants and qualified teachers in ESL and other subjects placed at Serian UK, Noonkodin Secondary School, in the rural Maasai village of Eluwai.

PREFERENCE OF NATIONALITY: All nationalities accepted. Non-native speakers of English should have IELTS 6.5 or above.

QUALIFICATIONS: Volunteers who want to be considered as independent class teachers of English should have the CELTA, TEFL or similar. Classroom assistants who work alongside a qualified Tanzanian teacher should ideally have completed a minimum of 1 year of undergraduate-level study in English, although school leavers with strong motivation and above-average qualifications will also be considered. Previous teaching experience in a school is strongly preferred, even if it is no more than a 2-week work experience placement. Maths and science teachers also needed.

CONDITIONS OF EMPLOYMENT: 2–3 months recommended for short-term volunteers though arrangements are flexible. Ideally 6–12 months from January or July for qualified teachers.

SALARY: Volunteers are asked to cover their living costs, $40–$50 per week, and are encouraged to carry out additional fundraising for the project.

FACILITIES/SUPPORT: Volunteers stay in a staff house at the school. Volunteers can also take up (at reduced rates) a range of additional activities such as walking tours, homestays in traditional Maasai boma or Swahili tuition.

RECRUITMENT: Applications can be made online. Pre-departure interview desirable.

CONTACT: Ms Charley Nussey, International Volunteer Co-ordinator (charley.nussey@gmail.com).

UGANDA

SOFT POWER EDUCATION (SPE)
UK: 55 Guildhall St, Bury St Edmunds, Suffolk IP33 1QF
Uganda: PO Box 1493, Jinja
+256 774 162541
volunteering@softpowereducation.com or info@softpowereducation.com
www.softpowereducation.com

British-registered non-religious charity improving quality of life through education. Among numerous other projects, SPE offers TEFL courses for men and women in the community.

NUMBER OF TEACHERS: 1 or 2 at a time based at the Amagezi Education Centre. Female teachers needed to work with women in Kyabirwa community near Bujagali Falls, Jinja.

QUALIFICATIONS: TEFL qualification and some experience preferable but not essential. Creativity and ability to work independently using one's own initiative essential.

CONDITIONS OF EMPLOYMENT: Minimum 3 months.

SALARY: None. Volunteers must cover their own living and travel expenses as well as a donation to the charity. Recommended amount is £75 a week.

FACILITIES/SUPPORT: Camping, dorms, private bandas or living within the local community. Guest houses in Jinja are also an option, but they are located some distance away from the Amagezi Education Centre, so travel costs would be higher.

CONTACT: Sharon Webb, Country Manager (sharon@softpowereducation.com).

ASIA

Although the English language is not a universal passport to employment, it can certainly be put to good use in many Asian countries where the demand for English teachers is substantial, even extraordinary as is the case with Korea and China, which have been described as 'black holes' for EFL teachers.

Conditions and remuneration differ wildly between industrialised countries, such as Japan, Korea and Singapore, with their western-style economies, and developing countries, such as Nepal and Cambodia, where both wages and the standard of living are lower. Thailand and Vietnam are in between. China combines rapidly industrialised cities with vast stretches of rural backwaters. A concerted job hunt in Asia will almost always turn up possibilities, and sometimes the difficulty comes in choosing among them. **Ross McKay** from Glasgow writes of his job hunt:

> *I was 50 and fed up for various reasons. So I wrote to about 500 institutions all over South-East Asia. Whilst waiting for replies I did a distance TESOL course and College of Further Education teaching certificate. I got three offers, one in Hanoi, one in Bangkok and I chose Jakarta as I knew nothing about Indonesia. My colleagues come from all over the English-speaking world and often become great pals. But there are some head-cases. I guess one has to be a little crazy to live this life, and a few people crack up. The great thing about life in Indonesia is that every morning you wake up and have no idea what the heck is going to happen next.*

The powerhouse economies of South-East Asia – Indonesia, Thailand, Malaysia, Singapore, Philippines and Vietnam – together with Brunei, Burma, Cambodia and Laos, are aiming to form the Asean Economic Community (AEC). The appointed common language for AEC is English, so the drive to raise linguistic competence in the region will only become more intense over the coming years.

In contrast to Thailand, Vietnam and Indonesia, with their strong demand for native English-speaker teachers, other countries between Pakistan and the Philippines (with a few exceptions) are not easy places in which to find paid work as an English teacher. The largest growth area has been in Cambodia, Vietnam and Laos, where a number of language schools employ native English-speaker teachers who can be paid a decent wage . . . or peanuts (or something in between).

Recruitment organisations such as Reach To Teach and Saxoncourt are active in the region. Saxoncourt recruits for the group of Shane English Schools in Japan, China, Taiwan, Vietnam, Korea (the most recent country to join the franchise) and (possibly in the future) Malaysia. The education broker Teach to Travel (see entry) fills vacancies in several Asian countries. TEFLOne is a free placement service for native English-speaking EFL teachers with a degree and a 120-hour certificate qualification in TEFL for reputable schools throughout China, as well as Taiwan, Japan, Vietnam and Indonesia. The package on offer normally consists of a monthly salary, end-of-contract bonus, paid return flight, free accommodation and welfare support (www.teflone.com). An alternative online recruiter for China, Hong Kong, Korea, Taiwan, Japan and Thailand is www.findworkabroad.com, based in Guangzhou, China. Another agency with its headquarters in Asia is Brightspark Teachers (www.brightsparkteachers.co.uk) run by an expat living in Kuala Lumpur. They advertise positions as English-speaking assistants for candidates with no formal qualifications.

In North America dozens of recruiters and agencies mediate between language schools in Asia and job-seekers, for example Footprints (www.footprintsrecruiting.com) and Reach to Teach (see entry below).

For American citizens and residents, both Princeton and Stanford universities have affiliated programmes that operate in various Asian countries and include TEFL teaching. Stanford's VIA (formerly Volunteers in Asia) has been providing international exchange opportunities since 1963 and continues to send volunteer English teachers to China, Vietnam, Indonesia, Thailand and Myanmar on short-term (summer) and longer-term (1 or 2-year) assignments. All programmes are open to college students or graduates over 18. Applications are due at the end of November or mid-January and the participation fee is from $1200–$1800 plus $850–$1900 for insurance. Further information is available online at www.viaprograms.org.

For information about the Princeton-affiliated programme, contact Princeton in Asia, 194 Nassau Street, Suite 212, Princeton, NJ 08542 (+1 609 258 3657; pia@princeton.edu; http://piaweb.princeton.edu). It currently places about 130 full-year fellows in 20 Asian countries. Applications, available on its website, are welcomed from recent college graduates from all universities. Suitable candidates will be invited to a compulsory interview in January or February in several US locations and a weekend's orientation in mid-May, on the Princeton campus. Teachers on the programme must also complete a TEFL training weekend in Princeton in April.

Exposure to the radically different cultures of Asia is fascinating. **Allison Williams** was writing from Korea about her exhilarating experiences and frustrations, but this could apply equally to much of Asia:

> *Among the highlights have been meeting and getting to know such awesome little people, by which I mean the kids! Some things here are so alien but then with other things you really do see that we are all pretty much the same. I've had quite a few of those whoa-man-I-live-in-Asia moments. For example you will have an old woman squatting on the road selling garlic right next to a couple that look like they just stepped out of Vogue magazine. I love eating all sorts of weird and wonderful things. Among the lowlights have been clothes that don't fit and being told you are a big size, lol. You get tired of not being able to do anything for yourself, like banking or simple things like exchanging a product. Of course it gets better the longer you stay. Accepting the hierarchy and educational views has sometimes been tricky, and it has been frustrating not being allowed to do more teaching on my own. All in all I am really happy with the whole experience, but after two years I'll be ready to go home. I'm excited about clothes that fit, being able to understand everything and eating cheese!*

One issue that rears its ugly head from time to time is discrimination on the grounds of age and also race. For marketing reasons in Asia, employers prefer their employees to look younger than 30, and many applicants have complained that too much emphasis is placed on the photograph requested at the time of application. Racism is also a potential problem, as highlighted by a contributor to a *Guardian* TEFL forum:

> *Myself and my girlfriend, both in our mid-20s and university graduates with good work experience, have been looking into TEFL in Asia for over a year now. We've gotten so far as getting interviews, but on several occasions we've been denied a job as my girlfriend is mixed race (Chinese/British). This hasn't been the explicit reason for not getting a job, of course, but it's been heavily implied. For instance, my girlfriend was asked whether she could dye her hair blonde in order to be considered for a job in a school in Hong Kong.*
>
> *I think that racism in Asia is hushed over by many, especially recruiting companies and advisors. It's a serious issue and one that affects many people applying for work in China, Hong Kong, Korea and Japan especially. If you don't 'look' western, you'll struggle significantly compared to your Caucasian brethren.*

LIST OF EMPLOYERS

ESLSTARTER LIMITED
Winnington Hall, Winnington, Northwich, Cheshire CW8 4DU, UK

☏ +44 161 818 2191
✉ info@eslstarter.com
🖥 www.eslstarter.com

NUMBER OF TEACHERS: Up to 100 interns, volunteers and teachers per country for China, India, Korea, Nepal, Thailand and Vietnam (among others outside Asia).

PREFERENCE OF NATIONALITY: All native English-speaking countries. Also, applicants with near native English fluency are welcome to apply.

QUALIFICATIONS: ESLstarter looks for applicants with a passion for teaching. Bachelor's degree is not always necessary.

CONDITIONS OF EMPLOYMENT: 4–12 months. Average 22 hours per week.

SALARY: Mainly volunteer or intern positions, e.g. Teach & Learn China pays a stipend of RMB2,000 rather than a regular teaching wage up to £1,300 monthly. Programme fees are usually charged, depending on country and whether the programme is government-sponsored or not.

FACILITIES/SUPPORT: ESLstarter assists applicants with the visa process. Either the accommodation is provided or assistance can be arranged to help teachers find accommodation on arrival.

RECRUITMENT: Application documents and Skype interview.

CONTACT: Philip Negus, Recruitment Director.

REACH TO TEACH

1606 80th Avenue, Algona, IA 50511, USA.
Also #319 Minsheng Road, Taipei, Taiwan

- +1 201 467 4612 (USA)/0203 286 9794 (UK & Ireland)/2 8011 4516 (Australia)
- info@ReachToTeachRecruiting.com
- www.ReachToTeachRecruiting.com

Reach To Teach is one of the largest human resource companies for teachers in Asia and all services are free to teachers. See separate entries in chapters on China, Korea, Taiwan and Thailand.

NUMBER OF TEACHERS: 500+ per year to work in Taiwan, Korea, China, Vietnam and a few countries outside Asia.

PREFERENCE OF NATIONALITY: In order to qualify for permission to work in Asia, you must be from one of the following countries: USA, Canada, UK, Ireland, South Africa, Australia or New Zealand.

QUALIFICATIONS: A positive, enthusiastic, dedicated and flexible attitude is the most important qualification. Most positions in Asia require a 120-hour TEFL certification. Teaching experience is a plus.

CONDITIONS OF EMPLOYMENT: All job placements are full-time positions and for 1 full year. Teaching schedules vary but are generally either mornings and afternoons or afternoons and evenings.

SALARY: Competitive packages that reflect the local market rate. Ability to save depends on lifestyle. Some job placements (especially Korea and China) offer free flights, free accommodation and bonuses.

FACILITIES/SUPPORT: Recruiter offers personal attention to every job placement. Through a partnership with a TEFL course provider, Reach To Teach can assist teachers in getting course discounts. All placements come with guidance on visas, flights, accommodation, etc and workplace teacher training. All teachers have the option of continued support throughout year-long placement.

RECRUITMENT: Applications submitted via Reach To Teach website. Interviews conducted over Skype, by phone or occasionally in person.

CONTACT: Carrie Kellenberger, Co-President (Carrie@Reach ToTeachRecruiting.com).

TEACH TO TRAVEL LTD

Room 4, Third Floor, Duru House, 101 Commercial Road, London E1 1RD, UK

- +44 20 7096 1214
- hr@teachtotravel.co.uk
- www.teachtotravel.co.uk

NUMBER OF TEACHERS: Roughly 100 positions in Hong Kong (see entry), Thailand, China and South Korea.

PREFERENCE OF NATIONALITY: Must be native English speaker.

QUALIFICATIONS: University degree and teaching qualification, such as TEFL/TESOL/CELTA/PGCE, required. Must be under the age of 40.

CONDITIONS OF EMPLOYMENT: Most jobs last 10 months, requiring 20–25 contact hours per week, 40 hours on site.

SALARY: £600–£1,300 per month (net).

FACILITIES/SUPPORT: Free accommodation in Hong Kong and Korea.

RECRUITMENT: Skype interview.

CONTACT: Geoffrey Thomas, Director (geoff.thomas@teach totravel.co.uk).

TEFL HEAVEN

Experience Teaching Abroad Ltd, Dr Fox's Building, Knightstone Causeway, Weston super Mare, North Somerset BS22 9DX, UK

- +44 20 8133 3885
- teachabroad@teflheaven.com
- www.teflheaven.com

NUMBER OF TEACHERS: Around 250 English teachers to be placed in Thailand, Vietnam and China as interns (among other countries).

PREFERENCE OF NATIONALITY: Teachers need to be of a native English speaking origin.

QUALIFICATIONS: TEFLHeaven programmes normally include an in-country TEFL qualification followed by a guaranteed job. For all paid teaching positions a Bachelor's degree is a requirement.

CONDITIONS OF EMPLOYMENT: 6-12 months is standard. 25-32 hours a week (with exceptions).

SALARY: Varies dramatically between countries and according to experience/qualifications.

FACILITIES/SUPPORT: If accommodation is not supplied as part of the package, assistance will be given in finding accommodation.

RECRUITMENT: Via direct marketing with universities, advertising online and word of mouth. Skype interviews mainly.

CONTACT: Ben Hesketh, Recruiter/Marketer.

CHINA

Recruitment of English teachers for the People's Republic of China is absolutely booming in the private sector. People inside and outside China keep wondering when this romance with the language will fade. However, jobs are not as easy to pluck from the vine because the authorities have begun to tighten up the visa regulations, making it far more difficult to pick up a teaching job on the spot and to sort out the paperwork later. This means that it is preferable to arrange a job in advance that allows you the chance to obtain the appropriate working visa before arrival. Fortunately the internet is plastered with any number of adverts from recruiters and language institutes. Cyberspace is a-buzz with new companies and organisations recruiting thousands of native English speakers to teach at schools and academic institutions around the country, in companies and in private language institutes. It is still the case that more positions are notified than there are foreign applicants to fill them, so the demand is huge.

English is compulsory for school pupils from the age of nine. Although optional, English is now even taught from kindergarten. A foreign language is a compulsory component of the entrance exam (*gaokao*) to enter higher education; of the more than nine million candidates who take this exam, the vast majority choose English over Russian, French, Spanish or Japanese. Unfortunately the *gaokao* does not test real acquisition of language, but requires the memorisation of vocabulary lists and grammar structures. The majority of candidates are not taught communicative English by native speakers, though this is slowly changing. Just as in Taiwan, Korea and Japan, the emerging middle class of China aspires to send its children for private tuition in English and in some cases 'real English' instead of exam English. Many students and teachers are very keen to improve their English to Cambridge Proficiency standard, in the hope of being accepted to study overseas. Competition can be cut-throat although children from the wealthiest families may be less inspired, knowing that they'll be going abroad eventually, whether their English is fluent or not. But most are eager to learn, even if the style of rote learning to which they have become accustomed can be difficult for foreign teachers to adopt.

English is ubiquitous. Many street and shop signs in the capital and other major cities are written in English as well as Chinese, though most Beijing citizens, especially the older generation, can say little more than 'What-a is-a your name-a?' It is easy to forget that, amid the well-reported stories of sprawling urban metropolises rising almost in the night, nearly half of China's population still lives in the countryside. **Sam Meekings** was surprised to discover that although he headed off to Beijing every other weekend to stock up on western foods and see the sights, most of his students had never left the small city of Hengshui; only 15 years previously it had all been farmland.

Bill Lehane was pleasantly surprised by his encounter with China:

> *I spent six months with my partner teaching teenagers at a school in Lishui City in Zhejiang province. As a journalist by trade with no prior interest in China or indeed teaching experience, I had perhaps an even steeper learning curve than most expat teachers in the Middle Kingdom. Undoubtedly switching the mild climes of Ireland for the hot and humid surrounds of provincial China is a big change, but I found the hours were good and the pay quite adequate as long as you stayed in-country. I would say the worst aspect for me was having to give a blood sample when I arrived, and the best was the ubiquitous, delicious street food. As a writer accustomed to hearing only bad things about communist China and its leaders in Beijing, I have to say I experienced a very different place on the ground. People are happy and friendly and have an interesting, varied and ancient culture.*

PROSPECTS FOR TEACHERS

'With just a university degree and a little determination anyone can find an opportunity to challenge themselves somewhere in twenty-first century China,' writes **Sam Meekings**, who taught in a state-run normal college (ie teacher training institute) before accepting an editing job with Oxford University Press in Shanghai (and is now a published novelist). However, the better schools have recently started to become more stringent in their recruiting methods and foreigners cannot simply walk into highly lucrative jobs in the same way that they did in the early days. Nevertheless, there are still schools in rural areas so desperate that they will employ anyone simply to have a 'token foreigner' and hence enhance their status.

Teachers are classified as foreign experts (FEs) who must have at the very least a university degree and, in some places like Shanghai where jobs are competitive, a master's degree in a relevant area (English, Linguistics, TEFL/TESOL, etc) and some teaching experience at the tertiary level. Teachers must have their dossier assessed by the State Administration of Foreign Experts Affairs (SAFEA) before a Foreign Expert licence will be granted. These days they want to see a TEFL Certificate and two years' teaching experience. China is the biggest market in the world right now for IELTS tests, so it is a good place to get trained and start testing. Once you are an official IELTS examiner, you can examine anywhere in the world, but have to keep your certification up to date by examining at least once every three months.

Most foreigners teach oral English rather than grammar, which means that younger candidates without qualifications may also find positions in Chinese schools but without FE status and with correspondingly lower wages or even as paying volunteers. This includes students on exchange schemes such as those run by gap-year organisations like Lattitude Global Volunteering, BUNAC (www.bunac.org/uk/volunteer/china/teach-english) and Project Trust, who are usually placed in primary schools, middle schools (public secondary schools, often boarding schools) or vocational schools. The more remote or deprived the area or the more hostile the climate, the easier it will be to find a job. But there are also plenty of vacancies in comfortable cities such as Kunming and Dalian, fewer in Shanghai and Beijing.

Even ordinary secondary schools employ native English speakers; applications can be made through provincial education bureaux. Writing direct to the Foreign Affairs Office (*waiban*) of institutes of higher learning may lead to a job offer. Chinese institutes seem to attach more weight to the letter of application than to the curriculum vitae, but the CV should still be sent and should emphasise any work or experience in education. Also enclose a photo, a photocopy of the first page of your passport, a copy of any education certificates and two references. Jessie Levene notes that schools seem to prefer female teachers, particularly for younger students, and as a result, she was given more and more classes, despite an already full timetable.

It is becoming increasingly common for schools to offer a job to an applicant but not guarantee employment until they arrive at the school. This is the result of foreigners having abused the system in the past, accepting numerous jobs in order to keep their options open. Many schools have also introduced a probationary period of between two and 10 weeks. Although this may sound a bit daunting if you have already paid for flight tickets, it can work in the applicant's favour, as it allows time to ensure that the school is suitable for you. It is always best, wherever possible, to visit a school before signing a contract and talk to other FEs, to make sure that the school is everything it says it is. After teaching in China and realising how great the demand for native speaker teachers is, **Caryn-Ann Langley** from Scotland set up a teacher placement agency. Her emphatic advice is:

> *Speak to other foreigners working at the schools! We cannot express how important this part of the application process is; it will save so much trouble if you can just speak with a foreigner. If there are none, ask to see the school's licence to employ FEs. If they won't show this, stay away because they probably don't have one. If the school is checked and you are found working, you may be deported for working illegally.*

FINDING A JOB

With the explosion in opportunities, the job hunt is more complex and varied than it was a few years ago, when most teacher applications were for state institutes and had to go through the Chinese Education Association for International Exchange (CEAIE) or one of its provincial offices. Nowadays, CEAIE leaves recruitment to online companies and private recruiters, foundations or China-linked companies eager to sign up native English speakers (with or without relevant experience) for an academic year.

Some of the tried and tested old schemes are still in place and still work. The British Council's Language Assistants Programme, in cooperation with the Chinese education authorities, places graduates in schools across China. TEFL training is provided on a two-week course in Beijing which is paid for by the British Council. Participants receive free accommodation and utilities and a flight back to the UK. Teaching experience and/or qualifications are not necessary. Details of the application procedure can be seen at www.britishcouncil.org/language-assistants/become/china. The British Council accepts applications up until the end of January. Applications are screened and then candidates are invited to attend an assessment day in February/March for positions starting in mid-August. The minimum requirement is a university degree, though a TEFL certificate and/or teaching experience, preferably abroad, improve your chances of acceptance. Opportunities are available in a large variety of cities throughout mainland China, though initial training and orientation take place in Beijing before teaching starts on 1 September. Wages are not brilliant on this programme, ie RMB3,000–4,500 (net) per month, but all teachers are provided with free accommodation. The required medical check in the UK must be paid for by the candidate as well as an International Child Protection Certificate which costs £60.

Most jobs begin with the school year in August/September and are advertised in the months beforehand. Schools hire teachers for the whole year, though one-term contracts are sometimes available. A couple of recruiters in the UK to try are Teaching English in China based in cardiff (www.teic.co.uk) and Flying Cows in Nottingham (www.flying-cows.com/teaching-china).

Any web search or a trawl of the major ELT job websites is bound to turn up plenty of contacts, such as www.jobchina.net, http://jobs.echinacities.com and www.cathayteacher.com, which have long lists of jobs, all dated and described in detail. Among the dozens of specialist online recruiters are Find Work Abroad (www.findworkabroad.com), based in Guangzhou in Southern China (see entry), which places many teachers in the cities of Southern China such as Zhuhai, Foshan and Shenzhen as well as Guangzhou. Candidates who do not have a BA in the field of education or a TEFL certificate are obliged to take an online TEFL course (£157). Other places to look on the web include www.networkesl.com, www.clickchn.com for jobs in public schools and universities, www.xhgjedu.com (New Time International Teaching Agency), LoveTEFL (www.lovetefl.com/jobs-in-china), www.teflpanda.com and Gold Star TEFL Recruitment (www.GoldStarTeachers.com), which advertises salaries at the high end, ie RMB6,000–17,000 per month. The classified sections of expat websites such as www.foreignercn.com, www.gochengdoo.com and www.thebeijinger.com/classifieds/english-teaching are also worth searching.

Tefl.chinajob.com offers a regular seven-day training course in Beijing and Guangzhou to graduates which enables them to claim FE status.

Demand for qualified teachers is so high that any who advertise their services online may get an instantaneous response, as happened to a teacher writing from Shanghai:

> *I put my CV on TEFL.com and the DoS of EF Academic Partnerships contacted me by email enquiring about my current location and availability. I replied that I was at home and currently seeking employment and asked for some more information. He promptly replied and we arranged an interview for the following Saturday morning.*

PRIVATE LANGUAGE TRAINING

An ever-growing number of private companies operate in the fields of media and education, especially English-language kindergartens and tutorial centres. **Jane Pennington**, who taught for four years in China, carried out a little research and estimates that there were about 100 private language companies in Kunming, only about 15%–20% of which were officially licensed. The ratio is better nowadays but there are still plenty of cowboy outfits. Such institutes are not authorised to invite foreign teachers, yet some persuade native English-speaking teachers to work for them without admitting that it is illegal. Like private schools everywhere, a number are run by unscrupulous entrepreneurs interested only in profit. Similarly there are independent recruiters and agencies that advertise vast numbers of vacancies and try to slot people in as quickly as possible so that they can collect their commission. If considering working in the private sector, try to find out the degree of professionalism of the company that has expressed interest in hiring you, and talk to other foreigners working there, especially with regard to payment.

International ELT organisations such as EF English First or Longman Schools (see entries) are expanding quickly and usually offer a solid introduction to life as an English teacher in China. Shane English School has more than 40 schools across China which recruit directly or via the Shanghai headquarters (recruitment@ shane.com.cn) or Saxoncourt Recruitment in London. Placement of teachers by Language Link (www. languagelink.com.cn) is concentrated on the Beijing area. The Taiwanese company Kidcastle specialises in teaching very young children; already it has 200 schools in mainland China, with new schools opening all the time. Recruitment of teachers is done centrally at http://ft.kidcastle.cn.

The internet is a prolific source of possibilities and expanding all the time. According to a leading news agency, China has more people online than the USA. Any web search or a trawl of the major ELT job sites is bound to turn up plenty of contacts. The long established www.eslcafe.com/jobs/china listed 16 new employers on the day this is being written (26th June 2015). In the private sector, some large companies (eg hotel chains) have their own language-training facilities for staff, especially if they are joint ventures with western companies. Most recruitment of teachers by business and industry takes place locally, since they do not offer accommodation.

PLACEMENT AGENCIES AND ORGANISATIONS

Many companies recruit teachers from abroad for China. Whereas many merely make the initial match, others have an ongoing relationship with their teachers. Australian **Shane Johnson** has been teaching all over China for the past seven years, and prefers to be hired through an agency, in his case Buckland International Education Group (see entry below), because they can sort out any problems that arise:

I have had a very smooth seven years and the only real problem was when I arrived at my current school to find that they wanted me to share an apartment and teach only Grades 1 and 2, even though they had assured me I would have my own apartment and my timetable would be Grades 3–6. It took only one phone call to my boss at Buckland before a second apartment was found and I had older classes added to my timetable. This is the reason I sign with a recruiter and not directly with a school. I have a contract with my boss/recruiter and they have a contract with each school.

A number of North American organisations involved in teacher placements in China have entries in the listings at the end of this chapter, including the Colorado China Council, Appalachians Abroad, East-West Education and the US-China Educational Exchange. WorldTeach (www.worldteach.org) is a non-profit organisation that sends volunteers to teach in secondary schools in Hunan province for a full academic year (August to July). Volunteers pay $500 for the year.

CONDITIONS OF WORK

With the rise of the free market many reward packages are now open to negotiation. Higher degrees or diplomas attract higher salaries, so if you have earned qualifications beyond a BA, take along the certificates to prove it. Employers generally offer to reimburse airfares or shipping costs. The general monthly salary range for most ordinary native English-speaker teachers should start from RMB5,000 ($800/£500) but can rise in the private sector (especially in sophisticated Shanghai and Beijing) to well over RMB15,000. Expect to pay a hefty fee if you are transferring renminbi to a bank account at home. Note that the renminbi is a non-convertible currency and foreigners have to negotiate a clause in their contract to be able to convert a certain percentage (up to a maximum 70%). When **Bradwell Jackson** arrived in Tangshan, he assumed that since so many foreigners are working in China as English teachers, it must surely be straightforward to deposit earnings in a bank at home (in the USA in his case). After some research he discovered that the Bank of China will make deposits into US bank accounts, albeit for a significant fee, especially if you don't have an account with them. An experienced teacher, Megan Eaves, wrote a book full of practical tips and insights specifically aimed at teachers, *This Is China: A Guidebook for Teachers, Backpackers and other Lunatics* (now a little out of date).

With the explosion of the English teaching market, dodgy operators have entered the fray and the number of complaints from teachers who feel badly exploited has escalated alarmingly. A good source of information on how to avoid this may be found at www.chinaforeignteachersunion.org, which calls itself a peer-to-peer blog site for foreign teachers and expats in China. It publishes a blacklist of poor employers and more usefully, a list of '*12 clauses every foreign teacher should insert into their contract before signing it*'. These mainly protect teachers from having to pay for things such as the invitation letter, school supplies or excursions, travel to off-premises lessons, and so on. All the big chains like EF (see entry), Disney (http://disneyenglish.disneycareers.com) and Wall Street Institutes (www.wsi.com.cn/career/en/index.aspx) have attracted complaints in the past, though problems are usually particular to a single branch rather than to the whole company so beware of attaching too much importance to negative feedback online.

The experience of teachers in the big cities is very different from that of native speakers who go to more obscure locations. Be aware that what are called cities in China are more like counties or small states, so even when you think you are going to a big city, you could in fact end up in a small town with few recreational outlets, as happened to **Dan Casaletto**:

> I was in a much smaller town than I had expected where there was no expat community. My fellow teachers were a bunch of Chinese men and women with whom I could not communicate. The few teachers who could speak English were friendly, but busy with their own lives. There was one other foreign teacher from the West and although we had little in common it was great to have a conversation in English and someone to commiserate with. The presence of a university nearby did give me a chance to make friends with English-speaking Chinese college students.
>
> I was living in a small town, where some of the more repugnant features of Chinese culture are brought to the fore (spitting, including indoors, children defecating on the sidewalk, yelling in confined quarters and market sellers charging grossly inflated prices for inferior merchandise). The school curfew was terrible, school gates were locked from 11.30pm to 6am. If I could do it again I would have demanded to be placed in a larger city.

Although higher wages can be earned in the big cities of Beijing, Guangzhou, Shanghai, the megalopolis of Chongqing and in the Special Economic Zones such as Hainan, life in Chinese cities has many drawbacks in terms of crowds and pollution. Kate Devlin, who taught at the China Agriculture University in Beijing, found the city 'polluted, very ugly and soulless'. For quality of life, South-Western China is probably better than much of the east. Yunnan province has a particularly congenial climate. This area is also reputed to be less money oriented than the east coast cities, which may have the drawback that it may be more difficult to find paying private students.

CARYN-ANN LANGLEY

Caryn-Ann Langley traded Scotland for China and wrote enthusiastically in June 2014 about her situation:

I was in a bit of a pickle about what I wanted to do next, so when a school friend posted on Facebook about teaching jobs in China, I decided to give this a go. In my first job in a government school. I was living in a hotel with my friend and two other girls. It got a bit much – whenever you walked out of your bedroom in your Spongebob PJs you'd come face-to-face with a half naked old Chinese man in the corridor. You can't move to a flat without the permission of the company you work for. After a bit of a breakdown in communication with that employer, I went onto a website called echinacities.com and found my new job here in Hainan, a tropical island of China, where I hope to stay for a long time. When I came down to Hainan I was apartment shopping within two days, and moved into this little place on the third. Such a difference it makes.

While most small cities in China are full of people who have never travelled far from their homes, Hainan is mostly populated by mainland Chinese people who have come for a more relaxed lifestyle on a tropical island. There are many local Hainanese people as well from small villages dotting the island, which makes communication very fun.

I don't have any teaching qualifications and neither do my friends teaching in Guangzhou and Kuitun. Working conditions in my kindergarten are really good for me. It is a private school so parents pay a lot of money and everything is clean and modern. The kids are four years old and spoilt rotten but I love them all. As long as they learn their new words in English and have fun, their parents are happy, and so is the school.

Foreign teachers generally earn double what the Chinese English teachers get, which is plenty to save for travelling unless you spend it on a lot of luxuries. I only work four hours a day, so I get to do what I want in the afternoons, like go to the beach. I get at least four weeks summer holiday with lots of other holidays as well. I can say I am in love with China.

Outside the major eastern cities you can live on less than RMB2,000 a month if your accommodation is provided. On his gap year, **James Butcher** from Portsmouth paid to join a programme called Teach and Travel China (www.immerqi.com), and taught for five months at a language institute in Zhongshan on the Pearl River delta. He was paid RMB2,900 a month – far less than a university graduate – but was able to save quite a bit for travelling around since his accommodation was provided free and the cost of living was low. However, those living in the major eastern cities are more likely to spend RMB3,000–5,000 per month, depending on their lifestyle. One highly qualified teacher in Shanghai estimated the cost of living out of a salary of RMB10,500 per month: RMB2,000 for a flat (not shared), RMB500 to cover bills and RMB2,000–3,000 on food. Inflation has been creeping up in China so hanging out in expat bars and taking taxis has become more expensive. In Beijing, the automatic charge for a taxi is twice as much as it is in Tangshan (two hours east of the capital).

The three or four-week holiday over Chinese New Year should be paid, as should vacation periods in state schools if you are contracted to continue teaching after it. Companies in the private sector may not offer payment during enforced breaks from teaching. **Paul Carey** identified the sudden six-week break from working and earning with little notice given by the employer as one of the low points of his experience with EF English First in Shanghai, which was otherwise '*a worthwhile experience both personally and professionally*'. Many employers offer free internet access and some offer free Chinese lessons. **Shane Johnson** appreciates the large number of holidays:

The Chinese are one of the most festive people I have ever known and they celebrate each festival with a lot of food, beer and a public holiday. In addition to all the school and statutory holidays, traditional festivals are celebrated such as Tomb Sweeping Festival and the Dragon Boat Festival. China is such a wonderful country to live in and life really is an amazing journey.

While teaching in a suburb of Shanghai, **Marybeth Hao** noticed many Chinese parents were more than willing to pay native English-speaker tutors high fees to tutor their children outside school hours. For her, one of the main rewards of teaching in Shanghai was to experience a culture in the midst of such dramatic and hurried changes.

Foreign teachers can be expected to teach anything from 15 to 30+ hours a week. A load of 20 hours is typical, though this sounds lighter than it actually is because there are bound to be extra duties. Often there is a heavy load of marking, not to mention marketing. Teachers in the private sector are routinely asked to attend student recruitment events, for example to hand out flyers or to appear at drop-in evenings whose main purpose is to rope in new clients. Some teachers are expected to staff an 'English corner' or English club, or deliver a weekly lecture on western culture. In out-of-the-way places, you might find yourself playing the part of 'token foreigner' at the many banquets you will be invited to when you first arrive. For **Dan Casaletto** one of the high points of his time in China was dancing at a nightclub on his birthday while a crowd chanted 'foreigner' and 'beautiful' in Chinese. He was enough of a rarity for one club to give him free drinks for four months on account of being a foreigner. He was humbled and amazed at the generosity of many whom he encountered and befriended.

In cases where teachers are given a huge number of classes, the administration's main ambition is to maximise your exposure, which may have the effect of minimising your usefulness. On the whole **Michelle** enjoyed her time in China, but she thinks that foreign teachers should be given more advice on what is required of them before they start teaching. It is not unusual for the school to leave it up to the teachers to find out if any national exams are looming for which you should be helping the students to prepare. Hours of teaching are unpredictable and the teaching days can be very long. Students get up at 6am and work at night in supervised sessions. Michelle was asked to take classes at weekends, which left little time for travel. If you want to keep your weekends free for travel and relaxation, firmly decline teaching hours on Saturday and Sunday, and be aware that it is all too easy to over-commit yourself in the first few weeks. It should always be your choice to take on extra hours and when you do, you should be paid accordingly.

Sam Meekings describes how attendance at several Chinese banquets can lead to a succession of nasty hangovers:

Every foreigner in China quickly becomes familiar with baijiu, *a sharp, clear liquor with a cloying aftertaste, which is measured out into shot glasses in front of you at the start of a meal. Though beer is increasingly popular, no large event is complete without* baijiu. *At any large banquet, especially with officials or high-ranking teachers at the school or college, you will be encouraged to drink with them. Your glass will be topped up throughout the meal, and often many people will wish to toast you, meaning you must once again down your drink as a sign of mutual respect. This is why, by eight or nine in the evening, restaurants begin to clear out – many diners are too wasted to do anything but go home and sleep. It should be noted, however, that women are usually exempted from this custom, and though I would have liked to have been spared the attention (and the subsequent hangovers), my female colleagues were not impressed that they were simply expected to sit and slowly sip beer or Coca-Cola while all the men went through the intricate tradition of getting each other as drunk as possible. Similarly, while almost all the male teachers in the college were heavy smokers (one of the best gifts to present to someone is a box of cigarettes), women smoking were frowned upon. Though these attitudes cannot be found in big cosmopolitan cities, I am certain that they persist throughout the smaller towns that make up the bulk of this vast country.*

On the other hand, you may find your colleagues and bosses bend over backwards to help and support you, as **Bradwell Jackson** reported:

I was offered a job with Aston in China on the basis of a telephone interview and I am very happy with this. Aston is good to me, and my co-workers scramble to help me whenever I have even a mild matter that needs attention. For example, when I told them I was looking for a kung-fu school, they took this as a very important issue and had many long discussions-cum-negotiations with each other in order to come up with the best option for me. I think it might be hard to convince a westerner to come and stay in an out-of-the-way city like Tangshan.

Really, I'm living the life of Reilly here. I've got nothing to complain about. The school has given me a free apartment complete with cable TV, washing machine, toaster oven, microwave and refrigerator. Whenever I'm hungry, I just mosey on down to the street vendors and get some proper Chinese food for a friendly budget price. Who can ask for more?

THE STUDENTS

There are not many corners of China these days into which foreigners, whether teachers or travellers, have not penetrated, although in Hengshui, three hours south of Beijing, **Sam Meekings** was amazed at the reaction he received from people in the town, who would stop and gape at him as though they had seen 'dinosaurs or dragons'. **Yasmin Peiris**, based in Shenzhen, one of China's newest cities, agrees that the attitude towards teachers is generally favourable, even though there is a language barrier. She chose to ask her students for advice on where to go at weekends and what to do (a foot massage, a little shopping and sampling tempting varieties of Chinese food were some of the suggestions). In Beijing, **Kate Devlin** reckoned that the students in her university classes came from very wealthy families and were spoiled rotten: *'Out of a class of 20–25 students, maybe five or six kids would listen to my lecture. Students would openly sleep, read, watch movies on their laptop or mostly talk. They were required to be in class so they were, but nothing more.'*

Perhaps the younger age groups are preferable. The students that **James Butcher** taught were not quite as he expected:

I think our general expectations are that Chinese students will be well behaved and silent in class, but this is far from the truth! They can be a rowdy bunch. But with the right methods they can be controlled. The younger grades are very enthusiastic and pick up things quite fast. I found the Chinese students to have a very positive, energetic attitude. They are also hilarious to watch and I guarantee they will put a smile on your face every day. The older grades are generally good too. They don't want to be treated like children, once they trust you they will enjoy your lessons and always run to give you a hug when they see you! I taught kindergarten for a few sessions at the start of my contract and discovered that age group wasn't for me so they assigned another teacher to that class. I found the children hard to control and much too young to learn English really. I had to teach kindergarten after a long day at school and I just didn't have the energy at that point!

Bradwell Jackson identified another interesting new trend in modern-day China from his experiences of teaching in a small city:

There is another interesting phenomenon in China, which is the syndrome of the 'Little Emperor'. Chinese children are well behaved, but they were even better behaved 10 or 20 years ago. With the advent of the one-child policy, some interesting changes took place. It seems that with just one child in the house, and especially if it's a boy, the child is much more likely to be spoiled and accommodated. Any English teacher here will probably get his/her small share of little brats who just can't understand why they can't do what they want.

I agree with the premise that a teacher has to be a bossy boots in order to establish the discipline straight off the bat. I certainly did this, maybe even a bit too much, so that now the (naughty) kids are just a tad bit resistant sometimes. The parents, on the other hand, are deliriously happy with me. They specifically love the fact that I'm strict with the kids.

Slowly, newer pedagogical methods are being accepted by students and administrators alike, although most teachers are warned not to stray into dangerous territory in their lessons, like politics and sex. **Bradwell Jackson** identified the three forbidden 'T' topics: Tiananmen, Taiwan and Tibet. One recent teacher struggled with the contradictions: '*We're invited here to teach Western Culture, then instructed not to behave like westerners*'. However, it is impossible to generalise, because in one place, techniques that smack of innovation will be greeted with blank stares, while in another, there can be lively class discussions.

Bill Lehane from Ireland blogged while he was teaching in China (http://sillybilly.travellerspoint.com) and gave an amusing account of a less than triumphant lesson:

The assignment, on the face of it, should have been simple. Choose your favourite foreign country, write seven sentences about it and then read your work out to the class the following week. The results were, well, pretty bad. Many of them obviously hadn't bothered to do the homework at all, and were just bluffing their way through about two and a half sentences in the hope they would get away with it. And many couldn't even do that much: at least one stood up and said: 'USA. I like NBA. Thank you'. And promptly sat down. X is for fail, mister! The most popular country was Canada, but only because loads of students had found a stodgy piece about it in their English textbook. The result of this was that I must have heard the same spiel: 'My favourite country is Canada. It is north of the United States. It is the second largest country in the world. It has a population of only slightly over 30 million people' – about 40 or 50 times over the course of the week.

Out of the 350-odd students, a few, to be fair, were quite good. One girl gave a presentation on Switzerland that could have doubled as a Wikipedia entry. One boy said his favourite country was South Africa because it had lots of gold, and that when he found it he would be very rich. A few chose Ireland but seemed not to know what to say about it except to ply me with compliments. They all passed! Many more in the middle ground had perfectly acceptable mini-speeches. Even where they just regurgitated what I had said in my introduction, I felt that they had done their job for what was an Oral English assignment.

Culturally, the exercise was instructive, despite the flawed results. Boys liking basketball while girls liking romance (or clothes!) seemed to be the benchmark of Chinese teenagerdom. In the end, then, my first foray into assigning homework was a bit of a mixed bag. But addling, lazy assholes aside, it's mostly a pleasant job being a foreign teacher in China I reckon. You draw up a simple lesson on PowerPoint and just run with it for a week, improvising and fine-tuning as you go along. And once you're plugged in to it, the work goes by really quickly, leaving plenty of time for fun.

Jessie Levene, reaching for some colourful similes, identifies the low point of her first teaching job was feeling like a 'robot' and a 'teaching monkey'. It seems that you may have to work fairly hard to introduce modern teaching techniques into the classroom, as from a very early age Chinese children are taught in a very traditional style, as **Nina Capek** found while teaching in a primary school:

The teaching style does take a bit of getting used to. The children are used to learning by rote and the general ethos is: whatever the teacher says, we copy. Teaching 'my name is . . .' to 50 six-year-old children proved very entertaining as they all copied me and said 'my name is Nina'.

A teacher who started work at Shanghai Lixin University of Commerce last year was delighted with the standard of students:

Their attitude has been excellent on the whole. I have only a couple of disruptive students, but they all seem to be very motivated to learn English and realise how important it can be to their future careers. I know little of their real expectations other than most are concerned more with fluency than complexity or accuracy.

At university, students expect to pass, as it has been difficult for them to get in, while some have paid to get in or used connections (*guanxi*), which means they expect to sail through. Don't be surprised if just before exam time your students ply you with gifts, expensive meals and even offer money. Teachers who accept these offers may find that their students expect high marks even if they do not turn up to the exam!

SAM MEEKINGS

Sam Meekings, like some other teachers, found that there is a demand for any English provided it is clearly enunciated. Imaginative interactive teaching methods can work, as Sam discovered when he had to teach a 60-strong class of university students, whose homework left something to be desired.

Each week I was supposed to go through the excerpts from Shakespeare or Dickens in the book, despite the fact that close to half of the class could barely communicate with me in English at all. Though the impulse was strong to follow the example of the Chinese teachers and teach only to the brighter students and hope the others kept quiet at the back, I soon found that it was much more enjoyable to try and work the material into games and activities that everyone could take part in. This took time, however, since some students were so used to either being ignored or simply learning by rote and repetition that they were too shy to speak up? This is a problem I have noticed even teaching in private school in bigger cities - students are often so heavily criticised for mistakes in their normal classes that they lack the confidence to risk answering a question or attempting to join a game or discussion in case they do something wrong.

It sometimes feels as if you are not only in a different country but also in a different century. None of the students I taught had any real concept of exploring or questioning an idea. When I set some homework essays for my literature class or set debate topics for my English speaking class to try to engage with, I was invariably met with 60 identical responses. Students are taught to pass exams in China, to memorise the single correct response and then repeat it when instructed - there is no concept of coming up with your own ideas. My students were all adamant that there was always one right answer and that everything else could therefore be discounted as wrong. This meant most essays and debates were very, very short. Coupled with the fact that we were not allowed to fail any students (even if they could not write more than their name on the biannual exam papers we had to set), it quickly became clear that we would have to set aside most of our preconceptions about education. Yet when students do finally open up or try something new, there is no better feeling.

REGULATIONS

As mentioned at the beginning of this chapter, the bureaucratic free-for-all of a decade ago is over. Enforcement of the new regulations is not universal especially in small obscure towns, but the state regulates foreign teachers much more tightly than it once did. If possible, try to jump through the hoops to regularise your status to avoid the possibility of punitive fines and being cheated by your employer.

Before leaving home or even buying a flight ticket, you should have in hand a signed contract and a Z-visa. For the letter of invitation to be approved by the authorities, you will need to supply scanned copies of your university degree and TEFL certificate (which can be an online course) and a medical report from your home country. The contract and letter of invitation from your employer must be taken to the Chinese Consulate or Embassy to apply for a Z-visa (work visa). Until July 2013, some teachers stayed in China on an F-visa (Business visa); however, that is no longer permitted.

People arriving with a Z-visa have 30 days to convert this to a Foreign Expert Certificate and Residence Permit from the Division of Exit-Entry Administration of the Beijing Public Security Bureau. SAFEA (State Administration of Foreign Experts Affairs) is trying to streamline and improve the process of recruitment and also to make foreign experts eligible to join the social security insurance system. Many positions, especially those working with children, now require police clearance. Keep receipts of all the visa expenses you incur because your employer might reimburse them at a later stage.

Requirements are more stringent in the popular destinations of Shanghai, Beijing, etc where Foreign Experts are expected to have two years' post-university working experience and/or an MA. In neglected regions like north-west China, the threshold will be much lower. Everything has to be officially stamped. If you are found without the appropriate documents you will be harshly fined. For example, a teacher whose papers were mostly in order but hadn't got the resident's permit was fined RMB3,000 (more than half a month's wages). State institutes of education usually do everything by the book but you shouldn't expect the same of private language schools.

A couple of summers ago **John Ramage** answered an ad on Dave's ESL Café and describes the application process and red tape requirements in detail:

> *I sent the agent a statement of interest plus the picture page of my passport plus my CV plus a reference letter plus photos. The agent then set up an interview with the private university, Huanghe College of Science and Technology in Zhengzhou (Henan Province). They called me on my mobile during a lunch break in the office, in Scotland. This was amazingly quick and easy and I got the job fast. The agent then sent me a long contract in bits and pieces, which made it a bit awkward and finicky.*
>
> *Before going to China, there were unexpected hiccups. Hiccup no. 1 was the medical. This is required for people teaching in China. A form is downloadable from the Chinese website which the doctor must complete. My GP flatly told me it was not NHS work. The MASTA Travel Clinic did help and promptly scheduled a comprehensive medical, exactly what the Chinese authorities were looking for, but it cost me £380.*
>
> *The second hiccup was the elastic time taken over visa processes. The Chinese Consulate suggests one month, but it can take much longer. I gathered my documents and sent them to the Public Security Bureau in China for processing. The college sent me the invitation letter and work permit to take to the Consulate to apply for the visa. Getting the visa took one week after that. My documents spent far longer than expected in the PSB. The agent made it worse by promising it would be over in several weeks, so I left my UK job. As the weeks turned to months, I got really annoyed. The agency seemed to have a mañana, mañana attitude (although they were Australian). Surely he ought to have known! Fortunately I didn't book my flight until after I got my Z-Visa, otherwise I could have lost money.*

LEISURE TIME

Foreigners who teach in Beijing can lead a standard expatriate life if they want to, socialising at expat bars and clubs. Life in the provinces will be very different. You may still be one of the very few foreigners that the local people have ever seen and are bound to be the object of curious stares (which will be even more persistent if you happen to be a non-white person).

The main way of socialising in China is going to restaurants, because a large banquet shared by many people is only marginally more expensive than cooking for yourself. However, as most people go out to eat around 6pm–7pm, restaurants do not usually stay open later than 10pm. Students in state institutions can be restricted by a strict curfew, but when everything closes at 10pm, native English teachers start to realise why the students are not so bothered.

In smaller settlements, there may be no restaurants even to rival the Chinese take-away in your home town; but the locals will be far more interested in you and perhaps even teach you to cook your own Chinese food. If there are several foreigners, communal dining facilities (often segregated) will usually be provided. Glutinous rice, soy beans and cabbage are staples and fresh produce may be in short supply in winter. In Tangshan, **Bradwell Jackson** reports that he can have a 'killer meal' of dumplings, quick and right off the street, for only 2 yuan (yuan is an alternative word for renminbi). Learning Chinese is the ambition of many teachers and is a great asset, especially outside cosmopolitan areas. Take a good teach-yourself book and CD/tapes, since these are difficult to obtain outside Beijing and Shanghai. Mastering Chinese characters is a daunting business, though the grammar is straightforward. Others prefer to study Tai Chi, Wushu or other exotic martial arts.

Despite China's rapid 'westernisation' in economic terms, its cultural differences remain both a challenge and a delight. Be prepared for noise and air pollution even in small towns, though it is usually possible to escape into the countryside by bicycle or bus. **James Butcher** found that everyone heads for the park to relax. His local one in a quiet town in Guangdong province had amusement rides and boating lakes. When it got really hot, everyone headed to the mall, where the air conditioning was on full blast.

School and college vacations take place over Spring Festival in or around February, when the trains are very crowded and the weather is cold. Chinese people are renowned for making last-minute arrangements, so be prepared for the frustration of finding out at the last minute when your holidays will be, by which time the trains may be booked up and flying is much more expensive.

Some cities such as Kunming have a good expat community to which the Chinese cater with western-style cafés and restaurants. There are plenty of films to watch (all pirated) and a couple of galleries to visit. Much of the time you will be responsible for your own amusement, so take plenty of reading matter, including *Wild Swans*, an astonishing account of life in the Cultural Revolution or perhaps *Under Fishbone Clouds* by Sam Meekings, quoted in this chapter, an interweaving of 20th-century Chinese history and folklore. **Jessie Levene** found lots to do in Chengdu: '*learn Chinese, take photos, enjoy the amazing Sichuan food, hang out with friends, go to bars . . .*'.

Bradwell Jackson would urge anybody to do TEFL in China:

> *My first impressions were that of a fascinating country with a splendid culture, and I wasn't even in a well-known city. The people are organised and respectful, and the food, of course, is a revelation. If you have just a little bit of travel experience to a non-western country, you should be fine and have no worries at all. There is certainly no problem with safety. My school has been very good to me. You will find that most schools bend over backwards to get you here. All you need is a fair amount of teaching experience (and a college degree) and the whole new world of China awaits you.*

American **Ed Flok** was similarly enamoured of teaching in China and in his third year began teaching at the North China University of Technology in Beijing:

> *Don't believe all the negative articles you read about China. Everywhere I taught the people were awesome, and very polite, reaching out to make me their friend. I ate at personal dinner tables, swam in the Yellow Sea with students, ate at restaurants, went bike riding and socialised. The best of this experience was actually teaching the students English, and seeing how fast they learn. To this day I keep in contact with some of my first students. They really get attached to you as a role model, and want you as their friend.*

LIST OF EMPLOYERS

AMITY FOUNDATION
71 Han Kou Road, Nanjing, Jiangsu 210008
- +86 25 8326 0836
- amitynj@amity.org.cn
- www.amityfoundation.org

A Chinese Christian NGO.

NUMBER OF TEACHERS: 40–50 for Young Adult Teaching Programme and 1-month summer programme.

PREFERENCE OF NATIONALITY: None, but must be native English speaker or have a high level of proficiency in English and language teaching experience.

QUALIFICATIONS: Ages 18–28 for Young Volunteer Programme. Teaching experience, a knowledge of Chinese or of living in Asia are useful but not essential. A Christian faith commitment is generally required, however, the 'mission' expected is to serve rather than to proselytise.

CONDITIONS OF EMPLOYMENT: 1-year placement in underdeveloped parts of China. Also Summer English Programme (SEP) for volunteers to provide oral English training to Chinese middle and primary school teachers of English in rural and minority areas, for 4 weeks from early July.

SALARY: None. Volunteers pay participation fee to cover orientation, admin, etc, eg US$3,200 for one year.

FACILITIES/SUPPORT: Accommodation is usually provided in the form of an apartment on the school campus.

RECRUITMENT: Teachers are recruited primarily through church sending agencies, ie mission agencies of various denominations in a range of countries including the UK, Canada and the USA. See above website for contact details of these organisations. Interviews in person are expected and generally take place in the applicant's own country.

CONTACT: Helen Zhao, Educational Exchange Programs (helenzhao@amity.org.cn).

APPALACHIANS ABROAD TEACH IN CHINA PROGRAM
Center for International Programs, Marshall University, Old Main 320, Huntington, WV 25755, USA
- +1 304 696 6265
- gochina@marshall.edu
- www.marshall.edu/gochina

NUMBER OF TEACHERS: 40–60 annually.

PREFERENCE OF NATIONALITY: American, Canadian and British.

QUALIFICATIONS: Bachelor's degree is essential; accepted ages range from new college graduates to early retirees.

CONDITIONS OF EMPLOYMENT: 10-month teaching contract from 1 September. Teaching 15–18 hours per week, at public and private primary and secondary schools and in institutes of higher education, mainly in Shanghai but other areas as well.

SALARY: RMB8,000–15,000 per month, up to 1 month paid winter school break and full international airfare paid on completion of teaching contract.

FACILITIES/SUPPORT: Accommodation provided free by hosting school. 4-day orientation in Shanghai in late August before arriving at Chinese host school.

RECRUITMENT: Internet adverts and phone or Skype-video interviews. Application deadline 31 March/16 April. Application fee is $100/£100; job placement and administrative fee is $1,250 which includes 9 weeks of online China TEFL training and 4-day orientation in Shanghai and 1-year travel and medical insurance card.

CONTACT: Ms QingQing Zhao, Director of China Projects.

ASTON ENGLISH
Dalian Head Office, Room 2003, Yue Xiu Mansion, No. 82 Xin Kai Road, Xi Gang Dist. Dalian, Liaoning Province 116011
- +86 186 9869 9349
- www.astonrecruiting.com

NUMBER OF TEACHERS: 300+ annually for about 100 schools mostly in Sha'anxi and Shandong but in 22 provinces altogether.

PREFERENCE OF NATIONALITY: American, Canadian, British, Irish, Australian, New Zealander and South African.

QUALIFICATIONS: University degree (any subject) and a TEFL certificate and/or TEFL experience. Candidates without a TEFL background can take a 1-week course in China which meets this requirement, at a cost of $315, which is part refunded on renewal of contract.

CONDITIONS OF EMPLOYMENT: Contract lengths of 6–7 weeks in summer or winter. Term-time contracts are for 6 or 12 months starting September and March, 7.5 or 13.5 months starting mid-January and mid-July. 19, 23 or 28 hours per week contracts.

SALARY: RMB7,000 for 28 hours, RMB6,000 for 23 hours and RMB4,800 for 19 hours per week. Varying flight allowances of up to RMB7,000 (approximately $1,100) based on hours and length of contract. Small deductions made for income tax.

FACILITIES/SUPPORT: Contracts provide teachers with private bedrooms in a 2 or 3-bedroom Chinese-style apartment. Teachers must pay for utilities. Proper documents provided for work visas before arrival and residence permit after. Chinese lessons provided.

RECRUITMENT: Via all methods such as internet, phone and drop-ins. Phone/Skype but not in-person interviews required.

CONTACT: Recruiter contact details in China and UK provided on website.

BEIJING TEACH

8 St. Marks Place, Roslyn, NY 11577, USA

✆ +1 516 535 9236

✉ info@BeijingTeach.com

🖥 www.BeijingTeach.com

NUMBER OF TEACHERS: 200 per year for partner schools in Beijing and region.

PREFERENCE OF NATIONALITY: Native English-speaking teachers preferred.

QUALIFICATIONS: Teachers must be energetic and patient because most pupils are young children. Teaching experience preferred but not required.

CONDITIONS OF EMPLOYMENT: 10-12 months. 25 teaching hours, 40 total work hours per week.

SALARY: RMB7,000-14,000 per month.

FACILITIES/SUPPORT: Free shared accommodation. Round-trip airfare reimbursement, free Chinese lessons, a free TEFL certificate, visa sponsorship and free lunches at place of work.

CONTACT: Eric Winder, Lead Recruiter (eric@beijingteach.com).

BERLITZ CHINA

211 Shimen Yi Lu, Unit 701-3, Wang Wang Plaza, Shanghai, 200041

✆ +86 21 5213 8393

✉ teaching.cn@em.berlitz.com

🖥 www.berlitz.com.cn

NUMBER OF TEACHERS: 140.

PREFERENCE OF NATIONALITY: USA, Canada, UK, Australia, New Zealand preferred.

QUALIFICATIONS: Bachelor's degree or higher, certification in language teaching (TESOL, TEFL, CELTA or equivalent preferred) and teaching experience preferred. Must have interest in teaching adults as well as children, and have organisational and communication skills. Instructors should be dynamic, mature, professional and culturally sensitive. Business experience, knowledge or qualifications also desirable.

CONDITIONS OF EMPLOYMENT: Minimum 1 year, but standard contracts are 2 years. Operation hours are Monday–Friday 8.30am–9.30pm and Saturday and Sunday 8.30am–4.30pm. Full time instructors are required to work 40 hours a week in shifts

during the operating hours with two days off (one weekend day and one week day).

SALARY: RMB14,000 per month.

FACILITIES/SUPPORT: First week's hotel accommodation is paid for overseas hires during which the centre staff help the instructor to find a place to live. Help given with red tape. Requirements vary among cities but always include Bachelor's degree or higher, 2 years post-university working experience. Approximate processing time is 1–2 months.

RECRUITMENT: Internal company postings, employee referrals, job fairs, as well as some international, national and local websites. Skype interviews.

CONTACT: Angelica Arango, Country Manager of Instruction.

BOND LANGUAGE INSTITUTE

2nd Floor, Bai Hui Zhong Xin, Lang Qing Xuan, Bo Ai 5th Road, Zhongshan, Guangdong 528400

✆ +86 760 8887 6667

✉ bond_ Institute@hotmail.com

🖥 www.tefl-bond.com/

NUMBER OF TEACHERS: 100+ including fee-paying interns.

PREFERENCE OF NATIONALITY: All major English-speaking countries.

QUALIFICATIONS: Preferably those with TEFL/TESOL certificates and college diploma and above. Ages 21–55.

CONDITIONS OF EMPLOYMENT: Usually a 6-month or 1-year contract. The maximum weekly workload is about 20 hours.

SALARY: Interns receive RMB2,900 (£300) a month; recruited teachers will be paid RMB6,200 or more.

FACILITIES/SUPPORT: Free accommodation; furnished apartment units equipped with major domestic and electric appliances. School is nationally accredited and authorised to employ western teachers and process work permits.

RECRUITMENT: By word of mouth and through partners throughout the world, eg the Teach and Travel China programme administered by ImmerQi in Beijing (www.immerqi.com). Interviews are essential and are often carried out in the UK and in North America.

BUCKLAND INTERNATIONAL EDUCATION GROUP

#78 Lane 1, Longyue Road, Yangshuo, Guilin 541900

✆ +86 773 882 7555

✉ bucklandping@gmail.com

🖥 www.bucklandgroup.org

Cultural Exchange Teaching Program.

NUMBER OF TEACHERS: 40 openings in 8 provinces for 2015/6.

PREFERENCE OF NATIONALITY: Native English speakers: British, American, Canadian, Australian, Irish or New Zealander.

QUALIFICATIONS: Bachelor's degree or TESOL certificate preferable.

CONDITIONS OF EMPLOYMENT: 5 or 11-month renewable contracts available. 15 teaching hours per week from Monday to Friday.

SALARY: RMB4,000–5,500 after tax per month. Taxes paid by the school. Bonus of RMB2,200 paid on completion of 1-year contract.

FACILITIES/SUPPORT: Free housing provided: furnished, private apartments with utilities (phone, TV, air-conditioning, western toilet, internet, etc). Up to RMB200 per month utilities allowance. Paid public holidays and up to 15 consecutive days of paid sick leave. Free visa service: work visa invitation letters, work permit and resident permit sponsorship and visa updates. Airfare reimbursement and assistance. Teacher training, cultural orientation and post-training teacher assistance. Mandarin lessons provided.

RECRUITMENT: Usually via the internet, eg www.tefljobs.net. No application fee. The first step is to submit a résumé in Word, recent full body photo and application form. Interviews not essential.

CONTACT: Ping Wang (bucklandping@gmail.com) or Owen Buckland (owenbuckland@gmail.com).

CLICK CHINA CULTURAL EXCHANGE CO LTD

Room 2308, Building#13 Wanda Plaza, Jiyuqiao, Wuchang District, Wuhan, Hubei Province

✆ +86 27 8275 1218

🖱 emilyclickcn@qq.com

💻 www.clickchn.com

NUMBER OF TEACHERS: Job agency that hires about 100 teachers for schools in Mainland China.

PREFERENCE OF NATIONALITY: North America, Oceania and European countries. Also jobs available for non-native speakers.

QUALIFICATIONS: Bachelor's degree essential, with TEFL/TESOL/CELTA or teaching experience from English-speaking countries preferred.

CONDITIONS OF EMPLOYMENT: 10-month contracts in public schools, with Monday-Friday hours 8am-12pm and 2pm-5pm. Language training institute contracts are for 12 months with most teaching taking place Wednesday to Sunday during the day and evening classes.

SALARY: In primary/middle schools: RMB6,000-13,000 (subject teaching positions up to RMB16,000); universities: RMB4,500-8,000; and language schools: RMB7,500-15,000.

FACILITIES/SUPPORT: Local teachers from schools help with finding housing. Agency sends teachers a detailed list of documents required by China Foreign Experts Affairs Bureau for work permits application. When documents are ready, schools apply for work permits and invitation letters from the Bureau, which normally takes 3-7 weeks, and then post them to the teachers who can then apply for a Z-visa at their nearest Chinese embassy.

RECRUITMENT: Email applications with resumé, photo, passport page and copy of degree and certificate. Interviews can normally be arranged within two working days.

CONTACT: Emily Liu, Senior Account Manager.

EMAIL: emilyclickcn@qq.com

COLORADO CHINA COUNCIL

4556 Apple Way, Boulder, CO 80301, USA

✆ +1 303 443 1108

🖱 alice@asiacouncil.org

💻 www.asiacouncil.org

NUMBER OF PARTICIPANTS: 15–20 per year in the year-long programme. Participants are placed at universities throughout China.

PREFERENCE OF NATIONALITY: North American with no discernible regional accent.

QUALIFICATIONS: Minimum bachelor's or higher degree (all majors and professional backgrounds considered, though English, TEFL, linguistics, business, accounting, economics and engineering especially welcome). Universities prefer that applicants have some teaching/public speaking/tutoring/seminar presentation background. People with a master's degree or PhD are strongly encouraged to apply, as are couples. Must be 60 or under at time of application and in excellent mental and physical health.

CONDITIONS OF EMPLOYMENT: Full academic year programme runs from September to June/July. 16–20 hours per week; 2-week intensive TESL and Mandarin Training Institute in Sichuan in August.

SALARY: Monthly stipend about RMB5,000–10,000 per month depending on university and academic or professional background. Free housing in FTs' complex, medical benefits, most or all of round-trip transportation costs reimbursed and 5–8 week paid vacation over Chinese New Year.

FACILITIES/SUPPORT: CCC provides full support if any problems or issues arise at any point. Most universities invite CCC's teachers to teach for a second year. Housing is adequate to excellent depending on city and university. CCC is the oldest non-religious China teaching, training and placement organisation in the USA which accepts people from all over the country. CCC has published *Yin Yang: American Perspectives on Living in China* (Rowman and Littlefield, 2012), which takes prospective applicants through the entire process of teaching in China, from attending the Summer Institute, through the joys and frustrations of the classroom, travel, making friends and how families cope with this challenging transition.

RECRUITMENT: Rolling admissions with fees from $2,950 rising every month after 1 January. For fees, application and detailed information, see www.asiacouncil.org.

CONTACT: Alice Renouf, Director.

413

Recruiting partner of Suman Education International (67 Ayres Road, Manchester, M16 9NH; +44 161 209 8118; tong.fu@suman.uk.com; www.suman.uk.com), a joint venture since 2003 with Jiangsu Provincial Department of Education.

NUMBER OF TEACHERS: 4 appointments for a year and about 16 short summer placements.

PREFERENCE OF NATIONALITY: Native speakers of English to teach Suman's partners and clients in Jiangsu, Beijing and Jiangxi. Britons preferred for ease of interview and training.

QUALIFICATIONS: Anyone with a bachelor's degree from a British or North American university can be considered. TEFL or teaching qualification preferred.

CONDITIONS OF EMPLOYMENT: Short contracts of 2–5 weeks at summer camps across China and longer contracts 6–12+ months available in Shanghai. Average 20 hours per week. Summer teachers get 1 day off per week.

SALARY: For summer positions, the cost of visa, plane tickets, accommodation and meals is provided by Suman Education International. Teachers are not paid for delivering lessons but will be given a £250 allowance for each week spent on the camp. For year-long jobs: RMB3,000–8,000 (£300–£800/$470–$1,250) per month, depending on the status of the schools/organisations. State schools or universities usually pay less than private language schools due to limited budget.

FACILITIES/SUPPORT: Accommodation provided in most cases.

RECRUITMENT: As soon as vacancies are notified by partners in China, they are advertised on website, TEFL forums, Gumtree, etc. Interviews are essential; for summer positions these take place before 21 May. Skype interviews are possible.

CONTACT: Jane Song, TEFL Teacher Recruitment Consultant.

Many franchise schools recruit directly (for example, see the next entry and adverts on tefl.com).

NUMBER OF TEACHERS: 1,000 a year for more than 100 EFL schools in China.

PREFERENCE OF NATIONALITY: Native English speakers.

QUALIFICATIONS: University degree, internationally recognised TEFL certification and teaching experience.

CONDITIONS OF EMPLOYMENT: 12-month contracts. Teaching 21 (real) hours between 9am and 9pm, 5 days a week.

SALARY: RMB13,000 (approx. $2,100) per month.

FACILITIES/SUPPORT: Shanghai, Beijing, Guangzhou and Shenzhen schools provide comprehensive benefits package including relocation assistance, flight allowance, health insurance, paid vacation, official working visa, Mandarin lessons and ongoing training and professional development.

RECRUITMENT: Via EF's Online Recruitment Centre at www.englishfirst.com/trt or send résumé and qualification details to efrecruitment@ef.com.

EF Changchun is quickly expanding, now with four branches in the city, and is the largest franchise school in China.

NUMBER OF TEACHERS: 50.

PREFERENCE OF NATIONALITY: USA, UK, Ireland, Canada, New Zealand and Australia.

QUALIFICATIONS: Bachelor's degree needed; TEFL or CELTA and 1 year of teaching experience are both desirable.

CONDITIONS OF EMPLOYMENT: 12 or 18 months. Evenings Monday–Friday (3pm–7pm) and all day Saturday–Sunday (9am–6pm). 2 consecutive days off during the week.

SALARY: RMB7,500–9,300 (net) per month (£700–£875) plus free accommodation, insurance, flight allowance (up to RMB10,000) and final bonus (equal to one month's salary).

FACILITIES/SUPPORT: Teachers are provided with their own furnished apartment (not shared) near the school. Hired teachers are sent the necessary paperwork to apply for a visa via courier. School then deals with all the necessary paperwork such as obtaining a foreign expert certificate, residency permit and so on. Costs are reimbursed after arrival. ERIKA insurance is provided by school, including medical and accident insurance, baggage and property insurance and liability insurance.

RECRUITMENT: Advertising on TEFL recruitment websites such as tefl.com and Dave's ESL Cafe, recruitment agencies and some local agents in different countries. Interviews by Skype.

CONTACT: Lynn, HR Specialist or Chris Marshall, Director of Studies.

ENGLON GLOBAL TEFL RESOURCING LTD
24 Hampshire Terrace, Portsmouth, Hampshire PO1 2QF, UK
(C) +44 2392 297144 or +44 203 435 6821
(at) info@globaltefl.uk.com
(computer) www.globaltefl.uk.com

NUMBER OF TEACHERS: 30+ for many locations including Shenzhen City in Guangdong Province, Hangzhou City, Zhejiang Province and Jiangsu Province.

PREFERENCE OF NATIONALITY: British, American, Canadian and Australian.

QUALIFICATIONS: Bachelor's or master's degree, TEFL certificate preferred. Internships available for those without degrees.

CONDITIONS OF EMPLOYMENT: One academic year from September in Chinese kindergartens, primary schools, secondary schools and colleges.

SALARY: RMB4,500–RMB8,000. The first RMB4,800 are tax-free.

FACILITIES/SUPPORT: Free accommodation provided. Return air ticket reimbursed.

RECRUITMENT: Via tefl.com, etc. Interviews held in the UK.

CONTACT: Polly Whitworth, Consultant; Ms Weidan Liu, Director (liuweidan@hotmail.com).

FIND WORK ABROAD
Office 1412, 6–8 Zhong Shan DaDao, Tian He, Guangzhou 510000
(C) +86 20 3730 3381 (China)
(at) apply@findworkabroad.com
(computer) www.china.findworkabroad.com

NUMBER OF TEACHERS: Recruitment agency deals with 1,000 applicants a year.

PREFERENCE OF NATIONALITY: UK, USA, Canada, NZ, Australia and South Africa.

QUALIFICATIONS: BA degree or higher. No experience is needed for most positions.

CONDITIONS OF EMPLOYMENT: 12-month contract. 20 hours per week Monday to Friday.

SALARY: RMB7,000–15,000 per month. Deductions of RMB300–600 unless school pays contributions.

FACILITIES/SUPPORT: Accommodation is usually offered, or a housing allowance given. Schools assist with work permits: after signing a contract, completing the medical exam and supplying copies of résumé, BA and certificates, the school will issue authorisation to get the working visa at the Chinese embassy.

RECRUITMENT: Adverts on ESL job websites. Interviews online if applicant is abroad, or in person.

CONTACT: Amy Wen, Office Manager.

GOLDEN APPLE CHILD EDUCATION (GROUP)
Floor 4, Bldg 6, Tianfu Xingu, 399 Fucheng Avenue, Gaoxin District, Chengdu, Sichuan 610041
(C) +86 28 8519 9369, ext 8079
(at) eslapplication@163.com
(computer) www.ga-education.com

NUMBER OF TEACHERS: 50+ for 33 kindergartens in Chengdu.

PREFERENCE OF NATIONALITY: American, British, Canadian, Australian, New Zealander, Irish and South African.

QUALIFICATIONS: Minimum bachelor's degree in any subject and 2 years' post-graduation work experience in any field, preferably teaching. Qualified teachers with PYP (Primary Years Program) experience needed for positions in two IB-accredited kindergartens.

CONDITIONS OF EMPLOYMENT: Standard 1-year contract. 20 teaching hours per week (ESL); 28 (PYP).

SALARY: RMB9,000–13,000 per month depending on hours and experience. (ESL Teachers) RMB14,000–22,000 per month, qualified kindergarten, primary, IB teachers/coordinators. Taxes are deducted from salaries over RMB4,800 per month.

FACILITIES/SUPPORT: School provides furnished accommodation or a stipend towards housing, and a FE's licence and working 'Z' visa. 7–8 weeks of paid holiday, one month's salary as contract completion bonus, RMB3000 arrival bonus and a 'cultural helper'. The procedure requires teachers to sign a contract with the school, and get a medical in their own country on the official Chinese embassy paperwork. The school then applies for a government invitation letter using the paperwork, which takes about a month or so to receive. An invitation letter to the teacher is then posted and teachers apply for a Z visa from the Chinese embassy.

RECRUITMENT: Through internet adverts, forums, ESL recruitment agencies and word of mouth.

CONTACT: Nigel Jones, Director of English Education.

GOLD STAR TEFL RECRUITMENT

1 Fl, 20 Lane 768, Nangang District, Taipei, 100 Taiwan

jim.althans@goldstarteachers.com or
apply@100goldstarteachers.com

www.GoldStarTeachers.com

English-owned and managed, independent TEFL recruitment
agent filling vacancies for a variety of English schools across
China including Inner Mongolia.

NUMBER OF TEACHERS: 25 a month.

PREFERENCE OF NATIONALITY: Native English speaker from UK,
USA, Canada, Australia, New Zealand or South Africa.

QUALIFICATIONS: Bachelor's degree, TEFL certificate
preferred, teaching experience preferred, plenty of passion and
energy.

CONDITIONS OF EMPLOYMENT: 1 year. 20 hours per week
(maximum 40). Choice of age from Kindergarten to adult.

SALARY: RMB7,700–17,000.

FACILITIES/SUPPORT: Schools provide accommodation, flight,
allowance, health insurance and Z-visa.

CONTACT: Jim Althans, Recruitment Consultant.

INTERLINGUA SCHOOL

Guiyang: 79 Wenchangnanlu, Guiyang, Guizhou 550001

+86 851 687 3853

Zunyi: Yangliu Street, Zunyi, Guizhou 563001

+86 852 825 6850

jobs@dyeduweb.com

www.interlinguaschool.com/eng

NUMBER OF TEACHERS: 20.

PREFERENCE OF NATIONALITY: British, American, Canadian,
Australian and New Zealander.

QUALIFICATIONS: Minimum bachelor's degree. ESL/EFL
qualification or 1 years' teaching experience essential.

CONDITIONS OF EMPLOYMENT: 1 year or longer. 30–36 hours
per week.

SALARY: RMB8,400–12,000, depending on qualifications
and length of contract. International trip allowance,
end-of-contract bonus, health care and travelling allowance
all paid.

FACILITIES/SUPPORT: Accommodation offered free of charge.
School applies for work permit from the provincial education
administration on arrival. Free Mandarin lessons.

CONTACT: Maosi Yan, Programme Director; Manuel Gomez,
Co-ordinator.

IST PLUS – TEACH IN CHINA PROGRAMME

Churcham House, 1 Bridgeman Road, Teddington,
Middlesex TW11 9AJ, UK

+44 20 7788 7877

info@istplus.com

www.istplus.com/teachinchina

NUMBER OF TEACHERS: 10–15 each year.

PREFERENCE OF NATIONALITY: Native English speakers; non-
native speakers must have near-native proficiency in English.

QUALIFICATIONS: University degree in any field essential. TEFL
training or experience is not essential but preferred. Maximum
age 65.

CONDITIONS OF EMPLOYMENT: 5- or 10-month renewable
contracts starting in either August or February, teaching 16–18
classes a week, which works out at a working week of 30–35
hours.

SALARY: RMB4,000–RMB10,000 net per month.

FACILITIES/SUPPORT: Free accommodation (usually on campus),
all-inclusive 7-day orientation in Shanghai on arrival including
basic TEFL training, accommodation, sight-seeing and airport
transfer. IST Plus arranges school/college placement, visa and
work permit, insurance and 24-hour emergency hotline.

RECRUITMENT: Deadlines are mid-December for February
departure and mid-June for August departure. Teach in China fees
are £1,100 for 5 months, £1,295 for 10 months. All teachers who
complete their contracts will receive a TEFL certificate.

CONTACT: Ralph Allemano, Director (rallemano@istplus.com).

LONGMAN SCHOOLS SHANGHAI

Rm 1901, Tower A, 388 West Jiangwan Rd, Hongkou
Plaza, Shanghai 200083

+86 21 6031 7131

shcareer@longmanschools.com.cn

www.longmancareers.com

Pearson bought the Wall Street English chain of language schools
in China in 2009 and proceeded to become the fastest-growing
English language provider in China with many new schools
opening, most recently in Nanjing and Suzhou.

NUMBER OF TEACHERS: 80+.

PREFERENCE OF NATIONALITY: Native English speakers.

QUALIFICATIONS: Minimum bachelor's degree, TEFL and 2 years'
teaching experience.

CONDITIONS OF EMPLOYMENT: 1-year contract. Approximately
36 hours per week with a maximum of 20 teaching hours. Paid
overtime available.

SALARY: RMB12,000–15,000 base plus paid overtime and year-end bonus.

FACILITIES/SUPPORT: Assistance provided with finding accommodation and applying for work permit.

RECRUITMENT: Usually via the internet and recruitment agencies. Candidates are asked to write a lesson plan prior to interview (carried out by phone if the candidate is not local) and submit a 3–5 minute video.

MIDDLE KINGDOM TEACHERS

Office in Xiamen, Fujian Province

apply@middlekingdomteachers.com

www.middlekingdomteachers.com

NUMBER OF TEACHERS: 50 each September.

PREFERENCE OF NATIONALITY: Native-speaking teachers of any origin.

QUALIFICATIONS: Bachelor's degree and good transferable skills.

CONDITIONS OF EMPLOYMENT: 10-month contracts. 12–20 teaching hours per week.

SALARY: RMB4,000–8,000 per month (depending on location and qualifications).

FACILITIES/SUPPORT: Each partner school provides a private apartment, a 1-year working visa and reimbursement of airfare. Seven-day orientation offered in August in China which leads to TEFL certificate and meeting up with other teachers in the new intake; inclusive cost of orientation of RMB2,500.

RECRUITMENT: University presentations, word of mouth, advertising. Skype interviews and then often an interview with a partner school.

CONTACT: Chris Thomas, Director (chris@middlekingdomteachers. com).

RAY ENGLISH TEFL RECRUITMENT

K.I. Business Building, North Street, Xi'an, Shaanxi Province 710075

+86 29 85515915

teachers@rayenglish.com

www.rayenglish.com

NUMBER OF TEACHERS: Agency that recruits more than 1,000 English teachers per year for jobs all over China including Mongolia.

PREFERENCE OF NATIONALITY: Native speakers of English from UK, Ireland, US, New Zealand, Australia, Canada and South Africa. Non-native speakers with exceptional English skills may also apply.

QUALIFICATIONS: University degree + TEFL certification. No experience needed. Applications from non-TEFL holders may be considered.

CONDITIONS OF EMPLOYMENT: 12-month contracts. Hours in the public system (middle schools, high schools, university) are Monday–Friday 8am–5pm, around 16–20 teaching hours per week. Hours are longer in private language centres (20–25 hours) and include weekends/evenings. 2 days off during the week.

SALARY: Depending on city and local living costs: RMB7,000–8,000 in smaller cities; RMB9,000–10,000 in larger cities; RMB13,000–16,000 for Beijing/Shanghai (since cost of living in those cities is wildly expensive). School deducts income tax of around 10%.

FACILITIES/SUPPORT: All public jobs and private language centres for younger learners come with free housing for teachers. Adult language centres in China give a housing allowance towards rent. Full support is given to find teachers modern places. School complies with Chinese law by sponsoring the work visas for teachers. Each school has a dedicated staff member whose assistance is free of charge.

RECRUITMENT: Skype interviews set up between teachers and schools.

CONTACT: Stuart Allen, Operations Director.

REACH TO TEACH

1606 80th Avenue, Algona, IA 50511, USA

+1 201 467 4612

info@reachtoteachrecruiting.com

www.ReachToTeachRecruiting.com/teach-english-in-china.html

For contacts in other countries, see entry at beginning of Asia chapter.

NUMBER OF TEACHERS: 200+.

PREFERENCE OF NATIONALITY: British, American, Canadian, Australian and New Zealander, Irish and South African.

QUALIFICATIONS: A full university degree (any discipline) is enough for most schools in the smaller cities or towns. Teachers in the bigger cities face much tougher requirements as the government will only issue work papers to those that have a TEFL qualification plus at least 2 years of work experience after leaving university (with one of those years being in a teaching or training-related field). Through a partnership with a TEFL course provider, Reach To Teach can assist teachers in getting course discounts.

CONDITIONS OF EMPLOYMENT: All job placements are full-time positions and for 1 year (and usually extendable). Teaching schedules vary but are generally either daytime, or afternoons and evenings.

SALARY: Depends on school, but commonly: reimbursed flights to and from China, free furnished apartment, salaries from RMB7,000–16,000 per month depending on qualifications and location.

FACILITIES/SUPPORT: China visa guidance, airport collection, teacher orientation, etc are provided. Teachers have the option of continued support and contact with Reach To Teach throughout their year-long placement.

RECRUITMENT: Applications submitted via website. Interviews conducted over Skype, by phone and occasionally in person.

CONTACT: Rick Goodman, Director of Recruiting – China (Rick@ReachToTeachRecruiting.com).

RECRUIT 4 CHINA
ZhongShan Road, Xugou, Lianyungang, Jiangsu
📞 +86 0518 81166999
✉ teachers@recruitforchina.com
💻 www.recruitforchina.com

Recruit 4 China is owned and operated by expats living in China, and provides a free service for teachers by teachers.

NUMBER OF TEACHERS: 100+ per year.

PREFERENCE OF NATIONALITY: Native English speakers from USA, UK, Canada, Australia, New Zealand and South Africa, although experienced near native speakers will be considered.

QUALIFICATIONS: Teachers must have a BA degree, which can be in any subject. Although TEFL certificates are preferred they are not essential.

CONDITIONS OF EMPLOYMENT: 1-year contracts. Typically 20–25 hours per week. In a tenth of schools, 15 additional office hours are required. If a housing allowance is provided, schools provide up to 2 weeks hotel accommodation and full assistance in finding a suitable apartment.

SALARY: RMB8,000–12,000 (net) per month, depending on qualifications, location and school type.

FACILITIES/SUPPORT: All schools provide either a free private apartment or housing allowance. Teachers are informed of the accommodation details upon applying. Work permits are obtained after teachers provide a copy of their résumé, photo, degree copy, TEFL certificate (if any) and passport copy. Applications will be made before a teacher's arrival and typically take 4–6 weeks to process.

RECRUITMENT: Via adverts on social media, referrals and ESL websites. Skype/telephone interview required.

CONTACT: Nathan Barker, Director & Foreign Teacher Manager.

SPEAKEASY
12 LingShiGuan Road, Wuhou District, Chengdu
📞 +86 1878 0298993 / +86 1862 8291690
✉ jb.englishtutor@gmail.com

NUMBER OF TEACHERS: 8.

PREFERENCE OF NATIONALITY: USA, UK, Canada, New Zealand, Australia. Others can be considered provided candidates have native pronunciation and fluency.

QUALIFICATIONS: TEFL qualified (CELTA, TESOL, etc.). Minimum 2 years relevant teaching experience (preferably both adults and children).

CONDITIONS OF EMPLOYMENT: 1 year contracts. Flexible hours, with teachers working on an hourly basis, as much or as little as they want. Teachers must provide a free demo class for prospective students, but no extra office hours are required.

SALARY: RMB160-200 per class hour plus signing/re-signing bonuses.

FACILITIES/SUPPORT: Teachers find their own accommodation. No help given with work permits.

RECRUITMENT: Word of mouth, online advertisements (e.g. on www.gochengdoo.com) and recruitment services. Interviews are essential, sometimes by Skype.

CONTACT: James Baxter, Headmaster.

TEACHING-INT LIMITED
Greigsford, Ellon, Aberdeenshire AB41 8QT, UK
📞 +44 1358 711764
✉ info@teaching-int.com
💻 www.teaching-int.com

NUMBER OF TEACHERS: Currently 5 per month, increasing with demand, for schools, universities and businesses, including oil and gas companies through sister company WellDrill Ltd.

PREFERENCE OF NATIONALITY: UK, USA, Canada, New Zealand, Australia, South Africa.

QUALIFICATIONS: TEFL or related as a minimum. South Africans must have at least TEFL and a BA degree. Articulate and creative school leavers welcome to apply.

CONDITIONS OF EMPLOYMENT: Minimum one-year contract, usually from February or August. Longer preferred. Maximum 40 hours per week.

FACILITIES/SUPPORT: Free accommodation provided but not utilities. Advice given on visas but no financial help.

RECRUITMENT: Mainly via social media. Candidates should submit full CV, photo, copies of all educational qualifications, even if only from secondary school, an up-to-date Criminal Records check, among others. Skype interviews conducted by Teaching-Int Limited or partner agency in China.

CONTACT: Carter Langley, Director.

TEACHING NOMAD

Kangding Rd No 1018, Yi Ge Bldg, 3rd Fl, Suite 306, Shanghai

☎ +86 21 5172 0484

✉ info@teachingnomad.com

🖥 www.teachingnomad.com

NUMBER OF TEACHERS: 20–25 per month.

PREFERENCE OF NATIONALITY: Americans and Britons preferred but applications from other 5 native-speaking countries also considered.

QUALIFICATIONS: ESL teachers must have BA, 120-hour TEFL qualification and two years' teaching experience. Teachers at International Schools need BA/MA, state teaching licence or QTS, plus 2+ years of relevant teaching experience.

CONDITIONS OF EMPLOYMENT: 15–25 teaching hours spread over the week including evenings, and weekends.

SALARY: RMB6, 200–20,000 per month, plus benefits.

FACILITIES/SUPPORT: Some client schools offer housing, others assist in finding an apartment.

RECRUITMENT: Online marketing, direct marketing, word of mouth, hosting events, conventions, etc. All candidates are screened and interviewed over Skype or in person.

CONTACT: Ginger de Ridder, Director of TEFL (g.deridder@ teachingnomad.com).

TOSIC INTERNATIONAL EDUCATION GROUP

Haidian District, Beijing 100086. Winter address: Suite 2A–2B, 525 Dundas St W, Toronto, ON M5T 1H4, Canada

☎ +1 416 356 8605

✉ tosic@careerinchina.ca

🖥 www.careerinchina.ca

NUMBER OF TEACHERS: 500 recruited for various schools on TOSIC (Teach or Study in China) programme.

PREFERENCE OF NATIONALITY: Canadian, American, British and Australian.

QUALIFICATIONS: Minimum bachelor's degree.

CONDITIONS OF EMPLOYMENT: Standard length of contract is 1 year. 20 hours per week.

SALARY: RMB5,000+ net.

FACILITIES/SUPPORT: Free accommodation provided. Affiliated to Applied TESOL certificate course (www.appliedtesol.com) which can be studied alongside earning in Guangzhou.

RECRUITMENT: Application can be made online.

US-CHINA EDUCATIONAL EXCHANGE

15 Locust St, Jersey City, New Jersey 07305, USA

☎ +1 201 432 6861

✉ edexchange@gmail.com

🖥 www.US-ChinaEdExchange.org

NUMBER OF TEACHERS: 200–300.

PREFERENCE OF NATIONALITY: Native English speakers: British, American, Canadian, Australian and New Zealander.

QUALIFICATIONS: Minimum bachelor's degree and commitment to teaching.

CONDITIONS OF EMPLOYMENT: 6 months or 1 year. 15 hours per week.

SALARY: Varies.

FACILITIES/SUPPORT: Schools provide free housing and send candidates visa approval documents.

RECRUITMENT: Internet and newspaper ads. Interviews always conducted by phone.

CONTACT: Dr. Yong Ho.

USIT IRELAND

19/21 Aston Quay, Dublin 2, Ireland

☎ +353 1 602 1742

✉ volunteer@usit.ie

🖥 www.usit.ie

Volunteer internship programme in Xi'an.

PREFERENCE OF NATIONALITY: Native speakers of English from Ireland, UK, US, Canada, Australia or New Zealand.

QUALIFICATIONS: No qualifications needed. Minimum age 18 years.

CONDITIONS OF PLACEMENT: Internship lasts up to 6 months. 15-20 hours of teaching a week (after training) plus attending Mandarin lessons for 6 hours a week, Monday to Friday.

SALARY: Nil.

FACILITIES/SUPPORT: TEFL Certificate provided at end of training, approx. 4-6 weeks into the placement. Accommodation is provided during the placement and intern receives a monthly stipend. Airport pick-up and orientation week in Xi'an included in programme cost, as well as a Chinese SIM card, welcome dinner and Xi'an Tourist Card.

RECRUITMENT: Placements are confirmed after an interview style discussion with USIT Representative to ensure participant is suitable for the internship. Interviews can also be held using Skype. Cost of programme from €1,299.

VERBAL EDUCATION CHINA

Room 728, Tongyuan Plaza, Qinghe Third Street, Haidian District, Beijing

📞 +86 158 1100 0581

✉ aken0810@qq.com or aken0810@163.com

💻 www.sinoteacher.com

NUMBER OF TEACHERS: Recruitment agency for many candidates, to teach oral English mainly to middle school students throughout China and Mongolia, from remote villages to large urban centres.

PREFERENCE OF NATIONALITY: English-speaking countries only.

QUALIFICATIONS: Bachelor's degree and teaching experience are required. TEFL/TESL/TESOL preferred.

CONDITIONS OF EMPLOYMENT: Minimum 3 months (September–December or March–June) but 1 year preferred. 18 teaching hours per week Monday to Friday.

SALARY: RMB5,000–8,000 depending on qualifications and experience.

FACILITIES/SUPPORT: Private accommodation provided and all meals at the school. Orientation given on arrival. Visa sponsorship and medical insurance provided.

RECRUITMENT: Via recruitment websites, eg www.cathayteacher. com. Interview required. Video of yourself needed.

CONTACT: Aken Wang, HR Director.

WELL INTERNATIONAL ENGLISH

133 Fuzhou Road North, Building 4, Suite 322, Shibei District, Qingdao, Shandong Province 266034

📞 +86 532 8569 9787

✉ well@wellenglish.cn

💻 www.wellenglish.cn

NUMBER OF TEACHERS: 10.

PREFERENCE OF NATIONALITY: American or Canadian.

QUALIFICATIONS: Bachelor' degree or higher. At least 2 year's teaching experience.

CONDITIONS OF EMPLOYMENT: 1-year contracts. 20/24 hours per week.

SALARY: RMB7,000–8,000 per month.

FACILITIES/SUPPORT: Free apartment. School will apply for a FE certificate and residence permit for the teachers once they provide a résumé, passport copy, diploma and certificate, medical report, 2-inch photo, reference letter, etc. Airfare reimbursed at end of contract.

RECRUITMENT: Via internet agencies such as RecruitForChina. com. Interviews are required.

XI'AN JIAOTONG-LIVERPOOL UNIVERSITY ENGLISH LANGUAGE CENTRE

No.111 Ren'ai Road, Suzhou Dushu Lake Higher Education Town, Suzhou Industrial Park, Suzhou, Jiangsu 215123

📞 +86 512 8816 1300/1345

✉ recruitment.hr@xjtlu.edu.cn; elc.sec@xjtlu.edu.cn

💻 www.xjtlu.edu.cn/en or www.hr.xjtlu.edu.cn

NUMBER OF TEACHERS: Approx 135 for fast-growing university. EAP. Specialists needed.

PREFERENCE OF NATIONALITY: Local visa rules restrict employment to the following nationals: UK, Ireland, Australia, New Zealand, Canada and the US.

QUALIFICATIONS: Tutors need an MA in TESOL/Applied Linguistics or equivalent, plus a teaching qualification (eg CELTA/ DELTA or BEd) and at least 2 years' experience.

CONDITIONS OF EMPLOYMENT: Renewable contracts for 1–3 years from August. Office hours are between 9am and 5pm with 20 hours of teaching per week (Monday–Friday only). Currently around 47 days of paid holiday per year.

SALARY: RMB14,898–RMB30,099 per month for a qualified and experienced tutor. Some lower-level tutor positions are available occasionally.

FACILITIES/SUPPORT: Housing allowance of up to RMB3,000 per month and HR will assist with finding local accommodation and applying for work permits. Travel allowance of up to RMB15,000 per year. BUPA health insurance (basic) paid.

RECRUITMENT: Usually via adverts on www.jobs.ac.uk and other websites. Applications are welcome all year round but main recruitment drives are in March and May each year. Interviews and some pre-interview tasks are essential and can be carried out over the phone or internet.

CONTACT: Dr Stuart Perrin, Director of Centre (stuart.perrin@ xjtlu.edu.cn) or Carly Ridyard, Deputy Director (carly.ridyard@ xjtlu.edu.ca).

XU BO ART AND CULTURE EXCHANGE

Room 2506, B Block, Lane 521, Wan Ping Road (South), Shanghai, 200032

📞 +86 21 5459 0999

✉ program.development@xubo.org

💻 www.xubo.org

NUMBER OF TEACHERS: 150 volunteers per year who come on (tourist) visas.

PREFERENCE OF NATIONALITY: None.

QUALIFICATIONS: None necessary.

CONDITIONS OF EMPLOYMENT: 1–3 months' volunteer work. Between 11 and 15 lessons per week (40 minutes). Summer camp work available.

SALARY: None. Programme fees from US$1,315 for 4 weeks.

FACILITIES/SUPPORT: Accommodation is arranged. No working permits are needed.

RECRUITMENT: Via overseas volunteer organisations including Travel to Teach based in Thailand (www.travel-to-teach.org); UK partner is www.planmygapyear.co.uk.

CONTACT: Jessie Duanmu, Programme Director (jiong.duanmu@xubo.org).

MONGOLIA

LIST OF EMPLOYERS

NEW CHOICE MONGOLIAN VOLUNTEER ORGANIZATION

POB–159, Ulaanbaatar–210646 A

📞 +976 11 314577

✉ info@volunteer.org.mn

💻 www.volunteer.org.mn

SANTIS EDUCATIONAL SERVICES

(Student Street, Ulaanbaatar), PO Box 1174, Central Post Office, Sukhbaatar District, Ulaanbaatar

📞 +976 11 318319

✉ mongolia@santis.mn

💻 www.Santis.mn; www.inlingua.mn

NUMBER OF TEACHERS: 5.

PREFERENCE OF NATIONALITY: None.

QUALIFICATIONS: Native speakers of English from UK, Ireland, USA or Australia with teaching skills.

CONDITIONS OF EMPLOYMENT: 2–12 weeks. 4–6 hours per day; 20–30 hours per week.

SALARY: Volunteers pay a fee of $945 for 2–4 weeks up to $2,045 for 9–12 weeks. Some possibility of paid work.

FACILITIES/SUPPORT: Accommodation provided with host families or in apartment. New Choice will apply for teacher's work permission and long-term visa.

CONTACT: Bayarjargal Damdindagva, Founder and Executive Director.

NUMBER OF TEACHERS: 12-20.

PREFERENCE OF NATIONALITY: None.

QUALIFICATIONS: CELTA or equivalent as a minimum.

CONDITIONS OF EMPLOYMENT: Annual commitment, variable hours.

SALARY: To be discussed, paid net in US dollars.

FACILITIES/SUPPORT: Accommodation is provided. All aspects of work permits are dealt with before teacher's arrival.

RECRUITMENT: Web (e.g. gooverseas.com), agency, word of mouth and local. Skype interviews.

CONTACT: Andrew Orgill, Director of the International Office.

HONG KONG

Since the former British colony became the Hong Kong Special Administrative Region (HKSAR) of the People's Republic of China on 23 June 1997, '*everything has changed and nothing has changed*', or so the saying goes. Only international schools and specialist 'ESF' (English Schools Foundation) schools offer a curriculum using English as the medium of instruction (EMI) though other government schools have been given more freedom to choose to teach in English rather than (or alongside) Putonghua (simplified Mandarin Chinese). Many parents are willing to spend vast sums on extracurricular English courses for their children and there is a high demand for native English speakers willing to teach children from as young as six months. Many of these companies have proprietary learning systems and systematic phonics programmes.

To meet the demand for English teaching, the Hong Kong government employs hundreds of English speakers to teach in the state education system and in non-government schools too as part of the NET (Native English Teacher) scheme described below.

It is illegal to enter Hong Kong as a tourist and take up work, so that those graduates who arrive on holiday and want to change their status are out of luck. However, it is possible to visit the city, find a teaching job and then apply for a work visa from a neighbouring country; Macao is the most convenient. The work visa is attached to the passport before entering Hong Kong. The authorities will expect to see a university degree, relevant work experience and/or a TEFL certificate and a corporate sponsor. Teachers who satisfy these requirements should have no difficulty obtaining a visa/entry permit.

FINDING A JOB

NET SCHEME

The NET scheme is administered by the Hong Kong Education Bureau (EDB) (NET Administration Team, Room 1110, 11th Floor Wu Chung House, 213 Queen's Road East, Wan Chai; +852 2892 6498; netrecruit@edb.gov.hk; www.edb.gov.hk).

The website carries full details of the scheme and an application form. Foreign Teachers, known as 'NETs', can interview for any school with a vacancy and have some control over where they're placed. The NET community maintains an online 'blacklist' of schools to avoid. The reason the scheme is so popular is that salaries and benefits are generous.

The competition has become much keener, partly because so many graduates and trainee teachers are looking for work outside their own countries. Acceptance is easier if you have a postgraduate diploma in education, though some categories of the programme are open to university graduates of language-related subjects with a TEFL certificate. The salary range for primary NETs is HK$24,380 (£2,000) to HK$49,515 (£4,000) per month and for secondary NETs even higher, HK$25,600 (£2,100) to HK$59,485 (£4,870). Superior qualifications are well rewarded in Hong Kong. Exact salaries are dependent on experience and qualifications. Every NET whose home is outside Hong Kong gets a monthly cash housing allowance of HK$19,081 (£1,500) which really bumps up the salary.

Also, there is a 15% gratuity on everything you earn, less contributions the employer has made into a pension fund, awarded at the end of the two-year contract, provided your conduct and performance have met with approval. Flights, medical allowance and baggage allowance are all additional perks.

Applications are usually accepted until mid-February, and term begins in mid-August. After working in the private sector for the Chatteris Foundation (described below), **Tom Grundy** became a Netter and compares the two teaching schemes:

The government NET programme is more highbrow and demanding but offers a better package and wage. However, you don't get the 'instant social circle' you would with an employer like Chatteris. NET is ideal should you decide to remain in HK and great if you already have a TEFL or PGCE qualification.

He recommends the 'NET Survival Guide' at http://en.wikibooks.org/wiki/NET_Teacher_Survival_Guide to answer any questions about the programme.

OTHER EMPLOYERS

Almost any English institute you locate on the internet will have a Recruitment or Careers page. The British Council has a teaching operation which has an ongoing need for certificate-qualified teachers with at least two years' experience, preferably with children. Hiring takes place on a rolling basis; details are at https://jobs.britishcouncil.org or you can apply locally for hourly jobs (www.britishcouncil.hk). Those applying for part-time hourly work should already have a valid Hong Kong work visa. The wage is about HK$400 per contact hour for Certificate-holders and more for teachers with a DELTA or PGCE. In 2014 the UK-based teacher recruitment agency Prime Teachers (www.primeteachers.com) was looking to fill a number of EFL vacancies on behalf of a Hong Kong client running a large programme teaching children aged 3 to 12.

One of the largest employers is the Chatteris Educational Foundation (see entry), which offers recent university graduates from English-speaking countries the opportunity to teach in Hong Kong. Like the government NET programme, this scheme has become more difficult to enter, although there are sometimes vacancies still being advertised in the summer for a mid-August start.

Tom Grundy completed the nine-month programme before he became a Netter:

The wages were just enough to live on and save some for travel. I saved hard and was able to travel for three months around South-East Asia afterwards, and even afforded two laptops. Chatteris has its problems and its 'charitable' status is questionable, but they support and train you. You'll be placed with another British, Canadian or American in a primary or secondary school, there'll be several dozen others who you'll train with and so you'll immediately have a big social network. With Chatteris, your emphasis will be on oral English with a 'non-formal' approach, ie games, crafts and other 'fun' activities.

The basic wage of HK$14,000 hasn't risen at all in the past few years and by about Christmas many CNETs (Chatteris Native-speaking English Tutors) conclude that their wages are exploitative. Furthermore you must pay a HK$2,000 deposit at the beginning against the completion of your contract, which will be returned to you at the end, minus bank charges. Participants often complain of an interfering management who require constant paperwork and attendance at workshops and meetings.

Ready to Learn is now in its 20th year in Hong Kong and sponsors a few teachers from the UK and elsewhere (see entry), although it is not interested in '*travellers seeing the world with a TEFL qualification or similar*'. It is looking for teachers who will commit longer term and take an interest in the company and its methods.

Dramatic English (see list of organisations) employs drama graduates on 10 or 12-month contracts, who are able to use their arts degree and possible performance skills to help children learn English.

Demand is very strong for native English speakers to work in English-speaking kindergartens, for which a degree and a TEFL qualification are generally sufficient. Adverts abound for TEFL-trained graduates to work for companies with names like Cheerful Kids, First Little Step, Blooming Buds or Kidz-n-us. English for Asia (www.englishforasia.com) in Kowloon is another major recruiter, though it can usually employ graduates of its own Trinity CertTESOL course (see Directory of Training Courses). Another reputable private language school which hires foreigners and also offers online TESOL training courses is Firstclass Intesol (http://intesol.firstclass.edu.hk).

Both internet adverts and the more traditional print-based means of advertising jobs are still going strong. For example the bumper Saturday edition of the *South China Morning Post* might contain some useful leads; its classified section often carries teaching posts and can be consulted online at www.cpjobs.com/hk. The online community http://jobs.asiaxpat.com carries many ads for teachers, though most will require that applicants already have a valid HKID/working visa. Another good searchable resource for jobs in HK is www. hk.jobsdb.com. The *Yellow Pages* are an alternative source of institute addresses or consult the list of English Learning Centres at www.englishtutor.hk. Landline calls within the city limits are free, so by phoning around you can easily get an idea of the possibilities. Although hiring is continuous, the summer months bring even more openings, while the Chinese New Year in January/February is a bad time.

Some companies specialise in recruiting and outsourcing teachers, saving schools the administrative burden of employing a foreigner. Elton Educational Services (see entry) provides English courses and English teachers to Hong Kong kindergartens and primary schools.

Freelance teaching can prove lucrative although it's always a risk for non-permanent residents, as work visas forbid foreigners to work for anyone other than their named sponsor. An attractive advertisement strategically placed in the letterboxes of the ritzy apartment estates in Mid Levels, Jardine's Lookout and Causeway Bay suburbs or in busy supermarkets might winkle out some private students. It is also possible to pick up tutoring work where you visit a family's home and help their child with homework/English games. The standard payment is £20–£30 an hour. Summer schools, English drama organisations and language schools are also options in Hong Kong, but all foreign workers doing paid or voluntary work require a work visa, so make arrangements with an employer beforehand.

Although Hong Kong is famous for its big-city smog and vivacity, there are quieter places and it is worth researching the exact place where you will be living and working. **J. W. Arble** worked at a secondary school in the New Territories in a suburban town 30 miles to the north of Hong Kong Island. '*I lived alone in a 12 by 16ft flat, 17 floors above a colossal shopping centre of six hundred stores, 30 restaurants and a single bookshop that mainly stocked self-help guides and comics. Everything shut at 10pm.*'

REGULATIONS

British citizens may visit the HKSAR as tourists without a visa for up to 180 days provided they can satisfy the immigration officer on arrival that they are entering as bona fide visitors with enough funds to cover the duration of their stay without working and, unless in transit to the Mainland of China or the region of Macau, hold onward or return tickets. USA citizens are given 90 days. The visa requirements are posted at www.immd.gov. hk. As already mentioned, visitors are not allowed to change their status after arrival.

Once you have an employer willing to sponsor you, it is relatively straightforward obtaining a work visa by submitting form ID990A (Application for Entry for Employment as Professionals in Hong Kong). After both parties have signed a contract, the employer sends this and all necessary documents including police checks, a medical certificate, academic certificates and references to the Immigration Department. The employer must do a lot of paperwork so teachers should try to honour their commitments instead of flitting off to a better-paying school after a month or two. The HKSAR Immigration Department is located on the 2nd Floor of Immigration Tower, 7 Gloucester Road, Wan Chai (+582 2824 6111; enquiry@immd.gov.hk). The work visa must be renewed annually.

Salaries are taxed at roughly 3% at the end of the year, because there is no PAYE system in Hong Kong. Nor is there any social security. However, after their first year, employees must pay 5% into the Mandatory Provident Fund (MPF), which is matched by the employer. Medical care is not free in Hong Kong, but as soon as the teacher is given an HKID card, he or she can use the Government hospitals for a nominal fee. A visit to a GP will cost HK$150–$200. Private health insurance is of course available.

CONDITIONS OF WORK

If you do not have an official contract and are picking up some teaching at a private institute, you are likely to be paid on an hourly basis and not very well.

Hong Kong children are usually well behaved, eager and well mannered, even though so many are under huge pressure from exams, extra tuition, band practice, kung fu, lion dancing and extra sports. It can be just as important for teachers to help their pupils enjoy English and gain confidence as to instil the finer points of English grammar. Hong Kong's British past can also lead to some interesting situations, as **J. W. Arble** discovered:

It is traditional for Hong Kong students to adopt an English name alongside their Chinese ones. These too have, in fact, become family names, passed down with little variation and as a result I found myself surrounded by ghosts from the Edwardian era, Sibyls and Mabels and Ethels and Normans and even an Algernon. Other students chose their own English names: King Kong was the moniker of one five-foot 14-year-old, School Bully was that of another, there was a Ferrari Vespa, an Ω – the student formerly known as Wong – and a Beckham, a 15-year-old covered in tattoos who literally slept through all my lessons undisturbed, who was rumoured to drive a minibus for the Triads. My favourite student name was Frozen Chicken Drumstick, belonging to a girl who had plucked it from a packet in the supermarket deep-freeze.

ACCOMMODATION

Hong Kong has overtaken Singapore (just) and Tokyo as the most expensive city in Asia, and rents keep climbing. Flat shares are obviously the cheapest option; check out http://hongkong.craigslist.hk/roo for listings. The outlying islands such as Lamma and Lantau and the New Territories are cheaper than the central areas; the same money can buy double the floor space. Even with HK's superb public transport system, the commute can be time consuming, so living in Kowloon just north of Hong Kong island might be a happy medium. **Tom Grundy** suggests that the best deals are in old walk-up buildings without lifts, where your money will buy comparatively more floor space. He goes on to recommend looking up flat shares on Asia Expat (the main expat community online: http://hongkong.asiaxpat.com) or Geo Expat (http://hongkong.geoexpat.com) in addition to the online communities mentioned above.

Areas in Kowloon that are considered to be quite poor are becoming popular with foreigners, such as Sham Shui Po or Tai Kok Tsui, as they are cheaper and still on the MTR red line, which goes direct to Central on HK Island. A decent room in a two-bedroom flat share will set you back at least HK$6,000 per month.

LEISURE TIME

Not surprisingly, culture shock is kept to a minimum in Hong Kong by the western affluence and the lingering British bias. Hong Kong is famed as a shoppers' paradise in which the cheap food, clothing and travel help to alleviate the problem of expensive accommodation. **Tom Grundy** concludes that Hong Kong is an ideal place to live:

In Hong Kong, tax is low to non-existent, it's super clean, has a huge expat community with lots of English clubs, activities, sports, events and the public transport is the world's best. It's very compact and all of Asia is on the doorstep (cheap flights and trains to China, Indonesia, Philippines, Thailand, Cambodia, Vietnam, Laos, etc). The territory has dozens of tropical beaches, temples, a mind-blowing metropolis at its heart, fantastic hiking and outdoor activities, 248 idyllic outlying islands, huge country parks (70% of HK's area is actually green) and everything's a good deal cheaper than home, what with China next door. It's an ideal balance of East and West, English is widely spoken and western food and luxuries are available everywhere. Though Hong Kong is an aggressively consumerist, capitalist society, it is 'tempered' with Chinese tradition and Buddhist beliefs.

TRINITY CERTTESOL & DIPTESOL IN HONG KONG

Trinity's position as a leading provider of international qualifications for TESOL teachers means that these qualifications are ideally placed to meet your professional teaching needs, no matter where you are in your teaching career.

The **Trinity Certificate in TESOL** is an initial teacher training qualification that will equip you with the basic skills and knowledge to take up a first post as an ESOL teacher. The CertTESOL is accredited at Level 5 on the UK Qualifications and Credit Framework (regarded as comparable in difficulty to the second year of an undergraduate degree).

The **Trinity Diploma in TESOL** is a qualification for experienced teachers of ESOL, designed to encourage the development of professional knowledge and expertise and refine practical teaching skills. The DipTESOL is accredited at Level 7 on the UK Qualifications and Credit Framework (equivalent to master's degrees in related subject areas).

Trinity's TESOL qualifications are accepted by employers worldwide. They are welcomed by the British Council for new and experienced teachers in their accredited teaching organisations in the UK, and in their own teaching centres worldwide.

In Hong Kong, Trinity's TESOL qualifications are registered under the Government's Non-local Higher and Professional Education (Regulation) Ordinance, and are accepted by the Hong Kong Education Bureau for the Primary NET teacher scheme.

English for Asia is Trinity's largest TESOL course provider outside of Europe and the only dedicated Trinity TESOL centre in Hong Kong. English for Asia is also the Trinity National Representative for ESOL and Drama in Hong Kong, Macao and Mainland China, working with over 1000 schools and organisations in the region, including the Hong Kong EDB, Macau DSEJ and Beijing Education Examinations Authority.

With a constant demand for qualified ESOL teachers in Hong Kong, China and other parts of Asia, most CertTESOL and DipTESOL graduates will be offered teaching placements soon after completing the course.

email: tesol@englishforasia.com; website: www.englishforasia.com

LIST OF EMPLOYERS

BERLITZ LANGUAGES LIMITED

Suite 807-809, 8/Fl., Harcourt House, 39 Gloucester Road, Wan Chai

✆ +852 2826 9223

🖱 career.hk@em.berlitz.com

💻 www.berlitz.com.hk

NUMBER OF TEACHERS: 7, increasing to 10.

PREFERENCE OF NATIONALITY: UK, US, NZ, Australia.

QUALIFICATIONS: TESOL/TEFL, Bachelor's degree, business experience. Teaching experience good but not essential.

CONDITIONS OF EMPLOYMENT: 1 year with option to renew. Depending on agreement, business hours are 7.30am–9pm Monday–Friday, and 9am–6pm on Saturdays and Sundays.

SALARY: Starting salary HK$100 per unit (40 minutes teaching time). Contribution to pension scheme is 5%, to a monthly maximum of HK$1,250. Low tax rates, paid annually to HK Inland Revenue Department.

FACILITIES/SUPPORT: No help with accommodation. Sponsorship for work visa is provided for full-time teachers only. Successful applications usually take 4–6 weeks.

RECRUITMENT: Ads posted online or in local newspapers. Interviews conducted locally or via Skype.

CONTACT: Ulf Behrendt, Manager of Instruction.

CHATTERIS EDUCATIONAL FOUNDATION

Flat A, 13F, Block 2, Camel Paint Building, 62 Hoi Yuen Road, Kwun Tong, Kowloon

✆ +852 2520 5736

🖱 hr@chatteris.org.hk, info@chatteris.org.hk

💻 www.chatteris.org.hk

NUMBER OF TEACHERS: 80–85 CNETs (Chatteris Native-speaking English Teachers) per year.

PREFERENCE OF NATIONALITY: Primarily British, American and Canadian.

QUALIFICATIONS: Bachelor's degree from the past 4 years or higher qualification in any subject, no teaching experience necessary. Undergraduates in their final year may also apply. Must have clean police record.

CONDITIONS OF EMPLOYMENT: 9-month contracts, 1 September–31 May (mandatory 3-week orientation begins mid-August). 8 hours per day with 1 hour lunch break, weekends free.

SALARY: HK$14,000. Must have enough funds on arrival to cover start-up costs and pay a refundable deposit of HK$2,000. Total recommended to have up front is about £3,750.

FACILITIES/SUPPORT: Accommodation is provided free of charge by Chatteris during the 3-week orientation period. During this time, flat-hunting workshops are provided to familiarise employees with the property system of Hong Kong. Chatteris office staff are also available for assistance with negotiation of rental agreements and any issues that may arise during this time. After acceptance into the programme support is provided to applicants regarding the organisation and processing of work visa. Chatteris will request a number of documents such as original degree certificates, police clearance checks, doctor's letter and employment visa form ID990A in order for the visa to be processed.

RECRUITMENT: Through online job postings and websites, word-of-mouth and seminars. Applications accepted from November; closing dates are 31 May and 1 July. Interviews are conducted via Skype or in person, and carried out in the UK during a recruitment trip in February/March, in Sydney in May and sometimes in the USA.

CONTACT: Daniel Chun, CEO (dc@chatteris.org.hk).

DEBORAH ENGLISH KINDERGARTEN & INTERNATIONAL PRE-SCHOOL

Kindergarten Tower, Beverly Garden, Tseung Kwan, Kowloon

✆ +852 2217 7933

🖱 dktko06@yahoo.com.hk or jobs@deborah-kindergarten.com

💻 www.deborah-intl.edu.hk or www.deborah-kindergarten.com

NUMBER OF TEACHERS: More than 60 for all schools; 8 kindergartens in HK and 2 in Shenzen, China.

PREFERENCE OF NATIONALITY: Canadian, Australian, British or American. Must be native English speakers.

QUALIFICATIONS: Any university degree or an early childhood certificate plus minimum 6-months' teaching experience.

CONDITIONS OF EMPLOYMENT: 2-year contract. School hours from 8.30am to 5pm Monday to Friday plus occasional Saturdays for special events. Must love children, since teaching children aged 2–6.

SALARY: From HK$16,000, depending on experience. Airfare, medical cover and 8–9 weeks' approx paid holiday provided.

FACILITIES/SUPPORT: Free shared accommodation per 2–3 teachers or HK$2,000 accommodation allowance. Visa sponsorship may be available.

RECRUITMENT: Via the internet, please send résumé/CV by email. Recruiting goes on year round. Interviews not essential.

CONTACT: Mr Anderson.

NUMBER OF TEACHERS: Around 40 full-time native-speaking teachers for Hong Kong (plus 10 for major Chinese cities).

PREFERENCE OF NATIONALITY: None but must be native English speakers.

QUALIFICATIONS: Company largely deals with recent drama and English graduates, as well as specialists in Early Childhood Development. Candidates should have a degree in theatre/drama, English or related field. ESL qualification/experience is preferred, but not essential. Non-degree tertiary qualifications adequate for Early Childhood specialists. Affiliated to Hong Kong TESOL Institute (www.hk-tesol.org) which offers 3-week, 60-hour training course for US$1,599.

CONDITIONS OF EMPLOYMENT: Contracts run for 10–12 months. Teachers may continue for another contract term. Working hours fall between 7.30am and 9.30pm with 9-hour working days, 5 days per week, depending on school programmes and timetabling.

SALARY: HK$20,000 per month starting salary plus end-of-contract bonus. Employees are required to pay their own taxes at the end of each financial year. There are tax-free thresholds, and due to the timing of contracts, first year employees end up paying little, if any tax.

FACILITIES/SUPPORT: Temporary accommodation for new teachers can be organised. Local staff are happy to support teachers who experience communication problems with local real estate agents and/or property owners.

RECRUITMENT: Via direct contact with universities, referrals and some websites. Phone interviews are essential. The company very occasionally carries out interviews abroad.

CONTACT: Luke Yick (yick.luke@gmail.com)

Recruitment agency that provides Native English teachers (NETs) to Hong Kong kindergartens, primary and secondary schools.

PREFERENCE OF NATIONALITY: UK, Australia, USA, South Africa, Europe.

QUALIFICATIONS: Good English pronunciation, experience and qualifications, i.e. degree, TESOL/TEFL, BA (Ed) or other teaching qualifications like PGCE/PGDE.

CONDITIONS OF EMPLOYMENT: 1 year, often extended. Hours are 8.30–4.30 Monday–Friday plus 1 Saturday morning per month.

SALARY: HK$18,000–HK$23,000 per month depending on experience, qualifications and duties.

FACILITIES/SUPPORT: Teachers are responsible for their own accommodation.

RECRUITMENT: Via Global English (online TESOL Provider), local media, word of mouth and internet. Face-to-face interviews in Hong Kong with agency and client schools necessary.

CONTACT: Toby White, Director.

British-owned and operated network of 12 schools around Hong Kong Island and Kowloon. The largest extra-curricular English school in Hong Kong.

QUALIFICATIONS: Degree and teaching certificate, eg TEFL, CELTA. Applications from those without a teaching cert will be considered if they have demonstrated experience of working with children in other capacities. Classes are limited to 4 students per class and are highly interactive, so potential teachers need to be energetic and friendly.

CONDITIONS OF EMPLOYMENT: To teach students aged 3–16. Minimum contract duration is 12–16 months. Generous completion gratuities reflect the importance of the contract. Saturday is a working day so working week covers Monday to Saturday with two long mornings off till 3.30 pm.

SALARY: Revealed to short-listed candidates. Monthly bonus paid.

FACILITIES/SUPPORT: Accommodation in Quarry Bay area provided (about 90% accept this option). School applies for visas on behalf of the candidates before arrival in HK.

RECRUITMENT: Applications must include a cover letter and CV with photo. Recruitment is done via telephone interviews throughout the year.

NUMBER OF TEACHERS: Nearly 200 Native English Teachers.

PREFERENCE OF NATIONALITY: None as long as they are native speakers. Company has links with universities in the UK, US, South Africa, Ireland, Australia and New Zealand.

QUALIFICATIONS: Minimum requirement is a bachelor degree (preferably in education or English-related subjects) or a teaching qualification (TEFL/TESOL/CELTA, etc).

CONDITIONS OF EMPLOYMENT: 12 months starting in September. Monday to Friday 8am-5pm.

SALARY: HK$18,000+ net.

FACILITIES/SUPPORT: Package available whereby accommodation is provided and a lower salary paid. Full assistance given with work permits. After the necessary documents have been received, Headstart lodges the visa application which normally takes 4-6 weeks to be processed.

RECRUITMENT: University recruitment fairs, paid job posting websites, referrals from teachers and social media. Skype interviews.

CONTACT: Julie Chu, General Manager; Dennis Leung, Officer Teacher Recruitment & Management (dennisleung@ headstartgroup.co).

HK INSTITUTE OF LANGUAGES
6/f Wellington Plaza, 56–58 Wellington Street, Central
☎ +852 2877 6160
✉ info@hklanguages.com
🖥 www.hklanguages.com

NUMBER OF TEACHERS: 5.

PREFERENCE OF NATIONALITY: British or American.

QUALIFICATIONS: University degree, CELTA or equivalent ESL teaching certificate plus state teaching certifications, eg PGCE.

CONDITIONS OF EMPLOYMENT: 1-year renewable contract with 20–25 contact teaching hours per week.

SALARY: HK$20,000 per month.

FACILITIES/SUPPORT: Accommodation provided for the first week then assistance is given to find suitable permanent accommodation. Sponsorship offered for work permits and all paperwork is taken care of.

RECRUITMENT: Usually via advertisements on corporate and professional websites. Interviews are essential.

READY TO LEARN HONG KONG LTD
1/F Wing Sing Commercial Building, 2–4 Wing Sing Lane, Yau Ma Tei, Kowloon
☎ +852 2338 1318
✉ frances.ma@rtlenglish.com (Human Resources)
🖥 www.rtl.edu.hk

NUMBER OF TEACHERS: 15–25 part-time and full-time for Educational Centres in North Point and Mong Kok as well as Kowloon, teaching children 3–18.

PREFERENCE OF NATIONALITY: Majority are permanent residents who have been in HK for some time. Teachers can be sponsored from English-speaking countries especially UK.

QUALIFICATIONS: University degree necessary for getting a working visa. 120-hour TEFL Certificate required; any ESL courses that emphasise grammar are useful. A willingness to teach a structured curriculum in the form of prepared and printed lesson books.

CONDITIONS OF EMPLOYMENT: Minimum 1 year, renewable. Full-time in Hong Kong is 19 hours, but overseas sponsored teachers usually work 30 hours. Teaching hours between 9 am and 7 pm, including weekends. Very structured material used for teaching, including a lot of grammar.

SALARY: Basic HK$17,000 per month. The teacher pays tax annually (on average about HK$5,500).

FACILITIES/SUPPORT: Return airfare paid (up to HK$6,000) if returning to home country. Up to HK$6,000 contribution to expenses during the first month. Help with finding accommodation initially can be given. New teachers will be met at the airport.

RECRUITMENT: Locally to find candidates who already have a working visa or permanent residence, internet advertising and word of mouth. Interviews necessary and can be by Skype.

CONTACT: Elaine Shannon, Principal and Founder.

TEACH TO TRAVEL LTD
Room 4, Third Floor, Duru House, 101 Commercial Road, London E1 1RD, UK
☎ +44 207 247 5820
✉ hr@teachtotravel.co.uk
🖥 www.teachtotravel.co.uk

NUMBER OF TEACHERS: Roughly 30–35 for positions around Hong Kong Island, Kowloon and the New Territories.

PREFERENCE OF NATIONALITY: Must be native English speaker.

QUALIFICATIONS: University degree and teaching qualification, such as TEFL/TESOL/CELTA/PGCE, required. Must be under the age of 40. Experience of 1 year is preferred but not necessary. Criminal background check needed, eg from www.disclosurescotland.co.uk in the UK or the FBI in the US.

CONDITIONS OF EMPLOYMENT: Most positions are in public and private kindergartens to teach children aged 2–6 though some are in language institutes. 10-month contract between 1 September and 31 July. Working week Monday to Saturday, 8.30am–4.45pm. In general, the more experience the teacher has, the closer to Hong Kong Island the placement is likely to be.

SALARY: HK$12,500 per month (net) with accommodation or HK$19,500 without.

FACILITIES/SUPPORT: Free accommodation provided, though teacher pays utility bills. Cost of flights reimbursed at end of contract. Orientation provided on arrival. Health insurance and work permit provided.

RECRUITMENT: Skype interview.

CONTACT: Geoffrey Thomas, Director (geoff.thomas@teach totravel.co.uk).

WORD POWER ENGLISH LEARNING CENTER

North Point Branch: Shop 102–103, 1/F, Island Place, North Point

📞 +852 856 5232

✉ manager@wordpower.edu.hk

💻 www.wordpower.edu.hk

NUMBER OF TEACHERS: 20.

PREFERENCE OF NATIONALITY: British, American, Australian and Canadian.

QUALIFICATIONS: 3 or 4-year full-time bachelor's degree plus TEFL/CELTA plus minimum 1 year teaching experience, preferably in Asia.

CONDITIONS OF EMPLOYMENT: 1-year contract. 120 contact hours per month.

SALARY: HK$20,000 per month (HK$240K per annum) subject to review after 3-month assessment. A gratuity of HK$10,000 paid on satisfactory completion of 1-year contract.

FACILITIES/SUPPORT: Help finding an apartment provided, soft set-up loan available to employees and also visa sponsorship.

RECRUITMENT: Via internet with interviews in Hong Kong.

CONTACT: Ken Chu, Manager.

MACAO

The lesser-known of China's two special administrative regions is Macao, a former Portuguese colony that lies west of Hong Kong across the delta of the Pearl River. The territory's economy is booming from its successful gambling and tourist industries. With a doctorate in Linguistics, **Joanna Radwanska-Williams** is an ELT professional at the Macao Polytechnic Institute and with MPI Bell (see entry) who makes Macao her home:

Macao is a very international city with a high standard of living. It's definitely a pleasant living environment, and the historic city centre is on the UNESCO World Heritage list. Macao feels like a 'happy place' and is welcoming to families and newcomers. Many people speak English as the international and regional lingua franca and there is a high demand for English. There is a lot of English-language local press. The health care is good. There are many churches, especially Catholic ones, and freedom of worship. It is basically a western-type setting, though with lots of Chinese tourists from the mainland.

The unusual factor – not necessarily a low – is the presence of the casino industry. This comes with incredibly luxurious shopping, good restaurants, etc. For the most part, we reap lots of benefits from this: good salaries, great public facilities funded by the government, such as parks, swimming pools, museums, cultural activities and tourist attractions. Macao has far surpassed Las Vegas in terms of revenue from the casino industry. To the extent that there is crime (much less so than in the US, I would think), it does not impact ordinary citizens. Macao is perfectly safe to walk in, day or night. The public transportation is great.

LIST OF EMPLOYERS

ENGLISH FOR ASIA LTD (MACAO BRANCH)

10E, Edificio Comercial Rodrigues, No. 599 Av. Praia Grande, Macao

- +853 2870 5784
- nathan@englishforasia.com or macao@englishforasia.com
- www.englishforasia.com

NUMBER OF TEACHERS: 10–15 (at present).

PREFERENCE OF NATIONALITY: Native English speakers of any nationality.

QUALIFICATIONS: Minimum bachelor's degree and TESOL certificate (or other equivalent teaching certificate). Minimum of 2-years' experience essential.

CONDITIONS OF EMPLOYMENT: 1-year rolling contracts (due to local labour laws). 27 teaching hours a week, plus an allocated 13 hours for preparation and admin work (40-hour working week). Hours usually stretch over 5 days, with 2 full days off per week. Operational hours are 8am–9pm; teaching schedule can accommodate teacher's outside commitments. Working during the weekends and summer months essential. Around 40 days of paid holiday per academic year (includes 2-week break at Christmas/New Year, 1 week at Chinese New Year, 5 days for Easter and a 5-day pre-summer holiday in June).

SALARY: HK$21,000 (depending on qualifications and experience). At current exchange rates, this is equivalent to £1,700, about double the average wage in Macao. Tax deductions are made quarterly and are very low (approximately £50 per quarter).

FACILITIES/SUPPORT: Teacher trainer on hand to give on-the-job coaching and guidance. Reasonably priced temporary accommodation will be provided upon arrival until an employee finds a home in the territory. No housing allowance is given. Visa sponsorship is given; teachers provide a copy of their CV/résumé and original certificates for inspection. UK syllabus is followed. The process can take up to 3 months and teachers will be required to pay a fee of around £10 upon collection.

RECRUITMENT: Usually direct application for teachers already in the region. Interviews essential.

CONTACT: Nathan Fox, Centre Manager.

HEADSTART GROUP LTD

Unit 2508, Nanyang Plaza, 57 Hung To Road, Kwun Tong, Kowloon, Hong Kong

- +852 21559602; Macao: +853 6268 6001
- juliechu@headstartgroup.co
- www.headstartgroup.co or http://hkmacau.headstartgroup.co

See entry above in Hong Kong chapter.

MPI-BELL CENTRE OF ENGLISH (BELL PARTNER SCHOOL)
Macao Polytechnic Institute, 3rd floor, Meng Tak Building,
Rua de Luis Gonzaga Gomes, Macao

(c) +853 8599 3162

mpibell@ipm.edu.mo or davidq@ipm.edu.mo

http://bellcentre.ipm.edu.mo

NUMBER OF TEACHERS: 11 in Macao plus 3 in Xinjiang,
China.

PREFERENCE OF NATIONALITY: None, but must be native
speaker of English.

QUALIFICATIONS: Minimum bachelor's degree, CELTA and 5
years' experience, preferably in China.

CONDITIONS OF EMPLOYMENT: 2-year renewable contracts.
Normally 20 contact hours per week over 5 days.

SALARY: Varies but approximately RMB400,000 gross per year.
Approximately 8% deductions.

FACILITIES/SUPPORT: Accommodation or accommodation
allowance provided. Work permit and visas arranged. End-of-
contract payment. 22 days' paid holiday per year plus public
holidays. Local medical insurance cover provided.

RECRUITMENT: Direct application.

CONTACT: David Quartermain, Deputy Director
(davidq@ipm.edu.mo).

INDONESIA

Indonesia is the fourth most populous nation on earth. The economist Jim O'Neill, who coined the term BRIC to represent the economic powerhouse nations of the early 21st century, has now identified the next wave. Indonesia conveniently provides the vowel in MINT (Mexico, Indonesia, Nigeria and Turkey). This nation embedded in Southeast Asia and with longstanding ties to China seems at ease with Western ways of doing business, and some predict that it could experience double digit growth in the coming years.

Schools are attracting professional ELT teachers from abroad with benefits packages and reasonable salaries of more than 16 million rupiah (£760). The best jobs continue to crop up in the oil company cities. Although oil production has been declining, the industry is still crucial to the country's economy. The so-called 'native English speaker schools' with multiple branches in Jakarta and the other cities continue to deliver English courses to the millions of Indonesians who want to learn the language. These organisations can still afford to hire trained foreign teachers and pay them about 10 times the local wage. EF English First is the biggest and most well known chain of the franchised language schools, with schools in Jakarta as well as on Sumatra, Java, Sulawesi and Bali. Wall Street English (www.wallstreetenglish.com.id) has several branches in Jakarta – including a plush branch on Jalan Jend. Sudirman, the capital's most prestigious thoroughfare. In their ads on tefl.com etc, they explain 'why teaching at Wall Street English is your dream job'. It has captured market share by targeting office workers using a highly flexible schedule, which means teaching schedules can be awkward. Over the past few years, the National Plus schools movement has been gaining ground. These schools for the children of the Indonesian middle class tend to follow an international curriculum, often with some local content, and the medium of instruction is English, or a mix of Indonesian and English. So far they have not proved much competition for private language institutes.

FINDING A JOB

The CELTA is highly regarded in Indonesia and anyone who has acquired the certificate has a good chance of pre-arranging a job in Jakarta, Surabaya, Bandung or Yogyakarta (arguably the most interesting city in Indonesia), provided they satisfy the other visa requirements. The government stipulates that teachers must be native English speakers from the UK, USA, Canada, Ireland, Australia or New Zealand in order to be awarded a work permit. Teachers are required to hold a bachelor's degree in a specified subject, ie Linguistics, English Language, English Literature or Education, to satisfy government visa requirements, and this is enforced, in spite of what other teaching or ELT qualifications (unless it is an MA in TESOL) the candidate might have.

Among the main schools in Indonesia it is standard to reimburse airfares and visa costs at the end of a successful contract. A number offer medical insurance and others offer free housing.

While some schools clearly favour either British or North American teachers, others express no preference, and there are also quite a few Australian and New Zealander EFL teachers in Indonesia.

EF English First advertises extensively and constantly for teachers in Indonesia. They are split into separate franchises, even within Jakarta, which are responsible for recruiting teachers for their own groups of schools, including the Swara Group with ten schools, the Depok Group, the Harmoni Group and so on. Employment conditions are fairly standard across the groups.

ON THE SPOT

More and more teachers are being hired on the spot, which suits the major schools, which then don't have to pay for airfares. Local recruits can negotiate shorter contracts, for example six months, unlike teachers recruited abroad, who usually have to commit for 12 months. Most teaching jobs start in July or September/October. With a Cambridge/Trinity or equivalent certificate and university degree in an approved field your chances of being offered a job are high. Under-qualified applicants would have to be extremely well presented (since dress is very important in Jakarta), able to sell themselves in terms of experience and qualifications and prepared to commit themselves for a longish spell or to start with some part-time work in the hope of building it up. Caution is advised at the interview stage, because promises are not always kept or the full extent of deductions mentioned.

Local schools staffed by Indonesians abound, many willing to hire a native English speaker at local wages, though they may not be in a position to arrange a work permit. There is no 'easy answer' for how prospective teachers should try to sell themselves, as **Ross McKay**, a long-term teacher in Jakarta, is keen to point out:

> *Each school has it own ethos. One place likes lots of chat but others are sober-sides who keep students' noses to the grindstone. I went to one interview and kept the class happy for an hour, only to be told that 'we're educators, not entertainers'. But another school didn't call me for interview because I'd stated that I took the job seriously and didn't go easy on students who habitually arrived late. Jam Karet, rubber-time, is a bad habit here, and you either adjust to it or get driven nuts.*

The Indonesian *Yellow Pages* is online at www.yellowpages.co.id and searchable in English under the heading 'Language Schools'. Opportunities exist not only in the large cities but in small towns too. Travellers have stumbled across friendly little schools up rickety staircases throughout the islands of Indonesia, as the German round-the-world traveller **Gerhard Flaig** describes:

> *In Yogyakarta you can find language schools listed in the telephone book or you just walk through streets to look for them. Most of them are interested in having new teachers. I got an offer to teach German and also English since my English was better than some of the language school managers. All of them didn't bother about work permits. The wages aren't very high but it is fairly easy to cover the costs of board and lodging since the cost of living is very low.*

Tim Leffel from New Jersey, USA noticed a large number of English schools in the Javanese city of Solo, and others have recommended Denpasar (Bali). Volunteer Programs Bali was set up in 2009 to recruit international volunteers to assist with English in local schools in Ubud (among other projects); a full table of fees (e.g. £525 for eight weeks) can be found at www.volunteerprogramsbali.org. At local schools unused to employing native English-speaker teachers, teaching materials may be in short supply. One of the problems faced by those who undertake casual work of this kind is that there is little chance of obtaining a work permit. It is difficult for freelance teachers to become legal unless they have a contact who knows people in power. The problem of visas doesn't arise if you teach English on a completely informal basis, as **Stuart Tappin** did:

> *In Asia I managed to spend a lot of time living with people in return for teaching English. The more remote the towns are from tourist routes the better, for example Bali is no good. I spent a week in Palembang, Sumatra, living with an English teacher and his family. You teach and they give their (very good) hospitality.*

If you get stuck job-hunting in Jakarta, go to Jalan Jaksa, a small but lively street where many teachers hang out.

REGULATIONS

The work permit regulations are rigidly adhered to in Indonesia and all of the established language schools and chains will apply for a visa permit on your behalf. Some even employ a dedicated visa coordinator and employ an agent in the Indonesian Embassy in Singapore where most people collect the visa. The Indonesian

Embassy in London issues 'General Information for Foreigners Wishing to Work in Indonesia', which starts with the warning: '*Please be informed that it is not easy for foreigners to work and stay in Indonesia since Indonesia has very strict and complicated immigration/visa requirements and regulations, and the process can be very long*' (www.indonesianembassy.org.uk). As mentioned, the Indonesian government limits work permits to teachers holding passports from the six main English-speaking countries (UK, Ireland, US, Canada, Australia and New Zealand) and with degrees in an approved field as listed above, which one school director called 'nonsensical', but that is the situation. Candidates are also expected to have three to five years of post-qualification experience and be aged 25–57, though these rules are more flexible.

If the job is arranged in plenty of time before you leave home, you may be sent a letter of sponsorship from your employer to take to the Indonesian Embassy in London and, subject to current visa requirements, it will issue you with a 60-day visa, £40 non-refundable. Alternatively, you may apply for a one-year Temporary Stay visa (VITAS), which costs £80.

It is possible to enter Indonesia on a tourist visa and, after being hired, have the school arrange the work permit, but for this you will have to leave the country after supplying your CV, originals of your TEFL course and university degree certificates, photocopies of your passport and application forms. You must also obtain a health certificate proving that you are free of HIV and of drugs. According to one school, the photos submitted must be in three different sizes and on a red background! The application is sent to the Indonesian Ministry of Education, the Cabinet Secretariat and the Immigration/Manpower Departments. If and when the application is approved, the work permit will be valid for one employer only and will be revoked and the offending teacher deported if work is undertaken outside the terms of the contract.

After your work permit and temporary stay permit have been granted (with a maximum validity of one year), the documentation will then be sent to the nearest Indonesian Embassy (normally Singapore), where the teacher can have it stamped in his or her passport. These visa runs only take a day or two and should be paid for by your employer, although some, such as Berlitz, consequently withhold 10% of your salary for the first six months, then reimburse the 10% monthly, starting in the seventh month, to ensure that teachers fulfil the year's visa.

It is possible to renew your tourist status by leaving the country every two months (eg flying to Singapore, or by ferry to Penang in Malaysia) but the authorities might become suspicious if you did this repeatedly. Anyone found working on a tourist visa will be deported and blacklisted from entering Indonesia in the future. Also, the employer would be in serious trouble.

CONDITIONS OF WORK

Salaries paid by the 'native English speaker' schools can provide for a comfortable lifestyle, including travel within Indonesia during the vacations. Most schools pay at least 12 or 13 million rupiah per month, after Indonesian tax of 7%–10% (on earnings of up to 25 million rupiah) has been subtracted. Although salaries with Wall Street English worldwide are usually at the lower end, in Indonesia it offers 16,000–18,000 rupiah in addition to a travel subsidy. Teachers with at least 5 years' experience were being recruited by TEFL One (wwww.teflone.com) not long ago on 20 million rupiah. As mentioned, reimbursement for airfares is commonplace, as described by **Bruce Clarke**, who worked for EF English First:

In addition to a decent starting salary, my school also agreed to reimburse me at the end of my contract for both the price of my plane ticket and my work visa. Basic living is relatively cheap. I spend about half my salary on western luxuries like beer, CDs, movies, etc. I bank the rest so at the end of my year I expect to head home with a few thousand dollars saved. Most of the teachers I meet are in their early 20s, and are generally still at the 'let's party every night' stage of their lives. They complain about constantly being broke because they tend to go clubbing two or three nights a week and waste a lot of money.

Many schools offer generous help with accommodation, ranging from an interest-free loan to cover initial rent payments or deposits, to free housing complete with free telephone, electricity and maid service. This perk may be at the expense of free choice though, and it is worth considering if you mind where you live/ who you live with. It is customary in the Jakarta housing market to be asked to pay the annual rent in a lump sum at the beginning of your tenancy, and so access to a loan from your employer is often essential. **Ross McKay** warns that housing contracts should not be undertaken lightly, since one of his ex-colleagues who refused to pay a year's rent on a house he had occupied for two months ended up behind bars and subject to a huge fine.

If you happen to work for a school which takes on outside contracts, you may have the occasional chance to work outside the school premises, possibly in a remote oil drilling location in Sumatra, for up to double pay. The majority of teachers, however, conduct lessons at their school through the usual peak hours of 3.30pm– 8.30pm, with some early morning starts as well. Many supplement their incomes with private students (provided their employer permits it). For example, Ross McKay was paid by a doctor to teach him while they drove into Jakarta in the morning, which boiled down to him being paid to be given a lift to work. Freelancers will have to get used to *jam karat*, which means 'rubber time', or the Indonesian habit of appalling time keeping.

THE STUDENTS

Outside the big cities, the standard of English is normally quite low, with students having picked up a smattering from bad American television. Classes also tend to be large, with as many as 40 students, all expecting to learn grammar by the traditional rote methods. According to a VSO volunteer teaching in Western Java (as quoted in the *Times Educational Supplement*): '*If I want to do something interesting, the students complain that it isn't in the exam.*' As is the case elsewhere in the world, the average age of English learners is getting younger, so anyone with experience of teaching children or teenagers will be appreciated. **Andrew Whitmarsh**, a teacher for Wall Street in Jakarta, enjoyed being able to entice his students into university-style discussions:

> *As I look back over my experience, I would say that the best times have come during the classes when I almost forgot I was a teacher and they were my students, and instead felt like I was leading a discussion group back at university. At the other end of the scale there were certainly days that some classes felt repetitive, but I got through these by being sure to make creative and engaging social clubs to balance it all out.*

LEISURE TIME

Although Jakarta is a hot, dusty, overcrowded and polluted city, there is a great deal to see and do, and most teachers end up more than tolerating it. After quitting his job in information technology at age 37, **Bruce Clarke** obtained a TEFL certificate from Winfield College in Vancouver and immediately landed a one-year teaching contract with EF English First in Indonesia and concluded that Indonesia is 'okay', though not quite as glamorous as he had hoped. He liked his school and staff, but found Jakarta just another big, crowded city. On a happier note, a past Director of Studies at Executive English Programs (EEP) writes:

> *Jakarta has moved on in leaps and bounds in many ways since I first arrived. The traffic may be viler than ever, but while it still certainly isn't Hong Kong or Singapore food-wise, the variety of good quality, reasonably priced restaurants is very impressive these days. Once you know your way around!*

Indonesia is a fascinating country and most visitors, whether short-term or long, agree that the Indonesian people are fantastic. Travel is cheap and unrestricted, and excursions are very rewarding in terms of scenery and culture. Travel by public transport can be time consuming and limiting for weekend trips, so you might consider getting a motorcycle, although Jakarta's traffic problems make this seem daunting. **Ross McKay** recommends using Bluebird or Express taxis in Jakarta as the most dependable and to use air-conditioned buses (but not after midnight). He also advises newcomers to arrive with crisp, new notes since banks are loath to handle creased or tatty foreign currency.

The draw for **Dan Quinn** from Cumbria was gamelan music, which he studied in his spare time from teaching in Jakarta, as well as climbing hills like Papandayan, Guntur and Cikuray, which are all within reach of Jakarta by Primajasa bus. He has gone on to run the website Quinn's World of TEFL http://worldoftefl.com. His favourite place to listen to music in Jakarta is the Iguana Dangdut bar in the Hotel Menteng.

Predictably, the community of expatriate teachers participates in lots of joint activities such as football and tennis matches, chess tournaments, beach excursions, diving trips and parties. Most teachers have DVDs but occasionally go out to see an undubbed American film. The pleasant city of Bandung might prove an attractive alternative to Jakarta and offers a good-quality lifestyle to teachers, with a good mixture of rural and city life. Since the opening of the toll road from Jakarta to Bandung, a journey time of two hours is possible. It's choked at the weekends, but fine during the week.

Speaking of weekends, **Andrew Whitmarsh** had no problem finding something to do, often with the help of his students:

This is one of the wildest and most wonderful countries I've worked in, so a lot of my time is spent getting out and seeing the city or jumping a train to check out the surrounding countryside. The traffic in Jakarta is tough to deal with and the air quality isn't great, but the opportunity for adventure and excitement is always just around the corner. Many of my students-turned-friends are great guides to the sights and always know the best nightclubs to visit, when the concerts are and where the best food is.

Bahasa Indonesian, almost identical to Malay, was imposed on the people of Indonesia after independence in 1949 and is one of the simplest languages to learn both in structure and pronunciation.

LIST OF EMPLOYERS

AIM FOR ENGLISH

Jalan Padang 5C, Manggarai, Jakarta Selatan 12580

📞 +62 21 8378 5238

✉ ian@aimjakarta.com/info@aimjakarta.com

🖥 www.aimjakarta.com/english

NUMBER OF TEACHERS: 11.

PREFERENCE OF NATIONALITY: British, American, Canadian, Australian, New Zealander and Indonesian.

QUALIFICATIONS: Must have a bachelor's degree in English Language, English Literature, Linguistics or Education. At least CELTA, and 3–5-years' experience (teaching adults, test preparation, Business English and Academic English).

CONDITIONS OF EMPLOYMENT: 12-month contracts. 24 hours' contact. 7 hours in the office 5 days a week. Some evening work. Teachers will also visit clients in their workplaces around Jakarta.

SALARY: 17 million rupiah (after tax), equivalent to around $1,275 per month.

FACILITIES/SUPPORT: Return ticket home, end-of-contract bonus and full health insurance. Ongoing career development. Visas and work permits taken care of: outsourced to a reliable agent.

RECRUITMENT: Through online advertising and word of mouth. Interviews essential, and can be via web-meeting (via Skype/Yahoo messenger with webcam). Face-to-face interviews preferred, as teaching a demonstration class is often necessary.

CONTACT: Ian Bishop, Managing Director.

BERLITZ LANGUAGE CENTRES

PT Berlitz, Hotel InterContinental MidPlaza Jakarta, Shopping Gallery R-26, Jl. Jendral Sudirman Kav. 10–11, Jakarta 10220

📞 +62 21 251 4589

✉ recruitment@berlitz.co.id

🖥 www.berlitz.co.id

NUMBER OF TEACHERS: 10.

PREFERENCE OF NATIONALITY: British, American, Canadian, Australian and New Zealander (essential for visa).

QUALIFICATIONS: Degree with a major in English (required). TEFL certificate (CELTA, Trinity or equivalent). 3 years' teaching experience. Minimum age 25.

CONDITIONS OF EMPLOYMENT: 12-month contracts. School hours: 7.30am–9pm, Monday to Friday; 7.30am to 3pm Saturday. Lessons scheduled as available between these hours.

SALARY: Approximately $1,000–$1,200 (net) depending on qualifications and experience.

FACILITIES/SUPPORT: Housing allowance paid and first month's housing arranged. Berlitz Instructor Training free of charge. Visa agent assists with permits and school bears the cost.

RECRUITMENT: Word of mouth, newspapers and via internet. Interviews by phone or held at nearby language centre.

CONTACT: Manager of Instruction.

EF ENGLISH FIRST

Indonesian Head Office, Wisma Tamara Lt. 4, Suite 402, Jl. Jend. Sudirman Kav. 24, Jakarta 12920

☎ +62 21 520 6477

✉ efrecruitment@ef.com

🖳 www.englishfirst.com/trt

NUMBER OF TEACHERS: More than 700 for 65 schools throughout Indonesia. New vacancies every week.

PREFERENCE OF NATIONALITY: British, Canadian, Australian, American or New Zealander (due to work visa restrictions).

QUALIFICATIONS: TEFL/TESL certificate preferred, indicating 120 hours of class work, observations and evaluated practice teaching. Teaching experience and/or bachelor's degree preferred.

CONDITIONS OF EMPLOYMENT: 12-month contracts. Usual hours are early afternoon until evening (1pm–9pm).

SALARY: Varies significantly between cities: 9.5–14.6 million rupiah per month (net) depending on experience.

FACILITIES/SUPPORT: Cost of airfares reimbursed. Most schools provide shared housing free or a monthly housing allowance. Teachers preferring to live alone are given advice and help but bear the contractual responsibilities themselves. Schools provide and pay for necessary working papers. Standardised induction programme on arrival, ongoing training and development, medical insurance and 10 days' paid holidays provided.

RECRUITMENT: Advertises heavily on main ELT sites like www. tefl.com. Via EF's Online Recruitment Centre or approaching groups of individual schools, eg via englishfirstjakarta.com.

CONTACT: Alan Davies, Senior Academic Operations Manager (alan.davies@ef.com).

EXECUTIVE ENGLISH PROGRAMS (EEP)

Jalan Diponegoro 7, Bandung 40115

☎ +62 22 426 3020

✉ dos@eepbdg.com

🖳 www.eepbdg.com

PREFERENCE OF NATIONALITY: British, American, Canadian, Australian and New Zealander.

QUALIFICATIONS: CELTA/Trinity certificate plus university degree in English, English Literature or Linguistics (as laid out in the Department of Education regulations) and at least a year's experience preferred.

CONDITIONS OF EMPLOYMENT: 1-year contracts to work a maximum of 28 hours per week.

SALARY: Minimum 11 million rupiah per month for in-centre training. Increments for higher duties, in-company work and specialised training projects. Contract renewal bonus operates. Salary includes 25 days' paid holiday per year and limited medical coverage.

FACILITIES/SUPPORT: Will provide documentation and assist in finding accommodation.

RECRUITMENT: Through local newspapers (*The Jakarta Post*). Local interviews almost always necessary. Local interviews preferred, although online interviews are also acceptable.

CONTACT: Ian Mulyana, S.Pd., MM, Director of Studies & Operational Manager.

KELT SURABAYA (formerly International Language Programs)

Jalan Jawa 34, Surabaya 63105

☎ +62 31 502 3333

✉ jawa@k-elt.com

🖳 www.k-elt.com

NUMBER OF TEACHERS: 25 in 3 schools.

PREFERENCE OF NATIONALITY: Must be classified native English speaker (to satisfy work permit requirements) ie British, American, Canadian, Australian and New Zealander. Most teachers are British

QUALIFICATIONS: Recognised EFL qualification required, eg CELTA or Trinity; short intro courses and online courses not acceptable. No experience needed.

CONDITIONS OF EMPLOYMENT: 1-year contracts, eg from July, October, etc. 20 hours per week, teaching 5 days a week, between 2.30pm/3.45pm/5pm and 7pm/9.15pm. Pupils from age 4.

SALARY: Starting salary is 13.5 million rupiah (net) per month with increments for experience.

FACILITIES/SUPPORT: Accommodation provided, including electricity and servants. Regular workshops held. 8 weeks' paid holiday.

RECRUITMENT: Adverts on the internet (www.tefl.com). Recruitment 4 times a year.

CONTACT: Ian Ramsdale (ian@k-elt.com), Academic Coordinator of Studies.

PRIME ONE SCHOOL

Jl. Jenderal Besar A. H Nasution No.88 A, Medan 20147

✆ +62 61 785 3630/785 3672

🖱 info@pos.sch.id

🖥 www.pos.sch.id

NUMBER OF TEACHERS: 4.

PREFERENCE OF NATIONALITY: American, British and Australian.

QUALIFICATIONS: Must have a degree and a minimum of 1-year's teaching experience.

CONDITIONS OF EMPLOYMENT: Standard 2-year contract. Minimum 30 sessions per week.

SALARY: 9 million rupiah before tax.

FACILITIES/SUPPORT: Shared accommodation in staff house provided. Assistance with work permits given.

RECRUITMENT: Writing test, interview and psychology test. Interviews via webcam.

CONTACT: Silvia Angkasa, BBA, Vice-Director of Admin, Finance and Operations.

SANG TIMUR

Karmel St No 2 Kebon Jeruk, Jakarta 11530

✆ +62 21 5302256

🖱 antorejekipurba@yahoo.co.id or sangtimur_smak@yahoo.co.id

🖥 www.smaksangtimur-jkt.sch.id

Catholic high school of East Jakarta.

NUMBER OF TEACHERS: 8 native teachers for Jakarta and also Medan, Pematang Siantar, Pekanbaru and Makasar.

PREFERENCE OF NATIONALITY: All native speakers, aged 22–40.

QUALIFICATIONS: Bachelor degree in any field. TESOL qualification preferred but school's British academic director will train fresh graduates in Jakarta.

CONDITIONS OF EMPLOYMENT: 1 year from mid-July, renewable to 3 years. 30 teaching hours per week is usual out of a 40-hour week, 5 days a week. 40 days of holiday per year comprising 15 Indonesian public holidays, 13 days at Christmas, and 12 days in summer.

SALARY: From $700 per month, up to $2,000, according to experience and qualifications. Tax deductions total 8%. Overtime paid in excess of 40 hours.

FACILITIES/SUPPORT: Free housing and transport to school, plus free lunches at school. Employer will assist successful candidates to obtain visa before arrival and then apply for and cover costs of a work permit, which takes 1–2 months. Agent in Singapore can assist with one-day pick-up of permit. Possibility of reimbursement for flights. Free insurance paid by affiliated foundation (Enormous Wishing Foundation).

RECRUITMENT: CV to be sent by email and then chat and interview by Skype (anto_rejeki).

CONTACT: Anto Rejeki Purba, Managing Director.

THE BRITISH INSTITUTE (TBI)

Menara Kuningan, Unit F1, Jl. HR. Rasuna Said Blok X7 Kav. 5, Jakarta 12940

✆ +62 21 3002 7988/9

🖱 recruit@tbi.co.id

🖥 www.tbi.co.id/native-teacher

TBI has 17 schools across Indonesia (8 in Greater Jakarta, 3 in Bandung, one each in Medan, Surabaya, Bali and Malang) and is the only CELTA centre in the country.

NUMBER OF TEACHERS: Approximately 150 expatriate and local teachers.

QUALIFICATIONS: CELTA or equivalent plus university degree in English-related subject minimum. TBI teachers must meet Indonesian education department criteria, eg be aged 25–57. One year's experience. Aspiring teachers with degrees in English disciplines approved by the Indonesian Department of Education may be considered for contracts that include CELTA sponsorship.

PREFERENCE OF NATIONALITY: British, American, Canadian, Australian and New Zealander only (for visa reasons).

SALARY: Base salaries vary and are based on relative cost of living and number of teaching hours per week (22–24). Monthly salary after tax ranges from 10 million to 15 million rupiahs. End-of-contract bonuses and airfare contributions are also paid.

FACILITIES/SUPPORT: Free health insurance coverage, settling-in loan, work permits and documentation paid. 6 weeks' paid leave per annum. Professional development programme of workshops and observed teaching with feedback. Good career development prospects, including supervisory positions.

RECRUITMENT: Local hire or distance. Local applicants must teach a demonstration lesson. Distance applicants must complete tasks and have a Skype/telephone interview.

JAPAN

After stagnating for some years, and then suffering the grievous blow of the earthquake and the tsunami in 2011, the Japanese economy is growing above expectations as of 2015, with the value of the yen recovering well. The marketplace in which English-language academies are now competing has shrunk since the glory days but is still flourishing. Groups of *eikaiwa* (conversation schools) remain in business, alongside thousands of independent English schools in Tokyo, Osaka and many other Japanese cities which hire *gaijins* (foreigners) to teach. Some are still willing to hire native speakers of English with no teaching qualification as long as they have a university degree and preferably some relevant experience.

The demand among Japanese people to learn English from native speakers will survive, no matter what. One of the booming areas of the market is the teaching of English to pre-school and primary-aged children. English has become compulsory for fifth and sixth grade pupils (from age 10) throughout Japan, and many parents are sending their children to cram schools in order to prepare them. Since 2013 some lessons in Japanese secondary schools have been taught using the medium of English. Japanese families devote a colossal percentage of their household income to promoting education, and English language schools are among the main beneficiaries.

The basic monthly salary of 250,000 yen for full-time EFL teachers has not risen for a dozen years, which is far less at the current exchange rate than it was a few years ago. A worrying trend is that schools in 2015 have been offering lower wages than they did in the past. Wages are of course meaningless without balancing them against the local cost of living, which is notoriously high. Another trend is the huge rise in part-time work at the expense of full-time jobs. People used to say that you can't expect to break even and begin to save before you've been in Japan for at least a year, but the cost of living has stabilised and many teachers who live frugally do manage to save. Developments such as the increase in the number of '100 yen shops' (the equivalent of 'pound shops' or 'dollar stores') have made it far easier to outfit an apartment or buy teaching materials at reasonable prices.

A university degree is a prerequisite for getting a teaching job, simply because it is a requirement for a work visa. However, despite the increase in competition for teaching jobs, there is still surprisingly little emphasis on TEFL qualifications. Image is of paramount importance to the Japanese and many employers are more concerned to find people who are lively and a touch glamorous than they are to find people with a background in teaching.

As long as your expectations are realistic, Japan should turn out to be a rewarding choice of destination. Native English speakers are hired in a surprising range of corporate and other contexts: in-house language programmes in steel or electronics companies, state secondary schools, hot-house crammers, 'conversation lounges' where young people get together for an hour's guided conversation, vocational schools where English is a compulsory subject, 'ladies' classes' (quaintly so-called) where courses called 'English for Shopping' are actually offered, and also classes of children from as young as two, since it has become a status symbol in Japan to send children of all ages to English classes. In fact, studying English for many Japanese is still more a social than an educational activity.

> Culture shock grips most new arrivals to Japan. Incoming teachers are often so distracted by the mechanics of life in Japan and the cultural adjustments they have to make to survive that they devote too little energy to the business of teaching. On the other hand, anyone who has a genuine interest in Japan and who arrives reasonably well prepared may find that a year or two in Japan provides a wonderful experience.

PROSPECTS FOR TEACHERS

Jobs teaching English in Japan can be looked for in a variety of establishments from kindergartens (increasingly popular) to universities (difficult to crack until you have been living in Japan for years). Most private language schools in Japan are looking for native English speakers with a bachelor's degree (any nationality) and possibly some TEFL experience. Although only a minority are looking for professional qualifications in their teachers, there has been a noticeable increase in the number of qualified EFL teachers (especially from Australia) looking for work, and naturally schools prefer to take them, over complete novices.

Old Japan-hand **Joseph Tame** reported on his blog that he was interviewed by an agency recruiting teachers: '*CELTA was once again highlighted by the interviewers as one of the main reasons they'd contacted me in the first place – it's good to know that it has an impact in the real world recruitment.*' Many schools have no set intake dates and serious applications are welcome at any time of the year, though most contracts begin in April and finish the following March (ie one year), which corresponds to the academic year.

The demand for Business English and TOEIC (Test of English for International Communication) preparatory courses is also considerable. Japanese workers who have paid employment insurance for over three years are eligible to take courses with accredited learning institutions and claim a portion of the cost back from the government. The growth in the demand for Business English is also due to companies expecting new recruits to be able to communicate in English in an increasingly global marketplace. In fact one maverick boss of a giant e-commerce company, Rakuten, decreed that all meetings and correspondence would be conducted in English.

The favoured accent is certainly American and to a lesser extent Canadian. In fact, not many Japanese can distinguish a Scot from a Queenslander, or an Eastender from an Eastsider. What can be detected and is highly prized is clear speech. Slow, precise diction together with a smart appearance and professional bearing are necessary to impress some potential employers. One way round this is that Skype and telephone teaching have penetrated the language-teaching market.

FINDING A JOB

With the decrease in vacancies at a sub-professional level, it is more difficult for university graduates to find a job before arrival, though this is clearly preferable because it means the employer can sort out visas and help with initial orientation and housing. The disadvantage is that the salary and working conditions will probably compare unfavourably with those of teachers who have negotiated their job after arrival; but most new recruits (*nama gaijin*, or raw foreigners) conclude that the trade-off is a fair one. Of course the pool of foreign job-seekers already in Japan is large enough that the jobs offering good conditions tend to be snapped up quickly. Some organisations do not welcome speculative applications from outside Japan, and quite a few advertisements specify that they will consider only candidates who already have the right visa.

One of the best ways of arranging a job in advance is to join the Japan Exchange and Teaching (JET) Programme, which is a prestigious government-sponsored programme that offers what many consider to be a 'dream job' for new graduates (described in detail below). Whereas at one time the majority of ALTs (Assistant Language Teachers) in the public school system entered Japan as JET participants, many are now hired by private language-teaching companies known as 'dispatch companies', which do not always enjoy a favourable reputation. In fact **Del Ford**, with nine years' teaching experience in East Asian countries, takes a decidedly dim view of this shift:

> *Now, many of the public school ALT jobs are filled by the poor saps who accept dispatch company contracts. These companies represent pure evil: low salaries, no benefits, no support system, no paid airfare, health insurance, etc. I really think a section in your next edition should include a blurb on the pitfalls of working for these gangsters. Some smaller eikaiwa outfits have this type of nonsense for ads: '200,000 yen per month,*

prefer experience, basic Japanese language ability, TEFL Cert., International Driving Licence, etc'. Simply put, it's gotten grimmer over the last decade.

A third route is to be hired directly as an ALT by a local education authority, as **Will Mercer** describes:

In practice, your roles and responsibilities are identical to that of the other ALTs but, generally speaking, the salary and benefits are more in line with that offered by the JET programme. As you are hired by your local education authority you tend to have a closer relationship with your bosses. In my case, I dislocated my knee at my school's judo club and had to have an operation. I stayed in hospital for over two weeks and missed several weeks of work but was given a very high level of support and help from both my fellow teachers and employers at city hall and was later able to return to my post. I'm sure that wouldn't have been the case if I had been employed by a private ALT dispatch company.

These direct-hire positions also have the potential for real longevity. Some of my colleagues had held their job for a number of years, certainly more than the maximum of five offered by the JET programme.

It seems that the proportion of direct hires is increasing over the number of dispatch-company hires, a trend that is likely to continue as education authorities realise they don't need a middle man. Direct-hire positions are not always well advertised. The first one **Will Mercer** got was after he made a speculative application, and the second position was posted on www.jobsinjapan.com.

These ALT positions tend to go to strong candidates who have already been in Japan for a couple of years. Entry-level applicants are more likely to be hired by one of the mass-market *eikaiwa* like Interac, which hired **John Ramage**:

After several frustrating trips to London a few years ago, I did manage to get a job, which seemed like falling through an open door. Interac interviewed me in Edinburgh, rather close to home, and it was a positive experience. I arrived in Japan just in time for the cherry blossom, and I met many memorable people. I started learning to write Japanese. My experiences were so vivid that my life back home and in the West generally seemed less real.

THE JET PROGRAMME

JET is an official Japanese government scheme aimed at improving foreign language teaching in schools and fostering good relations between the people of Japan and the 40 participating countries. The programme has been in existence since 1987 and is now responsible for placing about 4,000 native English speakers for a minimum contract of one year in state junior and senior high schools throughout Japan, with an increasing number in rural areas. Many consider the emphasis to be more on cultural exchange than on English teaching. After a period when the programme seemed to be in decline, the numbers have been again increasing. The 10-year plan is to provide native English-speaker teachers to all primary, junior high and high schools. The government is also moving towards making a Test of English as a Foreign Language compulsory for entry to and graduation from college, which would galvanise the demand for tuition.

The majority of JET participants are from the USA (contact details below). Britain annually recruits graduates to the programme and JET is among the largest employers of new graduates after the UK government. Acceptance has become more competitive and the prospects for people who become ALTs in English on the JET Programme are excellent. Any UK national who is under 40 with a bachelor's degree and an interest in Japan is eligible to apply.

In the UK the scheme is administered by the JET Desk at the Embassy of Japan, 101–104 Piccadilly, London, W1J 7JT (+44 20 7465 6668; ukjet@ld.mofa.go.jp; www.jet-uk.org). Non-British applicants should contact the Japanese Embassy in their country of origin for information and application forms. US applicants can obtain details from any of the 16 consulates in the USA or from the JET Office: Japanese Embassy, 2520 Massachusetts Avenue NW, Washington, DC 20008 (+1 202 238 6772/3; jetprograms@ws.mofa.go.jp; www.us.emb-japan.go.jp/JET).

The timetable for applicants from the UK is as follows: application forms are available online from early October; the deadline for applications is the last Friday in November; interviews are held in January and February; an intensive two-day orientation for successful candidates is held in London at the start of July and departures for Japan take place in late July/August.

Robert Mizzi from Canada worked hard on his application, which paid off since he was called to an interview:

> *The interview was probably the most difficult interview I have ever had. It was only 20 minutes, but a painful 20 minutes. Besides the usual 'why' and 'tell us about yourself' questions, I was asked to teach a lesson on the spot using dramatic techniques I would use in class. Stunned, I managed to get out of my seat and draw some pictures of the stars and moon on the board, taught them the meaning of those words and then proceeded to ask the interview team to stand up and learn a little dance to the song 'Twinkle Twinkle Little Star'. All I wanted to do was to create an impression and to stand out of the 300 people being interviewed. People remember you best when you are acting like a complete fool. When it is teaching English as a foreign language, the ability to act like a fool is one of the main requirements of the job. Getting Japanese men in suits up and dancing during a job interview with the prestigious JET programme was a half-crazed risk, but a successful one at that.*

Often government-run exchanges of this kind do not offer generous remuneration packages; however, pay and conditions on the JET scheme are excellent. In addition to a free return flight, JET participants receive 3,360,000 yen a year. This is the salary before income and inhabitant taxes have been paid (though some participants are exempt) and there are further social and medical insurance fees of 40,000 yen a month. The salary is standard for all JET participants. Contracts are with individual contracting organisations in Japan, so there can be discrepancies in working conditions. It is the luck of the draw that determines who goes where, although stated preferences will be taken into consideration. Any income tax deducted will be refunded at the end of your contract.

ALTs are theoretically expected to work a seven-hour day and quite often teachers are assigned an average of three classes a day; however, hours spent in the classroom will vary between placements. **Mark Elliot** feels that the JET programme is 'probably the best job in the world' and describes his situation:

> *I live on a wonderful island, three hours' ferry ride from Nagasaki, nearer Shanghai than Tokyo. There is a lot more to the job than teaching. After all, the programme is just as much about meeting people and participating in cultural exchange as it is about teaching.*

All JET participants teach in partnership with a native Japanese teacher so those without significant teaching experience are not thrown in at the deep end. The degree of responsibility varies depending on the relationship built with the Japanese teacher, with some ALTs effectively teaching the class in large part by themselves. Unfortunately this was not the case for **Charlotte Steggall** from Suffolk, who majored in Japanese and TESOL at university and is serious about pursuing TESOL at a master's level and as a career. She felt the ALT role to be of little actual value, but rather felt they were treated as 'singing, dancing white people to wheel out and show off in events in the town'. This was not what she signed up for, yet she loved the students and so agreed to stay on for a second year:

> *What I do depends on which teacher I'm working with. Some ask me to do a 10-minute game in a lesson, some ask me to be a living tape recorder, some ask me to do full classes. Training Japanese teachers to work with ALTs is very hit and miss, and most have no idea what to do with us. What we do has little meaning to the kids, who*

see us and say 'Yay! She's here today so we get to play games!' They would never ask us to do a lesson to prepare for a test, or anything else with responsibility. I love teaching. But we are here mainly to allow country kids to interact with us and to overcome racism for when they are older. When I try to help or do something more because I have passion, I am batted down again.

I have a lot of spare time at work. I study Japanese, read books, use the internet. After school, I earn more money and brush up my teaching skills by doing private lessons, which allows me to break free and try different teaching styles.

Other teachers are delighted with the easy timetable. As **Rabindra Roy** wrote from Shizuoka prefecture, '*I can think of very few jobs where a freshly qualified graduate with an irrelevant degree and no experience can walk straight into such a big salary for this little work.*' He also describes the programme as '*desperately well organised*'. But partly because of the variety in locations and schools and partly because Japan is such a weird and wonderful place, it is impossible to predict what life will be like, no matter how many orientations you attend. About two-thirds of JET participants renew for a second year, which indicates its success. A third of the second-years stay for a third year, with five years being the maximum a candidate can stay. The programme offers a tremendous amount of support and even those who are placed in remote or rural areas are usually within striking distance of other JET participants. In retrospect, **Susannah Kerr** who taught for a private company in Tokyo was not too sorry to have been turned down by JET because its teachers have little control over where they are sent and end up in small towns (however, she wouldn't have minded a JET salary).

IN ADVANCE

There are many other ways to fix up a job in Japan ahead of time, though these will usually require more initiative than signing on with JET. Some Japanese language schools have formed links with university careers departments, particularly in the USA and Canada, so anyone with a university connection should exploit it. Another possibility for Americans is to explore the Japanese-American Sister City Program which assists some native English speakers to find teaching jobs in the city twinned with theirs.

One or two language training organisations operate on a huge scale, with many branches and large numbers of staff. For instance AEON (see entry) has recruiting offices in New York and Los Angeles as well as Tokyo, and Interac interviews in cities throughout English-speaking countries. They want to interview anyone with a university degree and a perfect command of English. AEON's sister company, Amity Teachers, recruits many teachers of children for its 85 schools throughout Japan (www.amityteachers.com/teaching). Some chains have been described as factory English schools, where teachers are handed a course book and told not to deviate from the formula. They depend on a steady supply of fresh graduates who want the chance to spend a year or two in Japan. Often new recruits do not have much say in where they are sent and in their first year may be sent to the least desirable locations, as **John Ramage** discovered after a successful interview with Interac in the UK:

I was so keen to go to Japan that I accepted a job in a very rural location. I knew this could be problematic and I was right, it was. Coming with limited funds meant I could not afford to buy a laptop and have internet, which might have made things bearable. I tried to be frugal but found the isolation hard to take. Later I moved to Tokyo, with Shane English School and stayed for much longer. After suffocating small towns I found Tokyo positively exciting.

For its recruitment in the UK, Shane English Schools relies on its partner agencies like Saxoncourt Recruitment and TEFL in Japan (London W1; www.tefl-in-japan.com). An energetic agency operating mainly online is TEFLOne Recruitment (www.teflone.com), which recruits qualified teachers for posts in Japan as well as other countries in the Far East. A major employer is iTTTi Japan, which trades as Peppy Kids Club. The head office is in Nagoya but it has recruiting representatives in the UK, USA, Canada and Australia (see www.ittti.com/pkc) as well as an online application system. The company hires 350 native English speakers to work all over Japan, with the exception of Central Tokyo and the islands of Okinawa. The giant Gaba Corporation (http://teaching-in-japan.gaba.co.jp) operates 41 Learning Studios around Tokyo, Osaka and in Nagoya where clients are taught individually, and in off-site corporate settings. Gaba vigorously recruits year round.

Quite often schools and groups of schools will appoint a foreign recruiter. Many schools have no need to advertise abroad since they receive so many speculative résumés (the American term for CV is used in Japan).

Of course the internet is a valuable job-search tool. Using any of the popular household search engines, type 'English teaching in Japan' and dozens of job-related websites will appear. *O-Hayo-Sensei* (which means 'good morning teacher') has pages of teaching positions across Japan at www.ohayosensei.com. Many ads specify that 'candidates must currently reside in Japan'. Jobsinjapan.com is also excellent. *ELT News* (www.eltnews.com/jobs) lists ELT jobs around Japan, again mostly for candidates already in Japan, and the site carries news, classroom ideas, etc for ELT teachers in Japan. It is a good idea to send your CV to the big employers before arrival, make some follow-up calls and hope to arrange some interviews in your first week.

Once you have some international experience of teaching, particularly of IELTS testing, you can aim to fix up short lucrative contracts as **Steph Fuccio** and her husband **Evan** did for a three-month period:

> *Nagoya is a very 'livable' city, a million times more so than Tokyo was. My love for bicycling was rekindled along with a craving for sushi. We worked for a company called Westgate Corporation both in Nagoya and Tokyo. It's a very reputable, trustworthy organisation. I would do this programme again in a heartbeat, it's that easy and lucrative.*

The Westgate Corporation has been providing English-language instruction programmes for corporations, residents, public schools and universities since 1983 and operates an online application programme (www.westgate.co.jp) as well as advertising on www.tefl.com.

ON THE SPOT

As has been mentioned, native English speakers with a bachelor's degree have a chance of landing a job as an English teacher on arrival in Japan. The crucial question is how long will it take. The murderous cost of living means that job-hunters spend hundreds of dollars or pounds very quickly while engaged in the time-consuming business of answering ads, sending round CVs and going for interviews.

Travis Ball from Los Angeles set off on what he intended to be five years of world travels and chose Japan as his first destination because he had come to the conclusion that it would be one of the easier countries to find work teaching English without any experience or certificates:

> *I was basically sitting in my travellers' hotel room in Osaka sending out as many résumés as I could while attempting not to spend any money. I started by sending emails to every address listed in the chapter on Japan in your book and kept looking using the web and other resources. After filling out an online application and sending my résumé to a big chain, I was asked if I could attend an interview in Tokyo, which took place over two days and included a couple of tests and a mock 20-minute lesson we all had to prepare the evening before the second day. I was told that I had a job in a very small rural school (one other teacher who was Japanese and a manager). With hindsight I would probably have voiced my preference for a bigger city with more going on. That being said, I think it was my flexibility that helped me get the job in the first place.*

Joseph Tame from Herefordshire arrived in Tokyo with two big advantages, a working holiday visa and a Japanese girlfriend (now wife) with whom he could stay:

Having spent virtually all of my travel funds in my first 21 days in the city, I eventually decided to face the fact that I'd have to find a job, for a couple of months at least. What with all this talk of a global recession, I really didn't feel too positive. Furthermore I have virtually no experience teaching, have no teaching qualifications and indeed no university degree, which all employers insist on. My first stop was the Japan Association for Working Holiday Makers. I was fortunate in that as I was being registered, a phone call came through from a private English school who were desperate for a teacher. Thirty minutes later I had a job paying £17 an hour. The catch was that it was only four hours per week, but that was my pocket money taken care of. I actually spent time surfing the web in an attempt to remember what pronouns and adjectives are; I only ever remember that a verb is a 'doing' word.

Later Joseph Tame made good use of www.gaijinpot.com, which remains a superb resource for jobs, accommodation and news for foreign residents in Japan. He also recommends www.getstudents.net (formerly http://findateacher.net) for those wanting to teach English (or other languages). Other teacher–student matching services are at www.findstudents.net, www.hello-sensei.com and www.watashino-sensei.biz. You simply enter the relevant information about what you teach, what area of Japan you teach in, how much you charge, etc and the students will come to you.

GaijinPot (www.gaijinpot.com) is the largest job site for foreigners and has a near monopoly on the English teaching jobs in Japan among the English conversation schools, dispatch schools (for teaching in the public schools) and everything in between. The site stores more than 150,000 résumés, most of which are searchable by potential employers. GaijinPot is also a useful general portal for foreigners in Japan, with popular forums for sharing information, experiences and questions.

Other potentially useful sites are www.altTokyo.com and *Tokyo Notice Board* (www.tokyonoticeboard. co.jp). A typical advertisement randomly selected might read: *'We are seeking an energetic, gregarious and reliable job applicant who wishes to share their experience with Japanese Community. Part-time job (1,000–1,500 yen per hour free talk; 2,160 yen per hour for teaching a lesson) (3,000 yen for a dispatch lesson).'* A 'dispatch lesson' is a private lesson given at a company premises. You may also see ads for private teacher matchmaking agencies like Atlas (www.atlasp.net).

Few things could be more intimidating for the EFL teacher than to arrive at Narita International Airport with no job and limited resources. The longer the job-hunt takes, the faster the finances dwindle and the more nerve-racking and discouraging the situation becomes. One way to lessen the monumentality of the initial struggle would be to get out of Tokyo straightaway. Although there are more jobs in the capital, there is also more competition from other foreigners, to the point of saturation. Enterprising teachers who are willing to step off the conveyor belt which takes job-seekers from the airport to one of Tokyo's many '*gaijin* houses' (hostels for foreigners) may well encounter fewer setbacks. Osaka seems a good bet since it is within commuting distance of the whole Kansai area, including Kobe, which is 20 minutes away by train. In Osaka the cost of living is as much as a quarter less than it is in Tokyo. Another promising destination is Sapporo in the north, the fifth largest city in the country. **Ken Foye**, a reader of this book, chose to teach on Hokkaido, the northern island on which Sapporo is located:

I have been teaching here for a year and a half now and I would recommend Hokkaido to anyone, especially those who don't find living in a large urban metropolis very appealing. Here the people seem much friendlier than in Tokyo, the cost of living isn't as high, there's fresh air and the scenery is magnificent. And I probably would not have ended up here if not for your book.

After the large company that employed her collapsed, **Susannah Kerr** swiftly began 'on the spot' job-hunting courtesy of websites such as www.gaijinpot.com. She considered a large employer, Gaba (mentioned above), which specialises in one-to-one teaching and offers the advantage of being able to choose your hours. The disadvantage is that earnings are dependent on your popularity as a teacher, since students vote with their feet. Susannah was interviewed by a company called Balloon Kids (www.bkje.co.jp) which employs up to 20 teachers and pays 200,000–250,000 yen per month. Instead of working from its own institute, the company hires rooms in (for example) suburban shopping malls, where 12–15 kids show up. The teacher would be expected to go to an office to pick up teaching materials and a key, and then let him/herself into the room, so there would be no contact with other teachers. They also withhold 10,000 yen per month to be paid at the end of the contract.

The six-month contract that Susannah eventually accepted was with MLS (see entry for Model Language Studio), a school that uses a proprietary Drama Method to teach English. With 31 branches in Tokyo and Yokohama, it is a small company by Japanese standards. Susannah was impressed with the efficacy of the method, and because the teachers were '*interesting, creative, often musical types, the children were often engaged and excited, and their spoken English really did improve. The teachers were always trying to use attention-grabbing games like charades.*'

TOKYO

One of the most often recommended places to start a job hunt in Tokyo is the Kimi Information Center (Oscar Building, 8th Floor, 2 42 3 Ikebukuro, Toshima-ku, Tokyo 171 0014; +81 3 3986 1604; kimiinfo@kimiwillbe. com). Its website (www.kimiwillbe.com) carries teaching job adverts. Like so many postal addresses in Japan, it is difficult to find without a map (print one off from its website or follow these detailed directions: from Ikebukuro station take the West Exit, walk straight past the McDonald's for one block and turn right when you see Marui Department Store. Go three blocks past Sumitomo Mitsui Bank. Kimi is on the right across from the Post Office.)

The Kimi Center offers extensive services for foreigners such as a translation service, free guided tours with Japanese students as well as advising on cheap short and long-term accommodation, where tenants are not liable for key money. If you register with it online, you can receive information about new jobs daily. With this free service, Kimi can assist with searching for a suitable job and even setting up interviews.

Another useful source of guidance for new arrivals on a working holiday programme is the Japan Association for Working Holiday Makers (www.jawhm.or.jp/eng), whose services are available to those with the appropriate visa (see section on Regulations below). **Joseph Tame** was a satisfied customer when he was on the programme:

> *My first stop was the JAWHM, whose office was 20 minutes by bicycle from where I was staying. They were very helpful. After registering I had access to their lists of jobs. Essentially it's a job centre for foreigners. They also have the latest copies of all the relevant magazines and newspapers with sits vacant columns. They will advise on housing, etc.*

Even tourist offices such as the one at Hibuya station (exit A-3) have free noticeboards where private lessons may be sought or offered, as well as accommodation. **Amanda Searle** describes what she found in the newspapers when she was job-hunting:

> *Most companies give little idea in their adverts of the hours and salary, let alone the age and number of students or the textbooks used. They are not very willing to give that information over the phone, explaining that you will get the opportunity to ask questions if you are called for interview. I sent cover letters out with my résumé, explaining that I was looking only for full-time positions which offered visa sponsorship. I sent out about 20 applications and about 10 companies contacted me and I went to eight interviews. I ended up being offered two full-time positions and three part-time ones.*

The initial phone call is very important and should be considered as a preliminary interview. Since you may be competing with as many as 100 people answering the same ad, you have to try to stand out over the phone. Speak slowly, clearly, and be very *genki*, which means bubbly and fun. You may be asked to fax your CV to them; the cover letter should be short and intelligent, and the CV should be brief and interesting, emphasising any teaching experience. Always carry a supply of professional-looking business cards (*meishi*).

Demonstration lessons form an integral part of most job interviews in Japan, regardless of one's qualifications. Try to prepare yourself as much as possible, if only because travelling to an interview in Tokyo is a major undertaking which can take up to three hours and cost a lot of money; it would be a shame to blow your chances because of a simple oversight. Dress as impeccably and conservatively as possible, and carry a respectable briefcase, since books are often judged by their covers in Japan. Inside you should have any education certificates you have earned, preferably the originals, since schools have long since realised that a lot of forgeries are in circulation. Your résumé should not err on the side of modesty.

REGULATIONS

Britons, Irish, Canadians, Australians and New Zealanders (among a few other, non-English speaking, countries) are eligible to apply for a working holiday visa for Japan; details can be found at www.uk.emb-japan.go.jp/en/visa/working-holiday.html.

Applicants must be aged 18–30. Applicants must show that they have sufficient financial backing, ie savings of £2,500, or £1,500 and a return flight. Visa holders may accept paid work in Japan for up to 12 months, provided it is incidental to their travels. The quota of working holiday visas for Britons is 1,000. Note that applications are accepted from April and once the allocation has been filled, no more visas will be granted until April of the following year.

Some schools rely on a stream of Canadians, Australians and New Zealanders on working holiday visas, which they must obtain in their home countries through the SWAP Japan Programme. SWAP allows Canadians aged 18–30 to work for six months in the first instance but is extendable to 18 months. To qualify you must prove that you have $2,500 at your disposal.

For those ineligible for a working holiday visa, the key to obtaining a work visa for Japan is to have a Japanese sponsor. Documents which will help you to find a sponsoring employer are the original or notarised copy of your bachelor's or other degree and résumé. Most teachers are sponsored by their employers, although on rare occasions it is possible for the sponsor to be a private citizen. Not all schools by any means are willing to sponsor their teachers, unless they are persuaded that they are an ongoing proposition. If your visa is to be processed before arrival, you must have a definite job appointment in Japan. Your employer must apply to the Ministry of Justice in Tokyo for a Certificate of Eligibility which he or she then forwards to you. You must take this along with a photocopy of it, your passport, photograph and application form to any Consulate General of Japan. The regulations stipulate that anyone who works in Higher Education must have an MA in Education or TEFL. Sponsoring schools warn that the visa application process takes between three and five months.

The UK and US have a visa exemption arrangement with Japan whereby they can stay for up to 90 days with a possibility of extending for a further 90 days. It is possible to enter Japan, look for work and then apply for a work visa. Those found to be overstaying as tourists can be deported. Furthermore, employers who are caught employing illegal aliens, as well as the foreign workers themselves, are subject to huge fines, and both parties risk imprisonment.

Finding an employer to sponsor you for a work visa is very important. A number of schools advertising for teachers state in their ads that they are willing to consider only those who already have a work visa. Although immigration laws are being tightened, the government is making it easier for foreigners to get working visas. Whereas previously it was necessary for the teacher to leave the country, at great personal expense, to change their visa status (the Korean Visa Tour), these days the teacher need only take their Certificate of Eligibility into the local immigration office, where the visa will be processed. However, those on a student visa still need to leave the country to complete the visa process. According to **Alan Suter** the cheapest way is to take a ferry from Kobe to Busan, Korea. The work visa may be valid for 6 months, 12 months or 3 years.

After you have worked for one year on a work visa, you can renew it for a further three years. When renewing, one of the most important requirements is a tax statement showing your previous year's earnings. It is difficult to obtain a new visa unless you can show that you have earned at least 250,000 yen per month. Cash-in-hand and part-time jobs may be lucrative but they do nothing to help your visa application. If you break your contract with your employer, you will have to find another sponsor willing to act as sponsor the following year.

You are permitted to work up to 20 hours a week on a cultural or student visa. Cultural visas are granted to foreigners interested in studying some aspect of traditional Japanese culture on a full-time basis. In this case you must find a teacher willing to sponsor you. Cultural visas are often granted for *shodo* (calligraphy), *taiko* (drumming), karate, aikido, *ikebana* (flower arranging) and *ochakai* (tea ceremony). At one time these study visas were liberally handed out but nowadays you must produce concrete evidence that you actually are studying.

Teachers usually have the basic rate of national income tax in Japan (6%–7%) withdrawn at source.

CONDITIONS OF WORK

Despite the high cost of living, most teachers seem to be able to save money without having to lead too frugal an existence. Some even save half their salary in their first year by avoiding eating out and going to the cinema. **Antoinette Sarpong** spent one year teaching in Osaka and preferred to enjoy herself to saving:

> *I enjoyed Osaka's nightlife thoroughly. I also opted to save for travel, so I only put a small dent in my student loans. Having said that, I lived very comfortably and had a lot of friends who did save quite a bit of money because they stuck to a budget. Japan is an expensive country but it is possible to save heaps of money if you stick to a budget. I would also suggest living rurally, if you can – less temptation than the big cities.*

The longer you work in Japan the higher the salary and better the working conditions you can command. Rank beginners outside Tokyo and Osaka can earn as little as 200,000 yen a month, but the steady average of 252,000 yen persists almost everywhere. Perks such as increments for higher qualifications, end-of-contract bonuses, free Japanese lessons and travel tickets, etc are in fairly wide evidence, although it is always worth making sure that your contract mentions these perks. Teaching schedules can be exhausting. Teachers are increasingly asked to work 'outside their job description', helping out with advertising, student retention and the sale of study materials. Some companies organise informal conversation sessions with native speakers. The companies look for outgoing, reliable people to work as chat hosts who can lead lively conversations with a diverse clientele in exchange for a low hourly wage of 1000-1500 yen. One company called Leafcup (www.leafcup.com/job.php) is now stricter about the visa status of the people it hires.

Timetables may be announced at the last minute, though it is more difficult to opt out in Japan than in other countries because of the dedication Japanese workers show to their firms. (At best a Japanese worker gets 10 days' holiday a year and few take their full entitlement for fear of seeming lazy or disloyal to the company.) Some schools remain open all weekend and on public holidays too.

One of the advantages of working in state schools (as JET teachers and other ALTs do) is that they close for holidays, usually three weeks at Christmas and two weeks in August between semesters. Most schools offer one-week holidays (paid or unpaid or a combination of the two) at the beginning of May (the 'Golden Week') and in the middle of August ('O-bon vacation'). Holidays for those lucky enough to work in institutes of higher education are much more generous.

Private tutoring is still lucrative, paying from 3,000 yen an hour. **Susannah Kerr** managed to hold on to six hours of private teaching a week (teaching three children in one family), which netted her 18,000 yen, enough to eat. Occasionally you will meet someone who has been paid $100 just to have dinner with a language learner and converse in English, but these plums are few and far between.

THE STUDENTS

The stereotype of the diligent Japanese pupil has become somewhat outmoded. The younger generation of Japanese is not always willing to play by the rules that their elders lay down, and there is increasing tension in schools which may manifest itself in (mildly) unruly behaviour. But mostly teachers find their students eager, attentive and willing to confer great respect on their teachers, and in some out-of-the-way places even celebrity status. All teachers are expected to look the part and most schools will insist on proper dress (eg suits and dresses). But they do not want a formal approach to teaching.

Adults will have studied English at school for at least six years, and their knowledge of grammar is usually sound. They go to conversation schools in the expectation of meeting native English-speaker teachers able to deliver creative and entertaining lessons. Yet some are crippled by diffidence or excessive anxiety about grammatical correctness. **Michael Frost** is one teacher who experienced a clash of cultures when trying to encourage discussion in his classroom:

> *It is very difficult for Japanese students to come out and express an individual opinion. The best tactic is to get them in pairs, so that together they can work something out. They are more productive and open in pairs, and it takes the pressure off them. Then get the pairs into fours, to express a mini-group opinion, then work for a total group agreement. The thing to avoid at all costs is to stroll into class, saying, 'OK, today we are going to discuss environmental issues. Tetsuya, you set the ball rolling: What do you think of pollution?' It will not work.*

It is a popular myth that Japanese students have good reading abilities in English and require only conversation practice. This was not the experience of **Nathan Edwards**, a diploma-qualified teacher from Canada:

> *I am currently teaching at the Tokyo YMCA College of English, a pioneer in English teaching in Japan, established in 1880. The fact is that both reading and speaking in English present major challenges even to students with years of English instruction in the Japanese school system. It is highly advisable for teachers to bring a good supply of realia with them (various English brochures, used tickets, maps, coins, etc) and old lesson plans.*

Problems can arise in team-teaching situations if your Japanese colleague has not attained a high enough level of English. While teaching in the JET programme, **Robert Mizzi** came to admire Japanese culture, but he did find some aspects of his job frustrating:

> *A lot of times I cannot introduce a game idea because, literally, it will take 20 minutes for the teacher to understand (never mind the students).*

Amanda Moody worked in a small school in Nagoya, where she taught pre-school children using a mixture of the 'Gentle Revolution' and Rosetta Stone software:

> *My pupils were very smart and the children of successful Japanese. Some were the products of brain surgeons or music producers. Others were businessmen's kids. But most of them were reading and writing around the age of three. Their parents expected the world of both us and their children.*

Amanda loved her students, but thought poorly of her employer, who fined teachers for 'infringements' such as 'smelled strange and suspicious acting: 500 yen fine'. Among the many strange aspects of Japanese culture is one which most foreigners find particularly disturbing. A native English speaker who happens to have non-Caucasian features will almost certainly be discriminated against.

ACCOMMODATION

It is not uncommon for teachers who are hired overseas to be given help with accommodation, which is a tremendously useful perk, even if the flat provided is small and over-priced, with poor insulation and a badly equipped kitchen. If you are on your own, you may be forced to use a foreigners' rental agency. Rental costs are likely to range from 40,000 yen to 70,000 yen per person per month (more in Tokyo, less in more distant prefectures). When you find a place through an agency, you will have to pay a commission of one month's rent.

When looking for accommodation on arrival in Tokyo, pick up a list of *gaijin* houses from an information or tourist office and look for ones which charge a monthly rather than a nightly rent, since these are the ones which attract long-term residents. Apple House (www.applehouse.ne.jp/english/applehouse.html) is recommended for being affordable, friendly and in a good location. A good place to look is Fontana Co (+81 3 3382 0289; www.tokyocityapartments.net), which provides an excellent service. Because it is so difficult to rent flats, some teachers continue living in *gaijin* houses after they find work. Many foreigners live and work in the Roppongi district of Tokyo, which might therefore be a sensible place to base yourself.

A couple of years ago, **Susannah Kerr** rented a two-bedroom flat in a nice traditional Tokyo neighbourhood of Kagurazaka for 160,000 yen a month, but when her flatmates moved on and she had to pay the rent by herself, she decided to move. Even when accompanied by a local, using a local rental agency proved impossible so she used an English-speaking rental agency to find a one-bedroom apartment for 80,000 yen in Okubo, a bustling 24-hour-a-day area known as Koreatown, with a mildly sleazy reputation but gradually improving. Foreign letting agencies offer the advantage of not insisting that you provide a local guarantor. The Sakura House agency, which caters for non-Japanese accommodation-seekers (www.sakura-house. com), has become a prominent feature of the accommodation landscape in Tokyo, but there are many others. Expect to pay 65,000–75,000 yen for a '1LDK' which refers to a small apartment consisting of one main room with kitchenette and bathroom.

A sizeable deposit called 'key money' is payable on signing a tenancy agreement, which can cause problems, as it did to **John Ramage**:

> *A word of warning. I came to Japan with relatively little money. Interac will help you set up in a new place but they will offer you a loan because no one gets paid until they have been working for two months. It takes time for the loan to come through, and meanwhile there was a landlord on day one with his hand stretched out asking for £1,000 of key money. So, I used my credit card in an ATM. Bad move. My debt soared and this happened to other people too. Fortunately when I moved on to Tokyo, Interac returned part of the key money, and paid me the end-of-contract bonus, which was a great help.*

According to John, housing is more likely to be subsidised in Korea, Taiwan and China.

A further problem is the near total absence of furnished apartments because Japanese people do not like to use belongings that have been used by other people, which means you may have to go shopping for curtains and cookers on top of all your other expenses. Again, schools which normally hire foreign teachers may keep a stock of basic furnishings which they can lend to teachers. They may also have a member of staff willing to translate unpaid bills notices (a common affliction). If all this sounds too much hassle, perhaps staying in a *gaijin* house long term is not such a bad idea.

An alternative recommended by **Will Mercer** is a rental agency called Leopalace (http://en.leopalace21. com):

> *I stayed in several different places during my time in Japan, and on three occasions I stayed in an apartment owned by Leopalace, a huge company that owns flats all over the country. Their website can be accessed in several languages and you can arrange to move in from outside Japan (I think). Their flats are relatively expensive and although they don't have key money they nonetheless charge a large amount in other move-on costs and administration fees. They have something of a mixed reputation amongst the foreigner community.*

Personally, I think they're a good place to start. They go out of their way to rent to foreigners and provide services and support in English. Their flats come in a handful of styles and are virtually identikit. Their flats tend to be new, very clean and to come with furnishings such as a washing machine, fridge, microwave, TV, internet, etc. On the other hand they're generally pretty small and the walls are quite thin. I had to move from Gunma prefecture to Osaka at short notice and so chose Leopalace because it was the most convenient option. I saw the flat I wanted on their website and arranged a viewing over the phone. As I had lived in one of these flats previously I knew exactly what I was getting, in fact the flats were identical down to the tiniest detail, despite being located several hundred kilometres apart. As I didn't have time to visit the local estate agents it was the perfect solution for me, at least in that situation.

John Ramage paid an inflated rent for the convenience of staying in an apartment provided by Shane in Tokyo and suggests ways to keep the cost of living down:

In Tokyo internet cafés are expensive if you use them a lot, but an internet connection to your house is cheap. It took me a while to find the cheap shops. The 100-yen shops sell cheap stuff for the house and the recycle shop is where you get second-hand electric goods, which is helpful because Japanese flats tend to be unfurnished.

Obviously it is to your advantage to live as close to your place of work as possible but, as noted above, many teachers are forced to spend a sizeable chunk of their earnings and a lot of time commuting. Ask your employer to pay for your travel, preferably in the form of a monthly travel pass, which can be used for your leisure travel as well. If you're in Tokyo, bear in mind that city buses charge a flat fare of 210 yen.

LEISURE TIME

According to some veteran teachers, leisure time and how to spend it will be the least of your worries. Depending on your circumstances, you may be expected to participate in extra-curricular activities and social events which it would cause offence to decline and will eat up lots of your leisure time. Although **Bryn Thomas** enjoyed the sushi which his school provided for teachers still at work at 9pm, he was less keen on the '*office parties when teachers were required to dress up in silly costumes and be nice to the students*'. Most teachers are happy to accept occasional invitations to socialise with their Japanese colleagues or students, even if it does mean an evening of speaking very, very slowly and drinking heavily. Many teachers find the socialising with students fun if expensive. Knowing a *gaijin* is a considerable status symbol for many Japanese, many of whom are willing to pay good money just for you to go to their houses once a week and eat their food.

But it is not like that everywhere. A glut of westerners in Tokyo means that your welcome may be less than enthusiastic. In fact non-Japanese are refused entrance to some Tokyo bars and restaurants. Many people head straight out of Tokyo for the more appealing city of Osaka. **Julie Fast** describes the contrast:

I am still enamoured of Osaka; it is like a village after Tokyo. I am constantly amazed at the trees we see everywhere. I never realised in Tokyo how much I hated being constantly surrounded by people. I never had personal space in Tokyo. No one does – which explains the distant, sour looks on most people's faces. What a difference in Osaka. Osaka people have the roughest reputation in all of Japan. From a western point of view, they are the friendliest. I have been invited to houses for lunch, children say hello and people in shops actually talk to you. Which proves you can't judge a country by its largest city.

All cities are expensive. Any entertainment which smacks of the West, such as going out to a fashionable coffee house or a nightclub, will be absurdly expensive. However, if you are content with more modest indigenous food and pastimes, you will be able to save money. A filling bowl of soba noodles from a corner shop costs £3, though you may never take to the standard breakfast of boiled rice and a raw egg. Convenience stores sell tasty rice balls (*onigri*) which cost about 140 yen. Staying home to listen to Japanese-language tapes or to read a good book (eg *Pictures from the Water Trade*, a personal account of life in Japan) costs nothing. Obviously the more settled you become, the more familiar you will be with the bargains and affordable amusements. For example, while some Tokyo superclubs impose a cover charge equal to $40, **Susannah Kerr** found much cheaper ones and in fact one where she got to know the DJs was free.

Learning to live cheaply is easier in small towns, but there will be fewer entertainments. **Travis Ball** had to depend on his own resources to fill his leisure time:

> *Unfortunately, due to the rural nature of where I was living, there wasn't really a whole lot to do with my spare time. In addition to a lack of activities, the weather was much colder than what I was used to at home in California and this limited my getting around via bike and on foot. I tried to use the time to work on personal projects such as teaching myself how to cook and working on my photography. I was occasionally able to organise day trips with my co-worker and some students, but found myself on my own more often than not. I took the time to develop a personal travel blog for flashpackers (www.flashpackerhq.com) that I'm still working on to this day.*

Finding your way around is nothing if not a challenge in a country where almost all road and public transport signs are incomprehensible. On the other hand things are easier than they were 10 years ago, when finding a menu in English or anyone who could communicate in English was all but impossible. Even though there is more English signage around, many feel that it is worth making an effort to master at least something of the written language. There are three alphabets in Japanese: *kanji* (ancient pictograms), *hiragana* and *katakana* (the characters used to spell loan words from English). **Amanda Searle** is just one teacher who feels that kana can be learned through independent study, so that at least you will be able to read station names and menus. Learning some of the script not only impresses students and shows that you are making an effort to absorb some of the culture, it also helps you to survive. **Joseph Tame** signed up for Japanese lessons so he could get beyond 'large beer please' and 'I don't understand' to a variety of expressions to exclaim 'how much?' in disbelief.

Japanese addresses are mind-bogglingly complicated too: the numbers refer to land subdivisions: prefecture, district, ward, then building. When in doubt (inevitable) ask a friendly informant for a *chizu* (map). It is also a good idea to get a Japanese person to write your destination in both *kanji* and transliterated into *roma-ji* (our alphabet). Japanese people will sometimes go to embarrassing lengths to help foreigners. This desire to help is wedded to a reluctance to lose face which means that they may offer advice and instructions based on very little information, so keep checking. Young people in jeans are the best bets. Outside the big cities the people are even more cordial. Wherever you go, you don't have to worry about crime. Not long after **Will Mercer** arrived in Gunma prefecture, he went for a hike in nearby hills, as so many local people seemed to do at weekends. Unfortunately he had no map, and he was also unaware of how early it got dark, so it was no joke when he found himself completely lost. Using his mobile phone to illuminate his way, he finally stumbled out onto a road. A car stopped for him and insisted not only on driving him to the railway station (which turned out to be a very short distance up the road) but on giving Will a torch, later returned by post.

Travel is expensive. For example the 320-mile journey by bullet train from Tokyo to Kyoto costs over £100 one way. Yet the pace of a teacher's life in Tokyo or another big city can become so stressful that it is essential to get on a local train and see some of the countryside. Tour operators do sometimes have special deals on train fares. For example in 2015, JREast (which operates in Kanto in Northern Japan) was offering a three-day pass to foreigners for 8,300 yen, excluding all bullet trains (Shinkansen). Shopping around for package tours is another good way to get to see Japan at the lowest possible price. For example, a two to three-day hotel/transportation package could end up costing significantly less.

The alienness of Japanese culture is one of the main fascinations of the place. It is foolish to become bogged down worrying about transgressing against mysterious customs. But new arrivals soon discover that the Japanese allow foreigners a great deal of latitude. **Antoinette Sarpong** got better at her encounters with the local people after she realised that Japanese people do not like to say 'No' or directly express disagreement, so she gradually learned to read between the lines and to interpret their subtle communication style.

The expat scene is also not to everyone's taste, as **Antoinette Sarpong** from Canada described:

> One aspect of being here in Japan that was a little difficult was dating and body image. A conversation with a female mate from England the other day reminded me that it can be difficult for women first arriving in Japan, which is so patriarchal, and experience the highs and lows of the dating scene. However, for foreign men, it is often thought of as being much easier to meet women for relationships.
>
> Japan is a fascinating country, but don't expect to blend in or go incognito; it is very difficult to be 'accepted' by the Japanese.

Will Mercer is of the opinion that it would be misguided to aim for total acceptance:

> By sheer demographics you will, unless you have Asian features, stand out constantly. On more than one occasion a stranger opened a conversation with me by saying (in Japanese) 'wow, blue eyes!' This does not mean that foreigners will find themselves shunned or treated poorly. Rather, I think it is possible to be accepted within Japanese society, but always as a foreigner. You'll find it much easier to live comfortably if you accept just how exotic you appear to most Japanese. I didn't find it at all difficult to make Japanese friends and I found people, on the whole, to be very friendly, considerate and welcoming.

LIST OF EMPLOYERS

ACC ENGLISH SCHOOL

252 Genjishinmei-Cho, Hekinan-Shi, Aichi-Ken 447 0872

- +81 566 422 332
- info@acc-english.co.jp
- www.acc-english.co.jp

PREFERENCE OF NATIONALITY: Native English speakers for chain of schools in Aichi Prefecture (Nagoya, Anjo, Kariya, Handa, Hekinan, Nishio and Toyoake).

QUALIFICATIONS: University graduates. Teaching experience, basic Japanese language ability or TESOL training an advantage. Applicants must be prepared to teach all levels, from very young children to adults.

CONDITIONS OF EMPLOYMENT: 1-year full-time positions available to teach approximately 25 hours per week. Approximately 4 weeks of paid vacation. Part-time positions sometimes available.

FACILITIES/SUPPORT: 1-week pre-service training provided. Subsidised furnished accommodation arranged (monthly rent is around 40,000 yen).

RECRUITMENT: Speculative applications should be emailed/posted to the above address with a photo of yourself in business attire.

AEON CORPORATION

222 Sepulveda Blvd., Suite # 2000, El Segundo, CA 90245, USA

- +1 310 662 4706
- aeonla@aeonet.com

Also: 535 Fifth Avenue, Rm 413, New York, NY 10017

- +1 646 277 7333
- aeonnyc@aeonet.com
- www.aeonet.com

One of the largest chains of English conversation schools in Japan with over 320 branches.

NUMBER OF TEACHERS: 800.

QUALIFICATIONS: Bachelor's degree in any subject and a perfect command of the English language.

CONDITIONS OF EMPLOYMENT: 1-year renewable contract starting every month. 5 days a week. 40 hours/week work schedule.

SALARY: 270,000 yen per month.

FACILITIES/SUPPORT: Single occupancy apartment furnished to Japanese standards. Subsidised monthly rent of 55,000 yen. Accident and sickness insurance provided under Japan's Socialised Health Insurance plan. 3 weeks of paid vacation and paid training.

RECRUITMENT: 2 full-time recruiting offices in the US (as above). Group and personal interviews held on a regular basis in the USA, and 3 times a year in London, Toronto, Vancouver and Sydney. Positions start every month. Rolling deadlines. Initial applicants should send résumé and minimum 500-word essay entitled 'Why I want to live and work in Japan'. For up-to-date information regarding recruiting trips and application instructions see www.aeonet.com.

CONTACT: Lars Frank, Motoko Toki and Derek Johnson (Personnel Recruiters, New York office) and Andy Gadt, Yumiko Hamanaka and Tomoka Tsuchida (Personnel Recruiters Los Angeles office).

ARK FOREIGN LANGUAGE ACADEMY
4519–4 Innoshima Takuma, Onomichi, Hiroshima 722–2324
- +81 845 228511
- contact@arkgaigo.com
- www.arkgaigo.com/jobs

NUMBER OF TEACHERS: 3. Also part-time positions.
PREFERENCE OF NATIONALITY: None.
QUALIFICATIONS: Degree.
CONDITIONS OF EMPLOYMENT: 1-year contract with 6–8 working hours per day.
SALARY: From 205,000 yen per month. 1,600 yen per 40-minute lesson. Trainees are paid 1000 yen.
FACILITIES/SUPPORT: Accommodation provided free and sponsorship given for work visas.
RECRUITMENT: Interviews are essential.
CONTACT: Matt Winfield, Owner-Manager (matt@arkgaigo.com).

AUSTRALIAN CLUB
2F Manju Bldg, 8-banchi, San-ei-cho, Shinjuku-ku, Tokyo 160-0008
- +81 (0)80 5403 9246
- edu@australianclub.net
- www.100dreams.co.jp/au

Online school so teachers do not need to be resident in Japan.
NUMBER OF TEACHERS: 2–6.
PREFERENCE OF NATIONALITY: Australian teachers preferred.
QUALIFICATIONS: Applicants must be native English speakers with Australian citizenship. Must have TEFL/TESOL certificate, IELTS experience and experience with Japanese learners.
CONDITIONS OF EMPLOYMENT: No contracts; online teaching is on casual basis. Teachers nominate a 3-lesson shift (each lesson is 30 minutes in length). Shifts are on weekday nights or weekends (Japan time).

SALARY: 1,500 yen per 30-minute lesson (net).
FACILITIES/SUPPORT: No accommodation or work permits because this is an online school.
RECRUITMENT: Via TEFL/TESOL job boards. Skype interviews.
CONTACT: Rocco Nigro, Director of Studies.

BERLITZ JAPAN
Shin Aoyama Bldg., East 16F, 1–1 Minami Aoyama 1-chome, Minato-ku, Tokyo 107–0062
- http://teach.berlitz.co.jp

NUMBER OF TEACHERS: Over 1,200 for 63 locations, about half of which are in Greater Tokyo.
PREFERENCE OF NATIONALITY: None, must be native English speaker. For many vacancies, only candidates already in Japan will be considered.
QUALIFICATIONS: Minimum university degree, business experience and/or teaching experience needed for some posts.
CONDITIONS OF EMPLOYMENT: Choice of 3 contracts: semi full-time is open to all applicants; part-time and hourly contracts available only to people already in Japan with current visa. Working hours vary.
SALARY: Starting salary of 250,000 yen, plus possibility of a contract completion bonus.
FACILITIES/SUPPORT: Visa assistance given in some cases but for part-time openings teacher must be already resident and in possession of a visa. All new hires must attend a 6-day Berlitz Instructor Qualification Programme (unpaid).
RECRUITMENT: Via the above website. Interviews are essential and are conducted in Japan or sometimes by telephone and internet. Group interview sessions are organised at intervals.

BERNARD ENGLISH SCHOOL OF JAPAN
Shamotto Tsukuba 2F, 4–2-7 Matsushiro, Tsukuba City, Ibaraki-ken 305–0035
- +81 298 565093
- recruitment@bernard.co.jp
- www.bernard.co.jp

NUMBER OF TEACHERS: 15+ for multiple schools in the Tsukuba area.
PREFERENCE OF NATIONALITY: American, Australian, British and Canadian.
QUALIFICATIONS: Must have a 4-year university degree (any field), TESOL-type qualifications are a plus, must have a valid driver's licence (either a Japanese or an international licence).
CONDITIONS OF EMPLOYMENT: 1 year contracts from August, renewable on mutual agreement. Contracts are a salary/hourly

hybrid. Full-time teachers average about 90–100 hours per month, spread over 44 weeks per year, with 8 weeks of school holidays spread throughout the year.

SALARY: Base salary of 185,000 plus 2,300 yen per hour for those over 80 per month. Contract completion bonus of 60,000 yen.

FACILITIES/SUPPORT: Modern, fully equipped apartments are available for lease through the company. Staff are free to choose other lodgings, if desired. Visa sponsorship can be provided. Company cars are available for lease. A vehicle is necessary for travel between schools. Weekly Japanese language classes available for all teachers free of charge.

RECRUITMENT: Usually takes about 2 months from initial contact. Telephone interviews will be conducted. References are also required.

CONTACT: Frank Pridgen, Foreign Staff Manager.

THE BRITISH ENGLISH AND NEW DANCE ACADEMY

9–23 Hinodemachi, 3 chome, Sanyoonoda-shi, Yamaguchi-ken 756-0091
☏ +81 836 842390
✉ englishbenda@yahoo.co.uk or ennutton@gmail.com
🖥 http://bendaacademy.jimdo.com/esl-jobs

NUMBER OF TEACHERS: 6.

PREFERENCE OF NATIONALITY: Native English-speaking countries.

QUALIFICATIONS: At least a BA degree or 2-year college diploma. Experience is a plus.

CONDITIONS OF EMPLOYMENT: 12 months with option to renew. Teachers work a maximum of 24.5 teaching hours per week, with little or no office time.

SALARY: 245,000–260,000 yen per 98-hour month. National tax is paid from the first year and city tax from the second year.

FACILITIES/SUPPORT: Academy covers key money expenses for teachers' apartments. Teachers pay for their own rent, usually 40,000–55,000 yen. Employer provides work visa sponsorship which is mainly carried out in Japan, but requires the teacher to complete the process in his/her home country. Company car provided.

RECRUITMENT: After receiving applicant's documents by email and airmail, school will arrange telephone interview.

CONTACT: Ted Nutton, Principal (ennutton@gmail.com).

ECC FOREIGN LANGUAGE INSTITUTE

General Headquarters: 3rd Floor, ECC Honsha Building, 1 10 20 Higashi-temma, Kita-ku, Osaka 530-0044
🖥 http://recruiting.ecc.co.jp (for job applicants)
Kanto Management Centre Head Office:

9th Floor, Shinjuku Plaza Building, 1 3 14 Nishi-Shinjuku, Shinjuku-ku, Tokyo 160-0023
✉ ganative@ecc.co.jp
Chubu Management Centre Head Office: 8th Floor, Kanayama Building, 1 16 16 Kanayama, Naka-ku, Nagoya 460-0022
✉ nhr@ecc.co.jp
Kinki Management Centre Head Office: 8th Floor, ECC Honsha Building, 1 10 20 Higashi -temma, Kita-ku, Osaka 530-0044
☏ +81 6 6352 0090
✉ instruct@ecc.co.jp

NUMBER OF TEACHERS: 600+ at 165 schools throughout Japan.

PREFERENCE OF NATIONALITY: Applicants for whom English is their native language.

QUALIFICATIONS: Minimum bachelor's degree.

CONDITIONS OF EMPLOYMENT: 1-year contracts, ending yearly on 31 March; 29.5 total working hours per week, mostly evenings. To work 5 days a week with variable days off. 7 weeks' paid holiday per annum. Teachers work some Saturday or Sunday shifts. Opportunities for paid overtime are plentiful.

SALARY: From 252,000 yen per month.

FACILITIES/SUPPORT: Assistance with accommodation. Compulsory 50–70 hour pre-service training course over 2 weeks. ECC has been more sympathetic to teachers' unions than its rivals.

RECRUITMENT: Visit the website recruiting.ecc.co.jp for recruitment schedules. Main hiring period is September/October/November. UK recruitment: c/o ECC Recruitment (UK), P.O. Box 11985, Colchester, CO6 4XB; ukhiring@ecc.co.jp). Australia recruitment: AMAC Recruitment, www.amacrecruitment.com.au (+61 404 951271; ECC@amacrecruitment.com.au). Canada recruitment: ECC Canada Office, Suite 1801, Toronto Star Building, 1 Yonge Street, Toronto, Ontario M5E 1W7 (+1 416 524 7974; toronto@ecc.co.jp). Visa processing takes 2–3 months.

ENGLISH ACADEMY & HARVARD-KIDS ACADEMY

2-9-6 Ichibancho, Matsuyama 790-0001
☏ +81 89 931 8686
✉ marinbu@post.harvard.edu
🖥 www.eigo-academy.com

NUMBER OF TEACHERS: 7–9 including Harvard-Kids Academy in Yokohama.

PREFERENCE OF NATIONALITY: None.

QUALIFICATIONS: Teachers with at least a 4-year degree. Some experience in teaching is also helpful although training is given.

Native English speakers preferred. Experience with young children is preferred for Harvard-Kids Academy, which is an immersion kindergarten/pre-school.

CONDITIONS OF EMPLOYMENT: 18-month contracts. Hours 12pm–9pm, Tuesday to Friday, 10am–6pm on Saturday.

SALARY: Starting at 250,000 yen per month. Income tax is withheld and different arrangements are made for social security or health insurance depending on the circumstances of the teacher.

FACILITIES/SUPPORT: Help in finding accommodation and loan in making initial deposit. Academy has two apartments which require only minimal deposits. Help to apply for Certificate of Prior Permission for a work visa and in visa renewal when the time comes.

RECRUITMENT: Advertise in publications in Japan and sometimes at Ohayo-Sensei. Telephone and Skype interviews.

CONTACT: K Marin Burch Tanaka.

THE ENGLISH VILLAGE

4-2-1-113 Taihei, Sumida-ku, Tokyo 130 0013

+81 3 3624 3300

englishvillage@msg.biglobe.ne.jp

www.englishvillage.gr.jp

NUMBER OF TEACHERS: 7 for branches in Kinshicho (area of Tokyo) and Funabashi in Chiba.

PREFERENCE OF NATIONALITY: British.

QUALIFICATIONS: Degree (any discipline) and CELTA qualification or equivalent. Valid visa essential.

CONDITIONS OF EMPLOYMENT: 1 year renewable. 30–50-minute lessons per week and sessions supervising free conversation room. School specialises in teaching British English to adult learners.

SALARY: 250,000 yen per month plus 200,000 yen completion bonus.

FACILITIES/SUPPORT: Subsidised accommodation is arranged. New teachers are given a period of thorough training before they start teaching, followed by in-service training.

RECRUITMENT: British press adverts. Interviews in the UK.

CONTACT: Neil Pearson, Principal.

GABA CORPORATION

23F Shinjuku Front Tower, 2-21-1 Kita Shinjuku, Shinjuku-ku, Tokyo, 169-0074

+81 3 5338 5715

recruiting@gaba.co.jp

http://teaching-in-japan.gaba.co.jp

NUMBER OF TEACHERS: 1000.

PREFERENCE OF NATIONALITY: None.

QUALIFICATIONS: TEFL/TESOL experience and certification is preferred but not essential. An outgoing, adaptable personality with an interest in dealing with adult students one-to-one is a must.

CONDITIONS OF EMPLOYMENT: 6-month contracts, though instructors who require visa sponsorship are expected to stay 12 months. Busy times are weekday evenings and early mornings plus weekends. Instructors can choose their schedules on a monthly basis.

SALARY: Pay is on a per-lesson basis. Currently the rate is 1500-2200 yen per 40-minute lesson. Deductions are very low due to the contract type.

FACILITIES/SUPPORT: Accommodation is not provided but instructors can benefit from company links with established housing providers in Japan who may offer a discount. Help given with work visas, provided candidates have an accredited Bachelor's degree taught in English (any discipline) or else 3 years full-time English language teaching experience.

RECRUITMENT: Face-to-face or Skype interviews. Company holds regular recruiting events in the UK, USA and elsewhere where applicants can meet a recruiter and attend interviews.

CONTACT: Keri Sugiyama, Overseas Recruiting Program Leader.

HEART ENGLISH SCHOOL

310–0805 Ibaraki-ken, Mito-shi, 2–6–10 Chuo

+81 29 226 8010

info@heart-school.jp

www.heart-school.jp

Places teachers in public schools to assist Japanese teachers of English in Kanagawa Prefecture (including Yokohama and Kawasaki).

NUMBER OF TEACHERS: 300 Assistant Language Teachers (ALTs) per year, but varies by season.

PREFERENCE OF NATIONALITY: Native or near-native English speakers. Visa sponsorship possible only for passport holders of the US, Canada, UK, Ireland, Australia and New Zealand.

QUALIFICATIONS: Should already have working visa and live in the area. Key qualities are flexibility and a good personality with children. Experience is a plus but not essential if candidates have the right personality and are able to cooperate effectively with their Japanese co-teacher.

CONDITIONS OF EMPLOYMENT: Contracts are usually from the start date – normally April or September – through March, which is the end of Japan's public school year. If both parties agree, contract can be renewed in 1-year increments. Rarely, contract lengths are non-standard due to a specific school board request. In most cases the number of contracted hours is 4–5 per day, over 4 days a week.

SALARY: Pay depends on the municipality, and on number of working hours and days. Range from 160,000 yen per month to 240,000 yen. After rent, taxes, utilities and other compulsory expenses, an ALT earns the equivalent of $1,200–$2,400 in take-home pay, with an average of about $1,850. No payment when school is closed (as in August). Some companies provide a 100,000 yen stipend in these fallow periods, which is enough to cover rent, taxes, utilities and have enough left over for food, but not much else. Employees are expected to prepare for these lulls.

FACILITIES/SUPPORT: Housing can be arranged and subsidised in a private apartment, usually furnished. School cooperates with legalities, and does most of the leg-work in obtaining and renewing Instructor visa.

RECRUITMENT: Via Japan-specific recruitment websites or via university career fairs in North America, UK and Australia. Interviews are required in person or via phone or video connection online.

INTERAC CO. LTD.
Fujimi West 3F, Fujimi 2-14-36, Chiyoda-ku, Tokyo 102 0071
✆ +81 3 3234 7840
🖥 www.interacnetwork.com

Non-governmental provider of Assistant Language Teachers in Japan.

NUMBER OF TEACHERS: Over 2,000 full-time employees throughout Japan.

PREFERENCE OF NATIONALITY: None, though majority are Australian, New Zealander, Canadian, American, British, Irish and Jamaican.

QUALIFICATIONS: Minimum university degree, 12 years' education in the medium of English (all subjects taught in English at school for at least 12 years) plus a passion for teaching and a strong desire to live in Japan and work in Japanese public schools. Japanese language skills and teaching qualifications preferred but not a necessity. Driver's licence and willingness to drive are an advantage.

CONDITIONS OF EMPLOYMENT: 12-month contracts from early April to late March. Up to 29.5 teaching hours per week, Monday to Friday 8am–5pm; 7 months' contract available from late August to following year late March.

SALARY: Average monthly minimum of 230,000 yen; 10% deducted in tax.

FACILITIES/SUPPORT: Comprehensive orientation programme on arrival with follow-up training sessions. Company acts as guarantor for apartment contracts and visa sponsor. Private health

insurance cover available. Free Japanese lessons available in some locations. Company car available to lease.

RECRUITMENT: All recruitment is done through global online system. Interviews may be conducted in Oxford, Toronto and elsewhere. Intakes in late August and late March.

INTERNATIONAL EDUCATION CONSULTANTS/KULZ ACADEMY
Shin Yokohama, IK Bldg. 604, 2 12 12 Shin Yokohama, Kohoku ku, Yokohama shi, 222–0033
✆ +81 8033 135259
🖥 info@ieconsultants.co.jp
🖥 www.ieconsultants.co.jp

Language institute and cram school for young learners.

NUMBER OF TEACHERS: 4.

PREFERENCE OF NATIONALITY: Native English speakers.

QUALIFICATIONS: University graduate. Must be in the country and have work visa already.

CONDITIONS OF EMPLOYMENT: Approximately 100 hours per month. Lessons take place between 6am and 9pm but are mostly in afternoons and evenings, including Saturdays.

SALARY: Hourly rate. 2000 yen. Local taxes deducted at source.

FACILITIES/SUPPORT: No assistance with accommodation or visas. Transport is paid.

RECRUITMENT: Word of mouth. Face-to-face interview required.

CONTACT: Ulrich Kulz, CEO (ulikulz@ieconsultants.co.jp).

INTERNATIONAL EDUCATION SERVICES
Rose Hikawa Building, 22-14, Higashi 2-Chome, Shibuya-Ku, Tokyo 150–0011
✆ +81 3 3498 7101
🖥 jobs@iesnet.co.jp
🖥 www.iesnet.co.jp/english

NUMBER OF TEACHERS: 15–20 ALTs, Business English trainers and language teachers for specialised fields like engineering.

PREFERENCE OF NATIONALITY: Mostly from North America, UK, Australia and New Zealand.

QUALIFICATIONS: University degree required. An assessment of any candidate's English Language proficiency may be required as part of the hiring process.

CONDITIONS OF EMPLOYMENT: Initial annual contract with option for renewal. Majority of positions start in April and September. Total teaching hours vary per month but average 25–35 per week and associated travel time.

SALARY: Varies between the yen equivalent of about $30,000 and $45,000.

FACILITIES/SUPPORT: Administrative coordinator assists teachers in finding accommodation.

RECRUITMENT: Interviews are an essential part of the recruitment process and are sometimes carried out in the UK and the USA, but increasingly online. Applicants should apply 5 months before intended start date.

CONTACT: Damian Thomas, Academic Director (dthomas@iesnet.co.jp) or Jim Malian, Chairman (jmalian@iesnet.co.jp).

JAMES ENGLISH SCHOOLS

4-16-6 Teraoka Izumi, Sendai, Miyagi 981 3204

☎ +81 22 772 0161

🖥 www.james.co.jp/english

NUMBER OF TEACHERS: 50-100 for 15 branches in the Tohoku region of Northern Japan.

PREFERENCE OF NATIONALITY: None.

QUALIFICATIONS: Bachelor's degree and TESOL certificate required.

CONDITIONS OF EMPLOYMENT: 1-year contract. Expect teachers to stay at least 2 years. 30 teaching hours per week (average).

SALARY: 260,000 yen per month.

FACILITIES/SUPPORT: Loan provided for initial settling-in costs. Visa sponsorship. Training and regular professional development offered.

RECRUITMENT: Adverts on www.GaijinPot.com. etc. Application process completed through website. Skype interviews.

CONTACT: Mr Yoshi Kigawa, Owner and President.

JET PROGRAMME UK

JET Desk, Embassy of Japan, 101–104 Piccadilly, London W1J 7JT, UK

☎ +44 20 7465 6668

🖥 info@jet-uk.org or ukjet@ld.mofa.go.jp

🖥 www.jet-uk.org

NUMBER OF TEACHERS: Approximately 150 from the UK going to educational institutions all over Japan.

PREFERENCE OF NATIONALITY: UK passport holders only.

QUALIFICATIONS: Must hold a bachelor's degree by the time of departure and be under 40 years of age. TEFL training or experience preferred but not essential. Tattoos and body piercings are not well tolerated in Japan.

CONDITIONS OF EMPLOYMENT: 12-month renewable contracts starting in August up to maximum of 5 years. Normal working hours are 35 hours per week, although teaching hours are

between 15 and 20. Conditions of service vary according to the policies of different contracting organisations.

SALARY: Annual remuneration is about 3.36 million yen per year.

FACILITIES/SUPPORT: JET finds placement, organises visa and insurance, hosts 2-day pre-departure orientation day in London, beginners' TEFL training and basic Japanese language course, 2-day orientation in Tokyo, language books; return flights provided upon completion of contract.

RECRUITMENT: Application process begins in October. Deadline for application is the last week in November. Interviews in following January/February with decisions given in April. All application info is online or contact JET Desk with any queries.

KENT SCHOOL OF ENGLISH

Shoppers' Plaza 706, 1–4-1 Irfune, Urayasu-shi, Chiba Ken 279–0012

☎ +81 47 353 8708

🖥 kyagawa@tryon.co.jp

🖥 www.kent-english.jp/recruit

NUMBER OF TEACHERS: 8.

PREFERENCE OF NATIONALITY: None, but interviews held in London in July.

QUALIFICATIONS: Minimum university degree plus TEFL certificate or PGCE plus 2 years' TEFL experience. Must like children.

CONDITIONS OF EMPLOYMENT: 1-year contract. 23 contact hours per week. School is open Tuesday-Friday 1–10 pm and Saturday 10am–6pm. 5–6 weeks' paid holiday.

SALARY: From 260,000 yen per month (gross) plus outward flight provided. Tax and insurance deductions are less than 8%.

FACILITIES/SUPPORT: Subsidised furnished flats available, some shared, some single. All deposits/key money/gratuities paid, so teachers pay only the rent and utilities charges. Visa sponsorship and initial training.

RECRUITMENT: Adverts on the internet (eg www.tefl.com). Interviews held in the UK in the summer. Once contract is signed, permits are arranged and issued in mid-September.

CONTACT: Kaoru Yagawa, Principal.

KEVIN'S ENGLISH SCHOOLS

Iizawa 242–23, Minamiashigara Shi, Kanagawa Pref. 250-0122

☎ +81 465 744458

🖥 kevinsenglishschools@hotmail.com

🖥 www.eikaiwa1.com

NUMBER OF TEACHERS: 3.

PREFERENCE OF NATIONALITY: None.

QUALIFICATIONS: College or university degree and some extra training in how to teach English. A TEFL certificate and experience are pluses.

CONDITIONS OF EMPLOYMENT: 1-year contract. Most teaching hours fall in the afternoon and evening up till 9pm.

SALARY: 250,000 yen per month.

FACILITIES/SUPPORT: Apartment is provided for a rent of about 60,000 yen per month. Assistance given with all official paperwork.

RECRUITMENT: Via www.how-to-teach-english-in-japan.com. Interviews by phone or in person are essential; many candidates are interviewed by phone.

CONTACT: Kevin R Burns, Owner.

MODEL LANGUAGE STUDIO (MLS)
2–31–8 Yoyogi, Shibuya-ku, Tokyo-to 151–0053
+81 3 3320 1555
careers21@mls-etd.co.jp
www.mls-etd.co.jp/recruiting_e.html

NUMBER OF TEACHERS: 55 across 31 studio locations.

PREFERENCE OF NATIONALITY: All native speakers.

QUALIFICATIONS: Experience working with students aged 1–12. Valid Working Visa or minimum BA Certification in which case sponsorship is possible.

CONDITIONS OF EMPLOYMENT: 12-month contracts from April. Up to 30 hours per 5-day week (of which 25 are teaching hours).

SALARY: 255,000 yen (gross) per calendar month. Up to 80,000 yen end-of-contract bonus.

FACILITIES/SUPPORT: Company can temporarily house new arrivals. It has links to large number of apartments and can help staff source a suitable one (key money not required). Transport to and from work is paid. Various other monetary incentives. Long paid vacations and all national holidays paid. Company can help sponsor appropriate candidates for a visa before arrival in Japan.

RECRUITMENT: Via company website, www.gaijinpot.com and various Japanese recruitment agencies. Face-to-face interview essential. Non-Japan-based applications must include an mpeg/DVD of the candidate in action.

CONTACT: David Flynn, Instructor Management.

PEACE BOAT / GET UNIVERSAL
1-32-13-4F Takadanobaba, Shinjuku-ku, Tokyo, 169–0075
+81 3 5287 3192
getprogramme@peaceboat.gr.jp or pbglobal@peaceboat.gr.jp
www.peaceboat.org/english/?menu=110

Peace Boat is a Japan-based international non-governmental and non-profit organisation that travels the world on peace voyages.

NUMBER OF TEACHERS: 8-18 volunteer language teachers onboard each cruise, to teach as part of the onboard language programme known as GET (Global English/español Training).

PREFERENCE OF NATIONALITY: Aim to recruit a linguistically and culturally diverse team. Non-native highly advanced speakers of English and applicants with multiple language teaching ability are welcome to apply.

QUALIFICATIONS: At least 18 months of relevant full-time language teaching experience. Flexible, good communication skills and an interest in peace building and global education. A degree, qualification in language teaching and conversational Japanese ability are highly regarded. Average age is 27.

CONDITIONS OF EMPLOYMENT: Voyages depart 3 times a year, e.g. mid-December from Japan, and last approximately 100 days to circumnavigate the globe. Teachers can expect to teach 2-3 intensive classes and some private lessons as well as organising language-related events onboard. While in port, teachers normally have free time.

SALARY: None. Participation fee for the voyage, which covers meals, accommodation onboard and port taxes is covered by GET Universal Co. Ltd. Teachers must cover transport to and from Tokyo, and compulsory travel insurance.

FACILITIES/SUPPORT: Structured online preparatory study period of 4–6 hours a week over 2 months before departure. Intensive orientation lasting 3–4 days in Tokyo. Professional development workshops conducted onboard. Documents for the necessary visas are provided.

RECRUITMENT: Recruiting websites and the Peace Boat website as above. Deadline for applications is mid-August; interviews in Tokyo (or by Skype) in early September.

CONTACT: Nicholas Sutton, International Coordinator.

RED ROOF ENGLISH SCHOOL
Okinawa Prefecture, Ginowan City, Samashita 175–1-102 (Kasa G2)
+81 98 890 1228
job.info@redroof.jp
www.redroof.jp

NUMBER OF TEACHERS: 3.

PREFERENCE OF NATIONALITY: None.

QUALIFICATIONS: University degree is essential for visa sponsorship. Experience working with children is preferred.

CONDITIONS OF EMPLOYMENT: 1-year contract. Usual teaching hours between 1pm and 9pm Monday to Friday or Tuesday to Saturday.

SALARY: Starting from 185,000 yen to 225,000 yen per month depending on expertise; 40,000 to 50,000 yen deducted per month for rent and utilities.

FACILITIES/SUPPORT: Apartment with modest furnishings is provided. Assistance is also given with setting up telephones and banking, etc.

RECRUITMENT: Usually through the internet or word of mouth. Interviews are essential and can be held via webcam or occasionally in Canada.

CONTACT: Ken Nakamura-Huber, Director (ken@redroof.jp).

SHANE ENGLISH SCHOOL JAPAN (SESJ)

Kenkyusha Fujimi Building 4F, 2-11-3 Fujimi, Chiyoda-ku, Tokyo 102-0071

℡ +81 3 5275 6756

✎ drp@shane.co.jp or teflrecruitment@shane.co.jp

💻 www.tefljobsinjapan.com and www.saxoncourt.com/jobs-abroad/japan

Chain of language schools in the Greater Tokyo region that has been part of Japanese cram school company Eikoh Inc since 2010.

NUMBER OF TEACHERS: 400+ in 180 schools, especially Tokyo, Kanto areas, Nagoya and Osaka.

PREFERENCE OF NATIONALITY: Native speakers of British English, ie from Commonwealth countries.

QUALIFICATIONS: University degree required plus CELTA or Trinity CertTESOL.

CONDITIONS OF EMPLOYMENT: 12-month renewable contracts. Maximum 30 contact hours per week. Students from age 2. 5–6 weeks' paid holiday.

SALARY: Starting salary 252,800 yen per month plus possible bonuses. Deductions for income tax work out at about 6.5% of gross income.

FACILITIES/SUPPORT: Accommodation sub-lets provided for teachers who require it or information on guesthouses that accept long-stay foreigners. All documentation for work visas is provided. 1 week Young Learner teacher training given.

RECRUITMENT: Via face-to-face interviews in Japan or via recruitment agencies in the UK, ie Saxoncourt International (www.saxoncourt.com), TEFLOne or TEFL-in-Japan.com.

CONTACT: Director of Recruitment and Personnel (teflrecruitment@shane.co.jp).

TEFL IN JAPAN

76 Mortimer Street, London W1W 7SA, UK

℡ +44 207 079 3330

✎ tim@tefl-in-japan.com

💻 www.tefl-in-japan.com

NUMBER OF TEACHERS: 40 per year.

PREFERENCE OF NATIONALITY: None.

QUALIFICATIONS: University degree, CELTA/Trinity CertTESOL. Teaching experience not essential.

CONDITIONS OF EMPLOYMENT: 12 month contracts. 29.5 hours per week, to include approx. 25 contact hours.

SALARY: 252,800 yen per month.

FACILITIES/SUPPORT: Accommodation is found for teachers, and rent is deducted from salary. After sending documents to Tokyo that are processed, the teacher visits a Japanese Embassy to have the visa stamped into their passport; no need for notarised copies or medical reports!

RECRUITMENT: Web advertising and contacts at TEFL teacher training centres, leading to a face to face or Skype interview.

CONTACT: Tim Langley, Director.

VOLTA ASSOCIATES

Chiyoda Platform Square 1005, 3–21 Kanda Hishikicho, Chiyoda-ku, Tokyo 101–0054

℡ +81 3 3427 4227

✎ info@volta-associates.com

💻 www.volta-associates.com/recruitment.html

NUMBER OF TEACHERS: 5 corporate trainers to teach one-to-one.

PREFERENCE OF NATIONALITY: None.

QUALIFICATIONS: Bachelor degree with TESOL.

CONDITIONS OF EMPLOYMENT: 1-year contract. 4–6 lessons a day, 5 days a week.

SALARY: Approximately 230,00 yen.

FACILITIES/SUPPORT: Assistance given with finding accommodation (translating paperwork, finding estate agents, etc). TESOL course is provided (affiliated with American TESOL, www.americantesol.com).

RECRUITMENT: Online application to Human Resources department. Interviews are essential.

CONTACT: Benard Oppong-Kusi, President and CEO.

WESTGATE CORPORATION

Human Resources Department, Yushima Daido Bldg 2F, 3-17-1 Yushima, Bunkyo-Ku, Tokyo 113–0034

℡ +81 3 3836 0362

✎ westgate_recruiter@westgate.co.jp

💻 www.westgate.co.jp

NUMBER OF TEACHERS: 400.

PREFERENCE OF NATIONALITY: USA, UK, Canada, Australia, Ireland, New Zealand.

QUALIFICATIONS: Bachelor's or higher degree plus EFL/ESL teaching experience. 500+ hours of classroom teaching experience (including non-EFL/ESL) needed by applicants with EFL/ESL teaching certificate/degree and/or elementary/primary/secondary teaching credentials/ qualifications; or 1,000+ hours of classroom teaching experience (including non-EFL/ESL) for those without any of the above credentials.

CONDITIONS OF EMPLOYMENT: 3–5 months. 9 working hours a day including 4–6 teaching hours. Work available in universities.

SALARY: From 275,000 yen per month. Deductions made for income tax, employment tax, National Health Insurance premium, rent (if teacher lives in a Westgate-arranged apartment), and Nursing Care Insurance premium (for teachers over 40).

FACILITIES/SUPPORT: Westgate arranges a fully-furnished single apartment and sponsors all instructors to obtain the visa necessary to work in Japan.

RECRUITMENT: Online application form. Skype or phone interview.

CONTACT: Sachi Sasaki, Recruiter/HR Coordinator.

KOREA

Anyone who has witnessed the early-morning scramble by students and businessmen to get to their English lessons before the working day begins in Seoul might be surprised to learn that the motto for South Korea is 'Land of the Morning Calm'. Because Korea's economy is increasingly globalised, English is seen as essential for success in business. The level of affluence in Seoul and the other major cities is striking, and many of these ambitious young Koreans are not only keen but are also able to afford English lessons (or their parents can). An English proficiency test must be passed by all aspiring university students, which is why so many students of secondary school age study the language so feverishly. Both these groups have probably studied English for many years at school but need to practise conversation with native English speakers.

It is estimated that eight out of every ten students from primary school upwards study English after school, though a percentage of these are doing it online. The Korean government spends more per capita on English language education than any other country in the world. So the demand is insatiable. School and university vacations (July and January) often see a surge in student enrolment at private language institutes and at seasonal camps. The teaching of children is booming more than ever. This must be the only country in the world where it is possible to have your international airfare covered in return for teaching for a couple of weeks at a camp (see description below). Major language teaching organisations rely heavily on recruitment agencies abroad to fill their recurring vacancies for native English speaker staff. The market in Korea is ever changing. There are still lots of jobs around but it is becoming harder to find good positions, especially for male teachers and couples. Partly because of the difficult employment situation in their home countries, many teachers are staying in their jobs in Korea longer or finding new ones in Korea instead of returning home.

The bias is strongly in favour of North Americans, especially Canadians, and there are still relatively few British TEFLers in Korea, though this is gradually changing with the activities of UK-based recruiters such as Flying Cows in Nottingham (see entry), which recruits for positions in both the private and public sectors. Note that in the case of Korea, 'schools' normally refers to the state sector whereas 'institutes' means private language academies run as businesses. The number of small to medium-sized *hagwons* (private language institutes) in all Korean cities interested in hiring a few native English speakers is massive. One agency in Korea's third city, Daegu, estimates that there are 800 native speakers of English teaching in that one city. When dealing either with *hagwon* owners or recruiters, ask for the email address of a current English-speaking teacher and use it to ask about the school, students, the town/city and accommodation. (For an account of what can happen if you don't do this, see Emma Lander's story later in this chapter.) Fortunately the language industry's bad reputation for shamelessly exploiting foreign teachers seems to be slowly improving.

Of broader concern than the possible shark-like practices of some potential employers is the looming proximity of North Korea. Kim Jong-un has no intention of giving up Pyongyang's nuclear arsenal and his regime seems even more belligerent and ruthless than his father's. Recent events have done nothing to calm nerves in South Korea. **William Naquin**, a well-qualified American who taught in Kyunggi-Do, sums up the politics as he saw them when he was there:

> *Korea is a divided country. We were quite nervous that war might break out here between the two Koreas. The situation in the north is universally reported to be extremely bad, with summary executions and food riots. The North Koreans have nuclear missiles, nerve gas and chemical weapons, and are led by the most isolated, despotic lunatic and paranoid military strongmen in the world. Prospective teachers need to know that this is one of the most likely flashpoints for war on earth, and that coming here necessarily involves some degree of risk.*

For the curious, it is possible to visit the Demilitarised Zone (DMZ) between South and North Korea on a day trip (for about £30 from Seoul). However, it is not possible to enter the reclusive Democratic Republic from the south.

PROSPECTS FOR TEACHERS

According to long-term American expat teacher **Dwight Gauer**, globalisation and Tiger Mothers (so-called because of their vaulting ambition on behalf of their children) are the key drivers of Korea's fanatical pursuit of the English language. He has written a comprehensive and valuable book, *Teaching English in South Korea: A Guide And Critique*, published in 2013 and available on amazon.

> *As I used to watch new high-rise apartments being constructed around me, I was quick to notice that hagwons were fast to follow. In many cases, they are the first businesses to be constructed in the neighbourhood of new apartments. Some here, me included, call this the 'hagwonisation' of Korea. This is a billion dollar business.*

There are hundreds of *hagwons* in Seoul, the capital, Busan (Korea's second city, less than four hours south of Seoul) and in smaller cities. The majority of these are run as businesses, where profit is the primary or even sole raison d'être. ELT training is superfluous in the majority of cases. Native-speaker status and a bachelor's degree are usually sufficient to persuade the owner of an institute to hire an English speaker. Education is greatly respected in Korea and degrees generally matter far more to potential employers than specialist qualifications. For now, a bachelor's is sufficient and a master's (no matter in what field) counts heavily in one's favour. Having a TEFL certificate and/or teaching experience usually attracts more job offers, although some schools are suspicious of candidates with experience because they view them as potentially picky, plus they don't want to pay more than a basic entry-level salary.

If you wait until you get to Korea, it is easy to fix up a job, but the visa is more difficult to arrange (see section on regulations below). If you want to find a good job make sure you present yourself well. **Peter Burnside** offers three brief tips to people considering going to teach in Korea: '*follow your heart, trust your instincts and take insane risks*'.

FINDING A JOB

IN ADVANCE

The Korean government administers an official teacher placement programme, not unlike JET in Japan, which means that it is competitive to be accepted. EPIK (English Program in Korea) is run by the Ministry of Education and administered through Korean embassies and consulates in the USA, Canada, Australia and the UK, placing about 3,000 foreign graduates in state schools and education offices throughout the country. Private recruiters are also involved and are chosen as official representatives by EPIK every spring. For 2015/6, the agencies were Korvia Consulting in Seoul (www.korvia.com), Korean Horizons (www.koreanhorizons.com) Vancouver, Reach to Teach in the US (www.reachtoteachrecruiting.com) and Canadian Connection (see entry).

The annual salary offered on the EPIK programme is 1.8–2.7 million won per month (depending on qualifications and experience) plus free furnished accommodation, visa sponsorship, a settlement allowance of 300,000 won on arrival in Korea, 50% contribution to medical insurance and an end-of-contract bonus called severance pay. Applications for the autumn semester that starts on September 1st are accepted from 1 April until places are filled, usually in May or June, though the 2015 deadline was extended to July 15th, but documents can be submitted all year round in case of openings. The requirements have recently become stiffer for this programme. Unless candidates are certified teachers or have a BA/MA in Education, they must also hold a TEFL/TESOL/CELTA certificate. Details of the programme are available from the EPIK website (www.epik.go.kr). Applicants cannot specify the location in which they would like to live/work and couples cannot apply together. You can select a preference of metropolitan, provincial or Seoul, but with no guarantee that your request will be honoured.

A subsidiary government programme is called TALK (talkkorea@korea.com; www.talk.go.kr), which is open to people with at least two years of university education. The teaching here takes place in after-school clubs in rural primary schools, the commitment can be shorter (6 months is possible though a year is preferred) and the pay is lower (1.5 million won a month).

RECRUITMENT AGENCIES

Identifying the good recruitment agencies interested in more than collecting their commission from the hagwons is tricky. The fact that recruiters come and go indicates that some are just out to make a fast buck. Most private recruiters offer one-year contracts to English speakers with a university or college diploma. Candidates with additional EFL/ESL qualifications and teaching experience should be able to negotiate higher monthly salaries than the standard 1.8–2.1 million won. Recruited teachers are asked to commit themselves to teach 120 hours a month, which is a heavy load. Return airfares, free accommodation, paid holidays, contribution to medical insurance and completion bonus are all promised as a rule. Applicants who cannot be interviewed locally can do so by telephone or Skype. Note that recruiters should not charge teachers any fee since they earn their commission from the schools and institutes. An agency in the UK called Flying Cows, formed in 2004, aims to be as honest as possible about the rewards and drawbacks of teaching in South Korea (see entry).

Here is a list of Korea-based recruiters active at the time of writing, followed by a list for North American readers, all of which are located in Canada.

Daegu TEFL Job, Daegu (+82 10 254 4656; www.daegutefljob.com/tefljobs). Daegu Foreign Language Education Association consists of over 300 reputable private English language institutes in Daegu which employ foreign English teachers every year.
Korean Global Connections, Seoul (www.kgcesl.com).
Morgan Recruiting, Seoul (+82 070 8880 8855; www.morganrecruiting.com).
Park English Recruitment Agency, Seoul (+82 2 749 1011; www.parkenglish.wix.com/parkenglish).
People Recruit, Busan (www.peoplerecruit.com). Calls itself a 'Competent Persons Database'.
SeoulESL Recruiting, Seoul (+82 2 585 7871; esl@seoulesl.com; www.seoulesl.com).
TeachAbroadKorea.com, Top Placement Inc, Seoul (teachabroad 22@gmail.com, www.teachabroad-korea.com). Cooperates with recruiter in Salt Lake City in the US.
Think Outside, www.thinkoutsiderecruiting.com.

The following Canadian agencies are willing to place more than just Canadians provided they meet the requirements.

Adventure Teaching, Vancouver (www.adventureteaching.com).
Canadian Connection Consulting Agency (see entry).
Gone2Korea, ESL Employment Services, 2 Bloor Street W, Suite 700, Toronto M4W 3R1 (+1 416 642 6506; www.gone2korea.com).
I Love ESL, Toronto and Seoul (www.iloveesl.com). Korean ESL job placement agency.
Korea Connections (see entry).
Russell Recruiting, Vancouver (russell_recruiting@yahoo.co.ca; www.russellrecruiting.com). Caters to ESL teachers wishing to work in Korea. Agency made up of former and current teachers.
Scotia Personnel, Halifax (+1 902 422 1455; scotiap@ns.sympatico.ca or info@scotia-personnel-ltd.com; www.scotia-personnel-ltd.com). Refers Canadians with university degree to teaching English in schools in South Korea. Employer provides airfare, accommodation, competitive salary and more.
Teach Koreans, Cheongju (+82 10 4582 0247; www.teachkoreans.com).

Cara McCain found a good way of dipping her toe in the water of teaching in Korea without committing herself for a whole year. The camp she worked for paid round-trip airfares from the US and provided accommodation, food and a wage of 800,000 won for a commitment of three to four weeks. In order to apply, you need to have a university degree, no criminal record and be willing to jump through all the bureaucratic hoops to prove it in order to qualify for a C4 (short-term business) visa:

I was looking for a way to finance my trip to Korea, and a winter camp seemed like a perfect opportunity. Don't bother to apply unless you already have the documents, which include a notarised background check and an apostilled degree certificate. I contacted a couple of camps while I was waiting for my paperwork in the mail, but they turned me down flat because I didn't have the documents in hand. I was hired to teach a three-week intensive camp, seven hours a day with Sundays off. The camp that hired me was iHUFS [see entry] through a recruiter in Australia who worked with me over Skype and email.

The next step was buying my plane ticket. It was the winter holiday season, so airfares came out at about $1600. I told the recruiter that I didn't have the money to pay for my own ticket. He suggested that I just buy the ticket on a credit card, and the camp would transfer the money into my American bank account once I got to Korea. I took a leap of faith and it worked out fine. The camp went great. The staff was professional and took good care of all the teachers at the camp. We were picked up at the airport, and were given food and adequate accommodation. The students were great and enjoyed learning English. Couldn't ask for more. Overall the experience was a great way to jumpstart my ESL career. I gained relevant teaching experience, got to try the food, learned about the culture, and met people that I still keep in touch with to this day.

Another camp company to try is Camp Korea (hr@ck.co.kr), which pays 3,100,000 won (US$2,750) for a month from mid-July, but no travel. Vacancies crop up at the last minute so they are interested in hearing from native speakers already in Korea on a working visa (see their facebook page). The internet is well equipped to keep track of the volatile English-language market and many Korean employers rely exclusively on sites like http://koreajobfinder.com and www.hiteacher.com. More than one web page (eg http://blacklist.tokyojon.com) lists good and bad employers along with quite a few horror stories.

Another possibility for anyone with an MA or advanced TEFL/TESL qualifications is to work for the language department of a Korean university (of which there are several hundred). Universities probably offer the best-paid and most stable employment.

EMMA LANDER

Emma J. Lander's story is typical and may be instructive. In most respects the *hagwon* job she was assigned through an agency was satisfactory and certainly lucrative, but there was one defect she couldn't overlook.

I started working in South Korea in November 2012. Like most people who move to Asia with a teaching contract I had signed on the dotted line to stay there for 12 months, but it didn't work out and I was home in England again within four months. I have written this account of my experience in the hope that if you decide to teach abroad (which you really should, by the way) you will learn from my mistakes and avoid making them yourself.

I found the job through an online recruitment agency. I read the testimonials, all of which were great, and proceeded to send my CV. They found me a job within a couple of weeks and before I knew it a telephone interview had been arranged on my behalf. I had secured my TEFL qualification a year earlier and I had already had two short-term teaching contracts so I felt confident that this was the job for me.

I was offered the job the day after the interview and I asked if I could speak to the other foreign teachers at the academy. The principal refused, saying that she was confident that I would be happy in my new role. I had done a lot of research regarding working abroad and all the advice I had come across was the same: 'Never go to a school if they don't let you speak to the foreign teachers beforehand because it probably means they've got something to hide.' This should have been a red flag for me. I should have kindly refused the offer and looked elsewhere. I should have ... but I didn't. I was so excited that I had secured a job that I ignored everything I had researched and I accepted the position without a moment's hesitation.

When I arrived in Korea I was met at the airport by my agency and taken to my apartment. It was very small but comfortable and I soon settled in. I was due to start the next day and I spent two days observing classes and learning the ropes before being given my own students. My working hours were Monday-Friday 2pm-9.30pm, although we often worked much later. The school provided textbooks for me to work through but I was free to teach them how I wanted. For the most part my students were polite and appeared to genuinely enjoy learning English. I taught ages 7-16 and found that each age range presented its own enjoyments and challenges.

The wages I received were excellent; I was earning around £1,000 per month and my outgoings were small. The school paid for my apartment and my monthly bills came to approximately £20. I was in a position to save around £800 a month if I so desired and still have an active social life. I was lucky as my weekends were always free so I spent my spare time either exploring the city of Seoul, or going further afield to see temples and climb mountains.

My job was great fun for about two months; however, I started to encounter problems when it came to testing time. I had already advised the head teacher that some of my students should be moved down a class because they did not understand the lessons. My requests were ignored. When testing day came and I graded the papers the students I was worried about were only receiving 30%, but, instead of them being moved down, I was forced to mark them at 70% (the pass rate at the academy) and then watch as some of them were moved up a level! 'We have to do that to keep the parents happy', I was told, and that was when I decided I had to leave. The lowlight for me was watching my wonderful students struggle unnecessarily, simply because they were in the wrong classes. Seeing the academy put so much effort into making money and minimal effort into teaching was very sad.

You must be aware that if you break your contract the penalties can be harsh. I had to pay back my flight ticket and I lost 60% of my wages during the last two months. Even with the experience, I would (and will) do it again in a heartbeat. The highlight of my time in Korea was having the opportunity to explore a new culture and experiencing something entirely different to my life back home.

ON THE SPOT

Looking for a job on arrival is not recommended. The immigration laws stipulate that any foreigners who arrive in Korea to teach English must get their final visa processing completed in their own home country. There are all kinds of interesting conversations happening in Korea as to whether this regulation is really necessary, but the rules are mostly obeyed because the penalties for being caught are harsh. It is said that the government offers a reward to citizens who inform on offenders.

REGULATIONS

To reiterate, teachers must get their final visa processing completed in their home country if they are going to a *hagwon* job or even a short-term camp job, although some exemptions exist for visa processing in a third country if you are going to a public (state) school job. Anyone working without a visa risks fines and possible deportation. Similarly, the schools which hire freelance foreigners without permits can be closed down by the government. So, if at all possible, obtain a teaching visa (E2), which is available only to people with a 3 or 4-year bachelor's degree. The alternative C4 (short-term business) visa valid for single entry and maximum 90 days is also available only to degree holders. All must be native speakers of English and nationals of the UK, Ireland, USA, Canada, Australia, New Zealand or South Africa. Unfortunately some schools (such as Berlitz) want to hire only those with an F2 or F4 residency visa (for spouses of Koreans or people of Korean heritage) and will not accept E2 visas.

The procedures are ludicrously complicated. In the words of **Del Ford**, who has taught throughout the Far East for nine years: 'The application and immigration documentation requirements, especially for jobs in public schools, have entered the realm of Kafkaesque absurdity.' Recruiters and employers accustomed to the procedures will set them out as clearly as they can. Here is a summary: you must gather together the contract of employment from your prospective employer, your passport, your original degree officially notarised, which must be from an approved institution in an English-speaking country, a notarised criminal record/DBS check, medical certificate, ID and forms. After mailing these and other documents to the employer in Korea, they are used to obtain a visa issuance number. With a visa issuance number, you can proceed to apply for the E2 visa at the Korean consulate in your home country. The consulate officer may schedule a short interview that can be by phone and then stamp your passport with an E2 visa stamp. Within 60 days of arrival in Korea you'll have to subject yourself to a full medical, including blood and urine tests to check for HIV and any trace of illegal drugs, in order to qualify for an Aliens Registration Card. The medical exam will be at your expense and costs at least 100,000 won. Finally, your visa becomes valid and you may commence work immediately.

Emma Lander summarises the ordeal:

> *Securing the working visa for South Korea was a long and arduous process. I had to have my degree certificate verified, copied and signed by a solicitor and I had to acquire a background check and have that signed off too, none of which came cheap. I also had to get passport photos, copies of my CV and the contract, and complete a self-assessment medical check. It took roughly six weeks before my visa arrived. If you're going to work in Asia you must be committed because it takes a lot of effort on your part to get there.*

Since September 2010, Korean Embassies and Consulates General are accepting only notarised degree certificates and criminal record checks that have been affixed with the relevant 'apostille' (French for 'certification'). This can be done by specialist companies, for example in the UK see www.apostille.org.uk, where each stamp will cost £54 or £66. US nationals must obtain a criminal record check issued by the FBI rather than a state-level check, and these can take up to three months to process. Note that the Korean authorities do not return your submitted documents.

The E2 visa is valid only for employment with the sponsoring employer, which means that if you change employers, you must have your E2 visa officially endorsed, which is much easier than applying from scratch. So if you have obtained an E2 and completed your contract, you can transfer the visa to a new employer with minimal fuss. Freelance teaching is not permitted under the terms of your work permit and can (and does) lead to fines and deportation.

Teachers are liable to income tax from their first day of work. The rate of income tax for most teachers should be 4%–7%, so beware employers who try to hold back much more from earnings. Most teachers participate in the Korean National Medical Insurance Union; most employers pay half of the total, leaving teachers to pay about 2% of earnings.

CONDITIONS OF WORK

Discontentment seems to be chronic among English teachers in Korea. So many American teachers have fallen foul of faulty contracts, that the American Citizens Services Unit of the US Embassy in Seoul publishes guidance on its website (http://seoul.usembassy.gov/acs_teaching.html) with tips for avoiding the pitfalls. Here is an extract that addresses cultural differences head on:

> *Foreign instructors in Korea occasionally have contract disputes with their employers. Many have observed that in Korea, a contract appears simply to be a rough working agreement, subject to change depending on the circumstances. Many Koreans do not view deviations from a contract as a breach of contract, and few Koreans would consider taking an employer to court over a contract dispute. Instead, Koreans tend to view contracts as being flexible and subject to further negotiation. Culturally, the unwritten or oral agreement one has with one's employer is generally considered 'valid' as well. However, many employers will view a contract violation by a foreign worker as a serious matter.*

Whereas the internet reveals that a great many teachers end up disillusioned with *hagwon* owners who are variously branded crooks and rascals, a more considered view comes from a Scottish blogger called Lauren (http://livelauren.wordpress.com/tag/flying-cows) who taught in Korea through the Flying Cows agency after having been turned down for the EPIK programme:

> *I just want to point out that private schools are a much bigger gamble than public. A quick search online and you'll come across an abundance of horror stories about* hagwons *mistreating foreign teachers. But for every disreputable* hagwon *out there, there are a dozen decent ones. The best advice I can give you, if you decide to go down the* hagwon *route, is to speak with the current foreign teacher at the school and ask them any and all the questions you can think of, and if that doesn't put your mind at rest, then go with your gut and decline the job.*

The issue of severance pay (*taechikum*) is a sore point for many teachers. By law, anyone who completes a 52-week contract is entitled to one month's salary as severance pay. Employers have been known to make life quite unpleasant for their teachers near the end of their contracts, so that they're tempted to leave and forego the bonus. Bear in mind the quality of *hagwons* varies enormously. While some are excellent, others are run by sharks who may make promises at interview which they can't fulfil, and overfill classes to maximise profits. Many schools do not use recognised course books but rely on home-made materials of dubious usefulness. On the other hand, standards are rising in some schools and the experience of teachers in the private sector is not all bad.

ALLISON WILLIAMS

Allison Williams was accepted onto the government's EPIK programme, which she thinks is vastly preferable to teaching for a commercial institute.

I applied through the agency Gone2Korea, who accepted me onto the EPIK programme and gave me the opportunity to apply for whichever city or province I wanted. We arrived on 18 February for a week-long orientation which covered tips on teaching and advice. I really found it very useful. I also was able to make contacts with other people teaching in Daegu. Since then I have taken a 100-hour TEFL course while in Korea, which has resulted in a $100 a month pay rise.

I co-teach, which in Korea can be one of three options: you do everything, you do nothing or you do about 50%. Many of the Korean teachers' English ability is very low so their own lack of confidence inhibits them from interacting or working with the native teachers. When co-teaching, the experience is very dependent on the teacher you work with. Last year I did the 50% option. I prepared worksheets and games for the lessons, I taught about half of the class, monitoring or assisting for the other half. Because this year our school has to improve on its national English test scores, I'm pretty much doing very little to nothing. I don't prepare games for lessons any more as they have cut down on the games in place of tests. This is not the norm but it can happen. It is a bit frustrating going from being so involved to doing so little, but I'm looking forward to being more involved next semester again. We follow the national curriculum and the teachers don't deviate from it, even if the grammar and/or phrases are incorrect or inappropriate, though they do add supplementary materials.

Working conditions are great! Since my accommodation is provided and paid for by the government, I have very few living costs and can save $1,000-$1,300 per month, without having to eat beans on toast, or should I say instant noodles. The teachers and students are all fantastic, very welcoming and kind. From day one I felt like a celebrity and still do after 15 months at the same school. I have my own desk and computer and have been helped with everything from my personal bills to getting a cell phone. In terms of pay, hours, vacation and working conditions public schools are the way to go. If you are looking for autonomous teaching and complete control over what you teach then public schools are not always the best option. I think the biggest problem is that the government has come up with this idea to have native English speakers in every school, but at the level of the school they have little or no idea what to do with them.

The majority of Korean language learners are serious (some attend two-hour classes three or four times a week) and want to be taught systematically and energetically, though even those who have been studying for years often show precious little confidence in conversing. They also expect their teachers to direct the action and are not happy with a laid-back 'let's have a chit-chat' approach.

ACCOMMODATION

Most schools that recruit teachers from abroad will sort out accommodation for their teachers. If you are looking for accommodation independently, be prepared (as in Japan) to be required to pay a large deposit or even a year's rent in advance ('key money'). This should be returned to you at the end of your tenancy, though, as in Japan, disagreements can arise. If you don't hear about available flats from your school or other foreigners, check the English-language newspaper or find an English-speaking rental agent.

LEISURE TIME

Visitors are often surprised to discover the richness and complexity of Korean history and culture, partly because Japanese culture is far better known. Despite being a bustling metropolis of more than 10 million, Seoul has preserved some of its cultural treasures. Assuming your teaching schedule permits, you should be able to explore the country and, if interested, study some aspect of Korean culture such as the martial art Tae Kwon Do. The country's area is small, the public transport good, though traffic congestion at weekends is a problem.

Teachers often find that their students are friendly. Anyone homesick for the West will gravitate to the area of Seoul called Itaewon, where international restaurants and clubs are concentrated, not to mention a jazz club, a decent bookstore and other expatriate forms of entertainment. Teachers in the provinces will have to become accustomed to a very quiet life.

A contributor to a *Guardian* web forum on TEFL reported the following:

> Last year I worked in South Korea and it was the best year of my life. I have made friends all across the globe and loved every minute of my adventure in Busan, Korea's second largest city. It is a wonderful place and you can get to Seoul for a fun-filled weekend quite easily. The exchange rate is great and the free flights and accommodation allow for a high spending and saving lifestyle even though when the wage is measured against the pound it sounds fairly average. There are of course risks. But with Korea being a country unburdened by any large amount of crime and [with] a love for westerners, especially Brits, you are in good hands. Kids run around till midnight in the summer with no trouble. Old men drink soju all day and pass out on the benches at night; ajumas (old women) make you feel at home while joking about men and making harsh but delicious Korean treats. It's also wired up to the hilt with an extremely fast internet and a love for online gaming. Teaching can be challenging but it can also be a slacker's heaven, but I urge you to give it your all and you will feel better about yourself. Oh – and the beer is crap but you'll learn to love it.

LIST OF EMPLOYERS

BERLITZ KOREA CO. LTD

3F, Apple Tree Tower, 144-25, Samseong-dong,
Gangnam-gu, Seoul 135-090

☎ +82 2 3453 4266

✉ recruit@berlitz.co.kr or admin@berlitz.co.kr

💻 www.berlitz.co.kr/etc/JobOpportunities.asp

NUMBER OF TEACHERS: 40.

PREFERENCE OF NATIONALITY: Instructors must hold a passport from a country where English is a native language.

QUALIFICATIONS: Candidates with teaching and/or business backgrounds preferred, as majority of clients are professional people. Instructors must be professional, customer service-minded and able to teach using the Berlitz teaching principles.

CONDITIONS OF EMPLOYMENT: 1-year contracts. 3 types of schedule: morning block (6.45am–4.30pm); evening block (11.15am–9pm); split shift (6.45am–11.15am and 4.30pm–9pm). Instructors must be available to teach during their schedules, but if no classes are booked, attendance at the office is not required.

SALARY: Starting salary is 13,000 won per 40-minute lesson. Minimum guaranteed salary per month is 1,716,000 won (excluding housing). Monthly salary fluctuates, but is expected to average 2,500,000 won per month over the year. Tax deductions of 3–4% of earnings plus compulsory deductions for national pension and health insurance amount to 200,000 won per month.

FACILITIES/SUPPORT: Monthly housing stipend of 400,000 won per month. Loan for deposit for accommodation is available (up to 5,000,000 won). Staff member assigned to help find and organise the logistics of moving. All instructors must be in possession of a valid Korean working visa (F2 or F4) or be eligible for a new or transferred E-2 teaching visa.

RECRUITMENT: Berlitz Korea recruiting web page, current employee referrals, and recruiting websites such as www.worknplay.co.kr and www.eslcafe.com. Interviews are essential, preferably face-to-face at a Berlitz centre in Seoul, but can be done via Skype for overseas recruitment.

CONTACT: Vicky Hill, Country Manager of Instruction (vicky@berlitz.co.kr).

CANADIAN CONNECTION CONSULTING AGENCY

232 Merton Street, Suite 205, Toronto, ON M4S 1A1,
Canada

☎ +1 416 203 2679

✉ esl@canconx.com

💻 www.canconx.com

NUMBER OF TEACHERS: 300 per year.

PREFERENCE OF NATIONALITY: Canadian, American, British, Irish, Australian, New Zealander, and South African.

QUALIFICATIONS: Bachelor's degree in an English-related field, EFL qualification and teaching experience minimum.

CONDITIONS OF EMPLOYMENT: 1-year contract. To teach 22–30 hours per week.

SALARY: 1.8–2.5 million won per month.

FACILITIES/SUPPORT: Accommodation is supplied and paid for (teachers pay utilities). Agency handles all visa applications, teachers must supply documentation including notarised copy of their degree, criminal record check, 2 reference letters, passport photos, university transcripts and valid passport.

RECRUITMENT: Interview required.

CONTACT: Shane Finnie, Director.

CHUNGDAHM LEARNING INC

Chungdahm Faculty Recruiting Center, Baeksong Bldg,
5th Floor, Gangnam-gu, Cheongdam-dong 68–16 Seoul

☎ +82 2 6257 0256

✉ job@chungdahm.com or esljobs@aclipse.net

💻 www.teachinkorea.com and www.aclipse.net

One of the largest private language institutes in South Korea, with 120+ campuses teaching English to children. Aclipse Recruiting has offices in Boston and Seoul.

PREFERENCE OF NATIONALITY: Canadian, American, British, Australian, New Zealander, Irish and South African.

QUALIFICATIONS: College graduates, with clean criminal records (apostilled), from English-speaking countries. Candidates ideally have previous experience working with children, although previous teaching experience is not a requirement. Employer is looking for a professional, patient, flexible and outgoing demeanour. A strong desire to teach children overseas is required.

CONDITIONS OF EMPLOYMENT: 12 months. 4–5 days a week. Usual hours are 4pm–10pm for learners aged 10–16, or 1pm–7pm for younger learners aged 5–10. Hourly teachers work 120 hours per month, with a guarantee of 96 hours per month.

SALARY: Varies according to previous teaching experience, level of education and other factors, including performance on the Aclipse interview and evaluation. Standard range of salary is 2–3 million won for working 120 hours in a month. Hourly teachers are paid 25,000–35,000 won per hour. Teachers on a monthly salary are taxed at a rate of 7%–8% on their monthly income by the Korean government. Teachers on an hourly salary are taxed at rate of 3%.

FACILITIES/SUPPORT: Teachers on a monthly salary are given rent-free single furnished studio accommodation. Company pays half of compulsory health insurance and pension payments. On the hourly salary, ChungDahm Learning helps its teachers find housing either before they arrive or upon arrival, assists with the key money (security deposit), and the teachers then pay rent directly to their landlord each month. Aclipse in the US assists candidates with obtaining the E2 visa. Teachers are responsible for obtaining the necessary visa documents, such as a state-wide criminal background check and original diploma, which the Aclipse office in Boston checks and forwards to ChungDahm in Korea. The visa code is then emailed to the candidate, who takes it to their nearest Korean consulate and gets visa stamped in passport.

RECRUITMENT: Online advertisements, social media, career fairs and campus events/information sessions. Interviews are essential: initial interviews are typically done over the phone, with recruiters from the Boston office or by US recruiter Aclipse (www.aclipse.net) with offices in Boston and Seoul.

FLYING COWS
The Hive, Nottingham Trent University, Nottingham, NG1 4BU UK
📞 +44 115 824 0824
✉ placement@flying-cows.com
💻 www.flying-cows.com

Agency so-named because it aims to provide a service 'without the bull'.

NUMBER OF TEACHERS: Up to 30 teachers placed per month in schools throughout South Korea (as well as China and Colombia).

PREFERENCE OF NATIONALITY: Mostly British although can also be Canadian, American, Irish, Australian, New Zealander and South African.

QUALIFICATIONS: Minimum degree in any discipline. Experience of teaching or working with kids is a bonus. TEFL not essential but can help attract job offers (but not any financial advantage).

CONDITIONS OF EMPLOYMENT: 12-month contracts. 6 hours per day, with varying hours. Positions available in after-school academies and public schools.

SALARY: From 2.1 million won per month. Deductions made for health insurance and income tax.

FACILITIES/SUPPORT: School arranges and pays for the accommodation and flights. Assistance given for obtaining the relevant E2 visa. Support in all aspects of placement – contract negotiation, location advice, etc.

RECRUITMENT: Via ESL internet sites, university careers centres, media advertising and careers fairs. Applicants are usually interviewed by an FC representative over the phone, then by

the school also by phone. FC staff have personal experience of teaching in Korea. They recruit for spring and autumn positions, with deadlines falling 5–6 months in advance of the start dates.

CONTACT: Amanda McGillivray, Director/Senior Consultant.

i-HUFS ENGLISH CAMP
Recruited by English Beyond Borders, Toronto, ON Canada
✉ Camps@englishbeyondborders.org
💻 www.englishbeyondborders.org

HUFS is the acronym for Hankuk University of Foreign Students.

NUMBER OF TEACHERS: 40 teachers in summer, 20 in winter.

PREFERENCE OF NATIONALITY: Canadians only.

QUALIFICATIONS: Minimum Bachelor's of Education, and candidates must hold a Canadian passport.

CONDITIONS OF EMPLOYMENT: 2–4 weeks in January and July. Teachers work 46–48 hours per week, and get one day off each week depending on contract conditions.

SALARY: Airfare, accommodation in university residence and 2,000,000–2,500,000 won depending on contract duration.

FACILITIES/SUPPORT: Teachers are provided with contracts and supporting documents necessary for the work permit.

RECRUITMENT: All online. Summer recruitment completed in June. Telephone interviews are conducted.

CONTACT: Linda Lee, Recruitment & Global Mobility Specialist.

KOREACONNECTIONS EMPLOYMENT LTD
#71, 583–6 Tap-Rib-dong, Yoosung-gu Daejon 305–510
📞 +82 2 2058 2888
North American office: 211–3030 Lincoln Ave, Coquitlam, BC V3B 6B4, Canada
✉ admin@koreaconnections.net or jaymlee@korea connections.net
💻 www.koreaconnections.net

NUMBER OF TEACHERS: Approximately 150 annually for private and public schools.

PREFERENCE OF NATIONALITY: None; however, the Korean government only issues E2 visas to English teachers from UK, USA, Canada, Ireland, New Zealand, South Africa and Australia.

QUALIFICATIONS: Minimum bachelor's degree. BA in English, Education, Linguistics, TESOL or qualified teacher status is a plus though not mandatory. Clear spoken English and experience with working with young children.

CONDITIONS OF EMPLOYMENT: 1-year contract. Usual hours are 9am to 5pm Monday to Friday for public schools. Hours may be longer at private language institutes.

SALARY: Average basic salary is between 2.1 million and 2.3 million won at franchised private schools and can be between 1.8 and 2.7 million won at public schools, depending on experience and qualifications.

FACILITIES/SUPPORT: Accommodation is provided by the schools. Usually the housing is single accommodation within walking distance of work. Sponsorship and assistance provided when applying for E2 visas, and help is given with flight booking arrangements and airport pick-up.

RECRUITMENT: Usually via word of mouth, university career centre and online advertising. Interviews are essential and can be held over the phone or Skype. Face-to-face interviews can be arranged internationally depending on where the consultants are located at that time. Interviews have also been arranged while visiting TESOL conventions and job fairs in USA, UK, Canada and Ireland.

CONTACT: Jay Lee, HR Director.

KOREA GLOBAL CONNECTIONS

Ga-301 Daenong B/D, 35-50 Guui 2-Dong, Gwangjin-Gu, Seoul

✆ +82 2 452 9857

✆ kgcabc@gmail.com

🖳 www.kgcesl.com

NUMBER OF TEACHERS: 200 per year.

PREFERENCE OF NATIONALITY: The Korean government allows only people from native English speaking countries: UK, USA, Canada, Ireland, Australia, New Zealand and South Africa.

QUALIFICATIONS: Bachelor's degree in any subject.

CONDITIONS OF EMPLOYMENT: 12 months. Contracted hours are 25–30 per week.

SALARY: 2.1–2.2 million won per month (£1,200–£1,250).

FACILITIES/SUPPORT: Benefits include free one-way flight, free semi-furnished housing and an extra month's wages as bonus upon finishing 12-month contract. Full visa assistance given. Airport pick-up.

RECRUITMENT: Skype interviews.

CONTACT: Anna Jeon, Director.

PLANET ESL RECRUITING

#201 Bogwang-dong 3-154, Yongsan-gu, Seoul 140–822

✆ +82 10 9012 0579

✆ Jobs@PlanetESL.com

🖳 www.PlanetESL.com or

www.teach-english-korea.com

Recruiter for many schools in Korea.

PREFERENCE OF NATIONALITY: Teachers must be citizens of one of the seven designated English-speaking countries (Australia, Canada, Ireland, New Zealand, UK, US and South Africa).

QUALIFICATIONS: Bachelor's degree from an accredited university in one of the seven designated English-speaking countries.

CONDITIONS OF EMPLOYMENT: 1-year contracts are standard. Teaching hours range from 20 to 40 per week depending on whether it is a public or private institute. Private institutes normally operate an afternoon/evening schedule, while public schools have a 9.30am–4.30pm schedule.

SALARY: Average salary range 2–2.3 million won depending on experience and qualifications.

FACILITIES/SUPPORT: Accommodation is provided.

RECRUITMENT: Via online job postings and through recommendations. Interviews can be carried out by Skype or telephone.

CONTACT: Ms Jiyeon Kim, CEO and President.

REACH TO TEACH (SOUTH KOREA)

1606 80th Avenue, Algona, IA 50511, USA

✆ +1 201 467 4612

✆ john@reachtoteachrecruiting.com

🖳 www.ReachToTeachRecruiting.com/Teach-English-in-Korea.html

Also has contacts in UK, Australia and New Zealand (see entry at beginning of Asia chapter).

NUMBER OF TEACHERS: 200+.

PREFERENCE OF NATIONALITY: Canadian, American, British, Australian, New Zealander, Irish and South African.

QUALIFICATIONS: Teaching experience is a plus, but not a requirement. A 120-hour TEFL certificate is a requirement for most positions, unless candidates have more than a year of teaching experience, an MA, or a BA in English or Education. The agency has a limited number of placements for non-TEFL qualified applicants.

CONDITIONS OF EMPLOYMENT: Public (EPIK, etc) and private school positions. All job placements are full-time positions and for 1 year (and usually extendable). Schedules are generally either morning/afternoon (pre-school or public elementary, middle or high school) or afternoon/evening (elementary school).

SALARY: 2.1–3 million won per month (from $1,850–$2,650) plus reimbursed flights to and from Korea.

FACILITIES/SUPPORT: Free housing always given in a furnished one-bedroom apartment or studio. Teachers pay a deposit that is reimbursed. Teachers are also helped with work permits from beginning to end. All teachers are welcome at various teacher social events and gatherings (often held in Seoul).

RECRUITMENT: Detailed Skype or telephone interviews are essential. The company also carries out in-person interviews periodically in the USA and UK. Public school positions start twice a year (March and September) and the application process ideally needs to start 6 months in advance. Private school positions can be applied for year round and the time between application and arriving in Korea is often much quicker.

CONTACT: John Kellenberger, Co-President (John@Reach ToTeachRecruiting.com).

TEFA (THE ENGLISH FRIENDS ACADEMY)

733, Banghak-3 Dong. DoBong-gu, Seoul 132–855

℄ +82 2 3491 1431

✍ tefaenglish@yahoo.co.kr

NUMBER OF TEACHERS: Approximately 50 western teachers in 16 franchises throughout Korea.

PREFERENCE OF NATIONALITY: Must be a native English speaker of a nationality eligible for a E2 visa.

QUALIFICATIONS: Minimum 3 or 4-year bachelor's degree. Love of kids and mature, interactive outlook.

CONDITIONS OF EMPLOYMENT: 12-month contract. Less than 30 hours' teaching. School covers airfare, medical insurance, 10 days' vacation. End-of-contract bonus (1 month's salary).

SALARY: 2.2 million won per month (for newcomers to Korea).

FACILITIES/SUPPORT: Close to all amenities and the schools, free, fully furnished, single or shared accommodation. Well-resourced schools, supportive work environment, job security.

RECRUITMENT: Via email and phone. No recruitment agents used.

CONTACT: Jolie.

YBM EDUCATION ECC

YBM ECC Head Office, 28-2 Inui-dong, Jongno Gu, 8th Floor, Seoul 110–410

℄ +82 2 590 78217

✍ eccmain@ybmsisa.co.kr

🖥 www.ybmecc.co.kr

NUMBER OF TEACHERS: 200 at 31 company-owned ECC branches and about 450 at 74 franchise ECC schools that are not placed by YBM Head Office. YBM Language Institutes (see next entry) are for adults and offer slightly less advantageous terms of employment.

PREFERENCE OF NATIONALITY: Canadian, American, British, Australian, New Zealander, Irish and South African.

QUALIFICATIONS: Minimum bachelor's degree, criminal background check, academic transcripts. No teaching experience required but candidates must enjoy teaching young children using curriculum provided (training given).

CONDITIONS OF EMPLOYMENT: 12-month contracts. 26 hours per week. Schedule 1: 9.30am–6pm. Schedule 2: 1pm–8pm.

SALARY: 2 million to 2.4 million won per month.

FACILITIES/SUPPORT: YBM provides rent-free, furnished accommodation near the school plus prepaid airfare, medical, severance pay and pension compliance, guaranteed contracts backed by the YBM Head Office, and assistance with E2 visa.

RECRUITMENT: Job postings via internet, word of mouth referrals from previous teachers. Every applicant undergoes either a phone interview or a face-to-face interview if they are in Korea.

CONTACT: Danny J. Kim, HR Manager, YBM Education ECC Head Office.

YBM LANGUAGE INSTITUTES

YBM Building, 13th Floor, 820-8 Yeoksam-dong, Gangnam-gu, Seoul 135–080

℄ +82 2 3466 3519

✍ gregstapleton@ybmsisa.com or ybmrecruiter@ybmsisa.com

🖥 www.ybmhr.co.kr

NUMBER OF TEACHERS: Between 250 and 300.

PREFERENCE OF NATIONALITY: Canadian, American, British, Australian and New Zealander.

QUALIFICATIONS: Minimum bachelor's degree plus 1-year formal teaching experience with adult learners. Candidates with graduate degrees in applied linguistics or CELTA/TESOL certification are preferred.

CONDITIONS OF EMPLOYMENT: 1-year renewable contract, six 50-minute classes per day (30 hours per week).

SALARY: Depending upon academic qualifications and teaching experience, salaries range from 2.1 million won to 2.5 million won per month, plus 200,000 won housing allowance.

FACILITIES/SUPPORT: During the initial paid 5-day training period, teachers are provided with accommodation in a motel near the training centre in Seoul. Upon completion of training, instructors return to their school and are shown several apartments from which the teacher can choose. The school then provides up to 10 million won in key money (leasing) to secure the apartment plus a monthly housing stipend of 200,000 won. Visa processing costs are reimbursed. Instructor development and support is overseen by native-speaker English academic supervisors.

RECRUITMENT: Primarily through web-based job postings eg on teflsearch.com, followed by telephone/Skype interviews when candidates are outside South Korea. Candidates applying from within Korea must attend a face-to-face interview.

CONTACT: Greg Stapleton, National Academic Director.

INDIAN SUBCONTINENT

Although India's phenomenal economic growth has slowed, business and industry are charging ahead. One of the most notable by-products of globalisation has been the outsourcing of services to countries with cheaper labour costs, which has been accelerated in India by the widespread knowledge of English, a legacy of the Raj in the educational system. After a long period in which nationalistic sentiment tended to view British colonial rule and therefore the English language as a tool of enslavement, there has been a softening of attitudes, partly in acknowledgment that India's technology boom owes a huge debt to the country's English-medium education. The bias against English is weakening, and it is now taught in state schools from the age of six. Interestingly, it is especially popular among the marginalised castes (once called 'untouchables' and now called Dalit), who see English as a job skill that will help them achieve social and financial emancipation.

This does not mean that there is a huge demand for native-speaker teachers. Very few ordinary citizens in much of South Asia can dream of affording the luxury of English conversation classes. This is particularly true in Nepal after the horrendous earthquake that struck in April 2015, killing and injuring, 32,000 people and devastating the country's infrastructure. Few westerners could manage on the wages earned by ordinary teachers in India, Nepal, Sri Lanka, Pakistan, etc. However, those foreigners prepared to finance themselves and volunteer their time can find eager students by asking around locally.

Mainstream voluntary organisations are active in the region, especially providing skilled volunteers to teachers' colleges and vocational colleges. Unskilled volunteers can be placed in the Indian subcontinent and beyond by the main commercial volunteer placement agencies like Travellers Worldwide and Projects Abroad. A cheaper option for gap-year students and anybody else is available from the recruiter www. ESLstarter.com which sets up four-month teaching internships in Kerala for £590 (including free accommodation and meals provided by the school). For an extra £100, a 120-hour online TEFL training course with Global English can be added.

Grassroots organisations are also active, especially those concerned with improving literacy among women and children, such as Rajasthan-based Sankalp Volunteer (info@volunteersindia.org) which runs volunteer teaching programmes lasting up to 16 weeks in Jaipur, Dharamsala, Delhi and Bangalore and longer term ones in the first two. Other opportunities can be tracked down on www.omprakash.org which connects volunteers with grassroots organisations around the world. Plenty of paid language teaching also goes on, for example in business colleges, though usually with local teaching staff.

India

The emerging economy of India has some commentators predicting that, together with China, its capacity and markets will before long overtake those of the West. High standards of education in the dominant class and an entrepreneurial spirit have helped India to flourish. English has been the medium of instruction in the elite schools and universities since India was a colony, and now is spreading to many ordinary middle-class Indians who want to participate in the booming global economy. Much of the demand is met by English-speaking Indians rather than foreigners. Whereas at one time elite institutes such as the British Council looked to employ British English teachers they now prefer Indian nationals if possible. However, with 20,000 students at three British Council teaching centres in Chennai, Kolkata and New Delhi, hourly teaching is also available to expat teachers (see entry). The most exciting development at the British Council in India is its new programme to place teaching assistants in schools around the country; see entry for the Generation UK-India Programme.

Travelling English speakers have arranged to teach in the state sector simply by entering a school and asking permission to sit in on an English class. Provided they do not expect a wage, some teaching role could probably be found for them. A volunteer from Derbyshire teaching in several village schools in Andhra

Pradesh wrote that she and her teaching partner were in such demand that a busload of volunteers would find work. But it can be very challenging and discouraging. Facilities can be brutal, with no teaching materials and no space. The majority of local English teachers, who have not really mastered the language, are very badly paid and can be transferred without appeal at any time; it is not too surprising to find that most are demoralised.

A number of organisations in the UK send volunteers to teach English in India, including the main gap-year placement organisations. For example, Projects Abroad (www.projects-abroad.co.uk) arranges placements in Jaipur, Rajasthan; fees start at £1,145 for two weeks, up to £2,395 for three months. Postings are mainly to English-medium secondary schools. Just before **Raymond George** (age 62) started his official retirement from his job as a university physics lecturer, he noticed an advertisement on a college noticeboard for volunteer teachers with Travellers Worldwide. They were offering teaching placements in Southern India, a region he was keen to see, so he enrolled for a two-month placement teaching spoken English in a primary school. This proved to be hugely rewarding, giving him a wonderful opportunity to experience life in a family and local community with enough spare time to travel to see the amazing temples of South India. **Jenna Bonistalli** from New York City found an inexpensive volunteer option. She decided to use a windfall to fund six months off work to volunteer in India as a teacher:

> *Colleagues, friends and family were surprised upon hearing my decision to take off for half a year, especially when they learned my destination. The first three months were spent in the Himalayan hill town of Kalimpong in West Bengal. My boyfriend and I volunteered through HELP, the Himalayan Education Lifeline Programme, an organisation that places teachers in primary schools throughout Indian and Nepali Himalayan regions. We chose to go through them for a number of reasons, mainly location (we were both interested in going to this region mainly due to religious and cultural interest) and cost (their fees and donation requirements were very reasonable compared to some other outrageously high prices). This was after months of searching online, in books, on www.idealist.org and through recommendations. We had some choice in where we wanted to be placed and were able to read descriptions and see photos of the school and family, so this was helpful. There were no real requirements for being accepted, aside from an application form and references. Both of us had experience as educators in different capacities, so this made us more confident. Our experience in the Himalayas was unsurpassed – the setting, our students, the people we met; everything (aside from a bout of dysentery) was utterly amazing.*

The current combined admin fee and donation to HELP (see entry) is £480, plus volunteers contribute from £95 a month for host family or school hostel accommodation.

Jon Walker was surprised by how contented he felt living in rural India as a volunteer teacher, where the atmosphere struck him as entirely calm, peaceful and beautiful. He spent the month of January volunteering through Dakshinayan (www.dakshinayan.blogspot.co.uk), a grassroots development charity that works with tribal peoples in the hills of Rajmahal and nearby plains:

> *The children are of course what makes Dakshinayan so special. We were teaching Maths and English for three hours a day, and I really enjoyed the teaching. Although I had difficulties trying to translate to them what I wanted them to do, particularly to Class 2 whose English isn't so good, this was all part of the challenge. It was quite different from any teaching I had done before and meant that I really had to learn how to adapt lessons and make them the most beneficial. But we had some good fun along the way singing songs and playing games – educational of course! Their enthusiasm to learn is what motivates you every day and I miss their smiles and laughter that radiated around the school when they were there.*
>
> *Life at Dakshinayan is very simple and a way of life that I adapted to very quickly. Waking up at 5.30am and being in bed by 9.30pm seemed very natural. Initially I was apprehensive that I would get bored when we weren't teaching. But after planning our lessons and helping with the chores around the school, it was very easy to fill our time and the days flew by. We also learnt some Hindi on the way and it was good fun having conversation exchanges with Bansi and Shanku.*

LIST OF EMPLOYERS

BRITISH COUNCIL – NEW DELHI

17 Kasturba Gandhi Marg, New Delhi 110001

(C) +91 11 2371 1401

recruitment.englishpartnerships@in.britishcouncil.
org; careers.bcdelhi@in.britishcouncil.org

www.britishcouncil.in/about/jobs

NUMBER OF TEACHERS: The British Council has new Teaching
Centres across India and increased partnership and corporate
training. A large number of posts for freelancers to support
examination events across many cities.

PREFERENCE OF NATIONALITY: Indian nationals preferred.

QUALIFICATIONS: Minimum CELTA qualification and varying
levels of experience.

CONDITIONS OF EMPLOYMENT: Only hourly paid contracts are
available.

SALARY: Starts at approximately 1000 rupees per hour for
CELTA-qualified; more for DELTA qualified.

FACILITIES/SUPPORT: No help can be given with visas or
accommodation.

RECRUITMENT: Interview required. May be conducted over the
telephone. Applications accepted year round.

CONTACT: Head of Teaching Centres.

BRITISH LINGUA

1/48, Lalita Park, Laxmi Nagar, Vikas Marg, Delhi 110092

(C) +91 11 3258 5879/+91 11 4302 6787

britishlingua@yahoo.com

www.britishlingua.com

NUMBER OF TEACHERS: 1–2 to implement Spoken English
training to Mahadalit (the poorest of the poor) in Bihar state.

PREFERENCE OF NATIONALITY: None.

QUALIFICATIONS: University graduate.

CONDITIONS OF EMPLOYMENT: 1 year. 8 hours per day.

SALARY: Negotiable.

FACILITIES/SUPPORT: Assistance given with accommodation. No
help with visas.

RECRUITMENT: Local interview necessary.

CONTACT: Birbal Jha, Managing Director.

GENERATION UK-INDIA PROGRAMME

British Council, Bridgewater House, 58 Whitworth Street,
Manchester M1 6BB

(C) +44 161 957 7755

www.britishcouncil.in/generationuk; www.
britishcouncil.org/study-work-create/opportunity/
work-volunteer/teach-india

NUMBER OF TEACHERS: Sizeable number of Generation UK-
India teaching assistantships across India including the states of
Delhi, Gujarat, Madhya Pradesh, Maharashtra, Tamil Nadu, Uttar
Pradesh and West Bengal with most schools based in large or
medium cities.

PREFERENCE OF NATIONALITY: British only.

QUALIFICATIONS: Minimum age 18 and have completed at
least one year of higher eduction. Must have British passport and
permanent address in the UK. Positions available for all levels of
teaching experience. Formal or informal experience of working
with children, and ability to provide an overview of life in the UK
are needed.

CONDITIONS OF EMPLOYMENT: 2–6 months from the beginning
of July or October. Participants support English across the school
both in lessons and in extracurricular activities. 20 classroom hours
a week. Most schools are private or boarding schools. Must undergo
a child protection check (£60) and pay a £200 placement fee.

SALARY: Schools pay a monthly contribution of £150–£350 to
living costs.

FACILITIES/SUPPORT: Pre-departure briefing held in early June.
3-day induction provided on arrival. Accommodation and meals
provided free by host schools. Teachers are all assigned a mentor
teacher.

RECRUITMENT: Recruitment begins in January and again in
autumn. Applicants who pass initial screening will be invited to assessment days in March, held in Belfast, Edinburgh, Manchester,
Cardiff and London.

HELP (HIMALAYAN EDUCATION LIFELINE PROGRAMME)

30 Kingsdown Park, Whitstable, Kent CT5 2DF, UK

(C) +44 1227 263055

jim.coleman@help-education.org

www.help-education.org/volunteer.html

HELP recruits volunteer teachers to teach in primary and secondary schools in poor communities in the Indian Himalayas (Sikkim,
West Bengal, Ladakh and Uttarakhand) as well as Nepal. See
entry below in Nepal section. Volunteers pay an admin fee of
£180, a donation of £300 plus 9,300 rupees a month (£95) for
board and lodging (13,000 rupees in Ladakh).

CONTACT: Barbara Porter (barbara.porter@help-education.org).

LHA CHARITABLE TRUST

Temple Road, McLeod Ganj-176219, Dharamsala, Dist.
Kangra, Himachal Pradesh 176219

(C) +91 189 222 0992

office@lhasocialwork.org

www.lhasocialwork.org

479

NUMBER OF VOLUNTEER TEACHERS: 5 at any one time to work with Tibetan refugees in Dharamsala, India.

PREFERENCE OF NATIONALITY: No preference, but fluency in English is required.

QUALIFICATIONS: Native speakers with prior teaching experience preferred, but non-native speakers with a high level of English language skill and/or documented proof of completion of a TEFL course are accepted.

CONDITIONS OF EMPLOYMENT: Minimum 2 months, maximum 6 months. One or two hours of class time per day, Monday through Friday, plus any time needed for preparation and grading. Additional hours may be needed if teachers are also participating in Lha's one-on-one tutoring programme.

SALARY: None; these are voluntary positions.

FACILITIES/SUPPORT: Lha is unable to provide room and board for volunteer teachers, though advice and orientation are given.

RECRUITMENT: Volunteer applications through Lha website and via partner websites like www.omprakash.org. In-person interviews are not essential. All communication prior to volunteers' arrival is carried out via email or telephone.

CONTACT: Ngawang Rabgyal, Executive Director of Lha Charitable Trust.

MANJOORANS GROUP

Corporate Office: 3D, Metro Place, North End, Cochin, Kerala

☎ +91 484 2396816

✉ info@manjoorans.com; ceo@manjoorans.com

🖥 www.manjoorans.com

The group also has offices in Trivandrum, Kottayam, Thrissur and Kollam, and runs 10 schools with 15,000 students participating in an English-language programme called 'Speak Perfect'.

NUMBER OF TEACHERS: 50+ in ELT centres throughout the state of Kerala.

PREFERENCE OF NATIONALITY: British, American, Canadian, Australian, etc.

QUALIFICATIONS: TEFL, TESOL, etc with a passion for teaching. Anyone with a good command of spoken English is eligible even without professional qualifications. IELTS trainers need 1–5 years' experience.

CONDITIONS OF EMPLOYMENT: 6-month visas only are available. Hours of work are 9.30am–1pm and 2pm–4pm. To teach IELTS, TOEFL, conversational English.

SALARY: 10,000 rupees plus accommodation.

FACILITIES/SUPPORT: Accommodation provided. Assistance given with sorting out visas.

RECRUITMENT: ESL websites. References needed. Interviews not essential.

CONTACT: Babu Manjuran, CEO.

ROSE PUBLIC SCHOOL (RURAL ORGANIZATION FOR SOCIAL ELEVATION)

Social Awareness Centre, Sunargaon, PO Kanda, Bageshwar, Uttarakhand 263631

☎ +91 5963 241081

✉ jlverma.rosekanda@gmail.com or jeevanverma@rosekanda.org

🖥 www.volunteeringindiahimalaya.rosekanda.org

PREFERENCE OF NATIONALITY: None.

QUALIFICATIONS: None required. Experience of teaching or living in a developing country useful. Flexibility, sense of humour and positive thinker.

CONDITIONS OF EMPLOYMENT: Grassroots development project which organises range of activities to help this rural community in the Himalayan foothills. Projects include teaching children aged 2–8 between 7.30 am and mid-day, office computer networking, and other social projects.

SALARY: None. Volunteers contribute to their living and food expenses as paying guests (about £7 or 700 rupees per day). Also registration/admin fee 10,000 rupees.

FACILITIES/SUPPORT: Accommodation arranged in local homes as homestay. Hindi instruction. Cultural exchange available.

CONTACT: Jeevan Verma, Director.

VALUEPOINT ACADEMY

2nd floor, Shankar House, 1 RMV, Extension, Mekhri Circle, Bangalore, 560080

☎ +91 80 40793777

✉ hr@valuepointacademy.com

🖥 www.valuepointacademy.com

Four centres in Bangalore and one in Pune. Most students are from outside India especially the Middle East.

PREFERENCE OF NATIONALITY: None.

QUALIFICATIONS: Degree, preferably MA or PhD, in English plus preferably 5 years of teaching experience. English-language trainers must be passionate about the job.

CONDITIONS OF EMPLOYMENT: 1-year contract with a minimum of 6 and a maximum of 8 working hours per day.

FACILITIES/SUPPORT: Assistance can be given with finding accommodation and applying for work permits.

RECRUITMENT: Interview and demonstration lesson.

CONTACT: Ms Meenu Sood, Director.

Nepal

Just as Nepal was becoming more stable after emerging from civil war between pro- and anti-Maoists and then abolishing its backward-looking monarchical system, the country has been plunged into chaos by the destructive earthquake and its aftershocks of 2015. The people, among the poorest in Asia, are far more concerned with rebuilding at the moment than with learning English, so the casual English teacher may not find many opportunities. The British Council in Kathmandu closed its office to the public though re-opened part way through 2015. It should also be noted that the cost of living has been rising, even before the disaster, so that the price of basic food and travel has increased substantially over the past couple of years. In 2014, the Nepal Immigration authority introduced an online visa application system. Note that tourist visas can still be purchased on arrival for $100 cash and are valid for 90 days (shorter stays for less money are also available) and can be extended for $2 a day thereafter, up to a maximum of five months normally. Return is prohibited until the next calendar year. Note that a hefty fine or even prison sentence can be imposed on foreigners found overstaying their visas.

A range of organisations makes it possible for self-funding volunteers to teach. Of course living expenses are very low by western standards, though the fees charged by mediating or gap-year organisations as well as by Nepali agencies (some listed below) can increase the cost significantly. If you want to avoid a voluntourism agency fee, you can make direct contact with schools on arrival. A 2014 article in the *Guardian* revealed that some of the profit-making agencies are corrupt enough to fabricate profiles of children who, in some cases, are not really orphans but who have been lured into residential schools under false pretences; see www.theguardian.com/global-development/2014/may/27/nepal-bogus-orphan-trade-voluntourism.

Relevant organisations in addition to the ones in the directory are listed below.

Alliance Nepal (volunteerworkinnepal.org and on facebook). Opportunities to teach English, help in an orphanage, etc in the Pokhara Valley and Chitwan area for two weeks to three months. Prices from €200 for two weeks to €600 for 12 weeks.

Education & Health Nepal (www.ehn-nepal.org). NGO based in Kathmandu offering low-cost volunteering including teaching and orphanage work. £672 for eight weeks plus £80 admin fee.

KEEP (Kathmandu Environmental Education Project), Thamel, Kathmandu (www.keepnepal.org). KEEP is eager to recruit volunteers to help deliver English-language training to Nepalis who work in the tourist and trekking industry, government schools, etc. Volunteers stay with a host family and must be self-funding.

RCDP Nepal Volunteer, GPO Box 8957, Tasindole Marg 95/48, Kalaniki 14, Kathmandu, Nepal (www.rcdpnepal.org). Paying volunteers work on various programmes lasting 1–12 weeks, starting every other Monday, including teaching English. Volunteers stay with families in villages including with Sherpa families. Registration fee of $269 plus a weekly charge which goes down the longer you stay, up to $2000 for 12 weeks.

After **Melissa Evans'** placement in Kenya was cancelled at the last moment, her gap year agency, Adventure Alternative (www.adventurealternative.com), had to live up to its name and quickly find her an alternative adventure. It arranged for Melissa to fly a month later to Nepal, where she taught in a school:

It was very, very rewarding, as the children really thrived off the teaching from a foreign teacher. I found the teaching a challenge as the children struggled with English, and also pronunciation. Sometimes, I found myself unable to understand the children and vice versa. However, familiarity over the three months allowed the language barrier to break down, and conversing with the children was easier by the end of my placement, as I had learned a little Nepali and they had grown used to my pronunciation. Before my gap year I had the ambition of being a teacher. However, after travelling for the first time my ambition changed, and now I aim to found an orphanage.

Rachel Sedley spent six months between school and university as a volunteer teacher at the Siddartha School in Kathmandu, arranged through a UK gap organisation, and conveys some of the flavour of the experience:

The sun is shining and the kids are running riot. New Baneshwar is a suburb of Kathmandu, very busy and polluted, but of course so friendly. I do get tired of being a novelty, especially when I'm swathed in my five metres of bright turquoise silk (we wear saris for teaching) but I'm really loving it here. Already after one month, the thought of leaving the kids and my simple lifestyle is terrible. I find it funny that as a westerner I'm seen to represent infinite stores of knowledge and yet the servant girl is having to patiently teach me to wash my own clothes. And the general knowledge people have of the fundamentals of life makes me feel help- less and incapable. The children are so gorgeous (most of the time) and the Principal's family with whom I am living are lovely. It seems to me unnecessary to come to Nepal through an organisation. Everyone here is so keen to help.

Rachel's main complaint about her situation was that she was teaching in a private school for privileged children, when she had been led to believe that she would be contributing her time, labour and money to more needy children. While there, she met several people from various schools and orphanages who would love to have English volunteers.

LIST OF EMPLOYERS

HELP (HIMALAYAN EDUCATION LIFELINE PROGRAMME)

30 Kingsdown Park, Whitstable, Kent CT5 2DF, UK

📞 +44 1227 263055

📧 jim.coleman@help-education.org

💻 www.help-education.org/nepalschools.html

HELP enables young people from poor communities in Nepal (Kathmandu Valley, Pokhara and Chitwan) to improve their employment opportunities through education by providing financial and volunteer resources to their schools.

NUMBER OF PLACEMENTS: HELP supports some 25 schools in Nepal and the Indian Himalayas. Also a women's weaving cooperative in Pokhara.

QUALIFICATIONS: Ages 19/20–60+. Appropriate teaching experience and/or a basic TEFL qualification is essential. Volunteers should be mature and resourceful. Qualities needed include resilience and adaptability, an open mind and an interest in other cultures, good mental and physical health, plus tact and diplomacy. A love of and experience with children is vital.

CONDITIONS OF WORK: Minimum 1 month. Volunteers can stay for a maximum of 6 months (for visa reasons).

SALARY: None. Admin fee £180, donation to project £300 plus contribution to board and accommodation of 15,000 rupees (£95) per month. Accommodation is provided with host families or in school hostel.

FACILITIES/SUPPORT: Volunteers receive a briefing pack. Once in post, a local HELP representative is on hand to help with any problems.

RECRUITMENT: Applications accepted year round. Telephone interviews conducted after receipt of the online application form.

CONTACT: Barbara Porter, Volunteer Coordinator.

HOPE AND HOME TRAVEL

PO Box 119, Lazimpat, Kathmandu

📞 +977 1 443 9097

📧 info@hopenhome.org; Europe: volunteerhimalaya@ gmail.com

💻 www.hopenhome.org

Community-oriented volunteer opportunities for international volunteers with homestay and cultural exchange.

NUMBER OF PLACEMENTS PER YEAR: 55–60 in the Kathmandu Valley, Pokhara, and Chitwan areas of Nepal.

QUALIFICATIONS: Ages 18–35. All that is needed is a desire to help people.

CONDITIONS OF WORK: Volunteer opportunities lasting 2 weeks to 3 months are in the fields of teaching English, as well as community, health and environmental programme.

SALARY: None. Volunteer fees entirely fund programme and include homestay accommodation and food. From $400 for 2 weeks to $1,000 for 12 weeks plus registration fee of $200.

FACILITIES/SUPPORT: Language class, cultural information and project information provided.

RECRUITMENT: Online applications accepted year round.

CONTACT: Rabyn Aryal, Director.

INSIGHT NEPAL

PO Box 489, Pokhara, Kaski

+977 61 530266

info@insightnepal.org

www.insightnepal.org

NUMBER OF TEACHERS: 60 volunteers accepted each year for development projects mainly in the Pokhara Valley.

PREFERENCE OF NATIONALITY: All.

QUALIFICATIONS: Minimum A levels for UK volunteers, high school diploma for Americans. Age limits 18–65. Teaching or volunteering experience desirable but not necessary.

CONDITIONS OF EMPLOYMENT: Placements last 7 weeks or 3 months starting year round.

SALARY: None. Programme participation fee is $1,260 for 3 months, $850 for 7 weeks.

FACILITIES/SUPPORT: Accommodation and two meals a day provided, usually as homestay. Programmes include pre-orientation training, placement in a primary or secondary school in Nepal to teach mainly English or in community development projects, and a 1-week village or trekking excursion. The 3-month programme also includes 3 days of jungle safari in Chitwan National Park.

RECRUITMENT: Application forms, 3 photos and introductory letter should be sent 3 months in advance of proposed starting date.

CONTACT: Naresh Shrestha, Programme Coordinator.

TREK TO TEACH

PO Box 123, San Diego, CA 92103, USA

+1 619 405 8818

namaste@trektoteach.org

www.trektoteach.org

Achieved NGO status March 2012.

NUMBER OF PLACEMENTS PER YEAR: 3–7 (because programme is new).

QUALIFICATIONS: Minimum age 22. Schools want teachers who can teach English, Maths and Computers. The Nepali students want teachers who can teach them new hobbies and new ways of looking at the world. Candidates should be academically able with a degree or heading towards one and be passionate about life.

CONDITIONS OF WORK: Programme combines teaching in Himalayan Nepal with a family stay and trekking. Minimum of 3 months, maximum of 8.

RECRUITMENT: No deadline. Applications must be in at least 1 month prior to expected teaching date. Nepali school year is March–December. Telephone interviews necessary.

SALARY: None because this is a volunteer programme. Programme costs: first 3 months $3,100; 4–8 months $500 each.

CONTACT: Brad Hurvitz, Founder (Brad.hurvitz@gmail.com).

Pakistan and Bangladesh

The need for English in Pakistan and Bangladesh is frequently replaced by the desperate need for more basic aid, for example following the floods of 2010 in Pakistan. While the infrastructure in the devastated areas is slowly being repaired and schools rebuilt, deploying English teachers is the least of their concerns.

Prospects are further curtailed by the lack of remuneration and difficulty with visas. Most opportunities are available only to teachers willing to finance themselves and to work on a three-month tourist visa. Security clearance and visa processing can take months, and is very difficult unless you have someone to push for you.

The British Council employs qualified teachers at its own teaching centre in Dhaka, who are recruited in London. The centre also employs a number of hourly paid teachers who are recruited locally, but the demand for courses fluctuates so much that steady employment cannot be guaranteed. People who are established in Dhaka, such as spouses of expat managers, etc, sometimes manage to earn reasonable part-time wages teaching private classes.

Almost no gap year or volunteer placement agencies or educational charities send volunteers to Pakistan and Bangladesh, unlike India and Nepal. Few private language schools exist in Pakistan. The British Council organises exams, but does not run teaching courses. The US counterpart is the Pakistan American Cultural Center (PACC) with several branches throughout the country. Security concerns have escalated over the past year and the Foreign & Commonwealth Office advises against travel to many areas that used to be unproblematic, like Peshawar and the Karakoram Highway north of the capital, Islamabad. In 2013, ten foreigners and their local guide preparing to climb Nanga Parbat were shot dead by a Taliban group.

Opportunities for native English-speaker teachers are probably there for the taking, tutoring businessmen, university students and children, if teachers are respectful and resourceful. While loitering in a second-hand bookshop in Scotland, **Hannah Adcock** fell into conversation with a Pakistani university professor who promptly offered food and board in exchange for working at his wife's private school for children near Karachi. Having a native English speaker is apparently a real status symbol for a school.

LIST OF EMPLOYERS

BANGLADESH WORKCAMPS ASSOCIATION (BWCA)

289/2 Workcamp Road, North Shajahanpur, Dhaka 1217

- +880 2 935 8206/6814
- bwca@bangla.net
- www.mybwca.org

BWCA organises workcamps and longer-term projects for volunteers in rural and urban areas of Bangladesh.

NUMBER OF TEACHERS: 5 per year (roughly equally divided male and female).

QUALIFICATIONS: Native English speakers aged 18–30.

CONDITIONS OF EMPLOYMENT: Volunteers work 30 hours per week on placements which last 2–6 months on the RTYP (Round the Year Programme). Work can include teaching and developing English speaking and writing to primary and secondary school teachers, as well as to students. For example, a recent project was in a Dhaka kindergarten.

SALARY: Voluntary work. Registration charge of $300 for 3 months plus charge of $2.50 per day to cover food. Homestay or other accommodation is provided.

CONTACT: Abdur Rahman, Director and Organisation Secretary.

Tibet

Tibet (known as Xizang province in Mandarin), in the far west of China, has fascinated people in the West for centuries and until 1986 was inaccessible to the outside world. On the highest plateau in the world and encompassing a large section of the Himalayan mountains, Tibet offers something quite different from the rest of China. While there is a certain appetite to communicate with the outside world and learn English, there is also anxiety about incursions into Tibetan culture. The opening of a rail link from Lhasa to Beijing a few years ago has hastened and increased the influx of Han Chinese visitors and settlers, whereas the number of international tourists has been sadly decreased by the intermittent closure of Tibet's borders. Free travel is not permitted in Tibet and all visitors must have an authorised guide who holds the permit. Almost all NGOs that were active in the Tibetan Autonomous (so-called) Region have been expelled. The Chinese authorities have been made very nervous by the tragic spate of self-immolations by Tibetans (more than 130 since March 2011) as a final despairing act of protest against the occupation of their country and suppression of their culture. The security crackdown has been ferocious, particularly in Lhasa. So for the present time, there is very little chance of entering Tibet as a teacher. A brave charity based in Scotland called ROKPA UK (www.rokpauk.org) sends the occasional solo volunteer teacher for a year to teach in schools that it supports on the Tibetan Plateau, most recently to the country town of Jiantsar in the north of Huangnan Tibetan Autonomous Prefecture, Qinghai Province, where 70% of the population is Tibetan.

Despite a decision taken some time ago to change the medium of instruction used in Tibetan schools-in-exile from English to Tibetan, there are plenty of volunteering opportunities in places such as Dharamsala in the Indian Himalayas. Try for example the Lha Charitable Trust (see entry above in India section). Other NGOs looking for volunteer English teachers (who pay no fees) include Education Support Tibet (www.estibet.ch) which runs Kunpan Cultural School in a village near Dharamsala. The Buddhist nunnery Jamyang Choeling Institute in the same area looks for female volunteers (jamchoe@yahoo.com).

LIZZI MIDDLETON

Lizzi Middleton's gap year was spent teaching English in a completely unexpected setting.

Not quite believing that I was embarking on what was to be the biggest adventure of my life so far, I arrived in Delhi and a few days later caught a 15-hour overnight bus to McLeodganj in North-West India, seat of the Tibetan government in exile and home of His Holiness the Dalai Lama. It was a further hour's hair-raising bus journey down into the valley to my placement at the Jamyang Choeling Himalayan Institute for Buddhist women. The nunnery is in a very secluded area of the countryside, set in front of the stunning backdrop of the snow-capped foothills of the Himalayas. It was unbelievably picturesque and was a welcome relief after the madness of Delhi!

Finding out what we were meant to be doing, and where we were meant to be, was our first major challenge. Tibetans are notoriously vague - we had been warned about this but it was vague on a level that I've never experienced vague before! This was one of the real cultural differences that I had to adapt to. Having just completed my A levels and the careful structuring of time that they had required, and coming from a family where we always let each other know where we are, life at Jamyang Choeling was quite *a change. I had to learn to be very easy going, to not mind when a class just didn't turn up or when there was only half a class there.*

My classes were loosely organised according to ability but to be honest that didn't mean much. Lessons were fun - I realised soon after I arrived that these women needed their hour with me to be educational but light-hearted. They get up at 5am every day and apart from an hour for lunch and an hour for dinner they don't stop until 10 or 11pm - they're studying Buddhism all day. My first few lessons were pretty diabolical as I tried to find my feet in a completely alien situation. I had no idea of how I was going to learn the names of 90 women, none of whom had any hair and who all wore exactly the same clothes!

So the teaching was the reason that I was there but there were lots of other things to be done at the nunnery too. Cooking for more than 90 people three times a day is no mean feat and so every day from 10am to noon I cut up vegetables with a small team of nuns. I found that it was a great time for the nuns to practise the English that they were sometimes too shy to use in front of each other in the classroom, and it was also an opportunity for me to learn some Tibetan and to listen to their stories - often of escape over the Himalayas from Tibet. I made some amazing friends. Together we had a huge amount of fun - riding on the roofs of local buses, swimming in the river, shopping for food for our leaving party, teaching each other national dances (I'm afraid we ended up opting to teach the Macarena), blowing up balloons, and a lot of the time just sitting and chatting about the similarities and most of all the differences between our lives, religions and cultures.

Specialist tour operators may be able to advise. For example, Tibetan Wild Yak Adventures publishes a little information about volunteering on a page of its website (www.tibetanwildyakadventures.com/teach_english. htm), including in orphanages in Tibet, although it is likely the information is not up to date. The American-run Global Crossroads volunteer agency (www.globalcrossroad.com/tibet) used to offer volunteer teaching positions in Tibet but no longer can because of the visa issue.

Sri Lanka

In May 2009, the Sri Lankan government declared military victory over the Tamil Tigers, ending 26 years of civil war, and there is now free movement on the Jaffna peninsula. This opening up has fuelled a demand for English-language education. English is sometimes seen as a neutral choice between rival Tamil and Sinhalese and, as in India, is used in some elite private schools.

The British Council at 49 Alfred House Gardens in Colombo (www.britishcouncil.lk) has offices with libraries and teaching centres in Colombo, Kandy and Jaffna, with partner schools in Galle and Matara. The teaching centres offer classes to adults and young learners. Teachers need a minimum of two years' post-certificate experience to be considered. The Council runs a full-time CELTA course in August costing £1,800.

The Senahasa Trust based in London (www.senahasa.org) has been working in rural state schools in Southern Sri Lanka since 2005 and recruits a few volunteer English teachers for the four schools the charity rebuilt after the tsunami. Most of these are provided by the Project Trust (www.projecttrust.org.uk).

LIST OF EMPLOYERS

BRITISH TEACHERS ABROAD

Mulberry Studios, Mulberry Road, Canvey Island, Essex
SS8 0PR, UK

℡ 01268 695714

✉ info@britishteachersabroad.com

🖥 www.britishteachersabroad.com

NUMBER OF TEACHERS: Nursery and primary teaching
assistants for the British Teaching Academy in Bandarawela (south
central Sri Lanka).

PREFERENCE OF NATIONALITY: British or Irish.

QUALIFICATIONS: No special qualifications needed, although
CELTA and relevant experience would be helpful. Looking for
passionate candidates who are team players and can engage
students. Open to gap year students, graduates, retired people
and anyone wanting to gain experience.

CONDITIONS OF EMPLOYMENT: 9–12 month commitment. Up
to 25 hours a week.

SALARY: Volunteer stipend of 30,000–40,000 rupees per month
plus meals or a monthly food allowance of 10,000 rupees.

FACILITIES/SUPPORT: Accommodation provided with utilities and
internet. Visa is arranged. Teacher pays for the flights.

CONTACTS: Vincent Cox, Project Coordinator.

SCHOOLHOUSE ABROAD

Schoolhouse, Anderson Road, Ballater, Aberdeenshire,
AB35 5QW, UK

℡ +44 1339 756333

✉ info@school-house.org

🖥 www.school-house.org

Schoolhouse Abroad offers well-researched and well-supported
English teaching volunteering opportunities in a range of formal
and informal situations in Sri Lanka and Tamil Nadu in India.
Planning to extend to Myanmar.

PREFERENCE OF NATIONALITY: Must be native or fluent English
speaker. Ideally candidates can attend pre-placement training in
Scotland.

QUALIFICATIONS: Teaching qualifications are not essential as
there is a range of placements to match a range of skills and
experience. However, newly qualified teachers seeking experience,
those wishing to explore teaching with a view to training in the
future, teachers seeking a refreshing sabbatical or holiday
and retired teachers may be particularly interested. Volunteers
must be good communicators, be enthusiastic and open
to contributing to and learning from new and challenging
experiences.

CONDITIONS OF EMPLOYMENT: Volunteer English teaching
placements in government schools through the Ministry of
Education in Colombo and other organisations like children's
homes in Sri Lanka and Tamil Nadu. Placements last 1 month
to 1 year. Also organise 2-week English language camps in
summer.

FACILITIES/SUPPORT: A free (optional) 2/3-day residential
pre-departure training course is given at Schoolhouse premises
in Scotland. The course aims to prepare volunteers and enable
them to get the most out of their volunteer teaching experience,
both in terms of contribution and self-development. Volunteers
stay in campus accommodation, with selected host families or in
a shared house or flat with other volunteers.

RECRUITMENT: Applications welcomed year round. After
submitting the online application form (on the Schoolhouse site),
Schoolhouse will develop a rapport with applicants to ensure an
effective matching and good preparation.

COST: £750 for first month (covers placement admin, training,
airport pick-up, accommodation, most meals and ongoing support
during placement). Subsequent months go down to £650 and
then a further reduction.

CONTACTS: Alan and Cathy Low, Founding Directors.

Maldives

A country that is normally associated with celebrities' luxury holidays, the island nation of the Maldives in the Indian Ocean promotes the use of English and encourages native speakers to spend time working in schools. The government used to administer an International Volunteer Programme whereby volunteers spent an academic year volunteering in the Maldives. Since the violent removal of the democratically elected government in 2012, the volunteer programme has been suspended. As the founder of the UK organisation Friends of the Maldives confirmed: *'Sadly, since the coup in the Maldives, the programme has been dissolved. The new regime would prefer less outside influences.'*

A privately run scheme affiliated to a travel agency is called Volunteer Maldives (www.volunteermaldives.com). The two company founders offer a structured volunteering programme in various locations in the Maldive Islands, mainly involved with teaching and community programmes. Participants stay for a minimum of four weeks, up to three months. Possible extra activities include snorkelling trips, visits to uninhabited islands for swimming and sunbathing, and night fishing with the locals. Costs start at $1,600 for four weeks and rise to $3,400 for 12 weeks.

A similar programme is open to paying volunteers from Atoll Volunteers based on Naifaru Island (www.atollvolunteers.com); volunteers who enjoy working with children are assigned to primary and secondary schools on the various islands of Lhivayani Atoll, but mainly at Madhurasathul Ifthithaah. The fees here are a little more expensive: $1,750 for four weeks and $4,450 for 12 weeks.

When **Louise Sim** from Singapore was researching scuba diving in the Maldives, she chanced upon Volunteer Maldives and decided to apply as a pre-school teaching assistant. With minimal fuss she was assigned to Roashanee Pre-school and was billeted with a host who happened to be the principal and his family. Louise quickly picked up a few essential words of Dhivehi, especially when the little ones urgently needed the loo.

Like most children, they took time to warm up, but once they get to know you, they are very sweet, which will make you want to take up professional teaching for pre-schoolers. They were very creative in art and crafts, and some of them would want to bring me to the reading corner to select an English book to read together. A few of them were a little hyperactive and had tantrums, which required more attention. In my spare time, I hung out with the local children and families, attended barbecues, birthday parties and picnics, and swam in the sea. I learned about simple happiness and that you don't have to earn a lot to be happy. The heat was a trial – it is quite hot on the atoll of Naifaru as there aren't many trees.

Only a handful of English language institutes is active in the Maldives and they rarely advertise abroad. An exception cropped up recently, when the Language Learning Centre in the capital Male (www.llcmaldives.com) was advertising for teachers of young children. According to the advert on www.englishjobsabroad.com, the job was offering a monthly salary of US$1,000–US$1,300, reimbursement of airfare, accommodation and health insurance.

MALAYSIA

For the many Malaysian students who aspire to go to university in the UK, USA or Australia, intensive English-language tuition is an essential part of their training. The government has increased the profile of English as a medium of instruction in the state education system. Until 2012, CfBT (Centre for British Teaching) assisted the Malaysian Ministry of Education to improve the standard of English in rural schools; however, that programme has come to an end (www.cfbt.com.my), though they are still involved with the training of Malaysian teachers of English.

An in-service scheme that has taken its place is a government-backed mentoring programme. Native-speaker mentors work with local primary school teachers to develop English learning activities and to increase their confidence in using English. The three approved recruiters are Prime Teachers (www.primeteachers.com), the Kuala Lumpur-based Brighton Education Group (www.brightoneducation.org) and SMR HR Group (see entry). Extensive teaching experience is the usual requirement. Less experienced candidates may be eligible for the English Speaking Assistants programme offered by the agency Bright Spark Teachers (www.brightsparkteachers.co.uk). Native-speaking school leavers assist teachers in Malaysian state schools for six or twelve months as interns who receive 1,300 ringgits in total per month. Those who stay for a year have the cost of their flight reimbursed.

MICHAEL HUGHES

The Malaysian government has been investing generously in raising the standard of English in primary education. Michael J Hughes is the Project Manager for one of the companies that has the contract to oversee these mentors, and sent an account of the SMR programme (see entry):

As a long term resident in Malaysia I knew that the Government would be starting a scheme to hire foreign 'experts' to help with the pedagogy and personal language ability of primary teachers in Malaysia. As the contract has now been going on for nearly four years, we are finding that the processes for applications for visas are taking longer than when we first started, but I am given to understand this has been a common phenomenon throughout the immigration system.

On the whole, the mentors found it challenging to reach the Key Performance Indicators numbers required but they were not unrealistic, nor were they a barrier to us offering a good quality service to the teachers we were helping.

The mentors are given a great deal of freedom to arrange their own schedules, visits and which topics they will deliver at workshops and group gatherings. Mentors were issued with a car for their own personal use, along with allowances for housing, full medical insurance and salaries that were more than adequate to cover local expenses. The only slight drawback with regards money is the complicated tax laws, but the vast majority were able to obtain tax rebates and enjoy the fruits of their labours.

Generally there were very few (if any) problems with the mentors relating to the children. A vast number of mentors also became involved in the life of the school and the community by organising extra classes for needy children, or helping with local orphanages, extracurricular activities and sometimes collecting money for charities. Some mentors felt a little isolated away from the security of a normal school regimen where hours are fixed and colleagues and staff are regular, though many exchanged professional advice with other mentors located close by.

This seems to have been a good project for the vast majority involved in it, and for me personally it has been a privilege to have been a part of it for the past four years. One teacher wrote on Facebook: 'Do you realise we are being paid to do what most people pay to do?'

Two of the participating mentors sent positive feedback about the programme. Canadian **Amanda Stoddard** came across SMR's job posting on Dave's ESL Café, and is based in Taiping in the north in 2015:

The job consists of mentoring level 1 Malaysian English teachers in five separate elementary schools. The contract required 75 contact hours across 10 teachers, which included one-on-one meetings, lesson planning, demo lessons, events, workshops, assessment, observations and more.

The teachers we mentor are generally a bit nervous and reserved when we first start working together, but after a short time they warm up, open their minds and really enjoy sharing ideas, collaborating with other teachers and trying new techniques in their classrooms. A great part about the job is the emphasis on rapport building with the teachers and students. The flexible system allows mentors to truly assess the needs of each teacher, school and cluster and deliver assistance and training accordingly.

The salary is very good by Malaysian standards and the cost of living relatively low, so I am able to save between C$1000–C$1500 a month. In my spare time I explore different parts of Malaysia, visit other mentors, attend events with local friends and teachers, and sometimes just enjoy staying at home and enjoying the gorgeous Lake Gardens where I live in Taiping. During vacation periods I often hop off to another country in Southeast Asia for exploring, scuba diving, trekking, etc. The rewards of living and teaching in Malaysia are vast. I love the tropical climate and the tremendous number of things to do and experience. The people are generally very friendly and most speak English, which makes it easy to travel, live and make friends with locals.

Another mentor **Robert Sudy** was also favourably impressed and concluded that SMR is an '*outstanding company*'. The only thing that with hindsight he might have done differently was to leave the ties and suits at home and brought more short-sleeved dress shirts.

The British Council (www.britishcouncil.my) has teaching centres in Kuala Lumpur, Penang and Mutiara Damansara (near KL) that recruit teachers (minimum age 22) on an hourly or rolling basis; the former offers the CELTA course part-time (for 9,275 ringgits). As an employer the British Council is highly regarded, as long-time TEFLer **Steph Fuccio** from the USA reported after a stint of teaching in Kuala Lumpur at a different institute:

My husband and I moved to Malaysia right after we got married and worked for different branches of the same language school. After a lot of pondering and trying to make it work, we left after six months. While we were there the government switched from using English as the primary language in the schools back to Bahasa Malay. This switch apparently happens often, and with an unfortunate effect on the kids in the school system. Thus, there weren't as many jobs open to us as initially thought.

The British Council was by far the best-paying language school in town, pretty much doubling standard language school salaries, with more benefits to boot. We interviewed at many places and finally decided on another school because it offered set daytime hours, good pay (5,000 ringgits before tax), and they had locations near our apartment. Unfortunately, what we didn't bargain on was the materials that we were supposed to use, their own cut and paste versions of difficult grammar books, the method they wanted us to teach with (lecture, not communicative method) and just how penny pinching they were. My husband's school gave them a ream of paper each month for photocopies, my school had a copy tally. We were all 'talked to' monthly on lowering our copy numbers.

The government issues work permits only to highly qualified applicants. People caught working on tourist visas can expect to be fined and deported. Work permits can take a long time since the immigration department is slow to act; however, it is permitted to start work with an application pending. You will need to produce your degree and TEFL qualification certificates, university transcripts, reference letter from previous employer, medical report and passport photos. Also enquire about a minimum age stipulation, since the government has been known to limit the issuing of work permits to people over 27. Foreign workers who have been granted the Visa Pass Temporary Employment (VPTE) must also obtain the Visa With Reference from the Malaysian Embassy or the High Commission of Malaysia before entering the country. Without this, entry to Malaysia will be refused. Once you are earning, be sure to register at the tax office as soon as you start employment, and ensure your employer is taking taxes regularly from your pay. Otherwise you can be hit by a colossal bill when you leave, as happened to one of Steph's fellow teachers. Suddenly huge amounts were missing from his pay cheque with no itemisation, and they heard that this was not uncommon. The Erican Language Centre (see entry) offers teachers willing to relocate to various parts of Malaysia to teach children or adults an attractive package. Australians and New Zealanders are eligible for working holiday visas for Malaysia.

One aspect of life in Malaysia which can be difficult to accept is that racial Malays are accorded special privileges over other citizens of Chinese, Indian or tribal origins. For example, places at the universities are available exclusively to *bumiputeras* or '*bumis*', which means literally 'sons of the soil', ie ethnic Malays. Otherwise Malaysia offers a pleasant multicultural environment and teachers usually experience less culture shock than they do in some neighbouring countries. Kuala Lumpur is a model of modernity and efficiency when compared with the neighbouring capitals of Jakarta and Bangkok.

LIST OF EMPLOYERS

ENHANCE EDUCATION SDN BHD

Unit 3H-2-1 Straits Quay, Jalan Seri Tanjung Pinang,
Tanjung Tokong 10470, Pulau Pinang

(*) +60 4 890 3390 / +60 4 890 0726

careers@enhance-education.com

www.enhance-education.com

NUMBER OF TEACHERS: 22 for 4 schools in Penang State, two on the island, one each in Butterworth and Bukit Mertajam. Usually about 5 vacancies a year.

PREFERENCE OF NATIONALITY: None, provided they are native speakers.

QUALIFICATIONS: University graduate (any subject); CELTA or Trinity TEFL Cert (no on-line TEFL certs); minimum of 2 years full-time teaching.

CONDITIONS OF EMPLOYMENT: Minimum 2 year contracts. 40 hours per week of which up to 24 may be teaching hours. Working week is from Wednesday to Sunday with Monday and Tuesday off.

SALARY: Starting pay of 7,250-7,600 ringgits per calendar month + 12% pension addition + 500 ringgit monthly location allowance for mainland centres. Income tax banded from 11% to 25% for residents, 25% for non-residents. Teachers become residents once their work visa has been issued. No compulsory social security. Optional local pension scheme (EPF) at 11% but not compulsory for foreigners.

FACILITIES/SUPPORT: School assists and pays for teachers to obtain a valid work permit and to register as foreign teachers with the Malaysian Ministry of Education. Procedures take up to 3 months. Assistance with relocation and settlement costs is available including 14 nights in a hotel on first arrival and an interest-free car purchase loan. 36 days paid annual leave plus 12 local public holidays.

RECRUITMENT: Via Dave's ESL Cafe. Interviews by Skype after candidate sends a recent lesson plan they have taught.

CONTACT: Dr Tom Craig-Cameron, Principal (tom@enhance-education.com).

ERICAN LANGUAGE CENTRE

C-19–4 Megan Avenue II, Jalan Yap Kwan Seng, 50450 Kuala Lumpur

C +60 3 2164 9999

@ career@erican.edu.my

▢ www.erican.edu.my/LanguageCentre/career.php

Language education and training company with 20+ centres across the peninsula.

NUMBER OF TEACHERS: 5 full-time.

PREFERENCE OF NATIONALITY: British, American, Canadian, Australian or New Zealander.

QUALIFICATIONS: Minimum TEFL/TESOL or CELTA qualification and one year's teaching experience.

CONDITIONS OF EMPLOYMENT: 12–24-month contracts to teach children and adults. Usual working hours (25–30 per week) between 9am and 5pm Monday to Friday. Lots of IELTS preparation.

SALARY: Approximately $1,200 per month plus monthly performance incentive, less 10% deductions for tax and social security.

FACILITIES/SUPPORT: Free shared room in teachers' hostel is normally available or the teacher will be subsidised by the centre (typically 500 ringgits per month) for private accommodation. The centre applies for work permits and covers all required visa charges. The visa application process may take 2–3 months.

RECRUITMENT: Usually via online advertisements. Interviews are essential and are normally via online video conferencing.

CONTACT: Ki Chong, Director (Erican Education Group).

SMR HR GROUP

Suite 2A-23-1, Block 2A Level 23, Plaza Sentral, Jalan Stesen Sentral 5, KL Sentral, 50470 Kuala Lumpur

C +60 3 2279 9088/9199

@ michael@smrhrgroup.com or michael@smrelt.com

▢ www.smrelt.com

NUMBER OF TEACHERS: 120 for the government's teacher mentoring programme which is funded at least until February 2016 and probably beyond.

PREFERENCE OF NATIONALITY: Only requirement is native speaker English language competence.

QUALIFICATIONS: BA in any subject; ESL certificate such as CELTA, at least 5 years' teaching experience. Mentor programme requires at least 3 years' teaching young children. Other programmes may be more flexible. In most cases, trainers must have a driving licence. Minimum age 28.

CONDITIONS OF EMPLOYMENT: Contracts are allocated by the Malaysian Ministry of Education usually for 1–3 years, with a possibility of extension. Timetable is organised by the trainer in negotiation with the teachers they will be helping. Occasional out-of-school-time responsibilities but as a general rule around 20 full contact hours with teachers per week.

SALARY: Minimum 8,000 ringgits plus allowances which are RM1,500 per month. Additional settling-in allowance of RM4,000 and reimbursement of airfares. Tax laws mean 26% is deducted in the first 182 days, then reduced to variable amount depending upon salary and rebate paid on difference for first 182 days.

FACILITIES/SUPPORT: Zone Managers, Local Education officials, teachers and other mentors can assist with accommodation which is mostly found through word of mouth. SMR pays for first 10 days in a hotel while mentor finds a place to live. Full help given with visa procedure from initial application to getting visas for dependants.

RECRUITMENT: Personal recommendation, advertisements on popular ESL forums and recruiting sites. Interviews via Skype or in situ are essential.

CONTACT: Michael J Hughes, ELT Project Manager.

SINGAPORE

Malaysia's tiny neighbour clinging to the tip of the Malay peninsula is a wealthy and westernised city-state in which there is a considerable demand for qualified English teachers on minimum one-year contracts. Once a teacher gets established in a school, freelance teaching is widely available paying from S$32 an hour (US$24).

The Foreign Recruitment Unit of the Ministry of Education in Singapore (www.moe.gov.sg/careers/teach) recruits foreign teachers in English language/English literature, as well as geography, history and economics, on one to three-year contracts in secondary schools and junior colleges (Grades 7 to 12). The scheme is very competitive, so only suitably qualified applicants should consider this option, though there are other opportunities for people without advanced qualifications, including those with just A levels. Candidates should possess a relevant and very good degree, preferably with teaching/higher qualifications and experience. Interviews are held in July and August. Salaries for degree-holders start at S$3,010 (gross) per month plus an end-of-year bonus. Commercial schools tend to pay S$3,300–S$4,000 a month.

The British Council at 30 Napier Road has a teaching operation that hires qualified teachers especially for teaching young learners (and can also provide a list of approved language schools). The recruitment office for all of East Asia is located in Singapore; enquiries may be sent to eateacher.recruitment@britishcouncil. org.sg. Many private institutes are located in the ubiquitous shopping centres, especially along Orchard Road, for example Berlitz (391b), Geos Language Centre (Singapore Shopping Centre, near Orchard Road), Ikomo (350) and Goro (268). The majority of commercial language centres are Chinese-owned with a high proportion of teachers from Australia.

Not strictly an ESL programme, native English speakers are being recruited to teach literacy skills to children with a company called I Can Read. As with the government scheme, candidates must have either a university teaching qualification or a degree in a humanities subject such as English literature, linguistics or psychology, in order to qualify for the Employment Pass. Two-year contracts start in July/August (www. career.icanread.asia).

Singapore is not a recommended destination for the so-called 'teacher-traveller' who, without qualifications but with a smart pair of trousers, hopes to be able to impress a language school owner. Even people who have qualifications cannot count on landing a job without effort. However, persistent enquiries have resulted in the offer of hourly work. The Long-Term Visit Pass (LTVP), which may be applied for online, allows qualifying foreigners to look for work in Singapore. Once a job is found, a variety of Work and Employment Passes of varying grades may be applied for from the Ministry of Manpower; see www.mom.gov.sg for clarification. Students and graduates aged 18–25 from universities in the UK, US, Australia and New Zealand can easily qualify for the Work Holiday programme which permits participants to do any job for up to six months; the processing fee is S$150 and the total quota is 2000.

Once you have a sponsoring employer, the prospective employer must contact the Singapore Immigration and Checkpoints Authority (10 Kallang Road, ICA Building, Singapore 208718; www.ica.gov.sg) for an application form and approval letter, or simply apply online. The process usually takes between six and eight weeks, and it is necessary to wait for the approval letter before travelling as you will be required to present it at Immigration Control in Changi Airport.

Some teachers have reported that they have quickly tired of Singapore, coming to see it as one giant shopping mall. So if shopping malls and a repressive regime (for example there are signs threatening to fine you S$300 if you drop litter, jaywalk or fail to flush the loo) leave you cold, Singapore is perhaps best avoided.

LIST OF EMPLOYERS

INLINGUA SCHOOL OF LANGUAGES

51 Cuppage Rd, #10–12, Singapore 229469

+65 6737 6666

info@inlingua.edu.sg

www.inlingua.edu.sg

NUMBER OF TEACHERS: 8 full-time English teachers (62 teachers in total in 13 language sections). Also positions as interns for students on working holiday visas.

PREFERENCE OF NATIONALITY: Multinational team from the UK, USA, Canada and Australia. Teachers from the UK preferred.

QUALIFICATIONS: University degree and post-graduate teaching qualification required (CELTA, TESOL or TEFL). Experience is not necessary but candidates must be effective teachers who can work well in a team.

CONDITIONS OF EMPLOYMENT: Standard 18-month contract. 40 hours per week (8 hours per day maximum) on school premises. This includes up to 25 hours of teaching (30 lessons lasting 50 minutes each). Group lessons are usually Monday to Friday 9am–1pm but trainers may also have to teach until 9pm Monday to Friday and 8am–3pm on Saturdays.

SALARY: Starts at S$3,100 per month. After a 6-month probationary period and satisfactory performance, salary increases to S$3,300. 18-month contracts are taxed at around 3%. Teachers do not need to pay Central Provident Fund contributions.

FACILITIES/SUPPORT: Temporary homestay accommodation can be arranged for at least 1 month at a cost of S$900. Teachers are given help by school's admin when looking for more permanent accommodation.

RECRUITMENT: Please apply by email by sending detailed CV. Interview and demonstration lesson in Singapore preferred but not essential.

CONTACT: Graham Sage, School Director.

MORRIS ALLEN STUDY CENTRES

#03–02, Block 51 Bishan Street 13, Singapore 579799

+65 6258 3229

hrmgt@morris-allen.com.sg

www.morris-allen.com.sg

NUMBER OF TEACHERS: 40+.

PREFERENCE OF NATIONALITY: British, Australian, New Zealander, Canadian, American and South African.

QUALIFICATIONS: Minimum 3 years' experience plus degree in education; or bachelor's degree plus teacher training specialising in English, primary or early childhood education. Most teachers have classroom experience with children whose mother tongue is English.

CONDITIONS OF EMPLOYMENT: 2 years (1 year is available, extensions welcome). 28 teaching hours per week out of total working week of 35 hours. To teach Singaporese children aged 3 to 16 years, in an English-medium education system.

SALARY: S$3,500 per month, tax free plus bonus of S$3,000 at the end of 2-year contract.

FACILITIES/SUPPORT: S$700 per month per person provided for accommodation expenses in first year, S$900 second year, plus S$500 freight allowance. Medical insurance provided. 2 weeks' initial hotel accommodation and assistance given in finding an apartment. Employer will submit visa applications.

RECRUITMENT: Adverts in foreign teachers' journals and online, eg at www.englishjobsabroad.com. Face-to-face interview preferred; telephone interview possible.

CONTACT: Peter Scarrott, Principal.

NYU LANGUAGE CENTRE

The Adelphi 04–35, 1 Coleman St, Singapore 179803

+65 6338 3533

admin@nyu-online.com

www.nyu-online.com

NUMBER OF TEACHERS: 5.

PREFERENCE OF NATIONALITY: American, British.

QUALIFICATIONS: Degree with teaching experience in English.

CONDITIONS OF EMPLOYMENT: 1-year contracts. Hours are 9.30am–5.30pm, Monday to Friday.

SALARY: S$2,500–S$3,000.

FACILITIES/SUPPORT: Help given with work permits.

RECRUITMENT: Via advertisements or recommendation.

CONTACT: Nance Teo, Principal.

BRUNEI

Few people can locate Negara Brunei Darussalam (Brunei, the Abode of Peace) on a map of the world, let alone anticipate that there is a steady demand for qualified English teachers there. This wealthy oil state on the north shore of Borneo can afford universal education for its population of 415,000. The Ministry of Education has been implementing a bilingual educational system which '*ensures the sovereignty of the Malay language while at the same time recognising the importance of the English language*'.

Brunei, mostly covered in luxuriant tropical rainforest, has a pollution-free, healthy environment, few traffic jams and one of the lowest crime rates in the world. It provides a very pleasant place to live and work for those who like the outdoor lifestyle and don't crave a wide variety of nightlife. For water sports enthusiasts, the warm, calm waters of the South China Sea provide an ideal environment for diving, sailing and power boating. Most expatriates join one of the many sports and social clubs which provide excellent facilities.

Brunei has a rich cultural heritage and still boasts the largest water village in the world in the capital, Bandar Seri Begawan. There are many opportunities to participate in colourful cultural extravaganzas to mark national events such as the Sultan's birthday on 15 July and National Day on 23 February. In the rural areas there is an opportunity to see how the other indigenous groups celebrate their traditional harvest festivals. Although Brunei is a Malay Islamic monarchy, other religions are allowed to practise freely and Chinese New Year and Christmas Day are also national holidays, in addition to the numerous Islamic public holidays.

There are currently over 200 expatriate primary and secondary EFL teachers working in Brunei in state sector schools. CfBT Education Services (Block D, Units 5 & 6, Kiarong Complex, Lebuhraya Sultan Hassanal Bolkiah, Bandar Seri Begawan BE1318, Brunei; hr@cfbt.org; www.cfbt.org) recruits suitably qualified and experienced individuals along guidelines set by the Brunei Ministry of Education. All teachers must have Qualified Teacher Status, eg PGCE or equivalent, plus a degree, a minimum three years' experience including EFL/ESL and be under 52 (primary) or 55 (secondary). The package currently includes tax-free salary of B$3,500–B$5,500 a month, end-of-contract bonus, accommodation, flights, baggage allowance and other benefits. Contracts are usually for two years initially. A car driving licence is strongly preferred though some teachers can arrange to be driven to work by a spouse or a maid. CfBT also administers IELTS and runs a range of courses for teachers and the public including Cambridge ICELT, General English and ESP, ICT and Malay.

VIETNAM

The market in English-language training is very lively. Vietnam's economy is charging ahead and is now on target to achieve more than 6% growth this year. Student numbers are ever on the increase, and the established language schools are offering teachers a full timetable. Many urban Vietnamese want to learn English with a view to joining a profession such as banking or tourism or to have a chance of acceptance at institutes of higher learning overseas. From Ho Chi Minh City (HCMC) in the south to Hanoi in the north, opportunities abound both for trained professionals and freshly certified CELTA/TESOL graduates.

Although Vietnam is still a one-party socialist republic (which has been accused of blocking websites that are critical of the government), it bears all the trappings (complete with garish advertising hoardings and American pop music) of a capitalist society with an expanding young middle class who invest in electronic goods, luxury items and English lessons. The British Council offers many types of English course, from those aimed at primary school children to 'English for international business'. It employs 50 teachers and is always looking for hourly paid teachers, for its centres in HCMC and Hanoi.

FINDING A JOB

Prospective teachers in Vietnam should be aware that the country is becoming increasingly savvy about qualifications. A degree is often no longer seen as sufficient and EFL teaching qualifications are very desirable. Many employers are not impressed with online courses or those without a classroom component. However, it is still possible to get work in a local institute, gain experience and move up the ladder. The principal teaching organisations included in the list of employers are the most prestigious employers with relatively high standards and high pay. Both Hanoi and HCMC have at least 30 other language schools each which pay well enough and often employ staff within two weeks of arrival.

On the whole teachers are highly respected in Vietnamese culture, and it is not unusual for students to present their foreign teachers with flowers, presents and dinner invitations. However, caution should be exercised if you are advertising 'private English tuition', which can sometimes be misconstrued for other services. **Annabelle Laker** reported from Ho Chi Minh City that she got in a tangle when she went to meet a prospective student and he thought he could buy sex.

Vietnam is a good place to acquire the CELTA, since there are four course providers – Language Link, Apollo English in two cities and ILA Vietnam – all with entries at the end of this chapter. **Steph Fuccio** had no trouble getting work in Hanoi with Language Link after doing the CELTA course:

> *Language Link is a great place to do a CELTA and start working. They have all the usual trappings of an EFL job such as unpredictable schedules, weekend work and so on. But, they do have a huge amount of resources, keen students and there is real opportunity to build up your teaching skills quickly. In my second year I taught English for Academic Purposes and TOEFL-iBT along with my regular Business and General English classes.*

Often the best way to find work is simply to arrive in one of the major cities and look around. Check out Craigslist (http://vietnam.craigslist.org), which has scores of job ads and is useful for accommodation listings as well, and www.expat-blog.com/en/jobs/asia/vietnam, which is also good for posting private tuition ads. The site vietnamteachingjobs.com enables you to target your search for Academic English, Business English or General English. Other community sites for expats such as http://tnhvietnam.xemzi.com can be equally productive for jobs, accommodation, etc.

The teacher agent Jimmy Tran advertises often on the internet giving only his email address: jimmycali714@ gmail.com. The demand for Young Learners' English is rocketing. On arrival at her job with Language Link Hanoi, **Amalia Pesci** was taken aback to be told that she would be mainly teaching young learners, because all of her extensive experience had been in teaching Adult English. She coped with teaching children for her first year but found the parental pressure hard to deal with: 'The parents wanted their children to learn English in about six months.'

Originally, **Annabelle Laker** from Exeter had signed up to do an internship programme in Vietnam with a company called TTV found on the i-to-i TEFL website (www.onlinetefl.com/teaching-internships/vietnam). However, at just four days' notice, the internship fell through and, after a concerted effort, she got all her money back:

I was suddenly faced with no job, no apartment and no safety net for my first adventure overseas! I decided to travel to Vietnam anyway and see if I could make it work by myself. For my first two months in the country I travelled around and found voluntary positions by ringing up and visiting orphanages. Then I decided to settle in Ho Chi Minh City and printed out about 20 copies of my CV. I spent a few days running around the city dropping off CVs and copies of my TEFL certificates and degree at the head offices of language schools: I found this face-to-face approach worked better than sending emails or applying online for jobs. I was called for an interview a week later at a large language school called SuperYouth. Once they had seen that I could dress smartly and was a native speaker, I had the job so long as I worked the hours they wanted, ie 15 hours a week, almost all evenings and weekends. Friends of mine had clued me up to say I was currently being paid $20 an hour by private students and to use this to push up the original offer from the language school. In the end I was able to negotiate $17 an hour, but I did have to be quite firm to get this.

I work three jobs at the moment, which is very manageable and gives me variety which I love. The other two jobs I created really – I put up adverts on Craigslist and expat-blog as a private English-language tutor and from responses to these ads I now have a job with an agency as a conversation tutor for a group of four teenagers and as a Business English tutor for the reception staff at a western dental clinic based in the city.

By asking around you will soon discover which schools might be hiring. Some of the best-established companies in HCMC are ACET, which specialises in academic English, RMIT (affiliated to an Australian university), AUSP, VUS and many others like Compass Education, American Academy and Washington Language School.

In her late 20s, **Dawn Wilkinson** decided to use some money she had inherited to take a year off from her publishing job in the UK. After five months of travelling around South-East Asia with friends, she felt she wasn't ready to go home, so decided to find out how far her BA and MA in English would get her in landing a teaching job. After meeting up with a uni friend in Saigon – the old name for HCMC is still in wide use – and making friends with a few expats and locals, she decided to base herself there. After trawling through numerous ads placed by tutors looking for work, she finally stumbled across an ad placed by a wealthy French-Vietnamese woman looking for an English tutor for her seven-year-old daughter and Dawn got the job:

The family were lovely and, as the sessions were at their house, they always invited me to eat dinner with them afterwards. This family were middle class, I guess, so working for the two families gave me a great insight into Vietnamese life and I spent a lot of time chatting with the parents about their lives and to the girls about their hopes for the future (they were all keen to improve their English as a means to travel and work in Europe or America).

Exams are taking off in Vietnam and many students strive to obtain a good TOEFL score in the hope of going to America, while the Cambridge suite of exams and IELTS are popular with those wanting to take up scholarships to Australia and the UK.

SAMANTHA THORNLEY

Samantha Thornley shied away from joining the corporate world after graduation from college in Illinois and was delighted to be accepted by Teachers for Vietnam in the USA (see entry), which has a well-run programme; unusually, funding is available for qualifying volunteers.

I lived and taught in Vietnam for almost five months. I can honestly say that these were the hardest, scariest, best and most rewarding months of my life. The people that I met were the nicest, friendliest people I have ever encountered, and I was continually amazed at the generosity and hospitality of the Vietnamese people, especially my students.

On arrival I was continuously challenged by my surroundings. The first obvious problem I encountered was the language barrier. Simple things like ordering and paying for food, saying thank you or I'm sorry, it all got lost in translation. I took a crash course in Vietnamese - numbers, food, all the necessities for my daily needs. It turns out that I was capable of learning how to get by in a strange land. The more I explored Can Tho, the more I realised how fast English is becoming a second language for the locals.

My placement was as a volunteer English teacher at a university in Vietnam. I worked about 20 hours a week in class, although lesson preparation usually added at least another 10 hours a week. I also taught at a private English school at nights, which was my choice and just a way to meet more students and make some extra cash. In most places in Vietnam (especially Saigon and Hanoi) you can find private schools to work at and as long as you are certified or have experience you can teach there. Most of the smaller cities, such as mine (Can Tho) love to have a foreign teacher and are more than willing to find a way to accommodate you.

Another organised scheme, Teach and Travel in Vietnam (www.teachandtravelvietnam.com), charges substantial fees and is run by the English Language Company in Sydney.

CONDITIONS OF WORK

Base pay at the high-end schools and universities starts at $20 per teaching hour and rises to about $25, but a more usual hourly rate at language schools is $15, with private tuition paying $18–$20 and lessons delivered by Skype $16. This should allow a comfortable lifestyle since the cost of living remains low (for example, HCMC is much cheaper to live in than Bangkok), so Vietnam is a good country for those trying to save some money. ESL teachers are exempt from tax, so earnings are net of deductions.

Teachers often complain of the unsuitability of some of the teaching materials in use. Course books are often designed for European learners so materials have to be constantly adapted, as the cultural references mean nothing to Asian learners.

Annabelle Laker noted that lesson structuring tends to be very book focused in language schools, as opposed to in universities and international schools:

Language institutes want you to stick to the book and get through it. You have zero preparation time. You turn up to be given a printed schedule of room numbers and book pages to teach and review and away you go. Ad-libbing and thinking on your feet become your strengths. For one particular lesson I opened the book and it appeared to be some sort of song . . . I had no idea what the tune was meant to be and neither did the teaching assistant. Trying to think of a song tune on the spot felt a bit too much for me on this day . . . I wasn't feeling in jolly big purple dinosaur mode. Thankfully I had a light bulb moment and decided to turn the song into a clapping game! Turns out this is not something the Vietnamese kids are used to, so the whole concept was quite novel and exciting for them. It worked a treat. They learnt the song and we all had fun too. One successful lesson.

She goes on to explain why the best thing about the job for her is the students:

Although they are sometimes very naughty and hard to control or engage, for the most part they are a lot of fun and very cute. Some of the children have clearly never interacted with a 'real life' westerner before, which can initially mean they are very frightened. But it's not long before they are bouncing up to you saying 'Teacher, teacher, what's your name? Play game!' and stroking your arms.

REGULATIONS

New work permit requirements came into force at the end of 2013, making the process more difficult. You will need to submit the originals of your university degree, TEFL certification and recent police clearance certificate and notarised copy. The original or notarised documents are submitted to the immigration office with a medical report, and the work permit should be issued within about six weeks. It remains valid for two years.

Dawn Wilkinson commented that the laws are not always strictly observed though. Her employers assured her that it was fine to work on a tourist visa, as they were in the process of securing her a full work permit. In order to get this she would have to complete some kind of TEFL course, and was told that even a basic 60-hour/$200 online course would be enough to fulfil the criteria for a work permit. It is so costly for schools to obtain full work permits for their teachers that a lot of skulduggery takes place to avoid the hassle and expense, and rumours abound of schools paying off the authorities to turn a blind eye.

A degree certificate is obligatory for acquiring the permit, though the rules can be bent here too, as Dawn noticed:

Two friends in Saigon didn't have a degree and still managed to find long-term teaching positions. One of the guys had lied to a school that he had a degree and, I think, may have shown them a fake photocopy of a degree certificate (easily bought on Khao San Road in Bangkok) to get a job. He worked there for about 18 months with no problems and was a very good teacher. However, after the Vietnamese authorities became stricter, the school had to start applying for work permits, which meant submitting original documents. My friend had to admit that he didn't actually have a degree. I don't think they were very pleased about it at first but, as he had always worked hard for them, the school somehow managed to secure him a work permit – which he had to pay for himself (money can buy you anything in South-East Asian countries!).

LEISURE TIME

According to **Annabelle Laker**, a shared western-style apartment in HCMC costs about $200 per person per month. Teaching afforded her an 'amazing expat lifestyle' while still being able to save a third of her wages. The cost of living is higher in Hanoi than Saigon, with rents and wages following suit. There is a two-tier system for utilities and travel in Vietnam, which means foreigners pay substantially more than locals for almost everything. You will soon learn that the first 'western price' quoted will always be two if not three times more than the price westerners should actually pay. Bear in mind that what you see is not always what you get. Behind that charming Vietnamese smile is more often than not the intent to extract money. Of particular note are the numerous women in search of a foreign husband, a foreign passport and an airline ticket. Single men should beware.

Hanoi is smaller and more beautiful yet bustling and noisy, whereas HCMC is a Bangkok in the making. This sophisticated, sprawling commercial centre boasts a skyline already dotted with fledgling skyscrapers. The main complaints thus are traffic, noise, pollution and street hassle. Vietnam is a developing country and although the wealth of the nouveau riche classes in the cities is very visible, the countryside is still desperately poor. Countryside and cities alike experience frequent power cuts and things in general don't always work as they are supposed to. Internet access is widely available and improving although it is still unreliable, slow and government firewalls prohibit prying eyes from seeing things they don't want you to see.

As usual, the drawbacks of living in a large Asian city may begin to intrude, as happened to **Dawn Wilkinson**:

> *On the whole, I didn't find Saigon a particularly pleasant city to live in (apart from the fantastic food): it was either stiflingly hot or pouring down with rain, heavily crowded and polluted and had no green spaces at all. I tended to sleep through the day (directly in front of my fan!) or watch TV, then go out with friends late in the evenings after I'd finished working – Saigon does have a great, tight-knit expat social scene.*

The cities are wonderfully packed with cheap restaurants (*com binh dan*) and fantastic street food. Soon you will be addicted to *bun cha* (pork patty), *pho* (noodle soup), banana flower salad and *bia hoi* (draft beer). International restaurants and cafés are more expensive but still affordable for the average teacher. **Annabelle Laker** loves the chaos of street life in HCMC and the buzzing and vibrant nightlife, with many places offering free drinks for women on set nights.

Travelling round the region is very affordable, and has become more so with the rise of low-cost airlines such as Jetstar Pacific based at HCMC airport and Viet Jet Air, which flies from north to south for about $36. Regular tourist night buses are a great way to explore the country and cost just a few dollars for an eight-hour trip.

The *Reunification Express* is a train that runs the full length of the country (over 1,300km). The cheapest fare for the Hanoi–Saigon trip is about $55, though you will have to pay nearly 50% more for an air-conditioned soft sleeper.

Annabelle Laker feels that she wasn't really prepared for the assault on all her senses, but in an amazing way.

LIST OF EMPLOYERS

ACET (AUSTRALIAN EDUCATION AND TRAINING CENTRE)

187 Vo Thi Sau, District 3, Ho Chi Minh City

C +84 8 3932 6202

✍ recruitment@acet.edu.vn

💻 www.acet.edu.vn

ACET is a NEAS-accredited partnership between IDP Education and the University of Technology Sydney's language centre.

NUMBER OF TEACHERS: Approximately 50 for 3 branches in Ho Chi Minh City and 40 for 2 branches in Hanoi.

PREFERENCE OF NATIONALITY: No preference but they need to be able to obtain a work permit in Vietnam and have native English speaking ability.

QUALIFICATIONS: University degree and CELTA or equivalent teaching qualification (minimum 6 hours observed lessons) required. Preferred qualifications and experience: 1–2 years' teaching experience to adults with reputable organisations, demonstrated experience in teaching Academic English and/or IELTS preparation. Experience of teaching in Asia is a plus. A clean police clearance certificate is required.

CONDITIONS OF EMPLOYMENT: Teachers will be on term contracts (5 weeks) until they obtain a work permit. Then ACET has contract signings twice a year but most teachers stay for at least 1 year. Reliable and stable teaching schedules with minimal travel. Typical hours are Monday–Friday: 4-hour classes in the mornings and afternoons, and 2-hour classes in the evenings. Classes for teenagers are taught on weekend afternoons.

SALARY: Ranges from $23.50 to $32.50 per teaching hour, depending on qualifications and experience. Teachers are taxed according to Vietnamese laws; personal income tax is between 12% and 20%.

FACILITIES/SUPPORT: No help given with accommodation, though finding affordable accommodation is not a problem, from shared housing to villas. Opportunities for professional development, and academic support given. Full assistance given with visa application provided teacher has brought necessary documents (degree, teaching certificate and police check). Local costs are met by school.

RECRUITMENT: Advertisements posted on www.tefl.com, Dave's ESL Cafe, and the ACET website. Most teachers are hired locally but also some are hired overseas. Email applications should include CV with referees, covering letter, preferred start date and location (Hanoi or HCMC) and scanned copies of teaching certificate and university degree. All teachers will have an initial interview with the Director of Studies either face-to-face or over the phone.

CONTACT: Shannon Hopkins Rybacki, Country Manager or HR Team.

APOLLO EDUCATION & TRAINING

10 branches in Hanoi, Ho Chi Minh City, Danang and Haiphong.

C +84 4730 0299

✍ recruitment@apollo.edu.vn

💻 www.teachatapollo.com or www.apollo.edu.vn

Established in 1994, Apollo is affiliated to International House and offers training in English, professional development and overseas study consultancy as well as teacher training (Cambridge CELTA). Apollo also has an increasing number of younger learners and corporate classes in addition to partnership contracts with local schools.

NUMBER OF TEACHERS: More than 100 nationwide, more in the summer months.

PREFERENCE OF NATIONALITY: None, but must be native English speaker or have IELTS band 8–9 or equivalent.

QUALIFICATIONS: Teachers must have a CELTA or equivalent (ie 120 hours minimum with at least 6–8 hours of observed classroom teaching practice). Vietnamese work permit regulations stipulate that teachers must also have a degree.

CONDITIONS OF EMPLOYMENT: 1-year contract (some 3-month short-term contracts are available, particularly for the summer programme, and part-time positions). Teaching hours are between 7.45am and 9.45pm, Monday to Friday; 7.45am–8.15pm Saturday, 7.45am–6pm Sunday.

SALARY: From $1,200 per month depending on qualifications and a competitive package including 15 paid annual leave days, 11 paid public holidays, contract completion bonus and re-signing bonus.

FACILITIES/SUPPORT: $500 contribution to medical insurance, sponsorship plus visa and internal work permit costs. For 1-year contracts teachers are given agents' names and/or a Vietnamese member of staff can visit accommodation with the teacher to assist with translation and negotiation.

RECRUITMENT: Through http://ihworld.com, local adverts and internationally using posters, websites, etc. Interviews are essential and are occasionally carried out over Skype.

CONTACT: Ms Lee Nguyen, Nationwide Recruitment Coordinator.

ASIAN INSTITUTE OF TECHNOLOGY IN VIETNAM

Education Management Section, Building B3, University of Transport and Communications, Lang Thuong Dong Da, Hanoi

- +84 4 3766 9493 ext. 143
- linh@aitcv.ac.vn
- www.aitcv.ac.vn

NUMBER OF TEACHERS: 2.

PREFERENCE OF NATIONALITY: None.

QUALIFICATIONS: At least 5 years' experience and preferably a master's degree. TEFL cert also needed.

CONDITIONS OF EMPLOYMENT: Hours vary according to course availability. Classes last 2.5 hours. Mostly part-time.

SALARY: $22 per hour (diploma in TEFL/TESOL or TESOL certificate), $25 per hour (master's in TEFL or TESOL).

FACILITIES/SUPPORT: Some assistance with finding accommodation. No assistance with work permit.

RECRUITMENT: Word of mouth and interviews.

CONTACT: Ms Pham Ngoc Linh, HR Administrator.

ASTON EDUCATIONAL GROUP VIETNAM

614-618 3/2 Street, Ward 14, Dist 10, Ho Chi Minh City

- +84 8 3863 3654
- jobastonvn@gmail.com
- www.aston.edu.vn

NUMBER OF TEACHERS: Variable for several branches in HCMC with plans to expand the brand.

PREFERENCE OF NATIONALITY: Americans and Britons preferred.

CONTACT: Mr Minh.

AUSTRALIA-VIETNAM SKILLS & EDUCATION (AVSE-TESOL)

1300 Quang Trung Street, Go Vap District, Ward 14, Ho Chi Minh City

- +84 933883731
- peter@avse.edu.vn
- www.avse.edu.vn

NUMBER OF TEACHERS: 10–15.

PREFERENCE OF NATIONALITY: None.

QUALIFICATIONS: University degree and prepared to undertake an Australian government accredited TESOL programme in HCMC.

CONDITIONS OF EMPLOYMENT: 3, 6, 9 or 12 months. 20–25 hours per week.

SALARY: US$15–US$25 per hour (net).

FACILITIES/SUPPORT: Assistance given to teachers to find suitable accommodation in the local area. Help given with work permits.

RECRUITMENT: Interviews are essential.

CONTACT: Peter Goudge, Managing Director.

ILA VIETNAM

146 Nguyen Dinh Chieu St, Dist 3, Ho Chi Minh City

- +84 8 3521 8788 / 8 3838 6788
- recruitment@ilavietnam.com
- www.discovereltvietnam.com

NUMBER OF TEACHERS: 400+, with centres in Ho Chi Minh City, Danang, Vung Tau, Binh Duong, Haiphong and Hanoi.

PREFERENCE OF NATIONALITY: Native English speakers.

QUALIFICATIONS: Minimum requirements are university degree (any discipline), plus a CELTA, Trinity or equivalent. Preference is given to applicants who have experience with young learners. Also positions for untrained volunteers.

CONDITIONS OF EMPLOYMENT: Standard 12-month contract. Approx. 25 hours per week.

FACILITIES/SUPPORT: School provides an airport pickup and pays for initial accommodation at a guesthouse. Information and contact details for estate agents are provided. Other teachers are always on the lookout for flatmates and there is an accommodation board in each school. School provides a relocation bonus for overseas applicants as well as paying for and obtaining visas and work permits. Free health insurance and Vietnamese lessons plus quarterly social events are paid for by the school. Bonus paid on successful completion of contract.

RECRUITMENT: Via the internet (www.tefl.com; www.eslcafe.com) and recruiters. Telephone interviews for overseas hires; face-to-face interviews for applicants in Vietnam. Applicants must send CV with cover letter, supporting documents, passport details and realistic start date. Must bring recent police clearance certificate and certified copy. Local applicants must also provide visa details.

CONTACT: David Thompson, Teacher Recruitment Executives/Expatriate Human Resources.

LANGUAGE LINK VIETNAM (LLV)

62 Yen Phu St, Ba Dinh, Hanoi

- +84 4 3927 3399
- recruit@languagelink.vn
- www.llv.edu.vn/en/recruitment or www.schoolslinkhanoi.com

NUMBER OF TEACHERS: 100+ for 40 schools.

PREFERENCE OF NATIONALITY: Native English speakers.

QUALIFICATIONS: Bachelor's degree in any discipline plus 120-hour intensive teaching certificate with practicum (online certificates are not eligible).

CONDITIONS OF EMPLOYMENT: Minimum 1 year if hired from overseas; 6 months if already local. 70–100 contact hours per month. Teachers placed in primary and secondary schools for the academic year September to May.

SALARY: Hourly rate from $19 to $24; 70 hours minimum guaranteed after probationary period. Tax deductions 5%–30% on progressive scale, average 13%.

FACILITIES/SUPPORT: Advice given on finding accommodation and assistance with obtaining work permit. CELTA course offered on premises. Partial costs reimbursed for candidates who work for 1 or more months after the course.

RECRUITMENT: Internet advertising and local press. Local interviews necessary.

CONTACT: Alex Lorne Jameson, Teacher Recruitment and Welfare Manager (alex.jameson@languagelink.vn).

SHELTON DEVELOPMENT GROUP
73 Yen Lang Pho, Trung Liet Ward, Dong Da, Hanoi
- +84 4 7306 2688
- info@shelton.edu.vn
- www.shelton.edu.vn

NUMBER OF TEACHERS: 15.

PREFERENCE OF NATIONALITY: UK, Canada.

QUALIFICATIONS: Professionally qualified teachers as they tend to be substantially better trained than ESL teachers.

CONDITIONS OF EMPLOYMENT: 9.5 month contracts. Minimum 18 hours a week.

SALARY: $18–$25 an hour (net).

FACILITIES/SUPPORT: School advises on reliable landlords, helps negotiate issues and deals with local registration with the police. School covers two-thirds of the cost of obtaining the permits, but expects teachers to refund the difference if they leave after 1 year. No sick pay or holiday pay, and limited remuneration for cancelled lessons.

RECRUITMENT: Interesting cover letter, CV, scanned copies of qualifications, plus security and health checks to be sent. Interviews essential. Main hiring deadline for applications is mid-August.

TEACHERS FOR VIETNAM
PO Box 362, Salisbury, CT 06068, USA
- +1 860 480 5041
- info@teachersforvietnam.org
- www.teachersforvietnam.org

NUMBER OF TEACHERS: About 5 teachers of ESL for university posts in Vietnam to further Vietnam's educational development by increasing fluency of spoken English and to build bridges between people in Vietnam and the West, particularly the USA.

QUALIFICATIONS: Must be university graduate so most volunteers are over 21. Some experience and/or training in TESL needed, plus eagerness to live and work in Vietnam.

CONDITIONS OF EMPLOYMENT: Academic year from late August to May.

SALARY: Programme application fee $50. Programme pays for airfare, health insurance and travel during Tet holiday. Host universities pay a cost-of-living salary and in most cases provide free housing, usually a room or suite in a campus guesthouse.

FACILITIES/SUPPORT: In-country orientation session provided, which covers cultural issues as well as practical matters for foreigners newly arrived in Vietnam.

RECRUITMENT: Deadline for applications is 1 April. Face-to-face interviews in New York area required.

CONTACT: John Dippel, Executive Director.

VUS (VIETNAM USA SOCIETY) ENGLISH CENTERS
Head Office, 189 Nguyen Thi Minh Khai, District 1, Ho Chi Minh City
- +84 8 3925 9899 ext 165
- stephenthomas@vus-etsc.edu.vn; tutran@vus-etsc.edu.vn
- www.vus.edu.vn

NUMBER OF TEACHERS: Approximately 160 part-time and full-time.

PREFERENCE OF NATIONALITY: None.

QUALIFICATIONS: Minimum BA degree in any discipline and teaching certification (CELTA, TESOL, TEFL or equivalent). Teachers with prior classroom experience have priority but inexperienced teachers are encouraged to apply.

CONDITIONS OF EMPLOYMENT: 1-year contract. Full-time teachers can expect 80–100 hours per month of student contact. Weekend classes are scheduled between 8am and 9.30pm (with Sunday finish at 5pm). Weekday classes are from 5pm to 9.30pm and a small number in the mornings. Most classes are in 2-hour blocks.

SALARY: $17–$24 per hour (net) based on qualifications, experience and outcome of demonstration lesson.

FACILITIES/SUPPORT: VUS provides guidance in completing the work permit application process and reimburses the cost ($300). Additional benefits for full-time teachers include free Vietnamese lessons and vacation allowance. VUS works closely with an accommodation agency run by Americans and Canadians which has proven itself to be pro-active and supportive.

RECRUITMENT: Local recruiting and posting on sites such as Dave's ESL Cafe. Interviews are essential. Local interviewees conduct a demonstration lesson as part of the interview process. Overseas candidates must submit a lesson plan as part of the interview process. Interviews with candidates located abroad are conducted via Skype.

CONTACT: Stephen Thomas, HR Manager (Foreign Teachers).

ZACHARY KEESTER

Zachary Keester reflects on his experiences as an English Teacher with ILA Vietnam:

'I decided to teach English as a foreign language after I graduated from University in 2009. The economic climate in the United States was extremely volatile at the time, especially for an undergrad with very limited work experience. I looked around at my peers and myself and realised that there weren't any doors opening for us anytime soon. I wanted to live my life and see the world. Deciding to go into EFL teaching was the best and easiest decision I had ever made.

'Originally, the plan was to go to South Korea and work in their public school system through the EPIK programme. I had a successful interview with the EPIK coordinator and was all set to go. However, I was told the position would not be available until February 2011; it was August and I didn't want to wait. Meanwhile, my friend who had taught in Korea, Vietnam and had just come back after teaching in Turkey, told me about the CELTA training course offered at ILA in Vietnam. I looked online and discovered that the next available course started in early November. I enrolled and booked my round-trip ticket to Vietnam immediately.

'Two weeks into the CELTA at ILA, I cancelled my return flight and notified the school in Korea that I would not be teaching there in February. I would stay and teach in Vietnam.

'Directly after completing the CELTA course, I was hired by ILA on a full-time contract. It was great. I couldn't think of a better place to start my teaching career. ILA offers its teachers so much support and really encourages professional development. I knew immediately that it was the right school for me. It wasn't your run-of-the-mill EFL school that hired under-qualified backpackers off the street. It was highly respected by both teachers and locals alike.

'The best part about working for ILA in Vietnam is the hours and the location. As a full-time teacher you generally work on Saturday and Sunday, leaving you with five days off to relax or travel. As for location, Vietnam is centrally located, making travel to Thailand, Burma, Cambodia, Indonesia, Laos and Malaysia incredibly easy.

'I have recently completed a Young Learner course at ILA that was offered to me completely free of charge. I am currently planning on earning my MA in Education online, while I continue to develop my teaching skills and methodology by working for ILA. ILA hasn't just opened doors for me; it has opened the world to me.'

CAMBODIA

Cambodia is now a stable and welcoming country, having emerged from the shadow of its tragic past. The ELT market has been wide open to private enterprise in Cambodia for a number of years and is now well established. Yet the British Council does not have a presence in the country.

It is one of the last bastions for the so-called 'backpacker teacher' where a knowledge of the language is in many cases sufficient to land a job. Things have not changed all that much from the early days when it was possible to rent a moto for the day, take a spin around Phnom Penh and ask for teaching hours at one of the language schools to be found on most street corners. The standards are more professional in the reputable schools like ACE, but there are many others who are not very fussy and do not expect to see a qualification.

Cambodia operates on a dollar economy, so few wages are quoted in riels. People normally use the local currency only for items that cost less than a dollar, ie 4,000 riels. Wages at the upmarket schools start at $15 an hour, whereas most others pay about $10 regardless of credentials. Regulation of schools is non-existent. Prospective teachers should arrive with extra passport photos and buy a Business E visa on arrival for $50, valid for one month. This can be extended at the Ministry of Foreign Affairs for up to a year at a time for $280. According to some long-stayers, this bureaucratic laxity attracts a high proportion of misfits and dubious types. Girlfriend-hunting often seems to be a stronger motivator than education, rather like Thailand used to be. One commentator on www.asiapundits.com taught in Cambodia for more than a year and went further by saying that '*the country is a true degenerate's playground*'.

Of course there are plenty of serious teachers in the country too. A teacher placement agency in Phnom Penh (www.teachersincambodia.org) recruits for positions in primary and secondary schools starting in August/September. One of the longest established schools is the Australian Centre for Education or ACE (see entry), which is flourishing. Other commercial institutes in Phnom Penh include ELT (www.eess.edu.kh) and Home of English International (www.homeofenglish.edu.kh), while others have gone bankrupt. When experienced teacher **Bradwell Jackson** from the US visited, he ascertained that the American Intercon Institute at 217 ABCD Mao Tse Tong Blvd (+855 12 771 113; www.aii.edu.kh) is happy to hire foreign teachers who are in Phnom Penh.

Willing volunteers will find plenty of options, for example in one of the three rural schools run by the charity CESHEO (www.ceshe.org/volunteering.html) and also Savong's School (www.savong.com) for children who can't afford tuition fees. The upfront volunteering fee is $200. On her gap year **Pascale Hunter** from Cambridge noticed a flyer for Savong's School up in her hostel in Siem Reap and spent a short time teaching teenagers and younger children there. Although she found the experience interesting, she felt it was '*fairly commercial, with the kids clamouring for western souvenirs*'. However, plenty of other volunteers have enjoyed their visit and are impressed by the dedication of the students.

Another organisation to try is Volunteer in Cambodia (www.volunteerincambodia.org), which recruits volunteers to teach at Conversations With Foreigners (CWF), a local conversational English school in Phnom Penh (No 247C, Street 271, Toul Pumbung II). Money raised by the programme goes towards the Cambodian Rural Development Team, a local organisation working to improve livelihoods in rural communities. Volunteers stay three months (there are specific group starting dates) and do not pay to volunteer, though they do pay for their accommodation and meals, which currently costs $725 in the shared volunteer house for three months. Teaching qualifications/experience are an advantage, but not required.

LIST OF EMPLOYERS

AMERICAN EDUCATION CENTER

7E Mao Tse Tung Blvd, Sangkat Boeung Keng Kang I,
Khan Chamkarmorn, Phnom Penh

- +855 80 666345
- recruit@aec-cambodia.com
- www.aec.edu.kh

NUMBER OF TEACHERS: 6 part-time and full-time.
PREFERENCE OF NATIONALITY: None.
QUALIFICATIONS: BA in English or similar, or BEd, ESL experience.
CONDITIONS OF EMPLOYMENT: 1 year. 5 hours a day.
SALARY: Negotiable depending on experience.
FACILITIES/SUPPORT: No assistance with accommodation. AEC arranges for processing business visas.
RECRUITMENT: Via local advertisements in newspapers and on websites. Skype interviews are possible.
CONTACT: Janet English, Director.

AUSTRALIAN CENTRE FOR EDUCATION

46, Street 214, Sangkat Boeung Raing, Khan Daun Penh,
(PO Box 860), Phnom Penh, Cambodia

- +855 23 724204 or +855 23 881026
- recruitment.cambodia@idp.com
- www.idp.com/cambodia

NUMBER OF TEACHERS: 55 foreign teachers at two campuses in Phnom Penh and one in Siem Reap.
PREFERENCE OF NATIONALITY: Any native English speaker is acceptable, though Australians preferred.
QUALIFICATIONS: Undergraduate degree plus CELTA or 120-hour equivalent. 1 year's teaching experience, with proven ability to work autonomously. IELTS experience valued. Police clearance may be required.
CONDITIONS OF EMPLOYMENT: 21–23 hours of classes a week, but teachers are expected to attend at the school 40 hours per week. Minimum commitment 6 months for terms starting in January, April, July and September. Hours vary: the school is open 6am–8pm and on Saturday mornings. Teachers needed for general courses, English for Academic Purposes and ESP.
SALARY: $18–$25 per hour freelance; $1,700–$2,100 per month.
FACILITIES/SUPPORT: Advice given on affordable accommodation which is not hard to find in Phnom Penh (rents from $150 a month plus utilities). Assistance given before arrival on obtaining visas and school contributes to costs. The school is well equipped and resourced and a variety of professional development sessions are held at least once a month. School pays half of contributions to medical insurance.
RECRUITMENT: Web advertisements, word of mouth. Interviews are required, but can be over the phone and are carried out in Australia from time to time. Professional references are checked.
CONTACT: Theara Chea, HR Co-ordinator (theara.chea@idp.com).

CONVERSATIONS WITH FOREIGNERS (CWF)

#247c, Street 271, Sangkat Toul Tom Poung II, Khan
Chamcarmon, Phnom Penh

- +855 23 636 3040
- info@volunteerincambodia.org
- www.volunteerincambodia.org

Free 3-month voluntary programme to teach conversational English in Phnom Penh.
NUMBER OF VOLUNTEERS: 17–30.
PREFERENCE OF NATIONALITY: None. Must have a native level command of the language.
QUALIFICATIONS: TEFL or teaching experience not essential, though many come with some. Volunteers should have a real commitment to education and development and be capable of teaching English in a way that is sensitive to the development context and of encouraging the students to express pride in Cambodia. All ages from 18, with average in mid-20s.
CONDITIONS OF EMPLOYMENT: 3 months beginning in December, March, June and September each year. Volunteers teach up to 5 hours a day on week days. Classes can be any time 6–8am, 11am–1pm or 4–8pm.
SALARY: None. Volunteers fund their own living and travel expenses. Any profits go to fund the rural development work of partner agency, the Cambodian Rural Development Team.
FACILITIES/SUPPORT: Accommodation provided in volunteer house which costs $725 for 3 months including meals Monday to Friday, excluding public holidays. If volunteers prefer to live independently CWF can help with finding a place to stay. 2-week orientation programme includes lessons in Khmer language and culture, child safety training, teacher training and an optional trip to the province where volunteers learn more about rural development work and participate in a homestay. Assistance given in renewing Type E business visa which volunteers can buy on arrival.
RECRUITMENT: Direct application through website or through partner agencies: Working Abroad, LoveTEFL, Ecoteer or Volunteer Forever.
CONTACT: Volunteer Recruitment & Marketing Manager.

NUMBER OF TEACHERS: 40.

PREFERENCE OF NATIONALITY: None.

QUALIFICATIONS: Degree holders are preferred, but positions for non-degree holders are also available. In-house training is offered, and professional development is encouraged under guidance of the team leaders.

CONDITIONS OF EMPLOYMENT: 12-month contract. Students study in 3 shifts: morning session 7.30am–11.30am, afternoon session 1pm–5pm, and evening session 5.30pm–8pm. Teachers are offered a choice of classes within these time frames.

SALARY: $7 per classroom hour. Teachers submit a 5% tax return.

FACILITIES/SUPPORT: School has a library, computer laboratory and large play area which teachers may use during class time. All classrooms are air-conditioned.

RECRUITMENT: Via email to HR Dept.

LAOS AND BURMA

Laos was the last country but one in the region to open its doors to foreigners, while Myanmar (Burma) is the last. Over the past few years a number of English schools have opened in the Laotian capital of Vientiane, ranging from well-established institutions to small, shop-front enterprises staffed with locals or expats passing through on tourist visas. When English institutes first started opening in Vientiane, most were fly-by-night operations. But there are now several international English-medium schools such as the Lao-American College and the Vientiane International School (www.vislao.com), and also better-organised private language schools like ARDA Language Centres (www.ardalaos.com).

The visa procedures have settled down in Laos. If possible, a letter of invitation should be obtained from your employer before arrival which entitles the holder to enter Laos on a B2 visa (non-immigrant, business visa) instead of a tourist visa. With the B2 visa you can apply for a work permit which will cost around US$240 for a year while the resident card costs $90. Only the most elite schools will cover the cost of the visa, although most will assist you in obtaining it. In order to obtain the invitation, your sponsor needs a copy of your passport and probably copies of any educational credentials. Otherwise it is possible to buy a one-month tourist visa at the border for US$35. After arrival, the employer will have to make the invitation for a B2 visa. Then the teacher will be required to leave the country (usually across the border to Thailand) and re-enter on the B2 visa for a further fee.

Salaries and conditions of work can vary as much as the schools themselves. Vientiane College (see entry below) provides the best working conditions, staff development programme and benefit package. The majority of language schools pay by the hour, from as little as $5 up to $15 at the higher end of the range.

Demand for native English speakers also occasionally comes from bilingual schools such as the Oscar School and pre-schools or nurseries. Teaching opportunities also exist in the larger provincial centres such as Luang Prabang and Svannakhet and, in Vientiane, in larger companies and ministries for in-house teachers. Again, conditions vary greatly and there are often delays with payments and payments may be made in the local currency (kip).

Some volunteer opportunities exist in Laos, for example with the Thai organisation Openmind Projects (www.openmindprojects.org) and with the Sunshine School (see entry). The former programme costs €290 admin fee plus €340 for the first fortnight, which covers homestay accommodation, local meals and a three-day orientation in Nong Khai on the Thai-Laotian border. Stays can be extended for €85 a week.

Until a few years ago, there was almost no scope for teaching English in reclusive, repressive Myanmar. With Aung San Suu Kyi's wish to run for the presidency, hopes have been rising that military rule will slowly give way to a more open and pro-western system that would support English language schools. It is possible that Burma is shaping up to be the next EFL frontier. Although it remains the poorest country in Asia, with an average per capita annual income of not much more than $1,000, this is changing with increased industrialisation. For example Coca Cola has built two factories to supply a new local market. Business visas can be purchased on arrival at the airport for $50 but only if you have a letter of invitation. These are valid for 70 days and can be renewed by crossing the border to Thailand. To turn this into a one-year working visa will cost about $500, which some schools will reimburse at the end of the academic year.

The number of language schools that employ native speakers is still small, but rising. It is worth checking Asian teaching sites and also investigating possibilities at international and private schools such as Yangon Academy, which follows an American curriculum (www.yangon-academy.org), and Horizon International School, which has several branches and kindergartens around the capital (http://hism.co).

Several voluntourism organisations like Greenheart Travel in Chicago (www.cci-exchange.com/teach-myanmar) operate a Teach English in Myanmar programme that starts monthly and lasts a year. Participants pay varying programme fees of $1,085 for qualified teachers to $2,500 for those who take a TEFL training course on arrival, and earn a monthly salary of $800–$1,200. To be eligible you must be a native speaker aged 21–45 with a degree. Global Work Travel offers the same programme. Note that some agencies such as Thailand-based XploreAsia (www.xploreasia.org/teach-in-myanmar) promise only to facilitate interviews rather than guarantee placement.

NGOs are becoming more active in the country. The British Council has an expanding teaching centre in Yangon (formerly Rangoon), and was advertising for teachers with a TEFL certificate and at least two years of experience in summer 2015.

The lack of basic infrastructure in Yangon, such as faltering electricity, very slow internet and pot-holed roads makes everyday life difficult. The stock of rental housing has not kept pace with the influx of people, and what you can find is either very expensive or very grotty. This situation should improve as investment starts to flow into the country. Teachers in international schools earn decent salaries (eg $2,000+ a month) with few outgoings. Eating and drinking is very cheap (eg about $3 a day) and basic apartments can be found starting at $200 a month plus next to nothing for utilities.

For information about teaching programmes for Burmese refugees in Northern Thailand, see the chapter on Thailand.

LIST OF EMPLOYERS

21ST CENTURY SCHOOL OF ENGLISH
74/6 Sisangvone Rd. That Luang Tai, Vientiane, Lao PDR
+856 21 452500
info@21centuryeducation.com
www.21centuryeducation.com

NUMBER OF TEACHERS: 13.
PREFERENCE OF NATIONALITY: American, British, Australian, New Zealander.
QUALIFICATIONS: CELTA/TESOL/TEFL.
CONDITIONS OF EMPLOYMENT: 1-year or 6-month contract with 13.5+ teaching hours per week.
SALARY: $13–$17 per hour.
FACILITIES/SUPPORT: School will arrange 6- or 12-month work visas; payment terms vary.
RECRUITMENT: Usually via the internet or word of mouth. Interviews are essential and can be carried out from the UK or USA.

ARDA LANGUAGE CENTRE
13 South Road, Pakse, Champasak Province, Lao PDR
+856 312 14674 / +856 205 4090773
pakselc@ardalaos.com
www.ardalaos.com

NUMBER OF TEACHERS: 2-3 every two years.
PREFERENCE OF NATIONALITY: None.
QUALIFICATIONS: TEFL/TESOL/CELTA is mandatory.
CONDITIONS OF EMPLOYMENT: 1 year contract. 48 teaching hours a month.

SALARY: Volunteer role, though if the teacher does not have sponsorship, the school can support teachers up to $5,400 a year.
FACILITIES/SUPPORT: Assistance given with inspecting housing options and with negotiations with the landlord. One room apartments with bathroom cost $100-$120 per month. School admin staff assist with visa applications and school pays for the visa and work permits.
RECRUITMENT: Letter of interest, submission of CV & educational documents, references and interviews in Laos.
CONTACT: Biju Abraham, Centre Director (ardapakse@gmail.com).

BRAINWORKS SCHOOL – TOTAL GROUP OF SCHOOLS
280 U Wisara Road, Kamayut Township, Yangon
+95 01501976
hr@brainworksschool.com
www.brainworks-total.com

The Total Learning Academy has 9 K-12 schools.
NUMBER OF TEACHERS: Lots.
PREFERENCE OF NATIONALITY: USA, Canada, UK, Australia or New Zealand.
QUALIFICATIONS: TEFL/CELTA plus preference given to those with BA or MA. Must have one year's classroom experience and experience of living in a developing country.
CONDITIONS OF EMPLOYMENT: 12 months. 43-hour week, 24 contact hours.
SALARY: $1,200–$2,000 (net) depending on experience.

FACILITIES/SUPPORT: Shared air-conditioned accommodation provided. Employer takes care of all government taxes and registration requirements including paying for flights every 70 days to complete visa renewal process.

RECRUITMENT: Online advertising, eg www.asiateachingjobs.com. Applications by email then Skype inteviews.

MOTE OO EDUCATION

182/194, Hnin Si Condo A/B, 7th floor, Botahtaung Pagoda Road, Pazundaung Township, Yangon

☎ +95 931 115 669

✉ info@moteoo.org or moteooeducation@gmail.com

🖥 www.moteoo.org

Mote Oo Education works with civil society organisations and post-secondary schools in Myanmar and on the Thai-Burma border.

NUMBER OF TEACHERS: Varies according to number of requests for Learning Support Volunteers from partner organisations.

PREFERENCE OF NATIONALITY: Must have native/advanced level English language proficiency.

QUALIFICATIONS: Minimum 2 years teaching background. Enthusiastic, experienced volunteers needed, mainly over 24. Must be self-reliant, adaptable people who can fit into challenging environments and provide guidance and assistance to future community leaders, teachers and activists. As well as teaching English, suitable volunteers will assist with teaching social science and civic education courses, training teachers and helping with curriculum development.

CONDITIONS OF EMPLOYMENT: Minimum 3 month stay. 6–12 teaching hours per week.

SALARY: None. Where possible, host organisation provides a small stipend. Volunteer teacher must cover cost of travel, business visa, food, health insurance and accommodation (unless host organisation is able to provide).

FACILITIES/SUPPORT: Basic orientation package on Myanmar and its culture is provided. Advice given to volunteers on logistics, cheap accommodation and travel. Host organisation can usually issue visa invitation letter for business visa; tourist visa is fine for urban regions.

RECRUITMENT: Online advertising, websites, social media.

CONTACT: Josephine Nan Moo, Volunteer Coordinator.

SUNSHINE SCHOOL

Ban Si Meung, Vientiane, Laos

☎ +856 21 214522

✉ sunshinelaos@gmail.com

🖥 http://sunshineschool.tumblr.com/volunteer

NUMBER OF TEACHERS: Volunteers only.

PREFERENCE OF NATIONALITY: English-speaking countries.

QUALIFICATIONS: Creative approach to working with the kids is important; experience in teaching or experience with young kids are both good assets.

CONDITIONS OF EMPLOYMENT: 1–10 months (volunteers needed September–July). School hours include 7 teaching periods from 8am to 4pm on weekdays. Volunteers usually have 4–5 teaching periods a day (maybe less depending on the volunteer's needs), in kindergarten, primary or junior secondary classes. Volunteers may also be involved in creative activities with the children or teachers' classes or teaching village children and youth on the weekends

SALARY: Voluntary basis only. Long-term volunteers staying 6–12 months may get a small living allowance (max $100 a month) or help with housing, depending on the financial condition of the school at the time.

FACILITIES/SUPPORT: Long-term volunteers will be supported with working visas (which cost $250–$450). All volunteers get a vegetarian lunch provided on school days. No accommodation provided, but local guesthouses charge only $60–$90 per month.

RECRUITMENT: Direct application to school.

VIENTIANE COLLEGE

PO Box 4144 (Rue 23 Singha), Vientiane, Laos

☎ +856 21 414873/412598

✉ info@vientianecollege.com

🖥 www.vientianecollege.com

NUMBER OF TEACHERS: 40.

PREFERENCE OF NATIONALITY: Native English speakers from any region.

QUALIFICATIONS: Minimum bachelor's degree and CELTA. ESP/EAP experience preferred.

CONDITIONS OF EMPLOYMENT: Sessional and contract.

SALARY: From $1,500–$2,800 per month less 10% income tax.

FACILITIES/SUPPORT: Assistance with finding accommodation. School arranges and pays for work permit and residence visa. In-house training programme.

RECRUITMENT: Personal interview necessary.

CONTACT: Denley Pike, Director.

TAIWAN

The ELT industry is more than thriving in Taiwan, a country that remains a magnet for English teachers of all backgrounds. Part of the appeal of teaching in Taiwan is that the wages compare favourably with countries such as Japan, yet the cost of living is significantly lower. Equally important is that finding a job here is fairly easy. It used to be the case that schools were looking for only three things: a passport from an English-speaking country, a bachelor's degree and a pulse. These days, however, the better schools are becoming choosier, it is a little more difficult to get a working visa and many schools and local education departments are looking for an ELT qualification and prior experience. Nevertheless, the opportunities for teaching English in Taiwan are endless. Hundreds of private cramming institutes or *buxibans* continue to teach young children and high school students for university entrance examinations.

However, there is more regulation than there used to be. Only the reputable language schools, those that are fully licensed as foreign language schools, are permitted to employ English-speaking foreigners and sponsor them for visas, provided the teachers are willing to sign a one-year contract. Only native English-speaker teachers with a university degree (in any subject) are eligible.

The market for teaching children from age two seems boundless at the moment, so anyone who enjoys working with young children, ie likes to sing songs, play games and comfort little ones who miss their mums, may be able to find a job. However, government regulations require that teachers working in kindergartens be fully qualified kindergarten specialists. This means that CELTA-trained teachers can no longer legally work in kindergartens. Some do, and a few have been deported. Language organisations that specialise in teaching early primary school-aged children generally provide detailed lesson plans, which means that little time needs to be spent on lesson preparation.

FINDING A JOB

Taiwanese consumers of English have a clear preference for the North American accent because of strong trading and cultural links between Taiwan and the USA. However, many schools will hire presentable native English speakers, whatever their accent. Few want their staff to be able to speak Chinese; in fact one teacher reported seeing a sign in a *buxiban* window boasting 'Teachers Not Speak Chinese'. Language teachers and tutors working in Taipei are predominantly American; native English speakers of other nationalities tend to gravitate to Southern Taiwan. **Amanda Searle** from the UK felt only slightly discriminated against:

> *My employer claimed that they did not discriminate between people of different nationalities, but this is not what I have found. North Americans are the first choice when hours are allocated. I have had students complain that they wanted an American teacher because they wanted to learn 'real' English, though I have never had a student complain to the secretaries or me that my accent was difficult to understand.*

On the subject of discrimination, it seems that the ideal age for teachers is late 20s, and that both schools and agents are often accused of passing over older candidates, even those in their late 30s.

A few of the major organisations hire overseas either directly or via a North American agent. The Hess Educational Organization (see entry below), whose head office is in Taiwan, has a representative in North America who can send out information to enquirers. Interviews are conducted either in Taiwan or by telephone from Taiwan. The agency TEFLOne Recruitment (www.teflone.com) is one of many that recruit qualified teachers for posts in Taiwan as well as other countries in the Far East. The company Kid Castle (www.kidcastle.com.tw/en/jobs/apply.html) has more than 200 franchise schools in Taiwan that recruit individually, only after a face-to-face interview.

JAMES ROBINSON

James Robinson is one satisfied client of www.teflone.com and wrote from the small town of Taoyuan in Kaohsiung County in Taiwan's interior. After being made redundant as a welder/fabricator, he did a TESOL course, which he describes as 'the best move I ever made'. Soon afterwards he met the chief recruiter for TEFLOne, David Coles, to hear about opportunities with the Shane School.

My interview was a very positive experience. I knew that Shane would offer peace of mind, a highly efficient service and above all a friendly interview. It is for these reasons that Shane stood out from amongst the rest. Many other interviewers from other organisations sounded a bit officious and none of them offered as realistic and honest information about life in Taiwan as Shane did. It also sorted out all the administrative requirements such as work permits and bank accounts and patiently answered questions it had probably been asked a hundred times before!

My hours are currently about 25 a week, a lot more if you include the preparation, but a million times more interesting than welding! Most of the children are so eager to learn and I was astonished how the really young children retained new information.

Entertainment is the key. Yes, it was a learning curve and, yes, I made mistakes. But after a few weeks the preparation became far easier and it was a far more rewarding and positive experience. I think it's important to make things happen for yourself, eg to go climbing and cycling and participate in activities you like. This can be hugely rewarding for your inspiration as a teacher, to meet local people and get to know your new environment. As a result, my spare time is incredible. I still find it amazing that I can be out of the city and in the national park in 45 minutes, with its new aromas, wildlife and breathtaking scenery.

Many websites contain a wealth of detail about Taiwan and what it's like to teach there. Jobs and lots of information about teaching in Taiwan can be found at www.tealit.com (one of the best), www.taiwandeal.com, www.orseek.com and www.englishintaiwan.com. The US-based recruiter for Asia Reach to Teach (www.reachtoteachrecruiting.com) is very active in Taiwan, where its main centre is located. Another possibility is ESL Dewey (www.esldewey.com.tw) that posts ads.

Reports sometimes surface of teachers accepting jobs via an agent or directly before arriving in Taiwan, only to find that they have been placed not in Taipei as they agreed, but in some three-goat mountain village. Discrepancies also sometimes occur between the contracts given to teachers in English and those given to employers in Chinese. The Chinese part is the legal part of the contract, so it would be a sensible precaution to have this translated before signing.

Many people arrive on spec to look for work. This is straightforward for Britons, Americans, Canadians and a few other nationalities who can stay for 60 or 90 days (renewable once) without a visa. Finding a *buxiban* willing to hire you is not as difficult as finding a good one willing to hire you. If possible, try to sit in on one or two classes or talk to another teacher before signing a contract. (If a school is unwilling to permit this, it doesn't bode well.) Read the fine print of the contract to find out what the penalties are for breaking a contract.

On the strength of the TEFL course she had completed at the American Language Institute in San Diego and a year spent teaching in Poland, freelance photographer **Alicia Wszelaki** wanted a taste of teaching in the Far East. She joined a short summer teaching project in Taiwan for adolescent girls, run by the American Language Village (www.kidscamp.com.tw) that she had noticed on Dave's ESL Cafe. Teachers were housed in a hotel not far from the camp and she found working conditions to be very good although the hours were long over 10 straight days:

> *I realised a few days into the camp that this was indeed a summer camp and the kids were there not only to learn English but also to have fun. We played games, had lessons on pizza and hamburgers and other subjects that were more real world. The students really enjoyed these. There were lots of songs and dancing. If you choose to do a camp of this nature, bring lots of energy, smiles, optimism, an open mind and water. It was a wonderful and rewarding experience. The students were great and the teachers were some of the most incredible people I have met – a truly great blend of personalities and experiences.*

The best time to arrive is at the beginning of summer (the end of the school year), when Chinese parents enrol their offspring in English-language summer schools. Late August is another peak time for hiring, though there are openings year round. Word of mouth is even more important in Taiwan than elsewhere because there is no association of recognised language schools.

As always, travellers' hostels will be helpful, as reported by **Bradwell Jackson** from a trip to investigate the teaching scene:

> *I couldn't believe all the English schools in Taipei. I presumed that the market must be saturated by now and that it would be too difficult to find a job, but after talking to the people in the know at the Taipei Hostel (www. taipeihostel.com/teach.html), I found out that this was not the case. The hostel is English-teaching central for foreigners and the common room is where all the newcomers meet to get the latest on the English teaching situation. Once you get the low down from the old hands there, just pick a direction and start walking. After passing about three corners, you'll definitely see an English school, probably two. Have your introduction ready, march on in there and sell yourself.*

Apparently some hostels feature blackboards on which job vacancies are chalked up as the hostel manager is notified. A good noticeboard is located in the student lounge on the sixth floor of the Mandarin Training Center of National Taiwan Normal University at 129 Hoping East Road.

Once you have decided to approach some schools for work, make contact by email or telephone in the first place. Next you must present yourself in person to the schools. Many schools in Taiwan are used to and expect cold-callers. Take along your university certificate and any other qualifications, and take the trouble to look presentable. **Peter McGuire** was told point blank that your appearance and how you conduct yourself at interview count for everything, and concluded that '*all your experience in life or teaching in other countries really doesn't mean a thing here*'. **David Hughes** specifically recommends paying attention to your feet:

> *Bring plenty of socks/tights. You have to leave your shoes at the door of Chinese homes, and it's difficult to appear serious and composed with a toe poking through.*

Anyone with a high level of education (ie a master's degree or PhD) might find work attached to one of the scores of universities and colleges, where working conditions are very good. Foreigners are also allowed to work in public high schools, though it is difficult to function without knowledge of the language.

FREELANCE TEACHING

Work visas are valid only for employment with the sponsoring employer. However, many teachers teach private students, which pays handsomely from NT$700–$1,000 per hour. In a country where foreigners are sometimes approached in bars or on trains and asked to give English lessons, it is not hard to set up independently as an English tutor. **Peter McGuire** found the dream job of tutoring a travel agent three to six hours a day, seven days a week and then was invited to accompany his client on a trip to Hawaii: *'Some of my lessons are given at private clubs, saunas, in taxicabs and fine restaurants. Actually, it's kind of unbelievable.'*

Although it would be possible to make a good living by teaching privately, you will need to work for a school in order to obtain the visa. A helpful hint is to have business cards printed up, calling yourself 'English consultant'. It is even more lucrative if you can muster a small group of students and charge them, say, NT$300 per person. Women usually find this easier to set up than men. The main problem is finding appropriate premises.

Cancelled hours are a perennial problem. Freelancers will find it prudent to explain to students gently but forcefully that they will be liable to pay if they cancel without giving sufficient notice; most will not object. You can even request one month's fees in advance. Once you are established, other jobs in the English field may come your way such as correcting business communications, transcribing lyrics from pop tapes or writing CVs and letters of application for Taiwanese students hoping to study overseas.

REGULATIONS

Canadian, American, British, Australian and New Zealand passport holders are permitted to stay visa-free for 90 days (apart from Australians who can stay for only 30 days). If in that time you secure a job, your future employer will then apply for a work permit, which should take 3–4 weeks if the application is in order. After that the teacher will have to obtain a formal visitor visa before applying for the ARC (Alien Resident Certificate).

Information on visas should be requested from the Taiwan Economic & Cultural Office in your country of origin, all linked from www.taiwanembassy.org.

To stay legally in the country, teachers need to obtain an Alien Resident Certificate (ARC) from one of the many national immigration offices. Once you find a school offering a one-year contract, your school applies to the local education authority for a working permit, for which they will need a copy and translation of your degree diploma, contract, medical certificate (requiring various tests for HIV, TB, etc) and passport. Some employers (like Hess) insist on a criminal record check from your home country. Some schools may make a contribution towards permit costs, especially if you renew for a second year.

After the work visa has been issued, tax will be withheld from your pay. The tax rate for foreigners who stay in Taiwan for less than 183 days in one calendar year (category A) is 18%. After six months, the rate of tax drops to between 5% and 13% (normally 6%) but only on income beyond the standard exemption of NT$85,000.

CONDITIONS OF WORK

Most jobs are paid by the hour, and for the past three or four years the minimum hourly rate a teacher should expect is NT$550–600 (approximately US$18). For a monthly salary you should expect to receive between NT$50,000 and NT$65,000 (average US$1,800) for 25 hours per week. Occasionally the rate for cushy morning classes drops below, and unsociable hours are rewarded (if you're lucky) with a premium rate of

NT$600–$700. Rates outside Taipei (where the cost of living is lower) tend to be slightly higher due to the relative scarcity of teachers.

As usual some schools are shambolic when it comes to timetabling their teachers' hours. In a profit-driven atmosphere, classes start and finish on demand and can be cancelled at short notice if the owner decides that there are too few students to make it economic. When you are starting a new job, ask your employer to be specific about the actual number of hours you will be given and how scattered they might be throughout the day and evening. It is not uncommon for teachers who have been promised a full timetable at the point of hiring to find themselves with fewer hours than promised and a considerably lower pay packet.

Although exploitation of teachers (and students) is not as rife as in Korea, you should be prepared for anything, as **Rusty Holmes** had to be:

> *The real reason there was such a high turnover rate of staff at one school was because of the supervisor's habit of barging into class at unpredictable moments and accusing the teacher (especially my Scottish colleague) of mispronouncing words, when she herself could barely speak English. The worst incidents occurred when she beat her own children in the face for getting poor grades, when she engaged a parent in a fistfight over a tuition dispute and when she physically ran her husband out of the school, all right in front of our students.*

However, unacceptable behaviour can be found in the teaching population too, as Sesame Street's one-time HR Manager **Adrian Maskery** explained:

> *Foreign teachers in Taiwan don't have a good reputation amongst the local population here. Too many unskilled teachers take advantage of the situation. We have a word for being drunk and taking advantage of the local girls. This is what we are trying to change here, we would like to promote our image and turn things around.*

The usual problems which bedevil TEFL teachers occur in Taiwan, such as split shifts, often ending at 10pm, and compulsory weekend work, especially if you are teaching children. Few schools provide much creative training or incentives to do a good job. Like the educational system of China and so many other countries, Taiwanese state schools rely heavily on rote learning, making it difficult to introduce a more communicative approach, especially at the beginner level. Whereas some schools offer no guidance whatsoever, others leave almost nothing to the teacher. What is termed a 'training programme' often consists of a paint-by-numbers teaching manual. Here is an extract from the teacher's book of one major chain of schools:

> *How to teach ABCs (eg the letter K): Review A–J . . . Using the flash cards, say 'A – apple, B – boy, C – cat . . . J – jacket'. The whole class repeats after the teacher. Then say, 'A-B-C-D-E-F-G-H-I-J' and have the whole class repeat. Show the letter K flashcard. Say 'K' having the whole class repeat it each time you say it. Say 'K' 4 or 5 times.*

And so on. This certainly makes the inexperienced teacher's job easier but possibly also very boring. Not everyone will be comfortable with such a regimented curriculum.

LEISURE TIME

Flats are predictably expensive in Central Taipei so many teachers choose to commute from the suburbs by MRT where living conditions are more pleasant in any case. Rents tend to be in the region of NT$8,500–$20,000 per month per person. There are so many foreigners coming and going, and the locals are so friendly and helpful, that it is not too difficult to learn of flats becoming vacant. You will have to pay a month's rent in advance plus a further month's rent as a deposit or bond. Several schools will appoint a Chinese member of staff to chaperone new arrivals and translate on house-hunting trips.

Taipei has a rapid transit system that is far more enjoyable (and cheaper) than running a motorbike. Some teachers stay in hostels near the central station and commute to work in a satellite city where wages are higher than in Taipei (eg Tao Yuan and Chung Li). Without doubt, the biggest inconvenience and danger in Taiwan is on the roads. Taiwanese drivers often commit driving manoeuvres that would result in lynching in other countries. Red lights and traffic laws are more often than not ignored and foreigners compound the problem by riding too fast on scooters, with little experience, and often under the influence.

Not a single visitor to Taipei, which is one of the most densely populated cities in the world, fails to complain of the pollution, second only to that of Mexico City. Not only is the air choked with the fumes and noise of a million motorised vehicles, but there are also occasional scares that chemicals have infiltrated the water table, contaminating locally grown vegetables. One blogger maintains that you have to carry an umbrella to protect your skin and clothes from falling acid rain (www.roadjunky.com/article/654/teaching-english-in-taiwan). The weather is another serious drawback. The typhoon season lasts from July to October, bringing stormy wet weather and mouldy clothes. The heat and humidity at this time also verge on the unbearable.

Taipei is not the only city to suffer from pollution; Taichung and Kaohsiung are also bad. Even Tainan, the most historic city in Taiwan, with many old temples, has some pollution and far too many cars. Kaohsiung, on the south-west coast, is a large industrial city with a high crime rate by Taiwan's standards but has the advantage of being near the popular resort of Kenting Beach and within reach of mountain campsites such as Maolin. The geographical advantage of Taichung, further north, is proximity to the mountains as well as a good climate and cultural activities. The east coast is more tranquil, though some find it dull.

Wherever you decide to teach, one of the highlights of living in Taiwan is the hospitality of the locals. In fact some people report being smothered by kindness, since the Taiwanese will not accept a refusal of any food or drink offered, and even paying for meals or drinks can be a struggle. In general, apart from some petty crime, corrupt politicians and fairly well-hidden gang activity, Taiwan is virtually crime free, so you are free to follow your leisure pursuits without worry. Taipei has a 24-hour social scene that can seriously cut into savings. Heavy drinking is commonplace. Films are usually shown in English with Chinese subtitles. For the truly homesick there are some English-style pubs with pool tables and darts boards. For **Rusty Holmes**, the food was a highlight:

Eating out is just as much a pastime in Taiwan as it is in Hong Kong. There are countless little mom-and-pop restaurants that offer delicious and inexpensive food. My favourite is the black pepper steak. Considering the high price of food in supermarkets, it would be cheaper to eat out than to cook at home. Taiwan is also a fruit-lover's paradise, though most are expensive by American standards. My favourite is the outstanding sugarcane Taiwan produces.

LIST OF EMPLOYERS

GLORIA ENGLISH SCHOOL

22 Alley, 17–14, Lane 66, Huan-Nan Road, Ping-Jen City, Taoyuan

📞 +886 3 495 1751/2

✉ gloria@glo.com.tw; ges.job.tw@gmail.com

🖥 www.glo.com.tw

NUMBER OF TEACHERS: 100 for 18 cram schools in Taoyuan County (near Taipei).

PREFERENCE OF NATIONALITY: American or Canadian.

QUALIFICATIONS: Bachelor's degree, or 2-year college diploma and TESOL/TEFL certificate.

CONDITIONS OF EMPLOYMENT: 12-month contracts. Most classes are between 4pm and 9pm on weekdays and all day Saturday. Average minimum 20 hours per week; most teach 24–30.

SALARY: NT$650 per hour for teachers without previous teaching experience (approximately US$20). Deductions vary from nothing to 10% depending on length of employment. End-of-contract bonus of NT$25,000 plus other bonuses given throughout the year, including NT25–$30,000 bonus for contract renewal.

FACILITIES/SUPPORT: Rent-free accommodation at one of the school's dormitories provided for 15 months. School will provide assistance with all related visa paperwork, but teachers are responsible for paying for their work permits. Training given including one-to-one workshops.

RECRUITMENT: Online job postings, eg on www.mytefljobs. com, newspaper job postings, referrals by current or previous employees. Phone interviews are mandatory. If the applicant is already in Taiwan, in-person interviews are preferable.

CONTACT: Celia Chou, HR Manager.

HESS INTERNATIONAL EDUCATIONAL ORGANIZATION

No 107, Section 2, Minquan E Road, Zhongshan District, Taipei City 104

- +886 2 2592 6998
- hesswork@hess.com.tw
- www.hess.com.tw/en

NUMBER OF TEACHERS: 600 native English-speaking teachers in more than 150 branches throughout Taiwan. About 250 new teachers hired each year.

PREFERENCE OF NATIONALITY: American, Australian, British, Canadian, Irish, New Zealander and South African.

QUALIFICATIONS: Bachelor's degree (in any subject) plus desire to work with varied age groups and to experience Chinese culture. Those holding an associate degree are welcome to apply provided they hold a TEFL/TESOL certificate as well. Applicants must provide a criminal background check from their home country.

CONDITIONS OF EMPLOYMENT: 1-year renewable contract. Three contract options are available to suit each teacher's preference. 1) 20-hour Contract: 20 hours a week guaranteed minimum; teaching hours are generally between 1.30pm and 9pm, Monday to Friday and between 8.30am and 6.30pm on Saturdays; students aged 5–16; classes are 100 minutes. 2) 20M Contract: 20 hours a week guaranteed minimum; teaching hours are generally between 8.30am and 9pm, Monday to Friday and between 8.30am and 6.30pm on Saturdays; students are aged 2–16. 3) 25-hour Contract: same as 20M Contract except guaranteed minimum number of hours is 25 per week.

SALARY: NT$580 per hour (gross) starting salary. Tax rate is 18% for first six months then drops to 5%. A raise and bonus system is also part of the pay structure.

FACILITIES/SUPPORT: Airport pick-up and free hotel accommodation during initial 9-day training period. Full TEFL and curriculum training provided with 4 follow-up training sessions after 1, 3, 6 and 9 months. Assistance given to obtain work permits and accommodation. Application process should be started 3 months in advance to allow time to collect visa and work permit documents.

RECRUITMENT: Apply online through Hess website (www.hess. com.tw/en); 4 major new teacher intakes per year. Applications accepted year round.

CONTACT: Amy Simpson, North American, British and Irish Applications and Interviews Consultant, English Human Resources Department (amy.simpson@hess.com.tw).

JUMP START

6F, No. 3, Lane 334, JianGuo S Road, Sec 2, Taipei 106

- +886 2 2369 4128
- eric@jumpstart.com.tw
- www.jumpstart.com.tw

English immersion schools for children aged 2–12.

QUALIFICATIONS: Native English speakers. Early childhood education/elementary teachers needed, eg with degree, preferably BEd (especially early childhood or elementary specialists). Must be enthusiastic and enjoy teaching children.

CONDITIONS OF EMPLOYMENT: To start mainly from 1 July or 1 September but other dates are possible. Guaranteed hours with extra hours available. Planned curriculum with complete teaching materials. Teachers should arrive a week in advance in order to receive a 2–3 day induction.

SALARY: Depends on qualifications and experience.

FACILITIES/SUPPORT: Work visa and health insurance provided. Airport pick-up. Accommodation provided on arrival.

CONTACT: Eric Ma.

KANG NING ENGLISH SCHOOL

No. 39 Park Road, Jhudong 310, Hsinchu County

- +886 3 594 3322
- tammy.lin@kangning.com.tw
- www.kangning.com.tw

NUMBER OF TEACHERS: 13 native English-speaking teachers for Language Department and Kindergarten Department.

PREFERENCE OF NATIONALITY: British, American, Canadian, Australian, South African and New Zealander.

QUALIFICATIONS: Minimum bachelor's degree or 2-year associate degree (eg from US community colleges) and a TESOL certificate.

CONDITIONS OF EMPLOYMENT: Minimum 1-year contract from July/August or January. Working hours in the Language Department 12.30pm–9.30pm. Working hours in the Kindergarten Department 9am–6pm.

SALARY: NT$58,000–$66,000 per month, depending on professional and academic qualifications, with end-of-contract bonus, partial airfare compensation, performance bonus and additional overtime pay and bonus. Average tax rate 6%.

FACILITIES/SUPPORT: Free Chinese lessons, staff trips, free meals, health insurance and paid national holidays/vacation. Fully formed curriculum cuts down on preparation time. Free accommodation for the first month during compulsory training and assistance to find suitable housing thereafter. KNES will also help teachers to obtain an Alien Residence Card (ARC) and open a bank account.

RECRUITMENT: Via website. Interview and reference check required. Occasional possibility of interviews in the US.

CONTACT: Tammy Lin.

KNS LANGUAGE INSTITUTE

313 Wunxin Road, Gushan District, Kaohsiung

© +886 7 550 5611

✉ knsleon@yahoo.ca

🖥 www.kns.com.tw

NUMBER OF TEACHERS: 45 teachers over 6 branches, mainly to teach children.

PREFERENCE OF NATIONALITY: North American, though all native English speakers accepted (American, Canadian, British, Irish, Australian, New Zealander and South African).

QUALIFICATIONS: At least a bachelor's degree. Teaching experience, TESOL certification or BEd preferred. Applicants must pass a medical examination.

CONDITIONS OF EMPLOYMENT: 1-year contracts. Full-time hours 2pm–9.10pm, Monday to Friday, in one location. Regimented teaching system. 30 teaching hours a week.

SALARY: NT$580 per hour plus end-of-contract bonus of NT$42,000.

FACILITIES/SUPPORT: Assistance with accommodation, no-interest loans, 2-week paid training, paid work permit fees, health insurance, 3-week summer vacation.

RECRUITMENT: Via internet, university placement offices, etc. Interviews in Taiwan or via Skype. Deadlines are 15 January for spring intake, 15 July for autumn start and 15 April for summer. Teachers must arrive at least 2 weeks early for training and set-up.

CONTACT: Leon Ranger, Recruitment Administrator (knsleon@yahoo.ca).

KOJEN ELS

6F, #9, Lane 90, Sung Chiang Road, Taipei

© +886 2 8663 8287/2581 8511

✉ luisarecruit@hibox.hinet.net or elsjobs@ms54.hinet.net

🖥 www.kojenenglish.com

NUMBER OF TEACHERS: Around 300 for 21 schools in Taipei plus 4 in Kaohsiung and 2 in Taichung.

PREFERENCE OF NATIONALITY: American, Canadian, British, Irish, Australian, New Zealander and South African.

QUALIFICATIONS: Minimum bachelor's degree. ESL experience and/or TESOL/TEFL certificate will increase chance of employment.

CONDITIONS OF EMPLOYMENT: 1-year contracts. Afternoon, evening and Saturday work. Pupils range in age from 4 to 13 in the children's department.

SALARY: Starting wage NT$580–$590 per hour. Bonuses paid at end of contract, calculated according to number of hours taught for hourly teachers.

FACILITIES/SUPPORT: 1 week's free accommodation in shared apartments. Training provided. National health and labour insurance provided. Library has 6,000+ handouts.

RECRUITMENT: Direct application/walk-ins and online adverts, eg on www.teachergig.com. Local interviews compulsory for some applicants. Applicants may be asked to teach a sample lesson. The original university degree certificate must be brought to Taiwan.

CONTACT: Luisa Sia, Recruiter/Consultant or Christine Kwok, Personnel Coordinator.

MICHAEL'S EFL SCHOOL

261 Tong-Nan Street, Hsin-Chu City

✉ michaelseflschool@gmail.com

A small privately owned school managed by a Brit and his Taiwanese wife since 1985.

NUMBER OF TEACHERS: 3 native English speakers.

QUALIFICATIONS: Native English speakers with recognised university degree. Teaching/coaching experience/EFL qualifications are an advantage. References required. A genuine interest in teaching is essential. (Ideal for candidates considering teaching as a career.)

CONDITIONS OF EMPLOYMENT: Minimum 1-year contract. Afternoon and evening work only. Student-centred classes for 7 to 17-year-olds with average class size 7–10 pupils. School aims to offer parents a family-focused approach to education in contrast to the franchise schools.

SALARY: NT$600 per teaching hour.

FACILITIES/SUPPORT: 1-month (paid) induction course. 10 days' paid holidays, 10 days' unpaid. Gratuity fund. Free airport pick-up. Assistance finding accommodation. Work visa, national health care, ARC, all available through school.

RECRUITMENT: Via UK education newspapers and the internet. In first instance send dates of availability and photo plus CV. Interview with Michael Weatherley (School Owner) by Skype or in person.

REACH TO TEACH

1606 80th Avenue, Algona, Iowa 50511, USA. Also #319 Minsheng Road, Taipei, Taiwan.

- ✆ +1 201 467 4612
- ✉ info@reachtoteachrecruiting.com
- 💻 www.ReachToTeachRecruiting.com/teach-english-in-taiwan.htm

For contacts in other countries, see entry at beginning of Asia chapter.

NUMBER OF TEACHERS: 150+.

PREFERENCE OF NATIONALITY: American, Canadian, British, Irish, Australian, New Zealander and South African.

QUALIFICATIONS: Positive, enthusiastic, dedicated and flexible attitude are the most important qualifications. Teaching experience and/or a 120-hour in-class TEFL qualification will often lead to a higher salary or more job placement options. A TEFL certificate is often a requirement.

CONDITIONS OF EMPLOYMENT: 1 year full-time. Schedules are generally either morning/afternoon (pre-school) or afternoon/evening (elementary school). Pre-school positions start twice a year (February and August) and applications are needed 3 months in advance. Elementary school positions can be applied for year round.

SALARY: Salaries are competitive with most elementary and pre-schools in Taiwan. Salaries vary depending on teaching experience, qualifications, location and benefits. Salaries usually range between NT$55,000 and $70,000 per month.

FACILITIES/SUPPORT: Taiwan visa guidance and airport collection are provided plus teacher orientation/training (when available). Teachers have the option of continued support and contact with Reach To Teach throughout their year-long placement. Agency hosts teacher social events and gatherings (mostly in Taipei).

RECRUITMENT: Applications submitted via website. In-depth interviews conducted over Skype, by phone or occasionally in person.

CONTACT: Carrie Kellenberger, Co-President (Carrie@Reach ToTeachRecruiting.com) or Dean Barnes, Director of HR, Taiwan.

SESAME STREET / VIP ORGANISATION

No. 6, Alley 32, Chang Rung Rd, Tainan City
- ✆ +886 6 511 8086 ext 13
- ✉ service@sesamevillage.tw
- 💻 www.sesamevillage.tw (Chinese only)

NUMBER OF TEACHERS: 25–28.

PREFERENCE OF NATIONALITY: UK, South Africa, Australia, Canada, USA and New Zealand.

QUALIFICATIONS: Minimum of a BA degree and TEFL/TESOL certificate.

CONDITIONS OF EMPLOYMENT: 1 year renewable. Hours 2pm–8pm.

SALARY: NT$50,000 per month.

FACILITIES/SUPPORT: Handbook for new teachers written by recent teachers with advice on documentation, mobile phones, transport, food shopping, etc. Assistance given with finding but not paying for accommodation. Help given with applying for ARC, etc at local immigration department.

RECRUITMENT: Via websites or word of mouth. Interviews in Tainan required.

CONTACT: Kristian Chen (HR Manager).

SHANE ENGLISH SCHOOL

6F-1, 41 Roosevelt Road, Section 2, Taipei
- ✆ +886 2 2351 7755 ext 116
- ✉ john.yates@shane.com.tw
- 💻 www.shane.com.tw/sest

NUMBER OF TEACHERS: 180 in 61 franchise schools and 3 English-immersion kindergartens.

PREFERENCE OF NATIONALITY: Must be citizen of native English-speaking country.

QUALIFICATIONS: TEFL/CELTA/PGCE (dependent on position applied for) and honours degree.

CONDITIONS OF EMPLOYMENT: 1-year renewable contracts. Guaranteed salaries for 80 hours per month. 5 days per week schedule.

SALARY: NT$44,800–$70,000 per month depending on position, location and experience. Contract-completion bonus also paid.

FACILITIES/SUPPORT: Up-to-date facilities and teaching resources. Work permits, assistance with accommodation and comprehensive initial and ongoing training provided.

RECRUITMENT: Applicants can apply directly to arrange face-to-face or Skype interview. Saxoncourt in the UK (www.saxoncourt.com) also recruits for Shane Taiwan.

CONTACT: Steve Lambert, Principal; Johnnie Yates, HR Assistant Director of Studies; or Martin Black, Director of Recruitment at Saxoncourt.

THAILAND

The English teaching scene is flourishing, especially in schools that teach English to children. For several years the government has been making efforts to extend the instruction of English in state schools as well as private ones, by introducing 'EP' (English Program), a bilingual stream within Thai schools which involves the teaching of English and other subjects, preferably by native English-speaker teachers willing to accept a modest wage.

Knowledge of English is eagerly sought by most urban young people and, in the context of Thailand, 'urban' is almost synonymous with 'Bangkok', which is more than 20 times larger than its nearest rival, Nonthaburi. The *Bangkok Post* is a less fruitful source of vacancies than Thai-specific websites such as www.teachingthailand.com, www.teachteflthailand.com and www.ajarn.com described below. The latter is a treasure trove of teaching information, contact details and job advertisements.

In its aim to improve the quality of English teaching in Thailand and to ensure that 'fake' teachers cannot be so easily accepted into the expat community, the government has tightened up the visa regulations and issuance of teachers' licences, which might provide an incentive for people who do not qualify to consider joining one of the many volunteer teaching schemes that operate throughout the country.

PROSPECTS FOR TEACHERS

Only a small percentage of recruitment takes place outside Thailand. The major schools use foreign recruitment agencies and the internet to make contact with potential teachers, but most organisations depend on finding native-speaker teachers locally, including Thai universities and teachers' colleges, as well as private business colleges, which all have EFL departments. Hundreds of foreigners graduate from one of the many TEFL training courses offered in Thailand (see Directory of Training Courses) and many of them have links with local schools. One of the most active is See TEFL (Siam Educational Experience) (www.seetefl.com), which guarantees employment if graduating job-seekers follow nine steps.

Thailand also appeals to English speakers who would like a career break and find that teaching is the best job going. **Ed Reinert** worked as a salesman for 25 years before becoming a teacher in Thailand, while **Carlos Vega** was a computer technician who realised that teaching was the only job he would be able to find in Thailand. Whereas few language companies openly impose an upper age limit, some age discrimination does take place, especially with companies that specialise in the teenage market (a significant sector in summers).

Thais are exuberant and fun-loving people and their ideas about education reflect this. They seem to value fun and games (*sanuk*) above grammar, and an outgoing personality above a teaching certificate, although this attitude may be changing. Of course, there is already a nucleus of professional EFL teachers working at the most prestigious institutes in Bangkok. Many international and Thai bilingual schools look for individuals who can teach art, maths and science through the medium of English. Originally set up as teacher-training colleges, there are about 40 Rajabhat Universities around Thailand which are autonomous and hire their own English teachers. Some schools and language institutes may be more keen to hire women on the assumption that they are less likely to become distracted by the seamier side of Thailand's nightlife.

One thing to consider is that Thai salaries have not really increased in recent years, even though the government wants to attract more professional teachers. This is something of a sticking point, and teachers who want to make a good living in Asia would be better off looking at Korea or Taiwan. However, living costs are still fairly low in Thailand (Bangkok and tourist resorts excepted) and many teachers have such an exciting time that they don't give a thought to saving, or indeed to returning home.

FINDING A JOB

IN ADVANCE

Among the many teacher-placement agencies attempting to place suitably qualified candidates in schools throughout Thailand, try the following:

AYC Intercultural Programs Thailand, GOT Building, 9/197, 7th floor, Ratchadaphisek soi 29, 10900 Chatuchak, Bangkok (+66 2 556 1533; h_r@aycthailand.com; www.aycthailand.com). Native English speakers with a bachelor's degree are recruited for 90 schools in Thailand, and also for summer language camps. New teachers should arrive for orientation seminar in advance of semesters starting second week of May and November.

BFITS (Bright Future International Training & Services) – see entry.

Echo English Ltd, 90/165 Plex Bangna, Moo.15, Bang Na -Trat Road, Bang Kaew, Bang Phli, Samutprakarn 10540 (+66 863315751; echoteam@echo-english.com; www.echo-english.com/teachers). Intake of 40 teachers at beginning of term (late October/early November). One day induction in Bangkok is free; 3-day induction costs £80.

LoveTEFL, Leeds (+44 113 829 3300; www.lovetefl.com). Graduates recruited to teach English from May. Salary of 27,000–30,000 baht per month.

Teach to Travel Ltd, London E1 1RD, UK (+44 20 7193 2825; hr@teachtotravel.co.uk; www.teach totravel.co.uk). 70 teachers under the age of 45 are placed in government primary and secondary schools in South and Central Thailand. Wage of 25,000–30,000 baht per month for 12 months.

TEFL East/Global Training Academy, tefleast@gmail.com; www.englishjobsthailand.com. Affiliated to American TESOL Institute. 7-day teaching orientation in Bangkok (at a cost of $500) followed by placement throughout Thailand for 4–5 months, for degree-holders only. Monthly salary 30,000 baht per month.

Training Consultant Center (TCC), Bangkok (+66 89 500 2879 or 83 704 3854; training_tcc@ yahoo.com). Reputable teaching agency in Bangkok that has contracts at both private and government schools in Bangkok and the surrounding areas.

London-based exchange travel companies such as IST Plus (see entry) and Global Nomadic (www.global nomadic.com) arrange paid teaching jobs in Thailand but charge an administrative fee for their services. Global Nomadic's programme involves a two-week TEFL training course in various locations and job-placement package costing $1,390.

The British Council in Thailand (www.britishcouncil.or.th) runs the Thailand English Teaching (TET) Programme (www.tetprogramme.org) whereby 280 undergraduates and recent graduates from participating UK universities spend nine weeks over the summer or four months in the winter working as English Language Assistants in Thai education institutions across the country. The Ministry of Education has given permission for the programme to continue and expand. For longer-term teaching positions in the six British Council teaching centres, candidates will need a degree and at least 200 hours post-CELTA experience teaching EFL to kids (7–11) and/or teens (12–16). Applications should be submitted to the East Asia Recruitment Team located in Singapore (eateacher.recruitment@britishcouncil.org.sg).

The Anglo-Pacific (Asia) Consultancy (Suite 32, Nevilles Court, Dollis Hill Lane, London NW2 6HG; +44 20 8452 7836) is an educational consultancy that concentrates on recruiting teachers for schools, colleges and universities in Thailand as well as other Asian countries. Teachers are placed by APA, which welcomes graduates with a CELTA or Trinity certificate but also tries to place people with any TEFL background and/or appropriate personalities as long as they have a university degree. Their recruits are given briefing notes on their country of destination and a follow-up visit in their schools if possible.

One of the best all-round sources of information about teaching in Thailand, with an emphasis on Bangkok and inside information about the main hiring companies, is the website www.ajarn.com – *ajarn* is the Thai word for teacher – with stories and tips and current job vacancies posted on www.AjarnJobspace.com. The site is run and constantly updated by a teacher, Philip Williams, who has been in Thailand for many years. Various online recruitment sites such as www.teachteflthailand.com and www.totalesl.com carry current vacancies in Bangkok and beyond. The latter belongs to the Icon Group Thailand (IGT) of TEFL/TESOL websites providing educational resources and information to teachers, schools and students around the world with a special focus on Asia and the Middle East.

DAWN WILKINSON

Dawn Wilkinson taught from July to December at St Joseph Convent School in Silom, Bangkok, which she found through the BFITS agency advertising on www.ajarn.com.

Although it wasn't my favourite part of Thailand, I had made a few friends in Bangkok, so thought this would be the best place to live and look for work. I was surprised to discover how low teaching wages were in comparison to Vietnam; Thailand is so much more developed as a country (and living costs are much higher), but teaching wages far from reflect this, something that is complained about regularly on internet forums. There seemed to be hundreds of teaching jobs available in Bangkok. I only really looked at www.ajarn.com and, although I didn't struggle to find a job, I knew I could have got a better and higher-paid position if I had a TEFL qualification. After a successful Skype interview while in Vietnam, I accepted a full-time position as a Prathom (primary) grade 4 teacher in a prestigious Catholic girls' school in Silom. The agency arranged all my paperwork and visa, changing my tourist visa into a non-immigrant B visa which allows you to work while applying for your teaching licence (I wouldn't advise attempting to work in Thailand without the right visa – the authorities regularly catch and fine many people).

Teaching in Thailand seemed much more formal and serious than Vietnam. The Convent School was particularly strict in its enforcement of the 'proper' conduct and dress code of the teachers (no trousers or skirts above the knee for females, no sleeveless tops, no tattoos on show, etc). I taught more than 250 eight-nine-year-old girls, across eight classes, who were very sweet and affectionate, but who were also very hard to tell apart in their identical uniforms and French plaits (their self-styled nicknames, like Coffee, Ice and Bogey, also made me laugh somewhat!). I earned 35,000 baht a month, which, after 7,000 baht rent for a studio apartment (I lived in a cheaper 'Thai' rather than expat area), plus bills (3,000 baht), as well as the cost of travelling to work on public transport and food, didn't leave as much as I had had in Saigon. However, on the plus side, during just five months at the school I had about seven weeks of paid holiday – which I thoroughly enjoyed on the Thai beaches and islands!

Melanie Drake is another young teacher who landed a job in Thailand with ease, this one with ECC (see entry), after gaining a TEFL qualification at TEFL International Corinth in Greece:

My soon-to-be boss contacted me after he had spotted my CV on www.tefl.com. After several emails and a simple visa application process I was in Thailand. Culture shock all round. My job required me to teach in businesses, poor government schools with cramped, sometimes a bit unsanitary conditions and also in a local private language school. My tiny, basic but clean apartment was free and came with the job. My wages were more than satisfactory to save some as life was incredibly cheap. I was pretty lonely before I got to meet the other members of staff. I was living alone quite far out from the school and was unable to communicate with anyone due to language difficulties. I was terrified of dogs and it turns out that my city, Ayutthaya, had some of the highest numbers of stray dogs in the country, and dealing with this was easily my biggest hurdle. Classes were also over-populated in the schools, sometimes 60 to a class; with no air-conditioning. Students were for the most part quite lazy and more interested in the novelty of a foreigner than learning English. But, in hindsight, they showed more respect than the average British/American kid probably would.

VOLUNTEERING

For those who do not qualify for a salaried teaching position, the option of volunteering is attractive. Many worthy agencies operating internationally or at a grassroots level supply volunteer teachers to local schools who would otherwise not be exposed to native English speakers. To take one example, Gap Year Thailand (see entry) has a flourishing programme. The director, **David Lancaster**, explains: '*In our experience in Thailand, schools particularly want help from volunteers in spoken English. They usually have local teachers who are reasonably competent in grammar, vocabulary, spelling, teaching reading, etc, but value help from first-language speakers of English.*'

A charity founded by an American, Volunthai (www.volunthai.com), runs a teaching programme in rural North-Eastern Thailand. Teachers' accommodation is provided as homestays, and the fee is $375 for the first month and $200 thereafter. Small-scale charities such as this can respond flexibly to individual requirements. For example, Volunthai once incorporated an American family with four children aged 3–13, all of whom participated in school activities. Looking back on their experiences of travelling around the world, the **Battye** family concluded that becoming part of a rural Thai village through Volunthai was the highlight of the year for them.

In rural parts of Thailand, schools cannot afford to pay salaries to foreign teachers, and local children have little or no exposure to fluent English. Yet the children who dream of going to university and into the professions need to achieve a certain standard of English. To meet this need various organisations enlist the help of volunteer teachers including the following:

Gift School of English, see entry.
International Volunteer HQ, New Zealand (www.volunteerhq.org/volunteer-in-thailand). 250 volunteers placed in Thailand every year including English teachers for young children, especially among hill tribes around Chiang Rai. Sample price $1,320 for 12 weeks.
Mundo Exchange Organization, 1435 NW 30th Ave, Portland, OR 97210, USA (+1 503 227 8442; www.mundoexchange.org). Volunteers teach English and computer skills to disadvantaged children and/or adults mainly in Isan province in North-Eastern Thailand. Volunteers can be placed at short notice but 2–3 months' advance warning is preferred. The placement costs are $400 for the first week (which includes 2–3 day orientation), then $685 for 2 weeks, to $1,075 for 8 weeks, then $105 per additional week. Fees include pre-arranged accommodation, travel within the project and support before and during the stay.
Openmind Projects, 43000 Nong Khai (+66 8856 40734; www.openmindprojects.org). The fee for this volunteer teacher programme starts at €255 for the first fortnight, and is €85 per week thereafter. Three-day orientation included.
Starfish Volunteers (www.starfishvolunteers.com). UK voluntourism company that places volunteers of all nationalities in development projects in Thailand. The project on Koh Samui is called Teach & Beach. The 2015 fee is £1,235 for 8 weeks.

Travel to Teach, T2T, 77/4 Chaitalay Road, Prachuap Khiri Khan 77000 (+66 9 2818 5929; www.travel-to-teach.org). Thai-based organisation that provides volunteer teaching opportunities (among others) in various locations. Sample fees £515 for a month, £1,213 for six months.

Volunteer Teacher Thailand, 4/91 Soi Bang La-On, Moo 7, Khao Lak, Phang Nga 82190 (+66 845290616; volunteer.teachers@yahoo.com; www.volunteerteacherthailand.org). This charity continues the work of the now disbanded Tsunami Volunteer Centre. Registration fee of €60 and volunteers can join programme any Sunday.

The Karen Hill Tribes Trust, York, UK (+44 1904 612829; www.karenhilltribes.org.uk). Sends self-funding volunteers, including gap-year students, to North-West Thailand to work in upland and hill communities of Karen tribespeople, some as language teachers, for two, three or five months between November and March (fees respectively £650, £1,000 and £2,000).

Barbara Darragh also saw for herself how extremely popular English teachers are:

My first volunteer trip to Thailand was with an organisation set up after the tsunami. I then went to Chiang Mai for six months and after completing a month's TEFL course with SeeTEFL I offered my services to a local school. I loved working there and made many Thai friends who are always emailing me and asking me when I plan to return, which I hope to do again in September. It is very easy to find good, cheap accommodation and the Thai people are so friendly. The children are a delight to teach and are so excited when you go into the school. The poorer schools where I volunteer would never normally be able to afford an 'English' English teacher. There is also plenty of paid work and I did have a private student and if I had wanted I could have had a lot more. As soon as people realise that you are an English teacher they want you to teach them or their family. I have never felt so rewarded in a job before and the fact that I want to go back every year and work for nothing must say something.

The Burma Education Partnership (www.burmaeducationpartnership.org) is a specialist British organisation in-volved with teacher training in Mobile Teacher Units close to the Burmese border in order to support education in refugee communities that have been affected by war, hardship and oppression. About 120,000 Burmese people live on Thai soil. Volunteers can also work with displaced Burmese by following the links of the Burma Volunteer Programme's partners on http://burmavolunteers.org/local-partners. These organisations have few facilities for providing any training or orientation, so teaching volunteers should be prepared to hit the ground running.

ON THE SPOT IN BANGKOK

Any new arrival in Bangkok would be well advised to spend a week getting his or her bearings and asking for-eigners living in the city for inside information about possible employers. Many people say that the teaching scene has become somewhat exploitative and life in the city so unpleasant that it is better to leave Bangkok as quickly as you can. Others adore the buzz.

For those who feel strong enough to survive in Bangkok, language schools are generally easy to locate and approach on spec. As a long-term traveller, **Mark Wiens** claims not to make lots of cash, but he has discovered ways to make enough money to live overseas, partly by blogging at http://migrationology. com, and one of the strings to his bow is English teaching. While he was in Bangkok he noticed a billboard for English courses at the Wall Street Institute and simply went into the school and had a short friendly meet-ing with the HR manager, who just wanted to confirm that he would be someone that would respect and be patient with the students (though he did have a four-week TESOL certificate too):

My number one task was to elicit correct English from the students. The students studied the grammar using a computer program and it was my job to confirm their comprehension of what they learned. I worked from

11am until 8pm, five days per week in a very nice air-conditioned facility located in a shopping centre. The other teachers were a cool group of recent university graduates who enjoyed other cultures and experiencing new things. The low point was having to teach the same material day after day. Like any job, it became too much of a routine and I did get bored.

The best place to start is around Siam Square, where numerous schools and the British Council are located. The Council has a list of private and public universities, institutes, teachers' colleges and international schools throughout the country which have English departments and therefore possible openings for a native English speaker; but most job-seekers rely on the *Yellow Pages*, which include dozens of language school addresses. Note that the Thai school year ends in mid-March and restarts the second week of May. If you arrive after that, only the dregs are left.

The English-language daily newspaper, the *Bangkok Post*, is a possible source of job vacancies (http://job.bangkokpost.com) though the jobs listings on ajarn.com and Craigslist (http://bangkok.craigslist.co.th/edu) are more extensive. Many ads specify 'NES' status which simply means Native English Speaker.

DILYS EWART

Dilys Ewart discovered that the divide between voluntary and paid teaching is not absolute when she went as an unqualified volunteer to Thailand through Gap Year Thailand. Within two months Dilys had had three job offers for paid employment as a teacher.

During my introduction week in Thailand, we were shown many different aspects of the Thai culture. We were introduced to Thai food, Thai language and Thai schools. On our fourth day in Thailand we went to a nursery school based in Bang Saen; there were eight classes in the school with 15-20 students in each class. When we arrived we were given ideas and examples to make a lesson plan for a class. I had only ever done one lesson plan before and it was for a different subject. After an hour of preparation time I was given a classroom of 16 students for 45 minutes. There were three assistant teachers there to help with the translation for the students. I got the students to play English games and write letters from the alphabet. At the end of the day I was invited into the Director's office and was offered a job as an English teacher, with a contract for 1 year; she told me how much she was willing to pay me and also discussed accommodation. As I was going to my placement as a volunteer teacher a few days later I declined her offer.

In my volunteer placement, during lunch breaks I helped a 6th year girl for an English speaking competition which she was entering. When competition day came I went along with her for support and last-minute preparation. While she was being judged I was sitting outside on a bench when a Thai teacher approached me from another school. She asked what I was doing here in Thailand and where I was teaching. Then she asked me directly if I was interested in a job at her school as an English teacher. Once again she said how much they were willing to pay and said they would supply accommodation and some meals, with a six-month contract. I was very surprised, as she hadn't even seen me teach a class. As I was only a couple of weeks into my placement I declined the offer, but they insisted on giving me a number to call if I changed my mind.

I taught as a volunteer at Suan Pa Kao Cha Ang School for two months, through Gap Year Thailand. In my last week at the school I was offered a job with a year's contract with accommodation and reasonable pay, but again I declined the offer as I had plans for travelling. I feel if I need a job in Thailand I would be able to go out and use one of my job offers if I want. What can I conclude from this experience? Well, firstly, that there is massive enthusiasm in Thailand for learning English; secondly, that the schools are very keen to have first-language speakers of English as teachers; and thirdly, that it is obviously possible to start as an unqualified volunteer teacher of English and easily get offers of employment. I had thought I would go to Thailand and get some teaching experience but I never thought I would come home with three job offers - and one of the best memories of my life.

Travelling around this city of more than eight million is so time consuming and unpleasant that it is important to plot your interview strategy on a city map before making appointments. Also be sure to pick up a map of the air-conditioned bus routes, particularly if you are contemplating a job that involves travelling to different premises.

It may not be necessary to spend too much time researching the schools with vacancies. Many of the so-called back-street language schools (more likely to be on a main street, above a shop or restaurant) look to the cheap hotels of Banglamphu, the favourite haunt of western travellers in the north-west of Bangkok. There is such a high turnover of staff at many schools that there are bound to be vacancies somewhere for a new arrival who takes the trouble to present a professional image and can show a convincing CV supported with diplomas/certificates. As usual, it may be necessary to start with part-time and occasional work with several employers, aiming to build up 20–30 hours in the same area to minimise travelling in the appalling traffic.

The teaching of children is an expanding area; if you don't want to teach the alphabet, don't accept pupils under the age of 5. On the strength of her claim that she had experience of 'working with children', **Alison Eglinton** was soon earning a reasonable wage (and she suggests that anyone teaching young children should master at least one word of Thai: *hong nam*, which means toilet).

Ajarn (teachers) are respected in Thailand and are expected to look respectable. As well as dressing smartly for an interview, try to maintain a reserve in your manner while still projecting a relaxed and easy-going image. Too many gesticulations and guffawing are considered impolite and immature and will not earn you the respect of Thai people. When visiting a school, wear your posh clothes and carry CVs and passport photos to clip onto the application forms; otherwise you'll be asked to come back with the correct documents. Don't be surprised if the application form asks some weird questions, such as asking you to give the name, age and profession of every member of your family. You won't be hired on the spot but may well be contacted by phone within a day or two. Everyone who has ever had anything to do with teaching English in Thailand emphasises the need to dress smartly, as **Bruce Lawson** describes:

> The Thais like their pet farangs (ie foreigners) to look as much like currency dealers as possible. I bought a suit in Bangkok for £50 especially for the job hunt. Men should take out all earrings and wear a tie (thus risking asphyxiation in the heat and humidity of the hot season). Women should wear a decent skirt, not trousers.

Appropriate dress was also a problem for **Susannah Kerr**, who had been told by her sending agency (i-to-i. com) that T-shirts and flip-flops would be appropriate. But this was not the case at her school in Nakhon

Nayok (population 17,000), and she was promptly taken on a compulsory shopping expedition and obliged to spend money on smarter clothes that she didn't care for.

> *The busiest season for tutoring is mid-March to mid-May during the school holidays, when many secondary school and university students take extra tuition in English. This coincides with the hot season. Vacancies continue to be advertised through June, July and August. The next best time to look for teaching work in private schools is October, while the quietest time is January/February.*

ON THE SPOT IN CHIANG MAI

Teaching opportunities crop up in branches of the big companies such as ECC and AUA and in academic institutes. When approaching the bilingual (EP) schools, seek out the director for the 'bilingual' section of the school. Teachers are recruited for all levels from nursery school to kindergarten, primary to secondary, though in some cases a master's degree in education or a teaching degree will be required. When applying for jobs, it is best to visit the schools directly as they don't have time or the aptitude to answer endless emails. Most schools have websites, though they are not always easy to navigate.

There are seven international schools which may employ English teachers, though most of those hired are certified teachers recruited at international teachers' fairs such as those sponsored by the thorough and professional Search Associates (www.searchassociates.com), of which there is a long-established branch in Chiang Mai, run by Harry Deelman. Other jobs are available in the school holidays at summer and weekend camps held at resort hotels or at Chiang Mai's international schools and attended by rich children from Bangkok and other parts of Thailand. Getting into these and the summer camps run by the British Council and YMCA is by word of mouth, friends or advertisements. The advice of long-time Chiang Mai resident **Annette Kunigagon** is to be brazen, knock on doors, try hotels, shops catering to tourists, companies which export or have to deal with foreigners, pubs, restaurants, computer shops, large shops in the Night Bazaar area, etc.

Many private language schools can be found in the vicinity of Chiang Mai University and also in the area near the prestigious Thai secondary schools such as Montfort, Paruethai, Regina, Dara and Prince Royal College. The expanding expat community in Chiang Mai comprises many nationalities, most of whom use English as their second language and want to improve their skills.

ON THE SPOT IN THE PROVINCES

The number of teaching opportunities outside Bangkok has escalated; however, not many foreigners show an interest since the pay is much less than in Bangkok. The estimated four-fifths of teachers who are single males enjoying the nightlife in Bangkok are unwilling to move to a less exciting country town.

Competition for work is almost non-existent in lesser-known cities such as Nakhon Sawan, Khon Kaen, Udon Thani, Ubon Ratchathani and Pathumthani. For a job in a university you will probably have to show a higher degree or teaching certificate. The best places are Hat Yai and Songkhla. Hotels are always worth approaching, since many hotel workers are very keen to improve their English. If you find a place that suits and you decide to stay for a while, ask the family who run your guesthouse about local teaching opportunities. Sometimes the happiest and most memorable experiences take place away from the cities and the tourist resorts. **Brian Savage** returned to England after a second long stint of teaching in Thailand and describes one of the highlights for him:

> *My most rewarding experience was my week teaching English conversation in a rural high school in Loei province in North-East Thailand. These children had rarely seen and had certainly never spoken to a* farang

(foreigner) before. My work during that week and a subsequent second visit was really appreciated by the students. The first visit came about after I was introduced to a teacher at the Chiang Mai school where I was teaching. If travellers get away from Bangkok and the resorts, they too can have experiences such as this, especially in the friendly towns of the north and north-east. A little voluntary teaching can really boost the confidence of students who are usually too poor to pay to study with native speakers.

REGULATIONS

The goal posts keep shifting on the question of visas, and enforcement is inconsistent. The preferred alternative for people who have found a job from abroad is to apply for a non-immigrant B visa from any Thai Embassy. For this you will be asked to provide a copy of your degree certificate (essential), police clearance and various documents from your prospective employer in Thailand such as a contract of employment. With this visa, the applicant can stay in Thailand for no longer than 90 days unless his or her employer obtains a teacher's licence, for which you will need the original certificate of your bachelor's degree and transcripts or a letter/email of confirmation of graduation from your university. If your degree is in Education, that will suffice but, if in another subject, you will also need proof that you have a TESOL certificate of some kind. In addition you may need a criminal record check from your home country and from the Thai police and a medical certificate issued within the last month (obtainable from doctors in Thailand for a small fee).

To qualify for a full teaching licence, you must satisfy the requirements of the Teaching Council of Thailand, which means passing exams in Thai Language and Culture and also Professional Knowledge and Ethics. It seems that this is necessary only if teaching in a formal school that follows a Thai curriculum, so that non-formal schools, eg private language institutes and some employment agencies, are exempt, as are new teachers who may be granted a Provisional Teaching Permit instead of a full licence. A simpler alternative might be to qualify for the Educational (ED) visa by undertaking a course of Thai language and culture, which is valid for up to a year.

To upgrade a tourist visa to a Non-Immigrant B (Business) visa you must have a guaranteed job, the correct paperwork, patience and 2,000 baht for the fee. It is usually easier to apply for the Non-Immigrant B at a Thai embassy in another country. In this case the applicant must stay overnight and pick up the visa the next day. Most people take the overnight bus from Bangkok and arrive at whichever border town they're going to early the next morning, which makes the whole trip take at least three days. Before summer 2014 teachers used to do a 'visa run' every 90 days, i.e. leave the country and renew their tourist status on the way back into Thailand. However the authorities have mounted a strict crackdown on this practice.

The paperwork forum of www.ajarn.com is a very good place to read about the evolving red tape situation and its practical (rather than theoretical) implications.

Once a work permit is granted, tax will be withdrawn at a very modest rate, sometimes as low as 2%, plus up to 4% for social security contributions. However not all employers comply and some teachers take out private health insurance for instance through AIA (www.aia.co.th).

CONDITIONS OF WORK

In Thailand, the wages for *farang* teachers continue to be low. The basic hourly rate has risen only slightly over the past couple of years and is now in the 250–350 baht range (roughly £4.50–£6.50), while the monthly range is normally 27,000–35,000 baht in Bangkok, and on average 5,000 baht less in other cities. Company work can pay more depending on location, but in-company contract work is in short supply. The norm is for schools to keep their staff on as part-time freelancers while giving them full-time hours; this is primarily to avoid taxes. Most language institutes pay weekly in cash, but beware of schools that turn payday into a moveable feast.

The best remuneration is available from international schools such as the Bangkok Patana School (www. patana.ac.th). Note that the pay at international schools in Bangkok is as much as twice that paid by international schools elsewhere in the country. For a list of international schools in Thailand go to the website of the International Schools Association of Thailand (www.isat.or.th).

Few employers help with accommodation, which does not matter much since vacant apartments are not hard to locate and rental deposits not crippling as they are in Japan. Things are more relaxed in Chiang Mai, where a group of people can rent a house or live Thai-style in a studio room with attached bathroom for very affordable rents.

Remember never to touch a student on the head, which is difficult if you are teaching children. In class a show of anger will soon lose the students' respect since the Thais value a 'cool heart' (*jai yen*) and go to great lengths to avoid displays of negative emotion. They are great adherents of a 'no worries' attitude, called '*mai pen lai*' in Thai. Calm, smiling and enthusiastic personalities make all the difference. **Carlos Vega** thinks that there are two types of pupils:

> *Primary are nice and ready to learn every day. Secondary students mostly don't care and don't want to learn anything in a system that makes it impossible for any student to fail. No one really has to do any work in order to pass the grade, so why bother? Usually if the parents are involved with the school the student tends to do well.*

LEISURE TIME

It has to be said that Bangkok may be an exciting and lively city but it is not beautiful. It has very few parks, bad traffic congestion and polluted air. There is also a great deal of what some might consider moral pollution, and there is a certain element of the teaching fraternity in Bangkok who are there primarily for the easy availability of sex in the notorious Patpong district (despite the HIV/AIDS crisis in Thailand). Thai Labour Law stipulates that '*any employees who comport themselves in a manner which would embarrass or cause serious damage to employers' reputation may be terminated immediately, by employer, with no legal recourse available to employee*'. This applies on *and* off the clock. Many a *farang* man has been spotted in a 'night-time establishment' and been fired the next day.

With the ratio of foreign men to women teachers at least six to one, many women (although in great demand as teachers) do not enjoy the atmosphere in the city and leave as quickly as they can. Fortunately for teachers earning a low wage, the more innocent pleasures of Thailand, like street food, come cheap. Even part-time teachers should be able to afford to travel round the country, visiting jungle attractions such as Kanchanaburi, where you can ride an elephant along the banks of the River Kwai, and islands such as Koh Samet, Koh Samui and Koh Phangan where life is slow and the beaches are wonderful. Try to learn a little Thai, as **Bruce Lawson** did after getting fried battered banana when he thought he had ordered garlic chicken. He recommends organising word-swaps with students, which will also illustrate to them that they are not the only ones who have to struggle with alien sounds. Wherever you end up teaching you are sure to discover that Thailand is famously welcoming.

LIST OF EMPLOYERS

AMERICAN UNIVERSITY ALUMNI LANGUAGE CENTER

Bangkok: 21st Floor, Chamchuri Square Bldg, 319 Phyat-hai Road, Patumwan, Bangkok 10330

- ☏ +66 2 6576 411, ext 1271 or 1241
- ✉ sam.yi@auathailand.org
- 🖥 www.auathailand.org

Chiang Mai branch: AUA, 73 Rajadamnern Road, Amphur Muang, Chiang Mai 50200

- ☏ +66 53 211377
- ✉ chiangmai@auathailand.org

16 branches throughout Thailand (6 in Bangkok, 10 provincial).

NUMBER OF TEACHERS: About 175 in total: 40 at main branch, up to 20 at other branches.

PREFERENCE OF NATIONALITY: American, Canadian, British, Australian and New Zealander.

QUALIFICATIONS: Bachelor's degree and 120-hour certificate course, eg SIT TESOL, CELTA or equivalent. Teaching experience preferred.

CONDITIONS OF EMPLOYMENT: 1-year commitment preferred. 4–6 hours' teaching daily (considered to be full-time). Teaching year consists of 7 6-week terms separated by 1 free week (unpaid). Courses aimed at professionals aged 18–35.

SALARY: Starting rate is 400 baht per hour on weekdays, 650 baht at weekends, depending on experience/qualifications. Annual bonus may be paid on completion of contract. Free health insurance, 1-year work permit (paid for by teacher for first 2 years), 50% discount on Thai lessons.

FACILITIES/SUPPORT: Participation in pre-service training preferred before teaching hours are assigned. Mentoring programme for new teachers and in-service professional development.

RECRUITMENT: Adverts in the *Bangkok Post*, the internet and word of mouth. Initial applications to be made online. Face-to-face interview required.

CONTACT: Sam Yi, Bangkok (sam.yi@auathailand.org).

BELL EDUCATIONAL TRUST

UK: Hillscross, Red Cross Lane, Cambridge CB2 0QU

- ☏ +44 1223 275594
- 🖥 www.bellenglish.com/jobs

NUMBER OF TEACHERS: Vacancies occur from time to time in partner schools in Thailand, eg Assumption College Rama II in Bangkok.

PREFERENCE OF NATIONALITY: For visa purposes must be from UK, USA, Canada, Australia, New Zealand or South Africa, and be a native English speaker.

QUALIFICATIONS: Bachelor's degree and CELTA (better still Young Learner speciality, PGCE and/or DELTA). Experience of and/or interest in teaching English to young learners preferred. Candidates should have 2 years experience and be dependable and culturally sensitive team players.

CONDITIONS OF EMPLOYMENT: 1 or 2-year renewable contracts. Up to 21 contact hours per week (Monday to Friday). Much of the work is with young learners.

SALARY: 52,000–66,000 baht per month plus end-of-contract bonus.

FACILITIES/SUPPORT: One-way flight costs for teachers recruited outside Thailand. Hotel accommodation on arrival. Assistance in finding suitable accommodation. Visa and work permit arranged. 8 weeks' paid holiday per year plus public holidays. Health and medical insurance cover provided. Commitment to in-service training and professional development.

RECRUITMENT: Bell Recruitment, internet, newspapers, telephone and face-to-face interviews.

BERLITZ BANGKOK LTD

246 Times Square Building, 2nd Floor, Sukhumvit Road 12-14, Wattana, Bangkok 10110

- ☏ +66 2 255 6070
- ✉ careers@berlitz.co.th
- 🖥 www.berlitz.co.th

NUMBER OF TEACHERS: 60.

PREFERENCE OF NATIONALITY: Must have native proficiency in the target language.

QUALIFICATIONS: University degree. Professionalism and a strong customer service orientation are essential. Both new and experienced instructors are recruited, provided they show willingness to learn and use the Berlitz Method of instruction in the classroom.

CONDITIONS OF EMPLOYMENT: 1 year. Minimum availability required is 35 hours with weekend availability required. New instructors are assigned two consecutive weekdays off.

SALARY: New instructors are paid at a rate of 220 baht per 40-minute lesson, which results in a minimum salary of 35,000 baht (net) per month, with fluctuations. Higher earnings are achievable to those willing to make themselves available for more hours. Rate of income tax is 9%–10%.

FACILITIES/SUPPORT: Berlitz works with a reliable English-speaking estate agent who doesn't charge the instructor for arranging viewings of suitable accommodation and providing transport. HR representative assists with obtaining work permit by collecting the necessary documents from the instructor and processing the paperwork at the Ministry of Labour on the instructor's behalf. The company pays the 3,000 baht application fee.

RECRUITMENT: Websites, local recruiting classifieds (eg www.jobsdb.com, www.bangkokpost.com) and walk-in candidates who are welcome to leave their CV. If suitable, an interview will be scheduled.

CONTACT: Country Coordinator of Instruction.

BKS (BANGKOK SUCCESS GROUP)

184/73 Ratchadaphisek Road, Forum Tower, 16th Floor, Huay Kwang, Bangkok 10310

- +66 2 645 4300
- recruiting@bangkoksuccess.com
- www.bangkoksuccess.com

NUMBER OF TEACHERS: 80-120. Also for Myanmar.
PREFERENCE OF NATIONALITY: Native speakers only.
QUALIFICATIONS: 4-year university degree.
CONDITIONS OF EMPLOYMENT: 4.5 month stays. 25 classes of 50 minutes per week in office hours (between 7.50am and 4pm).
SALARY: 30,000–32,500 baht per month, less 3% for income tax.
FACILITIES/SUPPORT: Accommodation is ready and available at local prices (2,000–3,000 baht monthly). Dedicated Thai staff helps with work permits.
RECRUITMENT: Via online jobs sites, recruiting agents, and TEFL/TESOL training centres. Interviews are necessary and occasionally held in the US.
CONTACT: Jim Still, HR Department.

BR COMPUTER & LANGUAGE SCHOOL

73–75 Old Petchakaseam Road, Klongkrachang, Muang, Petchaburi 76000

- br.language@hotmail.com

NUMBER OF TEACHERS: 26 native English speakers.
PREFERENCE OF NATIONALITY: None.
QUALIFICATIONS: No preferences., though school recommends that candidates take at least an introductory TEFL course eg with UK-TEFL (www.uk-tefl.com). BR School hopes to offer its own TEFL training in future.
CONDITIONS OF EMPLOYMENT: 1-year contract. 18–25 teaching hours a week.

SALARY: 20,000 baht–35,000 baht a month for full-time teacher, less 3% for taxes.
FACILITIES/SUPPORT: Assistance given to teachers to find cheap accommodation (eg $30–$120 per month) and to obtain work permit if eligible. Internet access provided at school. Some schools provide free accommodation and/or free lunches. Meals in temple schools cost less than $1. Free or cheap internet access provided.
RECRUITMENT: Interviews not always necessary or can be conducted by phone. Written applications sometimes acceptable.
CONTACT: Noavarat (Nana) Tosuwan, Principal.

BRIGHT FUTURE INTERNATIONAL TRAINING & SERVICES (BFITS THAILAND)

SSP Tower, 11th Floor, 555/16-19 Soi 63 Sukhumvit (Ekamai), Sukhumvit Road, Klongton-Nua, Wattana, Bangkok 10110

- +66 2 711 4684
- hr@bfitsthailand.com
- www.bfitsthailand.com

NUMBER OF TEACHERS: 120+ for about a dozen full-curriculum partner schools.
PREFERENCE OF NATIONALITY: American, Canadian, British, Australian and South African. Primarily looking for native English speakers; non-native English speakers must provide TOEFL/TOEIC score.
QUALIFICATIONS: Bachelor's and TEFL certification. TEFL certification is not required for licensed teachers, teachers with degrees in education or English, or for teachers teaching content subjects such as mathematics.
CONDITIONS OF EMPLOYMENT: 1 year, May to February/March. 15–25 teaching hours per week for English conversation.
SALARY: 33,300 baht per month for English Conversation teachers; 35,300 baht for Intensive English, 40,300 baht for English Programme (Content) teachers. All positions come with yearly bonuses. Thai taxes are deducted at a rate of approximately 1,300 baht per month. End-of-contract bonus up to 34,000 baht.
FACILITIES/SUPPORT: Assistance given in locating accommodation and translating/negotiating lease, if needed. Teachers are given necessary documents with instructions on how to obtain a non-immigrant B visa plus 2 paid working days to travel to obtain it. BFITS takes care of all costs and processing of the work permit.
RECRUITMENT: Via www.TotalESL.com, www.TESall.com, www.ESLjobfeed.com and www.TeachOverseas.ca partner sites of BFITS. Applications to HR Department with CV, photo, degrees/certificates and professional references can be emailed with

contact information. Date of availability (or relocation date to Thailand) must be specified. Interviews by Skype or in person.

BRITISH-AMERICAN LANGUAGE INSTITUTE

Soi 58/1 Ladprao Road (Opposite Chokchai 4 Market), Wangtonlang, Bangkok 10310

- ✆ +66 2 933 5635/6/7/8; mobile +66 89 482 3577
- ✉ british.american1977@gmail.com
- 🖥 www.british-american.ac.th

NUMBER OF TEACHERS: About 25.
PREFERENCE OF NATIONALITY: Native English speakers.
QUALIFICATIONS: Enthusiasm and positive attitude are essential.
CONDITIONS OF EMPLOYMENT: Usually part-time, 4–6 teaching hours per day.
SALARY: Earnings usually approximately 30,000+ baht per month. Local rent for an apartment is approximately 3,000 baht monthly.
FACILITIES/SUPPORT: Provide details of recommended apartments. All the visa paperwork is done by the school, but the teacher pays for visa and out-of-pocket expenses.
RECRUITMENT: Advertising in national newspapers.
CONTACT: Jack Downes.

ECC (THAILAND)

Teacher Service Centre (English & Computer College), ITEC House, 1st Floor, 9 Rajdamri Road, Lumpini, Patumwan, Bangkok 10330

- ✆ +66 2 655 3333
- ✉ jobs@ecc.ac.th
- 🖥 www.eccthai.com/jobs.asp

50 schools in Bangkok and in most major centres outside Bangkok (including Chiang Mai and Phuket). Largest private language school in Thailand.
NUMBER OF TEACHERS: Around 500 native English speakers (usually recruit 10–15 new teachers each month).
PREFERENCE OF NATIONALITY: None.
QUALIFICATIONS: Bachelor's degree plus TEFL certificate (CELTA, Trinity or equivalent).
CONDITIONS OF EMPLOYMENT: Minimum 100 hours per month (average 25–30 hours per week), 6-day week, mostly in evenings and weekends. BUPA medical insurance, end-of-contract bonus of 12,000 baht, location allowance in Bangkok (3,000–5,000 baht per month). 5 days' paid holiday in April plus 13 statutory holidays.

SALARY: Depending on qualifications and experience 31,000–37,000 baht per month in Bangkok, 20,000–30,000 baht in the provinces.
FACILITIES/SUPPORT: Work permit and 1-year visa applied for after arrival. Assistance (non-financial) given with finding accommodation. Professional development with regular workshops, including a number of short courses that are free to ECC teachers: Teaching English to Young Learners and Teaching Business English. ECC offers the Cambridge CELTA course and an Introduction to TESOL course. BUPA health insurance plan.
RECRUITMENT: Adverts on the internet and qualified walk-ins.
CONTACT: Garth Marshall, Director of Study. (jobs@ecc.ac.th).

ECHO ENGLISH LTD

90/165 Plex Bangna, Moo.15, Bang Na -Trat Road, Bang Kaew, Bang Phli, Samutprakarn 10540

- ✆ +66 863315751
- ✉ echoteam@echo-english.com
- 🖥 www.echo-english.com

Also offers TEFL Internships via www.teflheaven.com.
NUMBER OF TEACHERS: 100.
PREFERENCE OF NATIONALITY: USA, Australia, United Kingdom, Ireland, Canada, New Zealand.
QUALIFICATIONS: BA is essential and a TEFL certificate is desirable. Relevant teaching experience is also taken into account as a possible alternative to qualifications.
CONDITIONS OF EMPLOYMENT: 1 school semester, i.e. about 6 months, with option to renew. Teachers must be at school all day Monday-Friday. Teaching time no more than 24 hours per week.
SALARY: 30,000 Thai baht per month.
FACILITIES/SUPPORT: 3-day TEFL programme run bi-annually costs £80. Advice given on finding accommodation.
RECRUITMENT: Online advertisements, through a TEFL course partner based in the UK, and through a 3-day TEFL programme Echo English runs in Bangkok twice a year. Candidates are interviewed via online video chat. Work permit costs including compulsory medical check-up are covered by the company.
CONTACT: Vicky Payne, Recruitment and Support Assistant.

GAP YEAR THAILAND

1 Vernon Avenue, Rugby CV22 5HL, UK

- ✆ +44 1788 552617
- ✉ davidgapyearthailand@gmail.com

Professional education non-for-profit organisation whose key team members have a background in teacher education in universities in UK or in the Rajabhat universities (teacher training universities) in Thailand. The programme is approved and endorsed by the South East Asian Ministers of Education Organisation.

NUMBER OF PLACEMENTS PER YEAR: 20+ volunteers to work as assistant teachers, teaching English (particularly conversational English) in schools or universities.

QUALIFICATIONS: Minimum age of 18, average age of 20s. Must speak English as a first language. Teaching qualification not needed.

CONDITIONS OF EMPLOYMENT: Minimum 2 months up to 6+ months.

SALARY: None. Programme cost: £980 including accommodation, which can be homestay with family or in a teacher's house.

RECRUITMENT: Applications accepted throughout the year. Telephone interviews. Pre-departure briefing weekend with some TEFL training, and further training in the orientation programme on arrival.

CONTACT: Dr David Lancaster, Chief Executive.

GIFT SCHOOL OF ENGLISH
Nakorn Pathom, Central Thailand
🖰 giftschoolofenglish@gmail.com
🖳 www.gift-school-of-english.com

NUMBER OF TEACHERS: 30 full-time and part-time native speaking teachers teach in small public and temple schools throughout Thailand, and at free summer camps for disadvantaged children.

PREFERENCE OF NATIONALITY: None

QUALIFICATIONS: Only a wish to gain experience in teaching English, Thai culture and travel.

CONDITIONS OF EMPLOYMENT: One-year contracts (renewable) to start May/June and October/November.

SALARY: None.

RECRUITMENT: Year round.

CONTACT: Nora Ying.

INLINGUA INTERNATIONAL SCHOOL OF LANGUAGES
4th Floor, Esplanade, 99 Ratchadaphisek Road, Dindaeng, Bangkok 10400
📞 +66 2 655 3333
🖰 teach@inlinguabangkok.com
🖳 www.inlinguabangkok.com

NUMBER OF TEACHERS: 140 full-time, 100 part-time. For 19 branches.

PREFERENCE OF NATIONALITY: Native English speakers: American, Canadian, British, Irish, Australian, New Zealander and South African.

QUALIFICATIONS: Candidates must have at least 2 of the following: bachelor's degree, TESOL/TEFL/CELTA, experience.

CONDITIONS OF EMPLOYMENT: 1 year. Children's classes are on Saturday/Sunday 9am–6pm. Teachers work a 6-day week or 5 for corporate work.

SALARY: Guaranteed minimum 35,000 baht for full-time contract teachers; possibly more, depending on workload.

FACILITIES/SUPPORT: Try to point staff in the direction of suitable accommodation. Full support given in work permit/visa applications. BUPA medical insurance.

RECRUITMENT: Internet adverts on www.ajarn.com. Applications welcomed on above email address. Mostly local hires.

CONTACT: Fraser Morrell, Director of Studies (fraserm@inlingua bangkok.com).

IST PLUS – TEACH IN THAILAND PROGRAMME
Churcham House, 1 Bridgeman Road, Teddington, Middlesex TW1 9AJ, UK
📞 +44 20 7788 7877
🖰 info@istplus.com
🖳 www.istplus.com

NUMBER OF TEACHERS: 20–30 each year for two programmes, one for paid teachers in state schools, supported by the Overseas Ed Group (www.oeg.co.th), and the other voluntary.

PREFERENCE OF NATIONALITY: None, although non-native speakers of English must have near-native proficiency in English.

QUALIFICATIONS: University degree in any field essential. TEFL training or experience is not essential but preferred. Maximum age 65.

CONDITIONS OF EMPLOYMENT: 5 or 10-month renewable contracts starting in either May or October, teaching 22 classes a week, which works out at a working week of 35–40 hours.

SALARY: Minimum 25,000 baht per month.

FACILITIES/SUPPORT: Free accommodation (usually on-campus), all-inclusive 7-day orientation in Bangkok on arrival including basic EFL training, accommodation, sight-seeing and airport transfer. IST Plus arrange school placement, visa and work permit, insurance and 24-hour emergency hotline.

RECRUITMENT: Deadlines for application are mid-March for May departure and mid-August for October departure. Teach in Thailand Programme fees from £995 for 5 months, £1,195 for 10 months. Teachers who complete 10-month contracts starting in May will receive a 20,000 baht bonus. All teachers who complete their contracts will receive a TEFL certificate.

CONTACT: Ralph Allemano, Director (rallemano@istplus.com).

KING'S COLLEGE OF ENGLISH

1093/19–21, 5th Floor, Central City Tower I, Bangna-Trad Road, Bangna, Prakanong, Bangkok 10260

- +66 2 745 6001
- kings.recruitment@hotmail.com
- www.kingsthailand.com

A group of 4 English-language schools in Thailand.

NUMBER OF TEACHERS: 35–40.

PREFERENCE OF NATIONALITY: Native English speakers: British (majority), Canadian, American, Australian, New Zealander, South African.

QUALIFICATIONS: University degree (any subject) plus CELTA or 120-hour equivalent. Preference given to applicants with qualifications or experience teaching young learners, and/or with experience at summer camps or primary schools. Support and extensive materials are supplied.

CONDITIONS OF EMPLOYMENT: 1-year contracts mainly from August. Contractual arrangement is 112 contact hours per month; preparation time is extra. Saturday and Sunday are working days. 2 consecutive days off a week.

SALARY: Approximately 34,000 baht per month depending on qualifications and experience. Yearly increment, paid holidays (13 days plus 13 statutory public holidays). End-of-contract bonus of 25,000 baht as contribution to flights.

FACILITIES/SUPPORT: Assistance with accommodation and non-immigrant B visa. Basic private health insurance provided by school. Free Thai language lessons plus Thai cookery and boxing programme.

RECRUITMENT: Local and web adverts and UK recruitment agency. UK applicants should send CV and photo in the first instance to John Hudson (john.hudson@firstwayforward.com or hudson.111@virgin.net). Interviews are usually by Skype and phone.

SIAM COMPUTER & LANGUAGE INSTITUTE

471/19 Ratchawithi Road, Bangkok 10400

- +66 2 247 2345 ext. 200/364
- adasm_1999@yahoo.com or recruitment@siamcom.co.th
- www.siamcom.co.th

NUMBER OF TEACHERS: 35 for client government schools in the greater Bangkok area and 49 at 38 external locations in the greater Bangkok area.

PREFERENCE OF NATIONALITY: Native English speakers.

QUALIFICATIONS: College degree required; CELTA or equivalent and experience preferred.

CONDITIONS OF EMPLOYMENT: 9–12 month contracts. Full-time internal teachers 6 days per week in air-conditioned facilities; 15 or fewer students per class. All ages. Full-time external teachers 5 days per week in Thai classrooms. 50 students per class from kindergarten to high school level.

SALARY: 33,000–40,000 baht per month based on experience. Bonus plans for external teachers. Hourly rates for part-time internal and external teachers.

FACILITIES/SUPPORT: Assistance with finding local accommodation. 15 paid Thai vacation days per year, assistance in obtaining a teacher's licence, work permit and 1-year visa. Complete teacher orientation and teacher training before starting in the classroom, with bimonthly teachers' meetings.

RECRUITMENT: Adverts in the *Bangkok Post* and on the worldwide web, and contacts with schools in Australia and the USA. Online application form.

CONTACT: Anthony Donnelly or Mr Bhudeb.

SIAM ENGLISH LANGUAGE SCHOOL

1199 4th Floor, Piyavan Tower, Phaholyothin Rd, Ari Samsennai, Phyathai, Bangkok 10400

- +66 5234 4713 or 2704 8244
- jones@siamels.org or contact@siamels.org
- www.siamels.org

NUMBER OF TEACHERS: 37 at 35 school locations in the greater Bangkok area and 49 at 38 external locations in the greater Bangkok area.

PREFERENCE OF NATIONALITY: Native English speakers.

QUALIFICATIONS: College degree required; CELTA or equivalent and experience preferred. Dynamic personality, aged 25–35.

CONDITIONS OF EMPLOYMENT: 1-year contracts. Full-time internal teachers 6 days per week in air-conditioned facilities; 15 or fewer students per class. All ages. Full-time external teachers 5 days per week in Thai classrooms. 50 students per class from kindergarten to high school level.

SALARY: 30,000+ baht per month based on experience. Bonus plans for external teachers. Hourly rates for part-time internal and external teachers.

FACILITIES/SUPPORT: Assistance with finding local accommodation. 15 paid Thai vacation days per year, assistance in obtaining a teacher's licence, work permit and 1-year visa. Complete teacher orientation and teacher training before starting in the classroom, with bimonthly teachers' meetings.

RECRUITMENT: Adverts in the *Bangkok Post* and on the worldwide web, and contacts with schools in Australia and the USA. Interviews in Bangkok required.

CONTACT: Ian Jones.

SINE EDUCATION
555 SSP Tower, 11th Floor, 555/50-51 Soi Sukhumvit 63, Sukhumvit Road, Bangkok 10110

📞 +66 2 711 4703

✉ hr@sineeducation.com

💻 www.sineeducation.com

NUMBER OF TEACHERS: Approximately 100.

PREFERENCE OF NATIONALITY: UK, Canada, New Zealand, USA, Australia, South Africa and Ireland.

QUALIFICATIONS: Minimum bachelor's degree from a recognised university. Must be enthusiastic and motivated.

CONDITIONS OF EMPLOYMENT: 10 months from 1 May. Max 24 teaching hours per week between 7.30am and 4pm. Positions are in public (government) schools, with large classes and few resources. Teachers follow the SINE system which involves standardised PowerPoints so preparation time is minimal.

SALARY: 33,000 baht per month. Maximum tax deduction of 5%.

FACILITIES/SUPPORT: Company assists teachers throughout the process and pays for permits to teach, work permits and final visas. Help given with finding accommodation. Training in the SINE method given.

RECRUITMENT: Internet, personal recommendation. Recruiting constantly via online form.

CONTACT: Keith James, Programme Manager.

SPENCER INTERNATIONAL
1st Fl., Muangthai Phatra Complex, 252/193 Rachadapisek Road, Bangkok 10320

📞 +66 2 693 2901

✉ stephen.l@spencer.co.th or recruitment2013@spencer.co.th

💻 www.spencer.co.th

NUMBER OF TEACHERS: 60. Also for schools in Cambodia, Vietnam, Myanmar, China and Indonesia.

PREFERENCE OF NATIONALITY: None.

QUALIFICATIONS: Professional educators need a 120-hour training course. Degree holders are preferred, but positions for non-degree holders are also available. Inexperienced and unqualified teachers

have opportunities to undergo formal or in-house training through a staff development programme.

CONDITIONS OF EMPLOYMENT: 10-month contract. Usual hours 7.30am–3.30pm Monday to Friday. Evening and weekend work are offered as overtime.

SALARY: Starting salary 32,000 baht with increments after 3 months, 6 months and 1 year. Tax is deducted at source.

FACILITIES/SUPPORT: Spencer International provides TEFL and TESOL courses in Bangkok, accredited through Chichester College, UK. Assistance given with finding accommodation in the school vicinity to suit teacher's lifestyle. School takes care of all work permit procedures for teachers holding the appropriate qualifications.

RECRUITMENT: Via TESOL training programmes or the internet. Interviews can be conducted by email, Skype or telephone.

CONTACT: Stephen Louw, Academic Coordinator.

SUPER ENGLISH
38/1–2 Bandon Road, Talad, Muang, Surat Thani 84000

📞 +66 77 213395

✉ teach@superenglishsurat.com

💻 www.superenglishsurat.com

NUMBER OF TEACHERS: 14.

PREFERENCE OF NATIONALITY: American.

QUALIFICATIONS: University degree essential. Must have the right attitude: a willingness to learn, be flexible about living in an eastern culture, able to think creatively and be patient. Must enjoy working with children and have a sincere desire to teach them English and to have an impact on their lives.

CONDITIONS OF EMPLOYMENT: Standard 1-year contract from October or May. Schedules vary greatly but usually 20–25 hours per week (and hours above 25 are paid overtime rate). Some teachers work in the mornings and have their afternoons off; others prefer late mornings and continuing through the early evening. Classes finish at 6.30pm. Weekends off.

SALARY: Current flat salary is 35,000 baht per month.

FACILITIES/SUPPORT: Shared, semi-furnished accommodation in Surat Thani provided free for first 3 months. Paperwork provided pre-arrival for a 3-month non-immigrant B visa. School will process that visa into a 1-year non-immigrant visa and will obtain a 1-year labour permit. 20,000 baht paid for holiday month of October.

RECRUITMENT: Adverts on www.eslcafe.com and directly via website. Interviews via Skype are essential.

CONTACT: Peter C. Meltzer, Owner and Founder.

THE AMERICAN ENGLISH LANGUAGE SCHOOL

29/492 Moo 2, Ransit Klong 3, Klong Sahm, A.
Klongluang, Pathumthani 12120

☎ +66 89 922 4126

✉ americanenglishthailand@gmail.com or
teacherfinder@hotmail.com

💻 www.americanenglishthailand.com

NUMBER OF TEACHERS: 40.

PREFERENCE OF NATIONALITY: All nationalities welcome.

QUALIFICATIONS: At least a bachelor's degree from an internationally accredited academic institution. BEd (or higher) degree holders will receive preference. At least 1 year's teaching experience required, preferably in Thailand.

CONDITIONS OF EMPLOYMENT: 1-year contract starting in early May, ending in late April. To teach Monday to Friday, 8am–4.30pm.

SALARY: Starts at 30,000 baht per month with no real ceiling. The AELS sends teachers to many levels of schools where top earnings are 50,000 baht and up. Taxes are 1,000–2,000 baht per month and 650 baht per month for health care coverage and social security (compulsory under Thai law).

FACILITIES/SUPPORT: Company helps teachers find a place that has a good location, for a good rent, with good amenities, and takes them to all the necessary offices, every step of the way, to get the necessary papers. Teachers pay for visa and work permit upfront, but will be reimbursed by AELS on completion of contract.

RECRUITMENT: By personal interviews and teaching demonstrations, followed by credential checks. Company rarely hires directly from overseas: three videoconferencing interviews have led to only one hire so far.

CONTACT: Jason Alavi, Owner & Director.

WECI TEFL (WORLD ENGLISH COMMUNICATION INSTITUTE)

70/145 Soi 112 Hua Na, Petchakasem Road, Tambon
Nhong Kae, Hua Hin, Prachuap Khiri Khan 77110

☎ +66 32 900464/mob. +66 96 883 1146

✉ info@wecitefl.com

💻 www.wecitefl.com

NUMBER OF TEACHERS: 15.

PREFERENCE OF NATIONALITY: Native English speakers.

QUALIFICATIONS: Minimum bachelor degree plus 120 hour TEFL training course (TESOL or CELTA).

CONDITIONS OF EMPLOYMENT: 30–25 hours per week. 1-year contracts.

SALARY: Minimum 30,000 baht (net).

FACILITIES/SUPPORT: Some schools provide housing; others help teachers to find accommodation. Full assistance given with correct visa. If applicant lacks necessary training, they can do it at WECI TEFL (as listed in Training Directory).

RECRUITMENT: Word of mouth, via universities. Interviews by Skype or email.

CONTACT: Darron Jenkins or Kannika Prakobphon, Office Manager.

LATIN AMERICA

Spanning 75 degrees of latitude, the mammoth continent of South America, together with the Caribbean islands and the eight countries of Central America, offers an eclectic range of teaching opportunities. With the important exception of Brazil, where Portuguese is spoken, South American countries have a majority of Spanish speakers and, as in Spain itself, there is a great demand for English teaching, from Mexican resorts where local people want to access jobs in the tourist industry to Punta Arenas at the southern extremity of the continent, south of the Falkland Islands.

The countries of most interest to the travelling teacher are Chile, Argentina, Colombia, Ecuador, Venezuela, Brazil and Mexico. Certain patterns emerged during the research for the various editions of this book, though sweeping generalisations are of limited value and will not apply to all countries and all situations. After problems with inflation, most countries (apart from Venezuela, where it ballooned in 2015) have brought the rates down to reasonable levels, which means that salaries do not lose their value as they once did. Although pay scales are sometimes quoted in US dollars, wages are almost always paid in the local currency.

Urban life in the big cities of Brazil, Argentina and Chile is more like that of Europe than of developing countries. In such cities, the greatest demand for English comes from businesses. Because of the strong commercial links between the two American continents, the demand tends to be for American English, though an increasing number of British and Australian teachers are finding work in these countries.

Among the providers of the English language are Bi-National Centers and Cultural Centers, the American counterpart of the British Council. There are scores of these centres in Latin America, many engaged in the teaching of English, including 17 IBEUs (Instituto Brasil-Estados Unidos) in Brazil alone employing more than 200 teachers. While the English Language Fellow Program administered from Washington requires teachers with an MA in TESOL from a US university to commit to 10-month contracts, there may be more informal local opportunities for others. A good point of contact is the relevant Regional English Language Officer (http://americanenglish.state.gov/locate-regional-english-language-officer-relo).

Britain also has cultural representatives in several Latin American countries; the longest-established Culturas Inglesas are in Argentina (founded 1927) plus Brazil, Chile, Mexico, Paraguay, Peru and Uruguay. Among them, these *Culturas* teach English to a quarter of a million students. Usually they require their teachers to have specialised ELT training and experience. Only a few recruit abroad, so it is worth making local enquiries on arrival.

Several South American nations have a number of British or American-style bilingual schools and *colegios*. Although this book is not centrally concerned with English-medium schools, which are usually looking for teachers with a PGCE or full teacher accreditation, international schools in South America are mainly for local nationals (rather than expatriates) who want a bilingual Spanish-English education and have a very strong emphasis on English-language teaching. Despite the prestige of these schools, some are willing to consider EFL teachers who have not done teacher training. For example, some accept school-leavers participating in gap-year projects.

Finally, there are private and commercial language institutes, from International House, which is not well represented in the continent (Argentina, Colombia, Ecuador, Mexico and Uruguay only), through to Berlitz (which is strongly represented in Latin America) to the cowboy operations where standards and wages will be extremely low. **David Hewitt**, a computer programmer from Yorkshire with no TEFL training or experience, was surprised not only to walk into a casual teaching job in Brazil but also to find himself giving lessons to the director of the school. In whatever kind of school you teach, or if you just give occasional private lessons to contacts, you will probably find the local people extremely friendly and eager to help. The ethnic diversity and Latin warmth encountered by foreign teachers and travellers throughout the continent usually more than compensate for low wages and (in the big cities) a high crime rate.

PROSPECTS FOR TEACHERS

In a land where baseball is a passion and US television enormously popular, American (and also Canadian) job-seekers have an advantage. The whole continent is culturally and economically oriented towards the USA. There is a decided preference among language learners for the American accent and for American teaching materials and course books, which explains why so many language institutes are called Lincoln and Jefferson. Business English is gaining ground throughout the region, particularly in Argentina, Chile, Colombia, Brazil and Mexico, and anyone with a business background will have an edge over the competition.

The academic year begins in February or early March and lasts until November/December. In the southern-most nations of Chile and Argentina, January and February are very slack months for language schools; while further north in Bolivia, for example, the summer holiday consists of December/January. The best time to arrive to look for work is a few weeks before the end of the summer holidays. But many institutes run eight to 12-week courses year round and will be eager for the services of a native English speaker whatever the time of year.

FINDING A JOB

Speculative enquiries from EFL teachers are less likely to work if sent before arrival than after, although sending a 'warm-up' CV may help your job search. What the principal of a girls' school in Lima wrote is echoed by many other institutes. '*Anyone interested in a job is welcome to write to me at any time. If they happen to be in Lima they are equally welcome to come into school.*' Unless you are very well qualified or have met your prospective employer before, you are unlikely to be offered a contract while out of the country. This is unfortunate since work visas are best applied for in the country of origin of the teacher (see below). On the other hand, **Miranda Crowhurst** had a Skype interview with an institute in Bolivia, and took up a position a month or two later, where she is still teaching.

IN ADVANCE

Not many Latin American language schools advertise internationally. Even the most prestigious schools complain of the difficulties they encounter recruiting teachers abroad, mainly due to the low salaries they can offer and the bureaucratic procedures for obtaining a work permit. When 20-year-old **James Gratton** was making plans for his first trip to South America, he wrote to all the embassies in London and received quite a lot of literature, including a number of lists of language schools, for Paraguay, Uruguay, Peru, Argentina, etc. Serious candidates might ask the cultural attaché for advice.

In addition to International House and Berlitz, already mentioned, EF English First and Wall Street English have quite a few branches. Saxoncourt Recruitment is occasionally active in Peru and one or two other countries of South America and sometimes recruits on behalf of Culturas Inglesas and international schools. Denver-based Bridge TEFL (www.bridgetefl.com) offers TEFL training courses in a dozen Latin American cities from Santiago to Playa del Carmen on the Caribbean coast of Mexico (at a cost of $1,995), many of whose graduates go on immediately to work locally. For language school listings and teaching information check http://thelajoblist.blogspot.com. A site called TeacherKick.com publicises a certain number of current vacancies throughout Latin America. TEFL training colleges in the US often have close ties with Latin American language schools, such as Transworld School, which sends large numbers of its graduates to posts in South America. Teaching House maintains an impressive database of teacher vacancies for CELTA holders; at the time of writing there were 285 listings for Colombia, 226 in Chile, 386 in Mexico and so on.

The British Council arranges for language assistants to work in five Latin American countries for an academic year: Argentina, Chile, Colombia, Ecuador and Mexico; details can be found on their website (www.britishcouncil.org/language-assistants/become/latin-america). Applicants must be undergraduates studying Spanish or graduates with a Spanish A level. The level of placements and the nature of the duties are more suited to graduates than undergraduates. Deadlines for application vary among the different countries.

The Association of American Schools in South America (AASSA, www.aassa.com) coordinates teacher recruitment for its 75 full and invitational members, all American international schools in 24 Latin American and Caribbean countries. Candidates who attend a recruiting fair in December must have a degree and generally be state-certified teachers. There is a $110 registration fee and if you are hired your school pays a further placement fee to AASSA.

Volunteers are widely deployed as teachers throughout the continent. The non-profit organisation South American Explorers keeps lists of schools that employ English teachers. It has a volunteer database for members to access with information about volunteering opportunities throughout South America. Many of the organisations listed will take on English teachers without TEFL certification. Membership costs $60 per year ($90 for a couple). Contact South American Explorers for further details (www.saexplorers.org).

Patient searching of the web will unearth opportunities for volunteering, perhaps through one of the mainstream databases like www.idealist.org or www.wwv.org.uk. Specialist websites like www.volunteersouthamerica.net and http://barefootatlas.com are always worth scouring for 'grass-roots, zero-cost volunteer work' in South and Central America. Another Latin American specialist website with a similar ambition is www.volunteerlatinamerica.com. To contact any of the organisations in their searchable directory of grassroots projects, it is necessary to join at a cost of £10 for two years' basic membership or £20 which includes personalised assistance.

Lots of commercial volunteer agencies have programmes in Latin America such as: i-to-i (www.i-to-i.com), which sends fee-paying participants to teach in Brazil, Costa Rica, Ecuador and Peru; Travellers Worldwide (www.travellersworldwide.com) with teaching programmes in Argentina, Costa Rica, Ecuador and Brazil. Knowledge of Spanish may be expected on some of these programmes and accommodation is usually with host families. The UK and Australia-based teacher recruitment agency TEFL Heaven (www.tefl-heaven.com) arranges jobs in Costa Rica, Peru and Guatemala normally involving an in-country TEFL training course.

WorldTeach at Harvard (www.worldteach.org) places paying volunteers as teachers of EFL or ESL for a year in Colombia, Costa Rica, Ecuador, Chile and (unusually) Guyana. There is also a summer programme in Haiti. The Spain-based online community www.culturegogo.com allows subscribers to arrange a live-in stay directly with a host family, many of whom are looking for English conversation practice. Listings for South and Central America include Colombia, Costa Rica, Chile, Mexico and Argentina. For a fee of €15, volunteers can sign up for a one-year membership and contact any registered families to teach them English in exchange for food and accommodation.

ON THE SPOT

The concept of 'job vacancy' is very fluid in many Latin American language institutes and, provided you are willing to work for local teaching wages, you should be able to create your own job almost anywhere. As throughout the world, local applicants often break into the world of language teaching gradually by teaching a few classes a week. Non-contractual work is almost always offered on an unofficial part-time basis. So if you are trying to earn a living you will have to patch together enough hours from various sources. Finding the work is simply a matter of asking around and knocking on enough doors. For those who speak no Spanish, the first hurdle is to communicate your request to the secretaries at language schools, since they rarely speak much English. Try to memorise a polite request in Spanish to pass your CV (*hoja de vida*) and letter (in Spanish if possible) to the school director, who will know at least some English. Check adverts in the English-language press such as the *Buenos Aires Herald*. English-language bookshops are another possible source of teaching leads.

Ask in expatriate bars and restaurants, check out any building claiming to be an 'English School', however dubious-looking, and in larger cities try deciphering the telephone directory for schools or agencies which might be able to use your services. There is more competition as well as more opportunities in the major cities (for example, it is said that up to half a million Americans live in Mexico City), so if you are having difficulties rounding up work, you could try smaller towns and cities off the beaten track.

The crucial factor in becoming accepted as an English teacher at a locally run language school may not be your qualifications or your accent as much as your appearance. You must look as neat and well dressed as teachers are expected to look, at least when you're job-hunting. Later your standards might slip a little: **Nick Wilson**, who taught for two years in Mexico, says that it is easy to spot the English teachers in banks and office buildings; they're the ones wearing jeans, T-shirts and carrying a CD player.

FREELANCE TEACHING

In most Latin American cities there is a thriving market in private English lessons, which usually pay at least half as much again as working for an institute. It is not uncommon for teachers to consider the language school that hires them as a stepping-stone to setting up as a private tutor. After they have familiarised themselves with some teaching materials and made enough contacts among local language learners, they strike out on their own, though this is far from easy unless you can get by in the local language and have access to suitable premises. If you are thinking of privately tutoring students you have met through a language school, check your contract carefully to make sure you are not breaking its terms. Clients can be found by advertising on online communities, by placing notices on strategic noticeboards or by handing out well-produced business cards. If the latter, use the local method of address and omit confusing initials such as BA after your name: teachers often call themselves '*Profesor*' or '*Profesora*'.

REGULATIONS

Of course requirements vary from country to country but the prospects are dismal for teachers who insist on doing everything by the book. It is standard for work visas to be available only to fully qualified and experienced teachers on long-term contracts. Often you will have to present an array of documents, from university certificates and transcripts to FBI police clearance, which have been authenticated by your consulate abroad or by the consulate of the host country. Although many schools will not offer a contract before interview and then will make it contingent on a work permit, the procedures should be started in the teacher's country of origin, which makes the whole business very difficult. All of this can take as long as six months and involve a great deal of hassle and expense, not least for the employer.

The upshot is that a high percentage of teachers work unofficially throughout Latin America. It is hardly an issue in some countries, for example virtually no one gets a work permit in Brazil, not even long-resident language school teachers. Teaching on a tourist visa or as a 'tourist' in countries where you don't need a visa is a widespread practice in Mexico and Peru. There are ways round the regulations, for example to work on a student/trainee/cultural exchange visa (as in Ecuador or Venezuela).

CONDITIONS OF WORK

Very few schools offer perks such as an extra month's salary or return flights to teachers who stay for a two-year contract. Contracts are fairly hard to come by and always require a minimum commitment of a year. The advantages are that you are guaranteed a certain income and you have a chance of applying for a work permit. Teachers without the CELTA or Trinity certificate are not greatly disadvantaged, partly because this qualification is not as widely known in Latin America as it is in Europe, although you can take the Trinity TESOL course at the Casa de Ingles in Chaco (Argentina), the British Council in Recife and Sao Paulo (Brazil), the Dickens Institute in Montevideo (Uruguay), ICLS in Guadalajara (Mexico) and Stael Ruffinelli de Ortiz English in Asuncion (Paraguay). Many institutes offer their own compulsory pre-job training (to be taken at the teacher's own expense), which provides a useful orientation for new arrivals.

One of the seldom-mentioned perks of teaching in Latin America is the liveliness and enthusiasm of the students. Brazilian students have been described as the 'world's most communicative students' and classrooms around the continent often take on the atmosphere of a party. You may also be dazzled by the level of knowledge of western popular culture, and should be prepared to have your ignorance shown up. Also be prepared to lose their attention if a lesson coincides with a major sporting event.

LEISURE TIME

Whether you are a serious student of Spanish or a frivolous seeker after the excitement generated by Latin carnivals, South America is a wonderful place to live and travel. Women teachers may find the machismo a little hard to take, but will soon learn how to put it in its place. If you want to travel around, the annually revised *South American Handbook* definitely justifies the initial outlay of £23.

ARGENTINA

The teaching market in Argentina is reasonably buoyant, with hundreds of institutes operating at varying standards. However, the economy as of 2015 looks stalled, though is not expected to go into recession, so the market may not expand over the next couple of years. The cost of living keeps rising, and many European visitors wonder how the local people can manage on the wages they earn, when eating out, taxis, etc are so expensive in Buenos Aires (but not basic services like public transport and haircuts). Teachers are far more likely to secure a job once they are in Argentina than by applying from their home country. Anyone with a recognised qualification like the CELTA will probably get snapped up, at least for a few hours a week initially, as Alan Chadwick did.

ALAN CHADWICK

Alan Chadwick completed the CELTA course in his home town of Cambridge, and exactly a year later set off for Argentina to work and travel.

He started in Buenos Aires and spent some time asking around and investigating teaching possibilities. But he found the city too hectic, not to mention too dangerous. Four or five mugging incidents were reported just by people in his hostel, and the final straw came when a young Finnish traveller who had set off one afternoon to catch a long-distance bus to her next destination returned within an hour having had all her bags, money and passport taken at gunpoint - possibly a toy gun but she couldn't be sure.

So Alan headed for Córdoba, second-largest city of Argentina, where he had an English friend managing a hostel. After handing round his CV to a few language schools, he was offered some hours of teaching within three days of arrival and at the first school he had approached, the British School, which has several branches around Córdoba. The wage was a decent £10 an hour. But it turned out that his teaching was to take place at a different branch, an hour and a half journey by public transport from where he was staying, which hadn't been spelt out at the interview.

His first exposure to his colleagues was a little challenging. Because he happens to be from Cambridge, home of the famous First Certificate English exam, they had lots of questions about the exam and the syllabus, with which he was almost totally unfamiliar ('To be honest, I haven't been teaching it very long ...') On the first day the director introduced him as 'someone from Cambridge - with a DELTA', which he hastily corrected to CELTA; it seemed that she was not familiar with the substantial difference between the two qualifications disguised by one letter along in the alphabet. When introduced in the staff room, he started shaking hands, and the staff (all middle-aged Argentinian women) laughed at him, telling him that in Argentina, you kiss.

In some respects Alan loved that everyone was 'super-relaxed' about everything: students routinely arrived 20 minutes late, no one was too bothered about targets, etc. But it wasn't so great on pay day, when he had to travel to the other side of the city to collect a quarter of the wages he was owed, probably due to gross inefficiency rather than anything more sinister. With some effort, and a strategic phone call to the head of his branch to vouch for him, he eventually received all the wages he was owed.

He was teaching a total of about 10 hours a week: two-three hours on four evenings. Because he didn't speak Spanish, he was assigned high-level adults. He taught FCE prep and a conversation class, which he really enjoyed. On the assumption that everyone likes to talk about themselves, he only needed to introduce a random question such as 'What have you done that has made you proud?' to prompt a cascade of conversation. The mixed bag of students asked him all sorts of questions about British culture, life in Cambridge, etc. He corrected some of their mistakes in English but not too many because he didn't want to discourage them.

After six weeks of working for British School, he told the boss that he needed more hours to make it financially viable or he would have to leave. She could not offer him any at that time, but suggested he try to piece together work from other schools that he knew would be possible. But by then he was finding the relentless 30-degree heat and the lack of greenery rather draining, so he decided to move 1,000km west to the coast of Chile.

Language schools are linked from www.inglesnet.com. Courses in Argentina tend to start in mid-March after the school summer vacation, and finish in early December, with the month of July off for school holidays.

Job-seekers should check community noticeboards such as Craigslist (http://buenosaires.en.craigslist.org), which includes a steady stream of teaching job ads, mostly part-time for people already living in BA. There is a useful noticeboard in El Ateneo, the English-language bookshop at 340 Calle Florida (the main shopping street). Schools of Spanish abound and often prove good contact points for foreign residents who want to teach on the side.

Some of the 14 Bi-National Centers or Instituto de Intercambio Cultural Argentino-Americano (listed at http://argentina.usembassy.gov/binational_centers.html) offer English courses, as do the three International House schools in the capital (located in Recoleta, Belgrano and San Isidro). To work at one of these, you usually have to have worked for IH before. A large number of full-curriculum private schools prepare students for Cambridge and other exams, such as the Belgrano Day School in Buenos Aires; www.bds.edu.ar, which has pupils from kindergarten to school-leaving age.

It is commonplace for Americans and Britons to move from learning Spanish to teaching English, as **Chris Moloney** from Queensland did (and along the way had a romance with a previous Miss Argentina), and as did also **Richard Ferguson**, a New Zealander who has travelled extensively in South America:

> There are heaps of English schools in Buenos Aires and everyone wants to learn English. I made a few basic signs in Spanish advertising conversational classes, stuck them around Palermo (a wealthier suburb) and sometimes I'd stand on a busy corner and hand out leaflets. I charged about 30 pesos an hour per student. I think any native speaker can teach here, better with experience and better still with qualifications. Either do as I did, approach some schools or look in the papers in the jobs section. I saw at least 15 in one edition of the Buenos Aires Herald.

The standard hourly freelance wage offered to qualified English teachers for in-company work is 90-130 pesos, while the rate at language institutes will be considerably lower.

One of the easiest routes into a job is to take a TEFL training course in situ (see Training Directory). For example US-based BridgeTEFL (www.bridgetefl.com) offers a 120-hour proprietary certificate qualification called IDELT in Buenos Aires and also a 60-hour online course leading to an Educator Certificate. For those who want everything guaranteed ahead, BridgeTEFL has an on-the-job training programme called Teach in Argentina which costs $3,000.

Luke McElderry from Texas and his girlfriend **Jenny Jacobi** spent hours researching potential teaching employers in Buenos Aires on the internet. After completing a training course locally, he sent a mass email with CV attached to at least 40 addresses and waited for responses to trickle in, and ended up hearing from about a quarter. He describes his job hunt:

> *The first interviews were varied, some in English, one in Spanish, but all fairly casual. Most take 30 minutes and they seem to care more about your availability than your experience. I was asked a couple of times if I had any visa/permit and said no, and the employers didn't seem to care at all. I have heard the biggest institutes are the ones who care, and ironically pay the least!*

Before long, they were working for an institute, Speak Spanish, which, confusingly, also teaches English (www.speakspanish.com.ar). They were sent out to teach 90-minute classes in businesses. Sometimes they were assigned to comfortable conference rooms with whiteboards, free photocopies, faxes and coffee. Luke and Jenny found that all went smoothly, apart from finding accommodation:

> *It is a real hassle finding an apartment as they want to charge you tourist rates and it is nearly impossible to get a lease as an expat. Accommodation prices depend on your ability to find a rental agency that doesn't require a garantiá from an Argentine property owner saying that you will pay the entire rental term in full; some places will let you pay everything up front, usually six months or more, but these places are very few and far between.*

Alicia Meta of ACM Business English, Buenos Aires (see entry), explains how the letting market works:

> *If you are renting on a short contract the agents will ask you to pay in full. For a short-term contract you also have to pay a commission to the real estate agency of about 8% of the total amount. For a one-year contract the commission is the equivalent of one and a half months of the rent to be paid. The deposit for a long-term contract (one year) is equal to two months' rent. It is always returned once the deal is over.*
>
> *It is difficult for tourists to rent an apartment and unfortunately I believe that there is no other way out. My advice would be to get some feedback before coming to Argentina, go to a hostel and then calmly try to look for the best option. Usually, apartments in the outskirts of Buenos Aires can be cheaper but the payment method might not differ.*

If you want to cast your net wider you can move to smaller cities where there will be fewer vacancies but also fewer applicants competing for the jobs. For example, Bariloche in Patagonia in the deep south of Argentina has an unexpectedly large market for English teachers because of its role as an international ski resort. Expect the cost of living to be much higher in Patagonia.

VOLUNTEERING AND CULTURAL EXCHANGES

Cultural exchange programmes will appeal to those willing to teach as volunteers in rural areas, normally in state rather than private schools. For example, Voluntario Global (see entry) feeds Spanish-speaking volunteers to worthy projects in schools, among others, in greater Buenos Aires, while Connecting Schools to the World (see entry) invites university graduates to live for one or two semesters in a *pueblo* or city, mainly in the Argentinian province of Córdoba. The programme fee covers homestay accommodation with a local family and a modest monthly stipend. As with all these programmes, participants are encouraged to take up various extra-curricular activities such as tango lessons, cookery and photography.

Other possibilities, some of them more like tour operators than exchange organisations, include the following.

Connecting Worlds, Buenos Aires: see entry.
EBC TEFL Training, Buenos Aires (www.ebcteflcourse.com). Offers a month-long TEFL training course for €1000 followed by a job placement programme.
Expanish, Buenos Aires (+54 11 5252 3040; www.expanish.com/volunteer). Spanish language school with Volunteer English teaching programme.
Road2Argentina, Buenos Aires (www.road2argentina.com). Places ESL interns for 4–24 weeks between March and November, as part of a cultural exchange and language-immersion programme. International interns are accepted without relevant training or experience to help in private or public school classrooms. Programme fees start at $675 for one month and include accommodation in a shared homestay. (Road2Argentina also offers its own 4-week TEFL training course for $1,400 in Buenos Aires.)

RED TAPE

UK and US nationals have to buy a tourist visa valid for 90 days on arrival; the cost is $120, and it can be extended for another 90 days at the Dirección Nacional de Migraciones. The tourist visa can also be renewed by crossing the border, most commonly by ferry to Uruguay for the weekend which costs about $60, which is up to ten times cheaper than an 'exchange visa'.

Working papers can be obtained from the National Direction of Migrations by employers, though a school will be willing only for long-term propositions. It will be necessary for the applicant to provide a contract of employment for a minimum of a year and birth certificate (notarised by a notary public in Argentina), as well as passport. Non-British passport holders must also provide a certificate of good conduct from the police authorities in his or her country or countries of residence in the five years prior to applying.

Irish and Antipodean young people are eligible for a six-month working holiday visa extendable by three months. Irish applicants should check out the service offered by USIT (www.usit.ie).

Most teachers are paid hourly by the language institutes employing them. Self-employed people are obliged to register in the *monotributo* system with AFIP (tax office) and pay approximately 15% of their full-time earnings in tax.

LIST OF EMPLOYERS

ACM BUSINESS ENGLISH

Viamonte 2660, Buenos Aires

+54 911 5025 4752

info@acmbusinessenglish.com.ar

www.acmbusinessenglish.com.ar

NUMBER OF TEACHERS: 3–4.

PREFERENCE OF NATIONALITY: American, British and Canadian. Note: A strong Australian accent is usually difficult for Latin Americans to understand.

QUALIFICATIONS: TEFL, ESL or equivalent. Experience teaching ESL to adults in companies needed. Candidates with a teaching degree are the most sought after. General knowledge and high intellectual level needed for training executives who will be dealing with native English speakers at headquarters.

CONDITIONS OF EMPLOYMENT: No contracts. Part-time work so people are self-employed. Most teachers intend to stay in the country for at least 1 year, starting in March. Courses in Argentina start in March and finish in December. Usually 2–3 hours twice a week teaching in different companies. Many companies are located on the outskirts of Buenos Aires, so it can take more than an hour to reach some companies from downtown (where most candidates live) by bus. In these cases, a block of 3 hours minimum in one place is offered.

SALARY: Around 70 pesos per hour, paid at the beginning of the following month.

FACILITIES/SUPPORT: No training given. No assistance with accommodation.

RECRUITMENT: Word of mouth/posting on international websites, and in the *Buenos Aires Herald* (local English newspaper). Interviews in Buenos Aires.

CONTACT: Alicia Meta, Director.

CIL – CENTRO INTEGRAL DE LENGUAS

Leon 1753, Maipu, Córdoba

+54 351 458 1727

info@cil-method.com.ar

www.cil-method.com.ar

NUMBER OF TEACHERS: 3.

PREFERENCE OF NATIONALITY: None.

QUALIFICATIONS: Experience of teaching a second language or English.

CONDITIONS OF EMPLOYMENT: 9-month contracts. Teaching takes place in the afternoons. School has developed its own methods.

SALARY: 45 pesos an hour. If the teacher can invoice school, social security contributions of about 200 pesos can be made.

FACILITIES/SUPPORT: No assistance with accommodation or visas.

RECRUITMENT: Via newspaper ads and local interviews.

COLONIAS DE INMERSION AL IDIOMA (CII)

Av Forest 1213, Caba, Buenos Aires 1427

+54 11 4553 8445

experienceargentina@ecolonias.com

www.ecolonias.com

Experience Argentina voluntourism programme.

NUMBER OF TEACHERS: 25–35 TEFL interns per semester who spend 20 hours per week assisting with English in a local school or camp, a few hours a week tutoring members of their host family and one weekend a month at a language camp for children and young people.

PREFERENCE OF NATIONALITY: Citizen of any English-speaking country.

QUALIFICATIONS: University students and graduates aged 20–26, no specific qualifications or experience required. Speaking knowledge of Spanish preferred and TEFL certificate.

CONDITIONS OF EMPLOYMENT: 3–12 months, preferably starting 10 March or 25 July. Most schools prefer applicants who can commit to at least a semester. Schedules vary from school to school. Total of 25 hours a week.

SALARY: Monthly stipend of 280–350 pesos plus 200 pesos for participating in weekend language camp. Early-booking programme fees of $2,495 for up to 6 months, $2,995 for up to 12 months includes homestay accommodation throughout with full board, Spanish coaching and opportunities to travel.

FACILITIES/SUPPORT: 60-hour Bridge TEFL online certificate course is compulsory for those who do not have a TEFL qualification (at a cost of $325).

RECRUITMENT: Through cooperating universities and the internet. Interviews sometimes carried out in the UK and Ireland.

CONTACT: Fernando Damián Carro, CII Director.

CONNECTING SCHOOLS TO THE WORLD

Luis Maria Campos 545 1 D; 1426 Buenos Aires

+54 11 4772 6724

connectingschools@gmail.com

www.connectingschools.com.ar

NUMBER OF TEACHERS: 20 teachers per year. All placed in different towns in the interior of Argentina for a period of one semester.

PREFERENCE OF NATIONALITY: People from any English-speaking country.

QUALIFICATIONS: College graduates.

CONDITIONS OF EMPLOYMENT: Teaching periods of 1 or 2 semesters. Up to 25 hours of work per week. First semester mid-February to 9 July and second 9 July to 15 December. Participants must wish to become part of the community and to make a contribution. They must also wish to learn the Spanish language.

SALARY: Homestay in Argentine family, private Spanish tutoring, round-trip bus ticket from Buenos Aires to location, $100 monthly stipend after fortnight of training and 1-week placement. Programme fee is $1,300.

FACILITIES/SUPPORT: Two weeks of intensive TESOL training on arrival in Buenos Aires while participants stay in a hostel (hostelpalermosuites.com). Supervision and help with lesson planning throughout the teaching period. 4 hours of private Spanish classes a week while teaching and homestay accommodation for 4 months arranged after initial 3 weeks. Volunteers teach on tourist visa (available at airport for $120 fee).

RECRUITMENT: Via internet. Résumé, list of references and a telephone interview with director required.

CONTACT: Cristina Rapela, Director.

CONNECTING WORLDS ARGENTINA
Marcelo T. Alvear 1459, Zip Code C1060AAA, Ciudad autónoma de Buenos Aires
+54 11 5199 5458 / +54 223 156 35 41 91
info@cwargentina.com
www.cwargentina.com

Argentine cultural exchange organisation.

NUMBER OF TEACHERS: Up to 20 per semester.

PREFERENCE OF NATIONALITY: UK, USA, Canada, New Zealand, Australia, Ireland, South Africa.

QUALIFICATIONS: TEFL/TESOL certificate and bachelors degree in any subject. Motivated to experience new cultures and promote English language; should be flexible, open-minded and willing to learn. Medical report and police clearance needed plus international travel insurance against sickness, accidents and third party liability. Minimum age 21; average 30-35.

CONDITIONS OF EMPLOYMENT: Semesters start in March and August. 3-4 months or 9 months. 15-20 hours a week Monday to Friday.

SALARY: Small stipend for personal expenses of $500 pesos.

FACILITIES/SUPPORT: Homestay with local family or young Argentine professionals is included, and all meals. Programme also covers cultural and activity programme, an intensive Spanish course (4 hours a week) and airport transfer.

RECRUITMENT: Facebook page, Goabroad and strategic partnerships. Programme costs are $1400 for 3-4 months, $1700 for 9 months. Applications processed 3 months before start date.

CONTACT: Lic. María Cristina Acuña, Director (cristinmdq@gmail.com).

FURTHER SCHOOL OF ENGLISH
Catamarca 1824, Buenos Aires 1246
+54 11 4941 0927
cv@furtherenglish.com
www.furtherenglish.com

NUMBER OF TEACHERS: 20 to teach in-company, children, teenagers and adults.

PREFERENCE OF NATIONALITY: British.

QUALIFICATIONS: University degree, TEFL/CELTA or similar, previous teaching experience. Some Spanish is a plus. Candidates should have outgoing personalities and be committed to the team.

CONDITIONS OF EMPLOYMENT: March to December. 25–30 hours per week scheduled in blocks.

SALARY: 85 pesos (net) per hour.

FACILITIES/SUPPORT: No assistance with accommodation or visas.

RECRUITMENT: Personal interview or via Skype.

CONTACT: Natalia A Garcia, Principal.

HOME INTERCULTURAL LEARNING
Calle 37 no. 1091 PB La Plata, CP 1900, Buenos Aires
+54 221 483 3575
info@homeenglishcourses.com.ar
www.homeintercultural.com.ar

NUMBER OF TEACHERS: Variable.

PREFERENCE OF NATIONALITY: None.

QUALIFICATIONS: Teacher training (CELTA, TEFL) or university degree needed for regular courses, other university degrees for fluency and multi-discipline consultancy work.

CONDITIONS OF EMPLOYMENT: Flexible hours and length of stay, according to teacher's wishes. School uses dynamic teaching techniques that emphasise conversation and make use of acting, singing, playing games, reading comics, listening to podcasts, etc.

SALARY: About 60 pesos per teaching hour. Teachers need to be enrolled in *monotributo*.

FACILITIES/SUPPORT: Spanish classes (and other languages) are offered at partner schools for special rates. Home Intercultural Learning has agreements with local hostels, but teachers must arrange accommodation on their own. Teachers are responsible for arranging their own permits.

RECRUITMENT: Skype interviews can be arranged.

CONTACT: Andrea Assenti del Rio, Director of Studies.

INTERACTION LANGUAGE STUDIO

Av. L. N. Alem 428 6 I, Buenos Aires 1003

+54 11 4311 7220

info@interactionls.com

www.interactionls.com

NUMBER OF TEACHERS: 5–8 foreign teachers and 40 local teachers.

PREFERENCE OF NATIONALITY: American and British.

QUALIFICATIONS: TEFL certificate and some teaching experience.

CONDITIONS OF EMPLOYMENT: Contracts from March to December. Usual hours from 3 to 20 a week; teaching in businesses.

SALARY: 65 pesos per hour (around $8).

FACILITIES/SUPPORT: 3-day training course for new arrivals.

RECRUITMENT: CV by mail, interview and mock lesson. Interviews essential.

CONTACT: Professor Virginia López Grisolia, Director of Studies and Owner.

LV STUDIO

Darregueyra 2394, Buenos Aires

+54 11 4637 9442

info@lvstudioweb.com, cvs@lvstudioweb.com

www.lvstudioweb.com

NUMBER OF TEACHERS: 20–30 for schools in Palermo, Abasto and Flores in Buenos Aires.

PREFERENCE OF NATIONALITY: None.

QUALIFICATIONS: TEFL/TESOL/CELTA and/or English teaching experience.

CONDITIONS OF EMPLOYMENT: 6–12 months. Variable contact hours; most teachers are part-time.

FACILITIES/SUPPORT: No assistance with accommodation or visas.

RECRUITMENT: Craigslist. Face-to-face interviews preferred.

CONTACT: Emily Miller, Assistant Director.

NETWORK IDIOMAS

Entre Rios 265, Avellaneda, Buenos Aires 1870

+54 11 4228 4900

teachers@networkinstitute.com.ar

www.networkinstitute.com.ar

NUMBER OF TEACHERS: 3–4 per year.

PREFERENCE OF NATIONALITY: None but must live locally.

QUALIFICATIONS: TEFL.

CONDITIONS OF EMPLOYMENT: Minimum 9 months (March to November); renewable for the next school year. Hours of teaching 5.30pm–8.30pm for regular courses; mornings and lunchtimes for in-company courses. Part-time openings also available.

SALARY: 85 pesos per hour for occasional teaching.

RECRUITMENT: Face-to-face interviews.

CONTACT: Cecilia Cicolini, Director.

SWITCH LANGUAGE SCHOOL

Avenida Presidente Roque Sáenz Pena 615, 7° Off. 716, Buenos Aires

+54 11 4393 4125

info@switchschool.com.ar

www.switchschool.com.ar or
www.consultoraswitch.com.ar

NUMBER OF TEACHERS: 25 for in-company training.

PREFERENCE OF NATIONALITY: None.

QUALIFICATIONS: Recognised TEFL Certificate.

CONDITIONS OF EMPLOYMENT: 9-month minimum contract.

FACILITIES/SUPPORT: No help given with work permits or finding accommodation.

RECRUITMENT: Interviews with a mock class carried out at the school are essential.

CONTACT: Mara France Garcia, Director.

VOLUNTARIO GLOBAL

Avenida de Mayo 1385, Buenos Aires

+54 9 11 6206 9639

jfranco@voluntarioglobal.org

www.voluntarioglobal.org

Argentinian NGO that aims to empower people from disadvantaged backgrounds by giving them education, training and support. Cooperates with range of projects such as the Pablo Nogués English School on the outskirts of Buenos Aires.

PREFERENCE OF NATIONALITY: Half of total are English native speakers.

QUALIFICATIONS: Experience teaching English, and people skills. Minimum age of 18, average age of 22.

CONDITIONS OF EMPLOYMENT: Teaching programmes start every Monday from March to November. Minimum stay 4 weeks. Usually afternoon hours 2pm–6pm.

SALARY: Unpaid. Donation fee to be paid, from $400 for 4 weeks (2016) to $700 for 12 weeks, $850/$2,080 with accommodation. Volunteers are responsible for travel and meal costs.

FACILITIES/SUPPORT: Rooms in a volunteer house located in downtown Buenos Aires. Orientation on arrival, with weekly follow-up and joint activities for volunteers working at different projects.

RECRUITMENT: Via websites and partner organisations.

CONTACT: Jesica Franco, Director.

BOLIVIA

A little known fact in Europe is that Bolivia's economy has been doing well of late. Instead of being the basket case it was once considered to be, it has raised the minimum wage by nearly 100% in eight years and thereby reduced poverty and inequality. The socialist president, Evo Morales, has recently been re-elected for a third term making him arguably the most popular leader in the world. He has decreed that the increase in national wealth be distributed in the form of a bonus to all workers: at the end of 2014 employers had to pay their employees the *aguinaldo*, an extra month's salary. With predictions that the economy will grow by 5% this year, Morales has legislated that at the end of 2015 workers will receive a *doble aguinaldo*, i.e. two months' extra wages. The bad news for foreign teachers is that the benefit does not apply to those on foreign contracts though teachers on hourly contracts are eligible.

The best hourly wage you can earn in Bolivia is probably about US$11 which is still considerably less than the equivalent in Santiago or Sao Paulo, but allows for a comfortable lifestyle in a country where a room in a hostel costs $3 and a meal in the market $1. Bolivia is still a poor country. Huge swathes of the population have no interest in learning English, since learning Spanish is more of a priority for those who speak an indigenous language like Quechua. Even among the middle classes, few need English for their jobs and fewer will have a chance to travel or meet English speakers, so the number of private institutes is limited compared to Chile or Argentina. Yet the demand for English exceeds supply and we have heard of several expats working on the idea of opening new schools, for example Panorama English in La Paz, and another one being hatched in Santa Cruz.

Many teachers touring South America prefer Bolivia to many other countries for cultural reasons. La Paz is a city with a low cost of living and a colourful social mix. The class structure is immediately apparent, with the upper class consisting of people of Spanish descent, the middle class or *mestizos* of mixed Spanish/Bolivian ancestry and the underclass of Indians still wearing their traditional costume. Bolivia may have preserved its traditional culture more successfully than other Latin American countries, but the inequality of wealth distribution led socialist president Evo Morales to implement stringent wealth-distribution measures, including nationalising much of the energy industry.

Language schools and a couple of *colegios* (private schools) are listed in the *Yellow Pages* (www.amarillas-bolivia.com, search 'Institutos de Idiomas') and they may be worth approaching before arrival, as **Miranda Crowhurst** did, while working in Tanzania:

> *I was lucky enough to bag myself a teaching job in Bolivia from abroad, spamming schools with my CV and picking up a couple of testing Skype interviews. My CELTA qualification and a couple of years' experience in education helped me to land a job at a reputable language school in Santa Cruz, the Cambridge College. An off-shoot of an English-medium high school, it runs English language courses for professionals and children.*

Many schools would be unlikely to commit themselves to hiring a teacher without meeting them first. Terms normally last from early February to early September, resuming at the end of September to the beginning of December. The biggest language school in the country is the ultra-respectable Centro Boliviano Americano or CBA (Parque Iturralde Zenón 121, La Paz; http://cba.edu.bo), with three other locations in La Paz, plus schools in other cities such as Sucre, Cochabamba (see entry below) and Santa Cruz (www.cba.com.bo). Despite its name it hires British and Irish native English speakers as well.

Colegios employ native English speakers for their English departments and tend to pay up to twice as much as the private language schools. Also, the hours of 8.30am–1.30pm are more convenient.

Make sure you do your research, online or on-the-spot, before pursuing a job. For example the recent negative feedback about one well-known centre in La Paz on the site www.eslwatch.info should serve as a warning:

This place is a complete joke of a school. It is owned and run by people who don't speak a single word of English... They didn't even have a working photocopier when I was there, and nobody could be bothered to fix it. The school is closed for 3–4 hours in the middle of the day, meaning there is nowhere to plan evening lessons. The boss promised to pay the fine for overstaying the tourist visa and then on the day of leaving, tried to wriggle out of it, but I pressured her and got it.

The Bolivia Volunteers teaching project (www.boliviavolunteers.webs.com/teaching.htm) supports a number of schools in Cochabamba and Santa Cruz that are often severely understaffed and rely on donations, small tuition payments from parents and the assistance of volunteers who pay from $750 for four weeks' food, accommodation and support while volunteering.

MIRANDA CROWHURST

Miranda Crowhurst is one teacher who fell immediately under the spell of Bolivia after arriving in the southern city of Santa Cruz and sent in her reflections in summer 2015:

I arrived in Santa Cruz, two and a half years ago, with no Spanish, and no real idea of what to expect. It's often swelteringly hot, and always chaotic, with few traffic rules and building regulations, and although it's definitely not a tourist destination, it's a great place to live. People are friendly and relaxed here, and proud of where they come from. Plus, there are some fantastic off-the-gringo-trail places to visit nearby, like national parks and local villages. Over the past thirty years, Santa Cruz has boomed from a sleepy backwater into a boom-town, and the contradictions are evident – there are horses and carts, and it's predominantly Catholic. Old men play chess under frangipane trees in the Plaza. But there's also a famously riotous carnival, and some serious worshipping of short skirts, gyms and enormous cars. Like all large South American cities, you do have to be aware of crime, and muggings are common. You have to watch yourself in public places, as girls can receive unwanted attention, too. Having said that, nothing serious has happened to me yet!

As for the teaching, schools vary hugely in their quality. While some pay peanuts, if you're a qualified and/or experienced native teacher, you should get a very good wage here (in Bolivian, rather than international terms). There is a real need for English teachers, as the ex-pat community is pretty small, so schools are always hiring. Teaching here is great, mainly because of the students. They may have a typically Latino attitude towards homework ('Tomorrow, teacher!'), and to time-keeping, but they are very chatty in lessons, keen to participate, and happy to have fun and laugh. If you'd rather strike out on your own, you can charge a decent amount for private lessons, once you get your name around. Since I arrived, I've really come to enjoy the chaos, and the easygoing, friendly atmosphere, where drinking, barbecues and dancing are compulsory. I'll be here for a while!

The college where Miranda teaches (Cambridge College) has treated her reasonably well. They collected her from the airport, and organised accommodation, orientation, Spanish lessons, medical insurance and a visa. The classrooms have equipment that is recognisable as being from the 21st century, as well as the good old-fashioned photocopier. Even if not everything in Bolivia runs with German-style efficiency, the good schools expect you to be prepared, organised and get good results. Miranda reports that it is possible to rent a room for $50 though a share of a nice flat in a trendy area will cost four times that amount. It is possible to live comfortably on $600 a month. Eating out is cheap – as little as $2 for a two-course meal. Miranda reports that they have the most amazing food 'all made with soul too'.

Historic Sucre is one of the most popular destinations for travellers. Although known as a city of students, there are only three or four language institutes. Other teachers have recommended the city of Cochabamba, because of the perfect spring-like climate. Among them is **Jonathan Alderman**, who concluded: '*if one wants to earn a decent wage teaching English in Bolivia, one has to turn to private classes.*' When he first arrived, he advertised in the local newspaper for private classes charging 30–35 bolivianos an hour. He says you can expect to be approached in shops and restaurants as well as by your students and asked about private classes, but this will generally come from people who would find it a hardship to pay even $2 an hour. One place to advertise private English lessons is the Sunday edition of the newspaper *El Diario* (www.eldiario.net).

Most teachers arrive on a tourist visa and should in theory apply for a work visa, though many continue to work on a tourist visa that will have to be renewed every 90 days by leaving the country. You are allowed four 90-day stamps in a year. **Miranda Crowhurst** describes the visa process as an '*obstacle race where officials often tell you to go back five obstacles!*' She recommends using a lawyer, especially if you don't speak fluent Spanish.

LIST OF EMPLOYERS

BRITISH ENGLISH CENTRE

No. 7916, Calle 13 de Calacoto (Entre Av. Ballivian y Bustamante), La Paz

☏ +591 2 2793320

✉ info@britishenglishcentre.org

🖥 www.britishenglishcentre.org

NUMBER OF TEACHERS: 5 native speaker teachers and 3 non-native speaker teachers.

PREFERENCE OF NATIONALITY: Preference for British and Irish teachers, though other native speakers are also hired.

QUALIFICATIONS: Minimum TEFL/CELTA qualified with preferably at least one year of EFL teaching experience.

CONDITIONS OF EMPLOYMENT: Initial contract is for one year, with renewal available (and preferred) for subsequent years. Teachers may choose to work a selection of hours between 7.30am and 9pm. Most classes take place 7.30–9am and 4–9pm.

SALARY: Minimum salary is $5.50 per hour, increasing to take into consideration qualifications and prior teaching experience. At the end of one year, a bonus is paid which is equal to half the amount spent on the visa.

FACILITIES/SUPPORT: Red tape assistance given. All teachers must apply for a 30 day *Visa de Objeto Determinado* followed by a 1 year temporary residence visa. We help teachers with the application process. Teachers must apply for a NIT (tax) number and present *facturas* (tax receipts) every month to the tax office, in order to reduce their tax bill. One month's shared accommodation is provided for new teachers who sign a contract; teachers pay only for utilities.

RECRUITMENT: Speculative applications in person or through the website. Occasional adverts on EFL websites such as tefl.com. Interviews are essential, and are carried out in person in Bolivia or through Skype.

CONTACT: Wilson Lacio Torrez, General Director (wlacio@britishenglishcentre.org).

CAMBRIDGE ESOL CENTRE/CAMBRIDGE COLLEGE

Residencias del Norte, Av. Beni entre 4to y 5to Anillos, Santa Cruz de la Sierra

☎ +591 3 341 6541

✉ rogerc@cambridge.edu.bo and marierenee@cambridge.edu.bo

🖥 www.cambridgebolivia.com.bo

NUMBER OF TEACHERS: 12.

PREFERENCE OF NATIONALITY: British.

QUALIFICATIONS: CELTA or 3 years' classroom experience.

CONDITIONS OF EMPLOYMENT: 2-year contract with working hours between 7am and 11am and/or 3pm to 9pm Monday to Friday.

SALARY: About $10 an hour, half paid in US dollars, the other half in bolivianos.

FACILITIES/SUPPORT: Assistance given finding apartments near the school and the school organises all the relevant paperwork for work permits and immigration.

RECRUITMENT: Usually via adverts on TEFL websites. Candidates submit their CV and a model lesson plan, and an interview is conducted through video conferencing/Skype. Interested candidates can also send their CVs directly to esolinfo@cotas.com.bo.

CONTACT: Maria Renee Canedo Landivar, Headmistress, or Roger Castaños, Centre Manager.

CENTRO BOLIVIANO AMERICANO – COCHABAMBA

PO Box 1399, Cochabamba

☎ +591 4 422 1288

✉ mblum@cbacoch.org or cba@cbacoch.org

🖥 www.cbacoch.org

NUMBER OF TEACHERS: 3.

PREFERENCE OF NATIONALITY: American and British.

QUALIFICATIONS: Proficiency in English. Work experience in schools/universities. International Examination Diplomas/TESOL/TEFL certificates.

CONDITIONS OF EMPLOYMENT: 2-year renewable contract. 6 hours chosen from the following teaching hours: 7am–8.30am, 8.30am–11.45am, 1.45pm–5pm, 2.30pm–3.45pm, 3.45pm–5pm, 5pm–6.30pm, 6.45pm–8.15pm, 6.35pm–9.45pm.

SALARY: Average of $4 per hour. Varies depending on academic background and teaching experience. Income tax of 13% is not deducted when the teacher submits invoices for the same amount each month. Social security deductions 12.21%.

FACILITIES/SUPPORT: Help given in finding accommodation at orientation. Health care provided. Assistance given with work permits. Teachers should come with a *visa de objeto determinado* valid for 30 days to start the paperwork for a work visa. If the teacher comes with a tourist visa, he/she has to change it to a *visa de objeto determinado* at a Bolivian consulate in a neighbouring country. After that he/she may start with the paperwork for a 1- or 2-year work visa. School also helps with additional procedure for a work permit that incurs an extra fee.

RECRUITMENT: Via adverts in newspapers. Local interview necessary.

CONTACT: Mery Blum de Schwarz, Academic Director.

BRAZIL

Expectations of Brazil becoming an economic powerhouse have been thwarted by the current recession that has seen austerity measures brought to bear. The euphoria over hosting the World Cup in 2014 and the Olympics in 2016 has turned sour, as the world's seventh biggest economy fails to grow. However you wouldn't guess that from the vigour of the English language market among the burgeoning middle class and business community. The school coordinator of a leading English School in São Paulo, who is responsible for recruiting, hiring and training a staff of 35 native and non-native teachers, wrote in July 2015 to say, 'It's a great time to be an English teacher in São Paulo; we are now hiring teachers every week, as we have students starting classes every week.' The company provides General and Business English Classes to adults, mainly from multinational companies.

Dozens of Culturas Inglesas in the Associacao Brasileira de Culturas Inglesas (www.culturainglesa.com.br) and many ICBEUs (Instituto Cultural Brasil-Estados Unidos) scattered all over the fifth-most populous country in the world employ several hundred teachers to serve thousands of students. Language-teaching chains like Wizard, the largest in the country, Britannia and Brasas are worth trying once you're in Brazil.

Schools in smaller places often notify cooperating institutes in the big cities of any job vacancies for native English speakers. But speculative visits to towns of any size are likely to succeed eventually. The distinguishing feature of Brazilian EFL is the high proportion of well-qualified Brazilian English teachers. Recruiting teachers from overseas is seen to be unjustifiably costly and also very difficult from the visa point of view. Only individuals with very specialised expertise are invited to work in very senior posts.

Visas are a major headache. You are permitted to stay no more than six months on a tourist visa, after which you will have to leave the country (usually across the Paraguayan border) or get an extension from the Federal Police. Training visas are an option for some. The Administrative Director of one of Rio de Janeiro's upmarket schools describes the difficulties:

> Unfortunately, teaching English is not an area the government considers a priority in issuing visas. There are only two situations in which foreigners can teach in Brazil. The first is to work illegally, since there are numerous small schools that can afford to run the risk of hiring illegal foreigners. As a result, pay is usually bad and employment unstable. The alternative is available only to specialists, and is extremely rare. Because we have a web page, I get requests from foreigners all the time. I basically tell them that it is an adventure here, only for the strong of stomach, and you have to be willing to subject yourself to the unsavoury experiences that go along with working without proper papers. I have come across dozens of foreigners who have been promised work-related visas. In 27 years of living in Brazil, I have never, not once, seen this happen. The only cases I know of where a person has taught legally, it has been when they enter the country with visas issued at the Brazilian consulate in their country of residence.

Occasionally language institutes in Brazil advertise on www.tefl.com and www.eslcafe.com. The latter is the site on which **Alexis Heintz** discovered that the Speaking School (see entry) had a vacancy:

> I contacted the school via email, then found them on Facebook and started chatting with the secretaries, teachers, and eventually the owner of the school, which included Q&A on both ends (from my side and theirs) about the job and my experience (I had volunteered as an English teacher a few months), and then I sent them my updated CV. The students all feel that English is very important for them to know and learn. However, since the majority are Engineering students at uni, they treat their uni studies as their number one priority and English falls into second place. The business professionals also have to put their career demands above their English studies, so I feel that most students do not spend much time studying outside of class. The low point for me is when you have a 7am class scheduled and your student does not show up and does not cancel in advance. You

don't get paid for the 30 minutes that you have to spend waiting around for the student before you can confirm that the class is indeed cancelled.

Useful information on teaching can be found on the site www.braziliangringo.com maintained by American Josh Plotkin. If you wait until after arrival to look for work, use the *Yellow Pages*, expatriate networks or informative websites such as www.gringoes.com, run by expats based in Sao Paulo; the latter has a good classified section with jobs for native-speaker teachers. Most adverts placed by companies with names like Executive English and Talking Business specify that applicants must already be living locally. In Sao Paulo a good source of teaching jobs is the newspaper *Folha de São Paulo* on a Sunday. Hourly wages at institutes in Rio and Sao Paulo hover around R$50 (reais) but can climb to R$80 for corporate classes, whereas the average in small towns is less. Some have predicted that as people involved with the Olympics begin to panic about the inadequacy of their English, rates for teachers will spike. When job-hunting, expect to go through quite a rigorous interview procedure, as **Jon Cotterill** discovered:

When you drop your CV in, the school may ask you to take a written English test on the spot. This can consist of anything up to 100 questions plus a composition section. If you pass the test, you may get invited to a group interview, a 'dinamica de grupo'. This consists of a group of potential teachers (usually Brazilians) and you having to perform various tasks in small teams or pairs. If you are successful then you may be asked to do a two-week training course (usually unpaid). Only after all of this will you be offered work.

Richard Ferguson, a New Zealander who has learned Portuguese, met an American who gave private English lessons in Sao Paulo charging more than $30 an hour. But he bemoaned the fact that the city was hard to get around (the Metro area has a population of about 20 million) and he insisted that you need to have the students pay in advance for a few lessons. This is because Brazilians are notorious for not showing up, being late or cancelling at the last minute (which they don't see as a problem), so you need to take some precautions so as not to waste your time. Demand for private tuition in Rio de Janeiro is sufficiently strong to prompt a local company On the Go Idiomas (www.onthegoidiomas.com.br) to try to match teachers to companies and to advise qualified expat teachers.

Although he is Swiss by birth, and arrived in Brazil assuming that Swiss time was a universal standard, **Hans Durrer** slowly adjusted to a different rhythm. He became familiar with the Brazilian way of life, made Brazilian friends, learned Portuguese and felt generally enriched. He attributes this to his open, curious and eager-to-learn attitude, and also to the warm hospitality of the school owners. He describes how rewarding it can be to tutor students with whom you develop a rapport, even when their attendance is sporadic, as happened when he spent two long stints working with Schutz & Kanomata (see directory entry) in Southern Brazil:

Two days ago, Reinaldo attended his last conversational English class in Santa Cruz do Sul. As usual, we talked about anything and everything, from corruption to the ways of perception, from travels to how best to live your life. He enjoyed my classes a lot and thought them interesting, stimulating and helpful, he said. He wasn't, however, too sure whether his English had improved, he laughed. Well, to be honest, it hasn't, I laughed back. Reinaldo is in his fifties and works in tourism. He's been around, from Bariloche to China, and often missed his private classes with me. But whenever he managed to attend, we had a ball. Among other things, I learned what a truly special place Easter Island is and that I really need to visit a certain fabulous hotel in the jungle near Manaus.

If you want to study Portuguese, you can apply for a student visa, which would make it easier to stay on. For example, many foreigners register at the Pontificia Universidade Católica in Rio de Janeiro. This is an excellent place to link up with students and advertise classes if you want to offer private lessons (which pay much better than working for an institute).

BARRY O'LEARY

Barry O'Leary, well-travelled TEFLer, arrived in Salvador (northern Brazil) just before Carnaval. (The best time to start work is following the Carnaval, which takes place during the week over Ash Wednesday every February.) He bought a map, borrowed a telephone directory from his hostel and walked round all the 25 language academies with his CV. His luck wasn't as quick as it had been in Ecuador (described later) because most academies couldn't tell how many students they would have until after Carnaval. But Barry managed to find an evening job at an academy outside Salvador and later found two other jobs.

I taught in three institutes: PEC (www.pec.com.br), Okey Dokey and AEC Idiomas. The business academy sent me to various offices that were all fully equipped and well organised. Generally working conditions were excellent and so was the pay; I received about $8 an hour, which was a good rate for Brazil. The students were a mixed bag, yet they all had a great sense of humour and participated in the lessons, though some students were there only because their boss wanted them to be and had little interest.

I worked at another academy one afternoon a week. The approach here was to teach English through music, followed by group conversation lessons. Each week the director would translate two or three songs for the students to sing along in English. The students enjoyed this immensely, and I thought it was a very original way to learn. Most students seemed to be more interested in asking me questions about England and my life rather than pay attention to the lessons, but it was a good way for them to improve their fluency. I found Brazilian students very happy-go-lucky people; they were always smiling and interested in learning English.

I was lucky enough to live in the old quarter of Salvador, called Pelourinho, which was the hub of the nightlife, but also the hub of any trouble. I lived in a house with 15 people including Brazilians, Nigerians, French and Irish, for which I paid $20 a month, and had a brilliant three months.

LIST OF EMPLOYERS

CalENGLISH SCHOOL

Rua Waldemar Faria Mota 85, Jardim Bongiovani, Presidente Prudente, Sao Paulo

📞 +55 18 3908 6361

✉ cris@calenglish.com.br or zac@calenglish.com.br

💻 www.calenglish.com.br

NUMBER OF TEACHERS: 4 per semester.

PREFERENCE OF NATIONALITY: USA or Canada.

QUALIFICATIONS: TEFL certificate, any teaching experience or any experience with children.

CONDITIONS OF EMPLOYMENT: 6 months, renewable. 20 hours per week, usually in the afternoons and evenings.

FACILITIES/SUPPORT: Rooms right beside the school may be rented.

RECRUITMENT: By email and Skype.

CONTACT: Cristiane Zagol, Director/Owner.

ENGLISH CAMP

Rua Barão de Capanema 220, Cerqueira Cesar,
Sao Paulo 01411-010

✆ +55 11 3061 0080

✉ englishcamp@englishcamp.com.br

🖥 www.englishcamp.com.br

NUMBER OF TEACHERS: 5 monitors and teachers per vacation season.

PREFERENCE OF NATIONALITY: None, provided they are fluent English speakers.

QUALIFICATIONS: Must have open mind, to teach international students. Minimum age 17/18.

CONDITIONS OF EMPLOYMENT: 2–4 weeks starting January and July. 6–8 hours a day. English language immersion camps also held throughout the year.

SALARY: None, volunteer positions only for those travelling on tourist visas. Full room and board provided free.

FACILITIES/SUPPORT: Letter of invitation sent so that volunteer teachers can arrive with tourist visa.

RECRUITMENT: Word of mouth from other teachers. Interviews can be conducted by Skype. Applications should be made at least 2 months in advance of January and July start dates to give time for a visa to be issued.

CONTACT: Sandra Goulart Urioste, Academic Director.

ENGLISH FOR BUSINESS

Rua Booker Pittman 303, Chácara Santo Antônio CEP:
04719-060, São Paulo - SP

✆ +55 11 35717706

✉ teacher@englishforbusiness.com.br

🖥 www.englishforbusiness.com.br

NUMBER OF TEACHERS: 20.

PREFERENCE OF NATIONALITY: UK, USA, Canada, Australia, New Zealand and Ireland.

QUALIFICATIONS: CELTA, DELTA and TESOL Certified Teacher as well as experienced professionals of other industries are welcome.

CONDITIONS OF EMPLOYMENT: 12-36 months. 3-32 hours per week.

SALARY: Ranges from R$600 to R$5000 net per month.

FACILITIES/SUPPORT: Advice on accommodation and visas given.

RECRUITMENT: Websites and agreements with English Schools in the UK and USA. Face-to-face or Skype interviews.

CONTACT: Pricila Gaffuri, School Coordinator.

ENGLISH ON DEMAND

Rua Pouso Alegre 2826, Santa Teresa, Belo Horizonte,
Minas Gerais 31010-514

✆ +55 31 3309 5590

✉ contato@escoladeingleseod.com.br

🖥 www.escoladeingleseod.com.br

NUMBER OF TEACHERS: 2.

PREFERENCE OF NATIONALITY: Native English speakers: American, British, Canadian and Australian.

QUALIFICATIONS: Minimum bachelor's degree. Must enjoy teaching even if lacking experience. Preference given to those with teaching experience.

CONDITIONS OF EMPLOYMENT: Minimum 12 months.

SALARY: Minimum $10 per hour. Extra payments depend on experience, attitude towards learning to teach and commitment to the students.

FACILITIES/SUPPORT: 1-bedroom house attached to the school can be made available to a qualified and approved teacher.

RECRUITMENT: Via internet. References will be taken up. Initial interview can be via Skype and also face-to-face interviews.

ENGLISH VOICE IDIOMAS

Edifício Barão de Monte Cedro, Rua Frei Caneca, 1407,
Conj 915, Consolação, Sao Paulo 01307-909

✆ +55 11 3266 6951

✉ paul@englishvoice.com.br or
comercial@englishvoice.com.br

🖥 www.englishvoice.com.br

NUMBER OF TEACHERS: 4.

PREFERENCE OF NATIONALITY: None.

QUALIFICATIONS: Teaching certificate needed, though 2 years' teaching experience would also be considered.

CONDITIONS OF EMPLOYMENT: 6-month contracts. 15–20 hours per week.

SALARY: R$40 per hour (net).

FACILITIES/SUPPORT: No assistance with accommodation. Help given with documentation.

RECRUITMENT: Via Gringoes (www.gringoes.com), a local expats community online newsletter. Most interviews take place face-to-face but in some cases can be by Skype.

CONTACT: Paul Major, Director.

IICA GLOBAL ENGLISH

Avenida 23, # 1274, Ituiutaba, Minas Gerais 38300-114

+55 34 3261 2141

iica@netsitecom.br

www.iica.com.br

Sponsors Intercultural Exchange Programme.

NUMBER OF TEACHERS: 15 intercultural interns.

PREFERENCE OF NATIONALITY: USA, UK or Canada.

QUALIFICATIONS: Should be aged 21–32 and either a student enrolled in last year of university or within 12 months of graduation at the time of application.

CONDITIONS OF EMPLOYMENT: 12 months. 34 hours per week. Monday–Saturday.

SALARY: Allowance of about R$1,000 (US$320) per month plus free family homestay.

FACILITIES/SUPPORT: Free homestay accommodation provided. Programme eligible for special trainee visa status after participants sign a contract and provide documentation as required by Brazilian Immigration Service. Global English will assist with visa process. VITEM-IV (student) visa fees are US$215 for Britons, US$160 for Americans and cannot be refunded in the case of a visa being denied.

RECRUITMENT: Screening based on candidate's CV. Intake months are February and August, and screening, based on candidate's CV, takes place 4 months in advance.

CONTACT: Professor Jacy Pimenta, Coordinator (jcjacy@hotmail.com).

KIWI BRASIL IDIOMAS

Av Pico da Bandeira, 1542, 1º andar, Água Verde, Alto Caparaó (Minas Gerais) 36979-000

+55 32 3747 2889

jander@kiwibrasil.com

www.kiwibrasil.com

6 schools located in small towns in Minas Gerais, teaching all ages and levels.

NUMBER OF TEACHERS: 7 on contract and freelancers.

PREFERENCE OF NATIONALITY: None.

QUALIFICATIONS: TEFL, TESOL, CELTA , DELTA or equivalent. 1 year's experience is required.

CONDITIONS OF EMPLOYMENT: Contracts from 6 months to 2 years. 30 hours a week.

SALARY: $500 a month (net) plus full accommodation.

FACILITIES/SUPPORT: Seminars and ongoing teacher training.

RECRUITMENT: Via TEFL jobs websites. Skype interviews.

CONTACT: Jander Kenedy Nogueira Soares, Director/Owner.

LINGUAE – PERSONAL LANGUAGE INSTITUTE

Rua Dom José de Barros, 152, 10th Floor, Centre, Sao Paulo 01038-902

+55 11 3255 7975; mobile +55 11 8784 4489

plinio@linguae.com.br or contato@linguae.com.br

www.linguae.com.br

PREFERENCE OF NATIONALITY: Native speakers. For 3 branches.

CONDITIONS OF EMPLOYMENT: In-company, part-time work.

SALARY: Hourly rates from R$35 to R$45.

RECRUITMENT: Candidates should be living locally.

CONTACT: Plinio Gherardi, Commercial Director.

NEW START COMUNICACOES

Rua Uruguiana 10/1211, Centro, Rio de Janeiro 20050-090

+55 21 2508 6917

newstart@newstart.com.br

www.newstart.com.br

NUMBER OF TEACHERS: 15–20 in-company teachers.

PREFERENCE OF NATIONALITY: Must be a native English speaker.

QUALIFICATIONS: Preferably CELTA or Trinity TESOL certificate and some classroom experience.

CONDITIONS OF EMPLOYMENT: Minimum 5 months' work.

SALARY: R$34 (£9) per hour.

FACILITIES/SUPPORT: Training in Business English.

RECRUITMENT: Direct application by CV via email and telephone.

CONTACT: Stephanie Crockett (stephanie@newstart.com.br) or Adam Reid (adam@newstart.com.br).

SCHUTZ & KANOMATA ESL & PSL

Rua Galvao Costa 85, Santa Cruz do Sul 96810-012

+55 51 3715 3366

eslinbrazil@asbi.org.br

www.sk.com.br/guests/sk-lcb.html

NUMBER OF TEACHERS: 5 every semester on Brazilian Language and Culture Exchange Program located in mid-sized town in southern Brazil.

PREFERENCE OF NATIONALITY: Canadian, American and British.

QUALIFICATIONS: Main qualification is personality; must be communicative, considerate and interested in making friends. ESL-teaching experience desirable. For visa reasons must be a student or recent graduate.

CONDITIONS OF EMPLOYMENT: 10–12 month contracts; semesters run 1 March–20 July or 1 August– 20 December. Occasionally 1-semester positions are possible. Up to 24 hours per week, mostly in the evenings.

SALARY: Accommodation provided in exchange for 5 hours of teaching (one a day) per week. Above that, the rate paid is R$20 for private lessons and R$25 for groups. Bonus of US$250–400 paid after one or $800 after two semesters.

FACILITIES/SUPPORT: Programme provides accommodation, Portuguese instruction and occasional weekend tours. Help given with obtaining study training visa valid for one year and extendable for a further year. This must be applied for in guest-teacher's own country for which enrolment on a Portuguese course is a requirement.

RECRUITMENT: Strong internet exposure. Also former teacher in Canada acts as agent. Candidates are chosen 3–4 months before semester start date, plus short-notice vacancies sometimes available.

CONTACT: Ricardo Schütz, Principal.

SPEAKING – CENTRO DE CULTURA AMERICANA
R. Cel. Renno, 321 Centro, Itajuba, Minas Gerais 37500-050
+55 35 3621 3354/+55 35 8846 1828
administracao@speaking.com.br
www.speaking.com.br

NUMBER OF TEACHERS: 5 per year.

PREFERENCE OF NATIONALITY: American, Canadian and British. Anyone with dual Brazilian nationality especially welcome.

QUALIFICATIONS: TESL or similar. Must be young, enthusiastic and committed.

CONDITIONS OF EMPLOYMENT: Standard commitment February to December. 40 hours per week, Monday to Saturday.

SALARY: R$17 (US$5) per hour net. Wage is enough for living in a small town in Brazil.

FACILITIES/SUPPORT: School provides a small, furnished house, or helps with living expenses.

RECRUITMENT: By email or via ESL websites such as www. jobstefl.com.

CONTACT: Dagmar Andrade, Director (dagmarandrade@yahoo. com.br); Paulo Phelipe, Pedagogical Assistant (pedagogico@ speaking.com.br).

CHILE

More than most other South American economies, Chile's is flourishing, with a modest unemployment rate of 6.1% (2015). In terms of market competitiveness, Chile ranks most highly among South American countries. As commercial, touristic and cultural contacts with the outside world have increased, so has the demand for the English language. The most booming market is for business English, though there is also demand for teachers of children, created largely by the Chilean government lowering the age at which English is taught in state schools from 7th grade to 5th grade.

The ongoing drive to raise the level of English-language teaching throughout the country continues with the Chilean Ministry of Education's major initiative, the *Programa Inglés Abre Puertas* or 'English Opens Doors Program'. The ambitious EODP programme aims to improve English-language education in state schools in cities and small towns throughout Chile by enlisting the help of native and near-native English speakers. University graduates work alongside local teachers in classrooms to help improve listening and speaking skills among students. Participants must be university graduates (aged 21–35) and stay for one or two semesters, normally from March/April or end of July but dates vary. Volunteers receive a small monthly volunteer allowance of 70,000 pesos (over $100) in addition to free room and board with a Chilean host family and domestic travel. Health insurance is provided. Prospective volunteers can apply directly via the Volunteer Centre in Santiago (+56 2 406 7191; voluntarios@mineduc.cl; www.centrodevoluntarios.cl).

Luke Harris was so enthusiastic about the EODP that after finishing his stint of teaching he moved into the office to help recruit further volunteer teachers:

> *Before doing the programme I had only volunteered as a teaching assistant a few hours per week in an ESL classroom. The application process is fairly rigorous. In addition to the application form and writing two essays, you must submit various documents and photos; that is followed with a Skype interview. Since you work in a public school, teachers and students are often not very motivated, which can be frustrating. Living with a host family was awesome! It is a great way to get a feeling for the community and culture, not to mention it allows you to learn a ton of Spanish.*
>
> *My students were extremely enthusiastic to have a native speaker for a teacher. For that reason they always received me with a great deal of warmth and appreciation. This made for a very comfortable and positive environment. However, students have a very low level of English. Despite many years of English courses most are not at a conversational level. Also, discipline can be difficult if you are used to an orderly classroom. In Chile classes are large and students have more freedom. Chileans are generally much more open and gregarious than people in the US. I was lucky to make many Chilean friends and spent a lot of time making barbecues with them, playing football and travelling on the weekends. I had not expected to receive so much attention for being a foreigner. This was great at times and difficult at times. For me, this has been a life-changing and self-defining experience. If you are a professional teacher though, and have your own ideas, styles and lesson plans, this programme could be somewhat unsatisfying in the classroom. The cultural experience is unparalleled.*

One of the advantages of the programme is that the Centro de Voluntarios will assist in the process for applying for the *residencia temporaria* before arrival, for which you will need a Criminal Background check, medical certificate and so on. As a volunteer, you're expected to teach 25 pedagogical hours (an hour is calculated as a 45-minute lesson in Chile) per week. In addition, you are required to spend 10 hours working on lesson planning with your head teacher as well as leading extracurricular activities.

Most other teaching opportunities in Chile are in the commercial sector and the majority of those are in the capital, Santiago, where there are scores of private language schools. Some relevant institutes can also be found in the Valparaiso-Viña del Mar area.

ALAN CHADWICK

Alan Chadwick spent six months in Valparaiso up to April 2014.

October was not the best time of year to start the hunt for full-time work, but he set to work dropping off his CV in many universities and schools, sending off multiple email enquiries and putting up posters offering private tuition (which brought no response). Eventually he got a few bites from potential employers impressed with his CELTA qualification, but deterred by the fact that he didn't have a working visa or a RUT (tax/NI number). He was lucky enough to be asked by an Englishwoman he knew to take over an evening class she taught to university students which met for three hours three times a week. This was the most enjoyable as well as the most lucrative of his several jobs. The hourly rate was 15,000 pesos per hour (£15) less about 20% for tax. Although the students were serious about achieving good scores on a Chilean language test connected with studying abroad, the classes were friendly and informal and often involved sharing food.

Another job he did was through the International Center in Viña del Mar (www.internationalcenter.cl) which Alan reckons is a good place for newcomers to try. Among other things, it hires teachers to work on occasional all-day immersion courses constructed round a theme and an excursion, for example wine-making. A large and disparate group of learners met in the lobby of a hotel for four hours of lessons before going by bus to a vineyard for a tour, a wine-tasting and lunch. After all that red wine in 30 degree heat, Alan was not sure how useful his lessons at the end of the day could be. In any case it was well paid.

Through a recruitment agent, Alan was eventually interviewed for a full-time job at the Naval Academy in Valparaiso which he got. He appreciated the civilised hours of 8am-1pm but it took a little while to get used to the no-nonsense discipline of the place, with its regulations and dress code and hierarchy. He had to get used to seeing the students doing press-ups for the slightest misdemeanour. He was conscious of the discrepancy between his respected role as teacher of future naval officers and his bohemian life in a big shared house on the hill (cerro) where he loved the frequent barbecues, proximity to the beach and the modest rent of £65 a month for a big room shared with his girlfriend.

Alan came away with the impression that there is a huge and growing market for English in Valparaiso and Chile generally and that Britons are in very short supply in Valpo.

There will be less competition for teaching vacancies and a lower cost of living in smaller places such as the aptly named La Serena in the dry north of the country, or other towns such as Arica, Iquique, Antofagasta, Talca, Concepción, Valdivia, Osorno and Punta Arenas, all of which have possibilities for teachers, albeit on a smaller scale. Some course providers in Santiago serve clients in Valparaiso/Viña del Mar, where there are three universities.

The Instituto Chileno-Británico de Cultura in Santiago (entry below) recruits qualified teachers and has a good library that incorporates the British Council's resource library for teachers; anyone prepared to pay the membership fee can borrow materials, though many schools in Santiago have good libraries themselves. Native English-speaker teachers are also hired by the Institutos Chileno-Britanico de Cultura in Concepcion (www.ibritanico. com), Arica (www.britanicoarica.cl) and Viña del Mar (www.icbc.cl). **Mandy Powell** noticed that there were relatively few teachers from her native Britain compared to North America and she speculated that this might have something to do with the high cost of the work visa for Britons. Perhaps because of their scarcity, the British accent is at a premium, in Mandy's experience, which makes work easier to find. She enjoyed the mixture of people, from students just out of university to people who had left work in search of a different pace of life.

South American language schools tend to prefer face-to-face meetings rather than emails and phone calls. **Heidi Resetarits** typed 'English schools in Santiago' into a search engine, came up with a huge list of language schools in areas she wanted to apply to and then dropped off résumés in person:

> *I actually got an interview on the spot at the second school I applied to . . . and I happened to just walk by it – it wasn't even on my list! Santiago is a very modern city and new schools are popping up all the time. It's worth it just to walk around town and see what's there. I know that South Americans appreciate face-to-face meetings rather than emails and phone calls, so I walked in and asked to meet with a director. I decided to stay and chat a bit with the receptionist, and he made me an appointment for the next day.*
>
> *The interview was a face-to-face with the director of the school. After we talked about my résumé and a bit about my teaching experience, we set up a teaching practice (he chose a topic and a student) for the next day. I got the job within three days.*

Doug Burgess went job-hunting in Santiago, armed with a CELTA he had acquired at home in England and some experience. He had an interview with a corporate training company and EF English First (see entry), who offered Doug a contract for 12 months with work visa and a rate of 5,500 pesos an hour, more if he had to travel more than two metro stations or worked at its other campus. In the end, Doug accepted another offer from the Instituto Chileno-Británico de Cultura. His contract was for 15 hours, which was enough to secure a work visa, although he had the option of working up to 30 hours or more. Before Doug secured a full-time teaching job, he participated in an exchange programme run by Woodward Chile. For every Spanish lesson he received, he gave an English lesson, and went from being a complete beginner in the language to fairly competent.

A further possibility is to teach at English-medium *colegios*, where a longer commitment will be necessary and a reasonable salary paid. Although they employ mainly certified teachers, often hired at recruitment fairs and through international advertising, they do need some native English speakers for their English departments. For example, **Eleanor Padfield** was determined to work abroad after finishing her A levels but did not want to go through an agency where she would be with lots of other British students. After spending the first half of her year in Salamanca, Spain, she sent emails in Spanish all over the world to find something to do, preferably in Latin America. Of the many schools and language schools she contacted, one of the few to reply was the Redland School, an upmarket private school. Although it told her that it didn't usually accept gap-year students (since so many previous gappers had left prematurely to travel), it made an exception for Eleanor when she promised to stick it out till the end of the term, beginning in March and ending in August. When June rolled round, she was tempted to leave early but her conscience (or her mother's exhortations) persuaded her to keep her promise, trying to see as much of the country as she could in her days off.

Heidi Resetarits was an English teacher for both the Universidad de Las Americas and Comunicorp, Santiago simultaneously:

I had two sets of students. My students from the institute were mainly businessmen who needed to learn English for work. These men were preoccupied with work but used their lunch breaks to take classes. They do want to learn, but more often than not, work took priority. I had a few women who were very dedicated and learned rather quickly.

I also taught 4th year college students how to write essays and give public speeches. They were at a different level than my business students (they were majoring in Teaching English) and they had a better grasp of the language. They were about 50–50 with effort and participation, but I could also have higher expectations for them. I really enjoyed working with these students.

The commercial institutes in Santiago vary greatly in size, reliability in their treatment of employees and teaching methods. Newcomers to the city quickly learn which are the better schools and gradually acquire more hours with them. In-company teaching usually takes place early in the morning; middle-ranking staff tend to be taught before the official working day begins, while directors and higher-ranking executives take their classes at a more civilised mid-morning hour. Most teachers enjoy the variety of off-site teaching rather than classroom teaching, which tends to be more textbook based.

The academic year runs from March to December with a two-week winter holiday in July and one-week recess in mid-September, so the best time to apply for a contract is the end of February. There are 19 British curriculum schools listed on the website of the Association of British Schools in Chile (www.absch.cl).

Non-contractual work is usually paid by the hour, starting at 5,000 pesos and rising to 8,000 pesos. Established teachers working for universities such as UNIACC in Providencia can top 15,000 pesos but this is rare. The cost of living is higher than in many other places on the continent but teachers can still support themselves. **Heidi Resetarits** says that '*you won't be able to do much saving in South America in general*', and recommends that you don't move to Chile without savings if you want to have fun and money to travel. Normally 10% of earnings must be paid in tax, which in some cases can be reclaimed the following April/May. After taking the first job she was offered by Bridge Linguatec, **Mandy Powell** assumed that all jobs paid roughly the same. However, later when she was working for EES (see entry) she discovered that there is a huge variation and wishes that she had looked for a better-paid teaching job sooner. It was especially tough trying to make ends meet in the quiet periods of January–February and July.

Usually the CELTA, Trinity or equivalent certificate is a minimum requirement for anyone considering working in the private sector. However, those looking to work within the state system of education will find that CELTA qualifications will not be accepted. In Chile a teaching degree takes five years, and school directors tend to look quite disparagingly upon one-month/120-hour courses.

A worthwhile volunteer teaching scheme is run by Voluntarios de Esperanza in Santiago (www.ve-global. org). VE works with partner institutions to place volunteers to work with at-risk children, including teaching English, for a minimum of four months beginning in September, January and May. The application process is competitive and no registration fee is charged.

RED TAPE

Most job-seekers arrive on a tourist visa valid for 90 days which is free for many nationalities (but not Australia). Once you find a job, the most common visa to apply for is the *Visa Sujeta a Contrato* (subject to contract visa), for which you will need to take a notarised copy of a contract from an employer that shows a minimum salary of 100,000 pesos a month to the Departamento de Extrajería. If you are able to commit yourself for a year, your employer may be willing to help you obtain the more flexible temporary resident visa. The total expenses for the permits will top £1,000 for Britons, whereas Americans pay next to nothing. After you get your work visa, you then need to register your address with the immigration police and obtain your ID card or *cedula*, which you require for joining the Chilean health care scheme, opening a bank account, etc.

Many British teachers delay applying for the expensive work permit until they are sure they are going to stay longer term. Others work for schools that are not keen to assist in the process. In this case it is necessary to leave the country before the 90-day validity of the tourist visa expires; most get a new 90-day tourist visa by crossing the border to Mendoza, Argentina. If you are from New Zealand, Australia or Canada you may be eligible for a working holiday visa that gives complete flexibility in job-hunting in Chile for one year.

Rarely, people are offered a job before arrival. If this is the case, there are two ways to obtain the appropriate visa permit. Either your employer submits the application at the Ministry of Foreign Affairs in Chile (Direccion de Asuntos Consulares y de Imigracion, Bandera 46, Santiago) or you apply at the Chilean Consulate in your country of origin. You will need a signed and notarised work contract and a full medical report. If granted, the visa will be valid for one year. After that you may be eligible for a *visacion de residencia* that allows an unlimited stay.

Almost everything you do in Chile requires you to present a national ID number, equivalent to National Insurance, known as RUN (Rol Único Nacional) but commonly referred to as RUT (Rol Único Tributario).

ADVERTISING FOR PRIVATE CLIENTS

The average rate for private lessons is about 10,000–12,000 pesos per hour though business people will pay up to 15,000 pesos. There are many ways to meet the expatriate community, from playing cricket at the Prince of Wales Country Club to frequenting the English-language bookshop Books and Bits on Av Apoquindo in Santiago (www.booksandbits.cl).

You can advertise for private clients in *El Mercurio*, the leading quality daily. Check ads on Craigslist (http://santiago.en.craigslist.org), mostly for part-time hours, or in the free ads paper *El Rastro*.

LEISURE TIME

Although Santiago is cosmopolitan and modern, there are pockets of poverty and the men can be aggressive, shouting across the street at women. However, Santiago is an interesting and on the whole safe city where young women can feel reasonably secure, even when out alone in the wee small hours. Pollution in the winter months can get a bit depressing. However, for the most part, the quality of life is enviable. **Mandy Powell** especially relished waking up after rain and seeing the fantastic mountains clearly against crystal-clear blue skies. **Heidi Resetarits** managed to keep herself pleasantly busy in her spare time:

> *I planned trips all over Chile at least once a week. I wrote for a magazine. I joined a gym and a swim team. I bought a bike and rode around town. I also spent a lot of time drinking coffee, pisco sours and/or wine on patios, reading or just enjoying the day. Santiago is a great city to spend time in, and it is very easy to get around in and relatively safe. The people are friendly and want to know who you are and where you are from. My favourite days were spent walking to a random café, meeting a friend and letting that meeting go into a warm summer Santiago night.*

LIST OF EMPLOYERS

ACADEMIA DE IDIOMAS DEL NORTE

Ramirez 1345, Iquique

📞 +56 57 411 827

✉ secretaria@languages.cl

💻 www.languages.cl

Swiss-owned.

NUMBER OF TEACHERS: 4.

PREFERENCE OF NATIONALITY: Native English speakers.

QUALIFICATIONS: Recognised TEFL certificate.

CONDITIONS OF EMPLOYMENT: 6–9-month contracts with 6 working hours per day. School is owned by a Swiss.

FACILITIES/SUPPORT: Information on homestay families, flats, hotels, etc is given. Shared apartments with other teachers sometimes available. Work contract provided in order to get work permits.

RECRUITMENT: Interviews are essential and usually held in Chile but can be conducted by telephone or Skype.

CHILENGLISH

Ramón Carnicer 81, Of. 607, Providencia, Santiago

📞 +56 2 665 1676

✉ oficina@chilenglish.com

💻 www.chilenglish.com

NUMBER OF TEACHERS: 15.

PREFERENCE OF NATIONALITY: None.

QUALIFICATIONS: TEFL-certified teachers with previous experience. Some opportunities for those who lack qualifications but have the right background and personality.

CONDITIONS OF EMPLOYMENT: Contract length is negotiable. Full-time is 25–30 hours per week with classes between 8am and 9pm, Monday to Friday. Some Saturday work available.

SALARY: Average 500,000 pesos per month.

FACILITIES/SUPPORT: Assistance given with work permits and guidance when filling in relevant paperwork.

RECRUITMENT: Interviews essential.

CONTACT: Craig Wilson, Director (cwilson@chilenglish.com).

COMUNICORP

Las Urbinas 68, Providencia, Santiago

📞 +56 2 234 1010

✉ dgreenst@comunicorp.cl

💻 www.comunicorp.cl

NUMBER OF TEACHERS: Approximately 30.

PREFERENCE OF NATIONALITY: None. Company prefers to have a wide variety of cultures and accents represented on the staff.

QUALIFICATIONS: At least one of the following: CELTA, TEFL certificate, MA in TESOL, MA in Education, MA in Communicative Disorders, and at least one year of classroom EFL experience, preferably with adult Business English students.

CONDITIONS OF EMPLOYMENT: New teachers are hired throughout the year, but most new positions begin in April, and finish mid-December. Late start may be available up to June/July. Hours are usually spread out during the day. Most business students prefer to have classes at the peak hours, which are: 8:30am–10am, 1pm–2.30pm, 6pm–7.30pm. Other students, who are more flexible, take classes during the off-peak hours from 10am to 11.30am and from 3pm to 4.30pm.

SALARY: Varies according to classroom experience, degree held, and time with the company. The lowest salary would be 500,000 pesos per month for 80 classroom hours. There are additional benefits such as a travel bonus at the end of the contract for those hired from abroad and a monthly transportation budget. Taxes are less than 5% and social security is not an issue if the teacher has a home pension plan.

FACILITIES/SUPPORT: Assistance with finding accommodation. School assists with processing the work visa. Spanish classes are available in exchange for English teaching hours.

RECRUITMENT: Internet and word of mouth. Applicants should send CV, at least one letter of reference from an employer and a recent photo.

CONTACT: Diane Greenstein, Academic and Human Resources Director.

EES EXECUTIVE ENGLISH SOLUTIONS

Luis Thayer Ojeda 0130, Of. 808, Providencia, Santiago

📞 +56 2 335 7781

✉ hspencer@ees.cl

💻 www.ees.cl

NUMBER OF TEACHERS: 30–40.

PREFERENCE OF NATIONALITY: None.

QUALIFICATIONS: 4+ year degree, TESOL, CELTA or TEFL and 1+ year's experience preferred.

CONDITIONS OF EMPLOYMENT: Standard contracts are 6–12 months. The usual hours are mornings, lunchtime and evenings, Monday to Friday. Normal allocation of hours is up to 18.

SALARY: 7,000–8,000 pesos per hour, 25–30 hours per week. Deductions of 10% refundable with filing of tax return.

FACILITIES/SUPPORT: Company will provide proof of employment for lease and rental agreement. All foreign employees receive a Chilean work visa.

RECRUITMENT: In-person interview.

CONTACT: Howard H. Spencer, Director of Studies.

ENGLISH FOR LIFE
Badajoz 130, Of. 1102 Las Condes, Santiago
7560908
- +56 2 2760 2206
- info@efl.cl; jrobertson@englishforlife.cl
- www.efl.cl

Associate Member of International House.

NUMBER OF TEACHERS: Around 15.

PREFERENCE OF NATIONALITY: None.

QUALIFICATIONS: CELTA, Trinity TESOL or IH certificate are preferred and English for Life also offers its own teacher-training programme. More experienced teachers have the possibility of moving into more senior roles or teacher training.

CONDITIONS OF EMPLOYMENT: Contract is initially for one academic year (9 months). The contract specifies an agreed number of contact (teaching) hours.

SALARY: Varies with number of contracted hours. Bonus may be paid depending on location of teaching in Santiago. Teachers are guaranteed a base salary, for example, for an 18-hour contract, with extra hours and bonuses paid in addition. 7% deduction for health insurance. Overtime paid on hours worked over 24 per week.

FACILITIES/SUPPORT: Accommodation and flights are not paid for by the school, although help and advice are given in finding suitable accommodation. Teachers enter on a tourist visa and then apply for a work permit/visa when they have signed the contract. Teachers are entitled to paid holiday and sick leave on a pro-rata basis. Full academic support is given; eg employer pays for teachers to attend meetings and teacher-development sessions that are run once a week by in-house teacher trainer. The school is easily accessible by metro and bus. School has a garden available to staff for lesson preparation, barbecues, etc. Free wi-fi access and computers. DoS willing to supervise teachers who wish to do the online DELTA or other career-development courses.

RECRUITMENT: Through IHWO (www.ihworld.com/recruitment), www.tefl.com or direct application throughout the year. CVs should be sent to the DoS (dos@englishforlife.cl), who will contact suitable candidates for interview.

CONTACT: Justine Robertson, School Manager.

FISCHER ENGLISH INSTITUTE
Calle Cirujano Guzmán 49, Providencia, Santiago de Chile
- +56 2 235 6667/9812
- contacto@fischerinstitute.cl
- www.fischerinstitute.cl

NUMBER OF TEACHERS: 30.

PREFERENCE OF NATIONALITY: USA.

QUALIFICATIONS: University degree and TEFL certificate or similar and 1 year's experience in teaching.

CONDITIONS OF EMPLOYMENT: Minimum 1-year contract, 20 hours a week.

SALARY: 8,000–8,500 pesos per hour.

FACILITIES/SUPPORT: None.

RECRUITMENT: References, preferably from school abroad. Interviews essential, carried out in Santiago.

GRANT'S ENGLISH
Londres 60, Oficina 4, Santiago 8330133
- +56 2 638 1128
- grants@grantsenglish.cl
- www.grantsenglish.cl

NUMBER OF TEACHERS: 20-25.

PREFERENCE OF NATIONALITY: USA, Canada, UK, Australia.

QUALIFICATIONS: Bachelor's Degree and TEFL/CELTA certification.

CONDITIONS OF EMPLOYMENT: 6-month contracts. 20-30 hours per week minimum

SALARY: 8,888 pesos an hour. 10% deductions for social security and tax.

FACILITIES/SUPPORT: Advice given on accommodation. Job letter given to teachers to be attached to a notarised copy of their degree, photocopy of their passport, entry stamp, photo and completed Temporary Residency form.

RECRUITMENT: Craigslist, Facebook, word of mouth. Face-to-face and Skype interviews.

CONTACT: Darshana Mahtani, Academic Director.

INSTITUTO CHILENO-BRITANICO DE CULTURA
Paseo Huerfanos 554, Santa Lucia, Santiago
- +56 2 413 2350
- edovas@britanico.cl
- www.britanico.cl

Other branches in Las Condes, La Florida, Maipu, Providencia and La Dehesa.

NUMBER OF TEACHERS: 10.

PREFERENCE OF NATIONALITY: None, but should be native English speaker.

QUALIFICATIONS: A degree in English or Modern Languages, plus a TEFL qualification. However, experience is valued more than TEFL qualification.

CONDITIONS OF EMPLOYMENT: 1 year, March to February. 30 teaching hours per week, mostly evenings.

SALARY: £700 per month.

FACILITIES/SUPPORT: Help with finding accommodation is provided. Teachers are provided with a settling-in grant towards their accommodation.

RECRUITMENT: Usually on the spot.

CONTACT: Eduardo Vasquez, General Manager.

INSTITUTO CHILENO-NORTEAMERICANO DE CULTURA
Moneda No. 1467, Santiago
- +56 2 2677 7167
- englishteachers@norteamericano.cl
- www.norteamericano.cl

NUMBER OF TEACHERS: 15–20, also for branches in La Florida and Providencia. Norteamericano branches in the regions (Valparaiso, Curicó, etc) recruit teachers separately.

PREFERENCE OF NATIONALITY: American and Canadian.

QUALIFICATIONS: BA in Education or TESL/TEFL and 6 months' teaching experience, or a bachelor's degree in related field with certificate in TESL/TEFL and some teaching experience.

CONDITIONS OF EMPLOYMENT: 1-year contracts starting in March. 30 hours per week. Peak hours of work early morning and early evening, and some Saturdays. Classes for adults, children, teens, Business and Academic English. Part-time openings for Friday evening and Saturday morning hours.

SALARY: Equivalent of US$1,100 per month in Chilean pesos.

FACILITIES/SUPPORT: Assistance given in obtaining visas. Training provided. Teachers' room with computers, email access and cafeteria privileges.

RECRUITMENT: Direct application by mail, email, phone or fax. Applicants should send cover letter, résumé, recent photo, copy of diplomas/certificates and letters of reference from recent employers.

REDLAND SCHOOL
Camino el Alba 11357, Las Condes, Santiago
- +56 2 959 8500
- secretaria_rector@redland.cl; jobs@redland.cl
- www.redland.cl

NUMBER OF TEACHERS: 72 in total.

PREFERENCE OF NATIONALITY: British or other nationalities with English as a first language.

QUALIFICATIONS: University degree and teaching qualification. Pre- and post-university students also considered for gap-year placements.

CONDITIONS OF EMPLOYMENT: 1–3-year contract, mostly starting late February for academic year March to December. Classes run from 8am to 3.30pm or 5pm. Pupils aged 4–18.

SALARY: On application. Increases are pegged to cost of living. 13th month salary given as bonus.

FACILITIES/SUPPORT: Assistance finding accommodation can be offered. Professional development opportunities and free lunches provided.

RECRUITMENT: Via email in first instance. Recruitment starts in August for following academic year.

TEACHING CHILE
Av. Vitacura 3355, Dept 113, Santiago
- +1 720 221 3831 (US phone number routes calls to Santiago office); +44 20 8150 6981 (UK phone number routes calls to Santiago office)
- info@teachingchile.com
- www.teachingchile.com

NUMBER OF TEACHERS: Approximately 90 native English-speaking teachers per year are placed by this recruitment agency.

PREFERENCE OF NATIONALITY: None. To date, TeachingChile has placed teachers from Australia, Canada, England, Ireland, New Zealand, Scotland and the USA.

QUALIFICATIONS: Varies among schools. Overall, applicants should be a graduate of a university or in their final year of undergraduate studies, ESL/TEFL/TESOL certification and teaching experience are desired but not required. Spanish language skills are not required for classroom instruction but elementary conversational language skills are recommended for the teacher's cultural enjoyment.

CONDITIONS OF EMPLOYMENT: Minimum 6-month contract; 10–12 months preferred. The majority of teachers choose a 1-year contract. All contracts are renewable directly with the teaching institution, assuming the school has positions available and the teacher has a good rapport with the employer and students.

SALARY: Minimum 445,000 pesos per month for a base of 18 hours of classroom time per week. For longer hours teachers earn more. Some schools deduct 13% for tax and an optional 7% for medical insurance, but salaries are adjusted accordingly and teachers make about the same net salary.

FACILITIES/SUPPORT: Guaranteed work contract, visa-processing assistance, and 3 weeks' rent-free accommodation. TeachingChile provides assistance with finding long-term accommodation and a pre-paid transfer from Santiago airport to the first night's accommodation.

RECRUITMENT: Via the internet, universities and ESL/TEFL/TESOL job placement websites. Applicants submit an application package available from TeachingChile's website prior to arrival and will be interviewed by telephone. Placement fee for full service is $1,395.

CONTACT: Bruce Thompson, Managing Director (bruce@ teachingchile.com) and Andrea Rodriguez, Programme Coordinator.

COLOMBIA

Since most people associate Colombia only with crime and violence, it is not surprising to learn that teaching institutes in that country sometimes have trouble attracting qualified foreign teachers. But this reputation is undeserved. Even the overly cautious US State Department admits that security in Colombia has improved significantly in recent years. Foreign teachers are extremely unlikely to become involved in any drug-inspired tensions but are guaranteed to be welcomed by the locals. Memories will be of a local carnival rather than of a neighbourhood shoot-out. **Dave Crowder** has nothing but praise for his adopted country:

> *I have found the people of Colombia to be universally friendly and helpful to strangers. Unlike the USA, the wel-*
> *come here is genuine, open and amicable, and the people are genuinely interested in the novelty of a stranger*
> *among them. There is no more drug trafficking in Medellín where I live than in any other major city anywhere*
> *in the world (I used to live in Miami, where there is much more drug gang activity). As a matter of fact, I will*
> *extend my comments about Medellín to every part of the nation that I have visited, which is everywhere but the*
> *few FARC/ELN-controlled areas in the boondocks.*

With the expansion of trade, interest in English has increased, as evidenced by the popularity of English-language media like newspapers and radio stations. The law that imposed quotas of foreign employees was abolished several years ago, so language institutes can now employ as many native speakers as they like, and many are keen to do so. The international chain Eurocentres opened in Barranquilla last year, its first outside the anglophone world.

For the Colombian Ministry of Education's new programme to encourage bilingualism, it is recruiting volunteer teachers to work for at least four months alongside local teachers mainly in secondary schools throughout the country. Although TEFL experience/qualifications and a basic level of Spanish are preferred, the only absolute requirements for acceptance are being a native speaker aged 21-50 and able to pay the refundable US$400 deposit. Various international recruiters are involved like Footprints in Canada (www.footprintsrecruiting.com) and Flying Cows in the UK (see entry). A monthly living allowance of 1,500,000 pesos is paid to participants in arrears.

Colombia is more strongly oriented towards the USA than elsewhere in South America, with an extensive network of Colombian-American Cultural Centers around the country. However, **Charles Seville** from Oxford, who spent a year as an English-language assistant at the University de Los Llanos in Villavicencio, was struck by how keen Colombians were to learn British English. There is a British Council Teaching Centre in Bogotá, whose market is primarily university students and young learners (www.britishcouncil.co/en) but which also runs conversation clubs. From time to time it advertises hourly-paid teacher vacancies.

It is possible to access the Colombian *Yellow Pages* on the internet (www.quehubo.com) which might provide a starting place for finding school addresses; search for *Instituto Idiomas*. Some global EFL companies have a strong presence in Colombia. EF Education First in Bogotá is based at the Edificio EF (Carrera 9, No. 78-57; +57 1 616 1130; www.ef.com.co) with about 16 branches, and Berlitz (www.berlitz.com.co) operates 41 centres, including five in Bogotá. The established company Inglés Bogotá (www.teachenglishbogota.com) offers a range of language services and is always looking for qualified teachers, and has opened offices in Medellin and Cali too. You can apply for an interview via a form on their website.

The main newspaper, *El Tiempo*, carries adverts for language schools in the capital. There are plenty of local language schools where untrained native English speakers can find work, but there are two main disadvantages. Wages and conditions can be very poor; many schools start teachers off at 10,000 pesos an hour (about $3.75), though the schools listed below offer more attractive salaries, with an upper limit of 200,000 Colombian pesos per month as paid by the respected institute Bogotá Business English to qualified teachers (see entry). One tip for anyone flying into Colombia is to have an address (e.g. a hostel) where you will be staying since you can be asked for this at the airport immigration desk. The immigration restrictions have become more manageable with the passing of several recent laws. It is no longer necessary to apply for a work permit from outside the country. The application with various apostilled documents can be made in Bogotá. Good employers will assist with the process and may even underwrite the $400 fee for a one-year visa. Check the website of the Ministry of Foreign Affairs (www.cancilleria.gov.co). If a teacher intends to stay in Colombia longer than three months, he or she must register at the Foreign Registry of Migration.

LIST OF EMPLOYERS

BOGOTA BUSINESS ENGLISH

Carrera 15 No.79-36 Oficina 402, Bogotá
+57 3 1136 99433
andrew@bogotabusinessenglish.com
www.BogotaBusinessEnglish.co

NUMBER OF TEACHERS: 40.

PREFERENCE OF NATIONALITY: None.

QUALIFICATIONS: CELTA/Trinity/TESL training with observed practice element or minimum one year experience.

CONDITIONS OF EMPLOYMENT: 1 year. Split shifts between 6am and 9pm; 2-hour classes.

SALARY: 2,000,000 pesos (approximately $750) per month.

FACILITIES/SUPPORT: Deductions for compulsory medical insurance. No tax. Assistance given with finding accommodation through various rental agencies. Support for one-year foreign worker visa which costs $400.

RECRUITMENT: TESL websites, direct from CELTA recruiters in Bogotá, word of mouth. Face-to-face interviews in Bogotá only.

CONTACT: Andrew Riordan, Academic Director.

FIRST CLASS ENGLISH

Carrera 12 #93-78 Of 407, 407 Bogotá
+57 1 623 2380
info@fce.edu.co
www.fce.edu.co

NUMBER OF TEACHERS: 24+ native English speakers.

PREFERENCE OF NATIONALITY: American and British.

QUALIFICATIONS: At least 1 year's teaching experience, preferably with executives/professional, CELTA, ICELT certification is a plus. But the bottom line is that the candidate must have 3+ years' college/university degree, hopefully in Business or related areas.

CONDITIONS OF EMPLOYMENT: Minimum 1 year, if volunteering

a minimum of 4 months. Up to 8 hours of teaching within the hours of 6am to 9pm.

SALARY: Contracted hourly pay from 15,000 to 18,500 Colombian pesos per hour, disbursed every 15 days. The retention (tax) deduction, specific to this type of contract, is about 7% of income.

FACILITIES/SUPPORT: Can assist with accommodation if necessary on a case-by-case basis. School provides paperwork for working visa; however, the teacher is required to activate the visa by travelling to a neighbouring country and going to the local consulate. This process can take up to 60 days in total from the moment the visa is requested.

RECRUITMENT: Email requests and walk-ins. An interview – possible by phone – is followed by 20-hour mandatory selection process. The process includes training, simulated class, teaching crash course and administrative instruction.

FLYING COWS

The Hive, Nottingham Trent University, Nottingham NG1 4BU, UK
0115 824 0824
placement@flying-cows.com
www.flying-cows.com

NUMBER OF TEACHERS: Up to 50 volunteer teachers per intake, e.g. from late July, for Ministry of Education programme.

PREFERENCE OF NATIONALITY: Mostly British although can also be Canadian, American, Irish, Australian, New Zealander, and South African.

QUALIFICATIONS: Having a TESOL certificate assists placement but is not essential. Experience of travelling in South America is valued.

CONDITIONS OF EMPLOYMENT: 5 months to work in state schools.

SALARY: 1,500,000 pesos per month.

FACILITIES/SUPPORT: School arranges and pays for the accommodation for first month, but after that teachers are independent. Visas are arranged.

RECRUITMENT: Ministry asks for a $400 refundable deposit against completing the programme.

CONTACT: Amanda McGillivray, Director.

FUNDACION EDUCATIVA PERSONAL GROWTH
Transversal 25 No 53C-15 Bogotá
- +57 1 541 1503
- info@pgrowth.com or academicdirection@ pgrowth.com
- www.pgrowth.com; www.teachincolombia. wordpress.com

Private international organisation with headquarters in the Cayman Islands.

NUMBER OF TEACHERS: 45.

PREFERENCE OF NATIONALITY: UK, USA, Australia, Canada and South Africa.

QUALIFICATIONS: Native speakers with or without experience. Teachers can take on-site TEFL course if needed.

CONDITIONS OF EMPLOYMENT: 1 year (February to November or August to June). 30–48 hours per week to teach one-to-one and in small groups (adults, teenagers and children).

SALARY: 3,000 Colombian pesos ($8.50) per 90-minute class, before tax. Teachers are responsible for paying their own health insurance.

FACILITIES/SUPPORT: Accommodation arranged with choice of homestay for $250 per month to private furnished apartment for $700 (including furniture, bedding and internet connection). Visa sponsorship promised with some jobs; working visa arranged after arrival.

RECRUITMENT: Usually via Craigslist or www.learn4good.com. Local or preliminary Skype interviews essential. If selected, candidates must give a demo class after arrival and have face-to-face interviews with Personal Growth and with the institution, and also a psychological test.

CONTACT: Sigfried Castell, International Academic Director.

INSTITUTO DE IDIOMAS (UNIVERSIDAD DEL NORTE)
Km 5 Via Pto Colombia, Barranquilla
- +57 5 350 9736/359 8852
- iidiomas@uninorte.edu.co
- www.uninorte.edu.co

NUMBER OF TEACHERS: Around 5 a year.

PREFERENCE OF NATIONALITY: None.

QUALIFICATIONS: Master's degree in TESOL, Linguistics, Psychology, English, Elementary/Bilingual Education, or related areas. Must have certified experience teaching EFL, preferably outside the USA. Must be a native English speaker; be able to teach and evaluate students effectively; and have experience using language lab equipment.

CONDITIONS OF EMPLOYMENT: Minimum 1 year. 8 hours a day depending on classes assigned. Most likely 9am–5pm.

SALARY: Depends on qualifications. Other benefits include a living allowance of around US$200 for rent, ticket and visa-issuing costs. The university pays in Colombian pesos.

FACILITIES/SUPPORT: University recommends a rental agency and will serve as a guarantor. When teachers arrive, the university pays for a hotel for 1 week. The university also provides transport and documentation needed for the working visa.

RECRUITMENT: Via internet websites such as www.studyabroad. com. Interviews through Skype or videoconferencing are required. References are also checked.

CONTACT: Lourdes Rey Paba, Academic Coordinator (arey@ uninorte.edu.co).

NATIVE TONGUE ENGLISH INSTITUTE
Cra. 4a Bis #35-05, B/ Cadiz, Ibagué, Tolima
- +57 8 264 6595
- infoibague@nativetongue.edu.co or ancusm@hotmail.com
- www.nativetongue.edu.co

Canadian-owned and operated company in its 13th year that operates a school in Pereira as well.

NUMBER OF TEACHERS: 10+.

PREFERENCE OF NATIONALITY: Canadians preferred, Americans accepted.

QUALIFICATIONS: Native speaker with at least 1 year overseas teaching experience. Spanish is an asset but not necessary.

CONDITIONS OF EMPLOYMENT: 11 months. Teaching hours 28 per week.

SALARY: Approx 1.5 million–2 million Colombian pesos (from CAN$750) less deductions of about 40,000 Colombian pesos ($19) per month.

FACILITIES/SUPPORT: Assistance given with finding accommodation, guaranteeing contract and a stipend. Help given with obtaining work visa outside of Colombia.

RECRUITMENT: Via web postings. Phone interviews acceptable. Face-to-face interviews occasionally carried out in Canada.

CONTACT: Shawn Miranda, Owner & Canadian Operations (Grimsby, Ontario).

TRAINING PEOPLE

Calle 46, No. 8–64, Piso 2, 001, Bogotá

✆ +57 1 4 660277

✉ sales@training-people.com

🖥 www.training-people.com

NUMBER OF TEACHERS: 5.

PREFERENCE OF NATIONALITY: British.

QUALIFICATIONS: TEFL certification (minimum 100 hours) such as CELTA, DELTA or even TESOL and TEFL (with approval of the Principal). Short courses such as TKT test are not acceptable. Candidates should be over 21. Degree plus TEFL preferred.

CONDITIONS OF EMPLOYMENT: 1 year. 40 hours a week, including Business English to adults.

SALARY: Approx $1,000 per month.

FACILITIES/SUPPORT: Assistance given with obtaining a working visa, but teachers normally arrange their own accommodation.

RECRUITMENT: Via teflcourse.net and other advertisements.

CONTACT: Jorge Gil Gomez, Director.

ECUADOR

Ecuador's economy has benefited since it was forced to adopt the US dollar as the national currency and it has been an oasis of political stability in the region for a long time. Teaching wages are still low, but obviously EFL teachers do not go to Ecuador to save money and it is still possible to live comfortably on the wages paid. For example, a night in a budget hotel costs from $10 and a tasty meal costs $3.

Demand for English continues to thrive, particularly for American English, in the capital, Quito, the second city, Guayaquil, and in the picturesque city and cultural centre of Cuenca in the Southern Sierra. The majority of teaching is of university students and the business community, whose classes are usually scheduled early in the morning (starting at 7am) to avoid the equatorial heat of the day and again in the late afternoon and evening. Many schools are owned and run by expatriates since there are few legal restrictions on foreigners running businesses.

BARRY O'LEARY

Barry O'Leary, on arriving in Quito, visited a tourist agency that had the addresses of all the possible academies and institutes. He started his first TEFL job-hunt armed only with a basic TEFL certificate and speaking very little Spanish. As luck would have it he found two jobs in 24 hours just by walking round the city with copies of his CV.

I can still remember the buzz I felt when José, my first employer, said 'Yeah we're looking for someone to start next week.' I couldn't quite believe it. With this institute there wasn't really a formal interview or application process. With another school I had a basic interview to make sure I could speak and wasn't a monster; they didn't even ask for my TEFL certificate. In Ecuador everyone I knew was working without a work visa. I remember being worried about telling them I was only staying for three months but they were just happy to have a native speaker teaching their students.

The teaching varied. In one school I was responsible for conversation classes. I had no guidance with the type of lessons they wanted so had to use resources from my course, the internet and my imagination. In every lesson a local teacher was there to help with any language barriers. The working conditions were very relaxed, no lesson plans or meetings. I was just given a timetable and left to get on with it. As long as the students were smiling I was seen to be a good teacher.

I was lucky enough to find an apartment with an Ecuadorian family through an advertisement in an internet café. I made enough money to pay for my rent, food and some social activities and even managed to travel a bit with my last pay packet - and the dollars went much further in Peru. The students were all great, the teenagers tending to be cheeky, a few times they changed the theme of the lessons to 'make the teacher dance like a fool' before they did any work, but this was all part of the fun. It was a very relaxed atmosphere most of the time. I really enjoyed working with local teachers and they were all very open and friendly and interested in my life in England, since many of them had never left Ecuador.

The highlight of Ecuador was helping my first students to prepare a presentation for the directors on their chosen topics of hooliganism, pollution and anorexia. The looks on their faces when they received their certificates were definitely worth all the hours of hard work we put in. The low point of my experience was unfortunately when I was held at knifepoint outside my house. Luckily I was not hurt and they did not steal anything but it should be known that certain areas of Quito are dangerous.

A qualified teacher can expect to earn from $400 to $800 a month, while the more prestigious institutes like the British School of Language (now affiliated to International House) pay $800–$1200 net per month. Accommodation is harder to find in Quito than in Cuenca. Qualified TEFLers should not accept less than $6 an hour, though the private institutes that accept unqualified teachers pay accordingly less. All teachers (both contract and freelance) have taxes withdrawn at source of between 5% and 12%. Quito is not as large and daunting a city as some other South American capitals and it should be easy to meet longer-term expats who may be able to give advice on teaching. The helpful British Council will give you a list of ELT schools throughout the country and will (unofficially) indicate which offer the best teacher support and modern teaching methods and resources. One possible source of information is the South American Explorers clubhouse (membership costs $60). In Quito the Club is at Mariana de Jesus Oe 3-32 y Ulloa. It includes language schools in Ecuador on its database and has a useful noticeboard.

As throughout the continent, charitable schools for children can always use voluntary help. The department of education in the country's poorest province runs a free volunteering scheme for native speakers with a basic knowledge of Spanish to teach in primary schools. If you want to spend at least three months between September and June in the Chimborazo region in the Andes, the poorest province in the country, go to http://ecuador.teach-english-volunteer.com for details. You Volunteer (www.youvolunteer.org) is part of a small registered British charity that offers volunteers the opportunity to work and teach in schools in the Amazon jungle of Central Ecuador as part of the Arajuno Road Project (see entry).

RED TAPE

Technically you shouldn't work on a tourist visa but there is little control. Britons and Americans can stay 90 days. If possible, teachers should get a 12-IX non-immigrant visa in their country of origin for stays of three to six months (fee $200), which can be extended by visiting a neighbouring country, usually Colombia. Most employers will help teachers who commit themselves for a reasonable stay to obtain a Cultural Exchange visa (Category 12 VIII), valid for a year. The requirements are as follows: a notarised copy of a police report, doctor's certificate (including HIV test) and birth certificate, letter of invitation and various other documents from an Ecuadorian employer, letter of financial support from a backer/inviter and so on. The visa fee for US citizens applying in the US is $50 plus a $30 application fee. The Centro de Educación Continua in Quito and CEDEI in Cuenca (see entries) both contract instructors as Cultural Exchange volunteers. For a proper teacher's work permit, a degree in English or Education plus a TEFL Certificate qualification are required.

LIST OF EMPLOYERS

ARAJUNO ROAD PROJECT

Casilla 16-01-803, Puyo-Pastaza, Ecuador

☎ +593 9 851 1638; UK: +44 1832 275038

✉ info@amazonvolunteerecuador.com

🖥 www.facebook.com/ArajunoRoadProject; www.ama-zonvolunteerecuador.com; www.youvolunteer.org

The Arajuno Road Project supports children and their families by providing quality English instruction, improving the infrastructure and environment of their schools and working on community development and conservation programmes in the Ecuadorian Amazon.

NUMBER OF TEACHERS: 2 Teaching Coordinator positions, 6 Teaching Volunteer positions and interns are accepted on a case-by-case basis.

PREFERENCE OF NATIONALITY: All nationalities encouraged to apply; however, all teachers must be proficient in English.

QUALIFICATIONS: Anyone over the age of 18 and in good physical/mental health is welcome to become a Teaching Volunteer. Teaching Coordinators must have a minimum of 1 year's work experience and must be bilingual in English and Spanish. It is highly preferred that applicants have previous experience working with children, working internationally, teaching and have a TESOL/TEFOL certificate. In addition, applicants should have excellent organisational skills, communication skills and people skills. Applicants should have the ability to adapt to diverse situations and be tolerant, patient and understanding.

CONDITIONS OF EMPLOYMENT: Minimum stay 2 weeks for volunteers, 10 weeks for coordinators. The schools run from 7.30am to 12.30pm Monday–Friday, including approximately 4 hours of English instruction. In addition, teachers travel up to 45 minutes to reach the schools. Teachers are also welcome to participate in non-formal English instruction in the afternoons and run cultural exchange activities as time and interest permit.

SALARY: None. Teaching Volunteers pay an at-cost placement fee and weekly fee covering food, housing, materials and support: $315 for first fortnight, $115 per week thereafter.

FACILITIES/SUPPORT: All teachers stay at the project's volunteer house, unless a host family is requested. No need for work permits; volunteers enter Ecuador with an automatic 90-day tourist visa, which can be renewed if needed.

RECRUITMENT: Via personal recommendations, social media/internet and partner volunteer organisations.

CONTACT: Laura Hepting, MSc, Director, Amazon Language & Conservation Exchange (laura.hepting@gmail.com).

CEDEI SCHOOL CUENCA

Gran Colombia 11-02 y General Torres Esq, Cuenca

☎ +593 7 283 9003

✉ jalban@cedei.org or english@cedei.org

🖥 www.cedei.org

NUMBER OF TEACHERS: 9.

PREFERENCE OF NATIONALITY: None.

QUALIFICATIONS: Teaching degree preferred, prior experience preferred. TEFL required if applicants don't have a teaching degree.

CONDITIONS OF EMPLOYMENT: 9 months from the last week of September. 20–25 hours a week with opportunities for extra tutoring and conversation classes. Usual hours between 7.30am and 1.45pm, teaching children from pre-school to 9th grade.

SALARY: $6.75 per hour ($7.75 on Saturdays).

FACILITIES/SUPPORT: 3-day pre-service orientation. Teachers are responsible for their own accommodation. School assists in obtaining an intercultural visa (not a work visa); teachers pay costs for the first year. Free Spanish and salsa classes.

RECRUITMENT: Through posts on websites and links with universities. Interviews by Skype/telephone.

CONTACT: Jessica Alban, International Coordinator.

CENTRO DE EDUCACIÓN CONTINUA DE LA ESCUELA POLITECNICA NACIONAL

Edificio Araucaria, Baquedano 222 y Reina Victoria, Quito

☎ +593 22 500068

✉ henryguygooch@yahoo.com and linguist@cec-epn.edu.ec

🖥 www.cec-epn.edu.ec

NUMBER OF TEACHERS: 160+.

PREFERENCE OF NATIONALITY: American, Canadian and British.

QUALIFICATIONS: BA in English, Applied Linguistics, TEFL, Drama, International Studies or a related field. TEFL certificate, 1-year experience.

CONDITIONS OF EMPLOYMENT: Minimum 1 year (40 weeks of teaching). 6 hours per day.

SALARY: Volunteers are not paid a salary, but are provided with a monthly subsistence allowance of $720–$885 net as required by law and written agreement.

FACILITIES/SUPPORT: Teachers must find their own accommodation. Instructors are contracted as Cultural Exchange Volunteers under the agreement the University maintains with the Ecuadorian Ministerio de Relaciones Exteriores.

RECRUITMENT: Word of mouth. Telephone interviews are conducted.

CONTACT: Henry Guy Gooch, Director of Linguistics and Cultural Exchanges.

CENTRO DE ESTUDIOS INTERAMERICANOS/CEDEI
Casilla 597, Cuenca
+593 7 283 9003
English@cedei.org
www.english.cedei.org

A non-profit institution dedicated to the study of American languages and cultures.

NUMBER OF TEACHERS: 50.

PREFERENCE OF NATIONALITY: Native English speakers.

QUALIFICATIONS: Minimum university degree in related field and TEFL/CELTA/TESOL certificate or university degree in TESL/TEFL. Experience in teaching EFL/ESL.

CONDITIONS OF EMPLOYMENT: Minimum 9-month stay, preference given to year-long commitments. Courses run from January to mid-March, early April to early June, end of June to early September and mid-September to the beginning of December. Teachers teach on average 20 hours per week. Most classes meet Monday to Thursday and there are also Saturday Intensives. To teach both classroom courses and individuals. In addition to classroom classes, teachers may elect to give tutorials and conversation classes to supplement their income.

SALARY: Approximately $325 per teenage/adult course, $260 per children's course, and $300 per Saturday class. Courses are 40–50 hours long and teachers are given 3–4 courses per term (10 weeks). This is a high salary by Ecuadorian standards.

FACILITIES: Apartments are very reasonably priced. Cost of living is low. Average rent for a shared apartment/house is between $90 and $140 per month. Free Spanish classes, dance classes and internet access for teachers. Beautiful school building. Very charming city in an Andean setting. Extensive help given with visas.

RECRUITMENT: Via the website www.cedei.org.

CONTACT: Elisabeth Rodas, Academic Director of English Programs (erodas@cedei.org).

EF SCHOOL OF ENGLISH – QUITO
Catalina Aldaz No. N34–267 y Portugal, Quito
+593 2 245 7289
www.ef.com.ec/quito

NUMBER OF TEACHERS: 20.

PREFERENCE OF NATIONALITY: None; school aims to have a mixture of nationalities and accents.

QUALIFICATIONS: CELTA or equivalent teaching qualification.

CONDITIONS OF EMPLOYMENT: 6 months to 2 years. 35 hours per week.

SALARY: Average $700+ per month after deductions of 12% for tax.

FACILITIES/SUPPORT: Accommodation arranged in local hostel, EF residence or with host family. Pre-arrival pack contains detailed information about the options. Free transfers on arrival.

RECRUITMENT: Via internet or worldwide network of EF schools. Teachers also recruited locally. For senior positions and long-term posts applicants may be asked to present themselves at a local EF centre.

FINE-TUNED ENGLISH LANGUAGE INSTITUTE
Macara entre Miguel Riofrio y Rocafuerte, Loja
+593 2578899/2563224/2574702
mpickup@finetunedenglish.edu.ec
www.finetunedenglish.edu.ec

NUMBER OF TEACHERS: 10.

PREFERENCE OF NATIONALITY: None.

QUALIFICATIONS: Minimum CELTA or equivalent.

CONDITIONS OF EMPLOYMENT: Minimum one semester. Minimum 20 hours per week, Monday-Friday.

SALARY: $6 per hour.

FACILITIES/SUPPORT: Institute finds temporary accommodation for teachers when they arrive, but does not offer financial assistance.

RECRUITMENT: Via email and Skype interviews.

CONTACT: Dr Michael Pickup, International Recruitment Officer.

IH GUAYAQUIL / IH QUITO
Kennedy Norte, Av. Luis Orrantia Mz 110 Solar 7, Guayaquil, Ecuador
+593 4 2684404
t.bolton@ihecuador.com
www.bsl.com.ec

PREFERENCE OF NATIONALITY: None but must be native speakers or non-native speakers with a CPE certificate or valid IELTS certificate at 9.0.

QUALIFICATIONS: CELTA/TrinityCert, DELTA/TrinityDip. Minimum 1 year experience.

CONDITIONS OF EMPLOYMENT: Minimum commitment 12 months; 1 or 2 year contracts. 20 contact hours per week, 80 per calendar month. Extra hours paid on top (excluding prep time, admin, marking and professional development).

SALARY: Start at US$800 (net) and reach US$1200 per month, depending on qualifications and experience.

FACILITIES/SUPPORT: Logistical support given on arrival. School obtains a non-immigrant visa upon completion of a one-month probation period, which is relatively straightforward; IH Ecuador does most of the leg work.

RECRUITMENT: Via www.tefl.com and www.ihworld.com. Skype interviews. Not financially, though we do offer logistical support before and upon arrival.

CONTACT: Tom Bolton, Director of Studies, IH Guayaquil.

INLINGUA

Sebastian Quintero N37–12 y Jose Correa (behind the Atahualpa Olympic Stadium), Quito

C +593 2 245 8763

✉ inlinguaquito@inlingua.com; academic@inlingua.com

💻 www.inlingua.com.ec

NUMBER OF TEACHERS: 25–30 mainly part-time.

PREFERENCE OF NATIONALITY: None, but native English speakers only.

QUALIFICATIONS: Recognised TEFL/CELTA and/or teaching experience (particularly Business English).

CONDITIONS OF EMPLOYMENT: Minimum 6-month part-time/full-time contracts. Hours vary. Full-time position totals 20/25 hours per week.

SALARY: $6.15–$7.35 per hour depending on experience and/or qualifications.

FACILITIES/SUPPORT: Full training on Inlingua's international programme and teaching resources provided. Spanish classes and health insurance offered at discounted rates for teachers.

RECRUITMENT: Applications by email, interview and induction in Quito upon arrival.

CONTACT: David Montenegro, Academic Coordinator (academic@inlingua.com).

MEXICO

The lure of the USA and its language is very strong in Mexico. The frenzy of American investment in Mexico after the North American Free Trade Agreement (NAFTA) saw a huge upswing in both the demand for English by businesses and the resources to pay for it. That boom is now over, but the market for English is still enormous in universities, in business, almost everywhere. Proximity to the USA and a tendency towards what Australians call the cultural cringe (in Mexico called Malinchism after the lover of Cortès who betrayed her people) means that there will always be an unquenchable thirst for English taught by native English speakers in Mexico. Foreign teachers are automatically respected and are often promoted almost immediately.

Companies of all descriptions provide language classes for their employees, especially in the early mornings and evenings (but seldom on weekends or even Fridays). **Roberta Wedge** even managed to persuade a '*sleek head honcho in the state ferry service*' that he needed private tuition during the sacred siesta and that busy executives and other interested employees of a local company needed English lessons at the same time of day.

It is not surprising that enrolment in English courses is booming, when some employees have been threatened with dismissal unless they master some English. A vet going to Dubai, a stockbroker doing deals with the New York Stock Exchange, housewives who have to go to parties with their executive husbands, teenagers with exam worries, all are keen to improve their English. After each six-year presidential term of office, the top layers of management in companies (especially oil and banking) are replaced by new staff that need new training, especially English. Elections always boost the demand for English not only in Mexico City and the border cities to which US industries looking for cheap labour have relocated, but throughout the country, including the Yucatan Peninsula and other unlikely places, at least one of which must remain nameless in order to preserve **Roberta Wedge**'s dreams:

> *After doing a 'taster' ESL course in Vancouver, I set out for Nicaragua with a bus ticket to San Diego and $500 – no guide book, no travelling companion, no Spanish. On the way I fell in love with a town in Mexico (not for worlds would I reveal its name – I want to keep it in a pristine time warp so I can hope to return) and decided to stay. I found a job by looking up all the language schools in the phonebook and walking around the city to find them. The problem was that many small businesses were not on the phone. So I kept my eye out for English school signs. I had semi-memorised a little speech in Spanish: 'I am a Canadian teacher of English. I love your town very much and want to work here. This is my CV.' Within two days I had a job at a one-man school.*

The British Council in Mexico City can provide the addresses of the 25 or so language centres attached to state universities. The British Council runs an English teaching centre in Mexico City; see www.british council.org.mx which mentions full-time and part-time teaching vacancies up to December 2018. Mexican-American Bi-National Centers employ scores of native English speakers, mostly on a local basis. The school year starts in early August and lasts for 11 months.

With a TEFL qualification and a year's experience in Indonesia, Canadian **Bruce Clarke** was in a good position to make use of the Mexico forum on www.eslcafe.com, where he learned of the vacancy at a state university in Oaxaca that he went on to fill. He reports that his students were pleasant and fun loving, though not particularly energetic or keen to complete homework. A further possibility is to work at English-medium schools modelled either on the American or British system. Many of these advertise internationally for certified teachers or recruit through recruiting fairs but, as in Chile, Peru and elsewhere, some are willing to interview native English speakers locally to work in the EFL department. Without a TEFL background or at least a solid university education you are unlikely to break into any of these more upmarket institutes.

CONDITIONS OF WORK

THE PRIVATE SECTOR

A host of private institutes supplies language training to business either on their own premises or in-company. The norm is for teachers to freelance and work for a combination of companies. There are also full-time school-based jobs with teaching companies such as Harmon Hall and Interlingua which have a national network of branches; the latter's website has an online application procedure (www.interlingua.com.mx) and seems to ask only that candidates speak English fluently, have a service-oriented personality and full-time availability; no teaching experience is required. A typical local branch of Harmon Hall might employ about 20 teachers, mainly of American English (as in Oaxaca). Hours can be unpredictable and a lot of time is taken up travelling from office to office. Getting three hours of work a day (early morning and early evening) is easy. Anything above that is much trickier. Freelance teachers must be prepared for frequent holidays cutting into earnings. Normally institutes do not pay for public holidays, sickness or annual leave. For example attendance goes into a sharp decline after Independence Day on 20 November, in the month leading up to Christmas, and there are no classes over Easter. Most courses run for three months and there may be a lapse of one or two weeks before another starts. Usually freelancers are paid cash in hand with no deductions for tax.

The spectrum of institutes varies enormously. At one extreme there is the employer who pays the equiva-lent of $5 an hour, never pays on time and who employs only Mexicans with poor English or native English speakers who have just arrived with their backpacks and no interest in or knowledge of teaching. The top of the range pays $15–$20 an hour, offers free training and gives contracts that aren't cancelled. These institutes are of course a lot more choosy about their teachers. Whereas a few companies want to control their teachers completely and send inspectors into classes, most leave teachers alone as long as the clients are happy. The typical institute consists only of four people: the owner who gets the contracts, a teacher coordinator, a secretary and an office boy.

Obviously a TEFL qualification is an advantage, though few employers are concerned about whether it is from a 130-hour or a 30-hour course. Business and financial experience is also beneficial, possibly more than a university degree. An ability to make a class interesting and patience are the two key qualities that many employers are looking for. As one of **Nick Wilson**'s bosses said: '*The most important thing is that the students enjoy their classes and think that they are learning English; don't just teach or we'll lose custom-ers.*' Word of mouth recommendations are very important in Mexican culture, and jobs are seldom filled by emailed applications.

Michael Tunison contacted half a dozen major teaching organisations from the *Yellow Pages* and was interviewed by Berlitz and Harmon Hall (www.harmonhall.com/bolsa-de-trabajo). Both offered tentative positions based more on his native English speaking than his American university degree and journalism background. In 2014, Harmon Hall were offering 80–90 pesos an hour though some of the chains pay considerably less. Obviously legitimate companies will hire only teachers with working papers. Other inter-national language companies represented in Mexico include International House, with schools in 12 cities, and Wall Street English (see entry). Try also Inter-Act speaking centers (www.interactmexico.com) with four branches in the Distrito Federal (DF), i.e. Greater Mexico City.

> Guadalajara and resorts such as Puerto Vallarta, Cancun, Acapulco and Mazatlan are places where a great many locals need to master English before they can be employed in the booming tourist industry, though wages tend to be lower than in the capital and the cost of living higher. Several independent US training organisations have set up TEFL training courses in Mexico; for example Teachers Latin America (www.teachers-latin-america.com) offers an 80-hour training course in Mexico City, followed by a job placement service.

American **Bradwell Jackson** had a go at funding his round-the-world travels by teaching English:

After reading Work Your Way Around the World, *I made the decision to quit my job, leave my home, give most of my belongings to charity and sell my car, so that I could wander the earth freely. I wondered if it was really possible to get a job teaching English so easily. Well I found out that it is. I was sitting at a metro stop in Mexico City, trying to figure out what school to go to for my first planned job enquiry. After I decided that the particular school I had in mind was too far away, I looked up and saw an English school right across the street. Providence, I thought. I was right. I sauntered on upstairs, cheerfully asked if they needed an English teacher, and about an hour and a half later, I was told when to start my training. It really was that easy.*

I teach a range of students including some teenage girls. For them I came up with the idea of asking them to talk about a popular soap opera. I also got them to pull out a teen magazine and tell me about the stars in it. I have also asked my students about popular Spanish songs and asked them to translate them into English for me.

Mexico is the first country I have visited on my world wanderings and I can't believe how lucky I've been. The people are top-notch and I certainly must count my blessings.

In 2014, Bradwell returned to Mexico after teaching elsewhere and then obtaining his CELTA in London. While he was in the tourist town of Oaxaca, he decided to investigate teaching possibilities. The Facultad de Idiomas of the local university Benito Juárez de Oaxaca employs 90 part-time teachers, five of whom were foreigners. All are paid less than 50 pesos (US$3) an hour, which is more than half of what you would expect in the private sector.

WORKING FOR YOURSELF

Private lessons are in great demand, and may be given informally in exchange for board and lodging. But it is also possible to teach on a more business-like footing. With so many clients seeking one-to-one tuition through institutes, it is worth considering setting up as an independent tutor and offering private lessons at a rate that undercuts the institutes. In the capital, a standard rate to charge students would be 200–250 pesos an hour. If you find clients who want two two-hour classes a week, you can do well. You can find students through the small ads on craigslist or segundamano. Teachers who are tempted to poach students from the organisation they work for should bear in mind that employers who find out have been known to set the immigration department on errant teachers. However, it is legitimate to advertise yourself in the press and distribute printed business cards. Teaching in companies sometimes produces lucrative spin-offs in the field of translation and editing documents in English.

REGULATIONS

The red tape situation in Mexico is difficult, although it is virtually unheard of for an English teacher working on a tourist visa to be deported. Officially of course visitors are not allowed to work or engage in any remunerative activity during a temporary visit. British and American citizens can stay in Mexico for 180 days without a visa as a tourist. Some employers may be willing to apply for an FM3 work visa (*no immigrante*) that will be valid for one year and renewable thereafter. As has been mentioned before, established schools are not usually willing to contract people without an employment visa, unlike private institutes. Private employers do not want to become involved with the hassle and expense of applying for teachers who are unlikely to stay long in any case. Some do deduct a small tax (recibos) which makes the teacher semi-official. Among the required documents are a CV in Spanish plus transcripts, diploma or certificate from your university, apostilled by the Mexican Consul or, in the US, by the Secretary of State, in the state where you studied.

LIST OF EMPLOYERS

AHPLA INSTITUTE

Juan Escutia No. 97, Colonia Condesa, CP 06140 DF

☎ +52 55 869016

✉ Kallen@ahpla.com

🖥 www.ahpla.com.mx

QUALIFICATIONS: Educated, flexible, willing to work with a team and travel. People skills and personality are a must.

CONDITIONS OF EMPLOYMENT: Minimum period of work 6 months. To work 7am–9am and 5pm–7pm.

FACILITIES/SUPPORT: No help with accommodation or flights, but assistance given with working papers after teacher has shown commitment to the institute.

CONTACT: Karen Julie Allen, Operations Manager.

BERLITZ (CENTRO INTEGRAL DE IDIOMAS)

Av. Benito Juarez No. 2005, Local Sub Ancla M Plaza Sendero, Colonia Estrella de Oriente, San Luis Potosí CP 78396

☎ +52 444 166 3570

✉ salvador.estrada@berlitzslp.com.mx

🖥 www.berlitzslp.com.mx

NUMBER OF TEACHERS: 20; also for centres in Saltillo, Aguascalientes and Tijuana.

PREFERENCE OF NATIONALITY: None.

QUALIFICATIONS: TESOL, TEFL, CELTA certification or a university degree in education.

CONDITIONS OF EMPLOYMENT: Standard 1-year contract. Hours mainly 7am–9am and 6pm–9pm, Monday to Friday, 8am–2pm Saturday.

SALARY: 55–75 pesos per 45–60 minutes of class.

FACILITIES/SUPPORT: School makes sure that the applicant has a place to stay after arrival.

RECRUITMENT: By email and telephone interview.

CONTACT: Salvador Estrada, Regional Academic Coordinator.

CULTURLINGUA JALISCO

Reforma #31, Col. Centro, Tlaquepaque, Jalisco

☎ +52 33 3344 9139

✉ info@culturlinguagdl.com

🖥 www.culturlinguagdl.com/teaching

Franchise of the Culturlingua group of schools with branches throughout the states of Michoacán and Jalisco in the Highlands of Mexico.

NUMBER OF TEACHERS: 4.

PREFERENCE OF NATIONALITY: Native English speakers.

QUALIFICATIONS: TEFL/TESOL certificate is essential and one year of teaching experience.

CONDITIONS OF EMPLOYMENT: Standard length of contract is 15 weeks with 30–32 working hours per week.

SALARY: 5,500 pesos per month.

FACILITIES/SUPPORT: Fully furnished accommodation is provided for teachers and included in the salary.

RECRUITMENT: Via internet sites such as Dave's ESL Cafe. Candidates successful with their CVs and cover letters are asked to submit a sample lesson plan and then a telephone interview will be organised.

CONTACT: Greg Davies, Owner or Nancy Garcia (nancygarcia@culturlingua.com.mx).

DUNHAM INSTITUTE

Avenida Coronel Urbina 30, Chiapa de Corzo, Chiapas 29160

☎ +52 961 616 1498

✉ academic-coordinator@dunhaminstitute.com

🖥 www.dunhaminstitute.com

NUMBER OF TEACHERS: 4.

PREFERENCE OF NATIONALITY: Native English speaker.

QUALIFICATIONS: ESL certified.

CONDITIONS OF EMPLOYMENT: Minimum 5 months from end of August or February. 3.5 hours in the afternoon and study Spanish in the mornings.

SALARY: None. Exchange of English teaching for free accommodation with a local family and 2 hours of Spanish tuition a day.

FACILITIES/SUPPORT: Work permits not required.

RECRUITMENT: Interviews are necessary.

CONTACT: Joanna Robinson, Director.

GLACE LANGUAGE CENTER

Francisco I. Madero 335, Zona Centro, San Luis Potosí CP 78000

☎ +52 444 8145526

✉ contacto@glacecenter.com

🖥 www.glacecenter.com

PREFERENCE OF NATIONALITY: All native speakers from English-speaking countries welcome.

QUALIFICATIONS: BA preferred. If the degree is not related to language teaching, must have TKT (Teaching Knowledge Test) core modules and at least 3 years' experience in a regular school and/or language school.

CONDITIONS OF EMPLOYMENT: Minimum stay: 2 years. Teachers sign contracts for each class with stated number of hours. Minimum 20 hours per week for teachers with full-time availability.

SALARY: 85–100 pesos per class, so monthly income can range from 6,800 to 8,000 pesos. Taxes are 8%–12%; no social security.

FACILITIES/SUPPORT: Assistance given in finding a reasonably priced place to live within walking distance of work.

RECRUITMENT: Interviews essential, at the centre or online.

CONTACT: Elvia Rico Zermeño, Academic Director.

HELP! HESLINGTON LANGUAGE PROGRAM

2 Norte 1210 Colonia Jacarandas Tehuacan, Puebla

☎ +52 238 384 6929

🖱 instituto-heslington@hotmail.com

💻 www.helpenglishmexico.org

NUMBER OF TEACHERS: 20 per semester, including paid teachers, volunteers and interns.

PREFERENCE OF NATIONALITY: None.

QUALIFICATIONS: TESOL/TEFL/CELTA Certification – no experience abroad required.

CONDITIONS OF EMPLOYMENT: 4 months. 25 hours per week.

SALARY: Monthly stipend of 4,000 pesos ($250) plus free housing (rent and utilities paid by school).

FACILITIES/SUPPORT: Free housing or host family arrangement.

RECRUITMENT: Via internet adverts (eg www.eslteachersboard.com) and word of mouth. Interviews carried out by Skype.

CONTACT: Matthew Poy (tehuacansupervisor@gmail.com).

ROBINSON SCHOOL

Blvd. Everardo Marquez #200 Piso 2, Colonia Periodistas, Pachuca, Hidalgo 42060

☎ +771 719 2247

🖱 luke@therobinsonschool.com or info@therobinsonschool.com

NUMBER OF TEACHERS: 3.

PREFERENCE OF NATIONALITY: None, must be native English speaker.

QUALIFICATIONS: ESL certificate preferred. Must be enthusiastic and politically and culturally open minded.

CONDITIONS OF EMPLOYMENT: 10 weeks. Individual schedules vary. Classes begin at 7am and finish at 8.30pm.

SALARY: 2,000 pesos per week (net).

FACILITIES/SUPPORT: Housing and/or furnishings can be provided and monthly rent deducted from pay cheque. Teachers will be assisted in acquiring necessary documents.

RECRUITMENT: Internet, word of mouth, newspaper adverts. Interviews are sometimes carried out in person in the USA but mostly conducted by phone.

CONTACT: Luke Robinson, CEO and Head of Recruitment.

UNIVERSIDAD DEL MAR

Campuses in Puerto Angel, Huatulco, Oaxaca de Juárez and Juquila

💻 www.umar.mx

NUMBER OF TEACHERS: 16.

PREFERENCE OF NATIONALITY: None but must be native English speaker.

QUALIFICATIONS: Degree-level education, TEFL teaching qualification (or an MA in TOEFL or related field) plus at least 1 year's experience working in a foreign country.

CONDITIONS OF EMPLOYMENT: 1-year commitment. Teaching hours are 8am–1pm and 4pm–7pm, Monday to Friday.

SALARY: 12,000 pesos net (more for candidates with an MA in TEFL or Education plus 2 years' experience), plus free medical service, Christmas and vacation bonuses, savings scheme and monthly shopping vouchers. Monthly deduction of about 2,000 pesos for tax and social security.

FACILITIES/SUPPORT: Teachers must arrange their own accommodation. University files paperwork for work permit on arrival; processing can take up to 3 weeks and teachers cannot start work without work visa.

RECRUITMENT: Most via internet ads and emailed CVs. Telephone interviews essential; short-listed candidates are telephoned.

CONTACT: Director of Languages.

WALL STREET ENGLISH MEXICO

Florencia 53 Col. Juárez, DF 06600

☎ +52 55 5533 8997/8

🖱 zonarosa@wse.com.mx

💻 www.wallstreetenglish.com.mx

NUMBER OF TEACHERS: 8 for 4 branches.

PREFERENCE OF NATIONALITY: None.

QUALIFICATIONS: CELTA or equivalent with a bachelor's degree with 1 year's experience preferably.

CONDITIONS OF EMPLOYMENT: 1 year. Full-time schedule, 35 teaching hours per week plus 5 hours every other Saturday.

SALARY: 14,000 pesos per month (gross), 12,100 pesos (net).
FACILITIES/SUPPORT: Wall Street helps teachers find an apartment near the branch where they will be working. Assistance given in obtaining a work visa. Teachers pay for the process but will be reimbursed after completing a year's contract.

RECRUITMENT: Via websites for ESL/EFL teachers. Candidates do 2 or 3 interviews with a demo lesson required in the second interview. Interviews are via Skype or Google Talk services..

PERU

Lima has in the past been considered one of the most stressful and dangerous South American cities in which to live; however, threats from guerrilla groups are a thing of the past and Peru has returned to the mainstream of destinations for English-language teachers. Modest wages and the difficulty of obtaining working papers mean that few professional teachers can be attracted to the private EFL sector. For those who are, it may be worth contacting the 11 Lima branches of the British-Peruvian Cultural Association, known familiarly as Britanico (www.britanico.edu.pe).

Yet the range of opportunities in Lima is enormous and the stampede to learn English is unstoppable. Many company employees have been told by their bosses to learn English or risk demotion. Some employers organise a course at their place of work, but most expect their staff to fix up private lessons, making the freelance market very promising at the moment. In-company training courses in all industries are often offered in English, so knowledge of the language is becoming essential for all ambitious Peruvians. The Peruvian economy is not in dire straits at present, as evidenced by the stability of its currency, the new sol.

A useful online resource is the LA Joblist (http://thelajoblist.blogspot.co.uk/2009/12/peru.html), compiled by an EL teacher, Sharon Hinojosa, who used to teach in Lima and researched all the schools. Although she has now left the continent to teach at a university in Korea, she still maintains the site. She stresses how much easier it is to find teaching hours once you are in Peru than when you're trying to fix up a job from home.

Many temporary visitors to Peru who lack a TEFL background end up doing some English teaching once they have established a base in the capital, usually earning about $5 an hour (three or four times above the Peruvian minimum wage). Some employers offer a free or subsidised training course to new potential recruits, at which native English speakers usually excel over the locals, whose knowledge of English is often very weak.

Ruain Burrows from Ireland turned himself from a long-term backpacker into a teacher in Lima working for Business Links (www.bl.com.pe) and English Life (see entry):

> *I had been travelling around South America for the best part of two years and was, inevitably, running out of money. I had just enough for a flight home, yet wasn't ready to go home, so decided to invest in a 120-hour online TEFL course (with i-to-i.com) after convincing myself that it was an easy way to continue living my dream. Three hundred US dollars and five weeks later, certificate in hand, I was ready to dive into the word of TEFLing. The application process was as simple as typing up a cover email, attaching my CV along with my new qualification and sending it out in bulk to all the institutes, colleges and temping agencies with which Google provided me. The interviews were really easy, the main requisite being fluency in English (being Irish, I just squeezed into this category) and being in possession of some sort of TEFL certificate. The recurring question was concerning my availability, because apparently a lot of foreigners pass through the doors of the institutes just looking for short-term work to fund a flight home or to fill a gap between stages in their lives and they were sick of this. Fortunately they didn't expect teaching experience because, prior to the application/interview stage, my teaching experience had been restricted to teaching my dog how to play fetch. Also, the institutes in Lima generally don't insist on permits or special visas but it is required if you intend on applying to the colleges or universities.*

Ruain taught as many hours as his employers were willing to assign him, and earned decent money, up to 2,500 soles a month (when the minimum wage in Peru is unchanged for 2015 at 750 soles). He found the cost of living to be relatively low, particularly since he earned free hostel accommodation by working as a barman in the evenings.

One tip he offers is never to give out your telephone number to students. When he did this to one of his female students she used him as her personal dictionary whenever she felt like it. He really enjoyed seeing the progress his students made: '*When you take on a student who can't even count to five, then watch them progress through the levels and go on to pass an exam like the IELTS or CAE, that to me is amazing.*' It is not difficult for him to identify an even better highlight, which was when he met his wife, with whom he has settled in Peru. So his summation of the experience comes as no surprise: '*The rewards of being a TEFL teacher in Peru are that the Peruvian people are amazing, the food is next to none and it's an intriguing country.*'

Plenty of opportunities exist for volunteer teachers in remote corners of the country. For example Vive Peru (www.viveperu.org) runs an English enrichment programme at public schools in northern Peru. A small family-run charity in the Andean region of Huaraz also deploys volunteer teachers (www.teachhuarazperu.org).

FREELANCING

Setting up as a freelance tutor is potentially lucrative. A standard fee is $10–$20 a lesson, though this can be reduced for clients who want to book a whole course. **James Gratton** put a cheap advertisement (written in English) in the main daily, *El Comercio*, and signed up two clients. This was straightforward in his case since he was staying at his girlfriend's house, where he had free accommodation and telephone. His new students were both employees of Petro-Peru, and soon other clients contacted James for lessons. He admits that freelancers do lose out to cancellations, though some of his students willingly paid for missed lessons. Freelancing is a continual process of advertising and getting new students to replace the ones that fall by the wayside.

REGULATIONS

Peruvian work visas are very rare and most people teach as tourists. British and Irish nationals, as well as US and EU citizens, do not require tourist visas for Peru; neither do nationals from EU countries. They are allowed to stay in Peru for up to 90 days, although they are required to possess an onward/return ticket. After that it is necessary to cross the Peruvian border. One reason which many people use to extend their stay is that they have formed a romantic attachment to a local woman/man.

In his quest for a work visa, **James Gratton** gathered together all the necessary documents, including contract, notarised certificates and documents translated into Spanish. All of this cost him a lot of money and time, and he still didn't succeed. He concluded that it would be possible only if you knew someone in the immigration department who could give your application a safe passage without having to pay fines (bribes) at every stage. Making key contacts is more important than gathering documentation. Care must be taken to keep on the right side of the tax office (SUNAT), to which about 15% of earnings are supposed to be paid. Many employers pay their staff under the table, sometimes by cash, personal cheque or via a *Recibo de Honorario* from a Peruvian friend, which uses their tax details and signature to receive your money.

LIST OF EMPLOYERS

BRITTANY ENGLISH SOLUTIONS

José Bustamente y Rivero Av, EEUU, Fl.1, Arequipa

✆ +51 54 422964

✉ brittany@brittanygroup.edu.pe

🖳 www.brittanygroup.edu.pe

NUMBER OF TEACHERS: 30 for several branches. Quite a few teachers teach remotely through 3G platforms.

PREFERENCE OF NATIONALITY: British.

QUALIFICATIONS: TESOL, TEFL, CELTA.

CONDITIONS OF EMPLOYMENT: 6–12 months. Teaching hours in afternoon.

SALARY: $600 a month.

FACILITIES/SUPPORT: Assistance given to teachers with finding suitable accommodation. School hopes to be able to offer its own accommodation to teachers in the future. Help given with permits.

RECRUITMENT: Web postings. Face-to-face interview is not necessary.

CONTACT: Christian Valdivia Chavez, Executive Manager.

NUMBER OF TEACHERS: 20 on self-employed basis (100% of staff are native speakers).

PREFERENCE OF NATIONALITY: None. School hires native English speakers only.

QUALIFICATIONS: TEFL certificate or similar, plus some experience is desirable.

CONDITIONS OF EMPLOYMENT: 6 months. Teachers are given part-time hours, on a class-by-class basis (3–15 per week).

SALARY: $8–$10 per hour.

FACILITIES/SUPPORT: No accommodation provided but advice can be given.

RECRUITMENT: People are invited for interview after submitting their CV. Interviews are essential and so applicants must be in Peru to qualify for an interview or employment.

CONTACT: Valerie Watson, Directora General and Owner.

NUMBER OF TEACHERS: 28.

PREFERENCE OF NATIONALITY: USA and Canada.

QUALIFICATIONS: TEFL, TESOL or CELTA on-site course, a bachelor's degree plus experience of teaching. Candidates without experience must have excellent natural teaching ability and 'people' skills.

CONDITIONS OF EMPLOYMENT: 4 months minimum; 6 months preferred. Normal working hours 7am–9am and 5pm–9pm. Centre operates a volunteer teacher programme.

SALARY: About $5 per hour.

FACILITIES/SUPPORT: Advice and contacts for accommodation given but teachers pay for their housing. Teachers come as legal TEFL interns.

RECRUITMENT: Paid ads online and university contacts in the USA. Interviews essential.

CONTACT: J. C. Larsen, BS Ed, MA Ed/TEFL, Executive Director or Alina Denham, Academic Coordinator (alinadenham@gmail.com).

One of 9 Bi-national Centres in Peru.

NUMBER OF TEACHERS: Fluctuating. North American students come as unpaid interns.

PREFERENCE OF NATIONALITY: American and Canadian preferred; others considered.

QUALIFICATIONS: University degree that qualifies candidate for teaching EFL/ESL. Experience not a necessity.

FACILITIES/SUPPORT: Can find apartments for teachers or arrange homestays. Help given with work permits for long-stay teachers.

RECRUITMENT: Via TESOL conferences and the internet. Interviews not essential.

Primarily a TEFL training provider.

NUMBER OF TEACHERS: 10–20.

PREFERENCE OF NATIONALITY: Must be native English speaker.

QUALIFICATIONS: Teachers must be TEFL, TESOL or CELTA certified from a training course of at least 100 hours with a minimum of 6 hours of practical teaching. Candidates must be dedicated, professional and passionate about teaching with a self-confident personality and a good sense of humour.

CONDITIONS OF EMPLOYMENT: 6-month contracts are the norm. Split shifts, generally with classes from 7am to 10am and 4pm to 9pm. Teachers teach 30 hours per week, Monday through Friday.

SALARY: $475 to $800 per month (net).

FACILITIES/SUPPORT: Teachers are responsible for their own accommodation, but school provides assistance in locating housing. Often the institute provides 5 days of free room and board in a family stay to a new arrival, while he or she finds more permanent housing. Work permits are available on a very limited basis, and only for long-term teachers.

RECRUITMENT: Via email and online advertising through www.goabroad.com, www.idealist.org, Dave's ESL Café and others. Many teachers are hired on graduating from Maximo Nivel's own TEFL/TESOL certification course in Cusco. In-person interviews are preferred, but interviews can be conducted via Skype or phone.

CONTACT: Ken Jones, Executive Director.

VENEZUELA

Largely because of the decline in the world price of oil, Venezuela's economy has been sliding into crisis, with 100% inflation recorded in 2015. Shortages of food and other essentials have led to social unrest, so this is probably not the best time to be thinking about a job hunt in Venezuela. For example the charity, Fundacion Aldeas de Paz, which had an entry in the 2015 edition of this book, has suspended its volunteer teacher placement programme 'until the social and political situation once again allows for a safe and enjoyable environment so that international volunteers and interns feel comfortable to come and join efforts in Venezuela'.

But not everyone will be deterred. Proximity to the USA and the volume of business which is done with El Norte result in a strong preference for American accents and teaching materials in Venezuela. Some corporations continue to hire in-company language trainers through Caracas-based agencies. But, as **Nick Branch** from St Albans discovered a few years ago, work is not exclusively for Americans, nor is it confined to the capital:

> *Merida is very beautiful and a considerably more pleasant place to be than Caracas. The atmosphere and organisation of the institute where I worked were very good. But alas, as with all the English teaching institutes in Merida, the pay is very low. Merida is three times cheaper to live in than Caracas, but the salaries are five to six times lower.*

Nick investigated most of the schools and agencies in Venezuela and worked for several of them, including one based in the Oriente coastal resort of Puerto la Cruz. Once again the pay was less than in Caracas but advantages such as easy access to the Mochima National Marine Park compensated. Opportunities for English teachers may even exist on the popular resort island of Margarita. For school listings try Craigslist Caracas or the Yellow Pages (www.pac.com.ve) under the heading 'Idiomas Academias'. Many institutes do not pay as much or as often as they promise at the outset. In fact, Caracas has more than its fair share of shady characters running language schools, so that newcomers should take their time about signing any contracts.

Chris Morvan had been a professional writer in the UK for 20 years, in journalism, advertising and PR. But when the recession hit, some of his freelance work dried up and this is how he coped:

> *I'm living in Venezuela, baking in the streets of Caracas and swimming in the Caribbean even in the cooler months here, rather than shivering in the UK. I applied for literally hundreds of jobs by the miracle of the internet and got nowhere. I put it down mainly to my age – I'm in my 50s and that's not a fashionable age. Then I met a Venezuelan woman through a dating website and we got married. With no prospects in the UK we examined my options and decided on taking an online course in Teaching English as a Foreign Language (TEFL). There are lots to choose from and I went for a 100-hour course with i-to-i. This consisted of 20 hours of 'grammar awareness', 60 hours about the science of teaching and smaller modules on teaching large classes, young people, with limited resources etc. In the meantime I moved to Venezuela, applied for three part-time jobs with agencies and got them all. This was even before I finished the course, but they don't bother about formalities like that out here. I found that I loved teaching. Most of my classes are one-to-one with adults in their offices, so it's early mornings, lunchtimes and late afternoons. You can get gigs with schools, teaching bigger classes and younger people if you want. The money is not great, to say the least, but it's a new career in which I am in demand, and that makes a change from ungrateful old UK. The course cost me a couple of hundred quid, but it was money well spent. If you have a good command of English, doing this can open doors for you.*

REGULATIONS

Most people work on a tourist card that is valid for 90 days and non-extendable. It is possible to apply for a multiple-entry visa if you can provide proof of employment, sufficient funds and a return ticket. A combined work/study contract or internship is the solution that some organisations have come up with but this is available mainly to US students.

Most long-stay foreigners take brief trips to Curaçao or Trinidad and Tobago and get an extension of their tourist card when returning to Venezuela. Work permits are available only if the employer has obtained approval from the Servicio Administrativo de Indentificacion, Migracion y Extranjeria (SAIME) and sent the necessary papers to a Venezuelan consulate in the teacher's country of residence. Even with a backer as well established as the British Council, the visa problem looms large.

Nick Branch described the process of getting a work permit in Caracas as a nightmare while **James Gratton** applied at the Embassy in London, with a definite job offer from a university extension department on Margarita Island and was turned down. His main complaint was that you hear a different story from every official. Even renewing his tourist card at the Immigration Office took a week and involved his having to present a typed letter in Spanish. Yet he managed to stay legally in Venezuela for nine months, leaving the country when necessary and returning without once being asked to show a ticket home as proof of his intention to leave the country. His most serious problem occurred when one of his employers threatened to report his tourist status to the police if he quit to look for a better job. (James did quit and the police were not called.)

LIST OF EMPLOYERS

CENTRO VENEZOLANO AMERICANO DEL CARACAS

Av. Principal de las Mercedes, Edif. CVA, Urbanización Las Mercedes, Caracas 1060-A

- +58 212 993 7911
- informacion@cva.org.ve
- www.cvalasmercedes.wordpress.com

CVA also located in the state of Zulia: Calle 63, No. 3E–60, Maracaibo, Estado Zulia

- +58 261 200060
- www.cevaz.org

Bi-National centre.

NUMBER OF TEACHERS: 100+.

PREFERENCE OF NATIONALITY: American, Canadian and Venezuelan.

QUALIFICATIONS: Bachelor's degree or teachers with EFL/ ESL experience. A written and oral test is given to all non-native English-speaking applicants. Also placements for university students studying modern languages.

CONDITIONS OF EMPLOYMENT: Minimum 6 months with renewals up to 2 years. Choice of children's courses (for ages 9–11), teens (12–15) and regular and Saturday courses for adults. Minimum 30 academic hours per week.

SALARY: Hourly rate plus housing bonus.

FACILITIES/SUPPORT: Assistance with obtaining accommodation, health insurance and visas. 2-week pre-service training course for interns is paid. Free Spanish course. Computer lab and access to cultural centre activities.

RECRUITMENT: Send CV and recent photo.

CONTACT: Human Resources Dept (telephone extension 114).

WALL STREET INSTITUTE (WSI)

Av. Francisco de Miranda, Centro Lido, Nivel Galeria Local 6–1, El Rosal, Caracas

- cv@wsi.com.ve
- www.wallstreetenglish.com.ve

NUMBER OF TEACHERS: Variable for 17 branches throughout the country.

PREFERENCE OF NATIONALITY: None.

QUALIFICATIONS: Teaching degree not necessary but some experience teaching English as a second language is helpful. WSI trains all teachers in-house.

CONDITIONS OF EMPLOYMENT: No contract but minimum of 6 months. 8 teaching hours.

SALARY: Local average.

FACILITIES/SUPPORT: Assistance with work permits.

RECRUITMENT: Word of mouth, advertising in local papers and via AIESEC.

CENTRAL AMERICA AND THE CARIBBEAN

If you keep your ears open as you travel through this enormous isthmus squeezed between two great oceans, you may come across opportunities to teach English, especially if you are prepared to do so as a volunteer. Salaries on offer may be pitiful but if you find a congenial spot on the 'gringo trail' (for example, the old colonial towns of Antigua in Guatemala or Granada in Nicaragua), you may decide to prolong your stay by helping the people you will inevitably meet who want to learn English. You might also find openings off the gringo trail. It is always interesting to hear from a part of the world that has never been included in this book before.

COSTA RICA

As the wealthiest country in Central America, Costa Rica is a good starting (and perhaps finishing) point for many native English teachers. It is government policy to teach English in primary schools, which has increased the demand for English teachers. Costa Rica Multilingüe (www.crmultilingue.org) is a non-profit foundation that seeks to provide the country's people with language skills that will help them gain access to employment and educational opportunities. Among its programmes are running local conversation groups led by volunteer native speakers and JumpStart Costa Rica (www.jumpstartcostarica.org) which provides 36 free intensive English camps for children in rural and low-income urban areas in January. Some Peace Corps volunteers are involved with the camp programme as well as being deployed in the state education system to teach English and train teachers. Although state schools can't afford to import expat teachers, they are often willing to accept an offer of voluntary assistance. The school year runs from 1 March to 1 December. The *Tico Times* publishes its job classified ads online at www.ticotimes.net, as do Craigslist for Costa Rica and www.insidecostarica.com. If you're lucky you'll spot an ad such as: '*The Swan English Learning is looking for Native English Teachers, for Heredia, San José & Ciudad Colon. Part and full-time. Excellent pay. Training and Free Spanish Classes*'.

The majority of teaching work is available in the capital, San José. After four years of teaching at different institutes in Costa Rica and now working as a director at Intercultura in Heredia near San José (see entry), **Lindsay Fair** is an established expat who feels frustrated with American attitudes whenever she visits her home country. She describes teaching in the corporate market:

> *Teaching corporate in Costa Rica has advantages and disadvantages. The biggest disadvantage is having to travel by bus most of the day, especially during the rainy season, wearing business clothes. The benefits of working corporates includes nice working conditions and well-behaved students. Classes are paid for by employers and success is monitored by the bosses, so the students are for the most part very responsible. They come from the upper-middle class of Costa Rica, so are generally educated and, after having worked for North American companies, knowledgeable about North American culture. My colleagues have been almost all North Americans, and most around my age (23–28).*
>
> *San José is not exactly what you think of when imagining Costa Rica; it's polluted, dirty and dangerous, and the closest beaches are a good two-hour bus ride away. But the company explained all that during the interview. Unfortunately, San José is where most of the work is, so the best part of living in Costa Rica is taking weekend trips to the beaches and national parks. Now that I know more about Costa Rica, I definitely recommend looking for jobs in Heredia instead of San José because it is much safer, nicer and an easier place to live for expats.*

Ex-teacher **Dev Parikh** stressed what he perceived as the dangers of travel round San José and the very high cost of living in the capital.

Bryson Patterson made use of contacts from the TEFL course he did at ALI San Diego to get his first job in San José but eventually moved away from the city:

> *After working for a time in the capital, I moved to a town called Jaco on the Pacific Coast where I worked at a high school and then at the Marriott Hotel. I was teaching English first to high school students (that was hell) then to the hotel staff, which was cool. A lot of people will tell you that there are no ESL jobs on the coast but they are wrong.*

If you want to teach in Costa Rica and support eco-tourism, a government-sponsored organisation called English Volunteers for Change (EVOLC; see entry) places native-speaker volunteers in various English-language teaching programmes for the tourism sector. Participants get a three-day weekend and plenty of cultural immersion. Programme costs including a homestay with meals are typically $750 per month for a six-month commitment.

Work visas and residency permits (temporary as well as permanent) are very difficult to get. Immigration requires that you get your birth certificate and state background check from your home region, get them notarised by a public notary and send them to the Costa Rican Consulate in your country to be authenticated. Once the documents are sent on to Costa Rica, you have to take them to the foreign ministry to be authenticated again, get a background check, get fingerprinted by the OIJ (Judicial Investigation Department) and pay a lot of money. Once all these steps are taken (and they must be taken within six months before the birth certificate and background check expire), you can bring your documents to immigration, whereupon it can take up to 18 months to get your passport stamped, and that stamp will expire. Because the process requires so much time, energy and money, schools are not generally willing to assist teachers on standard one-year contracts, who tend to opt for taking visa runs every 90 days to Nicaragua or Panama, making sure that they stay out of the country for at least 72 hours. Although it may be technically illegal for teachers to work without a work visa, the authorities routinely look the other way. Teachers with tourist visas only can register with the Caja Seguro Social (national health service), register with the Tributación (Home Office) as professional service providers, open bank accounts, get driver's licences, etc.

Allen Tracey has pursued an alternative route by becoming an 'Independent Contractor' with Pro Language (see entry). Foreign teachers can independently contract with an institute (by starting a self-employed business), which means that employers do not take on the obligations of hiring an employee. No taxes are paid, no benefits are received and there is no binding contract. However, for each class the teacher must sign an Assignment Sheet, and the services outlined become the teacher's subcontracted responsibility. The system does mean that you don't really get to know other teachers unless your institute organises group training sessions which you attend:

> *I have been very fortunate to have been assigned a wide range of interesting and motivated students in my time teaching for Pro Language over the past three years, including top executives who are as eager to learn as tradespeople. Aside from teaching the essentials like grammar from the textbook, I do try to find ways to make each two-hour class fun and entertaining. I am always searching for viable new teaching games because students just love games. I just can't seem to find enough really good teaching games that work. Of course, you get the occasional rotten apple students, who are there only because their employer requires it. A highlight was teaching a top Walmart executive who was a very interesting and appreciative student to invest time with . . . it's nice to be appreciated. A low point was having to deal with an extremely rude and controlling Venezuelan student who considered my lesson plans to be optional and negotiable.*

LIST OF EMPLOYERS

CENTRO CULTURAL COSTARRICENSE NORTEAMERICANO
San Pedro (Apartado Postal 1489–1000, San José)

☎ +506 2207 7500

✉ sharon.alvarado@centrocultural.cr

🖥 www.centrocultural.cr

NUMBER OF TEACHERS: Varies. Teachers also needed for centres in Heredia, La Sabana, Alajuela and Cartago.

PREFERENCE OF NATIONALITY: None, but must be native English speaker.

QUALIFICATIONS: Experience in ESL and/or EFL is indispensable.

CONDITIONS OF EMPLOYMENT: Standard 1-year contract. Minimum 16 hours per week.

SALARY: About 4,000 colones ($7+) an hour. Deduction of about $15 a month for voluntary insurance.

FACILITIES/SUPPORT: No assistance with accommodation or work permits.

RECRUITMENT: Via newspaper adverts, work fairs and internal recommendations. Interviews carried out at CCCNCR sites in Costa Rica after applications have been processed centrally.

CONTACT: Sharon Alvarado, Human Resources Assistant.

ENGLISH TO GO – INGLES SIN FRONTERAS
Apartado Postal 271–3007, San Joaquin de Flores, Heredia

☎ +506 2588 2204

✉ jobs@english2go.co.cr

🖥 www.english2go.co.cr

NUMBER OF TEACHERS: 15–25 contracted staff.

PREFERENCE OF NATIONALITY: Americans and Canadians; other native English speakers can also apply, as well as teachers of Spanish and Portuguese.

QUALIFICATIONS: 2 years' classroom experience teaching ESL in a foreign country or qualification like CELTA, TESOL, TEFL or others. BA needed. Must have professional appearance.

CONDITIONS OF EMPLOYMENT: Standard 6-month contract. Hours vary according to needs of students or companies with whom English to Go contracts.

SALARY: $10–$12 per classroom hour. $100–$300 bonus possible after first 90 days. Sub-contracted hourly work pays $9.

FACILITIES/SUPPORT: If needed on arrival, English to Go will help with finding housing but does not pay rent.

RECRUITMENT: Ads in Craigslist, ESL sites, newspapers, and website. Interviews essential.

CONTACT: Academic Director.

EVOLC
English Volunteers for Change in Costa Rica, Barrio Escalante Apartado Postal 11062–1000 San José

☎ +506 2248 0237 ext 102

✉ evolc@aliarse.org

🖥 www.evolc.org

NUMBER OF TEACHERS: Constantly taking on new volunteers.

PREFERENCE OF NATIONALITY: Any native speaker of English.

QUALIFICATIONS: University degree, TEFL certified or with teaching experience. Volunteers should be independent, willing to adapt, be responsible and able to organise, have experience of living in another country, have commitment to service and volunteerism and have the ability to communicate well with others.

CONDITIONS OF EMPLOYMENT: 5 weeks to 1 year with monthly start dates year round. 20 hours a week teaching, plus 20 hours preparing.

SALARY: Unpaid position. Volunteers pay a programme fee, eg $4,500 for 6 months, $8,000 for 12 months, that covers home-stay accommodation, where they are given 3 meals per day.

FACILITIES/SUPPORT: 3-day intensive orientation on arrival in San José. Visa application assistance given to participants who are staying for more than one year.

CONTACT: Chelsea Vasques, Programme Coordinator.

INTERCULTURA LANGUAGE AND CULTURAL CENTER
Apartado Postal 1952–3000, Heredia

☎ +506 2260 8480 ext 21

✉ ingles@interculturacostarica.com

🖥 www.inglesintercultura.com

NUMBER OF TEACHERS: 30–36 (depending on the semester).

PREFERENCE OF NATIONALITY: Native English speakers: American, British, Canadian, Irish, New Zealander and Australian.

QUALIFICATIONS: Minimum bachelor's degree, and TEFL/CELTA certification. At least 1 year's teaching experience is preferred.

CONDITIONS OF EMPLOYMENT: 1 year starting in July and January. Average 20–25 hours teaching per week. Classes last 1.5–3 hours and are held in mornings, evenings and some afternoons. Hours of teaching mainly Monday to Thursday evenings and Saturdays. Part-time contracts are for a minimum of 6 months.

SALARY: $800–$1,100 per month net.

FACILITIES/SUPPORT: Free Spanish lessons for full-time teachers, mentor programme and ongoing training/professional development opportunities. Help setting up a bank account and support for finding housing upon arrival. Classrooms with smartboards with internet and server access with lots of shared materials. No help with work visa.

RECRUITMENT: Local adverts and in-person or Skype interviews. Resumés accepted in April and October/November in time for the start of the semester.

CONTACT: Lindsay Fair, Foreign Language Department Director (lindsay@interculturacostarica.com).

MAXIMO NIVEL INTERNATIONAL COSTA RICA
De La Farmacia La Bomba, 75m South (left side), San Pedro-Montes de Oca, San José
☎ +506 2253 9220; Florida contact number +1 800 866 6358
✉ instructors@maximonivel.com
💻 www.maximonivel.com

NUMBER OF TEACHERS: 10–20.

PREFERENCE OF NATIONALITY: Must be native English speaker.

QUALIFICATIONS: Teachers must be TEFL, TESOL or CELTA certified from a training course of at least 100 hours with a minimum of 6 hours of practical teaching. Candidates must be dedicated, professional and passionate about teaching, with a self-confident personality and a good sense of humour.

CONDITIONS OF EMPLOYMENT: 6-month contracts are the norm. Split shifts, generally with classes from 7am to 10am and 4pm to 9pm. Teachers teach 30 hours per week, Monday through Friday.

SALARY: $475–$800 per month (net).

FACILITIES/SUPPORT: Teachers are responsible for their own accommodation, but school provides assistance in locating housing. Often the institute provides 5 days of free room and board in a family stay to a new arrival, while he or she finds more permanent housing. Work permits are available on a very limited basis, and only for long-term teachers.

RECRUITMENT: Via email and online advertising through www. goabroad.com, www.idealist.org, Dave's ESL Café and others. Many teachers are hired on graduating from Maximo Nivel's own TEFL/TESOL certification course in San José. In-person interviews are preferred, but interviews can be conducted via Skype or phone.

CONTACT: Paula Piazza (paula@maximonivel.com), General Manager Costa Rica, or Ken Jones, Executive Director.

PRO-LANGUAGE CORPORATE LANGUAGE SOLUTIONS
Edificio Langer, Of. #3, Zapote, San José
☎ +506 2280 6053 ext 11
✉ info@prolanguage.org
💻 www.prolanguage.org

NUMBER OF TEACHERS: 40 (for several branches in metropolitan San José, including in Escazu and Heredia).

PREFERENCE OF NATIONALITY: None, but native English speakers.

QUALIFICATIONS: TEFL certification or equivalent and a minimum of 6 months' experience.

CONDITIONS OF EMPLOYMENT: Minimum 4 months. Flexible part-time opportunities.

SALARY: $8 per hour.

FACILITIES/SUPPORT: Assistance with accommodation and work permits. Free Spanish lessons and free training.

RECRUITMENT: Newspaper adverts, internet and alliances with teacher training organisations. Candidates already in Costa Rica strongly preferred. Online application form.

CONTACT: Dawn Needham, Academic Co-ordinator or Mark Henker, Executive Director.

PROYECTO SAN GERARDO
600 M Norte de la Oficina de MINAE, Camino por Herradura, San Gerardo de Rivas, PZ, San José
☎ +506 2742 5356
✉ proyectosangerardo@gmail.com
💻 www.proyectosangerardo.org

Proyecto San Gerardo is a Rose Charities Canada project (www.rosecanada.info) providing English classes in three locations among other skills training to improve employment prospects for rural inhabitants of the Rivas area.

NUMBER OF TEACHERS: 3 volunteer English teachers plus English conversation volunteers.

PREFERENCE OF NATIONALITY: None, provided they are native speakers.

QUALIFICATIONS: Must have TEFL qualification or teaching experience. Some knowledge of Spanish preferred. Must be patient, creative and flexible with ability to adapt to a remote rural area with few city conveniences. Minimum age 21.

CONDITIONS OF EMPLOYMENT: Minimum stay 3 months, throughout the year except December/January when schools are closed. Teachers conduct children's classes for 2–3 hours in the morning twice a week plus afternoon/evening classes for youths and adults are held on weekdays 4pm–6.30pm.

SALARY: None, but homestay is subsidised. Homestay fee is $350 per month including meals, laundry, private room and shared bathroom.

FACILITIES/SUPPORT: Orientation to the homestay and support is provided. Volunteer Resource Guide and curriculum guidance given at the outset. Follow-up meetings are held bi-weekly or as needed. Short training on a Child Protection Policy is compulsory.

RECRUITMENT: Online via idealist.org, authentic volunteer recruitment websites, and via some ESL teacher training institutions.

CONTACT: Jenny Moss, Director.

SARAPIQUÍ CONSERVATION LEARNING CENTER
Apartado Postal 9241–001, Chilamate, Puerto Viejo de Sarapiquí, Heredia
☎ +506 2761 2082
✉ director@learningcentercostarica.org or commdev @learningcentercostarica.org
💻 www.learningcentercostarica.org

NUMBER OF TEACHERS: 3.

PREFERENCE OF NATIONALITY: English native speaking countries.

QUALIFICATIONS: TEFL, TESOL or CELTA certified, with teaching and group management experience. Intermediate level of Spanish, preferably with experience of community-driven organisations.

CONDITIONS OF EMPLOYMENT: 6 months. 18 hours of teaching, mainly 5pm–8pm. 22 hours in lesson planning and other duties at the Center.

SALARY: Unpaid positions. Room and board provided with a local family.

RECRUITMENT: Internet, volunteer websites, partnerships with language institutes in Costa Rica. Interviews can be by Skype.

THE SWAN ENGLISH LEARNING
Frente al Banco Costa Rica, Ciudad Colon Centro, San José Province
☎ +506 2249 3598
✉ info@theswanenglish.org
💻 www.theswanenglish.org

NUMBER OF TEACHERS: 13.

PREFERENCE OF NATIONALITY: None.

QUALIFICATIONS: TEFL, CELTA or equivalent. Experience preferred.

CONDITIONS OF EMPLOYMENT: Minimum 4 months. 20 hours per week on average.

SALARY: 4,000–5,000 colones ($7–$9) per hour, net.

FACILITIES/SUPPORT: Advice given on finding good, cheap, local accommodation.

RECRUITMENT: Via local paper, Craigslist, website, advertising in local university and word of mouth. Interview in person or via Skype.

CONTACT: Oliver Petersen, Owner and Director.

UNIVERSAL IDIOMAS
Avenida 2da, calle 9, San José
☎ +506 2257 0441; USA: +1 727 230 0563
✉ info@universal-edu.com
💻 www.universal-edu.com or www.ingles.co.cr

NUMBER OF TEACHERS: 10 English teachers. Also a large Spanish teaching operation.

PREFERENCE OF NATIONALITY: American, British.

QUALIFICATIONS: TEFL/TESOL, University diploma, a couple of years of experience.

CONDITIONS OF EMPLOYMENT: 1 year. Teaching hours mainly in evenings and on Saturdays.

SALARY: About $8 per hour. 9% deductions for social security.

FACILITIES/SUPPORT: Most teachers find their own accommodation, though homestay can be arranged at extra charge.

RECRUITMENT: Via internet ads. Local interview essential.

GUATEMALA AND HONDURAS

There are perhaps about a dozen institutes in the capital Guatemala City. But it is not nearly as appealing a destination as Antigua. Dozens of Spanish language schools in this backpacker honey pot have links with local communities that welcome volunteer teachers. To take just two examples, check out www.launion.edu.gt/volunteer-work/work-as-a-teacher and El Nahual Community Language School in Quetzaltenango (www.languageselnahual.com). Many travellers find that Lake Atitlán is the perfect place to use as a longer-term base. The small villages around the lake are all interconnected by launch boats, and the variety in atmosphere among these villages means that you can choose one that suits. Well-known party town San Pedro attracts many foreigners who come to attend one of the many Spanish schools. Hostel beds average about 50 quetzales (£4), though cheaper places can be found, and food is also very cheap.

ANNA LING

When Anna Ling was 20 years old, she headed to San Pedro while pursuing her main interests, writing and performing music. She decided to stay for a while and wrote at the time:

I am based at the Iguana Perdida hostel (www.laiguanaperdida.com), the first building near the launch stop. The local village is a wonderful place and home to the Amigos (www.amigosdesantacruz.org), a charity that has brought medical care and an outreach programme to the more remote villages. They have also built a library and a school offering free education to all children under 12, and scholarship programmes for older children. They are in the process of building a large new centre for vocational education. I went up to the village to see Pam, the current brains behind the operation, and within the hour I was teaching an English class. I was soon given a classroom and started an enrichment afternoon with the local kids, doing arts, craft and music projects. The organisation is so well run that anyone willing to give some time will be put to good use, whether in teaching, construction or any other interests.

Visas are not a problem at all, neither for work nor volunteering. No one even asks to see a passport. Language is no problem either. Personally I'm trying to live very much on a tight budget and paid language lessons (25-50 quetzals per hour) would push me way over my daily price watch. But volunteering at the school has been the best opportunity for learning Spanish I could imagine. I take up a dictionary and the kids speak really slowly and clearly and it has helped so very much.

Britons, Americans and other tourists are permitted to stay in Guatemala for 90-days. This can be extended by the same period at the immigration office, but when that 90-day limit expires you must leave the country and renew your visa on re-entry. Note that because Guatemala, Honduras, Nicaragua and El Salvador belong to the CA-4 border agreement pact, a harmonised visa regime, you must go to Mexico, Belize or Costa Rica.

Volunteer teachers who wish to go to Honduras can arrange a placement in La Ceiba, the third-largest city, through the fee-charging agency Volunteering Solutions (www.volunteeringsolutions.com), helping local people trying to get ahead in the burgeoning tourist industry. The cost is £1,292 for eight weeks plus a $225 application fee. It would be cheaper to work directly with the US-based charity that works in La Ceiba, Helping Honduras Kids (www.helpinghonduraskids.org), with whom you can arrange to become a volunteer teacher at a jungle school attended by marginalised children, for a one-off $100 fee plus $65 a week to cover homestay accommodation.

Another possibility is the Bilingual School in Cofradia (www.cofradiaschool.com) in northern Honduras, which relies on a team of internationally recruited volunteers to teach from August to June. The possibility of corporate teaching should not be discounted either. A company called Harris Communications (management@harriscom.org) employs native speakers with at least two years' experience and conducts conversation classes in the two northern cities of San Pedro Sula and La Ceiba.

LIST OF EMPLOYERS

BILINGUAL EDUCATION FOR CENTRAL AMERICA (BECA)

PO Box 229, New York, NY 10028, USA
+1 646 820 BECA (2322) in New York, +504 9964 5352 in Cofradia, Honduras
becaschools@gmail.com
www.becaschools.org

BECA exists to promote cultural exchange and affordable bilingual education in Central America. BECA's largest school is San Jeronimo Bilingual School in Cofradia, Northern Honduras.
NUMBER OF TEACHERS: 26 volunteer teachers.
PREFERENCE OF NATIONALITY: All nationalities welcome.
QUALIFICATIONS: BECA seeks motivated individuals who have completed a bachelor's degree. Average age is 24; most are 21–35.
CONDITIONS OF EMPLOYMENT: Minimum commitment 1 full year. Summer Institute begins mid-July and the school year finishes in mid-June of the following year. BECA schools operate from 7.15am to 2.15pm.
SALARY: All volunteers are provided with food, shared living accommodation and high speed Internet. Manager, administrators and second year teachers receive a modest monthly stipend in addition to food and lodging.
FACILITIES/SUPPORT: All volunteers have accommodation provided. 5-week training course provided for incoming volunteers, which covers training on different methods of language acquisition, classroom management, curriculum planning, cultural sensitivities, social and emotional development of the child plus complimentary Spanish classes. Volunteers come with a tourist visa to Honduras.
RECRUITMENT: Via websites such as idealist.org, through BECA alumni, and through promotion by various universities and colleges.
CONTACT: Sean Bell, Executive Director (sbell@becaschools.org).

MAXIMO NIVEL INTERNATIONAL GUATEMALA

6a Avenida Norte #16–16A, La Antigua
+502 7932 1500; +1 800 866 6358 (Florida contact number)
instructors@maximonivel.com
www.maximonivel.com

NUMBER OF TEACHERS: 10–20. Also organises volunteer teaching programme for paying volunteers.
PREFERENCE OF NATIONALITY: Must be native English speaker.
QUALIFICATIONS: Teachers must be TEFL, TESOL or CELTA certified from a training course of at least 100 hours with a minimum of 6 hours of practical teaching. Candidates must be dedicated, professional and passionate about teaching, with a self-confident personality and a good sense of humour.
CONDITIONS OF EMPLOYMENT: 6-month contracts are the norm. Split shifts, generally with classes from 7am to 10am and 4pm to 9pm. Teachers teach 30 hours per week, Monday through Friday.
SALARY: $475 to $800 per month (net).
FACILITIES/SUPPORT: Teachers are responsible for their own accommodation, but school provides assistance in locating housing. Often the institute provides 5 days of free room and board in a family stay to a new arrival, while he or she finds more permanent housing. Work permits are available on a very limited basis, and only for long-term teachers.
RECRUITMENT: Via email and online advertising through www.goabroad.com, www.idealist.org, Dave's ESL Café and others. Many teachers are hired on graduating from Maximo Nivel's own TEFL/TESOL certification course in Antigua. In-person interviews are preferred, but interviews can be conducted via Skype or phone.
CONTACT: Ken Jones, Executive Director.

NICARAGUA

LIST OF EMPLOYERS

ABC SCHOOL (American British College)

519 Calle El Consulado, Granada

✆ +505 55 2552 0812

✎ marlonabc@hotmail.com or abcorg@email.com

🖥 http://marlonabc.wix.com/school

NUMBER OF TEACHERS: 5 volunteers.

PREFERENCE OF NATIONALITY: North American.

QUALIFICATIONS: TEFL or equivalent, minimum 2 months' EFL teaching experience, some Spanish, some travel outside country of origin, interest in Nicaragua.

CONDITIONS OF EMPLOYMENT: Minimum stay of 3 months. 20 hours per week on weekdays between 3pm and 8pm and 3-hour classes taught on Saturdays and Sundays. School is open year round.

SALARY: Contribution of $160–$240 per month for housing.

FACILITIES/SUPPORT: Teachers are helped to find rooms to rent or homestays.

RECRUITMENT: Internet (including Facebook page) and word of mouth. Phone interviews.

CONTACT: Marlon Gutierrez, Owner/Director.

LA ESPERANZA GRANADA

Calle Libertad, #307, Una y media cuadras al lago, Granada

✆ +505 8913 8946

✎ info@la-esperanza-granada.org

🖥 www.la-esperanza-granada.org

NUMBER OF TEACHERS: 20–60 volunteers in total working in various aid projects, including some who teach English in primary schools and work in kindergartens.

PREFERENCE OF NATIONALITY: None.

QUALIFICATIONS: Knowledge of Spanish important for volunteers working with children.

CONDITIONS OF EMPLOYMENT: Minimum stay 1 month between February and November. Summer school projects run in December and January. Kindergarten hours are 7.30am–noon Monday to Friday. English team volunteers work Monday through Thursday 12.30–4pm or 1–4.30pm, and do lesson planning on Friday mornings.

SALARY: None. Volunteers pay a $20 administration fee and $5 for a project T-shirt.

FACILITIES/SUPPORT: 4 low-cost housing options available in centre of historic Granada: $23 per week in a dorm style room or $43 for a single room.

CONTACT: Pauline Jackson, Operation Director.

EL SALVADOR

After finishing high school in his hometown of Flagstaff, Arizona, **Kellen Brandel** knew that he wanted to take a year out. In his search for something affordable that would let him work on his Spanish, he settled on an NGO in the capital of El Salvador (see entry) which teaches English to local people and also supports some social justice projects around the country. Kellen spent a total of seven months in Central America and reflects on the benefits:

I mainly researched options using the internet and was most impressed with the one I chose (CIS: Center for Exchange and Solidarity) based on communication and quality of information, not to mention costs. I spent the first three months volunteer English teaching in CIS, a grassroots NGO founded by an American woman in the 1990s. I spent the next month backpacking through the countryside of El Salvador, Honduras, Guatemala and Belize before returning to San Salvador and spending an additional three months teaching again. While I volunteered abroad, I also studied the native language, Spanish, in a sister school at this particular NGO. The costs were quite reasonable. The average week consisted of spending about $80 for host family including meals and utilities, $57 for Spanish school, provided you were an English volunteer ($100 for passers-by) as well as a few additional expenses.

My volunteer position was that of an English teacher for adults, mainly in the evenings. The working conditions were great and the coordinators were very helpful in providing us with material, ideas and support. At first I was wary about teaching adults, as most of my students were in their late twenties and thirties. But I think I established respect with them and was laid back to the extent that the age difference didn't seem to matter. After that we were able to relax and eventually make jokes about my young age. It was professional, but the atmosphere at the CIS is also really laid back. Over the course of seven months I got to know my students on a much more personal level than many teachers get to, and that to me was really special. The low point would probably be the amount of English spoken. For many the balance is good, but since I already had a strong foundation in the Spanish language, I found too much English spoken at the CIS. But once I became more involved with locals outside school, that improved.

LIST OF EMPLOYERS

CIS – CENTRO DE INTERCAMBIO Y SOLIDARIDAD

Mélida Anaya Montes Language School, Avenida Aguilares y Avenida Bolivar #103, Colonia Libertad, San Salvador
US office: Los Olivos CIS, PO Box 76, Westmont, IL 60559–0076

- +503 2235 1330 / +503 2226 5362
- info@cis-elsalvador.org and volunteer@cis-elsalvador.org
- www.cis-elsalvador.org

NUMBER OF TEACHERS: 7–10 volunteer teachers at any one time.
PREFERENCE OF NATIONALITY: None.
QUALIFICATIONS: No teaching experience or certification needed. Must be committed to social justice and reciprocal learning between students and teacher.

CONDITIONS OF EMPLOYMENT: Minimum stay of 10 weeks for complete English cycle. Time commitment includes teaching English 3 days a week (Monday, Tuesday and Thursday) 5.15pm–7pm, weekly 2-hour teachers' meeting, plus time spent on lesson planning. Please contact for more details about rural volunteer placements and longer-term placements.
SALARY: None. Volunteers must also pay a one-time programme fee of $100.
FACILITIES/SUPPORT: The CIS has a host family network with whom volunteers can live: cost of homestay with breakfast and dinner starts at $80 a week. Training for teachers provided. Tourist visa ($10 at border) is sufficient. Volunteers are eligible to receive a half-price discount on Spanish classes.
RECRUITMENT: Word of mouth, internet, travel publications.

DOMINICAN REPUBLIC

A major tourist destination, the Dominican Republic (DR) provides some opportunities for native English teachers, although these may well be low paid (or volunteer positions) because the DR is still one of the poorest countries in the Caribbean. A useful resource is the Dominican Republic One news and information service (www.dr1.com) in English, which has a classified section and a message board where you can ask the online community for information. According to http://dr1.com/living/work/2.shtml:

> *If you would like to teach languages, particularly English, there are many immediate opportunities. For instance, the Instituto Cultural Dominico-Americano (+1 809 533 4191) is always looking for English teachers. Ditto for Universidad APEC's English Department (+1 809 686 0021). English Speaking Specialists (+1 809 547 7375) is an agency providing English teachers. It pays higher rates than the ICDA and provides all of the necessary materials. Look up language schools in the telephone book. Almost all of them will welcome you with open arms (if not pocketbooks) if you are a native, or a very good English speaker. Most of the primary or secondary bilingual or English-language schools need substitute teachers. A teaching certificate is not always required if you have a university degree or its equivalent.*

ICDA carries teaching information on its website (www.icda.edu.do) and invites applicants to submit CVs (to empleos@icda.edu.do).

A small not-for-profit organisation hosts summer volunteers to run an English summer school in the area around Ramón Santana; details are at www.supportingguasa.com/blog. A charity called Outreach 360 based in Arizona (www.outreach360.org) sends volunteers to participate in conversational English programmes with children in the Dominican Republic (and Nicaragua). This doubles as a fund-raiser for the organisation so, for example, a four-week summer stay costs $2,000. In the rural areas where the organisation works, access to native speakers of English is very limited. Volunteers are also needed to attend English-immersion summer camps. The charity Fundacion Aldeas de Paz (www.peacevillages.org) pulled out of Venezuela last year and has established a base in the Dominican Republic in the seaside town of Santa Barbara de Samana. It has set up a Teaching and Tutoring programme which deploys volunteers in after-school clubs and other contexts in Samana and El Cajuil in the north. The participation fee for eight weeks is $1200 which includes accommodation in the volunteer guesthouse.

LIST OF EMPLOYERS

ULAE (UNIVERSITY LANGUAGE EXTENSION) ENGLISH PROGRAM

UCNE (Universidad Cathólica Nordestana), Centro de Idiomas y Relaciones Globales (CIRG), Calle Restauracion esq. 27 de Febrero, San Francisco de Macorís, Provincia Duarte, (Apartado Postal No. 239), Dominican Republic

- +1 809 588 3505 ext 3200; +1 809 588 3151 ext 233; +1 809 290 3355.
- ulae@ucne.edu; darling.ulae@gmail.com
- www.cirg.webs.com; www.ucne.edu

NUMBER OF TEACHERS: 30 volunteer professors of language and literature.

PREFERENCE OF NATIONALITY: English-speaking countries.

QUALIFICATIONS: Ages 21–38. Should be graduate in education-related subject or with experience working with children. Should be able to adapt to life in the Caribbean and have a love of multicultural life and tourism. Intermediate Spanish needed.

CONDITIONS OF EMPLOYMENT: 6 months or a year from beginning of terms (second Monday in September or early January). Working hours are 8am–3pm Monday to Friday with lunches provided at 1pm daily at school.

SALARY: $650 per month (paid on the 10th of the month).

FACILITIES/SUPPORT: Shared apartment next to the school with utilities, phone and internet included; teachers have their own room. Access to beaches and aquatic sports on days off. Teachers meet regularly with the coordinator to prepare tests, evaluations and lesson plans.

RECRUITMENT: CVs to be submitted. Interviews by Skype.

CONTACT: Mr Darling J. Perez, Administrative Director ULAE English Program (coordinator.cirg@ucne.edu).

Just about every university and college in the major cities has an ESL programme, as do a range of government and charitable organisations. Commercial schools offer a wide variety of classes but tend to focus on survival ESL and EAP (English for Academic Purposes), with writing as a major component. Berlitz and Inlingua are represented throughout the USA and are a completely different type of commercial school, concentrating on conversational skills and foreign languages for business people. Embassy English (www.embassyenglish.com) has adult English schools in Boston, New York, Fort Lauderdale, San Diego, Los Angeles and San Francisco, plus a centre in Toronto. These may be worth applying to if you are well qualified, although they normally recruit locally. Details of summer teaching jobs in New York, Massachusetts, Florida and California can be found at http://jobs.embassysummer.com/usa-application.htm, which might be of interest to non-Americans who can obtain a J-1 exchange visa by joining the BUNAC Work America programme.

Bilingual/bicultural classes are run in thousands of high schools across the country. Many require staff who are not only state-certified teachers but also bilingual in exotic languages like Hmong or Gujarati. Most larger cities have at least one free or low-cost workplace literacy/vocational ESL programme that caters for immigrants needing assistance with the basics of English. Some of these programmes operate in outposts (eg churches, libraries) and many depend on local volunteers as tutors. Volunteer positions can conceivably lead to better things and are sometimes a prerequisite for ESL programmes abroad. The largest (and longest established) literacy organisation is ProLiteracy (www.proliteracy.org), which offers ten hours of training.

While many American English teachers set off to see the world, others like **Jeffrey Machado** move back to the US (after teaching in China in his case) to teach their language to incomers, as he explains on the forum of Cambridge English Teacher (www.cambridgeenglishteacher.org):

I have recently started volunteering with a literacy organisation here in my home country. I never fully understood the difference between ESL and EFL before this point. But, now, working with students who NEED English (rather than want to learn it for career purposes), the dynamic is completely different. I have found that students are less inhibited once they are here in the US.

There are some truly unique opportunities in the ELT field here in the United States. Just this weekend, I read an article about the state of Hawaii's difficulties retaining good teachers. Essentially, Hawaii with its English language learners, who mainly speak a combination of Hawaiian and pidgin English, represents not just a state, but an entire other country with unexplored opportunities. In addition, EAP careers are prevalent around cities and towns with large student populations. While not strictly EAP, there are also plenty of opportunities for TOEFL exam prep. The main downside is that the cost of living in the majority of these places is quite high whereas the pay for ELTs is rather paltry.

GEMMA PIRELLI

Gemma Pirelli tried to think of ways of achieving her desire to travel after finishing a degree in psychology, and spend time with people from different cultures. She carried out lots of research on the internet and made contact with the director of www.teachingenglishinitaly.com, Sheila Corwin, a fellow American. Not only did she enrol on a distance-learning course, but took steps to get some practical experience.

In addition to putting together a portfolio of all coursework I'm doing for my distance TEFL course (the International Certificate for Applied Linguistics), I tried to find some volunteering opportunities and classroom observations here in New Jersey. Therefore, I began to research local colleges/universities in my area as well as community centres accepting volunteers. I went back to my alma mater (Seton Hall University) and arranged a couple of classroom observations with the ESL adjunct. Because I wanted more involvement in the classroom, I decided to become a volunteer at a local community centre where they have programmes for adult learners. After connecting with the director, she was able to accommodate me in a Monday evening class, and have me float around different classrooms to observe various levels. I was able to teach one class of learners at intermediate level, which went very well, and I was able to use my knowledge from the course as well as lesson planning guided by Sheila. Eventually I was put in charge of advanced learners (only one to three at a time). There are no set books and little structure so I had to arrange lessons on my own ... There is no doubt in my mind that this experience will lead me to grand frontiers.

Although the demand for ESL teachers is enormous, it is very difficult for foreigners who do not have a 'green card' to obtain the necessary working visa. The J-1 visa is available to university students participating in an approved Exchange Visitor Programme (which are mainly for the summer) and to researchers and teachers whose applications are supported by their employing institution in the USA. Similarly it is extremely difficult to obtain the H-1B 'Temporary Worker' visa, which is available for prearranged professional or highly skilled jobs for which there are no suitably qualified Americans, an increasingly unlikely circumstance as more and more Americans are becoming qualified to teach ESL/EFL. Although more US organisations now recognise the Cambridge CELTA Certificate than before, the MA in TESOL still dominates the American EFL scene. Even for qualified American teachers, part-time work is the norm, often referred to as being hired as an 'adjunct'. Many contracts are not renewed, creating a transient English-teaching population. Pay is hourly and varies according to region, for example $20–$25 in Chicago, a little more in San Francisco. Part-timers almost never get benefits, which means no health insurance or vacation pay. Even full-time teaching openings may be for just nine months, with pay as little as $20,000–$25,000 in the Midwest.

Canada has a flourishing ELT industry; however, the difficulty of getting a visa is a major stumbling block for foreign teachers. People with experience might have expected to be able to do some casual one-to-one tutoring of new immigrants, but stiff competition makes this difficult. Two sources of possible contacts are Languages Canada (www.languagescanada.ca) and TESL Canada (www.tesl.ca). Member institutes will usually consider only Canadian citizens or those with work permits or landed immigrant status. The hourly wage starts at C$20–25 per hour.

TEACHING HOUSE NEW YORK

Lauren Harrington – Undergoing the Delta

'In an interview activity I did when I was on my Delta, I – teacher turned overnight pop star sensation – was asked if I was currently working on any new projects. Well, as a matter of fact, I confessed to my paparazzi classmates, I am currently undergoing my Delta. *Undergoing?* Interesting choice of words my interviewers noted.

'When I decided to do my Delta, I was at the point when I was no longer teaching just because I had somehow stumbled into it 12 years earlier. After college, I went to Romania for what was supposed to be a gap year. Six years later, when I returned to the US, I realised that teaching was not something I was doing until I figured out what I wanted to do with my life; it *was* what I wanted to do.

'Back in Boston, I found a teaching job that I loved and eventually started training teachers. I did not, however, have a teaching qualification that said that I was trained to do what I was doing. In the teachers' room, in between conversations about the broken photocopiers and unruly students, one colleague, having done his Delta years earlier, convinced me that this was the best next step for me. He told me that it would be both the hardest and most fulfilling thing I had done until then.

'I chose to do the Blended Delta because it gave me the most flexibility, as I needed to continue working while I was studying, and Teaching House was highly recommended to me by my boss/mentor. The Delta did not show me that everything that I had been doing in the classroom up until that point was wrong. In fact, it taught me that a lot of what I was doing was right and helped me to see why we do what we do.

'I am a more confident teacher now, which has both given me more control over the learning process yet has allowed me to relinquish complete control over the lesson, allowing the learners' needs to dictate where the lesson should go. This is what the Delta did for me.

'Considering that we usually undergo a huge transformation or treatment for something serious, *undergoing* my Delta doesn't seem as funny a phrase in retrospect as it did at the time.'

AUSTRALASIA

While Europeans tend to have a somewhat Eurocentric view of the world, the Antipodean English language industry has built itself into a giant. TEFL has a very high profile in both Australia and New Zealand. There are no fewer than 15 Cambridge CELTA training centres in Australia and nine in New Zealand, most of them attached to flourishing English language colleges. There are a further two Trinity TESOL centres in New Zealand, despite its tiny population of less than 4.5 million. **Neil Preston** of International House Brisbane has kindly contributed to this assessment of the ELT scene in Australia.

PROSPECTS FOR TEACHERS IN AUSTRALIA

The growth in student numbers and ELT schools has resulted in strong job prospects for TESOL qualified teachers. Approximately 80,000 students study English in Australia on student visas and the Australian immigration department estimates that another 60,000 students study on other visas, such as working holiday and tourist visas. This represents an increase of 80% over the past 10 years, although the last few years have seen shrinkage in the EFL student market, partly due to the strong Australian dollar and resultant high cost of living. Industry experts predict that the market will start to recover over the next year or two.

For obvious reasons of geography, the majority of Australia's international students are from Asia, although there are a growing number of students coming from further away, including Italy and elsewhere in Europe, plus a strong Latin America presence.

Australia has a strong market for longer-term students, eg Academic English students (20+ weeks) and English for high school students (20–30 weeks) who need to improve their English skills for entry into an Australian university or high school. However, the average number of weeks overseas students study is 12. This longer-term student market has resulted in relatively steady student numbers year round. Whilst Australia does experience a peak in student numbers over the warmer months (September to May), due to an influx of study tours, there is not the same dramatic seasonal fluctuation as in Europe.

There are approximately 100 English language colleges in Sydney alone, around 70% of which are accredited by the National ELT Accreditation Scheme (NEAS). The profession is strictly regulated in Australia and standards are high in both the private and public sector. The minimum acceptable qualification to teach at an Australian NEAS-accredited language school is a degree in any discipline (or 3-year full-time diploma) plus a recognised TESOL qualification and 800 hours of teaching experience. Alternatively you may be considered with a higher-than-pass grade in the TESOL qualification or if you can show references from your TESOL course director about your performance.

An acceptable TESOL qualification must have a practical component including at least six hours' supervised and assessed practice teaching in TESOL and involve no fewer than 100 contact hours in total (or the equivalent in Distance Education programmes). To check the current requirements and a list of 200+ accredited language schools see the NEAS website (www.neas.org.au). Some non-accredited schools will employ TESOL trained teachers who do not hold a degree or diploma. It is interesting to note that due to the strong demand for TEFL qualified teachers in Sydney, job-seekers with the CELTA but without a degree have still been offered positions by accredited schools.

Candidates (whether Australians or foreigners on working visas) are regularly offered employment in Sydney and in other Australian cities within a week or two of completing the Cambridge CELTA course. To find a list of English language schools throughout Australia, see the website of ELICOS (English Language Intensive Courses for Overseas Students – www.elicos.com). Job vacancies are posted at http://au.jora.com (search for ELICOS). Generally, teaching contracts are casual, as staffing is organised from one course period to the next, from week to week or month to month, depending on the college. Once a relationship has been built between school and teacher the teacher can opt to work long term with one school or short term with a number of schools. Annual salaries range from around AUS$40,000 for a newly qualified graduate teacher without experience to AUS$90,000 for a head teacher. The Fair Work Commission sets 'award rates' (agreed minimums) for different categories of TESOL teacher; these are normally reviewed in July. The median hourly wage is about $38.50.

Many foreigners teach English on a working holiday visa. British, Irish and North American travellers aged between 18 and 30 years can apply for working holiday visas for up to 12 months (renewable for a further 12 months provided visa-holders do a minimum of 88 days of fruit-picking in a designated rural area). For further information visit www.border.gov.au. One company that sometimes hires teachers with a WH visa is Lexis English (www.lexisenglish.com) with four schools in Queensland and one in Perth. When **Barry O'Leary** arrived in Sydney with a working holiday visa, he had very little money so needed a job fast. He had emailed a number of language institutes in Sydney in advance and fixed up an interview the day after he arrived. In addition to walking round all the schools he could find, he used Australian search engines such as www.seek.com.au, www.jobsearch.gov.au and www.mycareer.com.au to look for sessional positions. Soon he found a job with a college in an outer suburb of Sydney:

This was my first full-time job and I was thrown in at the deep end. Initially I was doing maternity cover and working 15 hours a week, but this later increased to 45 including preparation time. The wages were fantastic, I wasn't paying any tax because I set myself up as a contractor and I was paid AUS$30 an hour (the going rate then) and AUS$300 every two weeks for the evening business course I taught. I managed to save about AUS$8,000 in three months, which paid for a brilliant trip up the east coast of Australia. There was always a laugh in the staff room and a lot of banter between England and Australia. I really enjoyed the mixed classes because there was such a range of opinions and at times they were more challenging because each nationality would have different weaknesses.

LIST OF EMPLOYERS

ACCESS LANGUAGE CENTRE
72 Mary Street, Surry Hills, New South Wales 2010
℡ +61 2 9281 6455
✉ english@access.nsw.edu.au
🖥 www.access.nsw.edu.au

NUMBER OF TEACHERS: 16.
PREFERENCE OF NATIONALITY: None.
QUALIFICATIONS: Bachelor's degree plus TESOL certificate. Some experience essential.
CONDITIONS OF EMPLOYMENT: 4 weeks renewable to start.
SALARY: Depends on qualifications and experience.
FACILITIES/SUPPORT: No assistance with accommodation.
RECRUITMENT: Advertising and will respond to general enquiries about work while in Australia.
CONTACT: Tony Stock, Director of Studies.

AUSTRALIAN INTERNATIONAL COLLEGE OF ENGLISH
Level 3/303 Pitt St, Sydney, New South Wales 2000
℡ +61 2 9299 2400
✉ info@aice.nsw.edu.au
🖥 www.aice.nsw.edu.au

NUMBER OF TEACHERS: 15.
PREFERENCE OF NATIONALITY: Any native-speaking country.
QUALIFICATIONS: Recognised TESOL certificate/CELTA and a bachelor's or higher degree from a recognised university.
CONDITIONS OF EMPLOYMENT: 20 hours per week of teaching. Different class schedules, ie Monday–Thursday 9am–3pm or Monday–Friday 9am–1.30pm or 4.15pm–8.45pm.
SALARY: AUS$35–$45+ per hour (gross), based on state salary scale for English teachers. Deductions are made for tax and compulsory superannuation contributions.

FACILITIES/SUPPORT: Candidates with working holiday visas are welcome. No help given with visas or accommodation.

RECRUITMENT: Local advertising. Face-to-face interviews.

CONTACT: Heidi Reid, Principal.

ENGLISH LANGUAGE COMPANY

495 Kent St, Sydney, New South Wales 2000

✆ +61 2 9267 5688

✉ recruitment@englishlanguagecompany.com

🖥 www.englishlanguagecompany.com

NUMBER OF TEACHERS: 20.

PREFERENCE OF NATIONALITY: None but must already have right to work in Australia.

QUALIFICATIONS: University degree + CELTA or equivalent; though CELTA definitely preferred. (Under national industry regulations set down by NEAS, teaching qualifications must include 120 hours of face-to-face instruction and at least 6 hours of observed, assessed teaching.) One year's experience teaching adult learners.

CONDITIONS OF EMPLOYMENT: Most teachers start with a short contract of 10 or 12 weeks, as is common in Sydney. Teaching hours are 8.15am–4.15pm.

SALARY: Teachers are paid on a national step-based award system. Qualifications and relevant experience are factored to give a salary step. Salaries range from approximately AUS$41,500–S$60,000. Tax is deducted on a PAYE basis.

FACILITIES/SUPPORT: No help given with visas. Support to find accommodation given to teachers on working holidays.

RECRUITMENT: Applications with CV by email or post and then face-to-face interview is arranged. In certain cases the applicant is asked to do a demonstration lesson of 30–60 minutes using material given to them.

CONTACT: Lyn Scott, Academic Director.

ENGLISH UNLIMITED

Level 9, 138 Albert Street, Brisbane, Queensland 4000

✆ +61 7 3003 0088

✉ info@englishunlimited.qld.edu.au

🖥 www.englishunlimited.qld.edu.au

NUMBER OF TEACHERS: 5.

PREFERENCE OF NATIONALITY: Providing the applicant has the right to live and work in Australia and sufficient English language skills, teachers from any country of origin are encouraged to apply.

QUALIFICATIONS: Specific TESOL qualification, for example CELTA or Trinity CertTESOL are a requirement to teach within the private education industry, in colleges accredited by NEAS. TEFL training courses that are accepted must have a minimum number of hours input and a practical teaching component, which excludes online courses. University degree also required (in any discipline).

CONDITIONS OF EMPLOYMENT: Teachers are employed on ongoing sessional contracts, mostly on a casual basis. Most teachers work approximately 20 hours a week, 8.30am–2.30pm Monday to Thursday (5 contact hours per day).

SALARY: Teachers are usually paid based on a national scheme, according to qualifications and experience. Unfortunately, the majority of overseas experience is not counted, so teachers may well find themselves starting at the bottom. Salary range is from AUS$42.02 per hour at Level 1 to AUS$55 at Level 12 (less superannuation payments of 9% and income tax).

FACILITIES/SUPPORT: Teachers source their own accommodation but advice is available. No visa sponsorship is available.

RECRUITMENT: Via adverts on www.seek.com.au and www.onestopenglish.com, walk-in applications and teacher recommendations. Interview prior to appointment is essential for all positions including voluntary; paid employees must teach a demonstration lesson.

CONTACT: Ms Rufus James, Academic Manager (rufus@english unlimited.qld.edu.au).

INTERNATIONAL HOUSE BRISBANE

126 Adelaide St, Brisbane, Queensland 4000

Postal address: PO Box 13393 George St, Brisbane 4003

✆ +61 7 3229 3389

✉ neil@ihbrisbane.com.au

🖥 www.ihbrisbane.com.au

NUMBER OF TEACHERS: Approximately 20.

PREFERENCE OF NATIONALITY: Native English speakers.

QUALIFICATIONS: CELTA or equivalent and minimum of 1 year's experience.

CONDITIONS OF EMPLOYMENT: Variable length contracts. Up to 25 hours per week.

SALARY: Australian award rates ($41–$54 per hour).

RECRUITMENT: CV and interview. Interviews occasionally conducted overseas.

CONTACT: Neil Preston, Director of Studies.

MILNER INTERNATIONAL COLLEGE OF ENGLISH

379 Hay Street, Perth, Western Australia 6000

✆ +61 8 9325 5444

✉ dos@milner.wa.edu.au

🖥 www.milner.wa.edu.au

NUMBER OF TEACHERS: 25–35.

PREFERENCE OF NATIONALITY: None. Teachers from the UK and Canada can come on a working holiday visa if they are under 30.

QUALIFICATIONS: Degree plus CELTA (or equivalent).

CONDITIONS OF EMPLOYMENT: No contracts for casual teachers. School hours 9am–3pm.

SALARY: There is an award scale for EL teachers ranging from AUS\$38.55–\$50.46 per hour.

FACILITIES/SUPPORT: Teachers find their own accommodation.

RECRUITMENT: CV and interview.

CONTACT: Deborah Pinder, Director of Studies.

PHOENIX ACADEMY

223 Vincent Street, West Perth, Western Australia 6005

 +61 8 9227 5538

 robynne.walsh@phoenix.wa.edu.au

 www.phoenix.wa.edu.au

NUMBER OF TEACHERS: 30–35 across all English programmes.

PREFERENCE OF NATIONALITY: None, but candidates must have a working holiday visa or other appropriate visa.

QUALIFICATIONS: Minimum undergraduate degree in any discipline and a CELTA.

CONDITIONS OF EMPLOYMENT: Length of stay varies according to vacancy needs, eg it could be a 4-week summer course contract, a 12-week Business English or Cambridge course contract or a 6-month EAP contract. Permanent contracts occasionally available. Contact hours usually 20 per week plus 3–5 hours for other duties.

SALARY: Minimum starting salary AUS\$42,000–\$53,000 per year. School usually pays above this award minimum according to skills and experience. Tax reduces salary by about 20%.

FACILITIES/SUPPORT: On-campus residence available for new arrivals at a cost of AUS\$30 per night.

RECRUITMENT: Via teachers' websites and local advertising in newspaper media. Interviews essential and can be done by Skype for non-local applicants.

CONTACT: Robynne Walsh, Principal.

SYDNEY ENGLISH ACADEMY (SEA)

19/74 –78 The Corso, Manly, New South Wales 2095

 +61 2 9976 6988

 info@sea-english.com

 www.sea-english.com

NUMBER OF TEACHERS: 6–12 depending on time of year.

PREFERENCE OF NATIONALITY: None, provided they already have legal right to work.

QUALIFICATIONS: An undergraduate degree plus a CELTA or equivalent certificate (as an absolute minimum).

CONDITIONS OF EMPLOYMENT: Varies according to current needs but 12 weeks is typical. Hours normally 8.15am–3.45pm.

SALARY: Based on the New Federal Award. Depending on earnings, 25%–30% is deducted for income tax and the employers adds on 9% of earnings to pay into the employee's superannuation fund.

RECRUITMENT: Face-to-face or Skype interview necessary.

CONTACT: Samantha Milton, Director of Studies.

PROSPECTS FOR TEACHERS IN NEW ZEALAND

The English-language teaching market in New Zealand is fairly similar to that of Australia: highly developed, although subject to demand fluctuation. Demand from Chinese, Korean and other Asian students is very high. Also there are plenty of Saudis, South Americans and many others who can see the appeal of learning a foreign language in this beautiful country. According to Marty Pilott, on the National Executive of TESOLANZ (the New Zealand Association of ESOL teachers), plenty of local teaching applicants are available, which means that language schools are unlikely to hire teachers from abroad. However, anyone with a CELTA and several years' experience who goes to New Zealand to conduct a job hunt has a reasonable chance of success. One such, a few years ago, was **Mr Roy**:

> *When I came here, I'd never felt so popular. I was amazed how many jobs I got offered cold calling with a CV. I entered the country on a visitor visa that, as a British passport holder, gave me six months in the country. Before coming here I had looked on the internet for the addresses of English language schools and I brought a stack of*

CVs with me too. I just typed 'English language schools New Zealand' into the Google search engine and clicked on the second link, www.english-schools.co.nz, which gave me some useful information. I didn't jump at the first three jobs I was offered in Auckland because I wanted to check out Christchurch, the other main centre for EFL schools. There I was offered a few more jobs and decided to take up a post at Aspect [now Kaplan] at 116 Worcester Street in the city centre. The students are mainly Chinese, Korean and Japanese but there are notable groups from Taiwan, Switzerland and South America too. My school was helpfully willing to aid me with the visa bureaucracy and now I have residency. My school has a core of staff with open-ended contracts and a larger number of casual/part-time staff, including some British people with working holiday visas who work for some months and then continue travelling.

Private language schools are regulated by the New Zealand Qualifications Authority or NZQA (www.nzqa. govt.nz/providers/index.do). Its website lists all the educational establishments in New Zealand, but is worth looking through for leads (or search for 'language' to narrow it down). The national organisation of English language teachers, TESOLANZ (www.tesolanz.org.nz), provides a free listing for job-seekers and institutions offering work, while English New Zealand is an association of accredited private and state sector English language schools which posts current vacancies (www.englishnewzealand.co.nz).

British citizens aged between 18 and 30 can work in New Zealand through the working holiday visa scheme for up to 23 months (www.immigration.govt.nz/migrant/stream/work/workingholiday).

LIST OF EMPLOYERS

DOMINION ENGLISH SCHOOLS

8th Floor, 155 Queen St, Auckland (PO Box 4217)

- +64 9 377 3280
- dos@dominion.school.nz
- www.dominion.school.nz

NUMBER OF TEACHERS: Up to 20.

PREFERENCE OF NATIONALITY: None, but must be native English speakers.

QUALIFICATIONS: Minimum Cambridge/RSA CELTA or Trinity CertTESOL or recognised equivalent. Preferably also university degree and experience.

CONDITIONS OF EMPLOYMENT: Flexible contracts. Part-time hours 12.5 per week from 9am to 12pm. Full-time hours 25 per week, 9am–4pm.

SALARY: Starting wage approximately NZ$30 per hour.

FACILITIES/SUPPORT: Applicants must hold a valid work visa/permit.

RECRUITMENT: Local interviews essential.

CONTACT: Anne Lowerson, Director of Studies.

INDEX OF ADVERTISERS

Action English Language Training Limited 28
American Tesol Institute 58
British Council inside front cover
CLIC (Centro de Lenguas e Intercambio
   Cultural) 44, 233
English for Asia (Trinity Cert TESOL)
   Hong Kong 427
ILC France 37
International House Barcelona 17, 45
International House Lisbon 43
International House London 30
International House Madrid 47

International House Rome 39
International House World Organisation 77
ITTC/Beet Language Centre 31
NILE (Norwich Institute for Language
   Education) 32, 33
Oxford TEFL 9
Oxford University Press 114
Saxoncourt Teacher Training &
   Recruitment 18, 85
Teaching House 22, 49, 603, outside back cover
TEFL Org UK 24, 56
TEFL Worldwide 69